JULIUS CAESAR AND T

Julius Caesar was no aspiring autocrat seeking to realize the imperial future but an unusually successful republican leader who was measured against the Republic's traditions and its greatest heroes of the past. Catastrophe befell Rome not because Caesar (or anyone else) turned against the Republic or its norms and institutions, but because Caesar's extraordinary success mobilized a determined opposition that ultimately preferred to precipitate civil war rather than accept its political defeat. Based on painstaking reanalysis of the ancient sources in light of recent advances in our understanding of the participatory role of the People in the republican political system, a strong emphasis on agents' choices rather than structural causation, and deep skepticism toward the facile determinism that often substitutes for historical explanation, this book offers a radical reinterpretation of a figure of profound historical importance who stands at the turning point of Roman history from Republic to Empire.

ROBERT MORSTEIN-MARX is Professor of Classics at the University of California, Santa Barbara. He is the author of *Mass Oratory and Political Power in the Late Roman Republic* (Cambridge University Press, 2004), *Hegemony to Empire: The Development of the Roman Imperium in the East, 148–62 B.C.* (1995), and coeditor of *A Companion to the Roman Republic* (2006).

JULIUS CAESAR AND THE ROMAN PEOPLE

ROBERT MORSTEIN-MARX

University of California, Santa Barbara

CAMBRIDGE
UNIVERSITY PRESS

Shaftesbury Road, Cambridge CB2 8EA, United Kingdom

One Liberty Plaza, 20th Floor, New York, NY 10006, USA

477 Williamstown Road, Port Melbourne, VIC 3207, Australia

314–321, 3rd Floor, Plot 3, Splendor Forum, Jasola District Centre, New Delhi – 110025, India

103 Penang Road, #05–06/07, Visioncrest Commercial, Singapore 238467

Cambridge University Press is part of Cambridge University Press & Assessment, a department of the University of Cambridge.

We share the University's mission to contribute to society through the pursuit of education, learning and research at the highest international levels of excellence.

www.cambridge.org
Information on this title: www.cambridge.org/9781108932080

DOI: 10.1017/9781108943260

First published 2021
First paperback edition 2023

A catalogue record for this publication is available from the British Library

Library of Congress Cataloging-in-Publication data
NAMES: Morstein-Marx, Robert, author.
TITLE: Julius Caesar and the Roman people / Robert Morstein-Marx, University of California, Santa Barbara.
DESCRIPTION: Cambridge, United Kingdom ; New York, NY : Cambridge University Press, 2021. | Includes bibliographical references and index.
IDENTIFIERS: LCCN 2021024626 (print) | LCCN 2021024627 (ebook) | ISBN 9781108837842 (hardback) | ISBN 9781108943260 (ebook)
SUBJECTS: LCSH: Caesar, Julius. | Caesar, Julius – Influence. | Rome – Politics and government – 265-30 B.C. | Political leadership – Rome – History. | Rome – Kings and rulers. | Rome – History, Military – 265-30 B.C. | BISAC: HISTORY / Ancient / General | HISTORY / Ancient / General
CLASSIFICATION: LCC DG261 .M67 2021 (print) | LCC DG261 (ebook) | DDC 937/.05–dc23
LC record available at https://lccn.loc.gov/2021024626
LC ebook record available at https://lccn.loc.gov/2021024627

ISBN   978-1-108-83784-2   Hardback
ISBN   978-1-108-93208-0   Paperback

To Sara, Eric, and Matthew
again

Contents

Figures

Acknowledgments

My elder son was in middle school, I believe, when he asked me in all innocence whether my book on Caesar *was done yet*. He is now entering his senior year of college. At last I can reassure him that it *is* done. But this moment has been a very long time in coming. For their patience I express my gratitude not only to my beloved family but to my colleagues in the Department of Classics at the University of California, Santa Barbara (UCSB) and many others at this campus which has provided me with a supportive academic home for twenty-eight years now.

I often marvel at what a friendly and congenial community of scholars inhabits my corner of ancient history. Many friends and colleagues at other institutions have assisted me with salutary advice or answered difficult queries, read and commented on whole chapters and in some cases quite a bit more than one. Erich Gruen, Martin Jehne, Christopher Krebs, Sears McGee, Kit Morrell, Chris Pelling, John Ramsey, Nate Rosenstein, and Rex Stem all read preliminary drafts of one or more chapters and offered extremely helpful comments. Nate Rosenstein was also kind enough to read through the entire final manuscript on a tight schedule. Lindsay Driediger-Murphy, Chris Pelling, and John Ramsey generously allowed me to see parts of their own recent work in advance of publication, and Francesca Martelli drew my attention to some points I had hitherto ignored. To all I am more grateful than these paltry words can convey, and of course they are not to blame for the errors and imperfections that remain. I also wish to record my sincere thanks to the two anonymous readers for the Press, whose comments and criticisms I was not always delighted to read but ultimately spurred me to produce a far better book.

During the library lockdown of 2020, while I was polishing my final draft, Andrea Angius, Martin Jehne, and Francisco Pina Polo came to my rescue with scans of articles or other bibliographical assistance. John Ramsey generously fielded a whole series of sticky questions from me and shared parts of his forthcoming commentary on Asconius. Kenneth

Lapatin, Jens Daehner, Mary Beard, Christopher Hallett, and Hans Goette kindly shared with me their thoughts about the somewhat controversial portrait bust that graces the cover of this book. Professor Goette generously provided the photograph itself and Professor Andreas Scholl, the director of classical antiquities at the Staatliche Museen zu Berlin, graciously approved its use. To all I give my warmest thanks.

The ideas presented here in many cases received their first hearing in lectures or in seminars. I thank the alert audiences at UCSB, Stanford, Brigham Young University, and the UK Triennial Conference in Cambridge for their receptiveness to my arguments and their criticisms that have made them better. I also thank my former and current students, who in seminars have provided an ideal trial run for many of the arguments found in this book and through their dissertations or publications have clarified and deepened them. I am proud to be able to acknowledge some of their work explicitly in the chapters that follow.

A book of this size and scope on a subject on which dozens of scholarly articles and books appear every year cannot but be somewhat out of date the moment it is published. My manuscript was initially submitted to the Press in November 2018 and final revisions were completed in July 2020 during a global pandemic. In general I have considered a publication date of 2018 to be the cutoff point for full consideration here. While I was still able to make some limited use of some especially pertinent pieces published in 2019, these could hardly reshape my entire treatment, as perhaps they may have deserved to do. Readers may regard any reference to a scholarly work with a very recent publication date as a suggestion to explore further.

I have generally quoted foreign-language scholarship in my own English translation. I beg the authors' forgiveness if in any case I have ever erred or misled by my rendering.

This project was supported by various grants, the most essential of which was an American Council of Learned Societies Senior Fellowship in 2011 which gave me a full year of relief from teaching duties in which to write the initial draft of this book. (Little did the ACLS or I know how many more drafts would be forthcoming.) The University of California, Santa Barbara generously supplemented my ACLS grant and also gave me a further sabbatical quarter, as well as two Academic Senate grants to fund research assistants. From the series of chairs of my department through the time of the book's gestation I have received much kindly consideration in the timing of my teaching and departmental duties. My former student Noah Segal and my current student Chris Erdman both gave indispensable assistance in preparing a large and complicated manuscript.

I am deeply grateful to Michael Sharp, the Press's editor for classics and ancient history, who has been incredibly responsive and supportive of this project at every step of the (rather long) way. The whole team at the Press has been a model of kind consideration and efficiency in dealing with the many challenges of producing this book in the midst of the inconveniences, miseries, and tragedies of the pandemic. I also want to thank my copyeditor, Ami Naramor, for her sharp eye, good sense, and not least, sheer grit in working her way through an enormous manuscript despite the difficult circumstances.

I dedicate this book to my family – my wife, Sara Lindheim, and children, Eric and Matthew. They have borne the burden of my long preoccupation with this book with remarkable, loving patience. Sara finished her own book at virtually the same time, a coincidence that prompted many stimulating conversations which have broadened my understanding. I thank them all from the bottom of my heart for their unwavering support throughout this long ordeal and for putting up with my distraction without complaint.

I want to close with an expression of warm affection and deep admiration for my teacher and dear friend Erich Gruen. Since the time when I was a graduate student under his tutelage he has been my ideal of a scholar, teacher, and academic mentor. This book was in many respects inspired by his work and example. Despite its inevitable flaws I hope that its best parts at least might be seen as a tribute to Erich.

Abbreviations

Comprehensive lists of the standard abbreviations of ancient sources and of scholarly journals or resources may be found in the *Oxford Classical Dictionary* and *L'année philologique*.
The following abbreviations used in this book do not appear in those lists:

I.It.	*Inscriptiones Italiae*, Rome, 1931–1963.
Nic. Dam., *Bios*	Nicolaus of Damascus, *Bios Kaisaros, FGrH/BNJ* 90 F 125–139
OED	*Oxford English Dictionary Online* (December 2020 update).
OLD	P. W. Glare, ed., *Oxford Latin Dictionary*, Oxford, 1982.
RS	M. H. Crawford, ed., *Roman Statutes* (Bull. of the Institute of Classical Studies 64), 2 vols., London, 1996.
Sherk	R. K. Sherk, *Roman Documents from the Greek East: Senatus consulta and epistulae to the Age of Augustus*, Baltimore, 1969.

CHAPTER I

Introduction

What "new and true" can possibly still be said about Gaius Julius Caesar? A fair question. Even if one were to take a parochial view of the scholarship (for much of the most important work has been published in German), no fewer than four full-scale English-language biographies were published by top-rank scholars between 2006 and 2009, not to mention a weighty (and worthy) *Companion to Julius Caesar* also published in 2009, two interesting introductions pitched mainly to undergraduates and the general reader in 2015 and 2016, and now two book-length studies that emerged in 2017 and 2019 on the coming of the civil war.[1] A "companion" to the writings of Julius Caesar and a new compendium of his works with contextual essays covering a wide range of issues, historical, biographical, and historiographical, have recently appeared as well as an entire book devoted to Caesar's first consulship.[2] Caesar's own account of "his" civil war has recently become an especially fertile field for scholarly activity with the appearance of a new critical edition of the text together with its companion volume and a handful of monographs in English.[3] Since 2006 at least three important books have appeared on the reception of Caesar from the Augustan Principate to his status as a cultural icon today, while his assassination remains an ever-popular subject of books intended for a wider, nonspecialist readership.[4] We now even have a book that contests the traditional diagnosis of Caesar's illness as epilepsy, opting instead for

---

[1] Goldsworthy 2006; Canfora 2007 (original Italian edition published in 1999); Tatum 2008; Billows 2009; Griffin (ed.) 2009; Stevenson 2015; Wiseman 2016; Fezzi 2019. A new German edition of Gelzer's venerable biography has also recently appeared: Gelzer 2008. Because these volumes generally focus on a nonspecialist readership (not to mention their daunting rate of publication) they do not receive much attention in this book. For their merits and some criticisms see the following reviews: Osgood 2007; Santangelo 2010; Racine 2012; Zampieri 2016; Cornwell 2018.

[2] Grillo and Krebs (eds.) 2017, Raaflaub (ed.) 2017, and Chrissanthos 2019.

[3] Damon's OCT (2015) with Damon 2018 and Grillo 2012; Peer 2015; Westall 2018.

[4] Wyke (ed.) 2006, 2008; Devillers and Sion-Jenkins (eds.) 2012; Woolf 2007; Strauss 2015.

a series of small strokes.[5] The cascade of publications is overwhelming, impossible for any one scholar to master in full. Our culture's appetite for the story of the Roman dictator ensures that it will ever be fed, and doubtless never sated. This bodes well in general for another Caesarian project, but makes it difficult to stand out in such an eye-catching crowd.

This is not yet another biography of Julius Caesar. We have enough of them already, and anyway, if biography is a narrative of character, I doubt whether we have the necessary material to write one.[6] My interest here is not biographical but historical. What is distinctive about this book, I hope, is that it is founded on a combination of two crucial underlying premises, each of them the result of the development of historical scholarship on the late Roman Republic over the past half-century or so (although this analytic work has not always been well represented in the synthetic narratives that continue to be produced), and each of them still somewhat controversial. These are, in brief, the following: (1) that the Roman Republic was not an "oligarchy," as was so long supposed as a matter of course, but a participatory republican political order in which the People were partners with the aristocracy not only in steering political events but, more fundamentally, in determining what the Republic was and should be (which entails further that Cicero, whose voice has tended to shape not only our views of the dominant narrative of the Late Republic but even of the nature of the Republic itself, can hardly be taken to speak for the Roman People, or even for senators as a whole); and (2) that the teleological perspective that (often insidiously) dominates our narratives of both the "fall of the Republic" and that of Julius Caesar's political career is deceptive, and should be consciously challenged at every step. My hope and expectation in undertaking this project, which has proven so much more time-consuming than I originally imagined, is that a careful review of a selection of the key moments in Caesar's political career – many of which have become so encrusted by the standard teleologies and traditional interpretations of the late-republican crisis that it is difficult to see them in a new light – will yield a substantially new picture of this most controversial of ancient Roman historical figures. It should also cast light on the crises of his day, and on the beginning of the series of civil wars that would eventually transform the "Republic" into the "Empire."

Let us briefly review these premises.

---

[5] Ashrafian and Galassi 2016.

[6] Peter Brunt, whose undergraduate lectures I was lucky to attend in the early 1980s, was fond of pointing out that Cicero was the only Classical figure whose biography, in its full sense, could be written: Brunt 1988: 89.

The so-called democracy debate sparked by Fergus Millar's provocative articles of the 1980s is still percolating through scholarship and has not reached a definitive new orthodoxy.[7] Few have been convinced by Millar's classification of the Roman Republic as "a form of democracy," though of course the argument is bedeviled by the difficulty of defining this procrustean concept in a way that is acceptable to all. However, prevailing opinion among scholars over the past couple of decades generally acknowledges that popular participation in deliberation, decision-making, and ideology construction exerted a far more important influence on political events than had been accepted when we ourselves were students and giants such as Ronald Syme and Ernst Badian presided over what J. North facetiously called the "frozen waste theory of Roman politics." According to that conception, which had a stranglehold over the field at least in the Anglophone world until the revolution prompted by Millar, the People, not only in their deliberative function as participants in public assemblies (*contiones*) but also as *voters* who passed all legislation, elected all magistrates, and delivered a verdict in some trials, could safely be left out of the analysis of republican political life because these were regarded essentially as meaningless formalities (not unlike the lopsided and often near-unanimous "votes" that occur in many authoritarian and totalitarian regimes) whose outcome was determined elsewhere by coalitions of nobles and other powerful senators.[8]

It can fairly be said that this "theory" is dead, but consensus has not settled upon a replacement. On one hand Karl-Joachim Hölkeskamp accepts the broad freedom of Roman voters from formal relationships of dependency (e.g. the famous patron-client system) but still sees politics as dominated by the aristocracy, and therefore fruitfully explores *how* the Roman nobility won the "willing obedience" of the citizenry by projecting an image of meritocracy, wisdom, and success that produced a general consensus in favor of noble, even

---

[7] Millar's classic articles are now collected in Millar 2002, esp. 109–182; his Jerome Lectures (Millar 2002) offer something of a synthesis. The strongest reactions have been those of Hölkeskamp 2010 (although as noted in the text that follows he too shaped an important strand of contemporary scholarship on the Republic, giving special impetus to the swing toward "political culture") and Mouritsen 2017, defending and elaborating on his objections presented in Mouritsen 2001. For the main elements of the view presented here see Morstein-Marx 2004, with further development in 2013, 2015; also see the important, largely complementary work of Yakobson 1999, 2006, 2010, 2014, as well as Wiseman 2009. This is not of course a bibliography of the "democracy debate" as such, which has continued to generate contributions from leading scholars to the present.

[8] North 1990: 278: "Its implication was that voting behavior in the assemblies could be regarded as completely divorced from the opinions, interests, and prejudices of the voters themselves. In form, the popular assemblies still existed, but at least by the second century B.C., when we begin to have some limited grasp of the social conditions within which it was operating, power had been wholly taken over by an all-powerful oligarchic elite."

"oligarchic" domination of the Republic.[9] Henrik Mouritsen, however, min-imizes the political role of the citizenry, interpreting the popular assemblies not as actual decision-making bodies but as smallish groups of "Roman gentlemen" enjoying the perks of their leisure by listening to speeches and voting, and predisposed to ratify whatever the promulgator of a bill put in front of them in "a highly formalised and carefully choreographed ritual."[10] This is not the place to engage in detailed rebuttal; for my purpose here, it will suffice to point out that if the senatorial elite enjoyed the kind of "domin-ation" that Hölkeskamp supposes, or had the kind of stranglehold on voting assemblies that Mouritsen believes it did, then we should not be able to count more than thirty occasions between 140 and 50 BC on which voting assem-blies forced through "popular" legislation in the teeth of a strong senatorial consensus.[11] Clearly, the People in their constitutional aspect were hardly so deferential and submissive as many scholars have supposed. "Fear of the

[9] Hölkeskamp 2010 is a good entry point in English to that scholar's body of important work on Roman political culture, which may be explored further in Hölkeskamp 2004 and 2017 (summar-ized in English by Elkins 2007 and Eberle 2018).

[10] Mouritsen 2017: 61, 72, 68, and see the whole discussion of the assemblies as "consensus rituals" (following E. Flaig) at 58–72. Cf. p 72: "Most likely, comitial participation was considered a natural part of the lifestyle of the Roman gentlemen who frequented the Forum on a regular basis. When a bill was to be ratified, they probably obligingly performed their civic duty and spent some hours in the voting pens, conversing with their *tribules.*" Mouritsen's views about the "elite" character of the audiences of *contiones* and *comitia* were originally proposed in Mouritsen 2001, esp. 38–62. For criticism see Morstein-Marx 2004: 11–12, 128–136; Yakobson 2004: 203–206; Jehne 2006: 229–232.

[11] Morstein-Marx 2013: 39–42. Obviously I do not accept Flaig's and Mouritsen's interpretation of the voting assemblies as mere "consensus rituals" (see already Morstein-Marx 2004: 124). This fails to take into account that although the final vote on legislation was probably quite predictable come voting day, this was only because a bill that failed to win strong support in the crucible of numerous *contiones* over the three preceding weeks was thereby proven to be very likely to fail at the polls (or to be withdrawn beforehand). While this in a sense transfers the moment of decision to prior *contiones* rather than the actual vote, without the expectation of an upcoming decisive vote those *contiones* would not have the significance that they often did. Similarly, the presidential veto in the United States – also the final stage of the legislative process but one whose influence hangs over the congressional deliberations that precede it – is rarely used: only 3 percent of bills passed by Congress are vetoed even when the body is controlled by the opposing party. This is obviously not because the president's signature is automatic, ritualized, and therefore unimportant, but because the likelihood of a presidential veto has shaped Congress's deliberations all along, and there is usually little point in the cumbersome process of shepherding a bill through both houses if it is known in advance that the president will veto it. The lopsided proportion of signed versus vetoed bills would, taken in isolation, be utterly misleading evidence of the relative (un)importance of the presidential veto. Returning to Rome, while it is evidently true that a Roman bill was unlikely to survive long enough to be voted down by the assembly if it was not backed by the kind of overwhelming popular support that would predictably result in a favorable vote, this was not exactly unheard of: see the four known examples from the latter half of the second century listed by Mouritsen 2017: 59, plus Plin. *HN* 7.117 for another possible case in 63 (but cf. Cic. *Sull.* 65). Given the scarcity of detailed evidence about failed bills specifically (presumably less likely to be reported) and more generally about the fate of bills between promulgation and voting day, this does not seem to be a negligible number.

People" was a well-known and quite effective phenomenon in the Late Republic, not infrequently prompting the Senate despite its own objections to take action in the People's interest, or preventing it from opposing their will.[12] It was in fact long-established practice, validated by historical traditions such as the fifth-century Secessions of the Plebs, that the Senate ultimately had to yield to a sufficiently strong expression of the will of the sovereign People.[13]

I argue therefore for a nuanced conception of popular engagement in which senators were largely deferred to as experts in the running of the state (what one might call passive acquiescence by the plebs) but, when senatorial and noble failure became salient (e.g. during the Jugurthine and Cimbric Wars of the end of the second century, or again, during the rise of piracy and resurgence of Mithridates in the 70s and 60s), the voting citizenry was often aroused to action, checking (perceived) senatorial incompetence and arrogance and imposing its will on fundamental decisions of war-making as well as legislative remedies for (perceived) domestic problems.[14] Moreover, entirely in keeping with Polybius's tripartite model of this fundamentally divided political system, members of the political elite elected to executive magistracies might themselves break ranks with their social peers in the Senate and turn to the power of the popular assemblies when it seemed expedient, or right and just, for them to do so.[15] These observations suggest a complex model of popular participation in the Roman Republic in which periods of relative quiescence, during which the popular assemblies largely deferred to the superior political wisdom (as it seemed) of their senatorial leaders, might be promptly succeeded by others of "insubordination" and "course corrections" imposed by the voting assemblies, led and often prompted by individual members of the political elite who, usually only temporarily, dissented on

---

[12] Morstein-Marx 2019.

[13] In pursuit of this end even "sedition" was defensible: Cic. *De or.* 2.199 (M. Antonius speaking): *neque reges ex hac civitate exigi neque tribunos plebis creari neque plebiscitis totiens consularem potestatem minui neque provocationem, patronam illam civitatis ac vindicem libertatis, populo Romano dari sine nobilium dissensione potuisse.* Cicero himself had echoed Antonius's validation of popular "sedition" by reference to the Secessions: Cic. *Corn.* I frs. 48–49. In a famous chapter of the *Discorsi* [I.4] Machiavelli picked up on the idea from a different source: Livy, like Cicero, hardly a revolutionary firebrand. On the People's sovereignty, see n. 23.

[14] See Morstein-Marx 2015: 303–307, where I adjust my earlier emphasis on the ideological domination of the Roman aristocracy through its control of political speech (idem 2004: esp. 279–287) – no doubt a key reason for the usual quiescence of the Roman People during routine times – in order to accommodate the not uncommon instances in which the People, though typically rather deferential to aristocratic leadership, were roused to force major "course corrections" by means of their votes.

[15] This is of course the great truth expressed by Polybius's much-criticized tripartite model of the Roman "constitution," which otherwise tends to be represented in our sources (e.g. Sall. *Cat.* 38–39, *Jug.* 40–42) as a bipolar system consisting of Senate and People.

an ad hoc basis from the majority of their peers and superiors in the Senate. This dynamic bears more than a passing resemblance to the role of voters in today's relatively passive indirect (representative) democracies and republics, and some of the crises the Late Republic underwent therefore bear more than occasional similarities to some of the crises of "democracy" in our own age, making the Roman Republic arguably a more fruitful model for study by modern theorists than the "glories" of ancient Athens.[16]

Along with the thawing of the "frozen waste theory" and the new emphasis now put on the interventions of the popular assemblies in republican politics has come renewed attention to its ideological content, especially the speeches by which political leaders mobilized popular support and the values, principles, and goals that animated such speeches and therefore, presumably, at least in part motivated their audiences to act. T. P. Wiseman has rightly lamented a long, twentieth-century tradition of suppressing "the ideological content of republican politics," though in fact this way of thinking was largely spent by that century's end.[17] In this book I treat ideological issues both at the level of the individual bill or decree (Should there be an agrarian distribution? Should Caesar be recalled from Gaul?) and at the level of higher "constitutional" norm or principle (e.g. Where is the ultimate locus of decision, Senate or People? Must powerful senators be brought down to preserve "the Republic" and defend against *dominatio*?) to be central to the crises of the Caesarian age.

Since I have gone on record diagnosing an "ideological monotony" in the Late Republic this may seem to call for some clarification. The phrase "ideological monotony" was meant to express the demonstrable fact that "a nakedly 'optimate' stance was in straightforward contradiction with the *contio* as a rhetorical setting" but "*not* that all speakers sounded and behaved interchangeably when they climbed onto the rostra."[18] It emphasizes the narrowness of the range of ideological positions that was brought specifically *before the People* and characterizes somewhat negatively the

---

[16] According to Flower's disarticulation of "the Roman Republic" into six republics, the last of which (in her scheme) *ended* in 60 BC, the Roman Republic was not actually a republic any longer by the 50s (2010: 149), which also happens to be the only period for which we have copious contemporary evidence for the actual workings of the Roman Republic. I do not think this view is defensible on a normal conception of a "republic." On Flower's experiment in periodization see esp. Yakobson 2011: 155–156, and North 2010: 472.

[17] Wiseman 2009: 32. See (along with Millar's seminal works cited in n. 7) already Beard and Crawford 1985: 68: "Roman accounts of politics in all periods, but particularly the age of revolution ... systematically present political conflict as being about 'real issues,' about access by the people to the rewards of conquest and the creating of the political means to achieve this end."

[18] Morstein-Marx 2004: 239; 2013: 42–43. For criticism of the idea, which some others have embraced, see Tan 2008, Arena 2012: 79, and now esp. Rosenblitt 2016. Cf. Tiersch 2018 for another approach.

quality of public political argument, for an honest critique of *popularis* principles was essentially excluded by the circumstances of public deliber- ation. It expresses the fact that "popular" political values and principles went largely unchallenged in the public deliberation in the open Forum that led to decisive votes, which on one hand helped to sustain and reinforce *popularis* ideology, but on the other shifted the gravamen of debate from the public good (relatively uncontroversial) to a question of trust.[19] Yet none of this is meant to imply that there was no serious political argument or contestation in the public Forum, much less within the walls of the Senate. On the contrary, when we have evidence that laws were passed by the People, I assume (unless there are good reasons to the contrary) that a vote of the popular assembly does reflect a conscious choice by voters, not determined but at least informed by arguments that had been made to them, although of course voters were subject to all manner of rhetorical manipulation, and furthermore the institutions themselves were far from transparent mediators of the popular will.[20]

Thus I take seriously the popular perspective on the Roman Republic as revealed by their votes and imposed by the People in the form of laws and electoral choices.[21] And it is evident above all from those numerous occasions when a senatorial consensus was *rejected* by voters in the assembly that these "People" mobilized to impose their will not only where their material benefits were at issue (e.g. grain or land distribu- tions) but where the People's political rights (e.g. the rights of tribunes or the citizen's "due process" right of *provocatio*) were at stake, or corres- ponding constraints on the power of the Senate (e.g. the reassignment of command of major wars). The very fact alone that these latter categories of strongly supported "popular" proposals outnumber that of material benefits by a ratio of about two to one bespeaks a politically conscious voting population rather than an impoverished and easily manipulated proletariat interested only in "handouts."[22] In word certainly, and often

---

[19] Morstein-Marx 2004: 204–240.

[20] Morstein-Marx 2004, 2015. But scholars have tended to exaggerate the undemocratic features of the popular assemblies themselves: see esp. Yakobson 1999: 20–64; Morstein-Marx 2013: 32, 37–39.

[21] On the many meanings of "the Republic" see Hodgson 2017 (esp. pp. 46–60 on the "popular" perspective) and now Moatti 2018, whose semantic history of the concept reveals how it was co- opted as an anti-popular instrument by Cicero and other members of the elite. (Moatti 2017 gives an English summary.)

[22] Full argument and evidence presented in Morstein-Marx 2013; cf. 2019: 529–532. The very coherence of the principles involved in this body of "popular" legislation further suggests that it was not simply the wholesale creation of elite politicians jockeying for power (2013: 40–41) – that is that assemblies simply voted for whatever was put before them (Mouritsen 2017: 61, 66), as the elitist interpretation would have it.

in deed, the People were the final arbiters of political decision, using their votes to have the last word on legislation and (almost exclusively) choosing the magistrates and generals to lead them. In this specific sense we may call them "sovereign": even Cicero proclaims before the Senate that the Roman People "held supreme power in all (political) matters."[23] We should finally shed the antiquated notion that a politician's "popular" (*popularis*) stance responding to the interests and needs of the Roman People was in itself fundamentally at variance with the values and traditions of "the Republic."[24]

Something more radical follows from this. Manifestly there are moments in the political narrative of the last two centuries of the Roman Republic when we sense the opening of a yawning gap between what one might loosely call "senatorial" and popular perspectives on the very norms and proper functioning of the Republic: consider, for example, the sharp and fundamental difference between Cicero's oft-expressed view of the Gracchi brothers as subverters of the constitution who were justly struck down without any need for legal authorization and the "popular" one of those voters who flocked from "all Italy" to cast their ballots on the agrarian law, or

---

[23] Cic. *Har. resp.* 11: *populus Romanus, cuius est summa potestas omnium rerum.* Cf. (in a specifically electoral context) *Planc.* 11: *Est enim haec condicio liberorum populorum praecipueque huius principis populi et omnium gentium domini atque victoris, posse suffragiis vel dare vel detrahere quod velit cuique.* Cic. *Rep.* 1.39.1: *res publica res populi.* Cf. Liv. 25.2.7, 38.36.8; App. *Pun.* 112 (see pp. 11f.). The principle thrice cited by Livy that *quodcumque postremum populus iussisset, id ius ratumque esset* (7.17.12, 9.33.9, 9.34.6) is however probably only a principle to determine the validity of overlapping or conflicting laws, "not a general statement of popular sovereignty" (Crawford et al., *RS* 2.721, Tab. XII.5). For sharp criticism of some scholars' inclination to characterize this as "popular sovereignty" (if used technically, a modern concept anyway) see Hölkeskamp 2010: 12–22 with earlier literature cited at 13n6; also Mouritsen 2017: 15–21 (cf. Lundgreen 2011: 259–272); more favorably, see Straumann 2016: 119–129 and cf. Morstein-Marx 2004: 120n11. As will be clear from Morstein-Marx 2013, I think Hölkeskamp and Mouritsen go too far, overlooking the clear implications of the historical record of 140–50 BC (and before) while exaggerating the practical effects of the various forms of (mostly religious) obstructionism available to the Senate and magistrates. But this argument would usurp too much space here and must be reserved for another occasion.

[24] Morstein-Marx, forthcoming, where it is also noted that the assertiveness of the *populus* is by no means restricted to the Late Republic. (The plebiscites authorizing Scipio Aemilianus's consular election and takeover of the African command take the pattern back to 148, and earlier instances are by no means rare (*lex Flaminia de agro Gallico* of 232 BC, *lex Claudia de nave senatorum* of 218 BC, *lex Valeria* on full citizenship for Formiae, Fundi, and Arpinum of 188: Elster 2003: nos. 77, 83, 156). On *populares*, see Yakobson's recent summary in the *OCD*, with bibliography (2017). Classic discussions include Meier 1965, Seager 1972, and Mackie 1992. Robb 2010 concedes too much to their enemies by glossing the term as "*seditiosi*": see Yakobson 2012 and now Tiersch 2018: 62. Gelzer's description of *populares* in his classic biography of Caesar (first published 1921), clearly shows its age: "The populares sought to achieve a majority in the popular assembly. With this support they intended to replace the Senate and to govern the state from the Forum. In constitutional form, the magistrates were no longer to receive their instructions from the Senate, but to become the servants of the sovereign people" (1968: 14).

those who defaced the Opimian Temple of Concord with a *graffito* characterizing the slaughter as an "act of madness," or those who set up shrines at the locations where the two brothers were murdered.[25] Why should we assume the superior representativeness or legitimacy of Cicero's view, if the Roman Republic was composed not just of "the Senate" but also "the People of Rome" (*Senatus Populusque Romanus*), especially given the recognized primacy of the People in any matter on which they voted? If political legitimacy is ultimately and practically determined by society as a whole rather than a narrow elite, the popular conception of how the Republic worked and was supposed to work appears in fact to have the better historical claim to dominance, however philosophically superior Cicero's more elitist or even Cato's outright oligarchical views might be.[26] This will have obvious implications for our assessment of the clash between Caesar and Bibulus in 59, or the dispute over Caesar's *ratio absentis* that brought on the Civil War.

Correspondingly, the understanding has gained ground over the past couple of decades that Cicero cannot be regarded as the arbiter and touchstone of all things "republican." Late-republican Roman history from about 66 to 43 is often referred to as the Age of Cicero, not without reason. The nearly one thousand letters, fifty-eight speeches, and numerous political, rhetorical, and philosophical essays that come down to us from the pen of this towering figure of Latin literature cast into shadow virtually all of other sources for this period, mostly much later biographies and historical narratives (Plutarch, Suetonius, Appian, all imperial), and even those are frequently influenced by the record Cicero left behind. (Sallust departs our story early with his Catilinarian Debate, but in any case his account of that crisis is itself strongly colored by the Ciceronian tradition.) The only other substantial contemporary source, the war *Commentaries* by Caesar himself, are tightly focused military narratives that, though of extraordinary interest due to the identity of their author, usually only indirectly cast light on events in the capital (with a few, often problematic exceptions). It is impossible to escape entirely the shadow that Cicero casts over the history of this period. Yet we must try.

Here I am thinking not so much of the obvious distortions created by Cicero's personal perspective from a distinct locus of time and circumstance

---

[25] Plut. *Ti. Gracch.* 8.10; *C. Gracch.* 17.9, 18.3. On the graffiti, see Morstein-Marx 2012 and Hillard 2013.

[26] Morstein-Marx 2011: 276–278 and n. 30. To my mind, Drogula 2019 characterizes Cato's political leanings too readily as "traditionalist"; as will become more apparent in Chapters 3 and 4, I consider them *un*traditionally radical and reactionary. His attempt to restrict and redefine traditional military honors such as *supplicationes* and triumphs is similarly untraditional: Segal 2019: 165–226.

that was hardly representative of senators as a whole – that is that he was
a "new man" (*homo novus*) whose standing rested not on noble heritage,
military achievements, or awesome *auctoritas* but upon his eloquence and his
canny political leadership as *consul togatus* in the crisis of 63, subsequently
"betrayed" by the "optimates" whose savior he styled himself to be, sent into
humiliating exile by a tribune and the Roman People for his violation of law
and tradition, later a committed advocate of peace, even of accommodation
with a victorious Caesar, and finally a zealous defender of the morality of the
assassination and leader of a powerful attack against Caesar's first potential
successor. Such a brief résumé alone gives a hint of the specificity of the
Ciceronian perspective and how questionable it can be to extrapolate from his
many lamentations (or exultation) over current events to senators as a whole;
attentive readers of Cicero's letters will be familiar with how remarkably
closely Cicero's pronouncements about the "ups and downs" of the
Republic (mostly downs) track the vicissitudes of his own personal
fortunes.[27] More fundamentally, however, scholars have often been inclined
to adopt Cicero's perspective on the very nature of the Republic itself as if in
such matters he could speak for his entire society. But it should give us pause
to consider for a moment just how dubious it would be to do the same with
a modern politician's views, even those of an eyewitness participant possessed
of commanding authority such as Winston Churchill, not to mention lesser
figures who have nevertheless put their stamp on an age (e.g. Margaret
Thatcher or Ronald Reagan). Cicero may fairly be thought of as, on the
whole, a moderate senator, as is shown by his arguments in the *De legibus* in
support of "popular" institutions like the tribunate or the (mostly) secret
ballot, or his strenuous efforts to mediate the looming crisis of the Caesarian
Civil War. Yet the Roman Republic was "the Senate and People of Rome"
(*SPQR* – a formula interestingly inverted in its first two epigraphic appearances in the second century BC), and an important implication of the
resurgence of the People as a political agent in recent scholarship (as described
earlier in this chapter) is that the job of defining the nature or norms of the
Republic cannot properly be left to senators alone.[28] Scholars raised on

---

[27] Hodgson 2017: 105–162 traces Cicero's rhetorical self-identification with the *res publica* from the
consular orations to the late 50s. See, for example, *Red. pop.* and *Red. sen.*, passim; *Dom.* 73–76,
96–102; *Sest.* 136–147; *Prov. cons.* 2–3, 13–14, 45, and most interestingly, the retrospective exculpation
of Pompey and Caesar at *Fam.* 1.9.11–14. Griffin and Atkins 1991: xiii, rightly comment that Cicero's
talk of the "loss of the Republic" tends to be "an exaggerated way of expressing disappointment with
its present condition" (more or less identical with *Cicero's* present condition).

[28] *ILLRP* 514, lines 6–7; *AE* 2006.624. Cf. Polyb. 21.10.8. Moatti 2018: 260–269 (cf. 2017: 40–48)
provides a valuable review of the history of the formula, noting that it does not appear to be formally
fixed until Augustus.

Cicero's doctrines of senatorial hegemony, the common people's deference to their betters, and the need from time to time for the state's "defenders" to eliminate trouble-making demagogues by means of extralegal violence if necessary, may think it quite natural to equate "the Republic" with "dominance of the Senate," but what portion of politically active Roman citizens – the audience of the *contio*, urban political crowds, and voters – would have agreed with them?[29] We should be careful not to ascribe to an entire body politic a clear consensus on such matters. The voice of the Roman People too must be heard, which was not always in harmony with Cicero's.[30]

One of my objectives in writing this book has been to show how a proper integration of the popular perspective into an account of Julius Caesar opens up the possibility of critique and revision of the canonical picture both of the man and of the final years of the Republic that has developed over the years. No longer should the classic Ciceronian-senatorial analytical frame of Caesar's career be adopted as *the* "republican" view, as has been done so frequently, with inevitable distortion of key disputes such as that about the validity of Caesar's consular legislation or his claims and demands in 50–49. Once one internalizes the idea that the "republican system" was in essence an equilibrium of elite power holders policed by defenders of the Senate's authority armed with a dazzling array of obstructionist weapons it is no great step to interpret the rise of Caesar as an existential danger to that system. Instead, I would urge us to be receptive to an alternative, more popular view (but not, perhaps, for all that alien to most senators): that the "republican system" itself traditionally rested upon the community's proper allocation of honor (*honor* also in Latin, or *dignitas*), an essential part of the system of rewards and punishments that Polybius back in the second century had called "the bonds by which alone monarchies *and states* (πολιτεῖαι) are held together."[31] The People's exclusive right to confer honor was the engine that drove the republican "meritocracy," and in such matters they were sovereign. We are told that when the consuls tried to block a popular wave of enthusiasm to elect Scipio Aemilianus consul for 147 although he was some five years below the legal minimum age and at the time only a candidate for aedile, "the *demos*" (the People) cried that "by the laws handed down from

---

[29] Important recent work on the fundamental principles that animated the Roman Republic includes Arena 2012 (with some caveats sounded by Morstein-Marx 2014 and Steel 2014a) and Straumann 2016: 23–145.

[30] Morstein-Marx 2009: 115–117; 2011: 276–278, 2013; 2015: 303–307; forthcoming. Wiseman 2009.

[31] Polyb. 6.14.4–5: "For where discrimination of this kind happens not to be recognized or is recognized but handled badly, nothing can be administered rationally; for how is it right for the good and the bad to be held in equal honor?" Cf. 6.14.9: "The People give offices to the worthy – the finest prize of excellence in political life." See Morstein-Marx 2009.

Tullius and Romulus the People were the judges of elections, and ... they could set aside or confirm whichever they pleased of the laws pertaining to this matter."³² (A tribune followed up with a threat to deprive the consuls of the power to hold an election unless they "joined with the People [εἰ μὴ σύνθοιντο τῷ δήμῳ]," at which point the consuls and the Senate folded their hand and gave in.) Similarly, from the "popular" republican perspective, laws of the Roman People that deeply touched their interests could not simply be overruled by a senatorial decree, as notoriously occurred when Cicero executed the "Catilinarian" conspirators – an act illegally authorized by the Senate and legitimately punished by the tribune P. Clodius five years later.³³ An attempt such as this one to interpret Caesar as a republican leader necessarily entails taking the popular element of the Roman republican system seriously. The disinclination to do so in the past has inevitably tended to narrow the scope of interpretation of Caesar's political interventions, implicitly trivializing them from the outset as nothing more than demagogic machinations rather than as responses (typical in principle for Roman elite actors) to the perceived needs and demands of Roman voters, shaped by traditional norms to which virtually all Roman citizens subscribed to a greater or lesser degree.³⁴

As will be evident from my emphasis thus far on voters and voting, the "people" I am speaking of in this book are "the People" as a constitutional agent (hence the capitalization) – that is the people who showed up to vote in the assemblies to elect the magistrates who would lead them and pass the laws that would bind them: Polybius's *demos* or Sallust's and Cicero's *populus* or *plebs*, a variable and complex collective correspondingly difficult to define more precisely in sociological terms.³⁵ Unlike, for

---

³² App. *Pun.* 112/531 (148 BC): ἐκεκράγεσαν ἐκ τῶν Τυλλίου καὶ Ῥωμύλου νόμων (kings, to be sure, rather than noted "republicans," but authoritative foundational figures) τὸν δῆμον εἶναι κύριον τῶν ἀρχαιρεσίων, καὶ τῶν περὶ αὐτῶν νόμων ἀκυροῦν ἢ κυροῦν ὃν ἐθέλοιεν. Elster 2003: no. 202, pp. 425–426; see now Lundgreen 2011: 75–78. Similarly, Scipio Africanus is said to have declared, when his candidacy for the aedileship was being blocked (in this case by tribunes) because he was not yet of the required age, that "If all citizens want to elect me aedile, then I am old enough!" Livy 25.2.7, with Beck 2005: 335–336. Chapter 2, p. 60ff.

³³ Tatum's meticulous examination of Cicero's expulsion (1999: 151–166) gives (to my mind) too little emphasis to the crucial principles of law and popular rights involved that made this such an explosive issue.

³⁴ The crucial step was taken by Wiseman 2009, 2016, although his picture of Caesar is surely too uncritical. Stevenson 2015 strikes a better balance.

³⁵ There is ongoing argument over who exactly were "the People" represented in our accounts of *contiones* and voting assemblies. For *contiones* see Morstein-Marx 2015: 297 with references. Since laws in this period were typically passed by the tribal assembly, whose structure did not correspond to the timocratic bias characteristic of the centuriate assembly (on which see Yakobson 1999: 20–64), we may assume they plausibly reflected the preferences of the mass of Roman citizens who cast their

instance, the paradigmatic *popularis* politician P. Clodius, Caesar is not known to have possessed an organized urban network that he could mobilize to dominate the streets, the Forum, or the assemblies.[36] Caesar's following, if he had one in a strict sense rather than simply enjoying "popular favor," is therefore impossible to analyze in the kind of fine-grained detail that has been done with Clodius's "gangs." On some occasions it is apparent that he enjoyed substantial support from distinct sectors of society (e.g. the urban plebs or the soldiering class, townspeople, and councilors of Italy), and this will be duly noted in what follows, but in general it should be understood that "the Roman People" most often referred to in this book are the anonymous mass of Roman citizens below the senatorial and equestrian levels of society whose political role was expressed most commonly and significantly in the assemblies of the city of Rome, but also as citizen soldiers and townspeople of Italy on those occasions when they became significant determinants of political events.[37] I do not intend to imply here that the Roman People generally, or in any of these instances, thought and acted as one, and in fact I have written elsewhere of the "fundamental indeterminacy of the Popular Will," with specific reference to the confused immediate aftermath of Caesar's assassination before reflections on the traumatic events

vote. Mouritsen has rightly stressed the statistical "unrepresentativeness" of the voting assemblies relative to the entire citizen body, who resided (after 90) along the whole length of the peninsula (2001: 18–37, 2017: 55–58), but this does not disprove the impression gained from our sources that votes in the legislative assemblies still broadly reflected reasonably well the preferences of the mass of Roman citizens in the city and its immediate environs. It is clear that the results not infrequently conflicted with the majority view of senators, and the relative coherence of the content of "popular" legislation apparently reveals the social distinctiveness of the voters (Morstein-Marx 2013). Since one had to be in or travel to Rome in order to vote, the urban-rural balance of voters is likely to have varied greatly depending on which segments of the citizen population up and down the peninsula were directly touched by the bill under consideration; however, the exclusion of citizens who lived out of the City has in the past tended to be exaggerated. This matter deserves deeper investigation on another occasion, but in the meantime consider the obvious implications of, for example, Cic. *Att.* 1.1.2, *Phil.* 2.76; Hirtius, [Caes.] *B. Gall.* 8.50.2–4.

[36] On Clodius's urban organization based on tradesmen and workmen's groups as well as neighborhood associations centered on the cult of the *Compitalia* (*collegia* and *vici*) see Tatum 1999: 25–26, 117–119, 142–148, and Harrison 2008: 110–116; Courrier 2014: 509–533. On the *vici* see also Lott 2001: 28–60. See Chapter 9, n. 186 for Caesar's suppression of the "new" *collegia* as dictator and other anti-Clodian measures.

[37] For the constituents of the urban plebs, no doubt frequently but not necessarily the dominant element in the assemblies (n. 35), see esp. the rich recent study of Courrier 2014, who discerns a multilayered differentiation of social and economic circumstances behind the stereotyped elite representation of the urban "masses," at the top of which stood a relatively well-off *plebs media*, "not entirely plebeian, imperfectly aristocratic," which formed "a keystone for the entire system" (739); this elite of the urban plebs is likely to have played an important political role in the *contiones* and assemblies of the City. I. Harrison 2008 briefly offers a version of the darker picture that prevailed until recently.

reached a tipping point.[38] It may be possible in the future to develop a more sociologically nuanced analysis of Caesar's constituencies among the varied populations of Roman Italy than is found here, but at present it is often impossible to avoid speaking in rather general terms if we wish to trace the role "the Roman People" played in Caesar's political career.

A second guiding principle of this book is a strong skepticism toward the temptations of teleology and its twin sibling, hindsight. "Historians know the verdict in advance," wrote Ronald Syme, "they run forward with alacrity to salute the victors and chant hymns to success."[39] Nowhere is this professional vice more frequently in evidence than when scholars discuss the end of the Roman Republic. Erich Gruen kindled a firestorm of criticism in 1974 with his carefully crafted argument in *The Last Generation of the Roman Republic* that, contrary to what had been taught for centuries, Rome's political system was not on its deathbed in 50 BC.[40] Michael Crawford responded caustically with a review entitled "Hamlet without the Prince":

> It is precisely the possession of hindsight which is one of the distinguishing characteristics of the historian. It is only in the light of what happened and in the course of an attempt to explain what happened that some earlier events emerge as important and some as trivial.[41]

He has a point. Yet doubts also linger when we ponder Syme's "hymns to success." Ernst Badian responded to the Hegelian coloring of C. Meier's *Caesar* with a thought experiment:

> If some ... mistakes had not been made, and if the luck of the game had been different, the *res publica* would have been saved at that [sc. Caesar's] time, and quite possibly for a long time. We might have had scholars telling us today that the structure of the *res publica*, or mere fate, made it impossible for monarchy to be installed at Rome, however hard men like Caesar, who with all their genius did not see this, tried to do so.[42]

Is this obviously wrong? Can the explanatory power of history really depend essentially on however things turn out, which would seem to reduce it to a circular "just-so story"?

Though far from Rome, it is worth contemplating an actual case where within three decades the "verdict of history" reversed itself more than once.

---

[38] Morstein-Marx 2004: 151 and later in this volume (Chapter 9, p. 572f.).   [39] Syme 1958a: 1.435.
[40] Gruen 1974. See n. 77 of this chapter.
[41] Crawford 1976: 214. David Stockton nodded his assent: "Wisdom after the event is something which historians ought to exercise" (1977: 216).
[42] Badian 1990: 39.

England's first great republican political theorist, James Harrington, published his thinly veiled utopia, *Commonwealth of Oceana*, in 1656, during what would come to be known as the Interregnum, seven years after the execution of Charles I and the abolition by the "Rump Parliament" of both the monarchy and the House of Lords; but as fate or chance would have it, this was only three years before the stunning return of the Stuart heir from France. Harrington explained that crucial changes of the "balance" of property holding in England precipitated by the decline of the feudal nobility and the dissolution of the monasteries under the Tudors constituted the key cause of the Civil War by rendering England unfit for monarchy but ripe for a commonwealth:

> *The dissolution of this government caused the war, not the war the dissolution of this government* [italics original] ... Oceana [Harrington's fictitious name for England] ... must have a competent nobility, or is altogether incapable of monarchy. For where there is equality of estates, there must be equality of power; and where there is equality of power there can be no monarchy ... The balance of Oceana [i.e. between monarchical and popular government] changing quite contrary to that of Rome, the manners of the people were not thereby corrupted, but on the contrary fitted for a commonwealth.[43]

Harrington had shown, he believed, that "the dissolution of the late monarchy was as natural as the death of a man ... wherefore it remains with the royalists to discover by what reason or experience it is possible for a monarchy to stand upon a popular balance; or, the balance being popular, as well the oath of allegiance as all other monarchical laws imply an impossibility, and are therefore void."[44] He went so far as to predict that if the monarchy were restored in England it could last only a few years.[45]

"Until well into the winter of 1659–60" – that is three years after the publication of *Oceana* – "a betting man would have put money on the continuation of the revolution and of the exclusion of the monarchy," writes a leading scholar of the Revolution, Blair Worden.[46] But the Commonwealth crumbled with stunning swiftness and Charles II returned from exile in France the very next May. Twelve "commissioners" who had signed the death warrant for Charles I were hanged, drawn, and quartered,

---

[43] Harrington 1656/1992: 56, 60, 61, 62. Interestingly, Erich Gruen's well-known dictum, "Civil war caused the fall of the Republic, not vice versa" (1974: 504), seems to echo (while inverting) Harrington's formula italicized in the text.

[44] Harrington 1656/1992: 62.   [45] Hammersley 2012: 545, with 548n53.

[46] Worden 1994: 132. Yet historians still tend to frame the story as one in which "various factions [acted] out the hopeless endgame of the interregnum before an inevitable monarchical restoration" (Foxley 2013: 175).

while Harrington himself was thrown into the Tower. (Though soon released, he descended into madness and ill health which plagued him until his death in 1677.) The speed and astonishing ease of Charles's return and acceptance as king "made most men believe," the pious Earl of Clarendon later averred, "both abroad and at home, that God had not only restored the king miraculously to his throne, but . . . in such a manner that his authority and greatness would have been more illustrious than it had been in any of his ancestors."[47] Contemporary royalist historians, Clarendon among them, saw the Stuart Restoration as nothing less than a manifest example of Divine Providence – God's verdict in favor of "divine right" absolutism – with obvious implications for their interpretation of the fall of Charles I and the Interregnum.[48]

Yet the reorientation of "history" to fit the eventual outcome was not yet finished: the manifest "course of history" turned out to depend on where one decided to stop the clock. After the "Glorious Revolution" of 1688 put an end to the Stuart line (definitively, as it would turn out), and with it "absolute monarchy," Harrington's arguments could be "revised . . . to fit the new circumstances."[49] So in 1700 the Whig thinker John Toland, publisher of Henry Neville's *Plato redivivus* along with Harrington's *Oceana*, could claim in his preface that the very doctrines Harrington had invoked to demonstrate "that England was not capable of any other Government than a Democracy" were now employed by Neville "to the redressing and supporting one of the best Monarchies in the World, which is that of England."[50] And with the ultimate triumph of the Whigs in the eighteenth century it became perfectly evident for all with eyes to see that the events of 1688 had demonstrated the practical necessity of "limited monarchy" in England. "By deciding many important questions in favour of liberty, and still more, by that great precedent of deposing one king, and establishing a new family, it gave such an ascendant to popular principles, as has put the nature of the English constitution beyond all controversy," wrote David Hume, concluding his famous *History of England* in 1778.[51]

The important lesson for us appears to be that *historical outcomes* cannot supply straightforward retrospective verdicts about the relative weight of

---

[47] Clarendon 1857: 2:268.   [48] MacGillivray 1974: 220n72; Sharpe 2013: chapter 1, esp. 56–68.
[49] Hammersley 2012: 545.
[50] Toland 1700/1737: 551. Neville's latent republicanism shows through often enough to suggest that his "deference [to the regime] is a matter of presentation, not of substance" (Worden 1994a: 148). On Toland's own questionable commitment to the idea of a "limited monarchy," see Worden 1994a, esp. 182–183.
[51] Hume 1778/1983: 6:531. To be sure, Hume had earlier noted that "all human governments, particularly those of a mixed frame, are in continual fluctuation" (5:160).

the various causes that conduce to them. As Jonas Grethlein has pointed out recently, historical outcomes themselves also have a troubling way of changing their significance depending on *the viewer's vantage point in time*: a change of *telos*, or end point, retroactively changes the *teleology*.[52] But how, without begging the question, can a development substantially posterior in time – by years, perhaps by decades, conceivably by centuries – retroactively change the causal structure of an event or process in the past? All that has changed is the point of perspective. And to the objection that one simply *knows more* about that causal structure as time passes (as the "significance" of an event supposedly becomes more evident), what independent evidence would exist to show, with any degree of real conviction, that this newfound "significance" is not itself merely an artifact of the change, just as a river that has jumped its banks and settled into a new course soon makes the new path it has cut the "natural" one to all appearances? Once the state of the world is changed by an event in an important way (say, for the purpose of argument, the assassination of Caesar), causal chains stretch out from that event that appear to lock it in place – not necessarily because of some inherent quality of the event itself, but perhaps rather because *what has happened after it* is causally dependent on it, in what is already a different state of the world.

Like the modern historian Niall Ferguson, then, I would take a leaf from the physicists' "chaos theory" (for not even the scientists believe any longer in Laplacean determinism) and see history, in particular the history of events, as essentially "chaotic" in nature.[53] Although the physical world remains deterministic in theory (twenty-three stab wounds still kill Caesar), in practice historical events are extremely sensitive to slight variations of initial conditions. As I wrote these words, a striking example came in the *New York Times* obituary of Stanislav Petrov, perhaps the most

---

[52] Grethlein 2013: 6–9, aptly adducing how the early twentieth-century history of Germany changes depending on whether one takes as one's vantage point the economic crisis of 1929 or, alternatively, the Holocaust.

[53] Ferguson 1997, the preface to a volume on *Virtual History*, traces the intellectual history of the determinism debate and espouses a new kind of "chaostory" integrating the fundamental insight from physical chaos theory that even deterministic causation must still leave irreducible unpredictability in outcomes "even when successive events are causally linked" (p. 79). Walter dismisses what he calls "a postmodern chaos theory opening up space for arbitrary choice according to fashion" (Walter 2009: 33). But the deterministic underpinning of chaos theory actually is antithetical to postmodern "fashion": it does not subvert the common understanding of causation, undermine causal analysis, or reject an objective standard of truth. See also now Powell 2013, an entire volume devoted to hindsight and counterfactuals in the history of Greece and Rome, and Gallagher 2018, a history of "the counterfactual imagination" whose rich introduction provides a thought-provoking entry to the debate.

important person most of us have never heard of. On September 26, 1983, Petrov, then a forty-four-year-old lieutenant colonel in the Soviet air defense forces and duty officer at the Serpukhov-15 early warning center, prevented a nuclear war between the United States and the USSR when, five minutes short of the expected time of detonation, he decided that the satellite warning of an incoming missile strike by five Minuteman ICBMs received by his command center outside Moscow was *probably* (!) due to a systems malfunction. "The false alarm was apparently triggered when the satellite mistook the sun's reflection off the tops of clouds for a missile launch."[54] (The story itself was not widely known until it was revealed in a 1998 memoir by the former commander of Soviet missile defense.) To return to Caesar: if Mark Antony had not allowed himself to be turned aside at the door, if brave Marcius Censorinus and Calvisius Sabinus had been more successful in defending Caesar, or if the single death wound identified by his physician Antistius had not met its mark, does anyone really think subsequent history would have been essentially the same?[55] Or, to take a negative example, during the rout of Caesar's men at Dyrrachium in 48, if the panicked soldier who nearly killed Caesar as he tried to rally him had not been intercepted by a bodyguard, can anyone doubt that the course of history afterward would have been substantially different, perhaps drastically so?[56] In historical events, as in chaotic physical processes, a slight variation in initial conditions at particularly delicate moments can produce wildly divergent results, and since those slight variations in initial conditions can hardly be controlled, predicted, or in historical contexts even fully known, we call them "chance." And "chance" in this sense manifestly can have a powerful influence on history. Thus, as Syme suggests in the quotation with which I began this section, the fact that something happened does not mean that it had to happen ("the most elementary teleological error," observes Ferguson), or even that it was *most likely* to happen.[57] There is irreducible contingency in history, and it would actually be a serious *distortion* of history to fail to give it its due.[58]

---

[54] Sewell Chan, *New York Times*, September 18, 2017: www.nytimes.com/2017/09/18/world/europe/stanislav-petrov-nuclear-war-dead.html.

[55] Antony: e.g. Cic. *Phil.* 2.34 (other sources listed by Pelling 2011: 479). Censorinus and Sabinus: Nic. Dam. *Bios* 96, with Toher 2017: 354. Antistius: Suet. *Iul.* 82.3.

[56] Plut. *Caes.* 39.6–7: "Caesar was very nearly killed"; at App. *BCiv.* 2.62.258 the man is a standard-bearer, perhaps supported by Caes. *BCiv.* 3.74.1.

[57] Ferguson 1997: 79–90 at 87.

[58] Walter's stimulating essay on "'Chance and Contingency'" (2009) is now fundamental. I believe my characterization of "chance" differs not in substance from his definition of "Zufall" but only in my emphasis on the inscrutability of actual causation to the human observer.

Whether ultimately for good or ill, humans seem almost "designed" by evolution to overlook chance's role in precipitating events and the developments that unfold from them.[59] We are instinctive pattern seekers and tend to make sense of the world through *stories* – that is narratives – even (especially?) very simple or hackneyed ones, with characters whose motivations we feel we can understand, and which string together in a "meaningful" way the relatively few facts we actually have. "The confidence that people experience," comments the Nobel Prize-winning psychologist/behavioral economist Daniel Kahneman, "is determined by the coherence of the story they manage to construct from available information ... It is the consistency of the information that matters for a good story, not its completeness."[60] Narratives are (obviously) constructed on what we happen to know, not on what we don't: Kahneman and his longtime collaborator Amos Tversky dubbed this heuristic *WYSIATI*: "What you see is all there is."[61] We know the end point (the *telos*) that the narrative seeks to explain; in seeking an explanation, we naturally sift through the known prior facts, casting aside those that don't conduce to the chosen *telos* and seizing upon those that do. Furthermore, these facts have often *already* been selected by a process of cultural memory precisely because of their supposed explanatory power in reference to the stipulated *telos*. At each of these stages, those contingencies that *might have been* with equal or greater probability than what actually happened are trimmed off, so to speak, and lost to scrutiny, creating a narrative that is psychologically satisfying but logically circular. Kahneman pithily comments, "Our comforting conviction that the world makes sense rests on a secure foundation: our almost unlimited ability to ignore our ignorance."[62]

---

[59] "Almost" because, although sometimes vulgarly understood as itself a teleological process, evolution (not to be confused with "social Darwinism") is in fact antiteleological because it refuses to presuppose any ultimate outcome.

[60] Kahneman 2011: 87.   [61] Kahneman 2011: 85–88.

[62] Kahneman 2011: 201; see the whole discussion at 199–221. The problem of narrative in the forensic realm has received considerable attention by legal scholars: see Bennett and Feldman 1981; Brooks and Gewirtz 1996; Amsterdam and Bruner 2000; Meyer 2014. On the narrative fallacy, see also Nassim Nicholas Taleb's engaging bestseller *The Black Swan: The Impact of the Highly Improbable* (2010: 63–64), whose first edition was published in 2007 with implausibly perfect timing, just before the unpredicted market crash of 2008. In an anecdote that touches upon the point I am making here, Taleb describes the historical reading he did in his youth seeking refuge in a basement in Beirut during the first phase of the Lebanese Civil War. Familiar with the great works of the philosophy of history by Hegel, Marx, Toynbee, Aron, and Fichte that postulated a "logic" of history, a direction, Taleb found himself more influenced by William Shirer's *Berlin Diary*: "The journal was purportedly written without Shirer knowing what was going to happen next, when the information available to him was not corrupted by the subsequent outcomes." Readers of this book will think of Cicero's letters, an invaluable resource for precisely this reason.

Kahneman's disconcerting observation must be kept in mind when historians, as we inevitably will, protest with Crawford that hindsight is *necessary* in order to explain and understand the significance of events or changes. Historians as a class have a deep-seated "aversion to contingency" precisely because it threatens to undermine what we are after all trying to do – that is to *explain* the causes of things.[63] Knowing what happened afterward is indeed a very useful clue. But historians are not always humble in the face of what *we don't know* about the various causal strands in play in immensely complex interaction – of "our almost unlimited ability to ignore our ignorance" in typical WYSIATI fashion. Take, for instance, the almost universal opinion (so it seems) of experts that although the Caesarian Civil War of course did not *have* to break out in 49 (why not in 48, or 45, or 42?), still *some* such cataclysmic event would necessarily have brought down the Republic within a few years anyway.[64] I do not think anyone could really claim to know this with confidence or certainty. What we do know is that in 49 a civil war began that, in addition to whatever damage it wrought in itself, began a cycle of tightly linked civil wars that persisted – intermittently, but with great violence – for nearly two decades, including extraordinary traumas such as the assassination on the Senate floor, by men whose lives and fortunes he had spared, of a man whom many, perhaps most, living Romans thought of as one of the greatest heroes in their history; two battles on the Macedonian plain between two of the largest Roman armies ever assembled (some two hundred thousand legionaries); in Italy itself the proscription of perhaps three hundred senators and *equites* and the slaughter of many of them as they tried to escape; a revolt against the Triumvirs' expropriations, then Perusia starved into surrender, burnt (apparently by one of its own citizens), and its leaders subjected to savage reprisals.[65] Institutions do not run by themselves; they are animated by civil norms which rarely survive civil war (in itself the most extreme violation of civil norms imaginable) without crippling damage.[66] "War is a harsh teacher," and the civil wars of 49–31 appear quite sufficient in themselves to destroy the Roman Republic as a constitutional order – or to

---

[63] "Aversion of the historian to contingency": A. Heuß, cited by Walter 2009: 33. Wilhelm von Humboldt wrote of "the universal striving of human reason toward the annihilation of chance" (ibid., 36). See also Jehne 2009a: 147.

[64] See most recently Jehne 2009a, with a refinement of Meier's theory of an unstoppable "autonomous process" (esp. pp. 144–149; cf. Jehne 2006: 7–9). This serves as a kind of rebuttal to Walter 2009 in the same volume. Cf. Bleicken 1998 for a classic "political-structural" explanation of the "fall of the Republic."

[65] The whole tragedy is well told by Osgood 2006, with brilliant use of triumviral poetry to illuminate its psychological effects.

[66] On institutions and constitutional norms, see further Chapter 10.

transform it into something else.[67] Those who insist that the Republic could not have long survived even had the civil war of 49–45 not occurred overlook the tight causal nexus that binds that war with those that followed over the twenty-odd years to come – in particular, the violent emotion unleashed by Caesar's assassination under conditions that encouraged vengeance by Caesar's veterans, supporters, and heir – and to fall back on what seem to me to be entirely debatable counterfactual arguments of their own to defend their claim that the Republic's institutions and norms *would have failed* shortly (perhaps within a generation or so) even without the Twenty Years' War.[68] (The counterfactual mode seems inescapable even for those who shun counterfactual history.)

"Do not use this argument to avoid trying to learn from history," warns N. N. Taleb, quite rightly.[69] Hindsight is often invaluable; the danger is one of unreflective, simplistic reliance on hindsight, not that it is necessarily, inevitably deceptive. What is required above all is careful attention to those counterfactual possibilities (those, that is, of which we become aware: many, perhaps most, will be "submerged" below our vision) that suggest very different outcomes, and a healthy skepticism about the "grand narratives" that are often constructed on too little evidence in the usual WYSIATI fashion. In other words, we should always be prepared to exercise salutary skepticism against what may appear to be simply obvious. In fact, the unique nature of history, rooted in an unrepeatable past, *requires* us to be especially alert to the "alternative histories" that might have spun out from small changes in initial conditions (typically a human decision of some kind). The fact that historical inference (at least about events and their causes and consequences) cannot be tested against repeated experiments as is routine in the natural sciences means that the *only* test of our inferences will often be the care and sometimes the caution with which we assess the probability of outcomes different from the one that in fact ensued.[70]

Here a fraught methodological problem arises: if we allow consideration of counterfactuals, then what limit exists to control our most fanciful

---

[67] Βίαιος διδάσκαλος: Thuc. 3.82.2.

[68] See e.g. Jehne 2009a: 158–159, who also cites in support the alleged absence outside the "upper class" and especially the senatorial order of any strong interest in maintaining the traditional form of the Republic – a claim I dispute in what follows, pointing first to our recently heightened appreciation of popular participation in the political life of the Republic generally, then to the popular support manifested for legislation dear to the hearts of the Roman plebs in 59 and 58, later the widespread support for Caesar's (hardly revolutionary) claims at the outbreak of the civil war, and finally the manifest displeasure of the urban plebs with his arbitrary removal of the tribunes in 44, to name perhaps the most telling instances.

[69] Taleb 2010: 120; cf. 84 and the digression on history at pp. 195–200.

[70] Similarly, Walter 2009: 44–45, citing an essay of Max Weber.

speculations? Ferguson argues that to make an intellectually respectable basis for entertaining counterfactuals we should limit ourselves to those that are in fact considered in our evidence.[71] But this seems too limiting even for Ferguson's own argument, and applying this standard to ancient history would surely be too arbitrarily restrictive since the source material is so lacunose.[72] This would be to make counterfactual inferences too heavily dependent on the often arbitrary survival of evidence: they would spin out almost solely from the letters of Cicero. Counterfactuals such as "What if Cato in 62 to 60 BC had not simultaneously alienated both Pompey and Caesar as well as the *publicani* (publicly contracted tax gatherers) and their advocate, Crassus?" or "What if Bibulus had not resorted to an unprecedented theory of obstructionism against Caesar in his first consulship?" seem to me to be perfectly acceptable scenarios to contemplate, though I know of no ancient source that happens to attest explicitly to these alternatives. Counterfactual scenarios should indeed be limited to those that can be reasonably defended as realistic alternative possibilities – usually a human decision that evidently, given all our surviving evidence and our always incomplete knowledge of circumstances, might very well have gone the other way. Some of the charm of ancient history perhaps resides in the greater freedom granted to its practitioners not merely as a courtesy but of necessity.

More serious consideration of historical contingency as an antidote to our pattern-making instincts may help to put the whole story in a new light. A thought-provoking example from another historical period is Ferguson's rebuttal of the "hindsight bias" of traditional accounts of the outbreak of World War I. Today "everyone knows," it seems, that World War I was inevitable, a result of the entangled system of alliances that bound the major belligerents inescapably to war once the spark was applied

---

[71] Ferguson 1997: 86: "We should consider as plausible or probable *only those alternatives which we can show on the basis of contemporary evidence that contemporaries actually considered.*" (Author's emphasis.) This of course implies that "we can only legitimately consider those hypothetical scenarios which contemporaries not only considered, but also committed to paper (or some other form of record) which has survived – and which has been identified as a valid source by historians" (p. 87).

[72] Ferguson's own argument: "By narrowing down the historical alternatives we consider to those which are *plausible* – and hence by replacing the enigma of 'chance' with the calculation of *probabilities* – we solve the dilemma of choosing between a single deterministic past and an unmanageably infinite number of possible pasts. The counterfactual scenarios we therefore need to construct are not mere fantasy: they are simulations based on calculations about the relative probability of plausible outcomes in a chaotic world" (1997: 85). But "plausible" historical alternatives need not be only the ones explicitly acknowledged by authoritative sources. If, however, plausible historical alternatives can also be ones reasonably *inferred* on the basis of persuasive evidence (as, apparently, in Ferguson's argument about the stock market and World War I [see n. 73]), then we are in agreement.

by the assassination of Archduke Ferdinand. In such a frame, naturally, one takes more interest in the tangle than the spark. Yet, like today's nuclear deterrence, the point of the entanglement was precisely to prevent war. In a paper published in 2006 Ferguson asked why the bond market, which like other financial markets was highly risk-averse, was much less affected by the acceleration of the war crisis in summer 1914 than one would think if war was seen as truly imminent by lots of very smart people with skin in the game.[73] The answer must be that the risk of a major European conflict was generally perceived as low, controlled precisely by the system of alliances. "War, when it broke out in the first week of August, 1914, did indeed come as a surprise even to well-informed contemporaries. It was not the long-prophesied Armageddon depicted in so many histories."[74] As Ferguson and later C. Clark pointed out, the tangle of alliances was no "Doomsday Machine": the Austro-Hungarian Empire's aggressive response depended on the signals it received from Germany; Germany might, if better informed or less eager for a showdown, have assessed more accurately Russia's likelihood of intervening to defend its Serbian "brothers" on largely sentimental grounds; Serbia's government, by rejecting Austria's ultimatum, gambled everything on Russia's willingness to face a war with two major European powers; Russia's efforts at the very last moment to avoid the armed conflict with Germany that would result are well known; and so on, right down to the question whether Britain would, when the stakes were so high, truly honor its alliance with France or actually throw itself into the conflict if Belgium's neutrality were violated.[75] Ferguson and Clark move us away from a largely impersonal "structural" explanation of the outbreak of the war to one that stresses specific human decisions – human choices – made under conditions of radical uncertainty. It was not inevitable that a Balkan conflict would fail to be contained as earlier ones had been but would instead explode into a catastrophic world war. "Mistakes were made," and what in retrospect seems so notable is not how decision makers were trapped in a prison of their own making but how eagerly most of them embraced war as a solution.

To return at last to Rome, probably few today would still be so influenced by the impersonal, deterministic paradigm as to agree with Baron Montesquieu's famous dictum: "If Caesar and Pompey had thought like

---

[73] Ferguson 2006. See also Ferguson 1999, esp. chaps. 1–5.   [74] Ferguson 2006: 72.
[75] Ferguson 1999; Clark 2013. "I will not be responsible for a monstrous slaughter" was Tsar Nicholas II's comment upon receiving an anxious telegram from his cousin Kaiser Wilhelm II on July 29, prompting him to countermand the decision for general mobilization – only temporarily, as it turned out (Clark 2013: 512).

Cato, others would have thought like Caesar and Pompey; and the republic, destined to perish, would have been dragged to the precipice by another hand."[76] But Erich Gruen's controversial judgment that "Civil war caused the fall of the Republic, not vice versa" now no longer seems as radical as it once did.[77] Gruen's battle against the distortions of hindsight was timely, coinciding broadly with growing rejection of the nineteenth-century scientistic assumptions that had dominated hitherto. This is not the place to offer a résumé of the problems of the transformation of the Roman Republic, which demand to be revisited now that views of the nature and political culture of the Republic have significantly changed.[78] For the purposes of this introduction it is enough to say that this book is written in the spirit of Gruen's great work in the sense that it proceeds from profound philosophical skepticism toward the oft-repeated claim that the end of the Republic was imminent and inevitable. None of this is to deny preemptively that one could construct a plausible argument that various destabilizing conditions (periodic institutional dysfunction and frequent political violence, rural poverty, and powerful armies filled by supposedly disaffected peasants under the control of fairly unconstrained generals) made an imminent, serious explosion in 50–49 BC possible, if an occasion for serious political conflict supervened.[79] My point is simply that this should not be lazily assumed on the obviously fallacious principle of "what happened had to happen," but proven by better empirical arguments, which I think despite Gruen's challenge has still not actually been done.[80] In the meantime, it remains an open question whether the transformation of the Republic into

[76] Montesquieu, *Considerations*, chapter 11.

[77] Gruen 1974: 504. See Walter 2009: 28–31 for a review of more recent German scholarship that aligns well with Gruen's basic perspective (Baltrusch, Welwei, Girardet, Botermann, and, it seems, Walter himself). Contra, however, Jehne 2009a in the same volume).

[78] A brief synthesis in Morstein-Marx and Rosenstein 2006. Flower 2010 is to my mind too formalistic an exercise in historical periodization (see n. 16).

[79] The past two decades have been especially fertile for scholarship on demography and the agrarian question in the Late Republic, together with their effect on rural economy and society, in particular the state of the peasantry that supplied manpower to Rome's armies. The debates may be traced through Rosenstein 2004, De Ligt and Northwood 2008, Roselaar 2010, De Ligt 2012, and Kay 2014. The bibliography is extensive, the findings highly controversial, and at this time of writing they cannot be said to have yielded firm conclusions that would affect interpretation of the causes of the Caesarian Civil War (see Chapter 10, p. 605f.). Against the common, related assumption that late-republican legions were little more than quasi-mercenary "private armies" bound mostly by personal loyalty to their commander, see already Gruen 1974: 365–384, and the cautions expressed by Brunt 1988: 257–259; more recently, Morstein-Marx and Rosenstein 2006: 630–633; Keaveney 2007: 16–35; Morstein-Marx 2009 and 2011. See further Chapter 9, n. 190.

[80] Morstein-Marx and Rosenstein 2006: 629–635. Further bibliography in Walter 2009: 27–28n2. I note again that this book does not purport to resolve this much larger problem, but, I hope, to contribute to the debate.

the Empire is more meaningfully attributed to the ravages of twenty-odd years of nearly continuous civil war, as suggested earlier in this chapter, than to any inherent weaknesses of those institutions before the cycle of civil war began in January 49.

The Civil War itself is often treated as a nearly inevitable consequence of Caesar's tumultuous first consulship in 59 – yet, if we are going to trace the roots of that traumatic conflict so far back, it is more plausibly seen not as the result of systemic failure but of the aggressively inept prior decision by Marcus Cato to take up an uncompromising "scorched-earth" line of opposition against not just Caesar (a relatively minor figure at the time), but simultaneously against Pompey the Great at the zenith of his power and influence.[81] Even so, as this book will show, numerous opportunities to prevent the explosion that came in January 49 were rejected by those intent on a violent confrontation; Cicero and the many senators who to varying degrees sought to resist the "rush to war" demonstrate that there was nothing inevitable about it. Nor can we assume that the Caesarian Civil War of 49–45 irreparably harmed the Republic rather than the much more atavistic descent into blood vengeance unleashed by the treacherous, savage killing of Caesar on the Senate floor by his friends and those whose lives he had spared. Moral outrage made this a particularly potent fuel to drive cycles of bloodshed.

A second teleology that scholars have found even more irresistible (and neatly intersects with the first) concerns Caesar's own career and goals. Syme's comment about historians "knowing the verdict in advance" is doubly true, and doubly dangerous, for any student of Gaius Julius Caesar. The conception of Caesar as an aspiring autocrat who spent his life scheming to achieve that goal has over the centuries achieved something like the status of a cultural archetype (it is commonplace to compare US presidents to Caesar – with the intent to damn, not to praise them), and like all archetypes, this construct is hard to get out of our heads even as we approach the sources with what we feel is an open mind. As nearly all people think they know (and have thought they knew since the beginning of republican political theory), Caesar "marched on the Republic" and is widely held responsible for destroying it, while his heir and great-nephew Octavian is often seen as having completed his project of transforming the state into a stable autocracy.[82] The biographical tradition of Plutarch and Suetonius – both writing a century and a half after the fact, when the

---

[81] Drogula 2019: 107–127.
[82] See e.g. Machiavelli, *Discorsi,* 1.10, 1.17, 1.29, 1.34, 1.37, etc. See Christ 1994; Baehr 1998.

"verdict of history" had shaped their very world – expressed what would prove to be a highly influential teleology according to which Caesar was seen as seeking autocracy from the very beginning of his political life.[83] On this view, the end determines the beginning, rather like Tacitus's notorious portrait of the emperor Tiberius but without the dissimulation. This teleology dovetails perfectly with the other story about the "fall of the Republic," which in its traditional version assumes that the Republic "had" to fall about now, with monarchy as the only viable "solution." In fact, they reinforce each other, for Caesar is made to "see" the Republic for the anachronism it was and to strive actively to realize the necessary monarchic solution. A more recent twist on this old line has been to accept the former proposition but to deny that Caesar had any specific solution.[84] And while it is true that contemporary scholars have been much less disposed to tell Caesar's story as if its ending sets the goal toward which everything before it tends, I suggest that only by making full use of the revival of the "republican" paradigm in the study of the Roman Republic that has taken place over the past few decades can we banish the ghost of the old teleology.

A notorious utterance put in Caesar's mouth by the imperial biographer Suetonius illustrates how difficult it is to extricate ourselves from the deeply entrenched view that he was at some point (before or after the Civil War) frankly committed to the suppression of the Republic: "The Republic [or 'a state'?] was nothing, a name without substance or form" (*nihil esse rem publicam, appellationem modo sine corpore ac specie, Iul.* 77). This shocking statement (and Suetonius certainly means it to be shocking) is often solemnly quoted by first-rate scholars as a kind of revelation of Caesar's innermost thoughts: Matthias Gelzer, for example, ended his great biography with the quotation and a reflection on it, and nearly all modern biographers find the saying irresistible even as they acknowledge reservations about its authenticity.[85] Others have devoted considerable ingenuity to decoding what Caesar actually meant.[86] But we need to ask a more basic question: Who reported the alleged statement? Suetonius in this case happens to tell us, and the information turns out to be extremely relevant: T. Ampius Balbus, ultimately one of Caesar's bitterest enemies, a known adherent of Pompey and his legate in the Civil War whose partisan

---

[83] See Chapter 2.   [84] Meier 1982.

[85] Gelzer 1968: 333. Biographers: e.g. Canfora 2007: 138; Billows 2009: 283n7; Stevenson 2015: 171.

[86] Most notably Morgan 1997 – a brilliant tour de force which carries little conviction because it treats Ampius as an honest witness. Morgan rightly observes that the meaning of *res publica* is not restricted to a "republican political system" or "the (Roman) Republic" (see e.g. Cic. *Rep.* 1.39–44), which in itself undercuts the "anti-republican" interpretation that is often placed on the utterance.

pamphleteering (presumably around the beginning of the conflict) was so strident that it earned him the epithet *tuba belli civilis*, "war-trumpet of the Civil War."[87] In 46, the date of our last good evidence (a letter to him from Cicero), Balbus was hoping for Caesar's pardon, having now turned to a safer, laudatory variety of literary activity; it is likely that one followed soon thereafter.[88] Whether Balbus's purported revelations (he is not known ever to have been close to Caesar) were published in a kind of propaganda tract during the outbreak of the Civil War or, as some think, only after Caesar's assassination, it should be clear that no real weight should be given to this allegation by a notoriously outspoken enemy.[89] There was a lively market in slander and invective about the powerful in late-republican Rome. Caesar proved to be a specially attractive target, but not even Cicero was spared denunciations such as "tyrant," "king," or "butcher."[90] Scholars of ancient rhetoric have learned not to take this kind of thing literally and we should too.[91] Perhaps biographers and historians have been so taken with the Caesar quotation because it fits their preexisting conception of the man – which it then, circularly, buttresses. Once that interpretation of the man is itself in question, however, it can offer no independent support or illumination.

This book offers a different view: that Gaius Julius Caesar saw himself, and was seen by many if not all of his contemporaries, as a great *republican* leader – a powerful combination, as Rome had seen before especially in the Scipiones, of patrician pedigree, "popular" politics, and stunning military achievement, with values and goals consistent with ancient republican canons of *virtus, dignitas,* and *gloria,* who measured himself and was

---

[87] Cic. *Fam.* 6.12.3. Pompey's support for his failed consular bid and trial in 55: Cic. *Planc.* 25; Schol. Bob. 156 St; Cic. *Leg.* 2.6. We lose the scent of his civil war activities after 48 (*Att.* 8.11B.2, Caes. *BCiv.* 3.105.1), but unlike many other Pompeians his pardon did not come until late in 46 (Cic. *Fam.* 6.12; cf. 13.70 and Chapter 8, #61). This suggests some special offense that set him apart, and from Cicero's letter it seems evident that this must have been connected with his having served as the *tuba belli civilis*. See also *FRHist* no. 34; also see Chapter 9, n. 218.

[88] Safer literary activity: Cic. *Fam.* 6.12.5: *in virorum fortium factis memoriae prodendis.*

[89] Morgan 1997: 24, likes the idea that Ampius wrote only after Caesar's assassination, but since we know he was blowing the war trumpet for the civil war and that he had earned that title before 46, there seems to be no good reason to deny that the notorious phrase belongs then. It is tempting but fallacious to associate one piece of evidence with another (i.e. Ampius's further, perhaps simultaneous allegation that Caesar said it was stupid of Sulla to lay down the dictatorship and his assumption of the *dictatura perpetua* in February 44: see Chapter 9, n. 218) simply because they would go well together.

[90] Suet. *Iul.* 49–50, preserves a precious sampling of the anti-Caesarian invective tradition. On Cicero, see Cic. *Dom.* 75; *Sest.* 109; *Vat.* 29; *Sull.* 21–22; cf. *Phil.* 2.12–19; [Sall.] *Inv.* 3, 5–6; Dio 46.1–28.

[91] See Nisbet's wry remarks on the tradition (1961: 192–197); see Craig 2004, with lists of invective topoi.

measured by his contemporaries against models of leadership *in the past* rather than yet-unknown forms of autocracy that lay in the future (or, more precisely, in at least one of the indeterminate possible futures: the one that actually occurred).[92] Everyone will probably agree that Caesar possessed exceptional talents – he was an exceptional general, an exceptional speaker, even an exceptional writer, and by all accounts an exceptionally attractive personality, friend, perhaps even lover – but we should not suppose, for all these qualities, that he enjoyed a unique historical standpoint outside his time and place in the story of the Republic, exceptional foresight into the "course of history" and the imperial future, or an unconscious grasp of the movement of the Hegelian *Weltgeist* to give birth to "an independently necessary feature in the history of Rome and of the world."[93] Those who find it difficult to square Caesar's ultimate elevation to the "Continuous Dictatorship" shortly before his assassination with a pre–Civil War career dedicated to distinguishing himself as a republican leader might ponder the even more paradoxical trajectory followed by Oliver Cromwell in and after the English Civil War. An unexceptional Member of Parliament for the borough of Huntington, Cromwell would become the military leader of the armies of Parliament against the king's violation of the traditional English "constitution," eventually see to his execution, and die, shortly after refusing the crown, as Lord Protector of the Commonwealth of England, Scotland, and Ireland – virtually an absolute monarch. He professed an apparently quite sincere Puritan conviction that he had at every turn acted according to Divine Providence, but it is perfectly clear that he had not contemplated the removal, much less the execution, of the king, not to mention his own replacement of that monarch (though not as "king"), much before those events actually confronted him.[94] Events have their own logic and open up possibilities that had never been contemplated, and would probably have been vehemently rejected beforehand.

In general, as the criminal courts do, in this study I have tried to be as resistant as I am able to "character evidence" – that is the very human tendency to feel we *know* somebody's character traits well enough to treat

---

[92] Many great scholars before me have led the way for substantial portions of this book. I wish to note especially the debt of "my Caesar" to Erich Gruen (esp. 1974, 2009), Kurt Raaflaub (1974), Hinnerk Bruhns (1978), and, despite our divergence on many crucial points, Martin Jehne, with his large body of important work on Caesar, beginning with his still-fundamental dissertation on "'Caesar's State" (1987a). I have also often found myself in broad agreement with the approach of Zecchini (2001). Of recent biographies in English, Billows (2009) takes a comparable view but goes astray by overemphasizing Caesar as a "party man" of the "*populares.*"

[93] Hegel 1847/2001: 44.   [94] See Bennett 2006; Gentles 2011.

that acquaintance as evidence in its own right when we interpret that person's actions. People often feel they know Caesar quite well: an example, more explicit than most but not entirely unrepresentative, is Ridley's suggestion that we can be sure, "if we know anything about his personality," what would be Caesar's choice among the alternatives he faced before crossing the Rubicon.[95] One suspects that "we know" this because in fact that is what happened. But there is a good reason why the Common Law places such tight restrictions on "character evidence": what we think we know about the character of a person who is not our intimate may be nothing more than prejudice, or wrongly inferred from the result, or – in the context of historical study – a *communis opinio* so long established that it seems hardly open to question. We must not, I insist, allow assumptions about Caesar's "natural" inclinations, which are so easy to draw from hindsight and are inevitably but fallaciously colored by his assumption of the "permanent dictatorship" shortly before his assassination, to guide or determine our interpretations of his many actions and decisions over the two decades (roughly) that preceded that moment.

Much as I would like to establish a definitive new interpretation of Caesar as a historical figure, a more realistic goal for what follows would be to induce my readers to join me in a kind of thought experiment whose purpose would be to prompt a radical rethink by removing the encrusted patina of a hoary dominant narrative so persistent and enduring that it is hard even to envision any alternative, much less summon the will to challenge it. I hope to dismantle the tired, but still largely dominant dichotomy between Caesar and "the Republic" so that it may become possible to see him more clearly and accurately as a representative of Roman republican traditions of leadership in a regime combining popular power with aristocratic achievement. Caesar offers an illuminating test case for current debates about popular participation and the complex construction of republican legitimacy from popular as well as senatorial perspectives. These debates have been conducted thus far in a somewhat abstract way removed from the course of events; by painstakingly following Caesar's tumultuous career we can put them to a more satisfying empirical test and reveal their explanatory power in a connected series of concrete historical moments.

The focus on Caesar, even in relation to the Roman People, will seem misguided to some. Let me try to reassure them. This book is not a covert

---

[95] Ridley 2004: 152. Jehne 2009a: 142n4, is rightly cautious: "It is debatable how much we know about Caesar's personality." See n. 6 of this chapter.

plea for a return to nineteenth-century "great man history" according to which "all things that we see standing accomplished in the world are properly the outer material result, the practical realization and embodiment, of Thoughts that dwelt in the Great Men sent into the world."[96] Caesar and his political choices are of course very far from constituting the whole story of the transformation of the Roman Republic into the Empire, even of the crises of the 50s and 40s. Yet the experience of our own times may well convince us that men and women with their hands on the levers of power have often managed to wreak enormous havoc with institutions and human lives, and if that is so then they probably have also sometimes done some good. The hopes invested and the passions unleashed in our own national elections appear to prove that on the whole we are convinced that it actually does matter who is put in charge, even though we surely all recognize that deep, impersonal forces create the landscape in which leaders must operate, often blindly. But Julius Caesar played a central role in the crises of the 50s and 40s, and therefore a fresh look at his decisions and actions should cast considerable light on those crises, though it will of course not suffice alone as an explanation. This cannot be, and is not intended to be, a political history of the last two decades of the Republic: the actions of other major players, including his eventual rival Pompey as well as Cicero and Cato, are examined here only where they clearly impinge upon Caesar, and larger or deeper social and economic issues, interesting and important as they are, are subject to the same criterion of inclusion. A full reexamination of the transformation of the Republic (perhaps overdue) would require a much more comprehensive approach than I am able to offer here. Yet surely Caesar's role is an important part of that story, and I hope that when that comprehensive reexamination comes this study will prove useful.

The eight chapters that follow are arranged in a chronological series but are not intended to form a connected biographical narrative. They focus on key *historical* rather than biographical moments that I believe to be central to the interpretation of Caesar as a republican political leader; you will read little or nothing here about his famous capture by pirates or his controversial and paradoxical ("if we know anything about his personality") dalliance with the twenty-one-year-old Cleopatra in Egypt while the die-hard Pompeians regrouped in Africa. Various interesting topics that intersect with Caesar's story must here be laid aside in order to preserve my intended focus: you will have to look elsewhere for an examination of his attitude

---

[96] Carlyle 1911: 1 (lectures delivered in 1840).

and policy toward the Empire and the newly conquered domains east and west, including his many colonial projects, his Gallic or civil war campaigns, his qualities as a military tactician or strategist, his opinions on correct Latin usage or his (often alleged) Epicureanism, or the general topic of religious innovation, including the evolution of ideas about the deification of political leaders.

The book falls fairly evenly into two unequal halves broken by the coming of the Civil War in 50–49. I devote four chapters to each of these halves. In Chapters 2 and 3 I trace Caesar's rise as a patrician senator attentive both to popular and aristocratic traditions of the Republic up through his famous intervention in the Catilinarian Debate and its controversial aftermath; in Chapter 4 I examine his consulship of 59, which is frequently seen as the beginning of the end, setting the Republic on its inevitable course to self-destruction, and in Chapter 5 I turn to his activities in Gaul as seen from the vantage point of the Senate and People in the capital.

The second half of the book revolves around the Caesarian Civil War, whose influence on the fate of the Roman Republic was undeniably powerful if not determinative. First, in Chapters 6 and 7, I examine the development of the crisis that led to the war and the confusing "phony war" in Italy that ensued after Caesar returned to Italy, when despite the notorious "crossing of the Rubicon" it remained unclear for months whether a civil war was truly on. In Chapters 8 and 9 I look at Caesar's actions as leader and victor in the Civil War – first the famous but often misunderstood policy of "clemency," then his actions upon his return to Rome after the conclusion of the civil wars, which most scholars regard as forcefully foreclosing all hope of return to functioning republican government. I shall suggest that Caesar's focus in the months leading up to his assassination was on making the necessary preparations for his imminent Parthian war on an extremely tight time schedule rather than on constructing an autocracy, implicitly abolishing the Roman Republic. But I shall also argue that his preoccupied inattention to growing discontent, at both the popular and the senatorial levels, with the arbitrary actions he took toward this end made him vulnerable to an assassination that was justified, whatever the actual motives of perhaps sixty-odd conspirators, on plausibly "republican" grounds.

Caesar remains a fulcrum in Roman history, the nexus between the two great eras we refer to as "the Republic" and "the Empire." When we study the Republic we always have Caesar in mind as the end point to which we seem to accelerate; when we examine the Empire we are always casting a glance back at his example and precedent. This I believe sufficiently justifies the kind of thorough reexamination offered in these pages. Caesar is deeply implicated in arguments about republicanism and tyranny, and the "fall of the Republic" is often blamed on him. He stirs strong passions even today, which are likely to be provoked by the mildly revisionist spirit in which this book is written and which will grate on some as "apologia." Due to Caesar's centrality in the narrative of the very late Republic, the material that underpins the traditional views is extraordinarily copious, and a large mass of source material is itself buried by the accumulation of centuries of scholarly interpretation. An alternative view of a "republican" Caesar must be built up incrementally over a series of chapters, and I respectfully suggest that readers judge the coherence and plausibility of the whole only once the account is complete.

CHAPTER 2

The Early Caesar

Biographers are especially prone to scrutinize the early life of an extraordinary person for signs of the greatness or evil to come. Teleology comes naturally to the biographical mode and it was particularly congenial to ancient writers with their focus on character, often treated as more or less fixed early in life.[1] So it is only to be expected that the retrospective hunt for signs of future tendency proved highly productive in Caesar's case, magnifying aspects of his activity out of all proportion and even enhancing his importance among his contemporaries to a highly implausible degree. If we want to get closer to the historical reality of Caesar's early career we must accordingly subject all such references to relentlessly skeptical scrutiny, given the questionable historiographical impulse that likely gave rise to them.

Foreshadowing Tyranny

A famous anecdote nicely illuminates the tendency just mentioned and is therefore a good place to begin. In the version told by the Roman biographer Suetonius, writing roughly a century and a half after Caesar's death, Caesar, holding the assizes as quaestor during provincial service in Gades (modern Cadiz), Spain (thus in 69 or 68, when he was about thirty-one), happened to see a statue of Alexander the Great in the famous temple of Hercules/Melqart there. Heaving a great sigh, he expressed his dismay at reaching Alexander's age without yet having accomplished anything comparable. The next night he dreamed of raping his mother; the interpreters claimed that this portended that he would rule the world, inasmuch as the world was "the mother of all."[2]

---

[1] For Plutarch's Caesar, for example, see Pelling 2011: 21–22, 60–61. Gill 1983 issues an important corrective to the frequent modern assumption that ancient biographers and historians were rigidly committed to the idea of an unchanging, inborn *ingenium*, but their inclination remains clear enough.

[2] Suet. *Iul.* 7; likewise, Dio 37.52.2.

The Greek biographer Plutarch, an almost exact contemporary of Suetonius, tells a similar story, but this time Caesar is reading about Alexander's achievements in a book, the moment is transferred to Caesar's next Spanish assignment while praetor fully eight years later, and the incestuous dream is moved to a more meaningful point in Caesar's story: just before the crossing of the Rubicon, itself a crucial step in gaining the personal domination portended by the dream.[3] The ease with which Plutarch decomposes the story and reassigns its elements chronologically tells us something important that should be kept in mind as we approach the whole story of Caesar's early political career – one for which, in contrast to the rest of his life, we are almost exclusively dependent on the information provided by the biographers. Their objective was to reveal their subject's true character, and in doing so it was to them perfectly legitimate to extrapolate from the ultimate outcome to the earliest stages of his public life. Caesar's expression of impatience, exalted ambitions, and dreams of personal domination foreshadow that lust for monarchic power which would drive him to overthrow the "aristocratic" constitution and then cause and justify his death. The theme is struck again and again in the opening chapters of both biographies and gives them their unity and narrative direction.[4] The dominance of this leitmotif raises the suspicion that some actions, remembered and given their significance after the end point of Caesar's life had been reached, have been misleadingly set into a teleological frame or even in some cases manufactured wholesale.

According to Plutarch, Caesar "had sought dominion and power all his days," and it was this "passion to be king" (Plut. *Caes.* 60.1, tr. Pelling) that would ultimately get him killed.[5] This is a lifelong theme, the foundation of Plutarch's construction of the meaning of Caesar's life, and the biographer wastes no time in planting the idea, which appears as early as the third paragraph of the extant work (3.2–3 – curiously both biographies suffer from a lacuna at their beginning) and reemerges repeatedly thereafter in his account of Caesar's early career.[6] Caesar cultivates the multitude by his

---

[3] Plut. *Caes.* 11.5–6, 32.9.

[4] The stories may have originated in the early biography by Caesar's friend and agent C. Oppius: *FRHist* no. 40; Townend 1987; Pelling 2011: 49–50. Caesar's dream falls squarely in the category of "literary" dreams that William Harris, in his recent study of dreams in classical antiquity, considers of highly doubtful authenticity (Harris 2009: 91–122, note esp. his criteria 1, 2, and 5 on pp. 105–106. "It is evident at once that the historical and biographical writers of Greece and Rome are unlikely to provide us with many reliable dream-descriptions").

[5] Plut. *Caes.* 69.1; see n. 1.

[6] Pelling 2011: 21–24. Besides passages cited in the main text cf. Plut. *Caes.* 3.3, 4.6–9, 6.7. Plutarch is so eager to enlist the testimony of Cicero as well (4.8–9) in the matter that he explicitly moves this reference up anachronistically. Cicero later claimed to have become aware of the threat posed by

successful prosecution of corrupt senators, by his easy association with the citizens, and by generous banquets and daily extravagance (4.5–7); by displaying the portrait of the popular hero Marius in his mother Julia's funeral and his generous tribute to his wife Cornelia at her funeral, the first eulogy performed for a young woman (5.2–7); by going deeply into debt to finance improvements to the Appian Way and to put on spectacular shows in his aedileship of 65 (5.8–9). When in that capacity he also restored the splendid triumphal monuments of Marius destroyed by Sulla, some denounced this action as "pursuing tyranny" (6.3 τυραννίδα πολιτεύεσθαι), and the senior consular Q. Lutatius Catulus is said to have declared openly that Caesar was now "no longer undermining the walls of the Republic but trying to take it by storm."[7] His successful election only two years later to the high post of *pontifex maximus*, in preference to Catulus and another high personage many years his senior, made the Senate and the nobles fear that he would lead the People to the utmost recklessness (7.4), evidently resuming that "tyrannical purpose" which has been persistently suggested over the previous chapters.

If we turn again to Suetonius we find an even more strenuous effort to emphasize the theme of "tyranny" from the very start. Similarly to Plutarch, Suetonius states toward the end of the *Life* that ultimately his subject's overreaching *dominatio* justified his assassination (*Iul.* 76.1: *ut et abusus dominatione et iure caesus existimetur*). So the early stage of Caesar's life is made to point relentlessly in this direction from its very start. At the beginning of the preserved text, Sulla prophesies that Caesar will destroy the "optimate" party (*Iul.* 1.3);[8] Caesar rushes home from Cilicia after the death of Sulla and the beginnings of Lepidus's revolt, driven by "hope of new tumult," although in the event he did nothing (3); and Suetonius quotes a short (quite interesting) fragment of Caesar's funeral oration for his aunt in 69 probably not for its antiquarian interest but in order to point up strikingly the presence in the young politician of a combination of royal and even divine aspirations that would ultimately explain both his actions and his doom (*Iul.* 6.1). Next comes the story of Caesar's Alexandrian lament and incestuous dream with which we began this chapter.

The biographer continues to sound the drumbeat. On his way back from Spain, Caesar tries to exploit the aspirations of the Transpadanes for full

---

Caesar already in 63 (Cic. *Att.* 10.4.5 with Shackleton Bailey's n.), but even this is probably only an effect of Cicero's late attempt to link Caesar and Catiline. See in general Strasburger 1938: 45–72.

[7] Plut. *Caes.* 6.6: ἤδη μηχαναῖς αἱρεῖ τὴν πολιτείαν. Strasburger 1938: 68–69 thinks the remark historical: possible, given τὸ μνημονευόμενον (see Pelling 2011 ad loc.).

[8] Plutarch's version of the same scene has only the prediction that he saw "many Mariuses" in the boy (1.4), which Suetonius repeats.

Roman citizenship to stir up disturbance, and *would have* incited them to some act of daring had not the consuls withheld some troops destined for the East to meet the threat (*Iul.* 8); once back in the City he immediately "stirred up bigger things" by joining in a plot to assassinate the consuls (9.2).[9] Once again nothing happens after all, and historians have resoundingly rejected the whole story of the "First Catilinarian Conspiracy" in general, and in particular of Caesar's involvement in a murky pair of conspiracies in 66–65.[10] For us it is enough simply to note the authorities Suetonius cites for the story: the notoriously anti-Caesarian historian Tanusius Geminus, the inflammatory edicts of M. Bibulus, and the elder Curio's invectives – the substratum of an "invective tradition" on Caesar that Strasburger isolated and discredited long ago.[11] However, Suetonius is certainly convinced. Caesar, undeterred (and, be it noted, undetected) continues to seize every opportunity for sedition or seizing power: an *extraordinarium imperium* while only aedile to restore Ptolemy to his throne (*Iul.* 11). Nothing again came of it, however, and Caesar as an aedile can hardly have been more than a pawn in the contest; in any case Suetonius's story is a bizarre conflation of the events of 65 and 56.[12]

What is most notable in this farrago is how many items never actually issued in an observable result that could serve as at least minimal verification of the claim. Allegations of unfilled intentions are the most convenient slanders available against controversial figures (or those, like Caesar, who eventually became controversial). Without further anxiety we can dismiss on these grounds the Lepidan temptations, the Transpadane provocations, the abortive Egyptian adventure, and the "First Catilinarian Conspiracy," whose very existence nearly all recent authorities rightly reject. Suetonius is far from done, however. He continues by citing an alleged attack on the

---

[9] Among them his own cousin, L. Cotta, which Suetonius fails to mention.

[10] On Caesar specifically see already Strasburger 1938: 107–109; Brunt 1957; Gelzer 1968: 39. On the story of the "first conspiracy" generally see Seager 1964; Syme 1964: 86–102; Gruen; *CPh* 64 (1969) 20–24. Canfora 2007: 43–46 revives the old canard, and Billows 2009: 82–84 again refutes it.

[11] See Strasburger 1938: 36–39 on the powerful effect on the tradition of the "early Caesar" (esp. prominent in Suet. *Iul.* 9, 49–51) exerted by invectives (Bibulus, Curio, Memmius, and Dolabella), partisan pamphlets (Ampius Balbus and A. Caecina), and equally partisan histories (Tanusius Geminus), all composed no earlier than 59 and heavily influenced by the events of that year, not to mention Cicero's *De consiliis suis*, disseminated after Caesar's assassination, which contained various explosive allegations linking Caesar as well as Crassus to Catiline (Ascon. 83C; Plut. *Crass.* 13; Cic. 15; cf. Dio 39.10.2–3; Cic. *Att.* 2.6.2, 14.17.6; cf. Sall. *Cat.* 49; Marshall 1974: 807; Moles 1982: 136–137; Rawson 1982: 212–224). Drummond, in *FRHist* no. 44, 1:391–394, suggests that Suetonius relied heavily on Tanusius for his "depiction of Caesar as a restless opportunist of vaunting ambition and arrogance, never deterred by the frequent failure of his schemes or the opposition of his enemies or the optimates."

[12] Cf. Plut. *Crass.* 13 with Strasburger 1938: 113–114; Crawford 1994: 43–56; Drummond 1999: 154–156; Morstein-Marx 2004: 113–114.

authority of the *optimates* by restoring the monuments of Marius, Caesar's encouragement of the prosecution of Sullan bounty hunters for murder (ibid.), his suborning an accuser against the man who had nearly forty years before killed the tribune Saturninus under cover of the Senate's Emergency Decree (*Iul.* 12), and his victory – by means of massive bribery (*non sine profusissima largitione*) – over two extremely powerful competitors in the election of *pontifex maximus* (*Iul.* 13). These last items will be dealt with in due course; I mention them now only to give a fuller demonstration of the pattern.

It must be acknowledged that in ascribing a lifelong lust for domination to Caesar, the biographers were following a first-rate contemporary source: Cicero. When Suetonius reaches the beginning of the Civil War, a key moment in the development of this narrative, he notes that "some thought" Caesar had been looking for a chance to seize *dominatio* since his youth, and he cites in support (*Iul.* 30.5) a passage from Cicero's *De officiis*. Caesar, Cicero writes (3.82), "had conceived the desire to be monarch [or tyrant: *rex*] of the Roman People and master of the whole world – and actually attained his end." Now of course Cicero has a right to his opinion, but judicious readers of Cicero have learned to read his judgments on the rise and fall of the Republic (which coincide strikingly with periods of his own prominence or impotence) with a grain of salt, and likewise I think we should not set too much store by allegations the orator makes long after Caesar's early career, indeed *after* his assassination, about his lifelong pursuit of "tyranny." The comment just quoted, like a similar one in the contemporary *Second Philippic*, is part of a larger Ciceronian discourse of late 44 that pulled no punches in seeking to justify Caesar's assassination retroactively as "tyrannicide."[13] Yet if Caesar's "tyrannical" aspirations were so blindingly obvious during his early career, Cicero could hardly have effusively praised his achievements in the Senate in 56 and 55, defended his alignment with him in his famous, probably semipublic, letter to Lentulus Spinther in 54, or have spoken so glowingly of him in his private comments to Atticus and brother Quintus in the middle and late 50s, even binding himself to Caesar financially by taking out a large loan (HS 800,000) from him.[14] The same reservations apply to Cicero's quoted statement from a now-lost letter to his friend Axius at some

---

[13] Cic. *Phil.* 2.116 *multos annos regnare meditatus, magno labore, magnis periculis quod cogitarat effecerat.* This was the time also when Cicero was preparing for publication, or perhaps indeed published, his scurrilous secret history, the *De consiliis suis*, linking Caesar to Catiline (n. 11); cp. also Cic. *Off.* 2.84, also of late 44, with Dyck 1996: 478–479.

[14] Letter to Spinther: *Fam.* 1.9. Loan: *Att.* 5.1.2, 5.4.3; probably contracted early in 54 (*Q. fr.* 2.11.5).

unknown date after 59 that "in his consulship Caesar had established the
regnum that he had planned while aedile."[15] Yet there is no reliable sign of
such nefarious plans during Caesar's early career. Such statements, then,
may stand as Cicero's eventual judgment of the man, perhaps only after the
Ides of March but possibly at some moment of outrage no earlier than 59,
but they obviously cast little light on the contemporary reality of Caesar's
methodical and hardly hair-raising early steps up the ladder of offices (as
shown in what follows).

Suetonius is also impressed by Cicero's claim, made in the same passage
of the *De officiis* discussed earlier, that Caesar "could never stop quoting"
(*in ore semper . . . habebat*) Eteocles's lines from Euripides's *Phoenician
Women*, "If one must do wrong, it is best to do wrong for the sake of
absolute power, while being god-fearing in all else."[16] If indeed Caesar
"could never stop quoting" these disturbing lines given by Euripides to the
morally objectionable Eteocles, why did Cicero (and everyone else) fail to
bring this up before 44, the date of *De officiis*?[17] As it happens, we know
from Cicero's private correspondence with his friend Atticus that *he*,
Cicero, had this famous Euripidean passage in mind shortly after
Caesar's crossing of the Rubicon – yet he doesn't there claim that Caesar
himself quoted the lines, and the suspicion must be that they were more on
Cicero's mind than on Caesar's lips.[18] Again, little credence is due this kind
of retrojection at best, if not outright partisan fabrication.

Suetonius continues to pour it on. In a much later chapter focusing on
Caesar's supposedly kingly arrogance, he puts on record some notorious
sayings of Caesar's: "The Republic [*res publica*] was nothing, a name
without substance or form," and "Sulla had been an ignoramus [or alternatively, was 'illiterate'] because he had laid down the dictatorship" (*Iul.*
77). As we noted in the Introduction (p. 26ff.), these alleged pronouncements were collected and published by one of Caesar's enemies in the later
civil war. Serious scholars still spill ink over these statements, which of
course the standard teleology makes almost irresistibly seductive given that

---

[15] Picked up by Suetonius, *Iul.* 9.2. There once were two books of Cicero's correspondence with Axius
(White 2010: 171). As Suetonius infers, Cicero probably meant to insinuate involvement in the
fictitious "First Catilinarian Conspiracy" (n. 10). Strasburger 1938 is inclined to think, however, of
Caesar's spectacular aedileship (cf. *Phil.* 5.49), when Catulus is said to have complained that he was
assaulting the Republic (n. 7 and n. 52).

[16] Suet. *Iul.* 30.5, Cic. *Off.* 3.82 (Eur. *Phoen.* 524–525), which Cicero translates as *Nam si violandum est
ius, regnandi gratia / violandum est; aliis rebus pietatem colas.*

[17] Dyck 1996: 602–604.

[18] Cic. *Att.* 7.11.1: *honestum igitur habere exercitum nullo publico consilio . . . sescenta alia scelera moliri,*
"τὴν θεῶν μεγίστην ὥστ' ἔχειν τυραννίδα"? Gildenhard 2006: 199. Chapter 7, p. 381.

Caesar did in fact take up the dictatorship for life in 44 and that he is so often seen as the destroyer of the Republic. But however ingeniously explicated, the partisan or even propagandistic assertions of an enemy in a civil war deserve no credence; far worse was said of Cicero (Chapter 1, n. 90).

Already in 1938, in what remains the most thorough and sober sifting of the material yet undertaken, Hermann Strasburger showed persuasively that a revolutionary life plan was retrospectively constructed and imposed upon Caesar's early career only after the crisis year of 59, and probably a good deal later. Remarkably little concrete information exists about Caesar's early years, which in itself suggests that his contemporaries took relatively little notice of him, certainly not before his splashy aedileship of 65, probably not before his defeat of senior rivals for the high pontificate in 63, and not verifiably until his tumultuous consulship of 59. This can be demonstrated in some detail from the corpus of the works of Cicero, where Caesar is not so much as mentioned before a speech of 63 (the *Fourth Catilinarian Oration*) and does not intrude upon the rich and vivid observations of the correspondence until June 60 (*Att.* 2.1.6), during Caesar's consular candidacy. Later writers probably drew their scarce factual information on the period before Caesar took center stage from a rather thin biographical sketch which doubtless postdated his assassination and was bound therefore to have taken a teleological perspective. "The ancient authors' knowledge of Caesar's early plans and political role increases with their distance in time from him," Strasburger drily observes; by the time we get to the end of the series of authorities for Caesar's early life, Dio in the early third century AD "surpasses all his predecessors in his knowledge of Caesar's soul."[19] As for Cicero, had Caesar been disastrously defeated in his Spanish campaign of 61 and his future thrown on the skids, we may be fairly sure his ostensibly tyrannical tendencies would never have been discovered by even the keenest contemporary observer.

"Outsider"

Closely related to the biographers' assumption that Caesar was possessed from the beginning by a desire to overthrow the Republic is Christian Meier's notion that Caesar was an "outsider" (*Außenseiter*) to the aristocratic circles with whom the Republic was identified, and that he was

---

[19] Strasburger 1938: 140. Cf. pp. 50–71 (56: Cicero never even invented a mocking pseudonym for him in his correspondence to Atticus!), 72–73, 137–141.

therefore able to view the Republic itself with critical detachment as the sinking ship that it was, and indeed ultimately to look beyond it.[20] Yet the notion that a member of the patrician Julii – a family at the heart of the nobility that traced its line back to Aeneas and Venus and carried in its funerals the *imagines* of more than a dozen consuls – and the grandson of a noble lady who proudly claimed descent from the ancient king Ancus Marcius was an "outsider" to the Roman aristocracy is highly paradoxical on its face.[21]

Meier's view can only be sustained if by "the Roman aristocracy" he really means only the "Sullan oligarchy" whose dominance was forged by victory in the civil wars of the 80s, *and* if one follows Plutarch (but no one else) in attributing to Caesar's early political interventions a strongly partisan "Marian" flavor.[22] Both of these positions are highly problematic.

Regarding the first point, then – Caesar's ostensible alienation from the ex-Sullan noble clique that dominated the Senate in the 70s and 60s – we can acknowledge from the outset that after Sulla's victory Caesar was at first deeply compromised by his close Marian connections: nephew to Marius's widow, Julia, husband of Cinna's daughter, handpicked by the latter for succession to the recently vacated post of *Flamen Dialis*.[23] Sulla himself ordered him to annul his marriage to Cinna's daughter (perhaps to bind

[20] Some of Meier's (1982) most notable characterizations of Caesar as "outsider" and of his concept itself are: 8–11, 49–50, 71–72, 97–98, 131–135, 162. These are mostly rhetorical rather than analytical.

[21] Badian 2009: 12–16: fifteen to twenty consulships in the fifth and fourth centuries (some of them no doubt "doubles"); four more consuls between 267 and 90; a distant cousin of Caesar's was consul in 64. The Julii were far from unique among the Roman nobility in glorifying their origins in this way: the Antonii and Fabii claimed descent from Hercules, the Mamilii from Ulysses, and a whole host of noble families (Dion. Hal. 1.85.3 says about fifty of them) – including Marcus Brutus's – connected their family trees to the Trojan refugees who came over with Aeneas: for details see Erskine 2001: 21–22; Farney 2007: 53–65.

[22] Thus, for example, Meier 1982: 73. Badian trenchantly criticizes Meier's characterization, yet seems simply to redate it to the beginning of 58 (1990: 33–34). See further Gruen 1974: 50–53. Santangelo 2012 and 2014 has properly warned of the strict anachronism of the term *Sullani* after 78 and of the dangers of applying it loosely to explain the political developments of the 70s and 60s. Yet it remains true that the post-Sullan Senate was dominated by a narrow elite of nobles, most of whom had been Sullan loyalists (the "inner circle" described by Steel 2014b: 325–329). This elite frequently (though not always) cooperated to resist modification of Sulla's reforms or "popular" legislation and its influence seems undeniable as late as the arguments over the *leges Gabinia* and *Manilia* in 67 and 66 and the counterattack on the tribune Cornelius in 65 (Ascon. 60C). A "victory of the nobility" is trumpeted by Cicero in *Rosc. Am.* 16 (cf. 135, 138, 149) and the nontechnical use of the word "oligarchy" is justified, among other things, by the references to the *paucorum dominatio* and *factio* in the famous, indignant speech Sallust put in the mouth of the tribune of 73, C. Licinius Macer (Sall. *Hist.* 3.48.6, 8 M; see Rosenblitt 2016). On the state of Roman politics after Sulla see Rosenblitt 2019.

[23] Note, however, that Marius and Cinna had killed C. and L. Caesar (cur. aed. 90, cos. 90) – possibly distant cousins (see Billows 2009: xvii), but Caesars still – and displayed their heads on the Rostra (Livy, *Per.* 80; Cic. *De Or.* 3.10).

the young patrician to the new "aristocratic" regime by means of a new conjugal connection), and upon his refusal, stripped him of her dowry. Whether or not Caesar actually appeared on any proscription list (probably not), the bounty hunters were soon after him and he was forced into hiding, on one occasion (it was said) escaping only due to a substantial bribe.[24] But for one so close to the Marian core, what is more remarkable than the consequences Caesar suffered for defiance – pretty minimal compared to so many others – is how successfully he recovered his position, and by what means. Sulla called off the dogs after the Vestal Virgins and Caesar's relations, among them "the most distinguished and closest of his [Sulla's] friends," interceded for him.[25] Unfortunately the names of the six Vestals are not well known to us in this year, so prosopographical conjecture is limited; the important point for us is that their intercession as a body gives a suggestive indication of Caesar's social standing among the aristocracy as a whole.[26] Distinctively "Sullan" in character, however, are the names that Suetonius provides of two of Caesar's *propinqui et adfines* who interceded for him: the patrician Mamercus Aemilius Lepidus, consul in 77, and one of the three Aurelii Cottae prominent at this time (cousins on his mother Aurelia's side), probably the eldest, Gaius (cos. 75).[27] These two men (though there may have been more), men of authority in the circle of "Sullan" nobles who wielded great power in the Senate after the Dictator's death, would perfectly suit Suetonius's reference to Sulla's prominent associates who begged him to

---

[24] Plut. *Caes.* 1.4–7. See Ridley 2000, who however insists that Caesar must have been formally proscribed (221–222; cf. also Keaveney, 1982: 134n114; Badian 2009: 17). Under the circumstances he well recounts, however, formal proscription is hardly necessary to explain the manhunt (note Vell. Pat. 2.41.2: *magis ministris Sullae adiutoribusque partium quam ipso conquirentibus eum ad necem*), while Caesar's escape with a bribe no greater than the minimum reward for the killing of a *proscriptus* (Pelling 2011: 137) is more easily explicable if he was not one. Furthermore, neither Suet. or Plut. explicitly uses the well-established terminology of proscription (*proscribere*, προγράφειν), and it seems inconceivable that such a notable legal disability would go unmentioned in the mass of evidence, contemporary as well as posthumous, relating to Caesar's career, despite the continued controversy over the status of the sons of the proscribed right down to 44. Keaveney 1982: 133–134; Hinard 1985: 128–133 omits Caesar from his list (cf. 116n55).

[25] Suet. *Iul.* 1.2–3 *deprecantibus amicissimis et ornatissimis*.

[26] Rüpke 2005: 1.117: only Fonteia, sister to Cicero's client M. Fonteius, is certain (Rüpke no. 1733), but likely members include Licinia, kinswoman to Cicero's client (2218) Popillia, probably of the Laenates (2806), and Perpennia, probably daughter of Perperna (cos. 92). It is unclear when in the subsequent period down to 70 Arruntia (no. 722) and the patrician Fabia, half-sister to Cicero's wife Terentia (no. 1577), were selected. For what it is worth, this group comprises both high and low aristocracy with both probable Sullan and Marian ties. Sullan ties may be conjectured for Licinia and Fonteia; Perpennia's father was probably the Marian censor of 86, her brother possibly the Marian-Lepidan-Sertorian general put to death by Pompey, while Popillia's relative, the tr. pl. of 86, had carried out a notorious Marian execution (*MRR* 2.47).

[27] The precise nature of the relationship with Mam. Lepidus is unclear. Gaius Cotta: Gelzer 1968: 21. For the composition of the *Sullani* see Keaveney 1984: 114–150.

relent. Caesar's next step was to serve on the personal staff (*conturbernalis*) of the man Sulla had left in charge of mopping-up operations against the island of Lesbos, then briefly continued in Cilicia under another prominent Sullan, the consul of 79, P. Servilius Vatia.[28] Particularly notable in this context is Caesar's co-optation in 73 by the board of pontifices into the priesthood vacated by the death of his cousin, C. Cotta. The college was dominated by prominent former *Sullani*, including Q. Metellus Pius (cos. 80), Q. Catulus (cos. 78), M. Terentius Varro Lucullus (cos. 73), and also two of the old Sullan guard mentioned already, Caesar's relative and former intercessor Mamercus Lepidus (cos. 77) and his recent commander in Cilicia, P. Servilius Vatia (cos. 79), now endowed with the honorific Isauricus.[29] Meier maintains Caesar's "outsider" status by supposing that Caesar's friends in effect stood surety for him against the reservations harbored by the "ruling aristocracy," perhaps raising the hope that by such generosity "the establishment" could "draw this promising young nobleman on to its side."[30] But if, in view of what we have already seen, we decline to adopt the prior characterization of Caesar as an "outsider," then such conjectures are unnecessary. We might more straightforwardly interpret the college's action as a stamp of approval by "the cream of the Sullan establishment" (Jehne).[31] As Lily Ross Taylor put it, "it was . . . not through the popularity with the mob which is so much emphasized in the accounts of Caesar's early career but through the favor of Sullan aristocrats that Caesar obtained his first office."[32] When, after the death of Cinna's daughter Cornelia (probably in 67), Caesar was in the market for a new wife, his choice fell on none other than Pompeia, Sulla's granddaughter through his daughter Cornelia. Pompeia was niece of Sulla's living son Faustus, and granddaughter also of Q. Pompeius, Sulla's staunch "optimate" ally against Marius and Sulpicius in the fighting of 88.[33]

The idea of Caesar as "outsider," strained to the limit by his patrician status and remarkable lineage, simply fails to fit the facts. Yet what about

[28] Suet. *Iul.* 2–3: the Sullan character of Caesar's commanders is rightly stressed by Gelzer 1968: 22n2. Sallust's Macer described C. Cotta as *ex factione media consul* (*Hist.* 3.48.8 M).

[29] Vell. Pat. 2.43.1, with *MRR* 2.113–114, and Rüpke 2005: 1.122. Servilius's son was to be a notable Caesarian in the civil war.

[30] Meier 1982: 112.

[31] Jehne 2001: 20. "The nobility accepted him as one of themselves" (Gelzer 1968: 25); of course he *was* a noble, and a patrician to boot.

[32] Taylor 1941: 117–120, 1942, 1942b: 7–8; Gruen 1974: 77–78.

[33] Suet. *Iul.* 6.2, Plut. *Caes.* 5.7. The Pompeii had by no means given up pride in their Sullan heritage: Pompeia's brother minted a coin in 54 with a quite unusual pairing of portraits on the two sides of the coin, viz. Pompeia's two grandfathers: Sulla senior on one, Q. Pompeius (cos. 88) on the other: *RRC* 434/1.

Plutarch's stress on Caesar's cultivation of the legacy of Marius in the 60s among the still-smoldering embers of the civil wars? The key evidence here are the famous incidents in 69 and 65 when Caesar revived the public commemoration of Marius's honors and met with sharp criticism from the senior consular Q. Catulus and some others for doing so. Notably, Plutarch is the only one who reports the earlier of the two incidents, Caesar's display of Marius's *imago* and probably also that of Marius's son at the funeral of Caesar's aunt, Marius's widow and mother to the younger Marius (*Caes.* 5.2–3).[34] This bold action was bound to be controversial, for the two men had been declared public enemies by Sulla, and some now indeed cried foul; but Plutarch notes that "the People" shouted in opposition, applauding enthusiastically as they marveled at the return of Marius's honors after such a long time.[35] Seen through the lens of the still relatively recent civil wars and Caesar's own close association as a teenager with the Marian side, it is tempting to interpret this moment quite dramatically as nothing less than "[laying] down a definite line to follow in politics: espousal of the cause of Marius and Cinna."[36] That is no doubt what the objectors would have claimed, especially those, like the *princeps senatus* Q. Catulus, who had strong reason to hate Marius. (His father, who had claimed equal credit for the victory of Vercellae, had escaped execution after Marius's capture of the City in 87 only by suicide.)[37] On the other hand it was also probably already customary to include the *imago* of a deceased husband in the funeral of a noble lady.[38] Any "political" interpretation of Caesar's action could likely then be countered by one resting on the observance of social custom. Sulla's execration of the memory of the man once honored as the "third founder of Rome" was one of the pettiest of his cruel reprisals in victory; restoration of Marius's place

---

[34] If Reiske's emendation of the singular Μαρίου to the plural is right (it is consistent with the plural number elsewhere in the passage), then more than one Marius was represented: presumably there was only one other, Julia's son, Marius the younger (Pelling 2011: 150), since Marius was a new man *sine imaginibus*.

[35] From Plutarch's wording it does not appear as if Sulla legally banned display of Marius's image but rather that such display was de facto excluded for prudential reasons (Pelling 2011: 151, contra Flower 2006: 103 with n. 68).

[36] Billows 2009: 81 (who also assumes that Cinna's *imago* was carried in Cornelia's funeral). Similarly, Badian 2009: 21: "a powerful political proclamation" which "laid the foundation of Caesar's career as a champion of the People." Cf. Flower 1996: 124.

[37] Cic. *De or.* 3.9; Vell. Pat. 2.22.4; Val. Max. 9.12.4.

[38] Tac. *Ann.* 3.76.2, SC de Pisone Patre, lines 76–81, clearly imply that at least by the early Principate a husband's *imago* would be perfectly normal at a noblewoman's funeral; there is no obvious reason why this practice should not have gone back to the earliest *laudationes* for women, probably to be dated around the end of the second century BC. (As it happens, when the very first known *laudatio* of a woman was delivered – that of a certain Popilia – her husband, Q. Catulus the Elder [cos. 102], was still alive.) Cf. Flower 1996: 103, 122–123; Badian 2009: 21; Pepe 2018: 283–285.

in civic memory was presumably indeed seen by "the People" as a repudiation of Sulla's cruelty as well as long-overdue recognition for a Roman hero, but need not have been seen as an attempt to revive Marius's political cause and the divisions of civil war.

A more attractive reading of the event, then, is that this event was symbolic of the end of a politics chiefly defined by memories of the civil war: "It was high time that Romans put the violence and divisiveness of the Sullan years behind them," Erich Gruen observes.[39] Evidence of the gradual erosion of the Sullan-Marian dichotomy may be found in the steps by which the tribunes regained their former powers taken away by Sulla (including the law already of 75 sponsored by Cotta, a man Sallust regarded as *ex media factione*) and mixed criminal juries were restored in 70, as well as the very decision by the board of pontifices mentioned earlier to admit Caesar into its ranks in 73. Notable efforts to put an end to the penalties inflicted upon those on the losing side followed. First, the exile imposed on the remnants of Lepidus's followers who had fled to Sertorius was ended by a law of the People (probably in 70) with Caesar's predictable, but obviously not isolated support (his brother-in-law L. Cinna was one of the exiles).[40] Sulla's ban on future office holding for the descendants of "Marians" was widely conceded to be unjust but was maintained through the 60s and 50s even by moderates such as Cicero because it seemed politically necessary.[41] On the other hand other remnants of Sullan cruelty were targeted in the mid-60s not merely by Caesar but also by the likes of Cato, no advocate of popular politics or "Marian" anti-senatorial agitation. In 65, the year of Caesar's aedileship, and the following year efforts were made to bring Sulla's bounty hunters under the proscriptions to book for murder. Caesar himself predictably plays a leading role in this effort in 64, either as a prosecutor or as a presiding judge seconded to the court *de sicariis* after his aedileship.[42] But it was none other than Marcus

---

[39] Gruen 2009: 24–26.

[40] Suet. *Iul.* 5; note that Sall. *Hist.* 4.52 (McGushin) attributes the measure to the Senate, which suggests that it was supported by that body. Cf. Dio 44.47.4, Cic. *Verr.* 2.5.151–155. Date: McGushin 1994: 2:164–165.

[41] Crawford 1994: 201–207; Drummond 1999: 127–136, 157–158. Cic. *Pis.* 4 and Quint. 11.1.85 indicate Cicero's line of argument in his now-lost consular speech on the matter. Vell. Pat. 2.43.4 is obviously wrong to imply that Caesar already as aedile had managed to restore the right to stand for office to the sons of the proscribed: this was done only in 49 (Plut. *Caes.* 37.2; Dio 44.47.2, with Pelling 2011: 338; Hinard 1985: 87–100, updated in 2008: 107–120). Possibly Velleius has conflated this with the condemnation of the bounty hunters (see the next n.). Yet it is entirely plausible to assume that Caesar publicly supported lifting the ban already in the 60s (Gruen 1974: 77n125).

[42] Suet. *Iul.* 11; Dio 37.10.1–2; Cic. *Lig.* 12; Ascon. 90–91C names two of the most important men convicted, a centurion named L. Luscius and (for the murder of Lucretius Ofella) L. Bellienus, an

Cato – a man tied by various connections to the post-Sullan clique – who had opened the door to Caesar's action when as quaestor in 65, the very year of Caesar's aedileship, he had stripped the bounty hunters of their supposed legal cover under the proscriptions and forced them to repay the rewards they had received for their killings. According to Plutarch, "all" were delighted at Cato's punishment of these men and thought that by this action Sulla and his "tyranny" had been wiped away.[43] "The People" who applauded Caesar's restoration of Marius's *imago* were giving expression to the same potent sense of relief.

What is clear is that Caesar's actions on the problem of the proscribed were always in favor of "normalization" and reconciliation, in no case explicitly directed against Sulla's respectable followers as such. The public revival of Marius's memory fits easily into such a context: not a partisan political gesture but a return to normalcy in which the achievements of one of Rome's great heroes were properly recognized (while reflecting familial glory and the glow of *pietas* and patriotic duty back upon Caesar himself). Marius, let us recall, had been celebrated as Rome's "third founder" (Plut. *Mar.* 27.9), its savior from the terrifying Cimbric menace.[44] In a speech before the Roman People delivered in 66, even so cautious a rising "new man" as Cicero refers to Marius as the "sole hope of the empire" in the sequence of military crises toward the end of the second century; as consul in 63 Cicero praises Marius in a *contio* as "the father of our country . . . the founder of your freedom and this very Commonwealth."[45] Even addressing the Senate, facing its leader, Q. Catulus, Cicero includes Marius in a roll call of great Roman military heroes from Scipio to Pompey: "Let eternal glory attach to Marius, who twice saved Italy from attack and freed her from the fear of enslavement!"[46] But the memory of Marius was bound to raise some men's blood pressure – especially, for instance, the same

---

uncle of Catiline's. Broughton unfortunately perpetuates the myth that Caesar actually blocked the prosecution of Catiline on the same charge (*MRR* 2.162; cf. Gruen 1974: 77n124). Exactly in what capacity Caesar furthered these prosecutions remains unclear: Suetonius suggests that he was in charge of the court *de sicariis*, which leads to the inference that he presided over the court as ex-aedile in 64 (Gelzer 1968: 42, following Mommsen; *MRR* 2.162; Alexander 1990: nos. 215–216). Strasburger 1938: 117–119 suggests that he prosecuted the men (so too Gruen), but this is probably to take too literally the emphatic nature of our sources' language. Cf. Hinard 1985: 204–206.

[43] Plut. *Cat. min.* 17.6–7; cf. Dio 47.6.4. Santangelo 2014: 21: "The political realignment that brings to an end a major aspect of the Sullan age is made possible by a curious *union sacrée* that brings together Cato and Caesar." For Cato's connections, see Gruen 1974: 53. Despite his relative youth, the group of former *Sullani* seems partly to have reassembled around Cato after Q. Catulus's death in 61 or 60.

[44] This does not of course imply that he was awarded some such formal title: Muccioli 1994; Miles 1995: 104–105.

[45] Cic. *Leg. Man.* 60; *Rab. perd.* 27. Morstein-Marx 2004: 110–111.   [46] *Cat.* 4.21.

Q. Catulus, acknowledged leader of the Sullan Senate after the Dictator's death, whose hatred of Marius for his crimes against his father had probably not been much appeased by the perpetrator's demise.[47] But among the mass of the Roman People Marius remained a hero whose dark final days were largely cast into obscurity by Sulla's cruel victory. To bury Marius's fame in eternal ignominy was untenable in the long run, and Caesar must have judged the time right for restoring his great relative's memory – and of course, glorifying his own familial connections in the process. Despite Plutarch's emphasis on continuing Marian-Sullan partisan discord, we have positive evidence that Julia's funeral did not seriously exacerbate the old Sullan-Marian partisan division and that this dichotomy was not in fact the dominant frame of public perception of Caesar. As we have seen, when the young patrician widower remarried soon thereafter, he received the hand of Sulla's and Q. Pompeius's granddaughter, which hardly fits the partisan interpretation. Probably significantly, Plutarch passes over Pompeia's ancestry, which would indeed have been "embarrassing" (Pelling) for his "Marian" representation of Caesar.[48]

In 65, only four years after his aunt Julia's funeral, Caesar again engaged in an act of Marian rehabilitation, this time a good deal more conspicuously. Marius's victory monuments over Jugurtha and the Germans had been thrown down by Sulla after his victory, perhaps even literally buried.[49] As curule aedile, whose charge included the maintenance and restoration of public buildings and sometimes new construction, Caesar had the monuments – probably mostly new copies – restored in secret and under cover of night to their original place on the Capitol and in the Forum.[50] Our sources are unanimous in describing the outrage that Caesar's action unleashed among leaders of the Sullan nobility.[51] Plutarch is again fullest here: after the shining, gilded trophies come to light at daybreak, "some" attack Caesar for aiming at tyranny; "the Marians" on the other hand fill the Capitol, applaud enthusiastically, are moved to tears of joy as they look upon the representations of their great captain, and praise Caesar to the skies as the only one worthy of his kinship

[47] See n. 37.
[48] Pelling 2011: 152–153. Meier, equally embarrassed, is inclined to put the marriage outside of rational consideration as a "love-match" (1982: 142). Rightly, Jehne 2001: 24.
[49] Sehlmeyer 1999: 196, inferring from Catulus's use of the word κατορωρυγμένας.
[50] Suet. *Iul.* 11; Plut. *Caes.* 6 (§1: κρύφα, νυκτὸς §2 ἅμα δ' ἡμέρᾳ); Vell. Pat. 2.43.4. For the monuments themselves see Sehlmeyer 1999: 192–193, 196–197; C. Reusser, *LTUR* 5.91; Mackay 2000: 162–168; Morstein-Marx 2004: 111n192. Copies: R. J. Evans 1994: 4.
[51] Cf. Suet. *Iul.* 11: *quorum [sc. optimatium] auctoritatem ut quibus posset modis in vicem diminueret*; Vell. Pat. 2.43.4 *adversante quidem nobilitate.*

to the hero. In a senatorial meeting called to discuss the matter, however, Q. Catulus, the *princeps senatus*, long-standing chief of the remnants of the post-Sullan oligarchy, and scourge of Marius's memory, was moved to declare an opinion that was long remembered: Caesar was no longer simply undermining the walls of the Republic but was now taking it by assault.[52]

Scholars often interpret this moment, if not already the earlier one, as something like the open declaration of a "Marian" political stance and a declaration of open "warfare" against the "optimates."[53] It is true that the sources make clear how much displeasure was expressed by certain elements among the aristocracy, especially those clustered around Catulus, and it is also true that here Plutarch (uniquely) invokes the idea of a surviving party of "Marians" who applaud the revival of their leader's honors. But on careful consideration it becomes clear that Plutarch's dramatic story must at the very least be handled with some care.

A minor point first: it is simply impossible to imagine that Caesar as aedile would have been able to restore, or more likely, completely rebuild anew Marius's monuments *in absolute secrecy*. On the contrary: the sites, in two of the most hallowed locations of the City, would have to be cleared and demarcated, any religious obstructions cleared (Sulla would certainly have thought of that!), architects or restorers and workers hired, money raised and paid, and so on.[54] And even if Marius's trophies were considerably more compact than we generally suppose, it strains credulity to imagine that the work itself, undertaken in darkness, occupied only a single night. Then there is the fact that even according to Plutarch, once Caesar is called to account in the Senate he wins that body over despite Catulus's forceful complaints.[55] Catulus appears to have been relatively isolated in his fulminations, which may explain their hysterical tone.

Catulus's overblown statement raises the problem of "Caesarian exceptionalism" to which, as we have seen, the biographers are especially susceptible. In retrospect it was all too easy to pick out the signs that Caesar was head and shoulders above the rest, the future "Colossus" as Shakespeare's Cassius and so many book titles have it. At the time it seems very unlikely that anyone saw a mere aedile as such a threat to the Roman

---

[52] Plut. *Caes.* 6.3–6.6; n. 7. But see n. 77.

[53] Syme 1939: 65: "His ascension revived the party of Marius and the battle-cries of the last civil war, only thirty years before." More recently, Canfora 2007: 20; Tatum 2008: 35; Billows 2009: 85 take some version of this line. I myself have previously been too inclined toward it: Morstein-Marx 2004: 111.

[54] See Robinson 1992: 49.   [55] Plut. *Caes.* 6.7: ἔπεισε τὴν σύγκλητον.

system, however eye-catching his gladiatorial shows, however provocative his rehabilitation of the famous husband of his aunt.[56] In 65 the trials of the sponsor of the recent *lex Manilia* and of the controversial ex-tribune Cornelius, pitting the heart of the Sullan oligarchy against the rising master-orator Cicero in the first great test of the restored tribunician power, will probably have seemed much more momentous to those engaged in the political life of the City; likewise, the battle in this year between the two censors, Catulus and M. Crassus, involving major controversies over the possible annexation of Egypt and the rights of the Transpadanes. In these struggles Caesar played a miniscule role if any, visible only because of the spotlight shone on him by the late biographers.[57] Outside of Rome, Pompey was in victorious pursuit of Mithridates as far as the Caucasus as those whose achievements he had begun to cast into shadow – the deeply resentful Lucullus, Marcius Rex, probably joined in the course of the year by Metellus Creticus too – all brooded outside the city walls while their demands for triumphs were rudely put off. Much bigger things were in motion than an aedile's self-promotion.

Returning now to the Marian monuments, we may note that curule aediles, especially, it seems, patricians, liked to refurbish or restore what one might loosely call "family monuments" while they held this early office – for patricians, their first opportunity to draw the public eye as a magistrate. The clearest example we possess is that of Q. Fabius Maximus's restoration, while curule aedile in 57, of the *Fornix Fabianus*, a "triumphal arch" where the Sacra Via entered the Forum, which had been originally erected around 120 and commemorated the victory of Fabius Maximus Allobrogicus (cos. 121) in Gallia Transalpina. The *Fornix Fabianus* also contained inscriptions celebrating the achievements of kin outside the Fabian *gens* proper, such as Allobrogicus's grandfather, L. Aemilius Paulus, and his uncle, Scipio Aemilianus – a parallel, perhaps, for Caesar's implicit appropriation of some of the reflected glory due one who was not of his immediate family or line of descent.[58] At any rate, the kin connection did not of course go

---

[56] "Husband of his aunt": see Plutarch's careful phrasing at *Caes.* 5.2 (συγγενείας at 6.5). It remains unclear whether this kind of connection through marriage was perceived as being as close as that of an uncle and nephew related by blood or formal adoption. Suetonius does not so much as mention the kin relationship with Marius, in this context (*Iul.* 11) or any other.

[57] Seager, 2002: 22, 68–71 gives a usefully non-Caesarocentric picture. See n. 11.

[58] *ILS* 43–43a (*CIL* VI 1303, 1304, 31593). Less certain but likely later examples are M. Scaurus's (aed. cur. 58) restoration of his father's adornment of the entrance to the temple of Jupiter Optimus Maximus (Cic. *Scaur.* 47: *paternis atque etiam huius amplissimis donis ornati aditus Iovis*, presumably damaged in the fire of 83 BC; he is otherwise known to have erected the extraordinarily large and opulent Theatrum Scauri in his curule aedileship [Plin. *HN* 36.113–115]) and L. Aemilius Paulus's

unnoticed (see n. 56), and to that extent it would be understood that Caesar was cleaving to the good old Roman virtue of *pietas*, demonstrating his own adherence to the traditional value system, righting a wrong done to one of Rome's greatest heroes, a lingering reminder of the recent fratricidal wars, and of course connecting himself to the memory of Marius's greatest military victories (not, of course, his regrettable slide into bloody atrocities). "He celebrated the exploits of a great military hero and enhanced the profile of his own family by reminding the public of his illustrious heritage."[59] But it was only to be expected that Catulus, son of one of Marius's greatest enemies and victims, would have viewed Caesar's action in the frame of the civil wars a decade and more past, and have voiced strong objection. Suetonius and Velleius believe that he carried most of the *nobilitas* with him. Yet even in Plutarch's version of the story "the Senate" as a whole ended up siding with Caesar, not Catulus – hardly a likely result if Caesar's purpose was in fact to signal his assumption of the mantle of Marius in a conspicuous attempt to reverse the results of the civil wars.

Some scholars, including the great Ronald Syme, have been inclined to apply a Marian coloring to Caesar's entire career, which might encourage us to see the actions of 69 and 65 as the signal for the revival of a "Marian party." Yet there is no evidence whatever for a renascent Marian party at this time or thereafter. Syme did in fact argue on prosopographical and ideological grounds that Caesar's coalition in the civil war of 49–45 was just such a revived "Marian party," but H. Bruhns thoroughly refuted his arguments in 1978.[60] The two sides in the Caesarian Civil War are in no way coextensive with the battle lines of the 80s: too many descendants of Marians turn up on the Pompeian side, too many sons of Sullani on Caesar's. Restoration in 49 of the full civic rights of the sons and grandsons of the proscribed fits into a larger pattern that also includes many of those recently condemned in the courts; again the emphasis is on conciliation and the restoration of justice.[61] (Indeed, looking ahead, we may say that civil war reconciliation is a "red thread" that runs through Caesar's career from beginning to end.) The descendants of *proscripti* play no conspicuous role in the civil war itself and seem to have been beneficiaries of Caesar's victory rather than agents of it. Nor is Caesar known to have employed any distinctively Marian symbols or slogans in the Civil War. In his own account of his Gallic War campaigns Caesar never so

---

(aed. cur. 56?) restoration of the Basilica Aemilia (Cic. *Att.* 4.16.8 [ca. July 54]. *MRR* 2.216, 3.9; the basilica remains a vexed problem of the topography of the Forum: E. Steinby, *LTUR* 1.167–168).

[59] Gruen 2009: 25; cf. Jehne 2001: 26, "Familiensolidarität." Similarly, Blom 2016: 162.

[60] Syme 1939: 65, 86–94; Bruhns 1978: 71–88.   [61] For a summary see Pelling 2011: 337–338.

much as mentions his kinship relation with Marius even where it could be quite relevant, for example when he encourages his officers by citing Marius's victory over the Cimbri and Teutones, or his desire to avenge a bloody defeat in the Cimbric Wars.[62] We should remember that criticism of Sulla's cruelty was not in itself peculiarly "Marian" but a symptom of widely shared revulsion at his methods in victory.[63] (We shall return to the question of Marius's possible influence on Caesar as a model for his future career.)

Only Plutarch places such a strongly partisan emphasis on Caesar's rehabilitation of Marius's honors in the 60s.[64] His view is only superficially plausible and is fatally undermined by a more fine-grained analysis of the facts. We should give it up.

Bribery, Public Extravagance, and Indebtedness

In the biographical tradition both ancient and modern, a further aspect of Caesar's aedileship looms large: its fantastic munificence, or *largitio* (roughly, "bribery") from a negative perspective. As curule aediles, Caesar and his colleague M. Bibulus were jointly responsible for putting on the Megalensian Games in honor of the "Great Mother" and the Roman Games; although a modest public grant was made for this purpose, ambitious aediles had to supplement this grant with a heavy outlay from their own pockets. According to Plutarch, Caesar's extravagance in this office, in the form of gladiatorial shows, theatrical performances, processions and banquets, cast all his predecessors in the office into shadow and induced the People unanimously to seek out new offices and honors for him with which to reciprocate the favor (*Caes.* 5.9). Suetonius too marks Caesar's aedilician extravagance as a key moment in "winning the favor of the People."[65] Suetonius cites the impressive temporary structures around the Comitium and Forum built by Caesar (apparently to house displays in connection with his games), and the wild beast hunts, plays, and gladiatorial combats he put on. The biographer adds the bitter joke of Caesar's frustrated colleague, M. Bibulus, who received little public notice for their joint outlay: just as the Temple of Castor and Pollux in the Forum went popularly by the name of the

---

[62] Caes. *BGall.* 1.7.4, 12.4–7, 13.2, 40.5. See Grillo 2012: 154.
[63] Sall. *Iug.* 95.4 is illustrative. See Morstein-Marx 2004: 111–113.   [64] Pelling 2011: 156.
[65] *Iul.* 11: init. *conciliato populi favore*; cf. Dio 37.8.1: ἐν τῇ ἀγορανομίᾳ ἐπῃνέθη (note here no restriction to the People).

former alone, so their shared *munificentia* as curule aediles was credited to Caesar alone.[66]

The splendor of Caesar's gladiatorial shows deserves some attention. Gladiatorial *munera* were not a part of an aedile's official duties (not until 42 were they even made a part of the official festival calendar); these were funeral games held in honor of Caesar's long-dead father, which he had held off for twenty years presumably for financial and strategic reasons. This was therefore a "private" obligation of *pietas*, but it certainly made a splash, apparently setting a new standard in terms of the number of combatants provided – Plutarch says 320 – and the splendor of their weaponry.[67] A propos of the number involved, Suetonius adds that the number of fighters Caesar had collected was so great and so frightening to his "enemies" that a restriction was imposed (by a senatorial decree or magisterial edict?) upon the number of gladiators anyone could keep in the City, and he was forced therefore to present fewer than he had intended. Although the biographer implies that the restriction was prompted by fears specifically of *Caesar* (an interpretation in keeping with the monarchical interpretation Suetonius presses throughout these chapters), it seems more likely that only six years after the Spartacus rebellion had finally been put down concerns lingered about the concentration of large numbers of trained fighters in the City under *any* person's control.[68] In view of this consideration, which Plutarch passes over, it is legitimate to wonder whether the impressive number he gives of the contestants (320) was that which Caesar actually presented or only what he had originally intended.[69]

Given the well-known importance of aedilician generosity for future prospects in elections, there is no reason to doubt that Caesar pulled out all the stops as aedile to try smooth his path to the praetorship, at great financial cost.[70] Several stories cluster around the next step in his political career that emphasize the enormous magnitude of his indebtedness – doubtless the result of his aedilician extravagance and his near-simultaneous campaigns in 63 for

---

[66] *Iul.* 10.1; Dio 37.8.1.

[67] Plut. *Caes.* 5.9; Dio 37.8.1; Pliny *HN* 33.53 says that Caesar was the first to equip gladiators and *venatores* with silver armor; Suet. *Iul.* 10.1 adds that Caesar's temporary structures were designed to display the splendid equipment.

[68] Contra Pelling 2011: 155. Note *cuiquam* (Suet. *Iul.* 10.2). The Spartacan revolt had begun with a breakout of only about seventy gladiators from Batiatus's school in Capua: Livy, *Per.* 95; Plut. *Crass.* 8.2; App. *BCiv.* 1.116/539.

[69] Rightly, Meier 1982: 148. For what it is worth, Plutarch thinks the former.

[70] On the phenomenon in general, see esp. Yakobson 1999: 33–38. Gruen 1992: 188–193 cautions against exaggeration, but his criticism is largely focused on an earlier period.

the praetorship and high pontificate.[71] But once again we must not allow the biographers' narrow focus on Caesar and their teleological perspective to exaggerate his exceptional character in this regard.[72] Aedilician *munificentia* was far from unique to Caesar in this period.[73]

Cicero's rather extended discussion in *De officiis* of this very aspect of a young senator's self-promotion offers some useful points of comparison. Cicero surveys the high-water marks of aedilician extravagance and other *largitio*, but Caesar and his spectacular aedileship are now nowhere to be found, despite the anti-Caesarian animus that frequently motivates the work, written in the aftermath of his assassination. Cicero skips directly from the previous "record" set by D. Iunius Silanus (around 70) to P. Lentulus Spinther, curule aedile in 63, "who outdid all his predecessors."[74] "It is an old tradition of our community, observed even in the good old days, that the best men are called upon to spend lavishly in their aedileship," Cicero acknowledges.[75] Thus, he concedes, "public largesse" cannot simply be condemned outright: while extravagant, strategic *largitiones* are wrong by an absolute moral standard, in a Roman political context one must strike a balance corresponding to the circumstances and one's own fortunes. In speaking of his own case, Cicero quite explicitly excuses his large expenditure during his aedileship by pointing to the high offices he was able thereby to attain on the first attempt without losing a single tribe or century.[76] By the same standard, Cicero ought to have admired Caesar's investment! Nor was Caesar's fiercest critic, the elder statesman Q. Catulus, above treating the People to an extravagant spectacle: in 69, only a few years before, he had celebrated his dedication of the rebuilt temple of Jupiter Optimus Maximus with theatrical performances over which he had stretched a great awning (the first to do so) and whose stage building he had faced with ivory. He was

---

[71] To be dealt with later in this chapter. Plutarch indeed claims that he owed as much as 31 million sesterces *before his very first public office* (*Caes.* 5.8), but App. *BCiv.* 2.8/26 reports a similar debt after his praetorship (HS 25 million). Appian's sequence is far more plausible, since at the time when Plutarch sets the story Caesar's lavish spending was still to come.

[72] Rightly, Gruen 2009: 27.   [73] A convenient survey in Bernstein 1998: 298–308.

[74] Cic. *Off.* 2.55–60, esp. 57. Likewise in the survey at Val. Max. 2.4.6 (who also notes Spinther, citing his innovation in outfitting the stage equipment with silver).

[75] Cic. *Off.* 2.57.

[76] Cic. *Off.* 2.60, 59. Cicero himself offered three sets of games in his aedileship (*Verr.* 2.5.36; *Mur.* 40), partly financed by "grateful" Sicilians, whose gifts in kind also allowed him to lower the price of food in Rome (Plut. *Cic.* 8.2) Cf. also Cicero's public rationalization of Milo's lavish expenditure before his run for the consulship: *Mil.* 95 (but privately he judges this *stulte bis terque Q. fr.* 3.8.6, 3.9.2). In this case, be it noted, Milo dramatically failed to obtain the expected return on his investment of "three patrimonies"; apparently the Roman People could not actually be bought and sold in this manner.

supposedly accused in his own right of importing "Campanian luxury" into Rome.[77]

The biographers' vision of Caesar's "exceptionalism" must also be tempered when we consider the various juicy anecdotes they convey about his indebtedness at this time, which for their shock value have become irresistible staples of the undergraduate lecture hall and even scholarly biographies. For example, we hear that before even attaining his first public office, or more likely, just after his praetorship in 62, Caesar was mired in debt to the astonishing tune of 25–31 million sesterces.[78] In 63 he is supposed to have spent so lavishly in his successful effort to defeat two senior consulars for the position of *pontifex maximus* that he told his mother as he departed for the voting assembly that he must either come back victorious or not at all.[79] Still, we are told, after his praetorship his creditors prevented him from leaving for his province until M. Crassus agreed to guarantee his staggering debts to the amount of HS 20 million.[80] Entertaining stories, no doubt, but should we believe them? Who could have been an authoritative source for Caesar's words to his mother? What source would have been privy to Caesar's account books? The invectives that played such an important role in the elaboration of the tradition on Caesar's early career may have left their mark here as well.[81] And why would his creditors have tried to block the most reliable path to their repayment – Caesar's departure for Spain with the opportunity it provided for an aggressive governor to enrich himself?[82]

---

[77] Val. Max. 2.4.6; Plin. *HN* 19.23; Livy, *Per.* 98; cf. Amm. Marc. 14.6.25, who, as Münzer, *RE* 13 [1927] 2088 thought, has almost certainly mistakenly transposed the story to Catulus's aedileship. (Cf. also Bernstein 1998: 40n102; E. Papi, *LTUR* 5.31.) It remains uncertain whether under the disturbed conditions of the 80s Catulus ever held that office (*MRR* 3.131), but if he did, nothing is known of his tenure. For Catulus's commission to restore the temple after the devastating fire of 83 see S. De Angeli, *LTUR* 3.148–150, and n. 176 of this chapter.

[78] See n. 71.   [79] Plut. *Caes.* 7.3; Suet. *Iul.* 13.

[80] Plut. *Caes.* 11.1–2; cf. Drummond 1999: 154 and the speculations of Schulz 2002: 266–268.

[81] "Debt, whether caused by extravagant living or lack of means, was an eminently suitable topic for invective" (Crawford 1994: 248): cf. Cic. *In Clodium et Curionem* Frr. 8–12, with Crawford 1994: 248–250 (Clodius), *Pis.* 12 (Gabinius); *Phil.* 2.36, 44–46 (HS 6 million – it is sobering in this context to note that Plutarch takes this number from Cicero as fact: *Ant.* 2.5 with Pelling ad loc.), 50, 71–72, 78 (Antony) Dio 46.18.3 (Cicero in speech of Calenus). For the standard topoi see now esp. Craig 2004: 187–213. According to Suet. *Iul.* 46, *multi* (Bibulus? Curio? Ampius Balbus? Tanusius?) related that Caesar at around this time (*tenuem adhuc et obaeratum*) built a lavishly appointed villa at Nemi and then tore it down because it did not please him in every particular. Serious scholars have believed this (Gelzer 1968: 30; Shackleton Bailey 1965: 3.254, balking only at Suetonius's implied date; Billows 2009: 63), yet potlatch spending on villas is another popular *topos* of invective (e.g. Cic. *Pis.* 48, [Sall.] *Inv. in Cic.* 2, 4 [cf. Cic. *Att.* 1.16.10]; cf. Sall. *Cat.* 12.3, 13.1). Cicero (*Att.* 6.1.25) refers only to Caesar's building at Nemi 51–50; nothing about demolition.

[82] Reported in its fullest form by Plutarch (*Caes.* 11.1–2; cf. *Crass.* 7.6); Suet. *Iul.* 18.1, App. *BCiv.* 2.8/ 26, apparently all from the same source. A similar type of scenario is envisioned in a classic of

As a general phenomenon, senators' indebtedness was particularly acute and pervasive in the middle and late 60s due to a dangerous convergence of factors: the sharpening of political competition after Sulla's doubling of the number of lower magistrates, clearly much exacerbated by the expulsion of numerous high-ranking senators in the censorship of 70, many of whom immediately set about working their way back up the political ladder at great expense; and a wider financial and liquidity crisis created by the revival of the Mithridatic Wars, especially after the shocking defeat at Zela in 67.[83] In the already heated atmosphere of the 60s debt was a highly destabilizing factor in political life, notably helping to precipitate the "Catilinarian" Conspiracy of 63.[84] Of course the phenomenon may have looked more positive from below. It seems likely that one understandable political response to the financial crisis may have been that candidates *increased* electoral handouts to potential voters in the capital in a peculiarly Roman form of "stimulus spending." This may have lent an agreeable air of Carnival to the electoral season, but of course it further raised the cost of politics for all competitors and greatly increased what even Romans recognized as corruption, resulting in a flurry of *ambitus* legislation during these years.[85]

Caesar, then, was far from alone in his indebtedness. "The Roman senator, particularly in the early part of his career, was frequently in debt well above his wealth and disposable assets."[86] In a nice precedent for the "bailouts" for the rich in our own day, senatorial conservatives, led by Cicero, held the line against popular pressure for a general rescheduling of

---

invective, Cicero's *In Clodium et Curionem* (frr. 8–12, with Crawford 1994), yet there its authority is given very little weight (Tatum 1999: 87–88). I am hesitant to give the Caesarian anecdote any more credence. Blösel 2016 has interestingly discussed the declining profitability of holding a province at this time, but this seems to apply mainly to "unmilitary" provinces and the conquest of Spain was still promisingly incomplete (see his p. 77). Schulz 2002: 265–266 conjectures that Caesar's creditors were themselves invested heavily in Spanish debt and therefore stood to lose either way.

[83] On the phenomenon in general see Frederiksen 1966. Rosillo López 2010: 179–229. Financial crisis of 67–62: Cic. *Leg. Man.* 17–19; *Off.* 2.84 (next n.); Val. Max. 4.8.3. Andreau 1999: 103. Kay 2014: 257–260.

[84] See Cic. *De off.* 2.84: "Never was debt greater, nor was it ever paid off better and easier; for once the hope of cheating was removed there was nothing to do but pay up." (Cicero's insinuation in the following sentence that Caesar was behind the debt agitation of 63 is probably based on the tradition that he was an unexposed member of the "Catilinarian" conspiracy.) Dio 37.25.4 mentions a tribunician bill for χρεῶν ἀποκοπάς at the beginning of 63, and of course during his consular candidacy in this year Catiline associated himself with demands for debt relief (but not cancellation, as Giovannini 1995 persuasively shows). See also Drummond 1999: 136–147.

[85] Rosillo López 2010: 216–223 notes the focus on nonmonetary transactions in the *ambitus* legislation during the financial/liquidity crisis of 67–62; this is interesting, but does not seem to be strong evidence that less money was being scattered about.

[86] Frederiksen 1966: 128.

debts in 63 but then, during the instability of the Catilinarian crisis, lavished praise on one particularly powerful moneylender, Q. Considius for declining to press his claims on loans totaling 15 million sesterces to insolvent "rich" men – very likely including senators, as Rosillo López has suggested.[87] In 62 even Cicero, that scourge of debtors, was obliged by what he regarded as what was expected of his new station as consular to run up his own debts enormously; after purchasing Crassus's sumptuous house on the Palatine for the astronomical sum of HS 3,500,000, he grimly joked that he was ready to join any conspiracy that would take him.[88]

Caesar's level of indebtedness in the mid-to-late 60s was probably far from exceptional in his milieu, although it was probably higher than usual given the magnitude of the expenses he incurred in 65 and with not one but two electoral campaigns in 63. Yet his astonishing success in that very year should have proven to any anxious creditors that he was a good horse to bet on.

Caesar as *Popularis*: Military Achievement and Respect for the *Populus*

We have spent much time – necessarily – struggling against the general teleological and "exceptionalist" tendency of the biographers and making a case for what Caesar was *not* at this point in his career: he was *not* an aspiring autocrat, he was *not* signaling the revival of the "Marian party," he was *not* unique either in his aedilian extravagance or (probably) even in his indebtedness. What *was* he then?

In Cicero's *Fourth Catilinarian Oration* – his intervention as presiding magistrate in the midst of the debate about the punishment of the "Catilinarian" conspirators on December 5, 63 BC – Caesar at last emerges in a contemporary text, freeing us from our chafing dependency on biographers writing some sixteen decades after the events. Cicero crisply describes the now praetor-elect Caesar, author of one of the motions under discussion, as one who "has taken the political path that is considered

---

[87] Val. Max. 4.8.3; Rosillo López 2010: 201. On Considius see Nicolet 1966/1974: 848–849.

[88] Cic. *Fam.* 5.6.2, cf. *Att.* 1.13.6 (which notes, unless the text is corrupt [Shackleton Bailey], that the consul Messalla had paid HS 13,400,000 for a house; Clodius is supposed to have bought Scaurus's house for HS 14,800,000). Caesar's election to the high pontificate may have saved him this exorbitant expense since he was able then to move directly from his unimpressive house in the Subura to the *domus publica* (Suet. *Iul.* 46). It is by no means clear that this was "in a grand style" (Billows 2009: 93); indeed, in comparison to the extravagant luxury houses at the foot of the Palatine such as that excavated by A. Carandini, it seems to have been relatively austere. (Cf. R. T. Scott, *LTUR* 2.165–166 with E. Papi, *LTUR* 2.26, 4.25–26.)

popularis" (*Cat.* 4.9). With these words, the earliest contemporary notice of the man who would eventually become cloaked in ex post facto mythmaking, Julius Caesar first comes into the light of day for the historian.[89]

Caesar's speech on this occasion appears to have been his first major intervention in a senatorial debate, and a tour de force it was. However, the nature of the speech and its content merit separate and full consideration, which they receive in the next chapter. Here I wish only to use Cicero's contemporary characterization of Caesar in his *Fourth Catilinarian* as *popularis* to cast light backward on Caesar's early career, which I have labored to strip of the anticipatory accretions of the biographers.

What, first of all, does Cicero mean when he characterizes Caesar in passing here as a *popularis*? Caesar is, to be sure, "dear and pleasing to the People" (*Cat.* 4.11). Yet Caesar's specific way of being *popularis* is very carefully defined as anything but seditious:[90] his *dignitas* (here perhaps "proven worthiness" – i.e. earned status) and the splendor of his ancestry act as a sort of guarantee of his good faith to the *res publica*,[91] and his motion itself demonstrates the difference between a truly "*popularis*" spirit, which is actually devoted to the People's well-being, and the fecklessness (*levitas*) of demagogues.[92] Caesar is further distinguished from some unnamed senators who "desire to be thought *populares*" and therefore have absented themselves from an inevitably invidious senatorial debate.[93] On the contrary, unlike these others, who seem unable to be *populares* and also carry out their senatorial responsibilities, Caesar can do both things. He has not been shy about going on record in support of Cicero's actions instead of trying to preserve "deniability" before the People by absenting himself: he has made his position clear by being fully supportive of the previous decrees that handed over the men to

---

[89] The publication of the speech is traditionally dated three years later on the basis of *Att.* 2.1.3 (see Chapter 3, n. 38), yet even if that arguable proposition be accepted, it remains probable that it was written down shortly after actual delivery, as was usual. Nothing in the characterization of Caesar in *Cat.* IV would seem to imply its "contamination" by his praetorian activities or indeed consular candidacy in 60.

[90] On *popularis* and *populares* see Chapter 1, n. 24.

[91] 4.9: *habemus enim a Caesare, sicut ipsius dignitas et maiorum eius amplitudo postulabat, sententiam tamquam obsidem perpetuae in rem publicam voluntatis.*

[92] Ibid.: *intellectum est quid interesset inter levitatem contionatorum et animum vere popularem saluti populi consulentem.* See the classic treatment by Seager 1972: 328–338; Morstein-Marx 2004: 207–230.

[93] 4.10: *video de istis qui se populares haberi volunt abesse non neminem, ne de capite videlicet civium Romanorum sententiam ferat.* Possibly not Crassus, as usually supposed, though we know he was absent (Cic. *Att.* 12.21.1): Drummond 1995: 14–15. Yet no better candidate has been uncovered; Cicero would probably not have been so circumspect in attacking a junior figure like the tribunes Bestia or Nepos.

Cicero's custody, by joining the majority of the Senate in voting an honorific thanksgiving in his name, and by supporting rewards for the informers in the case.[94] He is even envisioned by Cicero as potentially playing a useful role as a kind of intermediary between Senate and People by joining the consul in the *contio* after the debate, there to use his popular influence to support the consul and to fend off any *popularis* attacks.[95] For after all, even Caesar has proposed an extremely severe punishment for the men, one that joins "want and poverty with every torture of mind and body;"[96] this stance, coming from "a man most mild and gentle," will help to shield Cicero and the whole Senate from any accusations of "cruelty" that so-called *populares* might make.[97] This may be a mischievous suggestion on the part of Cicero (seeking to instill anxiety in Caesar about the possible price to be paid for victory in the debate, namely, forfeiting at least some of his "popularity"), yet it is surely true that Caesar could not simply back away from his own motion if or when Cicero brought him before the People.

No doubt Cicero is being very careful here: he is constrained by the unwritten rules that govern senatorial debate not to appear to dampen senators' freedom of speech by manifestly taking sides in a debate despite his ostensibly neutral position as presiding officer.[98] So the passage should not be read naively as a sincere portrayal of Cicero's views about Caesar at the time. But that is not anyway what we are after; Cicero's characterization of Caesar in the *Fourth Catilinarian* can still stand as a valuable *public* representation of Caesar suitable for a *senatorial audience*, at a time when the great controversies of 59 had not yet made him a deeply polarizing figure. In a nutshell, here Caesar is represented as both a proud, noble senator *and* an advocate of the People. Not only are these aspects represented as united in Caesar but they are shown to be embraced by the consul (through his praise) and indeed to a non-negligible extent by the Senate – for even though Cicero makes no mention of the fact that Caesar's proposal had turned the tide of the

---

[94] 4.10: *iam hoc nemini dubium est, qui reo custodiam, quaesitori gratulationem, indici praemium decrerit quid de tota re et causa iudicarit.*

[95] 4.11: *sive hoc statueritis, dederitis mihi comitem ad contionem populo carum atque iucundum.* For bringing the introducer of a major senatorial motion before the People in the immediately subsequent *contio*, see Morstein-Marx 2004: 247–248. Cf. also §9: *fortasse minus erunt hoc auctore et cognitore huiusce sententiae mihi populares impetus pertimescendi.*

[96] 4.10: *ut omnis animi cruciatus et corporis etiam egestas ac mendicitas consequatur.*

[97] 4.10: *homo mitissimus atque lenissimus* (as Dyck notes ad loc., this was a "popular" virtue); §11: *facile me atque vos crudelitatis vituperatione populus Romanus exsolvet atque obtinebo eam multo leniorem fuisse.* Probably *eam* refers back to *Silani sententiam*, not *crudelitas* (so Dyck), which Cicero would not after all own.

[98] See Cape 1995 (though I sense no irony in Cicero's reference to Caesar's *dignitas*).

debate, any minimally informed reader will have known that at the moment
Cicero made his speech, the debate had begun to go very much in Caesar's
way. That is, his recognized political stance as *popularis* had not at all
undermined his credibility, or *dignitas*, as seen by a large number of senators.

This is important, but on reflection should not be surprising. After all,
many junior senators "played the popular card" on their way to the top,
not least Cicero himself.[99] *Popularis* stances or gestures were remembered
to have been made by some of the greatest heroes of the past, in particular
the two Scipiones Africani, the latter of whom was in fact embraced as
a model by *populares* of the present.[100] (Indeed, given the right – that is
popular – audience, Cicero is perfectly willing to assert that the *maiores*,
the "Forefathers," were themselves *populares*.)[101] As I stressed in the
Introduction, we must at last abandon the old tendency (influenced, no
doubt, by Cicero) to write as if being *popularis* was somehow to be
opposed to "the Republic." By the Late Republic, indeed, the popular
assemblies were in the habit of rebuffing the Senate in legislative controversies at least once every few years if not more frequently, yet there was
no movement to "democratize" the system as a whole, nor did the Senate
thereby lose its *auctoritas* or overarching legitimacy. On the contrary, the
sovereign assemblies functioned rather as a corrective, ultimately legitimizing rather than undermining the broadly paternalistic role enjoyed
by the senatorial elite.[102] No doubt conservatives in the Senate and even
among the People had their suspicions about the essential political
soundness of any man who set out on the *via popularis*, yet Caesar's
noble name and personal *dignitas*, as Cicero allows, served as a warrant of
his fundamental respect for the *mos maiorum* and made it highly implausible that his object was outright "sedition."[103]

Caesar's early actions in the public eye are entirely consistent with Cicero's
description. They suggest that he would have been seen by much of the
citizenry not as a fomenter of populist sedition but as a brilliant young
representative of the illustrious traditions of the Roman aristocracy.

Let us go back nearly to the beginning to construct an alternative story
more in line with Cicero's description here and avoiding the misleading
temptations of teleology. Although by Caesar's time the old requirement of
ten years' military service was in abeyance (if it truly ever existed: Polybius
6.19.4 is our only strong evidence), a now somewhat old-fashioned path to

---

[99] Q. Cicero (?), *Comment. pet.* 51–53, etc. On the phenomenon in general see Yakobson 2006.
[100] See n. 202.   [101] Cic. *Leg. agr.* 2.18 (cf. 2.26–27).   [102] Chapter 1, p. 4ff.
[103] Cf. Yakobson 2014: 287–290.

glory was that of military heroism.[104] In 221 BC Q. Caecilius Metellus, in his eulogy of his father, took pride in the fact that he had attained the ten "greatest and best things that wise men should spend their lives seeking." Among these the first mentioned was to be the foremost warrior (*primarium bellatorem esse*), but – interestingly stacking the deck in favor of the military virtues – two further and apparently distinct life goals were to be the bravest general (*fortissimum imperatorem*) and to win great victories while holding supreme command (*auspicio suo maximas res geri*).[105] This was the path on which the young patrician now struck out: we noted earlier that Caesar was awarded the *corona civica* for his role in the siege of Mytilene in 80 or 79, when he was only about twenty-one years of age on the staff of M. Minucius Thermus.[106] The *corona civica*, a crown of oak leaves granted for exceptional valor in saving the life of a citizen in battle, was an extraordinarily prestigious decoration comparable in public esteem to the US Congressional Medal of Honor or Britain's Victoria Cross, but probably much rarer.[107] According to Pliny, one decorated with the civic crown was entitled to wear it at all times, and all citizens, including senators, whatever their age and dignity, were obliged to rise when he made his way to his seat at the games (*HN* 16.13). The honor was thus also a highly conspicuous one in the great festival gatherings, the Roman *ludi*. E. Badian takes what one might call the "megalomanic" interpretation of the psychological impact of the award on Caesar.[108] A less teleological view, however, and one accessible to contemporaries, would tend to look back to the great *exempla virtutis* of the past rather than the unknowable future. By winning the civic crown Caesar joined a line of aristocratic warriors reaching back to the presumably largely legendary L. Siccius Dentatus, the "Roman Achilles" of the fifth century who supposedly had earned the

---

[104] Ten-year rule no longer observed: Harris 1979: 12n4 and see now Segal 2019: 30–112 with a pertinent review of the best-known careers of our period. Cicero's service of only two years suggests that some minimal service was still expected but that the bar was set rather low; even Caesar seems to have served only five years before his quaestorship. On the military path to public honors, see Cic. *Off.* 2.45; recent scholarship has shown that this was hardly the norm by Caesar's generation (convenient recent summary in Blom 2016: 55–59; Segal, op. cit., expands the argument).

[105] Pliny, *HN* 7.139–40 = *ORF* no. 6, fr. 2. On the speech see Flower 1996: 136–142.

[106] Suet. *Iul.* 2.

[107] See Plin. *HN* 16.7–14, Gell. 5.6.11–15, Polyb. 6.39.6. That Caesar reached the aedileship, praetorship, and consulship two years before the statutory minimum ages for those offices led Taylor 1957: 12–13 to adopt Helen White's suggestion in her 1950 dissertation (Broughton *MRR* 3.106) that the *corona civica* gave him the right to pursue office (at least from the aedileship on up) two years earlier than usual. Goldsworthy 2006: 106 and Billows 2009: 57 follow. But there is no substantial evidence for this privilege, and since Caesar apparently held the quaestorship at the usual age of thirty, I favor Badian's view (see n. 118).

[108] Badian 1990: 28–29.

corona civica no fewer than fourteen times, and the only slightly less legendary Manlius Capitolinus (six or eight times).[109]

For a young patrician starting his career in the 70s, however, more salient would have been the youthful military honors won by two of the greatest military heroes in the Roman pantheon, the Scipiones Africani, Elder and Younger. About 140 years before Caesar's feat, Scipio Africanus, also a very young man (aged about eighteen), was said to have been offered the civic crown after saving the life of his father, the consul, at the battle of Ticinus in 218. Scipio had declined the honor, presumably because of the family complications inherent in the circumstances and the apparent "conflict of interest" when a father decorated his own son, but the memory of the deed and the remarkable distinction he had earned remained.[110] The younger Africanus too (whom we usually know by his adoptive name Aemilianus) had won an even higher distinction for bravery and valor before his days as commander, though not at so young an age as his adoptive grandfather. As military tribune in Spain in 151 he had killed an enemy champion in single combat at Intercatia and then been the first to mount the town's wall in the assault, for which he was duly honored with the *corona muralis*.[111] Again, in the Third Punic War, having saved a surrounded force of four (or three) cohorts Aemilianus attained the highest Roman military honor available, the "siege" or "grass crown" for saving a multitude of citizens simultaneously.[112] The great Marcus Marcellus, although not a patrician, also stood out in the roll call of Roman military heroes for his youthful exploits: while still a very young man in the closing phases of the First Punic War, he had more than once killed his challenger in single combat and appears likely to have won the *corona civica* for saving his brother's life in a battle in Sicily.[113] If it was too

---

[109] Pliny, *HN* 16.13; cf. 22.9, Liv. 6.20.7.

[110] Pliny *HN* 16.14 (who however places the action at the Trebia); cf. Polyb. 10.3.4–7 with Walbank *HCP* 2:198–199; Livy 21.46.7–10. Zecchini 2001 notes the connection to Caesar (125) but fails to mention that Scipio *declined* the honor (Plin. *HN* 16.14; cf. 7.106). It is possible that the exploit or the story of its recognition is an invention (Weinstock 1971: 163; Beck 2005: 335), but even if it was only part of the Scipio legend, this legend is likely to have been influential in Caesar's generation.

[111] App. *Hisp.* 53–54; Livy *Per.* 48. For the context Astin 1967: 46–47. On the "mural crown" see Polyb. 6.39.5; Liv. 26.48.5; Gell. 5.6.16.

[112] App. *Pun.* 98–110; Livy *Per.* 49; Vell. Pat. 1.12.4. Pliny makes clear in his discussion of the *corona obsidionalis* (*HN* 22.6–13) that this honor was far rarer than the *civica*. Among its other republican recipients he lists Dentatus (again), P. Decius Mus, Fabius Cunctator, and Sulla, as well as one other military tribune besides Aemilianus and a single centurion. A recent review of the various Roman "crowns" in Bergmann 2010.

[113] Plut. *Marc.* 2.3: ἔτι νέῳ στέφανοι καὶ γέρα παρὰ τῶν στρατηγῶν ἦσαν. Later, of course, Marcellus was to win the *spolia opima*, though his military reputation was in the end somewhat tarnished by the rashness that brought about his death in 208. McDonnell 2006: 206–240 considers Marcellus the creator of a new ideology of *virtus* associated with popular appeal and attempts "to overcome

early to predict a glorious future for Caesar, it is likely that these were the kind of models that would naturally have suggested themselves to an ambitious young aristocrat who had won the *corona civica* at twenty years of age. (We may note in passing that Marius, though he clearly distinguished himself in his early military service under Scipio Aemilianus at Numantia, seems not to have won any of the major *coronae.*[114])

Caesar, then, first came to public notice in Rome not as a demagogue or "politician" but as a patrician warrior in the mold of the Scipiones. The tendency of ancient biographers and modern scholars is to characterize him implicitly or explicitly as one looking to the future (the end of the republican system) rather than aspiring to inscribe his name among the greatest leaders of the Roman past, but in fact a moment's reflection suggests that this has it precisely backward.

When Caesar returned to Rome in 78 he must have made quite an entrance at the *ludi*, with the whole audience, including the most exalted senators, rising to their feet in his honor. Capitalizing on his precocious military fame, in 77 and 76 he sought to bring himself more fully into the public eye by prosecuting two rather disreputable figures on charges of extortion in the provinces, Cn. Cornelius Dolabella, the Sullan ex-commander of Macedonia, and C. Antonius Hybrida, who had served in Greece as a Sullan officer.[115] The result of the trials was mixed (Dolabella acquitted, Antonius convicted but his sentence aborted), but this probably mattered little. More important was the reputation Caesar had won for championing justice and pursuing injustice as well as for the excellence of his oratory – a skill fundamental to traditional political leadership.[116] He furthered his reputation among the educated class by publishing the failed but highly regarded speech against Dolabella.[117] Plutarch is no doubt quite

---

traditional aristocratic restrictions on glory and power" (236); however that may be, the Scipiones more effectively realized this tendency in the memory of subsequent generations.

[114] Plut. *Mar.* 3.2–3. Surely one of the chief *coronae* would have been explicitly mentioned by "Marius" in his great speech if Sallust had known about it (Sall. *Iug.* 85.29: *hastas, vexillum, phaleras, alia militaria dona*). The tradition is in fact notably vague about Marius's youthful military action other than that he served with distinction: cf. Sall. *Iug.* 6.3–4; Val. Max. 8.15.7; Evans 1994: 27–28.

[115] Alexander 1990: nos. 140, 141; Damon and Mackay 1995; Blom 2016: 153–154. On Antonius's activities in Greece see now also Keaveney 2018: 54–56.

[116] On Caesar's reputed eloquence see Suet. *Iul.* 55.1–2; Plut. *Caes.* 3.2–4; cf. Cic. *Brut.* 252, 258, 261; Quint. 10.114; Tac. *Dial.* 21.5, 25.3, *Ann.* 13.3.4. Forensic speeches, esp. prosecutions, were an acknowledged way of demonstrating one's worthiness for a further career: see e.g. Cic. *Leg. Man.* 1–2, *Off.* 2.49–50, and Blom 2016: 26–33.

[117] *ORF* 121, frs. 15–23 (pp. 386–387). Blom 2016: 154–156. Dolabella is the author of the first dated public appearance of the notorious allegation that Caesar had been the Bithynian king's young lover, which would give Bibulus and Memmius good material for their invectives in 59: Suet. *Iul.* 49, with Osgood 2008.

right to claim that Caesar's oratory and advocacy won him great goodwill in Rome (*Caes.* 4.4); this was the path that Cicero also took to high office, with great success (*Leg. Man.* 1–2). What is out of order, however, is for Plutarch to tack on to this unexceptionable observation various sinister suggestions foreshadowing the *telos* to which his narrative tends: mention of his ingratiating manner and extravagant banquets leads directly to grossly anachronistic imputations of *dunamis*, "tyrannical" aspirations, and suspicion of revolution (4.4–9). Caesar had not yet been elected to his very first office.

Electoral success *suo anno* followed, perhaps with a statutory boost given to those of patrician status due to their omission of the tribunate.[118] Caesar's first electoral success was for a military tribunate in 72 or 71.[119] Suetonius strenuously assures us that in this minor office, while not yet even a senator, he strongly supported those seeking to restore the powers of the tribunate Sulla had taken away – a key popular demand which had been building through the 70s – but if that is so, no other source seems to have noticed, and in any case, the successful push did not come until the consulship of Pompey and Crassus in 70.[120] The quaestorship probably followed in 69, with assignment to Farther Spain, then the splendid curule aedileship in 65 which we have already discussed. An appointment as "Caretaker of the Appian Way," probably ca. 66, will have offered an opportunity to present an agreeable face to the populace: for instance, one L. Fabricius, as *curator viarum* a few years later, saw to the construction of the handsome bridge linking the Tiber Island to the City that still stands today.[121]

Apart from the unverifiable, insidious steps toward revolution dubiously reported by the biographers (see earlier in this chapter), Caesar's record in

---

[118] See Badian 1964: 140–156 for the view that this was a patrician privilege. Broughton demurs on the grounds that patrician careers are not well enough known to prove the point, and alone among modern authorities inclines to Mommsen's proposed date of 102 for Caesar's birth (*MRR* 3.105), rather than 100, which is clearly indicated by our most direct evidence (Suet. *Iul.* 88; App. *BCiv.* 2.149/620; cf. Deutsch 1914: 17–28 for full evidence) and is generally accepted among scholars today. Cf. n. 107. I leave out here the famous story of Caesar's capture by pirates in the winter of 74–73 (Plut. *Caes.* 1.8–2.7, Suet. *Iul.* 4, et al.; see Pelling 2011: 138–141; on the date, also Kallet-Marx 1995: 300n34). True or not, it seems most likely to be a product of the (late) biographical tradition and there is no evidence that the story was even known or public in the late 70s.

[119] The dates of the military tribunate and the quaestorship are plausibly inferred (Broughton, *MRR* 3.105–106; Taylor 1941: 120–123). Taylor conjectured that as military tribune Caesar served under Crassus in the Spartacan War.

[120] Suet. *Iul.* 5. See Butler and Cary 1927: 49; Pelling 2011: 149.

[121] *CIL* I² 751 = *ILS* 5892 = *ILLRP* 379, with Dio 37.45.3. Plut. *Caes.* 5.9; for the favorable publicity the road-building posts tended to give see Cic. *Att.* 1.1.2, Plut. *C. Gracch.* 7 (tribune).

these years reveals little sign of controversial populism. If he had supported the restoration of the full powers of the tribunate by the end of the decade of the 70s, so did most others, it seems, and its passage into law in 70 was by now apparently unstoppable.[122] Most likely Plutarch's statement – which he makes only in the *Life of Pompey* and omits from his *Caesar* – that in 67 Caesar was the only senator who spoke in favor of the *lex Gabinia* empowering Pompey to deal decisively with the problem of piracy is simply a conflation with his support of the *lex Manilia* in the next year.[123] But if indeed he, a mere quaestorian, was the only senator to speak in favor of the Gabinian Law in 67, as Plutarch claims, his role seems to have been fairly insignificant since he is entirely absent from Dio's detailed narrative of the passage of the law.[124] And to take a stand for the *lex Manilia* in the following year (66) would not have been terribly adventurous or controversial for a very junior figure since political cover was provided by no fewer than four senior consulars and Cicero himself – no rabble-rouser he – as praetor.[125] Caesar may well have been eager to attach himself to Pompey's rising star, but the advocacy of such a low-ranking senator as he was at this stage may have been little noted even by Magnus himself.

What is left, then, stripped of a great deal of ex post facto insinuation, is a quite unrevolutionary record of respectable self-promotion before the Roman People while steering clear of any conspicuous association with the more serious and risky *popularis* contests of the mid-decade: in 67, not just the Gabinian Law but, equally important, the tribune Cornelius's extended set-to with the consul, Piso; or in 65, the trials of Manilius and especially of Cornelius, where even Cicero stepped forward to justify the tradition of tribunician aggressiveness against the "optimate" leaders, Q. Catulus and Hortensius.[126] Caesar's magnificent aedileship in that very year won him much popularity but his only more overt political move – the restoration of Marius's monuments – was of essentially symbolic importance while he avoided exposure in the more serious struggle over the rights of the recently

---

[122] Gruen 1974: 28–35; Mitchell 1979: 130–132. For a somewhat more nuanced view see now Santangelo 2014: 5–10.

[123] Plut. *Pomp.* 25.8. Cf. Plutarch's shifting of the Alexander and dream anecdotes to more notable moments in the narrative. Strasburger 1938: 63, 100–101; Watkins 1987: 120–121n6; Heftner 1995: 192; Blom 2016: 163.

[124] Dio 36.20–37.

[125] Dio 36.43.2–4; Cic. *Leg. Man.* 68 lists the consulars, including Caesar's old commander P. Servilius Isauricus and another senior *Sullanus*, C. Scribonius Curio.

[126] See Asconius's sketch of the background, 57–62 C, esp. 60–61. It is true that Caesar was a sitting aedile and thus might have had scruples about associating himself directly with the defendant; but note that Faustus Sulla, a sitting quaestor, and C. Memmius, a sitting tribune, appeared as *supplicatores* on behalf of Scaurus the Younger in 54.

restored tribunes. Not that this caution should be surprising in an ambitious young patrician, who faced by the ideological and pragmatic constraints upon any senator seeking to climb to the top would have understood that his hopes of future *gloria* were likely to depend as much on the Senate as on the People. This is a surprise only to one who has internalized the teleological perspective of the biographers and imagines Caesar as one looking to a future beyond the Republic rather than to the Republic's past. As we shall see in due course, even to follow Cicero in describing Caesar as a *popularis* is a move not without difficulties and contradictions.[127]

So at last we come to the year 63, in December of which Caesar truly enters upon the political stage with his momentous speech on the punishment of the "Catilinarian" conspirators.[128] That speech marks a new, important phase in Caesar's career which will occupy our full attention in the next chapter; for now we will focus on the earlier events of the year, which Caesar will long have anticipated for quite another reason. For in the year we call 63 he knew he would be campaigning for the praetorship *suo anno* ("in his year"), seeking to win the office at the earliest possible date: a mark of preferment that would mark him as one of the favorites to win one of the two consulships three years later. As luck would have it, however, the aged *pontifex maximus* (the chief "pontiff" and thus the highest-ranking official in the state religious apparatus), Q. Metellus Pius, now died, and according to long-standing tradition his successor was to be elected by voters of seventeen of Rome's thirty-five "tribes" or voting units selected by lot. As was no doubt expected, two of the most senior and eminent members of the board of *pontifices* declared their candidacy for the prestigious position, the most eminent senior consular, Q. Catulus (cos. 78), whose personal hostility to Caesar was repeatedly noted earlier, and another senior consular and double *triumphator* (and Caesar's old commander), P. Servilius Isauricus (cos. 79). Caesar, also a *pontifex* but still a very junior senator, threw his hat into the ring – and won. The relatively youthful Caesar (actually thirty-seven, but this is a society in which a man in his thirties could be called *adulescens*: Cic. *Cael.* 1) therefore faced two elections in 63 and prevailed in both. (Unfortunately we do not know which came first.)[129] It was quite a year.

---

[127] Canfora 2007: 42 notes Caesar's departure from the "old, traditional politics of the *populares*."

[128] I leave aside the empty suspicion held by many that Caesar, with Crassus as senior partner, was pulling the strings behind the Rullan land bill (n. 148) or the bizarre machinations of the Rabirius trial.

[129] Jehne 2009: 56, thinks the pontifical election came first. There seems to be no solid evidence either way, since Dio's implication that it came after December 5 is clearly wrong (Broughton, *MRR*, 2.172n3); however, Ramsey's late date for the elections of 63 (2019: September) makes the priority of the pontifical election more probable. Describing the run-up to the P.M. election Dio mentions a law of the tribune Labienus (allegedly supported by Caesar) restoring in essence the *lex Domitia* of

Not only Caesar's victory in the pontifical election but his mere candidacy provokes astonishment among modern scholars, for his competitors, as the sources stress, were far his superiors in age and distinction.[130] Gelzer claims that this "highest religious honour in the Roman state" "had previously always gone to most respected consulars."[131] For once he is wrong. In the twelve elections for *pontifex maximus* held since 212 (our earliest known instance), in only three cases (which may be a consequence of the gaps in our evidence) does it not appear that at least one senior consular among the pontiffs was passed over in favor of the winning candidate. In five elections it is evident that the winning candidate was *much* junior in *dignitas* (a consulship at least a decade later) than at least one of his pontifical colleagues; in six cases the winner was not even a consular (although in half of these cases he was on the verge of the consulship), and in two famous instances he was not even yet a praetor.[132] The general picture then is very mixed, but there were also eye-catching precedents for victory by a *very* junior senator. As far back as 212, in the earliest election of a *pontifex maximus* of which we hear, the curule aedile P. Licinius Crassus Dives prevailed in an extremely contentious vote over T. Manlius Torquatus, twice consul and an ex-censor, and Q. Fulvius Flaccus, himself also an ex-censor then in his *third* consulship.[133] Our source, Livy, acknowledges the exceptional nature of this result but also notes that 120 years earlier, a candidate

---

104 (37.37.1–2), which instituted elections for the main priestly colleges rather than the ancient procedure of cooptation reinstituted by Sulla. Since Dio ascribes to Caesar the motive of improving his own chances in his run for *pontifex maximus*, there has been a tendency to assume that the *lex Labiena* changed the procedure for that election as well, but there is no evidence for that, and it is difficult to see why Sulla would have wanted to change a practice that had been part of the *mos maiorum* since at least the third century (Strasburger 1938: 102n30; Taylor 1942a; see more recently Drummond 1999: 166; North 2011). If indeed Caesar supported Labienus's law and this is not simply Dio's inference, a motive is not hard to seek: this was a "popular" move, and an attractive precedent could be found in Cn. Domitius's success in the election of *pontifex maximus* in 103, the year immediately after the passage of the *lex Domitia*.

130 Suet. *Iul.* 13; cf. Sall. *Cat.* 49.2; Plut. *Caes.* 7.1; Dio 37.37.2; Vell. Pat. 2.43.3. Jehne 2009: 57–58 attributes profound effects to this election by demonstrating Caesar's disregard for norms and aristocratic opposition, thus even accelerating the end of the Republic.

131 Gelzer 1968: 46. Gruen 2009: 23–24 was on the right track.

132 The evidence is contained in Rüpke 2005. The elections took place in 212, 183, 180, 150, 141, 132, 130, ca. 114, 107, 103, 89, and 81 (which I have counted as an election, though under the conditions this may be open to some doubt). Only in 130, 89, and 81 is it impossible in the state of our evidence to show that at least one pontiff was senior to the successful candidate (81 is a weak positive because *no* pontifex was even a consular). Winner much junior to at least one pontiff: 212, 180, 141, 132, and 103. Of course our evidence rarely reveals who were the candidates (212 is an exception: see next n.), but the assumption must be strong, especially if the common view has any validity whatever, that normally at least one of the most senior consulars among the pontiffs competed in the election. Winner not a consular: 212, 141, 132, 107, 103, 81.

133 Gruen 2009: 23. Livy 25.5.2–4; *ingenti certamine*. The great Fabius Maximus Cunctator, now cos. IV, was also eligible as a pontiff but did not throw his hat into the ring.

who had not yet even held curule office had become *pontifex maximus*: as rare as it was, then, in 63 the phenomenon had the patina of antiquity. More relevant to Caesar's success however is probably the case of Cn. Domitius Ahenobarbus, who as tribune in 104 had extended the traditional procedure for election of the *pontifex maximus* to *all* priesthoods: he was not only immediately elected *pontifex* on the new procedure but, in the very next year, elected *pontifex maximus*, despite the fact that his highest known *honor* up to this point was the very tribunate in which he had introduced the innovation. These precedents, especially this last, arouse the suspicion that on certain, relatively rare occasions the election for *pontifex maximus* was determined not by seniority but by a candidate's popular appeal – possibly actually increased rather than hindered by his relative youth.[134]

We may grant then that in 63 Caesar's victory was remarkable, if not unheard of, and rather humiliating for poor old Catulus and Isauricus (who may after all have split the votes of those who preferred seniority).[135] But the history of elections to the highest pontificate that we have just reviewed should make us think twice about the common assumption that the result could only have been produced by bribery on a massive scale. Our sources do not speak with one voice on the matter: Suetonius implies that Caesar in effect "bought" the election with massive expenditure (for bribery or splendor or both); Plutarch emphasizes not so much bribery as such but "the cost of doing politics," while Dio focuses rather on Caesar's shamelessly ingratiating *conduct* as candidate.[136] These all sound like plausible guesses and need not have been based on careful inquiry. It certainly would have been electoral suicide in this age to have rejected the great old Roman tradition of electoral "generosity." "Tokens of respect" were expected in an electoral campaign, and *ambitus* legislation, which did indeed tighten up considerably in the 60s in response to a felt need, persistently exempted gifts that could be plausibly construed as made in recognition of an existing social tie (i.e. to the members of one's own "tribe" or locality).[137] The sponsorship of public banquets, a popular form of

---

[134] Taylor 1942a: 423.   [135] As suggested to me by N. Rosenstein.
[136] Suet. *Iul.* 13, *non sine profusissima largitione*; Plut. *Caes.* 7.1–4, with Pelling 2011: 159; Dio 37.37.1–3.
[137] Rosillo López 2010. On Roman electoral "generosity," distinguishable from mere bribery in theory if not so much in practice, see esp. Cic. *Off.* 2.52–64. On electioneering and its regulation cf. Lintott 1990; Morstein-Marx 1998: 265–266 on *benignitas* (Q. Cic. *Comment. pet.* 41, 44, 49–50); Yakobson 1999: 22–43; Alexander 2002: 123–124, 132–134. Cicero's own brother (?) in the *Comment. pet.* recommends the same ingratiating manner that Caesar is alleged by Dio to have employed. Sall. *Cat.* 53.2–4 indicates that this behavior was remembered as characteristic of Caesar. For the unpleasant consequences of setting oneself against the tradition, consider Cato's failed consular run of 52, which was specifically attributed to this (Plut. *Cat. Min.* 49 [cf. 44.3–4]; Dio 40.58.3).

such gift giving, was entirely legal down to the *lex Tullia* of 63 (no evidence whether this was before or after Caesar's pontifical election), and even thereafter the force of the new ban was heavily undermined by the easy dodge of permitting one's friends to play host.[138] It was also the norm to show ingratiating condescension toward the voters as Caesar had done according to Dio.[139] Any popular election, even a pontifical election by a minority of tribes, symbolically involved "supplication" of the Roman People, and any time supplication of the People was demanded, popularity and "electioneering" – the wide range of practices by which a candidate tried to garner votes and orchestrate success on election day – must enter into the question.[140] Given the nature of our evidence it would be hard to decide which factor was the most important in effecting Caesar's victory, particularly since defeat deeply stung the *princeps senatus*, Q. Catulus, who had already spoken out against Caesar in the latter's recent aedileship.[141] Hostile observers and especially disappointed competitors typically raised the suspicion of bribery any time an electoral result went contrary to their expectations of the respect due to rank and privilege from the Roman voter, so we can be pretty certain how Catulus and those sympathetic to him explained Caesar's victory.[142]

"Bribery" pure and simple hardly seems to be the explanation, however. The curious procedure traditionally used for the election of the *pontifex maximus* (and now under the *lex Labiena* for those of all priesthoods), under which eighteen tribes were eliminated by lot from the vote, was one defense against the effects of money: one would have to bribe twenty-seven tribes in order to be assured of victory by this method, as opposed to "only" eighteen to gain the majority of the crucial First Class of voting units in a consular election.[143] Further, Caesar was never so much as charged with *ambitus* – either on this occasion or any other – although even a trial on such a charge,

---

138 See now the useful treatment by Rosillo López 2010: 49–85. Cf. Morstein-Marx 1998: 266 with n. 38; Yakobson 1999: 33–34.

139 Dio 37.37.3 θεραπεῦσαι καὶ κολακεῦσαι πάντα τινὰ καὶ τῶν τυχόντων. For Dio this was only a strategy to gain "power to come" (πρὸς τὴν ἐκ τοῦ ἔπειτα ἰσχὺν) over those toward whom he was currently adopting a servile attitude.

140 On "supplicating" the Roman People cf. Morstein-Marx 1998: 265–269, Yakobson 1999: esp. 211–225; Tatum 2018: 19–20, 264–266; Q. Cic. *Comment. pet.* 41, 44, 49–50 (*benignitas*). For elite distaste for the "carnivalesque" inversion of the social hierarchy, see Cic. *De or.* 1.112. Cic. *Leg. agr.* 2.18 *in eo* (*sc. pontifice creando*) *tamen propter amplitudinem sacredoti voluerint populo supplicari* shows that "supplication of the People" was expected even in elections for the *pontifex maximus*.

141 Catulus's bitterness is stressed by Sall. *Cat.* 49.2 and Vell. Pat. 2.43.3. Plut. (*Caes.* 7.2) says that Catulus tried to bribe (!) Caesar to leave the race.

142 Cic. *Mur.* 15–53, *Planc.* 6, 17, 51, with Alexander 2003: 124–125, 140–141.

143 Cic. *Leg. agr.* 2.21 implies that the sortition of the seventeen tribes would take place just before the vote, which is in any case the usual time for sortition to establish the tribal order of voting.

not to mention a conviction, would have been an efficacious way not only of reversing this result but of heading off any further high office if there were strong evidence that the law was broken.[144] Only three years before, a spectacular demonstration of the potential effectiveness of this tactic was given when the two consuls-elect for 65 were forced to step down after their conviction by rival competitors on a charge of *ambitus*.[145]

A hitherto unappreciated factor may be the fact that at the very time when the adventitious death of the *pontifex maximus* forced an election to fill the office, Caesar's campaign for the praetorship was either in full swing or may even have just successfully concluded. Canvassing for election to higher office was an opportunity to shine a spotlight on one's virtues, while on the other hand any senior consular who was competing might be ten or twenty years past his last great electoral contest. Looking back at our historical data, we find that in three of those cases in which the successful candidate for the highest pontificate was *not* even of consular rank, the election fell also *in the very year* – just as was the case for Caesar – of success in a major election, usually consular but in one other case praetorian.[146] Perhaps, then, Caesar was simply a more skilled, attractive, and zealous campaigner, assisted by fortuitously favorable timing. It would not be so surprising if the Roman voters simply liked what they saw in him – his peculiar combination of military *virtus*, aristocratic pedigree, and deference to the saturnalian claims of the Roman People – and preferred him to two pillars of the Sullan establishment whose consular elections and major achievements most voters will not have been old enough to remember personally. His eye-catching aedileship was a recent memory, as a result of which Plutarch himself said that "each and every man" of the People was disposed "to repay him with new offices and new honors" (*Caes.* 5.9); on the other hand Catulus had been on the wrong side of the Gabinian and Manilian debates and had spoken out forcefully against the long-overdue revival of honors to Marius.

As I have already noted, this was also the year of Caesar's successful candidacy for the praetorship (which passed without notice). We do not know whether it preceded the pontifical election (in which case it could have provided quite a boost) or, perhaps less likely, followed it (which would still have been beneficial for his chances in the pontifical election).[147]

---

[144] Billows 2009: 104, though it is a bit naive to assume that this proves Caesar's innocence.

[145] Alexander 1990: nos. 200, 201.

[146] P. Licinius Crassus Mucianus 132; Q. Servilius Caepio 107; probably P. Scipio Nasica Serapio 141 (praetorian: Broughton, *MRR* 1.478n2; 3.72).

[147] Dio 37.37.2 puts the pontifical election after the Catilinarian debate of December 5, when we know that Caesar was already praetor-elect, yet in this he is directly contradicted by Sall. *Cat.* 49.2. If

Of Caesar's other activities in 63 before the Catilinarian debates of December we hear little and know even less. It has often been supposed that he was one of the shadowy operatives behind the tribune P. Servilius Rullus's land bill combated so ably by Cicero at the beginning of his consulship. But he is never actually mentioned in this connection; his association with this event in some historians' minds seems to derive more from the irresistible magnetism of Caesar's name than from any actual evidence.[148] Indeed, the complete *silence* even of the ancient biographers on the matter calls for attention: if there had been significant suspicion of Caesar in this matter, it surely would have been mentioned somewhere (if only in Cicero's posthumous *de consiliis suis*) and put to service by the biographers in constructing their image of Caesar as a subtle but relentless agitator. It looks as if once again Caesar was not conspicuous where contentious *popularis* efforts were being made, now along the traditional popular path of agrarian reform. The same may be said of the debt agitation with which the year 63 had begun.[149]

Caesar's name does explicitly emerge in the confusing maneuvers surrounding the trial of the elderly senator C. Rabirius later in the year for the killing of Saturninus almost forty years before.[150] Rabirius could plausibly claim legal and political cover by virtue of the Senate's Emergency Decree, so the case necessarily touched upon the Senate's authority to advise the consuls to take emergency action against what it defined as acts of insurrection.[151] The tribune T. Labienus (Caesar's future lieutenant in Gaul) brought the charge under the ancient procedure of *perduellio* rather than the recent law of treason (*maiestas*), probably to ensure a hearing before the People rather than a jury of the well-off. According to Suetonius, Caesar had actually bribed Labienus to

---

Ramsey 2019 is correct to date the consular election of 63 to the last week of September, the odds are roughly three to one on present evidence that the pontifical election preceded it. Suet. *Iul.* 12–13 implicitly places the pontifical election after the Rabirius trial (for which see n. 150). Jehne 2009: 56 (cf. 2001: 29) suggests that Caesar put his entire political existence on the line by choosing to contest the pontifical election in addition to the praetorian in the face of extremely poor odds, when failure might have cost him the praetorian election as well and resulted in bankruptcy. This is probably overstating the case, and in any case we are not certain which election preceded.

[148] Strasburger complained in 1938: 114–115 that although no ancient source so much as mentions Caesar's involvement he had not yet found a modern treatment that expressed even the slightest doubt of Caesar's "authorship" of the measure. Yet the tradition continued in Gelzer 1968: 42–45; Mitchell 1979: 194; Meier 1982: 158; Goldsworthy 2006: 120; against: esp. Drummond 1999: 158–162; Morstein-Marx 2004: 196n148.

[149] Dio 37.25.4; Cic. *Off.* 2.84. See n. 84.

[150] Alexander 1990, nos. 220, 221; a recent summary in Lintott 2008: 120–125. Ramsey 2019: 242–244 now gives good grounds for dating the Rabirius trial to late July or early August.

[151] See Morstein-Marx 2004: 225–226. The decree is also often called the *s(enatus) c(onsultum) u(ltimum)* after Caesar (*BC* 1.5.3, where however the full phrase *illud extremum atque ultimum senatus consultum* makes clear that this was not a technical term).

bring the charge (*Iul.* 12). This is an easy but unverifiable allegation, which seems to overlook the fact that Labienus surely needed no bribe to avenge the killing of his own uncle in the Saturninus tumult and simultaneously to advertise his dedication to basic popular rights before the People.[152] The curious procedure of *perduellio* called first for a judge to pronounce sentence, followed, in the event of conviction, by a popular hearing and vote; this made conviction by the sole judge a virtually automatic formality in order to place the real decision in the hands of the People.[153] This was a natural way to proceed against a defendant alleged to have violated the cherished popular right of *provocatio* under the authority of the Emergency Decree: so too had Opimius, the consul who had first used the decree, been tried *apud populum* in 120 for having thrown citizens into prison without a trial and executed some of the Gracchans.[154] The parallel with the Opimian case is in fact rather close, since the issue in Rabirius trial, as in Opimius's, does not seem to have been the legality of use of the decree to suppress open insurrection as such but whether it gave impunity to a consul to kill and imprison citizens *after the tumult had been put down* and therefore the emergency had arguably passed.[155] Since this does not seem to have been a particularly salient political question at the time of the trial (certainly well before the arrest and execution of the "Catilinarians" in December), it is most simply interpreted as a bit of *popularis* image-making by Labienus, the tribune who played the central role. Naturally, Cicero, who undertook the defense, interpreted the trial as an attack on the authority of the Senate in general, but Labienus's sights need not in fact have been so high.[156]

---

[152] Q. Labienus: Cic. *Rab. perd.* 14, 18, 20–22.

[153] Hence Cic. *Rab. perd.* 12 *hic popularis* [Labienus] *a IIViris . . . non iudicari de cive Romano sed indicta causa civem Romanum capitis condemnari coegit.* So too in the legendary original trial for *perduellio* the *duumviri* consider their hands to be tied: Livy 1.26.7. For the curious role of the *duumviri* in the *perduellio* procedure see Tyrrell 1978, esp. 10–34. See also Drummond 1995: 61–62, acknowledging that the requirement to condemn was the "first-century interpretation" of the archaic procedure.

[154] Livy *Per.* 61, Cic. *De or.* 2.106; other sources at *GC* 50–51. On Opimius's trial see Ungern-Sternberg 1970: 68–71; note that he accepts Mommsen's emendation of Liv. *Per.* 61 *in carcerem coniecisset* to *in carcere necasset* or *in carcerem coniectos necasset,* which avoids the implication that the mere imprisonment of a citizen might be seen as contrary to the *lex Sempronia.*

[155] Brunt 1988: 16n16; Lintott 1999: 90 ("when it was held to justify extraordinary forms of trial *after order had been restored*" [my emphasis]); Morstein-Marx 2004: 109–110, 225–228. Note that contra Arena 2012: 200–220, who assumes that the legitimacy of the *s.c.u.* was fundamentally rejected by *populares,* both Sallust (*Cat.* 29.2–3) and Caesar (*BCiv.* 1.7.5–6) raise no doubts about the legitimacy of the so-called *s.c.u.* to suppress ongoing violent insurrection; both she and Golden 2013: 104–149 overlook the fact that the most controversial issue of its use in 121 and 100 was its application once the emergency for which it had been invoked had passed. The sources do not name the legal procedure under which Opimius was tried by the *populus*; perhaps *perduellio,* which would also make the choice of that procedure for Rabirius less curious.

[156] Cic. *Pis.* 4; Dio 37.26.1–3: Morstein-Marx 2004: 225–226; cf. Ungern-Sternberg 1970: 81–85.

Caesar enters the story only for a brief moment in the spotlight: he was chosen as judge, either by lot or by "the praetor," or perhaps both, if the praetor was obliged to name the man selected by the lot.[157] Unfortunately prosopographical research has thus far failed to identify the praetor involved (probably the urban praetor), but no source suggests that he had engineered some predetermined choice or acted as a pawn in some *populari*s game orchestrated by Caesar (or Labienus, for that matter).[158] L. Caesar, the consul of 64 and distant cousin of our Caesar, was also selected as a *iudex*, but there is no evidence for close political cooperation between the two Caesars at this time and nothing in his record suggests that this rather colorless and "safe" noble would have gone in for *populari*s posturing.[159] Inasmuch as Caesar's role as *iudex* is the *only* evidence available to corroborate Suetonius's claim that he was closely involved in bringing the accusation, it is surprising that so few scholars have been able to convince themselves that Caesar was *not* the driving force behind this trial.[160] The trial was sufficiently determined by its public relations value to the ambitious young tribune, Labienus. Conceivably, Caesar may have tried to exploit some of the publicity, though his formal conviction of Rabirius as *duumvir* does not amount to much since he could hardly have acted otherwise, and his non-*populari*s cousin did exactly the same. Nor did he play a prominent role in the trial; his name is not even mentioned in Cicero's defense. Rabirius was not even convicted. It is unclear whether the trial actually gave Labienus much of a boost, much less Caesar, who was well out of the limelight.

In 63 came the news that Mithridates had committed suicide. His long series of wars against the Roman People could now be declared over. The time was right for the supporters of Pompey, or opportunistic *populare*s, to celebrate the general's great achievements. The tribunes Labienus and T. Ampius Balbus successfully promulgated a law decreeing that Pompey

---

[157] Lot: Suet. *Iul.* 12. "The praetor": Dio 37.27.2.

[158] Identifications: Cicero's ally and client L. Valerius Flaccus has been the leading candidate (Broughton, *MRR* 3.212) until recently, when Ryan made a plausible case for L. Roscius Otho (1997: 239; but see Drummond 1999: 132). Both men seem to have been on quite good terms with Cicero: Flaccus would provide Cicero with his decisive evidence for the conspiracy later in this year and was defended by him later with much praise for his political sympathies (*Flac.* esp. 6–8, 94–105); Roscius was conspicuously defended against popular displeasure in this year by consul Cicero (Plut. *Cic.* 13.3–4; Cic. *Att.* 2.1.3). An older favorite was Q. Metellus Celer (see *MRR* 3.37), though his role in preventing Rabirius's conviction (Dio 37.27.3) argues against the assumption that the praetor was in on the scheme. Phillips's advocacy of P. Lentulus Sura (1974: 94) is patently circular.

[159] Gruen 1974: 135. Note that L. Caesar held firm for the death sentence in the Catilinarian Debate even after his cousin had spoken: Cic. *Cat.* 4.13, *Att.* 12.21.1.

[160] Exceptions are Strasburger 1938: 120; Ungern-Sternberg 1970: 82–83; Drummond 1999: 164–165. Phillips 1974: 93, 97–101 goes to the opposite extreme.

should wear a gold crown at the games and triumphal dress in the Circus.[161] Dio mentions neither tribune, but in accordance with his practice in his narrative of this year he cites Caesar as the one chiefly responsible for the honors.[162] The suggestion that Caesar here took the lead among so many peers and seniors may be questioned: other, more senior senators will have been as eager as was the consul Cicero to propose unprecedented honors for the victorious Pompey.[163] Like Plutarch and Suetonius, in his account of the year 63 Dio is repeatedly eager to foreshadow the future by dropping Caesar's name and crediting him with far more prominence in the matter than he is likely to deserve. There is every reason to assume that Caesar readily leapt aboard the bandwagon currying favor to the absent Pompey, but little reason to suppose that he was its driver.[164]

Some ancient authors allege that Caesar was a partner in the "Catilinarian" conspiracy of 63 who deftly evaded detection, or at least public condemnation, while at the same time almost succeeding in persuading the Senate to let the captured conspirators off with a punishment lighter than death.[165] Assessing this kind of argument judiciously is notoriously difficult: on one hand Caesar is not entitled to any "presumption of innocence," a judicial rather than a scholarly concept, but on the other we have seen how ready some ancient authors were to see Caesar lurking down every dark corner in this period and it is nearly impossible to prove a negative to a committed believer. The best approach, then, is to review the evidence methodically and ask ourselves in each case how determinative it appears to be, keeping in mind that in a matter that was by its nature secret we can do no more than judge probabilities.

Let us start with a simple statistic: approximately 2.5 percent or less of the membership of the Senate appears to have been seriously involved in the conspiracy.[166] In other words, without any further evidence explicitly

---

[161] Vell. Pat. 2.40.4; Dio 37.21.4 makes the crown laurel (a possible emendation of Velleius: Mommsen 1887: 1:427n.2); cf. Cic. *Att.* 1.18.6.

[162] Dio 37.21.4; Drummond 1999: 149.

[163] Cf. Cicero's proposal in the Senate for an unprecedented number of days of *supplicationes*, Chapter 5, n. 116.

[164] Syme 1938: 117. Cf. Gruen 1974: 79–80; 2009: 25.

[165] Sall. *Cat.* 49, Suet. *Iul.* 17. Many modern scholars have been tempted by the possibility of Caesar as a Catilinarian: esp. Canfora 2007: 39–41, 43–46, who is wedded to an antiquated notion of Sallust as dutiful Caesarian apologist, "vindicator of Caesar's memory." Billows 2009: 88 actually thinks Caesar would have supported Catiline since the latter would likely "follow policies more *popularis* than not." But see already Strasburger 1938: 120–125 and the demolition of the "First Catilinarian Conspiracy" (n. 10). For a judicious recent discussion see now Pelling 2011: 163–164.

[166] If we assume that *all* the senators Sallust confidently numbers among the conspirators were in fact guilty we reach the number eleven; adding a handful to allow for the possibility that some escaped denunciation, we reach roughly fifteen, or 2.5 percent of all senators. Sall. *Cat.* 17.3 lists P. Lentulus

mentioning Caesar we could assume that the probability of his being among the conspirators (or anyone else, for that matter) was no more than 2.5 percent. But in fact the conspiracy (or conspiracies) had very few high-ranking senators of Caesar's praetorian standing or higher. Apart from Catiline himself – who may in fact not have been an actual participant in the urban conspiracy that was rolled up on December 3 – only three known participants had been elected to high office before, and all of these had suffered major setbacks in their careers: P. Lentulus Sura, cos. 71, expelled from the Senate in 70 and thus forced to climb his way back up the ladder of offices, now praetor for the second time; P. Autronius, elected consul in 66 but immediately deprived of that office by conviction in the bribery court during his climb and expelled from the Senate; and L. Cassius Longinus, who had failed in his consular candidacy this very year.[167] Caesar, who had suffered *no* setbacks or electoral defeats but quite the contrary had enjoyed great success and public esteem both in his aedileship and in this very year, including a surprising victory over two of the most senior senators as well as election to the praetorship, simply does not naturally belong in this group of disappointed and probably increasingly impoverished also-rans. With his record of success, why ever would Caesar associate himself with an extremely risky plan to overthrow the system, which was working extremely well for him, and replace it with some kind of *dominatio* or junta over which he had no control?[168]

So much for general concerns, which in sum warn us not to be inclined to believe in Caesar's culpability without quite convincing evidence. Now for the evidence, such as it is: (a) Asconius's claim that Caesar supported Catiline in his previous consular campaign of 64;[169] (b) Sallust's report that

Sura (cos. 71, expelled in census of 70, pr. 63), P. Autronius Paetus (cos. des. 65 but convicted *de ambitu* and expelled from Senate), L. Cassius Longinus (pr. 66), L. Calpurnius Bestia (tr. des. 62), C. Cornelius Cethegus, P. Cornelius Sulla, Ser. Cornelius Sulla, Q. Annius Chilo, M. Porcius Laeca (apparently junior senators), L. Vargunteius (probably convicted *de ambitu* and expelled from the Senate), Q. Curius (expelled by censors in 70). See Gruen 1974: 418–419. Sallust's list corresponds closely to the roster of those clearly incriminated in the senatorial hearing of 63 plus those subsequently convicted in trials (Alexander 1990: nos. 229–233). L. Bestia is an exception, though named by Sallust he does not seem to have been formally charged or named in the senatorial debates: Syme is probably right to regard his inclusion as a malicious invention (1964: 132–133).

[167] Ascon. 82C; Q. Cicero(?), *Comment. pet.* 7. Catiline: Seager's persuasive demonstration (1973) that Lentulus's urban conspiracy should be distinguished from whatever Catiline had been doing remains unrefuted.

[168] For Cicero's suggestion (Cic. *Off.* 2.84, written in 44) that Caesar was scheming together with Catiline to cancel debts in 63 see nn. 84, 149).

[169] Ascon. 83C (bis). There is, incidentally, no evidence for the common assumption that Caesar (whether he acted as president of the court or as prosecutor) somehow engineered Catiline's acquittal in the trials of Sullan bounty hunters of 64.

Q. Catulus and C. Piso tried to prompt Cicero to implicate Caesar *falsely* (n.b.: *falso*) around the time of the debate, and failing in that attempt, had started a whispering campaign that he was involved;[170] (c) Cato's innuendoes or direct imputations against Caesar in his speech during the debate;[171] (d) the fact reported by Sallust and Plutarch that equestrian guards at the debate of December 5 were persuaded by these innuendoes or outright allegations to threaten his life as he exited the senatorial meeting;[172] and (e) Suetonius's report (partly backed by Plutarch) that after the debate (probably very early in 62) Caesar was named among the allies of Catiline both in court by the informer L. Vettius and in the Senate by Q. Curius, a "mole" in the conspiracy apparently relied on by Cicero who had turned state's evidence to reveal the details of the plot.[173]

None of these facts or allegations does much to increase the almost vanishingly low preexisting probability of Caesar's complicity in the conspiracy. (a) fails to distinguish between supporting Catiline in the election *the previous year* (64) and participating in a conspiracy to overthrow the Republic. Cicero himself may be adduced to defend him in the same terms he used to defend his protégé M. Caelius of a similar charge: Catiline enjoyed at one point the electoral support of many *optimi cives* before he was finally unmasked; even he, Cicero, had at one time been deceived by his appearance of virtue! In fact, among Catiline's most trusted friends even after his flight from Rome was none other than the *princeps senatus*, Q. Catulus, who seems likely to have endorsed him in this same election

---

[170] Sall. *Cat.* 49.1; similarly, Plut. *Caes.* 7.5, 8.4. Plut. *Cic.* 20.6–7 also mentions rumors of Caesar's involvement and seeks to explain why Cicero did not implicate Caesar; at *Caes.* 8.5, like App. *BCiv.* 2.6/20, he stresses more directly the immunity provided by Caesar's great popularity. None of these rumors was brought into the open enough to be refuted, and all of it appears to bear the mark of Cicero's *De consiliis suis*, a highly questionable source where Caesar is concerned (see nn. 11 and 175).

[171] Sall. *Cat.* 52.14–16; App. *BCiv.* 2.6/21; Plut. *Cat. min.* 23.1–2, implicitly relying on an account other than Sallust's (§§3–4).

[172] Suet. *Iul.* 14.2; Plut. *Caes.* 8.2, whose dating of the event is preferable to that of Sallust, *Cat.* 49.4, and therefore probably puts Cato on the hook as much as Catulus and Piso. Canfora thinks that the reaction of the overexcited *equites* "proves" how close Caesar was to the condemned conspirators. Suetonius seems to imply that the equestrian guard actually burst into the meeting (*strictos gladios usque eo intentans, ut sedentem una proximi deseruerint*), and some scholars have taken this view (Gelzer 1968: 53, Canfora 2007: 48). Yet Plutarch and Sallust seem very specific in placing the incident during Caesar's exit from the meeting, and had Cicero actually allowed the guard to intimidate senators during the meeting itself this would certainly have provoked much sharper adverse comment than can possibly be extracted from Cic. *Phil.* 2.16–17.

[173] Suet. *Iul.* 17. For the allegation made in court see Alexander 1990: no. 227 (only "threatened"); Novius's position, given by Suetonius as *quaestorem*, must surely be emended to *quaesitorem* (*MRR* 2.175). Cf. Plut. *Caes.* 8.5, who puts Caesar's defense in the Senate only a "few days" after December 5, although Suetonius says he avoided the Senate for the remainder of the year (twenty-five days). Pelling 2011: 171 rightly favors the latter. Q. Curius as Cicero's informer: Sall. *Cat.* 17.3, 23.1–4, 26.3, 28.2. Vettius as informer: n. 178.

(64); certainly, Catiline still enjoyed the conspicuous support of eminent senior senators during his trial in that year.[174] But the claim about Caesar's support for Catiline in 64 is further tainted by its likely origin in Cicero's posthumously published secret account of his consulship, which also contained wild allegations of Caesar's complicity with Crassus in plans for a coup d'état in 65 – part of the debunked myth of the "First Catilinarian Conspiracy."[175] (b) is explicitly labeled a partisan fabrication by Sallust (*falso*), and anyway charges spread at the time by two personal enemies of Caesar – Q. Catulus again, the *princeps senatus* humiliated by Caesar in the election for *pontifex maximus* earlier in this very year, and C. Piso, consul in 67, prosecuted or at least attacked by Caesar for his ostensibly illegal punishment of a Transpadane – hardly deserve much credence in themselves.[176] Instead, this very story alerts us to the opportunity provided by Caesar's ostensibly "lenient" motion (hardly: Cic. *Att.* 12.21.1 and Chapter 3) on the conspirators to exploit the occasion with imputations of guilt. Similarly, (c) Cato's insidious suggestions of sympathy or even complicity with the "Catilinarians" – if Sallust's version of the speech can be trusted this far – are an adroit, but it must be said rather unscrupulous, rhetorical move to undercut support for any sentence short of death by raising the fear that this would appear tantamount to a confession of guilt.[177] The equestrian guards (d) knew nothing independently; the sources make clear that they were responding to the allegations made by Catulus, Piso, or Cato. (b), (c), and (d) clearly form a cluster and surely fall together. (e) is no doubt the most serious evidence for Caesar's possible complicity in the conspiracy. There are indeed troubling features in the unfortunately very obscure references we have to these incidents: Vettius, whom Cicero later calls "that informer of mine" in a private letter to his friend Atticus, claimed to have an incriminating letter from Caesar to

---

[174] Cic. *Cael.* 12–15. Sall. *Cat.* 34.3–35.6, with Ramsey 2007: 155. (Catiline had notoriously avenged the death of Catulus's father.) Cic. *Sull.* 81–82 recalls the support of *consulares* for Catiline in his trials of 73, 65, and even 64 (Alexander 1990, no. 217; Barry 1996: 278, 296–298).

[175] Rejected, for example, by Brunt 1957; Gruen 1974: 138; Drummond 1995: 21; Lintott 2008: 135. On *De consiliis suis*, see Plut. *Crass.* 13.3–4; Dio 39.10, with Rawson 1982 = 1991: 408–415; Moles 1982; Marshall 1985: 285, 287. See also Dyck 1996: 478–479.

[176] Cf. Plut. *Caes.* 7.5–7 (cf. *Cat. min.* 22.5, Cic. 20.6–7), App. *BCiv.* 2.6/20. A good summary in Pelling 2011: 163–164. Drummond 1995: 19–21 has doubts about the historicity of Sallust's claim here: the story may even have been an invention of Caesar's *apologists*. But it hardly bolsters the allegation if it was merely an authorless rumor. The asymmetrical feud between Catulus and Caesar continued almost immediately with Caesar's proposal on January 1 (in the midst of the accusations under discussion) that his enemy's name be removed from the temple of Jupiter Optimus Maximus: Chapter 3, n. 84.

[177] See Chapter 3, n. 65.

Catiline; his evidence and Curius's too seemed sufficient to convict
a number of others; perhaps most troubling, Suetonius tells us that
Caesar punished Vettius quite severely for his revelations, destroying
some of his personal goods, allowing him to be roughly beaten by
a crowd at a *contio*, and throwing him into prison along with (so at least
Suetonius says) the *quaesitor* Novius himself (the latter for allowing
a superior magistrate to be brought before his court). How things got to
this state remains very unclear, but evidently the incriminating letter was
never produced, and Caesar's harsh treatment of Vettius, who was something of a professional informer, is consistent with Roman legal custom
protecting the dignity of magistrates and attitudes toward those who gave
false accusation, while Dio's account makes clear that there were serious
questions about Vettius's integrity that drew the attention and intervention of the Senate in particular (as would also be central to the incident to
come in 59), whether he was supplying names at someone else's bidding to
settle personal or political scores.[178] Several others were convicted on
Vettius's and Curius's evidence, so Caesar's avoidance even of a trial
appears significant.[179] To Curius's accusation in the Senate Caesar deftly
responded that Cicero himself attested that he (Caesar) had provided
information to him about the plot, and nothing further appears to have
come of it even with a possible trial in view, in a body that was hardly
disposed to ignore incriminating rumors.[180] Indeed, despite all the controversy that attached to Caesar's name in years to come, this allegation seems
never to have been repeated publicly in his lifetime or backed by more
credible evidence than (perhaps) Cicero's secret history.

In sum, although other scholars may rate the probative value of these
tidbits somewhat higher than I do, none of them does actually move the
needle very far past the exceedingly low general probability (<2.5 percent)
that Caesar was involved in the conspiracy of 63.[181] Neither, when there

---

[178] Dio 37.41.2–4 provides fuller information about Vettius's information than Suet. *Iul.* 17, but
without so much as mentioning Caesar (Alexander 1990: no. 226). Cic. *Att.* 2.24.2 *ille noster
index*; for the "Vettius Affair" of 59 see Chapter 4). Two other known instances of *pignoris capio*
are roughly comparable examples of the infringement of magisterial dignity (Greenidge 1901:
336–337; see also Butler and Cary 1927: 60–61). Vettius was "an informer of little repute" (Gruen
1974: 95–96).

[179] Alexander 1990: nos. 226, 228–232.

[180] If Plut. *Caes.* 8.5 refers to this incident (Pelling 2011: 171), a noisy demonstration pressed the Senate
to allow Caesar to leave. Note also that Caesar took one of the conspirators (Statilius) into his own
custody in accordance with a senatorial decree: Sall. *Cat.* 47.4.

[181] Suet. *Iul.* 17.2. Some readers may notice that in these pages, while avoiding for the most part
quantitative expressions of probability, I have followed the basic principles of Bayesian calculation
of conditional probability – the standard method for systematically updating probability estimates

were such strong motives for distortion, should one be impressed by the mere number of the allegations on the oft-fallible assumption that "Where there's smoke there's fire." As E. Gruen aptly comments in another connection, "After the execution of the Catilinarians in December 63, it was in any politician's interest to associate his enemies with Catiline. And after 59 the episode or episodes took on added significance as a means whereby to discredit Caesar and Crassus."[182] Insinuation of association with Catiline remained for decades a potentially useful line of attack against anyone one wished to discredit in the Senate or courts: not only Cicero's *bêtes noires*, P. Clodius and Antony for example, but also his own clients P. Sulla in 62 and M. Caelius in 56.[183] Even among those who were not Caesar's avowed enemies, by proposing a relatively "lenient' sentence of life imprisonment for the conspirators rather than death (see next chapter), Caesar naturally made himself a target for such suspicion and innuendo – quite unfairly, it should go without saying. When we add the impulse of the biographers and the anti-Caesar invective tradition to attach retrospectively every possible suspect action to his name, we have more than enough reason to reject this particular allegation.

To summarize, Caesar is nowhere to be seen in our accounts of the truly important *popularis* initiatives of the year, such as the Rullan land bill or a tribunician bill calling for relieving pressure on debtors. His role in Labienus's invidious trial of Rabirius was a minor one. It is hard to say even whether (as Dio thinks) he stood out very much among those lining up to shower Pompey with praises for his victory over Mithridates. Rumor swirled of his possible association with Catiline or with the urban conspiracy but no plausible evidence was ever produced and he was able to clear himself both in court and before the Senate; the rumors probably originated in Catulus's enmity and gained a specious plausibility because of Caesar's opposition to the execution of the conspirators. On the other hand Caesar's skill in cultivating popular support in electoral contests was amply demonstrated with his dual victories in this year, in one case against heavy odds. Ingratiating self-promotion in the pursuit of personal *dignitas*

---

in view of additional evidence. For nontechnical introductions to the method, see Lindley 2006: 79–100; Silver 2012: 240–250. Two notable lessons of Bayes's Rule are (1) that it takes powerful evidence indeed to change a prior *unlikelihood* appreciably (the <2.5 percent probability of *any* senator's involvement), and (2) "false positives" (in our examples: alternative, benign explanations for a piece of evidence adduced for Caesar's complicity) may greatly weaken an inference even when they are not in themselves actually very likely.

[182] Gruen 1969: 21.
[183] Clodius: Tatum 1999: 144–145, 277n117. Sulla: Cic. *Sull.* passim. Caelius: n. 174.

was Caesar's version of the *via popularis*, not invidious rabble-rousing, controversial reforms or outright sedition.[184]

Patrician *Popularis*

If this picture seems at odds with the one so familiar to us from the biographical tradition, it is also perfectly consistent with that which the contemporary Sallust provides us. Sallust's much-discussed "synkrisis" comparing Caesar and Cato, the two paragons of *virtus* in his day, is an important crux in the interpretation of the *Catiline*, but one central part of the characterization of Caesar deserves special emphasis in our context. After describing various emphatic divergences between Caesar and Cato in their manner of interaction and style of politics, where Sallust repeatedly stresses the contrast between Caesar's strategic, ingratiating dealings with others and Cato's strict moral code in the same realm, he attributes to each a larger goal. Cato's objective is to gain moral authority instead of pursuing *gloria*, "to be rather than to appear good";[185] Caesar's, however, was to seek "a great command, an army, a new war . . . that would permit his excellence to shine forth."[186] Now it is perfectly possible that Sallust is himself falling for the teleological perspective here, since of course Caesar would in fact turn out to be one of the greatest generals in the annals of Rome. Yet his imputation of Caesar's goal is well supported by the evidence we have reviewed in this chapter, as well as Roman reverence for *exempla virtutis* and the great military heroes of the past. Sallust is therefore probably right to suppose that Caesar's chief goal in his rise to high office was *not* demagogic rabble-rousing, subversion of the constitution, or pursuit of monarchy as his enemies, the biographers, and (retrospectively) Cicero claim, but obtaining the opportunity to demonstrate his *virtus* in the good old Roman way by martial feats.

Seeking an opportunity to demonstrate one's preeminent *virtus* through military leadership ("a great command, an army, a new war") is probably a repugnant idea to most of us, but for a noble Roman this was perhaps the most conventional and honorable form of advancement available. A great roster of Roman military heroes – not, of course, only the Scipiones whose

---

[184] My interpretation thus is close to that of Gruen 2009. Raaflaub 2010: 162, describing Caesar's methods in his early career as "unusual and aggressive," remains in my opinion too close to the traditional retrospective/teleological narrative.

[185] Sall. *Cat.* 54.6: *esse quam videri bonus malebat; ita, quo minus petebat gloriam, eo magis illum assequebatur.*

[186] Sall. *Cat.* 54.4 *sibi magnum imperium, exercitum, bellum novom exoptabat ubi virtus enitescere posset.*

youthful military exploits we have noted, but also many others, from Fabius Maximus and M. Marcellus in the Hannibalic War through L. Aemilius Paulus to the more recent *exempla* of Marius, Lucullus and now Pompey – all had "let their excellence shine forth" and won *gloria* in great, terrible, but ultimately victorious wars. "On the shoulders of every young man born into a leading senatorial family weighed the self-evident duty to strike out on a political path which was inextricably bound up with high military command."[187] Even Cicero, the *consul togatus*, had to acknowledge that "military excellence outstrips all other kinds of *virtus*" in the scale of values typical of the Roman voter.[188] The "Roman voter" is highly relevant here for in the Republic this means of self-advancement depended on a community of free men for its proper recognition in the form of *honor* (further offices) and *gloria* (in the collective memory).[189] If Sallust is right, then, Caesar had adopted an entirely traditional republican goal for himself; what was truly remarkable was how he proved to be up to it. (It is in fact Cato who is shown in the *synkrisis* to be the unconventional one by replacing the traditional pursuit of *gloria* with a rather untraditional emphasis on moral rigor.)[190] Caesar's pursuit of "a command, an army, a war" was a mark of adherence to the norms of the Republic, not of an intent to subvert them.

No doubt Caesar had models, *exempla*, from the great Roman past in mind as he climbed the ladder of political office, and no doubt he prompted some observers to consider such models as well. Scholars have nearly universally assumed that Caesar's primary model was his own relative by marriage, his aunt's husband C. Marius, whose memory and honors he had in fact restored.[191] Yet an act of *pietas* and historical justice (undoing acts of excessive vindictiveness by a personal enemy in civil war) does not imply, as we saw, any appetite for emulation except for Marius's extraordinary military achievements and victories. Beyond this the differences between the two men are more striking than any similarity. A huge social gulf separated the patrician Caesar, whose family boasted descent from Venus, Aeneas, and Romulus and whose consulships distinguished a score or more years of the *fasti* of the Republic, from the "new man" who

---

[187] Jehne 2001: 18 – a modest exaggeration by this date (Blom 2016: 55–59; Segal 2019 passim) but nevertheless a fair expression of the traditional importance attributed to this activity.

[188] Cic. *Mur.* 22–24 (*rei militaris virtus praestat ceteris omnibus*). Harris 1979: 10–41; Rosenstein 2006; McDonnell 2006: 181–240.

[189] Sall. *Cat.* 7.5–6. See Morstein-Marx 2009: 118–119.

[190] Morrell 2017: 114: "Cato valued moral excellence above military achievements in a manner atypical for a Roman."

[191] The idea is pervasive in the scholarship, but Zecchini 2001: 117–120 is rightly cautious: see n. 194.

hailed from rustic Arpinum. Marius furthermore had also proven fatally susceptible to *ambitio* and anger, had advanced himself by sharp attacks on the nobility as such, and had marred his glorious record with an unworthy end, a vindictive monster bathed in the blood of citizens.[192] It is impossible to imagine the aristocratic Caesar at any time in his career excoriating the nobility for its inertia, incompetence, and outright viciousness in the terms Marius used (at least according to Sallust) at the time of his first election to the consulship.[193]

Far more attractive models to a patrician who had set before himself the goal of attaining military *gloria*, especially after having won great honor already as a soldier, would have been the patrician Scipiones Africani, both the elder (the conqueror of Hannibal) and his grandson by adoption, the younger (destroyer of Carthage and Numantia, usually known to us as Aemilianus).[194] Their preeminence in the annals of Roman military achievement is clear.[195] Great nobles both, victors over Rome's greatest imperial rival, they were notable not only for the magnitude of their martial *res gestae* but also for their *honores*, *dignitas*, and massive popularity.[196] In fact they were the prime examples for the successful *use* of that popularity to attain the military commands that enabled them to win *gloria*. The elder Africanus had actually been elected to the aedileship at age twenty-two or twenty-three, well before the customary time ("If all citizens want to elect me aedile, then I am old enough": Livy 25.2.7), and gained his great opportunity to command the Roman theater of war in Spain when he prevailed in a special election to the post (*privatus* with *proconsular imperium*) at age twenty-five.[197] "Scipio's career

---

[192] Sall. *Iug.* 63.6: *postea ambitione praeceps datus est*; 64.5: *cupidine et ira, pessumis consultoribus, grassari*; 84.1: *antea iam infestus nobilitati, tum vero multus atque ferox instare, singulos modo, modo universos laedere, dictitare sese consulatum ex victis illis spolia cepisse, alia praeterea magnifica pro se et illis dolentia.*

[193] Sall. *Iug.* 85.

[194] Zecchini 2001: 124–126 persuasively stresses the usefulness of both Scipiones as models and precedents for Caesar. He focuses on his later career from the victories in Gaul onward, but there is no reason to think that the Scipiones had ever been absent from Roman minds.

[195] Various lists of Rome's greatest military leaders that appear in Cicero's speeches are instructive (esp. Cic. *Cat.* 4.21, *Planc.* 60, *Balb.* 40, *Sest.* 143, *Pis.* 58, *Rep.* 1.1): the Scipiones are the only men who make it onto all of the lists. Cf. Plutarch's comparison to the "Fabii, Scipios, and Metelli" at *Caes.* 15.3. Q. Fabius Cunctator was, as Ennius wrote, "the one man who saved Rome by delaying"; and see n. 112) but his essentially defensive posture made him a less natural model for emulation in this age.

[196] The Elder Africanus had been twice consul, censor, *princeps senatus*, and *triumphator* (twice if one includes the quasi-triumph of 206: Beck 2005: 344); his *imago*, extraordinarily, was preserved in the Temple of Jupiter Optimus Maximus (Val. Max. 8.15.1–2; App. *Iber.* 89; see Flower 1996: 48: "It is tempting to follow Valerius Maximus in interpreting this as a claim that the temple was in some special sense a home to Africanus during his lifetime"). The Younger Africanus was twice consul in an age when this may have been forbidden by law (Chapter 5, n. 239), censor, and twice *triumphator*.

[197] Liv. 26.18.4–11. See Beck 2005: 339–340 and his whole discussion, 328–367.

was the most extraordinary of the entire Middle Republic," observes H. Beck; he was, R. Feig Vishnia adds, "a new phenomenon: a member of the most distinguished patrician family, a brilliant and charismatic general who did not hesitate to turn directly to the people over the senate's head to achieve his goals . . . in short, a *popularis* in an age when the *via popularis* had not yet been defined."[198] Similarly, the younger Africanus (Aemilianus) moved directly from the military tribunate to the consulship at age thirty-seven in direct violation of the *lex Villia annalis*, although in fact he had been a candidate only for the aedileship. As we saw in the Introduction, massive popular pressure exerted through tribunes forced the suspension of the law ("by the laws of Tullius and Romulus the People were the judges of elections"), and when Scipio's colleague suggested the casting of lots for provinces, a tribune effected the assignment of the war with Carthage to Scipio by a law of the Roman People – apparently the first known case of thus forcing the Senate's hand.[199] When the cry rose up for Scipio to be chosen consul a second time to finish the drawn-out war with Numantia, contrary to custom and perhaps to law, the procedure was repeated, and once again senatorial resistance was circumvented by a law assigning him to the Spanish command as demanded by the popular will.[200] An "essential continuity in the fundamentals of Scipio's political position from 145 to 134 . . . is his continued ability to win and exploit popular favor."[201] No wonder later *populares* retroactively recruited him into their ranks.[202] For models of the kind of "cult of *dignitas*" that often strikes modern scholars as such a novelty in Caesar, contemporaries – and Caesar himself – need have looked no further than the two Scipiones.[203] But the Scipios were by no means antithetical to the Republic: on the contrary, they

---

[198] Feig-Vishnia 1996: 131; Beck 2005: 365.

[199] See Chapter 1, p. 11ff; App. *Pun.* 112. Elster 2003: no. 202, pp. 425–426, no. 203, pp. 427–428 (probably too cautious). Astin 1967: 61–69.

[200] Astin 1967: 135, 183–184; Elster 2003: nos. 217–218, pp. 450–452.

[201] Astin 1967: 182. Astin stresses a growing "readiness to circumvent or set aside constitutional impediments which were formally established in law" (186) and the rise of "popular demonstrations, of cheering and shouting crowds" (187). See also McDonnell 2006: 237–240.

[202] Cic. *Luc.* 13 with Meier 1965: 582–583.

[203] Cf. Feig-Vishnia 1996: 131 on the Elder Africanus: "Scipio would have fitted perfectly into the Roman political arena of the first century." Of the Younger Africanus, Astin 1967: 243 wrote in words that could have been taken from a (somewhat tendentious assessment) of Caesar, "with conspicuous success, he placed his own advancement above both usage and the law, that in the furtherance of his own ambitions he cultivated and exploited popular favour as an instrument with which to defy the Senate." Contemporaries of Caesar clearly began to draw the parallel with Africanus: note the surely fabricated claim that the elder Africanus declined the *dictatura perpetua* and lifelong consulship (Livy 38.56.12–13), and the tradition of his (figurative?) apotheosis (Enn. 5.23 V, Cic. *Rep.* fr. 3 Powell; Weinstock 1971: 294–295). It may not be merely a coincidence that Caesar's operative Oppius wrote a life of Scipio Africanus (*FRHist* 40, fr. 1–3) as well as one of Caesar (*FRHist* 1.381–382).

stand as paradigmatic examples of its strong tradition of achievement recognized by a voting populace, and if, at least in the case of the elder Africanus, their very success also inspired anxieties about their personal preeminence and retaliation, this did not, of course, remove them from the pantheon of Roman heroes or ban their virtues from emulation.[204] Cato the Elder was not the sole arbiter of Roman virtue: the peculiar combination of patrician blood, military achievement, and cultivation of the populace that we see emerging already in Caesar's early career was sanctioned by republican tradition and the Roman community's apportionment of *gloria*.

---

[204] The classic example of this leveling effect is the targeting (apparently driven by the elder Cato) of the elder Africanus (Gruen 1995; Briscoe 2008: 170–179; Rich, *FRHist* 3.352–358). Yet the strategy was not repeated with Aemilianus, and from even Cicero's perspective in the late 50s he deserved not to be taken down a few notches but to be elevated to some kind of extraordinary position, possibly even as dictator, to put the state in order (esp. *Rep.* 6.12.3–4; cf. 1.31.4) in a manner analogous to the *rector rei publicae/civitatis* described in the *De re publica* (*Rep.* 2.51.1; cf. *De or.* 1.211). For recent summaries of Cicero's political theory in the *Rep.* and the old problem of the *rector*'s place in it see Atkins 2013; Zetzel 2013; Hammer 2014: 76–79; Zarecki 2014; Hodgson 2017: 159–162; for Cicero's high admiration of Aemilianus see Mitchell 1991: 45–46. From a much later perspective, Caesar could be grouped not only with Africanus but also Camillus in an indictment of the Republic's inability to suffer the preeminence of truly exceptional men (Speech of Maecenas, Dio 52.13.3–4).

CHAPTER 3

Caesar's "Entry into History"
The Catilinarian Debate and Its Aftermath

More than once Cicero offered the Senate a theory to describe the overall arc of Caesar's career. "It is a law of nature, Members of the Senate," he declared in a speech delivered on January 1, 43, "that once a man has come to a perception of true glory and perceived that in the eyes of the Senate, the Roman Knights, and the entire Roman People he is a valued citizen and a benefit to the Commonwealth, he will think nothing comparable to this glory."[1] He goes on,

> I only wish it had been Gaius Caesar's fortune in early life ... to be highly valued by the Senate and the best of our community. Neglecting to win that esteem, he squandered his powers of mind, which were of the highest order, in irresponsible demagogy. And so, paying no consideration to the Senate and the honest men, he opened a path to his own aggrandizement such as the spirit of a free people could not tolerate.[2]

This is a partisan, retrospective view dating to the height of the deep crisis that followed the Ides of March, but it remains interesting for its implicit interpretive frame. Caesar, Cicero claims, went off the rails at some point and went down the path of "irresponsible demagogy," yet in some sense his natural place was with the Senate and "the best men," and had he won their esteem early on in his career perhaps the development of his character (*ingenium*) would have been very different.

Cicero had in fact articulated an interpretation of Caesar's turn for the worse that closely resembles this one many years earlier, during the debate

---

[1] (Shackleton Bailey trans.) *Phil.* 5.49: *Ea natura rerum est, patres conscripti, ut qui sensum verae gloriae ceperit quique se ab senatu, ab equitibus Romanis populoque Romano universo senserit civem c[l]arum haberi salutaremque rei publicae, nihil cum hac gloria comparandum putet.*
[2] (Shackleton Bailey trans.) Ibid.: *utinam C. Caesari ... contigisset adulescenti ut esset senatui atque optimo cuique carissimus! quod cum consequi neglexisset, omnem vim ingeni, quae summa fuit in illo, in populari levitate consumpsit. itaque cum respectum ad senatum et ad bonos non haberet, eam sibi viam ipse patefecit ad opes suas amplificandas quam virtus liberi populi ferre non posset.* Cicero has rhetorical reasons for this representation (Manuwald 2007: 2:718).

on the consular provinces in 56, when one option, which Cicero was strongly opposing, was to relieve Caesar of his command in Gaul.

> This [senatorial] order has never bestowed honors and favor on any man who thought that any kind of standing was preferable to that which he had achieved through you. Never was there anyone who could be a leader here who preferred to be a "Friend of the People." But some men, either lacking confidence in themselves because of their own unworthiness or pushed away from attachment to this Order because of the disparagement inflicted by others, have often almost been forced to throw themselves into those heavy seas. If, after serving the Republic well, they turn their gaze away from that popular course, with its tossing and turning, back to the Senate, and desire to be considered worthy of the highest prestige, which belongs to this body, they should not merely not be pushed away but even be courted.[3]

The principle is articulated in general terms, but it is clear that the example Cicero is seeking to call to mind is Caesar, the subject of the surrounding discussion. Caesar here obviously does not fall into the class of those who set their course into the stormy waters of popular politics because of diffidence in their own capacity but rather among the small number of men who were "pushed away from attachment to this Order because of the disparagement inflicted by others." This is clearly the moment, Cicero admonishes his fellow senators, to bring Caesar back to where he belongs.[4]

The picture of Caesar's early career developed in the previous chapter fits perfectly into this paradigm. An ambitious young patrician's natural milieu was the senatorial order. While conscious of the usefulness of the Populus in achieving high command and the honors that might follow from it, he would do well not to alienate the Senate. As we have seen, although Cicero counted him as one who had taken the "popular path" (*popularis via, Cat.* 4.9), this in fact consisted more in his manner of advertising his "worthiness" than in confrontational, high-stakes political gambles, more a matter of cultivating a "popular" public image than

---

[3] *Prov. cons.* 38: *Neminem umquam est hic ordo complexus honoribus et beneficiis suis, qui ullam dignitatem praestabiliorem ea, quam per vos esset adeptus, putarit. Nemo umquam hic potuit esse princeps, qui maluerit esse popularis. Sed homines aut propter indignitatem suam diffisi ipsi sibi aut propter reliquorum obtrectationem ab huius ordinis coniunctione depulsi saepe ex hoc portu se in illos fluctus prope necessario contulerunt. Qui si ex illa iactatione cursuque populari bene gesta re publica referunt aspectum in curiam atque huic amplissimae dignitati esse commendati volunt, non modo non repellendi sunt, verum etiam expetendi.*

[4] Cicero had had similar thoughts about Caesar in 60, just before Caesar's election to the consulship: *Att.* 2.1.6: *quid si etiam Caesarem, cuius nunc venti valde sunt secundi, reddo meliorem?*

courting controversy and provoking widespread animosity among senators.[5] (Catulus's hatred was of course an exception, but an ambitious nobleman might be allowed one great feud that perhaps only served to raise his stature). Even Cicero had built up his public image with stronger and more controversial stands before his candidacy for the consulship in 64.[6] At some point, however, in Cicero's retrospective view, Caesar turned away from what Cicero implies was his natural course of pleasing the Senate and the "good men," either through his own "neglect" (*neglexisset*) or because of disparagement by others (*propter reliquorum obtrectationem*). When was this turning point? The first passage points to quite an early stage, perhaps Caesar's aedileship.[7] On the other hand, the reference to "disparagement by others" suggests a later point in Caesar's career: his famous speech on the punishment of the "Catilinarians" and the backlash it provoked. It is to this crucial moment that we now turn.

The Debate and Caesar's Proposal

On the night of December 2–3, 63 BC, that "excellent consul"[8] M. Tullius Cicero rolled up the urban conspiracy hatched by the praetor P. Cornelius Lentulus Sura.[9] Five men were taken into custody without incident: two senators, Lentulus and C. Cornelius Cethegus; two *equites*, L. Statilius and P. Gabinius; and a certain M. Caeparius of Tarracina. Four others, L. Cassius Longinus (a noble ex-praetor, no less), P. Furius, Q. Annius Chilo, and a freedman, P. Umbrenus, had also been implicated, and the Senate ordered their arrest.[10] (We hear nothing more of them; it remains

---

[5] The metaphor of the *popularis* "path" (or "course," as at Cic. *Prov. cons.* 38) is noteworthy. Cicero's only other use of the term *popularis via* (*Att.* 9.6.7) shows that it need not entail adopting a distinct political program associated with *populares* (i.e. the *popularis ratio* or *causa*) but can mean simply "the course approved by the People" (i.e. "safe"). For a list of related phrases, see Meier 1965. For *populares* in general, see Chapter 1, n. 24.

[6] Specifically, his conspicuous advocacy in 66 as praetor for the Manilian law and his defense of Cornelius the next year against a dream team of *optimates*: Q. Cic. (?), *Comment. Pet.* 53 (cf. 5) and notes 96 and 97 later in this chapter.

[7] Note *adulescenti*, and cf. Suet. *Iul.* 9.2 (but see Chapter 2). For Cicero, Caesar in December 63 is already a *popularis*, though an unusually respectable one: *Cat.* 4.11, with Chapter 2, p. 55ff.

[8] *Optimus consul*: Cic. *Att.* 12.21.1 (Brutus); *optumo consuli*: Sall. *Cat.* 43.1.

[9] I am persuaded by Seager's argument (1973) that Lentulus's conspiracy should probably be distinguished from whatever Catiline was doing before his departure. Certainly there is no convincing evidence that Lentulus was carrying out Catiline's orders rather than making his own bid for *regnum* foretold, as he himself used to say, by the Sibylline Books (Cic. *Cat.* 3.9 with Dyck 2008: 179; *Sull.* 70; Sall. *Cat.* 47.2, etc.).

[10] Cic. *Cat.* 3.14.

uncertain whether the additional four were included in the Senate's decree imposing the death sentence on the original five, or if they were, whether they were ever apprehended alive.[11]) Lentulus, Cethegus, and Statilius were incriminated by the testimony of their erstwhile ally, a certain Volturcius, and the Allobrogian Gauls, as well as by the letters they had entrusted to the Allobroges on their return to their homeland but were then seized on Cicero's orders.[12] Gabinius[13] and evidently L. Cassius,[14] Annius, Furius,[15] and Umbrenus[16] were denounced by the Gauls as members of the conspiracy, but the source of the testimony incriminating Caeparius and Furius remains unclear.[17] Despite Cicero's claim (and that of Sallust's "Cato"), it is unclear whether any of the men had actually confessed in a meaningful sense to the conspiratorial actions alleged against them; certainly one man who was subsequently executed (Caeparius) had not even had an opportunity to give an account of himself in the Senate.[18] Some other men were also named besides these nine: for example, the Gauls claimed that L. Cassius had told them that P. Autronius (a disgraced senator expelled from the Senate after his conviction for corruption in the consular elections of 66) was in on the plot, though Cassius was apparently uncertain about P. Sulla (the other convicted consul-designate of 65), while Volturcius said that Gabinius had named Ser. Sulla and L. Vargunteius along with Autronius.[19] These additional figures were spared for the moment, probably, as Drummond suggests, because the evidence against them was still

---

[11] Drummond 1995: 76. Although nine men were covered by the consul-elect's original motion for the death sentence (Sall. *Cat.* 50.4), it appears that only the five in custody were executed (Cic. *Sull.* 33, probably more reliable than *Cat.* 3.14, which is on its face merely anticipatory).

[12] Cic. *Cat.* 3.8–13; cf. Sall. *Cat.* 44. Statilius allegedly had been given the job of arson, together with Gabinius (ibid., 43.2).

[13] Cic. *Cat.* 3.12; cf. Sall. *Cat.* 40.6, 44.1. He had acted as an intermediary with the Gauls and according to Sallust had been assigned the job of arson along with Statilius (43.2), according to Cicero a massacre of citizens (*Cat.* 3.13).

[14] Cassius had not incriminated himself in written form as had the other senators (Cic *Cat.* 3.9, Sall. *Cat.* 44.2), and he managed to slip out of the city before the roundup. He too is alleged to have had the duty of arson (Cic. *Cat.* 3.13, 14), in his case at his own request. The proliferation of arsonists is suspicious; it is reasonable to wonder whether this allegation was more useful than true (see later in this chapter).

[15] Cic. *Cat.* 3.14: Annius and Furius had been involved in approaching the Allobroges.

[16] A mere go-between according to Cic. *Cat.* 3.14 and Sall. *Cat.* 40.

[17] Cic. *Cat.* 3.14. Caeparius slipped away, allegedly to incite a slave revolt in Apulia, but was caught and brought back by December 5: Sall. *Cat.* 46.3–4, 47.4.

[18] Drummond 1995: 75–77: a sobering consideration. Cicero's claim at *Cat.* 3.13 is not borne out, at least to a skeptical eye, by his detailed narrative; cf. Sall. *Cat.* 52.36: *de confessis.* For Caeparius, n. 17. Likewise, the other four men covered by Silanus's proposed death penalty had obviously not had a chance to defend themselves. We do not know whether Cato's victorious motion left them aside for the time being (n. 11).

[19] Cic. *Sull.* 36–39; Sall. *Cat.* 47.1. Drummond 1995: 17n41 has doubts about Sallust here.

only hearsay; some were later indicted and condemned in the courts.[20] The next day (December 4) one L. Tarquinius dropped a bombshell, alleging that M. Crassus was also in on the plot, but the Senate, whether out of fear or some other, less sinister motive, rejected the allegation out of hand.[21] In the atmosphere of denunciation that surrounded such revelations it was no doubt correct to be alert to the possibility of scores being settled by suborned informers.[22]

When the populace was informed of the nature of the conspiracy, according to Sallust, they changed their minds radically and were now overjoyed as if they had been rescued from slavery; the historian adds that although earlier civil violence had been profitable for the plebs, the claim that the conspirators had intended to burn the city struck them as cruel and harmful to their own interest.[23] We must be careful here in dealing with what Drummond has aptly called Sallust's "patronizing cynicism about the plebs." Earlier Sallust had averred that all of the plebs fully supported Catiline's schemes because of their eagerness for revolution, from which the poor allegedly had nothing to lose and a great deal to gain.[24] But if the plebs were supportive of Catiline in his last electoral bid, it was surely because he had openly taken up the cause of the poor and dispossessed and had cast a friendly eye on plebeian cries for relief; there is no good reason to suppose that they would have been sympathetic to any plan for a violent coup in the City.[25] The ordinary inhabitants of the City who made up the urban plebs were in fact terrified by the memory of civil war and tended to be unsettled by potentially dangerous personal conflicts among the great, who often held their lives and livelihoods in their hands.[26] Whatever popular support Catiline had enjoyed during his consular campaign likely

---

[20] Drummond 1995: 23. See Alexander nos. 226, 228–234: Autronius and Vargunteius, along with C. Cornelius, M. Porcius Laeca, P. Sulla Ser.f. (RE 385), P. Sulla (cos. des. 65), Ser. Sulla. Of these, Autronius, P. Sulla Ser.f., and Laeca were certainly condemned; P. Sulla (cos. des. 65) was acquitted.

[21] Sall. *Cat.* 48.3–9.

[22] See Chapter 2 for the attempt to incriminate Caesar (Sall. *Cat.* 49). Cf. the "Vettius Affair" of 59 (Cic. *Att.* 2.24) discussed in Chapter 4.

[23] Sall. *Cat.* 48.1–2. Cicero indeed made this claim before the People in the speech Sallust alludes to (*Cat.* 3.8).

[24] Sall. *Cat.* 37. Cf. Morstein-Marx 2004: 68–118, an attempt to rehabilitate the civic values of the Roman plebs; also Morstein-Marx 2013. Courrier's comprehensive study (2014) casts further doubt on the antiquated stereotype of Rome's "urban mob" that has influenced elitist interpretations of popular political participation. Quote: Drummond 1995: 18.

[25] On Catiline's turn to *popularis* causes in his final campaign of 63 (and the fear and suspicion this prompted in senators like Cicero) see Cic. *Mur.* 49–52; Plut. *Cic.* 14.6; Sall. *Cat.* 35.3. Cf. Harrison 2008: 98–103, who casts an appropriately skeptical eye on Catiline's support among the urban plebs.

[26] Morstein-Marx 2004: 217 with 57. Add Dio 41.8.5, 16.2–3; Cic. *Att.* 10.4.8: *popularem esse clementiam* (all from 49 BC).

dissipated at the time of his electoral failure and then more or less evaporated after he abandoned the city in early November.[27] In any case, Catiline was not among the conspirators apprehended on December 2–3, and there is no reason to believe that the common people had any special affection for *them*. On the contrary, after hearing the consul's speech detailing the roundup of the conspirators and their nefarious plans, including massacre and arson, the poorer inhabitants of the City had every reason to be grateful to him and to trust him and the Senate to take the necessary measures to ensure their security. We hear of efforts by Lentulus and Cethegus to rouse angry mobs, but they seem to have fallen flat; they were evidently deterred in part by Cicero's countermeasures, but no source suggests that they enjoyed any popular sympathy whatever.[28] The wave of relief and enthusiasm for the consul had not subsided by the time of the senatorial meeting on December 5 at which the men's fate was debated.[29] Although we must always be on guard against Cicero's rhetorical construction of societal unanimity in his favor, in this instance he may not be so far from the truth when he claims that all ranks of society were united in supporting strong measures against the conspirators, including a great mass of poor citizens who (he says) had flocked to the Forum to show their support during the debate.[30]

All this is important because if the general sense was that the People supported the strongest measures against these apparently confessed traitors, murderers, and arsonists, this helps us to see why the death penalty was the only punishment entertained among the consulars, why none of them seems to have troubled himself to make much of an argument in its defense, and why before Caesar rose to speak no one had given any thought

---

[27] Consider Sall. *Cat.* 31.1–3 – a highly rhetorical passage, but one that stands in some tension with 48.1–2. Cicero himself proudly claims that his act of political theater on election day, when he descended to the Campus wearing a breastplate to suggest to "all good citizens" the danger of an armed attack, was highly effective (Cic. *Mur.* 52: *id quod est factum*). Cf. Plut. *Cic.* 14.7–8, Dio 37.29.4–5: ὅ τε δῆμος δεινῶς ἠγανάκτησε.

[28] See esp. Cic. *Cat.* 4.17–18 and note 29 of this chapter; Cicero's argument for urgency (§6) stresses the spread of the conspiracy in Italy and beyond rather than the prospect of urban violence. App. *BCiv.* 2.6/21–22 suggests that a crowd complicit with the conspirators cast a minatory shadow over the debate (cf. Plut. *Cic.* 22.4), and Cicero implies some such anxiety too at §§14; cf. 18. (See also Sall. *Cat.* 50.1–3, Dio 37.35.3.) On the other hand, Cicero also adduces the presence of many poor citizens in support (n. 30), while security was provided in part by the famous bodyguard of *equites* including Atticus: Cic. *Cat.* 4.15, *Att.* 2.1.7, *Sest.* 28; Sall. *Cat.* 49.4 (cf. Pelling 2011: 169).

[29] Drummond 1995: 18. Even after the execution of the men Cato was able to prompt the audience of a *contio* to cry out that Cicero had saved the state (App. *BCiv.* 2.7/24, Cic. *Fam.* 15.4.11; cf. 5.2.7, Plut. *Cic.* 23.3 – a more Cicero-centric version?) Morstein-Marx 2004: 144.

[30] Cic. *Cat.* 4.14–19, esp. 16: *omnis ingenuorum adest multitudo, etiam tenuissimorum.* Cicero's self-serving construction of unanimity: Morstein-Marx 2004: 119–159. However, Drummond 1995: 18–19 is skeptical, rightly dismissing Plut. *Cic.* 22.4 and App. *BCiv.* 2.6/21–22.

to the possibility of a strongly negative popular reaction once the immediate danger had passed. For according to Suetonius (who as we shall see offers valuable independent evidence on the thrust of the speech), Caesar "struck fear into those who were supporting harsher punishment by again and again demonstrating how much ill-will would await them *in the future* [my italics] on the part of the Roman plebs."[31] They would hardly need such a warning if the populace had been manifestly hostile to the men's execution. If on the other hand the people were for the present overwhelmingly supportive of the consul and the Senate, then the circumstances appeared prima facie to favor strong action, not caution and circumspection, and the failure of the senators at first to consider seriously the possibility of a popular reaction becomes more readily understandable. It further follows, then, that Caesar in this case was no populist weather vane, turning in stereotypically demagogic fashion in whatever direction the People wanted, but that he took what was at the moment an unpopular stance, not only among the senators but also among the plebs. (Note that none of the tribunes, whose duty it was to follow the will of the People, saw fit to answer Caesar's call for a tribunician veto against the part of the successful motion that called for confiscation of the men's property.[32])

Cicero summoned a meeting of the Senate in the Temple of Concord at the foot of Capitoline Hill for the morning of December 5 to discuss the punishment of the incriminated men.[33] According to current procedure, consul-elect D. Iunius Silanus was the first senator asked to state his opinion; he proposed that those held in custody as well as four others not yet apprehended (L. Cassius, Furius, Umbrenus, and Annius) should be executed.[34] (So, at least, all understood him to mean, but a humiliating and perhaps apocryphal embellishment of the story adds that subsequently, when influenced by Caesar, he decided to change his vote, Silanus explained that by "the maximum penalty" (*summum supplicium*) he actually meant

---

[31] Suet. *Iul.* 14.1: *identidem ostentans quanta eos in posterum a plebe Romana maneret invidia.* Arousal of fear of the People: Plut. *Cat. min.* 22.6.

[32] Veto: Plut. *Cic.* 21.5, with an explanation of the paradox (since Caesar had himself called for confiscation); Cicero himself is said to have dropped the demand for confiscation from the final vote on Cato's motion. (Drummond 1995: 74n55 [cf. 26–27] insists that Cato's motion did not include confiscation, but that is impossible to square with the Plutarch passage, which is our only good evidence for this detail. The context makes clear, contra Drummond, that Caesar was calling for division of *Cato's* motion, presumably in the hope of carrying out a maneuver like that of Munatius Plancus in 52 (Ascon. 44–45 C with Morstein-Marx 2004: 115–116). Duty: Polyb. 6.16.5; Plut. *Ti. Gracch.* 15.

[33] Sall. *Cat.* 49.4; Cic. *Phil.* 2.119 (with 19). Historical associations with the Temple of Concord – a monument of the bloody suppression of Gaius Gracchus, as August. *De civ. D.* 3.25 saw – are worth noting (Morstein-Marx 2004: 54–56, 101–103; Morstein-Marx 2012: 197–201).

[34] Sall. *Cat.* 50.4. See n. 11.

imprisonment in the case of a senator.)[35] Following Silanus, the other consul-designate (L. Murena) and all fourteen of the consulars supported the motion.[36] Only when Cicero had reached the praetorian level, beginning with the praetors-elect, did an alternative proposal emerge: Caesar's, which blew the debate wide open.[37]

The brilliant speech that Sallust puts in Caesar's mouth on this occasion cannot be regarded as an absolutely reliable representation of what Caesar actually said. Sallust (then only in his early twenties) was certainly not present in the Senate and may not even have been in Rome at the time. Further, there is no trace in his account of his use of any authoritative source for the speech other than Cicero's published *Fourth Catilinarian Oration*.[38] Consequently Cicero's speech rather than Sallust's must be our primary and overall best source for what Caesar said and proposed.[39] Even this, however, must be handled carefully because of Cicero's own efforts subtly to undermine Caesar's motion and to boost Silanus's. Particularly insidious is Cicero's great skill at willfully twisting others' words or actions in a rhetorically advantageous way

[35] Plut. *Cic.* 21.3, *Cat. min.* 22.6, supported by Suet. *Iul.* 14.1. Probably the hapless Silanus switched back again at the end to vote for death (cf. *consulares omnes*, Sall. *Cat.* 53.1); he had been lashed for his inconsistency by Cato (Plut. *Cat. min.* 23.1), a young man vastly junior to him, and very likely Q. Catulus too (who also intervened a second time to check the momentum in favor of Caesar: Plut. *Cic.* 21.4, *Caes.* 8.1–2). Silanus is hardly heard of again despite his consulship, and never after it; he probably died between 60 and 57 (Rüpke 2005: 2:1084n5). To make matters worse, poor Silanus was being cuckolded at this very time, according to the famous anecdote of the *billet doux* from his wife, Servilia, delivered to her lover Caesar in the midst of the debate – and read aloud to the body by Cato! (Plut. *Cat. min.* 24.1–3).

[36] Sall. *Cat.* 50.4; Cic. *Att.* 12.21. 1; Plut. *Caes.* 7.7. Plut. *Caes.* 8.1, *Cic.* 21.4 refers to a second *sententia* by Q. Catulus (Pelling 2011: 167–169); as a consular, he must have spoken for the first time before Caesar.

[37] The other main alternative, proposed by Ti. Claudius Nero (see later in this chapter), must have followed Caesar's speech (contra App. *BCiv.* 2.5/19: it is not mentioned by Cic. *Cat.* 4.7, and *designati* should have spoken first). Vretska 1976: 506–507; McGushin 1977: 238. Blew wide open up: n. 68.

[38] Drummond 1995: 23–50, a painstaking analysis of the historical authenticity of the speech. See also Ungern-Sternberg 1970: 103n100; Blom 2016: 164–165. It is often supposed on the basis of Cic. *Att.* 2.1.3 that *Cat.* 4, along with the other consular orations, was put into its final form only three years afterward (e.g. recently, Dyck 2008: 10–12; Lintott 2008: 147–148 [cf. 17–18], but cf. McDermott 1972; Cape 1995: 258–259; Cape 2002: 154). But this goes beyond the implications of *Att.* 2.1.3. Cicero could surely have anticipated a possible backlash (or been prompted by Caesar to contemplate one), so the final part of the speech need not be explained by retrospective revision. See Drummond 1995: 42; Dyck 2008: 208; cf. Ungern-Sternberg 1970: 96–98. On the general question of ex post facto "updating" of the *Catilinarians*, see Dyck 2008: 10–12; note that the published version of *Cat.* 3.9 retains a number for those punished that appears subsequently to have been wishful anticipation (n. 11) – a useful bit of positive evidence against thorough rewriting. It is often noted that *Cat.* 4 combines elements of a *relatio* and a consular intervention in the debate (see esp. Lintott 2008, also Dyck 2008), yet the echoes of a *relatio* are actually restricted to §6 (§§1–5 on the other hand make better sense as an interruption in the midst of the debate) and may simply represent minor amplification to provide readers with a proper introduction.

[39] Cic. *Cat.* 4.7–13. Other notable sources are Suet. *Iul.* 14.1, Plut. *Cat. min.* 22.5–6, *Caes.* 7.8–9, with Pelling 2011: 164–166.

under the guise of summarizing their position. It would be most credulous to accept as an honest reflection of Caesar's argument that although he "understands" (*intellegit*) that the Sempronian Law protects the lives of citizens, he also "understands" that an "enemy of the state" is no longer a citizen at all, and thus by implicit inference that such a person is no longer protected by that very law (Cic. *Cat.* 4.10). After all, in the same sentence Cicero also says that Caesar "understands" that the very author of the Sempronian Law, Gaius Gracchus, had rightly "paid the penalty to the Republic" by his death, which had been "ordered" in some sense by the People.[40] It is virtually unthinkable that Caesar actually said as much even if the sentiment might be welcomed by a senatorial audience. The core point Cicero is somewhat unscrupulously exploiting was that (in contrast to at least one, unnamed self-styled *popularis*, usually but not certainly identified as M. Crassus) Caesar, simply by attending the meeting and making a motion in that meeting, appeared implicitly to acknowledge that there were *some* circumstances (ongoing violent insurrection in the City, for instance) in which the protection of a citizen's life accorded by the *lex Sempronia* might not in fact be absolute.[41] That would indeed have been a nuanced interpretation of the law. Caesar may well have agreed with the law in principle while disagreeing with its application in this case;[42] in any case, in the event he of course took a quite different tack. But we may note that once again, Caesar is prepared to step away from an absolutist *popularis* position, unlike those *populares* who absented themselves from the debate in protest (presumably) against inflicting a capital sentence without a formal trial. Death was certainly in the air.[43]

The terms of Caesar's proposal are in principle easier to establish with clarity than the structure of his argument, though controversy has emerged

---

[40] Cic. *Cat.* 4.10: *ipsum latorem Semproniae legis iussu populi poenas rei publicae dependisse.* Drummond 1995: 43–44; see also Lintott 1968/1999: 170; Ungern-Sternberg 1970: 100, 106–107; Hodgson 2017: 131–132. The "evasive" (Drummond) word *intellegit*, like the frequently tendentious *vidit* (*Mil.* 15, 21, 25, 45; *Cael.* 53), describes an unverifiable mental phenomenon while studiously avoiding explicitly putting words in Caesar's mouth. Drummond goes so far as to suspect that Caesar did not actually invoke the *lex Sempronia* by name (see later in this chapter). There is no need to believe (Dyck 2008: 224) that Caesar actually conceded this much ground to "optimate opinion." For a later example of the trick, cf. e.g. Cicero's tendentious "explanation" of the attitude of the Senate and of Pompey toward the case in his defense of Milo (*Mil.* 12–21).

[41] Ungern-Sternberg 1970: 106–111. The unnamed *popularis*: Cic. *Cat.* 4.10 with Chapter 2, n. 93. Dyck 2008: 223 notes that several persons can be denoted by *non neminem*, despite the singular verb in the clause that follows.

[42] Ungern-Sternberg 1970: 107–110. The condition Plutarch makes Caesar express at Plut. *Caes.* 7.8 μὴ μετὰ τῆς ἐσχάτης ἀνάγκης unfortunately holds little weight given Plutarch's confusion about the precise nature of his proposal.

[43] Cic. *Cat.* 4.13, a reference back to the consular L. Caesar's call for Lentulus's execution at the prior meeting on December 3 (*nudius tertius*).

even here. An impressive list of scholars have supposed that Caesar in fact called *not* for permanent imprisonment, as is stated clearly by Cicero and Sallust (and strongly implied by Dio),[44] but, as Plutarch and Appian would have it, for merely temporary custody until the security crisis had passed and a proper trial could be held.[45] Normally we would not be inclined to prefer late Greek sources to contemporary Roman ones whose opposing political stances to some extent serve as a check on each other, but apparently some have felt that life imprisonment was such a radical departure from law and custom that Caesar cannot have advocated it, especially since his speech and his motion may be interpreted as "hewing to a constitutional and traditional line."[46] But for our purposes this is begging the question. The relationship of Caesar's argument as represented by Sallust to the actual words spoken on this occasion is itself problematic. A harder piece of evidence is the fact that our sources, including even Plutarch, agree that Caesar called for the confiscation of the conspirators' property so long as his proposal was still viable. That is very hard to credit as a mere prelude to a regular trial in a *quaestio*; it can only be construed as a penalty (indeed, one generally linked to execution).[47] The further stipulation that no one should be permitted to revisit the conspirators' punishment before the Senate or the People, on pain of being considered by the Senate to be acting contrary to the interests of the Republic, makes little sense in connection with an envisioned future trial in a *quaestio* (which Caesar would somehow have failed to mention in the Sallustian version), but it may have served as reassuring reinforcement for an untested penalty of permanent imprisonment, which was, as Cicero stresses, an innovation unsupported by custom and not prescribed by any statute.[48]

---

[44] Cic. *Cat.* 4.8, 10; Sall. *Cat.* 51.43; Dio 37.36.2: ἐπὶ τῷ μήτε ... ἔτι ... ποτε.

[45] Plut. *Cic.* 21.1, *Caes.* 7.9; App. *BCiv.* 2.6/20. Hardy 1924: 93–94; Syme 1964: 111n38; Gruen 1974: 281 with n. 79; McGushin 1977: 256; Ramsey 2007: 204; Billows 2009: 97.

[46] Gruen 1974: 281, preferring the late Greek sources as "more detached." But only Appian imputes to Caesar the regular judicial course of resorting to the *quaestiones* (for *vis*, presumably); Plutarch apparently still envisions *the Senate* judging the conspirators at peace and at leisure. Lintott 1968/ 1999: 170 interprets Caesar's proposal as "a capital judgment without the endorsement of the people" and thus an "infringement" of the *lex Sempronia* (accepted by Hodgson 2017: 132), but Ungern-Sternberg 1970: 106n11 (cf. 48–54, 68) points out that this position rests on no concrete evidence and conflicts violently with Caesar's apparent emphasis on that law (see later in this chapter). Cicero remarks on the "severity" of Caesar's proposal (n. 70) but would surely have pointed out any direct contradiction with the law.

[47] Plut. *Cic.* 21.1, 5. Rightly, Drummond 1995: 37 and Pelling 2011: 165–166. Plutarch may have been confused by Claudius Nero's proposal for continued custody of the prisoners while the debate was postponed (Suet. *Iul.* 50.4).

[48] Cic. *Cat.* 4.7: *vincula vero, et ea sempiterna, certe ad singularem poenam nefarii sceleris inventa sunt* (further information in §§8, 10; Sall. *Cat.* 51.43; cf. Dio 37.36.2). This stands in some tension with Sallust's representation of Caesar's warnings against an unprecedented penalty: n. 71.

Like the opposing motion for execution, his motion inflicted a severe penalty without resort to the courts, but by stopping just one step short of execution it avoided a direct conflict with the *lex Sempronia* (and other, more obscure laws that allowed for the death penalty to be averted by self-imposed exile).[49]

Reconstructing Caesar's actual line of argument is a much trickier proposition. It is possible that before an audience of senators it would have been prudent not to harp aggressively on the *lex Sempronia* or, more broadly, on the People's traditional right of *provocatio*, either of which might have alienated powerful members who were evidently in a heightened state of excitement;[50] and yet, as we have seen, this was necessarily the heart of the argument. What might seem to be the obvious recourse – allowing the men to be tried in the appropriate courts – got astonishingly little if any attention according to our sources.[51] What would be the purpose of the trial, since all senators, including Caesar, appear to have been fully convinced of the men's guilt on the basis of their confessions, supported by compelling documents and testimony?[52] The men would surely have been convicted in the courts, so insistence on taking that route would probably have been viewed as obstructionist if not treasonous.[53] Yet there was one very serious problem with proceeding along the regular judicial route: as Caesar would point out (at least in Sallust's version), various laws ensured that by this time a capital sentence was routinely evaded by the defendant's departure from the City followed by formal exile, and once they had departed they could be expected to make straight for Catiline.[54] This consideration must have weighed heavily on senators' minds and surely helps to explain the apparent neglect of the formal judicial option. Furthermore, there was a sense of urgency

---

[49] Plut. (*Caes.* 7.8, *Cat. Min.* 22.5) describes Caesar as objecting to the men's execution without trial (ἀκρίτους), but since the latter circumstance would also apply to Caesar's proposal even in Plutarch's mistaken version, the emphasis clearly falls on execution (cf. *Cic.* 21.1). Other laws: n. 54.

[50] Drummond 1995: 30, 36, 41–50 passim.　　[51] See nn. 45, 46.

[52] Cic. *Cat.* 4.7; cf. Sall. *Cat.* 51.20, 52.13. This is one of the few common elements between the *Fourth Catilinarian* and Sallust's speech for Caesar.

[53] Hence Cato's characterization of the incriminated men as analogous to *manufesti rerum capitalium* since they had confessed (Sall. *Cat.* 52.36); cf. App. *BCiv.* 2.6/21 as ἔπεισαν ὡς αὐτοφώρων ἄνευ κρίσεως. Drummond's polemic against Kunkel on the legal principle involved (1995: 57–72) must here be left aside. Nippel 1995: 69 rightly points out that the men cannot be understood to have confessed in a full legal sense. More than that, of course, they had not had the opportunity to summon their own witnesses and testimony had not been given under oath, nor were there a proper cross-examination, full-dress speeches, or sworn judges. The additional four men covered by Silanus's proposal of execution (and perhaps by Cato's successful motion) had not even had the opportunity to defend themselves at all. Yet no one seems to have been in any doubt of their guilt.

[54] The presence of this concern is apparent at Sall. *Cat.* 51.43 and 52.27 (a criticism that oddly does not fit Caesar's proposal). On the *lex Porcia aliaeque leges*, Sall. *Cat.* 51.22, 40 (cf. [Sall.] *Inv. in Cic.* 5 *sublata lege Porcia*). Drummond 1995: 28–32, 115–116; Ungern-Sternberg 1970: 104n100.

which Cato (according to Sallust) was to exploit to the fullest: it was clearly felt necessary to do something *now* that would effectively remove these men from play altogether.[55]

How did those who backed the ultimately victorious motion for the men's execution then square that decision with the law? Scholars have searched for a respectable legal argument that a modern jurist might countenance, and many settle on the notorious "Final Decree of the Senate" passed on October 21, which called upon the consuls to "see to it that the state suffer no harm."[56] However, this extrajudicial instrument, which had been used at least three times to suppress violent insurrection since its invention in 121, goes entirely unmentioned in Cicero's *Fourth Catilinarian Oration*, our best testimony to Caesar's argument and also a résumé of the argument for execution thus far. Cicero instead grounds his argument for execution on the superficially compelling commonsense idea that a citizen who has manifestly turned traitor has converted himself into a *hostis*, thereby forfeiting any legal protections of citizenship such as those provided by the *lex Sempronia*.[57] Nor does the *s.c.u.* appear in either of Sallust's speeches, including Cato's successful argument for execution.[58] In fact, none of our sources for the debate itself cites the Final Decree as a legal justification for the executions, although Dio, narrating P. Clodius's retaliation against Cicero five years later, implies that the Final Decree had laid the basis for the executions by "giving [the Senate] the power to do such things."[59] In this

---

[55] For Cato's speech, Sall. *Cat.* 52 and Plut. *Cat. min.* 23 are our main sources, which unfortunately do not neatly cohere; see also Vell. Pat. 2.35.3–4, App. *BCiv.* 2.6/21, Cic. *Att.* 12.21.1 *verbis luculentioribus et pluribus*. An authoritative record of Cato's speech may have been preserved (Plut. *Cat. min.* 23.3, unless Plutarch is conflating this with the speeches Cicero had had written down two days earlier: Cic. *Sull.* 42).

[56] Sall. *Cat.* 29.2; Cic. *Cat.* 1.4. Recently, Arena 2012: 202, 205, 208–211; Golden 2013: 130–133; Blom 2016: 166, following long and illustrious precedent. Persuasive against that traditional view are Ungern-Sternberg 1970: 100–101, 111–120 (who perhaps goes too far by envisioning the decree of December 5 as in essence a *hostis* declaration: cf. Drummond 1995: 101); Habicht 1990: 35–38; Drummond 1995: 95–105; cf. Lintott 1968/1999: 171–172 (also 52–66); Nippel 1995, and now Straumann 2016: 88–100, 68. Dyck 2008: 243–244 points out that if Ascon. 6C is counting inclusively the date of the Final Decree may be October 22.

[57] Cic. *Cat.* 4.10 (cf. 15): *qui autem rei publicae sit hostis eum civem esse nullo modo posse* (another thing that Caesar allegedly *intellegit*); note also 1.28: *nunquam in hac urbe qui a re publica defecerunt civium iura tenuerunt*. Cicero later liked to refer to the executed men as *hostes domestici* (*Sull.* 32, *Flacc.* 95, *Sest.* 11); for the nontechnical sense of his usage see Drummond 1995: 101. Cicero's related doctrine of "self-help against the enemies of the state" (Lintott) served him equally straightforwardly to justify the killing of Ti. Gracchus before the legal complications of the *lex Sempronia* and the *s.c.u.* (*Cat.* 1.3, *Dom.* 91, *Planc.* 88, *Off.* 1.76).

[58] Sall. *Cat.* 51.36: *per senatus decretum consul gladium eduxerit* is self-evidently a metaphorical allusion to the kind of death sentence passed by the Senate currently being contemplated, not to the *s.c.u.* of October 21 (Drummond 1995: 33–36).

[59] Dio 38.14.5. For the later reaction, see Ungern-Sternberg 1970: 123–129.

very compressed, retrospective comment Dio is probably loosely drawing a connection between two apparently similar decisions; Cicero himself in his later apologetics frequently emphasizes the Senate's moral responsibility for the executions by virtue of its decrees of December 3 and 5, but never actually takes shelter behind the *s.c.u.* of October.[60] The Final Decree, after all, had been passed more than six weeks earlier under very different circumstances and with a very different target in mind: Manlius's incipient insurrection in Etruria, with Catiline in the decree's sights only if and when complicity in that insurrection could be pinned on him.[61] If it authorized Cicero to act against any and all apparent threats to the Republic for the foreseeable future, it is not clear why he would have had to consult the Senate again; if that was because there was a serious question about its application to the new situation, then this surely should have been the chief point at issue in the debate. But it was not, so far as our evidence allows us to see.

None of our evidence for the debate suggests that it was lawyerly rather than political. The advocates of execution understandably avoided dwelling on the *lex Sempronia* protecting the lives of Roman citizens and how to get around this legal obstacle. Instead, to the extent that Cicero even feels a need for a legal justification for execution, he is satisfied to offer with the utmost brevity the rhetorically simple argument that a citizen who has turned traitor has lost his legal protections as a citizen. The argument, too often dismissed by scholars as laughable, has lost none of its power among ordinary citizens during times of national emergency, as has been shown since September 11, 2001, by the twists and turns of US law regarding the rights of due process retained (or not) by American citizens who have joined in active hostilities with non-state entities against their own country.[62] Cicero engages in no elaborate justification of this principle,

---

[60] E.g. Cic. *Fam.* 5.2.8, *Contra contionem Q. Metelli*, fr. 9 Crawford 1994, *Sull* 21, *Red. sen.* 32, *Dom.* 94, *Sest.* 11, 53, 145, *Mil.* 8. Cf. Cic. *Pis.* 14: *nam relatio illa ... fuerat consulis, animadversio quidem et iudicium senatus.*

[61] Sall. *Cat.* 28–29; cf. declaration of Catiline and Manlius as *hostes* at 36.2–3, with Lintott 1968/1999: 155n17. The target of a *s.c.u.* does not appear to have been named (Lintott 1968/1999: 152–153, contra Mommsen 1887: 3:2, 1242) – clearly to enhance flexibility, but at the cost of possible controversy over its targets and duration. On the stunning tendentiousness on this point of Cicero's *First Catilinarian* (*in te, Catilina,* §3; cf. *in te, Phil.* 2.51) see now Hodgson 2017: 122–127. Consciously or unconsciously, Sallust supports Cicero's claim that Catiline was the target of the *s.c.u.* by a chronological dislocation, placing Catiline's meeting at the house of Laeca and the alleged attempted assassination of Cicero *before* the passage of the decree; Syme attempts to defend him (1964: 77–81), but it is hard to avoid the conclusion that he has at least been confused by Cicero's rhetoric.

[62] The most recent important case involves the radical Islamist cleric Anwar al-Awlaki, killed by a drone strike in 2011. This is not to say that the US constitutional argument is as simplistic as Cicero's; a key distinction for the designation as an "enemy combatant" was that Awlaki was targeted abroad. See Powell 2016. Laughable: Drummond 1995: 100.

which we should expect if it was unique to him; as noted earlier, even Caesar probably accepted it in principle while demurring on its application to the present case (or at least on the political wisdom of applying it to the present case).[63] Indeed, in later speeches and treatises Cicero repeatedly regards it as given, requiring no special argument, that a citizen whose actions made him an enemy of the state could be killed with impunity even without *any* kind of official sanction.[64] The simple moral clarity of the *hostis* argument made it much more powerful in practice than a narrowly legalistic one. And Cato's powerful speech, whose weight in the debate even Cicero would later acknowledge, appears to have avoided legalistic justification altogether in favor of moralistic indignation, scornful attacks on supporters of Caesar's motion for irresolution or, worse, complicity in the conspiracy, along with a highly emotional amplification of the immediate danger still posed by the conspiracy despite its apparent decapitation.[65] If Catiline – who at the time was able to fit out only about one-fourth of his modest-sized band with proper military weapons while the others carried hunting spears, lances, or sharpened stakes (Sall. *Cat.* 56.1–2) – was, according to Sallust's Cato, "at our throats" or "looming over us with an army" in coordination with an undaunted band of traitors within the City, then Cato's rhetorical frame was one of war and imminent existential danger, and the decision to be taken was more a military and strategic one than a legal or constitutional one.[66] Furthermore, any senator could see that a vote for Caesar's motion could raise questions about his own involvement in the conspiracy, while a vote for the death sentence would be a fairly effective way of dispelling them. By these methods (if our sources do not mislead us) Cato stampeded those who had sided with Caesar in opposing the death sentence.[67]

---

[63] See n. 42.

[64] Lintott 1968/1999 171 with n. 2: *Dom.* 91, *Off.* 1.76, *Tusc.* 4.51, *Planc.* 88, *Rep.* 6.12 Powell (app. crit.).

[65] Sources of the speech: n. 55. For Cato's invidious imputations against the other side in general see Vell. Pat. 2.35.4 and cf. Sall. *Cat.* 52.35: *neque parari neque consuli quicquam potest occulte*; against Caesar specifically, Sall. *Cat.* 52.14–16, as well as Plut. *Cat. min.* 23.1–2, Cic. 21.4, *Caes.* 8.2, and App. *BCiv.* 2.6/21, who imply that the attack was much more direct. On suspicion of Caesar, probably prompted in part by his "mercy," see Chapter 2, p. 72ff.

[66] Sall. *Cat.* 52.35: *undique circumventi sumus; Catilina cum exercitu faucibus urget; alii intra moenia atque in sinu urbis sunt hostes, neque parari neque consuli quicquam potest occulte; 24 dux hostium cum exercitu supra caput est.* Note 3 *res autem monet cavere ab illis magis quam quid in illos statuamus consulare*; see also 4, 6, 12, 18. Drummond 1995: 53–56. Cic. *Att.* 12.21.1 confirms that Cato's speech stood out for its rhetorical power (*verbis luculentioribus et pluribus*). Plut. *Cat. Min.* 23.1–2 is consistent with Sallust, and seems to be drawing on an alternate source. For Cato's "demagogy" see also Vretska 1976: 2:606; Syme 1964: 108 is too sympathetic.

[67] Sall. *Cat.* 53.1: *consulares omnes itemque senatus magna pars sententiam eius* [sc. Catonis] *laudant, virtutem animi ad caelum ferunt, alii alios increpantes timidos vocant.*

Nevertheless, before Cato's blistering attack Caesar's speech had had an extraordinary impact on the body, apparently prompting many of those who had supported the death sentence before him to switch their vote or backpedal dramatically, to the point where Caesar seemed likely to prevail.[68] This strongly implies that the points he made had not in fact been carefully contemplated up to that point, and indeed our accounts of the debate suggest that no one bothered to make much of a speech before Caesar. Of course everyone will have known about the *lex Sempronia* going in, but if as I have argued there is good reason to believe, all orders of society, including the urban plebs, were united in their horror at the revelations of the plot to commit not only murder but arson within a tinderbox of a City, then senators may have thought that the law, which as we have seen was not absolute, offered no serious impediment to the most effective way of preventing any further mischief from the apprehended men and deterring any others from capitalizing on the disruption. But if Caesar's proposal drew their attention not to any strong current of popular outrage at present – they would hardly have needed to be reminded of that if it existed – but the danger of a popular backlash *in the future*, and the consequent risk *to the Senate's reputation and authority*, then we can make good sense of the surprising impact of the speech. Suetonius offers independent corroboration of Caesar's focus on the risk of a *future* reaction from the plebs, while the rest of these elements are clearly present in Sallust's version, a central theme of which is the wider community's reaction to the perceived errors of judgment (especially those made in anger or fear) made by those in authority, and the consequent imperative to preserve the Senate's standing in the eyes of the Roman People by avoiding such damaging mistakes.[69]

---

[68] Sall. *Cat.* 52.1, Dio 37.36.2; Suet. *Iul.* 14.2 (*obtinuisset adeo transductis iam ad se pluribus*); Plut. *Cic.* 21.2–4, *Cat. Min.* 22.6, and esp. *Caes.* 8.1 with Pelling 2011: 166–169, a careful summary of the various problems. Even Cicero's brother Quintus supported Caesar's motion (Suet., and n. 75). On consul-designate Silanus's embarrassing retraction see n. 35; Plut. appears to suggest that there were others.

[69] See esp. Sall. *Cat.* 51.25: *At enim quis reprehendet quod in parricidas rei publicae decretum erit?* (A question which would hardly need to be asked unless the plebs were perceived as fully on board.) *Tempus, dies, fortuna . . . .* 12–14: *qui magno imperio praediti in excelso aetatem agunt, eorum facta cuncti mortales novere. Ita in maxuma fortuna minuma licentia est . . . . Quae apud alios iracundia dicitur, ea in imperio superbia atque crudelitas appellatur.* 15: *plerique mortales postrema meminere, et in hominibus impiis sceleris eorum obliti de poena disserunt, si ea paulo severior fuit.* 7: *hoc item vobis providendum est, patres conscripti, ne plus apud vos valeat P. Lentuli et ceterorum scelus quam vostra dignitas, neu magis irae vostrae quam famae consulatis.* Note also Caesar's emphasis on initial popular enthusiasm for the precedents he deplores: §§29–34. Suet. *Iul.* 14.1: *quin et tantum metum iniecit asperiora suadentibus, identidem ostentans quanta eos in posterum a plebe Romana maneret invidia . . . .* The accuracy of Suetonius's brief description of Caesar's speech is strongly defended by Drummond 1995: 38–47. Cf. Plut. *Cat. min.* 22.6 φοβηθείσης [sc. τῆς βουλῆς] τὸν δῆμον, which is roughly on target but misses the focus on the future.

By carefully crafting a response that avoided direct violation of a law the People cherished (the *lex Sempronia*) but still dealt severely with the conspirators and blocked them from the escape route that the courts might permit, Caesar pointed a way forward that could maintain the dignity of the Curia and ward off the danger of an eventual popular backlash that could deeply undermine the broad support on which its authority depended (as would in fact happen five years later).[70] The proposal could also fairly be described as "popular" inasmuch as it preserved the integrity of the *lex Sempronia* but averted the anticipated charge of popular pandering, since in fact the citizens probably had few qualms about the death sentence for these particular men and supported the executions both when they were only in prospect and immediately afterward. The objection modern scholars often raise – that Caesar's own proposed penalty of permanent imprisonment was not recognized in Roman law and therefore arguably contradicts his own advice (according to Sallust) against creating a novel precedent in this case and inflicting an unprecedented punishment – does not seem to have troubled anybody very much under the circumstances; there is a difference between outright contradiction with a statute (Caesar's criticism of the death sentence) and an innovative penalty, which our sources treat as an appropriate effort to fit the punishment to the unique nature of the crime.[71]

Caesar's solution was thus a deft political compromise between the letter of the law and the need to take immediate, decisive action, between precedent and innovation, and between the Senate's power to act in an emergency and the prudence needed to maintain popular legitimacy. It further sought to mediate successfully between popular and senatorial perspectives – between the Senate's authority and the rights of the People – as well as between short-term and long-term senatorial and *popularis* strategies, seeking thereby a politically workable solution to what was potentially an intractable political-constitutional problem.[72]

---

[70] The "severity" of Caesar's proposal is attested more convincingly by Cicero's much later letter to Atticus (*Att.* 12.21.1) than his diplomatic response in *Cat.* 4.7, 10.

[71] Cic. *Cat.* 4.11: "In the case of such an atrocious crime, what punishment can be regarded as cruel?" Cf. Sall. *Cat.* 51.17: *quid enim in talis homines crudele fieri potest?* (also §23). To be sure, Sallust's wording, in which he makes Caesar twice reject "novel" or "unprecedented" penalties (§18: *genus poenae novom*; §8 41: *novom consilium*), heightens the sense of contradiction since Caesar's proposed penalty could also be described as *novum*. Ungern-Sternberg 1970: 102–103n97; Drummond 1995: 37.

[72] See also Drummond's elegant tribute to the speech we read in Sallust (1995: 50). In truth, one might doubt whether even Caesar's attempt to square the circle was likely to survive. Could an unprecedented verdict imposed by the Senate without force of law really stand, even buttressed by Caesar's demand for sanctions against anyone bringing up the conspirators' fate in the future? Such an injunction would have only the force of a senatorial decree and could not bind the Roman People as would a *lex*; later, as it happens, even Clodius's law containing a similar sanction against Cicero was

In the context of my argument in the previous chapter that Caesar was by no means predisposed to hostility toward the Senate, what is of particular interest to us here is that his proposal was no demagogic echo of popular sentiment but appears to have been grounded in an ideal of senatorial authority and leadership. It was Cicero who was the People's hero after the executions, not Caesar: the consul was escorted home through the streets by cheering and clapping crowds, his path illuminated by innumerable torches in the streets, doorways, and rooftops.[73] Caesar had warned of an *eventual* reaction from the plebs, not an immediate one. As for his advice on maintaining the "dignity" of the Senate, his argument (according to Sallust) partly rested on the idea that it was rightly entrusted with a lofty position of oversight and decision which, however, needed to be guarded and preserved against popular blowback. Caesar was an ambitious patrician, now praetor-elect, and in his position it made no sense for him to seek, as the hostile tradition would have it, to undermine or offend the very body that would determine so much of the future he desired, especially (according to Sallust) his chances for military achievement and honors.[74] The respectful stance toward the Senate that Sallust attributes to Caesar in his oration is confirmed not only by Cicero's (somewhat disingenuous) praise in the *Fourth Catilinarian* but also by the decision of Cicero's own brother Quintus, a fellow praetor-elect with Caesar and something of a hard-line optimate in Cicero's own portrayal, to side with his motion.[75]

Recriminations and Retaliation

As I noted earlier, the initial reaction of the people in the City to the execution of the conspirators, then, appears on its face to have been overwhelmingly positive: Cicero was the man of the hour. But once the atmosphere of fear had

not ultimately decisive. (Dyck 2008: 220–221.) Yet, as in that case, such a repudiation would have to stand the test of a full-scale popular vote, which was after all a pretty high standard to meet, and arguably even a proper one (as in Cicero's case): in effect, an appeal to the People, the sovereign power in the Republic. If Caesar actually reflected this far, that might not have seemed such a wicked or irresponsible thing.

[73] Plut. *Cic.* 22.5–6. Cf. Dio 37.34.3–4: ταῦτα καὶ τῷ δήμῳ ὁμοίως ἤρεσε ... τό τε θεῖον ἐμεγάλυνον καὶ τοὺς τὴν αἰτίαν λαβόντας δι᾽ ὀργῆς μᾶλλον ἐποιοῦντο. He appears to contradict himself promptly at 37.38.1, partly due to confusion about the timing of the pontifical election and partly misled by the criticisms of Cicero launched later in December. App. *BCiv.* 2.7/24: σωτὴρ ἐδόκει περιφανῶς ἀπολλυμένῃ τῇ πατρίδι γενέσθαι, χάριτές τε ἦσαν αὐτῷ παρὰ τὴν ἐκκλησίαν καὶ εὐφημίαι ποικίλαι. (See later in this chapter for Cato's *contio* supporting Cicero's actions.)

[74] Undermining the Senate: Plut. *Cic.* 20.6, *Cat. min.* 22.5.

[75] Suet. *Iul.* 14.2. Cicero presents Quintus as an implacable foe of the tribunate and the secret ballot in his dialogue *De legibus* (3.19–26, 34–37). Catulus predictably opposed the motion (Plut. *Cic.* 21.4, *Caes.* 8.1).

dissipated, as Caesar had warned, this apparent violation of *provocatio* was likely eventually to arouse public concern, especially if tribunes were willing to break ranks with the Senate and press the issue publicly. Contrary to the cynical view that the urban populace was more or less freely manipulated by demagogues, it has been shown that Roman voters were notably "politicized" and keen to defend certain core rights and interests, in particular the protections Roman citizens enjoyed from arbitrary punishment grouped loosely around the term *provocatio*.[76] In the last analysis, the life and person of the average Roman citizen depended on his right of *provocatio*, in particular the right enshrined in the *lex Sempronia* to a trial on a capital charge in a court constituted by the People. When the attack on Cicero's actions came, then, it would focus on the principle that citizens could not be executed without proper trial authorized by the People; his doing so was equated with *regnum* or tyranny, the overthrow of freedom itself.[77] It would be wrong to suppose that Cicero's standing with the plebs precipitately plummeted as an immediate consequence of the executions and remained persistently poor until his exile for this reason in 58.[78] But the popular reaction against the executions that P. Clodius was able to mobilize almost five years later suffices to show that the Senate's self-inflicted wound did not go away and that Caesar's warnings were on the mark.

Already in December popular rumblings were heard at the prompting of two of the new tribunes – both of them from proud noble families – Q. Metellus Nepos and L. Calpurnius Bestia. Dio says that Nepos came near to launching a prosecution of Cicero for executing citizens without authorization by the People, but that the Senate headed this off by decreeing a blanket legal immunity for those who had carried out the sentences and declaring that anyone who attempted to call them to account would be deemed an enemy. This astonishing decree in effect threatened those who questioned the Senate's treatment of citizens as *hostes* with being regarded as *hostes* themselves – if historical, a notable example of overreach by those who

---

[76] On *provocatio* see Lintott 1999: 97–99, and esp. Lintott 1972. On the prominence of *populi iura* among the issues that aroused the plebs to strong action see Morstein-Marx 2013: 39–41, with Cic. *De or.* 2.199: *provocationem, patronam illam civitatis ac vindicem libertatis* (Antonius) and P. Laeca's denarius (*RRC* 301).

[77] Sometimes the emphasis seems to be on the lack of a *proper trial* (Cic. *Fam.* 5.2.8: *indicta causa* [Nepos]; cf. *indemnati*/ἄκριτοι at Livy, *Per.* 103; Vell. Pat. 2.45.1; Plut. *Cic.* 30.5; App. *BCiv.* 2.15/54), sometimes on the lack of *authorization by the People* (Dio 38.14.4). The two issues were of course tightly connected since a trial in a *quaestio* constituted by statute met the requirement of *iussu populi*. Freedom: Arena 2012: 212–214. Hence P. Clodius's shrine to Freedom on the site of Cicero's demolished house: Tatum 1999: 159–166. For Cicero's "tyranny": Chapter 1, n. 90.

[78] Morstein-Marx 2004: 209–212.

held power in the Senate.[79] On the last day of Cicero's consulship Metellus used his tribunician veto to block him from delivering a speech to the People recounting his actions and permitted him only to swear the traditional oath that he had observed the laws – itself a questionable claim after December 5 – to which Cicero deftly added that he had saved the City and the Republic. Our sources are divided (as they often are in such cases) about the assembly's response: Cicero claims that it roared its approval and even somehow swore for its part that he had sworn rightly; Dio, our main alternative source, contends that the People themselves refused to let him say more than the oath, and the tribune Metellus was only an enabler, not an instigator.[80] Doubtless the People did not speak with one voice. Another of the new tribunes, M. Cato, had been able to prompt a *contio* to hail Cicero as "Father of his Country" (*pater patriae*); simultaneously, he also took care to pass a new grain law that by means of a very generous new grain subsidy demonstrated to the People in a timely manner his, and perhaps implicitly the Senate's, deep concern for their material interests.[81] The storm would not break over Cicero for a few years yet.

If I have interpreted correctly the nature of Caesar's intervention in the debate on the punishment of the conspirators, it is easy to see how stinging would have been the attempts of Cato, Catulus, and C. Piso to taint him with complicity, quite apart from the physical violence incited by their insinuations with which he was threatened as he left the Temple of Concord.[82] We hear that Caesar avoided the Senate for the rest of the

---

[79] Dio 37.42. Cf. Ungern-Sternberg 1970: 125n183; contra Golden 2013: 132, the decree did not restrict itself to existing laws. Surely Nepos and Bestia's position did not entirely lack support in the Senate as well: see Cicero's complaints about what Nepos' brother Celer said, or did not say, in the Senate during a brief visit back to Rome in December: *Fam.* 5.2.2, 4.

[80] Dio 37.38. Cic. *Pis.* 6–7, *Fam.* 5.2.7 on the other hand claim that the crowd overwhelmingly seconded Cicero's boast (similarly Plut. *Cic.* 23.1–3). Cf. *Sest.* 11–12; *Schol. Bob.* 82, 127 St. Cic. *Mur.* 81 shows that at least one tribune-designate (Bestia?) was already sowing dissent before the executions. Plut. *Cic.* 23.1–4 thinks that Caesar joined the tribunes, but this is clearly a mistake (Moles 1988: 170); although Moles is right to note that no source explicitly associates a second tribune with Nepos in this particular scene, others (*Schol. Bob.*, cf. Cic. *Sest.* 11) connect Bestia with his attacks on Cicero in general. More refs. at Berry 1996: 206. The traditional oath: Mommsen 1887: 1.625.

[81] Acclamation: App. *BCiv.* 2.7/24; Cic. *Fam.* 15.4.11; Plut. *Cic.* 23.3–4, with Morstein-Marx 2004: 144n136 – evidence that is sometimes doubted without good reason (Kaster 2006: 354). On the variability of contional audiences, each of which prima facie represented the Roman People, see Morstein-Marx 2004: 128–136. Q. Catulus described Cicero in the same way in the Senate around the same time (Cic. *Pis.* 6, *Sest.* 121); this need not have constituted the formal bestowal of a title and may have been simply a term of high praise, rather as Cicero had spoken of Marius at *Rab. perd.* 27. See Weinstock 1971: 201–202. Cato's subsidy: Plut. *Cat. min.* 26.1, *Mor.* 818d, *Caes.* 8.6–7, with Pelling 2011: 171–172. Very generous: see Rickman 1980: 168–170.

[82] Suet. *Iul.* 14.2; Plut. *Caes.* 8.2–3 adds that the elder C. Scribonius Curio (cos. 76) physically shielded Caesar with his toga (but see Pelling 2011: 170) and that Cicero called off the guards. Sall. *Cat.* 49.4 probably mistakes the date (Chapter 2, n. 172). Nearly two decades later Mark Antony would

month until he assumed his praetorship on January 1, 62 – but also that on his return to the Curia he faced explicit accusations of involvement in the plot brought by Cicero's informant (turned state's evidence), Q. Curius, which he was able to fend off by invoking Cicero's own testimony that he had supplied him with information about the plot.[83]

Caesar did not remain passive in the face of this dangerous sniping but vigorously fought back. On January 1, a celebratory day when the new consuls paraded about in the company of their supporters as they made their first appearance in their new office, Caesar publicly accused his old enemy, Q. Catulus, of embezzling funds granted him for the restoration of the Temple of Jupiter Optimus Maximus on the Capitol (rededicated with much pomp six years before) and demanded that he open up his accounts to public scrutiny, and further to transfer to someone else (Pompey was no doubt suggested) the remainder of the work – no doubt not much remained to be done, but most importantly the name of the replacement would have ended up in the blank space on the edifice. But he quickly dropped the proposal in the face of the united opposition of the *optimates*.[84] At some point in this context – possibly even spoiling Catulus's New Year's Day – Caesar forced him to attend a *contio* to defend his role in the restoration, and added the humiliation (literally) of not inviting him onto the speaker's platform but making him respond (inaudibly) from the floor of the Forum.[85] It seems unlikely that he was aiming at anything more than publicly embarrassing Catulus in retaliation for his attempts to incriminate or compromise him in the Catilinarian affair. More consequential was the new tribune Metellus Nepos's continued attack on Cicero and simultaneously on the Senate's handling of the insurrection, an escalation of the controversy in which Caesar would soon find himself entangled more than he would like.

The focus of attention had now shifted to Catiline's remaining band in Etruria. Metellus now proposed a bill to confer the command against Catiline on Pompey.[86] The Senate had threatened anyone who sought to

---

complain bitterly that Cicero's armed guards had intimidated the Senate (Cic. *Phil.* 2.16–17), a serious breach of the unwritten rules of the institution which Cicero then threw back at Antony (*Phil.* 2.8, 15, 19).

[83] Chapter 2, nn. 173, 180.

[84] Dio 37.44.1–2; Suet. *Iul.* 15.1 claims that Caesar formally promulgated a bill to this effect. Dedication: Chapter 2, n. 77. Cf. Tac. *Hist.* 3.72; *ILS* 35–35a.

[85] Cic. *Att.* 2.24.3 : *ex inferiore loco.* Pina Polo 2018: 111 plausibly suggests that this was the context and meaning of this memorable slight.

[86] Seager 2002: 72–77. The bill was probably introduced already in December (Plut. *Cat. min.* 26.2); a *trinundinum* must have passed before the assembly at which it was to be voted on in January (27.1).

reopen the question of the punishment of the conspirators on December 5, so Metellus now turned to an indirect approach that would have amounted to a strong public repudiation of the Senate's handling of the crisis in general and would have snatched the credit for the inevitable victory away from those who had chief responsibility for that policy (Cicero, Catulus, and Cato above all) and handed it to the popular hero to whom the Roman People had recently entrusted its most intractable problems. Catulus had feared that the *lex Gabinia* and *lex Manilia* would undermine senatorial claims to leadership of the Republic; to allow the operations against Catiline to be torn out of the Senate's hands just as victory was at hand would have been to erase its greatest recent success (as it seemed to men like Cicero) and to reinforce the ostensibly dangerous idea that Pompey alone was equal to the challenges the Republic now faced. Cicero had retaliated against Metellus's insulting treatment at his swearing-out ceremony on December 29 with a tough speech in the Senate the next day (January 1), and Metellus continued in kind in a *contio* two days later. Metellus was certainly not shy about continuing his rhetorical attacks on Cicero as he pushed his bill forward.[87]

On the day when the tribal assembly met in the Forum to vote on the bill, Nepos had brought Caesar onto the podium of the Temple of Castor, presumably to deliver one of the speeches in its support in the final *contio* immediately preceding the voting.[88] Scholars generally assume (as did Dio) that Caesar's object in lending his support to Nepos's bill could have been little more than to curry favor with Pompey at a time when he needed powerful allies.[89] The incentive to align himself with Pompey was no doubt strong, but we should also keep in mind that the bill was a natural

---

[87] Cic. *Fam.* 5.2.8. Cf. Plut. *Cic.* 23.4, who claims that the purpose of the bill was to "put down the despotism of Cicero" – perhaps a taste of Nepos's rhetoric. Nepos's brother Celer, then one of the commanders against Catiline in northern Italy, was shortly to complain of Cicero's excessive retaliation: *nec ratione nec maiorum nostrum clementia administrasti* (5.1.2). No senator can have thought that the men executed on December 5 deserved *clementia*, so Celer's comment presumably refers to Cicero's retaliation against Nepos.

[88] Plut. *Cat. min.* 27. Normal procedure involved final speeches pro and con immediately preceding the vote: Morstein-Marx 2004: 162–163 with n. 10, 179–186. Dio omits Caesar from his main account at 37.43 but implies complicity at 37.44.1 of the sort indicated by Plutarch. *Schol. Bob.* 134 St. also mentions Caesar's support, and cites another bill of Nepos's to authorize Pompey to run for the consulship in absentia. We hear nothing further of this. Cic. *Sest.* 62 tactfully makes no mention of Caesar.

[89] Cf. Dio 37.21.4, unsurprisingly giving Caesar exclusive credit for the privilege recently given to Pompey of wearing triumphal dress at the games and festivals. Dio is clearly proceeding on the law of Caesarian attraction traced in Chapter 2: in fact this was the subject of legislation promulgated in 63 by the tribunes Labienus and his colleague T. Ampius Balbus (Vell. Pat. 2.40.4, with no mention of Caesar).

development of Metellus Nepos's critique of the course that Cicero and the majority of the Senate had taken toward the crisis, for which Caesar was a natural spokesman because of his role in the debate. As will be evident from Cato's desperate veto of the bill, it had strong popular backing and it therefore may have seemed to Caesar an irresistible way to win vindication after the recent humiliating and dangerous defeat in the debate of December 5. The import of the law itself would also help to rebut any further charges of sympathy or complicity with Catiline or the others.

A violent confrontation followed, however, that for the first time nearly put Caesar directly in opposition to the Senate. Plutarch in his *Life of Cato the Younger* gives a long and detailed account of a fracas in the voting assembly from a strongly pro-Catonian perspective, whose ultimate source was almost certainly Cato's comrade Munatius Rufus.[90] Cato and his fellow tribune Q. Minucius Thermus, thrusting themselves through the crowd to the podium, sought to veto Nepos's presentation of the bill by physically preventing the herald from even reading it out to the assembly. Metellus then tried to read it himself, whereupon Cato snatched the text of the law from him, and when Metellus then tried to recite it by heart, Thermus physically gagged him – on its face, a blatant violation of tribunician sacrosanctity.[91] Metellus then, according to Plutarch, seeing the crowd wavering and turning toward the "more beneficial side" (i.e. Cato's side) summoned armed men to his aid and a confusing mêlée ensued in which most of the voters dispersed and the vote was aborted.[92]

[90] *FRHist* no. 37. Munatius is explicitly mentioned in the narrative as a companion of Cato in the fracas (27.5), which suggests that Plutarch's story was based on an eyewitness account; but since in the prelude to this moment it is Cato's tribunician colleague Minucius (Thermus) who accompanies him to the assembly the name may be suspected.

[91] Plut. *Cat. Min.* 28.1 (only Thermus, but the account is palpably pro-Catonian); Dio 37.43.2 (both men). Blom 2016: 218 notes a violation of sacrosanctity only later when Cato is driven violently from the assembly. Cornelius: Ascon. 60–61C; Alexander, no. 209. It is unclear whether Metellus had invited any opposition speakers to address the *contio* as was customary; it may be that he had invited Cato and Thermus (hence their ability to make their way through the crowd to the podium), who instead, aware of the inevitable outcome of a vote if it was allowed, turned to manhandling Metellus.

[92] Plut. *Cat. Min.* 28.2 τὸν δῆμον ἡττώμενον πρὸς τὸ συμφέρον καὶ τρεπόμενον. Plutarch claims that Metellus had occupied the Forum, or more specifically the platform of the Temple of Castor where the voting would take place, with "armed non-citizens and gladiators and slaves" (27.1, 5). Although we know little of magistrates' methods of providing what we would today call "security," this looks like an attempt to protect the proceedings on the steps and podium of the Temple from potential violence. The ὁπλῖται (§2: seemingly armed soldiers, different from or the same as these?) who respond to Metellus's orders later are posted at a small distance whence they are summoned at the moment of crisis and to which they withdraw immediately after order is again restored, although they are no help at all to Metellus when the opposing party suddenly rushes back and definitively takes over the space (§§3–5). All of this looks like the behavior of an armed guard to provide security for the voting: note, for instance, that Cato seems to have no difficulty making his way through this ring of fighters to reach the podium and then to hand up Munatius without apparent incident. Interpretation of these armed men therefore

To understand what was going on here we need to look back to the controversial history of the tribunate in the 60s.[93] The restoration of the traditional legislative powers of the tribunes in 70 had been a catastrophe for those like Q. Catulus who deplored active intervention by the popular assemblies in major issues of policy by means of tribunician legislation, thus on various highly contentious issues yanking the decision out of the hands of the senators where so-called *optimates* thought it belonged.[94] Only three years after the restoration of tribunician powers (67) they had been used first to place an unprecedented armada and an unprecedented command in the hands of Pompey to deal with the urgent matters of endemic piracy in the Mediterranean, and the very next year by another tribunician law overriding the Senate's assignment of provinces he was appointed to the command against the troublesome king of Pontus, Mithridates. Attempts by fellow tribunes to veto this nightmarish (to some) revival and expansion of tribunician power were completely futile in the face of the laws' overwhelming popular support: as had been argued and in fact demonstrated in practice by Tiberius Gracchus in 133, the veto power of the tribunes, invented to protect the rights of the plebs, could not properly be used to rob the very plebs of their legitimate demands especially when these were expressed (or about to be expressed) in the form of a vote.[95] The precedent of Gracchus's removal of a tribune who had tried to do just that was itself reiterated and reinforced when the tribune Trebellius tried to veto Gabinius's bill on the pirate command: Gabinius threatened him with an immediate vote on his continued exercise of the tribunate and Trebellius gave up his threat. Even Cicero – no optimate ideologue – defended Gabinius's reactivation of the Gracchan precedent: in such a serious matter relating to the welfare of the Roman People "he had not allowed the expressed will of a single colleague of his to be stronger than that of the entire citizenry."[96] (Particularly noteworthy is Cicero's dismissal of a tribunician veto as merely reflecting one

---

seems tainted by the pro-Catonian tendentiousness of Plutarch's source. Dio 37.43.3 notably describes the violence as two-sided, with sticks and stones "and even swords"; in Plutarch those sympathetic to Metellus *thought* they were being attacked by armed men (28.5).

[93] A thoughtful review in Millar 1998: 73–93. See also Steel 2010.

[94] On *optimates* see Morstein-Marx 2004: 204–207 and Yakobson 2017.

[95] A principle recognized at least as far back as Badian 1972: 706, speaking of M. Octavius's veto against Gracchus's agrarian bill: "The straining of the constitution by using the veto to prevent the People from deciding an issue closely concerning it had neither precedent nor justification."

[96] Cic. *Corn.* I fr. 31: *neque, cum salutem populo Romano . . . afferret, passus est plus unius collegae sui* [sc. Trebellius] *quam universae civitatis vocem valere et voluntatem.* The Gracchan precedent is a major reason why after 133 vetoes could not in practice be sustained against highly "popular" bills: Morstein-Marx 2004: 124–126. (The "precedent" I am speaking of is pragmatic; in Rome legal precedent was not law.)

man's will when it is faced with the unanimity of the Roman People.) In practice, then, so long as the Gracchan precedent held, the tribunician veto of a colleague's legislative proposal was not absolute but subject in the last resort to what was in effect ratification by the voters. Clearly the situation had become desperate for those hostile to "popular" legislation: if the tribunician veto could no longer be used effectively as a means of obstruction, how now was one to stop "popular" legislation in its tracks?

The first step in the reaction was to explore ways of physically interfering in the assembly with a tribune's steps in putting his bill to the vote. In 67, the same year as the *lex Gabinia*, the tribune C. Cornelius had proposed a bill forcing exemptions to law to be put before the People rather than decided in the Senate according to the cozy arrangement that had prevailed hitherto. This time a tribune P. Servilius Globulus, seeking to veto the bill, took a new route by blocking the herald from reading the law, as was formally required, to the assembled voters before their votes were cast. Cornelius then took the text of the law in his own hands and tried to read it, at which point the consul, C. Piso, exclaimed that tribunician sacrosanctity was being violated, sparking a riot which caused Cornelius to disperse the assembly. The attempt at obstruction was successful, since Cornelius in alarm went back and revised his bill into a more moderate version which was then passed without disruption. But in the second year after Cornelius's tribunate he was charged in court for having violated tribunician sacrosanctity. Despite the testimony provided by some of the heaviest hitters the oligarchy could offer ("leaders of the community who held the most power in the Senate," wrote Asconius, listing Q. Catulus, *princeps senatus* and cos. 78, Q. Hortensius cos. 69, Metellus Pius cos. 80, M. Lucullus cos. 74, M'. Lepidus cos. 66), Cornelius was acquitted with none other than Cicero arguing for the defense that the long history of popular agitation on behalf of the powers of the tribunate was beneficial – presumably, as his oratorical hero M. Antonius had argued at the trial of Norbanus in the 90s, because this was an indispensable defense of the People's freedom.[97] The *optimates* had overreached.

Against this background it becomes clearer what Cato and Minucius were trying to do. Just as Servilius Globulus had stopped Cornelius's herald from reading out the law, Cato stopped Metellus's herald from doing the

---

[97] The story of Cornelius's trial (Alexander 1990: no. 209) is recounted by Ascon. 57–62C; see also Crawford's commentary (1994). The historical argument: Ascon. 76–78C (Cic. *Corn.* I frs. 47–50 C). Antonius's defense of "sedition": Cic. *De Or.* 2.197–204. See also Steel 2010: 44–50.

same; just as Cornelius had done on that occasion, Metellus then took the document and began to read it himself. In 67, that had been enough: at the consul's vigorous protest the assembly had descended into disorder and was called off, effectively defeating the stronger version of Cornelius's bill and prompting his promulgation of a compromise version. But this time Metellus did not yield. Cato grabbed the scroll from him, so he began to recite the law from memory (he had, it seems, a good memory); but Minucius now covered his mouth. That prompted Metellus to summon his security detachment and the assembly predictably devolved into violence. Cato himself, ostensibly protected by tribunician sacrosanctity, was struck by sticks and stones thrown from the podium, and the opposing sides took turns rushing and seizing the voting space. In the end Cato's side prevailed, and so no law was passed that day. Thus Cato and Minucius had succeeded in their immediate aim, and the next step was to move matters to the Senate, where they were assured of a more friendly reception.

The Senate responded ferociously. Dio even claims that it passed the Final Decree, while Plutarch only says that it supported Cato's resistance to the law since it contributed to sedition and civil war.[98] It is hard to decide between these two: the *s.c.u.* would be an unprecedentedly heavy-handed response to something that appears to have been more a riot than an insurrection and seems not to have required any further police action to suppress, but since Nepos had so directly challenged the Senate's leadership in the ongoing Catilinarian crisis one can hardly rule out an extreme reaction. Suetonius adds that Nepos and Caesar as well (for his staunch support of the tribune) were actually removed from office by a decree of the Senate, which would also be a remarkable example of overreach since magistrates were elected by the People and did not serve at the Senate's pleasure.[99] But since Plutarch says that Cato himself successfully argued in the Senate against so severe a sanction as relieving Nepos of his office we should probably conclude that this extraordinary step was discussed but

---

[98] Dio 37.43.3; Plut. *Cat. min.* 28.6.

[99] Suet. *Iul.* 16; the reference to Caesar's "endorsement and vigorous backing" of Metellus's bill – which was not so very apparent on the day of the vote – may be to the speech *pro Quinto Metello* (Suet. *Iul.* 55.3: *Metellum seque adversus communium obtrectatorum criminationes purgantis*, with Strasburger 1938: 103–105; Blom 2016: 168n107; cf. 152). See also Butler and Cary 1927: 59. A surprising number of historians have accepted Suetonius's curious claim: e.g. Gelzer 1968: 57; Seager 2002: 73; Goldsworthy 2006: 144; Lintott 2008: 149; Billows 2009: 100. Gruen 2009: 29 is ambiguous ("nearly stripped of his praetorship" but "reinstatement by the senate itself"); Meier 1982: 177–178 implicitly rejects the story. A conspicuous and ill-omened precedent for the Senate's removal of a magistrate from office was the abrogation of Cinna's consulship in 87: Morstein-Marx 2011: 264–271. A possible later parallel for what is envisioned here is the decree against praetor M. Caelius in 48 (Caes. *BCiv.* 3.21.3: *ab re publica removendum censuit*).

not actually taken.[100] Instead, Nepos was given an exemption from the law
to allow him, though tribune, to leave Rome and join Pompey, and as we
shall see, Caesar lay low for a while. The main thing for Cato and like-
minded senators was that Nepos's proposal had been defeated – and in the
process Cato had shown them a way of defeating the wave of "popular"
legislation that had begun in 67. Never mind that it had required the
physical manhandling of a sacrosanct tribune (by another sacrosanct
tribune);[101] once violence had been provoked the assembly was likely to
descend into chaos, and when that chaos ensued the initiative would move to
the Senate, which was friendly ground for retaliation. With the Senate's
vigorous support, Cato scored a remarkable, almost unheard-of victory in
imposing a veto that, at the cost of some violence to popular constitutional
norms and principles, tumult in the assembly, and the expenditure of some
of the Senate's political capital, fatally undermined a bill that to all appearances the voters had strongly supported. It is a striking example of our
tendency, often quite unconsciously, to read late-republican history through
Ciceronian and even Catonian lenses that modern scholars tend to see
Nepos and Caesar (who had in fact done nothing, it seems, but agree to
speak in favor of the popular bill) as subversive mischief makers in this
episode, and Cato as a staunch defender of republican principles. As we shall
see in the next chapter, Cato had invented a strategy for subverting the will of
the People that would soon be developed further.

The reader will have noticed that Caesar played an almost vanishingly
minor role in the Nepos debacle: we do not hear of him giving a speech on
the day of the voting assembly and once the melee begins Caesar seems
nowhere to be found. Caesar does not so much as appear in Plutarch's
account of the Senate's stern reaction to the violence, and Nepos, not
Caesar, was the target for the (uncertain) *s.c.u.* mentioned by Dio, who has
the latter immediately go quiet in order to make sure that such a decree was
not passed against himself.[102] We have seen that Suetonius's idea that

---

[100] Plut. *Cat. Min.* 29.3–4. Note Cicero's assertion to Metellus's elder brother that he had himself
taken a lenient approach to Nepos (Cic. *Fam.* 5.2.9). Shackleton Bailey plausibly suggests (1965:
1:273) that *ut senati consulto meus inimicus . . . sublevaretur* refers not to reinstatement to office but
the grant of an exemption to allow Nepos to go abroad while a sitting tribune.

[101] The tribune's sacrosanctity was supposed to protect a tribune against all direct physical interference,
without which *auxilium*, a precious protection of Roman "civil rights," and *intercessio* itself would
have been in effect voided. Lintott 1999: 123–125; Cic. *Sest.* 79, *Tull.* 47; Liv. 3.55.7. However, law
and custom did not prescribe what should be done if the agents of such violation were tribunes
themselves. If Metellus cried out for help, this arguably activated the original oath of the plebs to
protect a tribune: Dion. Hal. 6.89.3; Fest. 318.35ff L.

[102] Dio 37.44.1–2.

Nepos and Caesar were actually deprived of their office is almost certainly false, which casts further doubt on the rest of his story, which has anyway always sounded a bit naïve: that Caesar continued to hold court despite the Senate's threats, but that when he heard that some were threatening to use violence to stop him he dismissed his lictors, laid aside his magistrate's toga (*praetexta*), and went home. When a great crowd assembled the next day crying out that it would win back his *dignitas*, Suetonius adds, he restrained them in a show of deference to the Senate, which (now meeting to discuss the demonstration) reciprocated by sending a deputation of its leading men to thank him and inviting him to a meeting where he was showered with praise.[103] It would be best to reserve judgment on this strange story. The best conclusion is probably that after Nepos was sent packing the new praetor (after making an initial defense in the Senate) backpedaled cautiously and gradually took steps to reassure the Senate that he had no intention of making further trouble. Any hopes Caesar entertained of an opportunity to hold a significant military command would depend on holding on to his praetorship and being included in the allotment of post-praetorian provinces. Similar efforts to mend fences were being made by Cicero and the Metellan clan in order to prevent Nepos's political extinction on one hand and a feud with one of Rome's most powerful families on the other.[104]

The "Stolen" Triumph

In the drawing of lots for the praetorian provinces Caesar obtained Hispania Ulterior (Farther Spain), one perfectly suited to his high military ambition. Dio, here echoing Sallust's judgment in the *Synkrisis* with Cato and speaking of precisely the same stage of his career, describes Caesar as "eager for glory and emulating Pompey and others before him who had won great power ... expecting that if he should achieve something then, he would be elected consul straightaway and would accomplish extraordinary deeds."[105] Another strong motive must have been the mountain of debts he had accumulated in his double electoral campaigns of 63: victory and plunder, not run-of-the-mill administrative corruption and profiteering, were what was needed to

[103] Suet. *Iul.* 16.1–2.
[104] Cicero made interesting back-channel approaches to Nepos's cousin (Pompey's wife) and also his sister-in-law (Cic. *Fam.* 5.2.6: none other than the famous Clodia) while seeking to explain himself to Nepos's powerful brother (Celer, cos. 60).
[105] Dio 37.52.1–2; cf. Sall. *Cat.* 54.4.

restore his strained finances.[106] Shortly before he was to make his departure
he deftly slipped out of entanglement in the Bona Dea controversy which
suddenly seized senators' attention at the end of 62 and beginning of 61 and
soon devolved into a significant contest, complete with riotous *contiones* and
an aborted voting assembly, between senatorial hard-liners ostensibly
upholding "senatorial authority" and their *popularis* opponents led by the
tribune Q. Fufius Calenus.[107] The religious celebration in question had taken
place in Caesar's house and a supposed adulterous liaison between P. Clodius
and Caesar's third wife, Pompeia, stood at the heart of the allegations of
sacrilege. This must have offered yet another tempting opportunity to
Caesar's enemies: he was a bigger fish than Clodius and may well have
been the initial target of the uproar and investigation. Yet Caesar deftly
slipped through the net by ruthlessly and shockingly divorcing his wife on
the grounds that she must be "above suspicion," delicately sidestepping the
question of her (and P. Clodius's) guilt yet falling far short of clearing them,
and thereby also distancing himself from any alleged sacrilege.[108] Clodius was
able to turn the affair, which consumed the attention of the capital for
months, into something of a *popularis* cause célèbre, but note that Caesar had
offered no help all. As we have seen repeatedly, he had always tended to
avoid what one might call *popularis* activism, and shunning this latest clash
he hurried off to Spain to pursue his main objective.

The details of Caesar's campaigns in Further Spain after his praetorship
(61–60) need not detain us.[109] It will suffice to note that he acted in the mold
of the great conquerors of old, disdaining the mundane frontier actions that
would have occupied the attention of less ambitious proconsuls and seizing
the capital of the Callaeci at Brigantium at the northwest limit of the

---

[106] Caesar's extraordinary indebtedness at this time is acknowledged by Sallust (49.3: *is privatim egregia liberalitate, publice maxumis muneribus, grandem pecuniam debebat*; cf. App. *BCiv.* 2.8/26). See Chapter 2, p. 53ff. Note, however, Rosenstein's observation (2011: 151–153) that Caesar may have restored his fortune not from war plunder but from pseudo-voluntary "gifts" from allied communities, as Suet. *Iul.* 54.1 reports (doubtless from a hostile source). Blösel 2016 suggests that the decreasing number of ex-praetors who accepted a province after their term of office in this period may be a mark of the declining profitability of provincial commands generally.

[107] The "Bona Dea affair" is usually interpreted as an effort by *optimates* to destroy the very junior P. Clodius. See Tatum 1999: 62–82; Lintott 2008: 154–159; Pelling 2011: 174–181.

[108] For the famous anecdote see Plut. *Caes.* 10.9 and other sources cited by Pelling 2011: 180. The idea that Caesar was "playing to the people" (Plut. *Caes.* 10.10) overlooks the fact that the divorce was prima facie quite damaging to Clodius and the declared agnosticism hardly helpful. Caesar's earlier rejection of intense political pressure to divorce his previous wife may have encouraged his enemies to think that this escape route was unlikely.

[109] See Schulz 2002 and now Osgood 2014. The details of Caesar's campaigns remain vague; for their modest place in the larger story of the Roman conquest of the peninsula see Richardson 1996: 83–149. For an archaeological survey of the Roman conquest of the region see Costa-García 2018.

peninsula by amphibious assault, thereby bringing the terror of the Roman name all the way to the shores of Ocean (the Atlantic).[110] Caesar claimed to have finished the conquest of Spain, forcing all those of wavering loyalty or who were not yet subjugated to submit to the *imperium populi Romani* (App. *Hisp.* 102/442), although as we know retrospectively much remained for his eventual heir to do in the peninsula.

Caesar hastened home the following summer (60) and naturally requested a triumphal celebration for his victories.[111] However, since he arrived outside Rome shortly before the consular elections for 59, which he also intended to contest *suo anno* ("in his year" – i.e. the first year he was eligible), his schedule was uncomfortably tight. It appears that the Senate did give its approval to a triumph – so say Dio and Appian, at least.[112] The difficulty for Caesar, however, was that the consular elections were upon him, which traditionally demanded the candidates' presence not merely in the environs of the City (where commanders customarily awaited their triumphal entry, and where the consular elections actually were held), but actually within the formal civic boundary (*pomerium*); yet the mechanics of *imperium* were such that crossing that boundary was tantamount to giving up hopes of a triumph, and of course it would take some time to arrange the celebration.[113] This would normally only cause difficulty for men of sub-consular status aiming for the consulship at the very same time they were also seeking to celebrate a triumph; in the recent past this had been the case only with Pompey and Crassus in 71 – and this had presented no

---

[110] Esp. Dio 37.52–54.1, Plut. *Caes.* 11–12. Cf. Suet. *Iul.* 18.1, 54.1 – a highly negative report "as certain men claim in their accounts." Plut. (12.4) and Suet. (54.1) suggest that Caesar extracted enough from his command to pay off his enormous debts (cf. n. 106). If so, this was lamentably unremarkable behavior for a Roman aristocrat. Cicero's model administration of Cilicia, with only modest military action, left him a sum of HS 2.2 million *legibus salvis* (Cic. *Fam.* 5.20.9, with Shackleton Bailey 1977: 1:471), perhaps including HS 400,000 as his manubial share of the booty (*Fam.* 2.17.4 with Shackleton Bailey 1977: 1:459; cf. *Att.* 5.20.5, where the figure seems likely to be corrupt (cf. Wistrand 1979: 27n4). Mitchell 1991: 224n63.

[111] Four of the seven triumphs celebrated since 71 had been for victories in one Spanish province or the other, and three of these were for men below the rank of consul (Pompey, Afranius, and Pupius Piso). Some uncertainty exists about the *provincia* of Afranius's triumph, but most authorities opt for Spain: Broughton, *MRR* 3.13; Itgenshorst 2005: no. 254; Rich 2014: no. 254.

[112] Dio 44.41.3–4 (cf. 37.54.1 τὰ ἐπινίκια without further ado; contra Morrell 2017: 115n102, μὴ τυχὼν δέ refers to the requested exception); App. *BCiv.* 2.8/28; Plut. *Caes.* 13.1 is ambiguous, focused as he is on the request for an exemption from the requirement to declare one's candidacy in the City. Ehrhardt 1987 argued "with some reason" (Pelling 2011: 187) that the references to the approval of the triumph are mistaken, but he does not explain away the precise circumstantial detail of Dio 44.41.3–4. See now Osgood 2014: 158–159 in favor of senatorial approval.

[113] A proconsul's *imperium* lapsed upon reentry into the City but was needed for the triumph itself. Drogula 2015: 114 goes beyond the evidence in asserting that the Senate had actually scheduled the triumph for a date after the deadline for declaring a consular candidacy.

difficulty at all, so far as we can tell.[114] In any case the requirement that a candidate be present even at the elections in the Campus was no hard-and-fast rule, as one can see from Cicero's attack on an identical provision in the Rullan *rogatio* of 63 as an invidious and insidious restraint on the People's power to vote for whom they chose, not to mention the waiving of that requirement in exceptional cases such as Marius's reelections to the consulship in absentia in 105 and 104 (though admittedly Marius's position was a much more exalted one than Caesar's at this stage).[115] Since much of the City was outside of the *pomerium*, including the site where the electoral assembly for consuls met, and Caesar was certainly present for his election, this cannot, except in the most narrow, technical sense, be called a request to stand in absentia.[116] A victorious commander just honored by the Senate's approval for his triumph was probably well within his rights to ask for exemption from a technicality that would cause an unnecessary setback in his career. Thus Caesar's request to the Senate to be permitted to fulfill the technical requirement by having "his friends" declare his *professio* within the City while he remained outside the *pomerium* to prepare and await his triumph was hardly so cheeky as is often suggested. A formal exemption from the law would need to be requested, yet exemptions from the details of electoral law, and much more significant ones at that, were nothing new when such complications arose. They might even be seen as honors, as testimony to exceptional merit, rather than as embarrassing affronts to the rule of law.[117]

Although the Senate granted the right to triumph, it did not in the end approve Caesar's request for an exemption allowing him to pursue his

---

[114] App. *BCiv.* 1.121/560–561; Plut. *Pomp.* 21.5–22.1. Contra Seager 2002: 46, we hear of no special legal dispensation given to Pompey (and Crassus) to be elected "in absentia." This supports the view of Linderski (1995: 93–94) that only after January 63 (Cic. *Leg. agr.* 2.24) was the declaration of candidacy *within the City* made a statutory requirement. That it was *customary* for a candidate to present himself formally to the Roman People (*professio*) within the City for a *trinundinum* before the elections seems clear (Kunkel and Wittmann 1995: 70–78), but until this was written into law ca. 63 a proconsular candidate who had not crossed the *pomerium* was not technically running "in absentia," for consular elections were held on the Campus Martius outside the *pomerium*. Thus ca. 63 a new, purely "technical" category of "in absentia" election was created that had not applied to earlier proconsular candidates in a position similar to Caesar's.

[115] Cic. *Leg. agr.* 2.24.   [116] A key observation of Linderski 1995 (see n. 114).

[117] Caesar's "friends": Plut. *Caes.* 13.1. Exemptions from other legal rules of election, such as the *lex Villia/Cornelia* regulating minimum ages and sequences for holding office or the old ban on reelection to the consulship, had also not uncommonly been granted, and without much ado. Cicero celebrates the far more sweeping exception granted Pompey from the requirement of holding *any* prior public office as testimony to Pompey's extraordinary *virtus* (*Leg. Man.* 62); cf. the various exemptions granted the Scipiones Africani (Chapter 2, p. 8off.). For the "popular" position that "by the laws of Tullius and Romulus [they] were masters of the elections and regarding these laws they could invalidate or validate whichever ones they liked" see Chapter 1, n. 32.

candidacy while remaining outside the religious boundary of the City, as Pompey and Crassus had done in 71. But neither did the Senate vote the request down. It was defeated (not for the last time) by a filibuster which Cato carried out when he observed that the Senate actually *favored* Caesar's request: when Cato saw that "many" senators were inclined to give Caesar what he wanted, he talked out the time of the meeting until sunset, requiring a formal end to the session without a conclusion, in effect denying Caesar's request despite being distinctly in the minority.[118] Caesar then gave up his request for a legal exemption and crossed the *pomerium* in order to make his formal *professio*, thereby abandoning a triumph already awarded by the Senate and with it, his first real stab at the military glory he so coveted.

The significance of this moment needs to be emphasized. The filibuster is a classic tactic of the *minority*, not the majority: Cato did not here represent the majority view of the Senate, presumably not even of the higher echelons of the Senate who normally held the most weight in deliberations.[119] As we saw, in 62 Cato had explored a new way of frustrating the popular will; now, in this first certain instance of the use of the filibuster – a tactic that would become his trademark over the next decade – he was evidently experimenting with new ways to undermine and perhaps ultimately to overturn the opinion of the Senate's majority.[120] This radical exploitation of the Senate's rules by a man who continues to be portrayed

---

[118] Plut. *Caes.* 13.2 ὡς ἑώρα πολλοὺς τεθεραπευμένους ὑπὸ τοῦ Καίσαρος ἐκκρούσαντος τῷ χρόνῳ τὸ πρᾶγμα καὶ τὴν ἡμέραν ἐν τῷ λέγειν κατατρίψαντος; *Cat. min.* 31.5 βουλομένων δὲ πολλῶν ἀντέλεγεν ὁ Κάτων· ὡς δὲ ᾔσθετο χαριζομένους τῷ Καίσαρι ... καὶ τὴν βουλὴν οὕτως ἐξέκρουσε. Suet. *Iul.* 18.2 says that *multi* spoke against Caesar's request, but his account here lacks the circumstantial detail that distinguishes Plutarch, including clear mention of the filibuster, which necessarily implies a minority position.

[119] A Roman filibuster differed somewhat from the modern congressional instrument in the United States. The Roman Senate could not pass decrees after sunset, so using up the remaining hours of daylight in effect killed a motion (bibliography at Pelling 2011: 188). But this does not mean that the device's power was absolute (so e.g. De Libero 1992: 15–22; cf. Drummond 1994: 124): it could be ended by the senators themselves overwhelming the speaker with their shouts (cf. Cic. *Att.* 4.2.4: Clodius, after three hours) or by the presiding consul having the speaker dragged off to prison (at the risk of a public relations disaster, presumably often the speaker's intent: Chapter 4). In an interesting discussion of the filibuster at *Leg.* 3.40 Cicero proscribes its use unless the Senate is about to make a serious error and no magistrate is prepared to step in. (Dyck 1996: 539 and Powell's OCT accept Bake's transposition of the text, which would blame the filibusterer in most cases for *ambitio*, but this must remain uncertain.) It must have taken extraordinary moral authority as well as physical stamina to carry off the filibuster (see Blom's rather too admiring discussion at 2016: 244, cf. 221); otherwise we would see it used any time a minority strongly dissented from the majority opinion of the Senate.

[120] Probably Cato's first targets for a filibuster were the *publicani* somewhat earlier this year. Cic. *Att.* 1.18.7 *neque iis a senatu responsum dari patitur* and 2.1.8 (Cicero's exasperation should be noted; cf. *Planc.* 34), with De Libero 1992: 16–17. "Trademark": Caes. *BCiv.* 1.32.3 *pristina consuetudine* (the

as "conservative" or "traditionalist" does not appear to be sufficiently appreciated. Who was here behaving more in keeping with the traditions of the Republic: the victorious commander respectfully asking the Senate and People for the *honor* his achievements were due, or the ex-tribune inventing a novel way to frustrate the will of the majority of the Senate in order to force that commander to sacrifice one or the other of the *beneficia* he had earned? Debates on the awarding of a triumph were often contentious, rancorous, and even petty, yet Roman history shows no precedent for the de facto denial of a triumph by means of a filibuster – a novelty again, and indeed Cato would also become in the 50s an isolated yet remarkably effective voice against the traditional Roman celebrations of martial virtue.[121] But by (in effect) taking away Caesar's praetorian triumph, Cato had ensured that he would set all the more store on his prospects for a consular one.

Martin Jehne has argued that everyone would have expected Caesar to accept the deferral of his consulship rather than to give up his sole shot (perhaps) at a triumph, and that his choice of the latter was a surprising gamble.[122] That is debatable. In any case, his choice was for the consulship. Caesar, Cicero judged, currently "had the wind at his back" (i.e. much popular support), so he chanced his consular election without the boost that a triumph would have given.[123] In accordance with a clause of the *lex Sempronia* the provinces for the consuls-elect were determined before the election, and according to Suetonius the *optimates* (a word he uses in this section to describe the group of conservatives now led by Cato after Catulus's recent death) had determined that the *provinciae* for the consuls of 59 would be trivial (*minimi negotii*), mere "forests and trails."[124] What precisely that meant must be reserved for a detailed discussion of the problem of Caesar's original provincial assignment in the next chapter, but Suetonius clearly understood it as an attempt to restrain his military ambitions, which the Spanish campaign and his request for a triumph had

---

context is 52 BC) *dicendi mora dies extrahente*. Plut. *Mor.* 804c is quite clear that this was Cato's strategy to frustrate not only the will of the People but also the prevailing mood of the Senate.

[121] Triumphal debates: see Bastien 2007: 249–311; Beard 2007: 199–214; Pittenger 2008, keeping Hölkeskamp's cautions in mind (2010). Cato's curious revisionism regarding supplications and triumphs: Cic. *Fam.* 15.4–5 with Morrell 2018: 106–116 and now Segal 2019: 164–226.

[122] Jehne 2009: 65–70. So too Seager 2002: 83.

[123] Cic. *Att.* 2.1.6: *cuius nunc venti valde sunt secundi*.

[124] Suet. *Iul.* 19.2. Death of Catulus between February 61 and May 60: Cic. *Att.* 1.13.2, 20.3; Rüpke 2005: 2.1122. It is remarkable that the *optimates* did not rally at Catulus's death around the consular Cicero (note his complaint at Cic. *Att.* 1.20.3), supposedly the hero of 63, instead of the merely tribunician Cato – another mark of the latter's curious charisma and the untraditional nature of his ascendancy.

clearly demonstrated. Earlier in the year there had been a serious war scare in Gaul across the Alps, which must have given Caesar some fleeting hope, but then the emergency seemed to have passed. Now the Senate's decree threw into doubt his best opportunity to replace the lost praetorian triumph with a consular one. And in the election, with the help of bribery sanctioned by Cato himself in order to counter the handouts being offered by Lucceius in Caesar's name as well as his own, the *optimates* managed to get Cato's son-in-law, M. Bibulus, elected as Caesar's colleague in the hope (Suetonius says) of checking his influence.[125]

Returning now in conclusion to the two Ciceronian retrospectives with which this chapter began, let us remember that both imply that Caesar's natural alignment, given his origin and heritage, was with the Senate: what needed explanation was why he would ever have fallen away from that natural allegiance toward "popular" demagogy. In the more general comments delivered to the Senate in 56, Cicero had reinforced this idea that the natural place of a man like Caesar was on the side of the Senate rather than turning to *popularis* political agitation.[126] We have seen in the previous chapter that Caesar's patrician birth and aristocratic connections fit that natural expectation, and that his early career shows no serious inclination toward "popular demagogy" (*popularis levitas*) as distinct from considerable skill in cultivating a popular public image. But something changed. In his address to the Senate in 43, Cicero declared to the Senate that it had not been Caesar's good fortune "to be highly valued by the Senate and all the best men" as a young man, and "neglecting to win that esteem" he had lapsed to *popularis levitas*. In the earlier speech of 56, he hinted more strongly that Caesar had strived to win the Senate's esteem and that of "all the best men" but had been "pushed away from attachment to this Order" by some "disparagement inflicted by others." Now on this occasion Cicero has specific rhetorical reasons to lay implicit blame for Caesar's change at the door of others, evidently those powerful senators who had driven him away from his expected natural allegiance to the Senate. It is quite clear that Cicero in this sentence is recalling to the minds of his senatorial audience the events examined in this chapter: the attacks on Caesar's standing that immediately preceded his "departure from this haven into the heavy seas" of "popular" politics in his consulship.

[125] Suet. *Iul.* 19.1: Lucceius is the grammatical subject of *pronuntiaret*: despite Caesar's restoration of his financial health in Spain, it was apparently Lucceius who had the money to spend on *largitio*. It is unclear whether *coitio* was illegal or simply frowned upon. This particular "ticket" had been in the works for some time: Cic. *Att.* 1.17.11, 2.1.9.
[126] Cic. *Phil.* 5.49, *Prov. cons.* 38 with full texts in nn. 1–3.

Cicero's conception of Caesar's involuntary turn toward *popularis* activism fits, at least in a broad sense, the facts we have traced over this chapter and the previous one.

By objecting to the illegal death sentence for the "Catilinarians," Caesar lost the "esteem" of the "Senate and all the best men" despite the fact that long-term prudence on the Senate's behalf would not recommend blatantly violating a law cherished by the People. "Disparagement" (*obtrectatio*) followed from powerful senators such as his personal enemy Q. Catulus, eager to settle scores with the young pup who had insisted on honoring the detested Marius and had humiliated him in the pontifical election, with the *optimates'* rising star Cato next up to take the lead in the fight. Caesar tried a somewhat aggressive response at the beginning of 62 but vanished from the fight over Metellus Nepos's bill (the closest he had ever come to a "popular" legislative battle), quickly running up the white flag. But the attacks kept coming even after he had returned from his victorious march to the Atlantic coast of Spain. Catulus had died but his place both as optimate leader and in his personal feud with Caesar had been taken by the *adulescens* Cato whose experiments with novel methods of obstruction in both the voting assembly and in the Senate were proving much more effective in blocking "popular" political initiatives and the projects of popular heroes (such as Pompey) than Catulus's *auctoritas* had been. Cato and his friends had already frustrated for two years Pompey's efforts to obtain senatorial recognition of his settlement of the eastern wars, his arrangements in Asia Minor and the Levant, and just reward for his veterans;[127] he had successfully filibustered M. Crassus's efforts on behalf of the tax gatherers; and now, though he could not prevent Roman voters from putting Caesar over the top in the consular election he could at least deprive him of his triumph in addition, as well as blocking the easy route to the kind of post-consular military assignment that would give him the chance to enhance his standing.

It would be an eventful year to come.

---

[127] Seager 2002: 75–82; Drogula 2019: 107–127; see also Gruen 1974: 85–87. Lucullus and Metellus Celer as well as Pompey's old rival M. Crassus joined in Cato's discomfiture of Pompey. Note Dio 37.49.2 (60 BC) "the optimates (δυνατοί) ... prevented these things from being voted on": the filibuster again. Cato's brusque rejection of Pompey's proposal for a double matrimonial connection upon his return (Plut. *Cat. Min.* 30.3–6, *Pomp.* 44) is remarkable testimony not only to his self-esteem but also to the uncompromising nature of the political warfare he was now waging: attempts at reconciliation were scorned as nothing better than bribes.

CHAPTER 4

Caesar's First Consulship

Within a generation Caesar's first consulship in 59, or more precisely, the formation of the triple alliance with Pompey and Crassus in the previous year, could be seen in retrospect as the beginning of the end of the Roman Republic. Already in the 30s BC the historian C. Asinius Pollio, a former Caesarian officer, had freighted the date *Metello consule* (60 BC) with this massive significance, which coincides suggestively with the "commonplace," attributed by Plutarch to Cato, that it was not the dissolution of the alliance between Caesar and Pompey that brought about the civil war but its original creation.[1] By the later first century AD, the Flavian historian Josephus could write that this moment marked not just the *beginning* of the end of the Republic, but its actual end (*AJ* 19.187). Varro's reference to the triple alliance as the "three-headed creature" – surely negative, with its allusion to Cerberus, despite Wiseman's recent attempt to sanitize the comment[2] – and Cicero's own repeated statements in his letters of the year 59 that the Republic was "lost" appear to lend some contemporary authority to such a judgment.[3]

---

[1] On Pollio's starting point (*Metello consule*: Hor. *Carm.* 2.1) see Drummond 2013: 1:437–438, and for an excellent, up-to-date summary of the related issues see the whole entry (pp. 430–445, no. 56). Plutarch attributes the sentiment already to Cato (*Pomp.* 47.4; cf. *Caes.* 13.5), while Drummond offers a string of Ciceronian references that are similar, though not exactly identical (e.g. *Fam.* 6.6.4; Drummond 2013: 1:437n52); it was "probably a commonplace before Pollio" (Pelling 2011: 191). Rising 2013: 216–221 blames Pollio for the partisan bias of our sources for this year, but Bellemore's emphasis on the influence of a eulogistic biographical tradition of Cato worship, starting with his admirer Munatius Rufus and extending all the way to Thrasea Paetus (major sources, as we know, for Plutarch's *Life of Cato the Younger*), seems more on the mark (2005: 225–227).

[2] App. *BCiv.* 2.9/33. Wiseman 2009: 117, cf. 139n43, 141, 147 (similarly, Gruen 1974: 95n36 and Pelling 2011: 188–189n3), overlooks both the unmistakable mythological allusion to Hades's terrifying guard dog and the literary precedent of Anaximenes of Lampsacus's satire (Paus. 6.18.5), as well as Varro's strong connection to Pompey and his service among the Board of Twenty implementing Caesar's agrarian law(s) (*MRR* 2.192). The work was likely written after the deaths of all three "heads" of the beast; for Varro's post-Pharsalus regrets see the correspondence with Cicero (*Fam.* 9.1–8). See also Rising 2013: 217n105.

[3] Cic. *Att.* 2.21.1[sc. *res publica*] *tota periit; Q.fr.* 1.2.15 *rem publicam funditus amisimus.* Cf. similar statements such as at *Att.* 2.17.1, 18.1–2, 19.2–3, 19.5 (*certi sumus perisse omnia*), 20.3–4, 22.6, 25.2.

Yet we must be careful. We have already noted how Cicero's lamentations for the death of the Republic tend to coincide closely with the dips in his own political fortunes; it often is palpable that such phrases express personal frustration but cannot be treated as an objective diagnosis.[4] Even Cato's well-known dictum carries buried within it more than a little self-exculpation since (unlike, for instance, Cicero) he ultimately bore considerable responsibility for driving Pompey and Caesar apart even at the price of civil war. (A critic might observe that it was he who had played a crucial role in bringing them together in shared frustration.)[5] As for Pollio, as a loyal Caesarian in the civil wars of 49–45 he seems unlikely to have taken precisely the same view as Cato did about the break-up of the alliance, but retrospectively from the 30s it would still have been perfectly reasonable to trace the causal chain that led ultimately to Philippi (through the crossing of the Rubicon and the assassination) back to Caesar's first consulship. But tracing the causal tree from leaf to branch to trunk is a deceptively simple matter, for there is always only one way to the trunk; but to go in the reverse direction – the one followed by the arrow of time – is a much more complex operation: in that direction every juncture leads to alternate branches, and more alternates, and so on until one reaches the minute twigs at the crown, so that one end point is not necessarily any more "natural" a destination than another. The two directions of the causal chain resemble each other, but one splits while the other converges: too many decisions had to be made, too many conditions had to be met along the way, for the end point to be predictable even in retrospect. We should try to look at the tumultuous year of Caesar's first consulship with fresh eyes, resisting as far as we are able, the easy but entrenched teleology after more than two thousand years of retrospective judgment often skewed not only by hindsight but also by the frequently uncorrected invectives and outraged denunciations of Caesar's enemies and critics.

In order to bring to the fore my critique of the standard interpretation of the significance of the year 59, I shall not review, piece by piece, all the historically significant events of Caesar's consulship, as would be appropriate and necessary for a survey or biography.[6] It is not unusual to interpret the events of this year as setting a course for the Republic from which there

---

[4] Chapter 1, n. 27.   [5] Drogula 2019: 107–127.

[6] A full account of the events of the year may be found in most of the biographies cited in Chapter 1, n. 1; see also now Chrissanthos 2019 (see esp. n. 73 of this chapter). Gelzer 1968, as always, stands out for his painstaking documentation, although his perspective is quite dated. Most recent work, including Billows 2009, Gruen 2009: 30–35 and 1974: 90–97, 397–401, Raaflaub 2010, Rising 2013, Stevenson 2015, Wiseman 2016, and Chrissanthos 2019, has been more sympathetic to Caesar's aims and perspective than was usual in the twentieth century.

was no real exit before the civil war that broke out ten years later.[7] I shall focus here on the central issues that underpin that rather sweeping judgment, specifically those that define the nature of Caesar's political leadership and its relationship to republican traditions and ideals. First come the formation of a political alliance with Pompey and Crassus and the struggle over Caesar's first agrarian law, which in many respects set the tone and drew up the battle lines for the entire year. Here, a central issue is whether Bibulus's use of obstructive devices to block Caesar's legislation, ultimately *for the entire year*, was remotely justifiable by republican precedent. Then we shall try to get below the rather general impression our sources give of Caesar's forceful political methods in this year – the basis for the widespread view that Caesar would "brook no opposition" to his initiatives, thereby ostensibly eliminating all republican constraint by institutions that lay at the foundation of the Roman political system and leaving the system more or less in ruins – by examining closely specific incidents that cast brighter and sharper light on the actual functioning of republican institutions than do the rhetoric and overall dark tone of our (rather biased) sources. Next, my analysis focuses on the *lex Vatinia* (supplemented by a decree of the Senate) that altered the unambitious provincial assignment given the consuls in the previous year (see previous chapter) and ultimately gave Caesar the military power and resources armed with which, according to a widely held view, he would finally become more powerful than the Republic itself. Finally, I conclude with a critical look at the claim that Caesar's legislation for the entire year was "technically" illegal, or at least that its legal status was ever seriously in doubt.

The Three-Way Alliance and the Presentation of the Agrarian Bill

We have just seen what Pollio retrospectively, and perhaps Cato at the time, made of the political alliance between Pompey and Caesar, who was able to bring in M. Crassus as well – an alliance which in modern times has come, quite misleadingly, to be called the "First Triumvirate." "Triumvirate" wrongly suggests a formally constituted body, as was the "Second Triumvirate" of Octavian, Mark Antony, and Lepidus created by the *lex Titia* of 43, and "first," of course, insidiously prefigures the legally authorized wave of murder and expropriation unleashed by the *Triumviri rei publicae constituendae* in 43. The very phrase therefore invokes a misleading teleology. Furthermore, it is almost

---

[7] For example, Jehne 2009a: 153–156.

impossible to use the phrase "First Triumvirate" without adopting some version of the view that it was a kind of conspiracy against the Republic. The word Suetonius uses when he describes its formation is the rather innocuous *societas* – that is, "alliance" (*Iul.* 19.2). Nomenclature matters, and in what follows I eschew the traditional "First Triumvirate" altogether in favor of locutions such as "the Three," "Caesar's allies," or the "triple (or three-way) alliance."

According to our best evidence (a letter of Cicero), in December 60 Caesar, as consul designate, was proposing to carry forward Pompey's well-known but thus far stalled agenda, but also insisting that he would follow Cicero's counsel; he also hoped, he said, to bring Pompey and Crassus together, which implicitly meant that he hoped Cicero would not stand in the way due to his deep suspicions about Crassus's political reliability.[8] There was clearly nothing revolutionary in this prospect. Billows points out with justice that the alliance of *optimates* surrounding Cato was in principle the same sort of grouping.[9] When Cicero reports the news to his friend Atticus, far from reacting with horror as one would expect if this were seen as some kind of conspiracy against the state, he describes it as an attractive prospect because it would ensure the closest association with Pompey and even with Caesar if he so desired, reconciliation with his enemies (he is probably thinking especially of Crassus here), peace with the masses, and a quiet old age.[10] On the other hand, he acknowledges, it

---

[8] Cic. *Att.* 2.3.3; cf. *Prov. cons.* 41 *consul ille egit eas res quarum me participem esse voluit . . . me in tribus sibi coniunctissimis consularibus esse voluit*. In general, on the formation of the political alliance, Gruen 1974: 88–90; Pelling 2011: 188–191. There is already a hint of a possible alignment between Pompey and Caesar in a letter written in the summer of 60, shortly before the elections, since while justifying to Atticus his flirtation with Pompey, he slips immediately into contemplation of making Caesar "better" as well (see n. 10 of this chapter). Caesar probably did enjoy the backing both of Pompey and Crassus in his consular campaign (so Dio 37.54.3–4) but only brought the two consulars together later, apparently after December 60, but clearly no later than the *contiones* on the agrarian law in January (Dio 38.4.4); thus Gruen 1974: 88 is strictly correct in denying a (public) "union of the trio" before that date. Relations between Cicero and Crassus had been fraught in 63 and thereafter (Sall. *Cat.* 48.8–9; Plut. *Crass.* 13.3–5; Ascon. 83C; Cic. *Att.* 1.13.3–4; cf. Chapter 2, n. 11). For Pompey's frustrations in pushing his objectives through after his triumphant return from the wars see n. 29.

[9] Billows 2009: 116.

[10] Cic. *Att.* 2.3.4: *coniunctio mihi summa cum Pompeio, si placet, etiam cum Caesare, reditus in gratiam cum inimicis, pax cum multitudine, senectutis otium*. Cicero thought he might even make Caesar "better" (2.1.6: *quid si etiam Caesarem, cuius nunc venti valde sunt secundi, reddo meliorem?* cf. §9), which clearly evinces suspicion of Caesar's political direction (unsurprising coming from the executioner of the "Catilinarians"), but also shows that he did not put him beyond the pale; it goes too far to conclude that wide sectors of the elite considered Caesar "a threat to the established order" (Raaflaub 2010a: 143). Rising 2015: 425 notes that "Cicero was a natural choice of 'ally' for Caesar in this matter"; similarly, Lintott 2008: 165, 168. Nothing corroborates Plutarch's assertion (*Cat. Min.* 31.7) that Cicero early on, along with (more plausibly) Lucullus, threw himself behind Bibulus and Cato in open opposition to the land law.

would not quite be consistent with the "aristocratic" (ἀριστοκρατικῶς – i.e. "optimate") political line he had taken since his consulship, and we know that in the end he did not accept the overture either now or later, when he was invited to serve on the agrarian commission for Caesar's agrarian law.[11] A political alliance with two consulars of Pompey's and Crassus's stature certainly put Caesar in a strong position for the beginning of his consulship, but it hardly merits the conspiratorial coloring retrospectively imputed to it by, for example, Dio, complete with mention of oath taking and a laudatory characterization of the alliance's eventual chief critic, Cato, as the only man "of that day who conducted politics with integrity and without seeking power for himself."[12] At least at the time, Plutarch comments, Caesar's effort to bring the two great men together had the appearance of something "altruistic" (presumably an allusion to the great scene of reconciliation between these two during their consulship), and Cato was considered an "ungenerous troublemaker" for his denunciation of it.[13]

In the same letter written to Atticus in December 60 that betrays Cicero's awareness of Caesar's alliance building, he also brings up the consul-designate's plans to promulgate an agrarian bill in January, and consults his friend about what position to take on it (*Att.* 2.3.3). That an agrarian law was long overdue and well justified, quite apart from Pompey's desire to reward his recently discharged soldiers, could not reasonably be denied. As far back as 70 the Senate had actually agreed to distribute land to veterans of the Sertorian War, but they were largely put off at the time for lack of funds.[14] These men were still for the most part awaiting consideration, while now Pompey's much more numerous

---

[11] Cic. *Att.* 2.19.4 (mid-July), 9.2a.1; Vell. Pat. 2.45.2; Quint. 12.1.16. Rising 2015 argues that Cicero was already at the end of 60 (2.3.3) offered membership on the high-ranking, select Board of Five consulars with judicial duties as well as the clearly attested occasion, circa July, when he was invited to replace a deceased member of the Board of Twenty. For Caesar's later offers of protection see n. 128.

[12] Dio 37.56–58 at 57.1, 3. Similar conspiratorial/revolutionary imputations at Plut. *Caes.* 13.3–6 (overtly "Catonian"; cf. *Cat. Min.* 31.5–7, *Crass.* 14.2–3, *Pomp.* 47.1–4), Liv. *Per.* 103. App. *BCiv.* 2.9/33 even thinks Pompey swore an oath to support Caesar in his consular campaign – a most implausible indignity for the senior partner. Cf. *societas* in Suet. *Iul.* 19.2 (based on the defensive principle of noninterference) and Vell. Pat. 2.44.1.

[13] Plut. *Caes.* 13.4, 6: ἔργῳ φιλάνθρωπον ἔχοντι προσηγορίαν ἔλαθε μεταστήσας τὴν πολιτείαν and δυσκόλου μὲν ἀνθρώπου τότε καὶ πολυπράγμονος . . . λαβεῖν δόξαν (key words tr. Pelling). Exactly when Cato made his complaint is unclear. Pelling 2011: 190 contrasts the strong emphasis of the later sources with the quieter tone of Cicero's contemporary evidence, and observes that "it seems that little was *ever* known about the coalition, and that contemporaries did not regard any such triple coalition as being of central importance."

[14] Dio 38.5.1–2 refers to a senatorial decree granting land to Pompey's and Metellus Pius's veterans from the Spanish wars of the 70s which was not put into operation because of the shortage of funds at the time. (Plut. *Luc.* 34.4, a piece of invidious rhetoric by a none too trustworthy speaker, Clodius,

veterans from his campaigns against the pirates and in the East had joined the queue. A strong attempt at agrarian legislation in 63 had been scuttled by Cicero's powerful oratory and a tribunician veto, and despite Pompey's return, another bill failed in 60, but the issue clearly was not going to go away. Many senators must have felt that it was now high time to make good on the promise made long ago to the long-suffering veterans, many of whom must have been away on campaign for several years and were surely losing patience.[15] Caesar now made sure to avoid the obvious pitfalls to which earlier recent proposals had fallen victim.[16] The law explicitly left untouched the controversial Campanian public land, and that this was a significant concession on Caesar's (and Pompey's) part is clear from the fact that later, after he could no longer hope for broad senatorial support, he went forward with a second bill distributing the *ager Campanus* to as many as twenty thousand further settlers drawn from the urban poor.[17] The commissioners to be chosen to administer the law might expand the available territory by means of purchase, not by compulsory sales or confiscations, and the purchases would be based on proper assessments, not sweetheart deals settled without public scrutiny. The necessary revenue would, of course, come from the windfall reasonably expected from Pompey's victories (a mark of the inevitable linkage between this law and the attempt to obtain ratification of Pompey's eastern arrangements).[18] To pass, however, the law needed to win the favor of the Roman People in their assemblies. It must therefore have stood to benefit the urban poor as

is weak evidence to the contrary: Seager 2002: 205n31 thinks "Clodius was lying"; alternatively he may have been grossly overstating a minimal implementation [Gruen 1974: 388].) Cic. *Att.* 1.18.6 may refer to the same measure under the name of the (*lex* or *rogatio*) Plotia – presumably promulgated by a tribune of 70 (Broughton, *MRR* 3.158). If so, the decree passed into law but was still frustrated.

[15] For the attempts of 63 (the *rogatio Servilia*) and 60 (*Flavia*), see Morstein-Marx 2004, esp. 190–202, 210–212. On the *rogatio Servilia* see now also Yakobson 2010: 297–300, and cf. the recent commentary on *Leg. Agr.* 2.1–46 by Walter, Geisweid, Hellweg, et al. 2013. Legal details in Ferrary 1988 and Ferrary in Crawford 1996: no. 52, pp. 757–760.

[16] Gruen 1974: 398: "The bill seems to have adopted the more salutary features of the Rullan and Flavian *rogationes*, while avoiding their errors." See his salutary review of its provisions: 397–401; also Crawford 1996: 763–767, who attributes to it the three extant clauses of the so-called *lex Mamilia Roscia Peducaea Alliena Fabia* (cf. Crawford 1989: 179–190), and Raaflaub 2010a: 144–145. Note the provisos under which Cicero himself had been willing to lend public support to the Flavian bill: n. 21.

[17] Cic. *Att.* 2.16.1 predicts that the second law would accommodate only five thousand, yet our other sources are quite firm about twenty thousand actual recipients, each of whom had at least three children (Suet. *Iul.* 20.3; App. *BCiv.* 2.10/35; cf. Vell. Pat. 2.44.4; Dio 38.7.3). As Gruen notes (1974: 399–400), as in the earlier *lex agraria* (Dio 38.1.2–3), such families will have consisted overwhelmingly of the urban poor rather than recently discharged veterans.

[18] In 61 the *publicani* had grossly overbid in their excitement (Cic. *Att.* 1.17.8–10, 2.1.8), probably a sign of the unexpected difficulties Pompey's arrangements had met with in the Senate.

well as Pompey's former soldiers; to the Senate Caesar could thus advocate it as a solution to the growth of an impoverished underclass in the City rather than simply a payoff to Pompey's veterans.[19] Caesar scrupulously made himself ineligible for service on the Board of Twenty to be named to administer the law. All in all, it was hard to find fault with this bill, and indeed none was actually found once it was brought before the Senate, as we shall shortly see.

The key question for Cicero, then, as he contemplated the new consular year in December 60 was what position to take on the upcoming agrarian bill. Familiar as we are with Cicero's (much later) tirade in *De Officiis* against all manner of redistribution schemes and his frequent exultation over the killings of the Gracchi, we are apt to consider Cicero the determined opponent of all land reform bills, but this is to misconceive his public persona before the People.[20] As consul in 63, he had publicly declared to the Roman People his ongoing commitment to agrarian laws (his private beliefs are a different matter), and as recently as March of this year (60) he had given qualified support in a *contio* to the agrarian bill L. Flavius had promulgated with Pompey's backing.[21] The Flavian bill had failed, but here was a new one specifically designed, it seems, to win over the critics of previous agrarian legislation. The political advantages of supporting the alliance (and thus the land bill) were tempting, and Cicero adds that "people say" Caesar had no doubt that he would.[22] Caesar's confidant, Balbus, had just visited Cicero to reinforce the point, adding, clearly as a further incentive, that Cicero would thereby obtain considerable influence over Caesar's plans.[23] Cicero was clearly undecided at the time he wrote Atticus.

Not only did Caesar hope for Cicero's support, but Dio says that he brought the measure before the Senate in the expectation that it would win support there as well.[24] According to Dio, Caesar *actually wanted to appear to be furthering the interests of the* δυνατοί (apparently more or less equivalent to the *optimates*) and therefore, to avoid provoking their opposition he "often" told them that he would propose nothing that was not also to their advantage (his advances toward Cicero here come to mind). And once he

---

[19] Dio 38.1.4–7, with Gruen's survey at 1974: 398–401.   [20] Morstein-Marx 2004: 207–212.

[21] 63: Cic. *Leg. agr.* 2.6–10 with Morstein-Marx 2004: 194–195. Flavian bill: Cic. *Att.* 1.19.4 with Morstein-Marx 2004: 210–212.

[22] Cic. *Att.* 2.3.3 *aut etiam adiuvandum, quod a me aiunt Caesarem sic exspectare ut non dubitet.*

[23] Cic. *Att.* 2.3.3 *is adfirmabat illum omnibus in rebus meo et Pompei consilio usurum.* See n. 10 on "making Caesar better."

[24] January is the likeliest month for Caesar's approach to the Senate, with passage of the law following in late January or February: Meier 1961: 69n2; Taylor 1968: 173–174. For the date of the law, see n. 73.

had drafted his agrarian law he stressed that he would not promulgate the measure unless they approved it.[25] He had the bill read out in the Senate and referred it formally to the senators to debate, promising to change or delete any clause that was objectionable to anyone.[26] According to Dio, however, this was mere pretense, and it caused great consternation among the *optimates* precisely because there was in fact no objection to be made to the bill as such (how sad!). The problem was simply that Caesar would win enormous prestige and power among the wider citizenry by means of successful passage of the law – which, Dio might also have pointed out, was a salutary and popular measure dealing with an increasingly pressing matter the Senate had resolutely ignored for a decade.[27]

This important moment calls for more analysis than it is usually given. Once again the "teleological fallacy," combined with certain misunderstandings or half-truths, does its work. Dio knows the end – a civil war launched (according to a certain perspective) against the Senate by a man aiming at supreme power – and therefore without serious reflection imputes to Caesar a hypocritical scheme to neutralize effective resistance, to embarrass the Senate, and to further his own aggrandizement ("fame and power over all men") by demonstrating its bankruptcy. Most scholars adjust Dio's imputations to bring out Caesar's subordination at this early stage of his career to Pompey's goals, but few seem to take his conciliatory gestures seriously.[28] But, to start with the most obvious point, if anyone's

---

[25] Dio 38.1.1–2. Bellemore 2005 rejects almost in its entirety the later tradition of Greek sources (Plutarch, Appian, and Dio) on the events of Caesar's consulship. Skepticism is certainly warranted, but she goes too far when she rejects Dio's apparently quite well-informed account of Caesar's presentation of his first agrarian law and of Bibulus's failed attempt to block it (38.1–6). Dio's evidence is not above all criticism, especially when motives are imputed or secret activities are reported as known facts, but it remains the most informative narrative of the events of 59 and is second in circumstantial detail only to Cicero's invaluable (because of its lack of prescience of the future) correspondence.

[26] Dio 38.2.1. Caesar's effort to assuage fears: see Raaflaub 2010: 162–165. This is probably the best place to refer to Pocock's interesting (1926/1967: 161–179) but ultimately unconvincing argument that most – perhaps nearly all – of Caesar's legislation actually was promulgated and passed through the agency of his allied tribune P. Vatinius, and thus that even the first agrarian law was really a *lex Vatinia* (162, 175–178). Apart from the lack of positive evidence other than the faulty assumption that consuls did not normally legislate through the *comitia tributa* (see e.g. the *lex Gabinia Calpurnia de insula Delo*, Crawford 1996: 1:346, lines 1–3; cf. the prescript of the *lex Antonia de Termessibus*, ibid., p. 333), this simply does too much violence to Dio's careful and detailed narrative of Caesar's presentation of the agrarian law to the Senate and then the People. Pocock *may* have a good point about the ratification of Pompey's settlement, possibly in part a piecemeal process for which Vatinius may have been responsible for some if not all elements (Cic. *Vat.* 29: see n. 121).

[27] Dio 38.2.2–3; cf. 1.2: ἐπλάττετο. Similar imputations by App. *BCiv.* 2.10/34–36, though note that he thinks Caesar was at first believed (πιστευθεὶς δ' οὕτω φρονεῖν, 10/35).

[28] See, however, now Gruen 2009: 32 and Raaflaub's remarks (2010: 162–165). Caesar's prior decision to "publish" in some sense the proceedings of the Senate is sometimes brought into this context as

potential "fame and power over all men" caused concern at this juncture, it was Pompey's – the conqueror of Sertorius, the pirates, and Mithridates, the recent triumphator over eleven peoples who had "made the *imperium* co-terminous with the world," whose return was the cause of much anxiety in 62–61, and whose subsequent attempts to influence the consular elections and to secure land for his long-suffering veterans of the Spanish and eastern campaigns, as well as to obtain ratification of his eastern settlement, had all been stoutly and so far successfully resisted.[29] Fear of Pompeian *dominatio*, not some far-fetched Caesarian autocracy, was causing some senators sleepless nights at this time (although Cicero seems relatively calm on this point).[30]

If, however, we make a slight correction to Dio's account and acknowledge that any real fears about overweening power will have been directed chiefly at Pompey rather than Caesar, we should still pause and ask why Caesar's bill should have provoked strong resistance in the Senate. After all, Dio also says, rather intriguingly, that, "since he wanted to appear to be pursuing the policy of the *optimates*, in order not to arouse their hostility [Caesar] repeatedly told them that he would not propose anything that was not in their interest."[31] Now, authorial imputations of what a character was secretly thinking are not deserving of any special reverence, but the remainder of Dio's assertion is a statement about publicly observed behavior and therefore at least theoretically verifiable or falsifiable. Thus it is reasonable to conclude that at the surface level of appearance at least, Caesar behaved with perfect correctness toward the Senate when he presented his agrarian bill to the Senate. So conditioned are we to see this moment in the light of what happened soon afterward that it is very easy to overlook this report altogether; yet note that Caesar had proposed the measure himself as consul, not used a tribune as intermediary (the by-now normal path for agrarian and, in general, "popular" legislation), and that he had brought the matter before the Senate, ostentatiously taking

a pressure tactic (to embarrass objectors by naming them publicly), but this probably overstates the "publicity" of these records: Morstein-Marx 2004: 249–250 with n. 51.

[29] Gruen 1974: 393–398; Seager 2002: 75–85; Rising 2013: 201–211 heavily qualifies the traditional view but is not entirely convincing. Eleven peoples: *Fast. Triumph.* a. 61; *I.It.* 13.1 pp. 85, 566 – the shortest of the lists: cf. Plin. *HN* 7.97–98; Diod. 40.4. *Imperium*: e.g. Cic. *Sest.* 67; cf. Kallet-Marx 1995: 332n173. Pompey had "triumphed" on all three continents of the *orbis terrarum*: Plut. *Pomp.* 45.5, Cic. *Pis.* 29, and *RRC* 426/4 (56 BC), with Crawford's commentary.

[30] Cicero's defensive tone in letters to Atticus (*Att.* 1.17.10, 2.1.7–8; cf. Lintott 2008: 161–165) about his cultivation of Pompey are a clear sign of the acute suspicions held by the self-styled *boni* in 60–59.

[31] Dio 38.1.1: βουληθεὶς δὲ καὶ τὰ τῶν δυνατῶν δοκεῖν, ἵνα μὴ καὶ δι᾽ ἀπεχθείας αὐτῷ ὦσι, πράττειν, εἶπέ σφισι πολλάκις ὅτι οὔτε γράψοι τι ὃ μὴ καὶ ἐκείνοις συνοίσει.

some pains to win its approval before moving on to the assembly ("and yet he pretended that he would not promulgate even this bill if it was not to their liking," Dio 38.1.2). When Caesar called upon them one by one (ὀνομαστί, Dio 38.2.1) to consider his proposed law, Dio says, the leading senators (δυνατοί) were aggrieved, but could find nothing to say openly against the law since their only real objection was that it would give excessive power to Caesar (§2–3).[32] "No one was able to bring any criticism against him."[33]

Viewed cynically, one might suppose that Caesar intended to put his opponents in the Senate in a bind and force them, out of "Fear of the People" if nothing else, to get on this bus before it ran them over.[34] But he would give them an honorable way to do this: this was an opportunity for the Senate to adopt symbolic leadership and demonstrate its solicitude for the interests (*commoda*) of the People – something that Cicero himself at other times insists that the Senate and the leading men of the Republic (*principes*) must always do.[35] Nor could Caesar's offer to amend the bill to meet senatorial objections have been entirely empty: after making a public pledge like that had objections indeed clustered around any specific clause he could hardly have expected to ignore them and still win senatorial approval. Senators, in short, were being given ample opportunity not merely to get on board the bus but to pretend to be driving it.[36] Had

---

[32] Some consulars must have spoken in favor of the law: Caesar surely did not fail to call on Pompey and Crassus or the "Pompeian" consulars M. Piso, L. Afranius (unless he had gone out to a province), and maybe M. Glabrio (cf. Gruen 1974: 131–133). For a list of consulars in 63 (minus Crassus and Pompey, of course) see Cic. *Att.* 12.21.1, to which the consuls of 62–60 would have to be added, and some, like Caesar's most prominent and persistent adversary, the recently deceased Catulus (Chapter 3, n. 124), subtracted. Gell. 4.10.5 seems to stress Caesar's careful observance of traditional protocol in calling upon senators (*quattuor solos extra ordinem rogasse sententiam dicitur*).

[33] Dio 38.1.2: οὐδεὶς αὐτῷ οὐδὲν ἐπικαλέσαι ἐδύνατο. 38.2.1 makes clear that Dio does not mean that the senators were intimidated or muzzled.

[34] See n. 52.

[35] Cic. *Sest.* 137: the Senate should "maintain and increase the freedom and benefits of the plebs," and "the People should not be induced to think that their interests were neglected by the leading citizens (*a principibus*)." Cf. *Rep.* 1.52.5. Aware of the public symbolism of such a claim, Cicero, of course, avows it before the People in *contiones*: esp. *Leg. agr.* 2.15, *Red. pop.* 24 (cf. Morstein-Marx 2004: 222–223). But every senator could agree with this principle, with the proviso in fine print (rarely explicitly enunciated before the wider public) that there was a crucial difference between what was truly in the People's interest and what they only *thought* was in their interest (*Sest.* 103; *Sull.* 25: *populi utilitati magis consulere quam voluntati*). Thus P. Scipio Nasica's famous cry, "Quiet, please, Citizens! – for I know better than you what is good for the Republic" (Val. Max. 3.7.3 = *ORF* 38.3, pp. 157–158) – was also believed by every senator (including Caesar) but, of course, rarely expressed so rudely in public.

[36] Cf. Raaflaub's suggestion that the agrarian law represented an "overture to his opponents and the whole senate," aiming at "perhaps nothing less than a 'grand coalition'," "an effort to overcome traditional patterns of rivalry among opposing groups in the senate and to encourage the resolution

they done so, especially had Caesar's colleague Bibulus joined him as cosponsor, as Caesar subsequently pressed him to do in the public assembly (Dio 38.4.2–3), they would have greatly diminished any personal debt to Caesar (or to Pompey) that beneficiaries might feel as a consequence and enhanced the Senate's current standing among the People to boot. Alternatively, of course, senators who failed to speak up against the bill in the coming debate would have undermined themselves in advance when the debate moved to the Forum, as it would do next as a matter of course. How could they then criticize the bill when they had remained quiet in the august council? If they did then criticize the bill, how could they avoid the accusation of sacrificing the public good out of mere personal antagonism?

But it would be reductive, I suggest, to explain Caesar's move entirely in terms of narrow tactical manipulation. A consular and senatorial resolution of the recent agitation for agrarian legislation was perfectly in keeping with other, successful interventions by consuls or other high magistrates in the post-Sullan era to bring, apparently with senatorial approval or acceptance, a politically acceptable, reasonably consensual end to a persistent source of popular discord: consider C. Cotta's removal of the disabilities of ex-tribunes in 75, Pompey's restoration of the full rights of tribunes in 70, and the remarkably salutary restoration of mixed criminal juries by Cotta's brother Lucius as praetor in the same year. When Plutarch complains, as he frequently does, that Caesar's behavior in his consulship, starting with the agrarian law, consisting as it did in what he regards as shameless pandering to the People, was more like that of a tribune than a consul,[37] he forgets that there was by now an old tradition of reformist, "popular" measures ostentatiously presented with the blessing of the Senate and intended, at least in part, to elevate the prestige of the Senate as a whole in the eyes of voters, soldiers, and the common people generally by visibly demonstrating its concern for those under its care.[38] Even Cicero agreed in his later treatise *On the Republic* that it was essential "the People should never be made to think that their interests are being neglected by their leaders."[39] And while it is true that never in recent times (so far as we know) had a consul promulgated a major agrarian law, given the consul's usual role of enacting

of an especially important issue through collaboration of leading senators from different camps" (2010: 162–165; 2010a: 143–147). He rightly asks: "What would have happened if the senate had allowed the bill to pass in the assembly without violent confrontations?" (p. 165).

[37] Plut. *Caes.* 14.2, *Cat. Min.* 32.1, *Pomp.* 47.5.

[38] Livius Drusus the younger (tr. pl. 91) is the obvious and most conspicuous example (e.g. Cic. *De or.* 1.24, *Mil.* 16; Vell. Pat. 2.13.3; Liv. *Per.* 70–71). See Morstein-Marx 2004: 233–236 for the elder Drusus (tr. pl. 122) and even Cato himself (with his recent grain law) in 63–62. See also n. 35.

[39] Cic. *Rep.* 1.52.5: *neque committendum ut sua commoda populus neglegi a principibus putet.*

the will of the Senate this could have been precisely the sort of gesture that might have assuaged popular doubts about the good faith of their leaders.[40] If we consider Caesar's patrician heritage, the widespread reverence for exemplary figures of the past in the mold of the Scipiones, and the arguments he seems to have made (at least according to Sallust) that the Senate should strive to maintain its authority among the People by taking wise, providential decisions in their long-term interest, it is possible to speculate that he saw his proposal as a way of elevating not merely his own "popularity" and prestige but also that of the Roman Senate.[41]

Knowing the eventual outcome of this initiative as we do, as well as all the terrible events that would follow in its causal chain, we may be inclined to dismiss the idea that Caesar could actually have hoped to win senatorial approval for his agrarian bill, and for good political reasons. Couldn't he see that the Senate could never allow a reformer to succeed for fear of the power that would accrue to him if he was allowed to succeed? Too easily do we treat the concerns of men like Cato as self-evidently valid – namely not that agrarian legislation would be a failure but that it would be a *success*, thereby throwing the senatorial equilibrium entirely out of kilter and producing a de facto *dominatio* of one man or a small faction who could claim credit for that success among the People. Caesar's eventual *dominatio* (or Octavian's) was not the product of *popularis* legislation but of military victory in civil war. Nor, despite much heated rhetoric about the *affectatio regni* of Tiberius Gracchus and others, had any prior *dominatio* in recent Roman memory – Marius, Cinna, Sulla – been a result of mobilizing massive popular support through legislative proposals rather than the clash of arms. Since the Senate could not legislate on its own and needed a consul (usually) to execute its will, at least some observers and participants cannot have been blind to the fact that the most promising way to neutralize the potential danger to senatorial equilibrium posed by the continuing aggravation of the agrarian issue would have been for it as an institution to associate itself conspicuously and enthusiastically with the project, ideally with M. Bibulus as cosponsor, thereby ensuring that neither Caesar nor even Pompey, who would have no official role in the passage of the legislation, could claim sole credit for championing the People's good against a grudging, carping aristocracy. In sum, by drafting a literally unobjectionable bill and bringing it to the Senate for real discussion before

---

[40] Pina Polo 2011: 290–307 surveys post-Sullan consular legislation. He is inclined to place C. Laelius's abortive plan to propose an agrarian law, quickly withdrawn in the face of strong opposition in the Senate (Plut. *Ti. Gracch.* 8.3–4), in his consulship of 140: not a strong precedent.

[41] See Chapter 3 on Caesar's Catilinarian intervention.

presenting it to the People, Caesar gave the body a chance to co-opt the cause of agrarian legislation in its own favor. Was its rejection truly a forgone conclusion? And how differently might the following decade have played out if more level heads than Cato's and Bibulus's (say, Cicero's) have prevailed?

At first, then, Cato, Bibulus, and other opponents of the bill were struck dumb. Although the δύνατοι could find nothing to object to in the law, they also did not lend their support to it, and this in turn induced the uncommitted to use various delays to duck the decision while reassuring Caesar privately that they would in the end pass the measure.[42] In view of his later, extremely sharp, indeed unprecedented opposition to the law, the silence of Caesar's colleague, the consul M. Bibulus, is remarkable; Appian (who, to be sure, is otherwise not very well informed) implies implausibly that Bibulus was taken in by Caesar's conciliatory speeches in the Senate.[43] Only Caesar's frequent recent adversary, M. Cato – still only of tribunician or at most aedilician rank – is recorded to have spoken up in opposition, not, to be sure, making any specific objection to the bill but simply calling upon the senators not to make any change in the current situation.[44] This is probably the best juncture to which to attach the famous story of Caesar's (abortive and perhaps not very serious) threat to haul Cato off to prison from a senatorial debate for his persistent filibustering.[45]

---

[42] An interpretation of Dio 38.2.3: τοῖς μὲν δὴ οὖν ἄλλοις ἐξῆρκει τοῦτο, καὶ ἐπηγγέλοντο μὲν ἀεὶ αὐτῷ προβουλεύσειν, ἐποίουν δὲ οὐδέν, ἀλλὰ διατριβαὶ καὶ ἀναβολαὶ τὴν ἄλλως ἐγίγνοντο.

[43] App. *BCiv.* 2.10/34–35. Not well informed: note especially all the conflation of the two agrarian bills and the sloppiness in saying that "the Senate" voted Bibulus into office (ἐχειροτόνησεν). Possibly Appian has moved Caesar's "conciliatory" pleas from the later *contio* back to the senatorial debate: cf. Dio 38.4.3.

[44] Dio 38.3.1: τοῖς μὲν γεγραμμένοις οὐδὲν οὐδ᾽ αὐτὸς ἐπεκάλει, τὸ δ᾽ ὅλον ἠξίου τῇ τε παρούσῃ σφᾶς καταστάσει χρῆσθαι καὶ μηδὲν ἔξω αὐτῆς ποιεῖν. In Dio's account Bibulus later takes up essentially the same cry in Caesar's *contio* (38.4.3, with Morstein-Marx 2004: 167). Plut. *Cat. Min.* 31.7 has Cato insist that he was not afraid of the distribution of land but of what its proponents would demand from the *plethos* as repayment; it is not clear whether he actually said this openly in the Senate. (Dio would seem to preclude this.)

[45] Dio 38.3.2–3 puts the story in this context, others, later in the year (detached from context but set in the Senate by Suet. *Iul.* 20.4, Gell. 4.10.7–8; Plut. at *Caes.* 14.11–12 connects it with the lex Vatinia, at *Cat. Min.* 33.2–4 with the second agrarian bill in April; Val. Max. 2.10.7, on the other hand, identifies the bill with that offering relief to the *publicani*). Bellemore 2005: 235–237 suggests that the Cato story was an insecurely contextualized, "free-floating" anecdote drawn from the biographical tradition, which may be true; see Pelling 2011: 201, and for the variations that plague the entire secondary literature on Caesar's consulship, pp. 194–195. (Canfora 2007: 80 misleadingly suggests that Caesar sent Cato to prison merely for speaking up in behalf of Bibulus in his plight.) Note that if this is the occasion Gellius refers to at 4.10.8, he has Cato make nothing more than the generalized objection that the proposal was not *e re publica*, it being left unstated whether this was because of its content (so Seager 2002: 86) or its effects on senatorial equilibrium (so, in essence, Dio).

Caesar relented, of course, as he had to do.[46] But it is important to remember that the filibuster is the tactic of the minority – a kind of "minority veto" – and thus that Cato was (once again) in the minority. If Caesar had been in a position to force a vote, the majority might well have come out in his favor.[47]

However, whatever senatorial support the three allies and their adherents possessed was too tepid to overcome Cato's filibuster, and Caesar's attempt to force the issue by ordering Cato's expulsion from the chamber doubtless inflamed feeling. The measure died without a vote. So Caesar in frustration moved the debate to the Forum and the People. Plutarch provides Caesar with a provocative exit line: "It was not by his own choice, he swore, that he was driven to the people; now he would court them, but it was the arrogance and inflexibility of the senate that were to blame."[48] Of course, the complaint was not unjustified. He had indeed offered the Senate a chance to act first, to take up much-needed reform with a bill that met every reasonable objection and would reassure citizens and voters that the senators had their interests at heart. It was not the first time he had tried to convince the Senate to rise to its responsibilities to the Roman People and to maintain or enhance its authority and dignity by taking a long-term view of its interests rather than a narrow, short-term perspective.[49] Caesar's proposal was carefully crafted to avoid the imputation of *popularis* radicalism (which was not anyway the mark of the man, as Cicero had emphasized in his *Fourth Catilinarian* [4.9]), but was perfectly consistent with the enlightened self-interest of the *optimates*.

Those shocked by the forceful methods Caesar would eventually employ to pass the law must consider how not only the fate of the bill in the Senate but also its public debate in the Forum further demonstrated in the public eye the vacuousness of the resistance offered by a few. What ordinary attendees of public meetings in the Forum (and eventual voters) thought of a long-awaited agrarian bill was probably a foregone conclusion, but Caesar anyway wanted to reassure voters that what they desired was nothing strange or unjust.[50] Thus he summoned a *contio*,

---

[46] Compare the recent, notorious instance of the tribune Flavius and Metellus Celer (Dio 37.50.1–3).

[47] Note that Caesar did not have the option, as do US senators, of calling for a "cloture" vote. Caesar's imprisonment of Cato was in fact the presider's only recourse for putting an end to a Roman filibuster (Chapter 3, n. 119). See Chapter 3, p. 113ff. on Cato's earlier filibusters.

[48] (Pelling 2011 tr.) Similarly, App. *BCiv.* 2.10/36, though conflating the first and second (Campanian) agrarian laws.

[49] Chapter 3.   [50] Dio 38.4.6. Cf. Yakobson 2010: 288–290.

requesting the presence and participation of a predictable opponent, none other than his fellow consul M. Bibulus.[51] The idea, Dio tells us, was to pressure some of the intractable leading senators to change their tack and support the law out of "fear of the multitude."[52] In other words, starting with their titular leader, M. Bibulus, they would be forced to defend a highly unpopular stance while confronting a lively audience of citizens, and their position would be made all the more untenable because they actually had no objection that they dared to make in public, at least not against the law in itself. Bibulus himself showed the utter bankruptcy of the opposition when Caesar pressed him before the People to join him in supporting the law. All he would say in response was that he would not permit any innovation (or "revolutionary" step: οὐκ ἂν ἀνάσχοιτο ... νεωτερισθῆναι τι) in his consulship, and when Caesar pleaded with him, calling upon the audience itself to join in vocally, Bibulus cried out in a great voice that they would not have the law in that year even if they were unanimous, and immediately departed.[53] If Bibulus was to be taken at his word, this clearly implied a threat to use his magisterial authority or influence to block passage of the law for the entire year, regardless of how much support it might enjoy among the People or indeed other senators.

This remarkable public outburst by Bibulus has not usually received much attention, but it is worth a moment's consideration not just because he made good on his promise (which helps to clarify the issue for us), but because it implicitly rejects a bedrock principle of the Roman Republic: the People were sovereign over legislation.[54] It was long-established tradition that the *contiones* before a vote on major legislation were precisely intended to allow the People to be instructed by the *principes civitatis* ("leaders of the community") on the matter on which they were soon to cast their ballots,[55] and it was a clear violation

---

[51] Dio clearly seems to distinguish at 38.4.4 the *contio* from which Bibulus ἀπηλλάγη and that to which, after some deliberation, Caesar "brought forth" (παραγαγών) his allies Pompey and Crassus. I therefore stick to my original view (2004: 264) against Blom 2016: 171n119.

[52] Dio 38.4.2: καὶ γὰρ ἤλπιζε μετεγνωκέναι τε αὐτοὺς καὶ πῃ καὶ τὸ πλῆθος φοβηθήσεσθαι. On "fear of the multitude," see Chapter 1, p. 4f. The episode is a paradigmatic example of a well-known contional tactic (*producere in contionem*) analyzed by Morstein-Marx 2004: 161–172 (with reference to this *contio*); see also now Pina Polo 2018.

[53] Dio 38.4.3: οὐχ ἕξετε, ἔφη, τὸν νόμον τοῦτον ἐν τῷ ἔτει τούτῳ, οὐδ' ἂν πάντες ἐθελήσητε.

[54] Rightly, Goldsworthy 2006: 170: "For a consul to express such disdain for the voters was a serious error"; Jehne 2011: 117: "Bibulus had denounced the basic consensus of the Roman Republic."

[55] Morstein-Marx 2004: 125, 162–163. See Cic. *Vat.* 24: *indicem in rostris ... quo auctoritatis exquirendae causa ceteri tribuni plebis principes civitatis producere consuerunt? Leg.* 3.11.8: *rem populum docento, doceri a magistratibus privatisque patiunto;* cf. Liv. 45.21.6–7.

of this norm for them simply to say no even if it was their intent ultimately to attempt to block a bill.[56] To rob the People of their power of decision in legislative and electoral matters, especially ones that deeply concerned them, was a blatant violation of the constitutional norm of popular sovereignty, a point driven home only a few years before by Gabinius's successful threat to submit Trebellius's veto to the voters, a move publicly applauded by none other than Cicero himself.[57] Even the tribunician veto was toothless in practice against any measure that enjoyed strong popular support unless, as Cato had managed to do in 62, one could manage by a physical confrontation with the presider to throw the assembly into chaos and violence.[58] Unlike Trebellius, Bibulus was a consul and therefore not subject to being voted out of office on the spot; yet consuls had no recognized right of veto over legislation, even of bills proposed by their colleagues; nor was the mere lack of prior formal approval by the Senate valid grounds for a veto.[59] Occasionally tribunes and or even consuls did have to be reminded that the People, not the Senate, held the power of decision over key issues of legislation and elections, but on known occasions when this occurred they swiftly conceded the point.[60] This was a republic with a highly participatory popular element, whose history over the previous century and more was replete with showdowns between magistrates, between tribunes and magistrates, and even between tribunes, which were typically, if not, always settled by

---

[56] Cf. Catulus's and Hortensius's recent (though fruitless) arguments against the lex Gabinia and lex Manilia (Morstein-Marx 2004: 179–183, 209–221; more recently, Yakobson 2009: 49–52 and 2010: 287–289; Arena 2012: 187–189; Jehne 2013; Morstein-Marx 2013: 44–45). To be sure, others in the past had expressed something like Bibulus's disdain for the imperiti, especially the second-century optimate hero, the leader of the mob that killed Ti. Gracchus, P. Scipio Nasica (cos. 138) (n. 35); eventually, however, he had to be removed from the public eye (Morstein-Marx 2004: 169–170, 229).

[57] Cic. Corn. I fr. 31 "He had not allowed the expressed will of a single colleague of his to be stronger than that of the entire citizenry" (Chapter 3, n. 96). For popular sovereignty, see Chapter 1, n. 23.

[58] Morstein-Marx 2004: 124–126; Chapter 3, p. 104ff.

[59] No consular veto against bills: Mommsen 1887: 1:285–286 (not to be confused with the rarely exercised right to veto decrees of the Senate advanced by a colleague or lower magistrate, whose last known instance dates to 95 BC (Ascon. 15C; see Mommsen 1887: 1:282n7). Lack of senatorial approval: n. 60 on the dispute of 188.

[60] See Liv. 38.36.7–9 (188 BC) on the response to preemptive tribunician veto of the bill to grant full citizenship with voting rights to Formiae, Fundi, and Arpinum: "It was the People's right, not the Senate's, to extend the right of suffrage to whomever they wished." (Similar objections to a premature veto at Liv. 45.21.6–7.) Cf. the cry of the People when tribunes tried to block Scipio Aemilianus's election to the consulship of 147: "by the laws handed down from Tullius and Romulus the People were the judges of elections" (App. Pun. 112/531; see Chapter 1, n. 32).

the sovereign voice and votes of the People.[61] The idea that one could simply stop a much-needed law – an *agrarian* law, in fact – without even engaging in public argument must have been particularly offensive to Roman voters; Cicero in 63 had at least respected the Roman People enough to argue at length in a series of *contiones* against Rullus's land bill, and the power of his oratory clearly was an important factor in the failure of the bill.[62] Bibulus had "made a mockery of the People."[63]

This is why it cannot be right to criticize Caesar at this juncture for failing to do "what any Roman senator was expected to do and normally did when he met determined resistance on the part of the senate's leadership – that is, to give in and accept failure."[64] That is to treat the standoff between Caesar and Bibulus as if it were merely a personal showdown and not a matter for the sovereign people to decide. If it were true that in a confrontation like this "any Roman senator was expected ... to give in and accept failure" we could hardly have so many examples of laws passed by the Roman People in the teeth of strong opposition by the Senate or senatorial leaders over the last ninety years of the Republic.[65] It is typical of republics based on a principle of fundamental division between parts that "check and balance" each other to engage in brinkmanship like this, and in Rome, at least in the Late Republic, for all the deference granted in more normal times to senior senators, the more conspicuous norm in highly contested cases where voters were strongly motivated to pass legislation that they saw as essential to their interest was for the Senate, together with one or both consuls, to yield to the People.[66] (Recent, conspicuous examples included the *lex Gabinia* and *lex Manilia* of 67 and 66.) It is, I think, an effect of the elitist-oligarchical interpretation of the Roman Republic that has generally prevailed until recently to assume that Caesar would have been expected at this juncture to do precisely the opposite, thereby abruptly abandoning the justified demands of highly expectant voters and citizens.

---

[61] Here Hölkeskamp's emphasis on the role of the Roman People as a third-party mediator of elite competition is also relevant (2010: 98–106).

[62] Morstein-Marx 2004: 191–193. See n. 15 for more recent bibliography.

[63] A phrase Sallust uses in a somewhat different contional context (*Iug.* 34.1: *ita populus ludibrio habitus*) to describe a comparable violation of the norm of public accountability.

[64] Raaflaub 2003: 46. (In fairness it should be noted that Raaflaub's criticism is two-sided: at the end of the paragraph he faults "Cato and his faction" for failing "to seek compromise rather than confrontation.") Similarly, Jehne 2009a: 153: "Caesar had proven in 59 that he was not prepared to summon up the willingness to compromise in the matter, without which the republican system could not function." Cf. also p. 156 for "Caesar's taboo-breaking."

[65] Chapter 1, n. 11.   [66] Chapter 1, n. 12 ("Fear of the People").

The Confrontation over the First Agrarian Law

Caesar knew what to expect: as in 62, Cato's friends would again attempt a tribunician veto in blatant opposition to the manifest popular will, and if they made it into the midst of the assembly, as Cato had done in 62, they would provoke a fracas which would either break up the assembly or give a pretext for invalidating the law due to violence. A sympathetic or alarmed Senate would be a powerful ally. Caesar, who had been on the losing end of the mess of 62, had resolved not to suffer this kind of paradoxical defeat again. His response was twofold. First, as we have seen, he sought to force the opposition into the open, making them take a public position on the bill and seeking to prevent them from disguising their resistance to the law as a legitimate and justifiable reaction to "sedition." Second, he would try to see to it that one or more tribunes would not succeed in playing the same game with him that had been employed against Nepos in 62. It was entirely predictable, given the nature of the law, that on the day of the vote supporters would overwhelmingly outnumber opponents. Since it was obvious to all that the People would pass the law if given the chance to take an orderly vote, it could be expected, given the precedents, that the opponents might resort to extreme measures to stop it, including violence. Thus any attempt to throw the proceedings into disorder would have to be anticipated and prevented.

Caesar now summoned his allies to another *contio* to proclaim their support for the bill.[67] He turned to Pompey with words that suggested that some were threatening to resist the bill with arms and violence, and Pompey replied that he would provide a shield if anyone dared to raise a sword in opposition.[68] This again tends to be viewed as either pure fearmongering or sheer intimidation, since after all Pompey would seem to have had many more swords at his beck and call than did the opponents of the law. But again, Cato's recent success against Nepos's bill was surely what Caesar (and Pompey) had in mind, and in this context it is worth emphasizing that Pompey promised a *shield*,

---

[67] It is likely that few, if any, in the audience at the *contio* knew beforehand of the three-way alliance: this was, in effect, its public debut.

[68] Plut. *Caes.* 14.4: παρεκάλει βοηθεῖν ἐπὶ τοὺς ἐνίστασθαι μετὰ ξιφῶν ἀπειλοῦντας; *Pomp.* 47.7: ἄν τις τοὺς νόμους βιάζηται < ... >, εἰς τὸν δῆμον ἀφίξῃ βοηθῶν; Πάνυ μὲν οὖν, ἔφη ὁ Πομπήϊος, ἀφίξομαι, πρὸς τοὺς ἀπειλοῦντας τὰ ξίφη .... Dio 38.5.3–4: ἐπήρετο εἰ βοηθήσοι οἱ προθύμως ἐπὶ τοὺς τἀναντία σφίσι πράττοντας ... εἶπεν ὅτι, ἄν τις τολμήσῃ ξίφος ἀνελέσθαι, καὶ ἐγὼ τὴν ἀσπίδα ἀναλήψομαι. Dio's version seems more precise than Plutarch's two, one of which has Caesar rather than Pompey first mention the idea of being threatened with swords (Plut. *Caes.* 14.4), and both of which make Pompey answer more threateningly by promising not only a shield, as in Dio, but also a sword.

not a sword. Pompey's response made clear that the assembly would be protected from armed attack; that voters should therefore hold firm and not disperse at the sight of trouble as they had in 62, thereby handing a paradoxical victory to the obstructionists. Plutarch goes on to add that "Pompey filled the City with soldiers and controlled everything by violence,"[69] yet these "soldiers" are conspicuously absent from the best description we have of the voting on the agrarian law (Dio's: see later in this chapter) and are hardly more evident in any other.[70] Since Pompey, a *privatus*, could hardly be commanding detachments of active-duty soldiers in the City, Plutarch may have been confused by a reference in his source to Pompey's *veterans* (no longer in active service), who, of course, had a strong stake in passage of this law and are likely to have flocked from all over Italy to join in the vote, as would anyway be normal for an agrarian law.[71] However, Plutarch's statement about "filling the City with soldiers" is echoed in two other of his *Lives* almost verbatim, but in connection with two other legislative moments of Caesar's consulship, so it is also quite possible that Plutarch has picked up some reference to Pompey's "soldiers"/veterans in a source but is not quite sure where to insert it.[72] On the whole, the context of the agrarian law seems the most natural for the reasons just described, but we must also be conscious of the uncertainty of its attachment to any one episode and thus of its questionable authority in principle.

[69] Plut. *Pomp.* 48.1: ἐμπλήσας στρατιωτῶν τὴν πόλιν ἅπαντα τὰ πράγματα βίᾳ κατεῖχε. Thus Tatum 2008: 72: "The Forum was packed with Pompey's veterans." Scholars sometimes cannot resist dramatic embellishment: Meier 1982: 210: "Pompey had summoned his veterans to Rome for the vote . . . They and others were organized into teams that were able to terrorize the public life of the city." Goldsworthy 2006: 171: "Whether those present felt intimidated – or even protected – by the burly men standing in groups around the Forum, is harder to say."

[70] App. *BCiv.* 2.10/35 claims that Caesar *secretly* (?) prepared a large "band" of armed men, but when he describes the assembly that voted on the agrarian law and the attendant violence, he says that those armed with "hidden daggers" were "the People" (ὁ δῆμος) – that is, the voters themselves (2.10/36, 11/38). This appears to be the only source in which Caesar rather than Pompey is presented as the agent. Appian is overall our least credible source for the events of this year, but see Chapter 3, n. 92 (Metellus Nepos in 62) for a possible precedent for an armed guard at a voting assembly. In the current case Caesar as consul held *imperium* and thus would have had the formal authority to command troops, as a tribune did not. For the use of armed guards by consuls: Cicero had posted an armed guard around the Temple of Concord and probably elsewhere in December 63 (Sall. *Cat.* 49.4 with Cic. *Att.* 2.1.7; Sall. *Cat.* 50.3: *dispositis praesidiis*, App. *BCiv.* 2.5/17); in 52 Pompey famously surrounded the *quaestio*, which tried Milo with an armed guard (*praesidio*: Ascon. 40C, cf. Cic. *Mil.* 1–4, 67); in both cases, an *s.c.u.* had been passed months before and therefore does not seem to have provided formal legal cover in scenarios far different from those that had called forth the decree. See also n. 168.

[71] Cf. famously Ti. Gracchus's land bill, for which "the multitudes poured into Rome from the countryside like so many rivers into the capacious sea" (Diod. 34/35.6); cf. App. *BCiv.* 1.10/41.

[72] Quoted in n. 180, in an examination of the question of military intimidation during the rest of the year.

On voting day, late in January or possibly February,[73] Bibulus descended to the Forum with three tribunes to block its passage.[74] Our sources
are ambiguous about the precise technical means he intended to employ
against the law. Suetonius (*Iul.* 20.1) says he intended to "obnuntiate" (i.e.
to postpone the assembly by declaring contrary omens),[75] while Cicero in
a letter written later in the year implies that he was trying to cast an actual
veto, probably through his attendant tribunes rather than his own consular
power.[76] Loretana de Libero has shown that obnuntiation was a frequent
"fallback" option if a veto was ignored, so it seems likely that Bibulus

[73] Date: Taylor 1968: 179–181 (January); but cf. Meier 1961: 69n2, apparently followed by Pelling 2011:
195 (February). Dio's narrative strongly implies an early date, probably January; Meier's strongest
argument for February is that Bibulus summoned the Senate after the passage of the law, which is
normally supposed to be a prerogative of the consul who "held the *fasces*," who was almost certainly
Caesar in January (contra Linderski 1965: who argued that *Bibulus* was *consul prior*); note that Caesar
had presided over the assembly, which may be a sign that it was actually he who "held the *fasces*" in
this month, despite the fact that Bibulus was evidently accompanied by *fasces* when he interrupted
the assembly (n. 82). In any case, the rotation of the *fasces* provides only a weak dating criterion
(Appendix 3). Dio's account, together with Cicero's expectation that Caesar's agrarian law would
come to a head in January (*Att.* 2.3.3) and the natural benefits of swift action, favors the idea that
Caesar would have promulgated the law immediately upon coming into office, submitting it to the
voters the statutory *trinundinum* (the passage of three market days, a period of seventeen to twenty-
five days: see briefly Kaster 2006: 393; Crawford 1996: 1:9–10 remains agnostic) later – that is, late in
January. Caesar would have wanted to act quickly since a long string of comitial days was available in
the second half of January, followed by a gap during the entire first half of February in which voting
assemblies were forbidden. Chrissanthos 2019: 130–133 dates the law precisely to April 4, which
seems inconsistent with Dio's narrative as well as with the nature and tone of Cicero's letters from
Antium (see p. 145ff), which must have begun only a few days later. In my view, he sets too much
store by questionable interpretations of the rotation of the *fasces* and of the calendrical rules that
governed meetings of the Senate.
[74] The tribunes were Q. Ancharius, Cn. Domitius Calvinus, and C. Fannius: *MRR* 2:189.
[75] Dio claims that Bibulus had already declared a ἱερομηνία blocking popular assemblies from meeting
for *the rest of the year* (38.6.1; cf. 6.5, which also makes clear that by ἱερομηνία he means *servatio* =
"watching the skies" (p. 142ff.) rather than a *iustitium* or *indictio feriarum*: see De Libero 1992: 62n51,
contra Shackleton Bailey 1965: 1:380, and Taylor 1968: 177–178, adhering to Mommsen's original
view on this [1887: 1:82n3] rather than his retraction [3:1058n2]). Dio clearly separates this act from
his retiring to his house for the rest of the year, which he places after the passage of the first agrarian
law and the Senate's refusal to annul it (38.6.5; so too Suet. *Iul.* 20.1, but other sources place his
withdrawal only after the passage of the *second* agrarian law: n. 102). Cic. *Har. Resp.* 48 asserts that
Bibulus said he had *always* "watched the skies" when Caesar's laws were passed, which seems to favor
Dio's view, although perhaps it should not be interpreted strictly. *Servatio* did not exclude following
up with obnuntiation in person, as was explicitly required afterward under the *lex Clodia* of 58
(p. 187ff.), although after he retired to his home Bibulus relied on obnuntiating at a distance by edict
(Suet. loc. cit.), an apparently unprecedented procedure. Thus there seems to be no compelling
reason to reject Dio's claim that Bibulus "watched the skies" even before the first *lex agraria*, but
retired to his home and relied on announcement by edict only after the second.
[76] *Att.* 2.16.2: *agrariam legem sibi placuisse, potuerit intercedi necne nihil ad se pertinere* (cf. also *Vat.* 5:
num intercessorem vi deiecerit). On the lack of a consular veto of legislation, see n. 59. Strangely,
Bellemore 2005: 239, asserts that "Cicero's evidence indicates that Bibulus did not offer any personal
resistance to the *lex agraria*." On the contrary, Cicero's references seem perfectly consistent with
Dio's account.

intended both.[77] According to Dio, who gives us the account that is not only the clearest and relatively impartial but also the richest in circumstantial detail, Bibulus was expelled only after he had forced his way through the crowd and climbed onto the podium of the Temple of Castor where the voting was to take place.[78] The similarity to Cato's and Minucius's actions in 62 is noteworthy, as is Dio's observation (again echoing 62: Plut. *Cat. min.* 27.6–7) that Bibulus and his company had only managed to get this far because people made way for him out of respect – and also because they did not believe he would resist them.[79] This, if true, indicates that the notion that Caesar deployed an intimidating armed presence to fortify the voting area and forcibly keep out the opposition is wrong or vastly overstated; we should note that Dio, our best source for this assembly, does not mention gangs of armed men or "soldiers" at all.[80] (Intimidation and exclusion were anyway hardly necessary to win the vote on an immensely popular agrarian law that opponents had not even made an attempt to debate.) Moreover, Bibulus, having made his way onto the podium, was actually resisted and maltreated only when he attempted (illegally) to interrupt Caesar while he was delivering his speech advocating passage of the law, then mounted on the temple's podium and began himself to address the People without the presider's consent.[81] Then, and apparently only then, he was pushed down the steps that ran down to the floor of the Forum and his *fasces* were shattered.[82] It is said that a bucket of manure was dumped over Bibulus's head – no pleasantry, to be sure, but also far from a lynching.[83] The tribunes

---

[77] De Libero 1992: 60–61, contra Taylor 1968: 179.

[78] Dio 38.6.2–3. App. *BCiv.* 2.11/40–41 also describes an attempt by Cato to throw the meeting into disorder by delivering a speech without the presiding magistrate's authorization, but in view of Dio's evident superiority as a source for the passage of the agrarian law (Appian fails even to recognize that there were two), I attribute this incident to the passage of the second (n. 132).

[79] Dio 38.6.2–3: τὰ μὲν αἰδοῖ τῶν ἀνθρώπων ὑπεικόντων οἱ, τὰ δὲ καὶ νομιζόντων αὐτὸν μὴ καὶ ἐναντιωθήσεσθαί σφισιν.

[80] Cf. nn. 69, 70.

[81] Dio 38.6.2: πρὸς μὲν τὸ Διοσκόρειον, ἀφ' οὗπερ ἐκεῖνος (sc. Caesar) ἐδημηγόρει, διέπεσεν (sc. Bibulus) . . . ὡς δὲ ἄνω τε ἐγένετο καὶ ἀντιλέγειν ἐπειρᾶτο. App. *BCiv.* 2.11/38: ἐνέβαλεν ἐς τὴν ἀγορὰν δημηγοροῦντος ἔτι τοῦ Καίσαρος. Bibulus's interruption of Caesar loosely parallels Cato's covering Metellus Nepos's mouth, but goes one step further in beginning to speak to the assembly without the presider's consent. For the relevant constitutional norms see Morstein-Marx 2004: 179–186.

[82] Dio 38.6.3; for his *fasces* see Plut. *Cat. Min.* 32.4, *Pomp.* 48.2; App. *BCiv.* 2.11/38. Cic. *Vat.* 5: *num consuli vim attulerit, num armatis hominibus templum tenuerit, num intercessorem vi deiecerit* all seem to connect Vatinius with this instance (unless they are to be attributed to another occasion when he tries to lead Bibulus off to prison).

[83] As had been threatened against the consul Piso when he tried to prevent passage of the *lex Gabinia* and apparently again (?) when he opposed the legislation of the tribune Cornelius: Plut. *Pomp.* 25.9; Dio 36.39.3. Manure: Plut. *Cat. Min.* 32.3, *Pomp.* 48.2.

accompanying him and some others were beaten or wounded, although Dio does not explicitly state whether weapons were used. It is no doubt quite likely that in the conditions of insecurity that frequently attended controversial votes by this time, many concealed weapons did, in fact, often find their way to the Forum on voting day; this will have provided material for the complaints against Caesar's methods that appear in the sources as well as plausible grounds for any subsequent attempt to annul successful legislation as being carried through violence (*per vim lata*).[84] But unless Bibulus and his tribunes had armed men at their side, it is unclear why weapons would even have been needed by the great crowd of supporters to push a relatively small group of men out of the Forum. Pompey's "shield" had not blocked Bibulus from approaching the focal point of the assembly, but it had proved effective in preventing him from breaking up the assembly.

Bibulus's violation of norms, both in his initial, mute rejection of the proposal and now in his attempt to quash an overwhelming consensus of the voters, helps to explain an important feature of the violence used against Bibulus: the breaking of his *fasces*. The breaking of the *fasces* was a ritualistic act of *symbolic* violence (the People thus disposing of tokens of the *imperium* that was in their gift) that substituted for direct *physical* violence against the person of the consul.[85] Martin Jehne plausibly connects this very specific and meaningful form of popular protest with Bibulus's statement of contempt for the People:

> The symbolism is not difficult to understand. The *fasces* stood for the official authority of Roman magistrates and they were deeply respected by the Romans even in times of conflict. Consequently, there are only a few acts of breaking *fasces* recorded, and all of them carry the message that the people refused to acknowledge the consular authority any longer. What Bibulus had done [viz., in the *contio*], was not acceptable. He had told the people that he did not respect its will ... So the people showed him at the next confrontation that he was no consul for them, if for him they were not the sovereign people. Bibulus had denounced the basic consensus of the Roman Republic and was punished accordingly.[86]

The violence, modest as it was by the standards of the day, was enough to give Bibulus hope that he might persuade the Senate to overturn the law

---

[84] Suet. *Iul.* 20.1 says *collegam armis Foro expulit.* Plut. *Cat. Min.* 32.4: βέλη, "things thrown," with "many" wounded; *Pomp.* 48.2: two of the tribunes wounded. Cf. also n. 70. Cf. the melee, with some use of small weapons, in the voting assembly for Metellus's bill in January 62. Precisely because weapons gave plausibility to the claim that a law had been passed *per vim*, their presence is apt to be emphasized and one-sidedly described.

[85] Goltz 2000. Note that Bibulus was accompanied by *fasces*: see n. 82.   [86] Jehne 2011: 117.

(Dio 38.6.4). In another echo of January 62, Bibulus now took the matter before the more friendly audience of the Curia. He summoned the Senate to meet the very next day, hoping for an annulment such as once had been passed against the legislation of Saturninus. But he got nowhere: "Everyone held their tongue because they were enslaved to the enthusiasm of the multitude."[87]

This important moment calls for some careful explication. First, despite some scholarly opinion to the contrary, Bibulus was certainly, as Dio says explicitly, attempting to *annul the law* (which was, after all, his larger objective), not to obtain an emergency declaration authorizing the use of force in the City (the so-called Final Decree).[88] The grounds of annulment would no doubt be that the law had been passed not in accordance with correct procedure (*non iure lata*) but "contrary to the omens and through violence" (*contra auspicia et per vim*).[89] But it is important to note what a long shot Bibulus was taking in seeking a senatorial annulment: only six reliable examples of this practice can be found in the Late Republic, nearly all concentrated in the period between Saturninus's first tribunate and the first phase of the Sullan-Marian Civil War, with only one instance in recent memory (Manilius's law on freedmen's voting tribes in 66).[90] It is not hard to see why annulment would be so rare since it carved out an exception to

---

[87] Dio 38.6.4: τῇ γὰρ τοῦ πλήθους σπουδῇι δεδουλωμένοι πάντες ἡσύχαζον. In Suet. *Iul.* 20.1 Bibulus can find no one who would dare either to refer the matter formally to the Senate or to make a motion (*nec quoquam reperto, qui ... referre aut censere aliquid auderet*); this suggests that Bibulus himself, as consul, could not submit the matter formally to the Senate but instead opened a more general debate and hoped, in vain, that a sympathetic member would raise it. Perhaps Vatinius's complaints about augural *adrogantia* "at the beginning of [his] tribunate" (Cic. *Vat.* 14) belongs to this debate.

[88] Dio 38.6.4: ἐπείρασε μὲν ἐν τῷ συνεδρίῳ αὐτὸν (sc. τὸν νόμον) λῦσαι. De Libero 1992: 61–62, 100 with n. 78. Suet. *Iul.* 20.1 is vague but entirely consistent with Dio, and almost certainly misunderstood by Gelzer 1968: 74 (where nn. 4 and 5 are transposed), who claims that Bibulus was trying to get a "state of war ... declared and dictatorial authority granted to him" (presumably the *s.c.u.*); surprisingly, some scholars have followed him (Goldsworthy 2006: 172 and Billows 2009: 114–115; cf. Meier 1982: 211).

[89] Lintott 1968: 140–142 argues that the *lex Caecilia Didia* of 98 gave this power formally to the Senate. The case is circumstantial, and De Libero 1992: 87–88 instead views the "right" as, like the *s.c.u.*, one in effect usurped in the "Revolutionszeit" since 133. There is some dispute whether the Senate could invalidate a law on grounds of *vis* alone (so Lintott 1968: 132–148; Heikkilä 1993: 142; but cf. De Libero 1992: 88–89 with n. 10), but since known relevant cases (see next n.) were almost always also associated with the charge of disregard of *auspicia*, as in our example, this makes little practical difference. Ryan 1996 speculates on the basis of Suetonius's wording and uncertain details of senatorial procedure. Surely no one yet had sworn the oath to uphold the law, thus the clause can hardly have foreclosed objections to the legitimacy of the *passing* of the law (*per vim lata*); cf. the first known legislative annulment, that of Saturninus's agrarian law, also famously protected by a *sanctio* (De Libero 1992: 91–96).

[90] De Libero 1992: 88–103, esp. 88n7.

the fundamental principle that the People had the last word on legislation. There was, let us recall, a long list of "popular" legislation that had been successfully passed and put into effect against powerful senatorial objections, which would be inexplicable if senatorial "cassation" had really been a relatively straightforward device for subverting bills of this kind after the fact.[91] The accepted grounds for annulment were fundamental procedural flaws (including violence that could throw into doubt the question of the People's actual will), not that the bill was pernicious or offensive to senatorial sentiment.

Finally, it deserves due emphasis that in this case the Senate *refused* Bibulus's demand. Bibulus had lost not only in the *comitia* but now in the Senate too. However ugly the scene at the Temple of Castor had been when Caesar's agrarian law was passed, the Senate now refrained from reaching a formal judgment that the passage of the law had been seriously vitiated by violence *or* disregard of religious objections. Certainly, it could hardly be claimed with a straight face that the passage of the agrarian law did not accurately reflect the will of the People. As for Dio's negative editorializing about the senators' being "enslaved to the multitude," most Roman citizens would probably have described this in more dignified language as exemplifying a proper respect for the "will and judgment of the Roman People."[92] This seems identical to what on some other occasions is described as a salutary "Fear of the People" (and by Dio himself earlier in his narrative: 38.4.2) which induces the Senate to make prudent concessions to a powerful popular consensus. We need not assume that the Senate was intimidated by "angry crowds."[93]

So, let us be clear about what had happened. After declining to discuss the agrarian law on its merits, the consul and three tribunes had attempted to make use, probably simultaneously, of the obstructive potential of religious objections (contrary omens) and the veto to prevent the Roman People from having the opportunity to pass, as they obviously were about to do, a law that they evidently considered strongly in their interest. They had failed, and Bibulus's last-ditch effort to overturn the law in the Senate had also failed. We would presumably say today that this was as it should be, yet it is not uncommonly implied that this moment somehow

---

[91] Morstein-Marx 2013: 32–38. Cf. Chapter. 1, p. 9ff. Senatorial "defunding," as was employed against Ti. Gracchus's land law and the decree/*lex Plotia* of 70 (n. 14), and was attempted against Caesar's second agrarian law in 56 (n. 273), was a more subtle and perhaps more promising senatorial response.

[92] *Populi Romani iudicium ac voluntas*: Cic. *Sest.* 106.

[93] So Tatum 2008: 72. See n. 52; Morstein-Marx 2019: 525–526.

represents a catastrophic, even fatal blow for "the Republic."[94] To be sure, Bibulus, Cato, and their ilk could claim, with some plausibility given the disorder and modest amount of violence that had broken out at the voting assembly despite Pompey's "shield," that Caesar had not given him the opportunity to announce (allegedly) contrary omens or even to address the People (although according to Dio, Bibulus had violated Caesar's right to preside over the assembly and indeed to finish his speech), and that the tribunes had been prevented from exercising their right of veto.[95] But should this line of argument have been decisive? The answer is surely no: this would be to treat the obstructive features of the republican "constitution" as if they were absolute, requiring no reasonable justification not only to the sovereign People but even to the Senate. On the contrary, de Libero showed in her monograph published in 1992 that "obnuntiation" (the announcement of contrary omens a la Bibulus) was in practice a manifestly ineffective obstructive device against legislation whose real value to opponents lay in triggering disorder and violence (which might force the voting to be called off altogether) or establishing a foundation for subsequent annulment of legislation by the Senate (which, as we have seen was exceedingly rare).[96] And the veto, as we have already noted, was impossible to sustain against a powerful popular consensus over the pre-legislative weeks of public meetings and regularly failed to block the voting on the day of an assembly.[97] In fact (as opposed to theory), such obstructive techniques were useful to opponents more often as a way of slowing down wildly popular legislation in the hope of inducing second thoughts or strengthening resistance in the Senate than as a way of stopping it altogether.[98] And in fact, in this instance, the Senate *had* yielded by refusing to accept Bibulus's request to annul the legislation on procedural grounds. Whether we see this as a case of republican "institutional restraint" or merely prudent recognition of the limits of the politically possible, this was the Senate's verdict on the matter: it had been given the

---

[94] Cf. Meier 1982: 211: "This meeting of the Senate clearly served only to write the illegal defeat of the *res publica* on the wall."

[95] Cf. Cic. *Att.* 2.16.2: *potuerit intercedi necne nihil ad se* (sc. Pompeium) *pertinere.*

[96] De Libero 1992: 56–68, who notes that obnuntiation was often a follow-up to an abortive veto attempt. Yet obnuntiation was always less effective than the veto; it was never immediately accepted and always subject to a later "ratification" by the Senate in the form of a vote for annulment, which as we have noted, rarely succeeded. Cf. Lundgreen 2011: 152–154, who exaggerates the likelihood of subsequent nullification by the Senate.

[97] Sustaining an intended veto: Chapter 3, n. 96. The only successful veto attempts on the day of voting known before this date were those in 67 and 62 in which the tribunes involved managed to throw the assembly into disorder: Chapter 3, p. 106ff. See De Libero's survey at 1972: 29–49.

[98] See n. 91.

opportunity to annul the Julian agrarian bill but there was no real political will to do so. The People had clearly spoken. Although Cato and his sidekick Favonius, along with Metellus Celer (inspired by the example of his kinsman Numidicus) and the opposing tribunes, stalled as long as possible against taking the oath to observe the law, which was incumbent on all senators, even they did so when the deadline came.[99] (We are not explicitly told what Bibulus did, which probably means he too swore the oath.)

Bibulus's Boycott

After the initial clash over Caesar's first agrarian law, our sources for the year 59 become frustratingly spotty: Dio's account, so valuable at the outset, declines into a series of vague vignettes, while Cicero's letters to Atticus do not resume until the senatorial vacation period of April (since both men had been in Rome), and even after that date, with one important exception (the second agrarian law), they do not offer the kind of detailed information about Caesar's legislative agenda that would free us from some reliance on our less insightful or informative sources (Suetonius's and Plutarch's biographies, Appian's thin narrative), for which nevertheless we must be grateful under the circumstances. An example of the blurriness that often absorbs our picture of the controversies of this year is the fact that we cannot be quite sure whether Bibulus immediately now withdrew for the rest of the consular year to his house to "watch the skies" for contrary omens whenever Caesar or his proxies brought legislation before the Roman People, or whether he did this only after Caesar and Pompey's radical decision to promulgate a second agrarian law expanding the distribution scheme to the "Campanian land," which had been seized in the name of the Roman People in the Second Punic War and specifically exempted by all agrarian laws up to now, including the laws of the

---

[99] The oath in the agrarian law is well attested as is Cato's ultimate decision to swear it: Dio 38.7.1–2; Plut. *Cat. Min.* 32.5–11; App. *BCiv.* 2.12/42; cf. Cic. *Sest.* 61 with Morrell 2018: 198n46. (Bellemore 2005: 227–235 places the oath in an altogether different context in 58. Rising 2013: 218 with n. 109 is confused: Cato *did* ultimately swear to uphold the first agrarian law, which was incumbent on all senators, but is not mentioned in connection with the second, presumably because he was not a candidate: n. 192). Plutarch interestingly puts in Cicero's mouth, while seeking to persuade Cato to give up his resistance to the oath, an objection that cuts to the heart of the matter: οὐδὲ δίκαιόν ἐστι τοῖς ἐγνωσμένοις κοινῇ μόνον οἴεσθαι δεῖν ἀπειθεῖν, "it was not just to believe that one, though only a single person, should disobey what had been decided by the community" (§8); yet, ever the *perfectus Stoicus*, Cato believed exactly that. Numidicus's refusal in 100 to take the oath to respect Saturninus's agrarian law (adduced explicitly by Dio and Plutarch) was evidently based on the idea that it had been passed *contra auspicia et per vim* and was therefore not a valid law (App. *BCiv.* 1.30–31/135–138; Cic. *Sest.* 37; cf. *Vir. Ill.* 62, 73).

Gracchi.[100] Dio and Suetonius both have Bibulus withdraw in response to the passage of the *first* agrarian law (probably late in January, possibly February),[101] yet Plutarch in his *Life of Pompey* offers the plausibly specific information that Bibulus shut himself in his house for eight months (beginning therefore around the beginning of May), and the early imperial historian Velleius – not an unimpeachable source, but earlier than the others and sometimes in possession of valuable tidbits – appears to suggest that Bibulus's retirement followed passage of the second law, which we know occurred in May.[102] Although neither Plutarch nor Velleius seems aware that there were, in fact, two agrarian laws, so confusion is certainly possible on their part, the biographer's eight-month figure is hardly likely to have been invented and fits only the later chronology, while Suetonius's and Dio's association of Bibulus's withdrawal with the first agrarian law may be a venial simplification of the narrative thread.[103] Furthermore, some evidence of public activity by Bibulus in the interval between the two agrarian laws supports the later timing of his withdrawal.[104] Cicero, in his correspondence to Atticus, certainly regards the *lex Campana* as a grave escalation in the confrontation of that year, as we shall see, which would at least make this an appropriate moment for Bibulus's extraordinary act of protest.

---

[100] The failed Servilian *rogatio* had attempted to make use of the *ager Campanus* (Cic. *Leg. agr.* 1.16–22, 2.76–82), but, as noted earlier (n. 17), this was untouched by Caesar's first agrarian law.

[101] Suet. *Iul.* 20.1, Dio 38.6.5. For the date of the first law, see nn. 24 and 73. I am unaware of any refutation of Shackleton Bailey's redating of Bibulus's withdrawal, which Pelling 2011: 199 also supports; yet all the biographies, both the recent ones and Gelzer's classic, repeat the traditional view.

[102] Plut. *Pomp.* 48.5, Vell. Pat. 2.44.5: *maiore parte anni domi se tenuit.* The second agrarian law was promulgated late in April (Cic. *Att.* 2.16, contra however Goldsworthy 2006: 175, who would place it perhaps a couple of weeks earlier) and therefore passed early in May. (App. *BCiv.* 2.12/45 has Bibulus retire to his house after the Vettius affair, dated from Cic. *Att.* 2.24 to mid-summer.)

[103] Shackleton Bailey 1965: 1:406–408, accepted by Pelling 2011: 199 and too easily rejected by Taylor 1968: 174. Modern biographers have all implicitly followed Taylor; Gelzer accepted Plutarch while still connecting the withdrawal with the first law (1968: 78).

[104] Cic. *Att.* 2.16.2: *de publicanis, voluisse [sc. Pompeium] illi ordini commodare, quicquid futurum fuerit si Bibulus tum in forum descendisset se divinare non potuisse* suggests that after the *lex agraria* Bibulus had again gone to the Forum to attempt to obstruct Caesar's legislation supporting the *publicani*. (Lintott 2008: 170 [with n. 19] objects to Shackleton Bailey's translation, but the grammatical construction is fundamentally ambiguous and either translation is difficult to reconcile with the idea that Bibulus was virtually a prisoner in his house.) Plut. *Caes.* 14.9 refers to *numerous* (πολλάκις) battles fought by Cato and Bibulus in the Forum with Caesar (rejected by Bellemore 2005). Cic. *Vat.* 21 refers to an incident involving Bibulus at the Rostra that may well belong after the first agrarian law. (See Coarelli 1992a: 55–56; Bellemore implausibly argues that this was the *only* instance in 59 when Bibulus and Cato actually bestirred themselves to active forms of resistance.) Grillo 2015: 247 states that Bibulus and the three tribunes cooperating with him (and joining him in "watching the skies," apparently from their homes: Cic. *Vat.* 16 with Schol. Bob. 146 St) also sought to obnuntiate against the *lex Vatinia*, but that does not appear in the sources.

"Watching the skies" (Lat. *servatio/servare de caelo*), like the other obstructive tactics mentioned earlier, was no silver bullet. Far from it. It is so rare (or so insignificant) a phenomenon that it is not very well understood: before 59 there seems to be no clearly attested instance, much less a record of its persistent use to abort a given law, not to mention an entire legislative agenda for the remainder of the year; the complete absence of the practice from the surviving books of Livy must give one pause.[105] The disputes that arose in 59 and shortly afterward over its legal effect and proper use must surely be explained by the extraordinary and unprecedented nature of Bibulus's exploitation of this practice whose rationale was to assess the gods' will before a binding vote, but was now being used blatantly as a political weapon.[106] The technically correct answers according to religious law, Cicero would later claim, lay in the "secret books" of the augurs, who divulged some of their relevant knowledge in a *contio* in the next year (58), and in that same year the procedure was clarified by a *lex Clodia*.[107] Yet, these very facts suggest that the details of the practice were obscure and its practical effect uncertain if challenged. In the sketchy state of our information, it is hotly disputed exactly what effect an announcement by a magistrate who had the power of *spectio* that he was "watching the skies" was thought to have: according to one plausible interpretation, that was in itself little more than a warning that obnuntiation was bound to follow and was "at best a delaying mechanism," while according to Lindsay Driediger-Murphy's recent reexamination of the evidence it essentially gave notice that the result of the inquiry into the gods' will was still pending and therefore, if a vote were nonetheless taken, this could be found to constitute a *vitium* (sacral flaw) providing a rationale for annulment.[108] Either way (and these two alternatives are not mutually

---

[105] "Watching the skies" seems to have been recognized or regulated in some way by the obscure *leges Aelia et Fufia* of the mid-second century (Cic. *Prov. Cons.* 49; Ascon. 8C with Cic. *Pis.* 9; see n. 287) – our only evidence of the existence of the practice before Bibulus.

[106] Rightly, Tatum 2008: 73.   [107] Page 183ff.

[108] Tatum 1999: 125–133, quoted at 128–129: "It has long been recognized that, in order to be valid from a narrowly technical standpoint, the bad omen perceived by *spectio* must be announced in person. The mere declaration *de caelo servasse*, while ordinarily sufficient to persuade a tribune or a magistrate not to waste his time gathering an assembly only to have it dismissed because of *obnuntiatio*, was not per se a binding restriction: since the possibility, however slender, of a fruitless *spectio* had to be assumed, a determined or rigidly scrupulous official might convene his assembly in any event. Hence the requirement to report the omen on the spot and in person." Driediger-Murphy 2019: 127–160 offers an attractive clarification of many points concluding with a useful collection of the evidence for this episode. Cf. the brief survey of De Libero 1992: 56–59. On whether the mere announcement of *servatio* sufficed to cancel a voting assembly, see p. 183ff. Cic. *Att.* 4.3.3–4 offers what appears to be a textbook example of how *servatio* was expected to function, although it is possible that the *lex Clodia* of 58 had introduced a significant change (n. 285).

exclusive), the declaration presumably tended to discourage a magistrate from calling a voting assembly *on that day*; but neither theory nor historical precedent laid down what should happen if the sky watcher carried on for days, weeks, and months on end. The embarrassing fact for those who treat Bibulus's attempted *servatio* as if it ought to have been decisive without further ado is that we have *no* well-attested instance *ever* of the successful use of the practice to prevent or to retroactively annul legislation, which surely means that the kind of indefinite, continuous sky watching Bibulus tried in 59 had never been attempted before.[109] In such a case, a determined magistrate had to decide for himself, and if that magistrate were both a consul and *pontifex maximus* he might feel he was in a position to reject such an unprecedented ploy. Even the much more common practice of obnuntiation had a dismal record of success when a law had a strong popular consensus in its favor.[110] Given Bibulus's abject failure to persuade the Senate to annul the first agrarian law after the fact, Caesar could reasonably calculate that even most of his senatorial peers could see through Bibulus's ploy and would recognize that this would be a dangerous precedent to set for all future legislation.

Bibulus does not seem to have made much headway by this method even among those who were not naturally disposed to see Caesar's actions in their most favorable light. Cicero, who liked to think of himself at this time as the true if rather frustrated leader of the *optimates* (*Att.* 1.20.3), may give us some valuable perspective. As we saw, Caesar himself had hoped he would support his agrarian law, not without reason, for Cicero was both eager to support Pompey and had after his consulship taken a notably less aggressive approach on agrarian legislation. When it came to a fight over the first agrarian law we hear nothing one way or the other about Cicero's attitude. When Cicero's correspondence with Atticus picks up, written from his villas at Antium and Formiae during the spring vacation period, their tone is quite different from the "gloom and doom" that suffuses the later ones in the year. The series begins with chit-chat about books, money, and villas, with a fleeting note of concern about what Cicero's enemy P. Clodius might be up to (Cic. *Att.* 2.4.2). (Clodius had already achieved his transfer to the plebs before Cicero had left Rome.)[111] Cicero proclaims

---

[109] De Libero 1992: 56n21.

[110] See n. 96. "Religious obstruction in the form of *servatio* und *obnuntiatio* was for the most part by far ignored in the popular assemblies" (De Libero 1992: 64).

[111] Indeed, scholars often interpret Cicero's absence from Rome at this time to his alleged offense to Caesar and the Three during his unsuccessful defense of Antonius, for which, Cicero claims, Clodius's transfer to the plebs was an immediate act of retaliation (within three hours!: *Dom.* 41;

himself finished for the present with playing a significant role in politics and insists he is resolved to give undivided attention to his books.[112] But in the very next letter he eagerly pumps his friends for political gossip from Rome – who were likely candidates for the consulship? was there any new legislation? – not, it must be said, with any air of great anxiety, and indeed with some humor as he indicates that the Three could perhaps buy his loyalty with an augurate, which had become vacant with Metellus Celer's recent death.[113] Clodius remains the chief concern of a political nature.[114] Curio piques his interest with talk of the combine and Clodius falling out among themselves (which Cicero considers "our only hope of salvation"),[115] and soon the news he receives about the growing unpopularity of the Three has him writing rather triumphantly that the political wheel of fortune was already turning full circle – that is, implicitly, the current sad state of affairs was about to change for the better.[116] Certainly, the Three are mentioned in disapproving terms, starting with *improbi* and moving with increasing frankness in the latter half of April to language of domination and tyranny, repeatedly employing the mocking name "Sampsiceramus" for Pompey.[117] But at the same time Cicero also makes clear that he did not approve of Cato's outright obstructionism, which to his mind had only "enraged" Caesar and Pompey and driven them away from their initial, conciliatory overtures.[118] Only the previous year, despite his natural sympathy with a Senate-dominated vision of the proper

---

Prov. cons. 42; cf. Dio 38.10.4–12.2; on the trial and Antonius's manifest guilt, see Alexander 1990: no. 241 and Morrell 2017: 143–144). So e.g. Tatum 1999: 103–108. But this interpretation relies too heavily on Cicero's heroic self-representation in the *De Domo*, delivered two years later after his exile, as one who bravely took on the Three and then paid a heavy price for it: Mitchell 1991: 114–120. We are never told exactly what Cicero said that was supposedly so offensive to Caesar at the time and yet did not cause him to withdraw his repeated offers of protection (nn. 11, 128); Cicero was on the whole a cautious man, and when the letters to Atticus resume in April we see no traces of such a dangerous vendetta. For the regular senatorial vacation period from early April to mid-May see Taylor 1968: 187n43.

[112] Cic. *Att.* 2.4.4, 5.2, 6.1–2, 7.1, 4, 8.1, 14.2, 16.3, 17.2 (cf. 10), Just how long Cicero envisions his withdrawal to endure is unclear. *qui etiam dubitem an hic Anti considam et hoc tempus omne consumam* sounds as if he is thinking, at most, of the rest of the year, but perhaps (since his decision soon was to move on to Formiae, then Rome: 8.2) he is only referring to the remainder of the April vacation.

[113] Cic. *Att.* 2.5.2. See nn. 178, 238. [114] Cic. *Att.* 2.5.1, 3., 7.2–3, 9.1, 3, 12.1–2, 15.2.

[115] Cic. *Att.* 2.7.3 : *una spes est salutis istorum inter ipsos dissensio*; cf. 8.1, 9.1, 12.1–2, 15.2.

[116] Cic. *Att.* 2.9.1–2; cf. 21.2. Bailey adduces *Planc.* 93 and *Rep.* 2.45. On 2.9.1 *id culpa Catonis*, see n. 118.

[117] *Improbi*: Cic. *Att.* 2.6.2; cf. 9.1: *improbitas istorum. reges*: 8.1 (perhaps quoting Curio; cf. *dynastae*: 9.1); *regnum*: Cic. *Att.* 2.12.1 (somewhat ironic), 13.2. ἐντυραννεῖσθαι (14.1), τυραννίδα συσκευάζεται (sc. Pompey, 17.1). "Sampsiceramus": 14.1 and often thereafter.

[118] Cic. *Att.* 2.9.1 *id culpa Catonis* (cf. §2 *illum ipsum qui peccavit, Catonem*, which makes clear that Cicero really is finding fault, not ironically giving Cato *credit* for the quick change for the better Cicero hopefully descries in current circumstances: see n. 116). Cf. 2.21.1 *nam iracundiam atque*

functioning of the Republic, Cicero had complained to his friend Atticus that Cato "expresses his opinion [in the Senate] as if he were living in Plato's Republic rather than among Romulus's scum."[119] Cato's hard line, with its blind neglect of the art of political compromise, had laid waste to the coalition of the "right-thinking" upper orders of society that Cicero felt he had painstakingly built up in his consulship.[120] There was therefore blame enough to go around. In general, in April Cicero's tone seems to be one not of alarm but of resignation, despite the fact that by this point Caesar had pushed through some highly contentious legislation, including of course the first agrarian law but also the revision of the Asian tax contract on behalf of the *publicani*, as well as allowing Clodius's *transitio ad plebem*.[121]

The turning point in Cicero's epistolary tone appears to be the passage of the *lex Campana* in May, followed by Bibulus's withdrawal to his house.[122] Cicero had in the past vehemently opposed any proposal to distribute the Campanian land,[123] and the decision of the Three to cross this red line must have seemed a blatant violation of their earlier assurances to him and to others. He is at first puzzled by the move: he had been expecting something that would not provoke further opposition, yet "if anything could further inflame better-class sentiment (*bonorum animos*), roused already as it evidently is, assuredly this will do it."[124] In retrospect, it made a travesty of Caesar's earlier assurances during senatorial discussion of the first agrarian law that he would scrupulously heed any concerns the senators had on the matter. And yet what public position did Cicero take on the *lex Campana*?

Plutarch may provide a clue. As always, we must be careful about the information provided by this late, biographical source, but when it goes notably against the grain it may be worthy of a more careful hearing. In his *Life of Cicero* Plutarch lists a series of Cicero's sometimes counterproductive witticisms. Among the many stinging jokes preserved here (not all of them

intemperantiam illorum sumus experti, qui Catoni irati omnia perdiderunt. Cato's filibuster of the first agrarian law is the most plausible "error" and source of "blame."

[119] Cic. *Att.* 2.1.8; cf. 1.18.7. "Dregs" (Wiseman 2009: 117n56) is probably too sanitized (cf. Shackleton Bailey's "cesspool").

[120] Mitchell 1991: 88–92. On Cato, see further *Off.* 3.88; n. 5.

[121] Cic. *Att.* 2.16.2, with n. 104. Cic. *Att.* 2.9.1 and 16.2 probably show that the ratification of Pompey's eastern *acta* had also been passed or at least promulgated by mid-April (so too Rising 2013: 211, but see Taylor 1968: 182). Rising follows Pocock 1926: 168–175 in attributing the law that ratified Pompey's *acta* to Vatinius (hence, properly called a *lex Vatinia*): see n. 26. This matters little for my purposes and in this chapter I shall refer only to the famous law on Caesar's command by that name.

[122] See n. 102. [123] See n. 100.

[124] Cic. *Att.* 2.16.1 (Shackleton Bailey trans). This letter and Cic. *Att.* 2.15.1 emphasize the partisan aspect of the law: more land had to be found for the "multitude," which would otherwise turn against the Three. Bellemore 2005: 240 oddly transposes Caesar's conciliatory gestures during the promulgation of the first *lex agraria* to the aftermath of the *lex Campana*.

very funny) is the following zinger: After Caesar had passed his bill to distribute the *ager Campanus* to "the soldiers" (a gross simplification at best) and many in the Senate were expressing their displeasure, the aged senator L. Gellius (cos. 72), who had reached the praetorship already in 94 and was therefore at least in his mid-70s – possibly, in fact, the oldest consular still attending the Senate – declared that this would not happen so long as *he* was alive. Plutarch says Cicero quipped caustically, "Let's wait, then; Gellius isn't asking for a very long postponement."[125] (Not Cicero's finest moment: it was this same Gellius who four years before had suggested that the Republic owed Cicero the *corona civica* for his suppression of the Catilinarian Conspiracy.)[126] Apparently, then, there was some critical discussion of the move in the Senate. More interesting is Cicero's riposte. Even if he sometimes had difficulty restraining his wit, it hardly seems conceivable that Cicero could have been so maladroit as to make cruel mockery of Gellius's *opposition* to the bill while he himself stood on the same side of the debate.[127] Perhaps Cicero was painfully constrained in public by Pompey's friendship and hopes for his protection (or Caesar's) against possible retaliation by Clodius. We know that as late as June Cicero was still considering an offer from Caesar of a place on his staff, or perhaps a religious commission, either of which would block an aggressive move by Clodius.[128] In mid-summer Cicero reports widespread revulsion against Caesar's methods and Pompey's complicity, but he remains unwilling to betray his friendship with Pompey and openly oppose him: he mostly steered clear of the fight while trying to maintain his self-respect as a senior consular.[129] Apparently candid observations like these show that at least on the surface Cicero was cooperating with – or at least not opposing – the agenda of the Three. This may qualify and even help to explain the vivid picture that he paints in his correspondence from the second half of the year of open revulsion and passive resistance.[130]

---

[125] Plut. *Cic.* 26.4. Apparently M. Perperna (cos. 92) was still alive at age eighty-eight, but is never mentioned in these years and surely had "retired" (Dio 41.14.5; Pliny *HN* 7.156).

[126] Cic. *Pis.* 6, Gell. 5.6.15; but see Weinstock 1971: 165n7.

[127] It seems just possible that Cicero could have been mocking Gellius for making an empty threat when actual resistance was called for, but this seems entirely contrary to our other evidence of his disinclination to cross Pompey publicly at this time.

[128] Cic. *Att.* 2.5.1, 18.3 (with Shackleton Bailey's nn.), *Prov. cons.* 41 *legationem* with Grillo 2015: 265. For the earlier offer(s) of a position on one or more of Caesar's land commissions, see n. 11.

[129] Cic. *Att.* 2.18.3 (June): *me tueor ut oppressis omnibus non demisse, ut tantis rebus gestis parum fortiter.* 2.22.3 (?August) *rem publicam nulla ex parte attingimus.* 2.23.3 *nos . . . publicis consiliis nullis intersumus.*

[130] Strictly speaking, one might question more than one usually does the candor of Cicero's remarks to Atticus in this year given his worries about betrayal of confidentiality (n. 136). Yet the ferocity of Cicero's criticisms in letters subsequent to *Att.* 2.20.5, including aspersions on Pompey's integrity

The second agrarian law was, it seems, a project of Pompey's.[131] When the bill was presented to the voters in May, it met little overt opposition in view of recent failures and the overwhelming support of the voters, many of whom were probably Pompey's (and other) discharged veterans: very likely Bibulus again "watched the skies" (though we have no direct testimony), and Cato made an invidious symbolic protest by attempting to speak against it, although without the consent of the presiding magistrate (as Bibulus had done before), and therefore illegally, until Caesar had ordered him dragged from the Rostra.[132] The remarkable provision in the law that candidates for office in 59 would have to swear an oath to respect the law sufficiently demonstrates that Caesar and Pompey were well aware of the dangers posed by their opponents' long-term strategy and sought to neutralize it in advance.[133]

On the view adopted here, Bibulus now took the drastic further step of retreating to his house and communicating with the public henceforth solely by edict. Cicero attests to the worsening of the mood in Rome: previously the *dominatio* had been pleasing to the mob and distressing, though not actually destructive, to the "good men" (*boni*); now it was so hated by all that Cicero expects the Three to start lashing out dangerously in anger.[134] Cicero's letters to Atticus now take a much darker turn than before, with repeated lamentations about the "lost" Republic, the end of "freedom," domination by a junta, aspirations for tyranny, and the like. Cicero tells his friend that the hostility against "those who control everything" is unanimous at every level of society, that although no actual opposition is offered to the Three, their embarrassment in public appearances is acute, and that people air their resentment constantly in private. Everyone thinks resistance will end in a massacre, and Cicero frets ominously that the potentates will react to their overwhelming unpopularity

---

(21.6, 22.5), continued mockery of the "Great" man as "Sampsiceramus" (23.3), and reference to the universal "hatred" of all (22.6, 25.2), show that the preserved letters at least were not written ἐν αἰνιγμοῖς (19.5).

[131] Note that Cicero was at first puzzled as to what *Pompey* intended by the new law (2.17.1): ὁμολογουμένως τυραννίδα συσκευάζεται. Cf. 15.1, 16.1–2. Vell. Pat. 2.44.4 also notes Pompey's advocacy of the Campanian law.

[132] Plut. *Cat. min.* 33.1–4, App. *BCiv.* 2.11/40–41; cf. Plut. *Caes.* 14.12 (who here sets the story in the context of the passage of the *lex Vatinia*, probably wrongly), also 14.9. Bellemore 2005: 235–237 rejects the story as a mere doublet of Cato's earlier trip to prison (n. 45), but Plutarch's and Appian's setting of the anecdote in a legislative popular assembly is in itself unobjectionable, and there is no reason why Cato should not have tried Caesar's patience twice in the two major venues for legislative debate. Cato had done this sort of thing before (in 61: Cic. *Att.* 1.14.5, with Morstein-Marx 2004: 187), quite apart from his disruption of Nepos's assembly as tribune.

[133] Cic. *Att.* 2.18.2.   [134] Cic. *Att.* 2.21.1.

with some kind of violence.[135] He even evinces anxiety about his letters to his friend falling into the wrong hands and warns him that if he is forced to use a less trustworthy carrier he would address his letters using the code names Laelius and Furius for himself and Atticus – on second thought, he adds in the next missive, he will only use a code name for himself – and cloak his comments in riddling language.[136] Yet, even now one must be careful not to go too far. For instance, in July, despite all the political worries weighing on Cicero's mind, he declares that "nothing distresses me more than Statius's [sc. Quintus's loyal slave] manumission" (!).[137] True, his brother Quintus's shocking indulgence toward his beloved slave was a real scandal in Cicero's eyes; but if this was more distressing (*molestius*) than the political situation it is fair to wonder just how calamitous that actually was.

"Watching the skies," as we have seen, was technically nothing more than an announcement that a magistrate was in the process of consulting the divine will, and it was entirely toothless in itself if a determined magistrate insisted nevertheless on going through with the assembly. And if the sky watcher – in this case Bibulus – could expect to be hindered from actually announcing the contrary omens in person on the spot it followed that it made little sense for him to subject himself to that unpleasant and fruitless experience. By remaining in his house and issuing his proclamations by edict he could instead dramatically press the point that a consul was being robbed of his "constitutional" powers. To be sure, it was his choice to close himself within his home; in fact, Caesar's allied tribune Vatinius once sent an attendant to try to extract him from his home and force him out into the public eye (presumably to make him account for himself before a rowdy *contio*).[138] This very fact reveals Bibulus's strategy: to remove himself from the normal ways in which popular opinion impressed itself on leading senators while hoping incrementally to erode Caesar's popular support by creating the invidious spectacle of a consul

---

[135] Cic. *Att.* 2.20.3: *neque enim resisti sine internecione posse arbitramur;* see also §§4–5 and esp. 21.1–5. Cf. further 18.1–2, 19.3, 22.6 (*eos qui tenent omnia;* cf. *illis qui tenent* 2.18.1), 23.2, 24.4, 25.2. An early hint of Cicero's worry at 14.1.

[136] Cic. *Att.* 2.19.5, 20.5. On *tabellarii* and code systems see White 2010: 11–15, 66–67 with 199n24.

[137] Cic. *Att.* 2.19.1. See *Q. fr.* 1.2.1–3.

[138] Cic. *Vat.* 22, where Cicero's claim that Vatinius had "driven" Bibulus from the Forum and Senate and forced him to take shelter in his house is obviously rhetorical; at the same time he attacks Vatinius for sending a *viator* to drag him forth. He is of course unlikely to have carried out his mission: Dio 38.6.6 states that Vatinius respected the intercession made by some of his fellow tribunes, despite the implication of *Vat.* 21. He mocked the three tribunes engaged in a similar protest in solidarity with Bibulus (n. 104) as having made themselves into "private citizens" (Cic. *Vat.* 16).

who was reduced by his colleague's refusal of recognition to the status of a private citizen and who apparently could not even risk leaving his home.[139] To counter his adversaries' claim that he sought to suppress the "voice and will of the entire citizenry," Bibulus now presented the image of the City dominated by one man's sole power, unchecked by a colleague of equal power and thus freed from the fundamental traditional constraints that distinguished the *imperium* of a consul from that of a *rex*. People joked that it was "the consulship of Julius and Caesar" (Suet. *Iul.* 20.2). By such means Bibulus probably hoped gradually to chip away at the popular support the Three enjoyed, and to judge at least from Cicero's comments about how eagerly people read Bibulus's posted edicts, full of Archilochean invective against both Caesar and Pompey, the home-bound consul appears to have made some headway.[140]

Yet again we must be careful not to over-interpret what Cicero says here. Were the people who, Cicero claims, showed their approval of Bibulus by eagerly crowding around his posted edicts in fact representative of "the People" – that is, in this context politically engaged members of the urban plebs (how many of these could read, or wanted to?) – or are these instead well-off citizens already hostile to Caesar's and Pompey's aims? When, in a famous instance, the actor Diphilus won a burst of applause and calls for encores at the festival of Apollo in July by turning a line of an unknown tragedy into apparent criticism of Pompey's lust for power ("by our wretch-edness you are great/*Magnus*"), did the acclamation truly come, as Cicero claims, from "the entire theater" (*totius theatri clamore*) or mainly from the senators and *equites* clustered most conspicuously in front?[141] Cicero had been fervently hoping for public opinion to turn against the forceful actions of the Three since early in the year, so it is likely that he was now engaging in some degree of wishful interpretation when he thought he discerned a swing

---

[139] Cf. Cic. *Fam.* 1.9.7: *qui Bibulum exire domo prohibuissent*; Cf. Vell. Pat. 2.44.5: *dum* [sc. Bibulus] *augere uult inuidiam collegae, auxit potentiam.* Note App. *BCiv.* 2.12/45: ἐκ χειρῶν ἅπαντα μεθεὶς οἷά τις ἰδιώτης οὐ προῄει τῆς οἰκίας.

[140] Cic. *Att.* 2.19.2, 5; 20.4, 6; 21.4–5: *admirabili gloria est*; for the "Archilochean invective" of Bibulus's edicts against both Caesar and Pompey, see esp. Cic. *Att.* 2.21.4 (*populo ita sunt iucunda ut eum locum ubi proponuntur prae multitudine eorum qui legunt transire nequeamus*), Plut. *Pomp.* 48.5, Suet. *Iul.* 9.2, 49.2 (*quibus proscripsit collegam suum Bithynicam reginam, eique antea regem fuisse cordi, nunc esse regnum*; on the notorious allegation that the young Caesar had served the Bithynian king sexually, see Chapter 2, n. 117).

[141] Cic. *Att.* 2.19.3: *nostra miseria tu es magnus* (cf. Val. Max. 6.2.9). Cicero also notes the weak reception given by the audience when Caesar entered, contrasting this with a standing ovation – begun by the *equites* – when young Curio, then an outspoken critic of the Three (n. 170), made his appearance. On the expression of public opinion in the theater, see esp. Vanderbroeck 1987: 238 no. 36 with 77–81; Flaig 1995: 118–124 and 2002: 232–242; and now Angius 2018: 60–80.

of sympathy toward their opponents. But on the whole we should probably assume that Cicero, an experienced senator and senior consular, was not so naïve in playing the complex game of reading the public mood that he completely misread the significance of a pathetically glum performance by Pompey in a *contio* on July 25 in response to Bibulus's edicts, and Caesar's own failure a little later to incite a *contio* to mount a demonstration at Bibulus's house when the latter postponed the elections by edict.[142] By midsummer it appears likely that even many ordinary residents of the City, having won the battles they had begun the year fighting for, were becoming increasingly disconcerted by the unusual appearance of the *res publica*, from which one consul and three tribunes had gone missing for weeks and now months while claiming to have been prevented from performing their public duties.[143]

Function and Dysfunction

But was the functioning of the *res publica* paralyzed by a kind of "lockdown" by the Three, or a virtual boycott or "strike" by their opponents? Did Bibulus truly renounce his public duties to create the disturbing spectacle of a City dominated by a "tyrant"? Was the Senate still meeting, and if so, was it reduced to a mere "rump" of yes-men who would decree whatever Caesar demanded of them? Were the assemblies still functioning or had they been reduced to a rubber stamp by voter intimidation and violence threatened by Pompey's soldiers? Was anything still getting done other than a hyper-partisan agenda controlled by the three powerful allies led by Caesar? It is no easy matter to answer these questions since our later sources (the biographies of Plutarch and Suetonius, the narrative histories of Dio and Appian, all of them separated from the events by a century and a half or more), dominated as they are by the larger political showdown between Caesar and his allies and Bibulus and his allies, lose much of their focus after the conflict over the

---

[142] Cic. *Att.* 2.21.1, 3, 5. Cicero at *Sest.* 113–114 argues that the true sentiments of the Roman People were indicated by the later electoral success of the three anti-Caesarian tribunes of 59, yet implicitly concedes that C. Alfius Flavus and Vatinius *believed* that they were taking the "popular" line. The creaky strains of Cicero's rhetoric are familiar.

[143] Cic. *Att.* 2.23.2 (probably August): *omnis illius partis auctores ac socios nullo adversario consenescere* suggests that the very lack of open resistance had lessened the zeal of Caesar's and Pompey's supporters. We must however take it with a grain of salt when Cicero goes on in the same sentence to assure Atticus that there had never been such a "universal consensus of talk and opinion" as that which now opposed the Three. (Canfora 2007: 80 goes too far when he adduces "the almost pathological unpredictability of the urban masses.") Tribunes: n. 138.

first agrarian law and tend to describe the rest of the year in unhelpfully broad-brush generalizations that do little more than emphasize the magnitude of polarization; Cicero's letters, on the other hand, though often eyewitness testimony, shine a spotlight on his mood at certain moments yet give little sense, except incidentally, of the day-to-day functioning of institutions, which would be rather boring for Atticus to read but would give us the best material for the present inquiry. To attempt to penetrate the fog we can only attend to some details of interest which our rather spotty evidence of this year lets slip almost despite itself. The results will satisfy no one completely: the evidence is too poor to exclude any but the most extreme conclusions. But I hope to show that the easy stereotype of "the consulship of Julius and Caesar" can be, and frequently is, taken much too far. It was, after all, originally a joke.

We can start with Bibulus. In fact, we know of one notable act he performed this year apart from the conspicuous act of political theater we have just been discussing: sometime in July, as we have just noted, he carried out by edict a threat he had been making since April to postpone the consular elections, moving them from their usual mid-summer date (July or August) to October 18.[144] Possibly his objective was to lessen "turnout" among less well-off citizens by separating the elections from the traditional summer season coincident with the Ludi Apollinares and placing them instead in a "lean month for festivals"; he may also have sought some advantage by pushing them to a month when he would (at least in a normal year) "hold the *fasces*" and perhaps be able to exert greater influence over them, if, that is, he saw fit to emerge.[145] As we saw, Caesar sought to prompt a crowd to protest the postponement but failed, and we have no grounds to conclude that by any other means he overturned Bibulus's decision about the date of the elections. Bibulus apparently let the consular elections go forward without an auspicial hitch, neither "watching the skies" nor obnuntiating against them, for no real cloud of illegality hung over the election of the consuls for the next year

---

[144] See n. 142: Cic. *Att.* 2.20.6, 21.5. April: Cic. *Att.* 2.15.2. July was the "normal" month for the consular elections, with roughly half the known examples, but it cannot be called the "usual" month since there are so many exceptions later in the calendar (now Ramsey 2019: 215–224; Drogula 2015: 299 is mistaken).

[145] "Lean month": Scullard 1981: 189. Linderski 1965 hypothesizes (1) that Bibulus was *consul prior* for 59 (contrary to all our documentary evidence, which Linderski explains as an artifact of Augustan recension of the Fasti, but see e.g. *non Caesare et Bibulo*, Suet. *Iul.* 20.2), and (2) that this automatically gave him the right to preside over the consular elections. Both are highly uncertain, the former indeed very doubtful. (On the latter, see the qualifications of Vervaet 2014: 41–42.)

(L. Calpurnius Piso and A. Gabinius).[146] Yet unless our sources are speaking loosely of Bibulus's absence for the rest of the year after his initial withdrawal, he does not seem in fact to have presided over the election, as under normal circumstances he presumably would have done in October.[147] (This was, of course, a far from "normal" year.) However that may be, the normality of the occasion seems to be highlighted by Cicero's acknowledgment that he himself not only turned up but served Piso in the honorific position of first vote counter assigned to the first century (the *praerogativa*).[148] Late in the year a young senator named C. Cato (not the more famous M. Cato) alleged in a *contio* that Gabinius had won the consulship by corrupt methods (no doubt funded by Pompey), but the audience would hear none of it, especially when Cato spiced his speech with harsh words against Pompey (*privatum dictatorem*). He barely escaped with his life, writes Cicero to his brother: apparently then the Roman crowd had not turned against Pompey, or perhaps they like Cicero considered C. Cato somewhat hare-brained.[149] In itself the allegation of *ambitus* was of course routine stuff: the same could be said of virtually every Roman election, including Bibulus's.

One can get the impression from our sources that – whenever exactly it was that Bibulus withdrew to his house – most senators boycotted meetings of the House in what was in effect a show of support for him and the three tribunes who joined in his protest, leaving only a "rump Senate" to do Caesar's bidding.[150] Plutarch specifically says as much.[151] Yet other sources fail to go this far, and closer scrutiny suggests that he has probably generalized broadly from a particular instance or episode.[152] A consul had

---

[146] For their election, see p. 164ff. and for the controversy over the legality of Caesar's legislation, see p. 183ff. We would certainly have heard about any serious irregularity in Piso's and Gabinius's election from Cicero, whose invectives against both men upon his return from exile were unrestrained.

[147] Plut. thought Caesar and Pompey called the shots (*Caes.* 14.8 τὸν δὲ Πείσωνα κατέστησεν [sc. Caesar] ὕπατον εἰς τὸ μέλλον; cf. *Cat. Min.* 33.6–7 ἀπέδειξαν ... ὑπάτους), but this need not refer narrowly to presiding over the election. There seems to be no solid evidence.

[148] Cic. *Pis.* 11, with Nisbet's comment ad loc. and Taylor 1966: 153n26 with pp. 79, 95–96 on *custodes*. Cicero was partly connected with Piso through his own son-in-law Cn. Piso, which may explain the special courtesy. As consul Piso called upon Cicero in the third place, again a mark of special favor (ibid.).

[149] *Adulescens nullius consili*: Cic. *Q. fr.* 1.2.15; cf. *Sest.* 18.

[150] So De Libero 1992: 73–76, who reports the alleged "boycott" as fact. Meier 1982: 212, 217.

[151] Plut. *Caes.* 14.13–15.

[152] Dio 38.6.6 refers to the "boycott" of their public duties by Bibulus and the tribunes who were acting in concert with him, which is evidently the main point of Suet. *Iul.* 20.2; Dio 38.8.2. App. *BCiv.* 2.11/37 describes a (dubious) meeting of the Senate at Bibulus's house during the voting on the agrarian law, and just before Bibulus's attempt to obnuntiate and veto in the Forum. Neither of these amounts to a general and long-term "boycott" of the Senate.

the right to compel attendance of the Senate, but Caesar seems never to have dared to go so far.[153] At most, as we saw, he tried to prompt a popular demonstration at Bibulus's house against his postponement of the elections, and presumably had favored Vatinius's effort to force him out, but both men had desisted, doubtless recognizing that more forceful measures would only backfire. Bibulus, then, was a lost cause. So too, at least according a later speech by Cicero, Cato stayed away from the Senate for the rest of the year, presumably after one or the other of the agrarian laws. Yet in the very same passage, Cicero acknowledges that he himself did not stay away.[154] His letters to Atticus of this year, though full of dismay about the political situation, particularly after Clodius's transfer to the plebs, contain no evidence that Cicero joined in any sort of boycott.[155] On the contrary, he notes that out of friendship with Pompey he is taking a "middle way" between association with the Three and opposition – which would be more in keeping with his principles – and Caesar's continued promises of a place on his staff or perhaps a religious commission corroborate the inference that Cicero had carefully avoided any such action that would overtly and irrevocably commit himself to Bibulus and Cato.[156] The letter recounting the Vettius scandal (discussed later in this chapter) attests to Cicero's presence in the Senate to hear Vettius's initial testimony.[157] Thus Cicero, a moderately "optimate" senator with links to both sides in the struggle, apparently chose not to join Cato's and Bibulus's boycott.

Other traces in our evidence also appear inconsistent with the simplistic idea that Caesar dealt for eight months of the year with a mere "rump Senate." Dio, to be sure, asserts that, at least after the People transferred to

---

[153] Cic. *Phil.* 1.12, with Ramsey 2003: 111.

[154] Cic. *Sest.* 63. Kaster 2006: 258–259, citing Plut. *Cat. min.* 32.1, notes that the comment about Cato is probably not "literally true," yet there seems to be no warrant on the other side for Canfora's claim (2007: 80) that Cato "kept up his opposition in the Senate" (the event he refers to probably belongs to the debate on the *lex agraria*). Cf. *Dom.* 8 with Kaster, loc. cit., for the objection that such boycotts in *minus bonis temporibus* only please those against whom their protest is directed.

[155] Pelling 2011: 202 misleadingly emphasizes the letters written from Antium and Formiae during the usual April vacation. *Publicis consiliis nullis intersumus* at *Att.* 2.23.3 can hardly be taken to mean that Cicero literally avoided the Curia in view of his open statement to the contrary in 56; of course, it can readily be translated broadly ("I take no part in political deliberations": Shackleton Bailey) in accordance with the implied contrast in the letter (politics vs. speaking in the courts).

[156] Cic. *Att.* 2.19.2: *utor via <media>*. Cf. 2.16.3, 18.3, 19.5. On the Ciceronian myth that in his defense of C. Antonius he had strongly criticized Caesar see n. 111. Caesar's offers: n. 128.

[157] Cic. *Att.* 2.24.2–3. Had he not been present at the meeting he would no doubt have given some hint of this in a letter to his friend. Nor is it likely that this degree of detail would have appeared in the *acta* that Caesar now began to publish. Note also Cicero's promise to support the Asian tax farmers in the Senate in their dispute over the *portorium circumvectionis* (16.4).

Caesar command of Cisalpine Gaul and Illyricum by the *lex Vatinia* (full discussion later in this chapter), Caesar was able to get anything he wanted, passed through a thoroughly cowed Senate, prompted by men eager to please him.[158] He makes this claim just before mentioning the Senate's decree to grant him the province of Transalpine Gaul in addition to Cisalpine Gaul and Illyricum, of which the last two provinces had been conferred by plebiscite. Now by chance, Suetonius reports an illuminating anecdote about a senatorial meeting very shortly after that one. First, the biographer, with rather different emphasis, attributes the Senate's cooperation to the desire to head off a further provincial reassignment by the People (a further example of the "Fear of the People" motif).[159] This in itself actually implies that the majority of the Senate was not taking orders from Caesar but seeking to preserve its prerogatives and dignity against the risk of further "popular" inroads, a strategic consideration also expressed in more normal times.[160] Then he writes that in another *well-attended* (*frequenti*) senatorial meeting a few days after that decree, Caesar crowed that he had obtained what he desired despite the lamentations of his adversaries and henceforth would "mount on everyone's head," a crude sexual expression implying oral penetration/rape.[161] When a heckler pretended to take the word literally and shouted that this would be hard for a woman to do (thereby presumably alluding to the old story of Caesar serving as homosexual plaything to King Nicomedes), Caesar deftly took up the thread and offered a rejoinder about the dominance once asserted by the Assyrian Queen Semiramis or the Amazons.[162] This is clearly a description of a rowdy meeting (explicitly a full meeting, thus hardly a "rump" session) at which Caesar's *adversarii* not only were present but were also actually prepared to hurl a crude insult to Caesar's face, which is hardly consistent with the picture of a browbeaten, docile Senate reduced to a rubber stamp

[158] Dio 38.8.4: οὐκ ἐν τῶι πλήθει μόνον ἀλλὰ καὶ ἐν αὐτῇ τῇ γερουσίᾳ. The date is uncertain but May or June seems most probable: n. 209.

[159] Suet. *Iul.* 22.1; cf. Dio 38.8.5. The motive is not implausible in itself: cf. Cic. *Att.* 8.3.3 gives Pompey the leading role in adding Transalpina to Caesar's provinces (*ille Galliae ulterioris adiunctor*), probably by proposing the motion. After Pompey had married his daughter Caesar called on him first in the Senate (Suet. *Iul.* 21; Gell. 4.10.5).

[160] Decrees on consular provinces were necessarily influenced by the risk of losing senatorial control over the process. See Cic. *Prov. cons.* 39 from the year 56.

[161] = *irrumatio*: Adams 1982: 200. *Frequens senatus* may have been a technical term for a quorate meeting (Ryan 1998: 13–51; but cf. contra Bonnefond-Coudry 1989: 425–435) but here Suetonius is probably using the phrase more generally.

[162] Suet. *Iul.* 22.2. On Semiramis (Sammu-ramat), who pops up elsewhere in contentious senatorial debate around this time (Cic. *Prov. cons.* 9), see Grillo 2015: 128. The admiring, near-contemporary account of Diod. 2.4–20 (Muntz 2017: 186–187; cf. 161–165, 206–209) suggests that the comparison may not have been entirely ironical.

for Caesar's decisions.[163] These political opponents, angry and obstreperous as they were, were evidently not too intimidated to voice opposition in no uncertain terms.[164] The anecdote seems to show that there were still senators present who were prepared to try to uphold the body's rights in determining consular provinces. That is consistent with another detail that is too little remarked on: when the Senate decreed provinces for the consuls to be elected in 59 for 58, these did not suit the ambitions of those eventually elected (L. Piso and A. Gabinius, allies of Caesar and Pompey, respectively), and thus the assignments were changed at the beginning of 58 by a law conferring upon them the more active (and lucrative) military assignments of Macedonia and Syria.[165] Why had this happened, if Caesar was able to make the Senate do his bidding? Or had he been cautious in the Senate because he doubted his ability to determine the results of the election? That alternative would in itself be of interest, and we shall return to the elections shortly.

The strongest evidence we have for intimidation is probably Plutarch's uncontextualized anecdote about the "brave" remark of the elderly senator Q. Considius. Plutarch says that after Bibulus's and Cato's original, failed attempt to block Caesar's legislation "very few" (ὀλίγοι παντάπασιν) senators would come to meetings any longer. In the Senate, Caesar put old Considius on the spot to explain why. Considius replied that it was because of their fear of "the weapons and the soldiers." When Caesar asked why this then did not deter *him*, Considius, the old man replied that his age made him fearless.[166] The anecdote is partly corroborated by Cicero, who writes sometime in August (perhaps) that recently "we" had actually feared "massacre" (*caedem*), but that this had been dispelled by "the speech of that brave old man, Q. Considius."[167] Two things, in particular, are worth noting about the anecdote. First, Caesar had to ask what was troubling the senators: apparently even though the story asserts that there were armed "soldiers" about, it was not blatantly obvious why senators should have feared them.

---

[163] Cf. De Libero 1992: 74 ("Rumpfsenat"), who seems to reject the anecdote because it does not fit with the "determined rejectionist stance of the senators at this time."

[164] Suet. *Iul.* 22.2: *invitis et ingementibus adversariis.* Billows 2009: 123 claims that Cato "objected vehemently" to the s.c., perhaps on the basis of Plut. *Cat. Min.* 33.5, but that story appears to be set in a *contio* preceding the vote on the *lex Vatinia* (mistakenly transferred to the agrarian law at Morstein-Marx 2004: 176). Note also the Senate's vote in favor of a supplication in honor of C. Pomptinus's victories in Gaul, which would hardly please Caesar (n. 227).

[165] Cic. *Dom.* 24. See *MRR* 2.193–194. Tatum 1999: 151–152; Kaster 2006: 173, 240.

[166] Plut. *Caes.* 14.14–15: φοβούμενοι τὰ ὅπλα καὶ τοὺς στρατιώτας. Cf. Shackleton Bailey ad Cic. *Att.* 2.24.4.

[167] Cic. *Att.* 2.24.4.

One might compare the beginning of Cicero's speech for Milo at his trial in
52 (Cic. *Mil.* 1–4), where the "fear" Pompey's armed guard inspired at the
trial is disputed: is it meant to intimidate the jurors or rather to keep the
rowdy, pro-Clodian popular audience under control? If Caesar had, in fact,
deployed some kind of armed guard or relied on Pompey's veterans to keep
order against those set on disrupting the legislative assemblies that took place
in a long sequence until at least mid-summer, this could, of course, in the
current environment arouse not unreasonable fears of its wider use against
dissenters and others sympathetic to Bibulus's and Cato's protests.[168]
Further, the fact that Considius's answer had done so much to put senators'
minds at ease implies not only that (1) the rest were too fearful to identify the
true cause to Caesar's face but also that (2) as soon as this was done, Caesar
(or rather, Pompey?) immediately responded in a way that removed that fear
by the time the letter was written in August. Either Caesar had had the
offending soldiers removed or perhaps he had clarified in some convincing
way that they were not there to terrorize political opponents but to maintain
security (Pompey's "shield") in the face of attempts to disrupt them.
Considius had only had to speak up for the fear to be removed. (The
evidence for the presence or participation of soldiers in the heated legislative
struggles of the first half of the year is examined later.)

     After this, we have useful testimony from an unusually informative letter
of Cicero's that the Senate returned to what to all appearances was its
ordinary functioning. This letter provides our most important evidence for
the murky scandal of mid-59 known as the Vettius affair, but more to our
point it gives a detailed description of a fraught and potentially contentious
meeting of the Senate perhaps in August.[169] L. Vettius, whom Cicero had
used as an informer against the conspirators in 63–62, came before that
body and alleged that the younger Curio, a conspicuous but still very
junior critic of the Three, had made threats against Pompey's life, and
furthermore that a number of other young senators had joined the plot
with support behind the scenes from none other than the consul
Bibulus.[170] Cicero expresses to his friend Atticus the opinion that Caesar

[168] There is a single reference to an armed band prepared by *Caesar* at the time of the first agrarian law
(n. 70) – unfortunately it appears in what is overall our least credible source for the events of
this year (Appian). On balance Considius's reference is more likely to have been to a substantial
turnout of Pompey's veterans (ex-soldiers), on which see further later in this chapter.

[169] The key evidence is Cic. *Att.* 2.24; *Vat.* 24–26 is thoroughly compromised by its invective, except
perhaps to show that none of Vatinius's allegedly nefarious plans came to fruition. A level-headed
review by Gruen 1974: 95–96.

[170] Cic. *Att.* 2.24.2; Vettius was *ille noster index* (in 63). For that episode, see Chapter 2, nn. 173, 178. For
the younger Curio's opposition to the Three, see Cic. *Att.* 2.8.1, 12.2, 19.3.

was at the bottom of the story, yet as has often been noted, Vettius's initial naming of M. Brutus among the plotters, subsequently retracted due to Caesar's pressure (it was thought), suggests the contrary.[171] One might suspect Pompey himself or his friends of manufacturing a scandal in order to deflect the growing odium onto Bibulus; Pompey often claimed to fear for his life.[172] Then again, Bibulus himself had ostensibly credited a story of a plot against Pompey and given him information about it.[173]

It would hardly be fruitful to dig into the morass of conjecture at this distance. Yet a few important points merit notice in the current context: the Senate was meeting; Cicero seems to have been present; and, most important, it did not act as an intimidated or "rump" Senate would have done. It took no rash action against the alleged plotters, nor did it exploit the information to "clean house" of the enemies of the Three. It shouted down (*reclamatum est*) the informer's request to turn state's evidence; senators soberly poked holes in the attempt to implicate Bibulus and pointed out the chronological impossibility of a crucial element of the story; finally the Senate, probably with Caesar himself presiding, passed a formal decree condemning the informer himself.[174]

Caesar next brought Vettius before a *contio* to relate his story (which had now changed a bit), which *may* imply that he sought to gain political mileage from it, although it could also have been unavoidable in a matter of this gravity, and advisable in order to tamp down rumor. In Caesar's *contio* (and almost immediately afterward in another one summoned by the tribune P. Vatinius) Vettius now stoked suspicions of Cicero, Lucullus, and L. Domitius (a candidate for the praetorship), none of whom he had mentioned in the Senate; yet, probably chastened by his reception in the Senate, he now seems to have soft-pedalled or dropped his allegations against Bibulus, while Cicero's report gives no suggestion that Caesar attempted to incite and mobilize the crowd as he had earlier in the summer when his colleague had postponed the election. The tribune Vatinius was probably less restrained, pressing Vettius to name

---

[171] Cic. *Att.* 2.24.2, 3. The ancient sources generally look to Caesar and Pompey, but Dio 38.9.2–10.1 suspects Cicero and Lucullus – perhaps only another sample of his frequent anti-Ciceronian bias. Why would Caesar entrust a scheme to Vettius, who had nearly ruined him in 63–62 with allegations of complicity in the Catilinarian conspiracy?

[172] Marshall 1987: 121–124. Note the link to Bibulus at §2. Pompey's suspiciously useful fears for his life emerge in 58, 56, and 52: sources and discussion in Marshall. Others have suspected P. Clodius (Seager 2002: 98–99; contra, Tatum 1999: 111–112).

[173] Cic. *Att.* 2.24.2.

[174] Cic. *Att.* 2.24.2–4: Vettius was to be put in chains as a confessed criminal until trial and anyone who released him (surely tribunes were in mind) would be considered to be acting *contra rem publicam*.

more names and promising to promulgate a bill to institute a special *quaestio* to try the suspects; yet we hear of no trials, and it looks as if the bill was dropped, perhaps after the key witness, Vettius himself, died in prison, officially of natural causes but according to rumor, murdered.[175]

The main point for us here is that, notwithstanding Cicero's understandable anxiety when he was implicated, nothing drastic against Caesar's and Pompey's political adversaries actually resulted from the scare. So far at least as we can tell, no wave of popular indignation arose against Bibulus or his allies and supporters, much less was one exploited; no discernable pressure was exerted to take preemptive vengeance on those who might have wanted Pompey dead; there were no "kangaroo courts," and in the Senate, no rush to condemn in order to please the powerful, such as one sees in a true *dominatio* (for instance in the Principate, with numbing regularity). The allegations were aired and for all practical purposes, discounted. The death of the informer is, of course, troubling (to us – nobody seems to have shed tears for Vettius at the time), but the *cui bono* question is here two-edged, and anyway much too much time has passed for anyone to get to the bottom of that mystery.[176] Contra Plutarch, then, the meeting on the Vettius affair, though its precipitating occasion was hardly normal, gives an impression of the Senate operating to all appearances in Caesar's consulship in the way that would be hoped for and expected. (Of course, as to what was truly going on under the surface, we need not assume it was any more high-minded than on other occasions of this kind.)[177]

Another sign that the alliance hardly held elite politicking in its grip is the failure of Caesar's loyal tribune P. Vatinius to be elected augur in the place Metellus Celer had vacated.[178] Because priestly elections since 63 had been returned to the People, and in a letter of April Cicero assumes this

---

[175] Cic. *Vat.* 24–26; note *rogatione* and *promulgarisne*, not *tulerisne*. Cic. *Att.* 2.24.3 suggests that Vatinius pressed the issue much more vigorously than had Caesar.

[176] Most sources are convinced that Vettius was murdered (Cic. *Vat.* 26: *fregerisne . . . cervices*; App. *BCiv.* 2.12/44; Dio 38.9.4), but note that Plut. *Luc.* 42.8, while tending toward this conclusion himself, acknowledges that Vettius was *said* to have died a natural death, but that this was doubted because of marks of strangulation and blows. The murder theory was fundamentally ambiguous since Caesar could suggest, not unreasonably, that Vettius had been murdered by those he had implicated in order to avoid conviction (thus Appian), while opponents of the Three could claim (somewhat less obviously) that Caesar or his allies had to dispose of Vettius once the charges had proven to be only an embarrassment to them and their own involvement was likely to be exposed (something like this in Cic. *Vat.* 26).

[177] Cf. Sallust's trenchant criticisms of the Senate's handling of allegations against Crassus in 63 (*Cat.* 48.3–9) or Pompey's encouragement of rumors against Milo in 52 (Ascon. 38, 50–52 C with Cic. *Mil.* 65–71).

[178] Cic. *Vat.* 19–21; cf. *Att.* 2.9.2 and 2.12.1 with Shackleton Bailey 1965: 1:374–75 and Rüpke 2005: 2:1357.

appointment would be in the hands of the Three, it is notable that such a "good soldier" as Vatinius had been in this year could not be put through handily; in fact, it appears that the Three did not manage to get any other ally or friend appointed in this year.[179]

What about outside the Curia? It is widely assumed that to work his will in the year 59, Caesar resorted frequently or persistently to armed domination of the public spaces, provided by Pompey's veterans. The idea is not made up out of whole cloth: we have already discussed the role of Pompey's "shield" in the passage of the first agrarian law – quite limited, it appears, and neither unprecedented nor entirely unreasonable in view of the new strategy of disruption explored by Cato in 62 and predictably pursued by Bibulus. But what about the rest of the year? It is curious and sobering on its face that *only Plutarch* mentions any employment of "soldiers" *tout court* (i.e. not simply voters carrying concealed weapons, which were not an infrequent phenomenon in the Late Republic) in the legislative assemblies that were the usual scenes of confrontation in this year. In three different *Lives* (*Pompey, Lucullus*, and *Caesar*) he introduces verbally nearly identical references to Pompey's "filling the City (or Forum) with soldiers/armed men" to push through controversial legislation in this year, but he sets them in three different contexts so it is difficult to decide what to make of this.[180] This may therefore be a "free-floating" report not anchored by Plutarch's source to any particular occasion and therefore placed by the biography where it best fits his narrative. We have seen that Plutarch is likely to have misunderstood or slightly misrepresented a reference in his source to Pompey's veterans rather than (active duty) "soldiers," and also that it is probably best contextualized in the struggles over Caesar's agrarian laws (see p. 135ff.). As we have seen, Caesar's laws do not seem to have lacked support from the voters to the extent that armed intimidation might become "necessary." The story Plutarch preserves (partly backed by Cicero) about old brave Considius's remark to Caesar's face in the

---

[179] Cic. *Att.* 2.5.2; at 2.7.2 Cicero anticipates a "squabble" over the augurate. Apparently no successor to Celer was appointed until 57, when the successful candidate was the younger P. Lentulus Spinther, son of the homonymous consul of that year (Rüpke 1:128–129 with 2:918, no. 1354n1). Shackleton Bailey 1965: 1:374 conjectured that M. Atius Balbus may have been "the 'triumviral' choice for the vacant Augurate," yet if so, he was not appointed.

[180] Plut. *Luc.* 42.6 (probably the earliest of these *Lives*: Pelling 2011: 37n84): πληρώσαντα τὴν πόλιν ὅπλων καὶ στρατιωτῶν βίᾳ κυρῶσαι τὰ δόγματα (in the context of the ratification of Pompey's eastern *acta*); *Caes.* 14.10: ἐνέπλησε τὴν ἀγορὰν ὅπλων καὶ συνεπεκύρου τῷ δήμῳ τοὺς νόμους (here the context is the passage of the *lex Vatinia* after Pompey's marriage to Julia: n. 209); *Pomp.* 48.1: ἐμπλήσας στρατιωτῶν τὴν πόλιν ἅπαντα τὰ πράγματα βίᾳ κατεῖχε (this context is the first *lex agraria*). See p. 135 at n. 72.

Senate seems to belong at some point before August; it may refer to men Caesar had brought in to prevent disruption in the assemblies, and of course, critics would have said, to intimidate opponents.[181] But by August, the senators' fears had apparently been dispelled (Cic. *Att.* 2.24.4).

Plutarch is not an unimpeachable source when it comes to points of detail; the eyewitness or at least hearsay evidence of Cicero is in general much more authoritative. But "soldiers" (or paramilitary "muscle") are less in evidence in Cicero than in Plutarch. Robin Seager notes that "the fear that Pompeius would in some way resort to violence first appears in Cicero's correspondence at the end of April" – which implies that this had not already happened.[182] The point appears to be corroborated by a letter of the very end of April in which Cicero imagines himself leveling a series of complaints against Pompey about his behavior in the year thus far: his tolerance of Caesar's refusal to allow a veto against his (first) agrarian law, his alleged ignorance of the fact that Bibulus had been "watching the skies" when King Ptolemy of Egypt had been confirmed, his pretended surprise that Bibulus was maltreated in some fashion when he went to the Forum to oppose the revision of the tax contract of the *publicani*.[183] Yet Cicero does not so much as mention Pompey's sending in the soldiers, which as a sin of commission rather than omission clearly belongs among the charges to which he would have had to answer. A bit farther on in the letter Cicero imagines Pompey making various excuses for thus far abetting Caesar, ending with the (imagined) threat that he (Pompey) would "hold you down with Caesar's (n.b.) army" (*exercitu*).[184] The meaning of *exercitus* here has prompted much inconclusive debate. In a literal sense, of course, Caesar did not yet command an "army," though even in April/May it hardly required clairvoyance to expect that he would have one after his consulship. If that is what Cicero's imaginary Pompey meant, he was looking ahead, not describing present circumstances (and, in any case, he was either being metaphorical or was playing an over-the-top "tyrant" type, for any "army" voted to Caesar would not be for use in the City.) Alternatively, perhaps Cicero was imagining

[181] See p. 157ff.

[182] Seager 2002: 94, citing Cic. *Att.* 2.14.1, 17.1. For earlier legislation see n. 121.

[183] Cic. *Att.* 2.16.2.

[184] Cic. *Att.* 2.16.2: *nunc vero, Sampsicerame, quid dices? vectigal te nobis in monte Antilibano constituisse, agri Campani abstulisse? quid? hoc quem ad modum obtinebis? "oppressos vos" inquit "tenebo exercitu Caesaris."* Pelling 2011: 200 offers a useful survey of opinion, concluding with the view mentioned first below; cf. esp. Meier 1961: 79–84, with Shackleton Bailey, 1965: 1.408. Lintott 2008: 170–171 believes the reference is to armed gangs with which Caesar is assumed to have dominated the assemblies, including Pompeian veterans, but apart from the *petitio principii* (for our purposes) his objections to the more common view are too legalistic.

Pompey to be referring to a metaphorical "army" of dedicated supporters and beneficiaries of the law, a figure of speech attested elsewhere in Cicero.[185] One thing "Pompey" could hardly be speaking of here, however, was his own veterans: he would hardly have called them "*Caesar's* army."

That is all we hear from Cicero on the subject. In April, he had dreaded the unleashing of violence by Caesar and Pompey, which he continues to anticipate through the summer – and indeed for the rest of the year, to judge at least from the surviving correspondence.[186] Cicero's "fear" rises, dissipates, or is projected into the future, but even in these private notes to his confidant, we never hear of any specific act that would validate such fears other than the legislative program itself, the frustration of its opponents, and suspicion of what the Three are ultimately aiming at.[187] The Vettius affair had seemed for a moment to be the trigger for the backlash Cicero had been dreading all year, yet again nothing came of it.[188] Nowhere else in his later speeches and hundreds of letters, in what is the best-documented decade in ancient history ultimately revolving around an armed confrontation with Caesar, does Cicero refer back specifically to any use of military or paramilitary force in his first consulship; others, to be sure, would threaten to bring Caesar to book, but even in that very highly charged context, our sources never specifically mention allegations of organized violence or illegitimate use of soldiers.[189] Caesar's actions as consul in 59 would be central to his enemies' case for civil war in 50, so the total absence of any clear retrospective reference to armed intimidation as that confrontation heated up should warn us not to build too much on

---

[185] E.g. Cic. *Att.* 1.19.4: *noster exercitus, hominum, ut tute scis, locupletium*; 2.19.4 *nostrum illum consularem exercitum bonorum omnium.* Cf. Gelzer 1968: 81.

[186] See *Att.* 2.19.2–3, 20.3, 21.1–2, 21.4–5, 22.6 (July to ?August).

[187] See nn. 134, 135 earlier in this chapter and the Considius anecdote (p. 157ff.). Use of "fear" by the Three is moved into the *future* at 2.19.2: *an metu necesse sit iis uti vereor.* Fear of much worse in store: 2.17.1: *quid enim eos haec ipsa* [sc. Caesar's legislation] *per se delectare possunt? Numquam huc venissent nisi ad alias res pestiferas aditus sibi compararent.* 2.22.3: *ut . . . ea contentio quae impendet interdum non fugienda videatur.*

[188] Cic. *Att.* 2.24.4: +*eam*+, *quam cottidie timere potueramus, subito exorta est.*

[189] For the general question whether Caesar faced serious threat of prosecution for his acts in 59, see p. 261ff. and Appendix 2. Those references that are at all specific about possible charges never explicitly cite the use of soldiers or even violence (Suet. *Iul.* 30.3; cf. App. *BCiv.* 2.23/87/88 with Plut. *Cat. Min.* 48.5–6). To be sure, Cicero (*Att.* 8.3.3) could eventually in exasperation blame Pompey for (among other things) "nourishing, building up, and arming" Caesar against the Republic (a charge sheet that on its face seems largely metaphorical) and for being his supporter or even instigator (*auctor*) in passing laws *per vim et contra auspicia* (in itself simply a repetition of Bibulus's complaint to the Senate after the first agrarian law, containing no specific indication of the instrument of the alleged *vis*). As this last reference shows (as well as Plutarch's repeated triplet cited earlier), *Pompey* was surely the source of those soldiers/veterans who joined (to an uncertain extent) in the tumultuous urban politics of 59.

Plutarch's rather isolated references to the presence of Pompey's "soldiers," or, more accurately, veterans, in some of the assemblies of the first half of the year in which nearly all of Caesar's legislation was passed.

But as I have had occasion already to note, military or paramilitary intimidation would hardly have been needed to win a fair vote on Caesar's laws. In fact (shifting his focus a bit) Plutarch claims that the voters, tamed by the bait of the agrarian laws, were passively prone for the rest of the year to cast their votes in stupefied silence for any project put before them.[190] But even our spotty and tendentious evidence for the year raises doubts that Caesar simply had his way even with the People. As we have already seen, we happen to hear of instances in this year when Caesar, Pompey, or their allied tribune Vatinius utterly failed to rally their popular audiences or mobilize demonstrations against their opponents.[191]

The elections provide a test of Pompey's and Caesar's domination of the assemblies. They had apparently anticipated trouble already in April–May (by which time Bibulus was already at work delaying the elections), for the *lex Campana* contained an oath binding the candidates to respect the Julian agrarian laws. A hopeful for the tribunate of 58, M. Iuventius Laterensis, actually gave up his candidacy rather than swear the oath.[192] As we saw, despite his withdrawal to his house, Bibulus did not forfeit all influence over the elections, and when he postponed them by edict until October 18, he was able to prevail against Caesar's pressure tactics. Intriguingly, the Three did not pursue the obvious and entirely legal slate of Pompey and Crassus, which had been generally expected in April.[193] Besides the ultimately successful candidates for the consulships of 58 only one other appears to be explicitly attested (L. Lentulus Niger, the *flamen Martialis*), but the names of Q. Arrius (pr. by 63) and Ser. Sulpicius Rufus (pr. 65, eventually consul in 51) had been ventilated early in the year as possible candidates favored by the Three, and we can infer interest among other figures with the necessary credentials such as the noble L. Marcius Philippus (pr. 62), who would soon marry Caesar's niece Atia and reach the consulship in 56, or the patrician M. Valerius Messalla Rufus (possibly pr. 62, eventually

[190] Plut. *Pomp.* 48.3.
[191] See nn. 138, 142. The year had begun with Caesar's failed, or perhaps not entirely serious, attempt to imprison Cato: Plut. *Caes.* 14.12, *Cat. min.* 33.1–4 with n. 45.
[192] Cic. *Att.* 2.18.2. On the oath, see now Bellemore 2005: 241–243; Pocock 1926: 127–128 conflates this oath with the earlier one. The oath did not stop the new praetors of 58 from leading an attack on the legality of Caesar's legislation early in 58 (p. 182ff.). Laterensis's posturing notwithstanding, it could be assumed that the oath would not necessarily deter Caesar's adversaries from pursuing their candidacy.
[193] Cic. *Att.* 2.5.2.

elected consul for 53).[194] When the elections were finally held in October, consuls friendly to the Three were indeed chosen: Caesar's father-in-law (or soon to be), L. Piso, and Pompey's consistent supporter, A. Gabinius.[195] But these two could certainly stand on their own merits in the judgment of the Roman People against competition such as this. Gabinius, though far from highborn, was a popular benefactor whose bold and effective solution for the pirate-and-grain crisis eight years before will not have been forgotten: Roman voters had probably benefited more directly by his law that freed the seas and city's grain supply from piracy than by any other single item of legislation in recent history, excepting, of course, Caesar's own agrarian laws of this year.[196] In a law presented to the People and passed in the very next year (58), Gabinius's law of nine years previous that had cleared the scourge of piracy is pointedly highlighted, while Pompey is not so much as mentioned; one might well mock this as self-praise (for Gabinius himself, cosponsor of this new law, was presumably looking over the shoulder of whoever drafted these very lines), but even if that is the case, it is still a fair reflection of how the Roman People will have regarded him at this time.[197] The noble L. Piso had been chosen quaestor, aedile, and praetor each time at the first attempt and was prominently endorsed in this year by none other than his future enemy Cicero; the marriage connection with Caesar forged in May or June may have been a consequence, not the cause, of his promise as a consular candidate in this year.[198] In any case, Piso's and Gabinius's electoral success need not be explained by heavy-handed intervention on the part of the presiding consul (assuming it was Caesar) or Pompey. If that was what won them the consulship, why then did it fail to prevent Cato's brother-in-law L. Domitius,

---

[194] Lentulus Niger: Cic. *Vat.* 25. Other names: Cic. *Att.* 2.5.2, 7.3 (Arrius had given up by April, not receiving the hoped-for support of the Three). C. Papirius Carbo (pr. 62) was taken out of contention by conviction in this year; Cicero's patrician client L. Valerius Flaccus (pr. 63) was probably too harassed in the courts to pursue the consulship in this year (Alexander 1990: nos. 243, 247; cf. Cic. *Flacc.* 1, 106). The future Augustus's father, C. Octavius, current husband of Caesar's niece Atia, was still in his province at the time of the elections (Cic. *Q. fr.* 1.2.7) and died before the end of the year.

[195] Caesar seems to have married Piso's daughter Calpurnia shortly after Pompey married Julia (ὀλίγῳ δὲ ὕστερον: Plut. *Caes.* 14.8), which probably occurred in late April or early May. Plut. at both *Cat. Min.* 33.7 and *Caes.* 14.8 weakly implies that Piso was already Caesar's father-in-law before he was elected, and Suet. *Iul.* 22.1 thinks that this was already the case at the time of passage of the *lex Vatinia* shortly after Pompey's marriage to Julia (n. 209). Pelling 2011: 198 is right to withhold final judgment, but on the whole, a marriage before the elections seems more likely, especially since they were postponed to mid-October.

[196] Gabinius: Badian 1959; Gruen 1974: 143; Yakobson 2006: 390.

[197] *Lex Gabinia Calpurnia de insula Delo* (Crawford 1996: no. 22, 1:346, lines 14–16): *praedones quei orbem te[r]rarum complureis [annos vastarint et fa]na delubra simul[a]cra deorum immor[t]alium . . . [compil]arint lege Ga[b]inia superatei ac deletei s[i]nt . . . .*

[198] Piso: Cic. *Pis.* 2, 11 with n. 148; Gruen 1968: 163–166, 1974: 143.

a confirmed opponent of Pompey and a predictable thorn in Caesar's side, from winning a praetorship along with C. Memmius (Catullus's future commander and Lucretius's future patron), both of whom celebrated the beginning of their term of office with a wholesale attack on Caesar's *acta* in the Senate?[199]

To close this section on governmental function and dysfunction we must consider the one law Caesar passed in this year that happens both to win the universal approbation of ancient jurists and modern scholars and yet to be completely ignored by our regular sources, fixated as they are on the tumult that surrounded Caesar's more controversial legislation: the Julian law on extortion in the provinces (*lex Iulia repetundarum*).[200] The *lex Iulia* reportedly contained more than one hundred painstakingly drafted clauses covering in detail a wide variety of shady practices that republican governors had raised to an art form and are well known to modern students through Cicero's excoriation of Gaius Verres in 70.[201] Over the previous century *repetundae* legislation had expanded its scope to cover not merely extortion per se by the governor but also judicial bribery, had made third parties liable under the law, had banned moneylending by the governor and virtually all "gifts" to him, had limited grants made to honor the governor with temples or statues, had set limits on requisitions, and had even imported clauses from the law of *maiestas* (usually translated "treason": in practice, serious violations of prerogatives of the Senate or People) prohibiting governors from leaving their provinces without authorization, and so on. But the Julian Law also innovated in various important respects: a governor's right to "crown gold" (*aurum coronarium*) or plunder from an enemy was tightly regulated, an ancient ban on ship-owning by senators was revived, "free cities" were protected from the abuse of military assets to collect debts, an elaborate system of recording the

---

[199] See n. 260. Domitius: Gruen 1974: 55–56. Memmius, a mercurial sort (Shackleton Bailey 1965: 1:331), was said to have turned against Caesar in April 59 (Cic. *Att.* 2.12.2). His praetorian invectives against Caesar were long remembered (n. 262). L. Antistius, tr. pl. in either 58 or 56, might be put down as another opponent of the Three elected in 59 if the earlier, traditional date is correct, though this now seems unlikely (Suet. *Iul.* 23.1; see Chapter 5, n. 157).

[200] Crawford 1996: no. 55, pp. 769–772. Cic. *Sest.* 135 brings up the law retrospectively only as a stick to beat Vatinius with: *haec optima lex* (cf. *Vat.* 29 *lex . . . acerrima*). Dio 38.7.5 does not explicitly mention the law on extortion but simply appears to cite it among miscellaneous further measures (ἄλλα πολλά) after the agrarian laws, the relief sought by the *publicani*, and Pompey's arrangements. The law was promulgated, though apparently not in effect, before the trial of L. Valerius Flaccus in this year (Cic. *Flacc.* 13), which may have been in September (Alexander 1990: no. 247, 2002: 279n6). Cf. Morrell 2017: 140.

[201] [Cic.] *Fam.* 8.8.3 (Caelius). Verres, of course, was far from alone and may have been the victim of selective justice: Stone 2018.

official accounts both in the province and in Rome was introduced, court procedure was tightened up – in sum Caesar made the law "more severe and scrupulously just" than its predecessors.[202] This carefully drafted statute on a crucial matter of imperial governance, typically providing the only legal check on the corruption of provincial governors, remained the fundamental law on extortion and related crimes into the Empire. Its drafting and passage, however, hardly fit well with the story our main sources wish to tell of this year, so a major achievement of Roman administration and imperial governance easily slips beneath the waves of narrative history.

Kit Morrell cannot believe that Caesar was the "instigator" of the extortion law given the apparent recovery of his finances during his proconsulship in Spain and his subsequent record of belligerence and rapacity in Gaul. She prefers to see Pompey as the motivating spirit behind the law, although he too had amassed an extraordinary fortune during his eastern campaigns of the 60s, probably surpassing even that of Marcus Crassus.[203] Still, it is as unnecessary as it is conjectural to divide credit for the law between the two men. As consul, Caesar was responsible for it, and thus for a notable advance in Rome's commitments to its Empire. Issues of basic justice to provincials were in the air, not simply the preserve of one side or the other of a partisan divide.[204] Other new measures promulgated by Caesar's allies appear to have attended to courtroom procedure: a law of the tribune Vatinius regulated the challenges of jurors while that of the praetor Q. Fufius Calenus laid down that the votes of each of the three different orders of criminal jurors (senators, *equites*, and *tribuni aerarii*) would be recorded as part of the verdict.[205] The first regulated an obvious abuse; the second imposed a degree of indirect accountability without violating the secrecy of the individual verdict. "This was not petty

---

[202] Cic. *Rab. Post.* 8. Morrell 2017: 129–135 gives an valuable survey of the terms of the law both in its tralatician features and its innovations; on the protection of "free cities" see n. 204.

[203] Badian 1968: 81–82: Pompey "could have bought Crassus out without feeling the pinch" (a nice turn of phrase but overly rhetorical). Kay 2014: 296 rates their fortunes as about equal (200 million sesterces).

[204] As Morrell 2017: 148–151 notes, the protection of "free cities" embraced by Caesar's law (Cic. *Prov. cons.* 7, *Pis.* 37) had recently been a project pursued by M. Cato in the Senate (Cic. *Att.* 1.19.9, 1.20.4, 2.1.10).

[205] Gruen 1974: 239–244; further sources in *MRR* 2.188–190, with fragments and reconstruction in Crawford 1996: 2:769–772. Calenus's law may have been an attempt to use shame to discipline the taking of bribes by equestrian jurors, whose legal immunity, a political hot potato, remained even under the *lex Iulia repetundarum* (Dio 38.8.1; cf. Cic. *Pro Rab. Post.* 12). From this standpoint the *lex Fufia* was complementary with the *lex Iulia* and remedied an awkward omission (Gruen 1974: 242, and now Morrell 2017: 153–176). Fufius's political allegiance: Cic. *Att.* 2.18.1.

politics."[206] It is a useful reminder that Caesar and his allies did not define their agenda in 59 solely by pursuing partisan advantage, and shows once again how selectively our regular sources have allocated their attention.

Gaul and the *Lex Vatinia*

Caesar's first consulship is distinguished by the passage of an impressive list of bills of a clearly or apparently salutary nature, at least from the standpoint of good governance or the interests of the *populus Romanus*: the two agrarian laws; the ratification at last of Pompey's eastern settlement, which had been locked down for years, doubtless creating undesirable uncertainty for Romans and provincials alike; the partial remission of the cost of the Asian tax contract, which the *publicani* had overbid (probably a conspicuous example of that uncertainty); and the extortion law.[207] "The triple alliance," observes Kurt Raaflaub, "represented large and important groups of Roman citizens whose needs and interests were consistently neglected by the ruling circles among the senatorial elite."[208] Yet no one would claim that Caesar was driven exclusively by altruistic motives, and the one law that addressed his own interest very directly was passed, probably in May or June, by his supportive tribune P. Vatinius.[209] The *lex Vatinia* gave Caesar the chance he had reportedly longed for, according to Sallust: "a great command, an army, a new war . . . that would permit his excellence to shine forth."[210] This would be his chance for "eternal glory" (*sempiterna gloria*), for a triumph even greater than the one he had earned in Spain – and then had been denied in a bit of Catonian sharp practice. The public esteem Caesar would eventually win from his nine years of campaigning in Gaul, the fears that this engendered, and the military resources placed in his hands over this extended period would create the conditions for civil war. And if we may be permitted

---

[206] Gruen 2009: 33.
[207] Conveniently summarized at *MRR* 2.187–188; add "P. Vatinius" on p. 190. Details in Rotondi 1912: 387–393. On the ratification of Pompey's eastern arrangements see n. 121.
[208] Raaflaub 2010: 164.
[209] The *lex Vatinia* was almost certainly passed no earlier than the beginning of May: according to Plut. *Caes.* 14.10 (also, implicitly, Suet. *Iul.* 22.1; Dio 38.8.5–9.1 however reverses the sequence, though he still appears to associate the two things closely in time) shortly after Pompey's marriage to Julia in late April or early May (Cic. *Att.* 2.17.1). (Meier 1961: 83–88 and Taylor 1968: 182–188 thought the law was promulgated as early as March on the basis of *exercitu Caesaris* at Cic. *Att.* 2.16.2, but this is an unwarranted interpretation of that passage [see n. 184], and Taylor anyway thinks the law could not be passed until late May because of the scarcity of comitial days.) In July, Caesar offered Cicero a legateship available to him under the *lex Vatinia* (*Att.* 2.19.5), which may also favor the later date. (See also Gelzer 1963: 2:206–214.)
[210] Sall. *Cat.* 54.4 with Chapter 2, p. 78ff.

to rise for a moment far above the historical horizons of any contemporary to view the matter *sub specie aeternitatis*, Caesar's conquest of Gaul would create a land bridge from the Mediterranean civilizations to the Celtic and Germanic peoples of the north that would ultimately, in millennia to come, lay the foundation for a new conception of Europe.[211] This is a big moment, whose ultimate historical significance extends far beyond the motives and intentions in play in 59 BC. Yet again, we must try to forget all this in order to understand the choices made under the circumstances of that year.

Caesar's massive military intervention in "Gaul across the Alps" (Transalpine Gaul) is apt to be seen solely in terms of his own desires and ambitions. But of course, the law that put him in a position to intervene in Gaul had to be justified not merely to the Senate but to the voting public, with reference not to Caesar's personal interests but to those of the Republic. And to understand the case that might be made for a major war in the north we have to step back a bit to sketch the background.

To an observer in 61 or 60, Rome's security arrangements protecting the province of Transalpine Gaul were in a pretty precarious state, if not quite yet a shambles. The evidence is scattered and not fully presented even in Caesar's own account in his military *Commentaries*, so the security concerns that invited or necessitated his intervention in Gaul tend to be obscured in most modern accounts, leaving the impression that it was an almost entirely arbitrary choice.[212] A brief survey of the immediate background will bring the issue into sharper focus.

Although "all Gaul" beyond the *provincia* (more or less modern "Provence," still *the* Transalpine province at this time) was not formally subject to Roman proconsuls, Romans were still apt to think of central Gaul – or at least, a broad zone around "the Province" – as part of the *imperium* of the Roman People.[213] Cross-border security of the *provincia*

---

[211] This is not, of course, to be laid to Caesar's credit: see the remarks of Canfora 2007: 122–123 comparing the "savage conquest of the New World."

[212] Hoffmann 1952: 16–20 is alive to the disastrous deterioration of the former security system in Gaul beyond the *provincia*, although he is rather too inclined to see the disturbances in Gaul in 58 as a complete surprise to the Romans. Dyson 1985: 149–170 offers a generally excellent survey of the history of the Roman frontier system in Gaul, yet his claim that "the frontier balance was restored" (170) by the time Caesar appeared on the scene is at variance with the evident facts. Similarly, Meier 1982: 237: "Everything had meanwhile [i.e. after 61 and 60] settled down." Canfora 2007: 98 is not quite correct to claim that in assessing the state of Gaul that confronted him "we rely exclusively on Caesar's version of the facts": as the survey cited later in this chapter shows, we have enough evidence from other sources to confirm Caesar's overall picture of the precariousness of the security structure in Gaul.

[213] Caes. *BGall.* 1.45.2–3. There is no need to suppose that Caesar is unduly stretching a point: the concept of the *imperium* was by no means restricted to the sum of the provinces: Kallet-Marx 1995: 22–29; Richardson 2008.

(as Caesar calls it) was anchored upon Rome's long-standing alliance with the powerful central Gallic state (*civitas*) of the Aedui (or Haedui) to the north, between the Doubs and Sâone Rivers, based on their capital, Bibracte (Mont-Beuvray). The Aedui had been honored with the title "brothers and kinsmen" (*fratres consanquineique*) of the Romans – probably a traditional Gallic diplomatic form – at least after the Roman conquest of the Transalpine province circa 121, but perhaps even before.[214] By 58, the Aedui could claim that they had performed many services for the Roman People, and no doubt the alliance played an important role in their ability to maintain a hegemonic position within Celtic Gaul, first as rivals of the Arverni in the Auvergne, then against the rising power of the Sequani to the east.[215] However, at some point in the 60s the Sequani, locked in conflict with the Aedui, had invited the German warlord Ariovistus to assist them; he had crossed the Rhine with a large contingent and in 61–60 crushed the Aedui in a series of battles.[216] Ariovistus shattered the dominance of the Aedui in central Gaul, and though it may have been some comfort to them that the Sequani themselves were soon increasingly under the German's forceful thumb, they were forced to pay tribute to him, give hostages, and swear submission to the Sequani as well as pledging that they would never again appeal to Rome for help.[217] Somehow the Aeduan Diviciacus, a Druid and nobleman who

[214] Caes. *BGall.* 1.33.2 (36.5, 44.9), with Cic. *Att.* 1.19.2 (cf. *Fam.* 7.10.4). See also Tac. *Ann.* 11.25.1; other references in Kraner, Dittenberger, and Meusel 1964: 1:33.2; Orosius 6.11.10 (*foedus*). Liv. *Per.* 61 supplies the date given in the text; Goudineau and Peyre (1993: 171–173) would take the alliance back as far as the early second century. The Arverni may have been similarly honored (ibid.) but lived largely within the Province (Caes. *BGall.* 1.45.2). The king of the Sequani had been named a *populi Romani amicus* (Caes. *BGall.* 1.3.4), a friendship that perhaps reached back to circa 100 (Plut. *Mar.* 24, with Hoffmann 1952: 16n43).

[215] Caes. *BGall.* 1.11.3, 1.31.3–4, 7, 1.43.6–7. Goudineau and Peyre 1993: 173–181.

[216] Caes. *BGall.* 1.31.4–9, 6.12.1–2. There were numerous battles (Caes. *BGall.* 1.31.6, 6.12.3 *proeliis . . . compluribus factis*) beginning in 61 (Caes. *BGall.* 1.35.4) through early 60 (Cic. *Att.* 1.19.2), when it is likely that Ariovistus inflicted a decisive defeat on the Aeduans and their allies (Caes. *BGall.* 1.44.3) probably at Magetobriga (1.31.12 [Glück]), unfortunately an unknown toponym. (Shackleton Bailey 1965: 1:334; the battle of early 60 was certainly not against the Helvetii, as Dyson 1985: 169 asserts.). Ariovistus's boast in 58 that his men had not slept under a roof for fourteen years (Caes. *BGall.* 1.36.7) cannot safely be used to establish the date of his crossing of the Rhine (Kraner et al. 1964, pace Gelzer 1968: 108).

[217] Caes. *BGall.* 1.31.7–12, 6.12.3–5, where *omni nobilitate Aeduorum interfecta* is an evident exaggeration given the subsequent prominence of Diviciacus and his brother Dumnorix; also 1.36.3–5, 1.44.2, 7.54.3–4. Nor had the Aeduan nation formally repudiated Roman friendship, as the nominal alliance of the Aedui with Rome during the Helvetic campaign of 58 and the service of Diviciacus and Dumnorix with Caesar's army shows, although it soon became clear that its allegiances were torn (1.9.3, 18–20). It is also important to remember that at the time of the Helvetic campaign, Ariovistus was a Friend of the Roman People (see n. 221) and thus posed no obstacle to the support the Aedui had rendered to Caesar.

had escaped being forced to give his own children as hostages, had fled to Rome to appeal for aid in 61 (he stayed as Cicero's guest), and the Senate had responded with a decree authorizing "whoever received [the province of] Gaul" to defend the Aedui and other Friends of the Roman People "as far as was consistent with the interests of Republic."[218] But Diviciacus failed to obtain any more forceful assistance, despite the nearby presence in Transalpina of a Roman proconsul, C. Pomptinus. Pomptinus had reason or an excuse for inaction since he was engaged in suppressing a dangerous revolt within the province itself by the once-powerful Allobroges. This had broken out very shortly after the failure of an Allobrogan embassy sent to Rome to complain of excessive fiscal exploitation (a mission well known to all Latin students because of its role in implicating the Catilinarian conspirators before Cicero and the Senate, a service for which they received little or insufficient thanks).[219] The Allobrogan revolt then was yet another blow to the Roman position in Gaul, but more dangerous still was Pomptinus's failure, despite the senatorial decree of 61, to avert final catastrophe for the Aeduans in early 60. (No doubt he would have claimed that his hands were full.) This cannot have escaped Ariovistus's notice, who must have concluded that the Romans no longer took very seriously their "brotherhood" with the Aedui.[220]

In fact, Ariovistus now made a move himself to supplant the Aedui as Rome's dominant friend in the Gallic frontier zone. In 60–59 he sent an embassy to obtain Roman friendship and to gain recognition of his status as king – and implicitly, doubtless, of his gains. It was in fact, Caesar himself who as consul introduced Ariovistus's embassy to the Senate and shepherded the diplomatic recognition of the German strongman through that body probably early in the year 59, when he received Rome's blessing as king and the title of "Friend of the Roman People."[221] Did Rome demand any concessions for their "brothers" the Aedui in return? Appian

---

[218] Caes. *BGall.* 1.35.4 *quod commodo rei publicae facere posset.* Diviciacus's embassy: 1.31.9, 6.12.5 *imperfecta re*; Cic. *Div.* 1.90; Panegyr. Lat. V 3.2–3.

[219] Cic. *Prov. Cons.* 32; Dio 37.47–48; Liv. *Per.* 103; Caes. *BGall.* 1.6.2–3 notes the dangerous aftermath of the Allobrogan revolt even in 58. Fighting occurred at least in part across the Rhone – that is, north of the Province as Caesar defines it in the Gallic War; the Allobroges held some territory north of that river (Caes. *BGall.* 1.11.5).

[220] He makes precisely this point at Caes. *BGall.* 1.44.9.

[221] Esp. Caes. *BGall.* 1. 35.2: *rex atque amicus a senatu appellatus,* 43.4, 44.5; cf. Dio 38.34.3. Ariovistus's initiative is stressed by Caes. at 1.44.5: *sibi ornamento et praesidio . . . esse oportere, idque se ea spe petisse.* Jehne 2009: 74 thinks that the embassy was dealt with toward the end of Caesar's consulship, but foreign embassies were traditionally presented early in the year, and by a *lex Gabinia*, passed probably in 67, February was set aside for such diplomatic business: Bonnefond-Coudry 1989: 294–320, 333–346. Bibulus may have stayed home.

thinks that at their request Ariovistus actually "withdrew from the Aedui" (whatever exactly that may mean, perhaps vacating some captured territory).[222] Yet Caesar makes clear that when he arrived in 58 the Aedui were still substantially under Ariovistus's domination, still paying tribute, and still bereft of the hostages they had given him, and it strains the imagination that Caesar would have omitted to add the German's failure to comply with a senatorial decree to his justifications for war if the complaint lay ready to hand. Possibly Ariovistus did make some token gesture of withdrawal to satisfy Rome's conscience and place a fig leaf over their abandonment of a long-standing ally. No wonder he was so surprised and indignant to find Caesar marching against him in 58. It is not hard to find signs of Caesar's bad conscience in his carefully constructed account of the prelude to the German campaign.[223]

But the collapse of the Aeduan perimeter, the rise of Ariovistus, and the revolt of the Allobroges were not all that will have troubled the Senate. An even more pressing adventitious development actually precipitated emergency preparations for an expanded war in Gaul in 60 itself (the very year, recall, of Caesar's election). In March 60, reports arrived that the Helvetii were raiding the Province (again, there is no sign of Pomptinus). This caused such alarm in Rome that the Senate suddenly changed the provincial assignments of the consuls to the two Gauls. Recruitment was ordered, military furloughs were cancelled, and an embassy was sent around to the Gallic communities warning them not to make common cause with the Helvetii.[224] By mid-May 60 the immediate war scare had died down, perhaps because of the internal strife among the Helvetii that Caesar records at the beginning of his work, but it would be surprising if the renewed preparations for the migration through Gaul that Caesar describes at the beginning of his work (unless these are pure fabrication) did not betray at least some sign of an impending confrontation in Transalpina over the next year and a half.[225] For the time being, the consul Q. Metellus

---

[222] App. *Celt.* 16: τοῖς Ῥωμαίοις κελεύουσι πεισθείς, ἀνέζευξεν ἀπὸ τῶν Αἰδούων; but cf. Caes. *BGall.* 1.31.15, 33.2.

[223] Consider how Caesar defers the information that Ariovistus was a Friend of the Roman People and indeed given diplomatic recognition through Caesar's own agency (first explicitly noted at 1.35.2) until *after* he has offered a compelling picture of the "barbarian's" violence and arrogance, not least against Rome's loyal friends the Aedui (1.31–34). By postponing this revelation he casts Ariovistus as one who has betrayed his friendship with Rome rather than the other way around. In general, see Christ 1974.

[224] Cic. *Att.* 1.19.2. Caes. *BGall.* 1.2–3 tells of diplomatic feelers allegedly put out by the Helvetic prince Orgetorix in 61 to leaders of the Sequani and Aedui.

[225] Caes. *BGall.* 1.2–5.

was disappointed at news of peace, his dreams of a triumph flitting away, and he does not seem to have gone to his province after the end of his year as consul.[226] Pomptinus seems to have been winding up his work against the Allobroges with at least enough success to make a plausible claim for a *supplicatio* early in 59 and, long after his return, a triumph in 54 – much delayed and in the face of strong resistance.[227]

This, then, was the situation across the Alps in the early summer of 60 when, as was normal according to the *lex Sempronia*, provinces were decreed for the consuls soon to be elected. As we noted toward the end of the previous chapter, Caesar was a shoo-in for the consulship, and Suetonius reports that "the *optimates*" had therefore seen to it that the Senate decreed provinces for the upcoming consuls that were characterized by "very minor duties (*minimi negotii*), that is forests and paths."[228] It is unfortunately very unclear what Suetonius has in mind here since *silvae callesque* does not otherwise appear in all our sources or narratives of the entire Roman Republic. A clue is provided by a reference in Tacitus to a province called *calles* given in AD 24 "according to ancient custom" (*vetere ex more*) to a quaestor, which led him to operate in the area of Apulia or (ancient) Calabria in southern Italy (*Ann.* 4.27.2). Possibly then under the Republic this *provincia* was normally assigned (when it was assigned) to a quaestor, which would explain its total absence from our relatively full record of consular provinces. But it is hard to believe, especially in view of the evidence soon to be reviewed of disturbances across the northern frontier at this time,

---

[226] See n. 237. A fragment of Nepos (fr. 15 Marshall) preserved by Pomponius Mela (3.45) and Pliny the Elder (*HN* 2.17) records the information that a king of the Suebi (*rege Sueborum* Pliny) or perhaps the Boii (Mela: *Botorum* or *Boorum* [Reinaldus]), gave some migrant Indians as a gift to Celer "while he was proconsul of Gaul." If Suebian, the king was probably not Ariovistus himself but perhaps an ally (cf. Caes. *BGall.* 1.37.3–4 with Kraner et al. 1964, 51.2, 54.1); if Boiian, this might be connected in some way with the invasion of Noricum (n. 243). If we knew Celer went out to a consular province we might date this to 59 (Fischer 2009: 439), but that is unlikely. Broughton sets the event during Metellus's praetorian proconsulship in Cisalpina in 62 (*MRR* 1.176). Helvetic strife: Caes. *BGall.* 1.2–4.

[227] Note that Pomptinus had been unable to capture the rebel leader, Catugnatus (Dio 37.48.2), while Cicero's polite reference in *Prov. cons.* 32 implicitly concedes that one might have criticized Pomptinus for not following up his victory very energetically. Caesar at *BGall.* 1.6.3 throws cold water on the idea that the Allobroges had been definitively pacified. For Vatinius's – and presumably therefore Caesar's – objections to Pomptinus's *supplicatio* in April 59, see Cic. *Vat.* 30 with Schol. Bob., 149–150 St., explicated by Taylor 1951: 263–264; cf. De Libero 1992: 108. The supplications must date in or before April: Cic. *Att.* 2.7.3 *epulo*, with Bailey ad loc. It was Cato who led the opposition to Pomptinus's triumph (Cic. *Att.* 4.18.4; Dio 39.65; Itgenshorst 2005: no. 259). Pomptinus seems to have been a relatively nonpartisan military man (*vir militaris*: Sall. *Cat.* 45.1–2): he first emerges as a legate in the Spartacan war serving under Crassus and would later serve in the same office under Cicero in Cilicia.

[228] Or "forest tracks," if hendiadys: *silvae callesque*. Suet. *Iul.* 19.2.

that the Senate truly could have been so blinded by fears of Caesar even
before his tumultuous consulship and so negligent of the larger security
issues as to order not just one but both consuls to patrol the southern
woodland tracks of Italy.[229] It is tempting therefore to conclude that *silvae
callesque*, introduced as it is with *id est*, is merely a dismissive characterization
of the duties involved in *Italia provincia* or possibly even an interpolated
gloss by a scribe provoked by the unspecificity of *minimi negotii*.[230] Long ago
J. P. V. D. Balsdon suggested that the province was actually "Italy" and that
in reality this was not the result of a factional plot to deprive Caesar (who had
after all not yet been elected) of a chance at military glory (Bibulus, the
optimates' favored candidate according to Suetonius, would likewise have
suffered the same fate), but a kind of "holding pattern" to allow the consuls
to respond, after authorization by law or senatorial decree, to any emergent
threat, which, by now could very easily be anticipated in Transalpine Gaul or
possibly even over the Alpine passes to the north or northeast.[231] Balsdon's
hypothesis is usually rejected, it seems, as inconsistent with the Senate's
normal practice, but Fred Drogula has recently argued with some force that,
because the *lex Sempronia* (normally) required the Senate to determine the
consular provinces far before the consuls-designate would actually take the
field (about eighteen months, in fact), "it became strategically more prudent
to assign consuls to permanent *provinciae* that were near to likely military
priorities, like Spain, Gaul, Macedonia, and (eventually) Syria. Instead of
guessing what enemies would pose the greatest threat in the next year, the
senate placed consular armies in areas where major fighting was likely, but
not certain."[232] In view of the many uncertainties in the exceedingly scarce
evidence, we might be excused a bit of speculation based on the intriguing
fact that we know that three legions stood in Cisalpine Gaul, the obvious
departure point for military operations either in Transalpina or Illyricum.[233]

---

[229] Balsdon 1967a: 67: "Senators often behaved with childish folly, but not with such childish folly as
that."

[230] Balsdon 1939: 181–182 remains fundamental; various views are aired at Gelzer 1968: 65n2 and
Townend in Butler and Cary 1927/1982: 157–158. The problem seems not to have attracted much
attention of late.

[231] Balsdon 1939: 182, a suggestion taken up in more recent times by Seager 2002: 84. For possible
threats see later in this chapter.

[232] Drogula 2015: 299–300. The difficulty of prediction was even greater than Drogula supposes, since
consular elections normally occurred at this time in July, not October as he thinks (n. 144). Vervaet
2006 argues that the law did not actually require the Senate to determine the provinces in advance
but in practice this appears to be the norm, unless a crisis supervened.

[233] At the beginning of Caesar's *Gallic War Commentaries* (March 58) three legions were in winter
quarters in Aquileia: Caes. *BGall.* 1.7.2, 10.3; Dio 38.8.5. Plut. *Caes.* 14.10 and App. *BCiv.* 2.13/49
give only the sum total of Caesar's legions (four) after the addition of Transalpina. Cf. *Gallicanae
legiones* (Cic. *Cat.* 2.5), with Brunt 1971a: 465. Domaszewski supposed that two of these three

Perhaps the consular provinces decreed in early summer 60 for the consuls soon to be elected were in fact the unglamorous but strategically crucial provinces of Cisalpine Gaul and Illyricum, which might be dismissed as mere "forest tracks" by those who wished for a more aggressive military posture and sought to tar the *optimates* with conspiring to prevent this.

In making that perhaps tendentious allegation Suetonius may be giving us a taste of the argument that the tribune P. Vatinius offered to the People before they voted on the bill he proposed to give Caesar the provinces of Cisalpine Gaul and Illyricum for five years. Given our survey of the troubled state of Gaul across the Alps, we can be fairly sure that Caesar already had his eye on the province where, as it turned out, he would in fact commit himself in his quest for glory.[234] Yet we happen to know that Transalpine Gaul was not in fact included in the law that the People now passed (the *lex Vatinia*), but that instead it was added by a *decree of the Senate*, probably on a motion submitted by Caesar's now son-in-law, Pompey. And an interesting consequence of the fact that this crucial province (as at least it would turn out) was assigned only by a senatorial decree and not by a law of the People was that the Senate could take it back at any time it wished.[235]

Why then did Vatinius not grab Transalpine Gaul, far the most likely trouble spot, while he was in the very process of putting before the assembly a law to define Caesar's provinces? To account for this puzzling omission it is widely assumed that Caesar was loath to take Transalpine Gaul from the man to whom it had (as is usually supposed) been assigned,

legions had been Caesar's in Spain, but there is no evidence (accepted by Ottmer 1979: 16n53; Fischer 2009: 437–438).

[234] Suet. *Iul.* 22.1 claims that "Gaul" was the focus of Caesar's attention from the start (*idonea … materia triumphorum*). In the anecdote that immediately follows (22.2), "what he passionately desired" (*quae concupisset*) was not just what had been given by the *lex Vatinia* but the whole package culminating in Transalpina (Maier 1978: 31).

[235] Pelling 2011: 200–201. The Senate's formal control by this means over Caesar's making war in Transalpine Gaul would be removed only by the *lex Pompeia Licinia* in 55. Suet. *Iul.* 22.1; Cic. *Att.* 8.3.3; cf. *Prov. cons.* 36 *quae pars provinciae sit cui non possit intercedi,* correctly interpreted by Butler and Cary 1924: 69: "The detachment of this province [Transalpina] from Caesar could have been simply effected by the appointment of a consular successor in accordance with the Sempronian Law, under which the tribune's veto was barred." Grillo 2015: 248 is slightly confused: it would be no violation of the Sempronian Law to reassign a province originally assigned under that law – nor, in fact, had Transalpina been assigned to Caesar under the *lex Sempronia* anyway. It is true that *quae pars provinciae cui non possit intercedi* appears to acknowledge implicitly that a veto *would* be permissible against reassigning Cisalpina; Butler and Cary are probably correct to infer that since such a decree would directly violate the five-year assignment under the *lex Vatinia* a tribune would be able to justify "defending" that province with a veto despite the *lex Sempronia,* a threat that could be backed up by a new bill overturning any senatorial reassignment of Cisalpina. On the *lex Sempronia* and the ban on the veto see Vervaet 2006.

Q. Metellus Celer, consul in 60 and a formidable aristocrat; but that when Metellus suddenly and providentially died early in the year, the province in which Caesar would in fact make his name was now open to be transferred to him, which the Senate was willing to effect now as a tactical concession to avoid inevitably being overruled by the popular assembly.[236] But the hypothesis is a house of cards. No source actually connects his death to the Senate's reassignment of Transalpina to Caesar. We do not actually know for certain whether Celer (rather than his colleague L. Afranius) had even been assigned Transalpine Gaul during the Helvetic scare of 60; in any case it looks as if he had never set foot in whatever province was assigned him, and our evidence suggests that C. Pomptinus simply continued undisturbed in his command of Transalpina well into 59.[237] Moreover, we hear that Celer was involved in the opposition to Caesar's first agrarian law (which not only places him in Rome early in the year but also raises the question why a prominent opponent would be treated with so much more consideration than were Lucullus, Cato, and Bibulus), and anyway he died in Rome in April, or perhaps already in March (so Metellus could have offered no hindrance to his province's transfer in a law passed almost certainly after his death).[238] Overall, then, as Broughton pointed out long ago, it is better to leave Metellus out of our interpretation of the *lex Vatinia* and its supplementation by senatorial decree.[239]

Our sources fail us on this point, so speculation is inevitable. In view of the immediate background of serious trouble in Transalpine Gaul, it is best to assume that Caesar intended all along to open up an avenue for intervention there. If that is so, the *lex Vatinia* assigning to him Cisalpine Gaul and Illyricum for five years provided a secure basis for extensive military action along the northern frontier without fear of

---

[236] The Metellus hypothesis goes back at least to Gelzer (1968: 85) and is still alive and well (e.g. Jehne 2001: 44; Goldsworthy 2006: 176; Billows 2009: 122). See p. 156ff. on Suet. *Iul.* 22.2. Date of Metellus's death: n. 238.

[237] Uncertain allocation of the provinces in 60: Cic. *Att.* 1.19.2, 20.5; Broughton, *MRR* 2.183 thinks Metellus "probably" received Transalpina but gives no reason. Metellus blocked from going out to his province: Dio 37.50.4. Pomptinus was voted a *supplicatio* for his "victory" against the Allobroges by April (n. 227); evidently the reassignment of the consular provinces for the consuls of 60 did go into effect, at least in Transalpina (*MRR* 2.185).

[238] Metellus had refused to take the required oath to Caesar's first agrarian law: Dio 38.7.1 with n. 99. (For the background of his resistance to Pompey's plans in 60 see *MRR* 2.183; Gruen 1974: 71, 85–87; Seager 2002: 81–82.) His death is best put in March: see Cic. *Att.* 2.5.2 (April) with Bailey's comment: if Cicero truly saw him on his deathbed (*Cael.* 59–60), March is the likely month since Cicero had left Rome around the beginning of April. The allegation of poisoning, if not merely Cicero's rhetorical fancy, may suggest that Metellus was taken away by a sudden illness. For the date of the *lex Vatinia*, see n. 209.

[239] Broughton 1948: 73–76, supported by Taylor 1951: 266.

removal,[240] but in return, as a concession to the Senate's dignity and presumably to appease some of the opposition likely in a year like this one, operations in Gaul across the Alps would require initial senatorial approval and at least tacit acceptance thereafter. The law saw to it that Caesar would possess significant military resources for a major campaign of conquest launched from northern Italy (three legions were in Cisalpina) without having to fear premature replacement while simultaneously setting a reasonable temporal limit.[241] The length of the campaign implicitly envisioned was by no means unheard of, even in more recent times than Marius's six-year run against the Cimbri and Teutones (105–100). A more immediate and exact precedent was provided by Pompey's five years of *imperium* prosecuting two related wars in succession (67–62). To Roman voters and even to senators such as Cicero, Pompey's commands were an unqualified success, hardly an erosion of the constitution. Indeed the temporal limits imposed by the *leges Gabinia* and *Vatinia* may have been a reaction to the excessive ambitions or recklessness shown recently by Lucullus and enabled or tolerated by his senatorial allies.[242] The kind of large-scale campaign implicitly envisioned by the *lex Vatinia* can hardly have been justified (as it had to be before the People) by anything less than the troubled state of Transalpine Gaul, although the recent invasion of Noricum and the attack on its capital, Noreia (only about 150 Roman miles northeast of Aquileia in what is now southern Austria), by the Boii, a central European Celtic people who subsequently turn up in Caesar's *Gallic War Commentaries* as subjects or allies of the Helvetii, may have also raised some alarms in

---

[240] It is usually supposed from Cic. *Prov. cons.* 37 that the law named an explicit date – namely March 1, 54 – before which replacement of Caesar in Cisalpina or Illyricum would be illegal (Pelling 2011: 285). It may be, however, that this date (which is less than five years after the likely date when the *lex Vatinia* was passed) was merely an improvisation in the debate of 56.

[241] See n. 233.

[242] Lucullus had commanded the war against Mithridates for no less than nine years and had to be extracted by a law of the People (74–66; see Cic. *Leg. Man.* 26: [Lucullus] *vestro iussu coactus qui imperi diuturnitati modum statuendum vetere exemplo putavistis*). Very long military commands had in recent times been enabled by the post-Sullan Senate rather by the popular assembly: cf. besides Lucullus, Q. Metellus Pius (cos. 80) in Farther Spain for no fewer than nine years (79–71), P. Servilius Vatia (cos. 79) in Cilicia for five years (78–74), C. Scribonius Curio (cos. 76) in Macedonia also for five years (76–72), and M. Aurelius Cotta (cos. 74) for five years in Bithynia (74–70), all regular senatorial consular assignments with corresponding prorogation. Pompey, by contrast, had wrapped up his three-year command against the pirates within less than one year and finished the job against Mithridates in three, for a stretch of *imperium* in toto of just over five years. In short, in the post-Sullan period "popular" laws had been a more effective means of keeping the length of generals' commands within limits than the Senate, which was predictably loath to put constraints on those it had in effect commissioned. Gruen 1974: 534–543 on the late-republican extraordinary commands is still worth reading.

Rome for the security of eastern Cisalpina.[243] The possibility of a forward
defense to the east of Cisalpina may explain the explicit assignment of
"Illyricum" under the *lex Vatinia*, which up to now seems normally to
have been thought of as part of a single north Italian security zone best
kept united under one command, that of Cisalpina; it rarely appears to
have been assigned separately at this time, on those occasions typically as
a praetorian province.[244] It is frequently supposed that the assignment of
Illyricum (and not of Transalpina) under the *lex Vatinia* shows that
Caesar's initial target was in the Balkan region until the Helvetic migration fortuitously supervened, but there is no evidence for a sufficient
threat to Roman security in that area at this time to justify committing to
it all readily available military resources at the very time when, as we have
seen, the situation in Gaul across the Alps was clearly precarious.[245]

The solution may be that Vatinius and Caesar were more restrained or
more cautious in their treatment of the Senate than we usually suppose,
influenced as we are by the sharply polemical tone of our sources for
this year. And yet there is really no good way around the conclusion that
Caesar and Vatinius *did* exercise restraint by not including Transalpina

[243] Caes. *BGall.* 1.5.4. Perhaps this is why three legions were wintering at Aquileia in 59/58 (n. 233).
Noreia (whose site is still not securely identified) was the ill-famed site of the first of the devastating
defeats the migrating Cimbri administered in 113 – disasters that still cast a distinct shadow over
Caesar's narrative in the *Gallic War Commentaries* (*MRR* 1.535; see 1.7.4, 10.2, 12.5–7, 13.2–14.5, 28.4,
33.4; 2.4.2–3, 29.4; 7.77.12–14.) For the Boii see also 1.25.6, 28.5, 29.2, and Göbl 1994.

[244] Shackleton Bailey, *Epp. Fam.* 1.353. Cf. Brunt 1971a: 429–430 with 432–433 (Table XIII), 463–466,
567–568, Dzino 2010: 81–83; Santangelo 2016: 104–105. There is no good evidence for the regular
assignment of Illyricum alone before Augustus.

[245] Initial target Illyricum: e.g. Brunt 1971a: 464; Maier 1978: 30–32; De Libero 1992:107–109; Williams
2001: 2; Jehne 2009: 71–73; Billows 2009: 126; Drogula 2015: 316; Santangelo 2016: 104 flirts with
the idea that Caesar intended to devote the "early phase" of his command to Illyricum but more
plausibly adds that "on the basis of the surviving evidence, it is not far-fetched to argue that the
addition of Illyricum to Cisalpina had an essentially preventive nature, and gave Caesar scope to
carry out military operations beyond northeast Italy" (if necessary, I would simply add). Scholars
often cite the rise of the Dacian king Burebista as a possible justification or pretext for intervention
(Hoffmann 1952: 8; cf. Timpe 1965: 193–194; Santangelo 2016: 104); however, there is no evidence
that his activities, still far to the east, provoked any Roman concern at all before the civil war (Dzino
2010: 82; cf. Zippel 1877: 180–223). Brennan 2000: 809n331 perceives a "threat from the Illyrians ca.
59," but can only adduce the modest raids of 53 and 52 (Hirtius ap. Caes. *BGall.* 8.24.3) – a *petitio
principii* for our purposes. The last non-negligible military activity we know to have been
undertaken by a (praetorian) proconsul of Illyricum took place in 78–76: C. Cosconius's capture
of Salonae (*MRR* 2.86–87). Hoffmann thought L. Afranius had won his triumph (Cic. *Pis.* 58)
fighting Alpine peoples in Cisalpina in 59, but the lack of space in a preserved section of the *Fasti
triumphales* shows that the triumph must be placed much earlier and now connected with Spain
(Degrassi, *I.It.* 13.1, p 565; Itgenshorst 2005: 349–350, no. 254; Rich 2014: 251, no. 254). Fischer 1985:
13–14 (cf. 2004: 311, 2009: 440) thinks that at this time Caesar concluded the treaty with the
"Iapydes" that Cicero mentions at *Balb.* 32 (along with treaties with various Gallic peoples,
including the Helvetii) in order to free his hands to march against Gaul, but this is pure speculation
since Cicero gives neither date, nor author, nor context of the treaty.

(a province ripe for military adventure if there ever was one) in the law. We are left to ponder why they would have done so. They may have been wary of adding to their *adversarii* in the Senate. The assignment of provinces by the popular assembly was always a bit of a slap in the face for senators.[246] But, it would lessen the insult if it was left to the Senate to pull the trigger on a major war effort across the Alps, and it was a notable act of trust to serve in Transalpina at the Senate's pleasure. Yet on the other hand, this was not a blind leap of faith on Caesar's part. Any attempt by the Senate to replace him before he thought his work was done was virtually certain to be blocked by a tribune (a veto against the regular senatorial determination of consular provinces under the *lex Sempronia* was impossible, but not a new law of the People adding Transalpina to Caesar's other provinces). Nor would his enemies, if they managed to extract him from Transalpina against his will, wish to contemplate his hovering in northern Italy for years or months with the three legions that had been Cisalpina's original complement, quite apart from the fact that major military activity in Transalpina would depend on close cooperation with the governor of Cisalpine Gaul.[247] If the Senate were driven by his enemies to reject the hand of conciliation he extended, he could, of course, resort again to the People to get what he wanted: this is in fact exactly what Suetonius says the Senate feared when they "gave" him the province of Gaul beyond the Alps.[248]

In short, under these circumstances Caesar had sufficient assurances that he would, in fact, get his "great command, an army, a new war ... that would permit his excellence to shine forth" (Sall. *Cat.* 54.4) and also that he would not be dragged back prematurely from it. He could therefore make a notable gesture of good faith to the moderate center of the Senate, which after all he could also hope and expect to win over by means of his success. The near-genocidal rhetoric Cicero indulges in a few years later (in 56) to persuade the Senate to allow Caesar to complete his conquest of the peoples of Gaul – "tribes which no one who ever lived would not wish to see crushed and subdued" (*Prov. cons.* 33) – shows that a great war against one of Rome's oldest and most dangerous foes, hated and feared since the

---

[246] See n. 236.

[247] Here "northern Italy" = Cisalpina. The administrative boundary did not prevent Caesar from regularly referring to the region as *Italia* in his *Commentarii*: Chapter 5, n. 52. Transalpina had at times been assigned as a unified command with Cisalpina in the past, most recently under Caesar's old enemy, the consul C. Piso, who fought the Allobroges in 67–65: Brunt 1971a: 465.

[248] Suet. *Iul.* 22.1: *mox per senatum Comatam* [= Transalpina] *quoque, veritis patribus ne, si ipsi negassent, populus et hanc daret.*

capture of the City by a Gallic band in 367, was bound to mobilize public support, both for the war and for a victorious commander.[249] Beating down "barbarian arrogance" was indisputably a *good* thing in the Roman tradition, so long as some fig leaf of justification could be excogitated to cover the nakedness of the commander's ambition.[250] Even so, the actions Caesar took across the Alps would have to be justifiable to the Senate on an annual basis. The clock was ticking: he would need to have impressive victories to show for himself at the end of each campaigning season in order to ward off any attempt to relieve him before he had achieved his goals.

Despite the evidence that the *lex Vatinia* was publicly justified by the need to assure the security of Italy and Gaul across the Alps and the reasonable assumption drawn from Caesar's past history (including his Spanish command and his "lost" triumph) that the command was personally motivated by his pursuit of *gloria*, it is sometimes suggested that the *lex Vatinia* was actually a means for extending triumviral dominance over Rome well into the future or a clever device to put off or even avoid altogether Caesar's prosecution for (supposed) legal or constitutional violations in his consulship.[251] (Or both.) But there was no realistic prospect of prosecuting and especially of convicting him, as I shall argue later in more detail.[252] Moreover, as we will see in the final section of this chapter, after the expiration of his consulship he remained away from his army (at the moment consisting of three legions in the northeast corner of "Italy," in Aquileia) and within easy reach of Rome until mid-March while with ostentatious correctness, he referred the question of the legality of his actions to the Senate. Caesar's army soon moved across the Alps and there is precious little hint in our sources that his military resources served to intimidate the Senate or individual senators until at least the major confrontation over his return in the late 50s.[253] To interpret Caesar's command at this early date as little more than a weapon of dominance

---

[249] Williams 2001: 2–3, 170–182 on the long history of the deep-rooted Roman fear of the Gauls, a sense of which can be taken from the fact that at three crisis moments of confrontation with Gauls from 228 to 114, a pair of Gauls were ritually sacrificed in the Forum Boarium (pp. 173–175).

[250] Collins 1972: 922–942; Brunt 1979; Riggsby 2006: 157–189.

[251] E.g. Tatum 2008: 45, 74; Billows 2009: 121–122. Meier 1982: 209 (cf. 213), on the other hand, sees the "violent and illegal means" by which Caesar "assert[ed] himself against the Senate" as the *consequence* rather than the cause of his need for an "extraordinary command."

[252] Chapter 6, p. 259ff. and Appendix 2.

[253] On Cicero's imaginary threat by Pompey *Att.* 2.16.2 *"oppressos vos" inquit "tenebo exercitu Caesaris"* see n. 184. Cic. *Sest.* 40 *exercitum in Italia maximum* is an invidious representation of *Clodius's* bluster, not Caesar's, and in any case belongs to the short period before the legions at Aquileia moved across the Alps.

over his (and his allies') enemies is to exaggerate the severity of the crisis of the year 59. Caesar's consulship had indeed been tumultuous and controversial, but the Republic was still far from teetering on the brink of civil war.

The Formal Validity of Caesar's Legislation

There is little doubt that Caesar's success in breaking through the legislative logjam created by years of persistent obstructionism ruffled a good many feathers. Bibulus's near boycott of public duties and disappearance from public view made for some pretty good jokes ("that was done in the consulship of Julius and Caesar," "I don't remember anything done in Bibulus's consulship"),[254] but such grim jocularity cannot overcome the impression that the unprecedented complete or nearly complete absence of one of the consuls for at least eight months of the year must have been deeply disconcerting even to some of those voters who had been enthusiastically passing the long list of bills that, while certainly realizing Pompey's and to a lesser extent Crassus's long-standing agendas (the two agrarian laws, ratification of Pompey's eastern settlement, and the partial remission of the cost of the *publicani*'s tax contract) as well as Caesar's own desire for a major command, were also in each case reasonably well-founded, readily justifiable responses to political issues and concerns that had merited serious attention over the immediately preceding years.[255] These laws in truth only take on the partisan coloring that they do in most of our accounts because the opposition adopted such an uncompromisingly rejectionist attitude toward them, in fact refusing almost entirely even to engage in public deliberation and to raise any substantive point against them,[256] and the Julian extortion law (virtually ignored for this very reason by our sources) demonstrates that Caesar's energy was not focused solely on a partisan agenda imposed by his powerful senior allies. (Even so, this did not deter Bibulus from seeking to invalidate this law as well as the others: he must have "watched the skies" during the passage of this one too, and when he prepared to return from his province of Syria in 50, he refused

---

[254] Dio 38.8.2: ὡς καὶ μόνος αὐτῆς [sc. τῆς πόλεως] ἄρχων; Suet. *Iul.* 20.2: *unus . . . omnia in re publica et ad arbitrium administravit.*

[255] See n. 207.

[256] Occasional tirades by Cato may have constituted an exception (Plut. *Cat. Min.* 33.2, 5; it is unclear whether Cato's "shout" described at *Caes.* 14.8 took place in an assembly or the Senate or perhaps neither), but Plutarch is so strongly influenced by the eulogistic tradition on Cato that these few scraps do not carry much conviction. Dio 38.7.5: "Even Cato made no objection" (οὐδὲ γὰρ οὐδ' ὁ Κάτων ἀντεῖπέ τι.

to file his accounts in the province as instructed by the *lex Iulia repetundarum*, evidently because he would not recognize its validity.)[257]

The opponents of the Three, of course, tried to capitalize on the unprecedented change of the public face of the Republic. Did Bibulus's steadfast "watching of the skies" (supposedly) during every legislative vote of 59 legally invalidate all of Caesar's legislation?[258] Some scholars have taken this bit of partisan cant much too seriously. As we saw in the aftermath of the passage of the first agrarian law, the Senate had the power to annul legislation passed *contra auspicia*.[259] Yet when it had its opportunity to do so at the beginning of 58, shortly after Caesar had vacated the consulship (and probably after he had formally crossed the city boundary and thus could no longer participate in the debate in person without losing his *imperium*), the attack on Caesar's *acta* launched by two of the new praetors, C. Memmius and L. Domitius Ahenobarbus, failed as utterly as had Bibulus's effort after the first *lex agraria*.[260] (It is noteworthy that the consuls, allies of Pompey and Caesar, did not block the praetors' unusual referral in the presence of both consuls – itself arguably a concession to the rights and authority of the Senate.)[261] The question

---

[257] Cic. *Fam.* 2.17.2.

[258] Apparently Bibulus's three tribunician allies had also joined him in "watching the skies" every day (*Vat.* 16 with Schol. Bob. 146 St.).

[259] For the debate of early 58 see also Chapter 5, p. 192f.

[260] Suet. *Iul.* 23.1 *Functus (sc. Caesar) consulatu Gaio Memmo Lucioque Domitio praetoribus de superioris anni actis referentibus cognitionem senatui detulit; nec illo suscipiente triduoque per inritas altercationes absumpto in provinciam abiit.* It is generally supposed (e.g. Ramsey 2009: 37) that the last words refer to his formal crossing of the *pomerium* on the grounds that Caesar delivered three speeches in rebuttal and therefore appears to have been present (Suet. *Iul.* 73.1; Schol. Bob. 130, 146 St.). Yet Suetonius pointedly says that Caesar *rescripserat*, which implies a written response to Memmius's invectives (n. 262; see Blom 2016: 173). Further, Suet. *Iul.* 23.1 and Schol. Bob. 146 St. both use language that implies that Caesar left the matter to the Senate with all formal correctness, probably therefore absenting himself. Finally, in this case we know that Caesar did not immediately depart for his province upon crossing the *pomerium* but waited outside the City at least until the promulgation of Clodius's law on *provocatio* (Dio 38.17.1; Plut. *Caes.* 14.17, Cic. 30.5) around mid-March (Caes. *BGall.* 1.6.4–7.1, with Plut. *Caes.* 17.5); in such a case *in provinciam abiit* is actually not identical to *pomerium transgressus est*. The evidence therefore is most consistent with the hypothesis that Caesar had already crossed the *pomerium* by the time of the senatorial debates, which probably, in view of Suetonius's phrasing, took place at the very beginning of the new year. Cic. *Sest.* 40 is too general to force the conclusion that the three-day discussion Suetonius mentions was still taking place at the time of Cicero's withdrawal. See Pocock 1926: 97 against the relevance of Cic. *Vat.* 15 to this episode.

[261] On the rarity of praetors summoning the Senate even while consuls are present in the City, see Mommsen 1887: 2:129–30 with n. 3; Brennan 2000: 115, 470, who assumes that the praetors made the *relatio* under the presidency of the consuls. Possibly Suetonius is using *referre* in a nontechnical sense for a *request* to put a motion to the Senate (i.e. *relationem postulare*), a practice Bonnefond-Coudry 1989: 454–461 describes. The fact remains that the consuls permitted a *relatio* proposed by the praetors to which they could be assumed to be hostile.

seems to have been fully aired since three days were consumed discussing the praetors' request before it was shelved.[262] The acrimonious discussion, however, led nowhere: another setback for Caesar's enemies who might have hoped to get farther now that their target was out of office.

The failure of the attack on Caesar's *acta* in the Senate of course did not amount to a full-throated endorsement of their legality or legitimacy. The issue of their legal validity gained enough traction to reemerge at crisis points throughout the decade as a way of at least annoying the proconsul of Gaul or his ally, Pompey.[263] But in lieu of a formal annulment, which had failed, Caesar's legislation henceforth was – and in a functioning legal system no doubt had to be – treated de facto as formally valid until specifically overturned.[264] Virtually all senators, including even Cato, had sworn an oath to uphold the first agrarian law after it was passed; an oath was not an easy thing to undo, even if one could try to resort to the tangled argument that the law that imposed the oath was "not a law."[265] Cicero (not the most objective source) insisted in one of his attacks on the legality of Clodius's tribunate that even without prying into the "secret books" of augural law, it was generally known that it was *nefas* to hold an assembly after a magistrate had announced that he was "watching the skies."[266] And indeed in 58, Clodius had invited some augurs (how many?) to a *contio* to declare their opinion that Caesar's *acta* were invalidated by his refusal to respect Bibulus's *servatio*; they thus expressed their expert opinion on religious law, but this was not a decree of the augural college, much less a formal decision of the Senate, which, according to an entrenched principle of the Republic, had to request and then execute

---

[262] Memmius published his invectives against Caesar, a sample of which is given at Suet. *Iul.* 49.2 (*ORF* 125.III, p. 403), a scurrilous reference to the old charge about Nicomedes that serves to remind us that Memmius's speeches significantly contributed to the anti-Caesar invective tradition. Caesar gave as good as he got and published no fewer than three speeches of apologia and invective (Suet. *Iul.* 73.1 and *ORF* 121.VIII, pp. 393–394). Cicero claims that the "Three" were deeply anxious about the fate of Caesar's legislation at this time (*Prov. cons.* 43, *Sest.* 40, *Pis.* 79).

[263] Most notably later in 58, at the instigation of Clodius (Tatum 1999: 167–174), and again in 56 (although this attack was ostensibly narrowly tailored to the *lex Campana*: see n. 273). Cicero claims to have used pro-Bibulan language in his defense of Sestius (*Fam.* 1.9.7), which, however, does not appear in the published version of the speech. Cf. *Sest.* 135, *Prov. cons.* 45.

[264] De Libero 1992: 58 (who however grants the protest too much weight "bei einem relativ geschlossenen Senat" [68, cf. 63n53, 100–101]). "The Senate" was hardly unified in the early 50s against Pompey, Crassus, and Caesar, all of whose *dignitas* was wrapped up with the preservation of Caesar's *acta*. Nor does it look right to say, with Goldsworthy 2006: 173, that "the Romans themselves" were uncertain whether Caesar's acta remained formally valid, unless and until they were formally invalidated.

[265] See n. 99.

[266] Cic. *Dom.* 39 *negant fas esse agi cum populo, cum de caelo servatum sit.* Cf. *Vat.* 15. See n. 108.

a priestly judgment for it to have legal effect.[267] Furthermore, quite apart from the larger practical question of the wisdom of allowing Bibulus's unprecedented expansion of this obstructive tactic to stand, it could be reasonably argued that he had not properly announced his *servatio*.[268] It appears to have been a rule of long standing that obnuntiation had to be performed in person, not by edict: "Ironically, Caesar was the traditionalist."[269] (Perhaps not really so "ironic": he was the *pontifex maximus*.) Driediger-Murphy has noted that there is no evidence in this entire episode that Bibulus ever actually reported any contrary signs seen by him during his persistent examination of the heavens throughout all of Caesar's legislative assemblies (Cic. *Har. resp.* 48); the vagueness is curious and unusual, and prompts the suspicion either that Bibulus did not follow up with a report of signs actually observed or, if he did, that they were not taken very seriously.[270] (A charge of "falsifying the auspices" was no small matter, as is shown by the censure [*nota*] against C. Ateius Capito imposed by the censor Ap. Claudius in 50, and the catastrophic consequences of such a misrepresentation of the divine will could fall on the entire community.)[271] Finally, the ceremony of *servatio* began at midnight before

---

[267] Cic. *Dom.* 40, *Har. resp.* 48. This declaration may have been the source for Cicero's "knowledge" just cited (n. 266). Cic. *Phil.* 2.81 shows that *servatio* was the only legitimate way to declare one's expectation of contrary omens in the future, but does not show that in itself the announcement sufficed in itself to abort an assembly. For the requirement of senatorial validation, see Beard, North, and Price 1998: 1:29; cf. 105–108. Cf. e.g. the Senate's decision to order the consuls of 162 to resign on the basis of a decision by the augural college (Cic. *Nat. D.* 2.10–11). Cicero therefore vastly exaggerates the power of a single augur at *Leg.* 2.31. Similarly, Antony's auspicial objection to Dolabella's election in 44 needed, according to Cicero, to be examined by the college of augurs as a whole (Cic. *Phil.* 2.83), evidently after referral to the Senate (2.88 and Chapter 9).

[268] Driediger-Murphy 2019: 136–137, 144 with n. 61: "Even Cicero never states that Bibulus actually made an *obnuntiatio* [which Driediger-Murphy applies to the formal announcement of a *servatio* as well as the more common announcement of contrary omens: 137], probably because his failure to do so in person meant that technically he had not." Cf. Linderski 1965: 425–426. See n. 284.

[269] Tatum 2008: 74. See his full discussion, pp. 72–74, and n. 108. More recent bibliography on the point in Driediger-Murphy 2019: 144n59.

[270] In Driediger-Murphy's view, what mattered was simply that Bibulus was watching the skies, not what he had seen (2019: 145–148). She makes a good case that "*servare de caelo* itself, when announced via a formally correct *obnuntiatio*, [was] technically sufficient to prohibit assemblies" (148), but a "technically sufficient" objection does not make it necessarily decisive, especially when the practice was used in an unprecedented, absolutist way. At p. 156 she acknowledges that "an actual sign would have been thought to carry more weight than a mere announcement of sky-watching" – that is, some kind of judgment of its authenticity and legitimacy would still be required.

[271] Cic. *Div.* 1.29–30. See Driediger-Murphy 2018 and 2019: 157: "In our revised view of sky-watching, as in other forms of augury, Romans did not endorse the outright fabrication or falsification of signs." Cic. *Phil.* 2.81–83 attacking Antony's alleged falsification of the auspices at the supplementary consular election of 44 (discussed in Chapter 9) demonstrates that one could be called upon to account for one's auspicial pronouncements with some specificity (*Quid videras, quid senseras, quid audieras?*), and that a failure to do so would undermine the claim.

a given assembly and would usually have been completed by dawn; perhaps its sacral validity could be extended into the following day, but it is hard to believe that anyone thought, in the absence of any clear precedent, that it was unproblematically consistent with custom or religious law for it to continue right through the following night, much less extended indefinitely (even if simply repeated every day).[272] Such shenanigans were self-deconstructing, particularly since they seem to have been unprecedented.

The half-hearted attempt in 56 to halt distribution of the Campanian land, whatever the true motives behind it, was publicly justified, it seems, not by reference to the legal status of the *lex Iulia* but by the state of the public coffers.[273] Pompey's eastern arrangements were never, so far as we know, challenged on the basis of Bibulus's continuous *servatio*, nor was P. Clodius's transfer to the plebs ever seriously thrown into doubt, though Cicero could toy gleefully with the notion.[274] In fact, it was none other than Cato who insisted upon the legality of Clodius's adoption in order to validate the legal basis of his own mission to Cyprus in 56, established by a law proposed by Clodius and thus potentially jeopardized by the question of Clodius's legal status: "It would be violently disruptive to vote to annul so many decrees and official acts."[275] In speeches of 56 Cicero not only treats Caesar's *repetundae* law of 59 as formally valid before a senatorial audience but calls it an *optima lex*;[276] while in 54, Cato himself, who when presiding as praetor over the extortion court could not escape taking a position on Caesar's new *repetundae* law, enforced the Julian laws while refusing to speak their name.[277] One would suppose that the *lex Vatinia*, which put such an important war and large military assets in Caesar's hands, would be a continuous target for Bibulus and his ilk. Indeed, when in 56 the provinces for the next consuls were being debated in the Senate, the possibility of replacing Caesar despite the *lex Vatinia* was for the first time seriously put on the table, yet both major motions that pursued this end were carefully crafted so as not to conflict with the *lex Vatinia*, even

[272] Driediger-Murphy 2019: 148–154.
[273] Cic. *Q. fr.* 2.6.1 with Lintott 1968: 135n2; Brunt 1971a: 316–317; Mitchell 1991: 177–178. (Of course, Caesar and Pompey could still not view the move with indifference (*Fam.* 1.9.9).) Cf. n. 91.
[274] Cic. *Dom.* 39–42, *Har. resp.* 48. For Cicero's formal objections to Clodius's election, including Bibulus's *servatio* and an alleged violation of the *lex Caecilia Didia*, see Tatum 1999: 104–108 with 125–133. This, of course, provided the basis (such as it was) for Cicero's frequent and fruitless complaint that Clodius's laws should be treated as invalid (e.g. *Prov. cons.* 45 with Grillo 2015: 286–294 with bibliography).
[275] Plut. *Cic.* 34.2; cf. *Cat. Min.* 40.2–3. Morrell 2018: 194–199 plausibly analyzes Cato's subtle legal thinking on this point.
[276] Cic. *Prov. cons.* 7; *Sest.* 135.   [277] Dio 38.7.5 with n. 200.

while their authors added the caveat (explicitly or implicitly) that they denied it really was a law.[278] If the Vatinian Law "was not a law," then the three legions Caesar had taken to Transalpina to form the core of his army there were not legally under his command, yet already by the end of 57 the Senate voted unprecedented supplications in honor of Caesar's victories against the Gauls and Germans.[279] Cicero concedes in his interrogation of Vatinius in the trial of P. Sestius in 56 that he "obeyed your laws, however they were passed."[280] If Cicero and Cato both went along with the laws of Vatinius and of Caesar, we can fairly assume that the rest of the senators did so as well – except, perhaps, for Bibulus. In July 50 Cicero pointedly urged Bibulus's quaestor in Syria to file his accounts as required by Caesar's extortion law despite the fact that his commander disregarded it on his own personal interpretation (*certa quadam ratione*); "I strongly urge you to observe it," he writes (*tibi magno opere servandam* [sc. *legem Iuliam*] *censeo*).[281] For Bibulus, it was something of a personal campaign to seek to undermine the legitimacy of *all* of Caesar's legislation (no matter how admirable). But his protests in 59 and later hardly "kept Caesar's legislation technically invalid," even if a great deal of ironical emphasis is placed on the word "technically."[282] This was a partisan interpretation not unlike modern partisan disputes over the legitimacy of presidential elections or nominations to the US Supreme Court; such judgments might cast a shadow over the results but hardly suffice to invalidate them.[283]

---

[278] Cic. *Prov. cons.* 36 [sc. alter]: *ostendit eam se tenere legem quam esse legem neget ... alter ... legem quam non putat, eam quoque servat.* (Grillo 2015: 245–246 suspects Bibulus was the author of at least one of these motions, but note that both in practice recognized the *lex Vatinia* as valid, if only for prudential reasons.)

[279] Caes. *BGall.* 2.35.4. *Terror iniectus Caesari de eius actis* (Cic. *Prov. cons.* 43), which apparently refers to the *contio* mentioned above (n. 267), looks like a Ciceronian exaggeration.

[280] Cic. *Vat.* 37: *praesertim cum ego legibus tuis, quoquo modo latae sunt, pare120.*

[281] Cic. *Fam.* 2.17.2; see n. 257.

[282] So Broughton, *MRR* 2.187. Less restrained are: Gelzer 1968: 79: "Without doubt, all Caesar's acts to date were formally invalid as his opponents maintained"; Meier 1975: 197: "According to traditional practice the Senate would have been able, or indeed would have had to declare Caesar's laws (together with the other legislation of the year) invalid"; Jehne 2001: 45: "All the laws that were passed in 59 had therefore come about in an illegal manner and in principle could be declared invalid by the Senate"; Raaflaub 2010: 164: "Most political actions of an entire year were legally invalid."

[283] Many US Democrats believe George W. Bush was elected unconstitutionally in 2000 and that the Senate's refusal to consider Merrick Garland's nomination to the Supreme Court in 2016 was also unconstitutional. But very few of these would actually assert that therefore Mr. Bush was not really president or that Neil Gorsuch was not really appointed in Mr. Garland's place. Cicero plays with the same rationale to deny the legality of P. Clodius's transition to the plebs, of L. Piso's and A. Gabinius's election to the consulship, and apparently of M. Cato's mission to Cyprus, but hardly expects to be taken seriously, and in any case he wasn't (Cic. *Dom.* 39, *Prov. cons.* 45, *Pis.* 30; Dio 39.22.1 et al.; cf. Tatum 1999: 104–105; Grillo 2015: 286–294).

It was certainly advisable to clarify the legal position in case something like this ever happened again. So, already in 58 Publius Clodius, who rarely receives due recognition as a lawgiver, proposed and succeeded in passing a law explicitly ruling out obnuntiation by edict or by *servatio* alone without following up in person with a formal announcement of the contrary omen.[284] The principle was salutary: if public business was to be called off on account of the gods' displeasure, surely such signs should actually be observed rather than merely in prospect. The new law appears to have been more of a clarification of long-standing practice and custom rather than imposing any radical new restriction upon the "religious veto";[285] it did not challenge the religious assumptions on which obnuntiation was based but simply insisted, by means of a procedure of the utmost simplicity, that a plausible connection be asserted between the public business at hand and whatever one thought, or said, one had seen to prevent it. Attempts at obnuntiation and even *servatio* continue after 58 and were often successful in elections while, as had always been the case, they remain generally ineffective against legislation.[286] Thus the religious veto was hardly eliminated despite Cicero's rather hysterical lamentations for Clodius's supposedly outright demolition of the *leges Aelia et Fufia*, "which have always incapacitated and suppressed the madness of tribunes": it was still possible for one so empowered to announce contrary omens if he could simply bestir himself to do so on the spot.[287] But Bibulus's irresponsible attempt to expand its scope beyond all recognition had, quite properly, been repudiated.[288] Jeffrey Tatum observes:

> For all its potential usefulness in menacing if not overthrowing Caesar's legislation, Bibulus's obstructionism set a precedent whose dangers must have been obvious even to Bibulus's staunchest supporters: the thought that a disgruntled magistrate or tribune could, without so much as leaving his

---

[284] Tatum 1999: 125–133, building on the work of Meier and Mitchell, is lucid and persuasive. Contra De Libero 1992: 65–68, who also believes that the initial announcement of a *servatio* could customarily be made *per edictum* (p. 57; contra Driediger-Murphy 2019: 144). See n. 268.

[285] De Libero 1992: 58n29; Fezzi 1997; Tatum 1999: 129.

[286] De Libero 1992: 64n58, with the survey at 62–68. Cic. *Att.* 4.3.3–4 (57 BC) is a clear example; see also Cic. *Sest.* 78 and *Phil.* 2.81, 83 with Ramsey 2003 ad loc. and Chapter 9.

[287] For the *leges Aelia et Fufia*, which regulated various religious restrictions on public meetings including obnuntiation, see Fezzi 1997: 305–310; Elster 2003: 401–405, and the clear survey by Tatum 1999: 126–128.

[288] De Libero 1992: 67 assumes, without evidence, that Clodius's law was soon repealed. If that had been the case, Cicero, who never let pass an opportunity to mock Clodius, would not have overlooked such a humiliating repudiation of his enemy by the Senate. The quotation is from Cic. *Vat.* 18, which incidentally implies that the *lex Clodia* was still in force in 56.

house, paralyze the government for a year will not have been a prospect to please anyone.[289]

Bibulus had sought to make of *servatio* an unanswerable and unaccountable obstructive weapon against not just one law or election but all the official actions of a colleague of equal power, and the People, the source of statutory law in the Republic, gave their verdict with the *lex Clodia*.

Cicero refers obscurely and tantalizingly in a speech of 56 to an offer ostensibly made (by whom exactly we do not know) to resolve the legal/constitutional issue of the disregarded auspices by allowing Caesar to repeat the voting on his legislation but this time without technical hindrance.[290] This may first have been mooted in the debate at the beginning of 58.[291] More than a few scholars have expressed surprise and dismay at Caesar's failure to take up the offer, a compromise said to demonstrate "remarkable flexibility" "in the old tradition of *concordia*" on the part of his opponents while his refusal raises doubts about his "attitude to the Roman order" and perhaps even definitively made him an "Outsider" alienated from the Republic.[292] They do not seem to recognize the seriousness of the insult to the People, whose manifest approval of the laws would now be nullified and made hostage to the goodwill of the very parties that had striven so mightily to subvert their will over the previous year. Those who had flocked to Rome to vote on the agrarian laws or had even simply crossed the City to stand in line for hours to cast their ballot might not be disposed to do it all over again (which may, in fact, have been precisely the point of the offer), especially since their

---

[289] Tatum 1999: 132. I would slightly adjust the wording: Bibulus's tactics did not in fact "set a precedent" since they had not actually succeeded. They *might have* set a precedent if they had been accepted in practice. Cf. Billows 2009: 116.

[290] Cic. *Prov. cons.* 46: *condicio C. Caesari lata sit ut easdem res alio modo ferret, qua condicione auspicia requirebant, leges comprobabant.* Meier 1975 is fundamental but highly speculative (we can hardly be sure given Cicero's penchant for rhetorical misrepresentation that the offer came from a unified front of *principes civitatis* including Hortensius, Cato, with Bibulus's implicit approval [197–199]; cf. Grillo 2015: 299 "impossible for us to identify"). Badian 1990: 27–28 freights Caesar's refusal with enormous significance ("Civil war would not have come, at least as and when it came, and Caesar might have gone on, like Aemilianus, to attain his level of *dignitas* as an honoured *princeps* within the Senate"); for Jehne 2001: 47, the episode proves that the break between Caesar and "the senatorial opposition" was irreconcilable. Lundgreen 2011: 154n434 rightly raises doubts about both the legal jeopardy imposed by Bibulus's actions and the significance of this rather obscure moment.

[291] Badian 1990: 27n6; Meier 1975: 201–202 had suggested summer or fall of 59 (which seems too early for Bibulus et al. to acknowledge that they had utterly failed to block the legislation altogether); Seager 2002: 104 (followed by Tatum 1999: 173) suggests mid-58, with a new conjecture involving Cicero; Lintott 2008: 207n85 moves the offer down to 56, in which connection cf. Cic. *Vat.* 15: *primum quaero num tu senatui causam tuam permittas, quod facit Caesar?* (present tense used in 56).

[292] Quotations 1 and 3 from Meier 1982: 218–219 (for deeper analysis in this vein see Meier 1975: 204), 2 and 4 from Badian 1990: 27–28. Jehne 2001: 47: "astonishing" at first glance.

votes on those occasions were now to be nullified on the strength of a handshake (as it were: no specific assurance is mentioned). And quite apart from the People's rights in the matter, after the events of the past year Caesar would have been a fool to entrust the fate of his legislation to the self-restraint of his embittered enemies. Moreover, agreeing to this proposal would be tantamount to accepting the legitimacy of Bibulus's injudicious attempt vastly to expand the "religious veto." Not surprisingly, Caesar did not go for the bait and can hardly be faulted for that.

"Caesar was a legislating consul," writes Francisco Pina Polo, not perhaps entirely approvingly, to judge from what follows: "He was at least partly a legislator who would bypass the senate and even confront it if necessary . . . In that sense, Caesar acted more like some tribunes of the plebs than as a consul was expected to act."[293] Yet the bills he introduced, from the first agrarian law to the *lex Vatinia*, were justifiable responses to the challenges the Republic faced in 59, and whether or not we find them truly unobjectionable, they were approved by the Roman People, in some cases (certainly the first agrarian law, doubtless others) with great enthusiasm.[294] As for "bypassing the Senate," the sole clear example we have is that of the introduction of the first agrarian law, in which, to be bit more careful, Caesar did not bypass the Senate but gave up trying to obtain its approval when it was paralyzed by Cato's filibuster; as for "confronting" it we actually have no certain example at all.[295] Bibulus and Cato (and no doubt others in their camp who saw themselves as acting in behalf of the Senate's authority) chose to confront Caesar, but there was nothing inherent in the situation that forced them to do so rather than, say, co-opt Caesar's plans to win credit for the Senate's benevolent concern for the People's *commoda*.[296]

It is a commonplace among historians to deplore Caesar's methods in pushing through his (on the whole beneficial) legislation – put another way, of course, his success – as amounting to nothing less than a wholesale "violation" of the "constitution," "dumping out" (as Cicero would say) a whole series of long-established senatorial checks on the powers of

---

[293] Pina Polo 2011: 299. The judgment echoes that of Plut. *Caes.* 14.2: εὐθὺς εἰσέφερε νόμους οὐχ ὑπάτῳ προσήκοντας, ἀλλὰ δημάρχῳ τινὶ θρασυτάτῳ.

[294] See n. 207.

[295] On the contrary, the Senate had refused to confront *Caesar* after the passage of the first agrarian law, and thereafter there is, as we saw (pp. 154–160), no evidence of a serious confrontation or clash over legislation or otherwise. The senatorial decree that gave Caesar his chance to intervene in Transalpine Gaul (p. 175ff.), however prudential it may have been, is more illustrative of cooperation than confrontation.

[296] See n. 35.

magistrates and the People that constituted the essence of republican government, not to mention the great senatorial tradition of prudent concession to peers in order to avoid passing the power of decision to the potentially uncontrollable People.[297] On this view, Caesar's destructive rampage in his first consulship made the Civil War virtually inevitable since it left the defenders of the senatorial "oligarchy" no choice but to strive over the following decade to bring him to book or even to bring him down decisively in order to correct the atrocious precedent he had set by his apparent (and, they hoped, illusory) success in that terrible year.[298]

But this is to elevate pure obstructionism to a high constitutional principle. It is true that obstructive devices can, when they are not used for their own sake, force joint deliberation and compromise, and at a minimum may slow or mitigate overly aggressive political action. That is their modern theoretical justification, although it should perhaps be noted that in the famous analysis by Polybius of the "checks and balances" of the Roman constitution religious obstructionism is nowhere mentioned, while in the same account the tribunician veto is categorized as a "popular" check against senatorial power, not vice versa.[299] Yet Bibulus and his friends had made absolutely clear that they were not interested in opening joint deliberation and compromise, or even slowing the inevitable vote in favor of the law that year "even if you all should want it."[300] They had, to judge from our sources, presented not a single serious counterargument to the People against a series of largely beneficial bills that they tried first to block, then to annul on questionable technical and religious grounds. It is manifest that Bibulus in 59 represents a continuation of Cato's recent attempts to discover a way to suppress the renewed and entirely "republican" power of the People exemplified by the revival of "popular"

---

[297] See Cicero's outrage in mid-April (*Att.* 2.9.1): *id culpa Catonis* (n.b.), *sed rursus improbitate istorum, qui auspicia, qui Aeliam legem, qui Iuniam et Liciniam, qui Cae<ci>liam et Didiam neglexerunt, qui omnia remedia rei publicae effuderunt* . . . .

[298] Meier 1982 (e.g. 222–223; cf. 211 on the "illegal defeat of the *res publica*" and 213 on Caesar's willful violation of "the constitution") and Jehne 2001 (e.g. 42: "the beginning of the end of the Republic"; 46–47: "If he got away with this . . . others too would imitate him, and the republican regime risked becoming obsolete"; cf. 42–43, where techniques of obstruction are placed at the heart of the "constitution") are perhaps the clearest advocates of this position. Meier 1975: 204–208 has some characteristically thoughtful observations along these lines. Anglophone scholars have at least of late been less inclined to characterize Caesar's actions in 59 bluntly as antithetical to the "constitution," but cf. Steel 2013: 164: "The year 59 was one of autocracy" (although "popular support" is adduced in the next sentence) or Tatum 2008: 127 (perhaps focalized through his enemies) "[sc. Caesar's] contempt, made unmistakably plain during his consulship, for the traditions and values of the senatorial class, . . . the prestige of the senate."

[299] Polyb. 6.16.5: "The tribunes must always carry out the will of the People and zealously pursue their wishes."

[300] See n. 53.

legislation due to the restoration of the full powers of the tribunes.[301] Pure obstructionism may have seemed to him and his blatantly oligarchical *factio* to be the last, best hope for senatorial domination of the *res publica*, but that does not make it a fundamental or widely recognized constitutional principle. The People no doubt felt very differently, and the historical record of the previous century at least backed them up.[302]

But the principle of popular sovereignty meant nothing to Cato and Bibulus. Stung by total defeat, they would work only harder to force a reckoning with the man who in their eyes had proven himself "stronger than the entire Republic."[303]

---

[301] Meier 1975: 208 rightly perceives the attempt toward the end of the 60s to develop the use of the tribunician veto to subvert the popular will in legislation. Billows 2009: 113: "It was the die-hard optimates who pushed the political process towards crisis, in their purely negative determination not to accept change of any sort."

[302] Morstein-Marx 2013. Not even Cicero was entirely on board, despite his hysterics about the indispensability of the *leges Aelia et Fufia*: see n. 118 on Cato's *culpa* and political shortsightedness (*Att.* 2.9.1).

[303] Cic. *Att.* 7.9.3 (retrospective): *plus valuit quam tota res publica*.

CHAPTER 5

Caesar in Gaul
The View from Rome

On January 1, 58 BC (~ December 8, 59 by the Julian calendar equivalent), Caesar was no longer consul.[1] However, he still lingered outside the City until the third week of March, first while the Senate debated for three days the validity of his legislation with no result, then while Clodius began his wave of popular legislation culminating in Cicero's expulsion from Rome.[2] It is suggested that he remained close to the City, just outside the *pomerium*, to deter the Senate or magistrates from dismantling his achievements in his consulship.[3] No doubt he did what he could to assert some influence over the tumultuous beginning of P. Clodius's tribunate, including the new tribune's assault on Cicero for having executed the "Catilinarians" without trial; Clodius's bill clarifying the procedures of *obnuntiatio* and *servatio* and implicitly repudiating Bibulus's attempt to undercut all the legislation of 59 must have been of particular interest.[4] But we should not

---

[1] Julian equivalents for the Roman civic calendar can be given for the 50s and early 40s with some exactitude; the calculations of Brind'Amour 1983 and Bennett 2003–2012 normally differ only by a range of two to three days depending on divergent theories about the starting date of the Julian calendar. Without taking a position on that detail I shall normally split the difference between these two estimates of Julian equivalents, whose variance therefore from a date qualified as "ca." is +/- only one or two days. Dates without the qualification "Jul." are given according to the civil calendar and so may be several weeks ahead of their solar/Julian equivalents.

[2] Chapter 4, p. 182ff. For the timing of Caesar's departure see now Raaflaub and Ramsey 2017: 11–12; also Shackleton Bailey 1965: 2:227; Kaster 2006: 396n7. Caesar says he left for Gaul when he learned of the Helvetic plan to muster near Genava on March 28 (*BGall.* 1.6.4–7.1, ~ March 25, Jul. after insertion of the intercalary month between February and March). It is generally accepted that 58 was an intercalary year: Brind'Amour 1983; Bennett 2003–12; Kaster 2006: 394; Raaflaub and Ramsey 2017: 1n2.

[3] Gelzer 1968: 97; Meier 1982: 227; Jehne 2001: 49. According to Meier (p. 229), when Caesar was prompted by the news of the Helvetic muster to leave the vicinity of Rome he at first left the three legions at Aquileia "in Italy, *ante portas* as it were, in order to exert pressure on Rome," and did not even summon them to Transalpine Gaul until the Helvetii had already plundered the land of the Aedui at the end of April (pp. 229, 239). The second part of this statement is clearly inconsistent with *BGall.* 1.10.3 (cf. 1.7.6); the first is most unlikely: Fischer 2004: 306–311 and Thorne 2007 have now both given convincing arguments for an old suggestion of Ferrero that Caesar immediately issued orders to the legions at Aquileia to march rather than waiting until after he had reached Genava.

[4] Clodius's laws and attack on Cicero: Tatum 1999: 114–167.

assume that Caesar's presence implies something much more serious than this, such as an attempt to intimidate the Senate with the threat of an army at his back. As we noted in the previous chapter, the three legions that in recent times had constituted the normal garrison of Cisalpine Gaul, and which Caesar had "inherited" with the passage of the *lex Vatinia*, were encamped more than 600 kilometers away around Aquileia on the Illyrian frontier.[5] Nor was Caesar simply tarrying in the vicinity of Rome when he would have been expected to rush immediately to his provinces to the north. Since the Roman civil calendar was more than three weeks ahead of the seasons at the beginning of 58, when Caesar laid down his consulship the normal opening of the campaigning season (to judge from his later practice) was still about six months away. Even when he did in fact set out for Gaul in mid-March after receiving news of the threatening Helvetic muster at Genava (modern Geneva) he was still at least three months from the usual time for the opening of campaigning even in the less mountain-ous areas of Transalpina.[6] Thus from a military standpoint there was nothing untoward about Caesar's remaining in the vicinity of the City for quite some time even after the senatorial debate on his *acta* had petered out. It is also sometimes supposed that Caesar was at least partly occupied during this period with repelling what is represented as the opening salvo of an attempt to prosecute him for his ostensibly illegal actions as consul; all we know, however, is that Caesar's quaestor (for 59 or 58?) was immediately dragged into a preliminary hearing regarding various unnamed charges. The context implies that Caesar was a target in some way, but the event is too obscure to draw any conclusions as to the specific actions that gave rise to the complaint; most significant for our purposes is that nothing came of it.[7]

As for Caesar's activities during this pause, our most substantial clue is that as P. Clodius's political attack on Cicero came to a head he called Caesar himself before an important *contio* held outside the *pomerium*

---

[5] Caes. *BGall.* 1.10.3. This should be kept in mind when assessing Clodius's threats about Caesar's army (see n. 8).

[6] See n. 2. For the normal opening of Caesar's Gallic campaigns see Raaflaub and Ramsey 2017 (esp. p. 24 on *BGall.* 3.9.2): roads typically became fully passable and there was sufficient forage for the horses and draft animals around late May to mid-June (Julian). Plut. *Caes.* 17.5 adds that this was the occasion of his astonishing eight-day journey from Rome to the Rhone (his actual route, as well as where exactly he reached the river, is disputed: see now Raaflaub and Ramsey 2017: 3n8, 6–7; cf. Pelling 2011: 216). Suet. *Iul.* 57 may refer to this speed record unless it is to be rejected (so Raaflaub and Ramsey 2018: 8).

[7] Badian 1974: 147; Tatum 1999: 139–140; Suet. *Iul.* 23.1 with Alexander 1990: 126, n. 256. Scholars have sometimes inserted at this point the reference in the same passage to an abortive attempt by a tribune, L. Antistius, to charge Caesar in court; but see contra n. 157.

(which the proconsul, it will be remembered, could not cross without relinquishing his *imperium*) to deliver his opinion on the tribune's bill imposing exile on those who had executed Roman citizens without authorization by a law of the People (i.e. Cicero). Asked about Cicero's execution of the "Catilinarians," Caesar could not but disapprove without gross inconsistency, but (it is too rarely noticed) he also explicitly rejected retroactive penalties. This last point, despite Clodius's blustering to the contrary, actually pits Caesar *against* Clodius with regard to any plan to target Cicero personally.[8] It is usually supposed, taking cues from our late Greek sources, that the expulsion of Cicero was as much a Caesarian project as a Clodian one, but then why exactly would Caesar have publicly registered his objection to the crucial clause targeting Cicero?[9] As we saw in the previous chapter, Cicero seems to have largely behaved himself in Caesar's consulship. Caesar's interest was surely to tie an eloquent potential ally to himself: hence his statement in Clodius's *contio* and the continued offer of a place on his staff still in the early months of 58. This may well explain Caesar's disinclination to leave for his province before the last possible moment. But if Cicero refused to take him up on his offer, he presumably saw no advantage in setting himself against the popular wave of revulsion skillfully set in motion by Clodius against "the tyrant" who had so grossly disregarded the most fundamental right of the Roman People.[10] That is quite different from a chilling plot to work hand in glove with Clodius to destroy Cicero.[11] Cicero was certainly not one to be reticent about those he held responsible for his exile, and the fact that even after the crossing of the Rubicon he does not level this charge unambiguously

---

[8] Dio 38.17.1–2, with Morstein-Marx 2004: 178n80. Clodian bluster: Cic. *Sest.* 39–40: *inimicissimus esse meae saluti ab eodem* [sc. Clodio] *cotidianis contionibus dicebatur* .... *His se tribus* [sc. Pompey, Crassus, and Caesar] *auctoribus in consiliis capiendis, adiutoribus in re gerenda esse usurum dicebat; ex quibus unum habere exercitum in Italia maximum* .... Cicero goes on to note that what Clodius said did not trouble him so much as the failure of the three to disavow it (40–41) – a different matter, of course, and understandably alarming.

[9] Plut. *Cic.* 30.5 skips blithely over the key legal point (noted by both Moles 1988: 177 and Lintott 2013: 177); see also *Caes.* 14.17, with Pelling 2011: 202–203. App. *BCiv.* 2.14/53, Dio 38.12.1–2 (cf. 14.7–15.6) both think that Caesar prompted Clodius to become tribune to keep Cicero in check, which, even if true ("prompted" or "permitted?") of course does not imply that he favored Cicero's expulsion.

[10] Cic. *Att.* 2.18.3, 19.5, *Prov. cons.* 41–42; Dio 38.15.2 and Plut. *Cic.* 30.3 with Moles ad loc. "Tyrant": Cic. *Dam.* 75, 94; *Vat.* 23; *Sest.* 109; cf. the crowd's plundering, burning, and destruction of Cicero's house and the erection of a temple of Liberty on its site: Tatum 1999: 156–166; Kaster 2006: 335.

[11] Clodius's relative independence of the Three has been generally recognized since Gruen 1966; see Tatum 1999. The contrary arguments by Mitchell 1991: 129–137 are not very persuasive; note for example his rejection of Caesar's reported disapproval of the retroactive clause: 136n113. Note Clodius's challenges somewhat later in the year to the legitimacy of Caesar's legislation (Cic. *Dom.* 40, *Har. Resp.* 48; Chapter 4, n. 267).

against Caesar in his private correspondence to his chief confidant, Atticus, surely indicates that he considered the man who had held out a lifeline to him for nearly an entire year only indirectly to blame, like Pompey, for enabling and tolerating the catastrophe which befell him.[12]

Across the Alps

With the news of Helvetic preparations for an incursion into Transalpine Gaul Caesar's opportunity had come at last to fight a "new war in which his valor could shine forth" (Sall. *Cat.* 54.4), to earn a triumph greater than the one that had been snatched from him, and to inscribe his name in the annals of Roman *virtus*. The Helvetic campaign issued organically in the war with the Germans under Ariovistus who had crossed the Rhine and defeated the Aedui, after which a series of entirely predictable challenges to the invading army drew Caesar ever deeper into Gaul to suppress what, after his boast of its complete pacification already by the end of 57, could be construed as revolt.[13] It is outside the scope of this book to trace the course of Caesar's campaigns in Gaul, but we should note that the initial stages of his intervention perfectly matched his political needs.[14] Each incremental step of his career of conquest over the four years during which his possession of the province of Transalpina depended on annual senatorial renewal (i.e. 58, 57, 56 and perhaps some part of 55) would have to be justified above all by its success, measured at the end of each campaigning season. Without such success, it would be all too easy for detractors to develop the theme, of which we find some traces already in the second campaign of 58, that Caesar was stirring up unauthorized and unnecessary wars solely for his personal glory. The predictable next step of escalation would have been a push for his replacement by a simple majority vote in the Senate during the determination of the consular provinces according to the *lex Sempronia* before each consular election in midsummer. Caesar would be walking a tightrope. The magnitude of his eventual success has largely screened just how precarious his position was during these early years of the campaigning in Gaul.

---

[12] Pace Mitchell 1991: 136n113. The closest Cicero seems to come to blaming Caesar (Cic. *Att.* 10.4.1 of April 14, 49) applies equally to Pompey – whom of course he did not directly blame for his exile. Rumor, it is true, found fault with Caesar as well as Pompey: Vell. 2.45.2. Cic. *Att.* 3.15.3, 18.1 show that in exile he hoped for Caesar's support rather than blaming him for his expulsion.

[13] Caes. *BGall.* 2.35.1: *omni Gallia pacata* (the basis for the first set of supplications), cf. 3.7.1. Explicit language of "rebellion" begins to appear at 3.10.2 (*rebellio, coniuratio*) but implicit characterization as such is no less clear (e.g. in the motivation for the great rebellion of 52: 7.1).

[14] The wars themselves are magisterially surveyed by Goldsworthy 2006: 197–356. Raaflaub (ed.) 2017 is now an indispensable guide to Caesar's own account.

Some scholars (mostly, it must be said, in older works) have tended to characterize Caesar as launching upon an "unauthorized," even an "illegal" war in Gaul; a natural corollary is the notion that Caesar's famous account of his first intervention in Gaul in the first book of *De bello Gallico* is an attempt to lay the groundwork of a formal defense against such charges, preemptively averting a day of reckoning in the courts for treason.[15] Yet there is not a shred of evidence that a trial (presumably for *maiestas minuta*, i.e. treason) was ever seriously mooted for Caesar's original intervention in Gaul – or, for that matter, for his subsequent actions in the province. In the next chapter we shall consider more directly whether a successful prosecution of Caesar after his Gallic proconsulship was ever more than an empty threat or pipe dream of his enemies, but for the moment I would just note that even the scraps that can be collected to support the notion of a serious threat of prosecution relate either to Caesar's alleged religious/procedural violations in his consulship or to his notorious slaughter of Germans arguably under diplomatic protection in 55, *not* to his decisions in 58 to pass the boundaries of his province to prosecute two wars against the Helvetii and Ariovistus.[16]

A critical tradition about Caesar's initial thrust into Gaul does indeed (barely) exist, though one can hardly say that it is very prominent in our evidence. In Cassius Dio's account of the first year of the war Caesar actively seeks out pretexts for an attack and delights in finding them against the Helvetii and Ariovistus.[17] Dio also relates a version of the Vesontio mutiny (or near mutiny) in which the soldiers allege that they were prosecuting an unnecessary and "unvoted" war for Caesar's personal

---

[15] Gelzer 1968: 103–104 for the second point. For the first see Meier 1982: 235, 236, 240, 258: Caesar had "no instruction to make conquests, nor authority to do so"; it was "a war undertaken on his own initiative," "without instruction or permission, and indeed quite needlessly, in contravention of the principles of Roman foreign policy," and one that "did not accord with the will of the Senate majority": "one man decided, without authority, to conquer the whole of Gaul." Bauman 1963: 105–117 imagines a *maiestas* charge, followed by Gruen 1974: 495. The general idea is by no means passé: Raaflaub 2017: 206 (by launching a war outside his province he "again violat[ed] the law and risk[ed] prosecution"), and see the rather fantastical charge sheet that Girardet 2017: 42 compiles for Caesar's (supposedly) anticipated trial, which includes, among many other terrible things, "beginning a war while abandoning his province since 58 without authorization of the Senate, and likewise conducting a *bellum iniustum* in Gaul." Jehne 2001: 54 rightly points out on the contrary that Caesar's departure from his province to assist Roman allies was "entirely consistent with the maxims of Roman foreign policy."

[16] Morstein-Marx 2007: 161. See further Appendix 2, #4.

[17] 38.31.1, 34.1–2, 34.6. This reminds us of Suetonius's well-known claim (*Iul.* 24.3) that after the extension of his command for five more years in 56–55 Caesar did not let slip any pretext for war against friend or foe. But note that this claim is evidently not made about the very beginning of the campaigns in 58: n. 197.

glory alone.[18] Unsurprisingly, such complaints are missing from Caesar's own account and it would be interesting to know where they came from. It is tempting to attribute this variant to Asinius Pollio, the eventual canonical historian of the Caesarian civil wars. Unfortunately we cannot be sure whether he narrated the Gallic campaigns in detail or instead only sketched them in the summary way familiar from Thucydides's *Pentekontaetia* or Polybius's *Prokataskeue*.[19] Another possible source is the contemporary anti-Caesarian historian Tanusius Geminus, who emphasized at least one discreditable action of Caesar's in Gaul also picked up by both Plutarch and Appian.[20] But it is not out of the question that Dio's story of the complaints of Caesar's troops was a plausible improvisation by the Severan historian himself; certainly, the long speech he now puts into the mouth of Caesar on this occasion (38.36–46) can only be regarded as substantially his literary creation, though conceivably built on some nugget of authoritative information found in a more recent instantiation, such as Livy's history.[21]

Since after L. Lucullus's recent debacle in Armenia there appears to be nothing implausible about the story in itself, for our purposes we may accept it with some caution as a possible sign of a contemporary undercurrent of criticism of Caesar's intervention in Gaul, whether or not it explicitly came into the open at Vesontio as Dio asserts, but Caesar implicitly denies.[22] Vesontio (Besançon) was more than 300 kilometers to the northeast of the Rhone frontier and only a few days' march from the banks of the Rhine: Caesar was now marching his army deep into hostile territory, and though he could again represent his actions as fully in keeping with a senatorial decree of 61 enjoining commanders of Transalpina to protect the Aedui, it was also

---

[18] 38.35.2: πόλεμον οὔτε προσήκοντα οὔτε ἐψηφισμένον διὰ τὴν ἰδίαν τοῦ Καίσαρος φιλοτιμίαν.

[19] Similarly, Drummond 2013: 438. Against a relatively full treatment by Pollio of Caesar's Gallic wars, note that not a single fragment of the historian survives on the subject, although Kornemann 1896: 673–674 isolated a handful of parallels between Plutarch and Appian in their handling of this material, a phenomenon frequently interpreted as a sign of their common use of the lost Pollio (Pelling 2011: 44–45; Drummond 2013: 1:439–440, is somewhat skeptical). Notably, one such "synoptic" parallel that diverges intriguingly from Caesar is the credit both give to Caesar's legate and eventual Civil War enemy Labienus for the initial victory over the *pagus Tigurinus* (Plut. *Caes.* 18.2 with Pelling 2011: 224; App. *Celt.* 1.3, 15; cf. Caes. *BGall.* 1.12). As is well known, Pollio criticized Caesar's *Commentarii* for some inaccuracies (Suet. *Iul.* 56.4), although it is unclear whether he was thinking of the *BGall.* at all (see n. 51), and in any case, there is no evidence that Pollio was an eyewitness to anything but perhaps the very end of the Gallic campaigning (Drummond 2013: 431).

[20] See nn. 113, 188.   [21] See now Burden-Strevens 2018.

[22] Lucullus: App. *Mith.* 90/409–412; Plut. *Luc.* 33.5–6; Dio 36.2.1. The mutiny at Nisibis as Lucullus was planning to take the war even further east into Adiabene makes this look like a plausible analog to the Caesarian near mutiny at Vesontio: Caesar is likely to have had it in mind as he wrote his account of his own deft handling of the crisis, and later writers can hardly have missed the parallel.

an awkward fact that Ariovistus had just the previous year – with the help of Caesar himself – achieved recognition as a "Friend of the Roman People."[23] So whether or not Dio actually had authoritative information or was simply making a reasonable inference, it makes good sense for the murmuring about "unauthorized" war to begin at this moment.[24] If this complaint was subsequently taken up by his adversaries in the Senate and by their friends among the tribunes, Caesar's worst fear might be realized: his replacement, repeating the fate of Lucullus.

This "political" line of attack is, however, something rather different from the legalistic complaint against Caesar's actions in 58 excogitated by some scholars – namely, that, in violation of the now standard principle, enshrined not only in the Sullan *maiestas* law but even in his own extortion legislation, that a provincial commander was forbidden to lead his army outside his province or wage war without formal authorization, he had illegally taken his army outside his province of Transalpina to fight the Helvetii and then Ariovistus.[25] Collins rightly noted that Caesar's account not only makes no attempt to hide his crossing of the boundaries of his province to wage war well outside them but even positively emphasizes these moments of literal transgression: it must follow that he had little reason to worry about the legal consequences of these facts, which he has himself laid on the table.[26] One reason was that the Senate had decreed two years before (61), during the earlier crisis that followed Ariovistus's inroads into central Gaul, that the commander of Transalpina should come to the aid of the Aedui "and other friends of the Roman People" if this was in the interests of the Republic.[27] Yet if that decree was so essential to Caesar's justification of leading his army outside his province to make war in potential violation of the *maiestas* law and his own new law on extortion, it is distinctly odd that he fails even to mention it when he takes the decision to leave his province in pursuit of the Helvetii; instead, he mentions this covering decree only after their defeat, when he is in the process of building his case for advancing on Ariovistus (a harder case to

---

[23] See nn. 27–28 and 36.

[24] See n. 18. Timpe 1965: 205–209 exaggerates any contrast between Caesar's policy (as it emerged) of "unlimited right to rule" and the traditional, defensive outlook held by his senatorial opponents. There is no sign of such a conceptual-ideological polarization in our evidence of the 50s, esp. Cicero's *De provinciis consularibus*, nor should the series of supplications voted by the Senate be downplayed on the dubious assumption simply that they were under Caesar's thumb (on which more later).

[25] For the prohibition *exire de provincia, educere exercitum, bellum sua sponte gerere, in regnum iniussu populi Romani aut senatus accedere* see Cic. *Pis.* 50 and now Morrell 2017: 135–137.

[26] Collins 1972: 926–927.   [27] Caes. *BGall.* 1.35.4 (cf. 1.10).

make, to be sure).[28] It looks as if he did not think he needed to offer his readers such a legalistic justification. And he was probably right. There appears to be no evidence that any provincial governor was ever actually found in violation of this clause and convicted.[29] Even A. Gabinius, who after years of controversy over the means whereby the expelled king of Egypt might be restored to his throne simply swept in from his province of Syria and did so in direct contravention of a senatorial decree on the matter, managed acquittal on the *maiestas* charge in 54, although he was subsequently condemned for extortion.[30] The advice Cicero had given in 56 to Lentulus Spinther, then governor of Cilicia and contemplating the very same kind of intervention on King Ptolemy's behalf, applied equally to Caesar when he crossed the Rhone boundary in 58: "Your policy will be judged by its results. If all turns out as we wish and pray, there will be universal praise for your good judgement and courage. If anything goes wrong, those same voices will say you acted ambitiously and rashly."[31]

At a fundamental level it is hardly likely that the clause forbidding making war outside one's province without authorization was actually intended to tie the hands of commanders confronting the challenges of policing boundaries in unsettled frontier zones often marked by raids and retaliation in both directions. The distinction between "waging unauthorized war outside one's province" and "advancing the frontiers of the empire" (*finium imperi propagatio*, a proud boast in Rome) might be a fine one that depended crucially on a successful outcome.[32] The details of the laws on treason and extortion did not pose a real problem for Caesar

---

[28] Reserving the detail until the confrontation with Ariovistus does serve the useful function of revealing with full effect the humiliating damage the previous proconsul's failure to act upon the s.c. had done to the *imperium*. Ariovistus himself points out that the Romans have done nothing to help the Aedui in the recent war against him (1.44.9); no wonder he had gotten it into his head that the Romans had no business in "*his* Gaul which he had conquered in war" (1.34.4).

[29] One *possible* recent case was that of C. Antonius in 59 (Alexander 1990: n. 242), but it is actually quite unclear on what charge he was tried. Gruen 1973: 304–305 (cf. 1974: 288; David 1992: 856 concurs) thinks *repetundae*, while Alexander sticks to *maiestas* (n. 2). Even if the charge was *maiestas* we have no idea whether Antonius was held in violation of the clause under discussion. As Alexander notes, citing the *Digest* (48.4.4), even military incompetence could be grounds for the *maiestas* charge.

[30] Alexander 1990: n. 296; cf. 303. It is true that the relevant clauses appeared both in Sulla's *maiestas* law and the *lex Iulia de repetundis* (Morrell 2017: 135–137), but given Gabinius's acquittal under the first of these laws and the emphasis on a 10,000 talent bribe in the *repetundae* case (pp. 169–170), we should surely assume (in the absence of any suggestion to the contrary) that it was actual extortion that tripped him up in that court rather than simply the clause shared with the *maiestas* law about leading an army outside his province.

[31] Cic. *Fam.* 1.7.5: *si cecidisset ut volumus et optamus, omnis te et sapienter et fortiter, si aliquid esset offensum, eosdem illos et cupide et temere fecisse dicturos* (tr. Shackleton Bailey).

[32] See Harris 1979: 122–123, 125.

as long as he could justify his intervention according to well-understood norms and principles. And this Caesar had no difficulty doing. No rhetorical heavy lifting was required to justify taking the fight to the Helvetii (who had so recently caused grave concern in Rome and Transalpina: Chapter 4), even after they had given up attempting to pass through the Roman province and were in fact receding from it, because it was always Rome's duty to defend its allies. When an embassy of the Aedui came to complain of the ravaging of the Helvetii in their territory Caesar had all the justification he would need to come to their aid.[33]

After the defeat of the Helvetii and the transfer of Caesar's attention to Ariovistus not only was he now headed for a conflict that was hardly envisioned (at least by others) when his command was conferred, but the German had only the previous year been recognized by the Roman Senate (with Caesar's assistance as consul!) as king and "Friend of the Roman People." Reading Caesar's own account in the *Gallic War Commentaries* somewhat against the grain, it is hard to miss Ariovistus's surprise and rising sense of indignation as he discovers incrementally, over discussions that escalate over a span of fourteen chapters, that he is not Caesar's friend at all but his target.[34] This, we may be sure, is precisely why Caesar is so careful to build up his portrait of Ariovistus as an arrogant "barbarian" who had the temerity to tell the Roman proconsul to his face where Romans could and could not go in Gaul, despite the latter's sweet reason and painstaking courtesy. Caesar's Ariovistus gradually defines himself as exactly the kind of *superbus* whom it was the Roman mission to beat down.[35] A clever rhetorical stroke on Caesar's part is to defer any mention of Ariovistus's status as Roman "Friend" until he has developed the portrait of the arrogant "barbarian" both by means of the information offered by the Aeduan Diviciacus (confirmed by the cowed silence of the Sequani) and by Ariovistus's own haughty reply to Caesar's first tactful plea: this information, damning on its face, diverts attentions from *Caesar's* behavior and highlights instead the appalling ingratitude of this ever more alarming figure.[36] It is Caesar who thus becomes the wounded party, deeply

---

[33] Caes. *BGall.* 1.11 (cf. 43.8). Of course, Caesar's reaction is morally "overdetermined" by the need as well to avenge past defeat, maintain the security of the Province, and check "barbarian" vaunting (1.7.4, 10.1–2, 12.5–7, 13.4–7, 14.3–5). For the s.c. of 61, 1.35.4. See Riggsby 2006: 175–189 for an excellent study of Caesar's self-justification against the background of Roman ideas of the "just war."

[34] Caes. *BGall.* 1.34–47. Christ 1974: 263 n. 47. Fischer 2004: 311–315 supposes that Ariovistus had been Caesar's chief target since the beginning of his intervention.

[35] Verg. *Aen.* 6.853. Dio 38.44.4 gives Caesar a good Vergilian rationale, but Caes. *BGall.* 1.31–47 implicitly does the same by stressing Ariovistus's *superbia, adrogantia,* and *crudelitas.* Jehne 2001: 55–57, 2009: 78–79 nicely sketches Caesar's rhetorical justification of the confrontation with Ariovistus.

[36] Caes. *BGall.* 1.35.2, 43.4, 44.5, and Chapter 4, p. 170ff. Contrast the effect of Dio 38.34.3, 43.

embarrassed before the Gauls who had just been brought back under the umbrella of Roman power, after he had given his word that he would be able to induce Ariovistus to do the right thing (Caes. *BGall.* 1.33.1).

Here, then, in Caesar's artful building up of the best possible case against his potential or actual critics it is legitimate to discern an undercurrent of preemptive defensive writing on the author's part.[37] Yet we should not exaggerate on these grounds the legal or even political precariousness of his position. Whether or not his soldiers grumbled at Vesontio about the nature of the war he was prosecuting, in a remarkably well-documented period of Roman history we hear not a peep of criticism otherwise of Caesar's decision to expand the theater of operations to include Ariovistus and indeed beyond.[38] We hear of no attempt to transfer the command in Transalpine Gaul before the unsuccessful effort of 56, though this could have been done according to the *lex Sempronia* with a simple majority vote in the Senate. At the end of Caesar's second year in Gaul (57), which had seen him march far to the north to confront the Belgae, he declared that "all Gaul was pacified" and *the Senate* honored him with an unprecedented fifteen days of supplications.[39] Success clearly was the most important thing, and though Caesar at the end of 57 had (as it would turn out) absurdly overstated the extent of that success (it is amusing how quickly, in 56, Gaul becomes *un*-pacified [3.7.1]) decisive victories on battlefields across Gaul – along with the largesse that derived from the profits of conquest, a matter to which we shall attend in due course – made his position virtually unchallengeable (so far as we can see) for the present.

What is in fact surprising is that Caesar was bold enough at the end of 57 to unfurl (prematurely) the equivalent of a "Mission Accomplished" banner, since of course that very claim, useful as it might be for the immediate present, could also invite awkward discussion of the termination of at least this portion of his command, just as analogous circumstances in 52–51 would do. We must assume that, since his command in Cisalpine Gaul and Illyricum still had two campaigning seasons to go, he was reasonably confident that he would be left in charge of assuring the security of the peace to follow. But confidence could not amount to

---

[37] Seager thus goes too far in claiming that the *BGall.* is "never in the least apologetic nor is there ever any hint that [Caesar] anticipated criticism against which he might feel compelled to defend his actions" (2003: 19). On the element of apologia, A. Powell 1998 and Riggsby 2006: 157–214 are excellent.

[38] On Suet. *Iul.* 24.3 see n. 17 and pp. 198ff. and 239f. Notable here too, however, is Suetonius's emphasis on the primacy of the criterion of success: *sed prospere cedentibus rebus . . .*

[39] Caes. *BGall.* 2.35.4; cf. Cic. *Prov. cons.* 25–27, *Balb.* 61, *Pis.* 45, 59; Plut. *Caes.* 21.1; Dio 39.5.2.

certainty, since at this particular juncture neither he nor Pompey, if he was still disposed to expend political capital on his behalf, could dictate the Senate's decisions.[40] Caesar took advantage of the winter lull to visit his legally secure province of Illyricum – perhaps in case of his immediate replacement – and it was Caesar's (not entirely unpredictable) good fortune that the Veneti and the peoples of the entire northern coast of Gaul took the occasion to "revolt" before, in the early summer of 56, the Senate would under the *lex Sempronia* be expected to determine the consular provinces for the upcoming elections.[41]

The idea that the war against Ariovistus or the later campaigns against the Belgae and others were *unauthorized* was anyway a matter for interpretation. Formal declarations of war by a vote of the Roman People had long been an institutional anachronism. The current and now rather venerable mechanism for beginning major military action, often extending for many years, was for the Senate, or in some cases, the People, to confer a province outside Italy on one or both consuls. Whatever other formalities may have accompanied the decision, this is how major recent wars such as the Jugurthine, Cimbric, and Mithridatic Wars (First and Third) had all been authorized.[42] Furthermore, a law of the Roman People had authorized Caesar's control at least of Cisalpine Gaul and Illyricum with its substantial army for five years; this was not for marching about on the parade ground. A major war was certainly going to be fought to secure some important portion of the unstable northern frontier;[43] against *whom* exactly may have been uncertain until the Helvetii began to make their move in March.[44] The main recent worry had been about Gaul across the

---

[40] See Seager's sketch of Pompey's circumstances toward the end of 57 and beginning of 56: 2002: 106–115. For much of this time, Pompey was preoccupied by the possibility of obtaining a special senatorial mandate to restore Ptolemy Auletes to his throne – a project in which he was frustrated.

[41] See n. 130. Cicero's *De provinciis consularibus* belongs in late June–early July (Grillo 2015: 12–13).

[42] Rich 1976: 14–15, 49–50.

[43] Dio 38. 41.4: "For what other reason did the People send you out here, why did they dispatch me here directly after my consulship? Why select me to hold command for a five-year term, which has never happened before? Why arm me with four legions? Why, if they were not fully committed to the belief that we would also have to fight? Surely it was not so that we might be fed in idleness."

[44] Interestingly, in the *BGall.* Caesar prefaces his intervention with a narrative of three years of Helvetic preparations for a migration covertly aimed at seizing "all Gaul" (1.2.2, 1.3.3–8; 1.5.1 shows that they continue to follow Orgetorix's basic plan even after his death). Clearly this is another bit of strategic writing, since it refutes preemptively from the outset the subsequent Helvetic claims that they intended only to travel innocently to a part of Gaul well outside of the Roman province (1.7.1, 7.5, 8.3), and thus undergirds in advance Caesar's eventual decision to leave his province to hunt down and annihilate a retreating enemy (1.7.4–5, 10.1–2, 11.2–6, cf. 14.3), even though strictly speaking he can only guess that their deeper objective is *totius Galliae imperio potiri.* The alert reader will wonder when exactly the alarming "backstory" recounted at 1.2–5 became known to Caesar and in what form; placed where it is in his narrative, however, it heightens

Alps (Chapter 4), and this turned out to be exactly where the first threat was realized. Ariovistus (and, for that matter, the Helvetii) had not been specifically named as military targets of the command, which though it gave an opening to critics (as Dio suggests) was hardly decisive, since a provincial commander was traditionally given great leeway to act against new, emerging, and unanticipated threats to the security of his province or ongoing military activities.[45] As long as Caesar was successful (unlike Lucullus), he was on pretty solid ground "constitutionally" (i.e. with reference to respectable and long-standing precedent) as well as politically. Dio's portrayal of the mutiny at Vesontio, for what it's worth, is the last we hear of the complaint about alleged lack of "authorization" of Caesar's Gallic wars before the passage of the *lex Pompeia Licinia* in 55, which at last gave Transalpina to Caesar by law (for another five years) and removed the necessity for ongoing senatorial approval of his tenure.

Were the *Gallic War Commentaries* "Political Instruments"?

Discussion of whether Caesar's offensive warfare in Gaul was "authorized" has led us to consider his self-justification on this point in the *Gallic War Commentaries*, which now raises an important question for our attempt to excavate "the view from Rome" and to ascertain how Caesar was able to shape his image in Rome during his nine-year absence. Were the *Commentarii de bello Gallico* intended, as seems universally to be supposed, to shape public opinion back in Rome during Caesar's long absence on campaign? Were they "propaganda" intended to be deployed in a contemporary war of words, either in the written form in which we read them today – say, as war dispatches to the Senate – or, alternatively, read out to the Roman People in public meetings, as T. P. Wiseman has suggested?[46]

---

dramatic tension while framing Caesar's reactions to the unfolding threat as diplomatic to a fault. There is no reason, though, to prefer Dio's superficial claim (38.31.1) that everything was "completely calm" in Gaul (ἀκριβῶς πάντα ἡσυχαζεν): see Chapter 4, p. 169ff.

[45] So Caesar replies (Dio 38.41) to the objection that the war has not been debated in the Senate or voted by the People. See Eckstein 1987 for generals' relative independence in the mid-Republic; more recently, note Metellus's and Marius's dealings with King Bocchus of Mauretania, Lucullus's invasion of Armenia (which backfired only because of failure), and Pompey's campaigns around the Caspian Sea, Armenia, and Syria.

[46] Gelzer 1968: 171: "An impressive and comprehensive edition (*Bearbeitung*) of the campaign reports, which Caesar had previously sent to the Senate." Mommsen 1894/1996: 4:720: "The military report of the democratic general to the People from whom he had received his commission" ("der militärische Rapport des demokratischen Generals an das Volk, von dem er seinen Auftrag erhalten hat" – not strictly correct, as we have seen, regarding the main theater of war, Transalpina). Wiseman 1998. Recent statements of the hypothesis that the *Commentarii* had the "urgent and

Most scholars today seem to agree that Caesar probably wrote up his campaigns in Gaul annually, season by season, devoting one book to each until he broke off the project after the climactic campaign of 52 as the crisis precipitated by his imminent return to Rome began to escalate. The older, alternative view is that the work was written as a whole in one unitary sweep and published for essentially propagandistic purposes between 52 and 50, as Caesar began to prepare in earnest for his controversial return home (possibly including – so at least Gelzer – the threat of facing a trial for his actions).[47] The arguments are involved and have a long history, but may be briefly summarized as follows. First, on purely a priori grounds, it seems obvious that Caesar must have written a detailed account of each campaign shortly after it concluded for the crucial purpose of serving as an "aide-memoire" for future uses of all types; thus it stands to reason that the seven Caesarian books of *De bello gallico* that were eventually published (the eighth was completed by Caesar's officer Hirtius) were surely very close to that record at least as regards content.[48] As it happens, there is good evidence that the final product reflects an origin in individual accounts written year by year after the conclusion of the annual campaigns that they describe. Most notably, some later books contradict statements made in earlier books, the easiest explanation for which is that the future was unknown to the writer of the annual reports and that little copyediting was done to iron out such inconsistencies before the final publication. A well-known case is the claim in the second book that Caesar in 57 virtually exterminated the Nervii, a Belgic people, although they manage

---

immediate purpose" to inform and to shape public opinion in Rome and Italy about the ongoing or just-completed campaigns: Riggsby 2006: 11; Raaflaub 2017: 205; Krebs 2018: 42. On "propaganda" Riggsby 2006: 207–214 is especially helpful; see also Krebs's working definition (2018: 30–31, from T. Qualter). I believe both use the term too expansively since their definitions would seem to include crafting a political image or even persuasive rhetoric. To my mind "propaganda" implies an organized, partisan effort by a political group, usually the one in power, to impose its distinctive, often polemical interpretation of issues and controversies. Cf. *OED*, s.v., 3: "The systematic dissemination of information, esp. in a biased or misleading way, in order to promote a political cause or point of view."

[47] Gesche 1976: 78–83 gives a brief review of the debate, conducted mostly in German, which spanned much of the twentieth century. For annual, serial composition see especially Ebert 1909, Barwick 1938: 100–123, Wiseman 1998, and the works by Adcock and Hastrup cited in n. 53. Riggsby 2006: 6–9, Krebs 2013, and Grillo and Krebs 2018: 3–5 offer recent updates. Mommsen was the father of the unitary theory (1894/1996: 4:720 n.), followed also by Gelzer 1968: 103–105, 132n1, 171 (n. 73) and Meier 1982: 253; its most influential modern proponent has been Rambaud (1966a: 9–12), but note that Levick 1998: 65 (cf. 72) still seems sympathetic. Defenders of the literary quality of the *Gallic War Commentaries* are inclined to believe that "however they were written, [they] were . . . finished off as a unitary narrative" (Kraus 2009: 160), but this seems somewhat at odds with the inconsistencies to be discussed shortly as well as Pollio's criticisms (Suet. *Iul.* 56.4).

[48] Bömer 1953: 248–249; cf. Riggsby 2006: 149.

to rise again quite formidably only three years later, in Book Five.[49] We have already noted Caesar's premature boast that "all Gaul had been pacified" at the end of the campaigning season of 57 (2.35.1), which he is forced to revise and explain away almost immediately early in the next book (3.7.1) and would provide further embarrassment in the face of the great revolt of 52 related in Book Seven. (In fact, in his account of the end of campaigning in 56 Caesar actually tries the phrase *omni Gallia pacata* one more time before abandoning it for the rest of the work.)[50] Imperfections such as these may have been part of what the historian Asinius Pollio had in mind when he wrote that the *Commentarii* were left in a rather unpolished state, with some glaring errors remaining: Caesar was surely going to edit and correct them, he thought.[51] All of this suggests (but in the nature of the case can hardly prove) that the *Gallic War Commentaries* were written up annually, presumably during Caesar's winter breaks, which he usually spent in North Italy rather than on the other side of the Alps.[52] I leave aside some rather weak textual counterarguments for the alternative theory of unitary composition after the suppression of the Great Revolt in 52, an account of which fills the last book in Caesar's own hand.[53]

As for the *publication* (rather than composition) of the work, we know almost nothing about it, which suggests that it does not seem to have made much of a splash whenever it happened. It is remarkable, for instance, that

---

[49] Caes. *BGall.* 2.28.1: *prope ad internicionem.* Cf. 5.39.3, 41.1, 5.42–52, 7.75.3. See Wiseman 1998: 2, 7n4, though the observation goes back at least to Ebert 1909: 14–15 (and countered already by Rice Holmes in 1911: 206: "perhaps . . . only a flourish"). Similarly, one might note that Caesar says he executed the entire senate of the Veneti and sold "the rest" into slavery at the conclusion of the war of 56 (3.16.4), yet they reappear among the reinforcements to be sent to Vercingetorix at Alesia (7.75.4).

[50] Caes. *BGall.* 3.28.1. *Pacatos/-a* at 4.37.1 and 6.5.1 refers more carefully to *parts* of Gaul (even then optimistic); the universal phrase is not tried again, though sometimes Gaul is made "calmer" (5.58.7) or even – just before the outbreak of the Great Revolt – "calm" (*Quieta Gallia,* 7.1.1). See now Krebs's forthcoming commentary to Book 7, ad 7.1.1.

[51] Suet. *Iul.* 56.4 = *FRHist* 56 F 8 *existimatque rescripturum et correcturum fuisse.* Unfortunately, it is uncertain whether Pollio was speaking of both sets or only the *Civil War Commentaries,* with which his own history would directly compete (so Morgan 2000: 58; contra, Drummond, *FRHist* 3.528).

[52] While his army was left in winter quarters across the Alps, Caesar spent every winter in Cisalpina except in 54/53 (Samarobriva/Amiens), 52/51 (Bibracte/Mont Beuvray), and 51/50 (Nemetocenna/Arras) (Caes. *BGall.* 5.53.3, 7.90.7, 8.46.6). The others he spent in Italia, as Caesar regularly calls Cisalpine Gaul (*BGall.* 1.10.3, 2.35, 5.1 et al.; the single exception [6.1.2] is pointed), occasionally with a brief visit to Illyricum (2.35.2, 3.7.1, 5.1.5–9); cf. Sherk 24A.

[53] See 1.28.5 (cf. 7.10.1) regarding the status of the Boii, and 4.21.7 (cf. 7.75.5–76.2; also 6.6.3) regarding the loyalty of Commius the Atrabatian. (Hirt. [Caes.] *BGall.,* 8 *Praef.* 6, is neither here nor there.) Sufficient rebuttal in English by Adcock 1956: 77–83; Hastrup 1957. In somewhat circular fashion, the assumption of composition and publication in 52–51 has often served as the basis of larger inferences as well (e.g. Maier 1978: 68).

despite Cicero's intense interest in politics, in Caesar, and in the progress of his campaigns especially after his brother Quintus had joined him as a legate, the massive Ciceronian corpus, including hundreds of letters and numerous speeches and essays from a decade about which we are consequently better informed than for any other in ancient history, gives no hint even of the existence of the *Gallic War Commentaries* before 46.[54] (It is perfectly possible that Cicero had just read them.) If, as one view has it, the publication of the work constituted an important move in a propaganda campaign to facilitate Caesar's return to Rome in 51, then it is odd indeed that this leaves no trace in our rather copious evidence of the approach to and beginning of the Civil War.[55] If on the other hand one prefers to think that individual books were released serially shortly after the completion of each year's campaign, the absence of any sign of the work seems particularly conspicuous at certain moments when it should be detectable. For example, Cicero's speech *De provinciis consularibus*, delivered in June or July 56, was specifically concerned with Caesar's success in Gaul in order to make the argument that Caesar's Gallic provinces should not be reassigned to others as part of the regular determination of consular provinces before the elections, yet it contains no discernible echo of the first two books of *De bello Gallico*, which relate Caesar's successes thus far (the triumphant campaigning seasons of 58–57).[56] Indeed, if Cicero had repeated the claim Caesar made at the end of his second book that "all Gaul had been pacified" it might have been disastrous for his case, for only a few months or weeks before the delivery of the speech, news of the "revolt" of the Veneti had arrived, a considerable setback which caused Cicero (informed by Caesar or conjecturing from reports) to retard the timetable for "binding all of Gaul with eternal chains" by one or two more seasons – that is, possibly as late as the end of 55.[57]

---

[54] Cic. *Brut.* 262. Note also A. Hirtius's reference to the *Gallic War Commentaries* as "published" (*editi*) in his preface to Book 8, evidently written between Caesar's death in March 44 and Hirtius's own in April 43.

[55] On "propaganda" see n. 46.

[56] Grillo 2015: 185 takes a different view, yet his comparison to the end of Caes. *BGall.* 3 is puzzling since that account of a campaign of ca. October 56 (Raaflaub and Ramsey 2017: 29) can hardly have been written until *after* Cicero had delivered (ca. end of June/early July: see n. 41) and probably published the *Prov. cons.* On Grillo's own showing there is significant tension between the speech and Caesar's own account of his rationale and justification for his campaign of conquest (p. 234 ad §32). Likewise, there is a palpable gap between Cicero's *paene confectum* (19) and Caesar's *omni Gallia pacata* (2.35.1) at the head of the last paragraph of the *BGall.* that would have been available to Cicero on the hypothesis here being rejected. (For another relevant point cf. also Krebs 2006: 116n22.) Of course, loose similarities between the two contemporary representations are only to be expected.

[57] Cic. *Prov. cons.* 34 (quoted n. 129); cf. 19. Although we have no good evidence for when Caesar learned of the dangerous rising of the Veneti (Caes. *BGall.* 3.7–16), Raaflaub and Ramsey 2017:

(Even this was probably transparently optimistic already at the time of the speech.) And the silence about any authoritative or "published" account of the campaigns from Caesar's pen is particularly conspicuous when Quintus sets about prodding Marcus to write an epic in honor of Caesar on the subject of the British expedition and offering him material about the *situs, natura rerum et locorum, mores, gentes, pugnae, imperator* – regarding all of which the British ethnography in the Fourth Book of the *De bello gallico*, written on the "serial" hypothesis by the end of the previous year (55), would have been an excellent source *de rebus Britannicis* even if Cicero intended to focus his narrative only on the second invasion.[58]

But whether written or published in a unitary fashion or not, Caesar's *Gallic War Commentaries* were not needed to keep the public, whether the political elite or ordinary citizens, informed about current events on the Gallic front, or even to shape Caesar's public image. There were a wide variety of more effective channels to employ for that purpose.

Let us start with Wiseman's suggestion, which some have found attractive, that the target audience for *De bello Gallico* was actually the Roman People assembled in their *contiones*, indeed "in the main piazza of every *municipium* and *colonia* in Italy," where (Wiseman suggests) Caesarian tribunes could read out portions of the *BG* to a "rapt audience."[59] Just how Caesar's achievements were presented to the *populus Romanus* over the ultimately nine years of his absence from the City is an interesting problem, to which we shall return. It is quite likely, even without explicit evidence, that impressive summaries of his *res gestae* featured in numerous *contiones* in some fashion across that near decade, stoking the popular enthusiasm for Caesar that emerges in our sources for this period from time to time. But the idea that large portions of the less than gripping narrative of *De bello Gallico* were read out at length to a standing audience with a taste for fiery denunciations and impatient of long-windedness is in principle quite implausible.[60] The *Gallic War Commentaries* were just not very well suited to "rousing the rabble"; even among Latin students, Caesar's text is actually a pretty hard sell except for hard-core fans of indirect discourse, gerundives, and ablative absolutes. The fact that in all our rather copious evidence for

24–26 argue that he set out from Cisalpina in June, so the news is likely to have come weeks or months before Cicero's speech. The subsequent campaigns in Brittany, Normandy, and Aquitania will have concluded probably in September (ibid., 26–29), well after *Prov. cons.* was delivered.
[58] Cic. *Q. fr.* 2.16.4; cf. 3.1.11, 4.4, 5.4, 6.3, 7.6; cf. Caes. *BGall.* 4.20–36.
[59] Wiseman 1998: 6. Objections at Riggsby 2006: 13–14; Jehne 2010: 316n19. Krebs 2018: 42 seems tempted, but thus far unconvinced.
[60] Norms of contional rhetoric: Morstein-Marx 2004.

contiones of all types in the Late Republic there is not even a single example of extended, detailed military narration of this type must clinch the argument.[61] Caesar's narrative of the Gallic War is vastly more detailed, much denser, and far, far lengthier than any narrative portions of contional speeches that we possess, which are typically quite brief.[62] Nor should one make too much of Caesar's frequent mention of the Roman People in the *Gallic War Commentaries*: this patriotic usage hardly implies derogation of the Senate.[63] More notable, I would judge, is the *anti*-demagogic tone Caesar adopts against populist methods of leadership where they enter obliquely into the narrative (e.g., in Gallic states whose leaders seek to exploit such methods for their own aggrandizement) and, on the other hand, the palpable admiration of his authorial persona for military hierarchy and properly constituted authority.[64] He is, after all, an *imperator* in the field.

None of this, of course, is to deny that Caesar's achievements must have been recounted in appropriate form and length in numerous *contiones*

---

[61] The closest surviving parallel for *military* narrative in a *contio* is, I believe, the brief narratives Cicero uses in *Leg. Man.* to support his argumentation (§§9–10, 22–26, 34–35). These are not even remotely comparable in narrative density to the long, detailed, and involved accounts of Caesar. The longest contional narrative we possess is Cic. *Cat.* 3.3–15, still much shorter than the Caesarian narratives and anyway a special case since it offers detailed information on an immediate crisis to an anxious, news-hungry audience.

[62] Note that *contiones* were typically short: Morstein-Marx 2004: 37–38 with n. 11. The longest surviving *contio* that was *not* part of the formal debate that immediately preceded a legislative vote (these appear to have been longer, for obvious circumstantial reasons) is the *Third Catilinarian* of Cicero, at twenty-seven pages in the OCT; Caesar's first and seventh books, which, containing the initial invasion of Gaul and its climactic defeat, one might fairly declare the most important, are much longer even than this at thirty-three and fifty pages, respectively. See also n. 73.

[63] Wiseman 2008: 3: "No fewer than forty-one times in Book I"; Krebs 2018: 38–39 counts eighty times in the whole work versus only sixteen of the Senate. But like any Roman general, Caesar was a commander *of the Roman People*, not of the Senate, just as the *imperium* itself was formally designated *populi Romani*, not *senatus*. (On the other hand, contra Krebs (p. 38), at least until 55 Caesar owed his appointment to command in *Transalpine Gaul* per se to the Senate, not to the People.) Even where it is not part of the traditional phrasing "the Roman People" lends solemnity and dignity, and in this sense it subsumes the Senate as part of the Roman community. Examples proliferate in a single Ciceronian speech before the Senate: *Prov. cons.* 9 *populi Romani imperator* and 3, 5 (bis), 31, 32 (ter), 33.

[64] See esp. Caes. *BGall.* 1.3.5, 9.3, 17.1–2, 18.3, 18.9 (Dumnorix the Aeduan); 7.4.3, 5 (Vercingetorix) (cf. also Hirtius 8.22.2), with Seager 2003: 26–30. To his examples add 7.42.1–4 (*plebemque ad furorem impellit,* sc. Convictolitavis the Aeduan) and 43.4 (*nihil se propter inscientiam levitatemque vulgi gravius de civitate iudicare,* sc. Caesar). In all these passages, Caesar exploits the language of anti-*popularis* rhetoric (cf. e.g. Cic. *Sest.* 96, 99, 104, 139), which becomes even more prominent in the *BCiv.* (1.5.1–3, 7.5–6). "The picture is thoroughly Roman and thoroughly respectable. Indeed, no optimate could have had more admirable views from Caesar and his secretary if only the Bellovaci had been the Roman people" (Seager 2003: 29–30). Riggsby acutely observes (2006: 91–96) that soldierly *virtus* in the *BGall.* depends ultimately on respect for hierarchy and surveillance from the top. Caesar berates his officers and men at some notable moments for their failure to follow authoritative command unquestioningly (Vesontio, 1.40.1; Gergovia, 7.52.1; cf. *BCiv.* 1.71–72, 3.74.2–3; see also Powell 1998: 118–119 on Sabinus at Atuatuca).

during his absence through the 50s. The question is rather where this sort of information could have come from, if not the *Commentarii* as most scholars seem to have assumed.[65] The first part of our answer is that Caesar was often enough not really all that far away – not so far, that is, that he could not talk face to face with senators and friends for several months every year in "Italy" itself. Caesar himself spent every winter season before 52/51 but one (following the disaster of November 54) in peninsular "Italy" – that is, Cisalpine Gaul (apparently Ravenna in particular, only 325 kilometers away from Rome – i.e. about four days by fast carriage).[66] His chief public duty during these winter visits to Cisalpina was to hold the assizes and thus give annual access to the governor's tribunal, but this seems to have occupied only the early part of his stay, and in any case he surely could have made time for important political visitors.[67] Unfortunately for us, it is only during his winter layover on the Italian side of the Alps in 57/56 that Cicero's correspondence gives us a glimpse at Caesar's appointment book: in March 56, the aspiring consular candidate Ap. Claudius (now governor of Sardinia) conferred with Caesar, probably at Ravenna, while Metellus Nepos, one of the consuls of the previous year and now proconsul of Spain, is also specifically named among those who met with him at around this time,[68] and in April Caesar met Crassus at Ravenna and then shortly thereafter met Pompey at Luca, apparently the southernmost city in Caesar's province, providing quick access from Rome because of its proximity to the north Tyrrhenian coast.[69] Indeed, before his return to the front in 56 Caesar is supposed to have held some kind of semipublic conference or series of meetings at Luca (the notorious "Conference at

---

[65] E.g. recently Goldsworthy 2006: 187–188; Osgood 2009: 350.

[66] See now Raaflaub and Ramsey 2017: 25n95. For Caesar's habit of wintering south of the Alps see n. 52. Luca was in fact closer to Rome by the sea route than Ravenna and therefore is mentioned as an alternative site for meetings (see n. 69), but this was less convenient for Caesar since it entailed crossing the Apennines. Perhaps, however, it was on his regular circuit of assizes.

[67] Political visitors: e.g. in November 58, the tribune-designate P. Sestius traveled to Cisalpina to meet with Caesar over the plans for Cicero's recall (Cic. *Sest.* 71, with Kaster 2006: 272 and 399n21). Assizes: Caes. *BGall.* 1.54.3, 5.1.5, 5.2.1, 6.44.3, 7.1.1. Cisalpina must have been unique among the provinces in the number of Roman citizens needing access to the governor's court; Caesar may therefore have been a good deal busier than was, e.g. Cicero in Cilicia, whose letters provide our most informative picture of this part of a governor's responsibilities. See Lintott 1993: 54–69.

[68] Claudius: Cic. *Q. fr.* 2.5.4 (for the date, *Q. fr.* 2.6.3), and Plut. *Caes.* 21.5 in the context of the Luca conference. Nepos is the other nonmember of the Three whom Plutarch names in that context as well. Whether or not they were actually part of that gathering, whose very occurrence is questionable (see n. 70), the fact that they are specifically named supports the idea that they did meet with Caesar around this time either at Ravenna or Luca, as did others (see Pelling 2011: 246). As recently as March 3 Caesar had been in Aquileia (Sherk 24A); he had spent some time as well in Illyricum: Caes. *BGall.* 3.7.1 and n. 128.

[69] Cic. *Fam.* 1.9.9.

Luca"), where he met with more than 200 senators – fully one-third of the
entire Senate, if the common source of Plutarch and Appian is to be
believed, attended by a retinue of 120 lictors.[70] The meetings of 56 may
have been the most intensive and extensive of the whole period of the war,
but Caesar's presence within a week's journey each winter must have
prompted many smaller versions of these gatherings over the course of
the 50s. |

When meetings of this kind were not possible, however, there were still
a great many lines of communication between the army of Gaul and elite
circles in Rome by which Caesar could keep friends and magistrates
informed of the progress of the war. Cicero characterizes these in his
speech *On the Consular Provinces* as "letters, rumor, reports" (*litteris,
fama, nuntiis* – note that the *imperator*'s own *Commentarii* are not
mentioned).[71] This is a bit vague and needs some explication. Caesar
must have been sending official letters to the Senate, both "laureled"
ones announcing major victories (and laying the groundwork for honorific
supplications) and what we might call "progress reports," probably toward
the beginning and end of each major campaign, of which in turn there
might be two or more in a year.[72] Extrapolating from Cicero's extant
reports on his campaigning in Cilicia and his personal letter seeking

---

[70] Plut. *Caes.* 21.5–7, with Pelling 2011: 246; *Pomp.* 51.4–5, *Crass.* 14.6; App. *BCiv.* 2.17/62; the meeting
is omitted by Dio and hardly corroborated by Cicero's reference to a meeting between *Pompey* and
Caesar at *Fam.* 1.9.9. This is not the place to discuss the historicity of this story (which Pelling
accepts, while Lintott 2008: 202 is nicely ironical; on the chronology see now Raaflaub and Ramsey
2017: 25–26), and whether indeed the number of 200 senators/120 lictors is supposed to have
assembled at once or cumulatively over the course of weeks. (Livy's story [3.36.4] of the shocking
vision of 120 lictors in attendance on the Decemviri may offer a clue about the story's origin.)

[71] Cic. *Prov. cons.* 22. For *fama*, cf. Dio 39.25.2 αὐτόματος ἡ δόξα; on *nuntius/-um* see *OLD* s.vv.
nuntium, nuntius 1b, 3; but in the present case messengers bearing official reports, as e.g. Cic. *Fam.*
8.10.2, seem most to the point. On Caesar's correspondence in and from Gaul see now Osgood 2009
and Krebs 2018: 32–33; cf. Rambaud 1966a: 15–16, 19–23; Maier 1978: 82–84.

[72] Each of Caesar's three sets of *supplicationes* followed immediately upon his letter at the end of the
campaign: *BGall.* 2.35.4, 4.38.5, 7.90.8. Dio 39.25.2; Plut. *Cat. Min.* 51.3 and *Crass.* 16.3 mention
other letters of Caesar to the Senate in 56 (which Pompey tries to prevent the consuls from reading
out!) and 55. For "laureled" letters announcing a victory and requesting a *supplicatio* see Halkin 1953:
80–87; e.g. Cic. *Prov. cons.* 14–15, 27, *Pis.* 39, *Att.* 7.2.6–7, *Fam.* 1.8.7 (with Shackleton Bailey's nn).
Such letters to the Senate were bound to be preceded or accompanied by a flurry of other letters to
influential individual senators: Cicero implies, for instance, that he wrote to all members of Senate
but two for his own *supplicationes* (*Att.* 7.1.8). Progress reports (*litterae publicae*): Cicero's two letters
from his province "to the Consuls, Praetors, Tribunes of the Plebs, and the Senate" (*Fam.* 15.1–2) are
the closest extant examples, which suggest that commanders were expected to send such reports at
least at key moments of their campaigns, especially their victorious ends (2.10.3). Failure to send
such reports could be damaging in the eyes of the senators (*Pis.* 38; Cael. [Cic.] *Fam.* 8.10.2 with
15.3.2, 9.3). Suetonius implies that Caesar's letters to the Senate survived down to his own day,
collected in the form of a *memorialis libellus* (Suet. *Iul.* 56.6: cf. Butler and Cary's n.). Note that he
draws no connection and remarks on no resemblance between this and the Gallic War *Commentarii*.

Cato's support for his application for *supplicationes,* we can suppose that Caesar too included in his "laureled" dispatches narratives of those victories for which the Senate voted him unprecedented numbers of *supplicationes* – though it is unlikely that these were of anything like the length and density of his Gallic War narratives.[73] As for letters of a more personal nature, the preserved correspondence between Cicero and his brother Quintus, who had set off to join Caesar as his legate in 54, shines a spotlight on a few small threads joining the Army of Gaul to Rome. In this year Cicero maintains a lively correspondence with Quintus and his protégé Trebatius Testa; as for the proconsul himself, Cicero received from Caesar not only frequent messages of a relatively informal nature but also what look like more extensive recountings in the style of Cicero's letter to Cato, especially at significant transition points in the campaigns.[74] During the campaign in Britain at the ends of the earth, Caesar himself wrote to Cicero no fewer than three times between August 23 and September 25.[75] Many other friends of Caesar must have been kept similarly "in the loop." "All told, though little survives now, the number of Caesar's letters to the Senate and to individual Romans was tremendous" – and this observation refers only to letters from Caesar himself.[76]

From this variety of correspondents, Cicero was in possession of a great deal of news, much of it containing much more current and more accurate information than anything that would eventually arrive in official dispatches to the Senate. For instance, Cicero learned from his brother of the poverty of Britain just *before* the invasion of 54 – apparently something

---

[73] Caesar's *BGall.* narratives are two to four times the length of any extant letter to the Senate or comparable epistolary narrative. This alone discourages adherence to Gelzer's view (1968: 171) that in 51 Caesar did little more than collect "the campaign reports which [he] had previously sent to the Senate" and publish them in "an impressive and authoritative edition." (See also the previous note on Suet. *Iul.* 56.6.) Our best comparanda are the letters of Cicero to the Senate from Cilicia: *Fam.* 15.1, 2 to the Senate do not surpass 97 lines in Watt's OCT, while the longest letter to the Senate preserved in the entire Ciceronian corpus (*Fam.* 12.15) extends to 111 lines. *Fam.* 15.4, though a personal letter, makes a case for a *supplicatio* and therefore may be more representative of the length of similar letters to the Senate; its narrative is 112 OCT lines long. (Sulpicius Galba's personal report to Cicero on the battle of Forum Gallorum (*Fam.* 10.30) runs to only 52 lines.) By contrast, Caesar's account in the *BGall.* of the campaign against the Nervii alone, excluding all preliminaries such as preceding victories against other Belgae, occupies some 289 OCT lines; the first British expedition alone, excluding entirely the earlier victory over the Germans, stretches to some 262 lines, and the Alesia campaign alone (again excluding all earlier stages of the Great Revolt) covers about 383 lines, including a 44-line speech in indirect discourse.
[74] Letters *from* Quintus: Cic. *Q. fr.* 2.14.2, 16.4; 3.1.8–14, 17–18; 3.3.1; 3.6.1–3; *Att.* 4.16.7 [cf. *Fam.* 7.7.1]). From Trebatius Testa: *Fam.* 7.7, 8, 10, 12, 13, 15, 17, 18. Caesar: *Q. fr.* 2.11.4–5; 14.1; 16.5; 3.1.8, 1.10, 5.3; *Fam.* 7.5.2–3; 17.2 *Att.* 4.16.7.
[75] Cic. *Q. fr.* 3.1.17, 25; *Att.* 4.18.5.
[76] Osgood 2009: 342 is an excellent résumé of the phenomenon.

the army knew from the first invasion in the previous year but kept quiet.[77] In August (~ July, Jul.) Quintus had written that the British campaign was not amounting to much (*Q. fr.* 3.1.10 *nec quod metuamus nec quod gaudeamus*), and Cicero must have been one of the first to hear about its conclusion, receiving two letters in Rome on October 24 (= ca. September 27, Jul.), one from Caesar himself and one from Quintus, both sent from the coast of the island on September 25 just before their return across the Channel: "The campaign was finished, hostages had been taken, no booty but a tribute had been imposed" are the headlines he passes on to Atticus.[78] Cicero heard from Trebatius of the dangerous revolt of the Eburones and Treveri very close to its outbreak after the close of the campaigning season of 54,[79] and he picks up a reference by Quintus to the Nervii in a letter of November 54 (= October, Jul.), *before* they had played a baneful role in Caesar's narrative (and nearly cost Quintus his life). Evidently Cicero's brother had written that he was to spend the winter in Nervian territory.[80]

Finally, there was *fama*. This might be defined as information passed along by others in Rome, ultimately derived from their own sources presumably comparable in quantity if not in quality to what Cicero had access to. Other senators of course received letters from Caesar and thus became conduits of *fama* to others.[81] Caesar's subtle operator, the Spaniard L. Cornelius Balbus, also must have been the source of much information about what was happening at the front; he was often on the move between Rome and the commander of Gaul, and at least in 54, when he was away he

[77] Cic. *Fam.* 7.7.1, *Att.* 4.16.7, with Shackleton Bailey ad loc. Osgood 2009: 344. Quintus had joined Caesar with the express intention of improving his financial situation: *Q. fr.* 3.6.1; more sources in Osgood (p. 342n76).
[78] Cic. *Att.* 4.18.5. Even from Britain, letters carried by Caesar's courier service took about a month to reach Rome (*Q. fr.* 3.1.13, 17, 25; *Att.* 4.18.5), though there were sometimes long silences (*Q. fr.* 3.1.25, 3.1 [40 days]).
[79] Cic. *Fam.* 7.10.2 (with Bailey ad loc.), probably written in November (Julian); 13.2, 18.2 (n. 18.4 *praesertim tam novis rebus* – a tone of some concern), with Shackleton Bailey's comments; cf. Caes. *BGall.* 5.26–38. (For the date of the disaster see n. 207.) Note also that Cicero was already teasing his friend Trebatius about his duties at Samarobriva (Amiens) starting from late November (~ October Julian) (*Fam.* 7.16.3, 11.2, 12.1); he would not have had to await Caesar's official reports or *De bello Gallico* 5.24.1, 47.2, 53.3 to learn of this outlandishly named outpost.
[80] Cic. *Q. fr.* 3.6.2 (cf. 3.4.4); Caes. *BGall.* 5.38–52.
[81] In the *ad Quintum* letters of 54, we hear by chance of a few – a tiny proportion – of Caesar's other correspondents in that year: P. Clodius, P. Vatinius, and P. Servilius *pater*, Caesar's old commander in Cilicia (*Q. fr.* 3.1.11, 20; 3.7.5). Clodius read out a letter of Caesar's in a *contio* (Cic. *Dom.* 22; the letter itself dated to 58 but the *contio* was probably in 57 or 56 [contra Pina Polo 1989: 299 n. 297], when Clodius was prepared to attack Cato's actions on Cyprus: Tatum 1999: 221, cf. Dio 39.23.4). There is no sign, however, that the letter conveyed significant information about Caesar's campaigns of that year, and it would be a mistake to generalize too much from this instance since it was a sensitive matter to make public the contents of a personal letter (Cic. *Att.* 8.9.1–2; *Phil.* 2.7–10 with *Att.* 14.13B; *Phil.* 13.22–48). A letter of Caesar's in behalf of Gabinius read out to a *contio*: Dio 39.63.4.

was frequently in correspondence with Cicero.[82] Other sources of *fama* would have been candidates for office sent from the army back to Rome for the elections (most notably, Marc Antony, q. 51, augur 50, tr, pl. 49, and P. Crassus), soldiers who returned from the army for elections, and indeed the many Roman citizens resident in Cisalpine Gaul who we know not infrequently made their way to Rome to vote in elections.[83]

Upon reflection it becomes evident that innumerable lines of communication carried news and information between the Army of Gaul and Rome. Cicero's situation cannot have been unique: many others at various levels of society will have been friends or family either to Caesar or to his officers or soldiers, and the information from this broad range of sources must have flowed outward constantly to a curious and concerned population. Caesar could hardly "control" this flow.[84] T. Labienus as well as Caesar had *tabellarii* going back and forth to Rome; given his eventual desertion of his commander, and his probable primary Picentine allegiance to Pompey, we should not simply assume that this channel of communication was subject to rigorous Caesarian surveillance or censorship.[85] Senators back in Rome also had their own, independent contacts in the war zone. Caesar makes Ariovistus assert that he had received many requests from Roman "nobles and leaders of the Roman People" that had made clear that he would be doing them a favor if he killed Caesar.[86] Since Ariovistus was a "Friend of the Roman People," recognized as king by the Senate and People only the previous year, there is nothing implausible about his exchanging communications with leading Romans even if the alleged contents of the exchange serve Caesar's rhetorical purpose too well to be uncritically accepted.[87] Another example is the Aeduan leader Diviciacus, who had gone on an embassy to Rome, as we saw in the previous chapter, and was even a guest-friend of Cicero's.[88] Suggestive too is the brouhaha, when Caesar requested

---

[82] Balbus and Oppius's role as mediators of information during the Gallic campaigns is evident from Cic. *Q. fr.* 2.10.4, 11.4; 3.1.8, 10–13, 18; *Fam.* 7.5.2, 6.1, 7.1–2, 9.2, 16.3, 18.3; *Att.* 4.16.8, 5.1.2, 7.4.2 (cf. *Att.* 7.3.11 and Cael. [Cic.] *Fam.* 8.9.5, 11.2). Gellius says that the two *rebus eius [sc Caesaris] absentis curabant* and describes the cipher system they employed for their correspondence with Caesar (*NA* 17.9.2), Oppius seems to have been in charge of the courier service between Caesar and Rome: *Q. fr.* 3.1.8. Note also Hirtius's visit to Rome in December 50, when he had been expected to meet with Pompey (Cic. *Att.* 7.4.2)

[83] See Chapter 1, n. 35. For dating Antony's quaestorship to 51 see Broughton, *MRR* 3.19–20.

[84] So, apparently, Osgood 2009: 346.

[85] Cic. *Q. fr.* 3.5.9, 6.2. Syme suggested that Labienus was "a Pompeian partisan from the beginning" (1938, 1939: 31n6), accepted by Gruen 1974: 63.

[86] Caes. *BGall.* 1.44.12.   [87] Caes. *BGall.* 1. 35.2, with Chapter 4, n. 221.

[88] Chapter 4. We last see him in action in 58 (Caes. *BGall.* 2.14–15; mentioned retrospectively at 7.39.1), but this does not affect the larger point.

a second set of supplications for his victories over the German Usipites and Tencteri in 55 (as well as for his first crossing to Britain), over the slaughter of a great number of Germans who, Caesar asserts in the *Gallic War Commentaries*, were treacherously exploiting a cover of peace but, according to Cato, had been sacrilegiously massacred. Cato's "facts" diverge crucially from Caesar's, and unless he was rather reckless with his own credibility we must suppose that he claimed verification by other reports – *fama*, if not *litterae* or *nuntii* – for the extraordinary demand he was making – namely, to hand a victorious Roman general over to the German enemy. Pelling is right to suspect that "evidently unfavourable reports were reaching Rome, and C[aesar] did not have total control of the flow of information."[89]

From a mix of all of these sources Romans – not only senators and *equites*, but also ordinary citizens and voters – learned about Caesar's campaigns in Gaul, assessed his "worthiness" for high honor (*dignitas*), and constructed his reputation (*existimatio*). At least the more important of his official communications to the Senate will have received an immediate public airing in *contiones*. Major victories will have been announced to the populace following initial receipt of the news in the Senate. The three sets of Caesarian *supplicationes* (in 57, 55, and 52, a total of fifty-five days) voted by the Senate would have been announced by the consuls in *contiones* directly after the relevant meetings, along with a brief statement of the grounds for each celebration. In itself the public declaration of the celebration by a consul, who will not necessarily himself have been friendly to Caesar, imposed a posture of communal consensus both within the Senate and between Senate and People.[90] The many days of thanksgiving, when business activity was set aside, the temples were thrown open, victims were sacrificed, and the Roman People as a whole – not merely male citizens but also their families – were called upon to visit the sacred homes of the gods and give thanks (in a striking exception to the quotidian norm), will themselves have afforded copious opportunity and leisure for discussion and admiration of the achievements that had given rise to the celebration.[91] Moreover, many contional speeches of the 50s – no doubt especially on the occasion of the promulgation and voting on the *lex Pompeia Licinia* extending Caesar's

[89] Mensching 1984: 53–57; Pelling 2011: 252. Sources in n. 188.
[90] The supplications of 57 must have been announced by Lentulus Spinther or Metellus Nepos, those of 55 by Pompey or Crassus, and those of 52 by Pompey or Metellus Scipio.
[91] See Halkin 1953: 83–109; for *contiones* following senatorial decrees see Morstein-Marx 2004: 246–248. For the "motive clause" of a decree of supplications Cic. *Phil.* 14.36–37 is our best evidence; cf. the "quod clauses" at Liv. 27.51.8, 37.47.4, Cic. *Cat.* 3.15. The most informative descriptions of *contiones* in which news of a victory and/or a decree of supplication was announced are Livian: see 27.51.5–8, 30.17.1–6, 30.40.2–4, 36.21.7–9, 45.1.6–2.8.

command in 55, or the Law of the Ten Tribunes of 52 – will have found occasion to describe Caesar's *res gestae* in Gaul in a concise but highly laudatory manner much like the descriptions of Pompey's victories in Cicero's *contiones* of the 60s.[92] From 54 the western end of the Forum began to be disrupted for the construction of *monumenta* of Caesar's victories, no doubt giving rise to further discussion (*sermo*) and evaluation.[93] In the Forum two notable Julian funerals of the late 50s (those of Caesar's daughter Julia in 54 and of his younger sister Julia in 51 or late 52) gave friends and family an opportunity in their eulogies to remind the public of the patriotic services of the absent conqueror of Gaul.[94]

Both senators and the Roman People, then, were kept well informed of the progress of Caesar's campaigns – and, what was most to the point, of their success – by much more current sources of "news" than the *Commentarii*, even if these were widely disseminated before the Civil War (which we don't know). The common assumption that the Gallic War *Commentarii* were "political instruments" by which, through "extremely careful writing," Caesar achieved the popularity in Italy to which the initial stage of the Civil War attests is in fact quite dubious.[95]

If, then, the common assumption of a narrowly propagandistic purpose for the *Gallic War Commentaries* does not fit well both with the complete absence of good evidence for their political impact through the 50s (and beyond) and with the fact that much more compelling evidence exists for different lines of communication between the Army of Gaul and Rome, then what, one might reasonably ask, *was* their purpose? I do not propose here to go too deeply into a debate that would quickly outgrow its relevance for our investigation, so I will state my answer fairly simply: *De bello Gallico* is not a short-term propaganda instrument aimed at shaping Caesar's public image back in Rome through the 50s (or in 51) but his stab at the "eternal glory" (*sempiterna gloria*) uniquely conferred by being inscribed in the genre of history – that is, in the annals of the Roman People.[96]

---

[92] Cic. *Leg. Man.* 27–50, *Leg. agr.* 2.49–55.   [93] See nn. 229–230.

[94] Daughter: n. 187. Sister: Suet. *Aug.* 8.1, with Wardle 2014: 109. The future Octavian/Augustus delivered the *laudatio* for the sister (his grandmother); Pompey would seem the best candidate to have done so for the daughter. Though her burial was evidently somewhat chaotic, that need not preclude the honor of a eulogy beforehand. Note that Caesar himself was somewhat innovative in his attitude toward *laudationes* for young females: Plut. *Caes.* 5.4 with Pelling's note.

[95] Welch's introduction to Welch and Powell 1998. The volume's subtitle is "the war commentaries as political instruments."

[96] The phrase comes from Cicero's own effort to persuade the historian (and senator) Lucceius to ensure the immortality of his fame by including him in his history: *Fam.* 5.12.6 (cf. also §1 *commemoratio posteritatis ac spes quaedam immortalitatis*).

It is often noted, rightly, that Caesar's *Commentarii* appear to have inhabited the space between the genres of *historia* proper and the various kinds of memoirs and memoranda collectively known as *commentarii*.[97] To be sure, Caesar's works have an undeniable *similarity* to "history" as his contemporaries conceived of it: for instance, the focus on military *res gestae*, a third-person "omniscient" narrator, ethnographic and geographic digressions, and so on.[98] And yet, for all of Caesar's syntactical precision and elegant Latinity, which make him an author of choice for second-year Latin courses or prose composition exercises, one must concede that his narrative is a rather austere thing, almost exclusively focused (in the case of *De bello Gallico*) on military maneuver and planning with no glimpse of high politics in Rome, lacking in stylistic grandeur and variation, smacking a bit too much of a traditional, lapidary "bulletin style," and largely eschewing that most dramatic (in both senses of the word) element of ancient historiography, direct speech.[99] There is a reason why his text tends to put general readers and undergraduates to sleep, despite the extraordinarily dramatic nature of the events recounted therein. When Cicero in his *Brutus* compares Caesar's *Commentarii* to nude, beautiful bodies, with the *ornatus* that we know he felt was fundamental to *historia* worthy of the name laid aside like so much clothing, he pays a gracious compliment to the work while at the same time making clear that it was not, after all, "history" in the fullest sense of the word.[100] Recently scholars have rightly rebelled against an older tradition of interpretation according to which Cicero was taken to be discreetly criticizing the work's (literary and rhetorical) "lack of finish," a criticism which (despite Pollio's criticism of

---

[97] Raaflaub 2017: 208: "Positioned halfway between a *commentarius* and a *historia*." Krebs 2017: 210 acknowledges that they "do not qualify as history according to either ancient or modern ideas of history."

[98] Handy résumés of such qualities proper to *historia* in Krebs 2017: 210–211 and Raaflaub 2017: 206–207. For Krebs, the "historical guise [sc. of the *Commentarii*] is a rhetorical ploy to lift them above the factional fray" (p. 211), but this presumes that they were *in* the "fray." For generic expectations of "history" Cic. *Fam.* 5.12 and Tac. *Ann.* 4.33.3 are the *loci classici*.

[99] Riggsby 2006: 141–142 rightly acknowledges that these formal qualities strongly differentiate Caesar's works from *historia* proper. For a recent survey of Caesar's style see Krebs 2018a. Fränkel 1956 shows that an important influence on Caesar's style was the rather dreary genre of official military reports, for which see also Odelman 1972, Mundt 2004, and Krebs, op. cit., 115–117.

[100] Cic *Brut.* 262: *nudi enim sunt, recti et venusti* [a pun since Caesar traced his descent from Venus], *omni ornatu orationis tamquam veste detracta*. For historiographical *ornatus* see Cic. *De or.* 2.51–64, esp. 2.54 *ceteri non exornatores rerum, sed tantum modo narratores fuerunt*. For *ornatus* as the polish that a worthy historian might apply to the bare record of *res gestae* see also Cic. *Att.* 2.1.2 *ut ornatius de isdem rebus scriberet*. (Closely related is the plea that the historian simultaneously *ornare* the "hero" of the work: *Fam.* 5.12.2 *ut ornes me postulem*.) On the "naked bodies" simile see also Kraus 2005, Pelling 2006, and now Nousek 2018, who also notes that "although the *BG* and *BC* are not without stylistic elegance, they lack precisely the type of *ornatus* that Cicero advocated" (108).

its factual accuracy) has been shown to be manifestly off the mark.[101] But this does not affect Cicero's central point, which (aside from its qualitative claim) is that the work was not actually *historia* in the full sense – that is, in all its grandeur and dignity – despite having a certain resemblance to that genre. Naturally, he cannot be rude, so he turns what might otherwise be taken as a criticism into a virtue (however disingenuously, perhaps): Caesar's work was "naked," yet like a beautiful body, it was actually best shown off unadorned. Cicero had employed a like simile fourteen years previously when comparing Atticus's "unadorned" *commentarius* on his consulship to women, "who seem to smell sweetest when they have no smell at all."[102]

If Caesar's *Commentarii*, therefore, are not quite history in the fullest sense of the genre, then why not? It is impossible to believe that Caesar could not have written the kind of full-dress *historia* that Cicero was calling for in the 50s had he intended to do so.[103] The basic problem, however, which Cicero emphasizes in his letter to Lucceius, was that to be the hero of your own history was like a victor crowning himself at the games (Cic. *Fam.* 5.12.8). *Historia* was the vehicle par excellence for attaining *sempiterna gloria*;[104] thus the historian was the gatekeeper of the path to glory, a role that required authoritative judgment, which in turn demanded impartiality – the impartiality of a judge dispensing praise and blame. The autobiographical historian, by contrast, would be "forced" to speak too modestly about himself and too generously about others' mistakes; furthermore his credibility and authority would come into question.[105] Better, then, to write up one's deeds in memoir fashion (*commentarii*) and make them available to historians to "embellish" (*ornare*), as we know Cicero tried to do not only with Lucceius but also earlier to Posidonius (in vain).[106] Cicero explicitly states that this was precisely the intention of Caesar's *Commentarii*, while Caesar's

---

[101] Krebs 2018a: 110. The common thrust of a wave of recent scholarship on Caesar (e.g. Welch and Powell (eds.) 1998; Krebs 2006; Riggsby 2006; Grillo 2012; Grillo and Krebs (eds.) 2018) is directed against this misapprehension.

[102] Cic. *Att.* 2.1.1: *ornata hoc ipso quod ornamenta neglexerunt, et, ut mulieres, ideo bene olere quia nihil olebant videbantur.* The recurrence of the basic idea reinforces the conventional nature of the compliment.

[103] The *loci classici* are Cic. *De or.* 2.51–64, *Leg.* 1.5–8, with *Fam.* 5.12.

[104] See Cic. *Fam.* 5.12.6 (also §1 *commemoratio posteritatis ac spes quaedam immortalitatis*), our closest document in time for the idea.

[105] *Fam.* 5.12.8: *haec sunt in hoc genere vitia: et verecundius ipsi de sese scribant necesse est si quid est laudandum et praetereant si quid reprehendendum est. accedit etiam ut minor sit fides, minor auctoritas, multi denique reprehendant et dicant verecundiores esse praecones ludorum . . . .*

[106] *Fam.* 5.12.10, *Att.* 2.1.2 (ὑπόμνημα – the Greek equivalent of *commentarius*). Ornare: *Fam.* 5.12.2, 6; *Att.* 2.1.2; cf. *De or.* 2.54.1: *exornatores rerum.*

continuator Hirtius says much the same.[107] Scholars tend to discount this idea out of hand, presumably because it seems inconsistent with the care Caesar manifestly lavished on his campaign memoirs; yet when Cicero sent Posidonius his Greek ὑπόμνημα/*commentarius*, it was adorned with "Isocrates' entire perfume-cabinet along with all the scent-boxes of his pupils, and some of Aristotle's rouge as well."[108] The master orator took pains to show off his best Greek style in this work; he submitted a copy to Atticus for his approval and anxiously awaited his verdict (or pretended to do so), while gently, and with more than a hint of condescension, criticizing Atticus himself for the *unadorned* nature of his own version. A *commentarius* was not necessarily artless, particularly if one hoped it would favorably influence the historian.[109]

Caesar, then, wrote his *Commentarii de bello Gallico* with his eye on "eternal glory" in the annals of the Roman People; he was indeed "thinking of history," as Kurt Raaflaub puts it, resisting a narrowly propagandistic interpretation of the work – but without (I would add) actually *writing* history (or *historia*).[110] He survived the conquest of Gaul by less than a decade and had not yet found his historian by the time of his assassination, only two years after Cicero's assessment of his work in the *Brutus*.[111] When Sallust took up his pen only a few years later his choice fell first on earlier moments of the crisis of the Republic which had planted the seeds of civil war, then on a sequel to Sisenna's admirable *Historiae* which had concluded with the death of Sulla in 78; he never reached the Gallic wars and perhaps had never intended to.[112] But Caesar's *res gestae* would only have to await Asinius Pollio (a Caesarian officer since the late 50s) for their proper historical elaboration in the 30s, and perhaps, for full treatment of the Gallic wars, Livy.[113] In the meantime, his elegantly written account

[107] Cic. *Brut.* 262: *dum voluit alios habere parata, unde sumerent qui vellent scribere historiam.* Hirtius *B Gall* 8 Praef., 5 *qui* [sc. *commentarii*] *sunt editi, ne scientia tantarum rerum scriptoribus desit.*
[108] Shackleton Bailey's fine translation of Cic. *Att.* 2.1.1. (Cf. 1.19.10, 20.6.)
[109] Hirtius's conventional compliment (*B Gall* 8 Praef., 5; cf. Cic. *Att.* 2.1.2) that Caesar's work was so beautifully crafted that it actually *deterred* future historians from working them up (*ut praerepta, non praebita facultas scriptoribus videatur*) should not be taken too seriously: Caesar's first historian would in fact step up within a decade (Pollio). See n. 113.
[110] Raaflaub 2017: 207.   [111] So Hirtius strongly implies: n. 109.
[112] Sisenna: *FRHist.* no. 26, with Cic. *Brut.* 228 and Sall. *Iug.* 95.2. Given his pro-Sullan tendency Sisenna surely made use of Sulla's memoirs (*FRHist.* no. 22), which would be a recent instantiation of the relationship between historical agent and historian suggested here for Caesar.
[113] Livy: The summaries of Books 103 to 108 give a sense of the large scale of Livy's treatment of the Gallic campaigns. Collins 1972: 925–926 remarks, with some exaggeration, that "the entire secondary tradition for the Gallic wars contains nothing but Caesar and smoke." Some important exceptions are Dio's criticism of the "unauthorized" war, Plutarch's and Appian's crediting of Labienus with the victory at the Arar (n. 19), Tanusius Geminus's story about Cato's proposal that

would also "shed some lustre" on his brilliant achievements among a relatively small group (in comparison to the Roman People) of interested readers.[114] And there is no reason to doubt that the letters and reports that arrived in Rome, at least from Caesar's hand, conveyed substantially the same image of Rome's *imperator* and his *res gestae* in Gaul as emerges from the pages of the *Commentarii*. Yet even Caesar's letters and bulletins had a good deal of competition from other news sources, and much of our tendency to exaggerate the proconsul's "control" over the news from Gaul derives, I think, from the questionable assumption that *De bello Gallico* was sent home from the front (either serially or toward the end of the campaigns) as a "political instrument" or even a work of propaganda.

The Response of Senate and People

Dio remarks on the enormous popularity Caesar had won by means of his victories in Gaul by early 56.[115] What is rarely equally stressed is how much progress Caesar had also made with the Senate by virtue of his success.

Caesar had requested *supplicationes* for his victories over the Belgae in 57 and received the signal honor of a longer thanksgiving to the gods in his name in a single grant (fifteen days) than had ever been celebrated before.[116]

Caesar be delivered to the Germans, Dio's mention of *decem legati* (both discussed later in this chapter), and Plutarch's powerful and poignant description of Vercingetorix's surrender (*Caes.* 27.9–10). See n. 19 for doubts whether Pollio covered the Gallic wars in detail. His was, of course, the canonical account of the Caesarian Civil War (Hor. *Od.* 2.1), which clearly underlies the accounts of Plutarch and Appian (Pelling 2011: 44–48; Drummond, *FRHist* 1.435–45; some papers in Welch (2015) dispute this unconvincingly), who besides telling the *whole* story of the civil wars beyond the end point of the *BCiv.* also contain many interesting and notable divergences from Caesar's own narrative (e.g. eyewitness accounts of the crossing of the Rubicon and the debacle at Utica, the "little boat" at Dyrrachium, or the casualties at Pharsalus).

[114] As Cicero hoped to do for himself with his ὑπόμνημα: *Att.* 2.1.2: *videtur enim posse aliquid nostris rebus lucis adferre.* We have virtually no clues about the readership of Caesar's *Commentarii.* Raaflaub 2017: 206 supposes that they "were probably intended to reach a very broad public that comprised all those who were not among his irreconcilable opponents." That would seem to include virtually the entire Roman People. Cf. also Krebs 2018: 41.

[115] Dio 39.25.1: ὁ δῆμος τά τε κατειργασμένα αὐτῷ θαυμάζων (cf. §3–4); cf. Plut. *Caes.* 21.2, also stressing the enthusiasm of οἱ πολλοί for Caesar at this particular juncture (although this could be mere editorializing: Pelling ad loc.).

[116] *Supplicationes* of 57: Caes. *BGall.* 2.35.4; Cic. *Prov. cons.* 25–26 (cf. *Pis.* 45, 59); Plut. *Caes.* 21.1–2; Dio 39.5.1. Caesar himself firmly fixes the decree toward the end of 57. (Halkin 1953: 42 thinks in September; Ramsey 2009: 39 thinks October; cf. Raaflaub and Ramsey 2017: 22.) The supplications mentioned in a letter of Cicero dated to March of the following year, 56 (Cic. *Q. fr.* 2.5.2) must be a different set, unless their performance was significantly later than their authorizing decree (so, apparently, Rice Holmes 1923: 50 and 83; contra Pocock 1926: 13n8). Pompey had enjoyed the honor of two sets of *supplicationes* in 63 and 62 totaling twenty days, but "only" ten for each individual celebration (Grillo 2015: 210–211 defends Manutius's emendation of *Prov. Cons.* 27, which appears in all standard texts, but see Hickson-Hahn 2000: 248).

Cicero himself appears to have made the motion, which clearly in itself was a way to stake a symbolic claim to respectability.[117] As Gelzer observed long ago, "this extraordinary honour paid to the proconsul of Gaul cut the ground from under the feet of [those] who maintained that since 58 Caesar had held his position illegally. By it the Senate recognized that Caesar's subsequent military achievements had cancelled out his earlier unconstitutional behavior."[118] Gelzer's larger point deserves to be underscored even though with his phrase "unconstitutional behavior" he adopts the language of Caesar's bitterest foes. The praetors Memmius and Domitius had failed to convince the Senate to invalidate his *acta* and his laws remained in full force, whatever his adversaries might say. "Controversial" they no doubt were – but for most senators as well as citizens, nothing that extraordinary services to the *res publica* could not redeem.

The supplications of 57 moved by Cicero were not the only sign that many senators were coming around. In late spring of the following year, 56, a series of decrees in Caesar's favor were passed, in all of which Cicero again claims to have played a conspicuous role.[119] First, the Senate voted to supply state funds to pay for the four additional legions Caesar had recruited in 58 and 57, despite the fact (or so Cicero asserts) that he could in fact have covered their expense out of the spoils of war.[120] This decree

---

[117] Cic. *Prov. cons.* 26, and further n. 119. Grillo 2015: 208 appears to doubt ("Cicero magnifies the role he played") the clear implication of Cicero's statement. Why?

[118] Gelzer 1968: 116; cf. 124, echoed by Grillo 2015: 209. Plut. *Caes.* 21.7–9 claims that the Senate was somehow "forced" to vote the supplications under protest, with Cato absent at Cyprus and Favonius helpless in his objections (μᾶλλον δὲ ἠνάγκαζον [sc. τὴν βουλὴν] ἐπιστένουσαν οἷς ἐψηφίζοντο). Special pleading is manifest: Caesar was in no position at this point to "force" the Senate to do anything. Similarly, Maier 1978: 86 downplays the importance of the honors by the senators by exaggerating their hostility to him (resorting even to anachronistic evidence such as Cicero's postmortem denunciations of Caesar's *regnum*) and emphasizing their hopes to share in Caesar's profits of victory. Inner motivations are always hidden to the historian, yet how could one hope to deny a triumph or even bring to trial (as is so often supposed) one whom the Senate itself had showered with more days and more sets of supplications than any Roman before him had received?

[119] Cic. *Prov. cons.* 26–28, with Butler and Cary 1924: 63 and Grillo 2015: 203–213; *Balb.* 61 *harum sententiarum et princeps et auctor fui.* Date: May or June (Kaster 2006: 404n41; Raaflaub and Ramsey 2017: 26n97). These decrees are usually supposed to have been a senatorial follow-up to the *de Caesare monstra* that some (tribunes, presumably) had promulgated by March 56, and which no tribune would veto (Cic. *Q. fr.* 2.5.2–3). Yet nothing assures the identification (Cic. *Fam.* 1.7.10, while suggestive, does not clinch the matter), and provisions for payment of the *stipendium* and the authorization of *decem legati* are unlikely subjects for legislation. The matter is too uncertain to form the basis of an argument that by means of the "Conference at Luca" Caesar had in effect forced the Senate's hand, although this is how it is usually represented. Note that the consul Lentulus seems to have been quite effective in quashing the "dangerous" bills of C. Cato and others (*sic legibus perniciosis obsistitur, maxime Catonis Q. fr.* 2.5.3; cf. Kaster 2006: 391), of which we hear nothing further.

[120] Cic. *Prov. cons.* 28; their recruitment is detailed at Caes. *BGall.* 1.7.2, 1.10.3, 2.2.1.

deserves a little more attention than it is usually given. Cicero's claim that the request was financially unnecessary but only a compliment to the general is a bit cheeky and made for a rhetorical purpose – namely, to suggest that the decree was a gratuitously bestowed honor to Caesar (*tum quoque homini plus tribui quam nescio cui necessitati, Prov. cons.* 28). In fact, by refusing until now to pay the legions Caesar had recruited in his provinces at his own cost, the Senate had "forced" Caesar to pay for the wars of the Roman People from the soldiers' plunder (or his share) – a risky and hardly painless expedient for whose negative effects he could hardly be held solely responsible.[121] The bill footed by Caesar thus far – one ultimately borne of course by necessity on the backs of the conquered – could have amounted to as much as 36 million sesterces.[122] Senators could no doubt complain that Caesar's recruitment of these supplementary legions had been done without their authority, and their disapproval may perhaps be measured from the fact that Caesar had to wait until this moment to receive any grant from the Senate to pay for them. Yet Caesar could make an excellent case for military necessity, and provincial commanders were traditionally given wide latitude to deal with emergencies.[123] Second, the Senate appears to have consented to his request that "ten legates" (*decem legati*) be sent to join him in organizing the settlement in Gaul, whose conquest he had announced at the end of the previous year. At least, so Dio says quite explicitly, and Caesar's own narrative asserts that at the end of 57 "all Gaul was pacified."[124]

Decem legati traditionally constituted a senatorial commission whose job was to assist the commander in arranging the details of the settlement of a major war. It may be supposed that they served to align the commander's decisions with the will of the Senate, thereby oiling the machinery of

---

[121] Rightly, Ramsey 2009: 39, contra Osgood 2009: 340: "Since he was already paying for these from his plunder, this [the decree of 56] was in essence pure profit for him."

[122] Quite apart from all the other associated costs of fighting a war, if the average annual cost of paying a single legion at this time was HS 6,000,000 (Crawford 1974: 696), for the four newly recruited legions this amounted to a debit for these two years of HS 36,000,000 = T 1,500 – no small sum! It would have been quite risky for Caesar to try to balance his books by failing to pay his troops during this period. Slave hauls like that Caesar conducted among the Atuatuci in 57 (*BGall.* 2.33.7) may have been "necessitated" by the failure of the Senate to pay the newly recruited legions.

[123] Thus, Goldsworthy (2006: 212) and Girardet (2017: 52 with n. 226, 55 with n. 241) surely go too far in suggesting that Caesar's recruitments were simply "illegal." (Girardet even adds this to his conjectural "charge sheet": p. 42.) Military necessity: Caes. *BGall.* 1.7–8 (Helvetic migration), 2.1–2 (Belgic *coniuratio*).

[124] Dio 39.25.1: ὥστε καὶ ἐκ τῆς βουλῆς ἄνδρας ὡς καὶ ἐπὶ δεδουλωμένοις παντελῶς τοῖς Γαλάταις ἀποστεῖλαι; Caes. *BGall.* 2.35.1: *his rebus gestis omni Gallia pacata*; 3.7.1: *cum omnibus de causis Caesar pacatam Galliam existimaret*. Cf. Plut. *Caes.* 21.3: εὖ θέμενος τὰ κατὰ τὴν Γαλατίαν; Cic. *Prov. cons.* 28; *Fam.* 1.7.10; *Balb.* 61.

subsequent senatorial approval. After his eastern campaigns in the 60s
Pompey had neglected to request or consult a senatorial commission of
ten legates, which may partly explain the great difficulties he encountered
when he tried to move his *acta* through the Senate. Caesar would then have
been avoiding Pompey's mistake and ostentatiously following the ancient
procedure last employed by a senatorial favorite, L. Lucullus.[125] This
request, then, looks like an attempt to avoid that kind of impasse and
consolidate the improvement of his position in senatorial opinion.
However, this has not been the favored interpretation of these *legati* in
recent times.[126] Even though there is no explicit evidence at all to oppose to
Dio's clear assertion, scholars have tended to agree that Caesar could not
have thus invited senatorial "meddling" in Gaul. Yet it fits perfectly with
Caesar's own claim that "all Gaul was pacified."[127] With this declaration at
the end of his second campaigning season, Caesar himself had returned not
just to "Italy" but to Illyricum for the winter – the alternative theater of
military glory which would remain to him under the *lex Vatinia* even if the
Senate now reassigned Transalpina – and that is where he was when he
received the disconcerting news of the "revolt" of the Veneti.[128] That rising,
however, swiftly made a dead letter of the idea by the time of Cicero's
speech *De provinciis consularibus*, and in the poisonous atmosphere of the
end of the decade it was not raised again.

By early summer of 56, however, it was clear that there was actually still
much to do in Gaul; in a speech before the Senate, as we have seen, Cicero
offhandedly estimates that perhaps one or two more seasons of fighting
would still be needed before Gaul could be thoroughly pacified, and we can
be fairly confident that he was putting the best possible face on the
matter.[129] With the consular elections for 55 approaching, for which

---

[125] On the institution of *decem legati* and Lucullus see now Yarrow 2012 and the standard work of
Schleussner 1978. On Pompey see Broughton 1946: 40–43.

[126] Balsdon originally accepted Dio's version (1939: 171–172), but he changed his mind by 1962: 138, and
since then scholarly consensus seems to have swung round to the idea that Dio is simply confused and
that the *legati* under discussion were simply personal legates – i.e. officers under his command (Balsdon
1962: 138; Shackleton Bailey 1977: 1:305; Pelling 2011: 248; Grillo 2015: 216; cf. already Gelzer 1968: 124n1,
Butler and Cary 1924: 65). A new wrinkle is Brennan's suggestion (2000: 810n344; apparently followed
by Yarrow 2012: 182–183), that *Caesar* was somehow depending on senatorial confusion of a request for
ten *personal legati* with the "established procedure of the Senate's 'Commission of Ten.'" None of this is
convincing; Dio's statement seems perfectly straightforward.

[127] See nn. 57, 124.

[128] Caes. *BGall.* 2.35.2, 3.7.1 (see p. 209ff.). Caesar's return not just to "Italy" but to Illyricum for the
winter of 57/56 may imply that at this time Caesar was considering his alternatives. Maier 1978: 54
suggests that Caesar may have been preparing to be relieved in Transalpina.

[129] Cic. *Prov. cons.* 34 *una atque altera aestas vel metu vel spe vel poena vel praemiis vel armis vel legibus
potest totam Galliam sempiternis vinculis adstringere.* See p. 206.

Caesar's enemy L. Domitius Ahenobarbus (who had already sought to overturn his consular *acta* at the beginning of 58) was known to be a strong candidate, the Senate was obliged by the *lex Sempronia* to determine the consular provinces for those elected.[130] For Domitius and other enemies of Caesar, this presented an excellent opportunity to sabotage his pursuit of *gloria* precisely where he had decided to stake his claim. Cisalpine Gaul and Illyricum were Caesar's by a law of the People, so these were effectively untouchable, but Transalpina, which had been assigned annually only by the Senate, could be transferred to one of the consuls of 55 simply by majority vote. And since under the *lex Sempronia* the decree on the consular provinces was not subject to a veto, Caesar could not block the move through the intervention of a friendly tribune.[131] To be ignominiously replaced in the midst of a revival of fighting that in itself refuted his boasts of the previous year would be a body blow to Caesar's political standing and would probably even throw his chances of a triumph into doubt. But Caesar was saved from humiliation by the *Senate*, a majority of which rejected the effort to replace him. Cicero once again played a leading part, delivering and publishing his speech for the occasion in Caesar's favor, yet it is not as if the Senate could be forced to do Cicero's bidding.[132] Rather, I suggest, the decision, in keeping with the series of decrees since the voting of supplications the previous year, reflects a rapprochement between the majority opinion in the Senate and the proconsul of Gaul.

It is common to undercut the apparent significance of the Senate's embrace of Caesar's agenda in 56 by stressing the revival of the Triple Alliance at Luca in April 56 and the broader effects of that realignment upon many senators, including of course Cicero: the Senate (so it is implied) was now in Caesar's, or the "triumvirs'," pocket.[133] The problem with this view is not merely that that last assumption is hardly borne out by the evidence – one might make an argument that the Senate was dominated by Pompey and Crassus in 55, but hardly in 56 – but, more concretely, that the beginning of the Senate's reorientation toward Caesar – the decree

---

[130] On the *lex* see Greenidge and Clay 1960: 37–38 and *MRR* 1.514, Vervaet 2006. Domitius: Suet. *Iul.* 24.1; Dio 39.31; Plut. *Pomp.* 52.1–2, *Crass.* 15, *Cat. Min.* 41.3–42.1; App. *BCiv.* 2.17/64. For the date of the *Prov. cons.* see n. 41.

[131] See Chapter 4, n. 235.

[132] Cic. *Prov. cons.* passim, esp. 3, 17, 36–38. The old controversy over whether the *Prov. cons.* was the *palinodia* Cic. refers to at *Att.* 4.5.1 (see now Grillo 2015: 14–16, contra Shackleton Bailey 1965: 2:233) can be set aside here.

[133] The revival of the Triple Alliance in early 56 and its effects are too well known to need recounting here: see especially the thoughtful narrative of Mitchell 1991: 168–190; cf. also Lintott 2008: 201–209. Gruen 1969a, esp. 89–96; Pelling 2011: 244–247.

ordering *supplicationes* of unprecedented magnitude in Caesar's name – came months *before* Luca, already in the fall of 57.[134] Furthermore, already in early March, about a month *before* Luca, P. Vatinius sharply criticized Cicero for having become Caesar's friend (probably by supporting the *supplicationes*) merely as a cynical response to his military successes.[135] Cicero's conciliatory moves toward Caesar and support for his *dignitas* clearly predate the revival of the three-way alliance in and around April 56, even if he tries to tell a more honorable story in his famous letter to P. Lentulus Spinther, written two years later in reply to his correspondent's pointed query, stressing his submission to Pompey's strong claims to gratitude and (implicitly) his realistic resignation to superior power.[136] If Cicero had begun making overtures to Caesar already in the fall or winter of 56, why shouldn't others, with less reason for grievance, have done the same?[137]

If we seek the reason for a change of heart among many senators, then, why do we need to look further than the obvious? Both Plutarch and Dio imply that the resounding acclaim among the Roman People that Caesar had won by his victories in Gaul made it more or less impossible to stand publicly in the way of his honors. Dio explicitly attributes the Senate's agreement to Caesar's requests for the ten legates and *stipendium* mentioned earlier to the People's admiration for his astonishing achievements

---

[134] See n. 116.

[135] Cic. *Fam.* 1.9.7: *dixissetque testis Vatinius me fortuna et felicitate C. Caesaris commotum illi amicum esse coepisse.* The occasion was Vatinius's *oratio* (*Vat.* 41) delivered in the trial of Sestius *de vi*, on which see especially Pocock 1926: 3–5, 134–145 (cf. 195–197); Alexander 2002: 206–217; cf. Lintott 2008: 27–30. Note that a request for a *supplicatio* was an occasion when a senator's *amici* were expected to pull out all the stops to defend their friend's *dignitas*: cf. Cic. *Phil.* 1.12, Cael. [Cic.] *Fam.* 8.11.

[136] Cic. *Fam.* 1.9. Lentulus had clearly asked Cicero to explain his reconciliation with Caesar, Ap. Claudius, and above all P. Vatinius (§4). Cicero probably greatly exaggerates the import of his motion of April 5 calling for a debate about the Campanian land in mid-May (i.e. after the return of the Senate from its traditional spring vacation). Even if it should be interpreted as actively supporting the earlier proposal by the tribune Rutilius Lupus to suspend distribution of the Campanian land in order to preserve funds for Pompey's grain purchases, Rutilius was pretty clearly aligned with Pompey and Cicero may have been confused by mixed signals emanating from Magnus himself. (A sampling of authoritative views includes Gruen 1969a, Mitchell 1991: 168–172, Seager 2002: 116–117, and Lintott 2008: 191, 202.) Furthermore, although Cicero claims in the letter to have made implicit but strong criticisms of Caesar in his speeches against Vatinius and Sestius (§7), none of the phrases he cites here made their way into the published version of the speeches, where on the whole he draws a careful distinction between the unspeakable actions of P. Vatinius as tribune and Caesar's as consul. See Alexander 2002: 215, with earlier literature, but also Kaster 2006: 151–152, 372–373, 377–378.

[137] Indeed, Cicero claims to have followed the senators' lead: *Prov. cons.* 25: *vos sequor, patres conscripti, vobis obtempero, vobis adsentior . . . postea quam rebus gestis vestras voluntatesque mutastis, me non solum comitem esse sententiae vestrae sed etiam laudatorem vidistis.*

and the high hopes they invested in him.[138] Caesar's glory had taken on a life of its own outside the Senate House, whether or not the consuls chose to lend a hand themselves by reading out his dispatches promptly within the four walls of the Curia.[139] The People were a force in the Republic, and in the face of this enthusiasm continued rearguard sniping against Caesar's highly popular actions as consul three years past was increasingly pointless. Already in March Cicero himself said (or represented himself in the published version of the speech as saying), "my true sentiment will now burst forth, and I shall say unhesitatingly what I feel!" – a great huffing and puffing to alert the audience that an important concession is coming – "if perhaps Gaius Caesar was too contentious in any matter, if the greatness of the struggle, his zeal for glory, his irrepressible spirit and high nobility drove him on," then that "should be tolerated in the case of a man of his quality and erased by the extraordinary achievements that he afterwards accomplished."[140] Put another way (as Cicero does a few months later), "I cannot fail to be a friend to anyone who has served the Republic well."[141] In a retrospective look at his realignment in the famous letter to Lentulus Spinther written in 54, Cicero emphasizes that Pompey and Caesar were, after all, hardly the kind of "evil scoundrels" (*improbi et perditi cives*) who had held domination with Cinna and his allies in the 80s. Implicitly he represents them as joined to the *causa* of the *boni* (revived by Spinther in his consulship) in a kind of "Grand Alliance" whose salutary effect was to block any inroads by a scoundrel (presumably such as P. Clodius).[142]

Even if most senators did not really believe in redemption, Caesar's stock was now extremely high at all levels of society, and it must have seemed to those senators with lingering reservations about the actions of 59 high time to make accommodations to political reality, especially if one could convince oneself, as Cicero claims to have done, that Caesar for his part was also prepared to return to a more harmonious relationship with

---

[138] Dio 39.25.1: ὁ δὲ δὴ Καῖσαρ αὐξανόμενος, καὶ ὁ δῆμος τά τε κατειργασμένα αὐτῷ θαυμάζων. Cf. 39.5.1 (with Cic. *Prov. cons.* 33); Plut. *Caes.* 21.2: ἡ πρὸς ἐκεῖνον εὔνοια τῶν πολλῶν.

[139] Dio 39.25.2: "[Pompey] attempted to persuade the consuls not to read Caesar's letters immediately but to conceal the facts as long as possible, until the glory of his deeds should prevail on its own" (μέχρις ἂν αὐτόματος ἡ δόξα τῶν πραττομένων ἐκνικήσῃ).

[140] Cic. *Vat.* 15: *deinde, – erumpet enim aliquando ex me vera vox et dicam sine cunctatione quod sentio, – si iam violentior aliqua in re C. Caesar fuisset, si eum magnitudo contentionis, studium gloriae, praestans animus, excellens nobilitas aliquo impulisset, quod in illo viro et tum ferendum esset et maximis rebus quas postea gessit oblitterandum . . . .* A slightly different but similar claim at *Fam.* 1.9.12 *etiam res ipsa publica me movit, quae mihi videbatur contentionem,* *praesertim maximis rebus a Caesare gestis,* *cum illis viris [sc. Caesare et Pompeio] nolle fieri.*

[141] Cic. *Prov. cons.* 24: *nemini ego possum esse bene merenti de re publica non amicus.*

[142] Cic. *Fam.* 1.9.11–12; 14: *nulli improbo civi locus ad rem publicam violandam esse potuisset.*

the Senate, "now that the Senate had recognized his splendid achievements by signal and unprecedented honours and marks of esteem."[143] It was now, in connection with the debate on the provinces for the consuls to be elected in summer 56, that Cicero intoned the words to the Senate quoted at the beginning of our third chapter:

> Never was there anyone who could be a leader here who preferred to be a "Friend of the People." But some men, either lacking confidence in themselves because of their own unworthiness or pushed away from attachment to this Order because of the disparagement inflicted by others, have often almost been forced to throw themselves into those heavy seas. If they turn their gaze away from that kind of tossing about on a popular course back to the Senate after serving the Republic well and desire to be considered worthy of the highest prestige, which belongs to this body, they should not merely not be pushed away but even be courted.[144]

Of course, money talks as well as success, and from quite early on in Caesar's Gallic campaigns (the winter of 57/56 and the prelude to the meeting at Luca, to be precise) Plutarch, echoed to some extent by Suetonius and Appian, begins to describe the general's attempts to cash in on his success through large-scale bribery, triumviral string pulling, and the like: "Candidates for office relied on him as their paymaster, spending his money on bribing the voters: they were duly elected, and they did everything they could do to increase his power."[145] The notorious (and questionable) story of a conclave of 200 senators with Caesar at Luca while 120 lictors cooled their heels outside is a key element in this same discourse of Caesarian corruption, implicitly demonstrating the extraordinary power the general supposedly wielded over city politics during his absence in the Gallic wars, through both his own resources and those of his allies.[146]

The apparent rhetorical function of the story should set us on guard. While the accumulating haul of plunder from Gaul clearly would ultimately make Caesar an astoundingly rich man, perhaps almost on the scale of

---

[143] Cic. *Fam.* 1.9.14 (Shackleton Bailey): *cum etiam Caesar rebus maximis gestis singularibus ornatus et novis honoribus ac iudiciis senatus ad auctoritatem eius ordinis adiungeretur.*

[144] *Prov. cons.* 38 (Latin at Chapter 3, n. 3). For the date of the speech see n. 41.

[145] Pelling's translation of Plut. *Caes.* 21.4; cf. 20.2–3; cf. *Pomp.* 51.4. Note that this is placed even before the revival of the alliance at Luca in April 56, though the phenomenon intensifies thereafter: *Caes.* 21.5–6. Cf. Suet. *Iul.* 23.2 and App. *BCiv.* 2.17/62, whose similarity suggests a common source (Pelling 2011: 236, 244); Appian sets the comment around the time of the meeting at Luca, but Suetonius is chronologically vague.

[146] The rather dubious story in its various instantiations is typically framed in the context of Caesarian influence (see n. 70). App. *BCiv.* 2.17/62 divides the two hundred senators into two groups: those who had *already* received "gifts" from Caesar, and those seeking money or favor.

Pompey,[147] it seems most unlikely that this was already the case in 57 and early 56, when as we saw Caesar was still paying out of his own purse (or rather, from his Gallic plunder) for the supplementary legions he had recruited.[148] Concrete, authoritative signs of the inflow of Gallic wealth seem to emerge only later, around 54; for example, that is when Caesar's large loan to Cicero of (at least) HS 800,000, which would prove such an embarrassment as the Civil War loomed, belongs;[149] this is also when Caesar and his agents began to purchase expensive land around the Forum for his *monumenta*, and a cluster of contemporary references to Caesar's wealth and generosity begins to appear.[150] Probably therefore the references of our late sources to Caesar's financial manipulation of large numbers of senators by means of his newfound *conquistador*'s wealth even before the middle of the decade are not only exaggerated but anachronistic.

Electoral Influence at Long Distance

How much influence did Caesar actually have on political events in Rome after he had marched away to his provinces? Was he able (as Plutarch's broad-brush account in the *Caesar* would suggest) not only to defend his position in the Senate but also to engineer consistently positive results in the popular assemblies? A little old-fashioned prosopography helps to put the matter in perspective. Careful analysis of the results of elections (i.e. lists of known magistrates) for 58 and 57 permits us to trace and, to some extent, to measure Caesar's influence on the voting assemblies in Rome. The magistrate lists for 58 and 57 are fairly complete because of the wealth of Ciceronian information we possess at this point in the narrative, due largely to his exile and his struggles to reestablish his position after returning to Rome. The electoral results, however, offer precious little confirmation that Caesar exerted *any* significant influence on the elections of 58

---

[147] See Appendix 1.   [148] See p. 220ff.

[149] We first hear of the loan on the eve of the Civil War, when the unpaid balance of HS 800,000 gave Cicero headaches (Cic. *Att.* 5.1.2 etc.), but in view of Cicero's frequent references to Caesar's generosity in the letters of 54 it is reasonable to suppose that this is when the loan was made (Gelzer 1968: 137; Mitchell 1991: 191n125).

[150] In 54, Cicero first describes Caesar's *opes* as *maximae* (*Fam.* 1.9.21 see Shackleton Bailey); also *divina liberalitas* (§12, 18). Cicero's appears to be the first of Caesar's known interest-free or cut-rate loans to senators (Suet. *Iul.* 27.1); these seem unsurprisingly to cluster around the end of the decade when his political future was at stake. For the *monumentum* see n. 229. See also Cic. *Rab. Post.* 41–44 (with Siani-Davis 2001: C. Rabirius Postumus (clearly connected somehow with Caesar's attempt to extract something out of Ptolemy's ill-fated bribe/loan); Cat. 29, line 15 *sinistra liberalitas*. More evidence and discussion in Appendix 1.

and 57, before the revival of the Triple Alliance gave him indirect influence through Pompey's candidates.

Among the major magistrates of 57 (i.e. those elected in 58), only the consul P. Lentulus Spinther can be convincingly shown to have enjoyed Caesar's support – yet Lentulus was anyway closer to Pompey than to Caesar, and his subsequent history in the office and in his province afterward shows no strong allegiance to Caesar.[151] No other magistrate of 57 is known for any inclination toward Caesar.[152] The consuls elected in 57 for the next year were both unfriendly. Two allies Caesar had enjoyed in the tribunician college during his consulship, P. Vatinius and C. Alfius Flavus, both fell through in their elections in 57 for aedile and praetor, respectively – a blow all the more troubling because two other members of the tribunician college who had vigorously *opposed* Caesar in that year, Cn. Domitius Calvinus and Q. Ancharius, both won their elections for praetorships in 56.[153] Vatinius's loss when running merely for the aedileship seems particularly notable since he had been Caesar's most important and conspicuous ally among the tribunes of 59 and had even carried the law that gave him his five-year command, while on the other hand the successful candidates, Calvinus and Ancharius, had enjoyed remarkably rapid advancement (only three years) from their tribunates to the praetorship.[154] The only bright spots for Caesar in the elections for 56 were the praetorian success of Caesar's recent legate, C. Claudius Pulcher (P. Clodius's brother) – though a Claudius would not feel beholden to any man for his election – and the

---

[151] Caes. *BCiv.* 1.22.4; other sources in Gruen 1974: 144–145. Even Lentulus's connection to Pompey did not forestall unpleasant friction over the restoration of King Ptolemy of Egypt in 56.

[152] The tribune Q. Numerius Rufus later turns up as a Caesarian legate in Illyricum (*MRR* 2.202), but since Caesar is known to have drawn men into his ambit through service with him (e.g. Q. Cicero) this is insufficient to justify labeling him as Caesarian in 57 (Gruen 1974: 187: "perhaps"; see Tatum 1999: 177; Kaster 2006: 278–279). His opposition to Cicero's return was enough to earn him the orator's scorn.

[153] Cic. *Vat.* 16, 38, *Sest.* 113–114; Schol. Bob. 151 St. Gruen 1974: 91–93: "Opposition was congealing, and the gains of 59 were soon to be overbalanced by greater losses in that and subsequent years." Cf. Ramsey 2009: 40. For the tribunician college of 59 see *MRR* 2.189–190. Alfius was probably running for praetor, though this is not explicitly stated (Broughton 1991: 35; contra, however, Mitchell 1991: 179). He probably attained the praetorship finally in 55 for 54 (Broughton *MRR* 2.222 with 227n3) during the brief revival of "triumviral" power in the consulship of Pompey and Crassus. At *Vat.* 38 the unnamed adversary whose success in the praetorian election Caesar is made to lament is presumably Domitius. Vatinius reached the praetorship in 55.

[154] Most praetors seem to take four to five years to cover this distance; in this period Domitius and Ancharius are beaten only by Metellus Nepos (tr. 62, pr. 60), Q. Fufius Calenus (tr. 61, pr. 59), and three "Pompeian" praetors elected under the unusual circumstances of 55 (T. Annius Milo [tr. pl. 57, pr. 55], C. Cato [tr. pl. 56, pr. 55? *MRR* 3.170], and M. Nonius Sufenas [tr. pl. 56, pr. 55? *MRR* 3.148). Domitius and Ancharius may have omitted the aedileship, or perhaps held it before their tribunates.

election of at least two supportive tribunes who advocated in his interest early in 56.[155] Although at least three of the tribunes of 56 were Pompey's men (L. Caninius Gallus, A. Plautius, P. Rutilius Lupus, and perhaps M. Nonius Sufenas), before Luca they could not be counted on to defend Caesar; one of them, P. Rutilius, actually worked against him.[156] Another hostile tribune was probably Antistius Vetus, whom Badian plausibly identified as the Lucius Antistius who sought to recall Caesar for trial in this year and was stymied only when the proconsul called upon the entire college of tribunes to support his plea that he was absent in the public service (*rei publicae causa*).[157] In short, Caesar certainly did not enjoy much success as an electoral string puller during the first two years of his Gallic campaigning, and he seems to have been largely dependent on Pompey's (and Crassus's) ability to get their men into important positions where they could also support his, Caesar's, interests.[158]

What about influence exerted indirectly through Pompey, then – Caesar's son-in-law until Julia's death in August 54? Erich Gruen's study of the limited success of the "First Triumvirate" of Pompey, Crassus, and Caesar in placing its men on the levers of power remains fundamental.[159] He found that the Triple Alliance was effective only in relatively brief bursts when extraordinary incentives to cooperation outweighed the

---

[155] Claudius: Cic. *Sest.* 41, probably referring to Gaius rather than Appius (*MRR* 2.198). Tribunes: Cic. *Q fr.* 2.5.3 (March), with n. 119. Crassus's follower Cn. Plancius is known to have had reason for gratitude to Caesar (Cic. *Planc.* 32, 34–35; Gruen 1974: 319). The entire college is known, or very nearly so: Broughton in the first *MRR* identifies all ten names but retracts Procilius at *MRR* 3.175 (see also Gruen 1974: 315n25 and Shackleton Bailey 1980: 185). "Cassius" at Cic. *Q. fr.* 2.1.2, should probably be emended to "Caninius" (Shackleton Bailey ad loc.) since the man is probably a tribune but the tribunates of known contemporary Cassii are all accounted for.

[156] By raising the issue of the Campanian land: Cic. *Q. fr.* 2.1.1. For stress in the Pompey-Caesar relationship in early 56 see Gruen 1968: 90–92 and 1974: 100. Gruen plausibly suggests a strategic design by Pompey to advertise his indispensability to Caesar, though it is also possible that Rutilius was acting on his own initiative, with the same result. Prosopographical data for all these men in Gruen 1974. On Nonius see *MRR* 3.148; Gruen 1974: 315. C. Cato abandons his hostile stance only after Luca and for the remainder of his tribunate becomes a strong supporter of Pompey, despite his former outburst in December 59 (Gruen 1974: 314–315).

[157] Suet. *Iul.* 23.1; cf. Cic. *Q. fr.* 2.1.3. Convincingly moved to 56 (and Suetonius's "L. Antistius" identified more fully as Vetus) by Badian 1974; cf. Shackleton Bailey 1991: 8–9 and *MRR* 3.17; Chapter 4, n. 199).

[158] Caesar's influence over elections remains limited for the rest of the decade until 51 and 50 as the contest over his eventual succession begins to heat up. Consuls: Gruen 1974: 143–159. Tribunes: C. Trebonius (tr. pl. 55), and M. Coelius Vinicianus (tr. pl. 53), but even in these cases we must remember that *subsequent* service as one of Caesar's officers does not imply that a man was a Caesarian partisan as tribune (too readily assumed by Gruen 1974: 187). Names of Caesarian officers who served in Gaul either before or after a magistracy in Rome are conveniently collected by Maier 1978: 90–91.

[159] Gruen 1974: 90–102, 143–150; cf. Ramsey 2009: 43–45. More detail in Gruen 1968. The broad outlines of the argument remain valid despite changes in scholarly fashion.

divergent personal goals of the principals, and that these bursts provoked coordinated reactions and novel coalitions among adversaries in the face of which they could not be long sustained. Even in Caesar's consulship the posturing of Bibulus and Cato had made headway by pushing the Three into uncomfortably forceful responses, thereby preparing for a showdown after the changeover of the magisterial colleges in the new year; even then, two men determined to challenge the legality of Caesar's legislation could not be kept from praetorship in 58. Of the consuls elected for 57 and 56, only one, P. Lentulus Spinther, can be considered friendly to the Three, and yet he soon competed with Pompey for the plum job of restoring Ptolemy Auletes; Pompey's ambitions were soon dashed by a coalition of nobles joined by a consul of 56 (Lentulus Marcellinus) while he endured incessant sniping from P. Clodius, who, encouraged by various prominent nobles, could not be reined in. Crassus smiled at Pompey's discomfiture, and Pompey in turn either prompted or failed to restrain his ally P. Rutilius Lupus from giving Caesar a fright over the Campanian land. Even after Cicero tightened his collaboration with Pompey and embraced Caesar anew, he could not be deterred from unleashing savage denunciations of Caesar's father-in-law, L. Piso, or Pompey's loyal ally, A. Gabinius. L. Domitius Ahenobarbus pursued his candidacy for the consulship, vowing to replace Caesar in Gaul; he was temporarily put off for the moment by the revival of the Triple Alliance and the election of Pompey and Crassus instead, yet these two were stymied for the remainder of the year 56 by the determined resistance of the consul Lentulus Marcellinus and by Domitius's persistence. As consuls in 55, Pompey and Crassus were able to exert a dominating influence on the elections for that year, but soon relented (or were foiled) in the elections still under their presidency for the very next year, when Domitius could no longer be kept from his consulship, nor even M. Cato from the praetorship of 54 after they had successfully frustrated his run for 55.[160] Crassus left for his province to the jeers of a tribune announcing unfavorable omens; Pompey's longtime ally A. Gabinius was denied a supplication for his successful restoration of Ptolemy to his throne in Egypt, then successfully prosecuted and sent into exile on his return to Rome. The triumviral candidates for the consulship of 53, M. Scaurus and C. Memmius, fell through. In the years immediately following Luca Cicero's letters contain

---

[160] Thus demonstrating the hyperbole of Cicero's claim that the Three had made up in their notebooks a list of future consuls as long as the *fasti* of past ones (*Att.* 4.8a.2). On Cato's campaigns of 55 see now Blom 2016: 224–228.

frequent references to Pompey's "sole domination" (a reminder, of course, that Caesar was not the dominant partner in Rome in his eyes), but the facts demonstrate that this was a gross exaggeration whose roots lay in the orator's own deep frustrations at his relative subservience to the great man in these years.[161] "The vigorous senatorial opposition that the triumvirs had provoked in 59 was evident again in 55 and 54 ... [T]he triumvirate could not control Roman politics even after Luca."[162]

It is worth pointing out, given Caesar's partly justified reputation as a *popularis* politician, that throughout the period of Caesar's absence in Gaul there is no evidence whatever that he was able to make use of the kind of urban political organization that Clodius had been able to forge in 58 and had maintained for some time thereafter. Indeed, even after Clodius's murder in 52 there is no sign that Caesar stood to inherit either that popular hero's organization or his followers. In a discussion of the popular following of Clodius and Catiline, Ian Harrison distinguishes between urban support "either in what might loosely be termed 'public opinion,' or in the form of a Clodian-type organization";[163] Caesar's urban support was entirely, it seems, of the former kind, and the precariousness of that support would be proven in the difficult years of the Civil War and after.[164]

In short, despite the retrospective exaggerations of some of our sources, especially Plutarch, Caesar was unable to control affairs in Rome in his absence, and his efforts to influence them indirectly through his son-in-law, Pompey, actually the senior partner in the coalition, enjoyed only intermittent success. In early 56, as his claim to have conquered Gaul was swiftly undermined by the rising of the Veneti as well as others and it seemed now likely that the job would take at best another couple of years, he had every reason to worry that he would not be left to complete the job, and that his attainment of *gloria* on the scale of the Roman heroes of old was gravely threatened. His command rested on the Senate's good will but now a strong candidate for the consulship had begun to talk of replacing him – a straightforward enough thing to do since, as we have seen, the Senate had only to decide that Transalpine Gaul was to be assigned to one of the consuls for 55, and no Caesar-friendly veto was even possible. On this

---

[161] Cic. 4.18.2 *unum* [Pompeium] *omnia posse, Q. fr.* 3.4.2 *unus ille omnia possit, Fam.* 1.9.11 *cum autem in re publica Cn. Pompeius princeps esset vir.* Cf. *Att.* 4.8a.2. On Ateius Capito's religious objections to Crassus's departure see now Driediger-Murphy 2018: not "curses" but "dreadfully unfavourable auspices (*dirae*)" which he would later be accused of fabricating (Cic. *Div.* 1.29–30).

[162] Gruen 1974: 95 and 101.   [163] Harrison 2008: 116.

[164] Consider the awkward interaction with the urban plebs in April 49 (Chapter 7, p. 410ff.), the popular demands and rioting instigated by Caelius and Dolabella in 48 and 47 (Chapter 9, p. 528ff.), and the clash with the tribunes in 44 (Chapter 9, p. 520ff.).

occasion his allies came together and prevailed in the debate at which *On the Consular Provinces* was delivered. But this only secured his command for one more year. The whole game would begin again in summer 55.

There is a tendency to regard the terms on which the Three renewed their partnership as essentially imposed by Caesar driving the whole process. This was explicitly Suetonius's view, and Plutarch's narrative implies much the same.[165] The familiar teleology is again suspect, for as matters would turn out, the extension of Caesar's command would give him the military resources with which he could fight a civil war. But under the *lex Trebonia* his partners would have themselves voted five-year commands in Spain and Syria – provinces where there was in fact no compelling justification for major military action – which would elevate them to military parity with Caesar.[166] In return, Caesar had only their word that they would follow through with an extension of his own command. In fact, it is not entirely clear that the terms of the Trebonian bill had actually been cleared with Caesar in 56: intriguingly, Dio asserts that it was a nasty surprise to Caesar's friends, who suspected that it was an attempt to overpower him after the imminent termination of his command, and that it was only then, in the course of 55, that the consuls actually committed themselves to a law extending Caesar's command in order to ensure the success of their own projects.[167] Whatever had been agreed in 56 was in any case kept secret for some time – even Cicero was left guessing – so perhaps its terms were never actually "leaked" but only extrapolated by other sources from the results, so that Dio's guess may be as good as theirs.[168] In the event, Pompey and Crassus did follow through, giving Caesar the assurance he needed by means of a joint consular law, the *lex Pompeia Licinia*, both extending his command for five years and at last removing the major theater of war from the Senate's control, where it had

---

[165] Suet. *Iul.* 24.1 [Caesar]: *Crassum Pompeiumque … extractos conpulit, ut … consulatum alterum peterent, fecitque per utrumque ut … prorogaretur*; see n. 146 on the "Conference at Luca." Gelzer 1968: 123 sees "the stamp of Caesar's genius" on the undertakings allegedly made at Luca. Syme 1939: 37 was right to place Pompey at the center (cf. Gruen 1968).

[166] More, in fact, for Syria than for Spain. Dio 39.33.2 mentions or imagines some recent disturbance in Spain (cf. 39.39.4) that might have served as weak justification for intervention. Regarding Crassus's project, the tribune Ateius Capito objected that the Parthians had done no wrong (Plut. *Crass.* 16.2–3; App. *BCiv.* 2.18/66), yet relations with the kingdom were in fact troubled since after the murder of the Rome-friendly king Phraates III by his own sons the Parthian kingdom had just gone through a major succession crisis and Roman action against the victorious Orodes had already been contemplated (See Dio 39.56.1–2, Justin *Epit.* 42.4.1–4, with Sherwin-White 1983: 272–273; Siani-Davies 2001: 26n88; and now esp. Weggen 2011: 56–66). Had Crassus been successful, a different narrative would have prevailed.

[167] Dio 39.33.2–4, rejected on insufficient grounds by Gelzer 1968: 128n2.

[168] Plut. *Caes.* 21.7, *Pomp.* 51.5; App. *BCiv.* 2.17/63; Suet. *Iul.* 24.1. Cicero: e.g. *Att.* 4.9.1.

recently become a dangerous temptation for consular candidates and Caesar's adversaries.[169]

Pompey and Crassus resorted to heavy-handed methods to force their election to the consulships of 55 – given the stout consular resistance to their candidacy in 56 they pushed the election into the year 55 – and in the year of their consulship, we are told, they ensured the defeat of the alliance's enemies and the success of their friends only through considerable violence and massive bribery. Cato, for example, was actually wounded in an ambush while defending his brother-in-law Domitius Ahenobarbus, a consular candidate who, as we have seen, was eager to replace Caesar (Domitius's torchbearer was killed), and Pompey once came home with his toga bespattered with blood after presiding over the aedilician elections, supposedly causing Julia to miscarry.[170] Dio implies that after much violence and delay the election of Pompey and Crassus was ultimately secured by soldiers that Crassus's son Publius, one of Caesar's legates, brought to Rome "for this purpose," and Plutarch also mentions the involvement of "many soldiers" in this election, without however explicitly referring to violence, and perhaps implying only that they were sent home to sway the assembly with their votes.[171] The prevailing view is that these soldiers were sent home to force the allies' election by engaging in violence and intimidation.[172] Which is it then? P. Crassus was not only Marcus Crassus's son but also the dashing hero of the Aquitanian campaign of 56 who was at this time not only giving a boost to his father's consular campaign but also presenting himself as a (successful)

---

[169] Dio claims that Caesar's command was extended for only three years (for a total of eight: 44.43.2); Pelling 2011: 247 suggests that a five-year grant from this date amounted to only three *additional* years. The common notion that the law forbade discussion or a decision allowing the reassignment of Caesar's provinces until March 1, 50 (Broughton; Pelling 2011: 286n10, 290–293) is wholly conjecture; that date is never explicitly linked to the law in our sources, and its chief basis is a statement by Pompey that can just as well have been a temporizing improvisation: Cic. [Cael.], *Fam.* 8.8.4–5, 9. See Morstein-Marx 2007: 175n78. It would be surprising that Caesar never explicitly condemns M. Marcellus (cos. 51) for pressing to break such a clause, or that no one mentioned the explicit illegality of an attempt to decide on Caesar's provinces in the senatorial meeting of September 51, described by Caelius (op. cit.).

[170] Plut. *Pomp.* 52.2, 53.3–4, *Cat. Min.* 41.6–8; Dio 39.31.1, 32.2; App. *BCiv.* 2.17/64. For a summary of the disturbances see Seager 2002: 121–125.

[171] Dio 39.31.2: καὶ προσέτι τοῦ Πο`υπλίου Κράσσου ... στρατιώτας ἐπ' αὐτὸ τοῦτο ἐς τὴν Ῥώμην ἀγαγόντος, οὐ χαλεπῶς ᾑρέθησαν. Plut. *Crass.* 14.7: τοῖς τε φίλοις γράφοντα [sc. τὸν Καίσαρα] καὶ τῶν στρατιωτῶν πέμποντα πολλοὺς ἀρχαιρεσιάσοντας; *Pomp.* 51.5: Καίσαρα συλλαμβάνειν αὐτοῖς, πέμποντα τῶν στρατιωτῶν συχνοὺς ἐπὶ τὴν ψῆφον. The two Plutarch passages are manifestly based on the same source. Furloughs for soldiers wintering in Cisalpina may not have been uncommon (cf. Dio 39.5.3, during an Alpine campaign in 57/56), but the soldiers would only be able to participate in elections if they were greatly postponed, as were those of 56 for 55. (Contra Meier 1978: 51, 90).

[172] E.g. Goldsworthy 2006: 264; Ramsey 2009: 43; Pelling 2011: 246. Maier 1978: 89–91, however, interprets the soldiers sent to Rome by Caesar from time to time as voters.

candidate for the augurate and possibly also for the quaestorship.[173] His sojourn in Rome, then, is not in itself untoward, and as for the troop of soldiers that accompanied him, we should recall that soldiers often played a significant electoral role in recommending candidates to the voters: presumably in this instance talking up young Crassus's accomplishments and his solicitude for his men.[174] We have no idea how many soldiers came with P. Crassus, but we certainly should not suppose that they swamped the *comitia*.[175] Indeed, our only other reference to electoral support offered by Caesar's soldiers (slightly later, in 54) explicitly uses the traditional electoral language of *recommendation* to voters (in this case Caesar's "recommendation" to his soldiers to support C. Memmius), not paramilitary thuggery.[176] Dio and Plutarch both mention the soldiers sent by Caesar in 56–55 in a context that probably implies the use of strong-arm methods, especially in the context of Pompey's and Crassus's tenuous control over the voting and their frequent resort to violence and bribery to impose their will. It is tempting therefore to think that the soldiers, then, not only endorsed young Publius's pursuit of the augurate and supported his father's (and Pompey's) election to a second consulship, perhaps by means of both their votes and intimidation, but may also have lent a hand in passing the Trebonian law and the consular law that together secured the military resources of all three allies.[177] But we should remember that it remains obscure to us what precisely Publius Crassus's troop was doing, and in view of the generally poor state of our evidence and the blurriness of Dio's own language it is best to remain cautious about the charge that its mission was to serve as the coalition's violent enforcers.

We would like to know more about the public debate that preceded the voting on the *lex Trebonia* and the *lex Pompeia Licinia*. Clearly the passage

---

[173] Augurate: *MRR* 2.220, Rüpke 2005: 2:1107, n. 2234. Quaestor 55?: *MRR* 3.119; Syme, however, objected (1980a, 1986: 271–272). P. Crassus may himself have been a *iuvenis gratiosus*, a young nobleman cultivating his influence among the voting units: Morstein-Marx 1998: 278. In 55 Publius's brother, Marcus, ran for (and won) the quaestorship (*MRR* 2.223); he would serve under Caesar.

[174] Cic. *Mur.* 38, with Morstein-Marx 1998: 269–270.

[175] Caesar could probably not spare large numbers of soldiers once he was making final preparations for the opening of the campaign (May in this year: Raaflaub and Ramsey 2017: 31).

[176] Cic. *Att.* 4.16.6: *ut ... Memmius Caesaris commendetur militibus*. In this way, Caesar acted as a *suffragator* for Memmius, as Suetonius says (*Iul.* 73); cf. Cic. *Q. fr.* 3.2.3: *quod Caesaris adventu* [sc. in "Italy"/Cisalpine Gaul] *se sperat futurum consulem*. See *OLD*, s.v. *commendo*, 4, esp. Suet. *Iul.* 41.2 and Hirt. [Caes.] *BGall.* 8.50.1. Pompey had summoned a *magna manus ex Piceno et Gallia* to resist C. Cato's legislation in February 56 (Cic. *Q. fr.* 2.3.4; for the *ager Picenus et Gallicus – not* part of Cisalpine Gaul – see Cic. *Cat.* 2.5, 26 and Brizzi, *DNP* s.v. *Ager Gallicus*), but it is doubtful that these were active-duty military units rather than personal *clientes*. Cf. Maier 1978: 51n33.

[177] For the (uncertain) dates of the *lex Trebonia* and *lex Pompeia Licinia* see nn. 178, 179.

of the Trebonian law was a major public event in which the tribune C. Trebonius gave even the staunch opponents of the law, M. Cato and M. Favonius, a total of three hours to speak against it – and presumably the time allotted to the proponents was at least as long. Our sources, however, concentrate not on the substance of the arguments on either side but almost wholly on the tactics of the opposition: Cato ran out the clock, "forcing" the tribune to drag him from the Rostra repeatedly and causing such delay and disruption that the vote had to be postponed until the next day.[178] And nothing whatever is recorded of the debate and vote on the *lex Pompeia Licinia*, except that Cato did not even try to speak against it.[179] But judging from the praises Cicero had sung only a year before in his speech to the Senate on the consular provinces, we can suppose that Pompey and Crassus, and perhaps Cicero himself, dilated eloquently on the magnitude of Caesar's achievements and the corresponding injustice of robbing him of the due rewards of honor, including the triumphal car, that awaited him;[180] on the long, checkered history of Rome's half-measures against the Gauls' barbaric arrogance and its current submission to Roman *virtus* (total, but not yet safely consolidated), exemplified in the very person of the proconsul who "has done enough to assure his own glory but not yet enough for the Republic."[181] Perhaps speakers repeated Cicero's rhetorical flourish: "Let the Alps" – which had so long protected the Roman *imperium* – "sink into the valleys! For Italy has nothing to fear beyond those high mountains all the way to Ocean."[182] Caesar's intention to overcome yet

---

[178] Dio 39.33.2–36; Plut. *Cat. Min.* 43.1–8 (with inflated provinces). Morstein-Marx 2004: 183–185: "As with Gracchus' and Caesar's agrarian laws, when the circumstances were so unfavorable to verbal discussion the opposition's hopes of turning the wave of popular support rested on symbolic acts of obstruction that would push their adversaries into repressive measures apparently contrary to Republican traditions." The hostile tribunes Ateius Capito and Aquillius Gallus were prevented from vetoing the overwhelmingly popular measure (as is implicitly conceded at Dio 39.34.3) by methods similar to those Caesar used in 59, presumably with similar justification. The law was probably promulgated after April 27 (Cic. *Att.* 4.9.1, with Shackleton Bailey's note). Note that Plut. *Crass.* 15.5–16.1 and App. *BCiv.* 2.18/65 say that the provinces were allotted to the consuls by chance sortition, which scholars have been loath to believe (e.g. Seager 2002: 229n23; but see Rosenstein 1995, criticized on the basis of the praetorian *fasti* by Brennan 2000: 760–763).

[179] Plut. *Cat. Min.* 43.8–9. Dio 39.36.2 seems to contradict this, but he names no one specifically. He also suggests that the *lex Pompeia Licinia* was passed virtually on the next day, which seems highly unlikely. It looks rather as if Dio is hastily winding up a narrative section.

[180] Cic. *Prov. cons.* 35, 38–39.

[181] Cic. *Prov. cons.* 33–35, esp. *cum vero ille suae gloriae iam pridem rei publicae nondum satis fecerit* (35).

[182] Cic. *Prov. cons.* 34 : *Quae* [sc. *Alpes*] *iam licet considant! Nihil est enim ultra illam altitudinem montium usque ad Oceanum quod sit Italiae pertimiscendum.* At *Pis.* 81–82 Cicero similarly celebrates the obsolescence not only of the Alps as a protective barrier for Italy but also the Rhine River; it is uncertain whether at the time he wrote those words he had information about the expedition across the Rhine of 55 (Nisbet 1961: 200); if so, the speech would date to September (civil) rather than August (see Cavarzere 1994: 157–163 rebutting Marshall 1975; cf. also n. 185).

another natural barrier, the Rhine River, in his first campaign of 55 may
already have been anticipated at the time of the passage of the Pompeian-
Licinian Law.[183] We hear of no active resistance to the bill: Cato must have
known that there was no hope of his persuading the People to reject the
extension of Caesar's command.

Soon thereafter there was yet more excitement as news came of Caesar's
triumph even over "Ocean" with his first expedition to Britain, and the Senate
reacted with a second set of *supplicationes* longer than ever before. Regardless
of the (relative) military insignificance of the crossings of the Rhine and
Ocean, Caesar had not only consigned the Alps to obsolescence but had
also leapt across two natural, even mythical boundaries in this year. "The scale
of Caesar's successes in Gaul were startling, even in a Rome so recently dazzled
by Pompey's achievements."[184] The "extraordinary and unprecedented marks
of honor" conferred in 57 were soon repeated in 55, or rather surpassed, since
this time the Senate set a new record in its decree of twenty days of supplications for the victories over the Germans and Britons.[185] It is about this time or
shortly afterward that the poet Catullus imagines his friends Furius and
Aurelius gaining a place on Caesar's staff in Transalpine Gaul, "visiting the
monuments of great Caesar, the Gallic Rhine, the harsh sea, and the Britons at
the ends of the earth."[186] The proconsul's standing among the common
people can partly be inferred from the fact that, when Julia, Caesar's daughter,
died in the following summer (54) her body was snatched up by "the People"

[183] Raaflaub and Ramsey 2017: 33–34 date the crossing ca. July 11, civil (~ ca. June 26, Jul.). Since it is
unlikely that the passage of the *lex Pompeia Licinia* was pushed very late in the year it would be too
speculative, with Stevens 1953: 17–21, to suppose that Caesar's British expedition, which immediately followed the German campaign at the end of August (Raaflaub and Ramsey 2017: 35), was
specifically intended to justify extension of Caesar's command.

[184] Goldsworthy 2006: 185. For the intense excitement created by the crossing to *ultimos Britannos*, "an
exploit of celebrated audacity" (Pelling trans.) see Plut. *Caes.* 23.2–3; Dio 39.53.1–2; Cat. 11.11–12,
Hor. *Carm.* 1.35.29–30, Vell. 2.46.1. Pompey had just celebrated the opening of his impressive
theater complex with a spectacular set of games in August or September (Davies 2017: 226–236; the
date is implicated in the question of the date of the *In Pisonem*: nn. 182, 185).

[185] For the phrase see n. 143. 55: Caes. *BGall.* 4.38.5; cf. Suet. *Iul.* 24.3; Plut. *Caes.* 22.4, *Cat. Min.* 51.1–5,
Comp. Nic. Crass. 4.2–3 (mistaken as to the number of days); Dio 39.53.2. The date of the
supplications of 55 is somewhat complicated. Caesar and Dio clearly place them after the conclusion
of the British expedition: thus in October (Raaflaub and Ramsey 2017: 36–37). Cic. *Pis.* 59:
supplicationes [sc. Caesaris] *totiens iam decretae tot dierum* should not be supposed to date the
speech after the crossing to Britain, which surely would have been mentioned explicitly at §81.
Perhaps the supplications of 55 were "worked in" retrospectively when Cicero wrote up the speech
for publication (Nisbet 1961: 201), or perhaps they are anticipated with certainty already on the basis
of the Rhine crossing. Caesar had probably been decreed supplications for his praetorian victory in
Spain as well as for those of 57, so there may have been enough instances already to justify *totiens*
(pace Nisbet 1961: 201 see *OLD* s.v., 2).

[186] Cat. 11.9–11: *sive trans altas gradietur Alpes, Caesaris visens monimenta magni, Gallicum Rhenum
horribile aequor ultimosque Britannos . . . .*

from her funeral in the Forum and buried in the Campus Martius, despite Pompey's own plans for her burial at his Alban villa and the opposition of "the tribunes" and the consul Domitius on the grounds that the hallowed site required special authorization by the Senate.[187] (Of course the popular demonstration must also have been partly on Pompey's behalf.)

Not that Caesar's actions in Gaul entirely escaped criticism. Most famously, or notoriously, Cato took the occasion of the celebratory mood surrounding the Senate's debate on supplications in Caesar's honor in 55 to propose that the Roman commander should be handed over to the Germans in expiation of his alleged violation of a truce, interpreted as a sacrilege that would otherwise draw the gods' wrath upon the Roman People.[188] But Cato's tirade fell on deaf ears and the supplications were not only passed but extended to the unprecedented length of twenty days. As dramatic as his proposal was, it was not much more than would be expected from Caesar's bitterest domestic enemy; the more important fact is that, as Plutarch drily adds, "no decree was passed" along the lines Cato proposed.[189] Senators could recognize personal enmity when they saw it, and if Cicero's speech *On the Consular Provinces* gives any

---

[187] Julia's death was probably late in August (about three weeks earlier by the Julian equivalent): Cic. *Q. fr.* 3.1.17, 25, with Pelling 2011: 259. Plut. *Caes.* 23.7; *Pomp.* 53.5–6; Dio 39.64; Liv. *Per.* 106; cf. Suet. *Iul.* 84.1, *AE* 1987, 65). Dio 44.51.2 states that Caesar's remains were later buried in an "ancestral tomb" (τὸ πατρῷον μνημεῖον); for the interesting question whether this was where Julia had been laid to rest see Coarelli 1997: 593, who however goes too far in interpreting this as a "dynastic" monument constructed by Caesar in his lifetime in the manner of Augustus's later mausoleum (cf. Suet. *Aug.* 95, who refers simply to the "tomb of Julia, Caesar's daughter"). Although the tradition seems to limit the grant of public property for burial to *viri fortes sive reges* (Serv. *ad Aen.* 9.272; cf. the Scipios who fell in battle in 210 or Sulla), note that the patrician Claudii had a publicly granted tomb beside the Capitol, presumably on the edge of the Campus like the surviving tomb of C. Poblicius Bibulus (Suet. *Tib.* 1.1, *ILS* 862). Caesar planned funeral games for his daughter (he was in fact the first to do so: Suet. *Iul.* 26.2), including a mass banquet, gladiators and Rome's first *naumachia*, but they had to await his return to Rome only to be deferred further until the illusory end of the civil wars in 46 (further Plut. *Caes.* 55.4; Dio 43.22.3). Perhaps this was the intended purpose of the gladiators Caesar was keeping in Campania in early 49 (Caes. *BCiv.* 1.14.4; Cic. *Att.* 7.14.2, 8.2.1; cf. Suet. *Iul.* 26.3). Julia's games seem to have been in some sense combined or identified with the *ludi Veneris Genetricis* that probably immediately followed Caesar's quadruple triumph of September 20–26, 46, and celebrated the dedication of the new temple that crowned Caesar's Forum (see Weinstock 1971: 89 with Ramsey and Licht 1997: 52).

[188] Chief sources are Plut. *Cat. Min.* 51.1–5, *Caes.* 22.4; App. *Celt.* 18.2 (generalized to *nonnulli dedendum eum hostibus censuerint* by Suet. *Iul.* 24.3) = *FRHist* 44 Tanusius Geminus, F3, with Drummond's commentary and Pelling 2011: 252–253. The two known precedents date to 321 and 136 BC. For Caesar's version of the incident see *BGall.* 4.1–15, on which see the excellent study by Powell 1998: 124–128.

[189] Plut. *Cat. Min.* 51.4: ἐκυρώθη μὲν οὖν οὐδέν. Powell, however, overinterprets ἐλέχθη μόνον ὅτι καλῶς ἔχει διάδοχον Καίσαρι δοθῆναι (1998: 127: "The majority opinion [of the Senate] was that Caesar should be recalled"). Plutarch gives no indication of how many people "said" this – or even whether more than one did.

sense of the public mood only one year before, most Romans (even senators) are likely to have regarded as absurd the idea that they should sacrifice to Cato's animosity their victorious commander who had "advanced the Roman Empire beyond the bounds of the human world" and hand him over to the Germans, some of Rome's most fearsome enemies.[190] One source (for what it's worth) says that "the People" dismissed Cato's objection to the supplications and was overjoyed with the celebration.[191] As Cicero had noted in his speech for Sestius in 56, "Hardly anyone has lost popularity among the citizens for winning wars."[192]

Caesar's enrichment of himself and his subordinates during the Gallic campaigns also inspired a mixture of envy and dismay, as all readers of Catullus will know. Contrary to some readings of the notorious poems targeting Caesar's chief engineer (*praefectus fabrum*) Mamurra, it is fairly clear that Catullus's objection was not to any singularly rapacious style of imperialism practiced by Caesar in Gaul but to the fact that the unworthy Mamurra, rather than he or his friends, was a conspicuous beneficiary on Caesar's staff.[193] Catullus's Poem 29 ("Who can watch this, who can tolerate it?"), dated around the time of Caesar's supplications of 55 or perhaps just a bit later in early 54, provides a good sense of the public perception of the bonanza now flowing into Caesar's pockets, and through them to his lucky and envied staff.[194] The impressionistic evidence we possess of this influx of wealth from Gaul is collected and evaluated in an appendix.[195] What here demands our attention is whether this wealth, or Caesar's means of getting it, excited unusual criticism other than that targeting the (supposedly) unworthy character of its recipients. Of that there appears to be little evidence. Suetonius, Caesar's Roman biographer, does say at one point in the *Life* that Caesar lacked *abstinentia* in general, and that in Gaul he "sacked shrines and temples of the gods packed with dedications as well as cities more often for the sake of plunder than for any offense they had committed, with the result that there was a glut of gold" which depressed prices throughout the empire.[196] It is

---

[190] Plut. *Caes.* 23.3 (Pelling trans.).

[191] Plut. *Comp. Nic. Crass.* 4.3 (cf. *Cat. Min.* 51.7 ἔξω [sc. τῆς βουλῆς] μὲν οὐδὲν ἐπέραινε). Krebs 2018: 35.

[192] Cic. *Sest.* 51: *ex bellica victoria non fere quemquam est invidia civium consecuta.*

[193] E.g. Konstan 2007. The poet's resentment of his own treatment by C. Memmius in Bithynia (and of his friends Veranius and Fabullus by L. Piso) provides the implicit point of contrast (Catullus 10, 28, 47). Mamurra is probably not to be identified with the author Vitruvius: *MRR* 3.133–134.

[194] On the date of Catullus 29 see Appendix 1, p. 619.   [195] Appendix 1.

[196] Suet. *Iul.* 54.2: *in Gallia fana templaque deum donis referta expilavit, urbes diruit saepius ob praedam quam ob delictum; unde factum, ut auro abundaret ternisque milibus nummum in libras promercale per Italiam provinciasque divenderet.* Appendix 1.

impossible to evaluate the underlying facts here with the evidence at our disposal, but the allegation hints at sacrilege as well as the violation of Roman norms of just warfare, so it is tempting to bring this into connection with Cato's attack on fundamentally similar grounds late in 55.

Aside from Cato's quixotic intervention criticism of Caesar's campaigning appears to have been fairly inconsequential. One oft-cited passage is sometimes adduced to the contrary: Suetonius comments that he was too belligerent in provoking "unjustified and dangerous" wars on any convenient pretext with allied as well as hostile peoples, so that the Senate actually sent envoys to investigate the condition of the Gallic provinces, "and some proposed that he should be delivered over to the enemy."[197] This sounds alarming but begins to fall apart on closer examination. We have just seen that Suetonius's phrase "some proposed" conveys a highly misleading and exaggerated impression of the actual senatorial response to Caesar's request for supplications in 55. What about the rest of it? One can well imagine some hand-wringing about "unjustified and dangerous wars" deep in hostile territory to which the proconsul had exposed his army, beginning with the intervention against Ariovistus discussed much earlier in this chapter. Yet since success always followed in due course, at the necessary decision points, this did not amount to much. In all our extensive evidence for this decade we do not hear of a single "unprovoked" attack (at least, by traditional Roman standards) on a peaceful allied people (*foederatis*).[198] There remains the charge of provoking needless wars with "hostile and

---

[197] Suet. *Iul.* 24.3: *nec deinde ulla belli occasione, ne iniusti quidem ac periculosi abstinuit, tam foederatis quam infestis ac feris gentibus ultro lacessitis, adeo ut senatus quondam legatos ad explorandum statum Galliarum mittendos decreverit ac nonnulli dedendum eum hostibus censuerint.* The second word of the quotation, *deinde*, probably marks time from the extension of Caesar's command in 55 (cf. 24.1, fin.), not the recruitment of the noncitizen Transalpine legion Suetonius has just mentioned (24.2), which would make little sense. Ottmer 1979: 20–21 plausibly suggests that the *Legio V Alaudae* ("Larks") was formed out of the twenty-two cohorts which Caesar's legate L. Caesar recruited in 52 in Narbonese Gaul (Caes. *BGall.* 7.65.1) and later appear in the Italian campaign of 49. (See Appendix 5, p. 642)

[198] Rome's key allies for most of Caesar's years in Gaul, the Aedui, joined the Vercingetorix revolt after Gergovia in 52 (Caes. *BGall.* 7.32–34, 37–43, 54–55, 63), and therefore were not "attacked," nor was provocation lacking when Caesar did operate against them. Given the direct reference to Cato's proposal at the end of the sentence, the object of the allusion may be the Usipetes and Tencteri, yet to call them *foederati* was surely wrong and in any case highly misleading since they had crossed the Rhine in great force, encouraging some anti-Roman Gallic peoples to enter into negotiations with them (Caes. *BGall.* 4.1–6; Plut. *Caes.* 22.1; Dio 39.47.1; App. *Celt.* fr. 18). Just possibly Caesar might have been criticized for making war on Britons who were in a relationship of *amicitia*, if not strictly "allies," due to their submission before his crossing to the *imperium p. R.* (Caes. *BGall.* 4.21.5–8, cf. 27.5; note App. *Celt.* fr. 19), but this was quite a stretch and there is no reason to think that Roman hearts would have bled for *ultimi Britanni*. Going back further in time, Ariovistus was a "Friend of the Roman People," and Caesar's attack on him could be seen by some as "unprovoked" as well as "unauthorized," but Caesar's own account shows that after the victory was won he had little to

savage peoples." If one is willing to disregard Caesar's own claims of justification throughout his text this charge might be attached to various occasions through his eight years of campaigning in Gaul, but few that are likely to have won much credit or sympathy in Rome. If, as seems likely, Suetonius has in this chapter passed along some of the essence of Cato's speech against Caesar's supplications in 55 (perhaps via the anti-Caesarian historian Tanusius Geminus), the basis of this last charge may have been precisely Caesar's expeditions in 55 across Ocean and across the Rhine – an occasion, it turned out, for widespread rejoicing, not for anti-imperialist self-criticism and atonement.

Caesar himself had no great difficulty explaining his interventions: "He knew that in nearly all the Gallic campaigns Britain had supplied reinforcements to our enemies," while the German Sugambri had offered succor to the Usipites and Tencteri, then refused to obey his ultimatum to set things right.[199] Everybody knew of course that both expeditions were driven in good part by the pursuit of glory, and they were singularly devoid of concrete results,[200] so Cato may well have hoped to find a vulnerable spot. And indeed, according to Suetonius, the Senate was ultimately moved "at some point" to send a commission "to investigate into the state of Gaul."[201] This isolated claim in the midst of a problematic passage has defeated all attempts to make sense of it. Some conclude that Suetonius is confused about the nature and even the chronology of the *decem legati* we have discussed above.[202] Alternatively, it may never have been sent, nor in any case did it have any recorded result.[203] Overall, the chapter gives the impression of an undiscriminating attempt to throw as much mud as possible in the hope that some of it might stick, perhaps as was speculated earlier reflecting the tone and nature of Cato's speech on the occasion of the vote on Caesar's request for a second set of supplications in 55. For our purposes what is important is that Suetonius himself wraps up the chapter

worry about on this score, and Suetonius's *deinde* would seem to exclude a campaign of 58 from consideration.

[199] Caes. *BGall.* 4.16, 20.1 (cf. 2.14.4, 3.9.10). See also n. 198.

[200] Results: After the Sugambri retreated into the hinterland Caesar considered Rome avenged and return across the splendid bridge he had built after only eighteen days (Caes. *BGall.* 4.19.2–4). Only two years later they proved themselves quite unchastened (6.35–42). Similarly in Britain Caesar declared victory and departed after an expedition lasting just two months (Raaflaub and Ramsey 2017: 39–46) after demanding hostages that were mostly not delivered, ostensibly necessitating his return the very next year (Caes. *BGall.* 4.36, 38.4; Dio 39.52.3; Plut. *Caes.* 23.4). Pretexts for glory: Plut. *Caes.* 22.6; Dio 39.48.3–4, 53.1.

[201] Suet. *Iul.* 24.3, quoted in full, n. 197. *Quondam* is a remarkably vague chronological indicator that could refer to almost any point in the nine years of campaigning.

[202] Butler and Cary 1927: 74.   [203] Gelzer 1968: 131; Morstein-Marx 2007: 161n6.

with the observation that Caesar's success was what really counted: "Since his projects were turning out well he obtained more thanksgivings, of more days, than anyone before him."[204]

Setbacks and Final Victory

Caesar was lucky that his command was secured and extended when it was, for his first major defeat in Gaul lay only a year and a half in the future and it was soon followed by considerably more trouble, including an exceedingly dangerous united revolt of Gaul which was a nearer-run thing than is usually acknowledged (another effect of the teleological bias). Already during the British expedition in the summer of 54 an unlucky storm had destroyed some forty ships, a loss that Caesar seems to minimize but probably had greater resonance back home since Suetonius picks it out as the first of three major setbacks in his Gallic campaigns.[205] The expedition itself had had rather disappointing results, apparently puncturing the get-rich-quick schemes of many an officer in the army along with his friends and relatives.[206] After returning from Britain, the Roman army was sent into winter quarters scattered about the land of the Belgae while Caesar himself prepared to return to Cisalpina as was his established practice, but late in the fall an entire legion plus five cohorts (the equivalent of half a legion) encamped at Atuatuca deep in northeastern Gaul (placed variously in recent years in the vicinity of Tongeren, Limbourg, and Liège in eastern Belgium) was eliminated almost to a man by the Eburones led by their king, Ambiorix, who went on to raise a revolt among the Nervii, where the legion commanded by Q. Cicero was in winter quarters only some 50–100 kilometers away as the crow flies.[207] This would doubtless have been destroyed as well but for Caesar's swift reaction to the initial disaster, Q. Cicero's steady nerves, and quite a bit of luck.[208]

A. Powell has acutely analyzed Caesar's artfully defensive writing about this major blot on his military record. "For every alert Roman the defeat of

---

[204] Suet. *Iul.* 24.3: *sed prospere cedentibus rebus et saepius et plurium quam quisquam umquam dierum supplicationes impetravit.*

[205] Caes. *BGall.* 5.10–11; Suet. *Iul.* 25.2: *in Britannia classe vi tempestatis prope absumpta* listed among the disaster in Belgium about to be discussed and the defeat at Gergovia in 52 (n. 224). A smaller maritime misfortune befell the first expedition to Britain: 4.29, 31.

[206] Disappointment is palpable in Cic. *Att.* 4.18.5, *Q. fr.* 3.1.10 (cf. §9: *nemo istorum est quin abs te munus fundi suburbani instar expectet.* See n. 200.

[207] Raaflaub and Ramsey 2017: 47 date the disaster "around 4 November" (civil) - ca. October 7 (Jul.). Tongeren: Pennacini 1993: 1065–1066; Limbourg: Grisart 1981.

[208] The narrative, certainly the most gripping in the *De bello Gallico*, is related at 5.26–52. For the numbers, 5.24.4, of whom only "a few" survived (5.37.7). Caesar defers the name of the site until 6.32.3–4.

Caesar's men by Ambiorix raised questions about Caesar's future political career, and about his military competence."[209] Caesar the narrator carefully fixes responsibility on the hapless, now conveniently dead legate Titurius Sabinus, who had – in an army council to which few if any surviving witnesses could attest – foolishly believed the promises of safe conduct offered by the enemy, and disobeyed Caesar's clear orders not to move without his permission.[210] Caesar's authorial scapegoating should set us on our guard. In particular, the question must be asked that must have been on many Romans' minds: where had Caesar been, whose standard practice, as we have seen, was to spend his winters south of the Alps in "Italy"? At this critical juncture Caesar himself mysteriously disappears from his own narrative. When the message sent him in desperation by Q. Cicero, smuggled heroically through enemy territory by a Gallic slave, reaches the commander we are left to infer (no location is stated) that he is still at or near Samarobriva (Amiens) where the text had left him, with the comment that he intended to remain in Gaul *until he knew that the legions were all safely quartered and their camps fortified.*[211] Yet on Caesar's own account that news had reached him a full fifteen days before Ambiorix made his first move, so although he says nothing to suggest this the inference is available that by the time Sabinus's camp was surrounded he had in fact already set out on his usual journey across the Alps.[212] That is in fact exactly how, in the tumultuous council that would decide the legion's fate, Sabinus counters the argument of his fellow legate Cotta, who had objected to accepting Ambiorix's treacherous offer to give them safe passage to the nearest Roman camp on the principle that the camp should not be abandoned without explicit orders from Caesar.[213] Cotta's argument is powerfully validated in the narrative by the horrific outcome, while Caesar's evasiveness about his location deprives Sabinus's not unreasonable counterargument of all of its force. But Dio and Plutarch both say that Caesar had already set out for Italy and had gone some way on his journey when the devastating news came.[214]

[209] Powell 1998: 123. Cf. Goldsworthy 2006: 300.
[210] Powell 1998: 115–124. See also Rambaud 1966: esp. 220–221, 238–242.
[211] Caes. *BGall.* 5.46.1; cf. 5.24.8: *quoad legiones collocatas munitaque hiberna cognovisset, in Gallia morari constituit.*
[212] Caes. *BGall.* 5.25.5: *certior factus est in hiberna perventum locumque hibernis esse munitum*; 26.1 (fifteen days). Raaflaub and Ramsey 2017: 47 with n. 152 believe it more probable that Caesar had not yet left Samarobriva at the time of the disaster. But it remains suspicious that Caesar leaves this crucial point obscure.
[213] Caes. *BGall.* 5.29.2; Cotta: 28.3–6.
[214] Dio 40.4.2: ἐς τὴν Ἰταλίαν ὥρμησεν ὡς καὶ ἐκεῖ παραχειμάσων, 9.1 μαθὼν οὖν ὁ Καῖσαρ τὸ γιγνόμενον (οὐδέπω δὲ ἐς τὴν Ἰταλίαν ἀπεληλύθει, ἀλλ' ἔτ' ἐν ὁδῷ ἦν). Plut. 24.1: αὐτοῦ δὲ πρὸς τὴν Ἰταλίαν, ὥσπερ εἰώθει, τραπομένου, 24.2 ὡς δὲ ἠγγέλθη ταῦτα τῷ Καίσαρι μακρὰν ὄντι,

Here, then, I think we can detect another example of Caesar's strategic writing. Some enemies back in Rome will have been inclined to find fault with the commander who had been so eager (so the argument would run) to rush homeward to safety and his political machinations, abandoning his men in a dangerously exposed position where communication with their commander through the winter months would be precarious at best and impossibly slow. Even friendly senators may have been troubled by the thought that (as Barbara Levick puts it), "the Eburones would not have attacked if Caesar had been present," and indeed that Ambiorix had chosen his moment precisely when Caesar would be expected to be en route to Italy.[215] In Caesar's telling, however, even the tiny glimpse we are given of this possible line of criticism is undermined by the fact that it is put solely in the mouth of the scapegoated and almost criminally foolish Sabinus, who actually comes off even worse for his unworthy assumption that his commander had abandoned the men in the camps for the more pleasant and safer surroundings of northern Italy. Caesar himself is further exculpated by the sudden (implicitly, therefore, quite unexpected and swift) nature of the revolt.[216]

The defeat at Atuatuca was disastrous and potentially catastrophic. Caesar himself acknowledged this at the time by refusing to cut his hair or shave his beard (marks of mourning) until he had taken vengeance for the "Titurian disaster" (*clade Tituriana*).[217] Caesar, "anticipating greater disruption in Gaul" (*maiorem Galliae motum exspectans*), thought it prudent to recruit two new legions and "borrow" one from Pompey, who had recruited it in Caesar's province of Cisalpina while consul in

---

ταχέως ἐπιστρέψας . . . . Pelling 2011: 260–261 assumes both were mistaken. Caesar had every reason to hasten to move closer to Rome: his daughter Julia, a powerful bond with Pompey, had died in August (see n. 187), leaving the urgent question of how to restore the familial bond between the two; in August (Jul.), just as Caesar was returning to Gaul from Britain, the sharply contested consular elections, in which candidates supported by Pompey and Caesar faced severe difficulties, descended into a chaotic bribery scandal, which had the effect of postponing the elections to the point that the year 53 began without consuls; Gabinius, Caesar's indirect ally, was under attack in the courts; while rumors swirled of a dictatorship for Pompey. Maier 1978: 68–69 (who overstates the case for friction between Pompey and Caesar); Seager 2002: 125–132; cf. Gruen 1974: 148–150, 331–337, 451–453.

[215] Maier 1978: 71; Levick 1998: 71. Cf. Sabinus's objection: *neque Eburones, si ille* [sc. Caesar] *adesset, tanta contemptione nostri ad castra venturos esse* (Caes. *BGall.* 5.29.2), and the Gauls' awareness of this vulnerability in their planning for the rebellion in 52: 7.1. (I thank Christopher Krebs for this observation.)

[216] Caes. *BGall.* 5.26.1: *repentini tumultus ac defectionis.* Naturally the provident commander is made to some extent to expect the unexpected (5.22.4): Maier 1978: 68n12.

[217] Suet. *Iul.* 67.2. Vengeance was presumably completed by the end of 53 with the devastation of the Eburones in 53 (Caes. *BGall.* 6.30–44). Indutiomarus of the Treveri had been killed early in the year (5.58; cf. 26.2).

55.[218] "War was being prepared on all sides": the Nervii, Atuatuci, and Menapii were already in arms along with all the Germans on the left bank of the Rhine, while rebellion was clearly brewing in central and northern Gaul (the Senones, Carnutes, and Treveri).[219] But the campaigns of 53 were largely frustrating: Ambiorix, clearly sheltered by the populations through whom he fled as a freedom fighter, persistently gave his hunters the slip; another Roman camp – poor Q. Cicero! – barely escaped mortal danger in a surprise incursion by the Sugambri (obviously not having learned their lesson in 55), while antagonism and defiance simmered on or just below the surface in central Gaul.[220] The attack of sixty thousand Nervii (according to Caesar himself) exposed how exaggerated the report of their annihilation in 57 had been, while the Menapii near the mouth of the Rhine gave the Romans an unpleasant reminder that they had never submitted despite prior Roman attacks in from 57 to 55. The only "good news story" that Caesar could send home in 53 was that of his second crossing of the Rhine – a mission, however, that again produced no result whatever: the Germans again withdrew into the interior, and since the Roman army could not be fed off the land (the Germans did not practice agriculture, allegedly) Caesar simply marched right back across his glorious bridge and broke it down immediately afterward.[221] Caesar was reduced to enhancing the deeply anticlimactic description of the actual campaign by inserting a lengthy ethnography of the Gauls and Germans, among other things explaining the differences between the two – thereby, not coincidentally, making a case that the Rhine was an excellent boundary.[222]

As bad as 53 had been, however, 52 began even worse.[223] We, like Caesar's original readers, know that the story will end with the stirring images of Alesia's double lines of circumvallation and Vercingetorix's noble surrender.

---

[218] Caes. *BGall.* 6.1, (Hirt.) 8.54.2. This legion would later play a role in the crisis of 50 as one of the two legions notoriously taken from Caesar to confront the possibility of a Parthian war. Since it was recruited *by* Pompey, though in Caesar's province and intended for service in Gaul, he would later claim it as his contribution for the anticipated Parthian campaign.

[219] Caes. *BGall.* 6.2.3.

[220] See Caes. *BGall.* 6.43.4 on Ambiorix's persistent escapes from Caesar's dragnet. Sugambri: 6.35–42. Central Gaul (Senones and Carnutes): 6.2–4, 44.

[221] Caes. *BGall.* 6.9–29. See Maier 1978: 72–75, who, however, again assumes too readily a change of plan due to domestic circumstances.

[222] Caes. *BGall.* 6.11–18, constituting almost half the book. The clear message is that Gauls can be integrated into the *imperium* but the Germans cannot. See Krebs 2006.

[223] It is notable that the winter of 53/52 – when the beginning of the Great Revolt had almost caught Caesar disastrously wrong-footed – was the last he would spend in Cisalpine Gaul until the end of the Gallic campaigns: n. 52.

But contemporary Romans will have heard first about the massacre of Roman traders at Cenabum, then of the first general rising of more or less all the Gauls in defense of their freedom under a charismatic national leader who had at last learned from the Romans how to conduct "modern" warfare, and of Caesar's second great defeat at Gergovia, where he lost almost seven hundred soldiers and forty-six centurions, this time indubitably under his direct command.[224] The final victory at Alesia throws into obscurity the awkward fact that after Gergovia, the defection of the Aedui, Rome's staunchest Gallic allies, and the massacre of the Roman garrison and traders at Noviodunum, Vercingetorix to all appearances had Caesar on the run. Just before the Gallic commander had hunkered down in Alesia, the Roman invader was not only to all appearances in full flight from central Gaul, but rushing to prevent disaster to the Roman province itself, now suddenly threatened by a Gallic counterattack.[225]

Yet it all came out right. Our knowledge of the victorious conclusion of the wars in Gaul and even the civil wars tends to invest Caesar with an air of invincibility. In toto he is said to have fought thirty battles in Gaul, suffering only two defeats in the field in all eight years of combat.[226] This astonishing win-loss record might give a misleading impression of the degree of control he could exert over his political fate in Rome. True, since all of his notable setbacks occurred only *after* the *lex Pompeia Licinia*, it may well be that up to and including 55 he had in fact achieved a certain reputation for invincibility, which no doubt helped his case for an extension of his command. Yet thereafter a certain vulnerability emerged even as he had begun to turn on the financial spigots to protect his position and attain his goals back in Rome. Caesar's position was far from unassailable, and his desire for an honorific return hung upon numerous imponderables – the most pressing of which was the future of his alliance with Pompey.

---

[224] Cenabum: Caes. *BGall.* 7.3. Vercingetorix's "learning from the Romans": most obviously, 7.30.4, but see Riggsby 2006: 96–105 on "the Gallic assimilation of *virtus*." Gergovia: 7.44–53, remembered as one of Caesar's three major setbacks in Gaul (see n. 205) and recalled by Caesar himself after a later defeat at *BCiv.* 3.73.6.

[225] Caes. *BGall.* 7.63–67 [sc. Vercingetorix]: *convocatisque ad concilium praefectis equitum venisse tempus victoriae demonstrat. Fugere in provinciam Romanos Galliaque excedere* (7.66.3). Caesar's victory in a major cavalry engagement as he made his way back to the province first turned the tide, forcing Vercingetorix to take refuge in Alesia. But the cavalry battle appears to have been much more dangerous for the Romans than Caesar admits, for the Arverni (Vercingetorix's people) displayed in Plutarch's time a dagger they said had been taken from Caesar himself (Plut. *Caes.* 26.8, with Pelling 2011: 269).

[226] App. *BCiv.* 2.150/627. A roughly comparable count by Plin. *HN* 7.92 gives Caesar's lifetime total of fifty battles (or fifty-two, emending from Solinus 1.106, as in Mayhoff's Teubner; but see contra Pelling 2011: 210). This made him the only Roman to surpass the record M. Marcellus had held since the late third century.

In the meantime, he could begin to secure his immortality in the traditional ways. Cicero had already spoken in 56 of the *dignitas* or "honorific position" that lay ahead for Caesar on his return, among which he clearly implied at least the celebration of a great triumph.[227] Though it would be deferred by civil war until 46 and it may sometimes have been in doubt (for instance after Gergovia in 52), it will have been evident to everyone from at least the time of his first *supplicationes* in late 57 and Cicero's *On the consular provinces* in 56, if not already from the time of the *lex Vatinia*'s passage, that a triumph for his *res gestae* in Gaul was a pressing goal for the conqueror of Gaul. Recall that because of Cato's filibuster in 60, Caesar had never yet ridden in a triumphal car, yet Pompey had triumphed three times, and even relatively minor figures like P. Lentulus Spinther and Caesar's rather underachieving predecessor in Gaul, C. Pomptinus, had been granted triumphs, an honor of which Cicero would not consider himself unworthy for his capture of a mountain fortress in Cilicia.[228] But to assure the survival of a triumph in Roman memory it would have to be inscribed in the very fabric of the City. Caesar began in 54 to move toward the public commemoration of his deeds with the purchase through his agents ("friends"), Oppius and Cicero himself, of exorbitantly expensive land around the northwest of the Forum with which to realize his aims of a worthy *monumentum*.[229] (No doubt the recent brilliance of Pompey's second consulship, with the opening of Rome's first great stone theater complex, was also on his mind.) Cicero anticipates creating a "most glorious structure" by widening the Forum and extending it toward the Atrium Libertatis; this would eventually evolve into the Forum Iulium dominated by a temple of Venus Genetrix.[230] A second project was to build a splendid new marble voting enclosure on the Campus Martius for electoral assemblies; it was to be girded round with

---

[227] Cic. *Prov. cons.* 35: *si ad eam dignitatem quam in civitate sibi propositam videt.* Triumph: §§29, 35. Also *Pis.* 59: *flagrat, ardet cupiditate iusti et magni triumphi* (cf. §60). Hirt. [Caes.] *B Gall* 8.51.3: late in 50 the people of Cisalpina Gaul give a preview of *vel exspectatissimi triumphi laetitia.*

[228] Dio 37.54.1 reasonably stresses the intensification of Caesar's desire for a consular triumph as a result of this praetorian disappointment.

[229] Cic. *Att.* 4.16.8 (July 54): HS 60,000,000. Suet. *Iul.* 26.2 and Plin. *HN* 36.103 quote a higher figure (HS 100,000,000), but Pliny also puts the purchase later (*Caesar dictator*) while Suetonius suggests that the purchases began only in 52; possibly they are quoting an eventual total.

[230] Cic. *Att.* 4.16.8: *efficiemus rem gloriosissimam.* Davies 2017: 257–260, with pp. 247–252, 271; for the Forum Iulium project see also C. Morselli and P. Gros, *LTUR* 2.299–307. The Temple of Venus Genetrix in the Forum would ultimately become something of a museum of Caesar's victories: Westall 1996. The identity of the Atrium Libertatis is unfortunately controversial: Purcell 1993 would identify it with the "Tabularium," but the traditional view that it was located on the saddle between the Capitol and the Quirinal probably still prevails (Coarelli, *LTUR* 1.133–135; Amici, *LTUR* 5.229).

a high portico a Roman mile in circumference and connected to the Villa Publica.[231] It is unlikely to be coincidence that the two projects monumentalize central popular spaces, one at the northwest end of the Forum near the Rostra, the preferred spot for magistrates and other senators to address the People, the other at the very place where the People chose their magistrates in elections. Yet these were both quintessentially republican political practices, and while these were certainly *public* spaces they were not exclusively *popularis* spaces.[232] The locations selected for adornment were central places of interaction in the relationship between the People and their leaders that characterized the Republic: where the People *chose* their magistrates and where they *listened* to those magistrates exercising their traditional role of leadership in the Republic.[233] But the patrician Caesar was no "democrat," any more than were his fellow senators.

The question of one further important honor emerges later than these: Caesar's desire for a second consulship, which lies at the heart of the dispute that led to the Civil War since his enemies were equally determined to deny it to him. After Pompey's assumption early in February (Jul.) 52 of a highly irregular third consulship (that is, not only before the statutory ten-year interval had elapsed but also without a colleague for at least two months) we also hear for the first time of the idea of a second consulship for Caesar to follow his return from Gaul. Only our late sources give any details about the emergence of the issue early in 52, and these remain murky, but both Suetonius and Plutarch mention that the matter of a second consulship for Caesar was raised, at least formally, first by others (certain tribunes in Suetonius, "the friends of Caesar" in Plutarch) in response to Pompey's assumption of a third consulship while he was simultaneously holding onto his provinces.[234] Now, by the time of

---

[231] Cic. *Att.* 4.16.8 with Davies 2017: 260–261. Further big plans for the Campus Martius, apparently actually begun shortly before July 45 but aborted after the assassination, are detailed at Suet. *Iul.* 44.1, Cic. *Att.* 13.33a (cf. 13.20.1). See also Chapter 9, n. 37.

[232] Eventually the Rostra would be moved to the west, apparently outside the area Caesar was purchasing in 54 (Chapter 9, n. 123). But Appian thinks that the Forum Iulium, the eventual culmination of the project, was still intended as a public space for interaction between magistrates and citizens: (τέμενος) ὃ ῾Ρωμαίοις ἔταξεν ἀγορὰν εἶναι, οὐ τῶν ὠνίων, ἀλλ᾽ ἐπὶ πράξεσι συνιόντων ἐς ἀλλήλους, καθὰ καὶ Πέρσαις ἦν τις ἀγορὰ ζητοῦσιν ἢ μανθάνουσι τὰ δίκαια (*BCiv.* 2.102/424). Appian's ethnography need not be correct for his characterization of the space to hold. Cf. Davies 2017: 259–260.

[233] Caesar would eventually move the Rostra/Comitium as well as the Curia itself, presumably in the service of the Forum Iulium project. But since the Curia had not yet been burned down (52) its replacement was hardly yet in mind (cf. Dio 44.5.1–2 with Davies 2017: 271); Cicero would surely not have approved (*Fin.* 5.2). See Chapter 9, n. 50.

[234] Suet. *Iul.* 26.1; Plut. *Pomp.* 56.1–3; cf. *Caes.* 29.1, App. *BCiv.* 2.25/96–97. Pompey's election occurred on the 24th of the intercalary month = ca. February 4, Jul. (Ascon. 36C). Dio 40.50.3–4

Pompey's election Caesar is likely already to have heard news of the massacre of Roman traders at Cenabum that touched off the great Gallic revolt, and consequently he probably departed for Transalpina within days (ca. February 8, Jul.).[235] Therefore if the thought had occurred to him or his partisans that he might declare victory in Gaul and join Pompey as his consular colleague later in 52, that idea was almost immediately overtaken by events.[236] The news of Vercingetorix's revolt naturally forced the commander to put aside domestic politics as soon as matters in Rome appeared to be under control and return posthaste to the province. This provides a suitable context for Suetonius's next comment, which is that after these tribunes called for Caesar to be made Pompey's colleague, Caesar asked them instead to allow him to stand for the consulship in absentia when his command was coming to its end "so that he would not have to return prematurely, with the war still not brought to a close."[237] The change of tack was surely a result of the troubling news from Gaul. Caesar's request, with Pompey's and Cicero's assistance, was soon granted (perhaps in March) by a bill promulgated in a great show of consensus by the entire college of ten tribunes (hence "the Law of the Ten Tribunes") against the predictable (and again fruitless) objections of Cato. This "gift" or "favor of the Roman People" (*beneficium populi Romani*) was therefore an improvisation to meet the exigencies of the moment, yet it would define the controversy that would ultimately erupt in civil war.[238]

Was a second consulship for Caesar at the end of his Gallic command as such (that is, setting aside for the moment the electoral privilege granted by the Law of the Ten Tribunes) a radical idea, an honor out of keeping with

alone suggests that talk of a consulship for Caesar preceded Pompey's appointment; he even makes it the chief rationale for Pompey's being chosen *sole* consul (so that Caesar could not be his colleague); see contra now Ramsey 2016: 310–312, also for the entire episode. Both Plut. (*Pomp.* 56.2) and Appian add a confusing alternative proposal for the extension of Caesar's command (see Pelling 2011: 283–285) – probably a misunderstanding of the sudden change of course necessitated by Vercingetorix's rebellion.

[235] Ramsey 2016: 310–311; Raaflaub and Ramsey 2017: 55. Caes. *BGall.* 7.6.1: *His rebus in Italiam Caesari nuntiatis, cum iam ille urbanas res virtute Cn. Pompei commodiorem in statum pervenisse intellegeret, in Transalpinam Galliam profectus est.* Deep snow nearly blocked the Cévennes (8.1–3).

[236] Pompey supposedly reported that Caesar had written to ask to be replaced in his command (Plut. *Pomp.* 56.2). *Quieta Gallia* (7.1.1), the opening words of Caesar's seventh book, suggest that before the massacre the Roman conquest had seemed complete (n. 7.1.3: *populi Romani imperio subiectos*) although in fact a larger Gallic rebellion had been simmering for more than two years (see Krebs's forthcoming commentary). Of course by the time Caesar wrote those words history had already shown the calm to be deceptive, thus he avoids the phrase *Gallia pacata* (see n. 50).

[237] Suet. *Iul.* 26.1 *quandoque imperii tempus expleri coepisset, petitio secundi consulatus daretur, ne ea causa maturius et inperfecto adhuc bello decederet.*

[238] See Chapter 6, p. 263ff. On the Law of the Ten Tribunes see Chapter 6, n. 9.

his achievements? No source suggests this. In itself the honor of a second consulship was not rare. In this very year Pompey was holding his *third* consulship, only three years after his second, while Crassus and Sulla had both held second consulships, and (leaving out the dubious precedents of L. Cinna and Cn. Carbo) Marius of course had been elected seven times, including an extraordinary run of five consecutive consulships during the Cimbric-Teutonic emergency of the end of the second century.[239] If we examine the consular *fasti* over the past two and a half centuries, we find that about one in eight consulars enjoyed this distinction over that period; it was therefore not exactly common, especially in recent times, yet hardly an exceedingly rare distinction viewed over the long term.[240] Most often, especially in earlier times, iteration of the consulship was the consequence of some kind of emergency, but in more recent memory – Marius in 100, Sulla in 80, Pompey and Crassus in 55 – a repeated consulship was essentially honorific in character, at least from the viewpoint of the voters.[241] It is therefore not in the least surprising that after his record-setting victories in Gaul (as could be directly measured by the unprecedented number of days of *supplicationes* granted) Caesar and his supporters thought he was worthy of joining the exclusive company of Marius, Sulla, Pompey, and Crassus, not to mention – reaching back to earlier generations – the Scipiones Africanus and Aemilianus, M. Marcellus and Q. Fabius Maximus the Delayer (the legendary "sword and shield of Rome" against Hannibal), L. Aemilius Paulus (conqueror of Macedon), and other great names in the honor roll of Roman generals.[242]

Repetition of the consulship was however somewhat constrained by a fourth-century law which barred iteration of any magistracy before an interval of a full ten years had passed.[243] But this rule had been suspended

---

[239] There is some evidence for an outright ban on repetition of the consulship dating to the middle of the second century, but this is not as well attested as one would like (Liv. *Per.* 56, with Astin 1958: 19n6 and Elster 2003: 408–409 n. 195; App. *Ib.* 84 is clearly jumbled to some degree and may simply be a doublet). If it is authentic it may have been largely forgotten after Marius, since we hear nothing further of it in connection with the iterated consulships of Sulla, Pompey, and Crassus.

[240] Over the entire period 290–53 (Beck's list at 2005: 97–99 provides a starting point), the rate of iteration (i.e. the proportion of all [non-vitiated ordinary] consulars in the period who repeated the [ordinary] consulship at least once) is about 12 percent.

[241] Emergency: the Second Punic War (Beck 2005: 101, and cf. Liv. 27.6.7) and the years of Marius's successive consulships until that of 100, when he was reelected *after* destroying the Cimbri at Vercellae (Plut. *Mar.* 28, Vell. Pat. 2.12.6: *sextus consulatus veluti praemium ei meritorum datus*).

[242] E.g. M. Aemilius Lepidus (cos. II 175), Ti. Sempronius Gracchus (cos. II 163), M. Claudius Marcellus (cos. III 152).

[243] On the law see Beck 2005: 44–51, 96–105, with references to earlier literature; also Astin 1958: 19n6. On *leges annales* in general see Kunkel-Wittmann 1995: 43–51. This law is distinct from the somewhat murky ban on iteration *tout court*: n. 239.

not infrequently when an exception seemed justified, most recently for Pompey's third consulship in 52 (a time of emergency) and, before that, to allow Sulla to place the seal on his "restoration of the Republic" only seven years after his first consulship despite the fact that he had just repeated the rule in his own new *lex Annalis*.[244] The relative ease and frequency with which the ten-year statutory rule was suspended (for this rarely provokes comment from our sources) often of course exemplifies nothing more than a salutary flexibility in the face of emergency, but in other cases it is clear that the People, who enjoyed the exclusive right to "give offices to the worthy, which is the finest prize of nobility in a state," chafed at times at the idea that their right to choose whomever they wished to lead them should be severely constrained by statute.[245] When in 148 Scipio Aemilianus presented himself for the aedileship but the voters decided to elect him consul contrary to the laws, the appalled consuls could in the end do little about it.[246] This is not to say that the law was simply disregarded; rather, in such cases the statute had been formally suspended in an orderly if notoriously abused procedure which was tightened up, but not abolished, by a law of the tribune C. Cornelius in 67.[247] The bar for such an

---

[244] App. *BCiv.* 1.100/466. Indeed, this historian claims that the People tried to reelect Sulla immediately as consul for the *third* time in 79 to honor him (θεραπεύων) but that Sulla did not permit this (App. 1.103/480). Marius's consular streak from 105 through 100 was another relevant precedent, the last of which could not be justified by a military emergency (n. 241). Exemptions from the rule are by no means a solely late-republican phenomenon, as Beck 2005: 97–99 reveals: thirty-one of the fifty-five second consulships since 290 BC must have required such exemptions, including those of such great names as C. Fabricius Luscinus, M'. Curius Dentatus (four times *triumphator*), M. Atilius Calatinus, L. Caecilius Metellus (cos. II 247, victor of Panormus), and Fabius Cunctator and M. Marcellus (both five times consul).

[245] Polyb. 6.14.9: καὶ μὴν τὰς ἀρχὰς ὁ δῆμος δίδωσι τοῖς ἀξίοις· ὅπερ ἐστὶ κάλλιστον ἆθλον ἐν πολιτείᾳ καλοκἀγαθίας.

[246] App. *Pun.* 112/531 (148 BC): "According to the laws of Tullius and Romulus, the People were masters of the elections and about these matters they could validate or invalidate whatever they wanted." See Chapter 1, p. 11ff. Cf. Livy 10.13.9 (298 BC), and 25.2.7 (214 BC); Plut. *Mar.* 12.1 (reelection of Marius in 104): "He was elected consul for the second time, although the law forbade that a man in his absence and before the lapse of a specified time should be elected again; still, the people would not listen to those who opposed the election." In a notable modern instantiation of the principle, in 1995, the US Supreme Court struck down term limits on congressional reelection imposed by the states on the grounds that "the people should choose whom they please to govern them" (*U.S. Term Limits, Inc.* v. *Thornton* [1995]).

[247] We hear of two procedures for lifting electoral restrictions. In 148 and supposedly again in 134, Appian claims, the tribunes, instructed by the Senate, introduced legislation rescinding the *lex annalis* and then (by another law?) reinstating it one year later (*Lib.* 112, *Ib.* 84: Elster 2003: 425–426, 450–451). Ascon. 58C seems to indicate that by 67 such exemptions had migrated exclusively to the Senate and tended to be "fixed" by a small number of powerful senators as an exercise in *gratia*. (Cf. also *Ad Herr.* 3.2.) The tribune Cornelius in 67 was able (after a significant clash with opponents, including the consul C. Piso) to pass a compromise law that left the decision in the hands of the Senate but required a senatorial quorum of four hundred members (Ascon. 58–59C, with Marshall 1985: 220–221). Flexibility in the face of such laws is not unheard of today:

exemption was not set very high (essentially, one needed the support of at least 201 senators), and there is no reason to think that Caesar could not have managed to obtain it before the elections of 51 or 50. Thus it seems doubtful that Caesar really intended to wait the legal and customary ten years before his second consulship, despite the fact that he claims exactly this in his *Civil War Commentaries* (which are designed, of course, to put his plans and actions consistently in the best possible light).[248] Such rigid adherence to a rule that was suspended not rarely seems particularly unlikely in the very year when it had been waived for Pompey. After his Gallic victories no one could persuasively claim that he was unworthy of it.

The right to contest the consulship in absentia is by its nature less easy to trace, and not entirely comparable since the requirement to present oneself personally to the voters in the Forum seems to have been an old norm but one only recently written into a statute.[249] (It will be remembered that this requirement was used to trip up Caesar's path to a praetorian triumph.) Marius's in absentia elections to the consulship for 104 and 103 provided a relatively recent precedent for extending this privilege to a commander still in the field, while his election in absentia in 102 for 101 as he faced the climax of his campaigns could serve as an even closer parallel to Caesar's situation; more recently, custom had also been set aside for Pompey and Crassus's election in 71 (for 70) without reentering the city boundary, and Pompey had also been elected technically in absentia for 55 and 52, although these latter circumstances were anyway exceptional in a variety of ways.[250] In sum, the electoral privilege extended to Caesar under a law promulgated by all ten tribunes was hardly an outrageous novelty.

cf. the US Senate's waivers in 1950 and 2017 (by a vote of 98–1) of the National Security Act of 1947, which mandates a seven-year gap between military service and appointment to secretary of defense in order to reinforce and preserve civilian control of the military.

[248] Chapter 6, p. 288ff.

[249] See Chapter 3, n. 114; for its tralatician adoption in Pompey's new legislation of 52 see Chapter 6, p. 265ff.

[250] Marius: see *MRR* 1.556, 558, 567. Pompey: consulships of 70, 55, 52 (see Girardet 2001; on the election of 70 see Linderski 1966 and Chapter 3, n. 114). Pompey was elected to his second and third consulships in absentia in the strict formal sense: almost certainly he did not cross the *pomerium* (and give up his *imperium*) before his election in 56–55 (cf. Dio 39.27.3), and in 52 it is clear that he entered the City only after his election (Plut. *Pomp.* 55.1; cf. Ascon. 34–36C). Possibly the rule that *imperium* lapsed automatically upon crossing the *pomerium* was more flexible than we usually suppose: in 56 Pompey crossed the boundary to give a character witness for P. Sestius, surely without losing his *imperium* (Cic. *Fam.* 1.9.7, with Shackleton Bailey 1977: 1:392), a curiosity that receives surprisingly little comment. It is not impossible that Pompey had been similarly excused to appear as Milo's advocate early in the same year (*Q. fr.* 2.3.1–2), but since this is likely to have been a *iudicium populi* it was presumably conducted outside the *pomerium* (Shackleton Bailey 1980: 176–177; Alexander 1990: 129, 266 n. 2; Kaster 2006: 110).

In the *contiones* that preceded voting on the law the tribunes must have based the case on Caesar's already extraordinary achievements in Gaul and the necessity to allow him to receive the fruits of his *dignitas* without dragging him back from the front and distracting him from the culmination of his years of campaigning on behalf of the *imperium* of the Roman People.[251] Caesar's hopes and expectations for a splendid triumph had been clear enough since at least the second year of his campaigns in Gaul.[252] The "in absentia" clause allowed Caesar to hope for a (literally) triumphal entry into the City on the first day of his second consulship; again, Marius and Pompey offered precedents.[253] Of course, celebration would not be the only item on Caesar's agenda in a second consulship: one could anticipate a strong push to reward his hardworking soldiers for their service. His very success in restarting large-scale agrarian distribution by means of his land laws of 59 could be expected to create difficulties since land would now surely have to be sought largely outside of Italy.[254] No doubt the idea filled Caesar's enemies with dread. But for now, the coming showdown in Gaul was doubtless foremost in most citizens' minds.

After the suppression of the Great Revolt of 52 yet another twenty days of thanksgivings were decreed in Caesar's honor.[255] By this time Caesar was indisputably a Roman hero on a historic scale, and while Pompey might well be envious and Cato still implacably hostile, the hard core of opposition and enmity to the conqueror of Gaul had dwindled to a couple of dozen senators by the end of the decade.[256]

The Other Side of Victory

Since so much of this chapter has necessarily been concerned with military victory as a political tool and token of "honor," let us at its close spare

---

[251] Caes. *BCiv.* 1.85.10 perhaps gives a glimpse of the argument.

[252] See n. 180 and p. 246. In 49, and surely before, it was obvious that this would be combined in some way with the second consulship (Cic. *Att.* 7.26.2, 8.11D.7, 12.2; note also Varro, *De Vita Populi Romani* 117 = Non., p. 147 M [apparently quoting Curio, tr. pl. 50, *before* he defected to Caesar]: *se obstringillaturum, ne triumphus decerneretur aut ne iterum fieret consul*).

[253] Morstein-Marx 2007: 168–169. Marius's first triumph was celebrated on the first day of his second consulship, Pompey's second on the day before he became consul for the first time: *Fasti triumphales ad annos* 104, 71: Degrassi, *I.It.* 13.1.561, 565. Marius's election to a celebratory fifth consulship shortly after his second triumph over the Cimbri and Teutones will have had a similar effect: Plut. *Mar.* 27–28 for the chronology.

[254] Roselaar 2010: 286–288.

[255] Supplications in 52 (probably December: Raaflaub and Ramsey 2017: 61): Caes. *BGall.* 7.90.8; Dio 40.50.4 (with a mistaken or corrupt number of days).

[256] Chapter 6, p. 294ff. Pompey's envy: n. 139. Note, however, that Pompey's modern biographer, Seager 2002: 130–132, sees little sign of tension between the two prime donne before 53.

a thought for Caesar's victims. *Res gestae*, the "deeds done" or, better, "achievements," of a Roman general were from our alien perspective usually blood-drenched acts of savagery. The scale of the carnage the conqueror of Gaul unleashed over eight years was horrific. Plutarch reports – in figures probably ultimately drawn from Caesar's own boasts written on the triumphal placards – 1,000,000 enemy dead, an equal number taken prisoner (which would mostly have meant sale to the slave traders who accompanied the army), the capture of 800 cities, and the conquest of 300 "nations."[257] C. Goudineau shows that the numbers, which at first appear exaggerated, are at least broadly consistent with the information provided piecemeal through Caesar's own *Commentarii*.[258]

Numbers can give a sense of the scale of devastation, but the savagery of the campaigns is best appreciated by rehearsal of a few details that Caesar himself coolly records in his narrative, but whose effect tends to be buried in the haystack of other information. As we saw, Caesar boasts (if a bit optimistically) that in 57 he had "nearly annihilated the entire people and name of the Nervii," who after their surrender claimed that they had lost all but 3 senators out of 600, all but 500 fighting men out of 60,000.[259] Then, because the Atuatuci (a Belgic people) had abused his "clemency" – for which there had been thus far precious little evidence in the text – and treacherously resumed the fight after submitting, Caesar sold every man, woman, and child of them to the slave traders who eagerly attended the army, to the number of 53,000.[260] When the "rebellious" Veneti were forced to their knees in 56, Caesar decided that the "barbarians" needed to be taught a lesson, "so he massacred the entire senate and sold the rest into slavery" (of course men, women, and children again).[261] When the "treacherous" German Usipites and Tencteri were routed in 55 (apparently believing a truce was in force), their women and children – for this was a mass migration – "began to flee in all directions; Caesar sent the cavalry to hunt

---

[257] Plut. *Caes.* 15.5, with Pelling 2011: 210–212. Pliny (*HN* 7.92) gives the seemingly more exact figure of 1,192,000, while Vell. 2.47.1 lowers the number to 400,000. App. *Celt.* 1.2.6 says 400 "nations." In general, the sources are fairly consistent and suggest a common source in the triumphal context. Pliny alone "criticiz[es] this particular record on humanitarian grounds" (Beagon 2005: 277); his distaste (*non equidem in gloria posuerim, tantam ... coactam humani generis iniuriam*) is probably explained by his distance in time and circumstance. A better index is Cicero's exultation in *Prov. cons.* over the crushing of Rome's ancient enemies: *quas nationes nemo umquam fuit quin frangi domarique cuperet* (33).

[258] Goudineau 1990: 308–311. The consistency of the figures of course may only mean that the numbers were drawn from Caesar's own notes, with which the *Commentarii* would naturally agree. Goudineau estimates Roman losses at about one-twenty-fifth of this number.

[259] Caes. *BGall.* 2.28.2.   [260] Caes. *BGall.* 2.33.7.

[261] Caes. *BGall.* 3.16.4 *Itaque omni senatu necato reliquos sub corona vendidit.*

them down."[262] They were hardly equipped for a slave roundup and must have slaughtered the helpless fugitives. In fact he implies in his account that nearly all of the migrants, to the number of 430,000, were cut down or drowned in the eddies of the Rhine.[263] After the loss of the fifteen cohorts at Atuatuca late in 54 to the treacherous attack of the Eburones, Caesar avenged the defeat by devastating their land and villages so thoroughly that he hoped – as he explicitly avers – to exterminate the Eburones' very "race and name." When the Romans had finished burning every building, driving off all their cattle, and consuming or destroying all their grain, he declares with evident satisfaction that any survivors would probably starve to death once the army withdrew.[264] Indeed, the name of the Eburones never reappears in our sources and it appears that the surviving remnant merged with the later occupants of the land, the Germanic Tungri and Ubii.[265]

When Caesar's soldiers captured Avaricum after a bitter and bloody siege in 52, he allowed them to vent their rage for the earlier massacre of Roman traders at another city (Cenabum) by slaughtering everyone – the elderly, women, and children. Out of a population of 40,000 at Avaricum, barely 800 escaped, according to Caesar's own record.[266] He had the "conspirators" and "rebels" – or, as the Gauls might say, "freedom fighters" – Acco and "Gutuater" executed "in the ancestral fashion" (*more maiorum*): they were placed, naked, with their neck in a wooden "fork" and beaten to death, after which they were decapitated.[267] At Uxellodunum in 51, since Caesar was confident that he had established such a reputation for "leniency" (*lenitas*) that he was free to punish the survivors harshly to deter further revolts, he cut off the hands of all who had fought against him and let them live so that they could serve as a striking example of the penalty for "wickedness."[268]

---

[262] Caes. *BGall.* 4.14.5.

[263] Caes. *BGall.* 4.15.1–3. Roymans 2018 believes he has found the remains of the massacre near Kessel in the southern Netherlands. However, this site is much farther to the north than Caesar's narrative would suggest, and in the absence of clear traces of Roman involvement Raaflaub and Ramsey 2017: 32n106 remain unconvinced.

[264] Caes. *BGall.* 6.34.5, 8; 43.2–3.

[265] F. Schön, *DNP* s.v. Eburones. The Eburones themselves seem to have been Germanic Belgae.

[266] Caes. *BGall.* 7.28.5.

[267] Caes. *BGall.* 6.44.2. (The name "Gutuater" may be corrupt: see Krebs's forthcoming commentary.) Hirtius (8.38.5) is more explicit about the mode of execution, but is also eager to excuse Caesar (*contra suam naturam*: the execution is conceded to the soldiery, outraged over Gutuater's supposed responsibility for the massacre at Cenabum). For *supplicium more maiorum* see esp. Suet. *Ner.* 49.2, *Claud.* 34.1 – a rare and exotic relic of ancient times.

[268] (Hirtius) Caes. *BGall.* 8.44.2: *Itaque omnibus qui arma tulerunt manus praecidit vitamque concessit, quo testatior esset poena improborum.*

Finally, in what is surely the most pitiable scene of the entire *Gallic War Commentaries*, Caesar describes how the residents of Alesia who were of no use in the fighting – the elderly, women, and children – were expelled from the town by the besieged Gallic army in order to save their dwindling supplies for the fighters, but were then turned back by the Romans when they reached the wall of circumvallation. "In tears, they begged and pleaded for them to take them as slaves and feed them. But Caesar posted guards on the rampart and forbade them to be received."[269] The story caught Dio's attention, who adds plausible (though clearly exculpatory) motivation for the cruel decision: "Caesar did not have sufficient food himself to feed others; and believing, moreover, that by returning the expelled he could make the enemy's lack of food more severely felt (for he expected that they would of course be received again), he forced them all back." The inevitable result, omitted by Caesar, is sketched by Dio: caught between the two armies, "these perished most miserably between the city and the camp, because neither party would receive them."[270] Presumably they slowly starved to death, succumbed to the elements, or killed themselves in the no-man's-land between the city and the wall of circumvallation, while the soldiers on both sides looked on.

Yet we know about most of these things only because Caesar himself chose to report them to his readers, including even the future guardians of his glory (i.e. historians). This reminds us that the actions he describes were in fact largely consistent with Roman notions of the laws and norms of war. A city that refused to surrender and "forced" the Roman army to capture it by siege or assault – which could extract a high cost in Roman lives – lost its claim to humane treatment and could be treated by the victor in whatever way military circumstances dictated.[271] This was harsh justice, and most of the examples of Caesar's severity seem in fact intended to demonstrate his *adherence* to this "duty," whose purpose of course was to ensure *Roman* victory and minimize the loss of *Roman* lives.

---

[269] Caes. *BGall.* 7.78.3–5; Dio 40.40.3.

[270] Dio 40.40.3–4. Since of course it was the Gauls themselves who had expelled the noncombatants and then refused to take them back, it could certainly be argued that by ancient standards of warfare it was they who bore most responsibility for the atrocity. The ferocity that this implies is emphasized by Caesar by the notorious speech of Critognatus advocating cannabalism (7.77) – the only extended direct speech in the entire *Gallic War Commentaries* – which in fact gives rise to the decision to send away the noncombatants. (Recent discussion in Riggsby 2006: 107–118). Is this Caesar's textual strategy to reshape the story so that it reflects mostly on Gallic responsibility and their own *singularis et nefaria crudelitas* (7.77.2) in their fierce determination to prevail?

[271] For the horrors of a Roman capture see Ziolkowski 1993, and now Levithan 2013: 205–227.

Men and women, surely even children, who are fighting for their freedom (as even Caesar acknowledges) will not part with it easily.[272] Let us not forget that when the revered Scipio soon-to-be-Africanus broke into New Carthage in 209, "he sent most of [his men], as is their [i.e. the Roman] custom, against the people in the city, ordered them to kill everyone they encountered and spare no one, nor to turn to plundering until the signal was given." "I think they do this," Polybius goes on, "to inspire terror; for when Romans capture cities by assault one often sees not only slaughtered human beings, but even dogs cut in two and the hacked-off limbs of other animals."[273]

As I have stressed (Chapter 2), even if fewer senators now pursued the path of military achievement than in the third or second centuries, successful war-making remained the most highly honored form of patriotic service demanded of Rome's leaders.[274] As that relatively un-military man, Cicero, declared in his defense speech for Murena, military success ranked even above excellence as a speaker in the minds of the Roman People (and voters in a consular election):

> Those who surpass the rest in military glory have the greatest "worthiness" (*dignitas*) [in Rome]. For they are believed to defend and strengthen everything that pertains to our empire and the condition of our City. They are also the most useful inasmuch as it is by their skill and acceptance of risk to themselves that we are able to thoroughly enjoy the fruits of our state and our private affairs.[275]

And so, perverse as it may seem to us, Plutarch relates the staggering numbers of enemies Caesar killed, enslaved, and captured in Gaul not to accuse him but to praise him. He introduces the figures in his *Life of Caesar* to reinforce in conclusion a laudatory paragraph that begins,

---

[272] Caes. *BGall.* 3.10.3: Caesar "knew . . . that all men naturally seek freedom and hate the condition of slavery" at the beginning of the very campaign which ends with the execution of the entire Venetian senate and (literal) enslavement of the whole population. For remarkably candid representation of the motives of Gallic freedom fighters and Caesar's own willingness to use the stark metaphor of "slavery" for Roman conquest and domination see also 1.17.4, 2.14.2, 3.8.4, with the insightful discussion by Riggsby 2006: 181–189.

[273] Polyb. 10.15.4–5.

[274] Rosenstein 2006; see also Brunt 1979; Harris 1979: 9–41. Segal 2019 traces the recent decline of the militaristic ethos in Rome among senators; however, public admiration for military achievement, and for the progressively fewer senators who successfully trod this path, does not seem to have diminished.

[275] Cic. *Mur.* 24; cf. *Brut.* 239, *Rab. Post.* 42, and Q. Metellus's eulogy for his father: Chapter 2, p. 59. To be sure, Cicero has a rhetorical purpose for emphasizing this truism. Elsewhere, and more privately, he objects (*Off.* 1.74); yet in the same essay urges his son first of all to win fame in war (2.45).

He showed himself as good a warrior and commander as any of history's greatest and most respected generals. One can compare Fabii and Scipios and Metelli; or Caesar's own contemporaries and immediate predecessors, Sulla, Marius, and both Luculli; or even Pompey himself, whose glory at the time blossomed through the whole firmament for every sort of military virtue. Caesar's achievements outdo them all.[276]

---

[276] Plut. *Caes.* 15.2–4, Pelling trans. "P[lutarch]'s admiration for the achievement is uncompromised" (Pelling 2011: 208).

CHAPTER 6

No Return

Caesar's Dignitas *and the Coming of the Civil War*

The approach to the Civil War of 49–45 is a notoriously complicated story bedeviled by seemingly irresolvable uncertainty about fundamental issues and a bewildering complex of alternative interpretations of crucial items of evidence. Naturally, therefore, it remains highly controversial, and it tends to be interpreted in diametrically opposed ways.[1] Yet it is possible to trace a coherent narrative through this complicated maze by focusing closely on Caesar's *ratio absentis* (literally, "consideration for an absent [candidate]") – that is, his right, according to the Law of the Ten Tribunes passed in 52, to be a candidate for the consulship in absentia (that is, without coming within the City walls).[2] Put simply, in order to provide a thread to follow through what at times may be fairly tough going, I will seek to demonstrate that the outbreak of civil war was not the fruit of a long-standing plan by either Caesar or his erstwhile ally, Pompey, to eliminate the other and thereby achieve domination over the Roman world but was instead the undesired result of an incremental erosion of trust between the two men over the years 52–49. This dynamic was aggravated by the fears and resentment of Caesar's enemies and adversaries, who probably sincerely believed that it was crucial for the Republic's sake to prevent the now-victorious proconsul from returning to a hero's welcome, together with Caesar's determination not to be "robbed" of an honorific return, complete with a long-deferred triumph and a second consulship worthy of the

---

[1] Hence, for example, Klaus Girardet has now (2017) expanded greatly on an earlier article (2000) in which he argued that on January 1, 49, Caesar finally effected a "Putsch" against the Republic that had been in preparation for years, a position almost diametrically opposite to my own view first presented in Morstein-Marx 2007. To avoid turning this chapter to an extended polemic I cite only a handful of our most serious disagreements while encouraging readers to consult Girardet's important work, which is distinguished by a magisterial grasp of the sources and the daunting history of scholarship on the many difficult questions. Raaflaub 1974 remains fundamental, standing somewhere between our two positions, but to my mind too charitable to the "prosecution theory" and to the view that Caesar's insistence on the defense of his *dignitas* was "an entirely personal matter" (p. 2; cf. Morstein-Marx 2009).

[2] See Chapter 5, p. 248.

magnitude of his achievements. At least until the very end of 50 the evidence does not show that either of the two principals, Caesar and Pompey, preferred a civil war to some kind of restored parity. Yet despite a last-ditch effort to avert the looming catastrophe, strongly supported by Cicero and taken seriously on both sides, ultimately their rapidly increasing mutual mistrust prevented either from staking his future on cooperation rather than confrontation.[3] In this sense the Civil War of 49–45 was a war that neither leader wanted – although the same cannot quite be said of Caesar's bitterest enemies clustered around Cato, who bear a heavy responsibility both for recklessly pushing the confrontation to war and for spoiling the final negotiations as Rome was going over the precipice.

Clearing the Ground: The "Prosecution Theory" and the Terminal Date of Caesar's Command

As we saw in the previous chapter, the idea that Caesar might be elected consul a second time after his return from Gaul appears to have been first mooted publicly as a response to Pompey's appointment to a sole consulship early in February 52 (Jul.).[4] During the tumult in the City that followed the murder of Clodius about two months before that crucial moment, pressure had built for Pompey to be named dictator in order to restore order. Caesar was then wintering in Cisalpine Gaul/northern Italy, to all appearances having settled matters in Gaul satisfactorily after the campaigns of 53, for news of the Vercingetorix rebellion did not arrive until about the end of January or the beginning of February (Jul.).[5] In order to head off talk of a dictatorship, two of Pompey's former adversaries, M. Bibulus, Caesar's former homebound colleague, and his father-in-law M. Cato, recommended his election to a third, sole consulship.[6]

---

[3] In Appendix 4 I show how this erosion of trust can be usefully modeled as a Prisoner's Dilemma (PD). The appendix may be skipped by readers impatient of the slightest whiff of game theory; the real-life effects of the PD can be perfectly grasped on an intuitive level without formal modeling as a "game." But readers willing to take the time to contemplate the formal model will probably appreciate better the central argument of this chapter.

[4] Chapter 5, p. 247ff. and n. 234.

[5] Raaflaub and Ramsey 2017: 55. See Chapter 5, n. 235. Clodius's murder occurred on January 18 by the civil calendar (= ca. December 8, 53, Jul.), but subsequent intercalation had now restored its alignment with the seasons.

[6] Dio 40.50.3–5; Plut. *Caes.* 28.7–29.1, *Pomp.* 54.5–8; App. *BCiv.* 2.23/84. Ramsey 2016: 308–318 examines the various impediments and disincentives to appointing a dictator, rejects the idea that the sole consulship was excogitated as a device to keep Caesar out of the office, and instead interprets it as a way to preclude Milo's likely (?) election to the consulship. But more likely the main point was to unify the highest *imperium* in one pair of hands during the duration of the crisis (an interval defined as two months at minimum (Plut. *Pomp.* 54.8).

This was a stunning turnabout in the difficult relations between Pompey and the Catonian hard-liners who had spent so much of the 50s making life difficult for him (and vice versa during Pompey's second consulship in 55). The realignment would immediately have set off alarm bells for Caesar, these very men's inveterate enemy who would later claim that it was in fact his friendship with Pompey that had caused these enmities.[7] After some tribunes began to press for Caesar to be elected as Pompey's colleague, Caesar – now preoccupied with the bad news from Gaul – weighed in from Cisalpina and asked that he be allowed instead to canvass in his absence for a second consulship toward the end of his Gallic command in order to avoid his being forced to rush home prematurely with the war not yet brought to a close.[8] In an impressive display of unanimity on the point, all ten tribunes sponsored this privilege – surely itself a sign of strong popular support – which was openly championed by Pompey and Cicero and opposed, unsurprisingly, only by Cato, who again made use of his favored tactic of the filibuster, the sure sign of a minority opinion in the Senate.[9] Any misgivings Caesar may have had about the support his old ally had won from Cato and his followers were perhaps thereby put to rest, at least temporarily. At the beginning of the seventh book of the *Gallic War Commentaries* Caesar uses quite generous language to describe Pompey's restoration of public order in Rome.[10] From this point on our sources treat the idea that Caesar would *be elected to* a second consulship upon his return from Gaul (not just *be allowed to stand*) as a matter of course, provided of course his candidacy were admitted.

---

[7] Caes. *BCiv.* 1.4.4, surely an allusion to his consulship.

[8] Suet. *Iul.* 26.1: *quandoque imperii tempus expleri coepisset, petitio secundi consulatus daretur, ne ea causa maturius et inperfecto bello decederet.* Chapter 5, p. 248ff.

[9] Esp. Cic. *Att.* 7.1.4, 7.3.4, 8.3.3; *Fam.* 6.6.5 (undermining Cicero's claim elsewhere [*Att.* 7.7.6, *Phil.* 2.24] to have tried to dissuade Pompey); also Dio 40.51.2 and Caes. *BCiv.* 1.9.2: *populi Romani beneficium.* Cicero even pressed his young friend Caelius, tribune in this year, to fall in with the idea (Cic. *Att.* 7.1.4). Cato's opposition: Caes. *BGall.* 1.32.3 *pristina consuetudine dicendi mora dies extrahente*; Plut. *Pomp.* 56.3; Livy *Per.* 107. The law was probably passed as early as March (civil and Jul.): Ramsey 2016: 311n50, 322. On the privilege itself see esp. Gruen 1974: 455–457, 475–477; Raaflaub 1974: 125–136; and now Gagliardi 2011: esp. 63–87. On the legal requirement of the *professio* see Kunkel and Wittmann 1995: 70–78, who persuasively interpret it not as a mere announcement of intent to the consul by the candidate, but his formal declaration of candidacy to the People within the City, customarily over a period spanning three market days. Whether or not personal *professio* within the city boundary was legally required only by 63 BC, this appears to have been a long-established custom (Chapter 3, n. 114). Note that commanders waiting outside the formal boundary of the City in order to prevent the premature lapse of their *imperium* (needed for the triumph) were in this technical sense "in absentia" if they sought the consulship, even though the relevant electoral assembly (*comitia centuriata*) met outside the *pomerium*: hence Caesar's notorious quandary in 60.

[10] Caes. *BGall.* 7.6.1: *cum iam ille* [Caesar] *urbanas res virtute Cn. Pompei commodiorem in statum pervenisse intellegeret . . . .* See n. 45 for a similarly friendly comment about Pompey in the context of 53 BC that supports the theory of serial composition of the *BGall.*

His combination of immense military prestige (*pro tuis rebus gestis amplissimis*, as Pompey himself would publicly acknowledge even at the beginning of the Civil War) and the profits from the conquest of Gaul made it a foregone conclusion that he would be elected, barring some chicanery.[11]

The original public rationale for the Law of the Ten Tribunes which granted Caesar the right to campaign for the consulship in absentia was, then, that Caesar should not be forced to leave his provinces, in particular at a moment of grave crisis for the Roman position in Gaul, simply in order to present himself for the election inside the City in the middle of the summer (the height of the campaigning season). But it is often supposed by scholars (not once, however, by an ancient source) that Caesar wanted this law for another, sinister purpose: for if he could avoid crossing the city boundary to declare his candidacy in order to run for election, then he could retain his *imperium* and remain outside the *pomerium* and thus out of reach of the courts during the interval of several months between his election and his entry into office on January 1, during which he would otherwise have been vulnerable to prosecution and even conviction. For this to be an important Caesarian objective, of course, the threat of successfully carrying out such a prosecution that would spoil Caesar's consular hopes and plans must have been a serious one, motivating such a strong response as the electoral privilege granted by the Law of the Ten Tribunes. The "prosecution theory" eventually became a widely accepted framework for understanding the nature of the crisis that led to the Civil War, explaining both the intensity of Caesar's enemies' desire to extract him from his army and province long enough to block his entry into the consulship and the proconsul's absolute determination not to give them this chance. But more than a decade ago, following a path blazed in the 1960s and 1970s by D. R. Shackleton Bailey and Erich Gruen, I laid out in detail the argument for giving up on this hypothesis, which has for so long been treated as if it were fact and typically made the keystone of analysis of the coming of the Civil War. I will here offer an abbreviated résumé to allow us to move forward while elaborating further on a few observations in an appendix:[12]

---

[11] Shackleton Bailey 1965: 1:39; Brunt 1986: 17: "With his prestige and popularity his election as consul, whether he stood in person or in absence, was a certainty." For the quotation: Cic. *Att.* 7.26.2. Certainty of election: Cic. *Att.* 7.4.3, 7.9.3, 7.15.3, 7.17.2, 7.18.2, 7.26.2, 8.11D.7, 8.12.2; Caelius ad Cic. *Fam.* 8.9.5, 8.8.9, 8.11.3, 8.14.2.

[12] Morstein-Marx 2007, with bibliography; see further Appendix 2. Girardet 2017: 287–289 attempts a refutation, summarizing a charge sheet of Caesar's alleged transgressions, including violations of the constitution as consul, illegal recruitment in his province, unauthorized initiation of a war outside his province, pursuit of a *bellum iniustum* in Gaul, breach of the rights of envoys, "etc." (p. 42). L Gagliardi 2011: 17–21 presumes without argument the validity of the "prosecution theory."

1) Although there are a few, fairly insubstantial references to a desire, entertained especially by Cato, *to bring Caesar to trial* after his return from Gaul (p. 623f.), the version of this idea that is specific to the "prosecution theory" – namely a realistic plan to "bring him to justice" in a trial during his period of vulnerability between election in the summer and the consulship he would take up the following January, and furthermore winning a conviction that would prevent him from entering into the consulship to which he had just been duly elected – is not only extremely implausible on its face after the Senate had decreed, and the City had celebrated, an unprecedented fifty-five days of thanksgiving *supplicationes* in honor of his victories, but is entirely absent from all of our sources, including our best sources, Cicero and Caesar. These would certainly have betrayed knowledge of such a scheme had it existed as more than a fantasy or remote possibility. Given the absolutely central role that the scholars who press this theory attribute to the plan in the various agents' strategies leading up to the Civil War (including passage of the Law of the Ten Tribunes), this seems inexplicable.

2) Furthermore, if this had indeed been Caesar's clever yet entirely predictable scheme to escape the noose his enemies had been trying to place around his neck since 59, why does this specific complaint nowhere appear in our sources for the year 52 and especially in connection with the Law of the Ten Tribunes itself, which on this view would have given him exactly the escape hatch he needed to evade his enemies' plans? For the law clearly gave him the right to be elected consul while still in his province and in command of an army, after which there was no requirement that he enter the city boundary of Rome and expose himself to a trial until he took up the office and regained immunity from prosecution. True, we have virtually no contemporary letters of Cicero that would shine light on the discussion surrounding the passage of the law, but in retrospect as the crisis reached its culmination and the seriousness of this (*ex hypothesi*) disastrous error was at least belatedly dawning on Caesar's enemies, we should be able to find in the copious Ciceronian correspondence from December 50 onward *some* complaint about this crux of the law more specific than grumbling about Pompey's inconsistency.[13]

3) The charges on which the scholars who adopt this theory suppose he would be tried are highly questionable. Our only (vague) reference to

---

[13] See n. 121 and Cic. *Att.* 8.3.3.

what Caesar might be charged with relate strictly to his actions as consul in 59,[14] yet a conviction for his disregard of the auspices or Bibulus's sky watching would be unprecedented and unthinkable after the passage of nearly a decade, *tantis rebus gestis*. As we have seen complaints against his acts as consul had never made much headway even within the Senate itself. Such a charge would never hold up even in a Roman court when popular pressure to acquit would be overwhelming and surely impossible for the narrow clique of Caesar's enemies to sustain, even with Pompey on board (which no source ever suggests he was).[15]

4) Finally, Caesar did in fact ultimately (during negotiations late in January 49) propose to lay aside the supposed protection from prosecution that the Law of the Ten Tribunes *ex hypothesi* provided him, and yet our information about the opposing side's response to his proposal, including even Cato's reaction, fails again to mention that he had thereby at long last given his enemies the opening they had sought to convict him before he stepped into consulship. If this was what precipitated the Civil War, this should have been noted by Cicero, who was present at the council that debated Caesar's response, even though the discussions ultimately proved abortive.[16]

In sum, the "prosecution theory" (or, more accurately, hypothesis) should be left aside. It cannot be regarded as the simple key to understanding the strategies of Caesar or his opponents during the development of the crisis that led to the Civil War.

If the Law of the Ten Tribunes should not be viewed as a lifeline thrown to Caesar to rescue him from a long-standing yet somehow unspoken plan to sabotage his political future before he stepped into his second consulship, then what great advantage did it offer him, so great in fact that he was willing in the end to risk civil war to avoid giving it up? The answer is not far to seek. A formal, legal exemption from the (recently encoded) requirement to declare one's candidacy within the city boundary would allow Caesar to finish his Gallic campaigns, which now necessitated suppressing the major revolt that had just exploded (deferring final victory, if that was coming, by an indefinite period) without having to forego most of the

---

[14] Suet. *Iul.* 30.3: *alii timuisse dicunt, ne eorum, quae primo consulatu adversus auspicia legesque et intercessiones gessisset, rationem reddere cogeretur.* See Appendix 2 (3–4).

[15] The precedent "many" cited of Milo's trial "surrounded by a ring of armed men" (Suet. *Iul.* 30.3) of course is not evidence that Pompey actually favored such a plan.

[16] Cic. *Att.* 7.15.2.

summer campaigning season to meet the deadline for the *professio* some three weeks before the consular elections, which normally came in mid-summer. Furthermore, by relieving him of the need to make his declaration of candidacy within the *pomerium*, the law also prevented a repetition of "Cato's dilemma" on whose horns Caesar become stuck in 60: he could prepare his eventual triumph at relative leisure without being forced to give up his *imperium* beforehand in order to compete in the consular election. (The election itself, in the *comitia centuriata* assembled on the Campus Martius, was outside the city boundary and therefore caused no such complication in itself.) He could certainly anticipate trouble from Cato; in recent years – probably most often due precisely to Catonian resistance in the Senate – the frequency of triumphs had slowed to a trickle (only two in the whole decade of the 50s), and those few that occurred were often held up for years while commanders waited idly outside the City, all the while banned from addressing the Roman People in the Forum and meetings of the Senate (unless by exception called outside the *pomerium*).[17] Cato, probably with Caesar very much in mind, had been committed in recent years to a one-man campaign to minimize or eliminate the traditional honors to victorious commanders for military achievement (*supplicationes* and triumphs both) and to replace them – bizarrely, given the long-standing traditions of the Republic – with honorifics and praises for morally upright administration.[18] The timing of the triumph would have to be carefully arranged, especially if, as is not unlikely, Caesar hoped for an especially celebratory beginning to his consulship with a triumph on the very day he entered into office on January 1, or on

---

[17] The two triumphs in the 50s were those of C. Pomptinus, Caesar's predecessor in Cisalpine Gaul, who triumphed in 54 after being kept waiting for five years, and P. Lentulus Spinther in 51, after two years. We are not well informed about the reasons for the delays, although the Bobbio Scholiast (149 St.) plausibly attributes Pomptinus's delay to Caesar's supporters (see Chapter 4, n. 227), we also happen to know from a chance mention in a letter of Cicero that in 54 Cato as praetor had claimed that Pomptinus would triumph over his dead body due to the lack of an enabling law (Cic. *Att.* 4.18.4). Of the last five triumphs before the outbreak of the Civil War, Pomptinus had waited the longest, but two *triumphatores*, L. Lucullus and Metellus Creticus, had waited for three years; only one triumph within sixteen years before 52 – Pompey's for the Mithridatic and Pirate victories – had actually been approved within a year of the commander's return *ad urbem*. See catalog in Itgenshorst 2005; Rich 2014: 235–237, 251.

[18] Cic. *Fam.* 15.4.14: *te non tam res gestas quam mores <et> instituta atque vitam imperatorum spectare solere in habendis aut non habendis honoribus* (cf. §11, 15), with Cato's answer and Cicero's rejoinder, *Fam.* 15.5–6. For Cato's invidious refusal to support Cicero's supplications (which did not stop him from moving an extraordinary twenty days in honor of his son-in-law Bibulus in this same year) see also Caelius, [Cic.] *Fam.* 8.11.2; Cic. *Att.* 7.1.7, 7.2.5 and 7, 7.3.5. For Cato's triumphal revisionism see Segal 2019: 175–209; for his attitude to traditional Roman conceptions of *gloria* see Morrell 2017: 261–267.

the day before, December 29 (the last day of the pre-Julian civil calendar).[19] But even if he was not aiming precisely for that goal, Cato in 60 had proven that the combination of a consular candidacy and a triumph was going to be a tricky thing to manage. The law was therefore a powerful signal of support for Rome's commander in Gaul who now had his hands very full with what was already a major crisis for the *imperium* of the Roman People across the Alps.

Some have doubted that the privilege granted by the Law of the Ten Tribunes remained legally valid after Pompey's passage later in the very same year of a law encompassing aspects of the duties of magistracies (*lex Pompeia de iure magistratuum*) which reiterated the existing legal requirement for the candidate to declare his candidacy (*professio*) inside the City. This might be interpreted as putting in jeopardy Caesar's electoral privilege just established by the Law of the Ten Tribunes, so (we are told) Pompey, claiming to have forgotten to exempt Caesar specifically in the text of the new law as passed, was moved to insert language explicitly protecting Caesar's privilege after the law had already been inscribed and placed in the archives.[20] A certain amount of ink has been spilled over this intriguing tidbit, to little result. It has been supposed that Pompey's law threw Caesar's privilege into a legal limbo, offering thereby a pretext to Caesar's bitterest enemies to treat it as annulled.[21] But this cannot be

---

[19] Morstein-Marx 2007: 168–169; Girardet 2017: 48. Marius's first triumph was celebrated on the first day of his second consulship, Pompey's second on the day before he became consul for the first time: *Fasti triumphales* ad annos 104, 71: Degrassi, *I.It.* 13.1.561, 565.

[20] Suet. *Iul.* 28.2–3: *quando nec plebi scito* [sc. the law of the Ten Tribunes] *Pompeius postea obrogasset* (on the text, see Butler and Cary 1927: 80, Kaster 2016: 65–66). *Acciderat autem, ut is legem de iure magistratuum ferens eo capite, quo petitione honorum absentis submovebat, ne Caesarem quidem exciperet per oblivionem, ac mox lege iam in aes incisa et in aerarium condita corrigeret errorem.* The subjunctive *obrogasset* should indicate that this was Marcellus's own rationale: even he acknowledged that the privilege had not been repealed, and therefore sought to render it superfluous by recalling Caesar prematurely (*ante tempus*). Dio 40.56.3: προσέγραψε [sc. Pompey] μὲν γὰρ τῷ νόμῳ τὸ μόνοις αὐτὸ [sc. canvass in absence] ἐξεῖναι ποιεῖν οἷς ἂν ὀνομαστί τε καὶ ἄντικρυς ἐπιτραπῇ has been interpreted as referring to the kind of belated correction described by Suetonius (cf. §§1–2), but according to Gagliardi 2012: 129–138 Dio's use of προσέγραψε implies that the correction was completely regular and made during the bill's discussion in *contiones*. This is uncertain but would be consistent with the suggestions of Lintott 2008: 435 and Morrell 2017: 214–215 that what was altered was not the final law as approved by the voters. In any case, even in Suetonius the upshot appears to be that Pompey's subsequent *lex de iure magistratuum* did *not* after all override the earlier law (*nec plebi scito ... obrogasset*) which is also what Cicero blandly states at *Att.* 8.3.3 (*quod idem ipse sanxit lege quadam sua,* where I think Shackleton Bailey 1965: 4:329 is mistaken to interpret *quadam* as "suggest[ing] a doubt as to the validity of Pompey's confirmation of the privilege"; he is merely being vague about by *which law* Pompey affirmed the privilege).

[21] Gelzer 1968: 153 and Seager 2002: 138–139 believe that Pompey's law did in effect annul the Law of the Ten Tribunes. Contra, persuasively, Gruen 1974: 456–457; see also Morstein-Marx 2007: 168n42, with references to earlier scholarship; Lundgreen 2011: 103–104; Pelling 2011: 287–289.

right. Caesar's electoral privilege can hardly have been overturned so uncere-
moniously only a few months at most after the Law of the Ten Tribunes was
passed with great fanfare: at least one of those ten tribunes would certainly
have vetoed the law if anyone could seriously argue that this was the import
of the *lex Pompeia*. Furthermore, and crucially, in all the highly partisan run-
up to the Civil War, no one is on record as having made or accepted such
a claim, which as far as we can see was quickly forgotten. Pompey himself
dismissed the problem as a mere oversight and sought to correct it, while
Cicero, in his many references in letters of 50 and 49 to Caesar's *ratio absentis*,
always treats the privilege as legally unimpeachable and essentially irrevocable ever since the passage of the Law of the Ten Tribunes, yet he could
hardly have been blind to any serious legal objection to the validity of
Caesar's electoral privilege.[22] The straightforward interpretation of the
story in Suetonius is that Pompey's new law changed nothing pertaining
to the general rule requiring *professio* within the City, which had stood in the
preexisting law and was now repeated in typical tralatician fashion. Before 52
the relevant statute on magistrates' elections had held that *professio* within the
City was required, and after 52 the new statute did the same. It may be that
someone (apparently not Marcellus himself) tried to make hay with the fact
that Caesar's exemption was not explicitly repeated in the *lex Pompeia*. But if
so, that argument went nowhere, and the exemption remained sufficiently
guaranteed by the Law of the Ten Tribunes whether or not we believe the
curious story about Pompey slipping in some correction ex post facto to
protect it.[23] The issue is a red herring.

There is one final sticky issue to get out of the way before we can begin our
analysis relatively unimpeded. Perhaps no problem in ancient history strikes
more dread into the hearts of students and specialists alike than that of the
terminal date of Caesar's command in Gaul. Although the *lex Vatinia*
spanned a length of five years, and its extension by the *lex Pompeia Licinia*
five more, we do not have reliable information on when these five-year spans

---

Gagliardi 2012: 105–149 (esp. 142–145) has recently argued that the *lex Pompeia* required henceforth
a senatorial decision *de novo* for each upcoming election, for Caesar just as for anyone else.

[22] Cicero *Att.* 7 passim, esp. *Att.* 7.7.6: *cum hoc aut depugnandum est aut habenda e lege ratio;* 7.9.2
amicis eius postulantibus ut e lege ratio habeatur. According to Cic. *Att.* 8.3.3, Pompey's own law
confirmed the privilege: *quod idem ipse sanxit lege quadam sua.* It is further telling that Cicero raises
no question of the validity of the law in his agonized lucubrations, and even in his indignant rebuttal
of Caesar's demands at 7.9.4. Cic. *Att.* 7.7.6 and 7.9.4 show that the only plausible objection Cicero
entertained to the *ratio absentis* was if one took the view that Caesar's military
command, which after all had provided its underlying rationale, had already expired.

[23] Note that Dio. 40.56.3 indicates that Caesar's privilege was sufficiently protected after the passage of
the *lex Pompeia* since he had in fact been exempted "openly by name" (ὀνομαστί τε καὶ ἄντικρυς).
Further, in Dio's version Caesar's supporters (§2) appear to have been fully appeased.

were deemed to begin, whether they were intended to fit like planks end to end, or whether instead they overlapped or were even separated by a gap. In fact, we are not absolutely sure whether the time intervals expressed a *maximum* limiting the duration of Caesar's *imperium*, or a *minimum* protecting him against premature recall or, even more fundamentally, whether a terminal date was explicitly stated in the law. Scholars have offered a variety of answers to these questions, and it is probably time to acknowledge that there will never be a consensus that would provide a basis on which to proceed securely on that question. Therefore it is best not to build our analysis on a controversial or perhaps even tendentious conclusion to any of these problems, and especially not to place exaggerated emphasis on a matter that our sources themselves fail to nail down securely.[24] The safest course is to suppose that ultimately it would be up to the Senate and People (the latter potentially by means of tribunician action) to decide when, within the fairly broad range of interpretation permitted by a five-year extension in 55, Caesar's time in Gaul would be reckoned to be "up." This was most likely to be decided in connection with the exercise of naming a successor to his command(s).[25] And because another *lex Pompeia* of 52 had revised the process of the Senate's annual determination of the consular provinces and lifted the ban under the *lex Sempronia* on the use of the veto, any reassignment of Caesar's provinces would have to be done with all due formality – that is, without triggering a veto, which should not be viewed in oligarchic fashion as a mere nuisance but as a fully legitimate means by which the

---

[24] As does, e.g., Girardet 2017: 21–29: the last day of December 50 (cf. Girardet 2000: 684–685, relying in part on Giovannini 1983: 103–146), or Gagliardi 2011: 23–61, who nevertheless argues that there were at least two plausible legal interpretations (March 1 and "December 31," 49, where, however, read December 29, the last day of the pre-Julian year) and concedes that even in antiquity there was no definitive solution (p. 59). Other recent scholarship has tended to follow Gruen 1974: 492–493 (with n. 153) in allowing for the possibility that no calendar date was strictly defined (cf. Morstein-Marx 2007: 175n78, Pelling 2011: 285–293, a recent, useful survey of the problem, and Steel 2013: 188; but cf. contra Lintott 2008: 433–436). Pelling strongly endorses the now fairly common view (e.g. also Shackleton Bailey 1977: 1:406; Vervaet 2006: 645–646 with n. 72) that the law explicitly stipulated that Caesar's provinces *could not even be discussed* by the Senate before March 1, 50, but while March 1 appears repeatedly in a fashion that suggests that it may be relevant (Cic. *Prov. cons.* 36–38; Hirt. [Caes.] *BGall.* 8.53.1; Cael. [Cic.] 8.8.9), that is by no means a necessary conclusion. Note that there is no independent reason to think that the *lex Vatinia* was passed as early as March 2, 59 (so Gagliardi 2011: 28n12, 33n22, on the grounds that March 1 was not a comitial day; cf. Chapter 4, n. 209). See further n. 127.

[25] Pelling 2011: 286 (with n. 10): "It was indeed anything but clear what a terminal date for the command would mean, or what would happen when it passed . . . Most provincial commands were granted not by law but by senatorial decree, and lasted not for a fixed time but until a successor was appointed and arrived. Analogy would suggest that a command granted by law would be similar, and C[aesar] would continue in Gaul until a successor . . . took over." Contra, Girardet 2017: 292–294, who does not take into account that Cicero's was a special case: he was determined to stay not a day longer than he had to in what he regarded as virtually an exile from Rome.

popular will or interest was recognized and defended.[26] Thus the decision to replace Caesar would ultimately be a political, not a juridical one: in a nutshell, it would not be a *Rechtsfrage* (so Mommsen) or even a *Machtfrage* (Syme), but a *Politikfrage*. This approach refocuses our attention where it should be: on the Curia and Forum, not on some nonexistent Roman Supreme Court.

When did Caesar and others expect him to make use of his electoral privilege? Suetonius says that the Law of the Ten Tribunes provided that his candidacy for a second consulship would be allowed "when the time of his command had begun to expire," a frustratingly vague phrase which again bespeaks a certain indefiniteness about the definition of Caesar's command's duration and appears to point loosely to one of the consular elections to be held after the upcoming summer of 52, when Caesar obviously had his hands full (the manifest rationale of the law) – that is, the elections of 51, 50, or 49.[27] Dio describes the law as permitting Caesar to stand in absentia "whenever this was consistent with the laws," which at first glance would seem to allude to the law requiring a ten-year gap between consulships and thus push the target date no earlier than the election of 49 for 48 (as Caesar himself would later claim he had intended all along).[28] Yet on second thought it is probably more likely that "the

---

[26] For the *lex Pompeia de provinciis* (as it is often called in scholarship) see Dio 40.56.1 (which may suggest that it formed a part of a comprehensive *lex de iure magistratuum*, discussed earlier), with Caes. *BCiv.* 1.6.5, 1.85.9; Cic. *Fam.* 3.2.1, with *MRR* 2.242–243 (proconsular assignments of Bibulus and Cicero) and Steel 2012: 85. The lifting of the *lex Sempronia*'s ban on the veto (Chapter 4, n. 235) is not explicitly attested but reliably inferred from the Senate's paralysis against Curio's veto in 50 of a replacement for Caesar. This, together with the fact that consular provincial appointments from 51 to 49 are clearly consistent not with the *lex Sempronia* but with the new law (cf. Caesar's complaint about assignment of provinces to *privati*), decisively refutes Giovannini's contention (1983: 105–127) that the new law did not replace the provisions of the Sempronian law for the assignment of consular provinces (accepted by Girardet 2000: 691, 699; 2017: 32–33, 64n288, and apparently Pina Polo 2011: 241, 298; rebuttal in Morstein-Marx 2007: 169–170n50; Pelling 2011: 287–289, Steel 2012: 84–88, Morrell 2017: 222). The reinstitution of the veto clearly shows that the law was not implicitly directed against Caesar, since at least from the passage of the Law of the Ten Tribunes it could be anticipated that his interests would be upheld by at least one tribune in the name of the People's rights. On the central provision of the purported *lex de provinciis* see now Steel 2012, who reinterprets it as an attempt to deal with the recent problem of a shortage of governors due to the increasing number who did not accept a province (on this, cf. Blösel 2016), and Morrell 2017: 214–236, who emphasizes the motive of improving imperial governance (see already Gruen 1974: 457–459) as well as the more traditional view that it was aimed at limiting electoral corruption.

[27] Suet. *Iul.* 26.1 *quandoque imperii tempus expleri coepisset, petitio secundi consulatus daretur.*

[28] Dio 40.51.2: ὅταν ἐκ τῶν νόμων καθήκῃ; Caes. *BCiv.* 1.9.2, 1.32.2, with Chapter 5, p. 249ff. Caesar's claim is probably therefore tendentious, a bit of ex post facto revisionism intended to demonstrate his rigorous adherence to the laws: Gruen 1974: 476; Girardet 2000: 681–689 (against an old consensus dating back to Mommsen: bibliography at Girardet 2000: 681n9); pace, however, Gagliardi 2011: 37, 51. But this must have been an arguable interpretation of the law(s), which

laws" Dio refers to were those on which Caesar's command rested (the *lex Pompeia Licinia* in combination with the *lex Vatinia*), which would make this simply another version of Suetonius's statement that the privilege was to be exercised when that assignment was coming to its end.[29] For it is clear from M. Caelius's letter to Cicero written in October 51 that at that time Caesar was expected to make use of his *ratio absentis* in the upcoming elections of summer 50 and it strains credulity to suppose that there was an overwhelming consensus at the time of the passage of the Law of the Ten Tribunes in favor of Caesar's remaining in his province and command for more than three further years (to the elections of 49).[30] Our evidence, then, suggests that the expected timing of the use of the privilege was not rigorously defined in the Law of the Ten Tribunes; if defined at all, it was in such broad terms as to allow a variety of interpretations (a typical feature of expressions of consensus). Lack of total clarity on this point seems to underlie the development of the crisis to come, yet at the time of the law's passage in 52 this was probably the price of keeping everyone (except Cato) on board.

The Law of the Ten Tribunes and the reiterated, record supplications voted by the Senate after the victorious conclusion of the Vercingetorix revolt (probably late October, Jul.) were, taken together, a powerful boost toward Caesar's hopes and expectations for an honorific return from Gaul.[31] In less than two years everything would change.

The Crisis Begins

Even after the suppression of the Great Revolt Caesar remained busy with mopping-up operations through the winter and early spring of 51, followed by the siege and capture of Uxellodunum in the Dordogne, which occupied the rest of the summer campaigning season. Caesar's staff officer (?) and continuator of his *Gallic War Commentaries*, A. Hirtius, states that it

---

supports the idea that the expected timing of the use of the privilege was as vaguely stated as Suetonius and Dio suggest.

[29] In this context it may be relevant that Dio thought the extension of the command according to the *lex Pompeia Licinia* was for *three* years "in actual fact" (39.33.3). He may only be making his numbers consistent with the eventual outcome (cf. 44.43.2; cf. Pelling 2011: 247), but the passage again lends plausibility to the idea that any terminal date was the product of inference and not explicitly stated in the law.

[30] Cael. [Cic.] *Fam.* 8.8.9, with Pelling 2011: 284 with n. 9.

[31] Caes. *BGall.* 7.90.8, 8.1.1 *omni Gallia devicta*. The story of the Great Revolt is expertly told by Goldsworthy 2006: 315–342. For the date see Raaflaub and Ramsey 2017: 61.

was general knowledge among "all the Gauls" that this would be Caesar's last summer of active campaigning in the province.[32] The natural expectation was, then, that Caesar would stand for election in 50, though still in absentia, remaining in one of his Gallic provinces while keeping a close eye on the still insecure peace in Transalpina.[33]

But one of the consuls of this very year (51), M. Marcellus, evidently exploiting Caesar's own recent declaration of victory and the Senate's answering thanksgivings, reasonably pointed out that since the war in Gaul had now been bought to a successful conclusion it was time to bring the victorious army home, along with, of course, its commander, even though this was manifestly well before the time envisioned (if not explicitly defined) at the time of the passage of the Pompeian-Licinian law.[34] This could, of course, render Caesar's electoral privilege moot. The effort failed, ultimately to a veto. But on September 29, Marcellus was able to win passage, avoiding a veto, for a decree requesting that the consuls of the following year (i.e. 50 BC) should open the question again in the Senate on March 1, a date that would leave time for Caesar to return and canvass in the consular election that would come no earlier than the summer of 50, if that was the way the debate fell out. The proposal was not an inequitable one; it was duly noted that Pompey declared that though it would have been *iniuria* to dispose of Caesar's provinces before that date, it would not be so afterward.[35] The fact that none of the tribunes who had vetoed a number of other measures that seemed inimical to Caesar's interests acted similarly to block this one shows that even Caesar's friends had to concede the point, though by a veto to a subsequent resolution they also gave

[32] Hirtius, [Caes.] *BGall.* 8.39.3. Unfortunately the text is somewhat ambiguous as to whether the summer in question is that of 51 or 50. But given the timing of the comment (late June–early July, to judge from the calculations of Raaflaub and Ramsey 2017: 64; cf. Raaflaub and Ramsey 2017: 185) and its relevance within its context (Caesar's need for an immediate, decisive response), the summer of 51, most of which was yet to come, is much more to the point than that of 50 (contra Kraner, Dittenberger, and Meusel 1964: 3:55; Girardet 2000: 683n19, 2017: 46; Raaflaub (ed.) 2017 ad loc.). Pelling 2011: 284n9 notes that the imputed judgment may be only the product of hindsight.

[33] See n. 30.

[34] Suet. *Iul.* 28.2 is explicit: *ut ei succederetur ante tempus* (so too Hirt. [Caes.] *BGall.* 8.53.1). The effort began around June 1, was persistently deferred due to lack of a quorum, and was finally defeated on September 29 (Caelius, [Cic.] *Fam.* 8.1.2, 4.4, 9.2, 8.5–9). Interestingly, there were rumors in May that Caesar was again in trouble in Gaul (8.1.4), which may also have taken some wind out of the recall effort.

[35] Cael. [Cic.] *Fam.* 8.8.5–6, 9: *se ante Kal. Mart. non posse sine iniuria de provinciis Caesaris statuere, post Kal. Mart. se non dubitaturum*. This is the strongest argument for the idea that the *lex Pompeia Licinia* specified Mar. 1 as a deadline for *discussion* of Caesar's replacement (n. 24); yet March 1 may have had a special significance in the senatorial calendar such as (as Balsdon suggested, now followed by Pina Polo 2011: 237–239) the beginning of deliberations on military assignments following the hearing of foreign embassies in February. March 15 was the ancient opening of the campaigning season (Chapter 9, n. 20).

notice that they still reserved the right to veto a decree when the debate was resumed on March 1.[36]

Cicero's friend M. Caelius, describing these resolutions in detail in a letter of September (Jul.) 51 to Cicero (who was now proconsular governor far away in Cilicia), conjectures that Caesar would leave his province (and, implicitly, his army) and return to Rome if he were elected consul in absentia at the next elections in the coming summer (50), but that if he were not allowed to run or was not elected, he would stay on in his province and therefore necessarily in command of an army.[37] However, Caelius also says that Pompey had made clear that he wanted Caesar to leave his province after March 1.[38] In two other letters written around the same time Caelius also says that Pompey was clearly against Caesar either *holding the consulship* while still in command of his provinces and army or, alternatively, *being elected consul* without first giving up provinces and army.[39]

At first glance it looks like Pompey was now disregarding altogether the law containing Caesar's electoral privilege passed with his blessing in 52, but a better interpretation is probably that he was simply pushing for its narrower application. As we have seen, it is clear that when the law was passed, it was envisioned that Caesar would make use of it while still in his province at the head of an

---

[36] Earlier in the year Pompey had resisted senatorial prodding regarding Caesar, but had delivered a conventional expression of allegiance to the Senate's will (8.4.4); now, at the end of September, he spoke as if he would consider a further veto to be a subversion of that will (8.8.9). Earlier in September Caesar's agent Balbus had been displeased by the proposed motion for the March 1 debate (8.9.5). The issues between Pompey and Caesar may have been complicated by the fact that Caesar was about to spend his second consecutive winter across the Alps (Hirt. [Caes.] *BGall.* 8.46.5–6), leaving no opportunity for direct consultation. Pompey had visited "his army" at Ariminum in late July (Cael. [Cic.] *Fam.* 8.4.4), while Caesar was fully engaged in Transalpina.

[37] Caelius [Cic.] *Fam.* 8.8.9 *alteram utram ad condicionem descendere vult Caesar, ut aut maneat neque hoc anno* [sc. 50] *sua ratio habeatur aut, si designari poterit, decedat.* Note that Caelius does not envision Caesar's running for the consulship *without* making use of his privilege. Schneider 2004 tries to open a space for the possibility that Caesar could hold on to his provinces without commanding an army, but has to acknowledge that this is unprecedented (146–147) and, I would judge, impossible. His reinterpretation of Cael. [Cic.] 8.13.2, rejecting the traditional emendations, is unpersuasive (see n. 85). See also Jehne 2017: 207–208n38.

[38] Cael. [Cic.] *Fam.* 8.8.4 *plane perspecta . . . voluntate in eam partem ut eum decedere post Kal. Mart. placeret.*

[39] Cael. [Cic.] *Fam.* 8.9.5 (September 51): *aperte Caesarem et provinciam tenere cum exercitu et consul<em fieri* (= to be elected) *non vult>*, the emendation of Boot accepted by Shackleton Bailey, or, alternatively, *consul<em esse>* (= to be consul, Lambinus). Cf. the question put to Pompey on September 29: *"Quid si . . . et consul esse et exercitum habere volet?"* (8.8.9). If Pompey was objecting to Caesar continuing to hold on to his army and province *while consul*, he was rejecting what he himself had done only the previous year, in his third consulship. The following April (8.11.3) Pompey's position seems to be rather that Caesar should not *be elected* consul while holding on to his province and army (*valde autem non vult et plane timet Caesarem consulem designatum prius quam exercitum et provinciam tradiderit*; cf. 8.14.2). Of course the best way to ensure that Caesar would not hold on to his army while consul was to require that he leave it before the election. See Morstein-Marx 2007: 170n54, with references.

army, for the stated rationale for the law was that he should not be forced to leave his province prematurely and leave the war unfinished.[40] Furthermore, the privilege would also be needed to protect Caesar's "right" to a triumph against "Cato's dilemma," for a commander waiting *ad urbem* to celebrate his triumph could not cross the pomerium to declare his candidacy (*professio*) without losing the *imperium* he needed for the triumph. Thus, the electoral privilege granted by the Law of the Ten Tribunes was still essential to Caesar's plans even if he left his province and most of his army and came to Rome to contest the election while awaiting his triumph outside the walls.[41] In making his recent push for Caesar to give up his province and army before election to a second consulship, Pompey was therefore not simply wishing away the Law of the Ten Tribunes, and he was able at least outwardly to maintain good faith toward his old ally.[42] Yet by simultaneously setting a deadline for his return he indicated that he was losing patience and did not wish to see Caesar's deferrals stretch on indefinitely. When at a meeting of the Senate on September 29, 51, someone asked Pompey what he would think if Caesar wanted to be consul while continuing to command an army, he blustered that this would be like his son taking a stick to him – though it is unclear whether this reply meant that this was unthinkable or that it would call for a good thrashing.[43]

It is clear enough that much of the impetus behind such fraught questioning was the desire of some senators already in 51 to use Pompey and his forces in Italy, such as they were, as a preemptive counterbalance against Caesarian pressure. Already in September 51 Caelius saw that things were shaping up for a showdown over the Gallic provinces which could be short-circuited by tribunician vetoes in Caesar's interests, leaving Caesar in Gaul "for a couple of years or more."[44] One obvious countermove was to

---

[40] See Chapter 5, pp. 252 and 260f of this chapter.

[41] For this "minimalist" interpretation of the *ratio absentis*, see Morstein-Marx 2007: 170–171 with 168n44 (now apparently accepted by Girardet 2017: 48, 72, 86–88, 99–100).

[42] Gruen 1974: 451–470 and Raaflaub 1974: 42–55 have effectively disposed of the old idea, too heavily influenced by e.g. Plut. *Caes.* 28.1, *Pomp.* 53.6–54.2 (also App. *BCiv.* 2.19/68), that Pompey had now turned against Caesar, at least privately, since Julia's death in 54. They convincingly show that Pompey took a scrupulously correct line to his old ally at least until March 1, 50, and recognize that he probably remained open to a settlement down to the last. Too much can be made of Pompey's opting not to accept Caesar's proposals for a renewed marriage connection in 52 (Suet. *Iul.* 27.1).

[43] Cael. [Cic.] *Fam.* 8.8.9. On *Pompeio cum Caesare esse negotium*, Shackleton Bailey ad loc. seems persuasive ("Pompey is having trouble with Caesar") against the interpretation of Balsdon and others that "a bargain had been effected between himself and Julius Caesar" (Gruen 1974: 469; also Girardet 2000: 697n84, 2017: 96–100), but due to the ambiguities inherent in Pompey's manner of expression and in Caelius's interpretation, the question must be left open.

[44] Cael, [Cic.] *Fam.* 8.5.2: *ita diu ut plus biennium in his tricis moretur* (cf. 8.9.2). Note that Caelius does not yet speculate about a military confrontation, an idea that first rises gently to the surface of the text in April 50 (8.11.3 *Caesar defendet intercessorem*) and only becomes explicit in July/August (8.14.2–3, n. 114).

try to enlist Pompey as the Republic's defender against "revolution" and, buttressed by his authority and troops, to deny Caesar outright the "honors" he was seeking: his election (in absentia or not), even a triumph. The strategy was well known to Cicero and cannot have escaped Caesar.[45] To be sure, the deterrent was essentially symbolic since it seems unlikely that Pompey at this time had more than the equivalent of one or two freshly recruited legions in Italy.[46] Nevertheless, it is remarkable that Cicero explicitly mentions this idea as if it was clearly in the air: Caesar's subsequently attested fears that his enemies were out to deny him "all honor" (*nullus honos*) were clearly not removed from reality.[47]

However, Pompey did not always appear committed to the role that others were scripting for him. In the summer and fall of 51 it looked to well-informed observers as if Pompey would after all move off to his province of Spain.[48] Soon a supervening confrontation with the Parthians added a new layer of complexity to the question. During Cicero's patriotic exile in command of Cilicia war with the Parthians had suddenly blazed up (much to his chagrin), and the invaders had actually wintered within the province of Syria in 51–50, raising the specter of a "major war" in the coming spring.[49] Already in September 51 there was talk of sending Pompey to deal with the emerging crisis, and around the turn of the new year Magnus himself wrote to Cicero to tell him that he would soon be taking over the command there.[50] This is an important reminder of how

---

[45] Cic. *Att.* 5.21.3 (February 50): *cum Pompeius propter* metum rerum novarum *nusquam dimittatur, Caesari* nullus honos *a senatu habeatur*; 5.11.3; 5.18.1 *vereor ne senatus propter urbanarum rerum metum Pompeium nolit dimittere* (here: against the Parthians). At 5.11.3 and *Fam.* 3.8.10 Cicero expresses anxiety lest Pompey go to Spain (again in the summer of 50: *Att.* 6.8.2); cf. the implied concern of the Senate at *Att.* 5.18.1. The retrospective comment at *Att.* 7.13.2 is more explicit: *praesidium, cuius parandi causa ad urbem* [sc. Pompeius] *retentus est.* For Caesar's concerns see Caes. *BCiv.* 1.85.8; cf. 1.2.3, 1.9.5 (all retrospective, of course). Note that in early 53 Caesar had been willing to excuse Pompey's remaining outside the city *rei publicae causa* (*BGall.* 6.1.2) – a concession that further supports the theory of serial composition of the *Commentarii*, since Caesar seems unlikely to have written this with partisan intent over the winter of 52/51 or 51/50.

[46] He had been authorized to recruit two legions in 52 (App. *BCiv.* 2.24/92), and in the summer of 51 Pompey had some kind of *exercitus* at Ariminum (Cael. [Cic.] *Fam.* 8.4.4). But given Pompey's lack of confidence in these troops in 49 they cannot have amounted to very much. For Pompey's military resources at the outbreak of the Civil War see n. 97.

[47] Cic. *Att.* 5.21.3.

[48] See n. 45. The fear seems to have reemerged in the summer of 50: *Att.* 6.8.2, with Shackleton Bailey's comment.

[49] For the grave concerns of Cicero and in Rome already in November (~ October, Jul.) 51 see the nearly simultaneous *Fam.* 2.10.4, Cael. [Cic.] *Fam.* 8.10.2. Cicero still fears a "great war" in April 50: *Fam.* 2.11.1, 13.57.1; *Att.* 6.2.6, and even as late as June (*Att.* 6.5.3). The threat seems to have dissipated only in July: see Appendix 3(d).

[50] September: *Att.* 5.18.1 (cf. Cael. [Cic.] *Fam.* 8.10.2). Pompey's letter: Cic. *Att.* 6.1.14 (which also seems to imply that Cicero expected Pompey to arrive by late summer); cf. §3. The letter is dated

contingent and labile the situation involving Caesar still was at this point. Had the Parthians continued their invasion in the spring, or had Pompey been less amenable to the pressures his new friends exerted, no one could have dreamed of stealing Caesar's honorific return from him, and it becomes easy to envision very different outcomes than the Civil War of 49–45.

When, in accordance with the s.c. of the previous September, the consuls raised the question of the provinces on March 1, 50 (~ ca. January 19, Jul., after the failure of the tribune C. Scribonius Curio's attempt to have an intercalary month inserted),[51] Curio cast a veto, or threatened one, against the attempt of the new consul C. Marcellus to pass a motion relieving Caesar of his command.[52] Ironically, Pompey's law of 52 had actually *opened the way* to Caesar to block simple reassignment of his provinces to a consul, since no veto of the consular provinces had been allowed under the *lex Sempronia*.[53] In response, as had long been anticipated, the consuls refused to consider the disposition of any of the other provinces (a great annoyance to Cicero, stuck in Cilicia, among others), leaving all provincial assignments frozen in place: this was a way of

---

February 20, 50 (ca. January 12, Jul.), at Laodicea, at a time when communications to that place from Rome must have taken well over a month. (Cf. §§1, 22.)

[51] Cael. [Cic.] *Fam.* 8.6.5: *levissime enim, quia de intercalando non obtinuerat, transfugit ad populum et pro Caesari loqui coepit* [sc. Curio]; cf. Dio 40.62.1–2 for details. While the civil calendar was now almost as misaligned with the seasons as it had been the last time intercalation was resorted to in 52 (see Brind'Amour 1983: 327–328; Bennett 2001–2012), the pattern of intercalation through the 50s thus far had been a three-year cycle (58, 55, 52: Shackleton Bailey 1977: 1:416 is incorrect), so it was arguable that it would have been premature in 50. The decision this year, however, was a political football, since Curio (who as a *pontifex* was on the board that decided the timing of intercalation) would have gained an extra twenty-two days for passing certain controversial bills he had proposed (Dio 40.61.3–62.1.) The nature of these bills is obscure: Caelius wrote late in 51 ([Cic.] *Fam.* 8.10.3–4) that Curio was expected to oppose Caesar in his tribunate (cf. Chapter 5, n. 252), but intended to propose something about the former public land in Campania that Pompey didn't like (but to which Caesar, interestingly, was thought to be indifferent); however, Dio describes the bills that Curio tried to save through intercalation as hostile to the interests of powerful senators cooperating with Pompey (40.61.3), and Caelius regards Curio as "deserting to the People" only *after* the failure of the intercalation proposal (Cael. [Cic.] *Fam.* 8.6.5; cf. §4: *Curioni nostro tribunatus conglaciat*). But an intercalary month would also have pushed back the March 1 debate by about three weeks and given Caesar correspondingly more time in his command. Possibly, then, this was the main stumbling block. The fifteen-man pontifical college which rejected Curio's intercalation, according to Dio, included Pompey's new father-in-law, Metellus Scipio, Caesar's great enemy, L. Domitius, P. Lentulus Spinther, and young M. Brutus (Rüpke 2005: 1:133). It also included the *pontifex maximus*, but we have no idea how Caesar's religious duties were performed during his long absence in the two Gauls.

[52] Cic. *Att.* 6.2.6 shows that the vetoes began in the first week of March. Girardet 2000: 699–700, 2017: 108–109 connects Caes. *BCiv.* 1.9.2 to this moment: but see n. 127.

[53] Raaflaub 1974a: 299–300; n. 26.

ratcheting up the pressure on Curio to lift the veto.[54] Curio had performed a remarkable political turnabout (at the time of his election he was expected to side with the *boni* against Caesar), and all could see that he was now operating in Caesar's interests.[55] The genius of Caesar's veto strategy was that it essentially pushed into the background the problem of deciding when precisely Caesar's extended command could be construed by law to have run its course. For until the Senate decided on the disposition of the Gauls with all due formality and correct constitutional procedure – that is, without incurring a tribunician veto, a fundamental republican institution – the current commander was free, nay arguably bound, to remain at his post until a successor was properly appointed.[56]

Curio's persistent veto against any attempt to replace Caesar would in the event hold throughout 50 – a novelty indeed, but hardly likely to have been sustainable without palpable popular support.[57] We need to give proper emphasis to this point. Caesar's cause was apt to be seen as the People's cause as well: the conjunction of ideas contained in Caelius's statement that Curio had "deserted to the People and begun to speak in Caesar's behalf" merits our attention.[58] Our sources tend to describe the crisis as it developed in the course of the year 50 almost exclusively in terms of the strategic decisions of the elite actors in a gradually escalating showdown, and in our own analysis we are forced largely to follow in their tracks both because these men were pulling the levers of power and because this is where our sources shed most light. Yet it is undeniable that our sources, whose authors were either senators themselves or later synthesizers of historical accounts that ultimately depended on senatorial sources, were much more interested in the interpersonal maneuvering within their own class than in the pressures exerted by popular opinion and popular

---

[54] Cael. [Cic.] *Fam.* 8.9.2, 8.5.2.

[55] The story of Curio's frustration and "desertion" to Caesar is well told by Gruen 1974: 477–482, although he probably exaggerates his independence after February (Morstein-Marx 2007: 160n3; Dettenhofer 1992: 45–62), when he suddenly "deserted to the People and began to speak in Caesar's behalf" (Cael. [Cic.] *Fam.* 8.6.5, Latin text, n. 51; cf. 8.4.2, 5.3). As we have seen (n. 44), Caesar's exploitation of a persistent veto to remain in his province was a maneuver that had long been anticipated; when Curio stepped into this role all will have understood what it meant. Consider also how Caesar's "friend" Balbus acts as Curio's "minder" during the discussion of Cicero's *supplicatio* in April (Cael. [Cic.] *Fam.* 8.11.2). None of this need imply that, as some ancient gossip held, Curio was "bribed"; sufficient motivation for his remarkable turnabout may be found in his quarrel with the consuls, the only motive actually mentioned by Caelius (8.6.5). But Curio may well have been encouraged by a generous loan around this time: Appendix 1, p. 620f.

[56] See p. 266ff.

[57] For the political impossibility of sustaining a *legislative* veto without popular support see Morstein-Marx 2004: 124–126.

[58] Cael. [Cic.] *Fam.* 8.6.5 (n. 51).

ideology.[59] The coming of the Civil War of 49–45 tends, for the reasons just mentioned, to be told in something of a *"populus*-free zone," and while this is mostly inevitable, we must not forget that tribunes in particular must have held numerous *contiones* throughout this year (which we hear about only toward its end)[60] in which Caesar's "just aims" and "deserved requests" were aired and perhaps debated – although interestingly, we do not actually hear of a single attempt by those opposed to Caesar to address the People in this year, a remarkable forfeiture of the public sphere by those who never tired of professing their dedication to "the Republic."[61]

Curio's persistent veto sharply escalated tensions and clearly heightened suspicion of Caesar's ends; it might well be called the true beginning of the crisis. Why did Caesar (through Curio) think it useful or necessary to make such an aggravating move at this time?[62] One might suppose that Caesar's interests were sufficiently secured by the fact that the Law of the Ten Tribunes specifically gave him the right to compete as a candidate in the consular election of 50 for 49 while remaining in his province – an election he would certainly win. Why now risk upsetting the delicate situation with a further escalation?

Perhaps in the end it was a mistake. But it is not hard to understand why Caesar would have thought he needed to make such a move. Let us remember what he would have known about his prospects in Rome. He knew that Pompey was still not in his province of Spain, which he had held in absentia for more than four years, and he will have known that even moderates like Cicero were eager to keep the proconsul of Spain in the environs of Rome as a possible counterweight to himself. It was of course manifest that Cato and Bibulus had effected a new rapprochement with Pompey, which hardly boded well for himself.[63] He will also have known that Pompey wanted him to be replaced in his provinces after March 1 and was hostile to his standing for election while still holding on to his

---

[59] See Morstein-Marx 2013: 31–32, 40–47 for a preliminary investigation of whether in this way our sources tend to reflect "a pleasant hegemonic dream with only a loose connection with reality." "Public opinion" is now receiving due attention: Rosillo López 2017; Angius 2018.

[60] See nn. 155, 172, 173, 196.

[61] This is presumably an effect of the well-known *popularis* bias of fully public speech in *contiones*: "a nakedly 'optimate' stance was in straightforward contradiction with the *contio* as a rhetorical setting" (Morstein-Marx 2004: 239), the basis of what I have called the "ideological monotony" of the *contio*. One might compare the failure of Bibulus and the "*optimates*" to articulate any rationale for their opposition to Caesar's laws in 59, or indeed the apparent lack of two-sided debate over Tiberius Gracchus's agrarian bill in 133 (ibid., pp. 172–175; cf. Flower 2013: 91).

[62] Here I am treating Curio's action as in effect Caesar's. See n. 55. Note that according to Girardet 2017: 111, Caesar had been persistently planning a "Putsch" since March 50, having laid the groundwork already in 51 ("Gewaltdrohung," p. 87).

[63] See p. 295.

provinces and army.[64] The modest military forces in Italy did not of course bear comparison with Caesar's large, battle-hardened army, but they might suffice to dominate an election if the proconsul of Gaul could be induced to leave his army and come to take his chances with the *comitia* in Rome (outside the *pomerium*, of course).[65] Under these circumstances it made good strategic sense to ensure that he was not replaced and forced to leave his provinces and army before he had secured his election.[66]

Caesar had little reason to entrust his future to Pompey's sense of scrupulous fairness, and he knew what Cato would like to do to him. Once he had been replaced and coaxed from his army his enemies would very likely attempt to block his candidacy (or possibly even, if allowed, refuse to accept the electoral result). This, rather than a supervening prosecution, is the method of foiling Caesar's plans that Caelius and Cicero repeatedly anticipate when they work through the likely future moves in the unfolding of the crisis.[67] The consuls had, at least in theory, considerable discretion to accept or reject candidates, recently demonstrated by the ability of the consul of 56, Cn. Marcellinus, to block Pompey's and Crassus's candidacies as long as he remained in office, and although this surely required some plausible legal justification, Caesar knew it would not be hard for his enemies to excogitate one: for example, the fact that only nine and not the statutory ten years had passed since his former consulship, or perhaps it could be argued that the Law of the Ten Tribunes was no longer applicable because on his own admission the war was over.[68] Especially after the experience of his first consulship he also had good reason to worry about attempts to exploit religious objections to sabotage his election.[69] Indeed, it was not impossible to take the view that the Law of the Ten Tribunes was now moot since active military operations no longer necessitated Caesar's absence. One key question would be where the consuls stood vis-à-vis Caesar. L. Aemilius Lepidus Paullus was a former adversary but was now reasonably friendly and already indebted to Caesar financially; there is, however, no sign

---

[64] See nn. 38, 39, 45. [65] See p. 272ff.

[66] As Caelius had seen already in September (Jul.) 51 ([Cic.] *Fam.* 8.8.9, text at n. 37). Cf. 8.14.2 (text at n. 114).

[67] See Appendix 2(2).

[68] Dio 39.27.3. Marcellinus apparently had a strong legal justification, but Caesar knew that it would not be too hard for his enemies to create one. Other examples in living memory of consular authority over the acceptance of candidates are those of C. Piso in 67 (who declared in a tumultuous *contio* that even if Palicanus won the ballot he would not authorize the result [Val. Max. 3.8.3: *non renuntiabo*]; Piso may have rejected Palicanus's candidacy due to its violation of Sulla's *lex annalis*, so the assumption that he had been praetor by 69 [*MRR*] seems unjustified) and L. Volcacius Tullus in 66 (who refused to accept Catiline's candidacy in 66 because he was facing trial for extortion: Ascon. 89C, Sall. *Cat.* 18.2–3).

[69] De Libero 1992: 64n58 (with a list) notes that in the 50s obnuntiation against *elections*, in contrast to its use against laws, was nearly always successful, at least in the short term.

that Caesar particularly trusted Paullus, and given his inconspicuous role in this crisis year it looks as if at best Caesar was able to secure his neutrality.[70] The other, C. Marcellus, despite marriage to Caesar's great-niece Octavia (and thus father to the first tragic "crown prince" of the Augustan future), was persistently hostile to his interests through his consular year.[71] When the elections of 50 do come, Caesar's continuator Hirtius explicitly states that Caesar's favored candidate, his former legate Ser. Galba, was robbed of the consulship although (so he claims) he actually had the most support *and the most votes*.[72] Even though the allegation is uncorroborated, it is a remarkable testament to the environment of mistrust that it is even conceivable. We do not know which one of the consuls would have presided over the consular election in this year, but Hirtius is accusing whoever it was of some kind of outrageous offense against the electoral norms of the Republic.[73]

In April (late February or March, Jul.), with the deadlock well and truly underway, Caelius judges that the Senate was eager to force Caesar to leave his province by the Ides of November (ca. September 30, Jul., corresponding roughly to the end of the campaigning season), and that Pompey seemed to be supporting the effort.[74] The November deadline was an attempt to draw a fixed deadline for Caesar's return now that the Gallic wars were evidently won.[75] It appears to be a compromise option backed by

---

[70] Which is in fact all that App. *BCiv.* 2.26/101 claims (though Dio 40.63.2 makes him an ally). Despite the gift or loan, L. Paullus neither opposes his colleague nor actively abets him in his anti-Caesarian actions (his support of Curio against Ap. Claudius's censorial zeal is explicitly explained as due to family relationship: Dio 40.63.5; n. 154): characteristic is App. *BCiv.* 27/103: καὶ Παῦλος ἐσιώπα. Pelling 2011: 297. It appears that Paullus had already made use of Caesar's money during his building projects in 54 (Plut. *Caes.* 29.3; cf. Cic. *Att.* 4.16.8), probably to improve his chances in his imminent run for the consulship.

[71] An awkward case for old-fashioned prosopographical inferences of political affiliation from family connections.

[72] Hirtius, [Caes.] *BGall.* 8.50.4: *ereptum Ser. Galbae consulatum, cum is multo plus gratia suffragiisque valuisset, quod sibi coniunctus et familiaritate et consuetudine legationis esset.* Some editors have suspected *suffragiis* (*suffragii*, offered by the β family of mss., is printed in Hering's Teubner; Kraner, Dittenberger, and Meusel bracket the word altogether), apparently because this would amount to rejecting the electoral result (1964: 3:125; the expression *gratia suffragii*, however, appears to lack any parallel). Yet that may be precisely the point. Cf. C. Piso's apparently decisive threat in 67 not to declare Palicanus elected even if he won the vote (Val. Max. 3.8.3) and Girardet's conjecture, next n. On Galba see n. 109.

[73] Girardet 2000: 704 (2017: 117–118) is prepared to countenance this and to infer that a hostile presiding consul (perhaps Marcellus) refused to announce formally Galba's election despite his having won the vote count.

[74] Cael. [Cic.] *Fam.* 8.11.3 *incubuisse cum senatu Pompeius videtur ut Caesar Id. Nov. decedat.* (The letter may date slightly later than April.)

[75] Cael. [Cic.] *Fam.* 8.11.3 expresses the concern that Caesar might exploit his privilege to remain in his province "as long as he likes." He had seen this coming at least since September 51 (8.5.2: *plus biennium . . . moretur*).

a majority of the Senate which now implicitly countenanced Caesar's use of his *ratio absentis* in the manner he wished – that is, while still holding on to his army and province – for one more election only (summer 50), but insisted that he must then submit to being replaced in the fall.

This was a significant concession from Pompey's perspective. Caelius adds that Pompey was fearful about Caesar's election while remaining in his province at the head of an army; yet he claimed to be doing right by his old ally (not very convincingly, Caelius implies) while blaming Curio for the rising tensions.[76] The compromise makes sense as an attempt to break the stalemate caused by Curio's vetoes. It would force Caesar to compete in the upcoming elections in the summer (perhaps while awaiting the results in Cisalpina), and it would make him give up his command and army before he took up his second consulship, but it would not force him to give up his plans for a brilliant triumph, perhaps coinciding with his entry into office. The proposal thus offered a possible route forward that should have eased many senators' suspicions of Caesar's intentions and might have frustrated the schemes of his most committed enemies. However, the suggestion went nowhere (we hear nothing further about it), which must mean that Curio refused to lift his veto to let it go through. Caesar's refusal to accept the offer appears to imply that he was unwilling to trust the consuls or Pompey, or both, to accept his candidacy in absentia in the upcoming elections even if he remained in command of his provinces and army. Why such deep mistrust at this critical juncture?

The fundamental basis of the answer has probably already been suggested: although Pompey had signed on to the compromise proposal, Caelius could see that he didn't like it; if Caelius could see this, Caesar's friends could also see that Pompey might find a way to subvert it. Mistrust was apparently already too deep to permit acceptance of even a compromise that had the potential to assuage both sides' greatest fears. Although each side made further strategic moves before the consular elections of late July or early August in which Caesar might have competed using his privilege as a candidate in absentia, that was not to be. Unfortunately because our chronology becomes blurry for these crucial months we cannot get a fine-grained picture of how these moves may have interrelated, and thus of how

---

[76] Cael. [Cic.] *Fam.* 8.11.3 (April? See n. 74): *tamquam Caesarem non impugnet sed quod illi aequum putet constituat, ait Curionem quaerere discordias; valde autem non vult et plane timet Caesarem consulem designatum prius quam exercitum et provinciam tradiderit.* Cf. 8.13.2 (May–June: Appendix 3[a]), 14.2 (August); *Att.* 7.9.3. Raaflaub 1974: 133n115; Girardet 2000: 701–702, 2017: 112–113. Pompey's new position is strictly consistent with the one Caelius had earlier inferred (that Caesar should leave his province after March 1: n. 38) but implicitly gives Caesar more time to wrap up affairs in Gaul, which in fact he did (after a short midsummer visit to Cisalpina coinciding with the elections in Rome) only perhaps around mid-October (Raaflaub and Ramsey 2017: 69).

and why the crisis intensified so dramatically. But we do at least know the main sources of contention and can look at them in sequence. Confusion and uncertainty about Caesar's intentions were probably quite pronounced even at the time, since for much of this period he was still in his winter quarters at Nemetocenna (modern Arras), some 1,700 kilometers from Rome and about as far to the north as he could possibly be while still in Gaul; a messenger's round-trip journey from Rome would have required about seven weeks, which must have left many large questions unanswered in the midst of the delicate and dangerous discussions.[77]

At some date between March and May that is unfortunately impossible to pin down with certainty, Curio first made his famous or notorious proposal ostensibly seconding C. Marcellus's motion to relieve Caesar of his command, but adding the proviso that if Caesar was to leave his army, then so should Pompey.[78] Although the chronology is uncertain, this ostensibly balanced proposal makes sense as a response to the recent push to declare a November deadline for Caesar's command. It was bound, of course, to appear utterly illegitimate to Pompey, for from a quantitative point of view a command that was clearly expiring could hardly be set on a par with one that had years left to run (perhaps as far as 45).[79] Yet it is also true that Pompey's lingering in Italy and indeed near Rome could not easily be explained or excused: if it could be argued that Caesar's job in Gaul was done, one might equally ask why Pompey's Spanish command should continue when he had not troubled even to go there over the five years since it had been assigned to him, a fact which effectively refuted any plausible claim that the command was necessary for the security of the province or the *imperium*. Thus the overall effect was to turn attention to Pompey and to highlight the fairly obvious efforts of those hostile to Caesar to use him against the victor of Gaul. To Pompey's reply that Caesar should be prepared to submit himself to the unconstrained verdict of the Roman People (implicitly, that is, without clinging to his army for assurance or leverage), Caesar's friends rejoined deftly that Pompey should be prepared to do the same.[80]

---

[77] Raaflaub and Ramsey 2017: 66n101. We do not know when he began the long journey back to Cisalpine Gaul to support Antony in his elections; Raaflaub and Ramsey think he waited until mid-July, but an earlier date seems more likely (Appendix 3[g]).

[78] App. BC 2.27/104–2.28/111; Dio 40.62.3–4; cf. Plut. Caes. 30.1. App. *BCiv.* 2.27/104: Κουρίων . . . ἐπήνει τὴν τοῦ Κλαυδίου γνώμην.

[79] Terminus of Pompey's *imperium*: a good summary in Pelling 2011: 281, opting for Gruen's suggestion of 45 (Gruen 1974: 459n36). Full discussion in Girardet 2001: 45–67 (to the end of 46).

[80] Plut. *Pomp.* 56.3 and *Caes.* 30.1, with Pelling 2011: 303 (although I do not see why both should not have made the same point about submitting to the voters, a commonplace). Pompey (presumably) had no electoral prospect as did Caesar, yet the mere act of returning to civilian life would subject

Curio's proposal was difficult to reject out of hand, especially when it was publicly put before an increasingly anxious People in *contiones*. Although Curio's intervention in this year tends to be painted in rather lurid colors by the imperial sources in particular and tends to be described by modern scholars as mischievous rather than a serious attempt to resolve the crisis, we should note that this very proposal would ultimately (with the threat of civil war looming, to be sure) be approved overwhelmingly by the Senate toward the end of the year.[81] If carefully handled by mutual friends such as Cicero (who was, alas, still away in Cilicia), the proposal might well have served as a formula whereby Caesar could have competed in the elections of 50 on Pompey's preferred conditions – that is, without holding on to his army and province.[82] For if Pompey had departed or given up his command in exchange for Caesar's, the latter would have been left with a much weaker public justification for his alleged fears for a fair election or his triumph; on the other hand, if Pompey's continued command was justified neither by a military emergency in Spain nor by fears of Caesar's army, then what legitimate purpose remained for it?

Such a compromise, then, would have required significant concessions on both sides, and would therefore have called for considerable trust to bridge the gap between the parties. Caesar's enemies must have been panic-stricken.[83] Luckily for them (and probably not without their forceful intervention) Pompey indignantly rejected the proposal on the grounds that a command that was clearly expiring could hardly be set on a par with one that had several years left to run.[84] But this in turn must have affected Caesar's own perception of the willingness of his erstwhile ally and long-standing enemies to cooperate in reasonable efforts toward a fair resolution.

---

him to the normal rules of competition for honor and esteem adjudicated by the Roman People. Caesar at *BCiv.* 1.9.5 makes a clear link between Pompey's continued presence on the outskirts of the City, long after he had received a Spanish proconsular assignment, with his anxiety about a free election: *proficiscatur Pompeius in suas provincias, ipsi exercitus dimittant, discedant in Italia omnes ab armis, metus e civitate tollitur, <u>libera comitia</u> <habeantur?* H. Fuchs, reported by Raaflaub 1974: 166n266> *atque omnis res publica senatui populoque Romano permittatur.* Cf. in the same vein Hirtius, [Caes.] *BGall.* 8.52.4 *fore eo facto liberam et sui iuris civitatem.*

[81] See p. 293ff.

[82] See, for instance, the acute analysis of Raaflaub 1974: 48–51, but cf. Pelling 2011: 302–303. Raaflaub is inclined to attribute an attempt by Curio to put the proposal to the vote in the Senate, as described by Hirtius at [Caes.] *BGall.* 8.52.5, to April 50 (1974a: 301–304). But it would be very odd for Hirtius to mention such an occasion and then to leave out entirely the actual vote on the proposal late in the year, which was so embarrassing for the anti-Caesarian forces. More likely Hirtius is confused or has misplaced and inaccurately reported that other episode.

[83] Cic. *Att.* 6.8.2 shows that Cicero had heard rumors in Ephesus that Pompey would leave Rome, perhaps to go to Spain (Shackleton Bailey ad loc.).

[84] See n. 79.

Their only answer to the impasse had been to reassert their right to arm themselves even in the absence of a corresponding military threat. The erosion of trust continued.

Probably a couple of months into the deadlock – May or early June by the civil calendar – the consul of the previous year, M. Marcellus, proposed a motion requesting the consuls to apply pressure on the tribunes to withdraw their veto. This was, however, heavily defeated, which in Caelius's interpretation indicated that the Senate had in practice now yielded the point that Caesar had the right to stand in absentia without giving up his province or army.[85] (Clearly the upcoming elections in summer 50 were those Caelius and others had now in mind.) But this may have been a somewhat tendentious interpretation of the senators' vote; in fact, they had merely declined to resort to extraordinary measures to break Curio's veto and thus allowed the deadlock to continue in preference to precipitating a major crisis at this juncture. As Caelius wrote to Cicero already in April, "our people, as you know well, were not inclined to dare to press matters to a full confrontation."[86] In the face of Curio's continued veto the greater part of the Senate was not inclined to force the issue immediately or to suppress, ignore, or arbitrarily reinterpret the Law of the Ten Tribunes. However, by this action the Senate had in a sense made itself complicit in the ongoing paralysis. Later in the year an exasperated Cicero, who did not appreciate being left high and dry in Cilicia, gives the so-called *boni* and the Senate a share of the blame for the fact that no decisions were put through about provincial commanders in the year 50.[87]

---

[85] Cael. [Cic.] *Fam.* 8.13.2: Caelius gives the motion as *agendum cum tribunis* [n.b. plur.] *pl.*, but *frequens senatus in alia omnia iit* .... *Transierant illuc, rationem eius habendam qui <neque> exercitum neque provincias tradere<t>*; cf. 8.11.3 *si, quod videntur, reformidarint, Caesar quoad volet manebit.* Cic. *Att.* 7.7.5 *senatum bonum putas, per quem sine imperio provinciae sunt (numquam enim Curio sustinuisset, si cum eo agi coeptum esset; quam sententiam senatus sequi noluit, ex quo factum est ut Caesari non succederetur).* For the date of the proposal see Appendix 3(a). Schneider 2004 argues unpersuasively that at 8.13.2 (where he also rejects the traditional supplement of the first *neque*) Caelius must be referring to a formal decree authorizing Caesar to exercise his *ratio absentis* while retaining command of his provinces, having given up his army. This seems to be a constitutional impossibility (n. 37), but in any case it is dubious method to make a remarkable novelty of great import depend on a questionable text. For *agere cum tribunis*, see Cael. [Cic.] *Fam.* 8.8.6 and 7 in the formal phrasing of the s.c., *de ea re ad senatum p[rimo] q[uoque] t[empore] referri*); Caes. *BCiv.* 1.2.7; Thommen 1989: 198; Kunkel-Wittmann 1995: 607.

[86] Cael. [Cic.] *Fam.* 8.11.3: *si omnibus rebus prement Curionem, Caesar defendet intercessionem.* Caelius acknowledges that *nostri porro, quos tu bene nosti, ad extremum certamen rem deducere non audeant.*

[87] Cic. *Att.* 7.7.5, quoted n. 85. The only senatorial decrees known to have been passed in 50 were those authorizing *supplicationes* for Cicero and for Bibulus (Cael. [Cic.] *Fam.* 8.11.1–2, Cic. *Att.* 6.8.5, 7.2.6–7), and the assignment of two legions to the expected Parthian War (App. *BCiv.* 2.29/114 incorrectly claims that this was the *only* decree passed this year).

A supervening complication about which we would like to know more details was that at some point in the summer that is unfortunately impossible to determine with precision (but probably well before the consular elections late in July or early August by the civil calendar),[88] Pompey fell gravely ill in Naples, then recovered after a great outpouring of public wishes and oaths throughout Italy for his recovery. Interpreting this as evidence of overwhelming political support in the face of Curio's sharp denunciations of his supposed *dominatio*, Pompey went so far as to promise in a letter from his sickbed to lay down his command before its term while praising Caesar's achievements; after his return to Rome he repeated the offer before the Senate, claiming that Caesar would also happily give up his command, return to the honors due him, and at last enjoy a rest after all his exertions on the Republic's behalf.[89] On its face, he had belatedly agreed to Curio's formula for mutual disarmament. But in the environment of heightened mistrust, the Caesarians suspected a trap: a mere promise in exchange for the actuality. Curio aggressively insisted that Pompey lay down his command first,[90] and the effect was to sabotage the idea. Any pretense of cooperation on the part of a deeply insulted Pompey ended. Again we get a glimpse of the emergence of a reasonable and fair solution to the growing crisis; again we may wonder at why it was not grasped. The answer must once again be the lack of trust to ensure both sides that they were not being duped and engineering their own destruction.[91] Again to Rome's great misfortune there was no one who could step forward as an intermediary to bridge the gap of mistrust. The two sides would not again come so close to public agreement on the mutual disarmament proposal, although Curio and Caesar still did not give it up for dead and it was to reemerge in remarkable fashion late in the year.[92]

It is best to interpret this series of proposals and counterproposals in the context of the approach of the consular elections in the summer (held in late July or early August),[93] which, as we have seen, presented Caesar with his final opportunity to make use of his electoral privilege without

---

[88] See Appendix 3(b) for the date of the elections, and (f) for the timing of Pompey's illness.

[89] App. *BCiv.* 2.28/107–109: ἐπὶ τιμὰς καὶ θυσίας [apparently the consulship and triumph] ἥξειν καὶ ἀναπαύσεις. This interesting move by Pompey is completely overlooked by Dio 40.62.4–63.1, who regards Curio's own proposal as designed to be rejected in order to establish a pretext.

[90] App. *BCiv.* 2.28/108–111, who characterizes Pompey's proposal unreservedly as a trick (σόφισμα) which Curio saw through.

[91] Appendix 4.

[92] Cael. [Cic.] *Fam.* 8.14.2 (early August, after the elections): *fert* [sc. Caesar] *illam tamen condicionem, ut ambo exercitus tradant.* See p. 293ff.

[93] See Appendix 3(b) for the date of the elections.

ratcheting up tension to the breaking point. In the end he would decide not to contest that election but choose instead to remain with his army and provinces for yet another year, despite the end of the wars in Gaul and the lack of any strong justification for his command. There can be no doubt but that this decision marks a new stage in the development of the crisis of 50, but unfortunately our sources again fail to give us an explicit explanation for why Caesar let this electoral deadline pass. Once again we must make an inference from the circumstances of the decision. As it happens, we know that on top of the atmosphere of steeply eroding trust that we have been tracing thus far came a new reason for Caesar to be on his guard – namely, the removal of two legions from his army in Gaul on what could be viewed as false pretenses and their transfer on even more questionable grounds to Italy and the consuls' command (ultimately to Pompey), where they would soon constitute in Caesar's eyes the core of a military buildup aimed at his destruction.[94]

The key decision was taken probably in the first half of April by the civil calendar (~ late February, Jul.).[95] The Senate, deeply concerned about a possible Parthian incursion, with ostensibly scrupulous fairness ordered both Caesar and Pompey to contribute one legion each for possible service in the east.[96] Since after the ambush by the Eburones in 54 Pompey had made up Caesar's loss by transferring to him one legion (recruited by Pompey in Caesar's province, however), he now requested it back as his own contribution, thus resulting in an overall debit to Caesar of two legions. (Caesar, to be sure, had many more at his disposal than Pompey.)[97] Caesar will have heard about the decree and Pompey's response by the end of April or early May

---

[94] Caes. *BCiv.* 1.9.4: *retineri legiones II, quae ab se simulatione Parthici belli sint abductae . . . . Quonam haec omnia nisi ad suam perniciem pertinere?* The complaint resonated outside Caesarian ranks: Cic. *Att.* 7.13.2: *duabus invidiose retentis* (for *invidiose* see Shackleton Bailey 1965: 4:305); cf. Caes. *BCiv.* 1.4.5: *infamia duarum legionum permotus* [sc. Pompey] *quas ab itinere . . . ad suam potentiam dominatumque converterat.* (For the language of *dominatio* cf. also Hirt. [Caes.] *BGall.* 8.52.4.) Hirtius stresses that the transfer of the legions made the intention of Caesar's adversaries clear to him (8.54.3, 55.1–2). Cf. also Caes. *BCiv.* 1.2.3, 1.32.6: *iniuriam in eripiendis legionibus.* Dio 40.65.4 ἤδει μὲν γὰρ τὸ γιγνόμενον. See n. 165.

[95] On the date of the decree see Appendix 3(d).

[96] App. *BCiv.* 2.30/114–116 (cf. 30/120); Dio 40.65.2–66.1; Hirt. [Caes.] *BGall.* 8.54.1–3; Caes. *BCiv.* 1.4.4, 1.14.3; Plut. *Caes.* 29.4–5; cf. Cic. *Fam.* 2.17.5.

[97] For the recruitment of "Pompey's" legion in Caesar's province see Caes. *BGall.* 6.1.2–4, Hirt. [Caes.] *BGall.* 8.54.2; Plut. *Caes.* 25.2 and *Pomp.* 52.4 show confusion (but not *Cat. Min.* 45.5: Pelling 2011: 262). Ottmer 1979: 39–50, esp. 47–48, estimates that at the beginning of the conflict, besides the two legions taken from Caesar and despite the apparent implication of Caes. *BCiv.* 1.6.1, Pompey had only some seventy to eighty newly recruited cohorts, not yet integrated into legions, scattered around Italy. If so, Pompey may have had no better choice, and the Senate would have known this when it passed its decree.

(mid-to-late March by the Julian equivalent), while still in his winter quarters at Nemetocenna.[98] Caesar's enemies had in fact been pressing Pompey to take back "his" legion since the previous summer, doubtless raising some suspicions, but the proconsul of Gaul now readily complied: note the absence of a veto.[99] Caesar's 1st and 15th Legions made their way south, but the Parthian threat unexpectedly evaporated over the summer, so after their arrival they were not embarked for the crossing to Macedonia but were ultimately sent into winter camps in Campania or Apulia.[100] Pompey still did not move off to his province of Spain, although with the dissipation of the Parthian threat the best pretext for his still lingering in Italy had gone; it was an open secret that Caesar's adversaries hoped to keep Pompey in Italy to establish a counterforce against him, and the retention of the two legions sent by Caesar will not have appeared innocent in light of that fact.[101] Echoes of the dismay felt by Caesar, and the scandal provoked by the decision even outside his circle, can be found not only in Caesar's own account but also in letters of Cicero.

Curio's withholding of a veto and Caesar's compliance with the decree cannot be treated as routine in this extraordinary year: in the context of the ongoing deadlock over the provinces, it must be seen as a strong (because potentially costly) signal of obedience and cooperation against what purported to be an authentic security threat. Pompey's sharp practice, which obviously undercut the pretense of scrupulous evenhandedness implied by the subtraction of one legion from each commander, presumably grated, but had to be accepted. In the current state of our evidence we do not know whether news of the legions' retention in Italy actually reached Caesar before he had taken his decision not to attempt to activate his privilege and be a candidate in the consular election held in late July or early August (~ late June, Jul.) 50.[102] But it is fairly certain that he had good reason to

---

[98] Cf. n. 77.

[99] Cael. [Cic.] *Fam.* 8.4.4: July 22, 51. Dio 40.65.4: Caesar "understood what was being done (ᾔδει μὲν γὰρ τὸ γιγνόμενον) but obeyed, not wanting to incur the charge of disobedience."

[100] The 15th Legion, presumably the one Pompey had levied in Caesar's province of Cisalpina, was still stationed in that province probably around Ravenna, where the 13th now replaced it (Hirt. [Caes.] *BGall.* 8.54.2–3). It may therefore have arrived at its destination in Italy considerably earlier than the 1st, apparently sent from the nearest likely winter camp in Transalpina in the territory of the Aedui. Where the legions lingered until sent to their winter camps in Apulia (Caes. *BCiv.* 1.14.3; Cic. *Att.* 7.12.2; App. *BCiv.* 2.31/120 says Capua) is unknown (possibly the environs of Rome? but App. 2.30/119 ἐς Ῥώμην should probably not be taken literally). See Appendix 3(d).

[101] See nn. 45, 94.

[102] Hirt. [Caes.] *BGall.* 8.55.1 (*cognoscit per C. Marcellum consulem legiones duas ab se missas, quae ex s.c. deberent ad Parthicum bellum duci, Cn. Pompeio traditas atque in Italia retentas esse*) misleadingly suggests that Caesar only learned the quite old news of the retention of the legions at the same time that he received news of the very current and much graver "Schwertübergabe." This cannot be true. For the chronological questions see Appendix 3(b), (c), and (d).

believe by that time that preparations were being actively made against him; Dio, for what it is worth, explicitly says that Caesar "knew what was going on" when he sent the two legions home (see n. 99). Once the legions left Cisalpina they must have been under the formal command of the consuls, which can only have given him even less reassurance than before that his privilege and other rights would be fully respected in the upcoming election.[103] As we have seen, Caesar would have had reasonable fears that the consuls could use some pretext to block his candidacy in this year, and now they could do so from a much strengthened military position.[104] Fear and mistrust again underlay an escalatory move; Caesar now declined or refused to be a candidate in the consular elections of 50.[105]

This is clearly a crucial moment in the development of the crisis, for by declining to exercise his electoral privilege on this occasion Caesar signaled that he was now aiming at the election of 49 for 48 (when the legal ten-year interval would have passed), which in turn raised reasonable fears that he intended to remain at the head of an army in his province until at least fall 49 – more than a year hence, when on any reasonable assumption the extension of his command, whether it was a minimum five-year guarantee or a maximum limit, had run its course.[106] Was he then intending to stay at the head of army indefinitely, blithely vetoing through his tribunician allies any attempt of the Senate to replace him, until such a time as he thought it optimal to extort his second consulship? It is easy to see how a relative moderate like Cicero, who abhorred civil war, could begin to wax indignant about Caesar's "impudence," not to mention what Cato and Pompey must have thought.[107] This decision must have torn or strained to the utmost whatever bonds of trust remained between the two principals; the center was hollowing out. After the elections for the first time Caelius speaks explicitly of his expectation of war within a year, and Cicero, on his way home from Cilicia, was clearly shaken by what he was hearing not just from Caelius but from Atticus as well.[108]

---

[103] Consular command of the legions is clearly implied by the "Schwertübergabe": n. 162.

[104] See p. 277.

[105] Gruen 1974: 477–480 suggests that Caesar simply needed more time to consolidate his settlement in Gaul. Contra, see Morstein-Marx 2007: 174.

[106] Girardet 2000: 705–708, 2017: 117–125 also emphasizes the importance of this "tipping point."

[107] References in n. 120. Cicero's use of the word is explicitly attested in the extant correspondence only in December.

[108] Cael. [Cic.] *Fam.* 8.14.2, quoted n. 114. Caelius claims to have made this point to Cicero "often" already, but we have no example in the surviving correspondence; perhaps he is inexactly recalling something like 8.11.3 (April, probably): *si omnibus rebus prement Curionem, Caesar defendet intercessorem.* At 8.13.2 (May/June) Wesenberg restored <*aut armis resistat*>, which Shackleton Bailey accepted, but a reference to armed conflict is by no means necessitated. Cicero: *Fam.* 2.15.3 (a reply to both 8.11 and 13 from Caelius), *Att.* 6.9.5, 7.1.2–4, 7.2.8 (Atticus).

"I Don't See Peace Lasting beyond the Year"

At last, perhaps in late spring, Caesar moved from Nemetocenna to Cisalpine Gaul to support his trusted legate and recent quaestor M. Antony in his tribunician and augural elections, as well as his former legate Ser. Sulpicius Galba (pr. 54) and apparently also L. Lentulus Crus in their bids for the consulship.[109] Caesar himself began (so he says) preparing for his own upcoming candidacy by cultivating the voters of the towns and colonies of northern Italy.[110] Antony prevailed in the augural contest over the senior consular (and avowed enemy of Caesar) L. Domitius in what Caelius and Hirtius both describe as an exceptionally partisan election, clearly a test of Caesar's popularity against what Hirtius calls "the oligarchy" (*contra factionem et potentiam paucorum*);[111] less remarkably, Antony was also elected tribune of the plebs for the coming year.[112] But the consular elections were less encouraging for the returning conqueror of Gaul. C. Marcellus, homonymous cousin of the consul of this year, and Lentulus came at the top of the polls, but in a remarkable turnabout, the latter become a forceful opponent of accommodation with Caesar at the beginning of his consular year. Galba, as we have already briefly noted, fell through; according to Hirtius, he was denied election after having actually won the majority of votes.[113] If true or even arguable, this would powerfully validate Caesar's concerns.

Hereafter, talk of war becomes for the first time explicit in our evidence. It was now clear to Caelius that Caesar would not allow himself to be separated from his army before his election to a second consulship, while on the other hand Pompey (and surely others) were equally no longer disposed to countenance his election – nearly a full year hence – while

---

[109] Antony: Hirt. [Caes.] *BGall.* 8.50.1–3, mentioning only the augural election, which Raaflaub and Ramsey 2017: 67–69 date ca. July 17. For the timing of Caesar's journey to Cisalpina, see Appendix 3(g). Galba: *MRR* 2.205: ancestor of the short-reigned emperor who would eventually join the conspiracy against Caesar's life. Suet. *Galb.* 3.2 claims that he resented *Caesar* for the defeat; perhaps Lentulus's success is part of the story. Lentulus as Caesarian: Cic. *Att.* 6.8.2: cf. Caes. *BCiv.* 1.1.3, and Caesar's attempt to detach him from his enemies in February 49: Cic. *Att.* 8.9a.2, 8.11.5, 8.15A.2).

[110] Hirt. [Caes.] *BGall.* 8.50.3–4: *tamen non minus iustam sibi causam municipia et colonias adeundi existimavit, ut iis gratias ageret, quod frequentiam atque officium suum Antonio praestitissent, simulque se et honorem suum insequentis anni commendaret petitione.* This is a striking example of the underappreciated phenomenon of voters traveling great distances to participate in electoral assemblies, here not just at the consular level but also at Antony's junior (but augural) level: see Chapter I, n. 35.

[111] Hirt. [Caes.] *BGall.* 8.50.2. Cael. [Cic.] *Fam.* 8.41.1: *magna illa comitia fuerunt et plane studia ex partium sensu apparuerunt, perpauci necessitudinem secuti officium praestiterunt.*

[112] Raaflaub and Ramsey 2017: 68–69 with nn. 198, 199 date the tribunician election slightly later than the augural election ca. July 17.

[113] Hirt. [Caes.] *BGall.* 8.50.4. See n. 72.

remaining at the head of an army and his provinces.[114] Caelius explains to Cicero what was at stake for Caesar as he saw it: Caesar was convinced that he would not be safe (*salvus*) if he left his army.[115] That is, Caesar feared that the only guarantee of his rights and just demands, as he saw them – namely, to stand for election in absentia under the protection of the Law of the Ten Tribunes and to receive a triumph for his extraordinary achievements in Gaul – was his army. Obviously, under the circumstances, the failure to achieve these important tokens of honor might well spell the beginning of the end for him: the resentful, self-imposed quasi-exile of Scipio Africanus only five years after his return from the glorious victory over Antiochus III would have come to mind, a cautionary tale about just how swiftly the mighty could fall.[116]

The end of the correspondence with Caelius as Cicero made his way homeward from his province leaves us mostly in the dark regarding the details of the further development of the crisis between the immediate aftermath of the elections and late November or early December (~ October, Jul.), when the next significant public step was taken. It was widely understood now that Caesar would not give up his army without first being elected consul – that is, not unless Pompey would do so too.[117] Rumors swirled about Caesarian troop movements in

---

[114] Cael. [Cic.] *Fam.* 8.14.2: *De summa re publica saepe tibi scripsi me <in> annum pacem non videre.... Propositum hoc est de quo qui rerum potiuntur sunt dimicaturi, quod Cn. Pompeius constituit non pati C. Caesarem consulem aliter fieri nisi exercitum et provincias tradiderit, Caesari autem persuasum est se salvum esse non posse <si> ab exercitu recesserit.* Cf. Cic. *Att.* 6.8.2 (October 1) *exercitum nullo modo dimissurum.*

[115] Caelius [Cic.] *Fam.* 8.14.2, quoted n. 114. The adjective *salvus* ("safe/healthy/well"; see *OLD* s.v., 1) may refer to the strength, standing, status, or security of a politician or group of politicians: cf. e.g. Cic. *Att.* 5.20.8 ("we are *salvi* if Caesar yields"); *Cluent.* 95 ("much less in these times ... would we be *salvi* without your wisdom and the verdicts of the courts"); Vell. Pat. 2.49.3 (on Lentulus as cos. 49, who "could not be *salvus* if the state remained *salva*"). There is no need to import here the much more specific fear of condemnation in the courts (*OLD* s.v., 4a) on which the "prosecution theory" rests.

[116] See the summary of Rosenstein 2012: 242–245; the complicated story is fully assessed by Gruen 1995: 85–86; Briscoe 2008: 176, Rich in *FRHist* 3.355–356. Africanus had become entangled (or perhaps had been complicit) in his brother's apparent misappropriation of funds; politically weakened over a period of three years by the drumbeat of accusations against his brother, he eventually was indicted as well and evaded the charges by withdrawing from Rome. The parallel with Caesar's situation was not very close, but it suggested the sort of fate that could await him if he stumbled.

[117] Cic. *Att.* 6.8.2. Girardet 2000: 708n21 and now 2017: 127–135, without sufficient reason, dates the letter mentioned by Suet. *Iul.* 29.2 to the immediate aftermath of the election and makes it into a blunt Caesarian "threat." This appears to be an overinterpretation of Suetonius's phrasing *cum ... videret ... designatos etiam consules e parte diversa*; the sentence immediately following shows that the context is the end of the year 50 and beginning of 49; since Suetonius knows of only one controversial letter of Caesar's, this must be the one read to the Senate on January 1 (Butler and Cary 1927: 83; Raaflaub 1974: 61n241).

Cisalpina and no doubt, on the other side, also about the meaning of the Senate's retention of the two legions in Italy.[118]

Cicero fretted mightily, and while his sympathies clearly lay mostly with Pompey and the so-called *boni* he also acknowledges that he wanted Caesar to be respected.[119] While he considered Caesar's demands "impudent," he thought they hardly justified the horrors of civil war, and in any case he appears to think that the *ratio absentis* could not be legally denied, even if Caesar desired to remain in command of a province and an army.[120] Furthermore, it was both inconsistent and imprudent for Pompey now to try to block Caesar from enjoying the privileges he had himself conferred, thereby building up his power to its current state.[121] Anyway, Cicero claims, most senators and *equites* wanted peace, not war.[122] Moreover, it was in the nature of things (as the example of Sulla showed) that victory in a civil war would bring a "tyrant" either way despite Pompey's claim to be defending the Republic.[123] There was also his debt to Caesar – impossible to pay off on the spot – and ingratiating letters reminding him of their friendship.[124] But it was also clear to him that the new year with the new consuls would bring a great push to deprive the proconsul of Gaul not only of his army but even of his *ratio absentis*.[125]

Pompey's patience, and we may be sure that of Cato and the rest of Caesar's enemies, was clearly at its end. Caesar was in effect taking the position that the *ratio absentis* was absolute and independent of the question of the duration of his command (and here it seems Cicero

---

[118] For the troop movements and rumors to which they gave rise, see Appendix 5.

[119] Cic. *Fam.* 2.15.3 (early August, from Cilicia): *Faveo Curioni, Caesarem honestum esse cupio, pro Pompeio emori possum, sed tamen ipsa re publica nihil mihi est carius.* Shackleton Bailey translates "I want to see Caesar respected," citing (ad loc.) *Verr.* 2.2.29.

[120] Cic. *Att.* 7.6.2; cf. 7.3.2, and §§4–5, 7.4.3, 7.5.4–5, 7.7.5 and §7, 7.9.3. Cicero sometimes strikes a more resolute tone (7.3.4, 7.7.6–7, 7.9.4), yet this is not his prevailing mood. See also Plut. *Cic.* 37.1, with n. 189. *Impudentia*: Cic. *Att.* 7.6.2, 7.9.4, 7.17.2; *Fam.* 16.11.2. To gauge the resonance of this word note that Cicero applies it, e.g., to the *publicani* during their request to renegotiate the contract for the Asian taxes (2.1.8), Brutus's agent Scaptius against the Salaminians (5.21.12), and Bibulus's request for supplications (7.2.6: *impudentissimas!*). Legality: esp. *Att.* 7.7.6: *sed cum id datum est, illud una datum est* (see n. 126).

[121] Cic. *Att.* 7.3.4–5, 7.6.2, 7.7.6–7.

[122] Cic. *Att.* 7.3.5, 7.5.4, 7.6.2, 7.7.5; this despite Caelius's prediction that Pompey would have the Senate and *equites* on his side (*Fam.* 8.14.3). Mention at *Att.* 7.3.3 of L. Volcacius (cos. 66) and Servius Sulpicius (cos. 51), who would in early 49 emerge as the consulars most ready to accommodate Caesar (Chapter 7), suggests that they had already begun to show their hand (see Shackleton Bailey ad loc.). By December 9 Cicero knew that Caelius was throwing in his lot with Caesar (*Att.* 7.3.6), which he could have anticipated since the summer (Cael. [Cic.] *Fam.* 8.14.3).

[123] Cic. *Att.* 7.3.4, 7.5.4, 7.7.7. Pompey managed to buck him up late in December: 7.8.4, 7.9.4.

[124] Cic. 7.1.3, 7.1.7, 7.3.3, 7.3.11, 7.8.5.

[125] Cic. *Att.* 7.1.4: *illa quae tum agentur cum venero, ne ratio absentis habeatur, ut exercitum dimittat.*

reluctantly agreed with him);[126] thus until he was formally and legitimately replaced (i.e. without triggering a veto in defense of his privilege assured by a law of the Roman People), for example under the proposed mutual disarmament arrangement with Pompey, he was within his rights to stay in his provinces at the head of his army.[127] The view that Pompey and Caesar's enemies took toward Caesar's claim can be gauged by the exasperated tone Cicero uses in a letter to Atticus written toward the end of December: "Could impudence go further? . . . The time is up, the time set not by law but by your own whim – but grant it was by law. The appointment of your successor is resolved. You obstruct and say 'admit my right to stand.' What about *our* rights?"[128] How, then, to stop him, when Caesar's privilege was enshrined in a law of the Roman People? The obvious strategy would be for the consuls to block his candidacy in the upcoming consular elections of summer 49 on the grounds that the rationale of the electoral privilege granted by the Law of the Ten Tribunes had lapsed, inasmuch as his command in Gaul, which alone justified his use of that privilege, could not plausibly be stretched into the summer: a full five years would have passed since its extension, and furthermore the war was manifestly over.[129] Yet any arbitrary, partisan interpretation of the Law of the Ten Tribunes was bound to be opposed by

---

[126] Cic. *Att.* 7.7.6: *cum id* [i.e. the *ratio absentis*] *datum est, illud* [its use in the upcoming elections of 49] *una datum est* is consistent with the rationale suggested in the text above, and, when combined with his assumption that the extension of Caesar's command must be considered to have lapsed by the elections of 49 (n. 129), this appears to show (Morstein-Marx 2007: 172n62; contra, Girardet 2017: 171n727) that Cicero himself accepted that Caesar's privilege alone assured him the right to be a candidate in 49.

[127] Caesar's rationale seems to emerge from his complaint at Caes. *BCiv.* 1.9.2, where he claims that the Senate's decrees of early January had shortened his command by six months. (Pace Girardet 2017: 106n443, the subjunctive of *extorqueretur . . . retraheretur* is not conative ["versucht hätten"] but demanded by the rules of indirect discourse, and refers to actual concurrent circumstance.) Interpretation of this passage is, however, bedeviled by ambiguities, even as to whether *proxima* refers to the *next* election (summer 49: Raaflaub 1974: 129 with n. 94, with most others) or the *last* one (summer 50: Girardet 2000: 688, 699–700; 2017: 45, 106–108) – and if the former, whether the six months are those of the second half of 49 (Mommsen's old view; so Raaflaub and recently Gagliardi 2012: 37, 103) or the first half, as I prefer (taking 1.9.2 to be a direct reference to Caesar's formal replacement at 1.6.5 following up on Scipio's motion at 1.2.6; cf. Gelzer 1968: 176n1). See Pelling 2011: 290n15 for further refs. See p. 266ff.

[128] *Att.* 7.9.4: *nam quid impudentius? . . . praeteriit tempus non legis sed libidinis tuae, fac tamen legis; ut succedatur decernitur; impedis et ais "habe meam rationem." Habe tu nostram.*

[129] The series of scenarios reviewed at Cic. *Att.* 7.9.2 all rotate around the admission or nonadmission of Caesar's candidacy in the elections of 49. Whatever the legal details, which are lost to us if they existed, Caesar's enemies clearly concluded that his command would no longer be legitimate certainly by those elections in summer 49, if not already by January 1 (Cic. *Att.* 7.7.6, 7.9.4).

a veto, since Caesar had at least one loyal tribune in Antony. Since he had not come this far just to submit to such injury, it was likely to provoke a fight.[130]

At some point in the latter half of 50 Caesar probably added the equivalent of more than four legions to the sole legion (the 13th) that had already been stationed in Cisalpine Gaul. But the inference that Caesar was already determined upon war and was now only looking for a plausible pretext goes well beyond the facts.[131] The two "stolen" legions were a clear sign that military preparations were being made in Italy *against him*; it would have been foolish for him not to try to neutralize any threat.[132] Saber-rattling is a standard, even arguably essential step in the pattern of looming confrontation, for somewhat paradoxically its "signaling" function is not uncommonly precisely what precipitates a breakthrough to resolution for it "proves" to each side how costly the conflict is likely to be.[133] Caesar will have heard from Curio and others that his cause was embraced by the Roman People and widely preferred even among senators to any hard-line stance that could provoke civil war.[134] Senatorial inaction against Curio's persistent threat to veto any attempt to recall or replace Caesar may well have given him some hope that the center might hold.[135] By clearly signaling his strength and his willingness to use it to defend his rights (as he and many others saw it), he could still hope to splinter the opposition to his triumphant return, and if that was the way things turned, the legions in Cisalpine Gaul were well placed to be brought to Italy proper, demobilized, and in part at least reengaged for Caesar's triumph. Conversely, however, if he did not show his strength in order to pressure the fearful majority of senators caught in the middle ground, the chances that his enemies would allow a fair election in 49 might become correspondingly slimmer.[136]

On the other side, however, Pompey saw his hand strengthening day by day. Apparently boosted by numerous vows taken and honorific decrees passed throughout Italy wishing for his speedy recovery from his illness, he is said to have openly mocked those who doubted his level of military preparations in case of war: it was apparently on this occasion that he

---

[130] See Cic. *Att.* 7.9.2–4.   [131] See Appendix 5.

[132] Müller 1972: 12: "um in Italien das Gleichgewicht der Kräfte herzustellen."

[133] Snyder (1977) esp. 95–101, still an excellent discussion of the diplomatic challenge of resolving a Prisoner's Dilemma–type crisis. See Appendix 4.

[134] For senators and *equites* see n. 122; for the city "crowd" and "the People" n. 243, and for ordinary citizens across Italy n. 244.

[135] Cic. [Cael.] *Fam.* 8.13.2; *Att.* 7.7.5.   [136] See p. 276ff.

delivered himself of his famous boast that he need only stamp the ground for legions to spring up anywhere in Italy.[137] He may well have felt that Caesar's intransigence and "impudence" were eroding his political standing daily, perhaps even with the urban plebs, but more crucially with the *populus Romanus* more generally across "all Italy" (*tota Italia*).

With matters already at such a delicate juncture, it was the consul C. Marcellus, Caesar's own affine kin, who, probably in late November or early December (~ October, Jul.)), made an aggressive new move in the standoff.[138] On his own authority, apparently without even senatorial sanction, Marcellus invested Pompey with responsibility for the defense of Italy and command over the two legions that Caesar had sent for the expected Parthian war but had been detained and sent into winter quarters in southern Italy.[139] Marcellus's action was clearly taken by all as a first open military move against Caesar (though whether offensive or defensive in character depended on which side one was on), and it is reasonable to interpret this action as marking a steep intensification of the crisis. Unfortunately none of our accounts of the senatorial meeting or meetings that immediately preceded and precipitated the action is contemporary, and all pose real problems for reconstruction. Consequently I shall try to refrain from dubious speculation about the details and hold fast to what, in the current state of our evidence, we know or can securely conjecture.[140]

Appian and Plutarch (in the *Pompey*) agree that Marcellus's investiture of Pompey was preceded by senatorial votes on the following motions and in the following order: that Caesar should be replaced in his command

---

[137] App. *BCiv.* 2.28/107–109; Plut. *Pomp.* 57; cf. Cic. *Att.* 8.16.1, 9.5.4; Vell. Pat. 2.48.2; Dio 41.6.3–4. In March 49 Cicero looks back bitterly to the apparent insincerity of these *vota* and *decreta* (Chapter 7, n. 370). Plut. adds that Pompey was also misled by the overconfident pronouncements of young Ap. Claudius (not the censor but perhaps his nephew, the future cos. 38: *MRR* 3.57) about the low morale of the two legions he had been delegated to bring back from Gaul (cf. App. 2.30/116–118).

[138] For the date see Appendix 3(c). For the *adfinitas* see p. 278.

[139] Hirt. [Caes.] *BGall.* 8.55.1; App. *BCiv.* 2.31/121; Dio 40.64.4, 66.1; on the confusion in Plut. *Pomp.* 59.1 see n. 158. See the varying interpretations of Gruen 1974: 486–488; Raaflaub 1974: 29–55; Ottmer 1979: 63–77. Only Appian mentions the picturesque detail of the sword, which has given the event the convenient but pseudo-*Staatsrechtlich* name of "Schwertübergabe" ("sword handover") in German scholarship. Bardt was inclined to regard the sword as apocryphal (1910: 345–346), but perhaps it was part of the ordinary ritual of deputizing or transferring command. On the transfer of the legions see p. 284ff.

[140] The episode itself has been somewhat neglected in recent scholarship: Botermann 1989 is an important exception, while Gruen 1974: 486–487 and Raaflaub 1974: 29–30 offer rather selective interpretations overlooking the anti-Caesarian motions presented by C. Marcellus and the senatorial support they won while emphasizing in isolation the famous 370–22 vote for mutual disarmament. The classic treatments remain Bardt 1910: 337–346 and Meyer 1919: 270–275.

(yes); that Pompey should be relieved of his command (no); and combination of these two (yes, with a precise vote count of 370–22 that is carefully recorded in both sources, while the vote count of the other two motions is not).[141] The combined motion will be recognized as Curio's long-standing proposal for mutual disarmament, the others as, in effect, a "division" of the two elements of that proposal.[142] Now, the outcome of the first two votes on the divided halves of the motion was entirely against the principle on which Curio had made the fundamental stand of his tribunate, so although we are not told this explicitly, it is hardly conceivable that he failed now to veto the successful motion that *Caesar be replaced*, as he had every earlier attempt to achieve this result.[143] There would then have been no formal decree of the Senate ordering Caesar's replacement, although awkwardly for Curio and Caesar it still would have been recorded as the Senate's *opinion* (*auctoritas*) and therefore could justify the claim that henceforth Caesar held his army and command against the will of the

---

[141] App. *BCiv.* 2.30/118–119 (cf. 29/112), Plut. *Pomp.* 58.5–10, in both cases simply referring to a "majority" (οἱ πλείους) voting in favor of Caesar's replacement. (Strictly speaking, Plut. seems to mention only two votes *in toto*, but he first appears to make the venial error of combining the *results* of the two motions described by Appian.) Plut. *Caes.* 30.5 and Dio 41.2.1 describe a similar vote in early January, but show no knowledge of the earlier vote, which encourages the inference that it is indeed a "doublet" rather than a second, almost identical vote (so Raaflaub 1974a: 306–311; cf. Pelling 2002: 107–108, 2011: 305; Caesar's silence about such a vote in his detailed account of the senatorial deliberations of early January is probably decisive). Hirtius [Caes.] *BGall.* 8.52, apparently describing this vote (see n. 82; 8.53–54 form a digressive analepsis intended to "clarify" the Senate's will) in good Caesarian fashion as a *magnum . . . testimonium senatus . . . universi* (53.1), separates it from the "Schwertübergabe" mentioned at 55.1. Strangely, Dio explains Marcellus's investiture of Pompey as precipitated by an entirely different proceeding in the Senate (the failure of a motion censuring Curio for an altercation with the overzealous censor, Ap. Claudius: cf. n. 154). Marcellus's action is much more poorly motivated in this version than in the majority opinion; presumably Dio has confused two moments of drama. (For attempts to work Dio's account into the more common narrative see Meyer 1919: 271–272; Raaflaub 1974: 29–30; Botermann 1989: 77–78.) Ap. Claudius's censorial vendettas during the latter half of the year also are a significant theme of Caelius's letters of August and September ([Cic.] *Fam.* 8.14.4, 8.12.1–3).

[142] Appian explicitly says that Marcellus *divided* a motion that was already under discussion (*BCiv.* 2.30/118: ἡ βουλὴ δὲ γνώμην ἕκαστον ᾔτει· καὶ ὁ Κλαύδιος πανούργως διῄρει καὶ ἐπυνθάνετο αὐτῶν παρὰ μέρος), which should therefore be Curio's proposal, the focus of Appian's attention from ch. 27 to 29, interrupted only by the story of the "Parthian" legions. "Dividing the question" was a well-known senatorial procedural tactic, often used to subvert a carefully crafted compromise resolution: the most recent and best-known example is described by Ascon. 44–45C, with Morstein-Marx 2004: 115–116. One unresolved question is whether Curio or Marcellus presided. Plut. *Pomp.* 58.4–5 seems to imply the former (although tribunes were empowered to make a *relatio* even when a consul was presiding: Mommsen 1887: 2.316n2, 3.954); yet according to App. *BCiv.* 2.30/119 it is Marcellus who *dismisses* the Senate. (Botermann 1989: 75 with n. 47 for some conjectures.) An earlier, failed attempt by Curio to pass a senatorial decree on his proposal, and apparently under his presidency, appears to be reflected at App. *BCiv.* 2.29/113; on Hirt. [Caes.] *BGall.* 8.52.5 see n. 82.

[143] This is the outcome of Dio's version of the vote in January (41.1.4–2.2, perhaps a doublet: n. 141).

Senate.[144] This represented a serious public relations setback for both men, so Curio had a strong incentive to undo the damage immediately by taking a vote on the recomposed motion (that both should disarm), which was now passed by the overwhelming margin mentioned earlier (370–22, or 94–6 percent of the votes cast).

Marcellus's apparent victory on the vetoed resolution now turned into a heavy defeat. What was the message that this somewhat contradictory set of votes sent? Partisans on both sides set to work spinning the results. For Caesar's friends, of course, the final vote was a clear testimonial of the Senate's preference for his proposal of mutual disarmament and rejection of any severe measure against Caesar that could provoke civil war; this is evidently how it was interpreted by the People in the Forum, who pelted Curio with flowers when he emerged from the meeting to announce it.[145] On the other side, however, it was certainly possible to argue that the earlier votes showed that the Senate did want Caesar to be replaced and did not want Pompey disarmed unless Caesar were simultaneously relieved of his command and army; therefore, if that outcome was somehow unthinkable or thought to be illegal, then it was Caesar who would have to yield.[146] Although our late sources probably offer no special insight, Appian's balanced judgment is worth quoting: "The Senate was now suspicious of both men, but they considered Pompey to be the more republican and they were angry with Caesar for his disdain for them during his consulship; some also thought it was in fact unsafe to disband Pompey's forces until Caesar had dismissed his own, for the latter was outside the City and had grander ambitions" (*BCiv.* 2.29/112).

The 370–22 vote count on the final resolution clearly shows how few – a hard core of twenty-two, probably no more than that *factio* of Caesar's personal enemies (*inimici*) on whom he was eventually to lay responsibility for the war – were actually prepared to take strong measures against him that

---

[144] Cic. *Att.* 7.9.4 and *Fam.* 16.11.2: *invito senatu*; cf. *Att.* 7.11.1 *habere exercitum nullo publico consilio*. For the recording of an *auctoritas* after a successful vote was vetoed see the decrees of September 29, 51 (Cael. [Cic.] *Fam.* 8.8.6–8). Nowhere is the vote of December described in our sources as constituting a formally enacted *senatus consultum*, and in fact the same matter is raised again in the meeting of January 1.

[145] See n. 155. The Caesarian interpretation is apparent from Hirt. [Caes.] *BGall.* 8.52–55 (cf. n. 82) and Caesar's own account of the alleged suppression of the true will of the Senate by his enemies in early January (n. 200). Plut. *Cat. Min.* 51.7 (τὴν δὲ σύγκλητον ... φοβουμένην τὸν δῆμον) interestingly suggests that the Senate's vote was determined by the "fear of the People" documented on other occasions (Chapter 1, p. 4f). App. *BCiv.* 2.30/119 however claims that most senators simply prioritized their personal over the public interest and shunned strife (ἐς τὸ συμφέρον ἀπὸ τῆς ἔριδος).

[146] The final vote thus hardly proves that the Senate had changed its mind since the first two (so Botermann 1989: 75).

ran a real risk of precipitating a civil war.[147] Who were these men? Hinnerk Bruhns compiled a list of twenty names who appear to have been the most committed enemies of Caesar at this time, starting with the most obvious ones drawn from the accounts of Caesar himself and Hirtius – Cato, Bibulus, Domitius Ahenobarbus, Metellus Scipio, and the consuls-designate for 49, Lentulus Crus and C. Marcellus[148] – and continuing with other prominent senators who took an anti-Caesarian line in this year or would soon join the other side – the other C. Marcellus (the current consul), Ap. Claudius, probably also M. Marcellus and P. Lentulus Spinther;[149] M. Favonius (an almost fanatical follower of Cato), a praetor-elect for 49, may safely be added, and one L. Postumius is further named among those hostile to Caesar in the Sallustian *Second Letter*.[150] These will more or less have constituted the "hard core" of the anti-Caesarians; Bruhns suggests eight more names on the basis of the commitment they show in the civil war to come and discernible personal interests: Sulla's son Faustus, and the ex-praetors L. Aelius Tubero, M. Aurelius Cotta, M. Considius Nonianus, A. Plautius, P. Sestius, Q. Voconius Naso, and M. Terentius Varro.[151] Bruhns's list of anti-Caesarians cannot of course be treated as a roll call of the twenty-two senators who voted against the mutual disarmament proposal in late fall 50, but it is likely to include most of them.

Cicero was later to describe how, when he came to Rome (he arrived in the outskirts on January 4 [civil], 49), he was bewildered to find himself in the midst of a war frenzy. He had "fallen into the midst of the insanity of men eager to fight," "an amazing fit of madness that made not only the wicked but even those considered 'good' (*boni*) want to fight as I cried out

---

[147] For the history of these enmities see Raaflaub 1974: 113–149; 2003: 40–46; Jehne 2009a: 151–153.

[148] Caes. *BCiv.* 1.1.2–4, 4.1–3, 6.5; Hirt. [Caes.] *BGall.* 8.50.4; Cic. *Att.* 9.1.4; cf. Dio 40.66.2–4. Botermann 1989 argues on the basis of possible allusions in Seneca that Cato was among the 370 rather than, as usually assumed, the hard core of 22; yet Seneca's glorification of Cato can hardly be accepted uncritically. (Jehne 2009b: 151n29; 2017: 203n18, 214–215; Pelling 2011: 305–306 is too charitable.) If Caesar's word (*BCiv.* 1.4.1) be insufficient, see Plut. *Cat. Min.* 51.7, a denunciation of Caesar apparently uttered in this very debate; also *Pomp.* 59.6, Vell. Pat. 2.49.3. Cato's son-in-law Bibulus was not among the 22 since he was returning from his proconsular service in Syria (Cic. *Att.* 7.3.5, 9.9.2), yet he certainly merits inclusion among the "hard core" of Caesar's enemies, as the (somewhat dubious: n. 150) Sall. *Ep.* 2.9 avers. L. Afranius would seem to be another solid candidate (Caes. *BCiv.* 3.83.2–3), but he was holding Pompey's province of Nearer Spain.

[149] For Ap. Claudius see Dio 40.63.2–64.1, with n. 141. For the consuls-designate see Bruhns 1978: 38–39, Cic. *Att.* 9.1.4, Caes. *BCiv.* 3.83.1; above p. 287 and Chapter 7. M. Marcellus, however, advised caution on January 1: Caes. *BCiv.* 1.2.2.

[150] Sall. *Ep.* 2.9, whose information in such a matter is likely to be good regardless of the dubious authenticity of the authorial attribution. For Favonius see Pelling 2011: 248–249.

[151] Bruhns 1978: 26–28. Faustus Sulla is specifically named by Caes. *BCiv.* 1.6.3. Pompey was outside the City and would not have voted for this and other reasons.

that there was nothing more lamentable than civil war."[152] Cicero's complaints are remarkably reminiscent, in fact, of Caesar's own famous representation of the actions of the hard-liners and the Senate at the beginning of January as driven by personal enmity, greed, and lust for power, prevailing only through intimidation and confusion (*BCiv.* 1.1–5). As we saw, while Cicero made his way back to Rome he repeatedly expressed his preference for peace even if it meant giving in to Caesar's "impudent" demands, in principle conceded long ago.[153] The lopsided senatorial vote taken only a few weeks before he stepped into the "madness of war" shows that this fiery emotion was far from representative of the majority of the Senate. Lucius Piso, Caesar's father-in-law but also at this time censor, the highest honorific position in the Roman aristocracy, had thrown his support behind Curio's motion.[154] And if that was the attitude in the Senate, we can suppose that popular sentiment was a good deal more Caesar-friendly, and correspondingly more anxious to preserve peace. We have already noted how Curio was greeted with applause and showers of garlands and flowers when he announced that pacific senatorial vote to the People in the Forum.[155] The detail is plausible. Not only were the common people typically terrified of civil war but, given the clear understanding in our contemporary sources that Caesar would certainly have been elected consul if the People had only been given the chance to express their will with their votes, we may suppose that they overwhelmingly favored the justice of Caesar's demands.[156] It looked as if Curio had found a way both to honor a Roman hero and to prevent armed conflict.

---

[152] *Fam.* 4.1.1 (to Ser. Sulpicius Rufus, ca. April 21, 49): *incideram in hominum pugnandi cupidorum insanias.* The language echoes earlier complaints to his intimates: *Fam.* 16.11.2 (to Terentia and Tullia, January 12) *incidi in ipsam flammam civilis discordiae, vel potius belli; cui cum cuperem mederi et, ut arbitror, possem, cupiditates certorum hominum (nam ex utraque parte sunt qui pugnare cupiant) impedimento mihi fuerunt.* *Fam.* 16.12.2 (to Tiro, January 27) *mirus invaserat furor non solum improbis sed etiam iis qui boni habentur, ut pugnare cuperent, me clamante nihil esse bello civili miserius.* Cf. *Att.* 8.11D.7 (to Pompey, February 27) *pugnandi cupidis hominibus; §8 illi armis disceptari maluerunt.* The retrospective view: *Brut.* 7 *quod si fuit in re publica tempus ullum, cum extorquere arma posset e manibus iratorum civium boni civis auctoritas et oratio, tum profecto fuit cum patrocinium pacis exclusum est aut errore humanum aut timore.* See further n. 190; Chapter 7, p. 386ff.

[153] See p. 289ff.

[154] Plut. *Pomp.* 58.6 (naming also M. Antony, tribune-designate). Piso's intercession for Curio (along with that of the consul L. Paullus) when his colleague in the censorship Ap. Claudius sought to expel him, is in Dio's account (40.63.5–64.4) the immediate precipitant of the "Schwertübergabe."

[155] Plut. *Pomp.* 58.9, *Caes.* 30.2; also mentioned by App. *BCiv.* 2.27/106, though without detailed context. This event should be added to Pina Polo's catalog of *contiones* (1989).

[156] The augural election of (probably) late July was evidently a strong sign of popular favor toward Caesar: n. 111. On the people's justified horror of civil war see Cic. *Att.* 7.8.5 (with n. 173), Dio 41.16.3–4, and Chapter 7, n. 413. For the certainty that Caesar would be elected if the people were given their choice see n. 11.

That peace did not after all break out can be laid firmly at the door of consul C. Marcellus. According to Appian, whose information about the meeting and its aftermath seems to offer the most precise details about this episode, Marcellus dismissed the Senate, crying, "You've won: take Caesar as your master"; then, presumably very shortly after (we are not told how long), when a false rumor came that Caesar had crossed the Alps and was actually marching on the City, he sought to obtain senatorial authorization to declare Caesar a public enemy and send against him the two legions taken from him.[157] Curio, claiming that the rumor was false, opposed him and apparently blocked the decree by threatening or casting a veto; Marcellus in turn declared, "If I am prevented from carrying out what is in the public interest by means of a vote taken by us in common, then I shall carry it out on my sole authority as consul."[158] The words are loosely reminiscent of those of Scipio Nasica when, in frustration at the presiding consul's refusal to propose a relevant motion, he led a band of senators out to attack Tiberius Gracchus in 133.[159] Marcellus therefore chose to regard Curio's veto as devoid of legitimacy inasmuch as it was manifestly cast (so he claimed) in collaboration with an enemy force marching on the City. In the supposed emergency Marcellus assumed a latent and implicit but overriding power as consul to protect the Republic from harm, though in these exceptional circumstances entirely without external authorization by the Senate because (so the argument would run) such authorization had been rendered impossible.[160] The senators then changed to mourning dress and attended him on his mission to Pompey, presumably at his *horti* (suburban villa) on the Campus Martius

---

[157] This rumor seems likely to have been precipitated by Caesar's final return across the Alps to Cisalpine Gaul in mid-to-late November: Raaflaub and Ramsey 2017: 70.

[158] App. *BCiv.* 2.30–31/119–121: "εἰ κωλύομαι ψήφῳ κοινῇ τὰ συμφέροντα διοικεῖν κατ᾽ ἐμαυτὸν ὡς ὕπατος διοικήσω" (§121). H. White in the Loeb and J. Carter in the Penguin translation both construe the dative ψήφῳ κοινῇ with κωλύομαι rather than with διοικεῖν; but in the context it is clear that ψήφῳ κοινῇ . . . διοικεῖν is put in parallel with κατ᾽ ἐμαυτὸν ὡς ὕπατος διοικήσω. That is, Marcellus is blaming Curio for preventing him (implicitly, by his veto) from serving the public interest (i.e., declaring Caesar a *hostis*) as defined by the collective vote (ψήφῳ κοινῇ) of the majority of senators and declaring that he would therefore act on his own sole authority as consul; he is not attacking the Senate for failing to agree with him (hence apparently Raaflaub's assumption [1974: 33] that Marcellus's action was contrary to the express will of the Senate majority; Gelzer 1968: 186 and Botermann 1989: 77–78 also overlook the veto or veto threat). Cf. Meyer 1919: 273. Plut. *Pomp.* 58.10–59.1 refers to the same rumor but seems to conflate Appian's two meetings into one.

[159] Plut. *T Gracch.* 19.5 "ἐπεὶ τοίνυν . . . προδίδωσιν ὁ ἄρχων τὴν πόλιν, οἱ βουλόμενοι τοῖς νόμοις βοηθεῖν ἀκολουθεῖτε"; Val. Max. 3.2.17: "*quoniam . . . consul dum iuris ordinem sequitur id agit ut cum omnibus legibus imperium corruat, egomet me privatus voluntati vestrae ducem offero . . . qui rem publicam salvam esse volunt me sequantur;*" cf. App. *BCiv.* 1.16/68: ἐβόα τε μέγιστον ἔπεσθαί οἱ τοὺς ἐθέλοντας σῴζεσθαι τὴν πατρίδα.

[160] Compare the rationale of Sulla's decision to march against C. Marius and P. Sulpicius in 88: Morstein-Marx 2011: 271–276.

just north of the City boundary, which sent a highly visible symbol of protest against the suppression of the Senate's will by Curio's veto.[161] In what may be regarded then as an improvised adaptation of the idea of the "Final Decree" (though without the actual decree!), Marcellus made his way to Pompey and declared that he and his colleague gave him command over all forces then in Italy (the two legions) and any others he might wish to levy; they ordered him to advance against Caesar in defense of the Republic.[162] The action was unprecedented and highly irregular: Helga Botermann not unreasonably describes this as "a kind of improvised coup from above."[163] Pompey accepted the order, though he expressed some reservations (sincere or not) by adding, "if there be no better course of action."[164]

Given the justification of this unprecedented action as a response to an existential emergency, it must have been embarrassing that Pompey in fact did not actually bestir himself before December 7 (civil calendar), and that when he did act, he moved not north as if a hostile army were speeding toward the City but south, to prepare the "Parthian" legions. The falsity of the pretext on which irregular emergency measures had been taken was now obvious; to collect the diverted legions to use against Caesar was now apt to look like blatant chicanery – and not only from the perspective of the other side.[165]

---

[161] Raaflaub 1974: 33. Plutarch's reference at *Pomp.* 59.1 to a (probably spontaneous) change into mourning dress by some senators (n.b. not "the city" as in B. Perrin's Loeb translation) may be a doublet of the final showdown with the succeeding tribunes, Antony and Cassius (below; so Pelling 2011: 306), but since it appears to have been a common tactic for ostentatiously expressing senatorial dismay at the frustration of its will by a tribunician veto (see n. 205) it is in fact perfectly apt here. For the *horti Pompeiani*, see V. Jolivet, *LTUR* 3.78–79.

[162] App. *BCiv.* 2.31/121: "κελεύω σοι . . . κἀγὼ καὶ ὅδε χωρεῖν ἐπὶ Καίσαρα ὑπὲρ τῆς πατρίδος· καὶ στρατιὰν ἐς τοῦτό σοι δίδομεν, ἥ τε νῦν ἀμφὶ Καπύην ἢ τὴν ἄλλην Ἰταλίαν ἐστὶ καὶ ὅσην αὐτὸς ἐθέλοις ἄλλην καταλέγειν." Cf. Plut. *Pomp.* 59.1. Dio clearly states (40.66.2) that, since this order had not been approved by the Senate and People, the validity of this consular action was construed as lasting only to the end of December; consequently Marcellus induced the consuls-designate to issue the same order, which they "believed" they were legally competent to do (καὶ τούτου κύριοι ἐνόμιζον εἶναι, 66.3; cf. Plut. *Pomp.* 59.2).

[163] Botermann 1989: 78. On the sword itself see n. 139.

[164] App. *BCiv.* 2.31 "εἰ μή τι κρεῖσσον."

[165] Caes. *BCiv.* 1.9.4: *Tota Italia dilectus haberi, retineri legiones II, quae ab se simulatione Parthici belli sint abductae, civitatem esse in armis. Quonam haec omnia nisi ad suam perniciem pertinere?* Cic. *Att.* 7.5.4 (mid-Dec.): *quos ego equites Romanos, quos senatores vidi, qui acerrime cum cetera tum hoc iter Pompei vituperarent! pace opus est*, with Shackleton Bailey 1965: 3:301; cf. 7.13.2 *duabus invidiose retentis*. For the background see n. 96. Pompey must have left the city about December 7 (7.4.2) and met Cicero en route on December 10 (ibid.), perhaps at Capua (Gelzer, in Shackleton Bailey 1965: 3:299); he was hastening back along the Via Appia when he overtook Cicero at Lavernium, near Formiae, on December 25, about four days out of Rome (all dates by the civil calendar). He clearly intended to be present just outside the *pomerium* on January 1. To be sure, the legions in Apulia constituted Pompey's only large organized military force; yet they still had not moved north by the second week of January (Caes. *BCiv.* 1.14.3, despite 1.2.3 [presumably rhetorical exaggeration, although some elements were soon be called up: 1.3.2]).

However that may be, this was the beginning of serious military preparations against Caesar, which by the end of the month of December were proceeding intensively.[166] The alarm on the Caesarian side is palpable and entirely reasonable: only Curio's veto had prevented Caesar from having been declared a public enemy on the basis of a false, perhaps fabricated rumor. Curio denounced the preparations in at least one *contio*, demanding that the consuls should countermand Pompey's recruitment efforts, but of course they did no such thing, and after his tribunate had run its course on December 9 Curio departed to join Caesar.[167] Having lost his tribunician sacrosanctity he may well have feared for his safety in Rome.

In Campania (perhaps Capua) on the very next day, December 10, Cicero met with Pompey and talked over the political situation for two hours. Pompey was now certain that there would be war: he took it as an especially bad sign (quite reasonably, given all that had happened) that although Caesar's friends Hirtius and Balbus had come to Rome, evidently as personal envoys, and had met with others on the 6th and 7th, they apparently had carried no instructions to meet with him. Yet it is notable that in this conversation Pompey cited this recent event as if until then even he had still required confirmation of Caesar's estrangement: even now, that is, there had been no public and definitive rupture between the two principals.[168] As it happens, we have a letter from Cicero to Atticus (dated within a couple of days before or after December 15)[169] in which he notes that the *boni* were hardly united, that he knew of many senators and knights who were bitterly critical of actions not conducive to peace, especially of Pompey's march south to assume command of the two legions and bring them back to Rome: for "what is needed is peace."[170] Capitalizing on this sentiment, on December 10 the new tribunes, Mark Antony and Q. Cassius Longinus, took up the cause.[171] Antony sprang into action by attempting to rally public opinion against Pompey's move to begin active military preparations against Caesar; probably in a *contio* he

---

[166] Cic. *Att.* 7.8.4 (December 25/26, 50): *cum audierit* [sc. Caesar] *contra se diligenter parari.* Hirt. [Caes.] *BGall.* 8.55.2: *hoc facto . . . nulli erat dubium, quidnam contra Caesarem pararetur.*

[167] App. *BCiv.* 2.31/123.

[168] Cic. *Att.* 7.4.2: *plane illum a se alienatum cum ante intellegeret, tum vero proxime iudicasse.*

[169] That is, between the previous and next letters in the collection (Shackleton Bailey 1965: 3:300), which Shackleton Bailey dates to ca. December 13 and ca. December 18.

[170] Cic. *Att.* 7.5.4 : *pace opus est.*

[171] This Cassius (*RE* 70) was *frater* to the future conspirator (*RE* 58, *Att.* 5.21.2; cf. 7.3.5), also tribune in this year: possibly brother, but the word can refer to a cousin. A brother of the Caesaricide named Lucius was a Caesarian in the Civil War (*RE* 65). Perhaps the distribution of the brothers between the two sides served as a kind of insurance policy (cf. the Thracian royal brothers at App. *BCiv.* 4.87, 103–104, 136).

urged – perhaps he even formally promulgated a law or threatened to do so – that the two legions in Italy should be sent on to Syria as originally intended, while removing from Pompey's control those currently being recruited.[172] A short time later, on the 21st, while Pompey was still on his military mission in the south, Antony delivered a *contio* in which he attacked Pompey's whole career from his adolescence, complained about the condemnations of 52 under Pompey's ad hoc laws, and dwelled on the imminent danger of war.[173]

The highly personal nature of this attack on Pompey suggests that he had now become Caesar's main rhetorical target. The reason appears simple enough: by accepting command over the preparations to oppose Caesar militarily, Pompey had made himself the figurehead of the hard core who had rejected the mutual disarmament decree of a few weeks past. Forced to make a choice between his new friends – Cato et al. – and his old alliance with Caesar, he had finally chosen the former.[174] Cicero's private conversations with the great man in December opened his eyes to the fact that Pompey was now firmly set on the path of confrontation and, if Caesar did not yield, war. On December 10, when Cicero had just arrived in Campania, Pompey had indicated that war was certain; he held out no hope of reconciliation.[175] When they met the second time on the 25th, in the aftermath of Antony's invective, Pompey, now on his way back to Rome, made it clear that he not only had no hope for peace but he had not even the desire for it.[176]

We should take in the full import of what Pompey was saying here. At a time when Cicero asserts that nearly everyone was in favor of giving

---

[172] Plut. *Ant.* 5.4. Plutarch's wording, διάταγμα γράψας, has prompted speculation about a tribunician edict, which causes constitutional difficulties (see Pelling 1988: 128). Whatever it was that Antony "wrote," however, it was quickly overtaken by events. At the very least, we may assume that Antony expressed fierce opposition, presumably in a *contio*, to the transfer of the legions and the recruitment effort.

[173] Cic. *Att.* 7.8.5 (December 25 or 26). *Terror armorum* might be interpreted to mean "*threats* of armed force" (so Shackleton Bailey's tr.), yet literally it means simply "fear of war" (cf. *terrore exercitus*, Sall. *Iug.* 37.3), which would certainly fit the context and indeed Caesarean "propaganda" (Caes. *BCiv.* 1.9.5: *discedant in Italia omnes ab armis, metus e civitate tollatur*). Whatever deeper motives one might attribute to Antony (or Caesar), it was hardly consistent with the Caesarian line to make direct threats of war, especially before a *contio*; the general *fear* of war was precisely the sensitive spot on which to press. Most probably then Antony sought to concentrate minds by delivering dire warnings of the imminent danger of war, which some ordinary citizens may have found hard to credit; cf. Antony's later prognostications at App. *BCiv.* 2.33/132.

[174] On Pompey's inclination toward Cato from 52 on see now Morrell 2017: 203–214, 267–268, 273–275.

[175] Cic. *Att.* 7.4.2: *mecum locutus est quasi non dubium bellum haberemus: nihil ad spem concordiae.*

[176] Cic. *Att.* 7.8.4: *quod quaeris ecquae spes pacificationis sit, quantum ex Pompei multo et accurato sermone perspexi, ne voluntas quidem est.*

Caesar what he requested in preference to fighting a civil war, he also tells us that Pompey took precisely the contrary view. Although before the elections at least Pompey had rejected outright only the idea that Caesar should be able to be elected consul *while holding on to his province and army*, now he took a much harder line, at least in private, and he was no longer disposed to countenance Caesar as consul a second time *even if he did give up his army.*[177] The trust needed to manage such a crisis had dribbled away in the rising tensions of the past year. The aggressive attacks of Caesar's tribunes – first Curio, then Antony – must have stung deeply and been interpreted as proofs of his former friend's alienation.[178] "What do you think *he* will do if he takes control of the state when this little twerp of a quaestor of his dares to speak this way?"[179] The great Pompey had had enough. He had come to believe that if Caesar should become consul for the second time it would mean "subversion of the constitution."[180] Nothing – not even civil war, apparently – was more to be feared than Caesar as consul again.[181] Caesar had been stronger than the entire Republic as consul the first time, but he was so much stronger now.[182] The mission placed upon Pompey's shoulders by C. Marcellus had now set him explicitly in opposition to Caesar as the defender of Italy, the City, and the Senate.

The bellicosity we observe in Pompey's statements in December 50 was absent from Cicero as he slowly made his way to the City's gates after his long absence of more than a year.[183] As we have seen, before his spine-stiffening interviews with Pompey his fervent hope had been for peace and reconciliation, a view that he claims was widely shared among senators and *equites.*[184] Even after his second, long discussion with the general on December 25, Cicero was quick to slip back to hopes of a settlement of the dispute if Caesar could only be induced to leave his army before his certain election to a second consulship. This, after all, was merely a revival of Pompey's offer before the worsening of the atmosphere over the summer. "All good men" would favor this solution to the crisis along with Atticus and himself.[185] But by late December it was also clear that such a settlement would no longer be accepted

---

[177] Cic. *Att.* 7.8.4.
[178] Here lies the core truth in Gruen's contention, following up on the hint in Vell. 2.48.3, that it was Curio who drove the two to civil war.
[179] Cic. *Att.* 7.8.5: *"cum haec quaestor eius infirmus et inops audeat dicere?"*
[180] Shackleton Bailey's translation of Cic. *Att.* 7.8.4: σύγχυσιν τῆς πολιτείας *fore.*
[181] Cic. *Att.* 7.9.3. Text n. 229.   [182] Cic. *Att.* 7.9.3.
[183] Cicero had reached Italy only on November 24 (Civil, *Att.* 7.2.1), perhaps just before the "Schwertübergabe."
[184] See n. 289.   [185] Cic. *Att.* 7.9.2–4.

by Pompey and others in the anti-Caesarian hard core,[186] even if Caesar himself could be persuaded to accept it – which seemed increasingly unlikely, even though from Cicero's perspective it would have given him everything he wanted.[187] Cicero was apparently blind to Caesar's reasonable doubt that his now-declared enemies would uphold such a bargain, which would leave him at their mercy if they reneged.[188] But Cicero did not give up, going even so far as to declare to the Senate in one of its meetings after his arrival outside the City on January 4, 49, that he would happily give up his own hope for a triumph and instead walk in *Caesar's* triumph if a settlement could be reached.[189] Within days he was at work on a last-ditch effort to broker a deal between the two sides.

Cicero – no apologist for Caesar – would later recall to his friend Varro, "I saw that our friends [i.e., Pompey and adherents] wanted war"; Caesar on the other hand "didn't so much want war as didn't fear it."[190] By the end of 50, for his part, Caesar could see that the hard core of his enemies was offering him a choice between war and humiliation (*ignominia*) rather than the *honor* he had had reason to expect, specifically grounded in a law of the Roman People.[191] It was not hysterical for him to feel that his political – perhaps now even physical – survival was at stake,[192] despite his magnificent victories in Gaul, not to mention the general understanding that the Roman People, if given the chance to vote on the matter as was their right,

---

[186] Cic. *Att.* 7.9.3: *ut quidam putant* (note pl.), *nihil est timendum magis quam ille consul.* Yet, Cicero goes on, *aliquis* (n.b. now singular, presumably Pompey) considers even this a "terrible thing." Shackleton Bailey ad loc. doubts whether the plural of *quidam* (if sound) could mean any more than Pompey, but surely Cato, C. Marcellus, the consuls-designate for 49, and Metellus Scipio could all be included.

[187] It would take some persuading (*Att.* 7.9.2; cf. §3), and Cicero seems by late December to concede that Caesar would probably never accept the proposal (§4), though earlier in the month he had still been quite hopeful (7.4.3: *non arbitror fore tam amentem ut haec in discrimen adducat*) and even later he expresses surprise at this (7.9.3: *idque eum . . . non facere miror*).

[188] The Prisoner's Dilemma helps to explain why: Appendix 4.

[189] Plut. *Cic.* 37.1, with Lintott 2013: 189. The meeting was probably the one held in the Temple of Apollo to which he refers at *Att.* 15.3.1 (cf. *Marc.* 15, perhaps Caes. *BCiv.* 1.6.1 *extra urbem*), which, like Pompey, he could attend without giving up his *imperium* because the temple was outside the *pomerium*. Cicero's right to a triumph was discussed but then postponed because of the crisis (Cic. *Fam.* 16.11.3).

[190] Cic. *Fam.* 9.6.2: *vidi enim (nam tu aberas) nostros amicos cupere bellum, hunc autem non tam cupere quam non timere. Att.* 7.8.5 [Pompeius] *non modo non expetere pacem istam sed etiam timere visus est.* At *Att.* 7.9.4 Cicero himself, after talking to Pompey, seems to have come around to his view, but the shift was temporary: later references in the letters consistently treat the war as a "war of choice" by a few hard-liners, even if Caesar's demands were "impudent."

[191] Caes. *BCiv.* 1.85.10: *in se uno non servari, quod sit omnibus datum semper imperatoribus, ut rebus feliciter gestis aut cum honore aliquo aut certe sine ignominia domum revertantur exercitumque dimittant.*

[192] Caes. *BCiv.* 1.9.4: *quonam haec omnia nisi ad suam perniciem pertinere?* Cf. p. 288.

was virtually certain to have elected him *consul II*. In these circumstances, to make a stand on *dignitas* was not to make the offensive declaration that one set one's purely personal interest above that of the state, but to defend fundamental Roman republican principles, both founded on powers and rights of the People: the right, the fundamental freedom, of the Roman People to perform its most important duty – that is, to bestow honor and confer *imperium* on those most worthy of it, and the power of the Roman People to pass laws binding on the community, including the Senate.[193] But Caesar's enemies were soon to give him yet another strong justification for resistance, for in the new tribunician college were two prepared to defend Caesar's claims: Antony and Q. Cassius.[194] The expected push for action on the first of January by Caesar's adversaries would no doubt have to confront a revival of Curio's vetoes, and the possibility that Caesar could use this as a pretext for war had been contemplated for months.[195]

Last Exit

Curio brought back from Caesar a letter which he delivered to the new consuls on the first day of the new year. Our sources agree that the consuls at first attempted to prevent the letter from being read out in the Senate, despite the vigorous protests of Antony and Cassius; ultimately the consuls yielded, perhaps because Antony went around them and had the letter read out in a *contio* over the consuls' continued objections.[196] According to our fullest summary of its contents, the letter "contained a solemn survey of all Caesar's deeds from the beginning and a declaration that he wished to lay down his command together with Pompey; that, however, so long as Pompey retained his command he would not step down but" – so Appian says – "would come with all speed to defend the Republic and himself."[197]

---

[193] For this interpretation of Caesar's *dignitas* claim see Morstein-Marx 2009.
[194] Cic. *Fam.* 6.8.2 with Shackleton Bailey 1965: 3:274. For Q. Cassius's relationship to Caesar's assassin see n. 171.
[195] Cic. *Fam.* 16.9.3 *Romae vereor ne ex Kal. Ian. magni tumultus sint.* Cf. Cael. [Cic.] *Fam.* 8.11.3; Cic. *Att.* 7.9.2.
[196] Caes. *BCiv.* 1.1.1; Dio 41.1.1–2; App. *BCiv.* 2.32/127; Plut. *Pomp.* 59.3–5; *Caes.* 30.3 (both here and in the *Pomp.* explicitly mentioning a *contio*); *Ant.* 5.5. Pelling 1988: 128, 2011: 304 is inclined to refer the *contio* to that of December 21 of which Cicero and Pompey complained, yet why should Antony not have resorted now to the People, as would any tribune stymied in the Senate? Note that *Pomp.* 59.5 explicitly states that L. Lentulus was already (ἤδη) consul. Plutarch's assertion in the *Pompey* that at first Lentulus "did not summon the Senate" (59.5) seems to be a misunderstanding of the attempt to suppress the reading of the letter.
[197] App. *BCiv.* 2.32/127–128: τιμωρὸς αὐτίκα τῇ τε πατρίδι καὶ ἑαυτῷ κατὰ τάχος ἀφίξεσθει; cf. Dio 41.1.3–4; Suet. *Iul.* 29.2, and the Plutarch passages cited in n. 196. On the probable "doublet" of the senatorial votes on Caesar's and Pompey's commands see n. 141.

This was tough language indeed, although it is important to remember that Caesar had just escaped being voted an enemy of the Republic about a month before, and military preparations against him were ongoing at this moment. Matthias Gelzer doubted Caesar could have used such threatening language in a formal letter to the Senate, but Cicero, who opposed Caesar's "impudent" demands while at the same time criticizing the rush to war on his own side, himself describes the letter as "bitter" and "threatening" in writing to his beloved freedman Tiro.[198] Some hard-liners in the Senate no doubt did regard the letter as a virtual declaration of war (ὡς ἐπὶ πολέμου καταγγελίᾳ, so Appian, *BCiv.* 2.32/129); yet if it had been truly that inflammatory the consuls would probably not have wanted to suppress it. Since in the letter Caesar was also reiterating a peace proposal that only about a month before had won overwhelming assent in the Senate, which had repeatedly shown its wobbliness when it came to hard measures against the proconsul, it is best to suppose that the tough language was intended to concentrate minds among the senators and nudge the majority to disavow the bellicosity of those currently prodding them in the direction of civil war.[199]

There follows the senatorial debate Caesar describes in detail at the beginning of *De bello civili*, in which moderate voices are drowned out by consular bullying and cowed by Pompey's string pulling and military intimidation: "Everything was done in hasty and disorderly fashion."[200] Caesar's compelling description is of course the product of a skilled rhetorician and deeply interested partisan. Yet the following facts appear to be beyond serious dispute. Already on January 1, the majority of the Senate

---

[198] Cic. *Fam.* 16.11.2 : *ipse Caesar, amicus noster, minacis ad senatum et acerbas litteras miserat.* It is interesting that Cicero also blames Curio for "inciting" Caesar; cf. similarly App. *BCiv.* 2.32/125. Girardet 2017: 183 (cf. 221) dates Caesar's "Putsch" to this precise date, when in his view he held on to his army and provinces "illegally" after the expiration of his command. The "Final Decree" is on this view a purely defensive response to the "Putsch," and the suppression of the tribunes' vetoes is an appropriate response to their blatantly illegal activity on behalf of an enemy of the state (228–230).

[199] Plutarch (*Ant.* 5.5) claims that many who heard Antony's reading of the letter thought the demands made in it were "just and moderate." Unfortunately we cannot be entirely sure whether here he is describing the effect of Antony's reading on senators or on the audience of a *contio* (n. 196). Note that Caesar himself claims that some in the Senate offered friendly, or at least less hostile, proposals until they were silenced by the consul's browbeating and their fear of Pompey's soldiers (*BCiv.* 1.2.2–6).

[200] Caes. *BCiv.* 1.5.1; see the whole account, §§1–4. For a critical review of the rhetoric of the episode see Batstone and Damon 2006: 41–55; for a trace of the Caesarian critique in Cicero's *Phil.* 2.52 (*quid cupide a senatu, quid temere fiebat . . . ?*). Although both consuls were present and perhaps technically presided in tandem (1.1.2: *referunt consules*; App. *BCiv.* 2.33/131), Lentulus plays far the more active role in the debate (Caes. *BCiv.* 1.1.2, 2.4, 4.1–3; Dio 41.3.2).

voted for a motion proposed by Pompey's father-in-law, Q. Metellus Scipio, calling on Caesar to dismiss his army before a certain date or be considered to be acting against the Republic.[201] That motion was then predictably vetoed by Antony and Cassius, and in response, a debate was immediately introduced (presumably by the consul Lentulus) on the veto itself – that is, on whether to pressure the tribunes to yield to the will of the Senate.[202] (This tactic, it will be remembered, was exactly what the Senate had *rejected* in late spring or early summer of the previous year.)[203] Probably the tribunes did not remain inactive for their part but counterattacked in the Forum in one or more *contiones*, as they had when the consuls had first attempted to suppress Caesar's letter. After an evening in which (according to Caesar) Pompey, excluded from the previous day's meeting because his proconsular command kept him outside the *pomerium*, sought to stiffen spines to take a hard line, senatorial debate resumed the next day, now clearly focused on pressing the tribunes to lift their veto.[204] An attempt to express senatorial dismay by passing a decree which called for a change into mourning dress was itself vetoed by the tribunes; the senators (or some portion of them) changed anyway in accordance with the Senate's *auctoritas*, and discussion of putting pressure on the tribunes resumed.[205]

---

[201] Caes. *BCiv*. 1.2.6–8; cf. Plut. *Caes*. 30.4: ἐν ἡμέρᾳ ῥητῇ, similarly Dio 41.3.4; Cic. *Phil*. 2.51. Scholars have been surprisingly inclined to assume that the *certa dies* was quite a distant deadline, perhaps even as late as July 1, shortly before the elections (Girardet 2017: 187 with n. 777, following many eminent scholars, including Mommsen; for further bibliography see Raaflaub 1974: 56n219 and Pelling 2011: 305, who suggest that an actual date may not have been specified but seem inclined to think that a late deadline was in the air). But bellicose haste is the leitmotiv of Caesar's account, and with all due allowance for his bias, why should we assume that in the midst of this rapid push for a resolution of the crisis Scipio actually wanted to give Caesar so much more time to push the Senate about? (Vell. 2.49.4 is hardly good evidence for a late deadline.) Note furthermore that according to Dio (41.3.3–4) the decree was *actually passed* immediately after the *s.c.u.* and about the same time as the declaration of a *tumultus*, neither of which implies a significant waiting period.

[202] In his own account, Caesar does not clarify what was done on the following days after the informal meeting with Pompey on the evening of the 1st (*BCiv*. 1.3) before the *s.c.u.* passed on January 7 (1.5.4). Dio 41.2.2 describes at least one day of inaction while the tribunes' veto stood (οὔτε ἐν ἐκείνῃ τῇ ἡμέρᾳ οὔτε ἐν τῇ ὑστεραίᾳ); this should be the 2nd, followed by the two comitial days on the 3rd and 4th on which the Senate did not meet (Caes. 1.5.4, with Carter ad loc.; cf. Müller 1972: 1–4).

[203] See n. 85.

[204] Cic. *Phil*. 2.52: *neque tu tecum de senatus auctoritate agi passus es? . . . cum te neque principes civitatis rogando neque maiores natu monendo neque frequens senatus agendo de vendita atque addicta sententia movere potui<sse>t . . . .*

[205] Caes. *BCiv*. 1.3–4; Dio 41.3.1; Plut. *Caes*. 30.6. See now Dighton 2017, who shows that the force of this symbolic weapon was to register a highly visible senatorial protest in the hope of undermining the popular support needed to sustain a veto. Raaflaub 1974a: 308 thinks that Plutarch regards the *mutatio vestis* as a protest against high-handed *consular* pressure, but Plutarch himself clearly motivates it as a response to the "discord" (διὰ τὴν στάσιν), which is easily interpreted in a manner consistent with Dio: a senatorial protest against the tribunician veto in keeping with the prior history of the practice.

In the midst of this story of the final senatorial deliberations in the first week of January – apparently between the 3rd and the 6th according to the civil calendar (~ ca. November 15–18, Jul.) – a remarkable initiative from Caesar supervened, who now proposed to avert the looming conflict by giving up all but two legions (presumably to balance the two legions Pompey had just taken over) and Cisalpine Gaul until he was elected consul.[206] Although modern scholars sometimes suppose that the offer was delivered publicly to the Senate, no source actually says this, and the information we have about the negotiations suggests instead that, rather like the meeting of the Pompeian "war council" at Capua that discussed Caesar's next offer about three weeks later, these discussions took place outside the Senate among a small group, whose principals on one side were Pompey, the consuls C. Marcellus and Lentulus, and Cato, and on the other probably the tribunes Antony and Cassius with Curio and perhaps M. Caelius, with Cicero, counted a friend by Caesar as well as Pompey and Cato, acting as mediator.[207] Pompey rejected Caesar's initial offer, in part because the two "Parthian" legions were of suspect loyalty. But Cicero was now able to persuade Caesar's friends to agree to his holding on to just one legion, while giving up even northern Italy – that is, Cisalpine Gaul, which would thus serve as a bulwark astride the line of march to Rome – and keeping only Illyricum. Pompey, we are told, was close to accepting this last offer but backed away from it when he was opposed by Lentulus (or both consuls) and chastised by Cato for allowing himself to be deceived "again."[208] Caesar was not, it is true, giving up his *ratio absentis* (without which any such deal was unworkable), but by offering to lower his military forces to half the size of

---

[206] Suet. *Iul.* 29.2; App. *BCiv.* 2.32/126–127; Plut. *Caes.* 31.1–2, *Pomp.* 59.5–6 (cf. *Ant.* 5.8); Vell. 2.49.4. Cic. *Fam.* 6.6.5 also probably alludes to this negotiation, in which Cicero is known to have played a prominent part, rather than that of late January 49 (cf. Shackleton Bailey 1977: 2:401); any arrangement by which Caesar obtained his second consulship was understood to involve Pompey's moving off at last to his province of Spain (*Att.* 7.9.3; see also the negotiations of late January 49 discussed in Chapter 7). There is once again a chronological problem: Appian dates the offer to the end of December 50, Plutarch to early January 49. See Appendix 3(h) for justification of the date given in the text.

[207] Pompey, Lentulus, Cato, and Cicero are explicitly named by Plutarch, "the consuls" by Appian. Cf. Vell. Pat. 2.49.3, naming the consuls and Cato possibly in this context. "Caesar's friends" (Plut. *Pomp.* 59.6, *Caes.* 31.2; App. *BCiv.* 2.32/126; cf. *Caes. BCiv.* 1.5.1 *Caesaris propinquis*, here denoting at least L. Piso and L. Roscius: 1.3.5) ought to include the tribunes and Curio. Caelius fled to Ariminum together with Curio and the tribunes after the veto was broken (Cael. [Cic.] *Fam.* 8.17.1, cf. Dio 41.2.1).

[208] Plut. *Pomp.* 59.6 (Lentulus and Cato), *Caes.* 31.2 (Lentulus); App. *BCiv.* 2.32/127 ("the consuls"); perhaps Vell. Pat. 2.49.3 (both consuls and Cato). Velleius (§4) appears to import mistakenly into this episode Caesar's later offer to give up his *ratio absentis* altogether and enter the city for the normal *professio*; this is hardly consistent with his retaining a legion and a province and is probably a conflation with Caesar's offer later in January.

Pompey's he attempted to remove altogether the sense of threat that his army of eleven battle-hardened legions had naturally created.

There is probably no strong reason to disbelieve the claim that Pompey now came within a hair's breadth of accepting a proposal that should in fact have averted the Caesarian Civil War, with all that that would have entailed. His trust of Caesar had certainly plummeted over the years 51 and 50, but the two men, kinsmen not so long ago, had a long history of collaboration behind them which was probably not yet entirely beyond remedy. This assumption is perfectly palpable in the first book of Caesar's *Civil War Commentaries,* where he repeatedly expresses his bewilderment and dismay at Pompey's preference for the friendship of his enemies rather than for their old connection.[209] On the other hand Pompey had spent most of his political life since his return from the East fiercely at odds with Cato and his ilk, whom he had no reason to trust in the longer term more than he did Caesar.[210] Indeed, Pompey, holding Italy with two legions and continuing his recruitment apace while continuing to hold Spain with seven more, would have had no reason to fear violence from Caesar, once suitably emasculated with only one legion and holding a single province outside of Italy until his election while the rest of his battle-hardened army was demobilized or placed under a successor. Those who suppose that such a reconciliation could never have happened should consult Cicero's correspondence of only the following year, where it is made clear that he at least believed that the two were about to come to a settlement still later in January (and perhaps later yet).[211] But it is also true that the deal would have saved Caesar from the political extinction his enemies hoped for, and in a second consulship he would have been (on Cicero's own later, sober analysis) not a *rex*, to be sure, but perhaps the most eminent of the *principes* or "leading men" in the Republic.[212]

The hard core of Caesar's enemies saw their plan crumbling before their eyes and leapt into the breach to ward off their nightmare scenario of a renewed alliance between the two powerful leaders. They had not coaxed Pompey this far only to have him save Caesar from just retribution at the last moment. Yet how different the story would have been had Pompey, torn between his old ally and his new "friends," neither of them entirely

---

[209] See n. 235.
[210] Plut. *Pomp.* 44, *Cat. Min.* 30 for Cato's original rebuff to Pompey on his return. Seager 2002: 76, 81–84. Pompey's second consulship brought further tension, including Cato's initial *repulsa* for the praetorship.
[211] He "had learned by experience [in 58] how hand in glove they were" (Shackleton Bailey tr., *Att.* 10.8.5). Rightly, Pelling 1982: 213. On the negotiations later in January see Chapter 7.
[212] See n. 232.

trustworthy from his point of view, had at this crucial moment broken in Caesar's direction rather than Cato's![213] Nor was this, as it would turn out, the last moment at which the conflict might have been prevented, since Caesar would make one more dramatic concession once he was in Italy.

But the warriors in the Senate had had enough. The consuls advised the tribunes to remove themselves from the meeting for their own safety, clearing the way for the passage on January 7 (~ November 19, Jul.) of the so-called Final Decree of the Senate which called on the magistrates and promagistrates to protect the Republic – only implicitly, but in fact manifestly against Caesar.[214] It was a point of contention whether the tribunes were actually manhandled or in effect driven out of the Senate, but significantly not even Cicero, in the invective against Mark Antony written after Caesar's death, could claim that the consuls had actually respected the tribunes' right of veto:

> [N]either the requests of Rome's leading men nor the warnings of your seniors nor the representations of a full Senate could move you from your corrupt, bought decision. Then it was, after much unsuccessful effort, when no alternative remained, that the stroke fell upon you which few before you have felt and none survived unscathed [the *s.c.u.*].[215]

Presumably their justification for such extra-constitutional action, if they had troubled to give one, would have been that a veto obstructing necessary action to protect the Republic was by that very fact illegitimate – more or less the same dangerously open-ended principle, as we have seen, as that on which C. Marcellus a month or so before had entrusted Pompey with the defense of Italy.[216] Collaborators with the target of the *s.c.u.* thus could be made into

[213] On Pompey's willingness to consider acceptance of Caesar's demand for a consulship rather than seeking to destroy him even by the end of December and early January, see Raaflaub 1974: esp. 42–55, 266–267, 321–322. See Appendix 4.

[214] Caes. *BCiv.* 1.5, 1.7.2–4; Cic. *Fam.* 16.11.2; App. *BCiv.* 2.33/131–132; Dio 41.3.1–2; Plut. *Caes.* 31.2, *Ant.* 5.8–10. Straumann 2016: 92n169 claims that the *s.c.u.* of January 7 was "against Caesar's tribunes" – not strictly against Caesar himself: cf. *in te, Antoni* (Cic. *Phil.* 2.51). Yet the matter was not quite so clear. Strictly speaking, an *s.c.u.* did not normally name its targets explicitly, thus leaving the magistrates some flexibility to interpret their order "to see to it that the state suffer no harm" (Cf. Cicero's identical prejudicial claim against Catiline in 63: *Cat.* 1.3). Girardet 2017: 207–223 points out that Caesar was the real target, as is implied in his own account (1.7). There is little reason to date the expulsion of the tribunes to January 5, with Müller 1972: 4.

[215] Cic. *Phil.* 2.52 (Shackleton Bailey tr.). Dio 41.3.2 plausibly suggests that the consul Lentulus advised the tribunes to leave before the vote of the *s.c.u.* On the expulsion of the tribunes, cf. Raaflaub 1974: 72–79, and 1974a: 321–326. Müller's defense (1972: 91) of Cicero's claim that the tribunes were *nulla vi expulsi* (*Fam.* 16.11.2) is inadequate.

[216] Girardet 2017: 228 with n. 916 believes that as a matter of law an *s.c.u.* could not under any circumstances be vetoed. There is no evidence for this view; there is no reason to think that *any* senatorial decision was immune from veto except where this had been explicitly authorized by a law

targets themselves: Cicero makes clear that the tribunes were in danger as soon as the decree was passed, and according to Appian, a detachment of Pompey's soldiers was already visibly posted around the Curia.[217]

Now Caesar's enemies had only one option left: what might be called in modern parlance "the nuclear option" of blatantly suppressing a tribunician veto. From their viewpoint, probably, Caesar's tribunes had used the veto not just to paralyze the normal exercise of senatorial functions such as provincial assignments but now, as they saw it, to subvert their defense against an existential danger. Yet from the viewpoint of those inclined to believe that the veto was cast in defense of a legitimate public interest, its suppression was as direct a violation of the customary rights of the Roman People as was imaginable. The association of tribunician rights with freedom in the civic ideology of the Roman citizen is strong and clear.[218] The hard-liners had handed Caesar a strong justification for war.[219] From a distant vantage point in time one might dismiss Caesar's defense of the tribunate as a mere pretext, as Suetonius does (*Iul.* 30.1–2); after all, it obviously supervenes upon a crisis that is already close to the breaking point. Yet surely Caesar's argument that his enemies had infringed the freedom of the Roman People by suppressing the rights of the tribunes had real force in its immediate context (why else would Caesar have emphasized it?), especially after those pushing the confrontation with Caesar in Rome had so far treated public opinion with such contempt. In his own account of the onset of the war, Caesar gives this outrage against the constitution the greatest weight in his harangue to the 13th Legion before ordering it to march into Italy. His men shout back at him that they are ready to avenge the injuries done to their commander *and to the tribunes of the plebs.*[220] Other contemporary or near-contemporary evidence corroborates the rhetorical and ideological power of this complaint even if it is also interpreted as mere pretext. Dionysius of Halicarnassus, the Augustan Greek historian, offers a summary that well highlights its political impact:

---

of the Roman People (e.g., the *lex Sempronia* on consular provinces). Yet there can be little doubt that the advocates of the *s.c.u.* – now apparently a majority of the Senate – will have viewed the veto as outrageous and illegitimate.

217 App. *BCiv.* 2.33/132; Cic. *Phil.* 2.51–53 *tum contra te dedit arma hic ordo.* Cf. Caes. *BCiv.* 1.2.3, 1.3.2.
218 See e.g. Cic. *Leg. agr.* 2.15, *Rab. perd.* 12; Sall. *Hist.* 3.48.12; Liv. 3.45.8; *RRC* 473/1. See Morstein-Marx 2004: 51–53, 217–220, 267; Arena 2012: 49–54. For the resonance of *libertas* in Caesar's self-justification and its connection with complaint about the treatment of the tribunes, see esp. Raaflaub 1974: 152–180 and 2003: 50–56; cf. also Weinstock 1971: 133–162, Dobesch 2000: 89–92.
219 *Causa belli*: Cic. *Phil.* 2.53, *Fam.* 6.6.5.
220 Caes. *BCiv.* 1.7.2–6, and §8: *sese paratos esse imperatoris sui tribunorumque plebis iniurias defendere.* (See below for Caesar's second major justification: the defense of his *dignitas.*) Cf. Cic. *Phil.* 2.53: *quid enim aliud ille* [sc. Caesar] *dicebat, quam causam ... afferebat, nisi quod intercessio neglecta, ius tribunicium sublatum, circumscriptus a senatu esset Antonius?*

And indeed the motivating cause, among many others, of the civil war among the Romans which occurred in my day and was greater than any war before it, the cause which seemed more important and sufficient to divide the common-wealth (ἡ κινήσασα πρόφασις ἐπὶ πολλαῖς ἄλλαις δόξασα μείζων εἶναι καὶ <μόνη> ἀποχρῶσα διαστῆσαι τὴν πόλιν), was this – that some of the tribunes, complaining that they had been forcibly driven out of the city by the general who was then in control of affairs in Italy, in order to deprive them henceforth of any power, fled to the general who commanded the armies in Gaul, as having no place to turn to. And the latter, availing himself of this excuse and pretending to come with right and justice to the aid of the sacrosanct magistracy of the people which had been deprived of its authority contrary to the oaths of the forefathers (ὡς ἀρχῇ δήμου παναγεῖ τὸ κράτος ἀφαιρεθείσῃ παρὰ τοὺς ὅρκους τῶν προγόνων αὐτὸς ὁσίως καὶ σὺν δίκῃ βοηθῶν) entered the city himself in arms and restored the men to their office. (Dion. Hal. *Ant. Rom.* 8.87.7–8)

Even if the complaint about the suppression of tribunician rights was essentially a pretext at this late stage, it would be hard to deny that that offense was emblematic of the larger contempt for the political rights of the People displayed by those who had pushed and were pushing for a military solution to their Caesar problem: their efforts to undermine or interpret away an inconvenient law of the Roman People, and above all, their manifest and overriding objective of using "every means necessary" to prevent the Roman People from electing Caesar to a second time, as everyone knew they would do if they were only allowed the opportunity.

As for the "Final Decree of the Senate" for whose passage the tribunes' veto had to be cleared away: its propriety could be and was vigorously disputed. Caesar complains in his *Civil War Commentaries* that the decree was intended to deal with urban violence and insurrection, not (he implies) disputes with proconsuls or stubborn vetoes; in any case, the Senate, he implies, was not its own master but was under constraint, browbeaten and intimidated by his personal enemies.[221] But there were in fact a few arguable precedents: the *s.c.u.* passed against Sulla during his return to Italy in 83, the decree used against the turncoat Sullan proconsul Lepidus in 77, perhaps also that which authorized action against Manlius and his allies in 63.[222] The key point for our purposes, however, is that the *s.c.u.* was in effect

---

[221] Caes. *BCiv.* 1.5.3, 1.7.5–6. It merits greater attention that, like Sallust (*Cat.* 29.2–3: *more Romano!*), Caesar does not object to the use of the *s.c.u.* in itself (Ungern-Sternberg 1970: 108–110). (Note that in 48 and 47 the Caesarian Senate passed the *s.c.u.* twice, albeit in Caesar's absence: Dio 42.23.2, 29.3, 32.1; Plut. *Ant.* 9.4.) This undercuts the idea that the *s.c.u.* was a strictly "optimate" instrument (Arena 2012: 200–220).

[222] Jul. Exsup. 7; Sall. *Hist.* 1.77.22; Sall. *Cat.* 29. Ungern-Sternberg 1970 remains fundamental for the history of the instrument; cf. recently Golden 2013.

a declaration of war. (Recall Cicero's language in the *Second Philippic* (quoted p. 308): "The stroke fell upon you which few before you have felt and none survived unscathed.") Unlike Scipio's vetoed motion, it was no longer simply an ultimatum: it did not take a conditional form, so it offered no alternative to conflict, nor was there any reason or precedent that would lead one to expect that any response whatever from Caesar would cause it to be rescinded.[223] Moreover, this "Final Decree" was almost immediately followed, according to Dio, by a formal declaration of *tumultus* or "state of war in Italy": the war was on, as far as the Senate was concerned.[224]

Note, then, that it was the Senate, not Caesar a few days afterward, that actually "crossed the Rubicon" on January 7 in the metaphorical sense of the phrase ("to take a decisive or irrevocable step at a critical moment of some undertaking or enterprise").[225] Since whenever Asinius Pollio penned his version of what was already then more than a decade of civil war (sometime in the 30s), historians and poets have focused their story of the opening of the Civil War of 49–45 on Caesar's physical crossing of the actual Rubicon River, the administrative boundary between Cisalpine Gaul, his province, and Italy, where the consuls' *imperium* was paramount. This is misleading in several ways, as I shall show in the next chapter, but one illusion this idea encourages is that by this powerful symbol of transgression Caesar is made to appear self-evidently as an aggressor. Upon reflection this makes little sense. The Senate's "Final Decree" of January 7 could hardly be interpreted by contemporaries as anything short of a declaration of war – surely the more decisive step in the triggering of the Civil War than Caesar's reaction to it.

"Saving the Republic"

It is clear that the engineers of the *s.c.u.* of January 7 sought Caesar's political if not physical extinction. What did they fear so much?[226] It is easy

---

[223] The only possible precedent for a *s.c.u.* that did not culminate in state-sponsored military action is the dubious case of 62 (Chapter 3, n. 98). If that single instance be excluded, all five known precedents for the *s.c.u.* had resulted in state-sponsored military action and violent conflict. (See Ungern-Sternberg 1970: 148 for a convenient list.)

[224] Dio 41.3.3: ταραχήν τε εἶναι ἔγνωσαν; cf. Suet. *Iul.* 34.1 with Butler-Cary 1927: 86; Golden 2013: 145n123. Rice Holmes 1923: 2:354 and Girardet 2017: 221 with n. 896. Note that Dio's implied chronology places the *tumultus* decree *before* news can have arrived of the Rubicon crossing (probably not earlier than the 13th), in which case it was proactive, not reactive.

[225] *OED*, s.v. Rubicon (phrases).

[226] The role of fear is explicitly cited by Cic. *Brut.* 7: *cum patrocinium pacis exclusum est aut errore hominum aut timore*, and is palpable in key passages such at *Att.* 7.8.4–5, 7.9.3. See Jehne 2001: 77, 2005: 39–40, and 2017: 203–204, 208–215.

to extrapolate from the experience of Caesar's first consulship that some of the very men who played a leading role in the rush toward war in 50–49 (mostly obviously and consistently M. Cato) had long sought an opportunity for a reckoning that would prove to Caesar himself and to all who came after him that no consul should escape the constraints imposed on him by his fellow senators by unleashing the largely irresistible power of the popular assemblies. From this perspective Caesar had not only escaped that reckoning during and after his consulship but he had also been rewarded with unprecedented tokens of glory (both popular and senatorial) during his long, successful wars in Gaul. Now he sought a hero's return, a second consulship, and a (no doubt) brilliant triumph that would render him untouchable for the near term at least. Denying him these rewards was therefore essential if they were to avoid living in his shadow for the rest of his life. From the perspective of Caesar's enemies the stakes could not be higher.[227] In their eyes Caesar had been "stronger than the whole Republic" in 59, and yet he was much stronger now.[228] "Nothing is more frightening than Caesar as consul [again]," the argument ran;[229] that, in these men's eyes, would be tantamount to "enslavement."[230]

It is likely that in this effort Cato and his followers were inspired by his great-grandfather's successful effort to bring down the Caesar of his age, P. Scipio Africanus.[231] As we have seen, the analogy between the two military heroes was clear. Starting with Pompey, the younger Cato had made the frustration of powerful military figures the guiding principle of his policy, steadfastly pursued by unparalleled exploitation of all the obstructive tactics available. He had failed repeatedly, even indirectly causing the alliance between Pompey, Caesar, and Crassus, until, in a remarkable example of politics making strange bedfellows, he and his faction had actually proposed Pompey's (strictly unconstitutional) sole

---

[227] Meier 1982: 1–2, 222–223, 346 (11, 275–276, 419 in the original); Raaflaub 1974: 20–21n24, 148, 317–327; Jehne 2001: 76–78 and 2005: 38–40.

[228] Cic. *Att.* 7.9.3: *"at tum* [in his first consulship] *imbecillus plus"* inquit *"valuit quam tota res publica. quid nunc putas."* The imaginary quotation is apparently of Pompey. Cf. 7.8.5 *"quid censes"* aiebat [sc. Pompeius] *"facturum esse ipsum, si in possessionem rei publicae venerit, cum haec quaestor eius infirmus et inops* [sc. Antonius] *audeat dicere?"*

[229] Cic. *Att.* 7.9.3: *ut quidam putant, nihil est timendum magis quam ille consul.* On *quidam*, see n. 186. Pompey, Cicero adds, was sure that a second consulship for Caesar would amount to the "subversion of the constitution" (Shackleton Bailey's tr. of σύγχυσις τῆς πολιτείας) even if he gave up his army (7.8.4).

[230] Cic. *Att.* 7.7.5 *sub regno;* 7.7.7: *"depugna"* inquis *"potius quam servias"* (Atticus's imagined interjection); 7.9.3 *"depugnes oportet, nisi concedis"* (an imaginary quotation of Caesar). *cum bona quidem spe, ut ait idem* (here apparently Pompey) *vel vincendi vel in libertate moriendi.*

[231] See n. 116. For Cato the Elder's role see Liv. 38.54.1–2.

consulship in 52. With this extraordinary revision of principle but with Pompey now recruited to the cause, he and his like could seriously contemplate Caesar's destruction. (Surely Pompey would have been next, if he did not exploit military victory to establish his own domination over Cato.)

The example of Scipio Africanus helps to focus our mind on just what kind of "enslavement" Caesar's enemies were talking about. This is clearly not literal enslavement, surely not even a "monarchy" or "autocracy" in a literal sense, although the word *regnum* had so often been used as the rhetorical justification for the assassination and extralegal murder of politicians (e.g. Tiberius Gracchus) who could be argued to be on the verge of escaping the restraints of the constitution. When Cicero, in a letter to one of the Pompeian de facto exiles in 46, retrospectively contemplates the possible future closed off by the Civil War, he describes it as one in which Caesar would have been "a distinguished civilian and a leading citizen, but would not have as much power as he now has."[232] His references to Caesar's possible second consulship imply that he assumed that he would have dismissed or separated himself from his army by the time he actually took office.[233] As outraged as Cicero was by Caesar's "impudent" disobedience to the Senate, he was generally consistent in viewing a future with Caesar preeminent as far preferable to the catastrophe of civil war, which as the wars of the 80s among Marius, Cinna, and Sulla had shown, was by its very nature bound to bring one master or another.[234]

This difference of opinion between men who thought like Cicero and those who thought like Cato needs to be highlighted because too often, it seems to me, scholars have failed to ask whether the fears of the latter were in fact fully justified. Cicero would in fact turn out to be correct; just how correct, one can only see with the benefit of hindsight. The state of civil war that Pompey, Cato, and their allies launched in 49 would, through its own internal dynamics, ultimately end only in 31 with Octavian's final victory, and among the casualties of the nearly twenty years of civil war would be

---

[232] Cic. *Fam.* 6.6.5 (to A. Caecina): *ea me suasisse Pompeio quibus ille si paruisset esset hic* [sc. Caesar] *quidem clarus in toga et princeps, sed tantas opes quantas nunc habet non haberet. Princeps* must here of course be read against the background of the republican conception of the word ("leaders of the state" or "leading senators": Morstein-Marx 2004: 263n83), not its later, euphemistic usage denoting the emperors. The passage probably refers to the final negotiations in early January (n. 206).

[233] Cic. *Att.* 7.8.4, 7.9.3.

[234] Cic. *Att.* 7.3.4, 7.5.4, 7.7.7 a complaint Cicero often repeats once military operations begin (Chapter 7, n. 270). Outrage: 7.9.4. Cicero's fear of civil war was exacerbated by his belief in Caesar's superior strength as well as the kind of people who would throw in their lot with him: 7.3.5, 7.5.5, 7.6.2, 7.7.6–7.

the Republic itself. Can anyone seriously maintain that a second consulship for Caesar would have been worse? Humans are of course not blessed
with foresight or future hindsight, so the question is somewhat unfair. But
even within the cognitive horizons of the historical actors of the year 49,
Cicero's skepticism about the "rush to war" he was witnessing suffices to
cast some doubt on the assumption, which seems to be widely shared
among scholars, that accommodating Caesar's demands in this case would
have been tantamount to signing the Republic's death warrant.

The change in Pompey must have been especially exasperating for
Caesar. It must have seemed obvious that if he could only regain the
trust of Pompey, who had cooperated with him for nine years – most of
that time as his son-in-law – Caesar would be able to gain all he wanted
without the terrible risks of war. Hence his persistent attempts upon his
march into Italy to meet Pompey and resolve their differences face to
face.[235] Caesar must have asked himself, as we know Cicero did, why
Pompey had built him up as recently as 52 if only to tear him down.[236]
Yet even Pompey may not have been sure where he stood with Caesar as
late as December 50.[237] As we have seen, even during the last-minute
negotiations of early January Pompey seemed open to averting the looming
catastrophe by means of an extraordinary concession on the part of his
former father-in-law, pressed by none other than Cicero, that would defuse
the military confrontation and divest Caesar of almost his entire army
while still allowing his candidacy in the next election (49 for 48).[238] Yet
Cato and Lentulus were able to prevent him from being "fooled again" by
Caesar; we must probably assume that Caesar's obstinacy through the year
50 (as he would have seen it) despite his own attempts at a reasonable
accommodation had pushed Pompey far in the direction of the hard-liners
and destroyed the trust on which any renewed cooperation would have to
be based.

In Caesar's own account of the meetings that led to the "Final Decree"
on January 7 the Senate is cowed and dominated by the hard-liners rather
than engaging in proper deliberation; since it is thus deprived of honest
agency, its votes lack authority and any true legitimacy.[239] The account is

---

[235] Caes. *BCiv.* 1.4.4, 1.7.1, 1.8.3, 1.9.6, 1.11.3, 1.24.5, 1.32.3; cf. his letter of March 49 at [Cic.] *Att.* 9.7C.2.
At the time of the negotiations in late January Cicero expected that the two were about to return to
their former collaborative relationship, for "I had learned by experience how hand in glove they
were" (Cic. *Att.* 10.8.5; Chapter 7, p. 344f.).

[236] Caes. *BCiv.* 1.32.3: *qui si improbasset* [sc. the Law of the Ten Tribunes], *cur ferri passus est? si
probasset, cur se uti populo beneficio prohibuisset?* Cicero repeatedly raises the question: see n. 121.

[237] See n. 168. Note also Pompey's conciliatory words to Caesar early in January (Caes. *BCiv.* 1.8.2–4).

[238] See p. 306ff.   [239] See n. 200.

blatantly tendentious, yet perhaps not a fundamental misrepresentation given the overwhelming vote in favor of mutual disarmament only a few weeks before and Cicero's evidence that the overwhelming majority wanted to avoid civil war. It is clear that Pompey continued to make subtle and not so subtle threats: toward the end of December he warned Cicero sternly against "the dangers of a false peace" – that is, allowing Caesar to become consul *even if* he gave up his army first – and gave him (and other senators) to understand that if they did not take a tough line he would withdraw to Spain and leave them at Caesar's mercy; Cicero himself worried mightily about being seen to part company with Pompey even though his real preference was decidedly for peace.[240] The majority of senators were probably alarmed by Caesar's apparent intransigence (and perhaps not very sensitive to his fears)[241] and, though hoping for peace, were increasingly resigned to some kind of forceful action to end the stalemate so long as Pompey could be counted on to protect them. By making a strong push at the top backed by reassurances of Pompey's support if they acted forcefully against Caesar (as well as sowing fear for what would happen if they did not) the anti-Caesar faction, here led by the consul L. Lentulus Crus, Pompey's new father-in-law, Q. Metellus Scipio, and M. Cato, was at last able to rally a senatorial majority in favor of two highly aggressive motions against Caesar, and simply to push the tribunes aside when the inevitable vetoes were cast. Yet as we shall see in detail in the next chapter, the Senate was in fact deeply divided once the confrontation devolved into military operations; a sizable minority of senators actually joined Caesar's side once war broke out, and many others (probably constituting a majority when added to the committed Caesarians) would reject Pompey's severe threats against all those who declined to leave Rome and Italy.

But in giving the Senate what they viewed as a necessary and salutary shove toward war, Pompey and Caesar's enemies crossed a clear red line. Most obviously they had trampled the rights of the tribunes, which were of

---

[240] Cic. *Att.* 7.1.4, 7.3.5, 7.6.2, 7.7.5–6, 7.9.3. "False peace": Cic. *Att.* 7.8.4: *de pacis simulatae periculis* (clarified by 7.9.3 *istuc ipsum "sic" magnum malum putat aliquis*). Spain: 7.9.3, more diplomatically stated by Pompey's new father-in-law, Metellus Scipio (Caes. op. cit. 1.1.4 *si cunctetur* [sc. *senatus*] *atque agat lenius, nequiquam eius auxilium, si postea velit, senatum imploraturum*). Everyone knew what he meant.

[241] Note, for instance, that Cicero himself cannot conceive of why Caesar does not just give up his army, come to Rome, and accept the (seemingly inevitable) consulship: *Att.* 7.9.3–4. It is common for adversaries in a crisis to underestimate the fears on the other side; after all, they know that *they themselves* are trustworthy and assume that the other side should be able to recognize this as well. Acquaintance with the Prisoner's Dilemma would have helped Cicero to understand.

course simultaneously cherished rights of the People (Polyb. 6.16.4–5). They never seem to have sought to make their case to the People that it was necessary to fight a war to preserve their "freedom" from Caesar,[242] and popular enthusiasm for peace had been clear, especially, for example, after the 370–22 vote in the Senate for mutual disarmament, which seemed at the time to ward off the threat of civil war. The violations of popular rights by the anti-Caesar hard-liners as they made their final push for war are rarely emphasized in modern accounts of the coming of the Caesarian Civil War, in accordance with now rather old-fashioned notions that equate the republican constitution with senatorial dominance. This is a mistake: not only does it encourage us to overlook what was certainly a highly signifi-cant factor in the development and culmination of the crisis, not to mention the Pompeians' rapid abandonment of Italy; it also inadvertently colludes in the suppression of popular agency which our elite sources share and against which we should be continually on our guard.

One very practical reason to consult the People about a war is to make sure they are ready to fight, but the anti-Caesar faction seems to have forgotten this bit of common sense at this dangerous juncture. Both before and after Caesar's entry into Italy the Roman *plebs* was seen to be entirely in Caesar's camp,[243] and wide swathes of Italy seem to have been remarkably welcoming to the "rebellious" proconsul as he swept into the peninsula – a fact that is easy to attribute to factors that have little to do with principle but gain force when we recall that even among *equites* and senators Cicero reports as late as mid-December a widespread willingness to grant Caesar's "impudent" demands.[244] Even after the outbreak of hostilities sympathy or support for Caesar remained strong among the urban plebs and all levels of society in the towns of Italy, while the social and political elites (*equites* and senators) were deeply divided. Hermann Strasburger's oft-repeated claim that Caesar's reaction prompted unanimous revulsion even among those in

---

[242] Rightly noted by Raaflaub 1974: 102–103, with 65n260; cf. idem, 2003: 53. In addition to Curio's *contio* cited in n. 155, pro-Caesarian *contiones* held in December by Curio and Antony are known from Plut. *Caes.* 30.3 (with *Pomp.* 59.3, *Ant.* 5.5); Dio 40.66.5; Cic. *Att.* 7.8.5. Plut. *Pomp.* 58.4: αἱ μέντοι Κουρίωνος ἀξιώσεις καὶ παρακλήσεις ὑπὲρ Καίσαρος ἐφαίνοντο δημοτικώτεραι surely implies that Curio held various *contiones* throughout the crisis since at least March, as we should anyway expect: he needed to justify his continuous veto.

[243] Cic. *Att.* 7.3.5, 7.7.6, 8.3.4–5 (*multitudo et infimus quisque*), 10.4.8, 10.8.6; Plut. *Caes.* 30.2, *Cat. Min.* 51.5 (cf. *Pomp.* 61.2); Dio 41.6.1. Further sources in Raaflaub 1974: 65n260; cf. Brunt 1986: 27n73.

[244] Sources n. 122; once military movements begin, see 8.3.4, 8.13.2, generally corroborating Caesar's account (*BCiv.* 1.12–15), which despite its partisan perspective seems therefore to be close to the truth. There is no reason why this should not actually reflect pro-Caesar feeling throughout Italy of the same intensity we observed in Rome in the mid-to-late 50s (Chapter 5; Morstein-Marx 2007: 176n83). See Chapter 7, p. 399ff.

Caesar's own camp depends on the assumption that only "respectable opinion" should count (thus effectively excluding those below equestrian status) and is even on its own terms a selective and insufficiently nuanced reading of the evidence – overwhelmingly Ciceronian in origin and perspective – on which his judgment was based.[245] The problems of morale and recruitment woes that the Pompeians suffered during the opening campaign of the war also bear out this suspicion and confirm the analysis. The leaders of the anti-Caesar strategy at the end of 50 and beginning of 49 did not trouble themselves to try to justify their "rush to war" to the Roman People. What would have happened on January 7, 49, if they had been given their say? Were they not entitled to that much according to the norms that governed the Republic?

The neglect, even abandonment of the public sphere by Caesar's enemies was no accident or slip of the mind. Had they tried to make their case publicly they would certainly have failed: the People would not have agreed to be saved from themselves. Before we dismiss this as a typical example of the shortsightedness of the mob, ever ready for a master (a stereotype into which the modern advocates of senatorial dominance sometimes risk falling), we should recall that Caesar was asking to be consul for a second time, not king, dictator, or tyrant. And among the basic ground rules of the Republic was the absolute right of the People to choose their officials.[246] The election of a Roman consul was not normally a contest of political ideologies but a contest of virtue – that is, of the candidates' "worthiness" (*dignitas*) for the "gift" (*beneficium*) of *honor* (normal Latin for an elected magistracy) that was conferred by the People's choice. It is through this nexus of ideas that Caesar's other main justification for standing firm against the assaults of his enemies – his right to defend his *dignitas*, by appealing to his army if necessary – needs to be understood.[247] For from the perspective of the ordinary Roman citizen, to attack Caesar's *dignitas* by taking away his right, established by a law of the Roman People, to be elected in his absence to a second consulship was not merely a personal affront to him but a violation of two fundamental rights of the Roman People, one legislative and one electoral.

---

[245] Strasburger 1968: 34–43, considered in detail in Chapter 7, p. 364ff.

[246] Polyb. 6.14.3–5; cf. §9: καὶ μὴν τὰς ἀρχὰς ὁ δῆμος δίδωσι τοῖς ἀξίοις· ὅπερ ἐστὶ κάλλιστον ἆθλον ἐν πολιτείᾳ καλοκἀγαθίας. "By the laws of Tullius and Romulus the People were sovereign over elections and could repeal or confirm whatever laws they liked pertaining to these things" (App. *Pun.* 112/531; Chapter 1, p. 11ff).

[247] For Caesar's well-known invocation (explicit or implicit) of his need to defend his *dignitas*, see Cic. *Att.* 7.11.1, 9.11A.2, Caes. *BCiv.* 1.7.7, 1.22.5, 1.32.2–6, etc. See Morstein-Marx 2009.

All Roman citizens were taught to hate *regnum*, the antithesis to the *libertas* every Roman citizen had cherished ever since the oath their ancestors had according to tradition sworn at the foundation of the Republic. This much is evident from our knowledge of the oratory of *contiones*, in which senatorial speakers who wish to mobilize popular resentment against anyone by preference turn to fearmongering about *regnum*.[248] Yet despite the fact that in the late Republic some senators (Cicero and Brutus most notably) developed the doctrine of "preventive tyrannicide" to justify the assassination of a series of popular heroes from the Gracchi to Publius Clodius on the grounds that they aspired to *regnum*, or were in practice already de facto *reges*, there is little evidence that the Roman citizenry as a whole adhered to the idea, often treated by scholars as if it were a constitutional axiom of the Republic, that no politician could be allowed to rise so far above his peers in the Senate that they could not control him collectively. Despite the prominence of this idea in some famous Ciceronian texts and its palpable presence below the surface in some famous historical episodes, including the second-century downfall of Scipio Africanus, in the Forum where the Senate met the People the policing of senatorial cohesion and of senatorial equilibrium is not conspicuously invoked in public communication and deliberation before and among the general citizenry.[249] This seems therefore to have been a largely internal, aristocratic norm, chiefly of concern to other senators. To judge from our evidence of fully public communication – mass speeches – the Roman People were able to distinguish between potential threats to the liberty of the *res publica* and potential threats to the full political independence of *senators*, and it was the former that interested them, the latter not so much.[250] To be sure, a politician who through his overweening popularity escaped the control of the Senate might conceivably become a threat to the People's *libertas*, but before 49 that would have required a rather abstract stretch of the imagination. There was no precedent for it. On the other hand, the threat to the People's *libertas* presented by *pauci potentes* ("the powerful few," = "the oligarchy") again and again from the days of Tiberius Gracchus to Sulla and beyond was clear enough to any *contio* goer and probably most legionary soldiers as well. *Regnum* was understood by the general populace in broader terms than mere "monarchy": domineering rule by a clique or junta was the kind of *regnum* the

[248] Morstein-Marx 2004: 208.

[249] The Ciceronian texts are well known, among them *Cat.* 1.3–4, *Mil.* 72–100, *Off.* 3.82–83. For Brutus see *RRC* 433/2, Ascon. 36C. See Lintott 1968/1999: 52–66 and Pina Polo 2006.

[250] Morstein-Marx 2009: 115–117. See Morstein-Marx 2004: 204–240 and 2013: 39–43 for complementary sketches of "popular ideology" drawn respectively from mass oratory and *popularis* legislation. Morstein-Marx (forthcoming) offers a recent survey.

Roman People had most reason to fear in history both ancient and recent.[251] The actions of the *pauci potentes* in the Caesarian crisis of 50–49 (arguably entirely of their own making) will hardly have encouraged public trust.

Those senators who were committed to Caesar's destruction in January 49 were therefore not self-evidently identifiable with "the Republic," although many modern scholars have not shied away from accepting their self-representation as such.[252] Caesar too could and did claim to be "defending the Republic,"[253] and he had in most respects the more credible case, certainly for the average Roman voter and *contio* goer. In justifying his part in the outbreak of the Civil War as a defense of his *dignitas*, Caesar invoked a fundamental republican ideal of reciprocal exchange between the People and their chosen leaders, in which the very purpose of the coin of *honor* and *dignitas* was to repay excellent service to the Republic (*merita in rem publicam* or *res gestae*). When Caesar declared that he set *dignitas* before life itself he was echoing a commonplace of Roman public life which would have come just as readily to the lips of a Cicero.[254] At the climactic moment of the whole *Civil War Commentaries*, just before the charge at Pharsalus, Caesar writes that his front-rank centurion Crastinus called upon his men to follow him and do their duty for their commander: "This one battle remains," he is supposed to have cried, "and through it he will recover his *dignitas* and we, our freedom."[255] Why "freedom"? The battle cry itself may be Caesarian invention, but it crisply encapsulates the complementary thrust of Caesar's two-sided republican argument. The *libertas populi Romani* had

---

[251] Morstein-Marx 2004: 218–219. Ancient: the *decemviri* of Roman historical legend, well known to contional crowds (ibid., 77, 183, 221) and clearly invoked by Cicero in his second speech *de lege agraria* (2.15 *decem reges*).

[252] See Chapter 7.

[253] App. *BCiv.* 2.32/128: τιμωρὸς αὐτίκα τῇ πατρίδι, and Caes. *BCiv.* 1.22.5, quoted n. 257. The Caesarian view is also reflected in Q. Tubero's speech against Ligarius (delivered in 46, ORF 175.I.4, p. 528): *inter quem* [sc. Pompeium] *et Caesarem dignitatis fuerit contentio, cum salvam uterque rem publicam vellet.*

[254] Caes. *BCiv.* 1.9.2, with Morstein-Marx 2009: 128 with n. 53.

[255] Caes. *BCiv* 3.91.2: *Unum hoc proelium superest; quo confecto et ille [sc. Caesar] suam dignitatem et nos nostram libertatem reciperabimus.* Cf. Cic. *Lig.* 18 *tua (sc. Caesaris) quid aliud arma voluerunt nisi a te contumeliam propulsare? Quid egit tuus invictus exercitus, nisi uti suum ius tueretur et dignitatem tuam?* The defense of *libertas*, along with other "mother-and-apple-pie" terms like *patria parentesque*, is a topos of battlefield exhortation (cf. Sall. *Iug.* 87.2, where *libertas*, if it denoted anything specific at all, could only have referred to the possibility of enslavement if captured), yet it is surely a mistake to dismiss its significance in a work that begins with the expulsion of tribunes, the intimidation of the Senate, and the servitude of the Roman People to a faction. Raaflaub 2003: 57n72 argued that Crastinus's *libertas* meant only citizenship; contra, Morstein-Marx 2009: 124–125. Against Mannsperger's redating to 48 or 47 of the famous "Palikanus" denarius with LIBERTATIS (and the Rostra) on the reverse (*RRC* 473/1), see now Woytek's recent defense of Crawford's date (45 BC): 2003: 306–307; this further weakens Raaflaub's suggestion (2003: 56f.) that Caesar abandoned *libertas* as a propagandistic talking point in the course of the Civil War.

been lost along with Caesar's *dignitas* when his enemies had exploited their factional and military power to attempt to suppress or get around the Law of the Ten Tribunes, tried to subvert his inevitable election as consul for the second time, refused to submit any accounting before the People for their moves against him, and finally had suppressed the tribunes' veto by intimidation or expulsion, a culminating act that crowned a series of offenses against the People's ancient rights.

Among the most dangerous constitutional crises for a republic or a democracy are those in which both sides are zealously animated by the certain conviction that they are right. Our own political moment shows us that little is more toxic than the conviction that the other side in a political dispute has cheated and will stop at nothing to use their partisan interpretation of the rules as a weapon against oneself. Instead of imagining that the mass of Roman citizens had lost their allegiance to republican government and demonstrated this by their embrace of Caesar we should suppose that they mostly embraced Caesar because they thought he was right.[256] So, when he returned to Italy at the head of an army in the late fall of 50 (by the Julian equivalent), Caesar was able to declare plausibly that "he had not left his province for the sake of doing harm but in order [among other things] to restore freedom both for himself and the Roman People after they had been crushed by an oligarchic faction (*ut se et populum Romanum factione paucorum oppressum in libertatem vindicaret*)."[257] Had this struggle been only about Caesar's personal honor, it is hard to believe that so many would have been prepared to follow him at enormous risk to their safety and fortunes. Whatever may have been Caesar's secret thoughts and intentions, the men who marched with him did not have to tell themselves that they were rebelling against the Senate or, worse yet, overthrowing the Republic. On the contrary, rather like Sulla and his army in 88, they would have told themselves that they were marching "to liberate it from a faction."[258]

---

[256] Raaflaub 1974: 171–172: "Practically the entire political argument of Caesar in the *Bellum Civile* rests directly or indirectly on decisions of the Roman People or takes their opinion and interests into account." For the view that ordinary Roman citizens were alienated from the Republic see esp. Brunt 1988: 1–92, 240–280, and in a larger frame, Morstein-Marx and Rosenstein 2006: 630–633.

[257] Caes. *BCiv.* 1.22.5. Here Caesar manifestly borrows from the topoi of invidious popular, especially tribunician, oratory in the *contio*, for which Sallust's speeches of Memmius and Macer are our best samples (*Iug.* 31, *Hist.* 3.48). Augustus echoes the assertion at the opening of his *Res gestae* (1.1), but Caesar should not be tainted retroactively by the cynicism of his heir's assertion.

[258] On Sulla see Morstein-Marx 2011. For a different assessment of Caesar's *dignitas* claim see now Peer 2015: 41–58. In my view, she downplays the republican history and resonance of the term. However I do not pretend to be able to penetrate Caesar's true, innermost motives.

CHAPTER 7

Taking Sides

It is customary for scholars to describe Caesar's crossing of the Rubicon River, which separated his province of Cisalpine Gaul from the administrative district of Italy, as an act of open rebellion against the Senate, the "Government," or even "the Republic" itself, with which Caesar, the clear aggressor, initiated the civil war that would have such weighty consequences for the Roman world. This deceptively simple statement of fact is, however, wrong or seriously misleading in virtually every respect. As we have already seen in the previous chapter, it was not Caesar's crossing of the Rubicon but the Senate's Final Decree of January 7, 49, that precipitated the military phrase of the crisis. Even so, despite this virtual declaration of war, and despite Caesar's swift reaction of crossing the Rubicon into Italy with one legion, I will show in this chapter that until Pompey's departure from Brundisium in mid-March it remained uncertain to contemporaries whether there truly was a war on or whether the military movements that ensued in Italy were the prelude to the conclusion of a settlement between the two former allies and *adfines*, now adversaries. Furthermore, we shall see that the Senate itself, true to its wobbly vacillation through most of the year 50, was deeply divided as senators were now forced to choose sides or find a safe middle ground between the two parties in contention. The rights and wrongs of the issues of the emerging conflict were by no means clear-cut even for senators, and how best to respond was even less so, as even the correspondence of Cicero – an *imperium*-holding general of the anti-Caesarian forces – will show. And the Roman People – not merely the urban plebs but, especially after Caesar made good on his claims not to engage in fighting a civil war with the savagery familiar from the recent past, citizens high and low throughout the peninsula – tended to support Caesar and turn their backs on the Pompeian war effort as the situation unfolded. Since, as we have seen in the previous chapter, a strong case could be made that

Caesar's enemies had tried to force a military conflict in defiance of the will of the People, of law, and of important republican norms, the failure not only of the People but of most senators to oppose Caesar's reentry into Italy under arms, or even to follow Pompey's lead, may be seen not simply as a pragmatic reflection of the military situation as Italy fell bloodlessly into Caesar's hands but as an unsurprising manifestation of an authentic division of political opinion. Caesar's enemies did not have an unproblematic claim to represent the Republic, the *Senatus Populusque Romanus*, and many Roman citizens must have felt that Caesar's claims were in fact the better ones.

Across the Rubicon

News of the expulsion of the tribunes and the passing of the Senate's Final Decree on January 7, 49 (~ ca. November 22, 50, Jul., for the civil calendar was now nearly seven weeks in advance of the seasons) must have flown up the Via Flaminia to Caesar, who was waiting about 350 kilometers away at Ravenna, the first significant city north of the administrative boundary of Italy.[1] The urgent message probably sped well ahead of the tribunes themselves: the best interpretation of our contradictory texts seems to be that Caesar met the tribunes only *after* he had reached Ariminum, the first city of Italy across the Rubicon, although he had received the news of the Final Decree *before* he had crossed.[2] We have no direct testimony of the date of the crossing, which is usually reckoned to have taken place on the night of January 10–11 because our texts suggest that a bit short of three full days of travel would constitute a very fast

[1] Caes. *BCiv.* 1.5.5: *eo tempore* [viz., the tribunes' flight to Caesar, January 7–10?] *erat Ravennae expectabatque suis lenissimis postulatis responsa.* Girardet 2017: 239–246 argues, against the plain meaning of that passage, that immediately after January 7 Caesar had moved to a location much closer to the Italian boundary – namely, Caesena just north of the Rubicon, from whence he claims the overnight dash to Ariminum began. Cf. also Appendix 5.
[2] Bicknell and Nielsen 1998: 138n3. Meeting the tribunes at Ariminum: Caes. *BCiv.* 1.8.1; Suet. *Iul.* 33, as well, apparently, as Dio 41.4.1, Caelius ad Cic. *Fam.* 8.17.1, and Lucan 1.261ff. for what it's worth. But Plut. *Caes.* 31.3 and apparently App. *BCiv.* 2.33–35/133–137 put the meeting north of the Rubicon. (Pelling 2011: 310 with n. 19 suspects there were two harangues; Bicknell and Nielsen 1998: 143–147 offer a partisan explanation for the discrepancy.) As for Caesar's address to the 13th Legion (*BCiv.* 1.7), it seems likely, given the need for secrecy, that he has moved this from Ariminum "back" to Ravenna in order to justify his movements to his readers in advance. Suet. *Iul.* 33 and Dio 41.4.1 plausibly place the harangue at Ariminum, and it was this tradition in defiance of Caesar's own account that inspired the pseudo-ancient inscription still standing in Rimini that purports to commemorate Caesar's address to his troops there (*CIL* 11.34*; Laurence 1999a: 188–189 Gregori 2015: 58–59, with a good photograph; Raaflaub (ed.) 2017: 315, however, describes it as a "copy" of an ancient monument). See n. 38 for another late forgery making a link with this famous episode.

(though not record-setting) pace for a high-ranking official to make the 300-kilometer journey from Rome.[3] Yet there is nothing sacred about this date, which might be a day late or possibly as much as a few days too early.[4]

The Crossing of the Rubicon has become an iconic moment subject to impressive elaboration in the mind's eye, various art media, and even popular culture. Probably most people (perhaps even some historians) picture it in a manner rather like this inspiring nineteenth-century illustration, with Caesar on horseback (preferably a *white* horse) fording a river in broad daylight at the head of his troops, perhaps even pointing the way with drawn sword:

Figure 7.1 "The crossing of the Rubicon" in the collective imagination. Illustration in J. C. Ridpath's *Cyclopedia of Universal History* (Boston 1885), vol. 1, p. 796

[3] See now Raaflaub and Ramsey 2017a: 180 and Ramsey and Raaflaub 2017: 188. Note that Caesar's travel between Ravenna and Ariminum took place in the night; had he been observed during the day he would almost certainly have found Ariminum closed to him (see nn. 7, 8). For the relevant travel times, cf. App. *BCiv.* 2.32/127 (Curio's three-day journey, ostensibly very fast, bringing Caesar's letter from *Ravenna*, some 50 kilometers closer than Ariminum, to Rome (the number of *stades* is given variously in the manuscripts); Caes. *BCiv.* 3.6 for L. Piso's and L. Roscius's request of six days in which to complete a round trip from Rome to Ariminum, including a meeting with Caesar. An urgent messenger with horse relays would have been faster; for some speed records see Laurence 1999: 81; cf. Raaflaub and Ramsey 2017: 6–8.

[4] Müller 1972: 7–11, reviewing earlier views, some of which run as late as January 12, 15, and 20. Note that when Cicero wrote from Rome to Tiro on January 12 he apparently had still not heard of Caesar's move to Ariminum (Cic. *Fam.* 14.11). If news of that event prompted the panicked withdrawal from Rome, this could place the crossing as late as the 13th or even the 14th.

Images very like this one have been put before our eyes again and again by artists such as A. Yvon (painting: *César*, 1875) and J.-L. Gerome (statuette: *César franchissant le Rubicon*, ca. 1900), not to mention the hugely successful HBO *ROME* miniseries of 2005. Yet all four of the key elements of the traditional picture are wrong: Caesar actually crossed the Rubicon *riding in a fast carriage*[5] *over a bridge*,[6] in the *dark of night*,[7] *long after* a band of troops that he had sent ahead to secure Ariminum in the night to ensure that it would not close his gates to him when he arrived.[8] Subterfuge and speed were absolutely essential if Caesar wanted to enter the first town across the provincial boundary in Italy peacefully and without incident; he had every reason to avoid bloodshed, as we shall see. And so, while on the previous day he had awaited news from Rome, Caesar conspicuously occupied himself until the prior evening not just across the provincial boundary at the Rubicon, where his lurking would certainly have been seen as ominous, but well back at Ravenna – probably at least

---

[5] A hired ζεῦγος driven at a gallop (δρόμῳ) in Plutarch and Appian (*Caes.* 32.5, 8; *B Civ.* 2.35/138–139, 141), in Suetonius (*Iul.* 31.2) a *vehiculum* pulled by mules liberated from a bakery.

[6] Suet. *Iul.* 31.2 *ponticulum*, despite Lucan's poetic license (see n. 24). Even without the testimony of Suetonius it could be inferred that a bridge must have carried the major military routes north and around the Adriatic to Aquileia across any significant watercourse or ravine, and that Caesar's carriage would have required a bridge in the middle of the night. The illustration above shows in the background the very bridge Suetonius mentions, yet bizarrely combines this with Lucan's idea of fording the river. Unfortunately, the identification of the ancient Rubicon is uncertain, and therefore so is Caesar's exact crossing point (see nn. 11, 12).

[7] Plut. *Caes.* 32.4, 8; App. *B Civ.* 2.35/138, 141. Suet. *Iul.* 31.1–2 has Caesar journey through the night and arrive at the Rubicon around dawn, but Appian and Plutarch are definite that he arrived at *Ariminum*, some 15 kilometers further, around dawn. In late November (astronomical) there would have been more than fourteen hours of darkness.

[8] App. *BC* 2.35/137; Plut. *Caes.* 32.3, with Pelling ad loc. (Suet. *Iul.* 31.1–2 offers a different, less plausible version in which Caesar *overtakes* the cohorts at the river [Carsana 2007: 132]; Plutarch's circumstantial detail, including the name of their commander [n. 20] is preferable.) The detachment, or perhaps only its vanguard, was dressed in civilian clothing (Appian) and carried no weapons beyond their swords (Plutarch), obviously to avoid provoking alarm; these must have been on horseback to remain ahead of Caesar's carriage. Perhaps this is the explanation of Orosius's odd statement (6.15.3) that Caesar had only five cohorts with him when he arrived at Ariminum, although Pelling 2011: 315 is right to observe that "it is rash to put much weight" on this information (as do Bicknell and Nielsen 1998: 159–161). Pelling 2011: 316, writes of the "assault" on Ariminum, but no sources speak of any fighting. The city had apparently not yet taken any special precautions, though Caesar had been just north of the river for some time; perhaps the *s.c.u.* was not yet known or fully absorbed in Ariminum and Caesar's night-time journey was intended to exploit this fact. Bicknell and Nielsen's attempt to impugn this particular element of the story (1998: 144–147) is unconvincing, although, as they suggest, Pollio's account probably betrays an apologetic tendency.

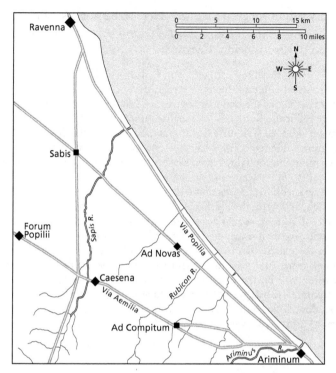

Figure 7.2 The three routes between Ravenna and Ariminum. (After Uggeri 1984: 413.) The longest route (ca. 62 kilometers) went south to meet the Via Aemilia at Caesena and then turned southeast to Ariminum; the shortest was the Via Popilia along the coast. Between these two routes ran a third, whose ancient name is unknown, bisecting the angle between the two others and joining the north-south route between Caesena and Ravenna at about its midpoint. This is the route between Ravenna and Ariminum shown on the Peutinger Map, with the Via Popilia perhaps in disuse by the later fourth century (Uggeri 1984: 404, 407). Caesar probably used the middle route.

35 kilometers from the boundary, and some 50 kilometers or so from Ariminum, normally two days' march for an army and a good day's journey even in a fast carriage.[9]

This last point in particular punctures the center of the famous scene recorded with only slight differences by both Plutarch and Appian and firmly attributable to Asinius Pollio, who was serving with Caesar perhaps

[9] See n. 1 and Figure 7.2.

as a military tribune or even a legate.[10] Here is the story as told by Plutarch in the *Caesar* (32.5–8): After a quiet day and a late dinner in Ravenna intended to divert suspicion, Caesar

> took one of the hired carriages, and first drove off in a different direction, then turned and took the road for Ariminum.[11] On his way he reached the river that marks the boundary between Cisalpine Gaul and the rest of Italy. They call it the Rubicon.[12] Thoughts came upon him on this very brink of danger, and he was turned this way and that by the [magnitude] of his enterprise. He reined in the horses, and ordered a halt. Silently, within his own mind, his thoughts veered first one way and then the other, and this was when his resolve was most shaken; and for some time he also spoke of the dilemma with his friends that were present, including Asinius Pollio – if he crossed, how great the ills that it would bring upon the world; how great the story of it they would leave among later generations. (Here Appian's synoptic version expands a little and seems to give greater precision:[13] "'He calculated all of the evils that would result if he crossed this river under arms. And pausing he said to those present, 'Friends, to stop this crossing will be the beginning of great evils for me; to continue, for all mankind.'" [2.35/139–140).]) Then, finally, as if with a burst of passion, he abandoned his counsels and hurled himself forward into the path that lay before him. As he went he uttered those words that so often serve as the

[10] Pollio: *MRR* 2.266; cf. Drummond, *FRHist* 1.431, 440 and PIR² A 1241. On Pollio's "autopsy" see Morgan 2000.

[11] Interestingly, the road system from Ravenna to Ariminum perfectly suits this diversion (Fig. 7.2): Caesar could avert suspicion by avoiding the most direct route to Ariminum, exiting Ravenna in the direction of Caesena, giving the impression that he was seeking the Via Aemilia and thus on what would be a *retrograde* path to join the 8th and 12th Legions somewhere to the northwest (Appendix 5). Then, after some 15 kilometers, he would have turned off in complete darkness onto the "middle road" toward Ariminum.

[12] The identification of the ancient Rubicon remains controversial. The name "Rubicone" was imposed on the stream called locally Fiumicino in 1933 by Mussolini, who was born only a few kilometers to the north. The Via Aemilia still spans this Rubicon by a picturesque reconstructed Roman bridge at Savignano, about 13 kilometers north of Rimini/Ariminum, but, sadly, Caesar likely took a more direct route (Figure 7.2, with nn. 6, 11). Some 11 kilometers further north along the Via Aemilia from Savignano is the crossing over the Pisciatello before Cesena; that this was identified as the Rubicon in the Middle Ages is indicated both by the forged pseudo-Roman law set into the bridge forbidding passage under arms (see n. 38), and by the position of the medieval church of San Martino in Rubicone along the upper stretch of the stream (see Pascucci 2007: 80–82 and the good map of the current river courses on p. 84). Complicating matters further, the lower course of the rivers in the plain traversed by the Via Popilia has evidently changed much over time; if the distance from Ariminum given by the Peutinger Map is correct, the lower stretches of the river must have flowed in or very close to the current bed of the Fiumicino (similarly, Pascucci 2007: 85).

[13] Which, incidentally, refutes the notion that in this case Appian drew the story directly from Plutarch (cf. Pelling 2011: 44–45) – unless he resorted to plausible confabulation.

prelude for some incalculable risk or audacious enterprise: "let the die be cast."[14] Then he moved swiftly to cross the river. He [rushed on for] the rest of the journey, and burst into Ariminum before dawn and took [over] the city.[15]

The dramatic pause and its accompanying utterance(s) before the aleatory rush across the Rubicon constitute one of that handful of Caesarian episodes that scholars tend to seize upon as a key to unlock the mysteries of this cryptic personality.[16] So, for instance, Christian Meier makes Caesar's resolution of the moral dilemma – shockingly unempathetic, by our standards – into a telling revelation of his true character:

> Caesar, solely for his personal interests, was risking a war that, if the worst came to the worst, would affect the whole of humanity .... [T]he misfortune that Caesar wished to fend off by embarking upon the war was solely his own ...... It seems monstrous and scarcely credible. How can an individual decide to inflict misfortune on all men rather than suffer it himself? How was it possible to conceive such an idea, to voice it, to act upon it, to persist with it? How could it be justified? Surely anyone who makes such a decision must be a desperado or not in his right mind, not just utterly isolated, but completely out of touch with the world he lives in? Or is it the mark of greatness? But then what is greatness?[17]

---

[14] App.: "He crossed in a rush like a man possessed, saying that common phrase, 'Let the die be cast!'" It is usually supposed that Caesar is quoting Menander (*Arrhephoros* fr. 59), but in fact the phrase seems to have been a commonplace already in Menander's time (Gomme and Sandbach 1973; Pelling 2011: 317–318] and certainly was in Caesar's, as both Plutarch and Appian imply. Plut. *Pomp.* 60.2 is explicit that it was uttered in Greek (Pelling, contra Drummond, *FRHist* 3.523); our famous Latin version, *iacta alea est*, comes from Suetonius's broadly parallel scene (*Iul.* 32), but Erasmus thought it should be emended to the third-person imperative (*esto*) to make it parallel more exactly the form Plutarch and Appian give in Greek (ἀνερρίφθω). Renehan 1969: 53–55, Beneker 2011: 86–87, and Pelling reject the emendation, since in Suetonius's narrative the phantom has already led the way and the simple perfect is therefore apt. (But cf. now Kaster's OCT.) The question of what appeared in Pollio's text is complicated not only by the near certainty that Plutarch and Appian got their Pollio in a Greek version (see Dobesch 2001: 327–330) but also by Caesar's own tendency to deliver some of his most famous lines in Greek (see n. 16). For the dicing metaphor see further p. 330ff.
[15] Translation after Pelling; words in square brackets are my substitutions. Plut. *Pomp.* 60.4 is highly compressed. Suet. *Iul.* 31–33 is quite similar, though it shows notable differences (such as the apparition on the bank that offers supernatural sanction for the crossing) that distinguish it from the fully synoptic version found in Appian and Plutarch.
[16] E.g. Caesar's supposed statement over the corpses strewn across the field of Pharsalus (following Pelling 2011: 370–372 on Plut. *Caes.* 46.2 over Drummond, *FRHist* 3.522–523), the self-damning pronouncements attributed to him by his enemy Ampius Balbus (Suet. *Iul.* 77), and the famous καὶ σὺ τέκνον; (Suet. *Iul.* 82.2, Dio 44.19.5), origin of Shakespeare's *et tu, Brute?*
[17] Meier 1982: 5 (p. 16 in the German original).

Others have written in a similar vein: it serves as a key, and for some, a rather appalling demonstration of Caesar's placement of his own self-interest – his *dignitas!* – before that of his community.[18]

The trouble is that such an event is unlikely ever to have occurred. For as Ernst Badian memorably put it, "the die had already been cast" – Caesar, as we have seen, had *already* sent several cohorts across the river to occupy Ariminum before dawn.[19] Advance elements of Caesar's army had *already* crossed the Rubicon when he arrived at the banks of the river, and were probably already taking possession of the town on the Italian side of the provincial boundary. (In fact, by a nice irony of history it was none other than Q. Hortensius, homonymous son of the great "optimate" orator and Cicero's rival at the bar, who actually first "crossed the Rubicon" in the van of Caesar's army.)[20] It strains credulity to suppose that Caesar brought his galloping carriage to a screeching halt at the edge of the Rubicon in the middle of the night after a journey of several hours, with yet more to come, in order to ponder whether after all to follow the advance detachment he had already sent into Italy, which he could hardly still call back from occupying Ariminum. Shouldn't he have thought this through earlier?

It is not hard to excogitate reasons why Pollio might want to *create* this dramatic moment. Boundary and river crossings had long offered temptation to historians: the most famous example is Herodotus's Xerxes bridging (then flogging and branding) the Hellespont. There the moment of crossing is also attended by a philosophical discussion about the hazards of great ventures.[21] Scholars have also noted that the prediction by Pollio's Caesar that this crossing would bring "great evils for all mankind" seems to

---

[18] Strasburger 1968: 34; cf. Raaflaub 1974: 213; Jehne 2009: 94 notes that Caesar's claims were hardly outlandish within the Roman value system but still stresses that marching with an army "against Rome and the Senate" was quite another matter. (As I will show, Caesar was not literally marching *on* Rome.) An antithesis between *dignitas* and *res publica* is usually constructed here, but on this see Morstein-Marx 2009 and Chapter 6.

[19] Badian 1990: 30. "The die had already been cast," however, only insofar as Caesar had already committed himself to occupying Ariminum; as the rest of this chapter will show, in reality even this was not the "point of no return" that Pollio retrospectively made it. See already Haller 1967: 142: "The thoughts that are supposed to have moved Caesar are in reality Pollio's own reflections." See also Morstein-Marx 2009: 140 and Ramsey 2009: 56n17.

[20] Plut. *Caes.* 32.3. See *MRR* 2.267, 3.103; *DNP* Hortensius (5); Shackleton Bailey 1960: 265–267. This is itself a small illustration that the war was not in fact between Caesar and *the nobility*, or even *the Senate* tout court, which was deeply divided (full discussion in what follows).

[21] Hdt. 7.33–36, 45–53; note esp. §50: "As each opportunity arises, if you were to take account of everything that is involved, you would never do anything" (Grene). Herodotus has Xerxes too employ a dicing metaphor (50.3, κινδύνους ἀναρριπτέοντες, "by risking dangers"; for the phrase, LSJ s.v. ἀναρρίπτω, II). Also see n. 32. Pelling 2011: 313: "River-crossings are often momentous in Greek and Roman historiography, from Herodotus . . . to Tacitus . . . and beyond."

carry an echo of another famous boundary transgression: the words of the Spartan herald in Thucydides at the beginning of the Peloponnesian War who announces to the Athenians just before the Spartan king Archidamus crosses the border, initiating the first invasion of Attica of the war, that "This day will be the beginning of great ills for the Greeks."[22] Slowing the narrative here heightens the drama precisely at the point of both literal and metaphorical transgression.[23] Lucan's treatment of the same moment demonstrates the phenomenon, and some of the attractions for dramatic history. The crossing fills forty-five hexameter lines with three speeches; to aggravate the transgression, "Patria" is brought on to the stage to remonstrate with Caesar, while by making Caesar *ford* the personified river against a raging current, Lucan converts the general's effortless ride in a carriage across a bridge into a hubristic violation of nature herself as well as his *patria*.[24]

Pollio at least does not go that far, but it is easy to see that any Classical historian worth his salt could hardly have let this moment pass without slowing it down and inviting us to dwell on its ultimately vast consequences.[25] All the more so because Pollio himself became a significant player in the events to follow and had himself lived through the "evils for all mankind" that had spread out from this moment in a continuous causal chain. Already in 43, in a fascinating letter to Cicero, Pollio declared that "my nature and pursuits lead me to crave for peace and freedom. The outbreak of the former civil war cost me many a tear."[26] How many more tears must he have shed by the time he was writing up that very story in the 30s![27] Pollio could recall from his own personal memory exactly those "evils for all mankind" that in the story lie in the future and are therefore obscured to Caesar's vision and rational calculation before he gives up and throws the die – the "Rubic κύβος," as John

---

[22] Thuc. 2.12.3, apparently first noted by E. Kornemann. Morgan 2000: 62; Pelling 2011: 317.

[23] Pelling 2011: 313 (cf. 2002: 327–328) remarks on the effect of the pause on the narrative. For other literary elaborations attracted to the Rubicon moment, note Caesar's "unspeakable dream" (Pelling 2011: 313–314) as well as the divine apparition Suetonius brings onto the stage at this point (with unconvincing, contrasting interpretations by Wiseman 1998a: 61–63 and Bicknell and Nielsen 1998: 152–156 ["The Pied Piper of the Rubicon"]; cf. also recently Rondholz 2009: 442–443; Beneker 2011: 85, 88).

[24] Luc. 1.182–227. See Rondholz 2009: 444; Beneker 2011: 91–92.

[25] Rightly, Pelling 2004: 318: "[Caesar's] hesitation dramatises the *moment* more than it characterizes the man, it brings out the immense importance for human history of this fraction of time."

[26] Pollio, [Cic.] *Fam.* 10.31.2 (Shackleton Bailey transl.): *natura autem mea et studia trahunt me ad pacis et libertatis cupiditatem. itaque illud initium civilis belli saepe deflevi.*

[27] Or perhaps the early 20s. On the time of writing and possible termini (43? Philippi? Actium?), see Drummond *FRHist* 1.436–439.

Henderson punned.[28] For Pollio, the crossing of the Rubicon, the ἀρχή κακῶν of the civil wars he was about to describe at length, led in a clear causal chain forward to Pharsalus, the great battle that should have been decisive but wasn't, the unexpected extension of the agony of civil war to the even more sanguinary fields of Thapsus and Munda and on, through Caesar's own assassination, the War of Mutina, the triumviral proscriptions, Philippi, Perusia, Brundisium – more than a decade of violence "without morality or law" as Tacitus would say, and more to come until Actium. The chain of disasters needed a starting point worthy of the narrative, and as so often, the crossing of the river that marked a key boundary was the natural choice.

The most arresting part of Pollio's story is the dicing metaphor with which Caesar precipitated these "evils for mankind." This must already have been the most memorable element of Pollio's story for Horace, who in his Ode celebrating (and cautioning) Pollio describes his history as a *periculosae plenum opus aleae*, a "work full of dangerous dicing."[29] To have Caesar pause at the banks of the Rubicon to contemplate the larger human costs of his choice, then – all too human! – give up on the imponderable calculation and throw himself, with a metaphorical roll of the die, "as if with a burst of passion"[30] into the causal chain that would ultimately entangle in death and destruction not just his enemies, but also himself and a good part of the Roman world – this was tragic, and *historia* worthy of the name.[31] Pollio's intention in writing up "the little scene" in this way was not partisan whitewashing, as has sometimes been suggested, but literary. It drives home a very traditional but still profound moral point about the catastrophes of human choice whose full consequences lie inscrutably over the horizon.[32] There has been long and interesting debate about the working methods and principles of Classical historians, sometimes exaggerating the freedom they

---

[28] Henderson 1998: 117n19.

[29] Hor. *Carm.* 2.1.6. See Nisbet and Hubbard 1978; Henderson 1998; Morgan 2000. Woodman 2003: 203–212, argues unpersuasively that *motum ex Metello consule* takes the opening of Pollio's history back to Numidicus in the Jugurthine War (Pelling 2006a: 271–272n31). See Jehne 2005: 40–41 for an interesting exploration of the dicing metaphor, and on the frequency of dicing metaphors in accounts of the Civil War see Pelling 2011: 318.

[30] Plut. *Caes.* 32.8: μετὰ θυμοῦ τινος ὥσπερ ἀφεὶς ἑαυτὸν ἐκ τοῦ λογισμοῦ πρὸς τὸ μέλλον (cf. *Pomp.* 60.4). Very similarly, App. *B Civ.* 2.35/140 οἷά τις ἔνθους.

[31] Pollio wrote tragedies (Hor. *Carm.* 2.1.9–12), and it is not fanciful to suggest that the genre influenced his presentation of the civil war past, replete as it was with its own cycles of violence and retribution (Henderson 1998: 121–123, 132–133). Pollio, like Sallust only slightly before him, was answering Cicero's call for a Roman *historia* worthy of comparison to that of the Greeks (Cic. *Leg.* 1.5–7, *De or.* 2.51–58).

[32] Croesus crossing another river, the Halys, to "destroy a mighty empire" comes to mind.

enjoyed to fabricate ostensible facts, but few scholars today will be scandalized by the notion that Pollio may well have taken some liberties in dressing up this key moment in the arc of the narrative on which he was now launching.

None of this is meant to deny that Caesar's entry into Italy did really involve a dramatic and weighty choice – only that he must have made that choice already, and was irrevocably committed before he himself reached the Rubicon. Pollio can be excused for desiring to dramatize that big decision at the actual moment of boundary transgression rather than days, weeks, or months earlier. Unfortunately, however, the power of this scene has tended to create the utterly misleading impression that by crossing the Rubicon *Caesar* made the essential decision that triggered the Civil War, and thus that he bore clear-cut and virtually exclusive responsibility for it.[33] As we saw in Chapter 6, however, after the Senate passed the Final Decree on January 7, Caesar no longer had a real choice whether to take the dispute regarding his return into the military sphere – unless, of course, he was simply to surrender and collaborate in his own annihilation. That question had been explicitly settled by the Senate's decree "that the consuls see to it that the state suffer no harm," which had always been understood as an authoritative request to the highest magistrates to take emergency military action. Caesar's weighty – and clearly, from the point of view of his adversaries, utterly astonishing – choice was to *advance* and engage immediately in Italy with the single legion he had with him rather than to fall back on his powerful Gallic army, or even just await the equivalent of four legions already marching to meet him.[34] The Senate's "Final Decree" had surely been intended to block his return to Italy, and to respond instead by *entering* Italy with an armed force was indeed to embark on a momentous and almost unbelievably risky endeavor. Therefore, while Pollio's "little scene" has some historiographical justification, it misleads by implicitly freighting the act with near-total responsibility for the consequent Civil War. (Of course, Pollio's context does not survive, and there is no strong reason to think that he overlooked the significance of the Senate's "Final Decree.")[35]

Even so, why does Caesar completely overlook the Rubicon crossing in his own narrative of these events in the *Civil War Commentaries*? Notoriously, Caesar's own narrative in the *Civil War* never so much as

---

[33] Even so, Caesar's thoughtful hesitation humanizes and mitigates (Morstein-Marx 2009: 140; Rondholz 2009: 448); compare Lucan for the opposite effect. Yet it can hardly be said that the result is a partisan whitewash.

[34] See n. 41. For the approach of the 8th and 12th Legions see Appendix 5.   [35] Cf. n. 2.

mentions the inconspicuous stream that this moment was to make famous. Instead, the general delivers a rousing speech to the 13th Legion (apparently at Ravenna [see n. 2]) and then immediately moves out to Ariminum, just on the Italian side of the Rubicon boundary, and subsequently "occupies" Pisaurum, Fanum, and Ancona along the Adriatic coast (*BCiv.* 1.8.1, 11.4). Scholars have often supposed that Caesar ignores his crossing of the Rubicon boundary altogether because he wishes to suppress quietly its "illegality" or "unconstitutionality."[36] But while some modern readers might not understand the significance of these movements without a specific reference to the River Rubicon made famous by Pollio, Caesar himself can hardly have expected his Roman readers not to realize without a reference to the obscure stream itself that Ariminum, Pisaurum, and Ancona were all Italian cities outside his province of Cisalpine Gaul. Caesar thus does not obscure the essential fact that by occupying these towns he had crossed into Italy proper.

It is often stated that it was *illegal* to cross that boundary without senatorial approval. So we are often told – but not by our reliable sources. The idea seems to appear first in some famous lines of the first-century (AD) poet Lucan: "Where further do you march? / Where do you take my standards, warriors? If lawfully you come, / if as citizens, this far only is allowed."[37] These very lines probably inspired the inscription, forged in the Middle Ages and set into the bridge over the Pisciatello River a few kilometers southeast of Caesena (modern Cesena, whose adjacent river was for centuries one of the major candidates for identification with the ancient Rubicon, partly on the strength of this very forgery), which purported to give the text of an ancient Roman law barring the crossing of the river under arms.[38] Baron Montesquieu in his *Considerations on the Causes of the Greatness of the Romans and Their Decline* (1734) believed the inscription to be authentic, despite its bizarre Latinity, and the youthful Theodor Mommsen apparently saw no reason to doubt it.[39] Now, it is true that the Sullan *lex Cornelia* and apparently Caesar's own *lex repetundarum* forbade leaving one's province or leading an army outside one's province

---

[36] E.g. Batstone and Damon 2006: 57: "It seems clear that Caesar wants to avoid calling attention to his legal status at this juncture," which was defined by the "fundamental illegality of Caesar's crossing the Rubicon" (p. 61). Westall 2018: 48–49: a violation of the *lex Cornelia de maiestate*.

[37] Luc. 1.190–192: *"quo tenditis ultra?/ quo fertis mea signa, uiri? si iure uenitis,/ si ciues, huc usque licet."*

[38] *CIL* 11.30*, a copy set into the bridge in 1545 to replace an earlier version seen already by Petrarch in the fourteenth century; Gregori 2015: 59–60. (For the doubtful identification of the Rubicon see n. 12). Amusingly, the forgery ultimately circled back to be cited in early printed editions of Lucan as independent evidence for the ban (CIL app. crit.)

[39] Montesquieu 1734/1965: chapter 11. Mommsen 1894/1996: 5:192.

unless ordered by the Senate, although, as we noted in Chapter 5, there is no evidence that this was regarded as an absolute injunction or that anyone was ever punished for breaking it; furthermore, we have no evidence that this specific boundary was singled out in this way.[40] But rather than falling down a rabbit hole in pursuit of the obscure details of poorly attested statutes, we need to step back a bit and consider the bigger picture. Caesar was *already* in the crosshairs of the "Final Decree"; he was *already*, from a formal point of view, holding on to his province and army in direct defiance of the Senate, which had shortly after January 7 assigned his province to L. Domitius (Caes. *BCiv.* 1.6.5). It is superfluous therefore to raise the cry of "illegality" when he responds to these belligerent declarations by immediately crossing the boundary of his province and entering Italy with an armed force, however small. What mattered was that he had surprised everyone by reacting with almost unbelievable celerity and boldness, in the process taking the war – or what seemed like war – directly onto Italian soil.[41] This is why not only Caesar but also Cicero, in his copious correspondence from this period, fails to mention the supposed "illegality" of the crossing of the Rubicon boundary.

The upshot, then, is that Caesar is not incorrect to focus attention on the Senate's "Final Decree" rather than on his reaction, the crossing of a boundary that no longer mattered now that the dispute had shifted from the legal/constitutional plane to a military/diplomatic one. Naturally, however, he does not fail to exploit the opportunity in his *De bello civili* to shape his narrative in the way that best serves his persuasive

---

[40] Cic. *Pis.* 50; for the *leges Cornelia* and *Julia* see also Chapter 5, nn. 29, 30. For Cicero's own departure from Cilicia (not under arms, of course) without senatorial authorization but apparently without fear of legal repercussions or the withholding of a triumph see Cic. *Att.* 6.5.3, 6.7, 6.6.3–4, 6.9.3.

[41] Jehne 2017 marvels that the anti-Caesarian war party made no serious preparations for an immediate invasion of Italy, yet the push for war under the new consuls took place shortly before the beginning of winter (mid-November by the seasons), and it can hardly be a surprise that no one expected Caesar to launch an invasion at such a time with only the single legion available to him before even a significant portion of his army had come up to join him. Whether or not Cicero, in his exhaustive review on December 27 of all contingencies concerning the prospect of war (*Att.* 7.9.2), even entertains the thought that Caesar might begin war almost immediately (note *statim nobis minus paratis*, which could mean simply immediately after his candidacy is rejected [*ob eam causam quod ratio eius non habeatur*] but before the elections [*aut tum comitiis*]), it is undeniable that he gives very little attention to this possibility and focuses instead on the period surrounding the elections, normally in July/August. The shock and panic created by Caesar's sudden entry into Italy is made perfectly clear by Cic. *Att.* 7.10–11, Plut. *Caes.* 33–34, and App. *BCiv.* 2.35/141, not to mention Caes. *BCiv.* 1.14 (not an unproblematic passage but not for all that apparently wrong about this). The anti-Caesarians were not suffering from the narrowed perspective of an "involutional city centre politics" (Jehne 2017: 215–223) but overly conventional military thinking against a bold adversary.

purpose. His narrative of the events in Italy that followed the Senate's "Final Decree" seeks to make the case that his entry into the peninsula was precisely not an aggressive *Blitzkrieg* preemptively opening the Civil War but an energetic and necessarily forceful attempt to press Pompey to meet him and thereby resolve their differences *before* it came to a civil war, which, he suspected, was being driven by a cabal of unscrupulous schemers around him.[42] He, Caesar, was troubled by the defection of his former son-in-law to the side of men who had long been mutual enemies of them both, but he felt that no effort should be spared to try to bring Pompey back to reason and pull the Republic back from the brink of civil war.[43] Not until the investment of Brundisium, after Pompey rebuffs Caesar's third and final request (in this phase of operations, at least) for a meeting to compose their differences, does Caesar in his explicit words accept that there really is a war on.[44] One of the central rhetorical strategies of Caesar's narrative of the Italian campaign of 49 is therefore to show that there *was no* point of no return – a "Rubicon moment" in the modern sense – that triggered the Civil War before *Pompey's* withdrawal from Italy. Even the Senate's "Final Decree," which formally initiated the military phase of the dispute, turns out to be inconclusive in Caesar's account, for no sooner does he reach Ariminum than an envoy from Pompey raises hopes for a possible settlement, and Caesar responds with a formal proposal for peace.[45] Obviously, Pollio's Rubicon story would not have fit well into this frame; according to Caesar's textual strategy, the situation is fluid, labile, and open right up to mid-March, more than two months after that episode.

[42] Caes. *BCiv.* 1.4, 8–11, and next nn. Batstone and Damon 2006: 41–74 offer an illuminating reading of the rhetoric of the *BCiv.*'s opening narrative.

[43] Caes. *BCiv.* 1.4.4: *Ipse Pompeius ab inimicis Caesaris incitatus . . . totum se ab eius amicitia everterat et cum communibus inimicis in gratiam redierat, quorum ipse maximam partem illo adfinitatis tempore iniunxerat Caesari.* Caesar's peace proposals (*saepius*: 1.26.6) at 1.9.3–6, 24.4–5, 26.2–6, 32.6; note his repeated emphasis on the necessity of a personal meeting (*colloquium*) with Pompey (see also 1.11.3; cf. Cic. *Att.* 8.15.3). (The negotiations of late January are treated fully in what follows.) Caesar's refusal to march directly on Rome and his repeated sparing of captured Pompeians (Domitius, Vibullius Rufus, N. Magius) reinforced the point (explicitly, Caes. [Cic.] *Att.* 9.7C.2).

[44] "So after having pursued this matter [a settlement] repeatedly in vain, Caesar finally decided that he must drop it and fight a/the war" (1.26.6: *ita saepius rem frustra temptatam Caesar aliquando dimittendam sibi iudicat et de bello agendum*). Up to this point Caesar had resisted using the word *bellum* for the dispute (cf. *controversiae* 1.9.1, 9.6, while at 1.25.3 *bello* means "military operations"). Similarly, Macfarlane 1996 notes that Caesar carefully avoids using *hostis* for his enemies in the Italian campaign: they are instead *inimici*, implying that matters had not yet reached the point of outright war. "Third and final": 1.9.6 (Ariminum: cf. 11.3), 24.5 (N. Magius, Brundisium: cf. Caes. ap. Cic. *Att.* 9.7C.2, 9.13a.1 with Shackleton Bailey 1965: 4:386–387), 26.3–4 (Rebilus and Libo, Brundisium). For his further proposals see Chapter 8, n. 69.

[45] Caes. *BCiv.* 1.8.2–11.4, discussed fully later in this chapter.

Is he wrong, or perhaps misleading his readers by some manipulative textual strategy? Despite the literally partisan nature of Caesar's own account in general and his known skill at putting himself in the best possible light, I think he was more right than wrong in depicting the highly uncertain nature of the conflict at this stage. We have a valuable check on Caesar's characterization: Cicero's correspondence is uniquely rich at this chaotic juncture, with nearly fifty surviving letters written during the first three months of 49 which give us an almost day-by-day picture of the great orator's perspective on the unfolding crisis. These letters are daunting in number, repetitive in their content, and generally try the modern reader's patience – precisely *because* they point to so many dead ends. Therefore few willingly take the time to work carefully through them; even when we do, the temptation is strong to reconstruct a linear narrative by pruning off all cogitations that lead away from the road actually taken.[46] But as I noted in the Introduction, if historians should take seriously as real alternatives in the chain of causation those counterfactual options and possibilities that left clear traces in the evidence (above all, those "which contemporaries contemplated," but not only those), these alternatives to civil war in early 49 need to be registered and thoughtfully considered, not suppressed simply because they did not actually come about ("the most elementary teleological error").[47] Cicero's letters from the first three months of 49 provide precious insight before retrospective pruning had reduced the story to the "essential" thread, and what they show actually supports the picture of indeterminacy and openness implied by the Caesarian narrative. Unless one adopts the view that Cicero was exceptionally obtuse, induced by a Caesarian disinformation campaign and his own personal abhorrence of civil war to believe that there were alternatives when in fact there were none – and some scholars may want to go down this path – the more likely interpretation is that the situation was radically open and fluid. Despite the ostensible finality of the "Final Decree" and Caesar's swift march into Italy, for most of the time until Pompey and the consuls shipped out from Brundisium it was probably uncertain to most senators and much of the Roman People whether civil war had indeed broken out.[48]

---

[46] See however now Zarecki 2014: 94–104, who paints a somewhat different picture from mine.
[47] Ferguson 1997: 87.
[48] For the atmosphere of uncertainty see already Raaflaub 1974: 77ff. For the military narrative of the Italian campaign and the basic facts see Goldsworthy 2006: 380–397; Westall 2018: 12–43.

War or Peace?

In the first shock of Caesar's occupation of Ariminum and the evacuation of Rome, Cicero writes as if a barbarian invader were ravaging Italy, threatening to sack and burn the capital.[49] After Pompey had given the order on the 17th Rome was abandoned in a panic by the consuls and most senators, including even Caesar's father-in-law, L. Piso.[50] Their flight implies that they expected Caesar to strike directly for Rome, and indeed Caesar says that it was precipitated by a rumor that Caesarian cavalry had been spotted close to the City.[51] But he ostentatiously did not – which Plutarch, Mussolini, and many modern interpreters both popular and scholarly have forgotten from time to time.[52] Caesar's own actions were such as to raise questions whether he actually intended to fight or rather, as he repeatedly said in a flurry of letters sent to friendly or relatively friendly senators such as Cicero through intermediaries such as Trebatius, to meet with Pompey to compose their recent differences in person. Caesar thus sent a signal that he did not consider himself at war after all, despite the Final Decree, and it was doubtless precisely due to that signal that the question of further negotiations almost immediately arose.

Caesar's own narrative of what followed is a notorious crux. Caesar gives the impression that, after occupying Ariminum and immediately meeting with envoys sent by Pompey (whom he then sent back with a formal peace proposal), he paused his advance, implicitly waiting for the outcome of the

---

[49] Cic. *Att.* 7.11.1 (ca. January 21, 49: see Shackleton Bailey 1965: 4. 297–298): *Quaeso, quid est hoc? aut quid agitur? mihi enim tenebrae sunt. "Cingulum" inquit "nos tenemus, Anconem amisimus; Labienus discessit a Caesare." utrum de imperatore populi Romani an de Hannibale loquimur?* In letters of January 23 to Terentia and Tullia and of the 27th to Tiro, Cicero expresses the fear that Caesar might sack and burn the city (*Fam.* 14.14.1, 16.12.1). Cf. *praedam* in *Att.* 7.13.1 (January 23), with explicit reference to "the kind of war this is."

[50] On Piso see p. 365ff. Pompey's evacuation order to the Senate and magistrates and his announcement that he would treat those who remained behind as enemies: Caes. *BCiv.* 1.33.2; Dio 41.6.2; Plut. *Caes.* 33.6, *Pomp.* 61.7; App. *BCiv.* 2.37/148; cf. Suet. *Iul.* 75.1; Cic. *Att.* 8.1.4. Pompey left Rome on the 17th, Cicero before daybreak the next day (*Att.* 7.10, 9.10.2 and §4, *Fam.* 16.12.2; Plut. *Caes.* 34.1, *Pomp.* 61.6; App. *BCiv.* 2.37/148; Dio 41.9). *pridie eius diei*) along with the consuls and the rest of the Senate (Caes. *BCiv.* 1.6.7, 14.1–3 with Cic. *Att.* 7.11.4, 12.2, *Fam.* 16.12.2; Plut. *Caes.* 34.1, *Pomp.* 61.6; App. *BCiv.* 2.37/148; Dio 41.9).

[51] Caes. *BCiv.* 1.14.1; cf. Plut. *Caes.* 33.6, *Pomp.* 61.5; App. *BCiv.* 2.35/141. However, Cic. *Fam.* 16.12.2 implies that the evacuation was prompted not merely by the arrival of Caesarian forces at Arretium (led by Antony) but also the push by some cohorts down the Adriatic coast to Pisaurum and Ancona.

[52] See especially Hillman 1988: 252, who also shows that Caesar's initial strategic movements in Italy were more tentative, limited, and conducive to negotiation than is usually thought. On Mussolini's exploitation of a nonexistent Caesarian precedent for his own "Marcia su Roma" on October 26–28, 1922 see Wyke 2008: 82–88, with a Fascist postcard of Caesar/Mussolini crossing the Rubicon exactly on the traditional lines discussed already. Our ancient sources are themselves sometimes confused (Plut. *Pomp.* 62.2; Dio 41.4.2 [contradicted at 41.10.1]), as are modern scholars now and then.

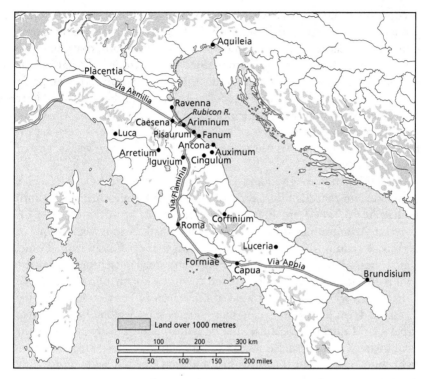

Figure 7.3 Italy: Area of operations, January–March 49

incipient peace discussions; subsequently, only *after* he had learned of the Pompeians' inadequate response (so Caesar states or implies by the sequence of his narrative), did he resume his advance, sending units over the mountains to Arretium and farther down the Adriatic coast to Ancona.[53]

However, it is clear that this picture is at best inaccurate, at worst seriously misleading. A surviving letter of Cicero implies that the Pompeian evacuation of Rome on January 17–18 was prompted by news that *in addition to Ariminum*, Pisaurum, Ancona, and Arretium had already been taken by Caesar's forces; even if rumor was somewhat exaggerated in the case of Ancona (as seems likely), this clearly places the

---

[53] *BCiv.* 1.8–11. The actual date of the occupation of Ancona is disputed (next n.). The meeting with the envoys cannot have been later than about January 16, since they were able to catch up to Pompey and the consuls at Teanum Sidicinum, 460 kilometers away (seven days by fast carriage: Stanford ORBIS), on the 23rd (Cic. *Att.* 7.14.1). Rightly, Raaflaub and Ramsey 2017a: 181.

occupation of these towns (with the probable exception of Ancona) before January 17 (see Figure 7.3).[54] But if this is true, that cannot have happened only *after* Caesar received word of the fate of his peace proposals, since we know from further letters of Cicero that the envoys brought Caesar's terms to Pompey and the consuls at Teanum Sidicinum in northern Campania on January 23, and that a larger war council considered them two days later at Capua; they can hardly therefore have reported back to Caesar at Ariminum before February 1 or so.[55] By then, of course, Caesar's men had been in control of Arretium and Ancona for about two weeks, give or take a few days.[56]

Something has to give, and obviously the weakest link is Caesar's implicit claim that his forces did not push at all beyond Ariminum until he had heard back from Pompey. In fact, almost immediately after his arrival in Ariminum he must have sent half the 13th Legion with Antony to occupy Arretium – only 200 kilometers up the Via Cassia from Rome, a move bound to give the capital a fright – and small detachments of single cohorts to occupy the Adriatic coastal towns up to Ancona (Caes. *BCiv.* 1.11.4). Even while the envoys were still in transit to Pompey in Campania Caesar had sent three of the remaining cohorts of the legion under Curio to expel Q. Minucius Thermus from Iguvium, almost halfway down the Flaminian Way toward Rome. This bore a risk of provoking an actual fight, but in the event Thermus fled and Iguvium was taken apparently without bloodshed.[57]

[54] Cic. *Fam.* 16.12.2 (written January 27). *Att.* 7.11.1 probably suggests that Cicero actually heard the news about Ancona only *after* leaving Rome, which would suggest a date for its fall closer to the 18th (Shackleton Bailey 1977: 1:484; cf. Gelzer 1968: 199n5) rather than the usual inference of ca. the 14th (Rice Holmes 1923: 3:377; Müller 1972: 13; Raaflaub and Ramsey 2017a: 181), but this does not affect the larger argument. Antony must have occupied Arretium with five cohorts on or about the 15th (Caes. *BCiv.* 1.11.4–12; Rice Holmes 1923: 3:377; Müller 1972: 13; Raaflaub and Ramsey, loc. cit.).

[55] Cic. *Att.* 7.14.1, 15.2–3 (Rice Holmes 1923: 3:378). Caesar mentions only the second of these two meetings (*BCiv.* 1.10.1). Given the need for haste, the envoys may have returned to Caesar directly after the first meeting on January 23 (Rice Holmes 1923: 3:377–378n10), yet the trip back to Ariminum, a distance of some 466 kilometers, would have required at least a further seven days or so by fast carriage. This rules out Müller's revival of Holzapfel's hypothesis (1972: 14–15, 17–22), based on a dubious interpretation of Dio 41.5.4: see n. 67), that the envoys undertook an *yet another* round trip from Rome to Ariminum and back between their meeting with Caesar and their trip to Campania. Against Holzapfel see already Rice Holmes 1923: 3:358–361; von Fritz 1941: 130–133; Shackleton Bailey, 1965: 4.444; Raaflaub 1975: 249n14.

[56] Pages 322–323, with n. 4.

[57] Caes. *BCiv.* 1.12.1–3, usually dated around January 19 or 20 because its fall is not known to Cicero as late as the 24th (*Att.* 7.13a.3: see Shackleton Bailey for the date of the letter). Cf. Müller 1972: 13; Raaflaub and Ramsey 2017a: 181. It is curious that Cicero nowhere seems to complain of the occupation of Iguvium, unless he refers to it in *loca occupare, vincire praesidiis* (*Att.* 7.18.2, February 3). Müller 1972: 30 assumes that this refers to the resumption of Caesar's advance to Auximum, but that is likely to be the graver news Cicero received two days later (7.20.1).

Evidently, then, Caesar has consciously or unconsciously suppressed the evidence that might have encouraged his readers to suspect that he did not give his own proposals a chance to bear fruit. Scholars are generally indignant.[58] Yet condemnation can go too far. Caesar was certainly not trying very hard to pull the wool over his readers' eyes – he makes the dislocation of chronology perfectly evident by *first* mentioning the Pompeian council at Capua at 1.10.1, in connection with the "negotiations" narrative, and then *only afterward* describing how it was that Pompey actually *came to be at Capua* – that is, the evacuation of Rome (1.14.1–3). Any reader can see that the military movements narrated between these two textual junctures cannot belong both after Pompey's retreat to Campania and before it. Caesar is no clumsy "propagandist," especially when he senses rhetorical danger; it would be hard to maintain that he is intentionally seeking to deceive the reader.[59] The most plausible inference is that Caesar wishes to emphasize his efforts toward a peaceful resolution at the outset of military operations, and that in order to do so he completes the important story of the negotiations *before* turning to the story of his pursuit of Pompey. He employs a common narrative technique by constructing compositional "blocks" which maintain narrative continuity by focusing the action on one sequence of actions or one of the two sides at a time, but often overlap chronologically.[60] This also would account for the other troubling chronological anomaly in this section of Caesar's narrative – namely, the impression created by Caesar's rather unspecific phrase *his rebus Roman nuntiatis* at 1.14.1 that Rome's panicked evacuation only *followed* news of Caesar's occupation of Auximum, which in fact

---

[58] Von Fritz 1941: 127–133 (128, "flagrantly untrue"); Carter 1991: 169: "an outright lie"; Bicknell and Nielsen 1998: 139–140, "Caesar's carelessness with the truth even in respect of what he chooses not to suppress forcefully"; Batstone 1991: 131–132: "one of the most egregious chronological distortions of the *Bellum Civile*"; cf. Rambaud 1966a: 135–136.

[59] Rice Holmes 1923: 3:383: "If Caesar had intended to deceive, he would have taken care to make his narrative consistent." Implausibly, von Fritz 1941: 128–129 supposes that Caesar "inadvertently told the truth [about Pompey's presence at Capua at 1.10.1] without noticing that it was inconsistent with the untrue part of his story." A new complaint is lodged by Girardet 2017: 239–240: by narrating his entry into Italy *after* the description of "den kriegsmäßigen Aufbruch der Regierung aus Rom" at 1.6.5–8 (sic), which actually happened on January 17–18 in response to Caesar's "attack," Caesar gives the impression that his march into Italy was a defensive reaction to the initiation of war by "die Regierung." But 1.6.5–8 describes the immediate aftermath of the *s.c.u.* of January 7 and includes only a passing allusion to the consuls' departure; the actual narrative of the panicked flight from Rome on January 17–18 is reserved for 1.14, where it appears to follow Caesar's advance on Auximum ca. February 4. (See n. 61.)

[60] On the composition by blocks see Wensler 1989: 252; Carter 1991: ad loc.; Raaflaub (ed.) 2017 ad loc. Cf. Syme's defense of Sallust's placement of the *s.c.u.* after the meeting at the house of Laeca: Syme 1964: 79–81.

occurred more than ten days afterward.[61] Yet one can hardly complain of a strategy to deceive.

As for the larger point at issue, though our chronology for the Italian campaign is imperfect it does in fact appear to be the case that after sending subordinate officers with detachments to seize the major communications routes leading from Ariminum to the south (or alternatively, seen defensively, screening those routes leading from the south *to* Ariminum) – that is, Arretium on the Via Cassia, Iguvium on the Flaminia, and Ancona on the coastal route – Caesar then paused his own and his subordinates' advance for some ten to twelve days until he had heard back from Pompey.[62] While the pause of course gave his 8th and 12th Legions time to draw closer – a prudent move since Caesar's single legion would be greatly outnumbered if the two sides really came to grips – it also opened a space for negotiation and discussion, even a meeting, if only Pompey would only agree.[63] T. Hillman observes:

> The evidence both direct and circumstantial strongly suggests that Caesar's passage of the Rubicon indicated a strategy of aggressive or forward defense rather than the first step of a plan for the immediate seizure of Italy and of absolute control of the Roman State. As such, it shows Caesar as more tentative in the initial steps of so momentous an undertaking, and perhaps as less inclined to force his will on the Roman State than is commonly assumed.[64]

Similarly, A. Müller has suggested that Caesar's thus-far modest advance was intended to strengthen his hand in the negotiations underway.[65] Even the capture of Iguvium, despite its risks, can be fit easily into this interpretation: he could not leave intact such a strong force (equivalent to half

---

[61] Contra Batstone 1991 and Batstone and Damon 2006: 61–63. No doubt, as they suggest, Caesar does gain some rhetorical advantage by suggesting that it was Auximum's refusal to fight Caesar, *bene de re publica meritum tantis rebus gestis*, that prompted the panic in Rome. But not a great deal turns on this.

[62] Caesar resumed his march about February 4, having apparently remained in the environs of Ariminum since about January 12 to attend to recruitment (*BCiv.* 1.11.4; cf. Cic. *Att.* 7.18.2 *acerrime dilectum habere*), thus not in a forward posture for an immediate advance, while his legates had seized Ancona (ca. 14th–18th), Arretium (15th), and Iguvium (19th or 20th). See Ramsey and Raaflaub 2017: 188–189.

[63] The 12th caught up with him shortly after Auximum opened its gates (Caes. *BCiv.* 1.15.3), thus somewhere between February 3 and 8 (cf. Ramsey and Raaflaub 2017: 189 with Rice Holmes 1923: 3:378n2; Ottmer 1979: 28), while the 8th is thought to have reached Caesar about the 17th (see also Müller 1972: 33, 49–50; Ottmer 1979: 28). Cf. Appendix 5. Recall that Pompey had in Apulia the two veteran legions returned to him by Caesar (and thus of doubtful loyalty, for which we have Pompey's own word ap. Cic. *Att.* 8.12A.2, 12C.2) and perhaps seventy to eighty cohorts scattered around the center and south of the peninsula, most of them newly conscripted and not ready to fight: Ottmer 1979: 39–48.

[64] Hillman 1988: 252.   [65] Müller 1972: 13.

of his own single legion) on the direct route between Rome and Ariminum should he be "forced" to chase Pompey into Campania. The impression Caesar gives that he tried to open up a space for a settlement after his defiant reentry into Italy is not, therefore, refuted by the facts. In fact, it looks as if it may be true.

We know that history would not smile on what Caesar presents as a last-ditch effort to avert all-out civil war. But it is important to note that contemporary observers did not know this. Although in the first shock of Caesar's advance, with no knowledge of the peace feelers already being put out, Cicero had written to Atticus (about January 21) that "people are now against any concession to Caesar" and complained that "the time for making terms has been let slip," it was only a few days later that he learned that a messenger, a cousin of the proconsul named L. Caesar, was bringing from Caesar a proposal for the resolution of the crisis.[66] Cicero's total ignorance of the fact that L. Caesar had initially been sent to Caesar by *Pompey* (as Caesar tells us in the *Civil War Commentaries*, 1.8.2–4), probably shortly after the passage of the "Final Decree," is intriguing. Shackleton Bailey plausibly inferred that Pompey had sent L. Caesar in a private capacity in all secrecy, hoping to avoid the suspicions of his new friends (particularly after the peace initiative of early January had shown how precarious was Pompey's commitment to his former ally's destruction) that he might abandon the cause and return to an accommodation with their enemy.[67] While the embassy made its journeys no blood worth

---

[66] *Att.* 7.11.4 (ca. January 21), 13.2 (January 23). A puzzle is Caesar's cryptic introduction of L. Caesar at 1.8.2 and his studied unclarity about *cuius rei causa venerat* (mysteries not entirely dispelled by Raaflaub 1975: 251n25). Perhaps Caesar did not wish to give Pompey any credit for initiating the peace discussion. For the terms and the counterproposal see Caes. *BCiv.* 1.8–9; Cic. *Att.* 7.13a.2 (January 24), 14.1 (January 25), 15.2–3 (January 26), 17.2 (February 2), 18.1–2 (February 3), 19 (February 3); *Fam.* 16.12.3 (January 27).

[67] Shackleton Bailey 1965: 4: Appx. III, pp. 441–447, strongly supported by Raaflaub 1975: 250–252. Further, L. Caesar, even if accompanied by the praetor L. Roscius, was a wholly implausible choice as a senatorial legate on such a weighty mission. (This L. Caesar, son of the consul of 64, is usually supposed to have been descended from the brother of our Caesar's great-grandfather, L. Caesar: see Münzer's stemma [*RE* 10 (1917) 183–184] reproduced in the front matter of Billows 2009 and by Sumner 1976: 343. On this assumption, the elder L. Caesar and the famous Caesar were third cousins, not second cousins once removed, as in Shackleton Bailey 1965: 4:442. The juncture between the two lines of ascent is, however, not conclusively proven.) The praetor Roscius was presumably a similarly suitable intermediary because of past Caesarian connections and his earlier offer to deliver the Senate's sentiments to the proconsul (Caes. *BCiv.* 1.3.6–7 – *rejected* by the Senate). Dio 41.5.1–3 explicitly says that Pompey had sent the men in an attempt to prevent the war "on reasonable terms" (ἐπὶ μετρίοις τισί) during a wave of remorse in Rome (also noted by App. *BCiv.* 2.36/143; Plut. *Caes.* 33.4); he also says that they were "volunteers" (αὐτεπαγγέλτους) and seems to imply that the mission was sent without consulting the Senate. However, Dio's chronology of the mission is muddled (after the arrival of Labienus!), and it is unclear what he means when he says that after their return from Caesar they were sent again (41.5.4; n. 55).

the notice of our texts had yet been spilt: the situation was still quite open. At first Cicero had been dismissive of the initiative, but after learning that Pompey and the consuls had already accepted the proposal in principle, his hope of a swift settlement was renewed: "Even an unjust peace is better than the most just of wars against one's countrymen."[68] On the very next day Cicero reported to Atticus that the terms were discussed at a council of many senators held by the consuls in Capua on the previous day (January 25).[69] Caesar's proposal renewed his earlier call for disbanding both armies, but in an extraordinary concession, he now waived his right to candidacy for the consulship in absentia, just as Pompey had long demanded, and offered to submit to the free verdict of the Roman People in the election. In return, however, he requested that Pompey withdraw his garrisons from Italy and at last go to Spain, where he would remain in command of the seven legions there.[70] The principals should meet to settle and confirm the terms, and to exchange oaths: "By discussion all their differences would be resolved."[71]

Here, it should be noted, Caesar had actually conceded the point on which he had stood firm through the crisis of the previous year at a time when Pompey had demanded it, and even during the abortive last-minute negotiations of early January 49;[72] however, as we saw, after Caesar's refusal to be a candidate in the consular election of 50, Pompey had toughened his stance and at least in private discussion had resolved against a second consulship for Caesar under any circumstances. Now that in addition the Senate had passed the "Final Decree" in effect outlawing Caesar, a dramatic concession was obviously required on his part. This looks like exactly that. At

---

[68] *Att.* 7.14.1, quotation from §3; cf. *Att.* 7.13a.2 (*absurdissimis mandatis!*) written only the previous day. In a letter to Cicero written from Rome on January 25 Atticus seems to have wind of some talk of a settlement (9.10.5); he must also have written him about the 22nd or 23rd that Caesar was not in fact marching on Rome (7.14.3). At this time the anxieties about Tullia and Terentia evinced in 13.3 give way to questions of appearances (see n. 91).

[69] Cic. *Att.* 7.14.1 reveals that Pompey and the consuls had already met with L. Caesar at Teanum Sidicinum on January 23 and approved Caesar's terms, with certain additional demands. The issue was then put before a larger council of senators at Capua on January 25 (7.15.2–3).

[70] The terms are related in Cic. *Fam.* 16.12.3 (January 27, to Tiro), with *Att.* 7.17.2; Caes. *BCiv.* 1.9.5. On the proposals and in particular the question of Caesar's sincerity, von Fritz's "indictment" (1941: 142) is sufficiently answered by Raaflaub 1975 (summary in 1974: 265–272). Seven legions: Caes. *BCiv.* 1.38.1, 85.6, with Ottmer 1979: 39–48.

[71] Caes. *BCiv.* 1.9.6: *fore uti per colloquia omnes controversiae componantur.* See nn. 43, 44.

[72] Raaflaub 1974: 268; 1975: 263, 265–268. Von Fritz indeed (1941: 145–146) considered this offer the best proof that Caesar was utterly insincere; Raaflaub gets around that implication by arguing that after disarmament in Italy and Pompey's departure for Spain, condemnation of Caesar would have been impossible. Fair enough, if it really ever was a serious possibility – which, I have argued, it was not (Chapter 6, p. 261ff. and Appendix 2).

the meeting called by the consuls in Capua, virtually all "desired" (*cupiebant*) Caesar to abide by his proposed terms (that is, they found them acceptable in principle). When Cato's sidekick Favonius complained that Caesar should not dictate terms to them no one paid him any attention: "Even Cato now prefers slavery to war."[73] On the other hand, they also imposed conditions of their own: that in keeping with Caesar's request that Italy be freed of arms, and in parity with his call for Pompey to disband his garrisons (*praesidia*), he too must withdraw his garrisons from all the towns he had occupied in Italy (presumably south of the Rubicon); also, and rather more troublingly, that the settlement be debated and ratified by the reunited Senate back in Rome, which implicitly suggested that after making the crucial concessions on the military front Caesar might find himself without a deal after all.[74] To be sure, Caesar's own language may have opened up this can of worms.[75] But Cato made a point of stating that he looked forward to participating in the senatorial debate – hardly an encouraging sign, recalling his history of filibuster and obstruction in all matters Caesarian.[76] And Pompey made no reply at all to Caesar's request for a face-to-face meeting and exchange of oaths, which his adversary understandably regards as especially damning but which may well have been prevented by the hard-liners' deep suspicion that the two men might actually be able to resolve their differences.[77] Caesar's former officer, T. Labienus, whom he had released from his service and sent along his property, had in the meantime made his way to Pompey at Teanum, arriving the very day before L. Caesar met Pompey and the consuls (January 22 and 23). He put much wind in their sails with the (apparently false) news he brought of the Caesarian forces' alleged demoralization; Cicero sensed Pompey's restored confidence.[78]

---

[73] *Att.* 7.15.2–3.

[74] *Att.* 7.14.1, 7.15.2; Caes. *BCiv.* 1.10.3–11.3, where it is claimed that Pompey insisted on Caesar withdrawing and disbanding his army *first*. "C[icero] ignores the crux of the matter, that Caesar was being asked to give up his military advantage without any real guarantee that the terms would be observed by the other side" (Shackleton Bailey 1965: 4:312); see also Raaflaub 1975: 276–280, 295–300; Brunt 1986: 21.

[75] I.e. Caes. *BCiv.* 1.9.5: *omnis res publica senatui populoque Romano permittatur.* Raaflaub 1975: 277–278 seems to regard this as calling for ratification of the peace by the SPQR, but more likely it meant only a return to the normal functioning of the state (cf. Augustus's famous line in the *Res gestae,* 34.1).

[76] Cic. *Att.* 7.15.2: *sed* [n.b. the adversative conjunction] *tamen ait* [Cato] *in senatu se adesse velle cum de condicionibus agatur.*

[77] Caes. *BCiv.* 1.11.3 (cf. 1.32.6). Raaflaub 1975: 264–265, 275–276, 279, 299.

[78] Cic. *Fam.* 14.14.2 (January 23; cf. *Att.* 7.11.1, 12.5, 13.1), *Att.* 7.13a.2 (January 24), *Fam.* 16.12.4 (January 27), *Att.* 7.16.2 (January 28). Raaflaub 1975: 281–285 lays great weight on Labienus's influence, not so much on Pompey's reply as on Caesar's decision to break off discussion. His release: Plut. *Caes.* 34.4–5.

For us, "aided" by hindsight, it is hard to see the deal as anything but a nonstarter at this point of the game, and indeed Cicero writes to Atticus on January 26 that "most people" don't believe that Caesar will actually "keep to his terms" (by this phrase Cicero overlooks the new conditions imposed by the Pompeians) but suspect that he was only seeking to slow their preparations for war.[79] Just before word came of the failure of the negotiations, Cicero also complained that even while L. Caesar was undertaking his peace mission Caesar had not stopped recruiting, or occupying new positions – though of course, neither had the Pompeians, doubtless on the grounds that they for their part had no guarantee that Caesar would carry out his part of the deal.[80] Yet when the Pompeian war council had first accepted the terms, Cicero was clearly optimistic. After all, "he [Caesar] has won" his point – his second consulship and triumph, now handed to him on a plate.[81] It was not only Cicero who was optimistic: Pompey himself took the huge risk of openly committing himself to the agreement in a public letter which at least in principle accepted Caesar's proposal "in recognition of your magnificent achievements" (*pro tuis rebus gestis amplissimus*), a laudatory phrase that was noted and commented on.[82] The letter was posted up (around Italy?) and read out in a *contio*, almost certainly in Rome.[83] Pompey was giving Caesar everything he wanted, Cicero judged, and he thought Caesar would be mad not to accept.[84] Cicero himself was preparing to be off to Spain with Pompey while Caesar would hold his consulship in accordance with the proposed deal.[85] Convinced that the old allies were about to restore their association, he took care not to be caught on the wrong side of Caesar when this

---

[79] *Att.* 7.15.3.

[80] Cic. *Att.* 7.18.2 (February 5). Note that Cicero both waxes indignant at Caesar's behavior *and* eagerly grasps at the (false) rumor that the Pompeians had recaptured Ancona. The Pompeians had explicitly refused to stop recruitment: Caes. *BCiv.* 1.10.4; cf. Cic. *Att.* 7.14.2, 16.2.

[81] *Att.* 7.15.3: *vicerit enim si consul factus erit, et minore scelere vicerit quam quo ingressus est.*

[82] *Att.* 7.17.2, 7.18.1, 7.26.2; 8.9.2; cf. 8.11D.7. This alone refutes von Fritz's claim (1941: 146) that Cicero simply allowed "wishful thinking" to take over his mind.

[83] *Att.* 7.17.2: *ut proponerentur in publico*; 7.18.1 (February 3): *grata populo et probata contioni esse dicuntur* (see Shackleton Bailey ad loc.: Rome); 8.9.2, where *in contione recitari* is treated as more or less equivalent to *in publico proponi*. The letter was actually composed by P. Sestius, about whose frigid style Cicero complains (7.17.2), as once Catullus had too (Poem 44). Did he think the letter should have been more gracious and fulsome, like his own later plea for peace (9.11A)? Possibly the letter was intended to compensate for Pompey's failure to make any movement toward an actual meeting, as requested by Caesar.

[84] *Att.* 7.17.2: *perspici tamen ex litteris Pompei potest nihil Caesari negari omniaque et cumulate quae postulet dari. quae ille amentissimus fuerit nisi acceperit.* Cf. 7.18.1: *quae quidem ille <si> repudiarit, iacebit; si acceperit <vicerit>.*

[85] *Att.* 7.18.2; cf. 7.17.1: *fuga ex Italia* is no longer anticipated.

happened. A few months afterward he lamented that he had been deceived: "I thought there would be peace. If that came about I did not want to have Caesar angry with me while on friendly terms with Pompey. I had learned how hand in glove they were."[86]

But at dawn on February 3, only a few hours after Cicero had written his previous letter by lamplight to Atticus, news came from his friend and others that Caesar would not accept the new Pompeian conditions.[87] Tragically, although both sides appear to have made serious and sincere concessions that had brought them remarkably close to agreement in principle, the intense mistrust between the two parties that is inherent in such a situation, exacerbated by the fluid military situation, left them unable in practice to take upon themselves the enormous risk of de-escalation.[88] There is nothing mysteriously fatalistic or inevitable about the fact that the result that prevailed was one that neither of the principals seems to have wanted. Simply put, once again the tragic pathology of the Prisoner's Dilemma had prevailed; the trust needed to encourage both parties to make the risky leap to a result that both might have preferred was in even shorter supply now than it had been at the beginning of January.[89] So, for the second time in a month, an entirely credible peace initiative failed to stop the halting slide toward open war.

By February 5, Cicero says, he had given up hope of peace.[90] The theater of military operations now moved quickly south along the Adriatic coast and the Apennines as Caesar set off in pursuit of Pompey. It is not even clear when the City itself came under the control of Caesarian forces. Caesar himself did not set foot in Rome until his return from the south at the end of March, after the consuls and Pompey had shipped out from Brundisium. How the City had been administered in the absence of the consuls is unclear. But Cicero's ruminations on whether and when to remove his wife and daughter (he did in the end, but despite much pumping of Atticus on the matter there seems never to have been any threat to their safety, and he seems almost equally motivated by fear of Pompeian criticism) and the absence of

---

[86] *Att.* 10.8.5 (May 2): *senseram enim quam idem essent.* See already 7.26.2 (ca. February 13), 8.11D.7 (February 27). The allusion to a lesson learned must be to his exile (cf. 7.26.2: *quod multo rectius fuit*, with Shackleton Bailey's note ad loc.). See Chapter 6, p. 306ff. for an earlier near reconciliation. According to Dio 41.5.3 other senators were sensitive to the same risk inherent in Roscius and L. Caesar's mission: that it would bring the two powerful men back and leave them critically exposed.

[87] *Att.* 7.19 (February 3). Cicero persists in overlooking the conditions placed upon Caesar's proposed terms. The envoys therefore must have made better time than Raaflaub and Ramsey 2017a: 181 (cf. Ramsey and Raaflaub 2017: 189) suppose – this letter implies that they had met Caesar substantially before February 3. See Rice Holmes 1923: 3:378: perhaps January 29.

[88] Raaflaub 1975: 276–300.   [89] See Appendix 4 on the Prisoner's Dilemma.   [90] *Att.* 7.20.1.

any sign of serious disorder in his daily correspondence with Atticus, who remained in Rome, not to mention the return to the City of senators and *boni* in the course of March, along with apparent signs of normalcy, suggest that the panic had quickly passed as Caesar had paused and made his intentions clearer, and no major disruptions in Rome had ensued.[91] It is remarkable that the physical occupation of Rome by Caesarian forces does not even merit a mention not only in Caesar's own account (who, it may be granted, could have had reason to pass this over in silence) but also in Cicero's letters; there is in fact no evidence that this had even occurred before Pompey's departure from Brundisium.[92] More positively, as late as a day or two before February 7 Pompey cannot have believed that Rome was under Caesar's control, since he now ordered the consuls to return to the City, apparently without a significant fighting force, and empty the Inner Treasury, which they had failed to do in the rushed evacuation.[93] Cicero,

---

[91] Terentia and Tullia: Cicero supposed that Tullia's new husband, Dolabella, would offer some protection – but that this might not be enough (*Fam.* 14.18.1, 14.14.1 [January 22, 23]). By January 25, Cicero seems mainly concerned that the ladies' remaining in Rome sent a bad signal (*Att.* 7.14.3), and by February 2 they had joined him at Formiae on their own (or Atticus's) initiative (*Att.* 7.18.1; cf. 7.16.3, 7.17.5). At this point Caesar's forces were paused at Arretium, Iguvium, and Ancona, and Cicero soon contemplated sending them back (7.23.2), but checked the impulse probably until he himself left Formiae for Arpinum at the end of March (Treggiari 2007: 100–108). Senators returning to Rome: nn. 103, 134, 135, 153, 325, 326.

[92] For Antony's and Curio's early movements to Arretium and Iguvium see nn. 54, 57. They quickly rejoined Caesar's main force early in February for the push south of Picenum (Rice Holmes 1923: 3:5–6, 378; Müller 1972: 23, 29), leaving no time, it appears, for securing Rome. Cf. Dio 41.10.1, which might be stretched to imply that Caesarian forces did take control of Rome until the military operations in Italy were over.

[93] Controversy arises over Caesar's statement at *BCiv.* 1.14.1 about the failure of Lentulus to empty the *aerarium sanctius* on January 17: *protinus aperto sanctiore aerario ex urbe profugeret*, which, interpreted as an abl. of attendant circumstance ("with the most sacred treasury [being] open"), has led many scholars to perceive a direct contradiction with *Att.* 7.12.2 (*aerarium clausum*) and thus to indict Caesar with another partisan fabrication or lie. (See the divergent interpretations of Müller 1972: 76; De Libero 1998: 120n42; B. Woytek 2003: 36–37; and now Westall 2018: 57–68, for whom *BCiv.* 1.14.1 is "perhaps the most striking instance of all of Caesar's mendacity that may be discerned" (304). On the *aerarium sanctius* itself see De Libero 1998: 112–113 and Woytek 2003: 32–34: probably one of the chambers of the *aerarium populi Romani* in the podium of the Temple of Saturn containing a special reserve accumulated by the 5 percent tax on manumissions as well as older treasure – according to tradition, the gold paid, then stripped from the fleeing Gauls in 387.) But it is easily translated as a normal verbal abl. absolute, as do Fabre and Rambaud in their edd.: "the treasury having been opened," standard Latin for "right after he opened the Inner Treasury." Caesar's point – still cutting, but in this form not a falsification – would be not that Lentulus forgot to close it again but that, even after opening the treasury, he was so overcome by panic that he failed to carry out his explicit order to *remove* the treasures. (For the senatorial decree see Dio 41.6.3 in addition to Caes., loc. cit.) De Libero 1992: 116–121 goes too far in dismissing the story as pure Caesarian fabrication: Cicero's letter sufficiently proves that Pompey considered the failure to empty the *aerarium sanctius* a serious mistake and supports the thrust of the Caesarian account that the Pompeians fled Rome so hastily that they failed to carry out an important duty imposed on them by the Senate and surely seconded by Pompey as well. (Cf. Cic. *Att.* 8.3.4.)

who reports the order, thinks the idea absurd, but apparently because they were likely to be cut off on their return.[94] (Lentulus declined unless Pompey should himself advance to Picenum.) It looks then as if Caesar completely bypassed the City during his advance down the "back" of Italy. He probably wanted to avoid assimilation to the intensely negative precedents of Sulla, Cinna, or Marius.[95]

No sooner had Cicero despaired of peace, however, than he received a letter from Caesar, written during the interlude, urging him to work for a settlement.[96] But Caesar had already begun to chase Pompey, ostensibly seeking to catch him and force him to a conference; Caesar's quarrel, he said, was not with Rome, which he claimed to be defending, but with his enemies.[97] Cicero does not know how to interpret Caesar's pursuit of Pompey: did he want to kill him?[98] Yet after the city fathers of Auximum had refused to block Caesar's entry to their town and Pompey's cohorts under Attius Varus had refused to fight, their lead centurion (*primi pili*), L. Pupius, who had fallen into Caesar's hands after being deserted by his troops, was immediately released.[99] This may be seen as the first act in his "leniency" policy, to be discussed in detail in the next chapter, but in the immediate circumstances it clearly sent a signal to Pompey and others like Cicero and Atticus that Caesar did not yet regard the dispute as a full-blown armed conflict, in which such a forfeiture of military advantage, however small, would make little sense. Despite Caesar's advance, then, Cicero was still not quite certain that there was a war on,[100] something which as late as February 17 he seems – with a rising sense of shock and horror – to be barely prepared to acknowledge.[101] But in that very same

---

[94] Cic. *Att.* 7.21.2: *urbe relicta redeant; quo praesidio? Deinde exeant; quis sinat?* Note also that in 8.3.4 Cicero complains not that Rome has been taken but that "the road to the capital has been left open."

[95] Cf. Dio 41.5.1, 8.5–6, 16.3; App. *BCiv.* 2.36/145. Cicero observes that the spectacle of Rome's *abandonment* by magistrates and Senate's was arousing anti-Caesarean indignation around Formiae (*Att.* 7.11.4).

[96] *Att.* 7.21.3 (February 8), 23.3 (February 10); Dio 41.10.2 mentions Caesar's letter writing "throughout Italy." Caesar's letter had been written before he "began plunging" – i.e. (apparently) before he resumed his advance with the capture of Auximum.

[97] *Att.* 7.20.1 (February 5). Dio 41.10.1–2.

[98] *Att.* 7.23.1 (February 10). Cf. similarly *Att.* 9.5.3 (March 10): n. 110.

[99] Caes. *BCiv.* 1.13.5; see Chapter 8, #1. In a similar gesture, Caesar released from his service those centurions he had promoted at Pompey's request (Suet. *Iul.* 75.1).

[100] *Att.* 7.26.3 (February 13?): *si enim erit bellum* .... To judge from Caesar's account, there seems to have been nothing rising to the level of *proelium* until the engagement at Auximum in which Varus was deserted by his troops (*BCiv.* 1.13.4).

[101] *Att.* 8.2.3: *hoc bello (sic enim iam appellandum est).* From the retrospective position of February 27, Cicero falls back to the original notion that they had been at war for some time (*Att.* 8.11d.7: *suscepto bello*).

letter, Cicero wonders if the next step is war or peace negotiations, and on the previous day (or perhaps two days before: February 15 or 16) he had allowed his hope of *concordia*, and his uncertainty whether they were really about to prosecute a war, to creep subtly into a letter he wrote to Pompey.[102] Meanwhile many so-called *boni* were voting with their feet and making their way back to Rome – clearly, their panic was over now that Caesar had shown that he was not repeating Sulla's march on Rome of 88, or any of the other marches that followed in the 80s.[103]

After the surrender of Corfinium on February 21 Caesar ostentatiously sacrificed military advantage and opted for a "bloodless" outcome in order to signal his bona fides and his desire for a settlement.[104] Cicero – despite his military command and his legal obligation under the Final Decree to treat Caesar as an enemy – in fact did anything but, instead writing to him to thank him for his clemency toward Lentulus Spinther, the other consular captured at Corfinium along with L. Domitius Ahenobarbus.[105] In the meantime, Cicero was tipped off by Caesar's envoy, the younger Balbus, about a secret peace offer being extended by Caesar to the consul Lentulus (Cicero didn't expect him to bite), and he was also being assured by the same intermediary that Caesar wanted nothing more than "to live without fear with Pompey as first man in Rome." (Cicero didn't believe it.)[106] On the Kalends of March, with Caesar rapidly closing in on Brundisium, both Cicero and, independently, Atticus were still holding out some hope for a meeting between the two principals to make peace.[107] But two days later

[102] *Att.* 8.2.4: *ad Pompeium, si de pace ageretur, profecturus; si de bello, quid ero? Att.* 8.11b: *tamen si, ut video, bellum gerendum est.* Eleven or so days later, Cicero acknowledges to Pompey that when he had written 8.11B he had still hoped it would be possible to restore peace (*concordia*), *qua mihi nihil utilius videbatur* (*Att.* 8.11D.1 [February 27]).

[103] *Att.* 8.1.3 (February 15 or 16). Many references follow in Cicero's letters to Atticus to the *boni* in Rome, sharply criticizing Cicero over their fine banquets for abandoning his political principles (e.g. 8.1.3, 8.2.3, 8.11.7, 8.16.1, 9.1.2–3, 9.2a.3, 9.5.3, 9.8.1: see esp. Bruhns 1978: 100–104). A curious case is that of the tribune L. Metellus, who after initially joining the Pompeians in Campania had returned to Rome, but then obstructs Caesar's actions at the beginning of April: *Att.* 9.6.3 (March 11), and p. 406.

[104] So Caesar asserted to his counselors Oppius and Balbus ([Cic.] *Att.* 9.7c.1, ca. March 5). Surrender: *Att.* 8.14.1; Cicero received the news at Formiae on the 23rd (8.8.2, with Shackleton Bailey 1965: 4:459). "Bloodless": Balbus, [Cic.] *Att.* 8.15A.3. Caesar's policy of "leniency" will be treated in full in Chapter 8.

[105] *Att.* 9.11A.3; cf. Caes. *BCiv.* 1.23.2.

[106] *Att.* 8.9a.2 (February 25): *principe Pompeio.* For the attempt to detach cos. Lentulus see also *Att.* 8.15A.2 (ca. March 1), where Balbus makes clear that he hoped Lentulus as consul would refer a peace proposal to the Senate with Cicero's support (*auctore te, illo relatore*). Curiously, he also claims that Caesar and he were grateful to Cicero for his approval of the plan (Cicero says nothing of this to Atticus). The gambit is interesting in light of Lentulus's own assertion as reported by Caes. *BCiv.* 1.1.3 that he might revert to his previous friendship with Caesar.

[107] *Att.* 8.13.1 (March 1), 15.3 (replying to a letter probably written March 1).

Cicero was again doubtful.[108] Yet he had also just received a letter from the elder Balbus asking him to lend his assistance to restore good relations between Caesar and Pompey and also urging him to help him vouch for Caesar's good intentions, and thus encourage Consul Lentulus to return to take up his duties in Rome.[109] After news arrived that Caesar was investing Brundisium and apparently turning his attention to a purely military solution, there follows another bout of remorse and self-recrimination.[110] Cicero now confesses to Atticus that he had been misled (and to some extent immobilized) by his hope (encouraged by Balbus) that a settlement would actually come about.[111] News of the consuls' departure from Brundisium, followed shortly afterward by (slightly premature) word that Pompey had sailed, crushed Cicero's hopes for a quick cessation of hostilities.[112]

Yet now, almost simultaneously, came a letter from Caesar himself asking for Cicero's "advice, influence, standing, and help in all matters."[113] Within a day or two Cicero heard again from Balbus, encouraging him with information about Caesar's desire to restore peace with Pompey and offering as evidence a letter *he*, Balbus, had received from Caesar written at about the same time (as it happens) as the just-mentioned letter Caesar had sent to *Cicero*.[114] The focus of their attention was Caesar's news that he had captured Pompey's Prefect N. Magius and immediately released him in the hope that they would "urge Pompey to prefer my friendship to that of those who have always been his and my bitter enemies, by whose machinations the country has been brought to its present pass."[115] Even Atticus had urged Cicero to

---

[108] *Att.* 8.15.3 (March 3).

[109] *Att.* 8.15a.1–2 (ca. March. 1). On the importance of intermediaries such as Balbus, Oppius, Trebatius, Caelius, and Dolabella in Cicero's epistolary exchanges with Caesar, most often at second hand see White 2003: 75–80.

[110] *Att.* 9.5 (March 10): §3: *intellego, serius equidem quam vellem propter epistulas sermonesque Balbi* (Shackleton Bailey 1965: 4:363 thinks "presumably before the outbreak of hostilities," but see *Att.* 8.15a, with 8.9a.2), *sed video plane nihil aliud agi, nihil actum ab initio, <nisi> ut hunc occideret.*

[111] *Att.* 9.6.2, 7 (March 11); cf. 9.10.3 (March 18), after Balbus's further approach but before Cicero committed himself publicly with his letter to Caesar. This retrospective acknowledgment actually seems to be true enough, and more or less conceded already on February 2 (*Att.* 7.17.4): *me tamen in praediis meis esse neque dilectum ullum neque negotium suscepisse. in quo quidem manebo dum spes pacis erit; sin bellum geretur, non deero officio nec dignitati meae.*

[112] *Att.* 9.6.3–4 (March 11). The news about Pompey was soon contradicted (9.11.3, 12.1, 13.1, 13a.1, 14.1, 14.3), and see n. 124. Cicero clearly understands that Pompey's departure would mean the end of his hopes to ward off "total war," including a probable blockade and invasion of Italy: 9.9.2.

[113] Caes. [Cic.] *Att.* 9.6A (sent from between Arpi and Brundisium, ca. March 5), received ca. March 11 (9.6.6).

[114] Balb. [Cic.] *Att.* 9.7B.1 (sent March 10 or 11), forwarding 9.7C from Caesar to Balbus (ca. March 5). Cicero included both letters in a bundle sent to Atticus on March 13 (cf. 9.7.3) and had doubtless received it either that very day or the previous one (March 12).

[115] Caes. [Cic.] *Att.* 9.7C.2 (see prev. n.), Shackleton Bailey trans.

step forward as a peacemaker.[116] Cicero put off his reply to Caesar while pondering the precise import of those words – *tuo consilio, gratia, dignitate, ope omnium rerum* – until on March 19 his good friend Matius (a loyal friend of Caesar's too, but still a "moderate and wise man") helpfully interpreted the letter for him as expressing the authentic desire to have Cicero's assistance in making peace.[117] Once again Cicero glimpsed a possibility that war might yet be averted, and despite the knowledge that the consuls had sailed from Brundisium and that Pompey was leaving any day, he went publicly out on a limb by writing on March 19 or 20 an open letter to Caesar professing his willingness to act as an ambassador for peace and *concordia*.[118] (His later response to Atticus when his friend informed him that the letter had "gotten out" is that he had expected this, even desired it.[119])

Ironically, by then it was actually too late – Pompey had at last set sail on the 17th – but Cicero did not know this, for his communications with the Pompeian forces had been cut off at least from the time that Caesar invested Brundisium on the 9th.[120] Within days he heard again from Balbus, hopefully forwarding along a note written by Caesar on the day he arrived at Brundisium (March 9) describing the continuation of discussions via Magius: the Pompeian officer had now returned from Pompey, met with Caesar, and was on his way back with his reply. Caesar does not report the nature of his reply ("I replied as I saw fit") but clearly suggests that he is still working for a settlement and might have some news on the subject at any moment.[121] Balbus was in agonies of suspense

---

[116] *Att.* 9.7.3 (March 13).   [117] *Att.* 9.9.3 (March 17), 11.2 (March 20).

[118] *Att.* 9.6A (the original letter from Caesar, ca. March 5), 11.2 (March 20), 11A (to Caesar, March 19 or 20). White's interesting examination of the exchange (2003: 80–86) overlooks, however, the central issue of peace, which both accounts for Cicero's interest and explains his problem of interpreting the precise nature of Caesar's request. It is also Cicero's desire for peace rather than "obliviousness of all but the addressee" or an ingrained "eagerness to accommodate" (White 2003: 88–89) that accounts for his adoption of the Caesarian line in *Att.* 9.11A.2 (p. 385ff.).

[119] See n. 294.

[120] Cic. *Att.* 9.13A.1 – from Balbus, sent from Rome March 22, received by Cicero on March 24 and then sent on immediately to Atticus back in Rome (9.13a, 14.1). Cut off: *Att.* 8.2.4 (February 17), 3.5 (February 18–19), 11D.1–5 (to Pompey, February 27).

[121] Caes. [Cic.] *Att.* 9.13A.1: *quae visa sunt respondi . . . . Cum in spem venero de compositione aliquid me conficere, statim vos certiores faciam.* (Cf. *mandata Caesaris ad consules et ad Pompeium* 9.15.4, with Shackleton Bailey's comment.) It is unclear whether the letter contradicts Caesar's assertion in the *BCiv.* 1.26.2 that Magius did not return from Pompey (thus ending this particular exchange), since it is possible that in his streamlined narrative in the *Commentarii* Caesar is simply leaving out one (fruitless) intermediate cycle of Magius's mission (Pompey – Caesar – Pompey, as described in the letter) and focusing only on the dead end (i.e. Pompey does *not* send Magius a second time). Nothing guarantees that Pompey had anything useful to say in response (after all, the consuls were *already* absent: cf. 1.26.5), and either way the exchange is terminated by Pompey. (The best analysis is that of Raaflaub 1975: 290–295, with references to earlier literature on both sides of the question. To the list of Caesar critics, add now Carter 1991: 178–179 and Batstone and Damon 2006: 68–69.)

(*torqueri*).[122] But Cicero heard from his own Caesarian informants (his son-in-law, Dolabella, and Caesar's nephew Q. Pedius) only of vigorous military operations on March 13 and 14 designed either to force Pompey out or blockade him in. By March 25 he was sure that Magius's mission had come to nothing (of course he blames Caesar) and reacted with despair and exasperation.[123] On the very next day, he learned that Pompey had sailed out of Italy on the 17th – two to three days *before* Cicero's politically risky letter to Caesar.[124] A cascade of depression, anxiety and self-reproach showers over the orator as he ponders the full import of what had occurred and what must now follow:[125] civil war, fought with Sullan ferocity, a war "savage and vast beyond what men yet see."[126]

Later in this chapter we shall return to the story told in Cicero's letters of his principled but by no means unwavering resistance to Caesar's pressure to come to Rome and support the cause of peace in the Senate, or to bolster his legitimacy. For the present argument, however, the important point is that for at least one contemporary witness whose day-to-day impressions and judgments we can actually trace because of the survival of his correspondence, and whose authority as a senior consular merits our close attention, the politico-military situation in Italy of early 49 was in a bewildering flux somewhere between a settlement and a "hot" war. If even Cicero was uncertain whether a war was well and truly on, then it is little wonder that town after town in Italy opened its gates to Caesar, "a commander who had served the Republic well and had won such splendid victories," despite the "Final Decree of the Senate," which ostensibly

---

Even if this is true, however, by telling the story the way he does in the *BCiv.* (1.24.4–5, 26.2–5) Caesar certainly avoids allowing any dissonant notes to spoil his emphatic self-presentation as the party who made every effort for peace while Pompey flatly refused to reciprocate. At *Att.* 8.15.1 Cicero appears to confuse with Magius the other captured Pompeian *prefectus fabrum*, L. Vibullius (Shackleton Bailey 1965: 4:354). Cf. the suggestion presented earlier about Pompey's initial peace feelers: n. 67.

[122] *Att.* 9.13A.2; cf. 9.13a. (March 24) and 14.2 (March 24 or 25).

[123] Cic. *Att.* 9.13.1–2 (March 23), 9.13a (March 24), 14 (March 24 or 25): *ubi est illa pax de qua Balbus scripserat torqueri se?* (§2).

[124] *Att.* 9.15a (March 25), quoting a letter from the Caesarians Matius and Trebatius. Earlier rumors had put Pompey's departure on March 4th and then the 15th (see n. 112).

[125] *Att.* 9.5.2–3 (March 10), 6.4 (March 11) 9.6.4: *nunc autem, postquam Pompeius et consules ex Italia exierunt* [the rumor was incorrect regarding Pompey, but not about the consuls' departure on March 4], *non angor sed ardeo dolore . . .. non sum, inquam, mihi crede, mentis compos; tantum mihi dedecoris admisisse videor*; 10.1–2 (March 18), 12.1 and 3–4 (March 20–21).

[126] Cic. *Att.* 9.10.2. Note that the "savagery" of which Cicero speaks is that of the Pompeians (9.6.7 *bellum crudele et exitiosum suscipi a Pompeio intellegebam*), with their strategy of starving Rome and Italy into submission, laying waste the cities and countryside, and confiscating the property of all those who had declined to leave with him (9.7.4, 9.2). See n. 269.

obliged them all to treat him as an enemy.[127] And Caesar's astonishing release of Domitius and the other senators captured at Corfinium becomes somewhat less surprising (though still remarkable) when we understand this uncertainty, and Caesar's own desire to emphasize that no "point of no return" had in fact been passed. Caesar's presentation of the character of this stage of the conflict thus turns out to be essentially vindicated; it is certainly much *less* misleading than any account (such as Pollio's, or more accurately, interpretations based on his "little scene" at the Rubicon) built on the idea that the crossing of the Rubicon on January 11 or thereabouts was the unambiguous beginning, much less the irrevocable beginning, of full-scale military conflict. The character of the conflict was in fact definitively clarified only by the departure from Italy of Pompey on March 17 (~ ca. January 25, Jul.). Although Caesar's occupation of Italy had been more or less "bloodless," Pompey's flight or escape now narrowed the range of likely alternatives more or less to a single thread.[128] A war "savage and vast beyond what men yet see" was now (but only now) virtually inevitable.

The Divided Senate

One effect of the slow-motion crystallization of the conflict over the first three months of 49 is that more people had more time to choose their course of action, as is forcefully demonstrated by Cicero himself, who allowed himself to be separated from Pompey's units on February 17[129] but on the other hand, at a meeting with Caesar on March 28 on his way from Brundisium to Rome, refused his request to return to the Senate,[130] then followed up by floating the question of leaving Italy to sit out the war in some neutral place; he appears to have formed his resolution to join Pompey physically only quite late in May.[131] But the dynamic could also work the other way. Senators of all sympathies seem to have fled the City in a panic when news first arrived of Caesar's entry into Ariminum – as we

---

[127] Quotation ostensibly of the city fathers of Auximum as reported by Caes. *BCiv.* 1.13.1. It is easy to suspect Caesarian fabrication here, but is there any circumstantial reason to deny that they spoke this way? (Cf. p. 399ff.) Cf. Caesar's earlier welcome in Iguvium and subsequently Picenum, even in Labienus's hometown of Cingulum (1.12, 15).

[128] Plut. *Caes.* 35.3: ἀναιμωτί. Not literally true, of course (Caes. *BCiv.* 1.13.3–4 [with App. *BCiv.* 2.35/141], 16.3 [with Dio 41.10.2], 26.1–2, 27 [with Dio 41.12.2–3, App. *BCiv.* 2.40/159]), but essentially correct.

[129] See n. 120.   [130] *Att.* 9.18 (March 28).

[131] He set sail on June 7 ~ ca. April 15, Jul. (*Fam.* 14.7). On Cicero's equivocation and ambivalence about leaving Italy see p. 390ff.

have already noted, these included even his father-in-law, L. Piso.[132] But many soon came back – some perhaps in response to Caesar's pleas through letters and intermediaries,[133] some drawing the reasonable conclusion from Pompey's conciliatory and honorific message to Caesar at the beginning of February, while others doubtless recognized that any immediate danger to the City had passed now that Caesar had clarified his purpose by veering off down the eastern side of the peninsula along the far side of the Apennines in pursuit of Pompey and treating the cities in his path with all respect.[134] Among those who (in addition to L. Piso) are known to have returned quickly, we hear in Cicero's correspondence explicitly about the similarly speedy L. Volcacius Tullus (cos. 66);[135] M'. Aemilius Lepidus (cos. 66), who returned to Rome in early March;[136] Ser. Sulpicius Rufus (cos. 51), who actually seems to have sent his son to join Caesar while he was pursuing Pompey to Brundisium;[137] and Q. Titinius, an elder senator and friend of Cicero's who is not known to have attained high office but

---

[132] Which Cicero chose to interpret as a clear-cut denunciation (*Fam.* 14.14.2, *Att.* 7.13.1) – surely mistakenly (see p. 365ff.). See Plut. *Caes.* 34.2.

[133] Dio 41.10.2; Cic. *Att.* 7.17.3 (Trebatius). Cicero's friend M. Caelius and his son-in-law, Dolabella, both Caesarians mentioned here as possible intermediaries, were in contact with him by early February: *Att.* 7.21.2–3.

[134] By February 15 or 16 (*Att.* 8.1.3; cf. 2.3, February 17), Cicero notes with irritation that Rome will soon be filled with *boni, id est lautorum et locupletum*: he specifically names M'. Lepidus (who, in contrast to the others, was probably not there quite yet: see Shackleton Bailey ad loc., with 9.1.2), L. Volcacius, and Ser. Sulpicius. The towns: see p. 399ff.

[135] Cic. *Att.* 9.10.7, 8.15.2 imply that Volcacius and Lepidus were sitting on the fence on February 22, probably at their country estates (see Shackleton Bailey on 9.10.6 *vos*; Lepidus is known to have been near Cicero at Formiae), but had made up their minds by March 3 – i.e. after Corfinium and Pompey's withdrawal to Brundisium. Thus Volcacius, like Lepidus, had almost certainly left Rome initially, contra Shackleton Bailey 1965: 4:325 (cf. *Att.* 8.1.3, 9a.1). The "bribed peacemaker" of 10.1.2–3 is probably Volcacius (so Shackleton Bailey ad loc, adducing 9.19.2). Shackleton Bailey (p. 401), probably rightly, rejects the traditional inclusion of Volcacius among those who had sent their sons to Caesar at Brundisium (see later in this chapter on Sulpicius's and Titinius's sons, bracketed together at 9.18.2 and 19.2; Bruhns 1978: 58 overlooks Shackleton Bailey's objection), which seems to be based only on the questionable ms. reading *tullium* [*sic*] at 10.3a.2. The appearance of Tullus instead of Titinius is indeed suspect here (Shackleton Bailey follows Koch in emending) and corruption of *Titinius* to *Tullium* may have come easily to one copying Tully's letters. (Shackleton Bailey thus corrects his earlier comment on the matter at 1960: 260n9, 264n10.) However, note also that a C. Volcacius Tullus – probably another son or nephew of the cos. 66 – served with Caesar from 53 to at least 48 (*MRR* 2: 232, 245, 283). On the spelling of the *nomen*, *MRR* 3.223. On Volcacius see further n. 152.

[136] See n. 134. *Att.* 8.1.3, 9a.1, 15.2, 9.1.2.

[137] First mentioned in the relevant correspondence at *Att.* 7.17.3 (February 2) in a context, as Shackleton Bailey notes, that "shows that Caesar and Sulpicius Rufus were personally on good terms" (313). See also 8.1.3, 9.18.2, 19.2, 10.1a, 3a.2, 14.3. Note that at 9.19.2, 10.1a, and 10.3a.2 Sulpicius is said to have *sent* his son to join Caesar. This becomes awkward for him once he discusses with Cicero the contingencies that would make him depart from Italy (10.14.3, May 8; cf. *Fam.* 4.1–2), but it is not denied.

was regarded by him and Atticus as an "optimate" all the same.[138] (His son too had been with Caesar at Brundisium.[139]) Men of this rank can hardly have stayed in Rome without attending the Senate, and the intention to do so is explicitly attested for the senior consulars Volcacius and Lepidus.[140] Cicero, who perhaps because of his military commission from Pompey seems never to have seriously contemplated emulating them, asks Atticus on March 14, "We too have heard that there are many senators in Rome. Can you tell me why they ever left?"[141] (About a month earlier he had joked – presumably – that if it hadn't been for his annoying lictors, i.e. his command, he would have joined them.)[142]

Cicero's mock query raises a serious question. Tradition has enshrined the shorthand description of the conflict as one between Caesar and "the Senate" or even "the Republic." Yet, when forced to choose a side, how many senators actually sided with Pompey? Or with Caesar? This is the sort of question prosopography is made for. The answers it gives may come as a surprise to those wedded to the old narrative. Already in 1960 Shackleton Bailey published a prosopographical study of the allegiances of the nobility in the "Second Civil War." He found that "in reality ... the nobility seems to have been fairly evenly divided so far as numbers go, the greater length of the Caesarian list (55, to 40 Pompeians) being offset by a somewhat larger infusion of questionable names" as well as some of doubtful standing, such as men who had "fallen foul of the law-courts," sons of proscribed Marians, and "young men, free of parental control."[143] Hinnerk Bruhns, in his valuable 1973 Köln dissertation on "Caesar and the Roman Upper Class," rightly noted that the question needed to be expanded to encompass the senatorial order as a whole. Once he did so, discriminating further by rank, a different picture emerged, most strikingly for instance in the case of consulars, of whom Bruhns would place just one who was not a recalled exile in Caesar's ranks (as were a further three) in comparison to ten Pompeians (and ten neutrals).[144] (Even so it may

---

[138] *Att.* 9.6.6 (with Shackleton Bailey's note); cf. also Gruen 1974: 197n136; Wiseman 1971: 266n433.

[139] *Att.* 9.6.6, 9.1, 19.2 ("Pontius Titinianus," thus presumably adopted by a Pontius: Shackleton Bailey 1965: 4:365); 10.3a.2, which strictly speaking seems to say that Titinius, like Sulpicius, *sent* his son to join Caesar.

[140] *Att.* 8.15.2.

[141] *Att.* 9.8.1. There is an old controversy on the precise nature of Cicero's military command, which here need not be resolved. Shackleton Bailey 1965: 4:438–440 argued that Cicero rejected the assignment of Capua, despite *Fam.* 16.11.3 but on the face of it in keeping with *Att.* 8IID.5 and 8.12.2, and accepted *only* the Campanian coast conveniently around Formiae (*Att.* 7.11.5, *Fam.* 16.12.5); Wistrand 1979: 206–211 insists that he accepted Capua "grudgingly."

[142] *Att.* 8.1.3.   [143] Shackleton Bailey 1960: 264–265.

[144] Ten consulars in the *Pompeianus senatus:* Cic. *Phil.* 13.28-29, with Bruhns 1978: 37. Caesar's one consular would be Cn. Domitius Calvinus, who turns up commanding Caesarian troops in Greece

come as something of a shock to some that fewer than half of the active consulars actually joined Pompey's senate-in-exile.) If we throw in praetorians as well to constitute a larger group of relatively high-ranking senators, Caesar is still left with only sixteen (as Bruhns counts them) out of sixty-nine (23 percent) to Pompey's forty-two (61 percent), with eleven neutrals (16 percent).[145] Like Shackleton Bailey, Bruhns noted a strong generational dimension to the conflict, with a relatively large number of young men of senatorial family, especially nobles, siding with Caesar (famous cases are C. Curio, Antony, and P. Dolabella).[146]

In this connection, however, a fundamental question is that of where exactly one should draw the line between "neutrals" and "Caesarians." Both Shackleton Bailey and Bruhns insisted on a fairly high standard of positively attested pro-Caesarian activity or sentiments in order to place an individual in the "Caesarian" column. Yet this is to tip the scales in a way that overlooks how the combatants themselves defined the issue – and the serious consequences in store for those making their choice in accordance with those definitions. For there was a key difference between Caesar and his adversaries in the way they defined the fate specifically of those in the middle: Caesar accepted the idea of "neutrality" for those senators who stayed in Rome or withdrew to the sidelines in some other place; Pompey, however, had explicitly declared that those who did not physically join him were to be treated as enemies. That is, in the Pompeian view *there were no* "neutrals," and those who remained in Italy after their own departure defined themselves as enemies, and thus "Caesarians," by that very fact.[147]

---

in 48 (*MRR* 2.277). Bruhns (1978: 40, following Syme 1964: 217) notes that even Calvinus may have been a recent exile who naturally drifted to Caesar's camp, for he had been indicted already for corrupt electoral practices before his consulship and may, like his consular colleague, M. Valerius Messalla Rufus, have been convicted afterward (see Alexander 1990: nos. 301; cf. 299, 329, 331). This is uncertain but would help to explain his surprising Caesarian allegiance in the Civil War after his record of sharp opposition in the 50s (Gruen 1974: 149, 290; Bruhns 1978: 39–40, n. 1). Note that in 44 the two men were to take over in sequence as *magister equitum* once Lepidus moved off to his province: Chapter 9, n. 283. The total number of consulars, excluding Pompey, Caesar, and the superannuated M. Perperna (cos. 92), who died early in 49, comes to twenty-four (Bruhns 1978: 37).

[145] Bruhns 1978: 31–63.

[146] Bruhns 1978: 48–49, 53, 62. There is some risk of exaggerating the real nature of the phenomenon because the defeat of the Pompeian side doubtless cut short or depressed the future career of some of its younger members, while those who bet on Caesar benefited accordingly. For the generational conflict see also Cic. *Att.* 7.3.5 (December 9, 50): *omnem fere iuventutem.* Further representatives of the *iuventus* attracted to Caesar (but "new men," not nobles) were Cicero's friend M. Caelius and Asinius Pollio; Caelius, Pollio, Curio, and Dolabella are all discussed below, p. 366ff.

[147] Cic. *Att.* 11.6.6: *omnes enim qui in Italia manserant hostium numero habebantur; Marc.* 18 *quidam* [sc. Pompeiani] *enim non modo armatis, sed interdum etiam otiosis minabantur; nec quid quisque sensisset, sed ubi fuisset, cogitandum esse dicebant; Lig.* 33 *te* [sc. Caesarem] *enim dicere audiebamus nos omnis*

Cicero himself was well aware of much threatening talk among the Pompeians of proscriptions and the like for those who remained in Italy; he was later to tell the complaisant Atticus that he too had been marked down for proscription.[148] This difference was rooted in the divergent views adopted by each side about the nature of the conflict: Pompey and the consuls had defined it in their original pronouncement upon evacuating Rome as a battle for the survival of the Republic itself against an enemy of the state, while Caesar defined the conflict as a regrettable quarrel between citizens and friends aggravated by a small faction of zealots, in which it was the part of patriotic citizens not to take sides gratuitously and to help patch it up as soon as possible. Those who exploited Caesar's tolerance of neutrality and stayed in Rome or stood outside the fray, however, made their choice in full knowledge that if Pompey won they were likely to be defined *as enemies*, as men who had made an unacceptable accommodation with Caesar and, despite the "with-us-or-against-us" declaration, had chosen not to be with them. Cicero clearly recognized this fact, and despite all the talk of emulating Q. Scaevola's behavior in the Marian-Sullan days, this is probably one major reason why in the end he betook himself to Pompey's camp.[149] It is therefore fundamentally misleading to carve out a category of "neutrals" from a list of what the Pompeians regarded as disingenuous Caesarians who had, in effect, staked their fortunes and even their lives on Caesar's victory.

It follows that those who stayed in Rome and Italy in accordance with Caesar's invitation or pleas recognized that for all practical purposes they were actually placing themselves in the "Caesarian" column, even if they did not lead Caesar's armies or receive *honores* from him.[150] Caesar's father-in-law, L. Piso (cos. 59), L. Volcacius Tullus, M'. Aemilius Lepidus (both cos. 66), and Ser. Sulpicius Rufus (cos. 51) all swiftly returned to Rome to

---

adversarios putare nisi qui nobiscum essent, te omnis qui contra te non essent tuos. See Raaflaub 1974: 230–232. For the proclamation see n. 50. According to Caes. *BCiv.* 3.83.3, L. Domitius proposed before Pharsalus that judgment should be passed not only on those who had remained in Rome but also on those who had fled to Pompey for protection, yet had made no contribution to the war effort.

[148] Cic. *Att.* 8.1.4, 8.11.4: <*singulorum proscr>iptio*; 8.16.2; 9.9.2; 9.10.2–3, 6; 9.11.3–4, 11.6.2; *Fam.* 9.6.3 (to Varro, 46) *crudeliter enim otiosis minabantur.* See Domitius's proposal, n. 147.

[149] Q. Scaevola the Pontifex (cos. 95), a widely admired mentor of Cicero's in his youth, had remained in Rome through the domination of Cinna despite his probable Sullan sympathies and was murdered in that regime's last gasp in 81 (Mitchell 1979: 88–90). Cicero frequently invokes him at this time as a possible model as he thinks through his options with Atticus (*Att.* 8.3.6, 9.12.1, 9.15.2).

[150] Badian 1964: 219: "When Caesar crossed the Rubicon, over half the consulars . . . either supported him or at least remained in Rome without opposing." "Quality," however, was another matter (Syme 1939: 61–62), unless that be a product of Cicero's alignment.

attend the meetings of the Senate Caesar had called for the beginning of April even as Pompey and the consuls were abandoning Italy with threats against those who stayed. Sulpicius had in fact, during the buildup of the crisis, urged acceptance of Caesar's demands in preference to the horrors of civil war, and lest anyone doubt that this revealed an accommodating attitude toward the proconsul he had, as we saw, even sent his son to join Caesar at Brundisium.[151] To place these four consulars in the "neutral" (or in Sulpicius's case, even "Pompeian") column is therefore quite misleading.[152] The reality was much less clear. As late as February 17 Cicero doubts that there are "really so many ['good men,' *boni*] with us" rather than lingering in their estates and villas near Rome, or soon to be.[153] Even after the consuls and the Pompeian army had started shipping out from Brundisium, Cicero balks at what he takes to be Atticus's suggestion that he should be with them, emphasizing that very few senators among them were not authorized by their position as magistrates or officers to go abroad, and even these (unlike himself) were nearly all men driven by personal enmity against Caesar.[154] The question was crucial, since Atticus had given Cicero the false impression

---

[151] Sulpicius's son: n. 137. Cicero recalls Sulpicius's advocacy of peace at *Fam.* 4.1.1, 2.3, 3.2, 6.1.6. He acknowledges that this served Caesar's interests at 4.2.3: *nam omnia utriusque [nostrum] consilia ad concordiam spectaverunt; qua cum ipsi Caesari nihil esset utilius, gratiam quoque nos inire ab eo defendenda pace arbitrabamur;* cf. also *Fam.* 6.1.6, 4.3.2. It is not entirely clear when Sulpicius took this position: *Fam.* 4.3.2 recalls a prescient warning about the costs of civil war during his consulship in 51, but 4.1.1 talks of his "provident defense of peace" both during his consulship and after, while *Att.* 7.3.3 of December 9, 50, suggests that Sulpicius (and Volcacius) was at this time known to favor accommodation of Caesar's demands (see Chapter 6, n. 122). Since however at *Fam.* 4.1.1 Cicero implies that when he himself returned to Italy he was isolated (*solus eram*) in trying to contain "the mad rush to war," he may have politely exaggerated Sulpicius's outspokenness in favor of peace. Still, it can hardly be doubted what the more zealous of the Pompeians thought of him in early 49. Wherever Sulpicius ultimately came down, in the early months of 49 his *actions* were those of a "Caesarian," one who, as Shackleton Bailey says, "[went] further in Caesar's direction than Cicero was prepared to go" (1960: 253[–254]n7). On Sulpicius see further p. 375ff.

[152] Volcacius is left out of Shackleton Bailey's calculations because he was not a noble (1960: 264n9; Wiseman 1971: 276–277, n. 506, notes that though Volcacius's family was of municipal origin (Perusia or perhaps Tusculum) he was no *homo novus*. Cicero already in December 50 saw Volcacius (and Sulpicius) as "soft" on Caesar (*Att.* 7.3.3), and his angry outburst in the Senate against Pompey after Caesar entered Italy was remembered (Plut. *Pomp.* 60.6–7: Pelling 2011: 324).

[153] *Att.* 8.2.3. See n. 103 and further p. 394ff.

[154] *Att.* 9.1.3–4 (March 6): Cicero suggests that Metellus Scipio, the Marcelli (the consuls of 49 and 51, but evidently *not* the consul of 50, who had unleashed a whirlwind toward the end of his consulship but was also the husband of Caesar's great-niece Octavia, Octavian's elder sister: Shackleton Bailey 1960: 261), and Ap. Claudius are all primarily motivated by fear of Caesar. The others are all subordinates and therefore had little choice, except for C. Cassius (tr. pl.), the future Caesaricide. Shackleton Bailey grasps Cicero's overt point that "everyone except Appius and C. Cassius has an official reason for leaving Italy" but Wistrand 1979: 103–104 rightly picks up on the undertone that "apart from himself, everyone else was forced to leave Italy whether they liked it or not," i.e. that he, Cicero, was actually under no public obligation to join them. Similarly, three days before Cicero had implied that there was a legal impediment to his leaving Italy (*Att.* 8.15.3, *neminem esse fere qui*

that he thought he should leave if Pompey and the consuls had left *bene comitatus,* "with a respectable company," but as on the occasion some two weeks before when he had jumped mistakenly to the same conclusion, he immediately begins to poke holes in the suggestion.[155] As we saw, on March 14 he says that he has heard that *many* senators (*multi*) were already back in Rome.[156] Ultimately Pompey was able to assemble some two hundred senators in Thessalonica, according to Dio (41.43.2) – which should mean that some three or four hundred or half to two-thirds were *not* there, some no doubt scattered around the Mediterranean, but many others still lingering in Caesar's Italy or even attending the Curia in Rome.[157]

Nor are the consulars just mentioned the only ones whose decision to stay aloof from the fighting, probably while remaining in Italy, must have deeply compromised them in the eyes of the Pompeians. The senior consular P. Servilius Vatia Isauricus (cos. 79), about eighty-five years of age at this time, was probably too old to be expected to perform heroics, but he had old ties with Caesar, and his homonymous

---

non ius habeat transeundi) although his Campanian assignment had surely been overtaken by events (n. 141, with Shackleton Bailey 1965: 4:355–356, Wistrand 1979: 100–101). Further updates at 9.6.3 (March 11), 9.8.1 (March 14). The letter of March 11 also mentions *tribuni pl.*, but C. Cassius is the only one known (8.15.3) and indeed the only known likely candidate, since L. Metellus stayed behind (first at Capua, then to Rome: 9.6.3). Shackleton Bailey is inclined to insert <*et praetores*> at 9.6.3, since quite apart from the questionable case of L. Torquatus (9.8.1 and Shackleton Bailey 1965: 4:342–343; this is the Epicurean spokesman in Cic. *Fin.*), three praetors of 49 are known to have been active in the Pompeian army in southern Italy (Shackleton Bailey 1965: 4:364; the report Cicero has on March 3 that Rutilius Lupus had taken up official duties in Rome is generally supposed to be wrong: *Att.* 9.1.2: see Shackleton Bailey 1965: 4:350). Of course Cicero did not yet know for sure who had crossed with Pompey and the consuls; he was eager to collect the names and would forward them to Atticus when he had them: 9.9.4, March 17 (note also 9.8.1, in response to a specific query: L. Torquatus and his uncle (?) Aulus, pr. ca. 70).

[155] *Att.* 9.2.1 (March 7): *ita si et Gnaeus bene comitatus conscendisset et consules transissent. utrum hoc tu parum commeministi, an ego non satis intellexi, an mutasti sententiam?* Earlier: 8.2.4 (February 17), corrected by Atticus in a letter dated February 19 (9.10.6).

[156] *Att.* 9.8.1 (March 14).

[157] It is usually supposed on the basis of App. *BCiv.* 1.100/468 that the size of the post-Sullan Senate was approximately six hundred, but note that this attests only to Sulla's *addition* of three hundred senators to a number depleted by the civil wars of the 80s (Santangelo 2006: 8–11). Since the Senate was apparently regenerated by the addition of twenty quaestors per year, an office held at or shortly after age thirty, life expectancy at age thirty would have to be thirty to maintain an average of six hundred members (e_{30} = 30). While this is most unlikely for the general (male) population (useful discussion in Parkin 1992: 67–90, with Appendix B), it may be in the right range for Roman senators. (Hopkins and Burton 1983: 75n55, 146–149, seem indifferent to the better survival prospects of the "healthy and wealthy" selected for the rigors of a senatorial career; cf. the historical life expectancy rates they cite at p. 71n52, as well as now Griffiths 2008.) Bruhns 1978: 60n43, Santangelo 2006, and Steel 2014 for different reasons suppose that the post-Sullan Senate stabilized from four hundred fifty to perhaps somewhere in the (low?) five hundreds, but for the reason just given I think this is too low. (I thank Cary Barber for discussion of his findings in his recent Ohio State dissertation on "Elite Losses and the Senate of the Hannibalic War.")

son – still under his *patria potestas* – soon emerged as a prominent Caesarian, the first "Caesarian" consul elected late in 49 beside Caesar himself under controversial constitutional circumstances.[158] L. Julius Caesar, the consul of 64, a distant cousin and old ally of Caesar's (also Mark Antony's uncle), who had served as legate under him in Gaul for the prior three years and may have retained this position at the time of Caesar's entry into Italy, can hardly have been viewed by Pompeians as solidly "neutral" when the crisis came, however circumspect his words and deeds in early 49.[159] (He would later be named *praefectus urbi* in 47 when Antony was forced to leave the City to attend to the legionary mutiny in Campania, a clear sign that he was considered a reliable member of the faction.) L. Aurelius Cotta (cos. 65) was another cousin of Caesar's whose family connection has emerged as a significant factor more than once in this study; he and L. Marcius Philippus (cos. 56), husband of Caesar's niece Atia, were both passed over for military command in the anti-Caesarian senatorial meetings of early January in view of their family connection to the enemy.[160] L. Aemilius Paullus, the recent consul of 50, was alleged to have been "bought" by Caesar for the price of 36 million sesterces; for good measure, he also happened to be the brother of Caesar's loyal praetor in 49 (M. Aemilius Lepidus, the future *triumvir*), who was key to Caesar's plans for holding consular elections for 48 and later, for enabling legislation for Caesar's first appointment as dictator.[161] C. Claudius Marcellus, Paullus's colleague in the consulship of 50 (thus not the homonymous consul of 49), despite his aggressively anti-Caesarian stance only the previous December, played a particularly wobbly role during the early months of the Civil War: he "regrets ever having been consul," writes Cicero, who proclaims

---

[158] For Cicero's dismay over the electoral procedure (since both consuls had abandoned Rome) see *Att.* 9.9.3, 15.2. As cos.-des. and cos. in the year of Pharsalus, Servilius adhered closely to Caesar's lead.

[159] Shackleton Bailey 1960: 261n3 (cf. 1965: 4:442); Bruhns 1978: 41. Legate: Caes. *BGall.* 7.65.1; *BCiv.* 1.8.2. His son, however, the peace envoy of January 49, became an active Pompeian and was the L. Caesar quite exceptionally put to death by Caesar after Thapsus: Chapter 8, p. 435. For the kin relationship see n. 67.

[160] For Cotta see Chapter 2, n. 27. For Philippus note Caes. *BCiv.* 1.6.5: *privato consilio*. Philippus received special dispensation from Caesar, perhaps to settle outside Italy as a "neutral" (Cic. *Att.* 10.4.10), but this is unlikely to have endeared him to the Pompeians. (Cicero's comment *sed veritus sum, quia ille a me nihil impetrabat* that Caesar suggests that he was in fact "getting something" out of Philippus in return.)

[161] For the bribe/loan see Appendix 1, p. 620f. Lepidus: n. 158, with Dio 41.36.1. Nothing is known about Paullus's actions in the Civil War. But note that he was a relative of Curio and acted forcefully in his behalf in 50 (Dio 40.63.5). Paullus and his son were probably (distant) cousins of the aforementioned M.' Lepidus (cos. 66), who returned to Rome and the Senate with unseemly alacrity.

him the only consular less timid than Sulpicius.[162] This cannot have
endeared him to the Pompeians, particularly when they considered his
relationship to Caesar by marriage.[163] He appears to have been intent on
remaining in Italy through the Civil War and reappears in 46 as an
intercessor for his Pompeian cousin in the Caesarian Senate.[164] The men
who had staked their lives on leaving with Pompey as a result of
Marcellus's belligerent saber-rattling seem unlikely, had they won, to
have viewed his enjoyment of his estates as merely "neutral."

All the supposedly "neutral" consulars, then, were compromised to some
extent, by their prior relationship to Caesar or his partisans or by their actions
in the early months of the war, demonstrating a willingness to accommodate
Caesar despite the threats of the Pompeians rather than (like Cicero, despite
his vacillations) ultimately taking a stronger stand that would deprive him of
the legitimacy their presence in Rome and Italy lent him. If, then, we revise
Bruhns's count of consulars accordingly, shifting Piso, Volcacius, Lepidus,
and Sulpicius into the "Caesarian" column and treating the "neutrals" as in
fact "compromised," the figures for the early months of 49 take on quite
a different look (Table 7.1). Five consulars, joined by the three known consular
exiles, may now be seen as "Caesarian" (33 percent); six more were "compromised self-proclaimed neutrals," who together with the more committed
"Caesarians," totaled fourteen out of the twenty-four ex-consuls (58 percent);
while the ten "Pompeian" consulars (42 percent) now take on a far less
dominant appearance. As for the representativeness of these proportions, we
must keep in mind that the option of "neutrality," or its appearance, seems to
have been a luxury of high senatorial status and therefore hardly representative
of choices farther down the hierarchy; lower-ranking senators had little to
bargain with and much less room to avoid taking sides.[165] (In the event, as
both Shackleton Bailey and Bruhns indicated, lower-ranking senators had
a notable tendency to break in the Caesarian direction.) A better estimate of
the schism in the upper ranks of the Senate might be obtained by adding to

---

[162] *Att.* 10.15.2; see 10.12.3, 10.13.2. Shackleton Bailey (1965: 4:350) rightly rejects inserting *C.* at
Att. 8.12A.4: that reference is to Gaius's cousin Marcus, on whom see Shackleton Bailey 1960:
253n7 (reliably "Pompeian"). Bruhns 1978: 42 offers a sympathetic and not implausible
account of Marcellus's lack of enthusiasm for Pompey's prosecution of the war with Caesar.

[163] See n. 154.

[164] Cic. *Att.* 10.15.2, where he is said to have gone so far as to press Antony not to let Cicero leave Italy merely
to make his own actions look better. 46: *Fam.* 4.4.3, 7.6 (Shackleton Bailey ad loc.: *frater* = cousin),
9.4, 11.1.

[165] See the "neutral" column on Bruhns's Table 7.1 (Bruhns 1978: 60), five-sixths of whom are consulars. It is
true that the great impetus to "neutrality" among the consulars appears to have been caused by Caesar's
gestures of mildness, but the Pompeians' threats will have made this an especially important
consideration.

the consulars those of praetorian status and known priests who had not yet reached a high magistracy: forty-six of the known seventy-eight names are Pompeian (59 percent), between twenty-five and thirty-one are Caesarian (32–40 percent, not including the exiles), and the rest (between one and seven = only 1–9 percent) neutral.[166]

Table 7.1 *Distribution of consulars between the two sides in the Caesarian Civil War. Three interpretations are given, concluding with my own (C). Names that shift columns according to at least one interpretation are printed in bold type.*

Pompeians	Caesarians	Neutrals
A) Shackleton Bailey 1960 (noble families only)		
1. M. Calpurnius Bibulus	1. C. Antonius Hybrida	1. **M'. Aemilius Lepidus**[167]
2. C. Claudius Marcellus (cos. 49)	2. Cn. Domitius Calvinus	2. L. Aemilius Paullus
3. M. Claudius Marcellus	3. A. Gabinius	3. L. Aurelius Cotta
4. Ap. Claudius Pulcher	4. M. Valerius Messalla Rufus	4. **L. Calpurnius Piso**[168]
5. L. Cornelius Lentulus		5. C. Claudius Marcellus (cos. 50)
6. L. Domitius Ahenobarbus		6. L. Julius Caesar
7. P. Lentulus Spinther		7. L. Marcius Philippus
8. Q. Metellus Scipio		8. M. Perperna[169]
9. **Ser. Sulpicius Rufus**[170]		9. P. Servilius Isauricus
B) Bruhns 1978		
1. L. Afranius	1. C. Antonius Hybrida	1. **M'. Aemilius Lepidus**
2. M. Calpurnius Bibulus	2. Cn. Domitius Calvinus	2. L. Aemilius Paullus
3. C. Claudius Marcellus (cos. 49)	3. A. Gabinius	3. L. Aurelius Cotta

---

[166] Bruhns Table 7.1 (Bruhns 1978: 60), adjusted with reference to Rüpke 2005: 1:133–134. C. Cassius Longinus, the future Caesaricide, and L. Marcius Philippus are left out of the count due to the uncertainty of their date of co-optation; in any case, their eventual partisan adherences balance each other out. It would be impractical, given the nature of the evidence, to filter out those figures who appear in the evidence for the Civil War only sometime after its beginning. Therefore in these statistics partisan affiliation is deemed to have reached back to January 49, though this in fact cannot be true in all instances.

[167] See nn. 134–136 and p. 356f.   [168] See p. 365ff.

[169] Perperna died in this very year aged ninety-eight (Plin. *HN* 7.156). His "neutrality" is therefore a given.

[170] See n. 151 and p. 375ff., especially n. 246.

Table 7.1 (cont.)

Pompeians	Caesarians	Neutrals
4. M. Claudius Marcellus	4. M. Valerius Messalla Rufus	4. **L. Calpurnius Piso**
5. Ap. Claudius Pulcher		5. C. Claudius Marcellus (cos. 50)
6. L. Cornelius Lentulus		6. L. Julius Caesar
7. L. Domitius Ahenobarbus		7. L. Marcius Philippus
8. P. Lentulus Spinther		8. P. Servilius Isauricus
9. Q. Metellus Scipio		9. **Ser. Sulpicius Rufus**
10. M. Tullius Cicero		10. **L. Volcacius Tullus**[171]

Pompeians	Caesarians	"Compromised self-proclaimed neutrals" (see pp. 355–360)
C) Morstein-Marx		
1. L. Afranius	1. **M'. Aemilius Lepidus**	1. L. Aemilius Paullus
2. M. Calpurnius Bibulus	2. C. Antonius Hybrida	2. L. Aurelius Cotta
3. C. Claudius Marcellus (cos. 49)	3. Cn. Domitius Calvinus	3. C. Claudius Marcellus (cos. 50)
4. M. Claudius Marcellus	4. A. Gabinius	4. L. Julius Caesar
5. Ap. Claudius Pulcher	5. **L. Calpurnius Piso**	5. L. Marcius Philippus
6. L. Cornelius Lentulus	6. M. Valerius Messalla Rufus	6. P. Servilius Isauricus
7. L. Domitius Ahenobarbus	7. **Ser. Sulpicius Rufus**	
8. P. Lentulus Spinther	8. **L. Volcacius Tullus**	
9. Q. Metellus Scipio		
10. M. Tullius Cicero		

The nobility was as divided as was the Senate. Caesar himself, we should recall, was not merely noble but patrician. Among the Roman nobles found on his side in the Civil War are men who bore illustrious names in the annals of Roman history such as Acilius Glabrio, Aemilius Lepidus, Antonius, Aurelius Cotta, Calpurnius Bestia, Cassius Longinus, Claudius Marcellus, Claudius Nero, Claudius Pulcher, Cornelius Cinna, Cornelius Dolabella, Cornelius Lentulus, Cornelius Sulla, Domitius, Fabius Maximus, Furius, Junius Brutus and Silanus, Licinius Crassus, Marcius Censorinus and

[171] See nn. 134–135, 140, 151, 152, and 318.

Philippus, Mucius Scaevola, Papirius Carbo, Scribonius Curio, Sempronius Atratinus, Sulpicius Galba and Rufus, Terentius Varro and Valerius Messalla.[172] Even if *more* of the "better" sort lined up with Pompey, it can hardly be said that Caesar suffered from a nobility deficit. This mattered in political disputes because noble names served as reassurance to those farther down the social ladder that the cause was not subversive of the Republic and the traditional order.[173] And indeed, to consider for a moment their own likely perspective, is it remotely plausible that men with these great names and long family traditions of service to the Republic had an interest in risking so much in order to assist in *overthrowing* the Republic and creating a *regnum* for one man – of a family not necessarily any better than theirs – rather than to take their rightful place (as they will have seen it) in due course as *principes civitatis*?[174] If the Sullan precedent was anything to go by, the nobles backing Caesar sought to improve their relative position and that of their families in a highly competitive aristocracy, not destroy it. It was, after all, to his opportune and valuable assistance to Sulla that Pompey himself originally owed his prominence, along with Scribonius Curio the elder, P. Servilius Vatia, Q. Hortensius, and other notable *Sullani*. From a certain, somewhat cynical perspective one might say that a Roman civil war was competitive politics by other means.

So it is after all fair to say, as Shackleton Bailey's study of nobility indicated, that the crisis of early 49 truly divided the Roman Senate,[175] as one would expect given its ambivalent showing in the immediate run-up to the war, even if it is also true – as is to be expected – that its less elevated and respected elements had special incentives to take sides against Pompey and the self-proclaimed *boni*.[176] As for these – the *boni*, in the sense of the wider Roman upper class, including *equites* – there was also a remarkable gap between their attested *attitudes* (so far as they can be inferred from the anxious or indignant comments of Cicero in his letters), and their *actions* during Caesar's occupation of Italy, when many, indeed most, do not leap with alacrity to throw in their lot with Pompey but rather return to Rome

---

[172] Shackleton Bailey 1960: 259–260. "Terentius Varro" is not the famous author and Pompeian legate but the quaestor of 46, tr. pl. 43.

[173] See Yakobson 2010 and now 2014.

[174] An important observation of Bruhns 1978: 171–172 and elsewhere: we find no evidence among contemporary sources that Caesar's partisans sought to change institutions, create a monarchy, or the like.

[175] Contra Raaflaub 1974: 244; Wistrand 1979: 163n1; Brunt 1986: 32.

[176] Hence the νέκυια (as Atticus cleverly dubbed them) of disreputable Caesarian followers, Antony at their head, who so scandalized Cicero in early 49: *Att.* 9.10.7 (with Shackleton Bailey's comment), 11.2, 18.2, 19.1, 10.10.5 (cf. *Phil.* 2.57–58).

and their estates.[177] One way to explain the gap would be to adduce the exigencies of war, in particular Pompey's rapid evacuation of Italy which may in some cases have left them on the wrong side of the battle lines without the chance for long deliberation.[178] Or they may have been "seduced" by Caesar's mildness, once he had demonstrated it repeatedly during his march southward and spectacularly proven it at Corfinium.[179] Perhaps, though, their actions speak louder than their words, or the motives imputed to them by others. In view of the conflicted feelings observable (as we shall see) even in Cicero, who was not merely a consular but currently an *imperator* specifically commanded by the Senate's Final Decree to "take care that the Republic should suffer no harm," we may suppose that the case was not so clear-cut after all: that given the zeal with which Caesar's enemies had pushed the Senate to war in evident violation of popular rights (the tribunician veto, the Law of the Ten Tribunes) and with questionable, perhaps even illegal manipulation of the Senate (the decrees of November–December 50, and the "Schwertübergabe"), in what could certainly be seen as a reckless bid to destroy a great noble, a patrician and a model of Roman *virtus* – that given all this, it was not palpably obvious that Pompey's was really to be seen as the "right" side, whatever one might say in conversation or in letters to Atticus (who remained in Rome!) or to Cicero.[180]

Did the Caesarians Have a Guilty Conscience?

These findings appear to contradict Hermann Strasburger's oft-cited demonstration that Caesar had "morally isolated himself" by entering Italy in defiance of the Senate's decree, and that respectable (i.e. elite) opinion sharply disapproved of Caesar's action. Strasburger examines the rich evidence mostly provided by Cicero's correspondence for the views of no fewer than twelve men associated with Caesar, among them even active "Caesarians" in the Civil War, and finds that "in their private utterances, without exception they disapproved of Caesar's decision to resort to armed

---

[177] Bruhns 1978: esp. 99–110.

[178] Bruhns 1978: 85–86, 93–95. Cf. Shackleton Bailey 1965: 4:365 on Titinius, Volcacius, M' Lepidus, and Sulpicius, "who professed republican sympathies while in reality playing Caesar's game." (According to my argument, however, "Caesar's game" was not inconsistent with "republican sympathies.")

[179] Bruhns 1978: 95–96. Detailed examination of the policy, Chapter 8.

[180] Bruhns 1978: 108 takes for granted that none of the *boni* questioned the rightness of Pompey's cause and is therefore particularly troubled by their failure to commit themselves to action. More likely, the gap between talk and action may be significant in itself.

force against the State," while on the other side not a single statement can be found *approving* of Caesar's action.[181] Let us set aside for the present the tendentiousness of the quotation, in which the role of the Senate's "Final Decree" on January 7 as initiator of the conflict is overlooked as well as the copious evidence that it was in fact Caesar's *enemies* who sought to precipitate a civil war in preference to seeing him elected consul a second time; further, as we have seen, to invest the Senate – in its January change of tone – with the hallowed term "der Staat" when it was arguably acting out of fear and intimidation, and certainly against the will, so far as this can be determined, of the Roman People, is to tip the scales before the weighing begins. But let us turn to the evidence Strasburger adduces for his judgment: the views, as far as they can be discerned (mainly from Cicero's correspondence), of the beginning of the Civil War taken by twelve men who might be expected to present Caesar's case in the best possible light.

Taking the men in the order Strasburger lists them, we can begin with Caesar's father-in-law, **L. Calpurnius Piso**, the consul of 58. Strasburger takes quite literally Cicero's approval of something Piso said or did at the time of the "optimate" evacuation of Rome which he, Cicero, describes in a letter to his wife and daughter as tantamount to condemning his own son-in-law for a crime.[182] Yet after this moment we hear not a peep further of this supposed propaganda coup against Caesar, and surely the most economical interpretation of the thin evidence is that in the general panic caused by rumors of Caesar's approach to Rome, potentially portending a bloody military capture of the City as had occurred several times in the civil wars of the 80s, Piso obeyed Pompey's order to senators to evacuate. This alone was hardly tantamount to condemning Caesar, particularly when the rumor driving the panic was shown to be false. We should also keep in mind that as the crisis had developed late in the year 50, Piso had twice at least intervened in support of Curio in a manner most unwelcome to the hard-core anti-Caesarians, and furthermore, just before the *s.c.u.* on January 7, had offered himself as an envoy to Caesar to explain to him the will of the Senate in what was obviously a last-ditch effort to prevent the war's outbreak.[183] The proposal was not taken up, and instead those eager to confront and crush Caesar proceeded immediately to the Final Decree,

---

[181] Strasburger 1968: 34–40, quotations at 34, 36.

[182] *Fam.* 14.14.2 (January 23): *Labienus rem meliorem fecit; adiuvat etiam Piso, quod ab urbe discedit et sceleris condemnat generum suum*; cf. *Att.* 7.13.1 (also January 23) *amo etiam Pisonem, cuius iudicium de genero suspicor visum iri grave.*

[183] Plut. *Pomp.* 58.6; Dio 40.63; Caes. *BCiv.* 1.3.6–7.

from which one can infer just how welcome Piso's proposal was to the hard-liners in the Senate.[184]

At just about the same time as Cicero's exultation over Piso's "condemnation" of his son-in-law, Cicero also learned that Caesar had asked their mutual friend C. Trebatius to write Cicero to ask him to remain near Rome, and Cicero infers that Caesar had written similar letters to Ser. Sulpicius and Piso.[185] This places Piso in a very select group of notable consulars close enough to Caesar for him to make such a request. And indeed, Piso next turns up in Caesar's Senate, almost certainly during the important meetings held at the beginning of April but certainly in December when Caesar returned from Spain. True, his presence is noted precisely because he was thought to have offended his son-in-law by proposing that envoys should now after all be sent in accordance with the unfulfilled decree of April.[186] But the independence he showed here is probably better interpreted as a mark of his continued high standing with Caesar rather than of any serious opposition to his son-in-law's actions, purpose, or "propaganda."

Strasburger supposes that **M. Caelius Rufus** "was always convinced at the bottom of his heart that Pompey's side had justice on its side, and was progressively more repelled by Caesar's character" until he openly rebelled in 48.[187] This is a much less mercurial, much more principled Caelius than we know from his fairly well-preserved correspondence with Cicero. The very letter to Cicero of January 48 that signals Caelius's recantation is perfectly consistent with his assertion before the war that he preferred the Pompeian *causa* but hated the men who took it up.[188] Although this could easily be dismissed as no more than what a friend *would* say to Cicero, on the other hand it is also true that Caelius had taken a rather conservative political line (e.g. supporting Milo in 52) until we find him bitterly feuding with those in the anti-Caesarian camp as the crisis came in 50. What has changed therefore by January 48 is that Caelius has now come to hate the

---

[184] Caes. *BCiv.* 1.3.6; cf. Caesar's complaint *nec docendi Caesaris propinquis eius spatium datur* (5.1). The praetor L. Roscius Fabatus, not Piso, does end up going on such a mission – *after* the Final Decree (8.4).

[185] Cic. *Att.* 7.17.3; the date of Caesar's request to Trebatius was January 22. On Sulpicius see further later in this chapter. A letter of Trebatius mentioned in Plutarch's *Life of Cicero* (37.4) is often identified as a distorted reference to this particular letter, yet its content is quite different, and there is nothing that prevents Plutarch's allusion from being one to another, later letter, written at the time when Cicero was known to be considering flight from Italy. Caelius suggested something very similar: n. 196.

[186] Plut. *Caes.* 37.1; this must be the occasion Dio refers to at 41.15.4, reinforcing his point by anticipating somewhat illogically an event later in the year.

[187] Strasburger 1968: 36.   [188] *Fam.* 8.17; cf. 12, esp. 14.2: *causam illam <amo> unde homines odi.*

Caesarians too.[189] According to the accounts we possess of the Caelian tumult of 48, it appears that this change of heart was prompted by the stifling of his ambitions after Caesar had elevated him to the praetorship.[190] Caelius's turnabout may also have something to do with the death at Utica of his close friend Curio, whose Caesarian allegiance had evidently strongly influenced his own initial choice of side.[191] (Caelius had even gone so far as to accompany Curio in his flight to Ariminum after the passage of the Final Decree.)[192] In sum, Caelius's choice of side in the Civil War appears to have had little or nothing to do with the rights and wrongs of Caesar's position as he saw them;[193] nor should his assertion that Pompey's *causa* was the better one (made to one he knew was deeply beholden to Pompey) several months *before* the conflict broke out – *before* the vote for mutual disarmament on his friend Curio's proposal, the expulsion of the tribunes, and the *s.c.u.* – be treated as definitive and fixed in stone. Indeed, the first letter (March 9) we have from Caelius after Caesar's entry into Italy exults in Caesar's success and Pompey's discomfiture, and shows no sign whatever of a bad conscience.[194] By early March Caelius was given several cohorts to suppress a midwinter rising in the mountains of western Liguria,[195] an important mission hardly to be entrusted to one whose loyalty was wavering.[196]

---

[189] *Fam.* 8.17.1: *perire satius est quam hos videre,* which echoes Atticus's and Cicero's outrage over the νέκυια. (Note how Cicero tries to embarrass Caelius on this ground at *Fam.* 2.16.7, May 2 or 3, 49.) In 48, however, Caelius's great foes are Gaius Trebonius, Cicero's respected friend (see e.g. *Fam.* 15.21 and Shackleton Bailey 1965: 2:189), and P. Servilius Isauricus the younger, a pedigreed noble.

[190] Dio 42.22.2 explains his disaffection as being due to Caesar's preferment of C. Trebonius to himself for the prestigious position of city praetor. Caes. *BCiv.* 3.20 describes him as "troublemaking" in classic *popularis* fashion by taking up the cause of debtors, and driven by the failure of his initial rabble-rousing to go to further extremes. Caesar's adoption in this narrative of traditional anti-*popularis* character types (3.21: *tabulae novae, ignominia et dolore permotus,* etc.) is notable and significant: he remains the patrician skeptical of demagogy that we have seen before.

[191] *Fam.* 8.17.1. Curio's desertion of the *boni* early in his tribunate may have been a significant impetus toward Caelius's comparable turn in the course of that year.

[192] Dio 41.3.2, confirmed by Cael. [Cic.] *Fam.* 8.17.1.

[193] This is in fact what he says at [Cic.] *Fam.* 8.14.3, though since in this case he is justifying the choice of Caesar's side it is easy not to notice that such a choice is eminently reversible.

[194] *Fam.* 8.15.1. Caelius claims to be deeply troubled about something he cannot commit to a letter (§1; Shackleton Bailey ad loc. is no less cryptic than Caelius), yet there is little reason to think that he had suddenly grown a political conscience.

[195] Cael. [Cic.] *Fam.* 8.15.2. Note that Caesar was now preparing for a dash along this route to Massilia and picked up Caelius on the way (16.4).

[196] Cael. [Cic.] *Fam.* 8.16 (ca. April 16) is an attempt, fully in accordance with Caesar's wishes, to deter Cicero from leaving Italy. Caelius's warnings that Caesar's mercy will shortly run out (§1) may not be disingenuous but must be read in that light: their rhetorical purpose here is to pressure Cicero, not to draw up an indictment of Caesar.

Strasburger believes Cicero's correspondence shows that his son-in-law, **P. Cornelius Dolabella**, and also the future historian **C. Asinius Pollio** joined Caesar at the outbreak of the war "against their political conviction, only for reasons of expediency."[197] But none of this is in fact suggested by the evidence if it is read with an eye to the intended readership – that is, Cicero. For Cicero, Dolabella is alternately an embarrassment (in the eyes of the Pompeians) and a source of reassurance (that his womenfolk and properties will be protected in Rome), but the young man's own letters to Cicero from the pre-Pharsalian stage of the conflict do not in any way cast doubt on his allegiance to Caesar, especially as far back as January 49. In an important letter of May 48, in the midst of the Dyrrachium campaign, by which Dolabella seeks to persuade his father-in-law to desert the Pompeian side, he is careful to represent Cicero's choice to him as honorable in view of his personal obligations and his own vision of the Republic, but one that had been overtaken by events now that Caesar's victory was virtually complete.[198] How else could one have hoped to influence Cicero? Note, however, that at the same time he represents Caesar's expected victory as bringing not the end of the *res publica*, but a different kind of *res publica* than the kind Cicero believed in; he clearly expresses his Caesarian allegiance by describing "the Republic" as being *with* Caesar rather than against him.[199]

Similarly, Pollio's fascinating *apologia* to Cicero of March 43, written in the midst of the War of Mutina, should not be read in a manner divorced from its immediate historical and rhetorical circumstances.[200] At this time Cicero was desperately trying to head off a revival of the Caesarian faction, and Pollio, who was probably in fact prevaricating, was seeking to reassure him about his own loyalties. But we also need to remember how this ended: entirely contrary to the spirit of the letter, Pollio *did* in fact end up joining

---

[197] Strasburger 1968: 37.

[198] Dolabella, [Cic.] *Fam.* 9.9.2 (note §1: *iam inclinata victoria*) *satis factum est iam a te vel officio vel familiaritati, satis factum etiam partibus et ei rei publicae quam tu probabas*).

[199] Ibid. §3: *reliquum est, ubi nunc est res publica ibi simus potius quam, dum illam veterem sequamur, simus in nulla.* The first-person plural form of *sequamur* should not be read in such a way as to make Dolabella too a man who still "followed the old Republic." He had in fact been fully active on the Caesarian side. Here he diplomatically imagines himself and Cicero as fundamentally like-minded, all the better to encourage him to jump ship.

[200] Zecchini 2001: 105–116 (cf. 1982: 1265–1296) and Bosworth 1972: 452–462 offer largely persuasive "Caesarian" readings of Pollio's letter very different from Strasburger's. I would temper their arguments only by pointing out once again that to be "Caesarian" in 49 was not to be "anti-republican." Dobesch 2001: 308–321 rightly emphasizes the ideological tensions in the letter, but does not make sufficient allowance for the influence on Pollio's rhetoric of the dangerous, uncertain political circumstances and of the highly partisan addressee. See also Haller 1967: 22–49.

Antony and helping to induce Lepidus to join Antony as well.[201] This was not really the time for Pollio to make a candid confession of his innermost thoughts about Caesar to Cicero, who had by now publicly committed himself to the idea that Caesar was unequivocally a tyrant whose killing was thoroughly justified. On the contrary, we should expect Pollio to reassure his correspondent by adopting the language and perspective of the kind of men with whom Cicero associated himself, the *boni*.

It may be helpful to compare briefly a more clear-cut case that shares notable elements with Pollio's: the celebrated letter written several months after the assassination to Cicero by his old friend **C. Matius**, who had also been a close associate of Caesar's. Matius stuck quite firmly to his personal loyalty to Caesar even after the Ides of March despite his old friendship with Cicero, and his own way of talking about the beginning of the Civil War helps us to see the rhetorical tack a loyal friend or follower of Caesar might take when prompted to give an account of himself to Cicero. Matius writes that

> It was not Caesar I followed in the civil war, but a friend whom I did not desert, even though I did not like what he was doing. I never approved of civil war or indeed of the origin of the conflict, which I did my very utmost to get nipped in the bud.[202]

Shackleton Bailey's comment on a later paragraph of the letter can be applied to the Caesarian *apologia* as well: "Its purport is to establish the writer as a thorough *bonus*, saving his loyalty to Caesar's memory."[203] This was the way Cicero and Matius worked around their differences and sought to remain friends despite deep political mistrust. Cicero was hardly taken in by their polite fictions, nor surely was Matius.[204]

Returning now to Pollio's account of his own role in the Caesarian ranks in the Civil War, we can see that he takes a quite similar line to Matius's

---

[201] Cic. *Fam.* 10.31–33; App. *BCiv.* 3.97/399.

[202] Matius, [Cic.] *Fam.* 11.28.2 (Shackleton Bailey transl.): *neque enim Caesarem in dissensione civili sum secutum, sed amicum, quamquam re offendebar, tamen non deserui, neque bellum umquam civile aut etiam causam dissensionis probavi, quam etiam nascentem exstingui summe studui.* Cf. Strasburger 1968: 39, who again overlooks the polite and diplomatic fictions that shaped such claims by Caesar's partisans after his assassination.

[203] Shackleton Bailey 1965: 2:490. Cf. Morgan 2000: 59, on Pollio's desire as historian to "distanc[e] Pollio the historian from the general for whom he actually fought."

[204] Cf. Cic. *Att.* 14.1.1 (April 7, 44): *nihil perditius!* Note also the negative comparison of Matius's attitude to Oppius's (*qui nihilo minus* [sc. *Caesarem*] *desiderat, sed loquitur nihil quod quemquam bonum offendat*): Matius evidently could not quite play the *bonus* convincingly after all. Cf. *Att.* 14.1.2: φαλάκρωμα *inimicissimum oti, id est Bruti.* See Hall 2009 on polite fictions in the correspondence; unfortunately, he analyzes only Cicero's letter in the exchange (*Fam.* 11.27: pp. 60–67), not Matius's reply.

after the Ides of March, with some "Caelian" personal animus mixed in and a heavy dose of respectable patriotic sentiment to establish his bona fides with Cicero in the current circumstances. Pollio asserts that

> My nature and pursuits lead me to crave for peace and freedom. The outbreak of the former civil war cost me many a tear. But since I could not remain neutral because I had powerful enemies on both sides, I avoided the camp where I well knew I should not be safe from my enemy's plots. Finding myself forced whither I would not, and having no wish to trail in the rear, I certainly did not hang back from dangerous work.[205]

Notably, both Pollio and Matius say nothing about "the Republic." That would either anger Cicero or compromise their own integrity. Both thoroughly "depoliticize" their decision to support Caesar. Instead, they both deplore "civil war" (here of course they aimed straight at Cicero's own known preference, at least on that occasion). But while doing so, Pollio does not quite distance himself from Caesar (in modest contrast to Matius, who at least expresses disapproval of his actions – apparently his part in bringing matters to the point of civil war). In fact, so far as Caesar himself was concerned, Pollio writes,

> I loved him in all duty and loyalty, because in his greatness he treated me, a recent acquaintance, as though I had been one of his oldest intimates.[206]

This single sentence offers precious insight into the immense personal appeal of Caesar – a sentence that helps us to understand the depth of the anguish and bitter resentment Matius expresses in 44 at the "terrible fate of his close friend and a great man": "I hope they [Caesar's killers] will regret what they have done. I want everyone to feel the pain of Caesar's death."[207] Note that Matius's indignation is expressed as an intensely moral one based on the killers' violation of some of the humane principles

---

[205] Pollio, [Cic.] *Fam.* 10.31.2 (Shackleton Bailey transl.): *natura autem mea et studia trahunt me ad pacis et libertatis cupiditatem. itaque illud initium civilis belli saepe deflevi. cum vero non liceret mihi nullius partis esse quia utrubique magnos inimicos habebam, ea castra fugi in quibus plane tutum me ab insidiis inimici sciebam non futurum. compulsus eo quo minime volebam, ne in extremis essem, plane pericula non dubitanter adii.*

[206] Pollio, [Cic.] *Fam.* 10.31.3 (Shackleton Bailey transl.): *Caesarem vero, quod me in tanta fortuna modo cognitum vetustissimorum familiarium loco habuit, dilexi summa cum pietate et fide.* On Pollio's use of "amatory" language see Hall 2009: 82. We possess earlier testimony from Cicero's own pen of the peculiar warmth Caesar was able to inspire in his friends: *nullum meum minimum dictum, non modo factum, pro Caesare intercessit quod ille non ita illustri gratia exceperit ut ego eum mihi devinctum putarem* (Cic. *Fam.* 1.9.21).

[207] Matius, [Cic.] *Fam.* 11.28.5: *quod hominis mihi coniunctissimi ac viri amplissimi doleo gravem causam* (cf. §6: *hominis amicissimi*). §4: *Sed quid mihi suscensent si id opto ut paeniteat eos sui facti? cupio enim Caesaris mortem omnibus esse acerbam.*

Caesar had exemplified: sparing one's enemies and respecting the autonomy of friends.[208] After all, then, Pollio and Matius integrate their admiration for Caesar as a friend into their story as reluctant civil warriors in
broadly similar ways. But Pollio plays down the personal attachment to
Caesar that appears so intense in Matius's letter, and adds, more in the
manner of Caelius, that his choice of side was ultimately "forced" by the
choice of his personal enemies to hew to Pompey's side. It was therefore
not a matter of personal inclination but a choice imposed by circumstance.

Pollio continues by protesting that in the Civil War he had done everything that lay within his power in such a way as to win the approval of
respectable opinion (*optimus quisque*), while what he had been ordered to do
he had carried out with transparent reluctance in a manner that revealed his
true principles.[209] He acknowledges that his service in the Civil War had
won him (unjustified) ill will, but he assures Cicero that this experience had
only taught him how pleasant a thing was freedom, and how wretched was
life subjected to another's domination.[210] To reinforce the point (and to hint
very strongly but probably disingenuously that he would take Cicero's side
against Antony, a suggestion he would very soon betray) Pollio rounds off his
apologia with a declaration of war against any man who would "again" seek
to usurp sole power: he would not shun any danger in defense of freedom.[211]

Pollio almost certainly at this point was trying to keep his options open.
No one – not even Cicero – could have expected him to offer a perfectly
candid portrayal of his thoughts on the outbreak and conduct of the Civil
War at this critical juncture, after the assassination of Caesar himself and at
a point when the remnants of the Caesarian party seemed to have been
crushed or co-opted. Instead, we can observe much the same self-
exculpatory strain discernible in Matius's Caesarian *apologia*. Both struggle
mightily to represent themselves to Cicero as men of excellent political
principles who were reluctant followers of Caesar for personal reasons in
the Civil War and therefore should not be suspected of any dark ambitions
in the current crisis. Their letters are useful documents for the ideological
dimensions of the War of Mutina, but cannot be interpreted as unguarded

---

[208] Matius, [Cic.] *Fam.* 11.28.2–3, 7.

[209] Pollio, [Cic.] *Fam.* 10.31.3: *quae mea sententia gerere mihi licuit ita feci ut optimus quisque maxime
probarit; quod iussus sum eo tempore atque ita feci ut appareret invito imperatum esse.* His exchange
with Cato when he arrived to drive him from Sicily seems perhaps inconsistent with his claim here:
see n. 212.

[210] Ibid. *cuius facti iniustissima invidia erudire me potuit quam iucunda libertas et quam misera sub
dominatione vita esset.*

[211] Ibid. *Ita, si id agitur ut rursus in potestate omnia unius sint, quicumque is est, ei me profiteor inimicum;
nec periculum est ullum quod pro libertate aut refugiam aut deprecer.*

confessions of their authors' true motives in a very different situation more than five years before. Only a few months after writing *Fam.* 10.31 to Cicero, Pollio, whom Velleius describes at precisely this juncture as "steady in his resolution, loyal to the Caesarian side and hostile to Pompey," deserted Cicero for Antony, Lepidus, and Plancus.[212]

C. Scribonius Curio had been instrumental in representing Caesar's interests in the run-up to the war and had directly associated himself with Caesar's cause during the outbreak of the war by personally delivering Caesar's "harsh and threatening" letter to the Senate on January 1 and afterward joining the flight of the two tribunes to Ariminum on the night of January 7.[213] Yet this man Strasburger sees as so shaken in 49 by the "conflict in his soul" prompted by his adherence to Caesar that he ultimately could only effect his escape from a "tragically squandered life" through a "Heldentod" at Utica in North Africa.[214] That is a highly romanticized interpretation of one who in fact never gives any sign of second thoughts about his role in bringing the crisis to a head. (One could just as easily accept Caesar's own romantic portrayal of Curio as one so moved by a sense of honor and loyalty to Caesar that he could not face him again after losing his army and so went bravely down with his ship.)[215] But it is best not to try to enter into Curio's thought processes as he was cut off by King Juba's horsemen and death loomed before his eyes. What we *can* say is that Curio played a prominent role in early military operations in Italy and subsequently in Sicily and Africa.[216] After Cicero met with Curio for the first time since the outbreak of hostilities, on April 14, 49, he reports no word of regret or disapproval of Caesar's actions thus far, even if Curio did speak darkly about Caesar's aiming at Pompey's death and warn Cicero as a friend about the limits of Caesar's patience, and the naiveté of supposing that his policy of clemency would continue forever.[217] His assertions that there was

---

[212] Vell. 2.63.3. His *Histories*, naturally had to adopt a more impartial perspective (Morgan 2000), though they were written under the Caesarian Triumvirate. Yet Pollio apparently gave himself a sharp Caesarian rejoinder to Cato's question on what authority he was sailing to Sicily (Plut. *Cat. Min.* 53.3, App. *BCiv.* 2.40/162) that is much like Curio's exchange with Cicero described at *Att.* 10.4.9. Pollio seems to have tempered the eulogistic tradition on Cato's suicide by adopting some elements of the Caesarian view: Rauh 2012: 281–284.

[213] Cic. *Fam.* 16.11.2; note *Curio meus illum incitabat*, with App. *BCiv.* 2.32/123–128. For Curio's role in the culmination of crisis of 50 see Chapter 6, p. 279ff. and passim.

[214] Strasburger 1968: 39–40.

[215] Caes. *BCiv.* 2.42.4: *At Curio numquam se amisso exercitu quem a Caesare fidei commissum acceperit in eius conspectum reversurum confirmat atque ita proelians interficitur.*

[216] Caes. *BCiv.* 1.12 (capture of Iguvium), 18.5 (Corfinium), 30 (Sicily); Pompey, [Cic.] *Att.* 8.12C.1.

[217] Cic. *Att.* 10.4.8–11. Curio clearly links the likelihood of such a "turn for the worse" to Caesar's recent loss of popularity due to the scene with Metellus (10.4.8, 7.3).

"no hope," no "escape," focalized as they are through Cicero, appear on their face to refer to *Cicero's* hope of avoiding a full-scale civil war, and should not be interpreted against the rest of our evidence as implying Curio's personal negative evaluation of the victory of the side he had chosen.[218] Nor should any great weight be set on Cicero's rejection, in a letter to Atticus of May 2, of the idea of delaying a departure from Italy until the outcome of the campaign in Spain became clear, on the grounds that "if [Caesar] is driven out, what sort of welcome shall I get or what sort of figure shall I cut joining Pompey at a time when I imagine Curio himself will go over to him?"[219] This is obviously not to be taken as a hint that Curio's loyalties are actually wavering, but rather a way of emphasizing the complete folly of the course of action under discussion, since if such a catastrophe befell Caesar *even Curio* would be changing sides. Cicero mentions Curio here precisely because he would desert Caesar only *in extremis.*[220] Other than this brief mention and the meetings we already noted, Curio comes up in the correspondence in this period merely in connection with Cicero's hopes that through his personal relationship with this prominent Caesarian he would be able to rely on his permission or connivance in slipping out of Italy.

Strasburger even suspects Caesar's "secretariate," the Spaniard **L. Cornelius Balbus** and **C. Oppius**, of nursing inner reserves over Caesar's actions and policies.[221] This looks very much like wishful thinking. Their joint letter to Cicero on March 10 or 11 makes clear that they are seeking to act in a way totally consistent with and dependent on Caesar's policy.[222] Balbus follows this up immediately with another missive citing new evidence that Caesar was eager to reestablish *concordia* with Pompey – and using the hope thus encouraged in Cicero to try to prevent him from turning definitively against Caesar.[223] (Note the loyalist exclamation Balbus allows himself here: "As I hope to die before Caesar!")[224] It seems that in a lost letter written in the first half of 49, Oppius had replied to a question Cicero had put to him about sailing to join Pompey or remaining in Italy with advice that he should take account of his *dignitas* in deciding what to do.[225] Five years later, after Caesar's

---

[218] Cic. *Att.* 10.4.9, 10.5.2.   [219] Cic. *Att.* 10.8.2.

[220] Some anxiety on Curio's part may be sensed at Cic. *Att.* 10.7.3. On Curio in 49 see further Dettenhofer 1992: 146–156.

[221] Strasburger 1968: 38. These two were prominent members of what Malitz called Caesar's "Chancellery" and Gelzer called his "Cabinet," on which see Malitz 1987.

[222] [Cic.] *Att.* 9.7A.   [223] [Cic.] *Att.* 9.7B (also March 10 or 11).

[224] Ibid., §3: *ita incolumi Caesare moriar!*, in Shackleton Bailey's trans. and with his note ad loc.

[225] The letter is recalled in Cic. *Fam.* 11.29.1 (*suasisti ut consulerem dignitati meae*), written to Oppius shortly before Cicero's planned departure for Greece in 44, five years later. Cf. Balbus's advice at *Att.* 9.7B.1–2.

death and under somewhat similar circumstances, Cicero recalls this advice in a letter to Oppius, and politely interprets it as implicitly recognizing his obligation to join Pompey, yet surely it can be read more ambiguously, and it should take more evidence than this to convince us that Oppius, no matter how friendly with Cicero, would offer advice directly contrary to Caesar's express position.[226] More likely, Oppius was simply seeking to satisfy simultaneously the demands of friendship with Cicero and with Caesar by offering a reply that Cicero could interpret in whichever way he inclined, in terms with which Caesar could hardly take exception.[227]

We have already interpreted **C. Matius's** fascinating letter of late 44 in connection with the strikingly similar professions of Pollio. Note, however that, whatever the real import of what he wrote to Cicero at that time, his behavior and discussions with his friend at the time of Caesar's occupation of Italy in 49 gave no signs of disaffection with his leader. After he paid a friendly call upon Cicero at Formiae on March 19, 49, Cicero describes him to Atticus as "a man of moderation and good sense. Certainly he has always been looked upon as an advocate of peace."[228] Yet that did not make him any less a Caesarian at a time when Caesar himself was repeatedly professing his desire for a settlement (to be advocated indeed by Cicero).[229] Cicero would have pounced on any utterance by his friend that was unambiguously critical of Caesar's actions, but all he can say is that "to me at any rate [Matius] seemed very far from approving what was going on, and very apprehensive of the Underworld, as you call them."[230] Yet there was much to deplore in the current situation without committing oneself to a partisan viewpoint, and tensions between the νέκυια and the more respectable Caesarians were only to be expected. None of this shook Cicero's understanding that Matius and another mutual friend with Caesar, **C. Trebatius Testa**, who was at this time traveling with Matius,

---

[226] Ibid. *ex quo quid sentires intellexi* seems to concede the surface ambiguity of Oppius's suggestion. In April Caelius is prepared to diverge from Caesar's line only to the extent of recommending as a compromise solution, if Cicero is "worried by what the optimates are saying," that he go to an *oppidum* – presumably outside Italy – far from the war: *Att.* 10.9A.5 = *Fam.* 8.16. But this is of course not the same as joining Pompey.

[227] See Cic. *Att.* 11.8.1 for Cicero's judgment that Balbus and Oppius were indeed well disposed to him while simultaneously influential with Caesar. Again, Strasburger does not attend sufficiently to the ambiguities and obscurities that "politeness strategies" create in Cicero's correspondence: see White 2003: 80–86, and 2010: 78ff.; Hall 2009.

[228] Cic. *Att.* 9.11.2 (March 20, 49).

[229] Cf. Balbus's constant talk of peace with Cicero documented earlier.

[230] Cic. *Att.* 9.11.2: *quam ille haec non probare mihi quidem visus est, quam illam* νέκυιαν, *ut tu appellas, timere!* (Atticus had darkly joked thus about the bad characters and opportunists who flocked to Caesar's side: n. 176.)

were solidly in Caesar's good graces, influential with him and usefully privy to his thinking.[231] Thus, for instance, shortly after his entry into Italy Caesar used Trebatius as an intermediary through whom to pass along his request to Cicero that he remain in the environs of Rome; this seems hardly the job for one whose loyalty or conviction was wavering.[232] Trebatius, whom Cicero praises in April and May in terms very like those he used for Matius (*vir plane et civis bonus*), may have allowed himself critical comments about some of Caesar's friends and supporters during a visit to Formiae on May 4, yet again there is nothing in Cicero's language to suggest that they were directed at Caesar himself, much less his political or military decisions. For example, among the *monstra* that he deplored was the appalling news that the Spaniard Balbus was hoping to enter the Senate![233] Such complaints seem to echo of the sort of thing Trebatius's good friend Matius had said about the νέκυια. Whatever their deeper feelings may have been on the topic of Caesar's recent actions, then, Trebatius and Matius are likely, when conversing with their old friend Cicero and others of a similar mind during the early months of the Civil War, to have stayed on the "safe" topic of the deplorable ambitions entertained by certain undeserving members of the Caesarian faction.[234] That old troublemaker Q. Fufius Calenus, on the other hand, was unrestrained by polite consideration of his host's feelings when, visiting Cicero on his way to Brundisium on March 9, he denounced Pompey as a criminal, and the Senate for its fecklessness and stupidity. ("Imagine the look of him, the arrogance!" Cicero writes to Atticus.)[235]

Ser. Sulpicius Rufus, the consul of 51, is a complicated case, as has already been indicated. He appears to have taken a neutral line during his

---

[231] Cic. *Att.* 9.15a (March 25), 17.1 (March 27): the two men helped prepare him for his interview with Caesar on March 28. For Cicero's patronal transferal of his protégé Trebatius to Caesar in Gaul *de manu, ut aiunt, in manum* see *Fam.* 7.5–15; Trebatius became friends with Matius while in Caesar's service in Gaul (7.15.2). See n. 185 for Trebatius's service to Caesar as an epistolary intermediary with Cicero.

[232] Cic. *Att.* 7.17.3 (February 2).

[233] Cic. *Att.* 10.11.4 (May 4) (with 12.1 of May 5); cf. 10.1.3 (April 3), which Strasburger again overinterprets (1968: 40): there is in fact no evidence at all that he "schimpfte ... weidlich auf Caesar," only that Atticus was delighted with something he had said or written. Praise of Trebatius in this letter as a *bonus vir et civis* is echoed at *Att.* 10.11.4 without any sign of criticism directed specifically at Caesar.

[234] Cicero himself "usually tended to think less badly of Caesar himself than of his adherents" (Shackleton Bailey 1965: 5:377). Trebatius would become an esteemed jurist of the Augustan age: Sonnet, *RE* 6 (1937) 2258–2259.

[235] Cic. *Att.* 9.5.1 (March 10). Fufius had supported Clodius against the attack of the *boni* in 61, had backed Caesar as praetor in 59, and served as his legate from 51: see *MRR* and Wiseman 1971: 232, n. 185. It is interesting that such an unlikely person would stop in to see Cicero at all.

consulship and afterward as the crisis regarding Caesar's return truly came to a head; his explicit advocacy of peace was expected to win Caesar's gratitude, and probably in fact did.[236] His son had actually joined Caesar's operations around Brundisium, and though Sulpicius himself probably tried to maintain a position of plausible deniability as to his own role in that matter, Cicero saw the father as completely implicated in the decision and thereby clearly taking a side.[237] Sulpicius remained in Italy, even returned to Rome as Pompey shipped out, and he played a prominent consular role in the meeting of the Senate called by Caesar for the Kalends of April.[238] Cicero politely credits him to his face with some plain speaking at that meeting "about peace and about the Spains," though privately to Atticus his tone is contemptuous.[239] However that may be, it was not enough to assuage Sulpicius's fears that Pompey was angry with him – quite understandably, given Sulpicius's prewar receptiveness to Caesar's demands (which the hard-liners will have seen as appeasement), not to mention the Pompeians' declaration that all who stayed in Italy, much less those who graced Caesar's Senate, were to be regarded as enemies.[240] In May, after putting out feelers to Cicero through Trebatius, Sulpicius journeyed south from Rome to confer with him at Cumae.[241] After their meeting on May 8, Cicero described Sulpicius to Atticus as paralyzed by anxiety and unable to restrain floods of tears.[242] He did go so far as to denounce Caesar's *audacia* – but also Pompey's *crudelitas*. Victory for either, he lamented, would be crowned by an assault on private property.[243] One thing he insisted on firmly: that he would go into exile if the condemned were recalled – presumably a matter of principle for

---

[236] See n. 151. Cicero tries to deny that Caesar showed Sulpicius any gratitude (*Fam.* 4.2.3), but this appears to be inconsistent with Caesar's famous or notorious attention to the friendly exchange of *beneficia* (Sall. *Cat.* 54.3–4).

[237] *Att.* 9.19.2: *erit immitissimus Servius, qui filium misit ad effligendum Cn. Pompeium aut certe capiendum*; Cicero consistently attributes to Servius Sr. the active role in the decision (cf. 10.1a, 3a.2). Shackleton Bailey is right to see *immitissimus* (i.e. toward Caesar's pressure) as sarcastic (ad loc.), and immediately undercut by the relative clause; Cicero's dismay at Sulpicius's action, which did not even have the excuse of fear, points the same way. Cicero expected Sulpicius to be chosen as the Senate's peace envoy to Pompey (10.1a). For the embarrassment his son's action later caused Sulpicius, at least when conversing with Cicero see 10.14.3.

[238] Cic. *Att.* 9.19.2, 10.1a (cf. 10.3a.2).

[239] Cic. *Fam.* 4.1.1 (note even here the sting in the wording *in senatum, sive potius in conventum senatorum*; cf. *Att.* 10.1.1.

[240] Cic. *Att.* 10.14.3 (May 8).

[241] Cic. *Fam.* 4.1 (ca. April 21), *Att.* 10.7.2 (April 22?); *Fam.* 4.2 (April 28 or 29), *Att.* 10.12.4 (May 5), 10.14 (May 8).

[242] Cic. *Att.* 10.14.1: *numquam vidi hominem perturbatiorem metu*, 3; cf. 10.15.2 *unum C. Marcello cognovi timidiorem*.

[243] Cic. *Att.* 10.14.1.

a famed jurist.[244] He may have been as good as his word. But "exile" is not the same thing as going to Pompey. We have no evidence that he did ultimately throw in his lot with Caesar's enemies, which surely, in view of his advocacy of accepting Caesar's demands and his conspicuous leadership in the Senate in April 49, would have been a very risky move – and even Cicero considered him a timorous man. Sulpicius next appears in isolation on Samos in 47 and, sometime in 46, taking command of the province of Achaea *for Caesar*.[245] On balance it seems more likely that, while expressing his displeasure by removing himself to an island in the part of the Empire dominated by Pompey, Sulpicius in fact played no role in the campaigns and kept a cautious distance from both sides until the aftermath of Pharsalus, when, accepting the verdict of what seemed to many to be the decisive battle, he allowed himself to be drawn into Caesar's emergent new regime.[246]

Sulpicius, then, is an interesting example of a consular caught in the middle, in some respects not so very different from Cicero.[247] His notable advocacy of peace must have been seen by the Catonians and Pompeians as pure appeasement. This is likely to have made Pompey's camp an unwelcoming place for him in 49 or 48, which is most likely the fundamental reason for Sulpicius's choice to remain in Italy and even return to the Senate after the departure of the consuls from Brundisium. But Sulpicius also ascribed *audacia* to Caesar, a strong term in a political or forensic context that can mean brazen criminality.[248] It would be reasonable then to infer that Sulpicius heartily disapproved of Caesar's decision to defend his

---

[244] Cic. *Att.* 10.14.3. Jurist: Cicero's witty putdown of Sulpicius's calling at *Mur.* 19–29 presumes that his dedication to this arena was well known. Curio had informed Cicero on April 14 that the restoration of "those condemned by the *lex Pompeia*" was as good as certain (4.8). 9.14.2 appears to indicate that by March 24 or 25 the recall only of those convicted under the *lex Pompeia de ambitu* was being floated. This would touch a fairly small number of senators, but some fairly distinguished ones: the praetorians M. Scaurus, C. Memmius, and P. Plautius Hypsaeus, and the consulars M. Valerius Messalla Rufus and Cn. Domitius Calvinus, the latter two of whom served Caesar with distinction in the Civil War and at the time of his assassination were queued up for future service as *magister equitum*: Chapter 9, n. 283.

[245] Cic. *Brut.* 156; *Fam.* 4.3–4; *MRR* 2.299.

[246] Late in 46 Cicero includes Sulpicius in a short list of "pardoned anti-Caesarians" advanced by Caesar (*Fam.* 6.6.10). This is the strongest evidence for classifying him as "Pompeian" (Shackleton Bailey 1960: 253n7 and 1965: 5:275, whose interpretation of Cic. *Phil.* 13.29 is rejected by Bruhns 1978: 37n25), but it is far from decisive. Münzer (*RE* 4A.853–55), Syme (1939: 45n1), and Bruhns (1978: 40–41) describe him as "neutral." Sulpicius's dignified letter of consolation to Cicero (*Fam.* 4.5, March 45) makes brilliant use of the idea of the "death of the Republic" in the Civil War, but it is not his purpose there to assign responsibility for the catastrophe that (according to Cicero) he had striven so mightily to prevent. Already in 46 he was Caesar's proconsul in Achaea (*MRR* 2.299).

[247] Cicero himself draws the comparison in April 49: *Fam.* 4.1.1. On Cicero see further later in this chapter.

[248] Cf. Cicero's angry denunciation at *Att.* 7.13.1 of *unius perditi civis audacia* (discussed further later).

position with arms, though like Cicero he probably also disapproved of the zeal for war evinced by the Pompeian side, not to mention its "cruelty."[249] Sulpicius did ultimately distance himself from Caesar by departing from Italy (perhaps into self-imposed exile), but note that according to his own words it was not apparently the "Final Decree of the Senate" or Caesar's unauthorized return to Italy under arms that made him do so, but Caesar's recall of the exiles, ostensibly the victims of Pompey's laws and trials in 52. For the great jurist, apparently, *that* was going too far – or at least, the final straw. Here, then, is a more independent, indeed more neutral view than those of the committed Caesarians we have reviewed thus far. Yet that is only to be expected, since he was never actually a *supporter* of Caesar's claims or an active partisan or officer once the conflict had begun – until, in 46 or perhaps 47, he took charge of the province of Achaea for him.

The eleventh of Strasburger's Caesarian witnesses, the historian **C. Sallustius Crispus**, need not detain us long. The old notion, still current in Strasburger's day, that Sallust wrote his historical works as a Caesarian partisan is now thoroughly discredited.[250] Nor, however, does any comment clearly critical of Caesar's actions in January 49 appear in the authentic surviving works. The first of the "Letters to Caesar" ascribed to Sallust, which Strasburger mined for his purposes at a time when its authenticity was generally accepted, is now widely regarded as a forgery, and whether or not that is so, it is certainly too dubious to lend any support to his case.[251] Sallust served Caesar loyally and effectively in the Civil War, and his reward was to be given charge in 46 of the new province of Africa composed of the former territory of the Numidian king Juba, defeated at Thapsus.[252] This was a strong mark of favor; if Sallust disapproved of Caesar, his commander must have been unaware of it.

Cicero's Anguished Lucubrations

There remains, of course, Cicero himself, who in the flood of letters poured out to Atticus and others during the first half of 49 has much to say, mostly

---

[249] "Doubtless" – inferred from Cicero's comments about Sulpicius's prewar policy and Cicero's lament to Sulpicius that upon arriving at Rome in January 49, *incideram in hominum pugnandi cupidorum insanias* (*Fam.* 4.1.1), a comment obviously not meant to apply exclusively, or perhaps even chiefly, to Caesar.
[250] Esp. Syme 1964.
[251] Strasburger especially stressed [Sall.] *Ep.* 1.3.3, 5. Gelzer too (1968: 276–277) accepted authenticity. Against see especially Syme 1958: 46–55, and 1964: 314–351; Koestermann 1970; E. Woytek 2004; and now Ramsey's revised Loeb ed. of 2013 (xxix–xxxi). See, however, Dupla, Fatás, and Pina 1994. W. Schmid's (1993) cryptographic defense of authenticity has not won acceptance.
[252] See now Ramsey 2013: xxiv–xxv.

negative, about Caesar's actions. The trouble is that he has *so much* to say, not all of it consistent as the circumstances and his anxieties change. For instance, in a painstaking analysis of Cicero's motives for (ultimately) taking the Pompeian side in the Civil War, Peter Brunt concluded that while a sense of personal obligation to Pompey for orchestrating his return in 57 seems from the letters to Atticus to have been the paramount factor determining Cicero's choice, this was greatly amplified by the fact that it coincided rather than conflicted with his view of the interests of the Republic.[253] On the other hand, Shackleton Bailey sagely remarks in his note to Cicero's letter to Atticus of March 6, 49, that "C[icero] knew that his obligation to Pompey was not in reality a very powerful argument, at least not in Atticus's eyes, and therefore puts it forward most emphatically when he is most averse to the course indicated."[254] The claim is conjectural, of course, but based on long and deep familiarity with Cicero's voice in the correspondence. And the principle it quietly presupposes is both salutary and radical indeed: that what Cicero writes even in these most private letters to his closest known confidant cannot be regarded as a window to his innermost soul.[255] One can legitimately take Shackleton Bailey's observation one step further (with a nod to contemporary cognitive neuroscience) and suggest that even if we *were* able to pry into Cicero's innermost soul we would be unlikely to find therein a coherent, consistent rationale that would explain his actions in such grave and ever-changing circumstances. It would probably be misleading therefore to disregard the ever-shifting strands of blame, worry, and self-exculpation in Cicero's correspondence in early 49 in an attempt to isolate a satisfactorily consistent thread. The great value of the letters, in fact, is precisely that they offer an almost unique glimpse of actual, chaotic, lived experience rather than the reductive artifice of retrospective

---

[253] Brunt 1986: especially 29–31. Note that Brunt's argument was implicitly directed against reductive explanations of Roman politics in terms of factional or kin allegiance; in so doing he (successfully, on the whole) shows that agents explained their choices to themselves and to others in terms of entrenched values and higher principles. That does not of course show that these did in fact determine their actions.

[254] Shackleton Bailey 1965: 4:360 ad *Att.* 9.1.4; cf., more pithily, "A man who gives a bad reason for doing what he knows he ought is excusing his own reluctance" (1965: 1:42). Brunt rejects the claim at 1986: 28–29: Cicero feared reproach for ingratitude.

[255] This aspect of the letters to Atticus seems generally underappreciated (but see Hutchinson 1998: 1–24). Even Jon Hall's excellent study of "politeness strategies" in the Ciceronian correspondence tends to leave aside Cicero's strategies of negotiation with his closest epistolographic interlocutor. Erving Goffman's "presentation of the self" seems clearly to be a feature of Cicero's correspondence even with Atticus, which is too often read as if it were free of rhetorical and social self-fashioning. On the contrary. See also Gazzaniga 2011, especially chapter 10 on the (ex post facto) "Interpreter" of consciousness and the "fiction" of rational agency.

narrative.[256] We should pay attention to relevant individual strands without suppressing any of them in the vain and misleading attempt to produce clarity where there was little or none. As anyone who takes the trouble to read through Cicero's anxiety-ridden letters to Atticus in early 49 will know, he was caught in a bewildering and rather terrifying flux of contingencies. It would be dishonest to reduce the confusion we find by suppressing the tensions and contradictions that abound therein.

Shackleton Bailey is not of course wrong to say that Cicero generally condemned Caesar "wholesale" – for his "most impudent" demands made of the Senate, for his "harsh and threatening letter" of January 1 while holding on to his provinces and army *invito senatu*, for "violating" and "making war on the Republic," and so on.[257] Civil war "has arisen not from a conflict in the civic body but from the recklessness of one unscrupulous Roman."[258] Cicero, who had seen the bloody civil wars of the 80s, contemplates the possibility that Caesar might even be "mad" enough to sack and burn the capital.[259] Was he a Roman general or another Hannibal?[260] Caesar was, or would be, a "tyrant" – whether in the mode of the unspeakably cruel Phalaris of Agrigentum, who supposedly liked to roast his victims alive in a giant bronze "bellowing" bull, or the gentler, but insidious Peisistratus of Athens, he would soon make clear.[261] A vivid impression of the tone of Cicero's denunciations in late January, before

---

[256] Chapter 1, n. 62.

[257] Shackleton Bailey 1965: 4:313, citing *Att.* 7.9.3–4 (*quid impudentius?* cf. 17.2 *impudentissime postulaverit*), 11.1 (below), 18.2 (below), *Fam.* 16.11.2 to Terentia and Tullia (*minacis ad senatum et acerbas litteras miserat er erat adhuc impudens, qui exercitum et provinciam invito senatu teneret*), and 12.2 to Tiro (*cum Caesar amentia quadam raperetur et oblitus nominis atque honorum suorum Ariminum . . . occupavisset*). *Att.* 7.17.2: *violata iam ab illo* [sc. Caesare] *re publica.* 8.5.1 *de salute rei publicae decernetur* (at Corfinium). Note that all of these letters were written before Caesar's act of clemency at Corfinium.

[258] *Att.* 7.13.1: *non ex civium dissensione sed ex unius perditi civis audacia.* (Shackleton Bailey perhaps under-translates both *audacia* and *perditus* here: cf. Sulpicius [n. 248], and 18.2: *o perditum latronem!*) Cf. 10.4.2: *ardet furore et scelere.* On the eve of the conflict he supposed that Caesar would be Cinna's equal in slaughtering leading senators and match Sulla in plundering the rich (7.7.7), that living under Caesar would be living under *regnum* (7.7.5, 7) and/or slavery (7.9.4; cf. 7.15.2).

[259] *Fam.* 14.14.1 (January 23), 16.12.1 (January 27); cf. *Att.* 7.13.1 (*non patriam sed praedam*), 8.3.4. For "madness" see also *Fam.* 16.12.2 (January 27) *amentia quadam.*

[260] *Att.* 7.11.1 (January 21?).

[261] *Att.* 7.20.2 (February 5); after Corfinium he had become simply "Pisistratus" (8.16.2, March 4). For Φαλαρισμός (Atticus's term) see 7.12.2 (already January 22). For Caesar as *tyrannus* see also 8.2.4 (February 17), 10.4.2 (April 14), 10.8.2 (May 2). On Cicero's use of the Greek (esp. Platonic) figure of the tyrant in his letters to Atticus of this period see Gildenhard 2006, who interestingly shows how Cicero was able to use it "to ennoble his wretched terms of existence in his correspondence with Atticus" (203), especially useful in fact during his fits of resolve to remain in Italy: "Cicero's Platonic self-fashioning . . . simultaneously condemns and encourages complicity with power" (205).

he had caught a glimpse of the possibility of peace, comes at the head of a letter to Atticus written probably from Formiae on or about January 21:

> Deluded wretch (*o hominem amentem et miserum*), with never in his life a glimpse of even the shadow of Good! And he says he is doing all this for his honour's sake (*dignitatis causa*)! Where is honour without moral good? (*ubi est autem dignitas nisi ubi honestas?*) And is it good to have an army without public authority, to seize Roman towns by way of opening the road to the mother city, to plan debt cancellations, recall of exiles, and a hundred other villainies "all for that first of deities, Sole Power (μεγίστην ... τυραννίδα)?"[262]

In early February, shortly after the collapse of the peace initiative of late January discussed earlier in this chapter, Atticus wrote to Cicero about his fears of a massacre in Rome; Cicero agreed that he had reason to be worried, such was the nature of Caesar's followers.[263] (Lamentably, of course, his own son-in-law, Dolabella, was among the worthless crowd of desperadoes!)[264] Such worries for the immediate future evidently abated after Corfinium in late February, yet by May Cicero "foresaw" such things again and a "Persian despotism" to boot if Caesar should be ultimately victorious.[265]

These kinds of exasperated outpourings are well known. Less noted, however, are the complaints Cicero has to make about those on the other side of the conflict. In his letters to Atticus he frequently gives free rein to his resentment of Pompey's strategic errors – building up Caesar when he was weak, then turning against him once he was strong; precipitately abandoning Rome; failing to come to Domitius's

---

[262] *Att.* 7.11.1, tr. Shackleton Bailey (cf. 7.17.2: *violata iam ab illo re publica illatoque bello*; 8.3.4; *qui rem publicam defensam velint*). Note that Cicero cannot cite any bloodshed or violence against Caesar: *occupare urbis civium quo facilior sit aditus ad patriam* is remarkably restrained phraseology for an invasion, as Caesar's move is usually styled. The Greek quotation is Eur. *Phoen.* 506, a passage that occurs to Cicero more than once when thinking about Caesar from 49 BC on: see Chapter 2, p. 38.

[263] *Att.* 7.22.1 (February 9); cf. 9.7.5 (March 13), 9.9.4 (March 17), 10.7 *colluvies* (March 18); 10.4.8 (April 14). Cicero professed to see the beginnings of proscriptions already in a military auction at Reate in March (9.8.1), and, in a dark mood, regards fine estates in Italy as "marked for destruction" (9.9.4 – by Pompey's men if not Caesar's?). Such worries are attested even before the conflict: 7.7.7 (December 19? 50). Mamurra, Caesar's notorious *praefectus fabrum*, may have been among the νεκυῖα (Cic. *Att.* 7.7.6 – mentioned in the same breath with Labienus and Balbus. But once Labienus turns his coat Cicero showers him with praise (7.13.1 [January 23]).

[264] *Fam.* 2.16.5, 7.

[265] *Att.* 10.8.2 (May 2): *caedem ... et impetum in privatorum pecunias et exsulum reditum* [cf. Sulpicius's similar worries: 14.1, 3] *et tabulas novas et turpissimorum honores et regnum non modo Romano homini sed ne Persae quidem cuiquam tolerabile*. For the lessening of such fears after Corfinium see Atticus's comment to Cicero on March 5 about how *sincere, temperate, prudenter* Caesar has behaved thus far (9.10.9). The warnings of Caelius (*Att.* 10.9A = *Fam.* 8.16.3, ca. April 16) and of Curio (*Att.* 10.4.8, April 14) surely contributed to the renewal of Cicero's fears.

aid at Corfinium.[266] Although these might be considered merely criticisms of execution rather than principle, I interpret them also as expressions of residual anger over the mad "rush to war" in the Senate that had suppressed his voice and that of other advocates of peace at the beginning of January 49.[267] It is striking how Cicero's criticisms broadly align with Caesar's overt or implied criticisms of Pompey and the hard-liners in his own narrative – criticisms that are partisan, rhetorical, and simplified, but despite that not necessarily unjustified.

While it is true that Cicero is generally inclined to identify Pompey's side as the *causa bonorum*, and that is of course where he ultimately ended up, yet already in mid-February, Cicero sharply rejects Atticus's suggestion that Pompey was the only hope of the Republic.[268] It was not merely that Pompey's plan for "restoring" the Republic seemed to entail first its destruction, using Sulla as a model.[269] Where lust for *dominatio* is concerned, Cicero once avers, there is really no difference between Caesar and Pompey, who aspired to a Sullan style of *regnum*; there will be no *res publica* as long as either one of them lives.[270] Outright fear of Pompey was also a factor, usually lurking under the surface of the epistolary conversation with Atticus but sometimes emerging clearly into our view.[271]

---

[266] At *Att.* 9.5.2 (March 10) Cicero acknowledges that he had actually been angrier with Pompey than with Caesar, since Pompey had enabled Caesar's actions. That was an old refrain going back to before the initiation of hostilities (see esp. 7.7.6, 8.3.3.).

[267] *Fam.* 4.1.1 (to Ser. Sulpicius Rufus, ca. April 21): *incideram in hominum pugnandi cupidorum insanias.* For other such references see Chapter 6, n. 152, and on Sulpicius's similar advocacy of "peace at any price" see n. 151).

[268] *Att.* 8.2.4 (February 17); to be sure, he may have misunderstood Atticus, as he certainly misinterprets his advice at this juncture (9.10.6). (I acknowledge with gratitude the work of my former student Derek Haddad, whose research project tracing the evolution of Atticus's advice to Cicero in the early months of 49 clarified my understanding of this phase of the correspondence between the two.) For *causa bonorum/optima* and similar judgments see *Att.* 7.20.2, 8.1.3 (with some irony: the City will soon be full of *boni, id est lautorum et locupletum*), 8.9a.1, 9.7.4.

[269] *Att.* 8.3.4 (February 18–19) (cf. 8.14.2, March 2); 9.5.2 (March 10): *omitto causam rei publicae, quam ego amissam puto cum vulneribus suis tum medicamentis iis quae parantur. Att.* 8.3, written literally as Cicero turned around in his half-hearted attempt to link up with Pompey, beautifully expresses his alternating views in the form of an academic dispute *in utramque partem*; in the first part, Cicero associates Pompey with the defense or restoration of the *res publica*, language which is undercut or omitted in the second part. Cicero even delicately undermines the "republican" claim in a testy *apologia* to Pompey himself (*Att.* 8.11D.6, February 27). For the Sullan analog see 9.6.7, 10.2 (*"Sulla potuit, ego non potero?"*).

[270] *Att.* 8.11.2 (February 27); 8.16.2 (March 4); 9.7.1, 3 (March 13) – yet even so, he concedes that the *causa* is *optima* (§4)!; 10.4.2–4 (April 14). Even before the conflict: 7.5.4 (cf. 7.3.4, 7.7.7); cf. Chapter 6, n. 234.

[271] *Att.* 8.11.4 (February 27), 8.15.2 (March 3), with Shackleton Bailey's note on *"Iovi ipsi iniquum"*; 9.2a.2 (March 8), 9.3.1 (March 9), 9.7.3–4 (March 13), 9.9.2 (March 17), 10.8.2, 4–5 (May 2). Certainly, Cicero was keenly aware of *others'* fear of Pompey's wrath: nn. 369, 371.

On a few occasions in his correspondence that are usually overlooked, Cicero moves further toward Caesar's line of argument. In a letter to Atticus dated February 2, Cicero describes those who in his view shared the blame for the Civil War as "envious" citizens (*invidi*) – envious, this must mean, of Caesar's accomplishments and of the honors to which he laid claim as a result.[272] Shackleton Bailey, noting that "as an expression of his private mind this passage is unique," was strongly tempted to emend the evidence away but ultimately decided that "the MSS may have the benefit of the doubt."[273] But this is not the only passage in the letters where this undercurrent of criticism of the motives of those who had driven the "rush to war" emerges. Cicero's emphatic advocacy of peace early in January had put him on the wrong side of the consuls and Cato; Pompey, he thought, had been "taken in by the same set of people" as had betrayed him in 58 – the so-called *optimates*, as Bailey rightly notes.[274] This too is not so far from the Caesarian line that deceitful intriguers had detached Pompey from Caesar's friendship.[275] In a retrospective passage of a letter written probably in October 46, Cicero writes that "My advice [viz., 'advocating the most inequitable peace as preferable to the most righteous of wars'] was overborne, not so much by Pompey, on whom it made an impression, as by persons who in reliance on Pompey's general-ship conceived that victory in such a war would be highly opportune for their personal affairs and ambitions."[276] The reference to the "ambitions" or even "greed" (*cupiditates*) of the zealous is no late revisionism but is cited already by Cicero in a letter to his wife and daughter of January 12 and reinforced elsewhere.[277] In fact, in a letter written to Atticus on March 20

---

[272] Cic. *Att.* 7.17.4: *tantum mali <est> excitatum partim ex improbis, partim ex invidis civibus.* Cf. Caes. *BCiv.* 1.7.1 (Caesar's address to the 13th Legion at Ravenna): *Omnium temporum iniurias inimicorum in se commemorat; a quibus deductum ac depravatum Pompeium queritur invidia atque obtrectatione laudis suae* . . . .

[273] Shackleton Bailey 1965: 4:313. Publicly, however, Cicero stated this quite directly in his letter to Caesar of March 19 or 20 (*Att.* 9.11A.2: see n. 290).

[274] Cic. *Att.* 9.13.3 (March 23): *ab eisdem illecti sumus.* Shackleton Bailey 1965: 4:384: "That Pompey was lured to disaster by the Catonian faction is certainly a tenable view, but it is not usually C.'s. He seems to have been seduced into it here by a rhetorician's desire to develop his similitude." This trivializes the complaint, which connects meaningfully with a series of similar observations by Cicero. Interestingly, Caesar makes *Cato* complain of being taken in by *Pompey* to fight an "unnecessary war" with inadequate resources (Caes. *BCiv.* 1.30.5).

[275] Caes. *BCiv.* 1.7.1; Balbus [Cic.] *Att.* 8.15A.1 *perfidia hominum*, 9.7C.2 (Caesar).

[276] *Fam.* 6.6.6 (to A. Caecina, 46): *peropportunam et rebus domesticis et cupiditatibus suis illius belli victoriam fore putabant.* For *homines irati et cupidi,* cf. *Fam.* 4.14.2 (to Cn. Plancius, 45); *Lig.* 18: *fuerint cupidi, fuerint irati, fuerint pertinaces*; *Brut.* 7: *iratorum civium. Fam.* 7.3.2: *rapaces.*

[277] *Fam.* 16.11.2: *incidi in ipsam flammam civilis discordiae, vel potius belli; cui cum cuperem mederi et, ut arbitror, possem, cupiditates certorum hominum (nam ex utraque parte sunt qui pugnare cupiant) impedimento mihi fuerunt.*

Cicero says that he would put no crime beyond Pompey's father-in-law, Metellus Scipio, and two other prominent Pompeians, Faustus Sulla and L. Scribonius Libo, "whose creditors are said to be convening" (i.e. to begin action for forfeiture and sale).[278] Once again he validates Caesar's own charges that some of the most prominent figures on the Pompeian side had a financial interest in inciting a civil war: "There was nothing respectable except the cause," Cicero was later to write to a friend.[279]

Cicero deserves more credit than he usually receives for adhering to his own principles in the face of harsh, potentially even deadly, criticism from the "optimates" and the anti-Caesarian coalition. Publicly he went out on a limb twice more in the early months of 49 in the hope of furthering the cause of peace. Late in January or early in February he wrote Caesar a "friendly" letter in support of the abortive peace initiative. Caesar circulated Cicero's letter to third parties, while in his own reply he urged Cicero to work for peace.[280] At the time this need not have been publicly embarrassing, since after all Pompey himself had written and publicly posted up more or less simultaneously a highly honorific open letter to Caesar to further these same negotiations, but there is some tension between Cicero's ostensibly insouciant claim that he would be happy if Caesar actually posted his letter publicly and the curious fact that he had not, it seems, even sent a copy to his confidant, Atticus.[281] Meanwhile, for the most part he remained quietly at his estate at Formiae, expecting a settlement and hoping not be hung out to dry as he had been once before

---

[278] *Att.* 9.11.4. Cf. *Fam.* 7.3.2 (to M. Marius, 46, explaining Cicero's fear of a *Pompeian* victory): *maximum autem aes alienum amplissimorum virorum.* Libo was or would soon become father-in-law to Pompey's son Sextus (Chapter 8, n. 289).

[279] Cic. *Fam.* 7.3.2 (to M. Marius, 46): *Quid quaeris? Nihil boni praeter causam.* Cf. Caes. *BCiv.* 1.4.2–3: the consul Lentulus's debts and Scipio's "fear of the courts" adduced to explain their eagerness for war.

[280] The letter does not survive, but Cicero describes it in a letter to Atticus written on February 17 (*Att.* 8.2.1), revealing incidentally that it was written at Capua in reply to a letter from Caesar about his gladiators. Cicero had been in Capua twice recently (January 25–28 and February 4–7), and Shackleton Bailey opts for the latter date (1965: 4:326), yet Cicero had learned of the collapse of the peace initiative just before that second trip to Capua (*Att.* 7.19, February 3), thus January 25–28 seems better. At 7.21.3 (February 8) Cicero refers to a letter of Caesar's written before he had resumed his march (*ruere coepit*) and urging Cicero to work for peace; this letter of Caesar's, which Cicero soon forwarded to Atticus on February 10 (7.23.3), must be a different one from the one about the gladiators, else Cicero would not have had to summarize its contents to Atticus at 8.2.1 (pace White 2003: 94). It is clear from loc. cit. ad fin. *non potui non dare [alteras litteras], cum et ipse ad me scripsisset et Balbus* that Cicero's "second letter" to Caesar sent on February 17 was a reply to a new letter from Caesar – the one Cicero had received by February 8. Caesar's gladiators may have been reserved for Julia's delayed funeral games: Chapter 5, n. 187; for criticism of Caesar's claim that Lentulus sought to enlist them see Westall 2018: 72–75.

[281] *Att.* 8.2.1. Pompey's letter: nn. 82, 83.

when the two great men reconciled, which he thought again likely.[282] Once military operations had resumed in earnest about the beginning of February, Cicero's quiescence looked less benign, and Atticus actually saw fit to warn his friend "not to appear inclined toward the worse (i.e. Caesar's) cause, which I [Cicero] might seem to be."[283] Caesar himself had written to thank him for his inactivity thus far and to urge him to continue the same.[284] Cicero's friendly language to Caesar in his letter (though he had avoided any censure of Pompey, and simply advocated a settlement) now aroused criticism among some hard-liners in Rome (!), prompting Atticus to probe for an explanation, even – the defensive tone Cicero adopts in his reply betrays the keenness of his sensitivity – going so far as to admonish his great friend to remember what he had "done, said, and written," probably especially in his recent *De re publica*, which, sure enough, Cicero soon quotes back to Atticus.[285] Meanwhile Cicero allowed himself to be cut off from the main force despite Pompey's urgent orders.[286] It is easy to see why Cicero's continued friendly contact with Caesar and advocacy of peace would now have attracted especially harsh comment in Pompey's council, where it was no doubt viewed as mere demoralizing appeasement at a time when they themselves were on the run.[287]

A month later, on March 19 or 20, Pompey having already slipped away from Brundisium (though he did not yet know it), Cicero tried again with a letter which does survive in the corpus.[288] Cicero's main point is ostensibly

---

[282] See n. 86.

[283] *Att.* 7.26.2 (February 13?): *ne propensior ad turpem causam videar, certe videri possum.*

[284] *Att.* 8.11.5 (February 27): *quod quierim, oratque in eo ut perseverem.* This must be a further letter of Caesar's written around the time of the surrender of Corfinium. It is unclear how Atticus learned of this further letter, which is not mentioned at what would be the appropriate place in the correspondence (ca. February 23) (Shackleton Bailey 1965: 4:340).

[285] *Att.* 8.2.1–2: *me hortaris ad memoriam factorum, dictorum scriptorum etiam meorum*; cf. 8.11.1 (February 27). Note that on February 17 Cicero is careful to enclose with his *apologia* to Atticus a copy of his new letter to Caesar (8.2.2).

[286] *Att.* 8.11.D.2; but n. 10.8.5 : *sed tamen (fateamur enim quod est) ne con<ten>dimus quidem ut possemus.* "It is hard to believe that every road was blocked to a resolute man" (Brunt 1986: 21n44). Wistrand 1979: 82–84 points out that there was hardly any real chance of being captured by Caesar's forces now that he had been brought up short by Domitius at Corfinium, however briefly as it turned out. But Shackleton Bailey 1965: 4:454–457 plausibly infers that a confusing sequence of letters from Pompey and Domitius led Cicero to return to Formiae on the mistaken belief that Pompey would now march to Domitius's relief and his presence was no longer urgently required.

[287] *Att.* 8.11D.8 (February 27): *neque enim ego amicior C. Caesari umquam fui quam illi* [! Cicero thus implicitly reminds Pompey of his own former relationship to Caesar] *neque illi amiciores rei publicae quam ego.* (Cf. cos. Lentulus's behavior toward his friend Balbus: 8.15A.2.) See also 8.12.2: *non solum ignaviae dedecus sed etiam perfidiae suspicionem fugiens.*

[288] *Att.* 9.11A.2, a reply to a letter of Caesar's written ca. March 5 (9.6A; cf. 9.9.3, 9.11.2). Yet in 9.9.2, written only a few days before, Cicero claims that the departure of the consuls had ended any reasonable hope of peace. (So too Caes. *BCiv.* 1.26.5–6.) Perhaps he had changed his mind (again).

to urge Caesar to open peace negotiations with Pompey (which was of course in line with Caesar's own stated policy up to this point, corroborated by Balbus) and to offer himself as a useful intermediary; his deeper purpose, however, may have been (as he wrote later) to put on public record his commitment to a peaceful resolution of the conflict, which could serve to protect his neutrality against the pressures he anticipated from Caesar.[289] He reiterates his established advocacy of peace, well known by now to Caesar and others, and to further his end he explicitly and publicly adopts the Caesarian line that "you were wronged by the decision to resort to war since your enemies and those envious of your achievements were striving to deprive you of an honor granted as a mark of favor by the Roman People."[290] Cicero even goes so far as to identify *Caesar* with the cause of the Republic: "If you are at all concerned to maintain our friend Pompey and win him back to yourself *and the Republic.*"[291] It is not too much to say, with Wistrand, that this constitutes a public "repudiation of the official ideology of the republicans" (although as I have noted several times it would be tendentious to grant that validating title exclusively to the Pompeian side).[292] Cicero claims that as the crisis came to a head he had been a defender of Caesar's *dignitas* and had even urged others to do the same.[293] This seems not far from the truth, save for the venial insincerity (for we know Cicero felt otherwise) of asserting simply that Caesar was the wronged party in the conflict. As Cicero explained to Atticus after the letter had become public in Rome, he had written as if he approved of Caesar's cause in order to lend his

For clarification of the previous exchanges in the Caesar-Cicero correspondence after the surrender of Corfinium see Wistrand 1979: 121n1; also, the useful list provided by White 2003: 94. By the date of the letter to Caesar, Cicero knew that Pompey was likely already to have left (8.15.3 [March 3], 9.6.3 [March 11]), though only on March 25 did he learn definitively of his departure on March 17 (9.15a.1). Wistrand 1979: 112–119 offers an extended analysis of *Att.* 9.11A.2, with too much emphasis (for my taste) on its lack of "sincerity." What matters for my purpose is the message it publicly communicated (n. 294) about Cicero's position in the conflict.

[289] *Att.* 8.9.1: *ea enim et acciderunt iam et impendent ut testatum esse velim de pace quid senserim.* Wistrand 1979: 106–108, 117, with *Att.* 9.7.3. By taking up this position publicly, Cicero began to build up preemptively a case against a request from Caesar that he return to an active role in the Senate. Caesar tried nevertheless to encourage him to return to Rome by exploiting his stated desire for peace (9.18.1; cf. 9.16.3), but Cicero had a ready answer based on the principle of strict neutrality he had suggested in his letter.

[290] *Att.* 9.11A.2: *iudicavique eo bello te violari, contra cuius honorem populi Romani beneficio concessum inimici atque invidi niterentur.* (The *beneficium* is the so-called *ratio absentis* granted by the Law of the Ten Tribunes in 52.) For *invidi* see n. 272. "Publicly": n. 294.

[291] *Att.* 9.11A.2: *si qua de Pompeio nostro tuendo et tibi ac rei publicae reconciliando cura te attingit.* Cf. Dolabella's remark in his letter to Cicero (Cic. *Fam.* 9.9.3, quoted, n. 199) that places "the Republic" with *Caesar.*

[292] Wistrand 1979: 114.

[293] *Att.* 9.11A.2: *eo tempore non modo ipse fautor dignitatis tuae fui verum etiam ceteris auctor ad te adiuvandum.*

suggestion greater weight. As for Atticus's and others' criticism of its laudatory language, Cicero was unrepentant. He again says that he would be happy for Caesar to make it fully public, not merely showing it around but having it read out in a *contio*; he had himself allowed others to make copies.²⁹⁴

Yet this time, since Cicero had to assuage even Atticus's complaints, the dismay of Pompey and his friends at Cicero's letter (or rumor of it, when it got out) can readily be imagined. No doubt encouraged by the letter, Caesar during his return trip to the capital visited Cicero at his villa at Formiae and now pressed him quite hard in person to come to Rome and lend his authority to a peace initiative he intended to launch through the Senate on April 1. But since Caesar made clear that he would not halt his military preparations to await an answer while Pompey mustered his forces and organized the expected invasion of Italy, Cicero stood firm and refused to be co-opted.²⁹⁵ By attaching conditions, Cicero no doubt hoped to avoid burning any bridges back to Pompey; anything less would have reeked of outright betrayal. (Alternatively, he may at this point have wished to step back from the highly exposed position in which he had put himself by means of the letter.) But these terms were obviously unacceptable to Caesar (as comparable restrictions upon his own military activity would equally have been to Pompey), and with good reason. Whatever his intentions, Caesar could not unilaterally suspend military preparations without any assurance of the same from Pompey. He was careful not to force the senior consular to attend the meeting he had summoned for April 1, and after it and others had taken place over the following days he reassured Cicero that he was not in the least offended, despite the fact that this was bound to be seen as a personal condemnation of his actions.²⁹⁶

²⁹⁴ *Att.* 8.9.1–2 (March 29 or 30): "to put on record what I thought about peace"; thus, an "open letter." Note the sharpness of Cicero's complaint against Atticus's and Sex. Peducaeus's hypocrisy at 8.9.2 (only, so far, in prospect, since Caesar had not yet reached Rome: see Shackleton Bailey ad loc.; in the event, their behavior earned Cicero's approval: 10.1a.1, but cf. 3a.1 a few days later). Cicero was probably provoked by Atticus's comments about his letter to Caesar. Earlier, Peducaeus had made a point of praising Cicero's quiescence: 9.10.10.
²⁹⁵ The story can be traced in *Att.* 9.16 (March 26), 17.1 (March 27), 18.1 (Caesar's visit to Cicero at Formiae, March 28); 10.1.3 (April 3), 1a (April 4, with a note of regret at not having participated in the senatorial meetings), 3 (April 7).
²⁹⁶ *Att.* 9.18.1: *damnari se nostro iudicio*; 10.3a.2 (April 7); cf. 9.15.1–3 (March 25), 17.1. Cicero later heard through back channels, however, that Caesar was not pleased: 10.8.3 (May 2). Cicero had been anxious at the beginning of April lest he be chosen as a peace envoy (10.1.3, 1a): had he not after all nominated himself in his letter of March 19 or 20? For the magistrate's right to coerce members of the Senate to attend see Mommsen 1887: 3:915–917. Caesar, of course, was not a magistrate (yet). The relevant meetings seem to have been summoned by the praetor M. Lepidus, whose authority to take harsh measures might be challenged – at the risk of offending Caesar.

Despite his formal military command, which he acknowledges he treated as a sinecure, Cicero was careful to keep friendly lines of communication with Caesar and the Caesarians open through Balbus, Matius, Trebatius, Caelius, and Dolabella in particular, as we have seen.[297] During the peace initiative of late January Cicero had actually written to Trebatius, a trusted intermediary with Caesar at this time, that he was simply residing on his estates and not undertaking any military preparations whatever, and would continue in this manner while there was hope of peace.[298] In fact, in his letter to Caesar of March 19 or 20 Cicero claimed not to have played any role at all in the war (*nec sumptis armis belli ullam partem attigi*); the claim, true enough, aroused predictable complaints among Atticus's optimate friends.[299] There is no reason not to accept Cicero's own explanation that his obvious lack of zeal in carrying out his military duties in the conflict with Caesar was motivated by his desire to lend greater authority to his calls for peace (the more public justification) or to avoid compromising his own position if, as he expected, Caesar and Pompey did come to terms (the more personal one).[300] As we saw, Cicero's lack of enthusiasm was noted both among Atticus's friends in Rome and in Pompey's camp at Luceria: Atticus had even felt compelled to warn his friend not to appear inclined toward "the worst cause."[301]

The letters that passed repeatedly between Cicero and Caesar from the beginning of hostilities characterized their relationship as one of continued friendship, apparently quite unaffected by Caesar's actions, including the Senate's Final Decree and the crossing of the Rubicon. After he gave up any pretense of joining Pompey in Brundisium and Corfinium had surrendered, Cicero's actions and semipublic pronouncements were in fact those of a neutral and friendly intermediary rather than a commander of an army hostile to Caesar. He had in practice capitulated, regarding his own military role as passé now that Pompey was set on abandoning Italy. Once cut off from Brundisium, Cicero makes no military preparations

---

[297] For Cicero's command see n. 141. Whatever was the precise nature of the command, he was of course formally committed (as he appears at last to remember on May 2: *Att.* 10.8.8) to carry out the Senate's Final Decree specifically calling on proconsuls along with consuls, praetors, and tribunes to protect the Republic, implicitly but clearly against Caesar (*Fam.* 16.11.2; Caes. *BCiv.* 1.5.3). On February 8, Cicero alone among the Pompeian generals has information that Picenum was lost – passed on to him in a letter from his Caesarian son-in-law, Dolabella (*Att.* 7.21.2). For the other Caesarian correspondents see p. 366ff.

[298] *Att.* 7.17.4, February 2. Note also Caesar's words of April 16, *ab eorum consiliis abesse iudicasti* (*Att.* 10.8B.1); also *Fam.* 2.16.1 *fin.* (Cicero to Caelius, May 2 or 3).

[299] *Att.* 9.11A.2; 8.9.1: *nam quod testificor me expertem belli fuisse, etsi id re perspectum est.*

[300] *Fam.* 16.12.5; *Att.* 7.17.4, 26.2; cf. 8.11D.7. Wistrand 1979: 69–81 and above.

[301] See nn. 283, 287.

or any move that could be construed as hostile to Caesar; indeed, rather than burying himself in Arpinum, which might give the appearance of avoiding Caesar on his return back to Rome, he remained in his villa at Formiae to meet with the "tyrant" himself.[302] Meanwhile he received the first of what would become a stream of Caesarian visitors: L. Balbus Jr., Curtius Postumus, Q. Fufius Calenus, C. Furnius, and C. Matius, culminating in the arrival of the imperator.[303] In this connection, the letter to Caesar of March 19 or 20, in which Cicero openly took the Caesarian line and explicitly described himself as *amicissimus* to Caesar as well as Pompey, may be seen as a formal capitulation.

Some will say that Caesar – directly or through his agents – was "playing Cicero like a violin": exploiting his known horror of civil war to detach an esteemed consular, to sap Pompeian morale, and to confuse the enemy with disinformation. All of which might be true – if we could be sure that Caesar did not actually mean what he said. Yet we have seen that it is perfectly consistent with all of our evidence leading up to the war and at its opening to infer that Caesar really did hope that civil war could be avoided by bringing Pompey back around – that in fact he found it almost inconceivable that Pompey, instead of returning to their old friendship and alliance, would prefer to throw in his lot with their old mutual enemies, his new, untested, and far from trusted "friends," and would do so at the price of civil war, for no better reason than to deny Caesar the honorable return he had earned. And it is dubious method to deny Cicero a reasonable grasp of the circumstances in early 49, when he is convinced that a settlement is probable (at the end of January) or at least possible (as late as March), and when even Pompey himself was prepared to take the great military risk of publishing his letter to Caesar accepting his terms in late January.[304] Even Cato may have had hopes for a settlement and hoped Cicero could facilitate it by remaining in Italy as a trusted intermediary.[305]

---

[302] *Att.* 8.16.2 (March 4), 9.5.1 (March 10), 6.1. 7.2; see Wistrand 1979: 103. On March 20 or 21, Cicero is moved to imagine a desperate intervention in the operations at Brundisium – but dismisses the thought as quickly as it arises (9.12.3). "Tyrant": n. 261 and now especially 9.4.2 (March 12).

[303] *Att.* 8.9a.2 (February 25), 11.5 (February 27); 9.2a.3 (March 8), 3.2 (March 9), 5.1 (March 10), 6.6 (March 11; cf. 6A), 11.2 (March 20). Balbus even went so far as to suggest to Cicero that he request a bodyguard from Caesar: 9.7B.2, March 10 or 11. Caesar's prominent officer Curio – on his way to lay claim to Sicily for Caesar – and his jurist-diplomat Trebatius freely enjoy Cicero's hospitality at Cumae in April and May: 10.4.7–11, 11.4, 12.1.

[304] Cicero reminds Pompey in his *apologia* of February 27 that he too had wanted peace in late January, or so he thought: *Att.* 8.11D.8.

[305] See Plut. *Cic.* 38.1, Cato's bitter welcome to poor Cicero when he had at last made his way to Pompey: he "would have been more useful to his country and his friends if remaining in Italy he

Ultimately, however, although Cicero allowed himself to become separated from Pompey's army in February and then in March to be left behind in Italy, he would sail to join him in Greece a few weeks after the spring equinox, not long after the seas opened.[306] It is naturally tempting to assume that the result that actually obtained was the goal to which Cicero was inevitably tending, at least unconsciously, as soon as the prospect of Pompey's departure from Italy came to be seriously entertained.[307] But that would be mistaken. The question emerges almost immediately after the evacuation of Rome. On January 21, three days after Cicero had fled the City along with most other senators, Atticus (who stayed behind, not only perhaps because he was a non-senator but because he was suffering from malaria) had written to his friend: "Let us see what Gnaeus is doing and where Caesar's plans tend. If your man abandons Italy, he will act wrongly and in my judgment irrationally; but then will be the time to change our plans."[308] Evidently therefore, the two friends were putting off the weighty question what Cicero should do if Pompey should abandon Italy: it was not a given that he should follow him. Two days later, on January 23, during the pause of military operations for negotiations, Atticus advised Cicero that if Pompey should depart from Italy he should actually return to Rome.[309] This is remarkable, given that only six days before those words were written Pompey had ordered the evacuation of Rome by all senators and threatened to threat as enemies all who disobeyed. Cicero quietly lets the idea drop for the present; Atticus adjusts his suggestions accordingly, over and over again reassuring his consular friend that the best course for him, even the morally

had stayed aloof from both sides and adapted himself to the war's outcome" (see Lintott 2013: 191). Once the war which Cato had played such an important role in precipitating had begun so unpromisingly, he may indeed have hoped for a quick settlement (Plut. *Cat. Min.* 53.5; Cic. *Att.* 7.15.2), though his intervention at Capua was hardly helpful. At Caes. *BCiv.* 1.30.5 Cato allegedly complains about Pompey's starting a *non necessarium bellum* (! n. 274).

[306] See n. 131; nn. 324, 335.

[307] Brunt 1986: 22 states that from March 3 Cicero "hardly wavered from the resolve to leave Italy," "initially" at least to join Pompey directly. Wistrand 1979: 97–112 believes that he finally made up his mind to join Pompey on March 4 and never wavered from this course [cf. 128], delayed only by the winter season and "practical difficulties" [135, 136, 139, 158–160].) Yet neither scholar seems to recognize that their evidence comes from a brief episode during which Cicero has again misunderstood Atticus, and that after his friend clarified his advice Cicero stepped back to await the decision point they had agreed on (n. 341). Even Shackleton Bailey exaggerates Cicero's resolution: "The question [regarding joining Pompey] was mainly one of ways and means, even though Cicero thought for a time of staying out of harm's way in Athens, Malta, or elsewhere" (Shackleton Bailey 1971: 155).

[308] *Att.* 9.10.4, from Cicero's dated roll of letters from Atticus which he consulted in anguish on March 18. Malaria: the "quartan fever" to which Cicero's letters in this period make frequent allusion (9.6.6).

[309] *Att.* 9.10.4 (January 23): *in urbem redeundum puto.*

and politically correct course, was to remain in Italy even if Pompey decides to leave. Pompey's departure, he writes Cicero, would portend a long and "truceless" war (*bellum* ἄσπονδον); despite the immense personal risks Cicero would hardly be in a position to do any service to the Republic, which he might retain if he stayed.[310] (Atticus may have written those words before Caesar had resumed his march.) Atticus picks up on Cicero's own repeated, exasperated description of Pompey's withdrawal before Caesar around this time as *fuga*, "flight," even calling it "dishonorable," presumably seeking to calm Cicero's palpable anxieties of shame and guilt at not standing with Pompey and sharing his fate unreservedly by coloring the "flight" as not only inexpedient but ignominious.[311] Later Cicero would acknowledge to his friend that "I was frankly incensed against [Pompey] . . . Considering these unparalleled disasters, or rather determining that they happened by his agency and fault, I was more hostile to him than to Caesar himself."[312] Nor was Atticus the only one to advise Cicero to stay on the sidelines: the future Caesaricide Cassius wrote to him from Pompey's headquarters in Luceria around this time to advise him to stay out of the conflict.[313]

Perhaps misled by Atticus's polite warnings to take care not to appear too inclined toward Caesar, Cicero on February 17 actually misunderstands his equestrian friend, inferring wrongly that he had inexplicably reversed himself and was now counseling departure with Pompey: this causes the consular to bristle, "I am not so convinced that in Pompey rests the sole hope of the safety of the Republic," and as for the idea of departing with him from Italy, "I do not think this would be helpful either to the Republic or to my children, nor even morally correct or honorable."[314] Atticus quickly and forcefully corrects

[310] *Att.* 9.10.5 (January 25 and February 7); cf. Cicero's reply at 7.23.2 (February 10).

[311] *Att.* 9.10.6 (February 11): *fugamne foedam*; (February 19) *nihil reliquitur nisi fuga, cui te socium neutiquam puto esse oportere nec umquam putavi.* Cf. Cic. *Att.* 7.13.1–3 (January 23), 17.1 (February 2), 18.3 (February 3), 20.1–2 (February 5), 23.2–3 (February 10), 24.1 (February 11), 26.1–2 (February 13?), 8.1.3 (February 15 or 16): *flagitiosae et calamitosae fugae,* 8.3.3 (February 18–19): *quid foedius, quid perturbatius hoc ab urbe discessu sive potius turpissima in qua sum<us> fuga?* 8.7.1 (February 21).

[312] *Att.* 9.5.2 (March 10, Shackleton Bailey trans, slightly modified): *vel potius iudicans eius opera accidisse et culpa inimicior huic eram quam ipsi Caesari.* Cf. 9.10.2 (March 18) *me illius fugae neglegentiaeque deformitas avertit ab amore.*

[313] *Fam.* 15.15.4 (August 47): *utinam primis illis quas Luceria miseras paruissem! Sine ulla enim molestia dignitatem meam retinuissem.* Shackleton Bailey 1977: 2:310. Cf. Cato, n. 305.

[314] *Att.* 8.2.4: *neque rectum neque honestum,* thus reinforcing Atticus's use of the language of moral debate (*honestum* vs. *utile*) in his letter of February 11 (9.10.6). Shackleton Bailey's translation of the first quotation is somewhat misleading: "I do not, as you do (*non ita*) judge him." There is no sign that Atticus referred to Pompey as the sole hope of the Republic in the correspondence of this period (or any other period for that matter). The choice of the verb *significas* ("you indicate"; cf. 9.10.6) shows that Cicero is *inferring* that Atticus was suggesting he leave with Pompey, not reporting something explicitly stated. Wistrand 1979: 110–111.

the mistake in his reply: "No, I never in any letter suggested that if Gnaeus left Italy you should leave with him, or if I did I was – I won't say inconsistent, but out of my mind."[315] But the temporary breakdown of communication is itself illuminating. This is one of the moments in this anguished correspondence when we come to see that Cicero's more consistent preference was to follow his friend's advice and remain in Italy, but that since he knew this was his correspondent's preference he did not have to defend it explicitly *except* when he suddenly fears that he has misunderstood him, or that Atticus has changed his mind. And conversely, at those times when his distress, fear, or shame temporarily overcome his mostly tacit agreement with his friend, *then* the ostensible strength of his commitment to join Pompey may be an effect of the shift in the conversation between friends to something more like an argument, for at these times Cicero is acutely aware that he was entertaining the thought of abandoning the course on which they had tacitly or explicitly agreed. In short, Cicero's ruminations, which seem when read in isolation to waver confusingly between the two main options, must be understood, as far as we are able to do, as his half of a developing, meandering, and sometimes even errant dialogue with Atticus, the other side of which must as usual be read between the lines, but in this brief period is also remarkably preserved for us (selectively) by Cicero's extensive quotations in a letter of March 18 from a scroll in which he had had his friend's letters glued together in dated sequence, to which he resorted at particularly anxious moments in order to reassure himself about the wisdom of the choices he was making.[316]

An example of this potentially confusing dynamic emerges on February 22, the day after the surrender of the Pompeian forces under L. Domitius at Corfinium. Atticus again urged his friend on that day to remain in Italy if other senior consulars like M'. Lepidus and L. Volcacius would stay: he could always join Pompey later, if he manages to establish himself strongly somewhere.[317] Cicero eventually replies that he did not think their example was good enough for him; Lepidus and Volcacius had indicated that they were not only going to stay in Italy but go to Rome and sit in Caesar's Senate.[318] He

---

[315] *Att.* 9.10.6 (February 19) (Shackleton Bailey trans.).

[316] *Att.* 9.10.4–10: *evolvi volumen epistularum tuarum quod ego signo habeo servoque diligentissime.* The quotations, with Cicero's comments, fill three pages of the Teubner text. Cicero later avers that he had quoted back so much of Atticus's advice to him "not to complain but to console myself" (9.13.3; n. 341). Only one week before Cicero had apparently read through the scroll for a similar "therapeutic" purpose: 9.6.5 (March 11): *tuas nunc epistulas a primo lego. Hae me paulum recreant.*

[317] *Att.* 9.10.7: *si salvus sit Pompeius et constiterit alicubi.*

[318] *Att.* 8.14.2 (March 2): *quod enim umquam eorum in re publica forte factum exstitit?* 8.15.2 (March 3). Lepidus actually left Formiae for Rome on March 7 (9.1.2) – he would be in Rome when Caesar arrived.

was already wavering in his resolution when – so Cicero thought – Atticus himself "wrenched him from our original position" with two letters written on February 28 and received by Cicero three days later on March 3.[319] Atticus had brought up Pompey's likely anger (presumably at any further delay in joining him) and the weighty significance of the consuls' imminent departure; Cicero replies, "I see what you think and what is morally correct, more or less" – that is, that he should join Pompey as soon as possible, in contrast to what Atticus had been recommending all along.[320] But once again Cicero had misread his friend's advice. On the day after Cicero wrote those words, in a letter that crossed in the mail with his friend's last, Atticus clarified: "I do not regret my advice about your remaining, and although very far from easy, still, thinking this as I do a lesser evil than departure with Pompey, I stand by my opinion and am glad that you have stayed."[321] Probably immediately after Cicero's letter of March 3 had arrived revealing his confusion, Atticus wrote again:

> After all I am not sorry that you are not with Pompey. Later, if desirable, it won't be difficult, and come when it may it will be acceptable to him. [Atticus here tries to correct Cicero's anxious interpretation of his last reference to Pompey's anger.][322] But I say this with the reservation that if Caesar continues as he has begun, with sincerity, moderation, and prudence, I shall think hard and look attentively to our interests.[323]

Cicero's response to what he mistakenly believes is his friend's change of course is once again revealing. Believing initially that Atticus had given him the green light to leave, on March 4 he immediately and for the first time describes his preparations for secretly crossing the Ionian Sea to Greece at the coming of spring.[324] Yet he also noticeably kicks back against the idea of tying himself to Pompey: he is not bound to Pompey, he writes, who has now proven to be an utter failure both as a politician and general, but he is driven by "the talk of men," specifically the criticisms of the so-called

---

[319] *Att.* 8.15.2 (March 3).

[320] *Att.* 8.15.2–3. For "*Iovi ipsi iniquum*" see Shackleton Bailey ad loc. Note that now Cicero is sure that leaving with Pompey would be *honestior*.

[321] *Att.* 9.10.8 (March 4). Cicero had last written on March 3.

[322] From Cicero's reply (*Att.* 9.2a.2) it seems that in this letter Atticus had warned him that Pompey's anger was surely great *at present* (*hoc tempore*). Apparently he suggested that with time it would wane.

[323] *Att.* 9.10.9 (March 5). Exchanges between Cicero at Formiae and Atticus in Rome normally took two to three days, as can be inferred from the dates of the known replies. A speedy journey begun early in the morning might be concluded by evening the next day (9.4.3, with Shackleton Bailey ad loc.).

[324] 8.16.1 (March 4). Atticus responded (9.5.1, probably March 7) with discussion of routes to the sea. Cf. 9.3.1 (March 9).

optimates.[325] But this is not good enough either, since we learn in Cicero's very next letter that the *optimates* are morally bankrupt: they criticize him over their dinner parties in Rome, and equate being a *bonus civis* with making war on Italy by land and sea![326] Those who have actually departed, Cicero adds, are driven largely by fear or have little choice in the matter.[327] So now, Cicero asserts, he is ready to take this fateful turn only out of a sense of obligation to Pompey![328] Rather than taking this direct self-contradiction as scripture, we should recognize it in its context as Cicero's way of placing blame and responsibility for the disastrous turn of events on Pompey while putting a moral gloss on his own motives at a very difficult time. But then Atticus's short letter of March 4 arrives, reiterating his recommendation that Cicero should stay – and thoroughly confusing his friend, who had interpreted his previous letter as advising him to leave, "provided that Gnaeus had embarked with a large following and that the consuls had crossed." Had Atticus forgotten, or changed his mind?[329] By the next day Cicero received a longer clarification.[330] Now he gets back on track, saying at the letter's end that he would after all wait to decide until word comes of Pompey's departure, but returning to his usual mode of poking holes in Atticus's advice while ostensibly adhering to it.[331] He is overwhelmed with guilt for abandoning Pompey in such a desperate time, but also staged a disputation *in utramque partem* for and against remaining in Italy under Caesar's "tyranny" when "liberation" would endanger the existence of his country or even threatened to exchange one "tyranny" for another.[332] Nothing was yet settled, even now.

Atticus now tried to soothe Cicero at his most sensitive point – that is, the court of public opinion – more precisely, that of the *boni*, against whose hypocrisy Cicero had recently been railing – by reporting that a respected friend named Sex. Peducaeus, and even the *boni* in general, approved of his

---

[325] *Att.* 8.16.1 (March 4); cf. 9.2a.3 (March 8): *ut appellantur, boni.*

[326] Cicero's rebuttal of the criticisms of the *boni/optimates* will be a major theme of subsequent letters (9.1.4, 2a.3, 5.3) until Atticus relents and assures him that after all they approve of his actions (n. 333) .

[327] See n. 154.   [328] *Att.* 9.1.4.   [329] See n. 155.

[330] *Att.* 9.2, 2a (March 8), anticipating, then responding to Atticus's letter of the 5th.

[331] *Att.* 9.2a (March 8): how wretched to beg Caesar's permission, how difficult to refuse his demand; Pompey should not be too angry with Cicero now, seeing that he was right about everything, but will be if he doesn't leave as soon as he can; how fearful he is of the charge of ingratitude; how unlikely that Caesar will be anything but a "desperado"! The moment of decision was soon pushed back just slightly to allow for an expected meeting with Caesar: 9.6.1 (March 11).

[332] *Att.* 9.4.2 (March 12), all in Greek. The cruelty of Pompey's strategy for recovering Italy becomes a major theme of the following letters: 9.7.4 (March 13), 9.9.2 (March 17): *tanta vis sceleris futura est*; 9.10.3 (March 18); 9.11.4 (Mar. 20); 9.13.3 (March 23): *tam pestiferum bellum.*

actions – that is, his quietude.[333] Meanwhile, as a solution to Cicero's anxiety about being forced by Caesar to participate in senatorial proceedings against Pompey, he urged his friend even now to step forward as an advocate for peace; this would naturally create a presumption of neutrality and would give Cicero respectable cover to remain in Italy at least temporarily.[334] Even while engaged in negotiations, Atticus suggests, Cicero could still slip away to Pompey when "the season for sailing" came – "as long as he [Pompey] is strong enough."[335] The proviso was crucial, however, and Atticus picked away at it as he questioned Cicero's exaggerated report of the number of men who had crossed with the consuls and Pompey, and asked for verification of the identity (or number) of the senators.[336] Implicitly answering Cicero's professions of loyalty to Pompey, Atticus subtly raised the question whether given the general's prior actions and "offences" against him (clearly alluding to Pompey's failure to save him from exile in March 58) he really deserved such devotion: if Cicero seemed so much indebted to Pompey, it was more because of his own pronouncements than because the man truly merited it.[337] Cicero agrees – "so far does gratitude for a service outweigh with me resentment of an injury" – but he continues to carry on his internal debate.[338] (Mark Antony was shortly to put the matter much less delicately: Pompey had first done him injury in

[333] The *boni*'s change of tune: 9.7.6 (from a letter written no later than March 11). Cf. n. 326. Sex. Peducaeus: *Att.* 9.10.10 (March 9; cf. 9.7.2, 9.13.6, 10.1.1). About this Peducaeus little is known: Shackleton Bailey 1965: 1.34, 4.306; Bruhns 1978: 51 (8), who reasonably supposes that, though of senatorial stock, this one was an *eques*.

[334] *Att.* 9.7.3 (Atticus's letter will have been sent about March 10): *video tibi placere illud, me* πολίτευμα *de pace suscipere.* Cf. *Att.* 9.2a.1–2 [March 8], 9.5.2 [March 10], 9.6.6 [March 11]. Cicero soon took up the peacemaking suggestion, as we have seen, once he was reassured by Matius that the move would be welcome to Caesar, though he knew Pompey would be very displeased and he perceived considerable danger from this quarter (9.11.2, March 20).

[335] *Att.* 9.7.5: *egregie probo fore ut, dum agamus,* "ὁ πλόος ὡραῖος" (a quotation of Leonidas of Tarentum [*Anth. Pal.* 10.1]; *Att.* 9.7.5, 9.18.3 with Shackleton Bailey's nn.) *obrepat. "si modo," inquis, "satis ille erit firmus."* The two had begun speaking frankly about routes to the sea: n. 324.

[336] *Att.* 9.9.2, 4 (March 17; Atticus's letter had been sent on the 13th). Cf. 9.6.3; the source of the mistaken number was L. Metellus's mother-in-law, a Clodia, surely one of Ap. Claudius's three sisters, plausibly identified by Wiseman 1974: 113–114 (cf. 182–183) not with Cicero's famous target but Lucullus's ex-wife (cf. Shackleton Bailey 1965: 5:412–413 with 413n2).

[337] *Att.* 9.9.1 (March 17; Atticus's letter was written on the 12th): *quod laudas quia oblivisci me scripsi ante facta et delicta nostri amici!* (Cf. 9.7.4, fin.) Whether Cicero had actually used such strong language (*delicta!*), Atticus's "praise" often seems to mark a rhetorical move: cf. 8.7.2, alluding to 7.1.4. Already about the 11th Atticus had laid out a defense to the charge of "ingratitude" (9.7.4); this was probably the beginning of the exchange on the subject. Perhaps about the 20th Atticus resumed the debate (9.13.3): *mea praedicatione factum esse scribis magis quam illius merito ut tantum ei debere viderer, est ita.* None of this is to say that Atticus went so far as to denounce Pompey: he too felt as if the "sun had fallen out of the universe" (9.10.3).

[338] *Att.* 9.9.1: *in decursu* θέσεις *meas commentari non desino; sed sunt quaedam earum perdifficiles ad iudicandum.* Note also §§2 and 4.

order to do him a favor.)³³⁹ The climax, at least of this phase of the
correspondence, comes when on March 18 Cicero, overwhelmed by the
idea that he had betrayed Pompey, passionately declares that he has been
"mad from the beginning" in not following his general like a good soldier
straight on to disaster – then talks himself back from the ledge by citing
historical precedents for declining to make total war on one's country,
however bad the regime, and finally by unrolling and consulting the scroll
containing Atticus's letters once more.³⁴⁰ Atticus bristled a bit at having his
words thrown back at him, and the consular had to assure his friend that he
had done so not to complain about his advice but to console himself that he
had in fact done the right thing in sticking to their resolution to remain in
Italy until the situation was clarified by what happened at Brundisium.³⁴¹

Yet this was not, in fact, the end of the anxious debate. Although Cicero
continues to announce here and there that he is determined to join
Pompey, Atticus continues to urge Cicero to temporize, to decline
Caesar's blandishments and evade his demands to return to Rome and
take up his seat again in the Senate.³⁴² Within days, then, Cicero declares
that he has decided to take up a position of *neutrality apart from both
camps*.³⁴³ Again his expression of apparent resolution to throw in his lot
with Pompey turns out to be a feint in an ongoing epistolary debate that is
hardly resolved. Atticus advises yet more temporizing, first to see the results
of the senatorial meetings of early April, then even to observe how things
turn out in Spain, for which Caesar had immediately departed after his
brief visit to Rome – that is, midsummer at least.³⁴⁴ Cicero dismisses that
idea and returns to the idea of neutrality, withdrawing to a neutral place
outside of Italy such as Malta.³⁴⁵ (Possibly Atticus himself had proposed

---

³³⁹ Ant. [Cic.] *Att.* 10.8A.2 (ca. May 1): *qui tibi ut beneficium daret prius iniuriam fecit.*
³⁴⁰ *Att.* 9.10; see n. 316.
³⁴¹ *Att.* 9.13.3 (March 23): *non est a me collecta ad querelam sed magis ad consolationem meam.* On
   March 24 (9.13a) Cicero signals that he has gotten back in line for the little time that remains (contra
   Shackleton Bailey): *maneamus ergo in illa eadem sententia.* For the agreed-upon decision point see
   9.15.3 (March 25), 18.4 (March 28; cf. already 9.6.1 [March 11]). The need to rethink the plan if
   Pompey fled Italy had been stipulated in the abstract since the evacuation of Rome (9.10.4, quoting
   Atticus's letter of January 21).
³⁴² *Att.* 9.18.4 (March 28): *extremem fuit*; 9.19.2–4 (April 1 or 2).
³⁴³ *Att.* 10.1.2 (April 3). Note that in early March Cicero had been angling for an invitation to stay at
   Atticus's estate in Epirus, though in the end he dismisses the thought because it is too likely to be in
   the way of *Pompey's* army (9.1.4, 7.7, 9.2, 12.1; 10.7.3). (This incidentally undermines Wistrand's
   judgment [1979: 120] that the Epirus idea was just a cover for joining Pompey.)
³⁴⁴ *Att.* 10.8.1 (May 2).
³⁴⁵ *Att.* 10.4.10 (April 14): *me recessum et solitudinem quaerere* (to Curio), but 10.7.1: *Melitae aut alio in
   loco simili <vel> oppidulo* (April 22?) shows that this is not just a "cover story" for Caesarians;
   10.9.1–3 (May 3), 18.2 (May 19). Cf. *Fam.* 4.2.4 (to Sulpicius Rufus, April 28 or 29), 5.19.2 (to

the idea.) Yet on May 3 he again fervently declares his resolution to join Pompey, only to inform Atticus the very next day that he had given up the idea, moved by the tears of his family, including his seven-months' pregnant daughter, who gave birth two and a half weeks later to a premature, sickly baby.[346] As late as May 12, Cicero was of two minds whether to join Pompey or to stay – or at least so he recalled with notable specificity in a letter written about three years later to his friend M. Marius.[347]

The letter of May 19 that conveys the news about the birth of Cicero's short-lived grandson ends the remarkable stream of letters to Atticus that has allowed us to follow the twists and turns of the two men's deliberation over the first five months of the year 49. Exactly nineteen days later Cicero embarked from Caieta to join Pompey "to defend the Republic together with those of my kind," as he writes on shipboard to his wife, Terentia, after a miserable night.[348] What exactly made up his mind finally to join the fray on Pompey's side, we do not know. Possibly Cicero gave up the idea of an ostensibly neutral withdrawal from Italy when he heard definitively through Atticus and Balbus that Caesar strongly disapproved, thus corroborating Antony's negative view rather than that of the friendly Curio and Caelius.[349] Cato's precipitate withdrawal from Sicily in early May may also have discouraged the idea.[350] Since so long as he remained in Italy he

Mescinius Rufus, ca. April 28), 2.16 (to Caelius, May 3 or 4; cf. Caelius's letter to which he responds, *Fam.* 8.16.5 = *Att.* 10.9A), with Shackleton Bailey's notes. Malta is explicitly mentioned at *Att.* 10.7.1, 8.10, 9.1, 3, 18.2. Wistrand 1979: 142, 156n3, thinks this was intended only to be a way station to Pompey, but this is nowhere stated or clearly implied. *Att.* 10.16.6 (May 14) may suggest that Cicero will next see Atticus in Greece but in view of the great uncertainties that cloud Cicero's plans at this time it should not be leaned on too heavily. The obscure and abortive "Caelian" project, which may have involved taking some dramatic stand to advocate for peace, was probably a separate matter: 10.12.2, 12a.3, 15.4, with Shackleton Bailey 1965: 4:461–69; Wistrand 1979: 151–152; Brunt 1986: 22.

[346] *Att.* 10.8.1–3 (May 2), with Shackleton Bailey's comment; 10.9.2 (May 3). The baby: 10.18.1 (May 19).

[347] *Fam.* 7.3.1 (prob. April 46): *quo tempore vidisti profecto me quoque ita conturbatum ut non explicarem quid esset optimum factu* (i.e. *si manerem in Italia . . . si proficiscerer ad bellum*: Cicero leaves out the extra-Italian neutrality option). The date is (broadly) corroborated by *Att.* 10.16.4.

[348] *Fam.* 14.7.2 (June 7): *me aliquando cum similibus nostri rem publicam defensuros.*

[349] *Att.* 10.4.10 (Curio, April 13) *Fam.* 8.16.5 = *Att.* 10.9A.5 (Caelius, ca. April 16; see Cicero's disingenuous reply, *Fam.* 2.16 [May 2 or 3]); *Att.* 10.8A and 10.10.1–2 (Antony, May 1?, 3?); 10.8B (Caesar, April 16). Cf. 10.9.1 (May 3) for Cicero's initial interpretation of Caesar's letter, 18.2 (May 19) for the last mention of the project, discouraged by Atticus's report of a conversation with Balbus. Note Cicero's worry that his departure from Italy might not be seen *by the Pompeians* as evidence of disfavor with Caesar (10.12a.1). It may be, as Wistrand 1979: 137 suggests, that Q. Cicero jr's visit to Caesar did indeed damage Caesar's trust in his uncle. Caesar had ordered Antony not to let anyone (any senator?) leave Italy (10.10.2). Ser. Sulpicius Rufus would also leave Italy for Greece – presumably not with Caesar's permission.

[350] *Att.* 10.16.3, May 14. For Cicero's surprise at Cato's withdrawal on April 23 without a fight see also *Att.* 10.12.2 (cf. 4.9, 7.3 for Curio's worries).

dreaded being pushed by Caesar into the Senate as a token of legitimacy,[351] there seemed after all then to be no space for a neutral option that would not incur the wrath of the Pompeians. Cicero expected a turn for the worse by Caesar whichever way the tides of war turned; early in May he reverts to the kind of harsh language with which he had characterized Caesar's initial move into Italy, predicting massacre, confiscations, the return of exiles, debt cancellation, political spoils for disreputable henchmen, and in a word, *regnum*.[352] But it had taken him – a general with *imperium* under the command of Pompey – more than four months after Caesar had defied the Final Decree of the Senate and entered Italy under arms to throw in his lot definitively with his own commander in chief.[353] Plutarch writes, prob-ably correctly, that the Pompeians assumed he had deserted to Caesar.[354]

If there is a pattern, then, it is a very complex one which reinforces the picture of confusion and uncertainty that can be extrapolated from Caesar's own, admittedly partisan, account. Atticus is quite consistent in insisting that Cicero wait at least until the outcome of Pompey's retreat is known; when that becomes clear he stalls, temporizes, and subtly criticizes the premises that would lead his friend to what he regards as precipitate action. Cicero, pricked by an acute sense of dishonor at his inaction (though he also defends this in the name of peace), chafes at Atticus's restraint, especially once he has allowed himself to be cut off from Pompey, and even leaps upon mistaken inferences that Atticus has changed his tune, only to come back into line once his friend corrects the misunderstanding. Cicero uses Atticus as his interlocu-tor as if in a disputation, and often appears to criticize his friend's advice most directly when in truth he appears to be searching for reassurance to stay the course:[355] in his most anguished moments Cicero seems to assuage his sense of dishonor for not sharing in Pompey's travails by telling Atticus that he fervently desired to join him.[356] It is hazardous to pin down a clear, stable hierarchy of Cicero's preferences in this terrible, confused, and confusing

---

[351] See esp. *Att.* 9.5.2 (March 10, 9.6.6 (March 11), 9.15.1, 3 (March 25), 18.1 (March 28); 10.1.3 (April 3), 10.1a.1 (April 4 – here Cicero seems to express some desire to return to the Senate, despite his deep misgivings); 10.8.3 (May 2); cf. 10.3a.2 (April 7), 10.8.3 (May 2). The "carrot" Caesar offered was the opportunity to advocate meaningfully for peace, but Cicero was afraid of being used and regarded the peace initiative in the Senate of early April as *simulatio aperta* (10.1a).

[352] Cic. *Att.* 10.8.2 (May 2), quoted n. 265. Cf. *Att.* 10.12.3 (May 6): *nihil inimicius quam sibi ipse* [sc. Caesar]. *illud recte times ne ruat. si desperarit, certe ruet.*

[353] Wistrand 1979: 157.   [354] Plut. *Cic.* 37.2.

[355] Most explicitly at *Att.* 9.10.10: *tu modo auctoritatem tuam defendito; adversus me nihil opus est, sed consciis egeo aliis. Ego, si nihil peccavi, reliqua tuebor. Ad ea tute hortare et me omnino tua cogitatione adiuva.* Cf. the quite different tone at the beginning of this very letter (next. n.).

[356] *Att.* 9.10.2: *amens mihi fuisse a principio videor et me una haec res torquet quod non omnibus in rebus labentem vel potius ruentem Pompeium tamquam unus manipularis secutus sim.* See prev. n.

time: Plutarch is not wrong in writing that he was "clearly distressed and much torn in both directions."[357] But if *Cicero* felt this way – a Pompeian general, eminent consular, and figurehead of the *boni* (as he saw himself) – then how must others less committed personally to Pompey and less wedded to senatorial dominance of the *res publica* have viewed the unfolding conflict of January through March of 49 BC? Cicero had supported Caesar's claim to a second consulship, elected in absentia if need be according to his legal right passed by the Roman People in 52, though he had disapproved strongly of Caesar's forcing his legal rights upon an unwilling Senate; he was shocked at the "rush to war" by Pompey and Caesar's enemies and highly suspicious of their motives, lust for *dominatio* in Pompey's case, envy and greed or opportunism for some of the others. On one point he is (mostly) consistent: that almost anything was preferable to outright civil war, and given the destructive cycle that this civil war would ultimately launch it would be hard in retrospect to deny that he was right.[358]

The Roman People

So now let us consider (so far as our evidence takes us) the rest of the Roman population of Italy: the citizens, soldiers, and voters without whose acquiescence or support, tacit or overt, no *dux* or *factio* could ever achieve their ends. Here we are reduced to reading "through" our texts for third-party judgments by the elite actors who authored the texts that survive to our time. It is easy to dismiss Caesar's representation of how he was warmly greeted in town after town as he "returned" to Italy more in the manner of a homecoming hero than an invader.[359] Yet how is it that Caesar was able to sweep through a long list of towns – Ariminum, Iguvium, Auximum,

---

[357] Plut. *Cic.* 37.2, citing at §3 the evidence of the letters. Contra: Lintott 2013: 190.

[358] E.g. *Att.* 8.11D.7 (to Pompey, no less): *primum enim prae me tuli me nihil malle quam pacem, non quin eadem timerem quae illi sed ea bello civili leviora ducebam.* For his advocacy of peace in December and January see Chapter 6, p. 289, 301f.

[359] Caes. *BCiv.* 1.12–15. Batstone and Damon 2006: 61–63 (cf. Batstone 1991), and especially Bruhns 1978: 81–88 are all highly skeptical of Caesar's self-serving but nevertheless credible account; Raaflaub 1974: 249–250 emphasizes Caesar's unexpected mildness and leniency rather than any preexisting pro-Caesarian feeling. Bruhns properly corrects Syme's claim that Italian Romans were actually enthusiastic partisans of Caesar's in a kind of replay of the Sullan-Marian civil war, but he goes too far in downplaying the evidence for pro-Caesarian sentiment through the peninsula. Cf. Brunt 1986: 18–19 for the likely Caesarian sympathies of "the rural poor among whom Rome always raised her legionaries" and the lack of enthusiasm for Pompey among "the ruling class in the Italian towns." In the circumstances, even to decline to take a side (as did the city fathers of Auximum, according to Caes. *BCiv.* 1.13.1) was hardly "neutral." Batstone and Damon stress fear of Caesar, which certainly must have played a role at the beginning of his march though there is little warrant for giving it primacy, and in any case such fear was dissipated, and goodwill perhaps redoubled,

Picenum, Cingulum, Asculum, Camerinum, Firmum, Sulmo – before he reached the first non-negligible resistance at Corfinium, despite the Senate's Final Decree which should have ruled neutrality strictly out of court? Could this have happened if he really was viewed by most Romans as a second "Hannibal"? But we are not forced to rely on Caesar's self-serving statements, for Cicero tells at least a recognizably similar story.[360] Before the outbreak of hostilities, he frequently points out that no one wanted war, and the "desperate city rabble" evidently favored Caesar: "The populace and the lower orders sympathized, as I myself observed, with the other side and many were eager for revolution."[361]

As we saw in the previous chapter, even the Senate was far from unified in its convictions toward the end of 50, despite the fact that the anti-Caesar *factio* was ultimately able to seize the reins at the beginning of 49; for most of the previous year, the majority of its members appear to have preferred peace to risking civil war by taking a hard line against him. A few days after the panicked flight from Rome, Cicero writes to Atticus from Formiae of the general outrage of the townsmen and others whom he met over the idea of Caesar advancing upon an abandoned and defenseless capital. The mood had swung against making any concessions to Caesar (which may suggest that the mood had recently been more conciliatory).[362] But having judged in December that the attitude of the urban plebs in Rome was pretty solidly in Caesar's favor, Cicero now urgently pumps Atticus for an update.[363] It was clear enough what the people's sentiments were when the honorific letter Pompey had written to Caesar, seeming to portend a quick settlement of hostilities, was read out to an enthusiastic audience, surely in Rome.[364] Cicero also reports that Pompeian recruiting among the *coloni* of Campania was not going well – in itself a kind of verdict of the soldierly class and the local notables on whom the recruiting officers necessarily relied.[365] Plutarch states explicitly that some flatly disobeyed the call-up, other unenthusiastically appeared, while "most cried out for a settlement"

---

after Caesar's ostentatious demonstration of his "leniency" in sharp contrast to what was expected from Pompey's wrath (p. 401). Cf. also Chapter 6, p. 316ff.

[360] Cic. *Att.* 7.3.5, 7.5.4, 7.6.2, 7.7.5 (cf. 7.8.4–5, 7.9.3), 8.3.4, 8.13.2.   [361] *Att.* 8.3.4.

[362] *Att.* 7.11.4 (January 21?): *mira hominum querela est.*   [363] *Att.* 7.11.5, 13a.3.

[364] *Att.* 7.18.1. See n. 83.

[365] *Att.* 7.13.2, 14.2, 21.1 (although now Cicero claims that *deficit enim non voluntas sed spes*, this seems to be a straw in the wind in view of the earlier observations and 8.3.4 later). Brunt 1986: 18–19. Some, perhaps many of the Campanian colonists had been settled under Caesar's agrarian law; however, many are likely to have been Pompeian veterans, while Pompey and some of his associates had also served on the Board of Twenty.

of the dispute.[366] In mid-February – *before* the surrender of Corfinium, be it noted – Cicero judges that Pompey's cause "aroused no passion either in any order or, overtly, among private individuals."[367] This appears to mark a real change since the first wave of indignation that Cicero had observed in Campania a few days after the *fuga bonorum* from Rome. (One might add that the kind of *municipales* and others who would converse with the great man in his villa were doubtless a self-selected group, nor would they necessarily have bared their souls to the military commander of the coast.) Then, after Caesar had conspicuously taken pains to spare not only the population of Corfinium but even the opposing army and its generals, Cicero perceived a great swing of the public mood in his favor. Two days after he had heard of Caesar's sparing of the general, officers, and army at Corfinium, Cicero writes that Caesar was earning "applause" in the worst cause while Pompey was earning only ill will in the "best."[368] On the first of March he adds that the "town and country people" (*municipales homines . . . [et] rusticani*) now "fear the man they used to trust [Pompey] and love the man they used to dread."[369] Three days later, Cicero complains that the towns are "mak[ing] a god of him, and no pretence either, as there was when they were offering their prayers to Pompey."[370] The towns were sending out welcoming parties and conferring official honors. Perhaps they were afraid, but they were much more afraid of Pompey than of Caesar: "They are delighted with *his* artful clemency and fear the other's wrath."[371]

Caesar's account of his reception in Italy therefore calls for some cautious revision, then, but not of a very radical kind. No one, it seems, wanted civil war. But there was no great interest in Italy or in Rome (outside certain circles of the Senate) in rejecting Caesar's prewar requests to be allowed to stand in the summer of 49 for a second consulship in absentia in accordance with the Law of the Ten Tribunes, and to triumph. It is likely that the eagerness of the anti-Caesar faction to bring matters to a fight bewildered the

---

[366] Plut. *Pomp.* 59.4; Brunt 1988: 269.

[367] *Att.* 8.3.4: *causa in qua nullus esset ordinum, nullus apertus privatorum dolor.*   [368] *Att.* 8.9a.1.

[369] *Att.* 8.13.1–2. "If he takes no lives and touches no man's property those who dreaded him most will become his warmest admirers."

[370] *Att.* 8.16.1–2; cf. 9.5.3.

[371] *Att.* 8.16.2: *huius* [sc. Caesar] *insidiosa clementia delectantur, illius iracundiam formidant.* (For skepticism about Caesar's *clementia* see 8.9a.2: merely a (deceptive) prelude to the *crudelitas* Cicero and Atticus had feared, presumably once it had achieved its object of softening resistance.) Pompey's "threats" had even managed to turn the judicial panel of 360 select *equites* against him (Shackleton Bailey). Cf. *Att.* 9.5.3: *his de victoria gratulationibus; 9.13.4 municipia vero et rustici Romani; 9.15.3* [*municipales homines ac rustici*] *metuunt ut crudelem, iratum.*

residents of Italy as much as it did Cicero. Once Caesar had entered Italy under arms in defiance of the Senate's decrees, a natural wave of apprehension and indignation appears to have swept through the peninsula. Past civil wars offered many frightening precedents to ponder. Yet Caesar conspicuously did not march on Rome, as had all civil warlords before him, and when by a spectacular gesture of mercy at Corfinium he made good his claim peace was his object, not total war in the manner of Sulla or Marius and indeed, the young Pompey, the towns of Italy warmed to him enthusiastically, while simultaneously repelled by threats of reprisals from the other side.

In such circumstances, who was to say that the men who had started this war to destroy one of Rome's greatest heroes and then had turned tail, refusing even to talk with their adversary in their headlong flight from Italy, truly represented the norms and ideals of "the Republic," as they claimed? Why should one suppose, as is done so often, that the partiality toward Caesar that emerges during his return to Italy, and becomes most conspicuous after Corfinium, was due simply to apathy or indifference to the cause of the Republic? One could easily argue, given the events we have traced, that "the Republic" appeared to be with Caesar rather than against him.[372] The consuls, it is true – traditionally an important marker of legitimacy – had set themselves against him.[373] But if one looked to the Senate in general, one saw that senators and nobles themselves split both ways, and the depth of the division itself will have raised reasonable doubt about the representativeness of the decrees of early January. *Boni* aplenty made their way back to Caesar's Rome rather than flocking to Pompey's camp or making their way to the nearest port.[374] Others, especially among the politically conscious urban plebs, may have been less inclined anyway to defer to senatorial opinion, especially in a matter in which the consuls and Senate seem to have grossly neglected the public forum, defied the manifest signs of the popular will, and finally trampled on the fiercely defended traditional rights of the tribunes to represent the popular interest. As we have noted before, the Roman People did not define "the Republic" solely from the senatorial viewpoint, much less the "optimate" one.

Return to Rome

On March 17 Pompey set sail from Italy. By March 27 Caesar, one day before meeting Cicero at Formiae on his route back to Rome from Brundisium, had

---

[372] See n. 291.   [373] Consuls as markers of legitimacy: Morstein-Marx 2011.
[374] E.g. *Att.* 9.13.4 (March 23), and above.

ordered notices to be put up in the towns around Italy summoning a full
senatorial meeting for April 1.[375] Cicero, as we have seen, begged off, but we
know that among the consulars, Ser. Sulpicius Rufus (cos. 51) was there as was
Volcacius Tullus (cos. 66), M'. Lepidus (also cos. 66), and probably also
Caesar's father-in-law, L. Piso (cos. 58). Surely others among the "neutral"
consulars who had not received special dispensation (as did L. Marcius
Philippus, perhaps uniquely besides Cicero) also appeared: perhaps, for
example, L. Caesar (cos. 64), who was both Caesar's (distant) cousin and
Antony's uncle.[376] According to Dio's impressively specific information, the
meeting was formally presided over (quite correctly) by the tribunes Antony
and Q. Cassius and (again with an eye to constitutional correctness) it was
held *outside* the sacred boundary of the city (*pomerium*) in order to allow
Caesar to be present without forfeiting his proconsular *imperium*.[377]

The tension of the moment must be appreciated, for in Caesar's own,
typically undramatic presentation one is likely to pass over it much too
easily.[378] The precedents were ugly. Sulla's first meeting of the Senate after
his capture of Rome by assault in 88 had, probably not entirely free of
intimidation, declared twelve men, including Marius, his son, and the
sitting tribune P. Sulpicius, enemies of the State, sending most (including
Rome's savior against the Cimbri and Teutones) into exile and precipitating the murder of the tribune, who was caught in flight. He then had
Sulpicius's legislation annulled. This would have been the kind of thing
that Cicero had in mind when he had first begun fretting about being
excused from attending the Senate.[379] Later examples were even worse.
When Marius and Cinna fought their way back into the City in 87, they
forced the Senate to lift the sentence of exile and unleashed a bloody
settling of accounts that left several eminent senators dead; the Senate
now declared Sulla an enemy of the state and his property confiscated. And
again in 82, after his final victory at the Colline Gate, Sulla delivered to the
assembled Senate his official report on his actions – while several thousand

---

[375] Cic. *Att.* 9.17.1. For the possible technical meaning of *senatus frequens* (= "quorate") see Chapter 4,
n. 161. Caesar must have relaxed the usual rule requiring a quorum of two hundred members, given
the departure of some two hundred senators.
[376] See n. 67.   [377] Dio 41.15.2.
[378] As indeed most scholars do. Gelzer 1968: 275 is an exception, with an uncharacteristic error as to
date (January).
[379] Cic. *Att.* 9.2a.1 (March 8), 6.6 (March 11): *ut absim cum aliquid in senatu contra Gnaeum agatur.*
Later in March Cicero began to worry more, it seems, about the possibility that Caesar wanted him
to add his voice as augur to a claim that a praetor could preside over election of consuls or name
a dictator, thus avoiding an interregnum: 9.9.3, 15.2. By then he had gotten hints from Balbus and
Oppius that Caesar would launch a new peace initiative once he returned to Rome (9.7A.1) and
Caesar had promised as much at their meeting on March 28 (9.18.1).

prisoners were clamorously massacred in the adjacent Villa Publica.[380] Immediately afterward he began the notorious "proscriptions" which gave a legalistic sheen to the slaughter and/or dispossession of some five hundred senators and *equites* – themselves a follow-up to the less restrained massacres his partisans had perpetrated since his recapture of the City.[381]

Caesar had not attended a meeting of the Senate for nine years, since the inconclusive send-off he had received at the beginning of 58 when two praetors challenged the legality of his acts and laws. The moment was a fraught one in this respect as well, for although many individual senators will have met him face-to-face in Cisalpina during the winters between Gallic campaigns, this was the first time in nearly a decade that they could watch him operating in this institutional context, and he, them. According to his own account in the *Civil War Commentaries*, Caesar now gave a speech defending his recent actions in which he recounted the injustices and injuries perpetrated by his enemies, pointed out that in seeking a second consulship after a lapse of ten years he had sought nothing irregular, condemned Pompey's inconsistency in supporting, then seeking to withdraw, his *ratio absentis*, and reminded the senators of his own proposal as the crisis loomed to lay down his arms if Pompey would only do the same. He dwelt on his enemies' hypocrisy in not themselves making a concession which they demanded from another, and their irresponsibility in preferring to turn everything upside down rather than give up their commands and armies. He recalled their "theft" of the two legions, their insulting and violent treatment of the tribunes, and their refusal of his peace efforts and pleas for a meeting.[382] As we saw in the previous chapter, these complaints were not without merit, and most senators who had returned to Rome would probably have tacitly acknowledged their force although various obvious objections and qualifications could not here be voiced.[383]

This kind of "charge sheet" might have been a prelude to a request for the Senate to take harsh action against Pompey. But instead of demanding that they vote Pompey, or Cato or any other of his *inimici* public enemies, Caesar now asked senators to step forward and undertake a mission of *peace*. Caesar called upon the Senate to do two things. First, he called upon the Fathers to "take up the affairs of the Republic and manage them jointly

---

[380] Plut. *Sull.* 30.3–4; Dio fr. 109; Livy *Per.* 88. An up-to-date review of the main events in Steel 2013: 94–107.

[381] Hinard 1985.   [382] Caes. *BCiv.* 1.32.2–6.

[383] Cicero's own public "peace letter" of mid-March had said much the same thing in more general terms: n. 290. Cf. Fufius Calenus's opinion, Cic. *Att.* 9.5.1.

with him." But he warned them that if they declined out of fear "he would trouble them no further and manage the affairs of the Republic by himself," clearly a threat intended to drive them on board.[384] Then he urged the Senate to send envoys to Pompey to try yet again to pursue a peaceful settlement. Pointedly criticizing Pompey's own recent objection in the Senate that a peace embassy to Caesar would be a sign of weakness, Caesar declared that he desired to prevail not merely in action but in justice and fairness.[385] This emphasis on his confidence in taking what might today be called "the high road" against the ostensibly short-sighted, self-interested machinations of his adversaries echoes the tone found in a letter he had written to Cicero about his generous treatment of those captured at Corfinium.[386]

In an exasperating echo of the last meetings Caesar had attended in March 58, not to mention those at the beginning of his consulship when he had sought to open debate on his agrarian law, three days of discussion in the Senate ensued with no real action on either of the two requests. To be sure, a proposal to send peace envoys to Pompey was passed, perhaps on the motion of L. Volcacius Tullus, but it is unclear whether envoys were then even named, and in any case they did not set out.[387] Caesar attributes the foot-dragging mainly to fear of Pompey's threats, not unreasonably.[388] Yet he must also have made clear that he would not slow military operations against Pompey in the meantime, which of course enabled the skeptical to see the initiative as purely specious and therefore their own participation as dangerously compromising.[389] Senators, of course, had no

---

[384] Caes. *BCiv.* 1.32.7: *Pro quibus rebus hortatur et postulat ut rem publicam suscipiant atque una secum administrarent. Sin timore defugiant illis se oneri non futurum et per se rem publicam administraturum.* Caesar's threat or warning substantially repeats his unpleasant parting shot at his private meeting with Cicero at Formiae on March 28: "If he could not avail himself of my counsels, he would take those he could get and stop at nothing" (Cic. *Att.* 9.18.3).

[385] Caes. *BCiv.* 1.32.8–9; cf. Plut. *Caes.* 35.4 : ἐπιεικῆ καὶ δημοτικὰ διελέχθη; Dio 41.15.2 πολλὰ καὶ ἐπιεικῆ. Caesar's claim that Pompey had objected in the Senate to a peace embassy is obscure; in the preserved text of the *BCiv.* he relates no such occasion (Pompey was not present at 1.3.6–4.1) although it could have been during one of the meetings held outside the formal boundary of the City after January 7 (1.6). Pompey did, of course, send envoys to Caesar soon after the *s.c.u.* was passed (n. 67); had he then opposed a peace embassy in the Senate but sent a private one instead?

[386] *Att.* 9.16.2: *neque illud me movet quod ii qui a me dimissi sunt discessisse dicuntur ut mihi rursus bellum inferrent; nihil enim malo quam et me mei similem esse et illos sui.* See Chap. 8.

[387] Plut. *Caes.* 35.4–5; Dio 41.15.4. Tullus: Cic. *Att.* 9.19.2 (cf. 10.1.2), with Shackleton Bailey's notes. Cicero expected or rather hoped that Sulpicius Rufus would be named the peace envoy, since he dreaded the possibility that he might be chosen in his absence (10.1a). Raaflaub 1974: 230–231, 276–278.

[388] Caes. *BCiv.* 1.33.1–2; Plut. *Caes.* 35.5; Dio 41.16.4.

[389] Note Cicero's own anxiety about the possibility of being selected for the mission. See *Att.* 10.1.3, 10.1a, and n. 351. Caesar cannot have hidden his intention to carry on the war effort unabated: see next n. Plut. *Caes.* 35.5 balances both motives (see Pelling's n.).

idea how the fighting would turn out and hedged their bets uncomfortably. It is possible that the allegedly timorous Sulpicius Rufus actually voiced some objection to Caesar's proceeding actively against Pompey while talking peace, unless Cicero is being overly polite in attributing such sentiments when he writes to him shortly thereafter.[390] Caesar also alleges that L. Metellus, a tribune who had popped up in Capua in mid-March (by which time the consuls had crossed to Dyrrachium and Campania was firmly in Caesarian control – so perhaps a Pompeian "deserter," like Furius Crassipes?), began to break up the proceedings and blocked further action, evidently by means of vetoes or threats of a veto.[391]

Caesar soon saw that the proposal was going nowhere and gave up the effort to achieve anything through the Senate. By the time Curio visited Cicero at Cumae on April 14, the senatorial peace initiative was a dead letter.[392] That is how Caesar himself treated it when, after he had wrested Spain from the Pompeians, he returned to Rome at the end of the year 49 on his way to pursue Pompey to Greece. His father-in-law, the consular L. Piso, sought to revive the decree and send envoys now, but Caesar threw his weight behind the objections voiced by P. Servilius Isauricus the younger, probably already consul-designate for 48, and we hear nothing further of this "senatorial" peace strategy.[393] As it happens, whether this was precisely what he had meant, Caesar was as good as his word: now that he was indisputably embarked on a civil war, he would necessarily have to fight it independently without relying on the Senate for guidance and consultation, just as Sulla and Marius and others before him had done. Some two weeks after the April meetings (April 14), Caesar's legate Curio

---

[390] *Fam.* 4.1.1, ca. April 21: *cui* [sc. *Caesari*] *quidem ego, cum me rogaret ut adessem in senatu, eadem omnia quae a te de pace et de Hispaniis dicta sunt ostendi me esse dicturum.* In the conversation with Caesar to which he refers he had (he claims) said that if full freedom were given him to propose in the Senate what he wished, he would propose *senatui non placere in Hispanias iri nec exercitus in Graeciam transportari* and would say much in Pompey's behalf. Caesar responded *ego vero ista dici nolo* (*Att.* 9.18.1).

[391] Caes. *BCiv.* 1.33.4; more than one veto or veto threat, probably: Cic. (Caelius) *Att.* 10.9A.1 = *Fam.* 8.16.1. It is interesting that according to Caesar there were *inimici* still in Rome in April, almost certainly senators who (unlike Cicero) had obeyed Caesar's summons to a *frequens senatus*. Metellus in Capua ca. March 10: n. 154. On Furius see 9.11.3, with Shackleton Bailey 1960: 259n6.

[392] Cic. *Att.* 10.4.8–9.

[393] Plut. *Caes.* 37.1; cf. Dio 41.16.4, and n. 186. It was not, however, Caesar's last attempt to open discussion of peace: see Chapter 8, n. 69. Plutarch mentions the consular elections last among Caesar's actions in Rome at the end of 49, but Caesar (*BCiv.* 3.1.1) puts them first. It will have been advantageous to hold the elections before any serious senatorial meeting, since the results would ensure that the first two men called upon to speak – himself and one other: P. Servilius, in the event – could be relied upon to say what Caesar wanted. And if Servilius was supposed to speak as Caesar's mouthpiece (so, roughly, Plut.), far better for him to do so as cos. des. than as a mere praetorian in the second rank of the speaking hierarchy.

told Cicero that Caesar had said "everything would come from himself" – that is, apparently, the Senate (which he "now hated much more") would be left no significant decision-making role.[394] A civil war, with its demand for centralized leadership and authority, inevitably and typically quite radically interrupts the routine peacetime functioning of institutions that disperse power outside the executive branches of government. Abraham Lincoln's presidency over the remaining half of the United States during the Southern secession is a notable exception, perhaps made possible by the federal nature of the US Constitution but itself not unblemished by some unconstitutional concessions to the exigencies of civil war.[395] Thus Caesar's threat to "trouble [the Senate] no further" should be understood in the context of waging (civil) war, not interpreted as in effect the permanent abolition of the Republic henceforth. It would be quite unsurprising if the complete failure of his effort to enlist the Senate to help negotiate a settlement with Pompey exhausted Caesar's patience with the body, whose weakness and fecklessness over the prior twelve months, despite some sympathy with Caesar's position, was manifest to all, but most particularly to the recent target of its decrees. Yet it is also true, as a matter of fact rather than inevitable consequence, that hereafter, that is through the Civil War and its brief aftermath until Caesar's assassination, the Senate did not again exercise independent agency except perhaps to confront a few emergencies that arose in Rome and in Italy while Caesar was far away in the East.[396]

What about Caesar's relationship with the People during this same visit – a moment which under happier circumstances would have been quite literally a triumphal one? Dio tells us that a *contio* was called for Caesar, again outside the *pomerium* (thus clearly for the same reason), at which he gave much the same speech to the assembled People as he had done to the Senate, adding a promise to distribute among them 300

---

[394] Cic. *Att.* 10.4.9: *"a me" inquit "omnia proficiscentur."* Curio was probably being somewhat alarmist with Cicero in order to deter him from making any awkward moves; he even tries to frighten Cicero with talk of *caedes* and *crudelitas* if Caesar's patience ran out (§8). Note that Curio represents Caesar as overruling his preference for even a nominal senatorial decision on the trivial matter of Curio's *fasces* (Shackleton Bailey n.). Caesar's "anger" (*iratus*) at the Senate is corroborated by Caelius, 10.9A.1 = *Fam.* 8.16.1; Caesar "has clearly been exasperated by these vetoes."

[395] Most notably his suspension of habeas corpus and disregard for the First Amendment (Chapter 8, n. 204) during the war.

[396] I.e. the rioting and insurrection led by Caelius and Milo in 48 and the similar disturbance set in motion by Dolabella, suppressed by an *s.c.u.* (!) (Chapter 9, nn. 182, 183). The Senate seems to have involved itself not at all in the great mutiny in Campania in 47 (Chrissanthos 2001).

sesterces and assuaging their fears for the grain supply, which Pompey threatened to cut, by announcing that he was sending for additional stocks from Sicily and Sardinia.[397] (The promise of a handout was clearly in anticipation of the Gallic triumph, which under normal circumstances would now have been celebrated but in view of present circumstances had to be deferred – until 46, it would turn out, when in compensation the sum was increased to 400 sesterces.)[398] It is of considerable interest that Dio's source stresses yet again that a meeting was held outside the formal city boundaries, thus in strict observance of the ancient custom (and statutory law) that *imperium* would lapse upon crossing the *pomerium*. This was not therefore merely a constitutional "nicety" that Caesar could safely ignore now as a military autocrat.[399] It made good sense for Caesar to remain outside the *pomerium*: why should he wish to put his own *imperium* in question and needlessly complicate his own legal position?

This small point has further implications, because the famous story recounted by Plutarch and, most famously, Lucan about the tribune L. Metellus's attempt to block Caesar's opening of the treasury places Caesar within the City boundaries. Dio too recounts the event, but consistently with his earlier statements about the *pomerium*; in his version it is not Caesar himself but Caesar's *soldiers* who break L. Metellus's intercession and cut the lock of the treasury doors.[400] B. Woytek then is probably right that at the very least Plutarch's source (perhaps Pollio again) has wrongly brought Caesar in person to the Treasury for the dramatic

---

[397] Dio 41.16.1 (cf. 17.1); Suet. *Iul.* 38.1. HS 300 seems to have amounted to nearly a third of a year's pay as a day laborer (Dyson 2010: 112) or perhaps one-sixth of what such a person might have to pay in rent in the capital (Suet. *Iul.* 38.2). Fear for the grain supply is confirmed by the many passages in Cicero's letters where he complains about Pompey's strategy to reconquer Italy. "The islands" must mean the nearby granaries of Sicily and Sardinia, both of them already in Caesar's hands (Caes. *BCiv.* 1.30.2–31.1). Strictly speaking, Dio does not say that Caesar announced the grain requisitioning in the *contio*, but it comes between two items that do apparently belong to it, and it was certainly important to ease the urban plebs' mind on this matter.

[398] Suet. *Iul.* 38.1; Dio 43.21.3.

[399] Pelling's objection (2011: 332) to Woytek 2004; Gelzer 1968: 209n5, preferred to reject Dio's explicit assertion that Caesar did not cross the *pomerium*. Other constitutional "niceties" observed by Caesar include (now) waiting for the consulship of 48 *legitimo tempore* and the eleven-day dictatorship to hold the elections. Shackleton Bailey (1965: 4:400) interprets Cic. *Att.* 10.3a.1 (*visum te aiunt in regia*) to mean that Caesar after all crossed the *pomerium*. Yet it is clear that he does not literally mean the building called the *Regia* just off the Forum, since he adds that he himself is subject to the same criticism (*quippe cum ipse istam reprehensionem non fugerim*). He must mean in "the palace" – i.e. "the presence of the *rex*," Caesar (cf. 10.7.1, 10.8.2, 10.8.8).

[400] Dio 41.17.2; cf. App. *BCiv.* 2.41/164 and n. 93. Pliny reports that Caesar extracted 15,000 gold ingots, 30,000 of silver, and 30 million coined sesterces (*HN* 33.56). Most well-informed sources do not restrict Caesar's withdrawal solely to the *aerarium sanctius*. The story found in Appian, Lucian, and elsewhere about the removal of the "Gallic gold" secured with a curse is probably either poetic license or propagandistic fabrication (De Libero 1998: 127–130).

scene which follows.[401] There was no need for him to be on hand – in fact it was better for the self-styled defender of tribunician *sacrosanctitas not* to be present at this difficult and risky moment. Thus Dio's version is surely better – which means no such weighty speechifying between the principals at the Treasury's door. Plutarch or his source has written it up however in a way that invests the clash with all its implicit ideological meaning. Metellus cites "certain laws" in support of his action;[402] Caesar makes the point that war is no time for free speech, but that once peace terms are agreed upon and arms are laid down, Metellus would have every right to address the People in opposition. For the present, he would waive the right of war only to the extent of not taking him captive (recall that Metellus had originally joined with Pompey before turning back to Rome), and proceeds to give orders to break down the door. When Metellus tries to block the way, Caesar threatened to have him killed, at which point the tribune at last steps aside.[403] A great story – but it probably never happened, at least not in this form.

The debate nicely encapsulates some key issues – authentic ones, I might add, whether or not they were explicitly voiced in any actual confrontation – namely, what civic rules apply when there is a war on – especially a *civil* war – and more especially when these civic rules are invoked blatantly as a weapon by a man who had actually chosen the opposing side?[404] But had Caesar not sought to show that he was not acting as one engaged in a civil war? Metellus forces the proconsul to acknowledge openly that he really was now fighting a civil war, which was bound to erode the cover of neutrality that he had extended to senators, and under which numerous senior senators had somewhat uncomfortably taken their seats again in the Curia.[405]

---

[401] Woytek 2003: 46–57. Goldsworthy 2006: 396–397 repeats the speeches in Plutarch as if they were history, though he actually concedes that Caesar himself may not have crossed the boundary, but the two propositions stand and fall together.

[402] These "laws" (νόμους τινάς) remain obscure. The dubious "curse" is not a law (n. 400). Perhaps the laws in question defined who was authorized to withdraw funds from the public treasury: presumably the quaestors, acting on the orders of a consul, both of whom were now in Greece. Caes. *BCiv.* 1.14.1: *ad pecuniamque Pompeio ex senatus consulto proferendam* shows that a s.c. had authorized the withdrawal and transfer of the money to Pompey, which could with some looseness describe as a "law." It would be hardly to the point *at this juncture* for Metellus to cite the laws protecting tribunician sacrosanctity (so Pelling), since here, at the first stage of the confrontation, Metellus is justifying his interception, not the right of interception in itself.

[403] Plut. *Caes.* 35.6–11.

[404] The justification of Caesar's enemies for expelling the tribunes who were vetoing the Final Decree would surely have appeared superficially similar, although in that case the war had not actually begun and the dispute was precisely about initiating it.

[405] See n. 44.

We hear from Cicero, who had it on the authority of Caesar's officer Curio, that Caesar had in fact been so angered by Metellus's actions (probably the senatorial vetoes as much as his interception at the Treasury) that he had wanted to have him killed.[406] (He evidently soon joined the Pompeians in Macedonia.)[407] We also hear from the same source that the matter of the Treasury had caused offense even among the plebs, which had so disconcerted Caesar that he had declined in the end even to hold a *contio* to mark his departure, presumably fearing further unpleasantness.[408] Curio (or Cicero) is inexplicit about the precise cause of the offense. We naturally think of Caesar's blatant rejection of a tribune's right of veto after claiming to be the champion of tribunician rights, but we must be careful. The right of veto was never absolute, after all, but depended on its justification in terms of the good (or will) of the People,[409] and in this case, since Caesar had made a generous pledge to them of HS 300 each, it may be that many among the populace were actually eager to see the treasury *opened*, an act which had probably been authorized by senatorial decree.[410] Indeed Dio makes no mention of any popular anger at the treatment of the tribune; instead he stresses their resentment because Caesar *failed to make good his promise* of a handout and instead used his funds for his soldiers and the war: "And far from receiving at that time the money which he had promised them, the people had to give him all the rest that remained in the treasury for the support of the soldiers, whom they feared."[411]

After nearly ten years' absence, and relying for his most recent information on the reports of the likes of Curio, Caelius and Antony, Caesar himself appears to have misjudged his public standing among both senators and the People and was deeply disappointed by his less than

---

[406] Cic. *Att.* 10.4.8; cf. Plut. *Caes.* 35.10; App. *B Civ.* 2.41/164. See Caelius's report of Caesar's anger at his *intercessionibus* (10.9A.1 = *Fam.* 8.16.1), apparently corroborating Caes. *BCiv.* 1.33.3. Caesar's own men Curio and Caelius seem to have been deeply impressed by Caesar's emotional response to being stymied in Rome: both speak of his *iracundia* (*iratus*) and the likelihood that he would soon turn openly *crudelis, saevus,* and *atrox.*

[407] Chapter 8, n. 85.

[408] Cic. *Att.* 10.4.8. Also 10.7.3: *iacere Caesarem putans offensione populari.* See n. 416.

[409] Morstein-Marx 2004: 124–126.

[410] Decree: Dio 41.17.2: ἀντεῖπε μὲν οὖν πρὸς τὴν περὶ τῶν χρημάτων ἐσήγησιν [= "motion:" LSJ s.v., II, Dio 36.38.5] ... καὶ ἐπειδὴ μηδὲν ἐπέρανε, πρός τε τοὺς θησαυροὺς ἦλθε . . . . . Caesar suggests that Metellus had used his veto power to block various proposals in the Senate (*BCiv.* 1.33.3 with n. 391); in this case, however, Metellus's opposition in the Senate seems to have no effect. De Libero 1998: 125 assumes that there was no authorizing decree.

[411] Dio 41.17.1: ὅσα ἐν τῷ δημοσίῳ ἦν πρὸς τὴν τῶν στρατιωτῶν, οὓς ἐφοβοῦντο, τροφὴν ἔδοσαν. Given the amount extracted from the treasury (n. 400) in the most conspicuous part of the Forum (the Temple of Saturn) their resentment is easily understandable.

acclamatory reception now. His long-delayed return to Rome after his glorious victories in Gaul was far from the adulatory homecoming he had wanted, expected, and ultimately fought for.[412] It is important to recognize that the Roman plebs was not, after all, slavishly devoted to the Conqueror of Gaul; through the culmination of the crisis in the year 50 they had shown their almost desperate longing for peace (remember the flowers tossed at the feet of Curio), and their refusal (along with most citizens up and down the peninsula) to *fight* Caesar as he returned to his homeland was not to be confused with any eagerness to plunge into the horrors of civil war. Ever since the Sullan-Marian bloodletting, civil war had been a peculiar horror of the Roman plebs, whatever rabid political sentiments their anxious "betters" like Sallust imputed to them.[413] *Clementia* on the other hand was "popular" – the Roman plebs was not usually so hostile toward the other side as to wish for its violent destruction.[414] Appian and Dio both plausibly represent the *contio* that met Caesar as preoccupied by the memory of Marius and Sulla, and thus both fearful and skeptical.[415] Cicero continues to grasp at any sign of possible popular discontent.[416] But no source, be it noted, hints at any, even covert expression of popular sympathy with the Pompeian cause. However offended the People may have been by Caesar's disregard of a tribunician veto (which could be excused or legitimated in various ways) or by his failure to fulfill immediately his financial pledge to the plebs, Caesar seems still not to have lost at least the appearance of popular favor for the defense of his rights against the Pompeian faction.[417] The People returned to civilian dress, putting aside their military cloaks (*saga*) to take up the toga again, which signified in the first instance the end of fighting in Italy (*tumultus*), but also rather hopefully implying a return to normalcy.[418]

---

[412] Evocative anticipation of the event in 56 at Cic. *Prov. cons.* 29–30: *ad gloriam devocant* [sc. Caesarem], *ad triumphum, ad gratulationem, ad summum honorem senatus, equestris ordinis gratiam, populi caritatem; 35 si ad eam dignitatem, quam in civitate sibi propositam videt . . . si in Capitolium invehi victor cum illa insigni laude gestiret . . . .*

[413] Morstein-Marx 2004: 68–70, 110–113, 216–217 with n. 57.

[414] Cic. *Att.* 10.4.8: *quod <putaret>* [sc. *Caesar] popularem esse clementiam.* Cf. App. *BCiv.* 2.41/163: Caesar makes much of his treatment of Domitius in his *contio* to the People.

[415] App. *BCiv.* 2.41/163; Dio 41.16.1–4.

[416] Cic. *Att.* 10.12a.3, (from Cumae, early May): Atticus had written of hostile demonstrations in the theater; Cicero adds that even legions in Italy were disaffected (cf. 9.19.1).

[417] Cic. *Att.* 10.4.8 note the *future* conditional of *si populi studium amisisset, crudelem fore.* Gelzer 1968: 210, goes much too far ("total loss of his popularity with the plebs").

[418] Dio 41.17.1. "War could exist without a *tumultus*, there could be no *tumultus* without war" (Lintott 1968: 153). For *saga sumere*, otherwise best attested during the Social War and the War of Mutina, see Lintott loc. cit. with n. 5; G. Manuwald 2007: 1:665–666; Golden 2013: 48–52. *Saga sumere* must be distinguished from the *mutatio vestis* (Dighton 2017).

After this unsettling conclusion to the Italian campaign (such as it was) Caesar abruptly departed for Spain and the next phase of the war against the Pompeians. The Senate and People (and Cicero, for that matter) had just seen a tougher face of Caesar, who had been forced to give up his "political" strategy and turn unambiguously to a military solution. Yet, as we shall see in the next chapter, even the "military" solution of a civil war had a crucial "civil" dimension.

CHAPTER 8

Caesar's Leniency

The most remarkable, most intriguing, and, on its face, most appealing of Caesar's qualities was his – to us and to his contemporaries alike – astonishing moderation in victory against his Roman adversaries in the Civil War. (His record against non-Romans, however, was quite another matter, although still not especially harsh by ancient standards.)[1] Through the millennia the most inflammatory and polarizing aspect of his assassination on the Ides of March, 44, was and remains that he had spared and even favored with political advancement many of those who plunged their daggers into his body on that day or, like Cicero, crowed in triumph after the bloody act. Caesar's "clemency" therefore has been from the start deeply contested ideological terrain: it provided a powerful moral counterpunch against the rather abstract political justification of "tyrannicide." Loyalists were outraged, pointing out that Caesar's very clemency had only brought about his destruction; his "respectable" agent C. Matius, a man moderate enough to remain Cicero's friend through the Civil War, seethed with indignation at the murder of a man who had spared his very assassins and longed for the day when they would bitterly regret what they had done.[2]

Little wonder then that Caesar's assassins and their apologists spared no time in undermining the moral status of his *clementia*. Already in the *Second Philippic* of 44, Cicero describes it as a mere pretense by which

[1] See Chapter 5, p. 252, for Caesar's often harsh practice in Gaul. In the civil wars, his savage treatment of the Thessalian town of Gomphi after it had defected to Pompey (Cic. *BCiv.* 3.80) is notorious; Caesar makes no attempt to hide the fact that he thereby sought to inflict *terror* among surrounding towns. The conclusion of the final Spanish campaign might also be cited for its savagery at Cordoba, Hispalis, and Munda (*Bell. Hisp.* 34–41). On the other hand, Caesar treated the people of Massilia, an ancient Roman ally, with considerable leniency given their determined resistance and the "stab in the back" they had inflicted on their former proconsul during the Ilerda campaign (*BCiv.* 2.22).

[2] Cic. *Att.* 14.22.1 (paraphrasing the Caesarians): *clementiam illi malo fuisse; qua si usus non esset, nihil ei tale accidere potuisse.* Matius, [Cic.] *Fam.* 11.28.3: *possum igitur, qui omnis voluerim incolumis, eum a quo id impetratum est perisse non indignari?*; §4: *id opto ut paeniteat eos sui facti . . . . Cupio enim Caesaris mortem omnibus esse acerbam.*

Caesar tried to bind his enemies to himself, and dismisses the *beneficium* of his own pardon in 47 as no more worthy of moral credit than a highwayman's "kindness" in not killing his victim: refraining from murder is not the same thing as saving a life.[3] In the first century AD the Neronian poet Lucan strains almost comically to subvert his demonic antihero's celebrated leniency: Caesar is figured as a bloodthirsty lion, he is bitterly frustrated by a victory achieved *without* shedding blood, he has to *force* great-hearted Domitius (not coincidentally, Nero's great-great-grandfather) to accept his mercy, he sets out tables to dine almost cannibalistically among the bloody corpses left on the field at Pharsalus.[4] Clearly, a lot was already at stake here. In more modern times the argument has continued. Baron Montesquieu dismissed Caesar's "clemency" as not so much "pardoning" as "disdaining to punish"; Frederick the Great of Prussia is said to have protested, "If all human actions are judged with such severity there is no longer any room for a heroic deed."[5]

As Frederick's riposte indicates, judgments of Caesar's clemency had inevitably become judgments about the possibility of benevolent autocracy – and in this context, the experience of fascist dictatorships and other personal authoritarian regimes in the twentieth century has tilted the balance decisively toward doubt and suspicion. Among scholarly treatments in English, the dominant view is probably still that expressed by Ronald Syme:

> When Caesar the dictator paraded a merciful and forgiving spirit . . . he did not endear himself to all men in his class and order. Clemency depends not on duty but on choice and whim, it is the will of a master not an aristocrat's virtue. To acquiesce in the "clementia Caesaris" implied a recognition of despotism.[6]

R. R. Dyer seconds the point: "To the Stoics, *as to any Roman noble*, clemency is not a virtue" (my italics).[7] More recently, Matthew Roller

---

[3] *Phil.* 2.116: *suos praemiis, adversarios clementiae specie devinxerat. Phil.* 2.5: *quod est aliud, patres conscripti, beneficium latronum nisi ut commemorare possint eis se dedisse vitam quibus non ademerint?* (This last objection is in the first instance directed at Antony, with whom as Caesar's representative in Italy in 47 Cicero had to deal upon his hasty flight from Greece, but Cicero applies the principle fully to his boss, as he makes clear in what follows – *si esset beneficium, numquam ei qui illum interfecerunt a quo erant conservati . . . tantam essent gloriam consecuti.*) Seneca echoes the point in his *De Clementia: non enim servavit is, qui non interfecit, nec beneficium dedit, sed missionem* (2.20.3). As regards the highwayman, of course, they have a point: refraining from (further) injustice can only be morally neutral, even if this be unexpected in a criminal. Griffin 1976: 185–186.

[4] Luc. 1.205–212, 2.439–446, 507–525; 7.792–795. On Domitius see the catalog, #3.

[5] Montesquieu 1734/1965, chapter 11; Frederick quoted by Meier 1982: 373.

[6] Syme 1958a: 1:414. Syme provided precious little evidence to support his oracular pronouncement, and some of it was flawed (see n. 300).

[7] Dyer 1990: 24. However, Flamerie 2011: 54–62 finds that the Stoics were by no means uncompromisingly hostile to clemency after all. Griffin 2003: 159–163 strikes an interesting but difficult balance

characterizes Caesar's clemency as (for the most part) a form of "symbolic violence," "a hostile offering, creating no good will but merely shifting the field of antagonistic exchange between the transactors."[8] These views are recognizably in the tradition of Montesquieu: "Caesar's Clemency" is seen not simply as devoid of moral credit in the manner of Cicero but actually *offensive*, a further way of humiliating and oppressing the already defeated enemy, and therefore offering at least part of the explanation, if not necessarily a justification, for the assassination to come. Thus in 2005 David Konstan went very much against the grain when he argued in a stimulating paper that on the contrary, "*clementia* was regarded as a wholly positive quality, whether in a general or in a statesman and ruler, both in the late Republic, when the term first seems to have become prominent on the Roman political scene, and under the principate of Augustus and afterwards."[9] "No one ... wants to be dependent on another's clemency. But it is defeat, not clemency, that galls."[10]

Konstan's paper remained largely on the philosophical plane, and perhaps as a result it has thus far failed to win very wide assent, at least among those who have dealt with the matter since.[11] But I think he is essentially correct, and that his central point can be strengthened by adducing a wider range of texts and by more historical contextualization in the Caesarian Civil War of 49–45. This chapter, however, is not primarily about the place of *clementia* in Roman aretology or about aristocratic values as such, but an attempt to gain greater historical clarity about Caesar's famously merciful

---

between the Syme-Dyer derogation of Caesar's *clementia* (182, "the Caesarian exercise of power by one supreme ruler pardoning his subjects"; note also the approving quotation of Plass on the *beneficium* of sparing an enemy, 179n64) and observations that seem to anticipate Konstan 2005, such as that "it was demonstrably the situation, not the word, that men like M. Marcellus and Cato resented" (160) or "*clementia* was the name of a virtue, so genuine clemency could not be discredited, only an insincere or otherwise specious parade of the quality" (164).

[8] Roller 2001: 182–192, quotations at 185, 183. Roller's real focus is on relations of reciprocity in the developed Principate, and his acute observations on that subject do not stand or fall on his interpretation of Caesar's *clementia*. Similarly Dowling 2006: 18: clemency was "unpopular among the elite," "an equivocal virtue, one that demonstrated a man's *virtus* but that could only be practiced on those he dominated"; 22: "to be *forced* [my emphasis] to receive freedom as though they were defeated barbarians," in essence to accept an ongoing status of subordination (17). See too Batstone-Damon 2006: 138–142.

[9] Konstan 2005: 340. German-speaking scholars have been on the whole much more generous than Anglophone ones in interpreting Caesar's "clemency" not as an expression so much of monarchical domination but as an invitation to former enemies to participate in the future *res publica*. See e.g. Jehne 1987: 318; Till 2003: 204–205; B. Woytek 2003: 202 (quoted n. 261).

[10] Konstan 2005: 341. Similarly, Dettenhofer 1992: 228 observes that it was not Caesar's *pardon* that made its beneficiaries subservient but Caesar's actual dominance. Both move any "resentment" to its proper place and thereby eliminate the obvious paradox that lies at the heart of this chapter.

[11] Braund 2009: 32n106 ("too one-dimensional") and 36n116 ("monolithically positive"). Zarecki too is unimpressed (2014: 183n30).

treatment of his erstwhile enemies in the civil wars that raged between 49 and 45 BC, and further to assess its implications for Caesar's conception of the postwar future. Syme's celebrated *sententia* has, for example, encouraged a "monarchic" or autocratic interpretation of the significance of "Caesar's clemency" which seems, excepting Konstan, to have largely prevailed.[12] But there is, I shall argue, good reason to open our minds to an alternative – namely, that the generous treatment of former enemies was a conspicuous attempt to "win the peace" by encouraging reconciliation after a war which, Caesar insisted, should never have been fought.

Caesar's leniency has too often been examined (at least in English) from an almost purely philosophical, ideological, or philological point of view, usually prompted for example by Seneca's famous tract of politico-moral advice, *De clementia*, or perhaps Caesar's brief comment in a letter to his agents Oppius and Balbus on his release of those who had surrendered at Corfinium ([Cic.], *Att.* 9.7C), without taking many pains to examine closely the empirical evidence of its application through the distinct phases of the Civil War. The facts are unclear and not easily grasped, trends over time are overlooked, the limits of Caesar's practice are not accurately perceived, contemporary reception (buried in Cicero's voluminous correspondence) is sometimes missed, and the scale of the phenomenon is not always appreciated. To be fair, the phenomenon itself is rather intractable because no comprehensive, systematic catalog of Caesar's acts of leniency toward citizens during or after the Civil War seems to exist or be readily available, although A. Alföldi, K. Raaflaub, and M. Jehne in particular have made important progress in registering the most important examples.[13] I have tried to collect their results in the catalog of individual acts of pardon which appears at the end of this chapter; this will provide us with a fundamental data set for our examination of the contemporary cultural meaning and historical purpose of Caesar's prominent, public cultivation of the "virtues of mildness." I urge readers to refer to this catalog for details which would have presented too great a distraction in the body of the chapter itself, but which are sometimes of considerable interest in

---

[12] Zarecki 2014: 116: "The problem with *clementia*, at least as it is presented in [Cicero's] *Pro Marcello* and *Pro Ligario*, is that it is incompatible with a republican government." See also Braund 2012: 89–90; also see Milnor 2012: 97n2. Flamerie 2011, an excellent survey of the concept that deserves wider attention among English-speaking scholars, proposes, with more attention than the others to changing historical circumstances between 49 and 44, an evolution from an essentially "republican" reception of *clementia* in the early stages of the Civil War to a more openly "monarchic" one at its end.

[13] See n. 262.

themselves and collectively should provide a preliminary empirical basis for the use of others who wish to reexamine the phenomenon in the future.

A related problem with the long tradition of assessment of Caesar's "clemency" derives specifically from the tendency of many scholars to *begin* with the classic later treatment of *clementia* by Seneca, penned for the teenaged emperor Nero in the second year of his reign (AD 56) – for this is where the classic definition appears – and then to work backward in a fairly straight line to Caesar.[14] This has the obvious effect of coloring the Caesarian (and late-republican) phenomenon with "monarchical" features drawn from the developed Principate.[15] But Nero's age, even the "golden quinquennium," was a changed world from that of the Late Republic. Seneca offers counsel to Nero in an explicitly autocratic context; the Roman state had become an institutionalized monarchy with already a considerable history of dissent, conspiracy, and treason trials which had made the exercise of imperial clemency a basic technique of autocratic rule. *Clementia* had already been advertised as what one might fairly call an "imperial virtue" on the famous *clupeus virtutis* presented to Augustus in his eighth consulship (26 BC, *ILS* 82), and with the development of the Principate it had taken on an increasingly distinctive monarchical color – or, more precisely, the preexisting monarchic strand of its usage which had arisen in response to Hellenistic kingship became more and more dominant as the emperors annexed the virtue. While imperial *clementia*, the lordly mercy the emperor sometimes showed to those who had angered him, operated within the context of a preexisting quasi-monarchic structure with an enduring and morally authorized hierarchy between a superior and his inferiors, Caesar's "clemency" was exercised toward fellow citizens, not subjects, in a republican civil war whose ultimate outcome was at first highly doubtful and still open to doubt even to its last battle in 45 at Munda. Nothing ordained that Caesar would win the war or even survive to its end, nor did its beneficiaries know what place they would hold in whatever postwar structures eventually emerged after the fighting ended. Further, when emperors employed *clementia* (rather than merely talking

---

[14] Sen. *Clem.* 2.3.1: *Clementia est temperantia animi in potestate ulciscendi vel lenitas superioris adversus inferiorem in constituendis poenis.* The emphatically hierarchical language misleads when we move back to the republican context; of course, "being in a position to punish," as is the victor in a battle, is a hierarchical position, though an unstable and often temporary one.

[15] Stacey 2014: 141 notes, "Seneca is extraordinarily prepared to acknowledge the depth of the changes to the structure of Roman politics which the imposition of monarchical government had caused." Stacey's article is an excellent explication of Seneca's project in *De Clementia*; for imperial *clementia* see also Roller 2001. Noreña 2011: 61 interestingly comments that *clementia* does not appear among the five most widely advertised "imperial virtues" on the coinage.

about it) they took virtually no risk that its recipient would simply refuse to reciprocate with subordinate behavior, the only choice available other than suicide. Until Caesar's civil war was definitively won, however, he took a very real risk – repeatedly realized in fact, as we shall see – that the man he spared today would face him again on the battlefield tomorrow. Thus the clemency of an emperor (particularly Nero, who had come to the throne more than eighty years after the Augustan settlement) to one accused of damaging his *maiestas* cannot be considered essentially the same thing as the typical "civic" examples of the virtue shown by a victorious general to a defeated enemy, a judge to a defendant, or indeed one friend and citizen to another. Caesar's "leniency" and Nero's *clementia* were very different, and we should therefore strongly resist the temptation (whether acknowledged or not) to interpret the former in the light of Seneca's advocacy of the latter.[16]

Late-Republican *Clementia* and Related Virtues of "Mildness"

Let us now review, reinforce, and expand somewhat Konstan's point about the virtue of clemency and its close relatives as they were recognized and valued in the republican context.

"Caesar's clemency" has proven to be a convenient shorthand to refer to Caesar's policy of sparing his opponents in the Civil War and in fact minimizing damage to their resources and standing. But when we analyze that policy it is misleading to restrict analysis to the word *clementia* and its place in ethical discourse, since in fact Caesar's practice was described by himself and others by means of various other, closely related words such as *lenitas* ("leniency"), *mansuetudo* ("mildness"), *misericordia* ("pity"), and *humanitas*.[17] In fact, in his *Civil War Commentaries* and letters preserved in

---

[16] A related idea is that Caesar first "establish[ed] *clementia* as a personal benefaction rather than a benefaction of the Roman state" (Braund 2009: 34–35; cf. 2012: 88), a point which seems to go back to Weinstock 1971: 239: "Clemency, in origin the virtue of the Roman State and its generals and exercised toward the defeated enemy, was now the virtue of an individual and exercised towards his fellow citizens." But "personal" and "individual" decisions of life and death were, of course, virtually inevitable in a civil war, and one might respond that what was truly novel here was that Caesar had introduced clemency to the civil war context whereas the "personal" and "individual" decisions of Caesar's predecessors in the civil wars of the 80s had overwhelmingly tended toward merciless punishment. Once again, critics have tended to retroject upon Caesar ideological constructions that lay in Rome's "monarchical" future history. In any case, earlier examples certainly exist of Roman commanders making "personal" decisions exemplifying clemency rather than punitive severity without prior senatorial authorization – e.g. Polyb. 10.17.6–19.7, 10.34–38.6, 40, 15.17.3–19.9, Vell. 1.12.5 (Scipio Africanus), Diod. Sic. 32.7, 30.23.2 (Scipio Aemilianus and L. Aemilius Paullus).

[17] For a concise survey of the cognate terms see Flamerie 2011: 16–22.

Cicero's corpus, Caesar never refers to himself in his own authorial voice as *clemens* or as demonstrating *clementia* specifically, nor does this appear in Sallust's famous character sketch in the *Catilina*.[18] Caesar prefers to characterize his actions as showing *lenitas, misericordia,* or by negation as the very opposite of *crudelitas*.[19] Sallust in his famous extended comparison of Caesar with Cato in the *Catilinarian Conspiracy* (the "*synkrisis*") also echoes the Caesarian preference for *mansuetudo et misericordia*.[20] It is Cicero, on the other hand, who heavily favors the term *clementia* when referring to Caesar's merciful actions in the Civil War beginning immediately with Corfinium and continuing right up to his extravagant praise for the quality in his speech *Pro Marcello* (most likely delivered in October 46). Probably not coincidentally, it was the word favored by Cicero that was adopted for the temple and cult of *Clementia Caesaris* after the victor's return from the civil wars.[21]

It is not easy to explain the divergence in terminology. The old conjecture that Caesar avoids the term *clementia* in his writings in order to suppress its supposed "monarchical" overtones has by now been pretty well discredited.[22] The idea that *clementia* was at this time a specifically or distinctively monarchical virtue is misleading, though one still finds this asserted now and then. True, *clementia* is especially desiderated in a monarch precisely because, as Aristotle pointed out, "the judgment of a single man is bound to be corrupted when he is overpowered by anger," while "it is not easy for everyone at once to get angry and go wrong."[23] Thus anger control and the practice of mildness by monarchs constitute an

---

[18] He uses the word only in the *BGall.*, where he has Gauls appeal to his proven *clementia ac mansuetudo* in the second year of the wars (2.14.5, 31.4).

[19] *Lenitas*: *BCiv.* 1.5.5, 1.74.7, 3.98.2, ap. Cic. *Att.* 9.7C.1: (*quam lenissimum*); *misericordia*: *BCiv* 1.72.3, ap. Cic. *Att.* 9.7C.1 (with *liberalitas*; for *misericordia* cf. *BCiv* 1.84.5, 85.3, also *BGall.* 2.28.3). Opp. *crudelitas*, ap. Cic. *Att.* 9.7C.1, 9.16.2; cf. *BCiv.* 1.32.6, 1.76.5, 1.85.4, 3.28.4, 3.32.3. (*Crudelitas* attributed to the "barbarian" chief Ariovistus, *BGall.* 1.31.12, 32.4, Gauls at 7.38.9, 7.77.3.)

[20] Sall. *Cat.* 54.2; cf. 52.27 (Cato's ironic characterization of Caesar's policy in identical words). Sallust also stresses *beneficiis ac munificentia* (54.2), which interestingly echoes Caesar's own reference to his *liberalitas* at Cic. *Att.* 9.7C.1. That the Sallustian First Epistle to Caesar eschews the Caesarian vocabulary for the Ciceronian *clementia* (1.3.3, 1.6.5; cf. 1.1.4) casts further suspicion upon its authenticity, pace Flamerie 2011: 86–88 (cf. 75).

[21] See p. 473ff.; on the date of the speech see n. 205. Cicero: *Att.* 9.16.1: *clementiam Corfiniensem illam*; cf. 8.9a.2, 8.16.2; *Marc.* 12, 18. This not to say that Cicero entirely avoided the cognate terms when speaking of Caesar's tendency toward "mildness" as far back as 63 and continuing into the civil wars. E.g. *mitis/mitissimus, lenissimus,* along with *clementissimus*: *Cat.* 4.10 (cf. 12 *clemens ac misericors*), *Sest.* 132, *Vat.* 22. *Mansuetudo*: *Att.* 10.8.6, (with *clementia*) *Marc.* 1, 9. *Clementia* with *lenitas, misericordia, Marc.* 12, *Lig.* 15.

[22] Griffin 2003: 159–163; on the "clemency" theme of the *BCiv.* see esp. now Grillo 2012: 78–105. Also Flamerie 2011: 82–86.

[23] Arist. *Pol.* 3.15.8, 1286a. Trans. after Barker.

important theme in the literature of kingship that underwent a notable development in the Hellenistic period with its proliferation of powerful kings, and in this discourse *clementia* was a key quality that could distinguish between a proper "king" and a "tyrant."[24] But the fact that certain virtues are especially recommended to monarchs because of their inherently dominant position does not thereby make them exclusively or necessarily monarchical in their connotations. (Compare e.g. justice, generosity, and so on.)

A variety of Ciceronian texts even as late as 44, when recent Caesarian experience must have colored its use, show that the word *clemens/clementia* was used in republican and civil contexts without the slightest suggestion of monarchic domination or subordination. Cicero describes "our ancestors" (*maiores nostri*) – those who made Rome great – as distinguished by their *clementia*, and Metellus Celer finds Cicero falling below the standard of *maiorum nostrum clementia* in a sharply worded complaint about the orator's harassment of his brother, Metellus Nepos, in January 62.[25] After Nepos, in the year of his consulship (57), had put aside his feud with Cicero and given his support to his recall, Cicero praises him with the (surely) honorable epithet *clementissimus*.[26]At the time of his denunciation of Catiline, Cicero professes that he himself wishes to be *clemens*,[27] and in the Rabirius case in his consulship he exploits the "popular" associations of *clementia* against the tribune Labienus.[28] Plutarch makes ἐπιείκεια – the usual Greek analog of *clementia* – a central characteristic of Cicero himself.[29] Even after "clemency" had become closely associated with the Dictator, Cicero writes in De Officiis that "nothing is more worthy for a great and distinguished man than a forgiving and merciful spirit (*placabilitate atque clementia*)," and recommends exercising *clementia* toward one's fellow citizens unless severity is demanded by the interests of the state.[30] Commentators often interpret this as an (ineptly included) vestige

---

[24] Harris 2001: 237–240; Braund 2009; Flamerie 2011. Since Plato at least, tyrants' cruelty was proverbial: e.g. Cic. *Rep.* 2.48, *Off.* 3.29-32; *Rep.* 1.50 is clearly paradoxical. On the contemporary saliency of the 'tyrant' archetype, see Gildenhard 2006: 200–201.

[25] Cic. *Leg. agr.* 1.19, dealing with the paradox of Capua (cf. *Off.* 1.35 for Corinth). Metellus: [Cic.] *Fam.* 5.1.2. In connection with the same incident Cato was allegedly praised by οἱ πολλοί for his φιλανθρωπία and μετριότης in restraining himself from excessive exploitation of his victory over Nepos (Plut. *Cat. Min.* 29.4). *Clementia* can also be a property of the *populus Romanus* in general: *Verr.* 2.5.74, 115.

[26] *Red. Pop.* 15. Cf. *Fam.* 5.4.2 to Nepos: *tua clementia*.　　[27] *Cat.* 1.4.

[28] *Rab. perd.* 13: *te hominem clementem popularemque* (ironic).

[29] Plut. *Cic.* 19.4–5; Berry 1996: 130.

[30] *Off.* 1.88: *nec vero audiendi, qui graviter inimicis irascendum putabunt idque magnanimi et fortis viri esse censebunt; nihil enim laudabilius, nihil magno et praeclaro viro dignius placabilitate atque*

of the Hellenistic genre of moral advice to kings, yet whatever its source, it is clear that Cicero himself, who is offering recommendations to young Marcus for his conduct in some kind of free republic, not a monarchy, sets this sentiment into a thoroughly civic context.[31] In this very passage Cicero stresses that among "free peoples with equality before the law" one must even adopt a placid, magnanimous response to perceived slights made (evidently) by one's political opponents or enemies.[32] The exception Cicero carves out at the end of this section for the application of *severitas* in defense of the Republic (obviously relevant for the defense of his actions in 63) equally shows with perfect clarity that, whatever its Panaetian origins, Cicero himself understood *clementia* to be a virtue operative in the civil sphere of political interaction between citizens.[33]

According to *De inventione*, Cicero's teenage treatise, which dates to just before the first Roman civil war (ca. 88), clemency was an instance of the larger virtue of *temperantia* and was a quality much appreciated by one's fellow citizens.[34] In Cicero's *De oratore* the great orator M. Antonius is made to observe that "clemency, justice, kindness, good faith, and bravery in the face of threats to the community are pleasing for the audience to hear about in speeches of praise, for all of these virtues are thought to be beneficial not so much for those who possess them as for the entire human race."[35] Clemency was a social and civic virtue opposed to cruelty and tyranny. Reference to the *clementia/crudelitas* dichotomy was readily mapped onto the *liber populus/rex* polarity, with "clemency" on the side of "freedom" and "cruelty" naturally associated on the other hand with kings and tyrants: thus, in such contexts *clementia* was often in real tension with

---

clementia .... Et tamen ita probanda est mansuetudo atque clementia, ut adhibeatur rei publicae causa severitas, sine que administrari civitas non potest.

[31] On the Stoic background of the passage see Dyck 1996: 224–230, touching upon the supposed "monarchical" element at 226–227.

[32] *Off.* 1.88: *in liberis vero populis et in iuris aequabilitate exercenda etiam est facilitas et altitudo animi, quae dicitur ne, si irascamur aut intempestive accedentibus aut impudenter rogantibus, in morositatem inutilem et odiosam incidamus*. Dyck supposes that *in liberis vero populis et in iuris aequabilitate* marks a transition from advice on *clementia* per se to "milder" offenses that call for (merely) *facilitas et altitudo animi* (on which see 1996: 227), yet the very next sentence picks up *clementia* again.

[33] For the *rei publicae causa* exception cf. also *Att.* 14.13B.3 and *Off.* 1.88. Presumably this would cover his objection to Brutus's *clementia* in the aftermath of the Mutina War (see n. 252).

[34] *Inv.* 2.164: *clementia* [*est*] *per quam animi temere in odium alicuius* †*iniectionis concitati comitate retinentur*. Lambinus proposed *inferioris*, probably influenced by the definition at Sen. *Clem.* 2.3.1, an emendation accepted notably in recent times by Griffin 2003: 160. (Braund 2009: 38 is agnostic.) G. Achard in his 1994 Budé edition prints *iniecti* [*concitati*].

[35] *De or.* 2.343. Similarly, the author of *Rhet. Her.* recommends citing instances of *clementia, humanitas,* and *misericordia* to win pity from judges (2.50).

monarchy.[36] *Clementia* is adduced especially frequently as an attribute of judges or provincial governors in their judicial and related administrative capacities: Cicero himself boasted to Atticus and others of his *clementia* in the handling of his responsibilities in Cilicia, along with his *mansuetudo, iustitia, integritas, abstinentia, continentia, facilitas,* and *fides*.[37] In a letter of early 45 that C. Cassius, the future Caesaricide, wrote to Cicero, he too attests to the great goodwill attendant upon *clementia* in sharp contrast to the hatred inspired by *crudelitas* when he praises Caesar's loyal officer C. Vibius Pansa, who was setting out to govern Cisalpine Gaul in January 45 immediately after his return from serving in the same capacity in Bithynia-Pontus.[38] And the other famed Caesaricide, M. Brutus, was not deterred by the Caesarian associations of *clementia* from championing the virtue in a sometimes sharp epistolary exchange with Cicero a year after the "tyrant's" death.[39]

As already noted, however, Caesar himself prefers other terms with a "family resemblance" to *clementia* such as *lenitas, mansuetudo,* and *misericordia*. These terms do not, like *clementia,* tend to suggest a context in which severe retaliation or punishment might be well justified but is thoughtfully rejected by one in a position or with some warrant to mete out such treatment. It may be that Caesar avoided the word *clementia,* with its suggestion of "forgiveness" of a prior wrong, precisely to avoid that hint of prior offense by its recipient.[40] However that may be, his policy cannot be framed narrowly within the concept of *clementia,* and thus a brief review of Cicero's comments is necessarily to give a sense of the late-republican valence of the virtues of mildness. The references range widely across social and political life but are quite consistent in being devoid of any "monarchical" connotation. Consistent with what we have seen regarding *clementia,* in the *Catilinarians,* the *pro Murena,* and the *pro Sulla,* Cicero

---

[36] Esp. *Rab. perd.* 13: *non modo suppliciis inusitatis, sed etiam verborum crudelitate inaudita violare libertatem huius populi, temptare mansuetudinem commutare disciplinam conatus es? namque haec tua, quae te hominem clementem popularemque delectant: "I, lictor, conliga manus," non modo huius libertatis mansuetudinis non sunt, sed ne Romuli quidem aut Numae Pompilii: Tarquinii, superbissimi atque crudelissimi regis, ista sunt cruciatus carmina.* See also *Leg. agr.* 1.19: *non crudelitate – quid enim illis fuit clementius . . . ?*

[37] Cic. *Rosc. Am.* 85, *Clu.* 202; *Planc.* 31. Cicero in Cilicia: *Att.* 5.16.3, 5.18.2, 5.21.5, 6.2.5, 7.2.7; *Fam.* 15.1.3, 15.3.2. Other governors: *Q. fr.* 1.1.25 (Quintus), *Fam.* 2.18.1, 13.55.2 (Q. Thermus).

[38] Cassius ap. Cic. *Fam.* 15.19.2 (cf. 15.17.3): *spero enim homines intellecturos quanto sit omnibus odio crudelitas et quanto amori probitas et clementia,* apparently without irony, despite mockery of P. Sulla in §3.

[39] See n. 252.

[40] See later in this chapter for Caesar's careful avoidance of characterizing political opposition, even in a *civilis dissensio,* as an offense in itself.

repeatedly stresses his own innate *lenitas* and *misericordia* and finds it necessary not to vaunt, but rather to excuse the *severitas* demonstrated by his treatment of the "Catilinarian" conspirators as a temporary and necessary expedient to secure the safety of the Republic.[41] In the *De Oratore* again, "Antonius" regards the type of speech characterized by *lenitas et mansuetudo* as a crucial means for winning over the jurors: in the fundamentally civic sphere of the courts one must make every effort to cultivate the image of a man who has "the qualities possessed by upright, unassuming men, not those of harsh, contentious, litigious, and bitter men; these win goodwill from listeners while their opposites repel them."[42] The ancient king Numa, by his attention to religious institutions and law, had moderated the aggressive and even "savage" hearts of the first Romans *ad humanitatem atque mansuetudinem.*[43] The Roman "masses," he adds in *De Officiis*, are deeply impressed by those virtues that are associated with mildness of character and affability.[44] In the *Pro Murena* of 63 Cicero expresses pretended regret that Cato, the more formidable of the opposing counsel in the case, had not learned more *lenitas* from his philosophy teachers.[45] Cicero exploits this educational gap in Cato's pragmatic ethics – his Stoic moral rigor – as the linchpin of his response, while characterizing the jurors on the other hand as reasonable men who understand the value of *mansuetudo* and *misericordia.*[46] Cicero further looks for "mildness" and its cognates outside the purely domestic sphere in military commanders or provincial governors. These constituted an important part of his self-praise as governor of Cilicia; Cato's own Stoic principles did not prevent him in fact from praising Cicero's *mansuetudo et innocentia* in the province, which had restored the goodwill of the allies.[47] The virtues of *temperantia, mansuetudo,* and *humanitas* are strongly desired even in a military commander, as Cicero stresses in the speech on the Mithridatic command, not least in securing a victory that will last: "Once victory has been won, we should spare those who were neither

---

[41] *Cat.* 2.6, 2.27, 2.28, 4.12 (cf. 3.14 *lenitate senatus*); *Mur.* 6; *Sull.* 1, 8, with Berry's comments ad loc.
[42] *De or.* 2.182–184; cf. 200, also 1.53.
[43] *Rep.* 2.27. Here Cicero invokes an opposition *mansuetudo – feritas* which is also found elsewhere – e.g. *Inv.* 1.2, *Leg.* 1.24 – and seems to echo the *clementia/crudelitas* polarity we have already noted.
[44] *Off.* 2.32. *Rhet. Her.* 2.25 suggests that such attractive qualities demonstrated by men in political power (*in potestatibus*) can go far to excuse their legal culpability on a formal charge.
[45] *Mur.* 64.
[46] *Mur.* 90 (J. Zetzel reasonably translates *mansuetudo* here as "civility"). For the appeal to jurors' *mansuetudo et misericordia* see also *Sull.* 93. On the rhetorical strategy in general see Craig 1986.
[47] Cato [Cic.] *Fam.* 15.5.1–2; cf. 15.3.2. See n. 36. See Morrell 2017: 98–128, esp. 111: the Stoics too believed in "mildness."

cruel or inhuman in the fighting."[48] Cicero here claims this as a long Roman tradition, citing the enfranchisement of the Tusculans, Aequi, Volsci, Sabines, and Hernici; he might also have adduced Scipio Africanus's generous treatment of Carthage after Zama, Flamininus's stance toward the Greeks after Cynoscephalae in 197, and Cato the Elder's defense of the Rhodians in 167.[49]

This collection of Ciceronian passages that adduce the virtues of mildness and generosity makes clear that even after all due allowance is given to the fact that Cicero's philosophical inclinations were exceptional for his class, "clemency" and the related virtues of mildness and generosity were indeed valued highly in the Late Republic, and also that they were regarded not only as consistent with a civic, republican milieu but also as fundamental to the benign operation of such a political system.[50] This should be no surprise since over the previous eighty-odd years Rome had had bitter tastes of the diametrically opposed type of behavior, not least the unleashing of personal enmity on a scale that exceeded all reasonable restraint and threatened to damage the public interest. Self-restraint against the temptations of anger and hatred must have had special salience not just for Cicero but for the political class in general.[51]

The cruelty (*crudelitas*) of the Sullan-Marian civil wars was a powerful reminder of the need for the virtues of "clemency" and mildness in the political arena. A brief review is in order of the atrocities that were in the living memory of virtually every senator or his father in 49 BC and thus will have shaped contemporary expectations of civil war. In 88, when Sulla captured the City by force, twelve of his adversaries were voted public

[48] Cic. *Leg. Man.* 13, 36, 42; *Off.* 1.35: *parta autem victoria conservandi ii qui non crudeles in bello, non immanes fuerunt* . . . . Here the idea seems to be based on Panaetius's theory of justified war, which stressed that war should be fought for the purpose of securing a lasting peace afterward (*ut sine iniuria in pace vivatur*). Cf. Dyck 1996: 137–141. The principle was hardly esoteric.

[49] Polyb. 15.17.4: πρᾴως . . . καὶ μεγαλοψύχως (cf. Liv. 31.31.16: *nimis facile victis ignoscendo*), 18.37.3, 7: δεῖ τοὺς ἀγαθοὺς ἄνδρας . . . νικῶντάς γε μὴν μετρίους καὶ πραεῖς καὶ φιλανθρώπους; Gell. 6.3.47, 52 (Cato too already invokes the *clementia* and *mansuetudo* of "the ancestors"). Sallust's Caesar also cites the Carthaginian and Rhodian examples in his famous speech in the Catilinarian Debate (Sall. *Cat.* 51.5). The destruction of Corinth, on the other hand, remained an embarrassment (Cic. *Off.* 1.35).

[50] Contra Dowling 2006: 17: "Clementia was an expression of a man's *virtus* on the battlefield and in the courtroom but could not be expressed in other fields of civic combat" because "it could not be fittingly or tactfully displayed to fellow citizens."

[51] On "anger management" in antiquity see Harris 2001: esp. 157–228 on its importance in civic relations. Note Cicero's rejection of the Peripatetics' advocacy of *iracundia* and concomitant criticism of *lenitas*: *Tusc.* 4.43–55, 77–79. An interesting Ciceronian passage is *Mil.* 35: *Quid enim odisset Clodium Milo . . . praeter hoc civile odium quo omnis improbos odimus?* Evidently, then, *civile odium*, unlike the common form of *odium* "falsely" attributed to Milo, does not lead to murder.

enemies to be hunted down and killed; most were, and probably more besides. When Marius and Cinna recaptured the City in 87 among widespread slaughter, the consul Octavius and a number of ex-consuls were killed and their heads exposed on the Rostra, while other ex-consuls and senators were driven to suicide. In 82, after Sulla's landing in Italy and his rapid march up the peninsula, he laid siege to Praeneste, and the situation of the remainder of the Marian-Cinnan regime in Rome became desperate. On the orders of the younger Marius, a praetor unleashed a massacre in the very Curia in which a former aedile and ex-praetor were killed in their seats, a senior consular was murdered at the door, and the *pontifex maximus,* Cicero's mentor and civil war model Q. Scaevola, was cut down as he tried to seek refuge at the Temple of Vesta, the hearth of the Roman People; their bodies were dumped in the Tiber. When Sulla captured the City in 82 a new wave of massacres was set off by the proscriptions: ultimately the toll of proscribed Marians and Marian sympathizers must have reached into the thousands, many of whom were hunted and killed while others were deprived of their property and means of subsistence, casting a dark shadow over the two decades to come. Sulla was said to have been directly responsible for the deaths of fifteen consulars and ninety senators;[52] Marius's buried remains were exhumed and scattered in the Anio River. After Sulla's final victory over the Marian-allied Samnites at the Colline Gate he coolly ordered the execution of some eight thousand of the prisoners from that battle while the Senate met next door listening to their cries. (Seneca, perhaps imaginatively, relates that to calm the "terrified" Senate Sulla said, "Let's get on with our business, Fathers. It's just a few rebels being killed on my orders.") It is reported that his epitaph on the Campus Martius proudly declared that "No friend outdid me in doing good, nor any enemy in doing harm."[53] Sulla thought he knew how to extinguish civil wars: with rivers of blood. This was the sort of thing Cicero, Atticus, and no doubt many others,

---

[52] See, however, n. 142.

[53] For the massacres see e.g. Liv. *Ep.* 77, 80, 86, 88 (eight thousand prisoners – or seven thousand: Sen. *Clem.* 1.12.2 – while the Senate met nearby); Cic. *De or.* 3.8–12; App. *BCiv.* 1.71–74, 88, 95–96; Plut. *Mar.* 43–44, *Sull.* 31; Dio fr. 109.4; Q. Cic. *Comment. Pet.* 9; [Sall.] *Ep. Caes.* 1.4.1; *Vir. Ill.* 68; cf. Greenidge and Clay 1960: 164–165, 172–177, 197–201, 207–208. For the slaughter of Q. Scaevola et al. see esp. App. *BCiv.* 1.88/403–404, Liv. *Per.* 86. The toll of consulars and senators: App. *BCiv.* 1.103/482. Efforts to appeal to the principals' clemency and moderation fell on deaf ears or were ignored in the event: Plut. *Mar.* 43.1-2; Dio 41.16.2–3. More generally on Sulla's *crudelitas* see Cic. *Off.* 2.27; on the tradition nevertheless crediting Sulla for some instances of *clementia* see Thein 2014. See Jal 1961. Also relevant is the sudden rise in the phenomenon of suicide (Rauh 2012). These episodes are recounted in standard narratives of the First Civil War – e.g. Seager 1994; Keaveney 2005; Steel 2013: 93–107. For the proscriptions see Hinard 1985.

expected and feared sooner or later once the Civil War was underway: sacking and burning of the capital, massacre, confiscations, and so on.[54]

Caesar's Leniency in the Civil War: The Factual Record

Apart from the various gestures Caesar made as he returned to Italy that seem manifestly intended to signal that his was no invading army (his letter-writing campaign to various senior senators, his pause at Ariminum, his march down the east side of the peninsula rather than heading straight for the capital, his behavior in the towns he had occupied), the first great example of his "leniency" came when three Pompeian legions under the proconsul L. Domitius (Caesar's designated successor in "Gaul") surrendered at the mountain stronghold of Corfinium.[55] Domitius, along with his young son, his quaestor, another consular (P. Lentulus Spinther), an ex-praetor, and at least one other senator as well as one of Pompey's prefects, L. Vibullius Rufus, and "many other young men along with a great number of Roman knights and decurions [town councilors]" fell into Caesar's hands, along with the three legions themselves (Catalog, ##2–9). Caesar let them all go; it seems he even returned to Domitius all or nearly all of his war chest, consisting of some 6 million sesterces of public money.[56] The soldiers were integrated without penalty or reprisals into his own army; they were later transferred to Sicily, which Cato abandoned without a fight, and then to North Africa for the Utica campaign.[57]

As we saw in the previous chapter, the magnanimous treatment of the surrendered Pompeians had an enormous impact on public opinion throughout the peninsula. Within days of the event Cicero writes that the townspeople of Italy now "fear the man they used to trust [Pompey] and love the man they used to dread."[58] Even Atticus was impressed: "if Caesar continues as he has begun, with sincerity, moderation, and

---

[54] See Cic. *Fam.* 16.12.1, *Att.* 7.22.1, 10.8.2, etc.: Chapter 7, p. 380.

[55] Chapter 7, pp. 336ff., 399ff. Behavior: see also Caes. *BCiv.* 1.13.5 (Auximum).

[56] Caes. *BCiv.* 1.23.4; App. *BCiv.* 2.38/149–150, 41/163; denied by Cic., *Att.* 8.14.3 (March 2), perhaps on the basis of an early, inaccurate report, or perhaps speaking only of a portion not returned. The very indignation Cicero evinces when he complains that Domitius has not received all his (public) money back speaks for itself. Scholars generally accept Caesar and Appian: Shackleton Bailey ad loc., Raaflaub 1974: 297n330; Alföldi 1985: 252. This remarkable instance is overlooked by Carter 1991: 1.177–178.

[57] Caes. *BCiv.* 1.23.5, 25.2, 30.2; 2.23.1, 25.1, 28.1, 29.3, 32.1–4, 32.7–10; Plut. *Caes.* 35.1; App. *BCiv.* 2.38/150; Dio 41.11.2–3. Cato leaves Sicily: Chapter 7, n. 350.

[58] *Att.* 8.13.2. See further Chapter 7, 401ff.

prudence, I shall think hard and look attentively to our interests."[59] Cicero immediately wrote Caesar a letter of thanks for his benevolent treatment of the man who as consul had brought him back from exile, Lentulus Spinther, although privately he suspected that it was only a trap (*insidiosa clementia*), a temporary gesture to divide and deceive his enemies, and that cruelty would follow soon enough.[60] However, nothing in this vein actually materialized, despite the anxiety of many when in April Caesar finally made his brief visit to Rome before rushing to confront the Pompeian legions in Spain.[61]

Within a couple of weeks of Domitius's release at Corfinium Cicero heard that he was back on his estate at Cosa, preparing to join the Pompeian forces either in Spain or Greece.[62] He was clearly left very much to his own devices, for right under Caesar's nose as he began his journey to deal with the Pompeian legions in Nearer Spain Domitius (no doubt funded by the public moneys returned to him at Corfinium) raised a small private army of his own slaves, freedmen, and tenant farmers and manned with them seven requisitioned ships with which he sailed to Massilia in southern Gaul to foment a revolt. This was a real setback even though the campaign would end successfully for the Caesarian forces, who were forced thereby to engage for several months in a hard-fought siege to the rear of their major offensive against Pompey's legions in Spain.[63] As for Lentulus, Cicero writes to Atticus that he was indeed grateful for the *beneficium*, yet he soon got over it, rejoined Pompey in Greece, and resumed the fight.[64] Vibullius for his part was immediately ordered by Pompey to join his forces in Spain.[65]

These three are the first examples of what would become a remarkably frequent story – that is, the more or less immediate return of spared and released Pompeians to their original colors to fight Caesar again another day. They appear to have been under no constraint whatever except that of their consciences, which were no doubt eased by the

---

[59] *Att.* 9.10.9 (Atticus): "*si hic qua ratione initium fecit eadem cetera aget, sincere, temperate, prudenter, valde videro et consideratius utilitati nostrae consuluero.*"

[60] *Att.* 8.9a.2, 16.2; 9.11A.3. More fears about a switch to cruelty at 10.4.8: Curio told Cicero in April that "it was not by inclination or nature that he was not cruel but because he reckoned that clemency was the popular line. If he lost favour with the public he would be cruel." Cf. Caelius [Cic.] *Fam.* 8.16.1, also in April.

[61] Chapter 7, p. 402ff.

[62] Cic. *Att.* 9.6.2 (March 11), with Shackleton Bailey's note; cf. 8.14.3 (March 2); App. *BCiv.* 2.38/150: μεθῆκεν ὅποι βούλοιτο ἀπιέναι. Caes. *BCiv.* 1.34ff.

[63] Caes. *BCiv.* 1.34.2–36.1. Massilia's defection lasted nearly five months (Ramsey and Raaflaub 2017: 191–194).

[64] Cic. *Att.* 9.13.7. See #5.   [65] Caes. *BCiv.* 1.34.1, 38.1.

conviction that they were fighting the good fight on behalf of the Republic. As their swift resumption of the fight shows, Caesar's repeated release of his enemies without harm or constraint was not free of serious risk for Caesar. He may have won a "propaganda victory" for the hearts and minds of Italy, but he also took a serious military risk that he would only have to defeat powerful senators and potential leaders like L. Domitius and P. Lentulus Spinther all over again. Had Caesar been Sulla, there might well have been no "revolt" at Massilia, and Domitius certainly would not have been at its head. And by treating so mildly those who had actually chosen to take up arms against him he imposed very little apparent cost on anyone who might yet make that choice.

Not unrelated to Caesar's gestures of "leniency" and "mildness" were his repeated peace proposals. These did not end with his offer at the beginning of January 49 to give up most of his army and provinces or even the failure of his proposal for mutual demobilization while dropping his demand for election in absentia made immediately after his takeover of Ariminum:[66] on the road from Corfinium to Brundisium Caesar captured another of Pompey's *praefecti fabrum*, N. Magius (Catalog, #10), and freed him with a peace message for Pompey: "If they [i.e. the two Prefects Caesar had captured in sequence, Magius and Vibullius] wish to show themselves grateful," Caesar wrote to his fixers Oppius and Balbus around March 5, "they should urge Pompey to prefer my friendship to that of those who have always been his and my bitter enemies, by whose machinations the country has been brought to its present pass."[67] This came to nothing again, but it was not Caesar's last attempt to draw Pompey into discussion of a possible settlement.[68] Caesar continued to try to draw Pompey into negotiations nearly up to their final confrontation. In January 48 Caesar sent Vibullius, who had by now fallen into his hands a second time in Spain, to Pompey with another proposal for negotiations, which again went nowhere, and as late as June Caesar tried again, this time aiming higher in the chain of command at Metellus Scipio, Pompey's father-in-law, operating in Macedonia as a commander with *imperium* in his own right and therefore less easily put off. But the result was no different.[69] Cicero verifies the factual basis of the first initiative (involving Magius as

---

[66] For these two offers see Chapter 6, 306ff., and Chapter 7, p. 341ff.

[67] Caes. [Cic.] *Att.* 9.7C.2: *ut malit mihi esse amicus quam iis qui et illi et mihi semper fuerunt inimicissimi, quorum artificiis effectum est ut res publica in hunc statum perveniret.*

[68] For Magius's abortive diplomacy see Chapter 7, n. 121; see also p. 405ff

[69] Caes. *BCiv.* 3.10, 15.6–18.5, 57. Carter 1993: 153: "This disingenuous proposal [Vibullius] ... indicates clearly Caesar's lack of real desire for peace"; but cf. contra Raaflaub 1974: 280–290.

intermediary), and it would be bold to deny the authenticity of the other two messages simply because they are reported by Caesar himself.

After the Pompeians shipped out from Brundisium and Caesar made his brief return visit to Rome, the focus of the conflict shifted to Spain. At the conclusion of the campaign of the summer of 49 in Nearer Spain all three Pompeian legates surrendered: L. Afranius (cos. 60) and M. Petreius near Ilerda, and the most learned of the Romans, the great antiquarian researcher and author Marcus Varro, at Corduba in Farther Spain (Catalog, #12–14). All three soon made their way to Pompey in Macedonia or Greece. In addition, our friend Vibullius Rufus was captured again by Caesar, but this time, as we just saw, he was brought by him to Epirus and sent back to Pompey with a peace message (#11). Caesar released from service the five legions commanded by Afranius and Petreius either immediately or when they had returned to the boundary with Gaul, apparently on their way home to Italy. He guaranteed that they would come to no harm and that no one would be forced to reenlist with his own forces; as a matter of fact, a sizable contingent would bypass their homes in Italy and make their way to Pompey in Greece under their former general Afranius to form the hard core of the Pompeian army at Pharsalus.[70]

Pompey's devastating defeat at Pharsalus (August 9 ~ ca. June 6, Jul., 48) was not, in fact, as costly in lives as its significance would suggest. Caesar in his own account claimed that fifteen thousand Pompeian soldiers died in the battle, but his officer Asinius Pollio trimmed this somewhat disconcerting number back to six thousand.[71] The relatively limited casualties must be largely thanks to Caesar's order to "spare all citizens" (*ut civibus parceretur*), obviously on condition that they surrender.[72] He claims in his *Civil War Commentaries*

---

[70] Caes. *BCiv.* 1.85.12, 86.3–4, 3.88.3–4; App. *BCiv.* 2.43/174; Dio 41.23.1. Curiously, Westall 2018: 105–106 sees only "paranoia" in Caesar's disbanding of the Afranian legions. Carter 1993: 211 deduces that the "Afranians" who formed the backbone of Pompey's line of battle at Pharsalus made up between seven and twenty-two cohorts, roughly one to two legions. Since the whole force must originally have constituted about fifty cohorts, this was a considerable portion of the former Pompeian army in Near Spain, especially when we note that their home in Italy (ostensibly but perhaps only notionally under Caesar's control) lay directly on the released soldiers' path to Macedonia.

[71] Caes. *BCiv.* 3.99.4; Plut. *Caes.* 46.3, App. *BCiv.* 2.82/346, with Carter 1993: 218–219 and Pelling 2011: 372. Note that Pollio does not dispute the number of dead but classifies nine thousand of them as noncitizens. (Pompey's army contained a large number of non-Roman troops, especially of course in his large force of cavalry [despite M. Cicero Jr.: Cic. *Off.* 2.45; cf. Caes. *BCiv.* 3.11.2–6], which may also help to account for the discrepancy.) Westall 2018: 217–218 suggests that Pollio was puncturing a central element of "the Caesarian myth" but in fact lowering the number of citizen deaths was entirely consistent with Caesar's rhetoric of leniency.

[72] Suet. *Iul.* 75.2: *proclamavit ut civibus parceretur*; Liv. *Per.* 111; Vell. Pat. 2.52.4–6. From at least late March 49, Caesar had declared that he would harm no one who was not bearing arms against him (Cic. *Att.* 9.14.2). By 45–44 *nemo nisi armatus* seems to have become almost a slogan (*Lig.* 19; *Dei.* 34; Sen. *Ben.* 5.16.5).

that some twenty-four thousand Pompeian soldiers surrendered at Pharsalus; they were spared and then enrolled into his own ranks.[73] Elite casualties were perhaps proportionately heavier, although this does not seem to have been caused by Caesar's direct agency. Appian says that ten senators and forty *equites* fell in the battle, but Caesar's old foe L. Domitius, who had already been released once only to cause much trouble and thus could have no hope in surrender, is the only one named by our sources.[74] Dio claims that Caesar now *killed* any senators and *equites* whom he had earlier captured and spared but now fell again into his hands. He gives no names (nor does everyone else), and his assertion directly conflicts with Suetonius's admittedly more general statement that throughout the civil wars he put no one to death outside the battle line; in fact we do have other, later examples of "two-timers" (*bis capti*) who were spared.[75] Thus Dio's claim is somewhat questionable, though it does not seem entirely implausible for all that. (Perhaps he has miscategorized deaths of armed combatants in battle.) Appian's number of ten senators, if true, would constitute a not inconsiderable proportion (5 percent) of the two hundred senators Pompey had allegedly rallied to his standards, many of whom (e.g. Cato, Cicero, Varro) were not even present at the battlefield.[76] We know for certain that no other consular than Domitius was killed at Pharsalus, and since no other name is known it is highly unlikely that any other prominent or high-ranking senator fell there.[77] Several Pompeian consulars died during the campaign in Macedonia and Greece in 48 for reasons apparently unrelated to the fighting, or (like Pompey himself) during their vain attempt to find refuge in Egypt, but these deaths cannot be ascribed directly to Caesar.[78] The combination of

---

[73] Caes. *BCiv.* 3.98 offers a striking description of the surrender, including Caesar's reassurance *de lenitate sua* and his guarantee that they would be unharmed. Enrolled in Caesar's army: Plut. *Caes.* 46.4; Dio 41.62.1.

[74] App. *BCiv.* 2.82/346. Domitius: Plut. *Caes.* 44.4 and App. *BCiv.* 2.76/316 (but see Pelling 2011: 365); Caes. *BCiv.* 3.99.5; Cic. *Phil.* 2.71. Shackleton Bailey 1965: 5:323 conjectured that the minor senator C. Valerius Triarius, who allegedly gave poor military advice to Pompey at Pharsalus (Caes. *BCiv.* 3.92.2), also died there; but this seems unlikely since his will was being discussed early in 45 (Cic. *Att.* 12.28.3).

[75] Dio 41.62.2. Suet. *Iul.* 75.3: *nec ulli perisse nisi in proelio reperientur* (cf. p. 435ff.). "Two-timers": most notably Varro (#21: not present, however, at the battle), and, later, Sex. Varus (#50).

[76] Two hundred senators (obviously a round number): Dio 41.43.2 and Chapter 7, p. 435.

[77] Lucan 7.582–585 ("Lepidi, Metelli, Corvini, and likewise Torquati") is, as usual, not to be taken literally; the names are almost certainly poetic fabrications that confer a patina of nobility.

[78] Among the ten "Pompeian" consulars, Bibulus and Ap. Claudius both succumbed to illness before Pharsalus (Caes. *BCiv.* 3.18.1–2, *MRR* 2.276) while the two Lentuli, Spinther (#5) and Crus, died in Egypt, the second certainly and the first probably by order of King Ptolemy (see n. 272). C. Marcellus (cos. 49) disappears from our evidence after the beginning of 48 (*MRR* 2.276) and may also have died before Pharsalus (Bruhns 1978: 39), but surely not in the battle (Shackleton Bailey 1977: 2:396).

these deaths with those directly connected with the fighting were enough to create a distinct sense of loss among contemporaries, at least on the Pompeian side, but this does not in itself reflect Caesar's practice of leniency toward his enemies.[79]

The corollary of Dio's claim that some senators and *equites* were killed if they had fallen into Caesar's hands now for the *second* time is of course that all of those captured now for the first time were released: one of these, for example, was Marcus Brutus (#33), who had fled to nearby Larissa and offered his surrender by letter from there.[80] Caesar further gave "his friends" permission to intercede for one of the captives: one known example is that of C. Cassius (#32), the future assassin, spared after his surrender through Brutus's intermediation.[81] (But note that Brutus himself had been an "enemy" at Pharsalus.) Caesar's pardons following Pharsalus were not confined to the battlefield, for many Pompeians were not even present at the battle, and those who were there fled in the rout, like Pompey himself, to places near and far from which sooner or later they negotiated their surrender from a distance. Thus the number of senators and other notables spared or pardoned in the aftermath of Pharsalus is quite impressive (thirty-one); they make up about half of all the names we know of the beneficiaries of Caesar's "leniency" over the five years of civil war. They include, most famously, Cicero, with his son, brother, and nephew (##-16–19); Varro again, Pompey's closest advisors Lucceius and Theophanes, and Publius Sestius, proconsul of Cilicia, who maintained his *imperium* and was soon to serve with Caesar's forces in Asia Minor (##21–23, 40); at least four other praetors or ex-praetors, including Cato's loyal sidekick Favonius and Scribonius Libo; Pompey's son Sextus's father-in-law (or soon to be) (##24–28); the future assassins C. Cassius, tribune of the plebs in the previous year, and Marcus Brutus (##32, 33); the sons of the consuls of 61, 57, and 54 (Pupius Piso, Cn. Domitius, Lentulus Spinther, ##36, 38, 39); and a number of other recent magistrates and officers,

---

[79] See Ser. Sulpicius's lament less than three years later ([Cic.] *Fam.* 4.5.4): *uno tempore tot viri clarissimi interierunt.* Cf. also Vell. Pat. 2.52.3.

[80] Caes. *BCiv.* 3.91.3; Liv. *Per.* 111, Vell. Pat. 2.52.6, Plut. *Caes.* 46.2, Dio 41.62.1–63.6 (43.13.3, 44.46.4–7). For the commonsense guideline see Jehne 1987: 319–320, it seems to have been known or understood among Pompeians at the latest after Pharsalus: Dio 42.10.3. Note that Varro and Cn. Domitius, son of Lucius, were given yet another chance, despite their having been released by Caesar once before (#21, 38).

[81] Suet. *Iul.* 75.2: *deincepsque* [sc. after Pharsalus] *nemini non suorum quem vellet unum partis adversae servare concessit* might seem to suggest that the practice was followed only *after* Pharsalus, but Dio 41.62.2 specifically mentions this first *at* Pharsalus and subsequently following the rout at Thapsus (43.13.3: n. 91).

running the gamut from tribunes through aediles and quaestors to one prefect (##29-31, 34-36, 42) as well as some less well-known senators and *equites* (#37, 43, 44). Ser. Sulpicius Rufus (#20), who after appearing to condone Caesar's actions at first had fled from Italy (surely in 49) for self-imposed exile on the island of Samos, was nevertheless brought around to Caesar's camp and given charge of the province of Achaea by 46, which might also be considered an act of "leniency" under the circumstances.[82] Furthermore, it was considered no small thing that when at Pharsalus Pompey's correspondence came into Caesar's hands, rather than using the letters to learn who were among his true enemies among those whom he had pardoned and others who had not yet formally thrown in their lot, he burned them without taking a look.[83]

After the victory the Senate granted to Caesar the right to deal as he alone saw fit with those who had been on the Pompeian side.[84] Since this came well after the victory itself, it obviously pertained not so much to battlefield pardons but to the final terms under which ex-Pompeians might (or might not) be reintegrated into the body politic, especially the restoration of their fortunes and their return to Italy, from which they had been banned during the conflict. Some in fact appear to have simply headed home to Italy without an official pardon: Caesar heard (incorrectly) that Cato himself as well as L. Metellus, the tribune who had caused him so much trouble in April 49, had returned to Italy after the battle and intended to live openly in Rome, and so he wrote to his deputy in Italy, Antony, that he did not approve of this lest it invite some disturbances (consider Domitius at Massilia). Antony should therefore block from Italy all those refugees whose cases he had not personally considered.[85] Caesar's letter and instructions to Antony are remarkable in that they seem to betray no surprise whatever that two of his bitterest enemies had taken the risk of returning to Italy uninvited; indeed, they even suggest (although without the document itself it is impossible to be sure) that Caesar expected nothing more coercive or punitive to be done in their cases than to prevent

---

[82] Chapter 7, p. 376ff.

[83] Sen. *Ira* 2.23.4; Plin. *HN* 7.94; Dio 41.63.5–6, cf. 43.17.4, 44.47.5–6: "This is a most astonishing fact and one without a parallel, that they were spared before they were accused and saved before they encountered danger, and that not even he who saved their lives learned who it was he pitied."

[84] Dio 42.20.1. This right may have been enshrined in a *lex Hirtia* in 48 (Cic. *Phil.* 13.32). Jehne 1987: 321–322; 1987a: 229–231, 433–434; B. Woytek 2003: 201–202 with n. 197, 209–211; Ferrary 2010: 14–16.

[85] Cic. *Att.* 11.7.2; cf. 11.9.1. The order caused Cicero great difficulty (see next n.) even though he pointed out that his Caesarian son-in-law, Dolabella, had written on Caesar's behalf to invite him to return "as soon as possible."

them from returning to the capital (as Antony was now doing to Cicero, miserably confined to Brundisium until Caesar's return to Italy in September 47) until he could meet and judge them individually.[86] (In the event, of course, Cato had instead crossed to North Africa and joined with the Pompeian remnants to carry on the war.)[87] However, Caesar's instructions also make clear that pardons were not to be automatic according to a fixed criterion but were a matter for judgment, and for his judgment alone, in person.[88]

Pharsalus and Pompey's subsequent death in his flight to Egypt might have been the end of the Civil War, and surely this was Caesar's hope and expectation. But some of his surviving enemies – most notably Metellus Scipio, Afranius, Petreius, Labienus, and of course Cato – had other ideas and carried the war to Africa, linking up with the Numidian king Juba, who had played the key role in destroying Curio's army in 49, massacred its remnants, and therefore faced a reckoning with the victorious Caesar.[89] Still, even after his further victory at Thapsus (April 6 - ca. February 6, Jul., 46) over the "diehards" who had not yielded after Pharsalus, Caesar did not abandon his policy of "leniency."[90] Dio, despite a series of critical comments about executions to be examined shortly, comments that he "spared many of those who had fought against him, partly on account of their own pleas and partly due to those of their friends," for as at Pharsalus he permitted third-party intercessions, which saved Marcus Agrippa's brother (#58) and probably Sex. Quinctilius Varus (#50), despite the latter's having fallen into his hands a second time.[91] We can list the names of only about half as many beneficiaries of Caesar's leniency after Thapsus (##45–59) as

---

[86] Cic. *Att.* 11.5–22, with Shackleton Bailey 1965: 5:298 and now Zarecki 2014: 108–112.

[87] Perhaps Caesar had heard some garbled version of the story in Plut. *Cat. Min.* 55.4 that Cato, who had passed the time of the battle with Cicero and other prominent Pompeians at Dyrrachium, first intended to carry those with him across to Italy before betaking himself to some place of self-imposed exile; he may well have had doubts as to his own reception. In the event he sent on Cicero and presumably some others from Corcyra while himself crossing to Africa at Cyrene.

[88] Of course it was not always easy to catch up with Caesar during the sequence of campaigns, and we hear later that Balbus and Oppius were normally empowered to make such decisions in his absence (Cic. *Fam.* 6,8.1, December 46).

[89] On the massacre see n. 153. For simplicity's sake I continue to refer to Caesar's opponents as "Pompeians," since "Republicans" is too tendentious a term to be granted by self-proclamation. The men mentioned in the text had committed themselves heavily to Caesar's destruction from the start; the fact that they were determined to continue to pursue that goal after Pompey's death does not make them "republicans." For a clear-eyed critical perspective see Cic. *Fam.* 9.6.3. Welch 2012: 73–75 relies too much on Lucan and Florus's late rewriting of the story.

[90] Vell. Pat. 2.55.2: *nec dissimilis ibi* [sc. in Africa] *adversus victos quam in priores clementia Caesaris fuit.*

[91] Dio 43.13.3: καὶ τῶν ἀντιπολεμησάντων οἱ πολλοὺς μὲν δι' αὐτοὺς ἐκείνους πολλοὺς δὲ καὶ διὰ τοὺς φίλους σώσας· τῶν τε γὰρ συναγωνιστῶν καὶ τῶν ἑταίρων ἑκάστῳ ἕνα ἐξαιτεῖσθαι, ὥσπερ εἴρηται, ἐπέτρεπε.

there were following Pharsalus (15 vs. 31), but the list is still substantial.[92] The known names include two ex-praetors (##46, 47), two ex-quaestors including Sex. Quinctilius Varus (##49, 50), a series of lower-ranking senators and *equites* (#51, 53–57),[93] and close family members of his enemies (namely, Cato's son [#52] and Pompey's daughter, wife of Faustus Sulla, together with her children [#59]), all of whom were left their property. Dio at least is convinced that he would have pardoned Cato had he had the chance (Plutarch was less sure).[94] And again he burned the opposing commander's correspondence as he had done after Pharsalus.[95]

Yet Thapsus and its aftermath were certainly a bloodier affair than Pharsalus had been. This is partly due to the evolved nature of the conflict. The Pompeian diehards who fought on had, from the Caesarian perspective, "pertinaciously" rejected the verdict of Pharsalus and insisted on the continuation of civil bloodletting; their own claim to public authority was tenuous and they relied on alliance with the foreign, even "barbarian" Numidian king Juba to fight against the army of the Roman People and their legitimate consul. For these reasons the legitimacy of those who continued the struggle was open to reasonable doubt, and Caesar himself was correspondingly "angrier" and evidently in a less forgiving frame of mind.[96] (These larger issues will be examined in detail following our survey.) Furthermore, some of their leaders had taken advantage of his leniency already once before, while others were driven by bitter personal hostility toward Caesar or political principle to reject any prospect of capitulation and reconciliation. Furthermore, Caesar lost control of his army at the climax of the victory itself, precipitating a massacre, and the flight of the defeated leaders to Spain was intercepted by the forces of a semi-independent freelancer, P. Sittius, leading to various deaths which cannot however be attributed with any certainty to Caesar himself.[97]

---

[92] Contra Nic. Dam., *Bios* 16: In the Thapsus campaign Caesar had pardoned very few "because in the previous wars they had not learned to behave." I omit here L. Caesar, killed somewhat mysteriously after a trial following his surrender (n. 101).

[93] Although the *eques* Trebianus was pardoned only in 45, since he had fought in Africa he might be included in this list (#62).

[94] Dio 43.13.4; Plut. *Caes.* 54.3 with Pelling 2011: 405; *Cat. Min.* 72.3. It is hard to imagine that Caesar could have refused leniency if Cato had requested it, but Caesar probably could be sure that Cato could never have brought himself to acknowledge his victory in this way.

[95] Dio 43.13.3–4; Plin. *HN* 7.94.

[96] Schol. Gron. 291 St.: *oderat eos vel maxime qui in Africa fuerant, quia iam non pro Pompeio pugnabat, sed pertinacia.* Cf. Cic. *Fam.* 6.13.3 (to Q. Ligarius, one of those whose pardon was delayed by the African rebellion: #55): *Africanae causae iratior diutius velle videtur eos habere sollicitos a quibus se putat diuturnioribus esse molestiis conflictatum.*

[97] On P. Sittius, a colorful and shady character who led a private mercenary army in North Africa outside of Caesar's command, see Berry 1996: 246–247 and Ramsey in Raaflaub (ed.) 2017: 660–661.

The suicides of the Pompeian leaders, Metellus Scipio (intercepted at Hippo Regius by Sittius's fleet), Petreius (in a death pact at a banquet with Juba), and Cato (at Utica) are well known.[98] Petreius had surrendered and been released once before, in Spain (#13), thus had no realistic expectation of pardon, while Scipio and Cato were evidently strongly motivated to choose death over surrender.[99] Aside from the suicides, a trio of executions followed the defeat at Thapsus, for which Caesar's responsibility or culpability was and is controversial; Suetonius remembered (probably not with total accuracy) three men – L. Caesar, Faustus Sulla, and L. Afranius – as the *only* notables in the entire Civil War killed neither in the line of battle nor by their own hand.[100] Caesar almost certainly bore direct responsibility for the execution of his own cousin Lucius Caesar, the messenger of January 49 and now Cato's (pro)quaestor. The details of his trial and execution are obscure: he was apparently first pardoned in the rout after the battle, but then tried and put to death (supposedly in secret), with various atrocious crimes imputed to him.[101] Even Cicero has some harsh words to say about L. Caesar, and it appears that few lamented his death, the single most blatant violation of Caesar's established practice.[102] Faustus Sulla (son of the dictator), and the consular L. Afranius (who had fought at Pharsalus despite being released at Ilerda [#12], after which he had made his way with a substantial remnant of his army all the way to Pompey in Greece), are somewhat less clear counterexamples to Caesar's general policy. They were both killed after being caught by Caesar's semi-independent ally, P. Sittius, en route to Spain

---

[98] Rauh 2012: 62–64, nos. 47–49, and on Cato, pp. 243–295 and 2018: these men were not therefore "killed" by Caesar, as stated by Schol. Gronov. 291 Stangl. (At *Bell. Afr.* 94.1 the manuscripts are unanimous that Juba killed Petreius rather than the other way around, but App. *BCiv.* 2.101/420 suggests that correction is called for; thus Raaflaub [ed.] 2017: 601.) A possible further suicide was Cicero's friend the Epicurean L. Manlius Torquatus (pr. 50 or 49: *MRR* 3.136; see Berry 1996: 18–20), who was sailing to Spain with Metellus Scipio (*Bell. Afr.* 96.1–2; cf. *MRR* 2.297–98; n. 162 and p. 455). Oros. 6.16.5 says Torquatus was killed, and Berry (p. 20) believes him; but Orosius also claims in the very next sentence that Caesar put to death Pompey's daughter and grandchildren (see #59): he is not noted for his restraint. Two other senators, P. Licinius Crassus Damasippus (cf. Caes. *BCiv.* 2.44.3) and one Plaetorius Rustianus, are known to have died at the same time and place as Metellus Scipio and L. Torquatus, but it is uncertain in precisely what manner.

[99] On Cato see p. 467ff.

[100] Suet. *Iul.* 75.3. Note, however, that in addition P. Ligarius had been executed *ob periuri perfidiam* after being captured a second time following his release after Ilerda (#15).

[101] See #45; also Suet. *Iul.* 75.3, Dio 43.12.3 (according to whom Caesar first ordered Lucius to stand trial but then had him put to death secretly in order to deflect responsibility), Cic. *Fam.* 9.7.1. Jehne 1987: 328: perhaps like Q. Ligarius, L. Caesar faced these additional charges only after he had first been spared. Suetonius claims that "some think" (*putant*) that none of the three men, including L. Caesar, were executed on Caesar's orders.

[102] Cic. *Att.* 7.13a.2 for Cicero's view of young Lucius "as an irresponsible good-for-nothing" (so Shackleton Bailey 1965: 4:445). For his less-than-solemn response to news of his death, *Fam.* 9.7.1.

to continue the fight.[103] We do not know whether Sittius was acting independently in this instance or on Caesar's orders, but Afranius at least was *bis captus* (as Suetonius thinks Faustus was as well) and thus had "used up" any expectation of leniency. In view of the apparently more careful accounting of Suetonius and Dio, we should probably not look beyond these three executions and the suicides mentioned earlier to explain Plutarch's vague generalization that although "a good many men of consular and praetorian rank survived the battle," "some" (οἱ μὲν) killed themselves while Caesar himself put "many" (συχνοὺς) senators and *equites* to death afterward.[104] While the killing of the three men, whatever the degree of Caesar's responsibility or deviance from his own general practice, will probably strike us as cruel, we should note that Suetonius does not consider this a significant mar on his record of *moderatio* and *clementia admirabilis* (*Iul.* 75.3). Suetonius is no doubt influenced by a (rather dismal) standard of imperial "clemency" established over the previous century and more, but even without retrospection his estimation would be justified in comparison to the recent bloody record of Sulla and Marius.

The greatest mar on Caesar's record of leniency toward his defeated citizen enemies was not so much due to his treatment of his elite peers but to the carnage his victorious army unleashed on the battlefield of Thapsus. When the tide of the battle turned Caesar's enraged men refused to recognize the attempted surrender of what remained of Scipio's army and slaughtered the broken remnants to a man, ignoring Caesar's attempts to regain control.[105] The anonymous author of the *Bellum Africum* describes a near-total breakdown of military discipline at this moment of

---

[103] *Bell. Afr.* 95.1–3 (see Raaflaub [ed.] 2017: 601, 13.95a); Suet. *Iul.* 75.3; Liv. *Per.* 114; Dio 43.12.2; further, late sources are listed by Alföldi 1985: 261n568 and Jehne 1987: 323n62. It is possible that, as Suetonius explicitly says, Faustus had been captured and released once already (p. 487).

[104] Plut. *Caes.* 53.7, with Pelling 2011: 404. Note Dio's curious claim, elaborating on his statement that L. Caesar was put to death "secretly," that Caesar had a practice of "disappearing" people who injured him (43.13.1–2). But L. Caesar seems to be the only named instance and otherwise there is not a breath of this kind of suspicion in our evidence; even the murder of M. Marcellus, for which at first suspicion of course fell on Caesar, was revealed to have nothing to do with him (n. 321). This kind of conspiratorial claim is of course bound to be murky. It does not say much for Dio's authority here that he seems to offer as another example of Caesar's allegedly insidious practice the deaths by a "friendly" hand in the battle itself, which *Bell. Afr.* convincingly describes as a spontaneous battlefield mutiny.

[105] *Bell. Afr.* 85.5–9: *armis demissis* (a less unambiguous gesture than *arma proicere*, Caes. *BCiv.* 3.98.1 [Pharsalus]). The anonymous author stresses that Caesar sought to restrain his men (85.9: *inspectante ipso Caesare et a militibus deprecante eis uti parcerent*; cf. §6: *non modo ut parcerent hosti non poterant adduci*) and adduces their rage (§6: *ira et dolore incensi*) and sense of impunity (§8: *immoderate peccandi impunitatis spe propter maximas res gestas*). Dio's excessively brief summary without circumstantial detail misleadingly suggests that the soldiers were operating under Caesar's orders: "Caesar gave no quarter to those who switched sides" (43.9.1). Várhely 2012: 117–118 appears

frenzied violence, claiming that Caesar's soldiers took advantage of a sense of impunity due to the magnitude of their victory not only to massacre the enemy but even to attack "urban notables" *on their own side* (*ex suo exercitu inlustris urbanos*), killing one ex-quaestor named Tullius Rufus and nearly taking the life of Q. Pompeius Rufus, who had to flee to Caesar's side to save himself.[106] Numerous senators and *equites* – on the face of it, not only those on the opposing side, who were after all trapped, but Caesarian ones as well – are said to have fled the battle at this point in a panic, so that no officers were present to restrain the soldiers as they proceeded to cut down their hapless adversaries while Caesar could only look on.[107] The result was no doubt a high body count on the opposing side, but our two sources (the anonymous author of the *Bellum Africum* and Plutarch) vary hugely between the high but plausible figure of ten thousand and a frankly unbelievable fifty thousand.[108]

The account cannot therefore simply be dismissed as an attempt to absolve Caesar of all blame – and in fact it does not. For that purpose the further step had to be taken of alleging (as Plutarch tells us some said) that he had been overcome by his epilepsy as he drew up his battle line and had entirely missed the actual fighting while removed in a state of incapacitation to a nearby tower.[109] The legions who committed this atrocity had been sorely tested by lack of pay and likely blamed Caesar's mildness toward his enemies for protracting the war and continuing their miseries; they had probably participated to a greater or lesser degree in the great mutiny of nearly all of his veteran legions in Campania in 47 before they

---

to prefer Dio: "[chose] to slaughter some ten thousand enemy soldiers." (For the number see n. 108.) Contra, Raaflaub (ed.) 2017: 596, 13.85i.

[106] *Bell. Afr.* 85.6–7; cf. Dio 43.13.1, apparently attributing the killing of some of his own men to Caesar himself. Tullius Rufus is otherwise unknown; Pompeius Rufus is probably the tr. pl. 52, restored from exile by Caesar. Bruhns 1978: 58, n. 29; 50–51 n. 22. *Illustres urbani* is an odd phrase, but must here mean "important men of the city" – i.e. not soldiers but members of the political and social elite, apparently identifiable with the *equites* and senators who fled from the battle. It is unclear what the author means by *quos* [sc. the *illustres urbani*] *auctores appellabant*. Bruhns suggests that the soldiers held these men responsible for *the war*, yet if that is the meaning it is very elliptically expressed in the absence of some such clarifying word as *auctores belli*. Perhaps the soldiers claimed that these men, presumably their officers, had authorized the massacre and then turned on them to validate their defense.

[107] *Bell. Afr.* 85.8: *complures equites Romani senatoresque perterriti ex proelio se receperunt.*

[108] *Bell. Afr.* 86.1, Plut. *Caes.* 53.4, with Pelling 2011: 403. The number in the *Bell. Afr.* is roughly comparable with the number reported at Pharsalus, where there had been no wholesale massacre. Perhaps Plutarch's number is meant to include Juba's losses while the Roman account focuses on the legions, as apparently had Pollio when he corrected Caesar's figures for Pharsalus.

[109] Plut. *Caes.* 53.5–6 (cf. Suet. *Iul.* 45.1: *bis inter res agendas correptus est*). Gelzer 1968: 268n3; Pelling 2011: 403, 449 seems to regard the excuse as genuine, yet it seems manifestly false, as again in connection with a later faux pas (Plut. *Caes.* 60.6–7; Chapter 9, n. 104).

had shipped out for Africa.[110] The state of their morale and discipline can
also be judged from Caesar's loss of control over the army at the battle's start:
his legates and veterans demanded an immediate attack, and though he
refused, a bugler nevertheless sounded the charge from the right wing and
the rest of the army followed despite the desperate attempts of their centurions to restrain them.[111] Caesar in his Gallic War *Commentarii* had presented
himself as a stickler for discipline in this kind of situation, and emphasized
the tongue-lashing he gave his troops at Gergovia when they had risked
everything by disobeying his orders not to engage: he needed restraint and
self-control from his soldiers as much as courage and valor.[112] The battlefield
massacre at Thapsus was a blow to Caesar's self-representation and self-
image even if he was not directly culpable. Yet this terrible incident also
stands as an outlier and can hardly be taken as representative of his regular
practice toward the citizens defeated in the civil wars.

Another controversial point was Caesar's treatment of three hundred
equites at Utica who had been induced to contribute money to Scipio's
cause, and had in fact functioned as a "counter-Senate." Appian curtly
asserts that after taking possession of the town Caesar killed (διέφθειρεν) all
of them, or at least all he caught.[113] Yet the *Bellum Africum* contains
a detailed description of how the "three hundred" were granted their
lives and allowed to "buy back" their confiscated possessions, while even
Dio notes that Caesar spared "most" of those whom he found at Utica,
who had surrendered.[114] It is more likely that the highly circumstantial
version of the *Bellum Africum*, supported by Dio and devoid of any obvious
hallmarks of propagandistic denial or *apologia*, is correct than that such
a heinous atrocity was mentioned by only a single source.[115]

Despite the fact that trouble was soon brewing in Spain after the sons of
Pompey and other committed holdouts from the remnants of Scipio's

---

[110] Chrissanthos 2001: 70–71 with n. 140. The 5th, 9th, 10th, 13th, and 14th Legions formed Caesar's
battle line at Thapsus; all were "likely" involved in the Campania mutiny (p. 71).
[111] *Bell. Afr.* 82.
[112] Caes. *BGall.* 7.52.3: *nec minus se ab milite modestiam et continentiam quam virtutem atque animi
magnitudinem desiderare.*
[113] App. *BCiv.* 2.100/416; cf. 95/397 σύγκλητον ἐκάλουν – which suggests a rather offensive travesty by
the anti-Caesarians – and Plut. *Cat. Min.* 59.2.
[114] *Bell. Afr.* 90. Dio 43.12.1, probably including the "three hundred" (cf. 10.2). For the activities of the
"three hundred" see also *Bell. Afr.* 88.1–2 and esp. Plut. *Cat. Min.* 59–71, both of which emphasize
the eagerness of these men after Thapsus to surrender themselves to Caesar.
[115] Alföldi 1985: 258–259 seems justified. Perhaps Caesar later put some of the "three hundred" he
captured out of the way quietly in the insidious fashion Dio alleges to have been his practice (43.13.2;
cf. 42.55.2 regarding the mutineers of 46); however, Dio's allegation is itself isolated, uncorroborated, and conveniently unfalsifiable.

former army had swiftly managed to escape and regroup there, the policy of leniency did not end with Thapsus, the second apparently decisive victory in the civil wars.[116] It does, however, now change its character somewhat as the numerous acts of surrender and pardon following the major battles of Pharsalus and Thapsus largely give way to more leisurely negotiations and accommodations for individuals remaining in de facto exile years after the last campaign in which they appear to have participated, if indeed they had participated at all. This last stage was splashily initiated in October 46, immediately after the quadruple triumphs and lavish spectacles that symbolically (and overoptimistically) celebrated the end of the wars, by the spectacular pardon of Caesar's old enemy M. Marcellus (cos. 51, #60), who in his consulship and the tense year that followed had pushed hard for his replacement in Gaul.[117] Marcellus had not played any conspicuous role in the Civil War, but after Pharsalus he had withdrawn to Mytilene and proudly declined to apply to Caesar to be allowed to return home, although his cousin and other relatives, along with Cicero, pressed the case in Rome. He remained therefore the last "holdout" among the Pompeian consulars after Thapsus, and thus his acceptance of pardon after the great Quadruple Triumph signaled the conclusion of the civil wars could be viewed as a great moment of national reconciliation, as well as a huge personal relief to Cicero, the only Pompeian consular who had up to that point come to terms with Caesar and returned to Italy.[118]

To mark the occasion Cicero broke his silence in the Senate to deliver a speech of thanks to Caesar, which he wrote up afterward as the *Pro Marcello*. In this speech Cicero publicly articulated an ideology of "Caesar's Clemency" and presented himself as its chief senatorial champion and advocate, following up over the course of the next year with a series of letters to the more prominent ex-Pompeians still languishing in exile in which he encouraged them to have good hope of Caesar's leniency and to look forward to returning to Italy and Rome in the near future.[119] Due

---

[116] Dio 43.28–31.1, *Bell. Afr.* 22–23, *Bell. Hisp.* 1, with Welch 2012: 99–105 (but on p. 104, read "April or May *46*").

[117] Cic. *Fam.* 4.4.3–4. On the date of the pardon see n. 205.

[118] Other than at p. 471f. and 475 the Quadruple Triumph itself will not be treated in detail elsewhere in this work. See the list of sources in *I.It.* 13.1, p. 567 and Butler and Cary 1927: 96–96; the analytic catalog of Itgenshorst 2005: 366–374; a summary in Gelzer 1968: 284–287; current scholarship and criticism in Pelling 2011: 410–414 and Davies 2017: 261–263 as well as evidence and perceptive observations scattered through important recent synthetic works on the triumph by Beard 2007 and Östenberg 2009 (see their indices, s.v. Julius Caesar). See also Havener 2014: 170-172 and Östenberg 2014: 186-192.

[119] On the speech and its vision of *clementia* see p. 465ff. The eagerness with which he takes up the cause of coaxing ex-Pompeians back to Rome is an important reason to be skeptical of the

precisely to this epistolary advocacy, representing a large proportion of Cicero's *Letters to His Friends* preserved from the years 46 and 45, we know something about a number of other notable figures who were either pardoned during the last stage of the Civil War or were awaiting Caesar's final decision on their case at its end: the ex-praetors A. Torquatus (#63), P. Nigidius Figulus (#67), T. Ampius Balbus (#61), the "trumpet of the civil war" who had attributed various "tyrannical" sayings to Caesar in a written invective, and C. Toranius (#68); also Cicero's former client, the ex-aedile Cn. Plancius (#69), and the *equites* Trebianus (#62) and A. Caecina (#57).[120] Thus from late 46 into 45 Cicero appears to have engaged in a systematic effort to restore as many ex-Pompeian senators of all ranks as possible to their proper place in the Curia.[121] Had Caesar explicitly prompted him to do so he would almost certainly have mentioned this in the many letters in which he encouraged the hope of former Pompeians for their imminent reinstatement. While Caesar presumably smiled on the effort to bring more of his former enemies back into the fold in Rome, Cicero had sufficient motive on his own to pursue this campaign: the reintegration of former Pompeians reduced his isolation and doubtless strengthened his hopes for a revived Senate, which would have to be at the heart of any *res publica* of which Cicero would approve.[122]

Meanwhile the final campaign of the Civil War in Spain culminating at Munda (March 17 [Jul.], 45) marks a sharp change in the application of the policy of leniency after each of the earlier victories. Pompey's sons Gnaeus and Sextus, supported by mostly native recruits, fought the final campaign of the Civil War overtly in the name of *pietas* ("loyalty") to the memory of their father. This inevitably had the appearance of a vendetta, and even former Pompeians such as C. Cassius trusted Caesar more than they did the younger Gnaeus Pompey.[123] Most of the soldiers on the opposing side,

---

widespread view that Cicero's speech was merely "ironical," even in some sense a fiercely oppositional attack on Caesar's "autocracy" (e.g. Zarecki 2014: 115–120). Recipients of these letters include Cic. *Fam.* 4.7–11 (M. Marcellus), 4.13 (Nigidius Figulus), 4.14–15 (Cn. Plancius), 5.21 (Mescinius Rufus), 6.1–4 (A. Torquatus), 6.5–8 (A. Caecina), 6.10–11 (Trebianus), 6.12 (Ampius Balbus), 6.13–14 (Q. Ligarius), 6.20–21 (Toranius), and 6.22 (Cn. Domitius).

[120] Figulus may have died in exile while awaiting the decision (#67).

[121] Of the thirty-two ex-praetors who served at one time or another on the Pompeian side (Bruhns 1978: 43–44), at least sixteen are known or very likely to have received pardon before the end of the civil wars; *no* Pompeian of praetorian rank is known to have survived the Thapsus campaign and yet been left out of this effort except for those who followed Pompey's sons to their deaths in Spain (Labienus, Attius Varus).

[122] See n. 248.

[123] Cassius ap. Cic. *Fam.* 15.19.4: *malo veterem et clementem dominum habere quam novum et crudelem experiri*. On *pietas* see the appearance of the elder Pompey's portrait on the sons' coins (*RRC* 470, 477, 479, the latter two with the explicit legend) with Welch 2012: 103.

apart from three legions drawn from Pompey's Spanish forces of 49 which now deserted to his son and one recruited from Roman residents in the province (out of a total of thirteen legions), were not actually Romans.[124] This gave the rebellion something of the character of a native revolt, an impression encouraged by images on the coins minted by the Pompey brothers during the campaign that evoked their partnership with Hispania and the Spanish cities.[125] Our sources indicate that the fighting was particularly savage: Munda itself was a close-run thing, and Caesar is remembered to have remarked after the battle that for the first time his very survival had been at stake.[126] The leaders of the Pompeian/Spanish forces fought desperately and with the notable exception of Pompey's younger son, Sextus, all – P. Attius Varus, T. Labienus, and the elder son Gnaeus – were killed on the battlefield or in the immediate aftermath. Some thirty thousand Pompeian/Spanish dead were supposedly left on the field, and while ancient casualty estimates, especially for the opposing side, are regularly inflated, Raaflaub seems correct to infer that "the rout was complete, most enemies were killed as they fled, and Caesar's soldiers showed no mercy."[127] Remnants were slaughtered at Corduba (twenty-two thousand!) and elsewhere; Caesar's reprisals were harsh by any standard against Spanish communities who had sided with the Pompeii brothers, and even against prisoners.[128] For the first time, it seems, Roman citizens could not expect pardon upon surrender as a matter of course, and only a few individual beneficiaries are known from the Munda campaign (#64–66), all of them minor figures.[129] M. Jehne remarks that "in Spain Caesar treated his adversaries as *hostes* in fact; that did not exclude leniency, but this was now consistent with the generous handling of foreign enemies and no longer represented special treatment given to citizens who

---

[124] *Bell. Hisp.* 7.4–5 with Raaflaub [ed.] 2017: 613n14.7d and Brunt 1971: 474. See also 34.2, Dio 43.36.1.

[125] *RRC* 469 (rev.), 470 (rev.), with p. 739.

[126] Plut. *Caes.* 56.4, App. *BCiv.* 2.104/433, on which see Pelling 2011: 418. Not strictly true since he had come close to being run through by his own standard-bearer in the rout at Dyrrachium (Plut. *Caes.* 39.7; App. *BCiv.* 2.62/258).

[127] *Bell. Hisp.* 31.9; Plut. *Caes.* 56.3, with Raaflaub (ed.) 2017: 630n14.31j. (The careless language of *Bell. Hisp.* 31.9 (*circiter xxx et siquid amplius*) does not inspire confidence.) Sex. Pompey for his part slipped away from Munda and resumed the struggle in northwestern Spain (Welch 2012: 107–108).

[128] *Bell. Hisp.* 34.5, 36.3–5; Dio 43.39. See Raaflaub 1974: 259–260, 300–301, with further references.

[129] The appeal for Caesar's clemency at Ucubis by the Roman citizen Ti. Tullius is interesting: Caesar answers that he will treat him as he has noncitizens (*Bell. Hisp.* 17.3: *qualem gentibus me praestiti, similem in civium deditione praestabo*). The episode implies that Roman citizens could no longer expect mercy as a matter of course (and Caesar's treatment of the native rebels had not been particularly generous), but it must be understood as an affirmative answer. In sum, it fits the picture we receive from our minimal evidence for "quarter" given to the Munda "rebels" suggesting that leniency was now the exception rather than the rule. See Raaflaub 1974: 259; Jehne 1987: 324.

had 'mistaken' Caesar's honorable aims or had joined the elder Pompey because of personal obligations."[130]

Jehne rejects the claim of Velleius, Suetonius, and Dio that shortly before his assassination Caesar offered a general amnesty to all remaining former Pompeians; he is probably right to suppose that Caesar will have continued to decide on a case-by-case basis.[131] In any case, after Munda only a few high-ranking ex-Pompeians seem to have remained in exile. These few would have had to take the initiative and plead for their reinstatement. But aside from the risk they ran that their property in Italy might be confiscated, they seem to have been left alone while they considered the step; thus, Marcellus had to be coaxed by Cicero in 46 to accept pardon, and appears to have been left in perfect peace for two years after Pharsalus on the island of Lesbos to contemplate his future.[132]

Finally, what about the property of fallen or unreconciled Pompeians? As a general rule, Caesar confiscated the property only of his *dead* enemies; living Pompeians, when pardoned, appear normally to have received back their property (or most of it) along with their right to resume their *dignitas*, or, if their property had already been confiscated and sold at auction – something that does not seem to have been done before Pharsalus – then the monetary value of their property.[133] Thus it is important to recognize that Caesar's pardoned former enemies were not, as a rule, simply spared and left their bare lives but also their property, which would be necessary for them to sustain future involvement in the Republic in a manner comparable to their past careers. According to the attractive hypothesis independently proposed by B. Motzo and A. Alföldi, funds from the auction of confiscated estates, including Pompey's (sold in October 47), were probably kept sequestered in the Temple of Ops, pending the pardon and reimbursement of

---

[130] Raaflaub 1974: 259–262; Jehne 1987: 324.

[131] Jehne 1987, 325, 329, and especially p. 335 against the wholesale acceptance of the claim in some of our sources (Vell. Pat. 2.56.1; Suet. *Iul.* 75.4; Dio 43.50.1–2, cf. 45.9.4, perhaps the only reference specific enough to carry any weight; but note Cic. *Phil.* 13.32). Cf. also Jehne 1987a, 230n15, 433–434n48; contra Alföldi 1985: 265. It was in the interest of those left high and dry by Caesar's assassination (perhaps Minucius and Coponius, ##71, 72?) to allege that a plan for such an amnesty was in Caesar's *acta*; this may be the origin of the idea.

[132] See #60. Jehne 1987, 325, 329. On Marcellus see p. 469ff.

[133] B. Woytek 2003: 201–217 offers the most comprehensive examination of Caesar's handling of the property of his Civil War enemies. Cf. also Jehne 1987: 331–332 and Brunt 1971a: 321–322, who gives a few notable examples of Caesar's restraint regarding the property of L. Lentulus, the consul of 49, Cicero, Pompey until 47 (next n.), and M. Marcellus. Consider also Varro (n. 284), Nigidius Figulus (Cic. *Fam.* 4.13.5–6, with Woytek p. 208), and even Cato (Val. Max. 5.1.10, with Woytek p. 213). Auctions of confiscated property seem to have begun in earnest in 47: Dio 42.51.2, with Woytek pp. 211–213.

any surviving former owners from these funds.[134] These funds would have comprised the lion's share of the HS 700 million allegedly remaining in the Temple of Ops at the time of Caesar's death.[135] While on the whole the property of dead Pompeians was open to confiscation, here too Caesar showed generosity by returning dowries to their widows and giving any children their portion of the patrimony, again in sharp contrast to Sulla's practice in the proscriptions.[136]

Caesar's policy about confiscation naturally offered an inducement to remaining holdouts to come to terms with Caesar and reintegrate themselves into the body politic, but the treatment of widows and children strongly suggests that it should not be seen in exclusively narrow strategic terms as a cynical war strategy aimed at sapping the enemy's will to continue their resistance. We should also recognize that this kind of generosity was far from cost-free. In his excellent article on the Great Mutiny of September, 47, Stefan Chrissanthos has well detailed how Caesar's soldiers had not only "rarely received their pay" even after Pharsalus, but that the bonuses their commander had repeatedly promised them, most recently after the great victory in Greece, had not materialized.[137] Thus Caesar's restraint with regard to his enemies' property was indirectly paid for during the duration of the wars by his increasingly disgruntled soldiers, something that was hardly in his interest from a narrowly military perspective. We must therefore seriously consider that Caesar's unprecedented policy of preserving the property of Pompeians still living, permitting inheritance in most cases to the survivors of the dead, and probably even temporarily sequestering the monetary equivalent of the confiscated property of deceased Pompeians in the Temple of Ops pending a future settlement, were all conceived as ways of "winning the peace" by limiting any permanent damage to those who had chosen the

---

[134] See now B. Woytek 2003: 324–332, with full bibliography, who strongly supports the suggestion, as does Jehne 1987: 333–335 and Jehne 1987a: 76–78. Date of the auction of Pompey's property: Cic. *Phil.* 2.64. The proceeds probably amounted to HS 200 million: App. *BCiv.* 3.4/11 with Dio 45.9.4; Cic. *Phil.* 13.12 (HS 700 million!) is doubtless a mistake (Shackleton Bailey 1986: 389): Jehne 1987: 334–335n136; Ramsey 2003: 256; Woytek, pp. 325n63, 330.

[135] Cic. *Phil.* 2.93a, 5.11, 12.12; Vell. Pat. 2.60.4. Varro's property, however, was not sold (n. 284), as was the case also for Cicero. It appears that Caesar refrained from taking harsh action in general until what he expected to be the "final showdown" at Pharsalus, after which he considered further resistance to be *pertinacia*. The sale of Pompey's property awaited Caesar's return from the East (prev. n.). One cannot exclude the possibility that the Temple of Ops also contained "the sale of booty in Caesar's conquests" (Ramsey 2003: 302) such as the HS 600 million in *pecunia* which Velleius says was carried in the Quadruple Triumph of 46 (2.56.2), and as Woytek observes, nothing prevented Caesar from using these funds with a free hand if he so desired (2003: 331).

[136] Dio 43.50.1–2; note the examples of Cato Jr. and Pompeia and her children (##52, 59).

[137] Chrissanthos 2001: 70. Cf. B. Woytek 2003: 171–173.

opposing side, or their heirs who had not, in most cases, had any real choice.

Having surveyed the instances of Caesar's "leniency" in the Civil War, we are in a position to make a few preliminary observations. First, our review shows that the practice clearly evolved through the series of major clashes that punctuated the Caesarian civil wars (Ilerda, Pharsalus, Thapsus, and Munda) and became more restrictive, at least as regards participants in the new clashes from Africa to Spain and especially those who insisted on renewing the fight again and again. This pattern will be examined and explained in the next section of this chapter, but for the moment it will suffice to note that evolving circumstances and even accident (e.g. the battlefield massacre at Thapsus) must be given their due when we are assessing and seeking to explain Caesar's policy of "clemency" or "leniency." While moments in the evolution of the policy may indeed be highly illuminating because of the unusual richness of the evidence they provide (for instance, Caesar's letter about Corfinium or Cicero's letters about the pardon of M. Marcellus, together with his speech *Pro Marcello*) the evaluation of the significance of any such moment (or others less well documented) cannot be made without consideration of its historical context in the larger story of the war and of the interests in play at each stage. In particular, we must avoid facile judgments driven more by tendentious prior assumptions about Caesar's goals (hindsight again) than the often complex empirical evidence. What happened at Thapsus, for example, hardly shows that Caesar's "leniency" was a sham, while what he did at Corfinium does not imply that he was impelled from the beginning by some militarily unrealistic ideal of mercy.

Second, the sheer scale of the phenomenon is impressive: we have the names of more than sixty notable individuals who saw fit to surrender to Caesar once and in some cases even twice, which should induce us to think twice about the implication of Syme's assertion, quoted at the beginning of this chapter, that the offer of "clemency" was an unwelcome imposition that implied "a recognition of despotism." There must have been in addition many others whose names are not reported by our sources, such as for example the many young men of senatorial family, equestrians, and decurions who were released at Corfinium (#9). Further down the social scale, the voluntary discharge of Pompey's army at Ilerda was remarkably generous (some of them reenlisted with Caesar's provincial garrison in Spain, but others traveled all the way to form the hard core of Pompey's army at Pharsalus), and of course the lack of reprisals against the many thousands of Pompeian soldiers who had surrendered at Corfinium and

Pharsalus is still worthy of note even if this was also to his military advantage.

Third, one of the most striking features of the phenomenon is the sheer number of "recidivists" among those Caesar spared and released, beginning with those pardoned at Corfinium – his confirmed enemy L. Domitius (the consul of 54) and his son, P. Lentulus Spinther (cos. 57), Sex. Quinctilius Varus (probably Domitius's quaestor), and Pompey's Prefect L. Vibullius Rufus – and continuing at Ilerda with Pompey's legates, L. Afranius (cos. 60), M. Petreius, M. Varro, and P. Ligarius, along with a substantial number of the "Afranian" cohorts whom Caesar allowed to be discharged from service unharmed but then made their way *beyond* their homes in Italy to join Pompey in Greece.[138] Indeed, among this group four were captured or surrendered and spared *yet again* (the younger Domitius, Varus, Vibullius, and Varro). After Caesar learned that Domitius and others had made use of their pardon by rejoining his enemies and carrying on the fight, he rather grandly assured Cicero that he was undisturbed: "Nothing pleases me better than that I should be true to myself and they to themselves."[139] Thus it seems clear that those who did accept Caesar's offer of leniency were under no powerful constraint against following their conscience or political allegiance and taking up the fight again against their ostensible benefactor; their "acquiescence" in allowing their lives to be spared, therefore, does not appear to have entailed any real or actual "recognition of despotism." This is one of the most important differences between Caesar's "clemency" and that of the *principes* of the future: its beneficiaries were left free to renounce it after the fact. Furthermore, as is shown especially by Domitius's case, such leniency could come at a high cost. We must free ourselves of the seductive, but anachronistically teleological assumption that somehow Caesar "had" to win the civil wars, and yet of course there are numerous moments (the pursuit of Pompey across the Ionian Sea, the nearly decisive defeat at Dyrrachium, the battle in the harbor at Alexandria, the legionary mutiny in Italy in 47, and the battle at Munda itself) where it might all have come crashing down in disaster. While it is true that generosity toward one's defeated enemies may sap the will of those remaining to fight and may have encouraged others to join one's side, repeatedly allowing prominent enemy generals and fighters to go back and try again, forcing one's hard-pressed soldiers to defeat them

---

[138] See n. 70. For the "recidivists" see Catalog ##2–5, 7, 11–15 (21, 38, 50).

[139] Cic. *Att.* 9.16.2: *nihil enim malo quam et me mei similem esse et illos sui* (Shackleton Bailey). The character he asserts for himself is his aversion to cruelty, stressed in the very first sentence of Caesar's letter.

again and again, is itself a heavy price to pay, and one which, history shows, victorious armies are rarely willing to bear. (We have noted a likely backlash against the policy within Caesar's own ranks in the Thapsus battlefield massacre, and as we shall see, his preservation of the property of his enemies sparked resentment among some of his strongest partisans.) Gestures such as the return of Domitius's war chest at Corfinium or Caesar's repeated destruction of his opposing commanders' correspondence (after Pharsalus and Thapsus) are even less convincingly explained by the pursuit of military advantage.

Fourth, the phenomenon is sufficiently consistent to merit the name of a "policy."[140] Cicero had fretted immediately after Corfinium that this was merely a trick that would soon be tossed aside (*insidiosa clementia*).[141] Yet in fact Caesar stuck to it with broad consistency overall even after Domitius's unfortunate intervention in the Massilian revolt and the aggravated circumstances of the African campaign, and while the nature of the final rebellion in Spain (as will be seen in the next section) virtually precluded many further acts of battlefield "leniency," he continued to favor Cicero's efforts to effect the return of those whose cases were still unresolved after Pharsalus and Thapsus at a time when continued generosity toward his erstwhile enemies offered little or no further military advantage. We shall return later to the question of the motivation of such a policy, which at first glance might appear implausibly altruistic.

Finally, it is worth stressing that the "leniency" policy had a real effect on the potential savagery of civil war, and that our sources have not simply made much ado about nothing. Statistics do not exist that would allow us to compare with any exactitude the human cost of the Caesarian civil wars with that of the Sullan-Marian conflict, but we can use some figures reported by our sources to gain at least an impressionistic view of their relative scale. Appian, as we saw, plausibly claims that ninety senators, including fifteen consulars, and twenty-six hundred *equites* were killed or exiled in the Sullan civil wars.[142] The Sullan proscriptions alone targeted perhaps eighty senators and four hundred forty *equites*.[143] The numbers are far from exact, but they should give a sense of perceived magnitude of the losses. In the Caesarian Civil War, besides Afranius (who was executed by

---

[140] Caesar [Cic.] *Att.* 9.7C.2 (already in March 49): *meo instituto usus sum; Bell. Afr.* 89.5 (Thapsus): *ex sua consuetudine.*

[141] Cic. *Att.* 8.9a.2 and n. 59.

[142] App. *BCiv.* 1.103/482. He claims that Sulla alone was responsible for these, but Mommsen showed that this was a slip (1894/1996: 4:102); cf. Gabba 1967: 284.

[143] Hinard 1985: 116–120.

the semi-independent *condottiere* P. Sittius), five Pompeian consulars including Pompey met violent deaths, two or three of them at the hands of Ptolemaic forces and one by suicide.[144] As for senators of all ranks, if it is true that ten Pompeian senators were killed at Pharsalus it is highly unlikely that more than twenty more died in the Thapsus or Munda campaigns, with their evidently diminishing numbers of elite Roman participants on the side opposing Caesar. Thus it looks as if casualties among the elite in the Caesarian civil wars amounted to perhaps one-third or at most one-half the number in the Marian-Sullan conflicts. Another figure that may be considered a proxy for the level of victors' savagery and losers' desperation is the number of known suicides in the two series of civil wars: Stanley Rauh's catalog of known Roman suicides includes eleven notable men who killed themselves in the civil strife of the 80s (five enemies of Cinna or Marius and six enemies of Sulla), perhaps only three of whom had any prospect of a better fate, while only four of Caesar's enemies did so (Cato, Metellus Scipio, Petreius, Quinctius Scapula), two of which might be considered "elective" suicides since they might have asked for quarter if they had been willing to accept it.[145] Again, the numbers, even as unreliable as they doubtless are, seem to reveal a scale of death among members of the elite in the Caesarian Civil War that was a mere fraction (one-third?) of the wars of the 80s. Of course such figures take note only of notable men of senatorial and equestrian rank. But it seems clear that Caesar managed to minimize casualties among enemy *citizen* soldiers through Italy, the first Spanish campaign, and the victory at Pharsalus (some six thousand, as Pollio claimed, actually lowering Caesar's figure), although his loss of control at the climax of the battle at Thapsus caused a substantially higher reported body count there (ten thousand +?), and as we have seen, for various reasons (some of which we are about to explore) quarter was not given at Munda and the remaining mop-up operations at Corduba and elsewhere. Overall, then, while it is clear that the final campaign in Spain was largely untouched by the "leniency" policy, it had up to that point

---

[144] Although Appian claims that ten senators fell at Pharsalus alone (n. 74) we know the names of only about sixteen senators (besides Pompey) who met a violent end while fighting on the Pompeian side in the entirety of the Caesarian civil wars: L. Afranius, P. Attius Varus, L. Caesar, M. Cato, L. Domitius, T. Labienus, Lentulus Crus, Lentulus Spinther (the elder), Licinius Damasippus, L. Manlius Torquatus [pr. 50 or 49], Metellus Scipio, Petreius, Q. Pompeius Bithynicus, Faustus Sulla, and probably A. Plautius [pr. 51] and C. Valerius Triarius. (Caesar had spared four, possibly five, of these once already.) Not all of them were killed by Caesar's men: apart from the three known suicides and the two executed by Sittius, four (including Pompey) were killed almost certainly on orders of Ptolemy XIV or his advisors (see nn. 78 and 272).

[145] Rauh 2012: 178–201, 207–213; see the catalog, pp. 47–56, 62–66.

saved many citizens' lives, especially in comparison with Rome's bloody recent history in the 80s.

The Evolution of *Lenitas*

As we have observed, at both the elite level and that of the rank and file, Caesar's policy of "leniency" evolved over the course of the four or five major civil war campaigns from one of quite remarkable generosity (Corfinium, Ilerda, and Pharsalus) to a more mixed record in Africa, after which the campaign at Munda against Pompey's sons and their Spanish allies was fought with ferocity and little or no quarter. At the elite level, our list of individual instances shows some forty-four cases to the end of the Pharsalus campaign (with twenty-nine after that battle alone), another nineteen after Thapsus and the victory celebrations of the fall of 46, and only three more from the Munda campaign, with perhaps six more belated pardons hanging over from the Pharsalus campaign datable to the end of Caesar's life, or pending at that moment.

A similar pattern is observable in Caesar's treatment of citizen soldiers who opposed him. No reprisals against defeated enemy soldiers at Ilerda or Pharsalus are recorded; Pompeian soldiers were spared after surrender as a rule and in the major conflicts were generally enrolled with Caesar's troops or, in the case of the "Afranian" cohorts who had surrendered at Ilerda, released altogether.[146] To be sure, Caesar in his *Civil War* is eager to stress his patriotic anxiety for the lives even of the Pompeian soldiers arrayed against him,[147] yet his actions at Corfinium, Ilerda, and Pharsalus gave substance to the claim. This behavior on the battlefield is consistent with the conspicuous respect Caesar evinced at the very beginning of the conflict toward those in Pompey's service, including even some who were permitted to leave his service and join his adversary during his

---

[146] See p. 429ff. Some of Afranius's veterans now reenlisted with Caesar's Spanish garrison, then at the beginning of the Munda campaign deserted to Cn. Pompey the Younger (Dio 43.30.4). Their numbers sufficed to form an entire legion (*Bell. Hisp.* 7.4, surely mistaken as to their origin: see Raaflaub [ed.] 2017: 613n14.7d, contra Brunt 1971: 474). Others joined Pompey at Pharsalus: n. 70.

[147] Most notably in the climax of the Ilerda narrative (Caes. *BCiv.* 1.71–77, 85–87), where, against the demands of his own officers for an immediate assault against the weakened enemy (esp. §§72, 81.2, 82.3), he prefers to avoid unnecessary bloodshed and instead forces them to surrender by cutting them off from their water source. (Chrissanthos 2001: 70 is mistaken: Caesar did not "quickly compl[y]" with his soldiers' demand for an attack.) The differing response of Caesar and the Pompeian commanders to the soldiers' fraternization further reinforces the point: Caesar is more solicitous of the enemy soldiers than are their own commanders. In a similar vein, note Caesar's release of the captured crews of some Rhodian ships (3.27.2) and the surrender of some twenty-four thousand at Pharsalus (3.98).

march into Italy, most notably Labienus and some of his own centurions whom he had promoted at Pompey's request. Similarly, after capturing Pompey's "front-rank" centurion L. Pupius on the march to Corfinium he had him returned unharmed to his commander.[148] By such actions Caesar further signaled that this was in fact a political dispute within a community, not a cataclysmic war *à l'outrance*, and implicitly expressed respect for citizens' autonomy in choosing sides.

But subsequent campaigns were clearly fought with greater savagery. At first glance Caesar's "leniency" toward the soldiers opposing him might seem to have been exhausted. Yet the massacre on the battlefield at Thapsus was apparently contrary to Caesar's orders; and the lack of quarter given at Munda would have been justified in Caesar's eyes by the fact that most of those opposing them (perhaps two-thirds of the whole) were not Romans but native Spaniards who had joined in a rebellion against the army and consul of the Roman People, while the remaining third composed of citizens (n. 124) had from a Caesarian point of view treacherously thrown off their allegiance to their benefactor after he had treated them generously at the conclusion of the Ilerda campaign, and thus were themselves in the same position as their social superiors who were "twice captured."

The limitations on "leniency" exposed by the Munda campaign are worth elaborating a bit further in order to understand better the evolution of Caesar's practice over the five major Civil War campaigns. Put simply, the withdrawal of Pompey, his followers, and army from Italy in March 49 meant that over the course of the following four years the anti-Caesarian forces were increasingly detached both from the sources of legionary recruitment (still citizens, and still overwhelmingly Italian, although citizens in the provinces and perhaps others were sometimes recruited in exigent circumstances) and from the sources of governmental legitimacy – the Senate and the People of Rome. Even the army of Scipio and Cato in Africa was heavily recruited from the province (perhaps more than half), and certainly did not consist exclusively even of Roman citizens, quite apart from the large Numidian contingent.[149]

Furthermore, the army's commanders depended for their *imperium* directly or indirectly on the decisions made while the Pompeians briefly held the reins of governmental authority in Rome against Caesar from November 50 to January 49, and these decisions had now receded into the

---

[148] Chapter 7, nn. 78, 99.
[149] Brunt 1974: 474 infers that just over half of the army had been "raised locally" and that "not all were Roman citizens of free birth," indeed that "the majority of the Pompeian legionaries may well have been non-Romans." Juba supplied four legions of the fourteen *in toto*.

distant past. Scipio, for instance, a *privatus*, had been named governor of Syria by the Senate immediately after the expulsion of the tribunes on January 7, 49 (there was a further requirement of a law passed in the name of the People, which may well have been overlooked in the crisis), yet at Thapsus he still claimed to hold *imperium* in North Africa when the Senate and popular assemblies had been in the hands of Caesar's men for three years.[150] We have no explicit statement by what public authority Cato, also a *privatus*, held his *imperium* from 49 onward, but we can fairly infer that this too was decreed by the Senate probably just before the abandonment of Rome in connection with his assignment to Sicily, a province he then gave up posthaste after Pompey's departure from Italy.[151] And so on.[152] Furthermore the Numidian alliance made the Pompeian diehards in North Africa especially vulnerable to patriotic Roman criticism, not only because Juba and his Numidians could be thought of as "barbarians" but also because Juba had much Roman blood on his hands for the massacre of prisoners he ordered after Curio's defeat at Utica, after which he was declared an "enemy of the Roman People."[153] (The willingness of some Pompeians to countenance an alliance with the "barbarian" Parthians after Pharsalus had already been a vulnerable point for critics.[154]) The public authority of the Pompeians in the final stand at Munda was even worse – in

[150] Caes. *BCiv.* 1.6.5. Scipio's appointment was only partly consistent with the new Pompeian law enforcing a gap between the consulship and a provincial assignment, since the gap was supposed to have been five years. (Morrell 2017: 222 resolves the inconsistency by supposing that the interval was shorter for consuls, but this probably exaggerates the Pompeians' punctiliousness in confronting the emergency.) For the legal requirement of a *lex* authorizing appointments under the *lex Pompeia*, see Cic. *Fam.* 15.9.2, 15.14.5. (This is almost certainly not the traditional *lex curiata*, on which see Kunkel-Wittmann 1995: 101n180.)

[151] *MRR* 2.263, 278, 289, 298; see Brennan 2000: 674–675. It is unclear whether the Roman People had formally conferred *imperium* on Cato or any of the others given new military assignments by the Pompeian Senate in January, 49 (nn. 150, 155).

[152] For further notables in the African campaign such as Faustus Sulla (apparently still *proquaestor pro praetore*) or Afranius and Petreius (both probably legates) see *MRR* 2.261, 300, 302.

[153] Caes. *BCiv.* 2.44.1–3; App. *BCiv.* 2.46/189; Dio 41.42.6–7. Cf. Q. Aelius Tubero ap. Quint. 11.1.78 = *ORF* n. 175, fr. 4: *Ligarium ... non pro Cn. Pompeio, inter quam et Caesarem dignitatis fuerit contentio, cum salvam uterque rem publicam vellet, sed pro Iuba atque Afris inimicissimis populo Romano stetisse*. Cicero disapproved as well: *Att.* 11.7.3: *iudicio hoc sum usus, non esse barbaris auxiliis fallacissimae gentis rem publicam defendendam*; and pace Shackleton Bailey, I suspect that in this context *Fam.* 9.6.3: *ad bestiarum auxilium confugere* does not refer to Juba's elephants but figures the Numidians as cruel enemies of Rome. (Cf. 7.3.3) Note that the author of the *Bellum Africum* stirs indignation by emphasizing the alliance, indeed subordination, of the Roman "diehards" to Juba (*Bell. Afr.* 8.5, 57.3; cf. Caes. *BCiv.* 2.44); for further examples see Cluett 2003: 121–124.

[154] Cicero expresses concern about the Pompeians' "barbarian" alliances already at *Att.* 9.10.3; cf. retrospectively 11.6.2: *tanta cum barbaris gentibus coniunctio*. Pompey and the Parthians: Theophanes, *BNJ* 188 T8d (= Plut. Pomp. 76.6-9, cf. App. *BCiv.* 2.83/349–351); Luc. 8.330–453; for a skeptical analysis, Hillman 1996. (Accepted however by Tempest 2017: 64). Note Caesar's tendency in the *BCiv.* to represent the Pompeians as corrupted by "barbarism" (Grillo 2012: 106–121).

fact, it was more or less nonexistent.[155] Caesar, on the other hand, was the formally elected consul of the Roman People when he led the army "of the Roman People" against Scipio and Juba in 46 and then against Pompey's progeny in 45, who must have been seen by many as pursuing a campaign of raw vengeance. (I am not here speaking of the underlying realities of such markers of public legitimacy, since Caesar's "elections" in 46 can hardly be taken naively as true signs of the popular will [see next chapter], but it is indisputable that such markers do have some weight, a fact Caesar's enemies had also exploited to the full at the climax of the crisis that led to the Civil War.) In his contemporary correspondence Cicero never speaks favorably of the political objectives of the Pompeian contingent in Africa and shows no sign of sympathy whatever with the cause of Pompey's sons at Munda.[156]

Taking these two factors together, then – that is, native, even "barbarian," alliances with the Pompeian die-hard remnants, and their lack of public legitimacy – it can be no great surprise to find that from the Caesarian point of view the African and final Spanish campaigns represent wars "against the Roman People."[157] The distinction was fundamental to the varying public recognition Caesar's victories received in the great sequence of triumphs that ostensibly but fallaciously concluded the civil wars in September 46. Pharsalus was entirely passed over; indeed Caesar had completely suppressed a formal announcement of that victory, and in 44 reerected the equestrian statue of Pompey "the plebs" had thrown down in the wave of public enthusiasm that had initially greeted news of the victory.[158] However, the African triumph had explicitly been authorized by the Senate for the victory "over Juba and the Romans who had fought

---

[155] Leadership at least nominally fell to the elder son of Pompey, who had perhaps been commissioned as a legate in Africa (*MRR* 2.291: "no title preserved") and gave himself the title of "Imperator" in Spain (op. cit., 2.298, 309). The two highest-ranking *imperium* holders were two praetorian legates, Labienus and Attius Varus, the origins of whose *imperium* at the beginning of the conflict is obscure and whose legateships apparently depended on Scipio's appointment in 47 (*MRR* 2.260, 268, 290–291, 310–311).

[156] Cic. *Att.* 11.7.3 of December 17, 48, describes his decision not to go to Africa as a rejection of the idea of "defending the Republic with the aid of barbarians of a most treacherous nation" (i.e. Numidians), although he acknowledges that if they meet with defeat it will be "more honorable" than his own. For the Munda campaign the letter of Cassius (*Fam.* 15.19.4) is illuminating, for he clearly presumes that Cicero will agree with his abhorrence of Gnaeus the Younger's cruelty. He professes indifference to the fortunes of Pompey's sons at *Att.* 12.23.1 (*quamvis non curarem quid in Hispania fieret*) and 37a, though his interest picks up when he hears a bit of contrary news (12.44.3).

[157] According to *Bell. Afr.* 91.2, 97.1, Juba and the Roman citizens at Zama had fought a war *contra populum Romanum*. So too Caesar, in his address at Hispalis with which the extant portion of the *Bell. Hisp.* concludes, describes the war as *contra populum Romanum* (42.6), an idea that shapes the entire speech (§§3, 4, 5, 7).

[158] Dio 42.18.1; App. *BCiv.* 2.101/419. See n. 209. Caesar himself notes that Pompey too had shown some restraint in celebrating his victory at Dyrrachium (*BCiv.* 3.71.3).

together with him."[159] It is not quite true that (as is often stated) triumphs could not be celebrated for victories in civil wars; it would be more precise to say that while a triumph for a victory won over Romans exclusively was novel and in principle unacceptable, one celebrated for a victory over foreign enemies *and Roman citizens* who had "treasonously" joined them in making war against "the Roman People" had relevant precedent reaching back to the 80s and the conclusion of the first round of Roman civil wars.[160] From a commonsense point of view, that is, those citizens who joined a *hostis* became *hostes* themselves.[161] So although the graphic nature of the depictions (probably paintings) of the suicides of Metellus Scipio, Cato, and Petreius that were carried in Caesar's African triumph seems to have distressed some viewers, they apparently did not violate any established rules governing triumphs or, certainly, the authorizing decree of the (Caesarian) Senate itself.[162] The same of course goes for Caesar's final triumph of the Civil War over "Spain" (Munda campaign) after his return to Rome late in 45. Plutarch says that "the most distressing thing of all to the Romans" at that time was the celebration of a triumph not over "foreign or barbarian generals" but over "the sons and the entire family of the man who had been the greatest of the Romans."[163] Plutarch may well be right about the emotional impact of the tragedy of the house of Pompey (though of course Sextus remained to cause much trouble in the future, while Pompey's daughter Pompeia, his grandchildren, and his wife, Cornelia, of course remained unharmed), but he is certainly misleading

[159] Dio 42.20.5: πρός τε τὸν Ἰόβαν καὶ πρὸς τοὺς Ῥωμαίους τοὺς μετ' αὐτοῦ πολεμήσαντας. Similarly, the Roman citizens at Zama who had "taken up arms against the Roman People" (*Bell. Afr.* 97.1; n. 157) suffered confiscation of their property. Jehne 1987: 322; cf. Raaflaub 1974: 259; 300n347.

[160] Namely, Sulla's triumph (formally) *de Mithridate* in 81, and Pompey's triumphs *de Africa* and *ex Hispania* in 81 or 80 and 71. See Havener 2014: 165–170 and Östenberg 2014. For the principle see Val. Max. 2.8.7. See Lundgreen 2011: 42–50 for a useful distinction between "rules" and "principles"; for its application to the triumph generally, 225–231.

[161] Jehne 1987a: 54n43: "wer als Bürger auf die Seite eines *hostis* tritt, stellt sich diesem gleich."

[162] App. *BCiv.* 2.101/419–420 alone describes the representations of the Roman suicides, on which see Jehne 1987a: 318–319n128; Dobesch 2000: 97–98; Beard 2007: 145; Havener 2014: 171; and especially Östenberg 2009: 246–261, who suggests that the εἰκόνες may have been dramatic tableaux with "human actors, who performed simple movements against painted settings" (or possibly tapestries).

[163] Plutarch *Caes.* 56.7–9: ὡς οὐδὲν ἄλλο Ῥωμαίους ἠνίασεν; Dio 43.42.1–2. Two of Caesar's legates, the suff. cos. Q. Fabius Maximus and Caesar's own nephew Q. Pedius, celebrated further triumphs *ex Hispania* somewhat later in the year. See *MRR* 2.304–305, 309, 311; Itgenshorst 2005: 374–380; Pelling 2011: 419–420. Rich 2014: 238, echoing Dio 43.42.1, stresses the "scandalous" violation of the "fundamental principle that only those who commanded under their own *imperium* and auspices could triumph." But the case is not so clear-cut. Before Caesar's arrival in Spain both Fabius and Pedius had operated independently of him as legates of praetorian rank (*MRR* 2.301–302), evidently with *imperium*, which in Pedius's case at least the Capitoline Fasti record as *pro consule*. The main thrust of Dio's complaint appears to be that they had achieved no triumph-worthy success independently of Caesar.

about the nationality of those whose defeat was being celebrated as well as about the questionable public legitimacy of those Romans who led the diehards' last hurrah in Spain.[164] Here it seems as if Plutarch's fine sense of tragedy has taken precedence over the more nuanced facts.

A further operative principle that seems to reflect a deeper rationale for Caesar's relatively lenient treatment of his enemies and account for its modalities is that since it was implicitly offered as an act of reconciliation, it could be forfeited by *pertinacia*. This word turns up repeatedly in this context to describe the kind of "fanatical obstinacy" that is expressed by the determination to continue Roman bloodshed beyond the first possible decision point (i.e. Pharsalus).[165] Caesar, as we have seen, sought to characterize the conflict as a "dispute among citizens" to be patched up with as little bloodshed within the community as possible. In a letter of 47 to Caesar's future assassin, C. Cassius, Cicero himself describes his own decision to bow out after Pharsalus in terms that clearly echo Caesar's:

> ... *uterque nostrum spe pacis et odio civilis sanguinis abesse a belli <non> necessari[a] pertinacia voluit ... . ut saepe soleo mecum recordari, sermo familiaris meus tecum et item mecum tuus adduxit utrumque nostrum ad id consilium ut uno proelio putaremus, si non totam causam, at certe nostrum iudicium definiri convenire. neque quisquam hanc nostram sententiam vere umquam reprehendit praeter eo<s> qui arbitrantur melius esse deleri omnino rem publicam quam imminutam et debilitatam manere. ego autem ex interitu eius nullam spem scilicet mihi proponebam, ex reliqui<i>s magnam ... . Equidem fateor meam coniecturam hanc fuisse, ut illo quasi quodam fatali proelio facto et victores communi saluti consuli vellent et victi suae; utrumque autem positum esse arbitrabar in celeritate victoris. Quae si fuisset, eandem clementiam experta esset Africa quam cognovit Asia, quam etiam Achaia ... . Amissis autem temporibus ... interpositus annus alios induxit ut victoriam sperarent, alios ut ipsum vinci contemnerent.*
>
> Both of us, hoping for peace and hating civil bloodshed, decided to hold aloof from persistence [*pertinacia*] in an unnecessary war. ... I often recall how in talking familiarly to each other ... we were both led to the persuasion that our verdict, if not the entire issue, might properly be decided by the result of a single battle. Nor has anyone ever fairly blamed us for taking this view,

---

[164] Rich 2014: 238 claims that "no such pretext [i.e. of 'cloaking' civil war victories as over foreign enemies] was available." On the contrary, both Fabius's and Pedius's triumphs were *ex Hispania* (Fasti Triumph. Capit. s.v. 45; Caesar's own triumph is broken off) and the overwhelming mass of the opposing soldiers were Spaniards. Incidentally, there is no sign that the younger Cn. Pompeius or other Romans were represented in this triumph. Possibly the mixed public reception of the African triumph had caused a rethink.

[165] Cf. Caes. *BCiv.* 1.85.4 and 3.10.3, characterizing the Pompeians' refusal to consider any opportunity to end the fighting.

excepting those who think the commonwealth had better be wiped out altogether than survive in an enfeebled and attenuated form. For my part I saw no hope (obviously) from its destruction, but great hope from its remnants. ... I confess my forecast was that, once the fated and final battle (*illo quasi quodam fatali proelio facto*) ... had been fought, the victors would turn their attention to the general survival and the vanquished to their own. At the same time I thought that both the one and the other depended upon swift action by the victorious leader.[166] Had that been forthcoming, Africa would have experienced the clemency which Asia came to know, as did Achaia also. ... But the crucial moments were lost. ... A year intervened, leading some to hope for victory and others to care nothing even for defeat.[167]

It has been argued that by the time of Caesar's return from Thapsus "Cicero and his correspondents had worked out a retrospective view of the civil war and the leading Pompeians that agreed to a remarkable degree with the account Caesar gave of them in his *Civil War*."[168] But the letter to Cassius shows that this view predates Thapsus, and given Cicero's deeply held objections to civil war and his well-known doubts about throwing himself into this one in particular, there is little reason to believe that this was a late epiphany. Cicero here expresses a conception of limited war which, as we shall see, is entirely consistent with Caesar's own stated rationale. He assumes that bloodshed should be restricted to the minimum necessary – one great battle – to settle the matter even among political enemies in the interests of preserving the remnants of a *res publica* rather than destroying it altogether. Persistence beyond that point was simply *pertinacia*, fanatical "obstinacy," unacceptable to those who had a patriotic regard for peace and an abhorrence for civil war and the shedding of citizens' blood. The African campaign was clearly driven by *pertinacia* in Caesar's eyes, and the final campaign of the civil wars in Spain (Munda),

---

[166] A complaint about Caesar's time-wasting diversion to Egypt, which gave his enemies their opportunity to regroup. For Cicero's fear and dismay as the diehards in Africa gained strength see Cic. *Att.* 11.7.3–4, 10.2, 12.3, 15.1, 16.1, 18.1. After Thapsus he would console Varro with the thought that "it was not duty, but despair (*desperationem*), that we abandoned" (*Fam.* 9.5.2). Cf. *Fam.* 7.3.3 (to M. Marius).

[167] Cic. *Fam.* 15.15.1–2, trans. Shackleton Bailey. See his note on the emendation. A similar rationale is given in a letter to M. Marcellus, *Fam.* 4.7.2 (September? 46): *cum spe vincendi simul abiecisti certandi etiam cupiditatem ostendistique sapientem et bonum civem initia belli civilis invitum suscipere, extrema libenter non persequi.* Cf. *Marc.* 10: *ut quidquid belli fortuna reliquum rei publicae fecerit, id esse salvum velis,* and *Fam.* 9.6.3 (to Varro). Contra Shackleton Bailey (followed by Dettenhofer 1992: 215n21), I think it is more likely that the earlier conversation with Cassius to which Cicero refers took place in February 49, as the stage was being set for what looked like a showdown at Corfinium, and both men are known to have met at Formiae (*Att.* 7.23.1, 24; cf. also *Fam.* 15.15.4: Chapter 7, n. 313), rather than in Greece after Pharsalus.

[168] Batstone-Damon 2006: 115.

with its majority of native levies and dearth of public authority, was even more open to interpretation as an utterly unnecessary prolongation of bloodshed after two great battles, each of which could and should (as even Cicero thinks) have been regarded as decisive.

Metellus Scipio and Cato had chosen to kill themselves rather than to ask for or presume upon the victor's "leniency," and as we have seen, along with Petreius (who had been captured and released once already), their suicides were brought vividly to the public eye in the African triumph of 46.[169] I have already explained why this was justifiable at least from a Caesarian point of view, but why did Caesar think this was *useful?* Although if Appian's account is to be trusted, the shocking display may have backfired somewhat, the best hypothesis to explain the intention behind it is surely that Caesar wished to offer these men's actions and fate as negative *exempla* of *pertinacia*. Appian stresses that Cato was shown "tearing himself open like a wild beast" (οἷα θηρίον) in a noteworthy echo of his description of the suicide itself: what was emphasized, then, if we take Appian or his source (probably Pollio) at his word, was bestial, irrational savagery, the very opposite of humane participation in a civic community.[170] The depiction of Cato's suicide in the African triumph is best regarded as powerful visual propaganda: an intentionally disturbing representation of what Caesar claimed to be up against. Since suicide is itself a transparent metaphor for the self-destructive animating spirit of civil war, the image also fits into the same ideological-conceptual framework as his reported utterance (according to Pollio) over the corpse-strewn field at Pharsalus – "this is what they wanted"[171] – and his agenda throughout the *Civil War Commentaries* of revealing the Pompeians as fanatically and cruelly determined to treat fellow citizens who did not agree with them as outright enemies.[172]

---

[169] See n. 162.

[170] App. *BCiv.* 2.101/420; cf. 2.99/412. Cf. Hor. *Carm.* 2.1.24: *atrocem animum Catonis*, which may not be laudatory (Nisbet and Hubbard 1978: 24 note that *atrox* is "complimentary only by way of paradox"; Harrison 2017: 54: "markedly less laudatory about Cato's suicide" than the other mention in the *Odes*). See Rauh 2018: 75–76, 83–85. "Backfired": "the People (ὁ δῆμος) groaned" at the reminder of their own troubles. On Cato's suicide see n. 94 and p. 467ff.

[171] Suet. *Iul.* 30.4: *Hoc voluerunt.* See Morstein-Marx 2007: 162–163 for fuller explication.

[172] The criticism, as we have seen, is not unfounded or unfair, given Pompey's order of January 17, 49, and the other threats of the Pompeians that followed (Chapter 7, nn. 50, 147; cf. Cic. *Att.* 11.6.6: *omnes enim qui in Italia manserant hostium numero habebantur*). The Pompeians' cruelty against soldiers on the other side is often stressed in the *BCiv.* (Batstone-Damon 2006: 93–94; Grillo 2012: 111–112), notably Petreius's execution of Caesar's soldiers caught fraternizing with his army (Caes. *BCiv.* 1.76.4–5), the massacre of the survivors at Utica (2.44.2, cf. App. *BCiv.* 2.46/189; n. 153), and Labienus's killing of prisoners taken at Dyrrachium (3.71.4); other, lesser atrocities are listed by Jehne 1987: 316n19). Cic. *Att.* 11.6.2 (*tanta erat in illis* [*sc. nostris*] *crudelitas*, cf. §6) and *Fam.* 9.6.3 (to Varro) shows that this is not just Caesarian propaganda. The Pompeian and future Caesaricide

Caesar's "Corfinium Letter": Winning the Peace

Somewhat curiously, while Caesar in his *Civil War Commentaries* represents himself as always avoiding cruelty, seeking to minimize bloodshed, and again and again trying (in vain) to open the door to peace, he does not actually lay out an explicit rationale for his practice of "leniency" even at its remarkable first appearance in his narrative of Domitius's surrender at Corfinium.[173] For insight into the motivation of the policy in his own words we must turn to a particularly interesting letter written early in March 49, while en route to Brundisium, to his "secretariate," Oppius and Balbus, and forwarded by them to their mutual friend Cicero ([Cic.] *Att.* 9.7C), whom they were trying to convince of Caesar's peaceful intentions. This immediately contemporary evidence is particularly valuable to us because it permits an analysis of Caesar's policy *before* his ultimate victory and consequent dominant position was known or even thought likely. Hindsight tends to color Caesar's "leniency" inevitably in "monarchic" terms, ostensibly revealed by its author's eventual "autocracy" after the end of the civil wars. But how would it have looked in March 49?

In the previous chapter we saw that in December and January 50–49 Cicero thought he knew what to expect of a Caesarian victory: Rome sacked or in flames, social upheaval, proscriptions, massacres, and confiscations in the style of Cinna and Sulla.[174] Which archetypal tyrant would Caesar turn out to be – a cruel Phalaris or a subtle Peisistratus?[175] When nothing of the sort materialized while Caesar marched down the "back" of Italy, Cicero was still unconvinced. But even Atticus conceded that the spectacular act of leniency at Corfinium called for a rethink.[176] A great wave of public approbation swept through Italy; Caesar, Cicero writes to Atticus, was "winning applause" despite representing the "most shameful cause" because he was thought to be the "protector of his enemies," while Pompey was causing offense despite the excellence of his cause because he was thought to be the "betrayer of his friends."[177] References to Sulla and

---

Cassius was appalled at Gnaeus the Younger's tendency to confuse cruelty with courage/resolution and was sure that Cicero shared his view ([Cic.] *Fam.* 15.19.4: *scis quo modo crudelitatem virtutem putet*). However, Pompey too had tried to gain some credit for leniency: n. 251.

[173] Caes. *BCiv.* 1.23.3 is downright laconic: *Hos omnes productos a contumeliis militum conviciisque prohibet. Pauca apud eos loquitur quod sibi a parte eorum gratia relata non sit pro suis in eos maximis beneficiis. Dimittit omnes incolumes.*

[174] Cic. *Att.* 7.3.5, 7.7, 13.1; *Fam.* 14.14.1, 16.12.1. See Chapter 7, p. 380ff.   [175] Chapter 7, n. 261.

[176] See n. 59.

[177] *Att.* 8.9a.1. Pompey's anger and threats against his own natural allies did not help (8.16.2, 9.10.6, 11.3, 15.3. Cf. 8.13.1–2, 8.16.2). As for Caesar, Caelius gloated to Cicero *eodem in victoria temperatiorem aut legisti aut audisti?* (*Fam.* 8.15.1).

his brand of cruelty now begin to pop up in Cicero's letters – but to characterize the attitude of *Pompey* and his chief advisors, not Caesar's.[178] The public response to the first great gesture of "leniency" is worth dwelling on because Syme's characterization of the policy as an irritant, a lordly act of mastery, tends to obscure the palpable reality that the victor's generosity was heartily applauded and admired as a virtuous act. It was not just peasants, townspeople, or ostensibly apolitical equestrians who joined in praise and gratitude but aristocrats themselves, even those on the opposing side. Cicero wrote personally to Caesar to thank him for "saving a man who had once saved me" – that is, P. Lentulus Spinther (cos. 57), the senior senator with Domitius's army at Corfinium, whose interview with Caesar from the walls was instrumental in encouraging the besieged to surrender the town (at least according to Caesar).[179] Lentulus himself wrote to Cicero effusively expressing his gratitude to Caesar, or so at least the orator informs Atticus.[180] That might be dismissed as disingenuous, but a letter to Atticus written only three or four days later states quite straightforwardly that Lentulus was "moved by Caesar's kindness (*beneficio*)" to give up the fight – though he was "moved even more by what he sees the future holds" (i.e. a Caesarian victory).[181]

True, Cicero soon reverted to skepticism, expressing to Atticus the fear "that all this piling up of clemency may be simply a prelude to the cruelty we feared."[182] And a little more than a week later, Cicero complains that Pompey is forfeiting the goodwill of the towns of Italy because of his anger and threats, whereas they "are delighted with [Caesar's] deceptive clemency (*insidiosa clementia*)."[183] It was, after all, exceedingly paradoxical – one

---

[178] First at *Att.* 8.11.2, written February 27, six days after the surrender at Corfinium. Also 9.7.3, 9.10.2 (*"Sulla potuit, ego non potero?"*), 9.10.6, 9.11.3. Cf. 9.9.4, *nec sine causa et eos qui circum illum sunt omnia postulantis et bellum nefarium times.* For the cruel nature of Pompey's strategy see Chapter 7, nn. 148, 270, 271, and n. 172 of this chapter.

[179] *Att.* 9.11A.3 (cf. 9.16.2: *meum factum probari abs te* [sc. Cicero]; Caes. *BCiv.* 1.22–23.3.

[180] *Att.* 9.11A.3.

[181] *Att.* 9.13.7 (March 23): *Pompeio nunc putat satis factum, beneficio Caesaris movetur, sed tamen movetur magis prospecta re.* See Shackleton Bailey's note. True, Cicero adds that Lentulus was mortified by the memory of his humiliation at Corfinium (something along these lines must be meant by διατροπὴν *Corfiniensem reformidat*: see Shackleton Bailey's note). Humiliating of course it was, in any case. Eventually Lentulus joined Pompey after all (n. 64).

[182] Shackleton Bailey's tr. of *Att.* 8.9a.2: *metuo ne omnis haec clementia ad unam illam crudelitatem colligatur*, with his n. ad loc. against emendation (e.g. Orelli's <*Sullan*>*am*, accepted by Alföldi 1985: 185). Grillo 2012: 152 assumes the reference is to Sulla nevertheless. Presumably Cicero adverts to the fears of massacre, plunder, etc. expressed in earlier letters.

[183] *Att.* 8.16.2 (March 4): *huius insidiosa clementia delectantur, illius iracundiam formidant.* Cf. *Att.* 8.13.1–2 (March 1): "*if* he kills no one or takes no one's property, those who feared him most will love him most."

could fairly say unprecedented – to release one's enemies unharmed, even permitting them even to take their war chest away with them.[184] Doubts about sincerity were therefore inevitable. Later letters of 49 continue to express anxiety about the possibility or even likelihood that Caesar would soon abandon his "leniency."[185] But he did not. In sum, Cicero recognized the propaganda value of Caesar's *clementia* in early 49 and assumed that it would turn out to be a sham.[186] But this is a far cry from regarding it as in itself an abhorrent, un-republican, monarchical gesture. On the contrary, while Cicero is skeptical about the authenticity and durability of Caesar's vaunted moderation, his fear was that it *would not last*, not that it, in itself, implied some kind of recognition of autocracy.[187]

Let us now turn to Caesar's letter. His friends and agents Balbus and Oppius had written him to thank him for his remarkable gesture; he now replies with a fairly short note written on the march to Brundisium around March 5, which they immediately sent on to Cicero as a warrant of his benign intentions. The bulk of the letter is worth quoting:

> *Gaudeo mehercule vos significare litteris quam valde probetis ea quae apud Corfinium sunt gesta. consilio vestro utar libenter et hoc libentius quod mea sponte facere constitueram ut quam lenissimum me praeberem et Pompeium darem operam ut reconciliarem. temptemus hoc modo si possimus omnium voluntates recuperare et diuturna victoria uti, quoniam reliqui crudelitate odium effugere non potuerunt neque victoriam diutius tenere praeter unum L. Sullam, quem imitaturus non sum. haec nova sit ratio vincendi ut misericordia et liberalitate nos muniamus.*

> I am indeed glad that you express in your letter such hearty approval of the proceedings at Corfinium. I shall willingly follow your advice, all the more willingly because I had of my own accord decided to show all possible mildness and to do my best to win over Pompey. Let us try whether by this means we can win back the good will of all and enjoy a lasting victory, seeing that others have not managed by cruelty to escape hatred or to make their victories endure, except only L. Sulla, whom I do not propose to imitate. Let this be the new style of victory, to make mercy and generosity our shield.[188]

---

[184] See n. 56. Sulla's release of L. Scipio after the latter's army deserted him near Teanum in 83 is hardly comparable (Liv. *Per.* 85; cf. App. *BCiv.* 1.85/383–387) and was in any case very much an outlier in that conflict; see Thein 2014: 169.

[185] *Att.* 9.14.2, 10.4.2, 4.8 (cf. 10.8.2, 8.6); Caelius, [Cic.] *Att.* 10.9A = *Fam.* 8.16.1;

[186] He returns to the theme of "pretended clemency" after Caesar's assassination at *Phil.* 2.116.

[187] Konstan 2005: 340–341.

[188] *Att.* 9.7C.1, tr. after Shackleton Bailey, replacing "reconcile" with "win over," "clemency" with "mildness" (*lenissimum*), and "conquest" with "victory" (*vincendi*) as justified in what follows.

Scholars sometimes seem to make this letter say more or less the opposite of what it says on its face, and to treat it as virtually a frank admission of coldly manipulative, strategic motives behind Caesar's exercise of clemency at Corfinium (and presumably elsewhere). For instance, by means of a painstaking philological analysis of some key phrases in the letter such as *diuturna victoria uti* and *nos muniamus*, M. Treu thought he found evidence that Caesar planned to assume a quasi-monarchic position after victory unlimited by republican collegiality and annual tenure but carefully distinguished from (mostly Greek) stereotypes of tyranny, such as the dependence on bodyguards for security.[189] More recently, Roller writes that "As Caesar presents it, his clemency and liberality are symbolic violence" since "they constitute a way of 'fortifying' himself against his enemies [*nos muniamus*] and are a 'new means of conquering' [*nova ratio vincendi*] with the aim of securing a 'lasting victory' [*diuturna victoria*]"; the very wording indicates that clemency is nothing more than a substitute for "the deployment of military force," something that "actually enhances its effects."[190]

All of this seems vastly overheated.[191] If Caesar really were nakedly confessing his aggressive and cynical exploitation of a traditional virtue to his friends Balbus and Oppius, why would they have thought it helpful to pass the letter on to Cicero, with the comment that "from it you will see how anxious is to restore good relations with Pompey, and how far removed from any sort of cruelty"?[192] Whatever game Balbus was really playing with Cicero at this juncture – was he truly seeking a reconciliation between Caesar and Pompey, or simply to immobilize or even detach Cicero from Pompey? (see Chapter 7) – the wobbly consular orator offered an important diplomatic opportunity to Caesar's "secretariate," and it surpasses belief that as cunning an operator as Balbus would have let the cat out of the bag and laid bare his commander's (ex hypothesi) cynical plans to a skilled reader who officially at least stood in the other's camp. A less confessional or cynical reading of Caesar's letter is preferable.

Scholars have often been struck by the military language sprinkled about the passage, especially the "fortification" metaphor and its references to

---

[189] Treu 1948, a paper that seems to remain influential.

[190] Roller 2001, 183. "Symbolic violence" is presumably here intended in the sense developed by sociologist P. Bourdieu – i.e. ideologically disguised usurpations of power by a privileged person, group, or class. It is "the violence which is exercised upon a social agent with his or her complicity" (Bourdieu and Wacquant 2002: 167).

[191] My interpretation of the letter is largely in accord with Raaflaub 1974: 311–316.

[192] (Shackleton Bailey tr.) *Att.* 9.7B.1: *ex quibus perspicere poteris quam cupiat concordiam <suam> et Pompei reconciliare et quam remotus sit ab omni crudelitate.* Similarly, Flamerie 2011: 79.

"victory," even "lasting victory." But it goes much too far to fasten upon these words in isolation, and against the tenor of the whole passage, as evidence of "symbolic violence." Other phrases clash head-on with that interpretation: *quam lenissimum me praeberem* ("show all possible mildness"), *Pompeium darem operam ut reconciliarem* ("to do my best to *win over* Pompey"), or *temptemus hoc modo si possimus omnium voluntates recuperare* ("Let us try whether by this means we can win back the *good will of all*"). Far from striking a martial tone, these phrases, like the explicit abjuration of cruelty (*crudelitas*) and Sulla's example, unmistakably evoke in the first instance the civic arts of peace: mildness, reconciliation, "winning back everyone's goodwill." Caesar states explicitly that the main purpose of the generosity he had shown at Corfinium was to "win over Pompey" – that is, to demonstrate to Pompey by a spectacular refusal to exploit his military advantage that his object was not in fact to *defeat* him by force of arms but, as he had been saying since he had entered Italy, to meet him and reach a "settlement" (*compositio*).[193] In its immediate context the "*lasting* victory" of which he speaks is represented as being not so much the result of force of arms (although at this moment they were evidently needed as a regrettable precondition) but of "win[ning] back the good will of all," which in the end cruelty like Sulla's could not anyway assure.[194] Here again it is important to remember that Oppius and Balbus forwarded the letter to Cicero to prove that Caesar was *eager to reconcile with Pompey*.[195] Far from "waging war by other means," Caesar is apparently falling back on the traditional wisdom that affection is more effective than fear for securing peace and tranquility – virtually the opposite of stereotypically tyrannical behavior.[196] In this connection, the blood-soaked Sullan victory secured at least in the short term by violence, but also deeply troubled by upheavals that it brought on (agrarian crisis in Italy, the deep

---

[193] Caes. *BCiv.* 1.9.6; Dio 41.10.1–2; Cic. *Att.* 7.17.3–4 etc.; similarly, the continuation of the letter at *Att.* 9.7C.2. (See Chapter 7.)

[194] Similarly, Raaflaub 1974: 296–297. On *diuturna victoria uti*, Treu's proto-monarchical interpretation (1948: 204–208) has been influential, but as Raaflaub notes, he presumes in Caesar an improbable degree of clairvoyance given that the date is early March 49, with Pompey not yet even out of Italy. Raaflaub rightly interprets the phrase from its immediate historical context rather than from the ambiguous philological parallels: Caesar naturally intended to *win* rather than lose a war if it had to be fought, but reflection on the moral barbarity of his predecessors in the First Civil War as well as on the transitory and precarious basis of their victories induces him to prefer what he expects to be a more effective approach, that of reconciliation (Raaflaub 1974: 315–316).

[195] See n. 192.

[196] Contrast Cic. *Off.* 2.23–29, where as part of his posthumous attack on Caesar Cicero implicitly attempts "to force Caesar and Sulla into the same mold" (Dyck 1996: 391–393). Cf. the "end-justifies -the-means" thinking of Cic. *Att.* 11.21.3: Shackleton Bailey ad loc.

wounds of the proscriptions, Catiline), posed a complex object lesson if any were needed for such a well-worn cliché, but Caesar, in keeping with the whole trajectory of his career since at least the "Catilinarian" speech if not before, explicitly rejects Sulla's model and implicitly suggests that that way of making victory last was unacceptable because it paid too high a price for its (only relative) endurance.

If this is the more natural way to interpret the letter, then we must be extremely careful in translating the famous (or notorious) phrase *nova . . . ratio vincendi*. It is more consistent with the tone of the letter and the ideas to which it alludes to translate it not as a "new means of conquering" (Roller) or even "a new style of conquest" (Shackleton Bailey) but a "new style of victory."[197] First, what is the nature of the "victory" he is speaking of? It was clearly much too early for Caesar to be speculating confidently about military victory, and in fact the letter itself speaks of "winning over Pompey" and restoring their friendship; he was now publicly urging a settlement to head off civil war and in this very letter describes how he had captured and returned two of Pompey's *praefecti* in the hope that they could act as intermediaries.[198] It appears therefore that the "victory" he envisions here would have been the realization of his goals – his honorific return to Rome with Pompey's blessing to a second consulship and a triumph – of which his enemies had tried by force to deprive him. That would indeed be a new style of "victory," and one that certainly could not be effected by Sullan methods. It was a style of victory that eschewed most of the traditional benefits or satisfactions or guarantees of winning a civil war – confiscations, abject humiliation of the enemy or his utter destruction, and so on. He totally forswears the language of "vengeance" or "punishment," the standard slogans of civil war.[199] All this is entirely consistent with Caesar's own framing of the Civil War as an unfortunate "quarrel (or dispute) between citizens" (*civilis dissensio, civiles controversiae*) that could and should be patched up, reunifying a civic community divided against itself.[200] From such a definition of the quarrel it followed that *misericordia* for the defeated was an appropriate response,

---

[197] For "style" cf. *OLD* s.v. *ratio*, 14b.

[198] §1: *Pompeium darem operam ut reconciliarem;* §2 *debebunt Pompeium hortari ut malit mihi esse amicus quam iis qui et illi et mihi semper fuerunt inimicissimi.* Chapter 7, p. 349ff.

[199] Jal 1961: 486. The article contains an appalling summary of the traditional, bloody-minded norms of civil war in Rome on which Caesar so strikingly turned his back; it is not Jal's purpose to reveal the distinctiveness of Caesar's practice.

[200] Caes. *BCiv.* 1.67.3, 3.1.3; Caes. ap. Cic. *Att.* 10.8B.2 (*civiles controversiae*); Hirt. [Caes.] *BGall.* Praef. 2; Matius [Cic.] *Fam.* 11.28.2. See Raaflaub 1974: 236–237. Cf. Cicero's reference to the *contentio dissensioque civilis* which had ejected him from Rome in 58 (*Fam.* 1.9.13). Q. Aelius Tubero similarly

perhaps the only proper one.[201] Cruelty, Caesar writes, could not restore stability; even Sulla's cruelty (if we may gloss a slight ellipsis in Caesar's thought here) had managed to sustain stability only by perpetuating the polarized division of civil war – in a sense, by *never ending* the war. Caesar professed to hope that *misericordia* and *liberalitas* could serve as a kind of fortification (*muniamus*) – a *defense*, be it noted, not an offensive weapon, and one that after all depended not on force but on goodwill.[202]

It is almost irresistible for thinking persons to regard Caesar's character-ization of his first great act of leniency at Corfinium without a certain degree of cynicism justified by personal and historical experience, even though it was written not for posterity but to his own "cabinet." That is perfectly appropriate, of course, given the desire of every victor to draw a veil over the less savory aspects of his triumph. And yet justifiable skepticism may sometimes go a bit too far, leading us away from a relatively simple answer right under our noses that is still very much in Caesar's interest.

There are various approaches to the challenge of ending a civil war. One extreme is that represented by Sulla's rivers of blood, ensuring (at least in the short run) the security of the victorious clique's domination so that its leader could even safely step down altogether from power and die in his bed. Another extreme was exemplified by President Abraham Lincoln toward the end of the American Civil War. Without suggesting any close analogy between the two civil wars and the two personalities, it is worth taking a moment to compare Caesar's challenge with that faced by the American president as the five years of horrific slaughter between "broth-ers" came toward its end point.

Early in the last year of the war, 1865, President Abraham Lincoln bucked hard-liners in the Northern-dominated Congress who were bent on severe punishment of secessionists and slaveholders and decided to offer the tottering South "amnesty" and "pardon." Whether from the perspec-tive of today, with hindsight of half a century of Jim Crow legislation which institutionalized racism in the South, this was actually a good thing can be and is argued over by historians and others. However that may be, Lincoln evidently hoped to bring a negotiated end to the carnage rather than impose a brutal military solution on the now-prostrate Confederacy

---

defined the Civil War as a *dignitatis contentio* (n. 153), implying the acceptance of "civil" limits on internecine warfare: Raaflaub 1974: 1–3 and p. 453ff. of this chapter.)

[201] Cf. Lepidus, [Cic.] *Fam.* 10.35.2.

[202] Cf. Plut. *Caes.* 57.8: "He regarded people's goodwill as at once the fairest and firmest protection." Hence Shackleton Bailey's "make . . . our shield." Literally, "to defend ourselves by means of mercy and generosity."

at the cost of an estimated ten thousand further American lives. This fundamentally generous hope was expressed at the end of his second inaugural address of March 1865 with words that still have a special place in the American heart: "With malice toward none; with charity for all; with firmness in the right, as God gives us to see the right, let us strive on to finish the work we are in; to bind up the nation's wounds; . . . to do all which may achieve and cherish a just, and a lasting peace, among ourselves, and with all nations."[203] Lincoln's eloquence is of a different type from Caesar's, yet in his reference to a "just, and a lasting peace" "with malice toward none, with charity for all" it is possible to hear a distant echo of the Roman's stated desire for a *diuturna victoria* not based on "cruelty" but "defended" by "mercy and generosity." Both men show a clear perception of the tragic paradox of civil war, in which the defeated must despite the bloodshed be saved, reconciled, and reintegrated in the hope of reconstituting by a just peace a civic community torn asunder.

In a letter Cicero wrote to one of those hoping for pardon, A. Caecina, perhaps in October 46, he stresses that Caesar and his supporters refrained from describing his adversaries as "bad citizens or wicked men" (*malos civis . . . aut homines improbos*), standard terms of invective deployed against political opponents.[204] As we saw in the previous chapter, in sharp contrast to the

---

[203] Abraham Lincoln Papers, Library of Congress: https://tile.loc.gov/storage-services/service/mss/mal/436/4361300/4361300.pdf. Accessed February 8, 2021. For the "Proclamation of Amnesty and Reconstruction" of December 1863 see https://tile.loc.gov/storage-services/service/mss/mal/284/2849300/2849300.pdf. Lincoln had gone so far as to meet secretly with representatives of the Confederacy at Hampton Roads in February 1865: Conroy 2014.

[204] Cic. *Fam.* 6.6.10. In the *Civil War Commentaries* Caesar is of course sharply critical of some secondary figures on the other side, though notably restrained toward Pompey himself (*BCiv.* 1.4 is an example), but he never descends to mere name-calling such as is the norm with political invective, including Cicero's. Caesar's *Anticato* is an interesting exception which must be set in the context of a public debate about Cato launched almost immediately after his suicide by Cicero's and then Brutus's eulogistic pamphlets: while Caesar's counterblast was highly scurrilous, I agree with Pelling 2011: 408 that "C[aesar] also deserves credit for encouraging an atmosphere where Cato's admirers felt free to write [n.b.: the civil wars were showing a disconcerting propensity to revive and were certainly not yet over], and the vitriolic elements of his own work were firmly in the imaginatively scurrilous tradition of Roman invective. The exchange was surely meant to signal a return to rhetorical normalcy, not tyranny," as Cremutius Cordus (or Tacitus, *Ann.* 4.34.4) was later to emphasize. For fragments of the two works see Jones 1970; Tschiedel 1981. The question of "freedom of speech" under Caesar's short domination (most of it while still on a civil war footing) is too large to be dealt with here. Hall 2009a fails to give due attention to the fact that the civil wars were still continuing at the time of the Cato debate and even when *Pro Marcello* was delivered and published. It is hardly scandalous that Cicero should feel *some* constraint in praising Caesar's most inveterate and obdurate enemy within months of his suicide, on which the official Caesarian line can readily be divined by its harsh representation in the African triumph in the midst of these literary skirmishes even as the Pompeian remnants regrouped in Spain. Returning for a moment to Lincoln, one might, for example, compare his outright violations of the First Amendment by jailing journalists and suppressing antiwar newspapers, including even the arrest for treason of Clement Vallandigham, a prominent antiwar politician, and his subsequent deportation to

Pompeian pronouncement at the beginning of the war and behavior afterward, Caesar did not choose to brand all those who chose the other side as "enemies": as Cicero puts it in the more or less contemporary *Pro Marcello* (presumably echoing the Caesarian official line), they had been misled by *error* (ignorance and perhaps empty fears), not motivated by crime (avarice and cruelty).[205] Some too, he claims in the same speech, had "erred prompted not by any kind of greed or immorality but by a sense of duty, perhaps foolish, but certainly not wicked, and by a certain appearance of patriotism."[206] As for Cicero himself, he declares that despite his abhorrence of civil war (true enough) he had chosen to follow Pompey purely out of personal obligation, not political duty (specious but arguable).[207] In this context we might note the respect that Caesar's agent L. Balbus accorded as far back as March 49 to Cicero's *fides et pietas* toward Pompey as an excuse for standing aside from the war.[208] Even Pompey continued to be honored by statues still standing in prominent places: apart from the one on the Rostra "the People" had thrown down in an intemperate outburst after Pharsalus in Caesar's absence and would soon be reerected on his order, there was also the one that dominated the senatorial hall of Pompey's own theater at the foot of which he would ultimately be assassinated, and these can hardly have been the only ones.[209] With its respectful characterization of the motives of recent enemies, Caesar's policy again may call to mind Lincoln's avoidance of triumphal exultation in victory, whether it be in his tragic vision of the inscrutability of God's purpose in his second inaugural address[210] or in his response to the crowd that gathered

---

the Confederacy for immediate arrest there as a Northern "alien enemy" (Holzer 2014). Speech is rarely, if ever, completely free in war, especially a civil war.

[205] Cic. *Marc.* 13. Cf. *Lig.* 19: *secessionem tu illam existimavisti, Caesar, initio, non bellum, neque hostile, sed civile discidium* ... On the *Pro Marcello* see also p. 465ff. Regarding its date, the senatorial meeting at which it was originally delivered (Cic. *Fam.* 4.4.3–4) has often been placed in mid-September (Shackleton Bailey 1977: 2:360, following Schmidt), but McDermott 1970: 319n6, with 1982/83: 227n20, points out that this was probably somewhat too early, which now seems confirmed by Ramsey and Licht's dating of the Quadruple Triumph to September 20–26, followed by splendid games (1997: 183–184). Since the civil calendar was now far out of alignment a mid-October date would actually fall in the height of summer (mid-August, Jul.).

[206] Cic. *Marc.* 20: *non cupiditate praesertim aliqua aut pravitate lapsis, sed opinione offici stulta fortasse, certe non improba, et specie quadam rei publicae.*

[207] Cic. *Marc.* 14: *hominem* [*Pompeium*] *sum secutus privato officio, non publico.* Chapter 7, p. 378ff.

[208] [Cic.] *Att.* 9.7B.1–2.

[209] Sehlmeyer 1999: 209–211, 219–221, 231–234. For the toppling of the statue on the Rostra and its restoration in 44 see Dio 42.18.2, 43.19.1–2; Suet. *Iul.* 75.4. Cicero elegantly declared that by restoring the statue on the Rostra, Caesar had "set up" not only Pompey's statues but his own (Plut. *Cic.* 40.5, *Caes.* 57.6).

[210] "Both [sides] read the same Bible, and pray to the same God; and each invokes His aid against the other. It may seem strange that any men should dare to ask a just God's assistance in wringing their bread from the sweat of other men's faces; but let us judge not, that we be not judged. The prayers

below the north window of the White House when news came of General Lee's surrender at Appomattox.[211]

Abraham Lincoln's pursuit of a "clement" policy toward the South in 1865 is not, of course, a close parallel to Caesar's task in ending his civil war except in the broadest terms. But the comparison helps to open our eyes to the idea that the great challenge facing a victor in civil war is that of "winning the peace," and therefore that Caesar's Corfinium letter is better read as an attempt to sketch the outline of a response to that challenge rather than a blueprint for autocracy. "Victory" in its usual military sense was far off and highly doubtful, and "autocracy," even if we were sure that was Caesar's goal, more so. Oppius and Balbus thought Cicero would be pleased, and that he would be persuaded that Caesar truly sought peace.[212] That is surely the nature of the more durable "victory" he claims he seeks to obtain through his remarkable act of leniency.

Gratitude

As befits an oration of thanks for the restoration of the consular M. Marcellus in October 46, Caesar's *clementia* and the proper response to it are a major theme of Cicero's *Pro Marcello*.

> There is no violence which cannot be weakened and broken by the power of the sword. But to overcome the will, to restrain anger, to exercise moderation toward the defeated; not merely to raise up a defeated adversary of distinguished nobility, talent, and courage but even to increase his former stature – I consider the one who does such things not merely comparable to the greatest men of history, but very like a god.[213]

---

of both could not be answered – that of neither has been answered fully. The Almighty has His own purposes." See n. 203.

[211] "We all agree that the seceded States, so called, are out of their proper relation with the Union; and that the sole object of the government, civil and military, in regard to those States is to again get them into that proper practical relation." Lincoln's last speech: http://www.abrahamlincolnonline.org/lincoln/sp eeches/last.htm. Accessed February 8, 2021). "That this was not the sort of speech which the multitude had expected is tolerably certain," wrote reporter Noah Brooks.

[212] One might still assume that the whole thing was an elaborate ploy to deceive Cicero as to Caesar's real intentions. But in such matters we must at a certain point ask ourselves why we should go to such lengths to explain away the evidence we have, while relying instead upon assumptions for which we lack evidence.

[213] Cic. *Marc.* 8: *Nulla est enim tanta vis quae non ferro et viribus debilitari frangique possit. Animum vincere, iracundiam cohibere, victo* [certainly preferable to *victoriam*] *temperare, adversarium nobilitate, ingenio, virtute praestantem non modo extollere iacentem sed etiam amplificare eius pristinam dignitatem, haec qui faciat, non ego eum cum summis viris comparo, sed simillimum deo iudico.* For the ideology of *clementia* in Cicero's Caesarian orations and the implied promise of deification as a reward see now Cole 2013: 111–134.

And thus, naturally,

> Your military praises, Gaius Caesar, will be sung not only by our authors
> and orators but by those of nearly every nation . . . yet somehow even when
> we read of deeds of this kind, they seem to be drowned out by the shouts of
> the soldiers and sound of the war-trumpet. But when we hear or read of
> some act of a forgiving (*clementer*), mild (*mansuete*), just, restrained and wise
> nature, especially in the midst of wrath, the enemy of reason, and in victory,
> which is by nature haughty and arrogant – how we burn with admiration,
> not only when the deeds are historical but even fictitious, so that often we
> feel affection toward men we have never even seen![214]

All the more so, then, will Romans praise, support, and feel gratitude
toward Caesar who sits among them, the focal point of their expectant
vision.[215]

Literary critics often warn us that the *Pro Marcello* can be read ironically,
and of course it is always open to readers (as it was to the original audience)
to do so.[216] But actual, public utterances have real consequences, and at this
exceedingly delicate juncture Cicero would have been singularly inept to
encourage Caesar or anyone else to think that he was speaking ironically.
Even if we had complete information about what Cicero privately thought
and intended at the moment of delivery or publication, "sincerity" is not
the most relevant hermeneutic principle here. But certainly in his letter to
his consular peer Ser. Sulpicius Rufus written very shortly afterward (*Fam.*
4.4.4), Cicero does not allow any hint of irony to creep in to his description

---

[214] Cic. *Marc.* 9: *Itaque, C. Caesar, bellicae tuae laudes celebrabuntur illae quidem non solum nostris sed
paene omnium gentium litteris atque linguis . . . sed tamen eius modi res nescio quo modo, etiam cum
leguntur, obstrepi clamore militum videntur et tubarum sono. At vero cum aliquid clementer, mansuete,
iuste, moderate, sapienter factum, in iracundia praesertim quae est inimica consilio, et in victoria quae
natura insolens et superba est, audimus aut legimus, quo studio incendimur, non modo in gestis rebus sed
etiam in fictis ut eos saepe quos numquam vidimus diligamus!*

[215] Cic. *Marc.* 10: *Te vero quem praesentem intuemur, cuius mentem sensusque et os cernimus, ut, quicquid
belli fortuna reliquum rei publicae fecerit, id esse salvum velis, quibus laudibus efferemus, quibus studiis
prosequemur, qua benevolentia complectemur?*

[216] See Dugan 2013 for a thoughtful exploration; see also Lintott 2008: 313–319; Gildenhard 2011:
223–233; Cole 2013: 111–126. Zarecki 2014: 115–122 interprets Cicero's intervention in altogether too
heroic terms ("Cicero, through his praise of the *clementia Caesaris*, does not highlight Caesar's
virtue but rather his position as autocrat," 117). To deliver and publish a speech "highlighting"
autocracy is a kind of self-refutation. Cicero does not so much brand Caesar as an autocrat in *Pro
Marcello* as argue that his job will be unfinished if he does not carry out Cicero's agenda (i.e. 27:
constituenda iudicia, revocanda fides, comprimendae libidines, propaganda suboles: Chapter 9, n. 2).
To interpret this as a kind of denunciation is completely inconsistent with Cicero's other public
actions at this time: the letter-writing campaign to fellow ex-Pompeians coaxing them to return (p.
439ff.) and his prominent role in voting honors for Caesar at the end of the Civil War (n. 246), such
that Antony could afterward accuse Cicero with some plausibility of having deceived him (Chapter
9, n. 100). Zarecki depends heavily on the dubious non-republican interpretation of *clementia*/
"leniency" (n. 11).

of the meeting of the Senate which culminated in the pardon of Marcellus and his own speech of thanks: there he describes the speech simply as one in which he "gave thanks to Caesar at considerable length" (*pluribus verbis egi Caesari gratias*) after "Caesar's magnanimity and the Senate's solicitude" (*Caesaris magnitudo animi et senatus officium*) had overcome his resolution to keep his silence "due to his longing for his former stature" (*desiderio pristinae dignitatis*). Indeed, Caesar's approval of the Senate's request had seemed to be "some kind of sign that the Republic was again coming to life, as it were" (*ut speciem aliquam viderer videre quasi reviviscentis rei publicae*, §3). And while the speech is of course marked by a fulsomely honorific tone befitting the dignity of the occasion, the praise Cicero accords to "Caesar's clemency" and his advocacy of it are entirely consistent with the tone of the letters he writes immediately thereafter to a whole series of high-ranking former Pompeians in which he conveys his optimism about their ultimately obtaining Caesar's pardon.[217]

The eagerness with which the recipients of these letters snatched at the hope of Caesar's pardon raises further doubts about the view that pardon was likely only to create resentment, or Roller's suggestion that Caesar's acts of ostensible leniency were actually a kind of aggressive "symbolic violence" that bound its beneficiary to future subservience inasmuch as he could hardly "pay off" the extraordinary "gift" of his very life. But there is actually precious little support anyway for this idea in the evidence we possess. One might adduce Cato's suicide because – according to Plutarch, following a blatantly eulogistic tradition – "I do not wish to owe a favor to the tyrant for his illegal acts."[218] Yet the simple truth is that, as in the case of most suicides, we really do not know why Cato killed himself; our sources provide different versions of his final preparations and last words, and it is evident that the whole story was much elaborated by later eulogists and

---

[217] Most explicit regarding the attitude of Caesar specifically are Cic. *Fam.* 6.13.3 (Q. Ligarius): *intellegimus eum cottidie remissius et placatius ferre* (i.e. after the conclusion of the African war; cf. 6.14.2); 6.6.8 (A. Caecina): *in Caesare haec sunt: mitis clemensque natura* ... §10: *in quo* (viz., never impugning the patriotism of the Pompeians: n. 204) *admirari soleo gravitatem et iustitiam et sapientiam Caesaris. Numquam nisi honorificentissime Pompeium appellat* ... . *Nos quem ad modum est complexus!* ... §13: *me amicissime cottidie magis Caesar amplectitur.* Cf. also Cic. *Fam.* 4.4.2 (Sulpicius Rufus): *nec id* [i.e. the miserable state of the defeated ex-Pompeians] *victoris* [sc. Caesaris] *vitio, quo nihil moderatius, sed ipsius victoriae, quae civilibus bellis semper est insolens.* (Cf. also §5.) The whole series, conveniently consulted in nos. 203–247 of Shackleton Bailey's editions, is characterized by Cicero's persistent optimism about Caesar's policy of leniency even as, naturally enough, he frequently expresses a melancholy sense of loss and anxiety about the ultimate outcome of the wars and uncertainty about Caesar's ultimate aims.

[218] Plut. *Cat. Min.* 66.2.

emulators in the succeeding age of emperors, not least by the "Stoic martyr" Thrasea Paetus whose own biography of Cato was probably Plutarch's major source.[219] Instead of playing a "martyr to freedom" as he would certainly become in the retrospective tradition of resistance to "tyrannical" emperors, it may be, for instance, that Cato felt honor-bound to pursue to its logical end the hostile policy he had adopted toward Caesar for at least a decade, that he was unwilling to survive defeat in a war for which he bore much responsibility, or simply that he could not bring himself to acknowledge as victor face-to-face a man he had demonized for so long. In his *De Officiis* Cicero – somewhat self-servingly no doubt, but with perfect plausibility and even psychological common sense – explains why Cato was more or less "forced" to kill himself rather than accept Caesar's victory while others were not.[220] Cato, then, hardly establishes a norm, especially when we recall the sixty-plus named individuals who, on the contrary, evidently preferred to experience Caesar's "leniency" to any of the alternatives.

If we set aside Cato's fate and its uncertain motives, little else might be adduced in favor of the "aggressive" interpretation of Caesar's policy of "leniency." Nicolaus of Damascus indulges in some interesting psychological speculation that among the conspirators, "many" actually hated Caesar for having spared them, even though he had treated them "irreproachably," because "the very thought of receiving as a favor the benefits which as victors they would readily have enjoyed, annoyed them very much."[221] The idea that recipients of Caesar's pardon resented not only their defeat but also their debt to Caesar for treating them almost as well as if they had been on the winning side is psychologically perhaps not entirely implausible, but it also obviously serves Nicolaus's agenda to depict the conspirators as morally vicious for their perverse reciprocation of Caesar's kindness. In that case it may be a damning imputation rather than authentic testimony. Somewhat similar perhaps was Q. Ligarius's source of resentment, who is reported by Plutarch to have been not so thankful for

[219] Plut. *Cat. Min.* 25.2, 37.1 = *FRHist* 2.1024–1029 (cf. 1.536): Paetus in turn relied heavily on the eulogistic biography of Cato by his loyal friend, Munatius Rufus. See Rauh 2018: 66–71, who notes that Plutarch's account "is a noteworthy example of the expansion of history" over time, in this case strongly influenced with so-called *exitus* literature recounting in laudatory fashion admirable deaths of aristocrats under tyrannical emperors (p. 67).

[220] Cic. *Off.* 1.110–112. Note Cato's criticism of Cicero when he arrived in Macedonia (Chapter 7, n. 305). "For himself [Cato] it would have been disgraceful to abandon the political line he had chosen from the beginning" (Plut. *Cic.* 38.1–2). Cf. Rauh 2018: 74–80.

[221] Nic. Dam. *Bios* 62. Toher 2017: ad loc.: "N. alone cites Caesar's clemency as a significant source of irritation that led directly to his assassination."

his acquittal by Caesar after Thapsus as he was angry at the power that had brought him into such danger in the first place.[222] Again, this statement is of uncertain evidentiary value (most likely, a simple conjecture to explain paradoxical action), but since the "power" described here was evidently the victor's power after Thapsus over the defeated, at its root we may again have a version of Konstan's "resentment of defeat" rather than of pardon or leniency as such. Ultimately there is no way to get into the minds of contemporaries to the extent that would be necessary to weigh seriously these kinds of hidden resentments against Konstan's rather straightforward suggestion that "it is defeat, not clemency, that galls." But it is surprising that in the absence of better evidence scholars have been so swift to embrace the theory that to be treated magnanimously in defeat was such a powerful source of hatred. However that may be, Caesar's assassination was certainly motivated by much more than this (Chapter 9).

More illuminating are the arguments Cicero makes in his letters to M. Marcellus as the groundwork was being prepared for the latter's pardon in October 46 (n. 205), apparently seeking to ensure that when the pardon came through he would in fact accept it. Since Marcellus was perceived as somewhat reluctant to cooperate although two years had passed since Pharsalus, this is where, if anywhere, the supposed obligation of beneficiaries of Caesar's "leniency" to submit to a state of permanent subjection would need to be addressed, however diplomatically. Cicero urges Marcellus to "come round to the view I take in my own case, that if there is to be some form of commonwealth, you ought to be in it, as one of its leaders in virtue of public opinion and reality, but of necessity yielding to the conditions of the time." And if there is to be no commonwealth, then it is anyway better to be in Rome than to be in exile, for there is nowhere that Caesar's domination does not reach.[223] But Cicero assures him that "even he in whom all power resides is well disposed towards talent; and as for birth and rank, he cherishes them so far as circumstances and his own political position allow."[224] There follow two further letters, still apparently before Marcellus's pardon was approved, in which Cicero continues to urge upon an apparently skeptical recipient only what he

---

[222] Plut. *Brut.* 11.2 ἀλλὰ δ᾽ ἦν ἐκινδύνευσεν ἀρχὴν βαρυνόμενος.

[223] Cic. *Fam.* 4.8.2 (perhaps August 46): *si sit aliqua res publica, in ea te esse oportere iudicio hominum reque principem, necessitate cedentem tempori* .... *Si enim libertatem sequimur, qui locus hoc dominatu vacat?* He reverts more expansively to this point in the next letter (4.7.4). Cf. 4.9.1: *ut in ea re publica quaecumque est quam primum velis esse.*

[224] Ibid.: *etiam is qui omnia tenet favet ingeniis, nobilitatem vero et dignitates hominum, quantum ei res et ipsius causa concedit, amplectitur.*

claims to be "conducive to your welfare and . . . not incompatible with your honor."[225] He had chosen a middle way, taking Pompey's side but holding aloof from the diehards in Africa, "but there is a limit, so at least it seems to me, to your present line of conduct; especially as I believe there is nothing except lack of will to hinder you from the enjoyment of all that is yours."[226] Cicero underlines his point by adding that "the personage in whose hands power lies" (i.e. Caesar) hesitates in authorizing his return only for "fear that you might not regard it as a favour at all."[227] Why? Perhaps he may not want to lay eyes on the current state of Rome?[228] But perhaps he is "afraid of having yourself to say things you do not mean, or do things you disapprove."[229] Here perhaps we finally come to the heart of the matter for a proud aristocrat and a consular. But note Cicero's response: first, yielding to necessity has always been a mark of the wise man (*sapientis*); second, "This particular evil, at present anyway, is not in the case. One is not free, it may be, to say what one thinks, but one is quite free to keep silence."[230] The victor now holds sole power and does as he wishes, much as Pompey would have done as well had he been victorious. "If he were now supreme, do you suppose he would feel any need of your opinions?"[231] Civil war is necessarily harsh, and victory is harsher still, for it makes even a mild victor crueler by necessity.[232] Pompey would have been cruel in victory; would Marcellus have stayed away then? "If refusal to supplicate the victor was nobility of spirit, are you sure it is not arrogance to spurn his generosity?"[233]

   It is clear that Cicero is working hard to make the idea of reconciliation more palatable to one who was not just a proud aristocrat but one with whom Caesar had been especially angry, and who had continued to manifest in exile an aloof coolness that the Dictator himself had characterized as "bitterness"

---

[225] Cic. *Fam.* 4.7.1: *et saluti tuae conducere arbitrarer et non aliena esse ducerem a dignitate.*

[226] Ibid. §3: *sed habet ista ratio, ut mihi quidem videtur, quendam modum, praesertim cum nihil tibi deesse arbitrer ad tuas fortunas omnis obtinendas praeter voluntatem.* Cicero insists further that Marcellus's property remains untouched (§5) – although it might not remain safe from "pirates" (*praedones*: presumably hungry Caesarians, like Antony, although Manutius thought of Marcellus's own relatives: Shackleton Bailey 1977: 2:396) for long.

[227] Ibid. §3: *quod vereretur ne tu illud beneficium omnino non putares.*   [228] Ibid., §4, 4.9.1.

[229] Cic. *Fam.* 4.9.2: *At tibi ipsi dicendum erit aliquid quod non sentias aut faciendum quod non probes.*

[230] Ibid.: *deinde non habet, ut nunc quidem est, id viti res. Dicere fortasse quae sentias non licet, tacere plane licet.*

[231] Ibid.: *non multo secus fieret si is rem publicam teneret quem secuti sumus . . . .nunc omnia tenentem nostras sententias desideraturum censes fuisse?*

[232] Ibid. §3: *omnia sunt misera in bellis civilibus . . . sed miserius nihil quam ipsa victoria; quae etiam si ad meliores venit, tamen eos ferociores impotentioresque reddit, ut, etiam si natura tales non sint, necessitate esse cogantur.*

[233] Ibid. §4: *Si fuit magni animi non esse supplicem victori, vide ne superbi sit aspernari eiusdem liberalitatem.*

(*acerbitas*) despite the distinct prospect of his restoration.[234] He does not try to pretend that defeat has no consequences. He acknowledges that at least for the present the complete independence of a proud consular is impossible. Yet note what he does not say. He does not say that Marcellus would be forced to abase himself or be browbeaten daily with reminders of his submission and ongoing demands for obedience. He would need to keep his counsel on some matters, but would not be forced to toe a line. Life for a consular in Rome is still better than in Mytilene. Nor does he suggest that the current state of affairs marked by the dominance of the victorious party in the immediate aftermath of a civil war is a permanent one. Eventually a proper *res publica* may return, and men like Marcellus and himself will be needed then; in the meantime, it is better to be at home in the enjoyment of his property than to remain in self-imposed exile. If acceptance of "Caesar's clemency" would have been an unthinkable act of abasement for a Roman aristocrat, Cicero could hardly have written to Marcellus (and the others) in the way he does.

Marcellus's cousin Gaius, the consul of 50 with whom at least before the war Caesar had as much reason to be angry as anyone, had for some time been urging him to reconcile; when Cicero had joined in urging this course, Marcellus had at last agreed.[235] The matter was resolved in a spectacular, even ceremonial way sometime in October after the celebrations that followed the series of four triumphs and the dedication of the Temple of Venus Genetrix.[236] In a meeting of the Senate Caesar's father-in-law, L. Piso, had raised the issue of Marcellus's restoration, and with C. Marcellus falling at his feet and the entire Senate rising up to join in making the request he had little choice but to approve the step.[237] After the matter was transacted Marcellus wrote to thank Cicero with a letter that, brief as it is, is also illuminating. Grumbling no more (except at the relative inertia of his other friends and relatives), Marcellus does not begrudge "his dearest friend" (*amicissimo*) Cicero a full measure of gratitude for his "good will" (*benevolentia*) and singular pursuit of his "well-being" (*salus*).[238] He graciously and flatteringly asserts that nothing else was of very great importance to him "given the times."[239] To return to Rome and the Senate where his recent enemy was triumphant and the role of senior consulars still quite unclear cannot of course

[234] Cic. *Fam.* 4.4.3; cf. 4.9.4, quoted last n. Anger: 4.6.10 (to Caecina): *Marcellum, cui maxime suscensebat.*
[235] Marcellus, [Cic.] *Fam.* 4.11.1. For *C. Marcellus frater* (= cousin) see 4.4.3; the consul of 49 was dead.
[236] For the games and banquets see briefly Itgenshorst 2005: 371–372; also n. 303. For the triumphs in general see n. 118. Dedication of temple of Venus Genetrix: Chapter 9, n. 50.
[237] Cic. *Fam.* 4.4.3.   [238] Marcellus, [Cic.] *Fam.* 4.11.1–2.
[239] Ibid.: *reliqua sunt eius modi quibus ego, quoniam haec erant tempora, facile et aequo animo carebam.* See Shackleton Bailey's n. ad loc.

have been an easy thing; Cicero acknowledges that there may be some people he would rather not lay eyes upon.[240] (As it happens, however, Marcellus never made it home.)[241] But if Marcellus or Cicero, who was already there, actually viewed returning to Rome as necessarily adopting a position of veiled or open servitude it is hard to imagine either that the latter (together with Marcellus's consular cousin) could have so earnestly advocated it, and the former to have been so gracious about receiving this boon. Somewhere in this correspondence, or in that which Cicero was soon exchanging with various other ex-Pompeians hopeful of their return, we should have come across something more like what Brutus was to write to Cicero a few years later about the prospect of returning to Rome by concession of Caesar's unworthy heir: "It would be better not to survive than to survive by his leave."[242]

Apparently, then, from Cicero's point of view and that of the senators who pressed Marcellus's restoration upon Caesar in that meeting of October 46, the victor's "clemency" was something worth seeking even for a consular of Marcellus's status. As Cicero's advocacy and the great mass of senators who stood up to plead Marcellus's case show, it was now not just the affected individuals in themselves who petitioned for their return but a larger circle of senators, perhaps even most of the Senate, who saw the restoration of the remaining ex-Pompeians as a good thing. The ideology of *Clementia Caesaris* as presented in the *Pro Marcello* delivered on this occasion may thus be interpreted as an attempt on Cicero's part to bind Caesar to a virtual amnesty of all those who had chosen the Pompeian side in the Civil War. Put simply, the "theory of *clementia*" he presents constructs a moral necessity for *Caesar* to consummate his glory with the full pardon of the former Pompeians, and to make this project appealing he imposes on its beneficiaries in return the strongest obligations of gratitude and abiding loyalty. However, as G. Flamerie de Lachapelle observes, even this implicitly "binding" form of "Caesar's Clemency" was intended not "to make of Caesar a monarch of the hellenistic type but to draw him back

---

[240] Cic. *Fam.* 4.10.2: *prorsus tibi ignoscerem si quosdam nolles videre.* Probably the exultant beneficiaries of Caesar's victory like Antony and Dolabella more than Caesar himself.

[241] See n. 321.

[242] Brutus, [Cic.] *Ad Brut.* 1.16.1: *atqui non esse quam esse per illum praestat.* The letter is among those condemned by Shackleton Bailey 1980: 10–14, but Syme 1939: 184n15, Moles 1997, and Osgood 2006: 88n91 accept authenticity. Caesar claims in his *Civil War Commentaries* that Pompey said something rather like this to his advisors when he rejected Caesar's last peace proposal in 48 (Caes. *BCiv.* 3.18.4). Caesar was not present and the scene is probably best interpreted as a bit of negative characterization: since Caesar was in fact not requesting his adversary's surrender at all Pompey comes off as almost pathologically intransigent.

to the Roman tradition of the good citizen, and to set him up as an example of the *sapiens*."[243]

After the last campaign of the Civil War, among the vast number of honors decreed to Caesar to make an auspicious start to the following peace, an official cult of "Clementia Caesaris" was established, complete with a temple, and celebrated on the coinage.[244] As we shall see in the next chapter, these rather extravagant honors cannot simply be assumed to have been initiated or even prompted by Caesar himself. Cicero's own *Pro Marcello* may reasonably be seen as the foundation document of the new cult, and Stefan Weinstock intriguingly suggested that the chief agent of the cult's institution may have been none other than Cicero himself.[245] Plutarch writes that Cicero "was foremost among those who advocated Caesar's honours and were eager to be ever saying something new about him and his measures,"[246] and it is indisputable that the honor with which Cicero is most prominently associated is the celebration of "Caesar's Clemency" toward the end of the wars. As we have seen, shortly after Thapsus, and then with greater intensity after articulating the ideology of "Caesar's Clemency" in the *Pro Marcello*, Cicero had thrown himself with notable passion into the effort to make this vision of leniency plausible to the exiles themselves in a long series of letters encouraging them to request pardon (directly or, like Marcellus, through other agents at home), to hope for it or for its full realization with his help, and, when this was forthcoming, to congratulate them.[247] This mass of correspondence provides no evidence that Caesar himself specifically prompted Cicero to take up this cause or given it his prior blessing; if that had been the case Cicero would have made the point conspicuously to the men he was seeking to coax, encourage, and reassure. Instead, Cicero "reads the signs" and interprets them for his correspondents; in general, he takes it as given that it suited

[243] Flamerie 2011: 93.

[244] *RRC* 480/21; Plut. *Caes.* 57.4 ('Επιείκεια), App. *BCiv.* 2.106/443, Dio 44.6.4; see Davies 2017: 255–256. It seems apparent that the new statue of Caesar wearing the *corona civica* placed on the Rostra in late 45 or the beginning of 44 was likewise an allusion to his leniency in the civil wars, assimilating the act of restraint in *sparing* errant fellow citizens to the kind of lifesaving heroism honored by the martial decoration: Sehlmeyer 1999: 231–234. The statue may also feature on the Dictator's coinage: *RRC* 452/1 (48 BC), now with B. Woytek 2003, 137n528. On the adjustment of the significance of the *corona civica* see Plin. *HN* 16.7 with Weinstock 1971: 163–167.

[245] Weinstock 1971: 238–239. Cf. also Griffin 2003: 163.

[246] Plut. *Cic.* 40.4–5; *Caes.* 57.2. Historians seem skeptical about Plutarch's assertion (Pelling 2011: 426; Lintott 2013: 196), yet the *Pro Marcello* itself and Cicero's praise for the restoration of the statues of Pompey and Sulla (n. 209) strongly suggest his prominence among those proposing honors for Caesar after his final return (Chapter 9, n. 100).

[247] See p. 439ff. and for a list of the main recipients, n. 119.

Caesar's ends to reintegrate the exiles and, among many lamentations of the state of the Republic that are hardly surprising in an adherent of the defeated side in a civil war, he occasionally allows his hope of a "revived" *res publica* to shine through.[248] In this light the new cult of *Clementia Caesaris* may be best interpreted as a (rather strenuous) effort by senators to reassure Caesar of their loyalty at the fraught moment of his return from the civil wars, and to define Caesar's victory in precisely the terms he had espoused at the time of Corfinium: a "new kind of victory" made more durable than the Sullan precedent by rejecting "cruelty" and relying on the "defense" provided by "mercy and generosity."[249] What had begun as Caesar's policy for winning the peace had become the Senate's means, in effect, of holding him to his promise.

It may be that, once safely restored to their fortunes and positions, some of the beneficiaries of this policy did actually come to resent the fact that they had been "forced" to make use of it. But the idea that leniency as such was something exceedingly *unwelcome* to those who took such full advantage of it seems, frankly, perverse, especially in the face of the large number (more than sixty) of those who seized upon it with alacrity or begged for it when it was less forthcoming. While such a large throng accepted it – a large proportion indeed of all known senators who took the Pompeian side – not a single case is known of a Pompeian rejecting Caesar's offer of leniency when it was given.[250] If Caesar's pardon had in itself been repugnant to republican aristocrats' sensibility, surely they would not have resorted to it so frequently and with such alacrity.

---

[248] Hopes may be glimpsed occasionally in the letters to ex-Pompeians written in the summer of 46: e.g. Cic. *Fam.* 4.4.3 (Sulpicius, September–October 46): *ut speciem aliquam viderer videre quasi reviviscentis rei publicae*; 6.10.5 (Trebianus): *ipsa causa ea est ut iam simul cum re publica, quam in perpetuum iacere non potest, necessario reviviscat atque recreetur*; cf. 4.8.2 (M. Marcellus, August 46): *si sit aliqua res publica, in ea te esse oportere*, 6.12.4 (Ampius Balbus, August or September 46): *nisi eam [spem] quam ab ipsa re publica, cum hic ardor restinctus esset, sperari oportere censerem.* Cicero's mood notably darkens after the revival of the wars in Spain, but even then he is still capable of envisioning some kind of "revival" of the Republic when writing to Torquatus in April 45 (6.2.2,): *si armis aut condicione positis aut defatigatione abiectis aut victoria detractis civibus respiravit* [sc. *res publica*], *et dignitate tua frui tibi et fortunis licebit.* In retrospect he could write to Brutus in July 43: *nullum enim bellum civile fuit in nostra re publica omnium quae memoria mea fuerunt, in quo bello non, utracumque pars vicisset, tamen aliqua forma esset futura rei publicae* (*Ad Brut.* 1.15.10). In 46 and later Cicero made much of his connections with Caesar's closest advisors: Shackleton Bailey 1998.

[249] See p. 458ff.

[250] Cato, of course, had not surrendered or been offered leniency. Bruhns 1978: 60 identifies eighty-nine "Pompeian" senators. Two instances are known when *Caesarian* soldiers or officers rejected Metellus Scipio's offer of leniency: Caesar's quaestor Petro (executed: Val. Max. 3.8.7 with *Bell. Afr.* 28, 44–46), and his centurion Titius (suicide: Plut. *Caes.* 16.8–9; cf. Suet. *Iul.* 68.1, with Pelling 2011, 213). Rauh 2012: 61–62 ##45–46.

Nor indeed would it be easy to make sense of Pompey's own, belated effort to win credit for comparable behavior, for before the battle of Pharsalus he made a public pledge, proposed by none other than Cato, to spare any Roman save those who met him on the field of battle, and not to plunder any provincial city. "This brought to the party of Pompey a good repute, and induced many to join it; they embraced his clemency and mildness."[251] And even after *clementia* had come to be associated so closely with Caesar that a temple of *Clementia Caesaris* had been decreed, after the killing of the "tyrant" it was Cato's nephew M. Brutus, the moral leader of the "tyrannicides," who argued the case for *lenitas* and *clementia* against Cicero's urging, in some of his last extant letters, to stop "trying to win praise [n.b.] by your clemency towards those you have defeated in war" and at last to put to death Mark Antony's brother Gaius, whom he had captured.[252] While Brutus had upheld Caesar's methods, Cicero vigorously rejected them: "If we want to be merciful, we shall never be without a civil war."[253] Caesar's own followers repudiated his policy in the aftermath of the assassination: "Clemency had been his downfall; if he had not practiced it nothing of that kind would have happened to him."[254] A century later Pliny the Elder more or less agreed while still granting that Caesar outdid all the great figures of Roman history in *clementia* and *magnanimitas*.[255] They did not mean of course that Caesar's "clemency" had been so insulting to its recipients that it proved counterproductive, but that his enemies had exploited his leniency to kill him. *Clementia*, that is, was indisputably a good for its beneficiaries, but there was a serious risk, especially if taken too far, that it might become an evil for the benefactor. That was the risk Caesar ran.

In large part because of Caesar's policy of leniency, this civil war was *much* less bloody than those of Sulla and his enemies, at least among the elite, and probably lower down the social hierarchy as well.[256] But by

---

[251] Plut. *Cat. Min.* 53.6: τὴν ἐπιείκειαν αὐτοῦ καὶ τὸ ἥμερον; also *Pomp.* 65.1. Cato had evacuated Sicily at the outset to spare it the ravages of civil war and later saved the pro-Caesarian population of Utica from Scipio's intended reprisals: Plut. *Cat. Min.* 53.4, 58.1–2 (implicitly conceded by *Bell. Afr.* 88.5).

[252] *Ad Brut.* 2.5.5, 1.2a.2, 1.15.10–11 (Shackleton Bailey 1980: 5, 6, 23). Note that these letters, unlike the two controversial ones, 1.16–17, are almost certainly genuine: Shackleton Bailey 1980: 10–14. Cf. n. 242.

[253] *Ad Brut.* 1.2a.2: *quod si clementes esse volumus, numquam deerunt bella civilia.* This time, he argued, the stakes were too high for *clementia* (1.15.10). Jal 1961: 489–491.

[254] Cic. *Att.* 14.22.1 (paraphrasing the Caesarians): *clementiam illi malo fiusse; qua si usus non esset, nihil ei tale accidere potuisse.*

[255] Plin. *HN* 7.93: *Caesari proprium et peculiare sit ... clementiae insigne, qua usque ad paenitentiam omnes superavit. Idem magnanimitatis perhibuit exemplum.*

[256] See p. 446ff.

carrying out this policy with such consistency and on such a scale, Caesar also took a very real and potentially serious risk that the liberal treatment of his enemies would not constrain their future behavior at all, and even ensured that not a few of them would simply exploit their good luck to fight him another day – or, after the peace, try to kill him, an eventuality against which he declined to protect himself by refusing a bodyguard.[257] Moreover, Caesar did not merely spare his erstwhile enemies but made haste after Pharsalus to *advance* some of them into positions of great responsibility. The ex-praetor P. Sestius, Pompeian proconsul of Cilicia, retained his *imperium* and immediately began service as a Caesarian officer in Asia Minor; the consular Ser. Sulpicius Rufus was soon put in charge of Achaea, where he was officially proconsul by 46; and most extraordinary of all, young M. Brutus, not yet even of praetorian rank, took charge of the militarily crucial province of Cisalpine Gaul while Caesar fought in Africa and Spain.[258] Upon his return from the last campaign of the Civil War, Caesar chose to initiate the postwar era with no fewer than four of his recent adversaries – Brutus, C. Cassius, M. Pupius Piso, and P. Sextius Naso – holding the praetorship, the stepping-stone to the consulship which they were thus encouraged to aspire to within only three years.[259] This might be dismissed as co-opting the opposition, but that understates the risk he took in placing recent enemies in positions that demanded a high level of trust. That Brutus held the prestigious post of *urban praetor*, for example, played no small role in the development of the conspiracy.[260] Caesar's policy of leniency thus greatly reduced the benefits (both property and *honores*) he would be in a position to distribute after victory to his loyal followers, men who had staked everything on him, while correspondingly increasing the number of people it would be necessary to gratify or placate. This was a dangerous dynamic to which he cannot have been blind: another risk, perhaps the greatest of all.

Caesar's famous policy of leniency has suffered from teleological hindsight even more than other aspects of his career. Retrospective projection from the imperial "clemency" of the Caesars, or even from Cicero's vision

[257] App. *BCiv.* 2.107/444; Plut. *Caes.* 57.7; Suet. *Iul.* 86.1; Dio 44.7.4; Nic. Dam. *Bios* 80.

[258] Sestius: *MRR* 2.278. Sulpicius had not taken a strong stand but had ultimately shown his Pompeian sympathies: Chapter 7. Brutus: *MRR* 2.301; n. 295. Cassius, the future Caesaricide, was quickly made a legate, something Cicero thinks worthy of emphasis to Caecina: Cic. *Fam.* 6.6.10.

[259] Bruhns 1978: 156; cf. 54, nos. 29 (*MRR* 3.199, n.b. App. *BCiv.* 2.113/474: ἐκ τῶν οἰκείων σφίσιν), 35 (Piso was evidently son of the homonymous consul of 61; *MRR* 3.177).

[260] Morstein-Marx 2012: 204–213.

of *clementia Caesaris* articulated toward the end of the civil wars even as Caesar's own pardons were sputtering to their end point, has resulted in various misconceptions. *Lenitas, clementia, mansuetudo,* and *misericordia* were not objectionable to the Roman aristocracy but were virtuous in themselves and welcomed by their beneficiaries. By employing these virtues in a war between citizens, Caesar was not attempting to humiliate his former enemies but to encourage them to take his view of the conflict, that it was a regrettable and forgettable disagreement among citizens (*civilis dissensio*) to be put aside as soon as possible. No doubt this had prudential, self-serving reasons: he hoped that this would shorten the war, just as did Lincoln with his policy of leniency toward the Southern Confederacy, though often at the price of immediate military advantage. But it is also credible that, like Lincoln, Caesar hoped the policy of "leniency" would lead to a more secure and lasting peace once victory had been achieved. This looks like a vision of peace that depends on the future participation of the defeated rather than on the imposition and policing of an ongoing state of subjection.[261] Would the actions of a staunchly "republican" victor in a civil war have been very different?

Catalog of the Beneficiaries of Caesar's "Leniency" in the Civil Wars of 49–45

The following list names the individuals (or in one instance [#9] a specific group of unnamed individuals), generally of senatorial families but including a few named *equites*, whom Caesar released after their capture or surrender, or pardoned after their defeat (or the defeat of the side they had taken). Nearly all the names are collected from the important prior studies by Alföldi, Bruhns, Jehne, and Raaflaub.[262] This is, I believe, the first such list and it cannot claim to be definitive. Six persons are known to have been released or pardoned twice and are therefore listed twice at appropriate points in the list. Note also that some of these individuals, especially those who appear toward the end

---

[261] The connection between Caesar's leniency and "the revival of the Republic" is made explicit in Cicero's letter to Sulpicius about the pardon of M. Marcellus: *Fam.* 4.4.3 (September or October 46). Cf. B. Woytek 2003: 202: "Caesar's *clementia* should be understood as the political conception of a far-sighted statesman who was aware that he would not be able to manage and govern the empire with his followers alone, and who therefore, in order to overcome the political division of the Roman elite, did not wish to eliminate or entirely crush his enemies but on the contrary to integrate them into the state."

[262] Alföldi 1985: 173–386 is fundamental, though somewhat vitiated by the author's Caesarian zeal. See also Raaflaub 1974, especially 293–316; Bruhns 1978: 30–63; Jehne 1987 and 1987a.

of the list, may not have been formally pardoned in Caesar's lifetime but (together probably with numerous others unknown) simply have been allowed to continue their lives without harassment.

Italy, 49

1) L. Pupius, *primus pilus* under Attius Varus, captured and returned to Pompey at Auximum (February 49): Caes. *BCiv.* 1.13.4–5.

2) L. Vibullius Rufus, an *eques* and one of Pompey's *praefecti fabrum* captured (for the first time) at Corfinium and freed with the others.[263] He made his way to the Pompeian forces in Spain and was there captured again (#11).

3) L. Domitius Ahenobarbus (cos. 54), freed after surrender at Corfinium (Caes. *BCiv.* 1.23 etc.).[264] In addition, Caesar probably returned to Domitius all or nearly all of his war chest, HS 6 million of public money.[265] After Corfinium Domitius returned to the fight first at Massilia, then, after abandoning the Massilians to their fate, he escaped to Pompey. He is recorded by Caesar and probably Pollio to have laid claim in Pompey's camp to Caesar's pontificate and to have urged in the war council severe reprisals against all who had remained in Rome or not given sufficient support to Pompey.[266] Domitius commanded the Pompeian left at Pharsalus and was killed in the rout.[267]

4) Cn. Domitius Ahenobarbus, son of Lucius (#3), the future cos. 32 and great-grandfather to Nero, was freed after the surrender at Corfinium and appears to have gone directly to join Pompey, unlike his father.[268] He was pardoned yet again after Pharsalus (#38).

---

[263] Caes. *BCiv.* 1.34.1: in Pompey's active service within days of his release. Although Bruhns 1978: 54 n. 28 identifies Vibullius as a senator, his absence from the list at 1.23.2 makes this improbable (Shackleton Bailey 1965: 4:320; Carter 1991: 1:173). *Praefectus fabrum*: implicit at Caes. [Cic.] *Att.* 9.7C.2; not noted at *MRR* 2.271.

[264] Lucan (2.507–525) makes Domitius the captive of his own troops and thus *forced* to surrender while actually *fearing* clemency and hoping for punishment. It is true enough that his troops handed him over to Caesar, but Lucan could have no idea of his true state of mind, and we may readily suppose that this is an attempt to minimize the humiliation of Nero's ancestor, about whose surrender some highly discreditable stories circulated (see Sen. *Ben.* 3.2; Plut. *Caes.* 34.6–8; Suet. *Ner.* 2.3, etc. with Pelling 2011: 327–328). Lucan can hardly be used to "suppl[y]" something of what Caesar leaves out" regarding the significance of the "pardon" (so Batstone and Damon 2006: 141).

[265] See n. 56.   [266] *BCiv.* 3.83; cf. Plut. *Caes.* 42.2; Pomp. 67.9; App. *BCiv.* 2.69/285.

[267] See n. 74.   [268] Münzer, *RE* 5 [1903], 1328). Ramsey 2003: 202–203.

5) P. Lentulus Spinther (cos. 57), freed after the surrender at Corfinium.[269]
Lentulus joined Pompey again after some hesitation and quarreled with
Domitius over Caesar's priesthood before Pharsalus, but he probably
was *not* the "Lentulus" who commanded a wing in the battle.[270]
Spinther fled Macedonia with Pompey; after being shut out of
Rhodes's harbor he may have sought Caesar's pardon through his
son's mediation, although it is possible that he declined to do so while
sending his son on to Alexandria to save himself (#39).[271] Lentulus *père*
was captured and executed probably by Ptolemy in the aftermath of
Pompey's murder in Egypt.[272]

6) L. Caecilius Rufus (pr. 57), freed after the surrender at Corfinium
(Caes. *BCiv.* 1.23.2).

7) Sex. Quinctilius Varus (q. 49), freed after the surrender at Corfinium
(ibid.). Varus fled to Africa, was ultimately captured a second time,
and again spared (#50), probably in 46.[273]

8) L. Rubrius, a senator, freed after surrender at Corfinium (ibid.).

9) "Many other young men [presumably of senatorial families] along with
a great number of Roman knights and decurions" were freed after
surrender at Corfinium (Caes. *BCiv.* 1.23.2).[274] (These will have included
Vibullius Rufus and the younger Domitius [##2, 4] among others.)

10) N. Magius, *praefectus fabrum* to Pompey, captured and freed with
a peace message to Pompey. Caesar already in March 49 describes
Magius's immediate release as "in accordance with my practice" (*meo
instituto usus*).[275]

---

[269] Caes. *BCiv.* 1.22–23.

[270] Caes. *BCiv.* 3.83.1; cf. Cic. *Att.* 9.11.1, etc. Pharsalus: App. *BCiv.* 2.76/316 with Pelling 2011: 265 (probably Crus, cos. 49 and still proconsul).

[271] Plut. *Pomp.* 73.9. Cic. *Att.* 11.13.1 with Shackleton Bailey ad loc.; cf. Caes., *BCiv.* 3.102.7; *Fam.* 12.14.3.

[272] Jehne 1987: 336n147, contra Vir. *Ill.* 78.9 and Bruhns 1978: 38–39 n. 4. Cf. the fate of L. Lentulus Crus (cos. 49, Caes. *BCiv.* 3.104.3, Plut. *Pomp.* 80.6 etc.), as well as of Q. Pompeius Bithynicus (Oros. 6.15.28).

[273] Caes. *BCiv.* 2.28.1, Cic. *Phil.* 13.30. Jehne 1987: 324. This was probably the Quinctilius Varus who killed himself after Philippi (Vell. Pat. 2.71.2, 2.119.3; but cf. App. *BCiv.* 4.74/313 "Lucius"), father of the cos. 13 BC (Publius) who committed suicide at Teutoburg Forest.

[274] Our manuscripts unanimously give the numeral "50" before the list of names (starting with five senators) given at Caes. *BCiv.* 1.23.2 and listed earlier. The numeral has usually been emended to *quinque*, which is in fact the number of senators Caesar lists (cf. Klotz's Teubner and Du Pontet's 1908 OCT), although Kraner and Hofmann retained *quinquaginta* and Damon's 2015 OCT rejects both. Batstone-Damon 2006: 24, however, retains "50." If that numeral is right, it would of course greatly increase the number of known examples of Caesar's clemency. Note also that Caesar mentions *senatorum liberi* (1.23.1) in the plural, although he mentions by name only the younger L. Domitius. The younger Lentulus Spinther seems another likely candidate: n. 271 and #39.

[275] Caes. *BCiv.* 1.24.4 (not at Corfinium, as per Batstone-Damon 2006: 67); Caes. ap. Cic. *Att.* 9.7C.2.

Spain, 49

11) L. Vibullius Rufus (#2), captured again, evidently in Spain, brought
by Caesar to Epirus in 48 and returned to Pompey with a peace
message, with whom he apparently remained.[276]

12) L. Afranius (cos. 60), legate of Pompey in Spain, surrendered and
released by Caesar with a pointed complaint about M. Petreius's
(#13) savage punishment of soldiers who had fraternized with
Caesar's army.[277] Afranius then rejoined Pompey with some of the
Spanish legions which Pompey thought the most reliable of his
troops at Pharsalus (Caes. *BCiv.* 3.88.3–4); he subsequently fled to
Africa, was captured by P. Sittius, and killed (p. 435f.).

13) M. Petreius (pr. 64), legate of Pompey in Spain, surrendered and
released with Afranius (#12). Joined Pompey in Greece, fled to Africa
after Pharsalus and committed suicide after Thapsus.[278]

14) M. Terentius Varro (*pr. incerto anno*), the great antiquarian and author,
legate of Pompey in charge of Hither Spain. Varro surrendered to Caesar
at Corduba and was released, since he soon joined Pompey (as did
Afranius and Petreius), and was pardoned again after Pharsalus (#21).[279]

15) P. Ligarius, an "Afranian" captured and released in Spain.[280] P. Ligarius
next joined Pompey and fled to Africa after Pharsalus, but was captured at sea and put to death *ob periuri perfidiam* (*Bell. Afr.* 64.1).

Greece, 48

16) M. Tullius Cicero, cos. 63.[281] One of only two senators from the
Pompeian side allowed to return to Italy immediately (Cic. *Att.*
11.7.2), although subsequently Cicero found himself confined by
order of Antony in Brundisium until he was explicitly authorized
to return to Rome.

17) M. Tullius Cicero, son of the preceding and cos. 30. Had commanded
a cavalry squadron (*ala*) at Pharsalus (Cic. *Off.* 2.45). After his pardon
he was invited to accompany Caesar to Spain for the Munda campaign (Cic. *Att.* 12.7–8), but his father dissuaded him. He later fought

---

[276] Plut. Pomp. 65.5; Caes. *BCiv.* 1.34.1, 1.38.1, 3.10.1–2, 3.18.4. Vibullius now disappears from history.
[277] Caes. *BCiv.* 1.84.5–85 (cf. 1.75–76); App. *BCiv.* 2.43/172–174; Plut. *Pomp.* 65.3; Dio 41.23.1–2.
[278] Vell. Pat. 2.50.4; Dio 42.13.3–4. See n. 98.
[279] Caes. *BCiv.* 2.20.7–8; Liv. Per. 110; Cic. *Div.* 1.68, 2.114; *Fam.* 9.5.2, 9.6.3.
[280] *Bell. Afr.* 64.1. See n. 100.
[281] Cic. Att. 11.5–7; Plut. Cic. 39.1–2; Dio 42.10.2. See Shackleton Bailey 1965: 5:270, and nn. 85, 86.

for Brutus at Philippi but held a suffect consulship in the first year of the post-Actian age.

18) Q. Tullius Cicero, pr. 62 and legate of his brother Marcus.[282]

19) Q. Tullius Cicero, son of Quintus (#18) (Cic. *Att.* 11.20.1).

20) Ser. Sulpicius Rufus, cos. 51. Sulpicius played no significant role in the war, but his failure to link up with the Pompeian army and to participate in its ordeal suggests that the Pompeians would not have regarded him as one of them.[283] Yet he had withdrawn from Italy to Samos before 47, surely in 49; thus his recruitment to become Caesar's governor of Achaea should probably still be considered an act of pardon and leniency.

21) M. Terentius Varro (#14) pardoned a second time after Pharsalus (he was among those who had remained at Dyrrachium), probably in 47.[284]

22) L. Lucceius (pr. 67), evidently a close advisor to Pompey, pardoned and his property returned after Pharsalus.[285]

23) P. Sestius, Cicero's former client, *pr. anno incerto* and *promag.* Cilicia. He joined the Caesarians and retained his *imperium*.[286]

24) L. Aelius Tubero, the historian, *pr. anno incerto* and *promag.* Africa, pardoned sometime after Pharsalus.[287]

25) Q. Aelius Tubero, son of Lucius (#24), the future jurist, also pardoned after Pharsalus (see n. 287).

26) P. Silius, *pr. anno incerto* and *propr.* Bithynia-Pontus 51–50.[288]

27) M. Favonius, pr. 49, Cato's loyal follower, fled Pharsalus with Pompey and was pardoned after Pompey's death. He eventually returned to Italy (Plut. *Brut.* 12.2).

28) L. Scribonius Libo, *pr. anno incerto*, chief advisor and probably legate of Pompey 49–48, already or soon to be father-in-law to

---

[282] Quintus and Quintus Jr. sailed after Caesar to make their peace: Cic. *Att.* 11.6.7, 8.2, 20.1.

[283] See Chapter 7, pp. 375ff.

[284] Cic. *Fam.* 9.1–6, *Phil.* 2.104; cf. Suet. *Iul.* 44.2. Shackleton Bailey 1977: 2:310–311; Jehne 1987: 320. His property appears to have been sequestered but not sold (Cic. *Phil.* 2.103–104), though Antony appears to have taken possession of his Casinum estate and still to have occupied it in May 44 (Jehne, p. 332). Varro's estate was eventually returned to him (Ramsey 2003: 312). B. Woytek 2003: 208.

[285] Cic. *Fam.* 5.13. Pompeian advisor, mentioned in same breath with Theophanes and Libo: Cic. Att. 9.1.3, 11.3, Caes. *BCiv.* 3.18.3. Lucceius had joined (unsuccessfully) with Caesar in a *coitio*, a kind of electoral "ticket" for the consular elections in 60 (Suet. *Iul.* 19.1).

[286] Cic. *Att.* 11.7.1; *Bell. Alex.* 34.5.

[287] Cic. *Lig.* 8–9, 20–29, in 48 according to Elvers, *DNP* Aelius I 14, or at least by 46 (Bruhns 1978: 45 n. 29). *MRR* 3.4. For the two Tuberones see Oakley, *FRHist* 1.361–364.

[288] Cic. *Att.* 10.13.3 with Bruhns 1978: 44 n. 10, contra Shackleton Bailey 1960: 265n2. Silius's pardon (already complete in early 45, if Shackleton Bailey rightly identifies this Silius as the man whose *horti* Cicero considered buying for Tullia's *fanum*: 1965: 5.407–409) might belong after Thapsus rather than Pharsalus. Whether our Silius had a cognomen (Nerva?) is uncertain: Shackleton Bailey 1965: 3:246.

Pompey's son Sextus. Eventually pardoned, probably after Pharsalus but in any case before December 46.[289]

29) C. Messius, aed. pl. 55, probably pardoned after Pharsalus.[290]

30) D. Laelius, tr. pl. 54, pardoned after Pharsalus (Cic. *Att.* 11.14.1). The only other ex-Pompeian senator besides Cicero immediately allowed to return to Italy (cf. #16).

31) L. Cassius, naval prefect?, whose surrender near the Hellespont is often confused with that of C. Cassius, the future conspirator.[291]

32) C. Cassius Longinus, the future Caesaricide, q. 53, tr. pl. 49 and naval prefect, at first withdrew to Rhodes but probably met Caesar and gained his pardon through the intercession of Brutus (#33) on his way to confront Pharnaces in July 47. Caesar made him his legate.[292]

33) M. Iunius Brutus (adoptive name: Q. Servilius Caepio), the Caesaricide, q. probably 54[293] and legate of Sestius in Cilicia in 49.[294] Already when Caesar set off for the African campaign in the fall of 47 he put Brutus in charge of the crucial province of Cisalpine Gaul.[295] M. Dettenhofer argues that Brutus "had become a committed Caesarian" and played an important role as mediator between Caesar and the defeated Pompeians.[296]

34) L. Mescinius Rufus, Cicero's quaestor in Cilicia in 51–50, was allowed to return to Italy between Pharsalus and Thapsus, but in April 46 still suffered under some disability. Perhaps he was not yet permitted to return to Rome.[297]

---

[289] Cic. *Fam.* 7.4. Shackleton Bailey 1965: 4:302; Pettinger 2012: 226–228 (but Libo's meeting with Cicero and Brutus on Sex. Pompeius's behalf dates to July 44, not 45); cf. *MRR* 3.187. Pompeian advisor: Caes. *BCiv.* 1.26.3–5; 3.15–18. Libo's daughter married Pompey's son Sextus at an uncertain date probably during the Civil War (Welch 2012: 114; cf. Gruen 1974: 108n63; Pettinger 2012,: 226n38).

[290] Bruhns 1978: 49; cf. *Bell. Afr.* 33, 43.

[291] *MRR* 2.283; Suet. *Iul.* 63, Dio 46.6.2, cf. App. *BCiv.* 2.88, 111 (but the future Caesaricide was operating off Sicily and southern Italy: Caes. *BCiv.* 3.101). Strictly speaking, we are not told what happened to this Cassius, but the stories clearly imply that he was spared in the usual manner.

[292] Dio 42.13.1, 5; Cic. *Fam.* 15.15.1–2; *Att.* 11.13.1, 15.2; cf. *Fam.* 6.6.10. Shackleton Bailey 1977: 2:309; Dettenhofer 1992: 214–18; Ramsey 2003: 202. Brutus: Plut. *Brut.* 6.6. Caesar gave each of his followers permission to intercede for one of the captives (presumably not covered by the other guarantees: Suet. *Iul.* 75.2; Plut. *Caes.* 46.4; Dio 41.62.1–3. Legate: *MRR* 2.290.

[293] *MRR* 3.112, correcting 2.229.

[294] Surrender: Plut. *Brut.* 6.1–2, 56.4; *Caes.* 46.4, 62.3; Dio 41.63.6; Vell. 2.52.5. Dettenhofer 1992: 194–197; Tempest 2017: 62–77.

[295] Plut. *Brut.* 6.6–7; App. *BCiv.* 2.111/465; cf. Plut. *Caes.* 52.2 with Pelling 2011: 400.

[296] Dettenhofer 1992: 204, cf. 197–211. Tempest 2017 more or less agrees.

[297] Cic. *Fam.* 5.21, 13.26. Shackleton Bailey 1977: 2:319.

35) T. Antistius, q. 50, supposedly an involuntary Pompeian caught by circumstance in Macedonia at the outbreak of the war, pardoned after Pharsalus (Cic. *Fam.* 13.29.3-4).

36) M. Pupius Piso, q. before 49, son of the homonymous "Pompeian" consul of 61, pardoned probably after Pharsalus.[298]

37) A. Terentius Varro Murena.[299]

38) Cn. Domitius Ahenobarbus the younger (#4), pardoned again after Pharsalus and allowed to return to Italy.[300]

39) P. Cornelius Lentulus Spinther the Younger, son of the consul of 57 (#5) and an augur, apparently pardoned after Pharsalus.[301]

40) Cn. Pompeius Theophanes of Mytilene the historian, Pompey's friend, advisor, and eventual *praefectus fabrum*, was present in Italy in 44 and thus probably pardoned not long after Pompey's death (Cic. *Att.* 15.19.1).[302]

41) Cornelia, Pompey's wife, permitted to return to Rome soon after her husband's murder on King Ptolemy's orders (Dio 42.5.7).

42) C. Lucilius Hirrus, tr. pl. 53, "cousin and faithful follower of Pompey" (Shackleton Bailey), sent by him to the Parthians to gain their assistance or neutrality and pardoned by Caesar by (probably) 46, since he is recorded to have given him six thousand moray eels for his triumphal banquets.[303]

43) Cn. Sallustius, equestrian friend of Cicero (Cic. *Att.* 11.20.2).[304]

---

[298] Joseph. *AJ* 14.231; Cic. *Phil.* 3.25. *MRR* 3.177.

[299] Caes. *BCiv.* 3.19.3, *ILS* 6075. Bruhns 1978: 55 n. 25.

[300] Cic. *Fam.* 6.22.2 with Shackleton Bailey 1977: 2:387. Syme 1958a: 1:414 mistakenly states that Cn. Domitius "refused the victor's pardon," presumably on the basis of Cic. *Phil.* 2.27: *spoliatio dignitatis.* Shackleton Bailey took this to refer to Caesar's failure to "rehabilitate" him, but Ramsey rightly notes that this may be no more than putting a rhetorical spin on Domitius's "failure to take an active role in political life" (2003: 203) under one who had been his father's mortal enemy.

[301] Cic. *Att.* 11.13.1, 12.52.2; *Fam.* 7.26.2. Shackleton Bailey 1965: 5:283. See #5.

[302] Santangelo 2018: 137–143.

[303] Caes. *BCiv.* 3.82.4; Dio 42.2.5; Pliny, *HN* 9.171; see Münzer, *RE* 13 (1927) 1642–1645, n. 25; Shackleton Bailey 1965: 2:209, 4.342, and 1977: 1:386–387; Dettenhofer 1992: 24 n. 61; Carter 1993: 205–206; Will, *BNP* Lucilius I 5; cf. however Hinard 1985: 472, who doubts the usual view, based on an emendation of Appian, that he was proscribed in 43–42. At *Fam.* 2.9–10 Cicero mocks poor Hirrus's speech impediment, which prevented him from pronouncing his own name correctly (see Shackleton Bailey's comments). The triumphs (pl.) will be those of 46 (and possibly 45) which were accompanied by enormous banquets, perhaps nominally in honor of Julia or Venus Genetrix (Suet. *Iul.* 38.2, Plut. *Caes.* 55.4 with Pelling 2011: 413; Chapter 5, n. 187). On Hirrus's embassy to the Parthians see Hillman 1996, especially 392–394.

[304] On whom see Syme 1964: 10–12: no known relationship to the historian. Bruhns seems to identify him with Bibulus's proquaestor in Syria (*MRR* 2.242, 247n2); Syme is skeptical.

44) P. Vestrius, *eques Romanus*, captured and released during the African campaign (*Bell. Afr.* 64.1).

After Thapsus

45) L. Caesar, Caesar's own distant cousin but now Cato's proquaestor, pardoned after Thapsus but subsequently killed under obscure circumstances.[305]

46) C. Vergilius Balbus, pr. 62, spared in the surrender of Thapsus. His property may have been confiscated and he was prevented from returning to Italy, at least at first.[306]

47) L. Livius Ocella, *pr. anno incerto*, near Utica.[307]

48) L. Livius Ocella *filius* (see #47).

49) M. Eppius, q. ca. 52, now leg., pardoned near Utica (*Bell. Afr.* 89.5).[308]

50) Sex. Quinctilius Varus (#7), q. 49, spared a second time probably after Thapsus, presumably through the intercession of a Caesarian.[309]

51) M. Aquinius, a minor senator, pardoned near Utica (*Bell. Afr.* 57.1–3, 89.5).[310]

52) M. Porcius Cato, son of Caesar's great enemy, spared near Utica and left his sizable patrimony.[311] Later killed fighting for the "Liberators" at Philippi.

53) C. Ateius, near Utica (*Bell. Afr.* 89.5).[312]

54) P. Atrius, an equestrian, near Utica (*Bell. Afr.* 89.5).[313]

---

[305] *Bell. Afr.* 88.3, 89.4–5. See nn. 101, 102.

[306] *Bell. Afr.* 93.3; Cic. *Att.* 12.51.2, 13.33.2. Shackleton Bailey 1977: 5:335–336 (ad 13.26), who accepts the identification of the legate of 46 with the praetor of 62; so too Bruhns. Cf. *MRR* 2.303 and 3.218.

[307] *Bell. Afr.* 89.5, as convincingly emended by Cichorius: *MRR* 3.126–127; Shackleton Bailey ad Cic. *Att.* 10.10.4. Bruhns 1978: 45 n. 30.

[308] Cf. *RRC* 461/1 LEG F C (perhaps *legatus fisci castrensis*: Crawford). *MRR* 3.85.

[309] See n. 273. After Thapsus Caesar's followers again had the right to save one person each: Dio 43.13.2–3. This was a repetition of the favor granted after Pharsalus: n. 292.

[310] *MRR* 3.25. Aquinius had held "received *honores* from the Roman People" but was still a *homo novus* and *parvus senator* (*Bell. Afr.* 57.3–4).

[311] *Bell. Afr.* 89.5; Val. Max. 5.1.10; Plut. *Cat. Min.* 73.1; App. *BCiv.* 2.100/416; Dio 43.12.1.

[312] Ateius is a plausible emendation of a corruption in the mss. Bruhns (1978: 49n7) identifies this man with Cicero's friend C. Ateius Capito, tr. pl. 55 (Cic. *Fam.* 13.29, *Att.* 13.33a.; *MRR* 2.332, 3.26, following Wiseman). But this is impossible to reconcile with Cic. *Fam.* 13.29.3, 6. (Shackleton Bailey 1965: 2:218).

[313] Cf. *Bell. Afr.* 68.4. A certain "Antius" may be mentioned at *Att.* 4.17.4 (Shackleton Bailey however emends to "Ateium" and refers to Cicero's friend Ateius: n. 312), and an Antius was proscribed in 43 (App. *BCiv.* 4.40/167).

55) Q. Ligarius, sen., spared after Thapsus at Hadrumetum. His property and senatorial rank were retained, but he was not allowed to return to Italy until after delivery of *Pro Ligario* late in 46.[314]

56) C. Considius *filius*, spared after surrender of Hadrumetum (*Bell. Afr.* 89.2).[315]

57) A. Caecina, spared after Thapsus but not allowed to return to Italy immediately (*Bell. Afr.* 89.4–5). Probably ultimately pardoned in full.[316]

58) M. Agrippa's brother, saved through the intercession of Octavius, Caesar's great-nephew.[317]

59) Pompeia, daughter of Pompey and wife of Faustus Sulla (killed after Thapsus), was released along with her two children (Pompey's grandchildren) and their property was returned.[318] Along with the treatment of M. Cato Jr. (#52) and Cornelia, wife of Pompey (#41), this was another conspicuous example of the general rule Caesar followed of not punishing the close relatives of his most prominent enemies.[319]

After the Quadruple Triumph, 46

60) M. Marcellus (cos. 51), who had withdrawn after Pharsalus to Mytilene, pardoned October 46.[320] Murdered by a deranged friend in Athens's harbor during his return journey to Italy in 45.[321]

[314] *Bell. Afr.* 89.2; Plut. *Brut.* 11.1–3; App. *BCiv.* 2.113/474; Cic. *Fam.* 6.13–14; Cic. *Lig.* Jehne 1987, 322n55.
[315] To be distinguished from his father, C. Considius Longus, *pr. anno incerto*, but hardly to be identified with C. Considius Paetus, mintmaster in Rome the same year, *RRC* 465.
[316] Suet. *Iul.* 75.5; Shackleton Bailey ad Cic. *Fam.* 6.6 (1977: 2.399). Note Cicero's correspondence with Caecina at end of 46 and beginning of 45 in which he encourages him to hope for pardon in the very near future (ibid., 6.5–8; cf. 13.66). At the time Caecina seems to be biding his time in Sicily.
[317] Nic. Dam. *Bios* 16: taken prisoner apparently at Utica and released after Caesar's return to Rome. Cf. Jehne 1987: 324n68.
[318] *Bell. Afr.* 95.3; App. *BCiv.* 2.100/416; cf. Dio 43.50.2. Flor. 2.13.90, Oros. 6.16.5 falsely and invidiously claim that Pompeia and her children were slaughtered by Caesar's order. Jehne reasonably doubts that Pompeia and her children were allowed to join her brother Sex. Pompeius in Spain, though this is explicitly stated by App. *BCiv.* 2.100/416. Because Pompeia and her children by Faustus Sulla were unharmed, Pompey's line (and Sulla's) would include several consuls of the Augustan and Tiberian ages, including four consuls *ordinarii* and two *suffecti* over the next few generations, not to mention others descended from her later marriage to L. Cinna (Syme 1986: 261–262, and Tables xiv, xvi).
[319] Damasippus's children were also spared (*Bell. Afr.* 89.5).
[320] Cic. *Fam.* 4.4.3, 4.7, 4.9–11; *Marc.* 3; see n. 205 for the date. *Fam.* 4.7.5 appears to show that his property had not been confiscated (Brunt 1971a: 321).
[321] Sulpicius [Cic.] *Fam.* 4.12, Cic. *Att.* 13.10.3; Liv. *Per.* 115; Val. Max. 9.11.4.

61) T. Ampius Balbus, pr. 59, the *tuba civilis belli*, encouraged by Cicero late in 46 to hope for pardon, which he probably eventually received.[322] Balbus is the source of the famous lines about *res publica* and Sulla's dictatorship attributed to Caesar.[323]

62) Trebianus, an *eques* who had fought against Caesar in Africa. Pardoned 45, but part of his property may have been confiscated (Cic. *Fam.* 6.10–11).[324]

63) A. Manlius Torquatus, pr. 70?, had fled to Athens. He was pardoned and his property returned in 45 after Caesar's return from Spain.[325]

Spain II (Munda)

64) Ti. Tullius, a Roman of uncertain status who surrendered to Caesar before Munda and was spared not so much for his citizen status but simply as a suppliant.[326]

65) C. Subernius Calenus (*eques*) and

66) M. Planius Heres (*eques*), formerly serving in Varro's army, spared by Caesar at beginning of Munda campaign but not yet (around beginning of 45) granted right to return to Italy.[327]

Finally, a few cases in which we know Cicero was actively encouraging pardons but we cannot be certain whether these were actually granted before Caesar's assassination in March 44:

67) P. Nigidius Figulus, pr. 58: Cicero's correspondence includes a letter of late 46 encouraging hopes for a pardon, but Figulus died in exile in 45. It is unclear whether a decision had yet been taken.[328]

68) C. Toranius (aed pl. probably by 64 and *pr. anno incerto*) was the recipient of another letter of the same kind written in 45. It seems likely that Toranius was pardoned before the Ides of March.[329]

---

[322] Cic. *Fam.* 6.12, 13.70.   [323] Suet. *Iul.* 77; Chapter 1, p. 26ff.

[324] Cic. *Fam.* 6.11.2: *plus acquisisti dignitatis quam amisisti rei familiaris*, with Alföldi 1985: 256, B. Woytek 2003: 207. Alternatively, perhaps Cicero refers to Trebianus's property or capital losses in the war (Jehne 1987: 331n110).

[325] Cic. *Fam.* 6.1–4. Shackleton Bailey (1977: 2:413) observes on the basis of *quo veniam* (6.2.3) that Torquatus had already by ca. April 45 received permission to return to Italy, but not to Rome.

[326] *Bell. Hisp.* 17–18.2. Raaflaub 1974: 259 and n. 129. Tullius was not, presumably, Cn. Pompeius Jr.'s "legate" but only an envoy from the town.

[327] Cic. *Fam.* 9.13, a letter in which Cicero requests his Caesarian son-in-law Dolabella's assistance in obtaining their *reditus*, though Caesar had already granted them their *vita* (§4).

[328] Cic. *Fam.* 4.13; Jer. *Chron.* p. 156; Helm. Della Casa 1962: 37–53.

[329] Cic. *Fam.* 6.20; Suet. *Aug.* 27.1. See Fündling, *DNP* Toranius 1; Ryan 1996a: 207–210; cf. *MRR* 3.207.

69) Cn. Plancius, aed. cur. 55? and Cicero's former client, also received such letters written early in 45. Plancius disappears from our evidence thereafter.[330]

A few further individuals are likely to have received pardon for taking the Pompeian side in the civil war either in Caesar's final months or shortly thereafter:

70) A certain senatorial Sextius Naso was an ex-Pompeian present in Rome to join the conspiracy against Caesar, thus evidently among the pardoned.[331]

71) Q. Minucius Thermus, Cato's tribunician ally in 62 and praetor sometime before 51.

72) and C. Coponius (pr. 49), were present in Rome by 43 and therefore probably had been granted formal pardon, although we cannot be absolutely certain.[332]

One important case remains uncertain. Faustus Sulla, proq. 49–48, son of the dictator and son-in-law of Pompey, is said by Suetonius to have been one of only three prominent men put to death by Caesar outside the battle line. Suetonius seems to say that Faustus had already been spared once before Thapsus (*Iul.* 75.3: *post impetratam veniam rebellaverant*), yet Dio 42.13.3 explicitly says he joined Cato and Sex. Pompeius in the Peloponnese in the aftermath of Pharsalus. Since Dio's testimony seems solid and Suetonius's arguably tendentious, it is probably best to reject the idea of an earlier surrender, although strictly speaking this could have occurred even after Thapsus, as was the case with L. Caesar.[333] Perhaps a better case might be made out for Q. Lucretius Vespillo, a Pompeian naval commander who eventually reemerges as consul in 19 BC under Caesar's heir.[334]

---

[330] Cic. *Fam.* 4.14, 15; cf. 6.20.1. For 55 as the date of the aedileship see *MRR* 3.158 and Alexander 2002: 130–132.

[331] App. *BCiv.* 2.113/474, usually now identified as the P. Naso who was pr. 44 (*MRR* 2.322; cf. 3.199, but contra, Manuwald 2007: 2:414).

[332] Bruhns 1978: 117n7. It is not clear whether in the fluid situation after the Dictator's assassination, and especially after Antony's departure for Gaul, anything prevented those who had not yet been formally pardoned for their choice of sides in the Civil War from returning to Rome.

[333] Jehne 1987: 323 seems more open to the idea that Faustus was *bis captus*.

[334] Shackleton Bailey 1965: 2:202; Bruhns 1978: 55 n. 11.

CHAPTER 9

En Route to the Parthian War

Since Cicero's copious writings largely shape our understanding of the political life of this age it comes naturally to us to see things through his eyes. In the summer of 46, in his speech to the Senate thanking Caesar for extending pardon to M. Marcellus, Cicero declares that what remains upon the conclusion of the Civil War (which would actually be deferred a year by the Munda campaign) was "to put the Republic in order, and for you first of all to enjoy the greatest quiet and peace."[1] Caesar should "set the courts in order, restore good credit, repress sexual excess, increase the birthrate, and bind everything which has collapsed and washed away with tough laws."[2] This was a fairly conventional to-do list that closely resembles what Cicero had imputed to Pompey in 52.[3] In neither case, however, does Cicero seem to have been asked, and in any case Caesar turned out to have different priorities. By the time he returned from Munda in late September 45, his mind was clearly set on a great expedition against Parthia to avenge the devastating defeat of Crassus at Carrhae in 53 and restore Rome's imperial prestige on a frontier which had since then invited at least two notable Parthian invasions of the province of Syria and real war scares in 51–50, 47, and 46–45.[4]

Preparations for the Parthian War

Pompey had considered seeking military assistance from Parthia at the beginning of the war and was said to have contemplated fleeing there for

---

[1] For the date of the *Pro Marcello* see Chapter 8, n. 205.

[2] Cic. *Marc.* 27: *haec igitur tibi reliqua pars est; hic restat actus; in hoc elaborandum est, ut rem publicam constituas, eaque in primis summa tranquillitate et otio perfruare.* 23: *constituenda iudicia, revocanda fides, comprimendae libidines, propaganda suboles, omnia quae dilapsa iam diffluxerunt, severis legibus vincienda sunt.*

[3] Cic. *Mil.* 78: *in spem maximam et, quem ad modum confido, uerissimam sumus adducti, hunc ipsum annum, hoc summo uiro consule, compressa hominum licentia, cupiditatibus fractis, legibus et iudiciis constitutis, salutarem ciuitati fore.*

[4] Malitz 1984 is fundamental. See also Jehne 1987a: 447–462; Zecchini 2001: 89–103; Sommer 2010.

sanctuary after Pharsalus. The idea of a Parthian expedition had emerged in Caesar's councils already after Zela in 47, but it was then put off because of disorders in Rome and the revival of the civil war in Africa.[5] Serious trouble soon erupted in the summer of 46, when Q. Caecilius Bassus, an equestrian officer under Pompey, took advantage of rumors of Caesar's troubles in the African campaign to prompt a mutiny there by the legions left in Syria under Sex. Iulius Caesar's command. After the proconsul's murder Caecilius took command and installed himself in Apamea, near the Syrian coast, for most or all of the year 45, where he was soon besieged by modest Caesarian forces drawn off from Syria and Cilicia, while fears rose of an imminent Parthian invasion in support.[6] A Parthian war was clearly now on the agenda once Caesar returned from Spain. Cicero was unhappy with the interruption: in May 45, shortly after news reached Rome of Caesar's victory at Munda, he wrote a draft of a "letter of advice" (συμβουλευτικόν) to the Dictator urging that the Parthian project should be subordinated to settling affairs in Rome.[7] Caesar's agents Oppius and Balbus insisted on vetting the letter and irritated Cicero by informing him (citing letters from Caesar himself) that this was the Dictator's plan anyway: he would not embark on the Parthian War before he had taken care of matters in the capital; to another of Cicero's sources (P. Sestius) Caesar expressed concern that his laws might be neglected in his absence.[8]

Yet Caesar's mind had evidently changed by the time he returned to Rome, and with good reason, it seems, given the troubling reports coming in from Syria.[9] After the unwelcome recent surprises in Africa and Spain Caesar would have recognized the risk of an even more dangerous continuation of the civil wars if the rebellion and its Parthian enablers were not

---

[5] Dio 44.46.3, 45.29.4; App. *BCiv.* 3.77/312, 4.58/250. Pompey: Plut. *Pomp.* 76.6–9 = Theophanes, *BNJ* 188 T8d; App. *BCiv.* 2.83/349; Dio 41.55.3 (but cf. 42.2.3–5); Justin 42.4.6; Hillman 1996. Chapter 8, n. 154.

[6] See esp. Dio 47.26–27, with Sherwin-White 1983: 301–302; *MRR* 2.297. News of the troubles had already reached Cicero in Rome by mid-September 46 (*Fam.* 12.17), which shortly thereafter rose to the level of a *bellum* (12.18.1, 19.1); for Parthian fears, *Fam.* 12.19.2.

[7] Cic. *Att.* 13.27.1 (May 25). Caesar had now been Dictator continuously since the aftermath of Thapsus (see n. 198): on his use of the office see Jehne 1987a: 15–38 and, concisely, Gardner 2009: 57–60. Since this special magistracy unified the highest *imperium* in one pair of hands, the advantages the position offered to one fighting a civil war, or settling one after the precedent of Sulla, need no elaborate explanation. For Cicero's *sumbouleutikon* see also 12.40.2 (May 2), 13.26 (May 14), 12.51 (May 20), 13.2 (May 24), 13.28.2–3 (May 26) with Hall 2009: 100–103 (who seems to overlook the fact that Oppius and Balbus irritated Cicero not by contradicting his preference but by asserting, in effect, that Caesar needed no such prompting).

[8] Cic. *Att.* 13.31.3 (May 28): *se nisi constitutis rebus non iturum in Parthos.* Sestius: n. 34.

[9] He returned to Rome probably in September: n. 21.

fairly swiftly dealt with.[10] But we can readily imagine that the change of plan was an unpleasant shock to Cicero and others who felt, as he did, that the "restoration of the Republic" should be Caesar's first priority, and it is a fair guess that the hothouse atmosphere in which the Dictator soon found himself over the months following his arrival in Rome was due in large part to this clash between the hopes and expectations of many powerful men within and outside his faction and their sudden deferral due to the emergence of the extraordinarily ambitious Parthian project. In December 45 a large Parthian force under the king's son, Pacorus, crossed into the Roman province to lift the siege of Apamea and rescued Caecilius.[11] News of this invasion appears to have been slow in reaching Rome (Cicero seems to have heard of it only the following April), yet even if Caesar had died before it reached him the fact of the invasion itself is suggestive of the deteriorating situation on the eastern frontier. Our sources for the early months of 44 are obsessed with the question of Caesar's desire for "kingship," but his own preoccupations were evidently very different.

The buildup of forces for use against Parthia had already been going on for some time. In the context of his narrative of the events in Rome of early 44 Appian says that Caesar "was sending forward" (imperf. tense, προύπεμπεν) across the Ionian Sea no fewer than sixteen legions (about half again the size of the army Caesar had led in Gaul, and almost half of the entire Roman army throughout the *imperium*; nominally about eighty thousand men, perhaps in fact closer to seventy thousand) plus ten thousand cavalry.[12] Probably Appian should be interpreted to mean that the force slated for the campaign was sixteen legions strong *in toto*, including ten legions already in the East (Asia Minor and Egypt) and thus not needing transport out of Italy, yet this still leaves six legions that had certainly had to be shipped across the Straits of Otranto in late 45 into early 44, some, but not all of them, veterans of the Spanish campaign.[13]

---

[10] Zecchini 2001: 94. Cic. *Fam.* 12.19.2, referring to a letter from Syria written probably in October–November 46.

[11] Cic. *Att.* 14.9.3, referring to a letter written from Syria on December 31, 45.

[12] App. *BCiv.* 2.110/460. Caesar seems to have initially intended to attack the Getae/Dacians on his way to the East (Suet. *Iul.* 44.3, *Aug.* 8.2; App. *BCiv.* 2.110/459, 3.25/93; Vell. Pat. 2.59.4; Strabo 7.298C; see Malitz 1984: 54–55; Zecchini 2001: 90–91) – but App. *Ill.* 13 suggests that at the last moment they had opted for a gesture of submission, abandoned after Caesar was assassinated (Malitz rejects the chronology but does not give his reasons: 45n122).

[13] Malitz 1984: 44–45; cf. Brunt 1971a: 479–480; McDermott 1982/83: 224; Jehne 1987a: 357–359 (who rightly observes [n. 107] that the eastern provinces could hardly have been stripped for the campaign and therefore suspects that if Appian's number is correct some legions are not accounted for in our evidence); Pelling 2011: 438. Malitz lists the six legions in Macedonia at 44n119; they need not all have

This was to be the largest Roman army engaged in a single campaign since the Second Punic War.[14] Some of the legions gathered in Macedonia must have been recruited in Italy in late 45; we happen to hear quite fortuitously of one legion recruited in 45, but as Brunt noted, "there must have been many more."[15] The six legions across the Ionian Sea were currently under the command of M. Acilius Caninus, Ser. Sulpicius Rufus's successor as proconsul in Greece and Macedonia.[16] Caesar's eighteen-year-old great-nephew, C. Octavius, the future Augustus, had shipped out for the staging point at Apollonia in Epirus late in 45, probably in December or even earlier.[17] Caesar had already sent ahead his war chest for the campaign, much of which is said to have reached Asia Minor by the Ides of March while the rest had gotten no further than Demetrias in Thessaly.[18] Money and supplies were still being gathered in Brundisium and shipped over to Macedonia at the time of the assassination.[19] Caesar himself had been in Campania in mid-December on unknown,

been veterans (see later in this chapter). The legions on their way to Syria at the end of 46 (Cic. *Fam.* 12.19.2) will have been sent to confront the Caecilius Bassus crisis and need not imply that Caesar had already decided on a major invasion. Brunt 1971a: 480 speculated that Caesar had transported one of the four legions in Egypt by early 43 in preparation for the Parthian campaign. Cic. *Att.* 14.5.1: [*legiones*] *quae fuerunt in Hispania* (April 11, 44) probably refers to legions brought from Spain after Munda (Shackleton Bailey).

[14] Pompey had twelve legions against the pirates and Mithridates; Caesar ultimately had eleven (or thirteen), plus a few cohorts, in the Gauls (see Appendix 5). See conveniently Brunt 1971: 449.

[15] Brunt 1971a: 477; Cic. *Fam.* 10.24.3: *bima* in 43. On Brunt's reckoning (476–478), thirty-seven to forty legions were in the field after the remnants of Pompey's army were integrated; it is possible that two additional non-Italian legions were recruited in the East, but the ten "Gallic" legions were discharged by 45. This would leave twenty-seven to thirty-two legions empire-wide, but at least thirty-four legions were in the field in March 44.

[16] Nic. *Dam. Bios* 41; Cic. *Fam.* 7.30.3, with Shackleton Bailey 1977: 2:435–436; *MRR* 2.285n8 and 3.1–2.

[17] Nic. *Dam. Bios* 37 (December); App. *BCiv.* 3.9/32 (October, by inference) with Malitz 1984: 39n97. Mommsen's restoration of *Fasti Capit. Cons. sub anno* 44, making Octavius *magister equitum designatus* for 44, has now been disproved by the newly published fragments of the Privernum Fasti (Zevi and Cassola 2016: 299–303, 306–309; cf. App. 3.9/30; Dio 43.51.7; Plin. *HN* 7.147; see already Malitz 1984: 39n95; cf. Toher 2017: 226–227). It remains possible that he was designated *mag. eq.* for 42, as Dio says; Cassola suggests that this may have been in anticipation of a triumphal return in that year. It is intriguing that on the night of December 18 Caesar stayed near Puteoli (or Cumae) at the house of Octavius's stepfather, L. Marcius Philippus, who was at this time mentoring and advising his young stepson (Cic. *Att.* 13.52.1, with n. 20; cf. 14.11.2, 15.12.2; Nic. Dam. *Bios* 34, 51–54; Suet. *Aug.* 8.3, Vell. Pat. 2.59.3, 60.1–2). Perhaps he had escorted Octavius part of the way to Brundisium.

[18] Nic. Dam. *Bios* 55, with Toher 2017: 261; App. *BCiv.* 3.63/259. Malitz 1984: 46 plausibly speculates that the massive output of coinage early in 44 is connected with the huge outlay the campaign demanded. See B. Woytek 2003: 332–335, who picks up on Motzo's suggestion that the transport of such enormous sums gave rise to the rumor that Caesar was transferring the capital to Alexandria (Suet. *Iul.* 79.3: *translatis simul opibus imperii*).

[19] App. *BCiv.* 3.11/39. Some units of course remained in Brundisium attending to these duties: ibid., and §10/35.

apparently military business, and his own departure date from the City was eventually set for March 18, 44.[20] J. Malitz conjectures that Caesar must have made known his Parthian plans at the latest about the time of his return to Rome in the latter half of September 45.[21] Given the magnitude of the undertaking, an earlier date is attractive.

You might think that after more than four years of civil war, Romans would not be particularly eager to begin a new "war of choice" with one of their most dangerous neighbors. Apparently you would be wrong. Dio writes (in a context of the end of 45 and beginning of 44):

> While Caesar was thus engaged, a longing came over all the Romans alike (πᾶσι τοῖς ῾Ρωμαίοις ὁμοίως) to avenge Crassus and those who had perished with him, and they felt some hope of subjugating the Parthians then, if ever. They unanimously voted (ἐψηφίσαντο) the command of the war to Caesar, and made ample provision for it. Moreover both so that he might have more men to employ as his assistants and also that the city should neither be without officials in his absence nor, again, by attempting to choose some on its own responsibility, fall into strife, that the magistrates should be appointed in advance for three years, this being the length of time they thought necessary for the campaign. (Dio 43.51.1–2, tr. after Cary)

The main points of this important passage need to be underscored. First, in Dio's representation, the Parthian campaign was, if not necessarily prompted by others ("the Romans," the Senate and perhaps also People), at least fully consistent with a broadly felt public demand. Indeed, if we take his version at its word, there was an actual comitial vote for war or one appointing Caesar to the command (presumably as his *provincia*), which in recent times had amounted to the same thing.[22] Dio's enthusiastic description of the Parthian plan endorsed by "the Romans" themselves is remarkably different from Appian's rather jaundiced view that Caesar had conceived the project (ἐπενόει) in the midst of the frustration of early 44, with Caesar "either renouncing his hope [i.e. of monarchy], or being tired out, and wishing by this time to avoid this plot and odium, or deliberately giving up the city to certain of his enemies, or hoping to cure his bodily

---

[20] Campania: Cic. *Att.* 13.52.1 (December 19). Caesar was accompanied by two thousand soldiers, making his visit more an ἐπισταθμεία than a *hospitium*. March 18: App, *BCiv.* 2.111/462, 114/476: the assassination was on the *fourth* day (inclusive) before his planned departure. We don't know when this date was set, but it may reflect the traditional opening of the military campaigning season. From the Second Punic War to 153 BC, the consuls had taken office on the Ides of March (Liv. *Per.* 47, with Pina Polo 2011: 13–15), although the actual time of their departure varied widely (ibid., pp. 208–218).

[21] Malitz 1984: 39–40, dating Caesar's arrival between September 13 and very early October.

[22] Jehne 1987a: 127n80.

ailment of epilepsy and convulsions, which came upon him suddenly and especially when he was inactive."[23] But Appian entirely overlooks the fact that the expedition had been actively pursued for several months by this time and was no sudden whim or council of desperation. He clearly does not understand (or chooses to downplay) the importance of the Parthian campaign to Caesar and (to judge from Dio) "the Romans," and inverts the true state of affairs when he treats it as wholly secondary and adventitious in comparison to the matters leading up to the assassination that in retrospect appear to be of much greater moment.

It is possible, of course, that Dio may be indulging his creative imagination here. But we should have evidence to think that before we dismiss what appears to be, on the whole, our most informative guide to the events of late 45 and early 44. As I shall try to demonstrate, there is on the contrary a good deal of evidence lurking just below the surface of what was eventually constructed as the primary narrative of these months that the Parthian campaign was Caesar's greatest priority, and that should open the door to consideration of the idea that, at least on the surface, the Republic's institutions were gearing up as well for a great patriotic war to wipe out the dishonor of Carrhae and restore the security of the eastern marches of the *imperium*.

Second, for the sake of the Parthian War, Caesar and "the Romans" were prepared to tamper radically with one of the most hallowed traditions of the Republic – the election of officials in one year to take office the next. Dio says that Caesar was given the right to appoint the magistrates *for the following three years* (i.e. 43, 42, 41) in anticipation of his absence on the Parthian campaign. (Appian, incidentally, twice says *five* years.)[24] Whichever it was, by the time of the assassination Caesar had exercised only part of his right under this provision – all magistrates for the coming year, 43, but only consuls and tribunes for 42 – which is likely a reason for discrepancies and vagueness in the sources.[25] Such a radical

---

[23] App. *BCiv.* 2.110/459. Cf. Syme 1939: 53: "Caesar postponed decision about the permanent ordering of the State. It was too difficult. Instead, he would set out for the wars again . . . ." Suet. *Iul.* 86.1 reports rumors that Caesar was sick of life, which do not seem consistent with his vigorous preparations for an immense expedition abroad. On Caesar's state of health see n. 212.

[24] Dio 43.51.2–3 (who appears to indicate that the right was given formally by "all the Romans" [§1 πᾶσι τοῖς Ῥωμαίοις, §2 διενοοῦντο] – i.e. the Senate and People); cf. App. *BCiv.* 2.128/537, 138/574, put into the mouths of two opposing figures, Antony and Brutus. Dio in general seems the better-informed source for Caesar's stay in Rome; Toher 2017: 317 suspects that Appian may be retrojecting the period of the triumviral appointments of Octavian and Antony.

[25] Dio 43.51.6; Nic. Dam. *Bios* 77 (remarkably accurate); Cic. *Att.* 14.6.2, 15.6.2; Suet. *Iul.* 76.3. Cic. uses the title *cos. des.* already in 44 for both men chosen by Caesar for the consulship of 42, L. Munatius Plancus and Dec. Brutus (Cic. *Fam.* 10.3.3, 11.4–7).

innovation probably had to be validated by a *lex populi Romani*, which is in fact what Dio seems to imply: "the Romans" are the implicit subject of "voted" and "decided"; and though it seems possible that with "decided" Dio moves on to a second, supplementary decision, its agent appears to remain the same. Nicolaus also appears to make mention of a δόγμα, here seemingly a law, giving Caesar this right.[26]

We shall deal in due course with the political fallout of this astonishing innovation when it was actually acted on shortly before the expected date of Caesar's departure. For now, two things need to be said while putting off more extensive discussion until its appropriate place. First, the law (or decree) clearly implies that, whatever grandiose title he gave himself, Caesar must have feared that he would not be able to control elections in Rome in his absence. Second, and more important for our larger argument, this law is itself proof of the absolute centrality of the Parthian campaign among Caesar's current aims and objectives, for only this can explain such a forceful and necessarily painful disruption of the traditional patterns of republican political life – *spreto patrio more* indeed, as Suetonius writes.[27] The projected settling of accounts with Parthia was fundamental and determined other dramatic moves in turn that no doubt greatly intensified political tensions in the months before Caesar's assassination.[28] Cicero, perhaps, had hoped for a restoration of some plausible version of traditional political life before any foreign adventures were undertaken, yet it should be (and should have been) perfectly clear that once Caesar had chosen to give priority to the Parthian War there was no time for a return first to politics as usual. Whatever might be hoped for later, nobody can any longer have seriously expected that an authentic "restoration of the Republic" after the Civil War would be fit into the few months of military preparations between September 45 and March 44.[29] All of this Caesar took on board with his Parthian decision.

---

[26] Nic. Dam. *Bios* 77: ἀρχαιρεσίαι δ᾽ ἦσαν ἐνιαύσιοι ὑπὸ Καίσαρος ἀγόμεναι· αὐτὸς γὰρ εἶχε τὴν τούτων ἐξουσίαν, ὥσπερ ἐκέλευε τὸ δόγμα. Which decree he means is unclear, since that of §76 pertains to the return of the exiled tribunes. Perhaps it is a reference back to §67. The election of a *sequence of future* magistrates one or more years ahead of time very likely would require special legislation. Toher 2017: 317 (cf. 287) thinks the reference is to the *lex Antonia*, but as Dio 43.51.3 ἐν νόμῳ τινὶ indicates, that appears to have been quite distinct (n. 35).

[27] Suet. *Iul.* 76.3.

[28] Zecchini 2001: 94–95, who assumes, however, that only the timetable of Caesar's constitutional adjustments would have been different, not their substance. That is doubtful.

[29] Dettenhofer 1992: 194–222, 226–227 makes a good argument that as late as August 45, both M. Brutus and Cassius also had high hopes for Caesar to restore fundamental elements of the traditional republican order, presumably along similar lines to those Cicero called for in his *Pro Marcello* of the previous year. Caesar's reversal of priorities may have come as a shock to them as well.

If we wish to resist the tendency of hindsight to reorganize the narrative and thereby occlude unrealized alternatives and much contemporary experience, it is better to invert the usual account of Caesar's last months and place the preparations for the Parthian War firmly at the center, in sharp contrast to the way the story is usually told by our (late) literary sources. His assassination, and the ideological and real battles it unleashed, have for obvious reasons focused the attention of our sources on that event and its prelude, in particular the series of public incidents which (I shall argue) cumulatively eroded Caesar's standing both with senators and People, but this has had the effect of turning our attention on other people's projects rather than the Dictator's own, thus suggesting a certain lassitude on his part in the area where they, and consequently we, expect to see the most effort. So, for instance, Appian's presentation of the Parthian campaign as a sort of "escape" from the seemingly irresolvable problems that greeted Caesar in the city of Rome has been highly influential – much too influential – on modern scholarship, providing specious textual support, for instance, to Christian Meier's conception of a Caesar quite alienated from "the judgement of Roman society," "increasingly driven on by an urge to escape from the transient," fixated on a plan that "was thus an expression of helplessness in the face of Rome and her society."[30] But the fact that Caesar's priorities were not Cicero's hardly suffices to show that the Dictator was, at least in this matter, alienated from "the judgement of Roman society." Dio on the contrary claims that it was Cicero, not Caesar, who was out of touch with the priorities of "the Romans" at this time (whoever exactly they were), to whom settling accounts with the Parthians appears to have had great appeal. It may be that the "healing effects" of a unifying campaign of revenge against the Parthians for the worst defeat against a foreign enemy in half a century (since Arausio in 105) did not have to await Mark Antony and Augustus, both of whom would appreciate the strategic importance and the patriotic appeal of belated retribution against the Parthians, turning Roman weapons outward rather than inward in a heartening manifestation of renewed concord and vitality.[31] Even on the purely military and diplomatic plane, it was perfectly apparent that Rome's failure to retaliate after the defeat

---

[30] Meier 1982: 455–458. Contra, see already Malitz 1984: 40n99; Jehne 1987a: 447–448.

[31] Zecchini 2001: 98–103, whose speculative argument that the Parthians could take over Carthage's old role of providing a *metus hostilis* to restore concord does not undermine the larger point that a Parthian victory would lend legitimacy to Caesar's resolution of the Civil War (and demoralize any remaining political opposition: Sommer 2010: 136). Cf. also McDermott 1982/83, attributing considerable strategic vision to Caesar's plan, despite our unfortunate lack of crucial details. For ideological exploitation of the Parthians in the Augustan age see *Res gestae*, 29.2; Hor. *Epist.* 1.12.27–28, Ov. *Fast.* 5.593–594, etc. with Gruen 1996: 191–192. Gallus's fragmentary poem (n. 32)

had invited persistent Parthian invasions, raids, and interventions in the provinces of Syria and Asia Minor. The recent instability of the eastern frontier was a serious problem for the *imperium populi Romani*, not something Caesar had engineered to open an escape hatch from the toxic atmosphere of the City.

In view of Caesar's preparations to embark on the most ambitious military campaign of his life, the impression some scholars have conveyed – that he was in some sense weary of life and of struggle – seems far wide of the mark. On the contrary, he is likely to have seen this as his crowning achievement in a lifelong pursuit of *gloria*. It is unlikely that he wanted his final and greatest victory to be one in civil war. By now defeating the Parthians he might become, in a poet's only somewhat hyperbolic phrase, "the greatest part of Roman history."[32] The Parthian War was an undertaking on an enormous scale, requiring a corresponding effort of planning which must have been at the forefront of Caesar's attention throughout the period of his stay in Rome – his longest, in fact, since he had left for Gaul in March 58, and probably for this very reason.[33]

But other important projects also urgently demanded his attention. As he began his long march to Rome after Munda he had written a letter to P. Sestius expressing anxiety lest his laws be ignored, as he claimed his "sumptuary" law (probably) of 46 had been.[34] Whether this implies the

---

may suggest something similar going on in 45–44. C. Pelling has drawn my attention to Plut. *Pomp.* 70, the reflections of wise observers at Pharsalus on how much better it would have been to turn seventy thousand Romans against "Parthians or Germans."

[32] *Maxima Romanae pars eri<s> historiae*, from the papyrus fragment of Cornelius Gallus (Anderson, Parsons, and Nisbet 1979: 140 = *FRP* 145). With the conquest of Gaul, victory in the Civil War, and defeat of the Parthians under his belt, Caesar's achievements would indeed dwarf all others' both in volume and magnitude. Scholars have overwhelmingly followed Anderson, Parsons, and Nisbet in identifying the campaign projected in the lines as Caesar's Parthian project: see (selectively) Putnam 1980: 49–56, Petersmann 1983, and most recently Gagliardi 2014. Jehne's skeptical warning (1987a: 276–277) should be kept in mind, but chiefly as a restraint against overly exuberant extrapolation.

[33] Malitz 1984: 38n86. The enormous mass of business to which Caesar and his staff had to attend in this brief window of time is well conveyed by Malitz 1987, especially 62, 69–70. The plan for the campaign, which according to some late sources was to be prefaced by an attack on the Getae or Dacians, remains largely in the realm of speculation, sometimes quite grandiose (India or Ocean, the latter actually accepted by Dobesch 1980: 35ff., 1998. Nic. Dam. *Bios* 95; Dio 44.43.1; Plut. *Caes.* 58.6–7 with Pelling 2011: 436–438). For a down-to-earth suggestion, see Zecchini 2001: 90–91, 96–97. Surely there were also strategic questions to discuss with Cleopatra and her fifteen-year-old brother-husband, who together with the two-year-old Ptolemy Caesarion had been visiting Rome from late in 46 until shortly after the assassination. To judge from Dio 43.27.3 (cf. Eusebius, *Chron.* a. 46), she had obtained formal recognition of their title as "Friends and Allies of the Roman People" early in her stay. Cf. Gelzer 1968: 287n2; Osgood 2006: 29n69.

[34] Cic. *Att.* 13.7 (June 10). On the sumptuary law, which pertained not only to the dinner table but also to extravagant construction of houses and tombs: Yavetz 1983: 154–156; Jehne 1987a: 86–88.

intent to add to the flurry of his earlier legislation (mostly passed, it seems, in 46) is unclear, but several notable laws seem to belong to his final sojourn in Rome. A law of the Dictator conferring so-called Latin Rights – a sort of half-citizenship – on Sicily, a *lex Cassia* augmenting the number of patricians available for offices and priesthoods exclusive to them, and the *lex Antonia* giving him the formal right to name half of all the magistracies except the consulship all appear to belong to late 45 or early 44, the last certainly so.[35] A separate law surely was required to enable the advance elections of the magistrates for 43–41; laws probably also had to be drawn up in order to expand the college of praetors to sixteen, that of the aediles to six, and the quaestors to forty.[36] Meanwhile, an immense building project in the very center of Rome was now underway, which involved a radical redesign of the Campus Martius and the diversion of the Tiber to allow most of its activities to be shifted to soon-to-be adjacent Vatican hill.[37]

Quite apart from the somewhat obscure legislative projects of these months, it must be recalled, Caesar was also still in the midst of settling his newly demobilized veterans on land in Italy and abroad. He had made the task of settling his demobilized veterans much more difficult for himself by eschewing mass confiscations in the manner of Sulla.[38] The large project of discharging and resettling his Gallic War legions must have begun before the end of 47 and picked up speed after Thapsus in 46, but even if seven legions were fully settled by now, which seems doubtful, three

---

[35] Yavetz 1983: 97–98, 126–127; on the *lex Antonia*, Jehne's discussion (n. 260) supersedes that of Yavetz. Jehne plausibly shows (contra Bruhns 1978: 159, and apparently Yavetz) that the *lex Antonia* was distinct from the law enabling the "Vorauswahlen" for the expected time of Caesar's absence (1987: 127–128n80). A convenient summary of Caesar's legislation as Dictator is Gardner 2009: 61–65.

[36] It is not entirely clear whether Caesar's augmentation of the number of praetors, aediles, and quaestors required one or more new laws (Yavetz's *leges Iuliae de magistratibus creandis*, 1983: 109–110; Jehne 1987a: 372–373), although the model of Sulla's *lex de XX quaestoribus* (Crawford, in *RS* 1.293–300) might point to an affirmative answer. Tantalizingly, the mime-poet Laberius seems to have made a joke about the prodigious (?) appearance of six aediles (Gell. *NA* 16.7.12, with most recently Panayotakis 2010: 305–307).

[37] The project seems nearly incredible but is apparently soberly attested by Cic. *Att.* 13.20.1 (citing a bill *de urbe augenda* promulgated in the summer of 45) and 13.33a. (I thank F. Martelli for drawing these letters to my attention.) This should doubtless be associated with the mile-long enlargement of the Saepta anticipated in 54 (4.16.8) and the projected temple of Mars "of record size" to be built, according to Suet. *Iul.* 44.1, on the site of the *naumachia* used in 46. One might speculate that the temple was to be dedicated to celebrate the expected triumph over Parthia, and that Augustus later adapted the idea for his temple of Mars the Avenger. Coarelli 1997: 580–590 has little to say about the ambitious project, presumably because, like most of Caesar's other rather fantastical "final plans" (Chapter 10, n. 19), it was never realized. Cf. Yavetz 1983: 160 and esp. Liverani 2008: 49–50, with a conjectural plan (reproduced in Davies 2017: 266).

[38] Brunt 1971a: 319–326.

others had served in the Munda campaign and thus can only have been
demobilized late in 45.[39] "The work was still not complete on Caesar's
death," observes Brunt.[40] At the time of the assassination "many" demobilized veterans were present in and around Rome who had received their
assignments and were awaiting imminent departure to their new homes –
men who boosted the strength of the "Caesarian" leaders in their maneuvering after the Ides of March.[41] But Caesar's colonization projects went
beyond accommodating the needs of his veterans. Suetonius says that he
was actually able to resettle the astonishing number of eighty thousand
residents of the city of Rome itself in colonies abroad; we know the names
of some eighteen to thirty-four Caesarian colonies, including the major
foundations at Corinth and Carthage, probably only some of which had
gone beyond the planning stage by the time of Caesar's death.[42] But the
planning of the colonies was itself probably the most onerous part of the
business for the Dictator.[43] Because of Cicero's intervention on behalf of
his friend Atticus, who had his estate nearby, we know about one colony
thus slated for settlement in 44 or 43: Buthrotum in Epirus. In response to
this pressure, Caesar adjusted his plan shortly before his assassination.[44]
Similar interventions can be readily imagined elsewhere; even colonies

[39] Brunt 1971a: 320, 377; Keppie 1983: 49–58; Chrissanthos 2001: 74. See Jehne 1987a: 147–152 and
2000: 161–162n77, who argues strongly that the *lex Iulia* mentioned in the *lex Ursonensis* (clause 97)
dates to 46 and authorized the huge colonial effort. (Crawford, *RS* 1.397 does not seriously consider
this alternative and presumes that the *lex Iulia* is Caesar's agrarian law of 59). Cic. *Fam.* 9.17.2
(August or September 46); App. *BCiv.* 2.94/394–395.
[40] Brunt 1971a: 377.
[41] App. *BCiv.* 2.119/50, 120/507 ("billeted in temples and sanctuaries under one standard and one
resettlement officer of the colony, having sold their possessions for their departure"), 125/523 ("if
anyone should not secure for them their assignments which had either already been made or
promised"), 133/557 ("many thousands" were in Rome who had been "assigned to colonies according
to their original units"); cf. 135/565, Dio 44.34.2, Cic. *Att.* 14.14.2, 16.16A.4. Nic. Dam. *Bios* 49 (cf.
§103) mentions only the arrival in Rome after the assassination of veterans *already* settled in "nearby"
colonies, presumably to insist on protection of their rights. Antony made it a priority to restart the
Caesarian resettlement program with his own agrarian law in June 44 (Brunt 1971a: 324–325);
"the main interest of their [sc. Antony's commissioners] proceedings is in confirming that some
of the veterans had not even been assigned lands before Caesar's death" (ibid., 325).
[42] Suet. *Iul.* 42.1. C. Bearzot 2000; Zecchini 2000. On the extra-Italian colonial program in general,
see Yavetz 1983: 143–150; Jehne 1987a: 343–347.
[43] For the execution of his plans of land distribution Caesar relied on a board he had appointed, three
members of which are known from the Buthrotum dossier (cited n. 44): the praetor-designate
L. Plotius Plancus (*MRR* 3.158–159; natural brother of cos.-des. for 42, L. Munatius Plancus),
C. Ateius Capito, tr. pl. 55 (*MRR* 2.332), and a relative nonentity named C. Cupiennus. Others
may have belonged to the board; these three may only have been those particularly concerned with
Buthrotum.
[44] Cic. *Att.* 16.16A–F of July 44, especially 16A, which reveals that Caesar ultimately agreed to spare
Buthrotum but wanted to keep the decision secret until the settlers were already transported out of
Italy.

whose planning was far advanced, such as this one, needed some attention. In view of the "thousands" of veterans still billeted in and around Rome on the Ides of March, it is reasonable to assume that many other colonies and settlements were still on the drawing boards at that time. Whatever time was left over from preparations for the Parthian War, including recruitment of new legions and the selection and formal election of magistrates for three years in the future, as well his latest legislative projects, must have been quickly filled by the resettlement and colonial plans of the Dictator.

Caesar was a very busy man. Cicero, and perhaps many other senators, urgently desired him to clarify as soon as possible his status against the constitutional framework of the Roman Republic, but he does not seem to have shared their priority.[45]

Caesar's "Passion to Be King"

The ancient narratives of the background to Caesar's assassination – Plutarch, Appian, Dio, Suetonius, and Nicolaus of Damascus – preface the assassination with strikingly similar accounts of a series of incidents seen as holding clues to the great question of whether Caesar wished to be "king." There are enough differences of detail between the narratives to reassure us that they represent more than a single original source, and indeed it is clear that the assassination's importance prompted quite a few writers to try their hand at it or to offer their varying insights.[46] Our main sources do not quite agree on the sequence of these incidents, but reasonable inferences may be drawn about their correct order, and what follows adheres largely to the order generally accepted by scholars.[47] The inherently polemical nature of the ancient narratives, however, whose underlying purpose was evidently that of judging whether Caesar was "justly killed," must be kept in mind as a warning to the historian; also we are hampered by the near-complete absence of Cicero's correspondence for this period, our most valuable source and almost constant companion up to now.[48] As a result, although our reconstruction of basic facts and chronology often is frustratingly murky, we cannot shake entirely free of the broad outline of the story on which our

---

[45] Similarly, Gardner 2009.   [46] Pelling 2011: 51–52.

[47] See Appendix 6. I place the Forum Iulium incident slightly later than most scholars (January 44 rather than December 45), but in the same sequence of the key events that raised the issue of *regnum*.

[48] Suetonius expresses most clearly the underlying question: *Praegravant tamen cetera facta dictaque eius, ut et abusus dominatione et iure caesus existimetur* (*Iul.* 76.1). Both Cicero and Atticus were evidently both in Rome from September to mid-December 45, and little light is shed on this period by the few letters that belong to it in the *Ad Familiares* corpus, the most notable exception being *Fam.* 7.30 to M'. Curius on the election of a suffect consul on the last day of December.

main sources insist. The canonical narrative, as we might call it, focuses on the following key moments: (1) the offense Caesar gave when an unparalleled package of honors was presented to him in his new Forum Iulium; (2) the clash with two tribunes that grew out of the incident of the diadem on Caesar's statue and the quasi-royal acclamation "*rex!*" that greeted his return to the City from the Latin Festival on January 26; and (3) the famous moment at the Lupercalia festival when Caesar's colleague in the consulship, Mark Antony, offered him the diadem ("the crown"). The traditional narrative is at least reasonably coherent, and while we may doubt the validity of the frame of monarchical probing and tyrannicide into which it is set by the late sources, it plausibly tells the story of a progressive and steep erosion of Caesar's public position among senators and the People in early 44, a precondition for any rational plot to remove him from power.

The Forum Iulium Incident

On what appears to be a series of different occasions extending from late 45, following Caesar's return from Spain to Rome, into early 44, the Senate voted the Dictator an enormous number of honors, in many cases entirely unprecedented and even showing a degree of ingenuity in excogitating eye-catching novelties.[49] On one day in this period (setting aside for the moment problems of relative and absolute chronology) the Senate – of course in Caesar's absence, to demonstrate its "independence" (n. 113) – had passed an unusual number of extraordinary honors even by the exuberant standards of the day; its members immediately set forth in a procession of the entire Senate, led by the consul or consuls and the whole descending sequence of other magistrates, to the Forum Iulium, still under construction, and the temple to Venus Genetrix within it, which Caesar had dedicated a little over a year before.[50] The purpose of the parade was to announce the decrees in

---

[49] On the specific honors see Jehne 1987a: especially 191–225; Till 2003; Ferrary 2010. Weinstock 1971 remains an important work of reference, although driven by an interpretive agenda that goes far beyond the evidence; a similar interpretation in Dobesch 1966 (on which see Balsdon 1967).

[50] Dio 44.8, who claims that only Cassius and "some others" had voted against the honors (§1) – which must have lent an air of legitimacy to the majority (they apparently suffered no consequences: Dettenhofer 1992: 249); Plut. *Caes.* 60.4–8; App. *BCiv.* 2.107/446; Nic. Dam. *Bios* 77–79; Suet. *Iul.* 78.1. Date of dedication (September 26, 46): Degrassi, *I.It.* 13.1.183; 2.48. If 45 is in fact the correct date for the swearing of oaths according to the treaty with the Cnidians (*SEG* 59.1207), this is our earliest testimony to the conducting of public business in the Forum Iulium (November 8: A, line 2). Recent discussions of the Forum Iulium incident include Zecchini 2001: 57–63 with Ferrary 2010: 21n45; Pelling 2011: 448–450; Toher 2017: 318–322. Both Appian and Plutarch mistakenly place the incident at the Rostra: *BCiv.* 2.107/445, *Caes.* 60.4; see Appendix 6, n. 13. It would be good to know where the Senate had met and thus the course of the procession; my guess would be the Temple of

person to Caesar there: according to Nicolaus, the only source who specifies what the Dictator was doing, he was letting the contracts for the construction of the unfinished Forum surrounding the temple.[51] Lictors pushed a way for the procession through the crowd on each side, while in the rear followed "the whole People," an enormous multitude of citizens "unparalleled in size" according to Nicolaus.[52] Nicolaus too emphasizes the awe the procession inspired in observers: the foremost men of the Republic, in whose hands so much power was concentrated, were making obeisance to another who was yet greater![53] When the great procession arrived, Caesar was sitting and conducting his business on the elevated temple platform, perhaps in the forecourt (*pronaos*) of the temple itself (Dio) or at the front of the high podium (Suetonius).[54] But Caesar took no notice of the deputation and apparently (according to Nicolaus again, the only source who offers this level of detail) continued speaking with those beside him and handling his documents until one of his friends drew his attention to those approaching him on the floor of the Forum below.[55] Plutarch and Suetonius cite somewhat contradictory stories about two of these friends: L. Balbus, who urged Caesar to stay seated though he wished to rise ("Remember you are Caesar!"), and Cicero's old protégé C. Trebatius, mentioned only by Suetonius, who on the contrary advised him to stand but received a dark look from the Dictator for his pains.[56] The contradiction clearly reveals a controversy over the interpretation of Caesar's action (no doubt current already at the time), some further strands of which emerge to view in Caesar's own excuses put in shortly afterward.[57] Whatever his motive, he did not rise

Jupiter Optimus Maximus on the Capitol, given the solemnity of the occasion, possibly the celebratory first of the year, an attractive date for the event (Appendix 6, p. 645). See nn. 89, 90. The new Curia in the Forum Iulium was hardly completed at this date (Chapter 5, n. 233).

[51] Nic. Dam. *Bios* 78: ἀγορὰν κατεσκεύαζε μεγάλην καὶ ἀξιοπρεπῆ ἐν Ῥώμῃ, καὶ τοὺς τεχνίτας ἀθροίσας τὰ ἔργα εἰς τὴν κατασκευὴν διεπίπρασκεν.

[52] Nic. Dam. *Bios* 77–78: μετὰ δὲ . . . εἵπετο καὶ ὁ πᾶς <δῆμος> ἄπειρος τὸ πλῆθος καὶ ὅσος οὐκ ἄλλος.

[53] Nic. Dam. *Bios* 78: πολλὴ δὲ ἥ τε ἔκπληξις ἦν καὶ τὸ ἀξίωμα τῶν πρώτων, εἰς οὓς τὰ συμπάντων ἀνήρτητο κράτη, θαυμαζόντων ἄλλον κρείττω. Not only senators but also the People are said to have been strongly affected by the subsequent perceived insult: Dio 44.8.2 and Plut. *Caes.* 60.5.

[54] Dio 44.8.1; cf. Suet. *Iul.* 78.1: *sedens pro aede*. The podium stood some 5 meters above the floor of the Forum (Morselli, *LTUR* 2.302). Conducting business: App. *BCiv.* 2.107/445: χρηματίζοντι; Nic. Dam. *Bios* 79: διὰ τὸ τοῖς ἐκ πλαγίου ὁμιλεῖν . . . διοικῶν ἃ [sc. τὰ γραμματίδια] ἐν χερσὶν εἶχεν.

[55] Nic. Dam. *Bios* 79. Contra Pelling 2011: 450 ("as they were coming up at an angle"), I infer from ἐξ ἐναντίας προσιόντας that the procession was approaching Caesar's party frontally; it was *Caesar* who, being distracted, was turned aside (διὰ τὸ τοῖς ἐκ πλαγίου ὁμιλεῖν).

[56] Plut. *Caes.* 60.6, 8; Suet. *Iul.* 78.1. In Nicolaus, the intervention of a "friend" is limited to drawing Caesar's attention to the procession in front of him (*Bios* 79).

[57] See n. 104.

even once his attention had been drawn to the solemn procession but received it as if he were dealing with mere "private persons," and (thus exacerbating the insult) delivered the opinion that his honors should be reduced rather than increased (Plutarch).[58] The procession dispersed almost immediately, greatly dejected (Plutarch: μετὰ δεινῆς κατηφείας, 60.5), and Caesar rose himself to go home, drawing his toga back and crying out to his friends (n.b.) that he was ready if anyone wished to cut his throat.[59] In doing so he not only showed his awareness of the negative effect his action had had on its participants and witnesses (so Plutarch) but also of the danger to which it exposed him; perhaps he even blamed his "friends" – for the surprise, or for their advice. All sources are agreed that the insult to the Senate (and thus to the Republic) was perceived as severe, creating intense indignation against him, validating suspicions of his objectives, and providing a pretext for assassination.[60]

This was not the first time the Senate had showered Caesar with honors. In fact, this had become something of a ritual, since after each of the great Civil War victories – Pharsalus/Pompey's death, Thapsus, and Munda – the Senate had passed a large package of extraordinary distinctions. Inasmuch as Caesar had fought the war to defend against an assault on his *dignitas* (Chapter 6), this was of course natural and, from a certain perspective, appropriate – repaying him in the coin he preferred, as it were. A brief look back at this background will help put the Forum Iulium incident in its proper perspective.

The honors, so profuse that a list must be relegated to the footnotes, notably included (post-Pharsalus) the right to make war and peace over any he chose without referral to the Senate and People, the tribunician power for life, presidency over the elections of all but the plebeian magistrates (tribunes and plebeian aediles),[61] (post-Thapsus) a record-setting *supplicatio* of forty

---

[58] Plut. *Caes.* 60.4: ἀλλ᾽ ὥσπερ ἰδιώταις τισὶ χρηματίζων ἀπεκρίνατο συστολῆς μᾶλλον ἢ προσθέσεως τὰς τιμὰς δεῖσθαι.

[59] Plut. *Caes.* 60.6: ὡς ἕτοιμος εἴη τῷ βουλομένῳ τὴν σφαγὴν παρέχειν. Note that at *Ant.* 12.6 Plutarch transfers the outburst to the Lupercalia (Pelling 2011: 449). For the gesture, cf. App. *BCiv.* 2.11/39 (Bibulus in the tumultuous assembly that passed Caesar's first agrarian law).

[60] Plut. *Caes.* 60.5: οὐ μόνον ἠνίασε τὴν βουλήν, ἀλλὰ καὶ τὸν δῆμον, ὡς ἐν τῇ βουλῇ τῆς πόλεως προπηλακιζομένης. Suet. *Iul.* 78.1: *praecipuam et exitiabilem sibi invidiam hinc maxime movit* (cf. Plut. *Caes.* 60.1). Dio 44.8.2: ὥστε ἐν τοῖς μάλιστα πρόφασιν τῆς ἐπιβουλῆς τοῖς ἀποκτείνασιν αὐτὸν παρασχεῖν. App. *BCiv.* 2.107/446 τοῖς διαβάλλουσιν αὐτὸν ἐς τὴν ἐπιθυμίαν τῆς βασιλικῆς προσηγορίας καὶ τόδε παρέσχε. Nic. Dam. *Bios* 79 συνόντες οὖν αὐτοῖς οἱ ἐπιβουλεύοντες ⟨ἤχθοντο⟩ τὸ γεγονὸς καὶ τοὺς ἄλλους τῆς πρὸς αὐτὸν δυσμενείας ἀνέπλησαν καὶ αὐτοὺς ἤδη ἀχθομένους.

[61] After Pharsalus (strictly, the death of Pompey): Dio (42.20), after noting that he is omitting honors that were not unprecedented involving "images, crowns, front seats, and things of that kind" or those which Caesar did not "confirm," leaving only those that "had some special and extraordinary

days, the dictatorship for ten years and (either post-Thapsus or post-Munda) now the appointment of *all* magistrates,[62] and a further fifty days of supplications after Munda, as well as various quasi-divine honors that hinted at assimilation to the gods.[63] Dio explicitly notes that Caesar did

importance and were confirmed" (42.19.3–4, cf. 21.1), lists the following: the right to dispose of the Pompeians as he alone wished; the power of war and peace over any he chose without referral to the Senate and People (Dio adds that the revival of the Pompeian party in Africa was the pretext for this); the right to serve as consul for five years in succession (Ferrary 2010: 13 interprets this, however, as an exemption for five years from the ten-year statutory interval) and as dictator for a full year (rather than the traditional six months), as well as the tribunician power for life "as it were" (thus presumably *perpetuo*; note that, somewhat mysteriously, Dio and Appian appear to date a grant of tribunician sacrosanctity after the end of the civil wars: 44.5.3, *BCiv.* 2.106/442; the best solution is probably that Caesar declined the full tribunician power: Jehne 1987a: 102–104, but cf. Ferrary 2010: 16), along with the right to sit among the tribunes and in all respects to be included with them; presidency over all elections except those of the plebs; the assignment of praetorian provinces without casting of lots (ostensibly the Senate retained the power of assigning the consular provinces); and the right to hold a triumph over Juba and whatever Romans joined with him (Ferrary, p. 14, interprets this as the right to triumph even if another general won the victory, which would seem presumptuous; either way, of course, it is literally preposterous but credible as a loyalist acclamation: Jehne 54–55n44). These honors, including the second dictatorship, must have been passed late in November (September, Julian equivalent): n 68.

[62] After Thapsus: Dio 43.14.3–6 (again with a note on the omission of honors that Caesar declined, 43.14.7): forty days' supplications; his triumphal chariot (in the triumph over Juba already decreed: n. 61) to be drawn by white horses; the right to be accompanied by the total of all the lictors who had ever attended him (including his recent dictatorships, presumably!); to be the overseer of morals for three years, and dictator for ten; a curule chair in the Senate along with those of the consuls, and the right always to deliver his opinion first; the right to give the signal at all the games in the Circus; to appoint also the People's magistrates (but cf. 43.45.1 and nn. 63, 260); a statue of him in a chariot to be set up on the Capitol facing that of Jupiter; a bronze statue of him to be erected standing on the world, bearing the inscription that he was a demigod (after the triumph Caesar has the inscription erased, however); to substitute his name for that of Catulus on the Temple of Jupiter Optimus Maximus.

[63] After Munda: (Dio 43.42.2–3) a thanksgiving of fifty days, the festival of the Parilia celebrating the foundation of the City on April 21 to be given permanent annual games in the Circus Maximus because news of the victory in Spain had come on the previous day (more than a month after the battle was fought); (43.43.1) the right to wear triumphal clothing at all the games and to wear the laurel crown on all occasions; (43.44.1–3) the title "Liberator" and erection of a new temple of *Libertas*; "imperator" as a permanent title to be handed down to any eventual sons and grandsons (not actually used except by Octavian); (43.44.6) a house on public property, and a special kind of thanksgiving to be given in his honor whenever a victory was won even if he had no role in it. Dio considers the honors enumerated thus far to be "not unrepublican," even if unprecedented and excessive, but the following as undisguised declarations of "monarchy" (43.45.1): selection of the offices traditionally elected by the Plebs (although this already seems to have been granted after Thapsus; furthermore at 43.47.1 he appears to indicate that Caesar declined to appoint any magistrates other than the consuls, who were ostensibly elected "by the People according to ancestral custom," though in fact named by Caesar himself), appointment as consul for ten years continuously (note, however, that Appian dates this later and explicitly adds that this was declined [2.106/442, 107/447]), the exclusive right for him or his nominees to command soldiers or use public funds; an ivory statue of him and a chariot to be presented in the procession at the Circus along with the statues of the gods; a statue to be placed in the Temple of Quirinus inscribed "to the unconquerable god" (cf. Cic. *Att.* 12.45.2, 13.28.3, both written May 45), and another to be placed among the statues of the kings on the Capitol (43.45.2–4; cf. Suet. *Iul.* 76.1).

not accept *all* of these honors, but does not tell us exactly which ones, and furthermore he notes that he will not trouble to mention *all* the honors that were voted, all of which makes the job of historians considerably more difficult.[64]

Our source for the details of these exuberant outpourings is the third-century AD Severan historian Cassius Dio.[65] This, of course, raises questions. Dio was of course himself a product of the fully developed imperial system of honorific exchange, which involved as a matter of course the voting of extravagant honors by the Senate to demonstrate loyalty to the Emperor, balanced normally by a show of reluctance and restraint on his part adopted to display due observance of the "honor code" of (authentic) *virtus* on the part of the First Citizen (*Princeps*). One might therefore worry that Dio may have adopted in passages like these an anachronistically "imperial" perspective. Yet that would not force us to reject the facts that he reports; we might note, for instance, that in contrast to his descriptions of some later examples, such as for instance his justly famous account of the Senate's reception of Octavian's announcement of his decision to retire in 27 (53.11–16), there is no prompting, feinting, or dissimulation on Caesar's side. As for the insight into the dynamics of acclamation that he offers, one might venture in his defense that he was an experienced connoisseur of such performances. His interpretations should not, perhaps, be rejected out of hand.

Here then is his picture of the Senate's first honorific outburst after it was at last convinced that Pompey was really dead. Dio writes:

> At last they openly praised the victor and abused the vanquished, and proposed that everything in the world which they could devise should be given to Caesar. And not only in this respect was there great rivalry among practically all the foremost men, who were eager to outdo one another in fawning upon him, but also in voting such measures. By their shouts and by their gestures they all, as if Caesar were present and looking on, showed the very greatest zeal and thought that in return for it they would get immediately – as if they were doing it to please him at all and not from necessity – one an office, another a priesthood, and a third some pecuniary reward. (Dio 42.19.1–2, trans. E. Cary)

---

[64] Dio 43.46.1: although Caesar declined some of them "emphatically" (μάλιστα), he seems to regard even these as still formally ratified because he claims that Caesar in truth intended to use them eventually despite his denials.

[65] Jehne 1987a: 102–104. Ferrary 2010: 9–11 offers a broadly favorable assessment of the third-century historian's information about Caesar's honors, although he rejects without good reason Dio's emphasis on the point that the honors were initiated by senators rather than prompted by Caesar himself.

Above all, Dio here stresses the self-serving motivation of these honors – to gain "an office, . . . a priesthood, . . . some pecuniary reward." Second, he stresses the feverish competition among senators to outdo each other in formulating honors that would produce these benefits for themselves. He adds interestingly that "because they wished still to appear to be free and independent citizens, they voted him these rights and everything else which it was in his power to have even against their will."[66] Dio is in the first instance making a point about the emptiness of this competition when Caesar was in his view in a position to take what he wanted for himself (here Dio may be exaggerating the strength of Caesar's position in his absence from Rome as the African situation looked more and more threatening), but notable also is the suggestion that by taking these initiatives that gave the impression of acting as "free and independent citizens" senators were able to flatter their sense of self-importance – of still *mattering*.[67] A further motive not explicitly stated but clearly implied by Dio is that of putting one's loyalty on record. The majority of senators were frantic to do so as it was now becoming clear that there would be a follow-up campaign against the "diehards" in Africa, so they decreed a triumph for Caesar before he had earned it – in fact (Dio claims) before he was even aware that a war would have to be fought![68] He develops this idea further in his account of the new volley of honors that followed the victory at Thapsus: the votes were a way of assuaging senators' own "fear and suspicion" of Caesar at this fraught moment, thereby encouraging his "magnanimity" upon his return from what had been a most unwelcome campaign.[69] The gesture pays off, for Caesar begins with a reassuring speech upon his return, which (along with statements made later to the People as well) "somewhat relieved them of their fear," and despite their fears and doubts ultimately he managed to "please them" by consulting the

---

[66] Dio 42. 20.2: πολῖταί τε γὰρ καὶ αὐτοτελεῖς ἔτι δοκεῖν εἶναι ἤθελον. Although Dio's remark is directly prompted by the second item in his list (power to make war with any he wished), it evidently applies to the entire list as indicated by ταῦτα . . . τἄλλα παντα.

[67] Valerius Messalla's (in)famous protestation of his "independence" while flattering the emperor Tiberius (Tac. *Ann.* 1.8.4) comes to mind.

[68] Dio 42.20.5: [a war] "which Caesar did not yet know was going to happen." References to the upcoming war in Africa at 42.20.1 and 5 show that these decrees belong *after* news had reached Rome of Scipio's and Cato's flight to Africa (described at 42.13.4), but not very long afterward since Caesar is supposed still to be ignorant of this (§5). The first mention in Cicero's letters of the regrouping of his allies in Africa is on December 17 (ca. October 11, Jul.), 48 (*Att.* 11.7.3). The previous letter to Atticus, dated November 27, would certainly have included some allusion to Africa if Cicero was aware of the regrouping of Caesar's enemies there. Since in that letter Pompey's death is relatively recent news, the series of senatorial honors Dio describes are roughly contemporaneous. (For Cicero's own grave anxieties at this time about the buildup in Africa see Chapter 8 n. 166.)

[69] Dio 43.14.2: μεγαλοφρονούμενος with *LSJ*, s.v.; cf. 43.15.1, 21.4.

Senate on various reforms.[70] This was quite a change from his disposition when he had set out for Spain in April 49, and, frustrated by senatorial inaction and obstruction, had declared that he would "manage the affairs of the Republic by himself."[71] Perhaps it was observed that this kind of "exchange" worked.

The most important thing for us to note here is that Dio describes a context in which the hysterical flurries of honorific votes by the Senate at celebratory moments in the Civil War are not actually prompted by Caesar himself (who in each case was of course absent) but the product of competitive rivalry of senators for self-interested motives – i.e. seeking to gain security, dignity, and political position or material benefit by their actions. The competitive aspect neatly explains the inevitable tendency toward excess as well as the sheer volume of honors. Given the powerful incentives in play, the only effective constraint was exercised by Caesar's *refusal* of some honors (rarely are we told explicitly which ones, unfortunately) and positive expressions of *displeasure* toward others. Yet, as can be seen from the Forum Iulium incident itself (discussed further later) both of these kinds of response were not cost-free for Caesar, since such interventions, like the rejection of a gift, could be viewed as disrespectful of the prestige of the august council of the Senate and even the People. Therefore we cannot unproblematically divine *Caesar's* policy from the "free and independent" actions of cringing, opportunistic senators. Caesar had "emphatically" rejected numerous proposals, and while as a rule Dio insists that he will report only those honors Caesar actually accepted, even this does not offer in itself a clear sign that they were all equally welcome to him.[72] So, for instance, immediately after the long list of honors decreed after Pharsalus and Pompey's death, including the twelve-month dictatorship (in contrast to the traditional six-month limit), Dio writes that Caesar immediately assumed the office, making clear that in this instance this was indeed a priority for him rather than empty flattery excogitated by obsequious senators frantically jockeying for position.[73]

---

[70] Dio 43.18.6 (speech at 43.15.2–18.5), 27.2 (see 25–27.1). The reforms included the restriction of juries to the elite orders of senators and *equites* (i.e. the removal of the less illustrious *tribuni aerarii*), a sumptuary measure limiting extravagant expenditure, rewards for large families, limitation of the term of provincial governors to one or two years, and of course the great calendrical reform. On the other hand, Dio tells us, this goodwill was somewhat squandered by his restoration of some men condemned by the courts, his admission of some "unworthy" elements to the Senate, and the arrival of Cleopatra (43.27.2–3; for Cleopatra see above, n. 33).

[71] Caes. *BCiv.* 1.32.7; Cic. *Att.* 10.4.9. See Chapter 7, p. 405.

[72] Dio 42.19.3–4, 43.14.7; cf. 42.21.1, 43.46.1, 44.7.2. See also nn. 61–63.   [73] Dio 42.21.1; cf. 20.3.

The avalanche of honors we have been tracing culminated in the incident at the Forum Iulium, to which we now at last return. The event itself may belong late in 45 but is more probably placed in January.[74] All our major sources in their narratives of the assassination treat this as a tipping point or galvanizing event in the rise of general hostility and resentment against the Dictator. Despite many obscurities it demands close attention as we explore the themes of senatorial initiative and the fraught complexity of Caesar's response to the cascade of honors which appears to have largely defined Caesar's relationship with the Senate during the years 48–44.

Unfortunately no source states exactly which honors were contained in the omnibus decree the senatorial procession brought to Caesar, but we can make some reasonable conjectures.[75] One way to go about the problem is to assume that the much shorter list of honors supplied by Appian just before he narrates the Forum Iulium story is intended to convey those that were most relevant to it.[76] These include the senatorial authorization of many statues of Caesar (one of them wearing the *corona civica*),[77] the title *parens patriae* ("Father of the Fatherland"),[78] the new office of *dictator perpetuo*,[79] the consulship for ten years (which, Appian explicitly adds, he

---

[74] Date: Appendix 6, p. 644f.

[75] Besides the unspecific reference in Dio (44.8.1), cf. Suet. *Iul.* 78.1: *plurimis honorificentissimisque decretis* and 84.2: *senatus consultum, quo omnia simul ei divina atque humana decreverat* (86.1: *novissimo illo senatus consulto*); Plut. *Caes.* 60.4: τιμάς τινας ὑπερφυεῖς; Liv. *Per.* 116: *plurimi maximique honores*. For the content of the decree, see Dobesch 1966: 29–34; 2001: 1:407–426. App. *BCiv.* 2.106/441–443 (cf. 107/445: τῶν προλελεγμένων τιμῶν) and Dio 44.4–7 give long lists of the honors conferred after Caesar's return too lengthy to enumerate here. Dio clearly marks off four distinct clusters, each apparently followed by an interval in which Caesar's reaction can be assessed (4.2: τὰ μὲν γὰρ πρῶτα ... 5.1: ὡς δὲ ταῦτα ἐδέξατο ... 6.2: κἀκ τούτου ... 6.3: καὶ ἐπειδὴ καὶ τούτοις ἠρέσκετο ... 6.4: καὶ τέλος .... 7.1: ἅμα τε ταῦτα ....). The honors presented to Caesar at the Forum Iulium had been voted on a single day and constituted "a great number and the grandest" (44.8.1) of a list that has filled four chapters. Despite a slight indefiniteness in Dio's account (ποτε) it would stand to reason, given the unpleasant aftertaste of the Forum Iulium incident, that the honors presented formed the culmination and end point of the series.

[76] App. *BCiv.* 2.106/441–443; note 107/445: τὸ ψήφισμα τῶν προλελεγμένων τιμῶν.

[77] Cf. Dio 44.4.5. New statues of Caesar on the Rostra were props in the diadem incident of late January (n. 123). For the novel association of the civic crown with "clemency" see Chapter 8, n. 244.

[78] Cf. Dio 44.4.4, Suet. *Iul.* 76.1. Jehne 1987a: 191–196. There is reason to believe that the denarii that bear the legend *parens patriae* (*RRC* 480/19) are not posthumous, as was formerly claimed, but belong before the Ides of March (B. Woytek 2003: 424–428, pace Crawford ad loc., who follows Alföldi on this point).

[79] Caesar still had to abdicate his serial dictatorship (Zevi and Cassola 2016: 295–296, line 10: *abdic-(avit) ut perpet(uo?) [dict(ator) fieret?]*; *Fasti Cons. Capit.* ad ann. 44) and be appointed/elected (Dio 44.8.4: ἀποδειχθεὶς) to the continuous dictatorship before he actually took up the office shortly before February 15 (see Appendix 6).

afterward declined, and in fact had probably already done so),[80] tribunician sacrosanctity,[81] a throne of gold and ivory (chryselephantine),[82] the triumphal dress whenever he performed sacrifice,[83] celebration of Caesar's victories as public holidays,[84] public prayers for his safety and oaths sworn by magistrates to uphold his acts,[85] the renaming of Quintilis, the month of Caesar's birth, to Iulius ("July"),[86] many temples to him as a god, and one jointly for him and Clementia.[87] These final items in Appian's list roughly coincide with those that Dio places at the end of the long series of honors: a vote (presumably by the Senate) to recognize Caesar as Divus Iulius, to erect a temple to him and to his Clemency (with Antony to be inaugurated as *flamen*), and the right to place his tomb within the religious boundary of the city (*pomerium*) – an honor which, as C. Till points out, is appropriate to a "hero" and founder figure, not a god.[88] Dio adds that the Senate had these decrees inscribed in gold letters on silver pillars and set up at the feet of the statue of Jupiter Capitolinus.[89] This was probably "the decree of the Senate in which it had proposed for him everything divine and human," which, Suetonius says, Antony read out at Caesar's funeral, and which "some think" had given him false confidence in the senators' loyalty.[90]

---

[80] App. *BCiv.* 2.107/447. Dio 43.45.1 mentions the ten-year consulship as being among the earlier pack of honors voted immediately after Munda, and it would seem to be rather cast in the shadow by the continuous dictatorship. Furthermore, it would directly conflict with Caesar's actual plans for the office in his absence. I conclude that Appian is right that this was declined, but would put this not long after Munda.

[81] Cf. Dio 44.5.3. For tribunician *potestas* since 48 see 42.20.3 and n. 61.

[82] Cf. Dio 44.6.1, for whom (as in the Latin sources) the chair is simply golden. See n. 230.

[83] Since it appears that what Caesar was wearing at the Lupercalia was indeed "triumphal dress" (n. 230), Appian is here perhaps referring to the formal grant of this right.

[84] Somewhat obscure: it is tempting to associate this with the institution of the *ludi victoriae Caesaris*, which according to an old theory were instituted in 45 by moving to July, Caesar's birth month, the *ludi Veneris Genetricis* begun in 46. Yet Ramsey and Licht 1997 have now argued strongly that this change occurred only after Caesar's death in 44.

[85] Cf. Dio 44.6.1.   [86] Cf. Dio 44.5.2. Cf. Cic. *Att.* 16.1.1, 4.1.

[87] Cf. Dio 44.6.4. Till 2003: 92–93 infers from the coins that Dio has been overenthusiastic: the temple was to *Clementia Caesaris*, and Caesar was only a σύνναος. On the Temple of Clementia see Chapter 8, p. 473.

[88] Till 2003: 87–88, 208. Dio 44.6.4–7.1 (καὶ τέλος ... ἅμα τε ταῦτα); cf. Cic. *Phil.* 2.110: *quem is honorem maiorem consecutus erat quam ut haberet pulvinar, simulacrum, fastigium, flaminem?* In a recent, probing study of these honors, Koortbojian 2013: 15–49 concludes that they were not decreed within Caesar's lifetime; this may be going too far (note Cicero's use of the pluperfect tense), but his emphasis on the distinction between "honors" and formal deification is salutary. Dio 44.6.4 implies that Iuppiter Iulius was the cult name, but Cic. *Phil.* 2.110 is clear: Dobesch 1966: 17–28, 2000: 101–102; Zecchini 2001: 57–58.

[89] Dio 44.7.1: ἅμα τε ταῦτα.

[90] Suet. *Iul.* 84.2, 86.1: *novissimo illo senatus consulto*, which evidently refers back to 84.2 and thence to 78.1.

We observe immediately that, with the exception of the authorization of a "continuous" or "permanent" dictatorship and the ten-years' consulship (which may already have been declined), what is left is what a cynic might call a lot of "happy talk" – honors in the fundamental sense that they conferred no new powers but instead fulsomely expressed approbation and gratitude even to the point of deification. None of these gave Caesar greater legal authority or resources to manage the difficult and pressing tasks he had before him before his departure on the Parthian campaign, probably already set for only two months hence. On the other hand, while ever more fervent protestations of loyalty and gratitude were presumably not unwelcome in themselves, it was also clear to all, even to Caesar, that these excesses were also potentially dangerous, especially so now that the Senate had chosen to break through the fraught line between mortal and divine. To be formally acknowledged as a god was pretty close to being acknowledged as a "king," although at the same time it can also be seen as a highly diplomatic way of *avoiding* the odious name.[91] The legislation assimilating Caesar to the status of a god would inevitably have brought in its train all manner of unwelcome criticism, with little or nothing to be gained from it after the deluge of recent honors. Much as the divinity question has exercised modern scholars because of its great importance for Caesar's heir, for the development of a central imperial ritual, and for the history of Roman religion, the evidence suggests that it was far from a priority for Caesar and probably under current circumstances a nuisance, and a dangerous nuisance at that. Anything that was truly important to him had to be taken care of before his departure – especially the choice of dozens of magistrates for the next few years of his absence, quite apart from the ongoing preparations for the Parthian campaign and other administrative and legal work detailed above. Yet notoriously, Antony, though *appointed* as Caesar's *flamen* in the original decree (and presumably legislation) had still not been inaugurated by the Ides of March; moreover, the addition of a god to the Roman state pantheon would presumably have required a decree of the Senate, which we know had not been passed at the time of the assassination.[92] This looks like a hot potato that Caesar preferred not to handle.

---

[91] In Hellenistic Greece "the significance of the classification of the ruler in divine terms is that it disguised the novelty of the monarchies" (Price 1984: 52).

[92] Dio 44.6.4; Cic. *Phil.* 2.110. If the flaminate of *Divus Iulius* was modeled on the Flamen Dialis (44.6.4), we may wonder whether Antony was eager to take over the job and the many crippling restrictions that attended it (not to remarry – already a problem – not to leave the City for a single night, or to mount a horse, or to lay eyes on an army, etc.). The Clementia temple project was celebrated on coins (*RRC* 480/21; Plut. *Caes.* 57.4), which, however, are probably posthumous; it was presumably replaced after the assassination by plans for a temple of Divus Iulius. Formal deification

Dio's preliminary remarks before he relates this final wave of honors passed by the Senate provide useful commentary upon the Forum Iulium incident:

> [By the time of his death Caesar] had aroused dislike that was not altogether unjustified, except in so far as it was the senators themselves who had by their novel and excessive honours encouraged him and puffed him up, only to find fault with him on this very account and to spread slanderous reports how glad he was to accept them and how he behaved more haughtily as a result of them. It is true that Caesar did now and then (n.b.: ἔστι μὲν γὰρ ὅτε) err by accepting some of the honours voted him and believing that he really deserved them; yet those were most blameworthy who, after beginning to honour him as he deserved, led him on and brought blame upon him for the measures they had passed. He neither dared (ἐτόλμα), of course, to thrust them all aside, for fear of being thought contemptuous, nor, again, could he be safe (ἀσφαλής) in accepting them; for excessive honour and praise render even the most modest men conceited, especially if they seem to be bestowed with sincerity.[93]

Later Dio returns to the theme, this time shining the spotlight more closely on the proposers' incentives:

> When they had begun to honour him, it was with the idea, of course, that he would be reasonable; but as they went on and saw that he was delighted with what they voted – indeed he accepted all but a very few of their decrees – different men at different times kept proposing various extravagant honours, some in a spirit of exaggerated flattery (ὑπερκολακεύοντες αὐτόν) and others by way of ridicule (οἱ δὲ καὶ διασκώπτοντες). . . . Others, and they were the majority, followed this course because they wished to make him

came only sometime after Caesar's death (Suet. *Iul.* 88.1; Plut. *Caes.* 67.8 with Pelling 2011: 490; App. *BCiv.* 2.148/617; Till 2003: 93–94nn386, 389, 168n149, follows Gesche in putting the formal apotheosis no earlier than 40/39). Till offers a survey of the evidence and scholarship on Caesar's quasi-divine and divine honors (pp. 74–97, 170–172); see also n. 88. Wardle 2009: 107 puts it well: "a tentative, uncertain groping by the Senate for appropriate forms of honors by which to celebrate the achievements of Caesar." For a thoughtful exploration of the ways in which Cicero worked out ideas of the deification of exceptional mortals from his *De lege Manilia* to Caesar, see now Cole 2013.

[93] E. Cary trans. of Dio 44.3.1–3. The exceptional interest of Dio's analysis here merits reproducing the original: οὐ γὰρ δὴ καὶ ἀναίτιον πάντη τὸ ἐπίφθονον ἐκτήσατο, πλὴν καθ' ὅσον αὐτοὶ οἱ βουλευταὶ ταῖς τε καινότησι καὶ ταῖς ὑπερβολαῖς τῶν τιμῶν ἐξάραντές τε αὐτὸν καὶ φυσήσαντες ἔπειτα ἐπ' αὐταῖς ἐκείναις καὶ ἐμέμφοντο καὶ διέβαλλον ὡς ἡδέως τέ σφας λαμβάνοντα καὶ ὀγκηρότερον ἀπ' αὐτῶν ζῶντα. ἔστι μὲν γὰρ ὅτε καὶ ὁ Καῖσαρ ἥμαρτε, δεξάμενός τέ τινα τῶν ψηφισθέντων οἱ καὶ πιστεύσας ὄντως αὐτῶν ἀξιοῦσθαι, πλεῖστον δὲ ὅμως ἐκεῖνοι, οἵτινες ἀρξάμενοι τιμᾶν αὐτὸν ὡς καὶ ἄξιον, προήγαγον ἐς αἰτίαν οἷς ἐψηφίζοντο. οὔτε γὰρ διωθεῖσθαι πάντα αὐτὰ ἐτόλμα, μὴ καὶ ὑπερφρονεῖν νομισθείη, οὔτ' αὖ λαμβάνων ἀσφαλὴς εἶναι ἐδύνατο·τὸ γὰρ ὑπερβάλλον τῶν τε ιμῶν καὶ τῶν ἐπαίνων χαυνοτέρους πως καὶ τοὺς πάνυ σώφρονας, ἄλλως τε κἂν ἀληθῶς γίγνεσθαι δοκῶσι, ποιεῖ. An otherwise similar analysis by Nic. Dam. *Bios* 67 omits the risk of offense by *declining* excessive honors.

envied and hated as quickly as possible, that he might the sooner perish. And this is precisely what happened, though Caesar was encouraged by these very measures to believe that he should never be plotted against by the men who had voted him such honours, nor, through fear of them, by any one else.[94] (Dio 44.7.2–4, E. Cary tr.)

As we saw in our discussion of the prior votes of honors, Dio again places the initiative squarely on the shoulders of the senators; these extravagant gestures are not prompted or solicited by Caesar.[95] He gives a glimpse of plausible motives, first and foremost "exaggerated flattery," of course, whose potential advantages are obvious, especially for those seeking to safeguard themselves vis-à-vis an all-powerful figure; "mockery" makes less sense, unless it be interpreted to mean such extravagance that it invites mockery of its recipient – covert, of course, and deniable by its initiator. And again Dio stresses the danger to Caesar that the honors posed, as well as their deceptive quality, for he again represents the Dictator as misled, thinking that the honors were sincerely motivated, while at the same time attracting ill will and thus undermining his political position. Yet he could not reject them en masse because then he would be perceived as acting "contemptuously" (i.e. with "tyrannical" *superbia*).

The process was evidently driven by the competitive dynamics discussed earlier which would now, with Caesar known to be preparing to depart within perhaps only two months, have reached a fever pitch. The window of opportunity was now rapidly closing in which senators would be able still to gain from the Dictator in person what they wanted: "an office . . . a priesthood . . . [or] some pecuniary reward," to quote an earlier but still relevant passage.[96] They courted the Dictator's favor ever more fervently in the few remaining weeks before his departure – a time when, as will be seen, their own fortunes over the next few years would be decided – and they ultimately, inevitably, overshot the mark: "The result was that they rendered the man offensive and loathsome even to the most mild-mannered of observers, so extravagant and bizarre were the decrees."[97] The Senate, in short, was being a nuisance, and a potentially dangerous nuisance at that.[98] Some sources go so far as to claim that Caesar's *enemies* took the lead in proposing these decrees, precisely to bring odium upon

---

[94] Dio's points are echoed by Nic. Dam. *Bios* 59, 67, 80 and Plut. *Caes.* 57.2–3. Nicolaus presses the idea that Caesar was naïve and lacking in political experience, evidently in order to reveal a contrast with his hero, Augustus (see Toher 2017: 34–35, 283–285). See n. 108.

[95] For the opposite view, Dobesch 2000: 105: "die vorzüglich geformte, sehr klare Ideologie trägt die Handschrift Caesars." Similarly, Ferrary 2010.

[96] Dio 42.19.2, p. 504.   [97] Plut. *Caes.* 57.2 (Pelling tr.).   [98] Zecchini 2001: 59–60.

him.[99] This presumably could only have been inferred securely after the fact. It is intriguing that some sources hint that Cicero, the most prestigious of the senior consulars of Caesar's Senate, played a leading role in proposing these honors: Antony would later accuse him of "deceiving" Caesar, apparently on these grounds.[100]

This, then, may offer sufficient explanation for Caesar's refusal to stand: to express his displeasure with this last, over-the-top, invidious yet empty gesture. If we are to take our sources seriously it is also clear that this was no pre-orchestrated piece of political theater (or at least, not with Caesar himself). Appian and Nicolaus make clearer than the others that Caesar was interrupted while he was *busy*: "Having gathered together the builders [sc. of the Forum], he was selling off the contracts for its construction."[101] As we saw, Plutarch and Suetonius both paint a picture in which Caesar was *surprised*, being of two minds whether to stand or remain seated as his friends and advisors offer their contradictory advice.[102] Dio echoes the sense of confusion and extempore improvisation, resorting to explanations such as "some heaven-sent fatuity or even … excess of joy" for Caesar's failure to rise.[103] According to Plutarch, Caesar himself later offered his epilepsy as an excuse, while Dio alleges that Caesar's friends adduced an attack of diarrhea.[104] Not a single ancient source takes the line of defense taken up in modern times by Weinstock – namely, that Caesar was under no obligation to rise before the magistrates and Senate because, as Dictator, he was the superior magistrate, or, similarly, because he was after all now by their own admission a god (Dobesch).[105] On the contrary, one thing we do

---

[99] Most notably Nic. Dam. *Bios* esp. 67; see also Plut. *Caes.* 57.3; Dio 44.7.3, 9.1. Yet Dio also claims that Cassius had spoken *against* the most extravagant of the decrees (44.8.1: n. 50) – possibly a case of "rewriting history." Note that Nic. Dam. alone has Cassius and P. Casca try to prompt Caesar to pick up the diadem at the Lupercalia (§72, Toher 2017: 309).

[100] Chapter 8, p. 478 with n. 246. Plut. *Caes.* 57.2–3 "The first honours were proposed to the senate by Cicero"; cf. *Cic.* 40.4–5 (Cicero) "was foremost among those who advocated Caesar's honours and were eager to be ever saying something new about him and his measures." Antony: Cic. *Phil.* 13.41: *deceptum autem patrem Caesarem a me dicere audes? Tu, tu, inquam, illum occidisti Lupercalibus.* Cf. Brutus's similar complaint to Cicero, if authentic: n. 108.

[101] Nic. Dam. *Bios* 78 (note that at §79 a friend has to draw Caesar's attention to the procession); cf. App. *BCiv.* 2.107/445: χρηματίζοντι.

[102] See n. 56.   [103] Dio 44.8.2.

[104] Plut. *Caes.* 60.6–7; Dio 44.8.3. The "diarrhea defense" might be a "scatological parody" of the epilepsy excuse Dobesch 2001: 1:284–285; Pelling 2011: 450), though if so Dio has no idea of it. Dio himself throws up his hands, but interestingly allows as one of the two authentic alternatives that Caesar was actually thrilled: εἴτ᾽ οὖν θεοβλαβείᾳ τινὶ εἴτε καὶ περιχαρείᾳ (44.8.2). Cf. Chapter 8, n. 109.

[105] Weinstock 1971: 275–276, on which see Pelling 2011: 449. Dobesch 2001: 1:279–280. Similarly, Jehne 1987a: 280: "Caesar dokumentierte auf diese Weise die realen Machtverhältnisse."

know (from Plutarch) is that he said in response that "the honours needed to be cut down, not increased."[106]

From what we have seen of the game senators had been playing, this appears to be an utterly rational and perfectly honest, if undiplomatic, response. Caesar had been put in a "no-win" position, and our sources are agreed that the particular form his expression of displeasure took proved gravely damaging to his public standing – and not only among those looking to discredit him. Plutarch points one way when he describes Caesar as addressing the magistrates and Senate "as if he were dealing with private persons" (ὥσπερ ἰδιώταις τισὶ χρηματίζων), implicitly (to draw in Balbus's probably invented advice) that he demanded "to be courted as a superior" (ὡς κρείττονα θεραπεύεσθαι).[107] Dio says that the general impression people had was that he had become "over-proud" (ὑπεραυχεῖν) and so hated him for his arrogance (ὑπέρφρων: note the repetition of ὑπερ elements).[108] Appian and Nicolaus make the underlying danger more explicit: Caesar's reaction "made himself vulnerable to those attacking him on the grounds that he desired the title of King" and caused the "hatred" against him to spread much more widely than just the small circle of those already plotting against his life.[109] Indeed, Plutarch adds that indignation even spread to the People, who had constituted an important part of the audience for the spectacular misfire: in Plutarch's words, it "distressed the people as much as the senate: they thought that an insult to the senate meant an insult to the whole state."[110]

The ten-year consulship, if it had not already been declined as I am inclined to think, was immediately dropped.[111] The deification plan was put on a back burner. Nevertheless, rather than gaining approbation for such acts of moderation, Caesar's "insulting" refusal to stand before the representatives of the Roman Senate and People opened him to the charge

---

[106] Plut. *Caes.* 60.4.   [107] Plut. *Caes.* 60.4, 8.

[108] Dio 44.8, esp. §§2, 4. Dio adds that if he was arrogant, they had made him so by their extravagant honors. Cf. the complaint of Brutus (on the letter's authenticity see Chapter 8, n. 242) written to Cicero in 43: "It is this weakness and despair (*ista vero imbecillitas et desperatio*), for which the blame rests no more with you than with everybody else, that brought Caesar to dream of monarchy" (*in cupiditatem regni impulit*, [Cic.] *ad Brut.* 1.16.3).

[109] App. *BCiv.* 2.107/446; Nic. Dam. *Bios* 79. Plutarch too introduces this story by reference to Caesar's "lust for kingship" (*Caes.* 60.1).

[110] Plut. *Caes.* 60.5: οὐ μόνον ἠνίασε τὴν βουλήν, ἀλλὰ καὶ τὸν δῆμον, ὡς ἐν τῇ βουλῇ τῆς πόλεως προπηλακιζομένης (Pelling tr.). Dio 44.8.2: ὀργὴν ἐκ τούτου πᾶσιν, οὐχ ὅτι τοῖς βουλευταῖς ἀλλὰ καὶ τοῖς ἄλλοις. Nic. Dam. *Bios* 78 is attentive to the awesome effect of the procession on the great crowd, but conspicuously omits their reaction to Caesar's reception. Suet. *Iul.* 79.1 sees only the Senate: *adiecit ad tam insignem despecti senatus.*

[111] See n. 80.

of having assumed a tyrannical arrogance. The various awkward excuses
put about perhaps at the time, and Caesar's own great gesture of dismay
(n. 59) – itself perhaps an allusion to the possible fate that awaited anyone
successfully labeled a *rex* in Rome – seem to have had little effect on the
general sense of embarrassment and indignation.[112]

It seems clear, not only from the public relations disaster that ensued
but from the accounts of the event themselves, that Caesar and his
attendants on this occasion (no less than Balbus and Trebatius) were
caught completely by surprise. Yet he had known to stay away from the
senatorial meeting at which these honors had been decreed,[113] and anyway the consul or consuls involved (whether Antony alone or the pair,
Fabius and Trebonius), as well as the mass of senators at this point, were
of course to varying degrees supporters of Caesar in the recent wars.[114] It
is remarkable, even astonishing, that they do not seem to have communicated and coordinated with their chief or with his closest advisors, of
whom Balbus was certainly one. This scene takes the form of
a confrontation not only between the Senate – led by its Caesarian consul
or consuls – and Caesar but also within Caesar's "Cabinet," who are given
important supporting roles in the drama as they stand with the Dictator
and offer their conflicting advice in response to the unwelcome or
unexpected *démarche*. This moment may represent an eruption of the
tension that J. Malitz discerned between senators of the old type (e.g.

---

[112] Excuses: n. 104. It will be clear that I have virtually no common ground with Dobesch's theory (e.g.
2000: 112) that the idea of kingship was reflected in virtually every respect of Caesar's self-
presentation at this time and was "an integral part of his ideology." This makes nonsense of his
strenuous efforts to avoid the label *rex* and overlooks the intense resistance to hints of monarchy
both among senators and People. Furthermore, Dobesch strains belief when he suggests that during
his few months in Rome, preoccupied by preparations for the Parthian War as we have seen, Caesar
put together a remarkably coherent and all-encompassing monarchical ideological system (pp.
121–122), especially since our sources make clear that the initiative for this monumental series of
honors, whose coherence Dobesch overstates, came from senators engaged in competition with
each other to win Caesar's favor, and that they often manifestly overshot the mark. Dobesch 1966
laid out the foundations of his case that Caesar actively pursued a divine monarchy and developed
them further with the important further studies collected in Dobesch 2001, including one focused
on the Forum Julius episode (1:275–361) and another that is highly relevant (ibid., pp. 407–426).
While my interpretation is fundamentally different from his, Dobesch's painstaking work remains
among the most detailed analyses of the individual episodes examined in this chapter, and any
reader interested in pursuing the subject at a deeper level is recommended to study these important
pieces closely.

[113] Dio 44.8.2: "They transacted such business in his absence, in order to have the appearance of doing
it, not under compulsion, but voluntarily." On Caesar's manner of "consultation" with the Senate
in this period see Jehne 1987a: 440–446.

[114] Dio 43.47.3; Syme, *RP* 1.98. Cf. Cic. *Div.* 2.23: *in eo senatu, quem maiore ex parte ipse cooptasset.*
Fabius was a "newer" Caesarian than Antony and Trebonius, yet he had played a conspicuous
enough role in the Munda campaign to earn a triumph (Chapter 8, n. 163).

Cicero) and the Caesarian "Chancellery," between traditional republican forms and practices and those that reflected the concentration of power in the hands of a single man.[115] We should also remember that there were Caesarians on both sides of this confrontation. This may be our first sign of the fragmentation of the victorious Caesarian party, a phenomenon that has rarely received the attention it merits. Toward the end of this chapter we shall consider clearer evidence of Caesar's inability to control his former officers tightly now that they had achieved victory – probably the only shared goal they had.

The Removal and Expulsion of the Tribunes

On or very shortly before January 26, and probably within just a few weeks of the unpleasant scene in the Forum Iulium, occurred the next notable moment in the story of disaffection – this time in particular, of *popular* disaffection from Caesar.[116] The flare-up with the tribunes plays a significant role in all the major narratives of Caesar's final months. Although the story is fairly well known, a brief review of the facts will help us see the salient points.[117]

It is relevant to observe that even apart from the confrontation with L. Metellus in April 49, this was not Caesar's first case of trouble with tribunes. Suetonius, in an unfortunately isolated anecdote, reports that a certain tribune named Pontius Aquila declined to stand as Caesar passed the tribunician benches when he celebrated one of his triumphs, probably that of early October 45 for the final victory of the civil wars at Munda.[118] We have some evidence that this triumph was at least latently controversial since it was celebrated over an army which, though apparently consisting mostly of local Spanish levies, had nevertheless had a citizen core and was certainly *led* by Romans.[119] According to Suetonius (our only source for

---

[115] Malitz 1987. Unlike Malitz, however, I would emphasize not the resemblances between these latter forms and those that would eventually characterize the Principate – something that could only become apparent from historical hindsight – but those that would be familiar from observers' own historical experience of *dominatio*, especially Sulla's. Cf. Tac. *Ann.* 1.1.1.

[116] Date: see Appendix 6.

[117] See recently Pelling 2011, 455–457, Morstein-Marx 2012: 208–209, and now Toher 2017: 292–301. See also Dobesch 2001: 1:101–143.

[118] Suet. *Iul.* 78.2. For the date of the triumph see Appendix 6, n. 7; other sources for the triumph: Dio. 43.42.1–2; Plut. *Caes.* 56.7–9; Quint. 6.3.61. Strictly speaking, nothing absolutely excludes a date in 46 for Pontius's tribunate rather than 45, but since App. *BCiv.* 2.113/474 suggests that Pontius Aquila had taken the Pompeian side in the Civil War his election is harder to imagine before Thapsus than after it.

[119] Plut. *Caes.* 56.7–9 (cf. Dio 43.42.1). Jehne 1987a: 281, and Chapter 8, p. 440.

this event) Caesar is said to have been so incensed by Aquila's gesture of disrespect that he challenged him, a mere *homo novus*, to "take back the Republic" from him, and for some days sarcastically qualified every pledge he made with the proviso "with Pontius's permission."[120] If this is so, Caesar chose to interpret Aquila's action as an invidious bit of republican grandstanding intended to arouse odium against himself. Yet, as he had done earlier in connection with the suicide of Cato, Caesar seems to have kept the dispute on the level of words rather than deeds. We hear of no further retaliation, in sharp contrast to the dispute with the tribunes of 44 about to be examined; nor did Caesar's anger make life unbearable for Aquila. We are still a long way off from the day when a caesar's denunciation left suicide as the only honorable option.[121] But the incident offers a kind of preview of Caesar's angry reaction to a more open kind of "republican" demonstration by the tribunes Flavus and Marullus in the last days of January 44.

On or just before January 26 a diadem (the ancient symbol of royalty, in fact only a glorified ribbon tied around the head) threaded through a laurel "crown" (strictly, a wreath) was spotted at dawn's light on one of the new statues of Caesar on the new Rostra, reconstructed by Mark Antony at the (north)west end of the Forum.[122] This new monument complex entailed a radical intervention in one of Rome's most tradition-laden spaces (among other things, by tearing down the old Rostra along with the hallowed monuments of the ancient Comitium and relocating it some 35 meters to the west) and included an unparalleled commemoration of Caesar: two statues at least, apparently gilt, one bearing the "civic crown" and the other the "grass crown" (*corona obsidionalis*), both associated with Caesar's new

---

[120] Broughton identifies the tribune and later conspirator against Caesar (always called Pontius Aquila) as the "Pontius" whose Neapolitan estate was confiscated during the civil wars and sold at a bargain price to Caesar's former lover Servilia (Suet. *Iul.* 50.2; Macrob. 2.2.5; Cic. *Att.* 14.21.3), and also with an L. Pontius of Trebula who entertained Cicero in the *ager Trebulanus* (*MRR* 2: 308). Both assumptions are quite doubtful for different reasons (Münzer, *RE* Pontius, nos. 1, 11, and 17; Shackleton Bailey 1965: 1:295, 3:191, 6:241; Jehne 1987: 331–332n116 and 1987a: 282n71). The closest match for the name appears relatively early on a list of pontiffs in the triumviral colony of Sutrium in southern Etruria (*CIL* 11.3254, col. II.13 L. Pontius Aquila; note also a L. Pontius P.f. at I.16; cf. Wiseman 1971: no. 335), yet our Pontius Aquila's eventual role in the conspiracy against Caesar makes it improbable that this is he.

[121] As e.g. for Cornelius Gallus under Augustus (27 or 26 BC); indeed, Aquila apparently lived to become one of Caesar's assassins. We would have heard of it if Pontius had been relieved of his tribunate, as Flavus and Marullus were later.

[122] Dio 44.9.2–3 (λάθρᾳ); App. *BCiv.* 2.108/449; Plut. *Caes.* 61.8; *Brut.* 9.8 (νύκτωρ); Nic. Dam. *Bios* 69 (κρύφα). For concealment by night, a common phenomenon of popular interventions such as graffiti against the "public transcript," see Morstein-Marx 2012: 198. Even so, the tribunes would later claim to have discovered the culprit (App.).

status as *pater patriae*.[123] It stands to reason that the appearance of a diadem on one of these statues would be understood by spectators the next morning as in some sense a response to the new monument and what it represented. As for the curious, mixed form of the "crown," while this could be explained on largely functional grounds as providing some structural integrity for the diadem to be threaded around, this may also have suggested an assimilation of the traditional sign of royalty with the symbolism of republican leadership, for a successful *imperator* wore a laurel wreath, and after Munda Caesar had been granted the honor of wearing the laurel "crown" at all times.[124] Returning to our story, then, we hear that when the wreath with intertwined diadem was discovered, the tribunes L. Caesetius Flavus and C. Epidius Marullus – absolute nobodies both – took it upon themselves to have the diadem removed from the wreath and to arrest the (alleged) perpetrator with alacrity.[125] If we are to believe Plutarch (with some corroboration from Dio), the tribunes' zealous defense of the Republic even sparked a popular reaction, for after they had imprisoned the supposed culprit, "the People (ὁ δῆμος) followed them with applause, saluting them as 'Brutuses' because Brutus was the man who had ended the succession of kings and transferred the power of the

---

[123] Dio 44.4.4–5. For the Antonian Rostra and its statues see also Dio 43.49.1–2 and App. *BCiv.* 2.106/441; Coarelli 1992a: 238–245; Sehlmeyer 1999: 231–234; P. Verduchi, *LTUR* 4.214–217; Till 2003: 68, 167; Davies 2017: 268–269. It is fairly certain that the Rostra on which the statues stood was the new one: the old Rostra and Comitium, already damaged by the fire of 52, must have been a work site, if not entirely demolished by this time. Nic. Dam. *Bios* 69 alone says that the statue was gilt – not by now so very unusual for a high honor (Cic. *Phil.* 5.41, 9.12, with Manuwald 2007, ad loc.) Plut. *Caes.* 61.8 speaks of the decoration of a plurality of statues with diadems, probably a needless complication (cf. *Ant.* 12.7). On the *corona obsidionalis* see Chapter 2, n. 112, and n. 124 of this chapter.

[124] The "crown": App. *BCiv.* 2.108/449 and Suet. *Iul.* 79.1 (with Kaster 2016: 82); note that Plut. *Caes.* 61.5 and Nic. Dam. *Bios* 71 describe the "crown" presented to Caesar at the Lupercalia as exactly the same type. It has sometimes been supposed that the laurel was for concealment (Ramsey 2003: 285; Pelling 2011: 454; Toher 2017: 307–308), but this appears dubious since it was completely unsuccessful on both occasions. Grant after Munda: Dio 43.43.1; Suet. *Iul.* 45.2 (an earlier grant for Pompey: Vell. Pat. 2.40.4, Dio 37.21.4). There has been a great deal of interest in the variety of "crowns" associated with Caesar. For a useful review of the controversies, see now Bergmann 2010: 115–131. Bergmann rejects both Kraft's interpretation (1969) of the distinctive wreath/"crown" worn by Caesar in the portrait that appears on the obverse of a large series of coin issues in 44 BC (*RRC* 480/1–20) as an archaizing Etruscan/Roman symbol of royalty and Crawford's view that this is nothing other than the triumphal *corona aurea* granted after Munda (n. 230; cf. now Till 2003: 189–192); her own identification of the numismatic "crown" as the *corona obsidionalis* (pp. 126–131, c. 190–191, 197–198) is not unattractive but lacks strong positive evidence.

[125] App. *BCiv.* 2.108/449 mentions only the arrest; Dio 44.9.3 (also Nic. Dam. *Bios* 69) only the removal of the diadem; Plut. *Caes.* 61.8 and Suet. *Iul.* 79.1 mention both, the latter interestingly specifying that the *fillet* (diadem) was removed *from* the wreath (*coronae fascia detrahi*), thus seemingly implying that the laurel wreath was left in place in accordance with the honors mentioned earlier. Both were new men, Caesetius possibly from Campania: Wiseman 1971: nos. 84, 161.

monarchy to the Senate and People."[126] They then explained their action
before the People in a *contio*, stressing that Caesar himself had no desire for
kingship and had already shown his displeasure with those who spoke of
the subject.[127] From what we have seen thus far, these ought to have been
irreproachable statements from Caesar's point of view. Yet their *actions*,
like Aquila's, could be seen as invidious, and intentionally or not they had
sparked a popular reaction in which *they* were figured as heroes of the
Republic against some hidden hand furthering *regnum* which, in the
poisoned atmosphere of the aftermath of the Forum Iulium incident,
might well be supposed to be guided by the Dictator himself. Something
was going on, and the tribunes made much of their standing up against it.
Caesar would doubtless have preferred to let the thing blow over quietly in
a manner that did not raise further questions about his role or preferences –
and did not suggest that the Republic needed a Brutus.

On January 26 – possibly the same day as the incident of the diadem,
perhaps immediately thereafter – Caesar's return to the City after performing the traditional sacrifices on the Alban Mount for the Latin Festival was
celebrated in an especially honorific fashion in the form of an *ovatio*, or
lesser triumph.[128] This event is remarkable inasmuch as it had, it seems, not
been granted for any specific military achievement, as had always been the
case for past *ovationes*; the precise character of this innovative use of the
honor is therefore unclear.[129] Perhaps it was intended as a symbolic act of
closure to the series of civil wars as a whole, but emphasizing the victor's
role as the dispenser of *clementia* and preserver of citizens' lives instead of
martial achievement.[130] G. Sumi has recently noted that this *ovatio* seems

---

[126] Plut. *Caes.* 61.9. See also Caesar's insult of "the People" (τὸν δῆμον) as *bruti*: p. 523. Morstein-Marx
2012: 209n68.

[127] Dio 44.9.3: καὶ προσέτι καὶ ἐπαινεσάντων αὐτὸν ἐν τῷ πλήθει ὡς μηδενὸς τοιούτου δεόμενον;
App. *BCiv.* 2.108/449: ὑποκρινάμενοί τι καὶ τῷ Καίσαρι χαρίζεσθαι, προσαπειλήσαντι τοῖς περὶ
βασιλείας λέγουσιν.

[128] *I.It.* 13.1, *Fasti triumph. Capit.* an. 44, which alone attests that the form of the honor was the *ovatio*.
On the relative chronology of the diadem episode, see Appendix 6.

[129] The pretext for the celebration is ignored by all our sources. Dio 44.4.3 only briefly mentions in
passing, among the enormous package of honors granted toward the end of 45 or the beginning of
44, the right to "ride on horseback into the City from the Alban Mount after the Latin Festival."

[130] Weinstock's treatment of the *ovatio* (1971: 326–331) is informative but, as often in that book, goes
rather too far in the direction of divinization. There is no evidence, for example, that Caesar wore
the dress of the Alban kings when he entered Rome, and none of the many sources stress anything
exceptional in Caesar's appearance. Caesar's *ovatio* may have been the first in which the general rode
on horseback rather than walked, but Weinstock probably makes too much of the variation from
ancient custom forbidding dictators from riding a horse (Mommsen 1887: 2:159; Kunkel and
Wittmann 1995: 2:675–676): exemptions had often been given, and in any case Caesar had no
doubt spent a great deal of his Alexandrian, Pontic, and Munda campaigns (all as Dictator) on

to establish a (transitory) connotation as a "bloodless triumph," which of course the Caesarian civil wars hardly were, strictly speaking, although due to the victor's remarkable use of *clementia* the bloodletting was minimized.[131] As Caesar entered the City, then, "some men" called out to him as "King" (*rex*), to which the Dictator responded by turning the dreaded word into a joke: "My name is not King [*Rex*, the name of the noble family to which Caesar's grandmother belonged] but Caesar."[132] With a typical kind of variation that pervades our narratives of Caesar's final fraught months, our sources diverge significantly about just who had addressed Caesar as *rex*: Suetonius blandly, or perhaps innocently, attributes the acclamation to "the *plebs*," but Dio makes those who cried "*rex*" a relatively small minority while Appian and Plutarch emphatically *separate* these men from "the People," who in fact "groan" or are "disturbed" at the outburst.[133] But the action of the tribune Marullus is in keeping with this more discriminating perspective, since he ordered his attendants to bring before his tribunal "those who had begun" the shouting, suggesting that (in keeping with known practice in public demonstrations) the chant had been begun by a claque in an organized manner.[134] Both of our more detailed sources (Appian and Dio) clearly state that the tribune (or tribunes) *initiated a prosecution* of the man (or men).[135] It is hard to say what kind of trial these sources are thinking of, but given the highly political nature of the complaint and the fact that one or more tribunes were the instigators of the projected trial, it is not impossible that the charge would have been *perduellio* and the procedure would then be a trial before the assembly

horseback. We have explicit attestation of this at Munda (Dio 43.37.3; Vell. Pat. 2.55.3) and during his trip through Campania in December 45 (Cic. *Att.* 13.52.2).

[131] Sumi 2011: 93–94; cf. Rich 2014: 238 (213–214n82, 215n92), who argues that the tradition had no historical foundation and was invented by late-republican scholars, most likely Varro. See Pliny, *HN* 15.125; Gell. 5.6.21–22; Plut. *Marc.* 22, Fest. 213L. Already in 40 both Antony and Octavian celebrated *ovationes* for their avoidance of civil war in the Peace of Brundisium (*Fasti triumph. Capit.* an. 40). If the *ovatio* was a way of defining the conclusion of the civil wars as a triumph of *clementia*, this might give added point to the decoration of the statue that bore the *corona civica*.

[132] Dio 44.10.1 (τινες); App. *BCiv.* 2.108/450 (ἑτέρων); Plut. *Caes.* 60.3 (with Pelling ad loc.); Suet. *Iul.* 79.2. Early in his career Caesar had vaunted his descent from the Marcii Reges: Suet. *Iul.* 6.1.

[133] App.: τοῦ δήμου στενάξαντος; Plut.: τοῦ δὲ δήμου διαταραχθέντος. Dio seems to imply that the shouters were actually members of the growing conspiracy (44.9.1, 10.1), but prominent men will hardly have been arrested by Marullus without leaving a trace of their names.

[134] App., who attributes the response to Marullus alone. Dio, less plausibly, has the tribunes (n.b. the plural) call to account the *one man* who had begun the shouting. Note that both authors say that the tribune(s) summoned the man or men *for trial*; they did not throw him into prison (the fate of the perpetrator of the diadem – another reason to infer that Plut. *Caes.* 61.8 conflates the two incidents [cf. Pelling ad loc.]). For organized chanting and claques in the Late Republic see Morstein-Marx 2004: 134–136.

[135] Dio 44.10.1: δίκην τῷ πρώτῳ αὐτὸν εἰπόντι ἔλαχον. App. *BCiv.* 2.108/451: ἐκέλευον ἄγειν ἐς δίκην.

(*iudicium populi*), as in the trial of Rabirius in 63 with its three *contiones* and the *populus Romanus* standing in judgment; this would of course ensure maximal publicity for the tribunes and whatever cause they claimed to represent.[136] But however that may be, even if the intended prosecution was "merely" to take place in a standing criminal court (*maiestas?*) or even some less elaborate judicial proceeding reserved for defendants of low standing it becomes easier to understand why at this point Caesar's patience snapped. He "no longer restrained his anger," Dio says, "and expressed outrage that these men themselves were stirring up party strife against him."[137] It is unclear whether Caesar spoke thus before the Senate or the People in a *contio*. However that may be, he still took no official action against the tribunes until they escalated the confrontation by posting an edict in which they declared that they were being denied the freedom to speak openly on behalf of the *res publica*.[138]

Perhaps the tribunes were not gratuitously making trouble for Caesar; perhaps, as Pontius Aquila had done, they were testing the limits of the new post–Civil War environment. Yet they had acted in a way that left Caesar no good choices. He could have stayed his hand and thereby shown his willingness to live by "republican" rules, at the price of letting a tribunician prosecution go forward, inevitably with much further public ventilation of the inflammatory topic of *regnum* – a dangerous subject which the Dictator repeatedly showed he preferred to suppress. Or he could crack down and retaliate against the tribunes for their "trouble-making" behavior in "stirring up ill will against him," thereby violating their sacrosanctity (which he claimed to have fought the Civil War in part to defend) and simultaneously both validating their complaint about the infringement of their "freedom of speech" and lending credence to the rumors about his own desire for *regnum*.[139] That he grasped the latter horn of the dilemma seems at first almost incredibly inept, or openly "tyrannical." Sheer exasperation may well have played a part: our sources

---

[136] Jehne 1987a: 421 with n. 24. For the institution of the *iudicium populi* see conveniently Lintott 1999: 152–154. The last known *iudicium populi* was the prosecution of Milo in 56 by P. Clodius as curule aedile (Alexander 1990: no. 266). The case was clearly not a civil one since the plaintiffs were not themselves harmed.

[137] Dio 44.10.1. The standard translation of προσστασιάζειν, "to stir up to sedition," is not in itself incorrect but might here subtly encourage too "monarchical" a reading of the allegation: cf. Dio 38.37.1.

[138] Dio 44.10.2, translating ὑπὲρ τοῦ κοινοῦ somewhat differently from E. Cary in the Loeb ed. ("on behalf of the public good"). Appian leaves out this important escalation by the tribunes.

[139] Stirring up ill will against him: Liv. Per. 116: *invidiam ei tamquam regnum adfectanti <concitantibus*: Rossbach >.

emphasize the emotional intensity of Caesar's response.[140] His anger is understandable if not politically excusable: as J.-L. Ferrary observes, Flavus and Marullus had turned Caesar's efforts at a *recusatio regni* into evidence of *affectatio regni*.[141] The earlier ugly episodes involving L. Metellus in 49 and Pontius Aquila only a few months before suggest that he had no patience with what he would likely have seen as tribunician efforts to paint him as a "tyrant" before the Roman People; if that definition stuck, Caesar knew that he might as well cut his own throat.[142]

Caesar now chose to make a forceful demonstration of his institutional power, the most dramatic since the Civil War began. Summoning a meeting of the Senate in the Temple of Concordia (often a bad sign), Caesar personally accused the tribunes themselves of placing the diadem on his statue and seeking, by their zealous pursuit of the alleged instigators, to raise the suspicion that he desired *regnum*. He suggested or actually asserted that by these actions they were endangering his very life.[143] However (he went on) he would be satisfied with their expulsion from the Senate, which was indeed effected after they were deposed from office by action of their own tribunician colleague, the ill-fated poet Helvius Cinna. (This may refer to a prior Gracchan-style abrogation of the men's tribunate in the popular assembly.)[144] The men were also sent

---

[140] Dio 44.9.3–10.2: ἰσχυρῶς ἐχαλέπηνε . . . οὐκέτι τὴν ὀργὴν κατέσχεν, ἀλλ' . . . ὑπερηγανάκτησε . . . περιοργῆς ἐγένετο. App. *BCiv.* 2.108/452: οὐκέτι ἐνεγκών. Plut. *Caes.* 61.10: παροξυνθεὶς . . . ἐφυβρίζων. Suet. *Iul.* 79.1: *dolens . . . graviter increpitos.*

[141] Ferrary 2010: 29.

[142] Cf. n. 59. Caesar's fears are plausibly represented by Nic. Dam. *Bios* 69; Vell. Pat. 2.68.4.

[143] Dio 44.10.2; App. *BCiv.* 2.108/452: ὡς ἐπιβουλευόντων οἱ μετὰ τέχνης ἐς τυραννίδος διαβολήν; Vell. Pat. 2.68.4: *dum arguunt in eo regni uoluntatem*; Val. Max. 5.7.2: *quod is* [Caesetius] *tribunus pl. cum Marullo collega inuidiam ei tamquam regnum adfectanti fecerat* (almost identical phrasing in Livy *Per.* 116); Nic. Dam. *Bios* 69: εἴ πως δύναιντο εἰς τὸ πλῆθος αὐτὸν διαβαλόντες ὡς ἂν δυναστείας παρανόμου ἐρῶντα καὶ αὐτοὶ ἐξάρχοντες νεωτεροποιίας ἀποκτεῖναι. Nicolaus's assertion that Caesar attributed to the tribunes designs on his life is supported by Appian's and Dio's information that he (or others) gave the opinion that they deserved to be put to death. For the "bad sign" see Chapter 3, n. 33.

[144] App. *BCiv.* 2.108/452: μόνης δ' αὐτοὺς ἀφαιρεῖσθαι καὶ παραλύειν τῆς τε ἀρχῆς καὶ τοῦ βουλευτηρίου. In fact, however, the men were banished as well. Cinna (ironically, the man mistakenly lynched by the crowd after Caesar's assassination): Dio 44.10.3: [sc. ὁ Καῖσαρ] προσαπαλλάξας δὲ ἐκ τῆς δημαρχίας διὰ Ἑλουίου Κίννου συνάρχοντος αὐτῶν (cf. 46.49.2; Iul. Obs. 70). See Morstein-Marx 2012: 212n82. Suet. *Iul.* 79.1, Plut. *Caes.* 61.10 suggest that Caesar acted on his own, but they are probably omitting legal niceties. Vell. Pat. 2.68.5 has Caesar punish the tribunes solely by virtue of his censorial powers (whose nature remains a point of scholarly controversy; Jehne 1987a: 80–95); this fits Dio's statement that he "erased them from the Senate," yet he does appear to have obtained a senatorial decree authorizing his action (ψῆφον ἐπήγαγε, Dio; συνδόξαν τῇ συγκλήτῳ). Jehne (90–91) suggests that Velleius should not be taken too literally and that the tribunes automatically lost their place upon being deposed by the assembly, perhaps in accordance with the *lex Cassia* of 104.

into exile.[145] It would be hard not to take the view that the affair amounted to an unambiguous and extreme violation of tribunician sacrosanctity.[146] The ugly confrontation left its traces: at the first consular elections after the tribunes' banishment their names were found to have been written on quite a few of the ballots in a disturbing revelation of the "hidden transcript" of dissent.[147]

Throughout the Late Republic, the tribunes remained a potent symbol of the political rights of the Roman Plebs.[148] This was still true in January 44: perhaps the most powerful iconographic representation of the association of "freedom" with the tribunes is the great denarius of Palicanus, best dated to 45 BC, emblazoned with *Libertas* on the obverse and a representation on the reverse of a tribunician bench (*subsellium*) atop the Rostra on the reverse.[149] Caesar himself had made the defense of the *tribunicia potestas* central to his self-justification in the Civil War. Appian puts the clash with the tribunes in the context of "the People's" disappointment in their hope that he would "restore the Republic to them" – hopes in which (he implies) they had been at first encouraged by Caesar's clemency and political generosity toward his former opponents.[150] When the royal acclamation was given at the *ovatio*, Appian says that "the People" groaned, thus making clear that he considered those who addressed Caesar as "king" a small minority;[151] he explains the "anger" the incident aroused by referring to the "title of king" and the fact that "the power of the tribunes was sacrosanct in accordance with an ancient law and oath."[152] In the speeches Appian embeds in his narrative after the assassination and before Philippi in order to represent the public justifications offered by the

---

[145] Nic. Dam. *Bios* 69 says by senatorial decree. App. *BCiv.* 2.108/452 and Dio seem unaware of the banishment, which however Suet. *Iul.* 80.3 confirms.

[146] App. *BCiv.* 2.108/453, 138/575–576. Ninety years before, the city plebs had been troubled even by Ti. Gracchus's removal of a sitting tribune by means of their vote: Plut. *Ti. Gracch.* 15.

[147] Suet. *Iul.* 80.3, with Butler and Cary 1927: 144; Dio 44.11.4, dated shortly after the Lupercalia. Our sources seem to conflict about whether the tribunes had been recalled by the time of Caesar's assassination: so explicitly Nic. Dam. *Bios* 76, with the information that the praetor L. Cornelius Cinna, brother of Caesar's second (or perhaps first) wife (see n. 305), who as a Marian and Sertorian himself had tasted exile and restoration, effected their restoration by means of a δόγμα (here probably law), having requested this as a favor from Caesar (Toher 2017: 315–316). But App. *BCiv.* 2.122/514 says that the conspirators recommended the tribunes' restoration in the immediate *aftermath* of the assassination.

[148] Morstein-Marx 2004: 266–270; Arena 2012: 47–54.

[149] *RRC* 473/1, illustrated also at Morstein-Marx 2004: 52. Crawford's date of 45 BC has now been reinforced against Mannsperger by B. Woytek 2003: 306–307.

[150] App. *BCiv.* 2.107/448: ὁ δῆμος ἤλπιζε καὶ τὴν δημοκρατίαν αὐτὸν αὐτοῖς ἀποδώσειν.

[151] App. *BCiv.* 2.108/450: ἑτέρων δ' . . . βασιλέα προσειπόντων καὶ τοῦ δήμου στενάξαντος.

[152] App. *BCiv.* 2.108/453: ἥ τε τῶν δημάρχων ἀρχὴ ἱερὰ καὶ ἄσυλος ἦν ἐκ νόμου καὶ ὅρκου παλαιοῦ.

"liberators" Brutus and Cassius, Caesar's mistreatment is highlighted among his most conspicuously "tyrannical" actions before popular or military audiences.[153]

Obviously these kinds of judgments of the popular mood are hardly precise. Dio, for example, traces the signs of popular displeasure a little farther back, to the Forum Iulium incident, after which his narrative describes a progressive accumulation of "hatred" against Caesar without distinction of classes.[154] Plutarch, more vaguely, says that Caesar's "yearning for kingship" gave even "the multitude" (οἱ πολλοί) their chief cause for "open and deadly hatred" against him and he clearly marks the affair of the tribunes as a major step in the development of dissent and resistance to Caesar's increasingly "unrepublican" behavior.[155] He also describes, as we saw, a popular demonstration in support of the tribunes after their initial action regarding the diadem in which they invoked the name of Lucius Brutus the Liberator, in mocking reply to which Caesar – so Plutarch says – responded after he had punished the tribunes by called them *bruti* (idiots) and "Cymaeans," insulting thereby not merely them but the People (τὸν δῆμον) too.[156] Suetonius, after briefly describing the conflict with the tribunes, says that Caesar "was unable to shake off the accusation that arose from this that he actually desired the title of 'king.'"[157] Appian is more emphatic than the others about Caesar's loss of popular support at this stage, but the picture of our main sources is broadly consistent. Only the friendly Nicolaus of Damascus insists that ὁ δῆμος remained wholly infatuated with the Dictator, demanding that he cease his hesitation to become king.[158] He is alone in this and his protestation is suspect in itself.

The aftermath of this debacle is the probable context for another important phenomenon noted by most of our major sources for the prelude to the assassination: a series of writings or graffiti, produced in

---

[153] App. *BCiv.* 2.138/575: οὐχ ἱερὰν καὶ ἄσυλον ἄρχοντες ἀρχὴν ἐξηλαύνοντο σὺν ὕβρει; 4.93/389: οἴκτιστον ἁπάντων . . . τοῖς δημάρχοις ὑμῶν ὑβριζομένοις.

[154] Dio 44.8.2: οὐχ ὅτι τοῖς βουλευταῖς ἀλλὰ καὶ τοῖς ἄλλοις (cf. §§3–4 τοὺς πολλούς). 44.10.4: ἐκ τούτου διεβλήθη. 44.12.2 οἱ πολλοί.

[155] Plut. *Caes.* 60.1, 61, 62.1: οὕτω δὴ τρέπονται πρὸς Μᾶρκον Βροῦτον οἱ πολλοί. See Pelling 2011: 422 for the theme.

[156] Plut. *Caes.* 61.9–10: ἅμα καὶ τὸν δῆμον ἐφυβρίζων; cf. Dio 44.12.2. See Pelling ad loc. for an explanation of the second insult.

[157] Suet. *Iul.* 79.2: *neque ex eo infamiam affectati etiam regii nominis discutere valuit* . . . .

[158] Nic. Dam. *Bios* 70. Nicolaus presses this line consistently at the Lupercalia incident, against all other sources: Morstein-Marx 2004: 145–146. For Nicolaus's crafting of his picture of Caesar in relation to his heir see Toher 2017: 29–38. Nicolaus presents Augustus as wiser than Caesar (above all, having learned the lesson of his assassination), but this does not lead him to endorse any of the sharp justifications of the Dictator's assassination familiar from our other sources.

secret at night and revealed in public places in the day, which played a key role in prompting Marcus Brutus to fall in with the plot.[159] Plutarch, who as a biographer is particularly interested in the motives that led the young Brutus to kill his friend and benefactor, gives the fullest information, which is, however, largely corroborated by others.

On the Capitol among the group of statues of the Seven Kings in front of the Temple of Jupiter Optimus Maximus there stood, providing a kind of closure to the royal group, an image of Lucius Brutus, who according to tradition had expelled the Tarquin dynasty and became the first consul of the Republic.[160] Plutarch interestingly claims that Brutus was depicted holding a drawn sword, which is not easy to explain since he was no tyrant slayer in the strict sense; perhaps he had been assimilated to the Greek vision of the tyrannicide, or alternatively someone in the chain of transmission mistook the dagger (*culter*) Brutus had pulled from Lucretia's breast for a tyrannicide's "drawn sword."[161] However that may be, early in 44 BC, and probably on more than one occasion (to judge from Plutarch's use of the imperfect tense), the base of this image was marked with graffiti that read "If only you now lived, Brutus" and "If only Brutus were alive."[162] But of course, a Brutus *was* alive, the young protégé of Cicero pardoned by Caesar after Pharsalus and given the prestigious urban praetorship for this very year, so in fact the graffiti on the base of the statue were simultaneously a lament and a shaming exhortation: if Marcus Brutus were truly a Brutus, he would emulate the spirit of his ancient ancestor.

---

[159] Morstein-Marx 2012: 208–209; Hillard 2013: 112–113; and now Montlahuc 2019: 205–212. Although there are no precise chronological indicators, note that the graffiti, like the incidents with the diadem and the acclamation, participate in the same discourse of kingship and emphatically develop the connection with L. Brutus that was perhaps first introduced by those events. Furthermore, Plut. *Brut.* 9.8 appears to place the graffiti *after* the diadem incident.

[160] For the statues see Weinstock 1971: 145–146 (Brutus); J. D. Evans 1990; Sehlmeyer 1999: 68–74; Coarelli, *LTUR* 4.368–69; Cadario 2006: 38–41. (Tempest 2017: 87 mistakenly places the statues in the Temple of Concord.) Their dates are commonly placed within a few decades of 300 BC, but Weinstock is inclined to put the statue of Brutus at least as late as the mid-second century.

[161] Plut. *Brut.* 1.1: ἐσπασμένον ξίφος. For divergent views see Weinstock 1971: 146; Welwei 2000: 53; Walter 2004: 145. No need to doubt its existence, as does Sehlmeyer 1999: 73. Ghirlandaio's famous fresco at the Sala dei Gigli of the Palazzo Vecchio in Florence shows how easily the mistake could be made.

[162] Plut. *Brut.* 9.6 (ἐπέγραφον); Dio 44.12.3 and Appian *BCiv.* 2.112/469 provide close echoes of the phrases, and Suet. *Iul.* 80.3 probably preserves the original of the first (*Utinam viveres!*). I infer from Suetonius's verb (*subscripsere . . . statuae*) that the *graffito* was written on the statue base. This certainly seems the easiest and quickest method of applying a message to a statue, but one could instead hang or affix a *titulus* on it (Dio 61.16.2a; Suet. *Nero* 45.2). The graffitists were not the only ones "looking for Brutus": see Cic. *Att.* 13.40.1 (August 45): *ubi igitur* φιλοτέχνημα *illud tuum* (sc. Attici) *quod vidi in Parthenone, Ahalam et Brutum?* Dettenhofer 1992: 210. See n. 170 for further graffiti on Brutus's tribunal.

The corollary of the stated counterfactual was of course that Marcus Brutus was really *not* a descendant of Lucius as his clan always claimed, and indeed one version of the incident says that further graffiti declared explicitly that "Your descendants are unworthy of you," and even "You [now addressing the living Brutus] are no descendant of *him*."[163] The accusation is especially neat in its precise physical setting, since the statue was itself a kind of touchstone of Brutan identity by the Late Republic. Descent of living Bruti from the "Father of the Republic" was challenged by malicious souls who awkwardly pointed out that since Lucius Brutus had executed *both* his sons, his named bloodline ended there.[164] But the statue itself was adduced by the Bruti of the Late Republic as evidence, for Plutarch tells us on the authority of Posidonius that they used to point to the similarity between the statue's features and their own to substantiate their claim of descent from the first consul of Rome.[165]

Suetonius intriguingly adds another, otherwise unattested graffito in this connection, a couplet inscribed on the base of a statue of Caesar himself, as follows:

> *Brutus, quia reges eiecit, consul primus factus est;*
> *Hic, quia consules eiecit, rex postremo factus est.*

> Brutus became the first consul, since he had expelled the kings;
> This man at last became king, since he had expelled the consuls.[166]

Given the allusions in the first line, it is most attractive to suppose that this statue of Caesar was the very one set up on the Capitol as recently as the end of 45 BC right next to that of L. Brutus which Suetonius mentions in the same breath – and, of course, also next to those of the ancient kings of Rome.[167] An odd juxtaposition at first blush, even perhaps mischievous like some of those "honors" to which our sources allude. The placement of the statue gave more than the suggestion of monarchy, yes, but on the other hand proximity to L. Brutus "saved" it: perhaps, as Weinstock suggested, Caesar was being paired with L. Brutus

---

[163] App. *BCiv.* 2.112/469, where σου and τοῦδε seem to require their placement in the immediate proximity of Lucius's statue rather than Marcus's tribunal in the Forum.

[164] Plut. *Brut.* 1.4–5; Dio 44.12.1. The philosopher-historian Posidonius had leapt to the defense, stating that a younger third son had survived (*BNJ* 87 F 40). This was likely the line Atticus also took in the genealogical monograph commissioned by M. Brutus (Nepos, *Att.* 18.3). Brutus had himself made clear reference to his ancestry on his coins of ca. 54: *RRC* 433/1–2.

[165] Plut. *Brut.* 1.8 = Posid. *BNJ* 87 F 40.

[166] Suet. *Iul.* 80.3. Angius 2015: 272–276, 2018: 97–114 comments on the stylistic features of the language of popular protest as exemplified in graffiti, chants, and mime.

[167] Dio 43.45.4; Sehlmeyer 1999: 229–230. See Morstein-Marx 2012: 204–206.

as a liberator.[168] But the hostile were free to "read" the statue in the most negative way, and indeed this very statue is said to have played a role in spurring Marcus Brutus on to conspiracy, while a comment in Cicero's *Pro Deiotaro*, delivered before Caesar himself, acknowledges (if ostensibly by way of rebuttal) the indignation it inspired among some.[169]

This was not all: the tribunal and seat in the Forum where Marcus Brutus, urban praetor in 44, held court were another focus of the graffitists' attention. More than once (it seems) Romans woke up to find them "covered" in the night with goading phrases like those on the statue of the founder of the Republic: "Brutus, are you asleep?" "Brutus, are you dead?" "Brutus, have you been bribed?" and – now in an explicit denial of the bloodline – "You are not a true Brutus."[170] (The story is well known from Shakespeare, though the Bard, following North's and ultimately Bishop Amyot's translations of Plutarch, misconceives these as "papers" laid in Brutus's chair.[171])

Who were the authors of these graffiti? It is in the nature of graffiti written secretly under cover of night that no one except the perpetrators could be entirely sure who the culprits were. Many will remember the cynical plan of Cassius in Shakespeare to influence Brutus with "writings" "in several hands . . . as if they came from several citizens," and may suspect that the graffiti were actually produced by the conspirators themselves or like-minded members of the elite.[172] Yet we have seen that (with the exception of the ever-faithful Nicolaus) our sources on the contrary describe increasingly bitter popular alienation from Caesar at this stage, especially after the deposing of the tribunes. There is no real need, then, to explain away the indications in our sources that the graffiti were indeed popular in origin, "hidden transcripts" of popular displeasure at Caesar's recent, ostensibly "unrepublican" behavior.[173] Plutarch *in propria persona* describes the graffiti unambiguously as expressions of the

---

[168] Weinstock 1971: 145–147. The title had just been given to Caesar after Munda: n. 63.

[169] Cic. *Deiot.* 33.

[170] Plut. *Brut.* 9.7: (εὑρίσκετο μεθ' ἡμέραν), cf. 10.6, *Caes.* 62.7: (νύκτωρ δὲ κατεπίμπλασαν), imperfect tense in both places; App. *BCiv.* 2.112/469: (λάθρᾳ); Dio 44.12.3.

[171] Shakespeare, *Julius Caesar*, I.3.142–146; cf. I.2.312–317 and II.1.36ff. See Morstein-Marx 2012: 206–208 and Pelling 2011: 463. Modern translators of Plutarch seem often to have been influenced by Shakespeare here.

[172] Shakespeare (I.2.315–317) may have been guided to the idea by Plut. *Brut.* 10.6 (n. 174), but the notion that the notes really derived from the conspirators themselves and ultimately from Cassius is apparently his alone (Humphreys 1984: 127 ad 1.3.142–146).

[173] Morstein-Marx 2012 for the full argument against elitist views that suppress ideological autonomy and political agency among the lower orders (cf. Morstein-Marx 2013). Already Jehne 1987a: 321–322 had acknowledged that the graffiti were at least in part authentic expressions of popular views.

People,[174] Appian is quite explicit that the agents were ὁ δῆμος (entirely consistent with his view that the People first hoped that Caesar would return the Republic to them, "groan" when some address him as *rex* on his return from the Latin Festival, applaud his refusal of the crown at the Lupercalia, and now prompt M. Brutus to act),[175] while Suetonius lists the graffiti among a series of anonymous critical responses to Caesar's actions that exemplify how "not even the People were any longer pleased with the present situation but both privately and in public they objected to (his) domination and cried out for liberators."[176] Our sources for the events of early 44 are therefore perfectly consistent with what we know about the practice of political graffiti and comparable writings (such as satirical placards attached to statues), which shows that they were regarded, and rightly so, as "popular" forms of political communication as a rule.[177]

On my interpretation, then, the disastrous conflict with the tribunes had prompted a kind of underground, popular "graffiti campaign" which exploited the references to L. Brutus, Father of the Republic, that had emerged in the conflict with the tribunes shortly before. The focus of the campaign on Brutus's namesake or (supposed) descendant, the praetor of 44, is probably sufficiently accounted for by the invocation of his great ancestor and M. Brutus's own tendency, at least before the Civil War, to advertise his heritage as a "liberator."[178] The graffiti, coming on top of the well-attested popular dismay over the punishment of sitting tribunes for ostensibly defending republican principles, are important evidence of the worsening political environment for Caesar at a time when his focus must have been on preparations for the upcoming Parthian campaign. The faux

---

[174] Plut. *Brut.* 9.5: οἱ πολῖται, *Caes.* 62.1: οἱ πολλοί (with Pelling 2011: 422) (cf. ὁ δῆμος 61.9–10). For the arguably contrary evidence of a synoptic passage in both Appian (*BCiv.* 2.113/472) and Plutarch (*Brut.* 10.6) see Morstein-Marx 2012: 210.

[175] App. *BCiv.* 2.107–108/448–449, 108/450, 109/457–458, 112/469.

[176] App. *BCiv.* 2.112/469: ἐρεθιζόμενος καὶ ὀνειδιζόμενος μάλιστα ἐς τοῦτο ὑπὸ τοῦ δήμου; Suet. *Iul.* 80.1 : *ne populo quidem iam praesenti statu laeto, sed clam palamque detrectante dominationem atque assertores flagitante.* To be sure, not all of the other protests that he lists apparently in support of this assertion (§§2–3) are necessarily and exclusively popular in origin: a placard (*libellus . . . propositus est*) and jingle attacking his induction of new senators, including (allegedly) newly conquered Gauls (but note *vulgo canebantur*); the derisive shouting that greeted the suffect consul Fabius Maximus in the theater (note *universis conclamatum est*); or the "many" voting ballots in the consular elections marked with the names of the deposed tribunes. But there is manifestly enough of a popular character to this series to justify Suetonius's point in §1 about popular expressions of alienation.

[177] So too Hillard 2013. The *locus classicus* is of course the popular graffiti that called on Tiberius Gracchus to "take back" the public land for the poor: Plut. *Ti. Gracch.* 8.10, with Morstein-Marx 2012: 201–202.

[178] The coins of ca. 54 (n. 164) suggest a certain emphasis on the lineage. In 52 Brutus had published a fictional defense of Milo that argued that his murder of P. Clodius was *pro re publica* (Ascon. 41C).

issue of "kingship" had become a dangerous distraction, and signs were now emerging of deep alienation among the more politically involved elements of the urban plebs – a political constituency that had until the civil wars been overwhelmingly friendly to Caesar.

The notion that Caesar, so often associated with *popularis* causes, was always and even now the darling of the People remains fairly strongly rooted in contemporary scholarship. Not uncommonly one reads that the *populus* were indifferent whether they had a *rex* or not, or even desired Caesar to be that *rex*, and that the conspirators were victims of "wishful thinking" in supposing otherwise.[179] But this is to infantilize the Roman plebs, and to assume that the Republic had entirely lost the allegiance of ordinary Roman citizens (a proposition for which there is no evidence). Our narrative sources in fact – whether tendentiously or not is hard to say – make noises repeatedly about the people's displeasure with their condition during the Civil War years and at times with Caesar himself.[180] Civil war – even when fought partly in their name – was not a pleasant experience for the Roman People. Whatever the precise nature of the clash with the tribune L. Metellus over the treasury in April 49, it is clear that it aroused some discontent and lowered his standing among the city plebs.[181] In a matter very close to the plebs' heart, the debt crisis of the Civil War years, Caesar cannot have been very popular. Caesar's debt legislation of 49, widely admired today, was clearly perceived among those suffering under the burden of debt as much too friendly to the lenders, since in 48 M. Caelius as praetor, and in 47 much more dramatically P. Dolabella as tribune, dared to defy the new rules openly in a way that our sources describe as "cancellation of debts."[182] Popular resentment exploded, and

---

[179] E.g. Woolf 2007: 34; Billows 2009; Wiseman 2009: 218–219. Jehne 1987a: 286–331 draws up a detailed balance sheet of Caesar's standing with the *plebs urbana* during and immediately after the Civil War. While his conclusion is somewhat more positive than mine, he also stresses that the Dictator's record was highly mixed: not the stuff of passionate, resolute loyalty.

[180] Dio 41.16.1–17.1 on Caesar's first *contio* in April 49; 42.26–28 on popular dismay in 47 at Caesar's incessant warring and Antony's imperious behavior; 43.19.2–20.3, 24.1–3, 42.1–3 with various critical comments by anonymous observers of the triumphs of 46 and games in honor of Julia (counterbalanced, it must be added, by other, positive impressions: esp. 43.20.1); very similarly, App, *BCiv.* 2.101/420, and on the Spanish triumph, Plut. *Caes.* 56.7–9. These last examples are all good examples of what Pelling calls "characterization by reaction" (2011: 25) and therefore may not depend on actual testimony.

[181] See Chapter 7 p. 410f.

[182] Caelius: Dio 42.22–25.3, Caes. *BCiv.* 3.20–22.4. Dolabella: Dio 42.29–33, Plut. *Ant.* 9.1–5. Bruhns 1978: 123–137; Dettenhofer 1992: 156–175; Welch: 1995; Jehne 2000: 157–160; on Caelius see also Cordier 1994. For Caesar's debt legislation, a prudent compromise between the interests of debtors and creditors – therefore inevitably disappointing to the urban poor – see Caes. *BCiv.* 3.1.2–3 (cf. 20.1), Dio 41.37–38, Suet. *Iul.* 42.2, App. *BCiv.* 2.48/198. Despite Cicero's howls of outrage (*Off.*

when the crowd barricaded the Forum so that Dolabella could pass his debt legislation Antony, Caesar's Master of the Horse, backed by a decree of the (Caesarian) Senate, brought the situation under control by a deployment of massive force within the city walls, perhaps authorized by a *senatus consultum ultimum*; hundreds were killed, some even (it is said) hurled off the Tarpeian Rock.[183] The poor of the City, then, saw their champions humbled, their hopes dashed, by Caesar's deputies working hand in glove with *the Senate*, and even authorized by the "Final Decree" (!); Antony was "hated by the multitude" for this, and it strains credulity to assume that Caesar's reputation was untainted by his deputy's action in defense of his own legislation and against their own clearly demonstrated demand for relief. When Caesar at last returned from the East in October 47, "the multitude," now in more orderly fashion, pressed their claims again for dramatic debt relief (χρεῶν ἀποκοπάς); he now made concessions both on debt and on rent (another urban issue Dolabella had championed), and by these measures – more dramatic on the latter than the former – Dio assures us that he belatedly won them over.[184] Perhaps. But what then did they think in 46 of his striking of 170,000 names – more than half! – from the list of those entitled to receive the free grain distribution in Rome?[185] Or his outright abolition of the new-style *collegia* that P. Clodius had developed into the crucial mechanism for mobilizing crowds in support of "popular" political action, which very likely had formed the backbone of Dolabella's debt and rent agitation in 47?[186] By a law passed in 46 Caesar excluded

---

2.84), "Caesar's policy on debts was not especially revolutionary" (Yavetz 1983: 136). One might even doubt whether it was "popular": Caelius bitterly comments to Cicero in early 48 that in Rome only the moneylenders support Caesar ([Cic.] *Fam.* 8.17.2. Pelling 2011: 338–339 gives a brief summary of the debt legislation, Jehne 1987a: 243–250 (cf. 2000: 158–159) elucidates the facts and the politics, and B. Woytek 2003: 57–72 offers a full examination of the measures in the context of the debt crisis, concluding that they "attest to deep understanding of economic conditions" on Caesar's part.

[183] Liv. *Per.* 113 (800!); Dio 42.32.3; Plut. *Ant.* 9. 4–5: τοῖς μὲν οὖν πολλοῖς ἐκ τούτων ἀπηχθάνετο. S.c. u.: certainly passed in 48 (Dio 42.23.1–2; notably absent from Caesar's own version, *BCiv.* 3.21.3) and almost certainly again (αὖθις) in 47 (42.32.1; Plut. *Ant.* 9.4).

[184] Dio 42.50.4, 51.1–3: remission of all unpaid interest since the beginning of the Civil War, increased valuation of property forfeited in payment of the debt, release of one year's payment of rent. For the rent remission (remarkably recorded on the Fasti Cons. Ostienses, but under the year 48, probably the retrospective beginning of the rent-free period: *I.It.* 13.1, pp. 182–183) see Yavetz 1983: 133–137; Jehne 1987a: 293–294, 2000: 159–160.

[185] Suet. *Iul.* 41.3, Dio 43.21.4, App. *BCiv.* 2.102/425 and Plut. *Caes.* 55.5–6 are clearly synoptic and would seem to go back to Pollio – troubling because they both perpetuate the misunderstanding that the *recensus* was of the whole citizenry rather than the registry for the grain dole. (See Appendix 6, n. 13 for another mistake probably traceable to Pollio.) Yavetz 1983: 153–158; Jehne 1987a: 91–94, 304–308; B. Woytek 2003: 186–189; Pelling 2011: 414.

[186] Suet. *Iul.* 42.3, with Yavetz 1983: 85–96; Jehne 1987a: 308–310. For Clodius's use of the newly reorganized *collegia* see Chapter 1, n. 36. Cf. Tatum 1999: 242 for Dolabella's imitation of Clodius.

from the juries of the criminal courts the *tribuni aerarii*, whom Dio explicitly describes as belonging to "the crowd" or "common people" (ἐκ τοῦ ὁμίλου), in order (Dio says) that only the "purest part of the population" (τὸ καθαρώτατον: senators and *equites*) would sit in judgment; whatever its motivation – Dio implies that it was purely to enhance the "respectability" of the juries – this must have been felt as a gratuitous insult to those just below the equestrian census who, according to C. Courrier's recent, persuasive demonstration, formed an elite among the urban plebs and thus served as a key nexus between senators and the multitude for the various forms of popular political mobilization in the City.[187] In sum, if the politically active elements of the urban plebs in Rome had expected Caesar to act like a traditional *popularis* politician – that is, as their patron and protector of their interests, both material and political – they must by now have been quite disillusioned.[188] By these actions, together with the brutal repression by his deputies and Senate of the Caelian and Dolabellan disturbances of 48 and 47, Caesar had not only ensured that he would not inherit Clodius's urban organization but had also made himself into something of an "anti-Clodius."

Moreover, the Dictator's heavy hand in controlling all elections, and presumably legislative votes as well, had deprived the People of the substance of their traditional and ancient right to influence, and sometimes to determine the political agenda and outcomes, in a manner even more domineering than had the Pompeians at the outbreak of the Civil War; this might have been excused during the rolling series of crises that defined the war, but now no longer.[189] Appian explicitly attests to this popular grievance even among soldiers originally recruited by Caesar; while that may attest more to his belief than verified knowledge, the evidence should

---

[187] Dio 43.25.1–2; Suet. *Iul.* 41.2. See Chapter 1, n. 37.

[188] To judge from the past history of the enfranchisement of Italy and long-standing Roman reservations about the cultural identity of Cisalpine Gaul in particular (Williams 2001: 120–127), Caesar's grant of citizenship to "Gauls" north of the Po (perhaps in 49: Yavetz 1983: 66–70; Jehne 1987a: 153–154 with n. 8) is also unlikely to have won him much credit with the Roman plebs. Note the jingle chanted *everywhere* (*vulgo*), "The Gauls have shed their trousers and donned senators' togas!" (Suet. *Iul.* 80.2).

[189] Other sources ignore this aspect, while Nic. Dam. *Bios* 67 brings it up only as a grievance of the *powerful* (n. 270), but this is transparently a result of their pervasive elitism. Here I part company from that excellent guide, Jehne 1987a: 310–312, 416–422. For popular activism and the vigorous defense of popular rights in the Late Republic see Morstein-Marx 2013, especially p. 40; cf. also Courrier 2014: 471–477 on the *dignitas* of the People. Consular elections with a predetermined result were not utterly unprecedented (Pompey had been elected sole consul in 52 without facing a competitor: see now Ramsey 2016), but not since Sulla had the outcomes been determined by the will of a single man.

not be dismissed out of hand.[190] Close examination of our sources reveals that it is only the Augustan (and therefore in principle pro-Caesarian) loyalist Nicolaus of Damascus who again insists that the Roman plebs wanted Caesar to be "king."[191] Caesar's standing with the plebs had already weakened over the years of civil war that had followed the heady days of his Gallic victories, and the conflict with the tribunes in January 44 caused it to slump further to a nadir in his political experience.[192]

The Lupercalia

"I saw Mark Antony offer him a crown . . . he put it by once; but for all that, to my thinking, he would fain have had it."[193] The strange affair at the festival of the Lupercalia on February 15, 44 – one month to the day before the Ides of March – is the best-known today of the public scenes whereby according to Plutarch, Shakespeare, and the "common knowledge" of people everywhere, Caesar tested the waters for an open assumption of "kingship" in the months before the Ides of March; yet, celebrated as it is, it remains puzzling and as susceptible to contradictory interpretations as it evidently was to contemporaries.[194] Suetonius, for instance, apparently saw the Lupercalia affair as an attempt *to discourage* damaging rumors that Caesar wished to be king, and some of the other versions seem to line up with this, while Nicolaus chooses to emphasize the confusion of the

[190] App. *BCiv.* 4.91/383 (Cassius before Philippi): χειροτονίας ἀρχῶν ἀπὸ τοῦ δήμου ... ἐς ἑαυτὸν περιφέροντα, 93/388: ἀλλ' οὐκ, ἀφ' οὗ Καῖσαρ ἐδυνάστευσεν, οὐκ ἀρχήν τινα, οὐ στρατηγόν, οὐχ ὕπατον, οὐ δήμαρχον ἐχειροτονήσατε ἔτι; cf. 2.138/574 (Brutus's Capitoline oration) and n. 153. Appian stresses the power of the "republican" motivation of Brutus's popular audience and Cassius's soldiery one (4.133/559–560; n. 206). Cassius's complaint closely resembles that put in Cinna's mouth for another military *contio* at 1.65/298–299, on which see Morstein-Marx 2011: 266–271; especially noteworthy is the complaint in both speeches that the loss of electoral power meant that successful candidates for office *no longer owed anything to the People* (1.65/299 and 4.93/388). Against the assumption that by the 50s and 40s Rome's soldiers had no part in republican civic values and were largely disaffected toward the Republic see Chapter 1, n. 79.
[191] Nic. Dam. *Bios* 64: τοῖς μὲν πολλοῖς ἐθαυμάζετο, 70: ὁ δὲ δῆμος ἐβόα βασιλέα τε αὐτὸν εἶναι καὶ ἀναδεῖσθαι (sc. with the diadem) μηδὲν ἔτι μέλλοντα *even after* the clash with the tribunes, 72–73 (the *demos* and *hoi polloi* shout at the Lupercalia for him to accept the diadem and become "unambiguously" king); cf. n. 158. On Nicolaus's divergence from the others see Morstein-Marx 2004: 145–146; Toher 2017: 300 and n. 158.
[192] Cic. *Att.* 13.44.1 (July 28, 45) took heart at the news that "the People" had not applauded Caesar's statue when it was carried in the procession at the victory games celebrating Munda. Cicero had been wrong before about the significance of these things and would be again, but the fact itself is of interest.
[193] Shakespeare, *JC* I.2.235–239.
[194] Cic. *Phil.* 2.85; Nic. Dam. *Bios* 71–75; Liv. Per. 116; Plut. 61.7; Suet. 79.2; App. *BCiv.* 2.109/456–458; Dio 44.11.1–3 (cf. 46.19.4). Morstein-Marx 2004: 145–146; North 2008: 158–159; Pelling 2011: 450–451. Toher 2017: 301–315, especially 312 on παντοδαπαί μὲν φῆμαι ἐν τῷ ὁμίλῳ ἦσαν. See now also Buttrey 2015.

spectators about what exactly the point of the political theater was, and leaves his readers in the same state of uncertainty.[195]

An essential part of the background to the Lupercalia incident we have not yet examined is Caesar's very recent assumption (within a few days) of the unprecedented "continuous" or "permanent" dictatorship (*dictatura perpetua, dictator perpetuo*).[196] This new title is often given a great deal of emphasis in scholarship as a stimulus for the assassination plot, so it deserves extended consideration in itself apart from its significance in the festering "kingship" controversy.

First, a word about the meaning of the title. Our best sources for this – Cicero and coins minted during the short remainder of Caesar's life, as well as a few minted by his heir – give it as *Dictator perpetuo*, with one relatively small issue of coins bearing the legend *dict[ator] in perpetuo*.[197] *Perpetuo* means "continuous": the new title explicitly focused on the fact that the dictatorship was now to be a single, uninterrupted office. This gains point when we observe that after Thapsus Caesar had been granted a ten-year dictatorship, or more strictly, ten successive iterations of the one-year dictatorship enumerated sequentially; we know from the variations of Caesar's titulature during the ten-year dictatorship (*Dict. III, Dict IV designatus, Dict IV*, which he was still holding at the beginning of 44, are all attested before the transition to *Dict. Perpetuo*) that he was "designated" (presumably formally "elected" or "appointed") to each individual annual dictatorship in the ten-year sequence, as for example "Dictator for the third time, appointed for a fourth time," attested both in an epigraphic and a literary source.[198] The notion of an annual sequence (with whatever ritual

---

[195] Suet. *Iul.* 79.2: *neque ex eo infamiam affectati etiam regii nominis discutere valuit, quamquam ... Lupercalibus ... diadema reppulerit.* This is consistent with Fufius Calenus's version at Dio 46.19.4 and apparently with Appian. Nic. Dam. *Bios* 72–74.

[196] Cic. *Phil.* 2.87; see Appendix 6, where it is suggested that legislation appointing Caesar to this last office was promulgated shortly after the procession to the Forum Iulium. Jehne 1987a: 32n65 is persuasive against 'Alföldi's theory that Caesar was "only" Dict. IV at the time of the Lupercalia. The date of Spurinna's prophecy – probably February 13 or 14 (n. 230)– is often taken to be the day on which Caesar actually assumed the *dictatura perpetua* (e.g. recently Ferrary 2010: 26), yet in fact we only know that this was the first day on which he sat on his golden seat in his purple toga (Cic. *Div.* 1.119; Plin. *HN* 11.186; cf. Val. Max. 1.6.13) – not necessarily his first day in the new office. There is some (weak) evidence that the initial appointment was enacted by a vote by the People: Dio 46.17.4–5: πάντα δὲ αὐτῷ τὸν δῆμον μετὰ τῆς βουλῆς εἴκειν, οὕτως ὥστε τά τε ἄλλα καὶ δικτάτορα αὐτὸν διὰ βίου εἶναι τῇ τε σκευῇ τῇ τῶν βασιλέων χρῆσθαι ψηφίσασθαι. But see n. 378.

[197] Cic. *Phil.* 2.87; *RRC* 480/6–14: *dict[ator] perpetuo* (169 obv. dies); 15–16 (15 obv. dies). *Dictatura perpetua*: Suet. *Iul.* 76.1.

[198] Sherk 26 b.7–8 [Caes.] *B Hisp.* 2.1, both quoted n. 224. For details of the sequential dictatorships see Broughton, *MRR* 2.256–257, 272, with Jehne 1987a: 15, and for "designation" see n. 224. Caesar's first two dictatorships were the eleven-day tenure in 49 for the purpose of elections and the

and legal procedures were required to effect the renewal) was now replaced by one of continuation without a designated end point. This aspect of the new office naturally likely drew the most attention: this dictatorship, in contrast to the others, was "permanent." Not incorrectly, then, Greek translators and historians rendered the phrase (*in*) *perpetuo* as διὰ βίου, as was recently confirmed by an official document from Sardis in Asia Minor.[199]

The possession of permanent authority was, of course, understood to be a key criterion of kingship.[200] Not surprisingly, it is tempting therefore to seek here the real significance of the new titulature. Since the date of the termination of Caesar's dictatorships had been lifted, one might suppose with Martin Jehne, who sees the continuous dictatorship as the cornerstone of Caesar's new regime, that its assumption was chiefly "a demonstration by which he made it clear that his position of dominance should not be seen as a transition towards the goal of restoring the traditional *res publica* to health: the *dictatura perpetua* signaled rather the permanent transformation into an autocratic regime."[201] On Jehne's view, probably accepted by most scholars, this was "the official proclamation of [Caesar's] sole rule," which constituted a breaking point for many of the conspirators.[202]

There is some evidence to support the suggestion, most notably Plutarch's comment in his *Life of Caesar* that "the Romans," "thinking

---

absentee, twelve-month dictatorship voted him after Pharsalus, probably late in November 48 (*MRR* 2.272, 3.106–107; see now Jehne 2000: 166–167n110; Ferrary 2010: 11, and n. 68). The recently published treaty with Lycia dating to July 24, 46, names Caesar as *Dict. III* as the Senate had decreed after Thapsus (*SEG* 55.1452 = *AE* 2005.1487, lines 2–5); this date more or less coincides with the date of Caesar's actual arrival in Rome (*B. Afr.* 98.2, where the reading of one manuscript would coincide perfectly [overlooked by Kantor 2014] while the others put it one day later – i.e. July 25). It is unclear whether the third dictatorship was strictly limited to twelve months despite the massive intercalation added for the initiation of the Julian calendar (see Broughton, *MRR* 3.107, Jehne 1987a: 31n62). See also n. 224.

[199] *AE* 1989.684 = *SEG* 39.1290, line 5 (March 4!). Cf. *OLD*, s.v. *perpetuus*, 1, 2. The (relatively rare) legend on the coins *in perpetuo*, assuming it was not a mistake, unambiguously has the same meaning. See Jehne 1987a: 34.

[200] Cf. Cic. *Rep.* 2.49: *nostri quidem omnes reges vocitaverunt, qui soli in populos perpetuam potestatem haberent* (cf. 2.43), written a decade before February 44 and thus free of Caesarian "interference."

[201] Jehne 1987a: 38.

[202] Jehne 1987a: 451. For Jehne (see especially 15–38, 186–190, 448–451) the permanent dictatorship constituted the capstone of a carefully constructed new, essentially monarchical regime. Cf. similarly Syme 1939: 52–57; Gelzer 1968: 320; Dettenhofer 1992: 242; Dobesch 2000: 112; Zecchini 2001: 32–34; Ramsey 2003: 90: "must have dashed all hopes in the minds of contemporaries that Caesar intended eventually to step down from power and restore the Republic. It served as catalyst to hasten the plot against Caesar's life." But see contra Gardner 2009: 60: "The picture that emerges of the years 48–44 is one of haste and improvisation in times of crisis, rather than the execution of some long-premeditated plan . . . to make himself autocratic sole ruler over Rome and its empire."

that monarchy could afford a respite from civil war and national calamities ... proclaimed him dictator for life. This was acknowledged tyranny: he already enjoyed a monarch's unaccountability, and now he had a monarch's permanence as well."[203] Yet it is only Plutarch, and only in this one passage of his three main accounts of the assassination, who attributes such epochal significance to the new position above all other irritants; curiously, he fails even to mention it in his other most relevant *Lives*, that of Brutus [!] or the *Antony*.[204] For Suetonius, the continuous dictatorship seems to be simply one among many "excessive honors" that showed that Caesar was justly killed; similarly, Appian is aware of it but like Suetonius buries it without comment among a host of other honors voted Caesar shortly before his death.[205] In the two great "republican" speeches Appian dedicates to the "Liberators" in the ensuing tumult (Brutus's famous *contio Capitolina* immediately after the killing and Cassius's address to the soldiers before Philippi) the extended dictatorship is omitted while Caesar's tyrannical transgressions are detailed, with considerable attention given in both speeches to the violation of the tribunes' rights and of the People's electoral privileges.[206] Nicolaus too ignores the new title altogether. Dio on the other hand asserts that it was actually the placement of Caesar's statue among those of the kings that chiefly motivated Brutus to plot against his life; in his account of the conspiracy, in fact, the "dictatorship for life" barely features.[207] Not even Cicero gives the office the kind of prominence that would be consistent with "the official proclamation of sole rule" in his posthumous tirade against Caesar in the *Second Philippic*, written only months after the assassination, and he leaves it entirely aside in the contemporary *De Officiis*.[208] The fact that the assassination came only one month later is an example of the *post hoc propter hoc* fallacy and proves nothing: that also came one month after the Lupercalia incident, very shortly before the unprecedented elections for future years, and as we shall

---

[203] Plut. *Caes.* 57.1 (Pelling tr.). Dio 44.8.4 says that his appointment to the new office "increased the suspicion" that he had become "arrogant" (ὑπεραυχεῖν) and exacerbated the "hatred" already felt toward him on this account.

[204] For instance, in the *Ant.*, Antony gave the conspirators their "most respectable pretext" for the assassination – the offer of the diadem at the Lupercalia (*Ant.* 12.1; cf. Cic. *Phil.* 13.41 [n. 100]), not the acceptance of the continuous dictatorship.

[205] Suet. *Iul.* 76.1; App. *BCiv.* 2.106/442.

[206] App. *BCiv.* 2.137–141/570–591, 4.90–99/377–422. See nn. 153, 190.

[207] The statue: Dio 43.45.4: ἐκ τούτου ὅτι μάλιστα ὁ Βροῦτος ὁ Μᾶρκος κινηθεὶς ἐπεβούλευσεν αὐτῷ. Dio mentions the new title only once: it "heightened suspicion" (44.8.4).

[208] To be sure, at *Phil.* 1.4 Cicero praises Antony for abolishing the office of dictatorship because of the "recent memory" of the *perpetua dictatura*. For *Phil.* 2.87, the only other mention in all the *Philippics*, see n. 239.

see, only a few days after Dolabella's election as suffect consul. In short, while there is every reason to believe that the *dictatura perpetua* was, as Suetonius, Appian, and perhaps Dio indicate, a conspicuous additional irritant among many, there is little reason to follow Plutarch in singling out the new office as the decisive precipitant of the conspiracy, and much less to go beyond even Plutarch and interpret it as something like an explicit abolition of the Republic.

Strictly speaking, the removal of the traditional temporal limitation on the office of Dictator was not unprecedented: Sulla's dictatorship too had been temporally indefinite, yet this had not prevented him from abdicating it within about a year.[209] Caesar held no more power with the new dictatorship than his earlier decennial version, which he was still far from exhausting. Until 36 BC (the terminus of the ten-year grant after Thapsus) Caesar would not have gained any powers under the continuous dictatorship that he had not had before. He continued to hold *imperium* superior to that of the consuls and other magistrates (and not delimited by a *provincia*), he still presumably had no more than twenty-four lictors, and he probably remained formally subject to tribunician intercession and *provocatio* (though in practice such things had not been tried, and after the banishment of Flavus and Marullus they probably would not be), but the powers of the office had not increased one whit by becoming "continuous."[210] Moreover, 36 BC was a full eight years hence. By then Caesar, at sixty-four years of age, would be pushing beyond the average life span of a Roman senator anyway.[211] Two

---

[209] App. *BCiv.* 1.99/461: χειροτονοῦσι τὸν Σύλλαν, ἐς ὅσον θέλοι, τύραννον αὐτοκράτορα. *MRR* 2.66–67, 3.74–75.

[210] I am persuaded by Jehne 1987a: 29n58 that Caesar's *dictatura perpetuo* was not defined further as *rei publicae constituendae*, which some have inferred on the basis of Gasperini's restoration of *AE* 1969/70.132 (Broughton, *MRR* 3.107–108; Badian 1990: 34–35, Zecchini 2001: 32–33). The inscription may anyway honor the younger Caesar (Sordi 1969: *rei pub. const.* was never part of the official titulature of the dictator and does not seem to appear on inscriptions other than the *fasti*. Sordi also points out rightly that there is serious tension between the open-endedness of the designation *perpetuo* and the temporal restriction implied by *rei pub. const.*

[211] The life expectancy of senators is a notorious minefield, but some sense of the probabilities may be gained by considering the twenty-six consulars alive at the beginning of the Civil War (including Caesar and Pompey: Bruhns 1978: 38–40), but at the end of a long period of relative internal peace marked by little violent mortality among consulars. Of living consulars in 49, those of Caesar's age cohort (i.e. cos. 57 or earlier, for he had held the office two years earlier than usual) make up just over half (54 percent) – that is, at age fifty, five years before the present moment, he was more or less at the median age of living consulars. And if the peacetime age distribution of 49 be taken as a norm, five years later in 44 he would have joined the eldest third of living consulars. Only two superannuated consulars living in 49 had held that status longer than seventeen years, which strongly suggests a very rapid die-off around age sixty. Caesar was now a few months from age fifty-six and his Parthian expedition was expected to keep him away at least until he was fifty-nine if, of course, he survived its rigors and dangers.

months after the assassination Cicero was to complain that the Dictator never should have been assassinated because "he never would have returned" from the Parthian expedition; given Caesar's record of military success, this seems an odd thing to say unless it was a reference to his musings on mortality and less than perfect health at this stage.[212] When someone warned him to beware of Brutus, the Dictator is supposed to have said, "Brutus will wait for this flesh": evidently, that is, Caesar could not be expected to live very much longer.[213] Given the monarchic teleology that propels the narrative of Caesar's life at this point, it is not surprising that Plutarch (or his source) interpreted the comment as a reference to Brutus's worthiness *to succeed* Caesar and *to rule* after his death; surely it is at least as likely in its original context that he was alluding to the looming end of his irregular *dominatio* and Rome's return after his death to the normal rules of the republican game.

The obvious question then is: why change the serial dictatorship to a "continuous" one? Why was a ten-year dictatorship with eight more years on the clock not enough, just before the departure for the great eastern campaign that was expected to require less than half of that time? I do not think anyone has solved this puzzle. It is likely, to judge from what the other sources have to say, that the answer is much more mundane than Plutarch claims. The better path to understanding the "continuous dictatorship" is probably to view it within its immediate context of the outpouring of extravagant honors that greeted Caesar's return to Rome, reviewed earlier in this chapter, and to interpret it accordingly as an *honor* rather than a novel form of executive power.[214] It was, after all, decreed by the Senate *as an extraordinary honor* (as Suetonius explicitly calls it: *eximios honores*), probably among the culminating package of honors presented to him by the great procession to the Forum Iulium.[215] Seen strictly from the standpoint of the

---

[212] Cic. *Att.* 15.4.3 (May 24): *ille enim numquam revertisset.* At the time of the assassination Caesar was suffering from *valetudo minus prospera* (Suet. *Iul.* 86.1, cf. 81.4), apparently marked by fainting spells (epileptic fits?) and sleeplessness (45.1, with Butler and Cary's note), though he can hardly have been on his deathbed in view of his ambitious military plans. See also App. *BCiv.* 2.110/459, quoted n. 23.

[213] Plut. *Brut.* 8.3–4: "οὐκ ἂν ὑμῖν δοκεῖ Βροῦτος ἀναμεῖναι τουτὶ τὸ σαρκίον"; cf. *Caes.* 62.2–6, with Pelling 2011: 462. Caesar's consciousness of approaching mortality is a significant theme in the story of his last years: Cic. *Marc.* 25–26: "I have lived long enough for nature or glory" (*satis diu vel naturae vixi vel gloriae* – but the architect of the Parthian campaign had evidently changed his mind); App. *BCiv.* 2.115/479: (ὁ δὲ Καῖσαρ) λόγον ἐπὶ τῇ κύλικι προύθηκε, τίς ἄριστος ἀνθρώπῳ θάνατος (cf. Plut. *Caes.* 63.7; Suet. *Iul.* 87).

[214] See p. 500ff.

[215] Suet. *Iul.* 76.1: *honores . . . nimios recepit: continuum consulatum* (in fact probably declined: n. 80), *perpetuam dictaturam praefecturamque morum, insuper praenomen Imperatoris, cognomen Patris patriae . . . .* etc. Probably to be dated in January: Appendix 6, 644ff.

accrual of power, the new title meant little, as we saw, but seen as an honor it greatly surpassed its predecessor, not merely in the extension of duration (perhaps not much anyway) but in its complete removal of any externally imposed terminus, thus leaving its termination entirely to the gods and Caesar's sole discretion. Such a possibility is obliquely hinted at in the newly published fragment of the Privernum Fasti, where Lepidus is described as having been appointed "Master of the Horse *perpetuo*" yet also only "so long as Caesar would be Dictator."[216] None of this, however, would preclude Caesar's eventually making use of the dictatorship as an instrument of reform, as Cicero in his *De re publica* of 54 had supposed to have been the destiny of his potential *rector* ("director," "guide," or "ideal statesman"), Scipio Aemilianus, had he not been prematurely cut off.[217] On a favorable estimation, he might, like Sulla, abdicate it once he thought his job was done, perhaps after the kind of reform of political life that Cicero himself had been crying out for but that Caesar had now put off for the immediate future in favor of the Parthian project.[218]

The "continuous dictatorship" may thus be best understood in the context of other "excessive" honors, such as his deification, that elevated Caesar in some ineffable but awe-inspiring way above and beyond the established structure of Roman governmental institutions.[219] Like deification, the continuous dictatorship could be seen as a kind of monarchy *manqué*, a way for the Senate simultaneously to honor Caesar quite extravagantly, to acknowledge even more emphatically his dominant power, and yet simultaneously define it (and perhaps verbally tame it) as "non-monarchy."[220] Senators could tell themselves that the annals of

---

[216] Zevi and Cassola 2016: 295, line 12: *quoad dict(ator) Caesar esset*, more careful phrasing than *quoad Caesar viveret*.

[217] Cic. *Rep.* 6.12, using Scipio Aemilianus as a "specific instance of the need for a single person of authority at moments of great crisis" (Zetzel 1995: 229). On Cicero's ideal of the *rector* see now Zarecki 2014: 5–8 and esp. 77–131, who emphasizes both its centrality to Cicero's thinking about the Civil War and Caesar's failure to rise to his standard.

[218] For the apparent lack of a terminal date for Sulla's dictatorship see n. 208. For Cicero's call for reform and disappointment at the priority Caesar gave to the Parthian problem see p. 488ff. The oft-quoted quip "Sulla was illiterate, for he laid down the dictatorship" (Suet. *Iul.* 77) is too often adduced as reliable evidence of Caesar's intentions in taking up the *dictatura perpetua*, without sufficient notice of the fact that it derived from the pen of one of his Pompeian enemies, T. Ampius Balbus, called the "trumpet of the Civil War" (*tuba belli civilis*) (Chapter 1, p. 26f., Chapter 2, p. 38f.) and the fact that we do not know the date of the comment, which seems likeliest much earlier: a *tuba belli civilis* will not have waited until 44 to complain about Caesar's lust for power, and Caesar did not actually have to hold the dictatorship to be imagined saying such things.

[219] Deification: see nn. 88, 92.

[220] C. Pelling suggests to me a possible parallel in the proposal of the sole consulship for Pompey in 52 (by Bibulus and Cato, no less) as a palatable alternative to the dictatorship, which was "in the air" (Ascon. 35–36C, etc.). In early 44 "kingship" was clearly in the air, even if there is no reason to think

Roman history had taught that the Republic was incredibly successful and that periods of personal *dominatio* had proven brief and transitory even in tumultuous, recent times; why should Caesar's time of dominance be different?[221] His own followers were champing at the bit to return to republican "politics as usual," as we shall soon see in detail. Far from "signalling the permanent transformation into an autocratic regime," the adoption of the continuous dictatorship was followed within only a few weeks by Antony's defiance of Caesar in the most public way possible, and Caesar's answer was not to bare the iron fist of autocracy but to summon a meeting of the Senate to discuss the problem.

The redefinition of Caesar's dictatorship(s) as no longer an annual series but a single continuous office may have held additional supervening benefits in view of his projected absence for at least three years on the Parthian expedition.[222] J. Jahn suggested long ago that the motive for the change to "continuous" or "permanent" dictatorship – or at least, Caesar's motive for *accepting it* – was some kind of formal, technical reason relating to his upcoming prolonged absence.[223] We do not know what formalities actually attended the "designation" of each successive dictatorship in the former decennial sequence (which was entirely unprecedented), but it would not be a surprise if given the novelty of the situation the reappointment or renewal of an annual dictatorship was thought to call for his presence in Rome.[224] Already in 48 there had been a temporary hang-up when in Caesar's absence the augurs at first refused to countenance

that it was sought by Caesar, and in that environment the continuous dictatorship could emerge as a palatable alternative.

[221] Tac. *Ann.* 1.1: *non Cinnae, non Sullae longa dominatio; et Pompei Crassique potentia cito in Caesarem, Lepidi atque Antonii arma in Augustum cessere.*

[222] Dio 43.51.2.

[223] Jahn 1970: 187–188. Jehne 1987a: 34–38 rightly rejects some of Jahn's assumptions and arguments, but his fundamental idea that the change may have had essentially to do with the advance elections for 44–42 remains attractive.

[224] Jehne 1987a: 31n62, 37–38. Dio seems to note the irregularity of Caesar's taking up his second dictatorship outside of Italy in 48 (42.21.1: καίπερ ἔξω τῆς Ἰταλίας ὤν); it seems likely that the formal requirement of a *lex curiata* confirming *imperium* was at least partly responsible for the norm that dictators assumed their office in Rome (Mommsen 1887: 2:152–153; see now F. Cassola in Zevi and Cassola 2016: 308–309). It is possible but not certain that Caesar began his third dictatorship before his return to Rome (n. 198), while his fourth dictatorship began after his departure for Spain (*B. Hisp.* 2.1 with *MRR* 3.107, Jehne 1987a: 31n62). Examples of "designation": Sherk 26 b.7–8: δικτάτωρ τὸ [τ]ρίτον, καθε[σταμένος τὸ τέταρτον] (note that this case is particularly important in suggesting that *some* kind of date or ritual of entry into office was awaited after appointment before the magistracy formally began); [Caes.] *B Hisp.* 2.1: *dictator tertio, designatus dictator quarto*; cf. Joseph. *AJ* 14.211: δικτάτωρ τὸ τέταρτον ὕπατός τε τὸ πέμπτον, δικτάτωρ ἀποδεδειγμένος διὰ βίου = *Dict. IV, Dict. perp. designatus*). ἀποδεδειγμένος τὸ δ' has been thrice restored in recently published documents from Phrygia (*SEG* 59.1479 [A–B]), but this does not seem to be required by anything on the stones.

Antony's unprecedented appointment as Master of the Horse for more than six months; with his renewable annual dictatorships Caesar was already on uncharted territory, which could prompt novel objections while he was far away.[225] Attention was still being given to technicalities that may seem superfluous or irrelevant to us at this distance: for instance, we happen to know from the consular *fasti* (no less) that Caesar had formally to abdicate his fourth dictatorship to take up the new "continuous" one, thereby necessitating his Master of the Horse, M. Lepidus, to abdicate and be reappointed likewise, which raises the question whether the transition between dictatorships involved ritual or institutional complexities that remain obscure to us.[226] The "continuous" dictatorship may also have been desirable in order to forestall any religious or constitutional objections to Caesar's presiding over the absolutely unprecedented election of consuls and other magistrates well into the future – not just for the following year but for 42 and 41 – the latter of whom would take office more than a year after Caesar's current office (Dictator for the fourth time) would have come to an end.[227] The ten-year sequential dictatorship was itself utterly unprecedented and it would be little wonder if the newly invented procedures governing its perpetuation were in flux and called for clarification or adjustment in order to deal with complications created by the magnitude of the upcoming Parthian campaign.

Still, even if the new office did not obviously change anything, at least for the near future, it was new and unfamiliar, and the removal of any temporal limitation would certainly prompt questions. What sort of thing was Caesar's new "continuous" or "permanent" dictatorship? Was it, as Matthias Gelzer opined, merely a novel form of *rex* – a tyrant in all but name?[228] It is certain that contemporaries too were almost as puzzled about the meaning of the unprecedented title *Dictator perpetuo as* modern scholars have been. This in itself helps us to see what was likely going on in the famous moment of political theater at the festival of the Lupercalia on February 15.

[225] Dio 42.21.2.
[226] Zevi and Cassola 2016: 293, 295: *C. Iulius Caesar IV dict(ator) abdic(avit) ut perpet(uo ...); Fasti Cons. Capit.* sub anno 44, *I.It.* 13.1, pp. 56–57. Jehne 1987a: 380–382. The new Privernum fragment states that Lepidus would remain *magistri equitum* "as long as Caesar would be Dictator" even though others were to take up the post in Rome; it is unclear how we are to understand this doubling of *magistri equitum* (Zevi and Cassola, pp. 296–303).
[227] Jehne's objection (1987a: 36) to Jahn's suggestion on this point is not entirely cogent. We do not know for certain when in 45 Caesar's fourth dictatorship had begun, but it does not seem to have had very long to run when he was assassinated.
[228] Gelzer 1968: 320.

Caesar's appearance on February 15, resplendent atop the high platform of the Rostra, at the culmination of the Lupercalia – an ancient pastoral festival associated with Romulus and Remus and the foundation of Rome – may well have been his first appearance before the *populus Romanus* in that office.[229] This may help to explain his eye-catching outfit, combining several striking visual symbols of his prestige: he sat on a golden chair, wearing an all-purple, triumphal (or "dictatorial") toga and a gilt "crown" probably to be identified as the triumphal *corona Etrusca*.[230] The Rostra, as

[229] Major sources: Cic. *Phil.* 2.84–87; Dio 44.11.1–3; Plut. *Caes.* 61.1–7, *Ant.* 12; App. *BCiv.* 2.109/456–458; Suet. *Iul.* 79.2; Nic. Dam. *Bios* 71–75. A complete list at Toher 2017: 301, who rightly judges that "it is impossible to point to any one source as providing an accurate account of what happened at the Lupercalia" (42–43). For religious aspects and the cultural context of this occasion see now North 2008, who emphasizes the connection of the ritual with the idea of re-foundation by way of the allusions to Romulus and Remus, and by highlighting the carnivalesque character of the ritual effectively disposes of the old notion that this could ever have been intended as an authentic "coronation." Similarly, Zecchini 2001: 12–17. "Atop" the Rostra: rightly Pelling 2011: 452–453. Suetonius's *pro rostris* is a common imperial usage for "on the Rostra" (and probably near the front, thus visible): see Festus 257L: *"pro" significat in, ut pro rostris, pro aede, pro tribunali*; cf. Taylor 1966: 44, and for a familiar example, Tac. *Ann.* 2.81.1 with Goodyear ad loc. Height of platform: ca. 3.5–3.7 meters (*NTDAR*, 336; P. Verduchi, *LTUR* 4.215).

[230] Cic. *Phil.* 2.85; Plut. *Caes.* 61.4, *Ant.* 12.1; Dio 44.11.2; App. *BCiv.* 2.109/456; Nic. Dam. *Bios* 71. Toher 2017: 304–305; Pelling 2011: 453; and on Caesar's outfit, see now Till 2003: 180–188. The *toga purpurea* and *sella aurea* (Cic., Val. Max. 1.6.13) were granted perhaps late in 45 (Dio 44.6.1; cf. App. *BCiv.* 2.106/442); they were to be carried in the games together with the gold, bejeweled "crown" (44.6.3), whose formal conferral is not mentioned in our sources unless it be identical to the grant after Munda of the right to wear the triumphal crown at all times (Dio 43.43.1; Suet. *Iul.* 45.2; cf. the earlier grant to Pompey: Vell. Pat. 2.40.4). (The golden chair was also brought in for senatorial meetings over which he presided: Dio 44.17.3.) This very ensemble reappears at the Lupercalia, this time worn or used by Caesar; whether this was the first time he appeared thus accessorized or had already done so on one or two days before (on the occasion of the prophecy of Spurinna [Cic. *Div.* 1.119; Plin. *HN* 11.186; Val. Max. 1.6.13], dated February 13, 14, or even 15 on the basis of Val. Max. 8.11.2: Ramsey 2000: 445–446; cf. Jehne 1987a: 223; Till 2003: 180), it would have been a novel sight for most spectators at the Lupercalia. The identity of the gilt "crown" (Cic. Phil. 2.85; Dio 44.11.2), probably that which appears resting on a *sella curulis* on Octavian's denarius (*RRC* 497/2), is a notorious problem. Kraft interpreted it as an archaizing Etruscan/Roman symbol of royalty (1952/ 53 = 1969), but Bergmann 2010: 117–119 more persuasively identifies it as the *corona Etrusca* associated with triumphs (cf. pp. 37–108). Bergmann also rejects (126–127) Kraft's argument that the crown of the Lupercalia is that which appears on Caesar's head in the great coin series of 44 (n. 124), and further argues against Alföldi in particular that the *toga purpurea*, which Dio explicitly describes as στολή ᾗ ποτε οἱ βασιλῆς ἐκέχρηντο (44.6.1), was in fact the standard triumphal dress, derived, of course, from that of the ancient kings but not thereby distinctively monarchic in its semiotic implications (257–259n416; cf. Till, pp. 183–185). Indeed, it may be that the *toga purpurea* was the standard wear for dictators, inherited, it was often supposed, from the ancient kings. (Dion. Hal. 10.24.2 [Cincinnatus] and Lyd. *Mag.* 1.37, though Mommsen 1887: 1.419n1 argued on the basis of Liv. *Per.* 19 that dictators wore "only" the *praetexta* – an uncertain inference since Glicia had been forced to abdicate). If so, Caesar's toga was no different from what he had worn since 46. Thus the ensemble, though eye-catching, may not have been so far out of ceremonial norms as to have summoned "monarchy" to the minds of Caesar's spectators rather than the "trappings of a *triumphator*" (Rawson 1975: 155; cf. Plut. *Caes.* 61.4 "in rich triumphal dress," with Pelling 2011:

mentioned previously, was the new replacement of the old speaker's platform, formerly located a little to the northeast, and now bearing Antony's name as dedicator.[231] The most notable feature of the Lupercalia was the run undertaken by the so-called *Luperci* around the Palatine (almost certainly) and up and down the Sacred Way through the Forum; the Rostra was thus toward the end of the course.[232] Caesar, in his gorgeous garb and placed at the new focal point of the Forum, must have been the cynosure of all eyes as the runners made their way through the elongated square. One of the *Luperci*, in fact a member of a supplemental college newly constituted as an honor to Caesar (the *Luperci Iuli*), was Caesar's own colleague as consul in 44, Mark Antony.[233] Antony approached the Rostra, climbed up on the high platform, and presented Caesar with a diadem, apparently wound (again) through a laurel "crown" (Plut., Nic. Dam.).[234] Our sources diverge in describing the onlooking crowd's reaction, which given the nature of crowds is not very likely to have been unanimous anyway, giving large scope to writers to give their own tendentious twist to whatever eyewitnesses may have seen and heard.[235] Our sources also differ about whether Antony (alone or with the help of others) tried to press the diadem on Caesar only once, twice, or even thrice.[236] What all agree, however, is that Caesar rejected it; in Dio Caesar himself adds an explanation: that "Jupiter alone was king of the Romans."[237] Caesar

---

453) or those of a dictator with some recent, Caesarian enhancements. Beard 2007: 276–277 rightly observes that antiquarian distinctions would have been lost on spectators.

[231] The "new" Rostra: n. 123.   [232] North 2008: 156 for details.

[233] On the *Luperci Iulii* and Antony see Dio. 44.6.2, 45.30.2; Suet. *Iul.* 76.1.

[234] Plut. *Caes.* 61.5, *Ant.* 12.3; Nic. Dam. *Bios* 71. For discussion of the detail see Ramsey 2003: 285; Pelling 2011: 454; Toher 2017: 307–308; see n. 124 for the same detail regarding the diadem found on the statue in January. This "crown" is of course distinct from the *corona aurea* on Caesar's head at that moment: n. 230.

[235] Morstein-Marx 2004: 145–146; cf. 123, 135–136.

[236] Toher 2017: 312–313. Nicolaus diverges most notably from the other accounts in working in immediately prior attempts to prompt Caesar to take the diadem by a certain "Licinius," and Cassius the conspirator, with P. Casca, another of the conspirators (*Bios* 71–72). See Toher (pp. 306–307, 309), suggesting that L. Cinna (pr. 44) may lurk behind the manuscript "Licinius," and that "Publius" Casca may be a mistake for Gaius (tr. 44). Toher rightly points out that Nicolaus's version cannot be summarily rejected, but notices a suspiciously neat pattern: "N. has introduced into the Lupercalia as the prime agents of the episode's *invidia* three of the magistrates of 44 who were also Caesar's assassins" (p. 301). Sordi 1999 takes Nicolaus's hint and argues that the approach was organized by Caesar's enemies, including (secretly) Antony himself.

[237] Dio 44.11.3. North 2008: 158 interprets Liv. *Per.* 116 *in sella reposuit* to mean that (on this account) Caesar *accepted* "his status as deity" on the analogy of a similar ritual marking a god's presence. This, I think, is to read too much into the rather pathetic summaries offered by the *Periochae*, generally little more than a table of contents which cannot be supposed to reflect Livy's original very accurately.

ordered the diadem to be dedicated to Jupiter Greatest and Best and the following text to be inscribed in the official calendar (*fasti*): "M. Antony, consul, offered monarchy by order of the People (*iussu populi*)[238] to Caesar, *dictator perpetuo*; Caesar refused to accept it."[239] That is, taking this strange charade at its word: Caesar's Rome was *not* a *regnum*, even though some might have thought it looked that way with a "continuous dictator" at its head. Only Jupiter could be "king" among the Romans.

To be *dictator perpetuo* was on this view defined as *not* to be a *rex*, a wearer of a diadem, and Caesar remained a Roman magistrate, if one with a novel absence of legal terminus. The drama was played out on the Rostra before the eyes of the Roman People at the time and place where it would get maximal publicity before Caesar's departure. It was, then, most likely a piece of "political theater" intended to impose a more benign interpretation on the new office and provide a direct answer to the critics of the recent redefinition of Caesar's office, who with some prima facie plausibility could have claimed that to be *dictator perpetuo* was actually to be a *rex*.[240] The response was to assert that the *dictatura perpetua* remained a republican magistracy, if a novel or even unprecedented version of the dictatorship, to be distinguished from the odious name

[238] Dio 44.11.2 (cf. 45.31.2–32.4) gives Antony words to this effect, Nic. Dam. *Bios* 72, the crowd. *Iussu populi* looks like an honorific fiction (Cic. *Phil.* 2.86; Dio 45.32.1–3). Ferrary 2010: 29 attractively suggests that the reference is to the popular acclamations (e.g. Nic. Dam. *Bios* 70); it was traditional for politicians to dignify shouts of contional and other crowds as "the will and verdict of the Roman People" (Morstein-Marx 2004: especially 119–128).

[239] Cic. *Phil.* 2.87; cf. Dio 44.11.3; Nic. Dam. *Bios* 73; Suet. 79.2; Plut. *Caes.* 61.7. Ramsey 2003: 287 rightly suspects that Cicero intends to suggest that Antony is the implied subject of *iussit* and thus gave the order to enter this note into the calendar. Whether the suggestion is true, given Cicero's rhetorical purpose, is doubtful; for what it is worth, Dio attributes the order to Caesar. The versions of Plut. *Ant.* 12.7 (not the *Caes.*) and Nic. Dam. 75, in which the diadem is now placed on a statue of Caesar, evidently reflect some contamination by the similar story of the discovery of a diadem on a statue on the Rostra (cf. *Caes* .61.8; Pelling 1988: 147, 2011: 455–456; Toher 2017: 302). Dobesch 2000: 103 suggests that since Caesar was now deified as an avatar of Jupiter, he was in effect keeping the "crown" for himself.

[240] Intended by whom – Caesar or Antony? Strictly speaking, we cannot know. To judge from a speech Dio puts in the mouth of the Antonian (and former Caesarian) Fufius Calenus, Antonian propaganda excused Antony's action by claiming that this was his carefully considered plan to deter Caesar from his desire to become king (46.17.4–8, 19.4–7). This seems too blatantly apologetic to be taken seriously, especially since there is no evidence whatever of that supposed desire and plenty of public repudiation of it by Caesar. As suggested in the text, the move makes good sense as a Caesarian public relations effort to smooth over the recent assumption of the *dictatura perpetua*, and if that is the case, why should it not have been coordinated with Caesar if not his idea? Yet, in view of Antony's virtual rebellion in a month's time, and the likelihood that it was he who was at the head of the procession to the Forum Iulium, it is possible that he was again putting Caesar on the spot in an unexpected, unwelcome, and potentially dangerous way.

of *regnum* and thus not subject to the sanction of the legendary "oath of Brutus."[241] Although the distinction may have seemed an over-fine one to some, especially those already ill disposed, it might be noted that the office had no doubt been authorized by the Senate and perhaps by the People; there is no evidence that the tribunes were legally subject to the dictator's *imperium* or formally deprived of their right of veto (although the fate of Flavus and Marullus was ominous); the basic Roman "civil right" of *provocatio* probably remained intact, so the dictator had no recognized right to carry out extralegal executions or punishments of citizens.[242] Nor, of course, did a *dictator* have any presumptive right to name their successor (and of course Caesar had not done so) – a crucial buttress of monarchic power in practice.[243]

But if the purpose of the drama at the Lupercalia had been to calm anxieties and indignation, it seems to have been a failure. Dio says that as a result Caesar was now "bitterly hated" – exactly by whom, he neglects to say.[244] Appian too describes a rising sense of danger from the time of the removal and expulsion of the tribunes, and this of course supervened upon the ill will generated by the disastrous incident in the Forum Iulium.[245] Not long before his assassination Caesar had acknowledged to his and Cicero's mutual friend Gaius Matius that he was sure the senior consular hated him (he had kept him waiting for some time to see him on an errand for a friend) – and since Cicero was of all people one of the most easygoing, he now "had no doubt how greatly hated he was."[246] The vignette seems to cast light on Caesar's consciousness of the rising hostility to him generated by his very presence, or rather, the fraught interactions with

---

[241] That the Lupercalia was intended as a spectacular *recusatio regni* to put the idea permanently to rest is no longer novel and has perhaps become the prevailing view: Zecchini 2001: 25–27; North 2008: 159; Ferrary 2010: 26–27. Sordi 1999 mainly differs in suggesting that Caesar's enemies engineered the incident in order to arouse hostility against him. The old view that the occasion was intended to establish a new monarchy based on Hellenistic, Roman, or some kind of mixed model is best represented by Dobesch 1966 and 2000, Weinstock 1974, and Alföldi 1985. Sordi 2003 (= Sordi 2000) speculates that Caesar had in mind a novel kind of *civile imperium* which he sought to contrast with traditional models of kingship and autocracy.

[242] Jehne 1987a: 21–29.

[243] The ancient *Roman* monarchy had been theoretically elective according to canonical tradition, but ultimately the hereditary principle asserted itself in the Tarquin dynasty. Octavian had been designated as heir to Caesar's name and fortune, but no constitutional means existed of making him a "successor."

[244] Dio 44.11.3: δεινῶς ἐμισήθη (cf. also 8.4 [sc. οἱ πολλοὶ] ἐμίσουν, 10.4 and 12.2).

[245] App. *BCiv.* 2.109–110/454–459.

[246] Cic. *Att.* 14.1.2: "*ego dubitem quin summo in odio sim, cum M. Cicero sedeat nec suo commodo me convenire possit? atqui si quisquam est facilis, hic est. tamen non dubito quin me male oderit.*" The moment was *proxime* to the date of the letter, April 7.

key constituencies – individual senators, the Senate as a whole, and the People – which were continually forced upon him by his presence in Rome. Paradoxically, perhaps, his projected lengthy absence may itself have looked like a solution.

The Elections of 44 and the Implosion of the "Caesarian Party"

Scholars' eyes have understandably been fixed on the spectacle of "kingship" played out at considerable length in all our sources. As a result, they tend to overlook something that must have been a greater preoccupation among all those who had contributed to the Caesarian victory or hoped for something from it – even former Pompeians like Brutus and Cassius who had made their peace at the opportune moment and been rewarded with high responsibility and position. For in preparation for his imminent departure on a long campaign expected to keep him away from Rome for three, perhaps five, years, Caesar had decided to appoint the major magistrates to cover the expected years of his absence – and it seems to have been exactly now that this bizarre sequence of elections was in full swing.[247] As we already observed, before the assassination the full set of magistrates had been chosen for only one year (43), while for 42 only consuls and tribunes had been elected.[248] Yet Caesar was scheduled to leave Rome as soon as March 18 (more or less the traditional opening of the campaigning season).[249]

We must pause now to consider the implications of this remarkable step. Through the years of civil war, since campaigning around the Mediterranean often kept Caesar from being in Rome at the right time, elections were typically postponed until he could be present. No curule elections (i.e. those for the higher magistracies: consul, praetor, or curule aedile) were held in Caesar's absence, except for the somewhat ceremonial occasion in which the Dictator himself was elected sole consul in 45 in an

---

[247] See p. 493ff. Nic. Dam. *Bios* 77 and Dio 44.11.4 date the elections after the Lupercalia, which fits our information that at the time of the assassination even the three-year sequence had not been completed, perhaps a demonstration of "restraint" (Jehne 1987a: 128–129) or, alternatively, a result of the unexpected delay caused by Antony. Dio 43.51.2–4 is doubtless a prolepsis rounding out his account of preparations for the Parthian War (Ramsey 2000, 447n32; note, however, that Nic. Dam. 76 is hardly definitive about the timing of the restoration of the tribunes from exile [n. 147], which anyway was not a precondition for the subversive write-in ballots.) Jehne, p. 117–118n34 reasonably supposes that the elections, which would have required no fewer than nine comitial days, all of them presumably before Dolabella's election, must have reached into March. In fact, since the first half of February was virtually all *nefastus*, Caesar must have used nearly all the available comitial days between the Lupercalia and the Ides of March (February 18–20, 22, 25, 28; March 3–5 or 6, 9–12).

[248] See n. 25.   [249] App. *BCiv.* 2.111/462: n. 20.

assembly presided over his own deputy, M. Lepidus, Master of the Horse. Most notably, for example, the year 47 went without consuls (nor were consuls elected for the next year) *until* Caesar returned from the East at last in October. Evidently none of those he left in charge of Rome during his absences felt they were in a position to hold consular or other senior elections in Caesar's absence; the persistence of the pattern throughout the wars sufficiently shows that this was clearly understood to be his policy.[250] Apparently he did not feel he could trust his nominated subordinates to maintain full control over the elections and the disorders to which electoral competition so often led.[251] The potential for trouble may be measured by the republican-style *popularis* uprisings led by ambitious Caesarians (the praetor M. Caelius, the tribune P. Dolabella – a patrician "transferred" to the plebs à la Clodius, no less) in 48 and 47, complete with street battles, the "Final Decree," and many dead.[252] Anxiety about the city "falling into strife" in Caesar's absence was entirely warranted, and now he would be even farther away.

Yet the pressure building for these "advance elections" must have been intense. Caesar, a patrician himself, had been careful not to alienate his noble followers, and had shown a traditional preference for nobility in his appointments to the consulship and other high magistracies during the Civil War years. Hinnerk Bruhns showed long ago that while, as Syme stressed, Caesar's consular appointments from 48 to 44 show a greater proportion of "new men" to men of senatorial family and *nobiles* (perhaps three *novi* out of nine, though *all* of these held the office only for the last three months of the year), his apparent adherence in general to the minimum age requirement before 44 and the relatively low number of reliable nobles available suggest that, contrary to common opinion, he showed no special favor to *novi* as a class but actually did his best to adorn the *fasti* with reassuringly aristocratic names: five of the nine were *nobiles*.[253] Bruhns also made the excellent point that Caesar's noble

---

[250] Bruhns 1978: 142–144, 160; Jehne 1987a: 124–125, 198–203, and 2010. This rule did not necessarily apply to tribunician elections, which could not be held by Caesar (as a patrician) and in any case were by long tradition the prerogative of tribunes.

[251] Dio 43.51.2: ἡ πόλις μήτ' ἄνευ ἀρχόντων ἐν τῇ ἀπουσίᾳ αὐτοῦ γένηται μήτ' αὖ καθ' ἑαυτὴν αἱρουμένη τινὰς στασιάσῃ. Bruhns 1978: 159.

[252] Bruhns 1978: 123–136. See n. 182. "Final decrees": n. 183.

[253] Bruhns 1978: 141–154. Cic. *Fam.* 4.8.2 (to M. Marcellus, 46): *[Caesar] favet ingeniis, nobilitatem vero et dignitates hominum, quantum ei res et ipsius causa concedit, amplectitur. Nobiles:* P. Servilius Isauricus (cos. 48), M. Aemilius Lepidus (46), Q. Fabius Maximus (suff. 45), M. Antonius (44) and P. Cornelius Dolabella (suff. 44). *Novi:* Q. Fufius Calenus (perhaps), P. Vatinius (47), C. Trebonius (suff. 45). Senatorial non-noble: C. Caninius Rebilus (suff. 45). Bruhns rightly

followers – as we saw, men with great names like Aemilius Lepidus, Antonius, Cornelius Cinna and Dolabella, Fabius Maximus, (Dec.) Iunius Brutus, Marcius Philippus, Servilius Isauricus, or Sulpicius Galba – can hardly be supposed to have cast in their lot in a civil war at huge risk to themselves in order to establish a *rex* over their heads.[254] The nobles who had joined themselves to Caesar and had thus come out on top can hardly have seen themselves as embarking on some radical post-republican future; rather, as Dolabella had written in 48 across the battle lines to his father-in-law, Cicero, they saw their side as "where the Republic is now."[255] What was different now was that they had won – and Caesar *owed them*.[256] Dolabella's resumption of old-time tribunician agitation in 47 as if there was no Caesar is a good indication of the expectations and ambitions of this class of men.[257] With the end of the Civil War the hopes and expectations of both Caesar's partisans and co-opted former enemies would have been greatly aroused, and now, due to his imminent departure for the Parthian campaign, everything (at least over the near term) would be settled. Over the course of just a few months the men were to be chosen who would hold scores of magistracies, among them the great prize of the consulship, over the period of Caesar's absence, and once this intense blast of political activity, amounting perhaps to as many as fourteen separate elections, was past, the Campus would fall silent for three years. What was a Roman aristocrat supposed to *do* for those three years?

criticizes Syme for taking too wide a view of *novi*, including men with senatorial forbears such as Caninius Rebilus and possibly Fufius Calenus.

[254] See the lists in Shackleton Bailey 1960 and Bruhns 1978: 30–63. Bruhns 1978: 172: "Caesar acknowledged that he had begun the Civil War and fought it to defend his *dignitas*; his noble supporters had not joined with him in order to make him into a ruler." Similarly, Dettenhofer 1992: 223: "They would actually have had a special interest in preserving the *res publica*, for that was the foundation of their ambition" (223; see especially 223–230, 318–319, 327–330 with detailed biographical surveys of Dolabella, Antony, M. and Dec. Brutus, and Cassius).

[255] Cic. *Fam.* 9.9.3: *reliquum est, ubi nunc est res publica, ibi simus potius quam, dum illam veterem sequamur, simus in nulla.*

[256] Bruhns 1978: 170–172, who aptly cites Antony's pretended riposte to Caesar in Cic. *Phil.* 2.72: *a me C. Caesar pecuniam? cur potius quam ego ab illo? an sine me vicit? at ne potuit quidem.* These debts heavily constrained Caesar's own freedom of action, as Cicero noted in a letter to Paetus in 46 (Cic. *Fam.* 9.17.2): *qui si cupiat esse rem publicam qualem fortasse et ille vult et omnes optare debemus, quid faciat tamen non habet; ita se cum multis colligavit.* A common refrain in 46: Cic. *Fam.* 4.9.3: *multa enim victori eorum arbitrio per quos vicit etiam invito facienda sunt*; 12.18.2: *bellorum enim civilium ii semper exitus sunt ut non ea solum fiant quae velit victor sed etiam ut iis mos gerendus sit quibus adiutoribus sit parta victoria.* Cf. *Lig.* 15, *Dei.* 35.

[257] Dio 42.30.3 claims that in fact in the early stage of the quarrel the tribunes expected Caesar to die and never return, but when on the contrary it was reported that he was on his way homeward they were checked only briefly. Of course, similar rumors were bound to swirl during the projected Parthian campaign.

Worse yet: the fact that the elections were very much now in Caesar's hands necessarily focused all hope, expectation, and resentment on him alone. There would be no time to earn trust, honor, and standing either with Caesar or the Roman People by means of the age-old parlaying of *virtus*, *dignitas*, and *gratia*. Everything would depend on how one stood with Caesar now. In the good old days one could soothe resentment by tactfully blaming aberrant electoral results on random circumstance or mistakes in the People's judgment, a face-saving, diffuse target;[258] now the Dictator would determine the outcome of the elections alone and the resentment aroused by "wrong" results would be focused directly on one man. His electoral powers were now utterly dominant if not absolute. We hear of two major kinds of legal privileges granted him in this area: one, the practice of sending around personal recommendations of candidates to the tribes,[259] the other, a right actually to appoint half of all the magistracies *except* the consulship (and probably the tribunate) by virtue of a *lex Antonia* passed by Mark Antony's brother Lucius, tribune in 44.[260] By this law Caesar "divided" with the People the recently doubled number of the magistracies (except for consulship and tribunate), which suggests that these two innovations may belong together: the People may have retained their formal rights over all the pre-Caesarian number of magistracies (thus avoiding the impression that they had "lost" control of any), while Caesar in effect appointed his candidates to the new, supplementary number.[261] The sources make clear that the elections under Caesar had become a formality, a ritual of ratification for decisions already made by the Dictator. We hear of no defeated candidates

---

[258] Cic. *Planc.* 11; *Mur.* 35–36.

[259] Suet. *Iul.* 41.2: *edebat per libellos circum tribum missos scriptura brevi: "Caesar dictator illi tribui. Commendo vobis illum et illum, ut vestro suffragio suam dignitatem teneant."*

[260] Cic. *Phil.* 7.16: *sua* [sc. L. Antoni] *lege qua cum C. Caesare magistratus partitus est suffragium sustulit.* Dio 43.51.3: ᾑρεῖτο δὲ τῷ μὲν λόγῳ τοὺς ἡμίσεις ὁ Καῖσαρ, ἐν νόμῳ τινὶ τοῦτο ποιησάμενος, ἔργῳ δὲ πάντας. Cf. App. *BCiv.* 2.129/540. On the *lex Antonia* see Jehne 1987a: 110–130. Dio 43.14.5 seems to say that already after Thapsus the Senate offered Caesar the unrestricted right to fill all magistracies without election, which many (e.g. Bruhns 1978: 158–162) have taken at face value. Jehne, however (pp. 119–123), offers cogent reasons to be skeptical of that interpretation (see especially Dio 43.47.1), suggesting instead that Caesar was formally empowered to send nonbinding *recommendations* to the People which then had the effect of determining the timing of elections (since they were impossible until the recommendations were made) and de facto, the results. Yet there is no sure evidence for such nonbinding recommendations – at least, none certainly before the *lex Antonia*. Possibly Dio 43.14.5 refers to one of the honors Caesar declined, despite the historian's stated principle (n. 72): Ferrary 2010: 27–28, cf. Jehne pp. 102–104.

[261] For the more or less twofold increase of the number of the magisterial colleges see n. 36. The hypothesis need not require perfect doubling in all cases in order to satisfy the meaning of *partitus est*: the number of aediles did not quite double (increased from four to six by doubling only the *plebeian* college: Dio 43.51.3), while the last increase in the number of praetors was only incremental (fourteen to sixteen), though the final number was in fact double their pre–Civil War number.

for office, which suggests that no one offered himself as a candidate without receiving Caesar's blessing.[262]

Yet a certain punctiliousness on Caesar's part about maintaining constitutional appearances is still evident. For instance, the secret ballot was apparently still in use, and exploited by some malcontents to express dissent: at a consular election held in late February or early March – probably the one for the consuls of the next year (43: Hirtius and Pansa) – some ballots "were found" bearing the names of the deposed tribunes.[263] And when on the last day of the year 45, just before the *comitia tributa* was summoned to vote in the quaestorian elections, word arrived at the Campus Martius that the suffect consul, Q. Fabius Maximus, had suddenly died, Caesar at once converted the assembly to a consular election and spent almost four hours presiding over the voting in order to have a second consul for the rest of the day and one night.[264] This prompted Cicero to make various bitter jokes (the one-day consul, C. Caninius Rebilus, was so stern a moralist that no one dared to have a party or sleep during his entire tenure of office[265]) and, rather more seriously, to complain about Caesar's indifference toward the technicalities, since Caesar had taken the auspices for a tribal assembly but then presided over a consular election. Yet Caesar's insistence on having a second consul in place even as the year closed may also have been justified according to constitutional principle: might he not have come under equal or worse criticism if he had done nothing?[266] Note also that apparently enough voters had turned up for the expected quaestorian election to require almost four hours for the proceeding under the Dictator's direct presidency. In certain respects, then, traditional forms were ostentatiously followed despite the radically changed circumstances, which presumably gave Caesar's unprecedented actions some veneer of constitutionalism.[267] And the *populus* still cared about forms: when late in 45 the great noble Q. Fabius Maximus, made "suffect consul" for the last three months of the year in an early experiment

[262] Jehne 1987a: 126. Cic. *Att.* 14.6.2: *consules et tribunos pl. . . . quos ille voluit*; Nic. Dam. *Bios* 67; App. *BCiv.* 2.129/540, etc.
[263] See n. 147. On these elections see Jehne 1987a: 116–118.
[264] Cic. *Fam.* 7.30.1: from the second to the seventh hour. (At the end of December a Roman hour lasted approximately forty-five of our minutes.)
[265] Ibid. The joke is picked up by Dio 43.46.4; another at Plut. *Caes.* 58.3 ("Let's hurry [viz., to congratulate Rebilus] or his consulship will be over").
[266] Weinstock 1971: 276, criticized by Bruhns 1978: 155n65. Bruhns, p. 154n62 and Jehne 1987a: 280–281 suggest that the point of the exercise was merely to have one more (rather dubious) consular. This would be more in line with Plutarch's view (*Caes.* 58.2), yet this shows only one side of the story. A balanced view in Pelling 2011: 433; Pina Polo 2018a: 102.
[267] Note that Caesar himself personally took the auspices for the relatively minor quaestorian electoral assembly on December 31, 45: Cic. *Fam.* 7.30.1, with Jehne 1987a: 417–418.

of a practice that would become routine under the Principate, he was greeted with shouts that he was not really a consul.[268] The respect Caesar showed for nobility, and even for the *lex annalis* (violated, so far as we can tell, only in 44 to put forward two crucial Caesarian nobles) would also have sent a signal of normalcy and traditionalism.

But for the unprecedented elections of magistrates far in advance for 43, 42, and 41 (projected) in a blast of activity before the expected date of Caesar's departure there could be little pretense of "constitutionalism." It is evident there was latent senatorial dismay at Caesar's tight control of the elections in any case, and the rapid-fire elections in advance that took place before the assassination certainly exacerbated anxiety and resentment.[269] Indeed, according to Nicolaus, Caesar's usurpation of the People's right to choose the magistrates in general was "what offended men of rank the most" out of all "the decrees and laws passed" at that time.[270] Note that Nicolaus wishes to stress the effect of this change not on the People, but on "men of rank," οἱ ἐν τέλει.[271] The passage is thus a nice example of the synergy of the republican system between aristocratic status and popular adjudication: loss of the latter precipitated a crisis of *dignitas* for the former. The passage alludes to the fact that the People's real, sovereign discretion over elections was central to the aristocracy's sense of identity and self-worth, inasmuch as only it could constitute an acceptably fair field for their competition in *virtus, dignitas*, or even *gratia* plain and simple, and the removal of this crucial source of validation deconstructed the ideology of *dignitas* itself: *honores* obtained as a personal favor rather than by a judgment of the People were in fact no

---

[268] Suet. *Iul.* 80.2. The difference from the situation of the late-elected suffect consuls of 47 was that Caesar *stepped down* to give Fabius the final three months: this was indeed a constitutional novelty (Dio 43.46.3; Suet. *Iul.* 76.2, slightly confused about 47: Butler and Cary 1927: 139). For a noble this kind of sham advancement may have appeared especially disgraceful. For Caesar's use of the suffect consulship see Jehne 1987a: 374–379 and now Pina Polo 2018a: 101–103.

[269] General: In addition to Cic. *Fam.* 7.30.1–2 (cf. Plut. *Caes.* 58.2) discussed previously, see especially *Phil.* 2.80; Nic. Dam. *Bios* 67 (discussed further later); App. *BCiv.* 2.138/574, 4.93/388. For the advance elections in particular, see especially Cic. *Att.* 14.6.2 (April 12, 44): *quid enim miserius quam ea nos tueri propter quae illum oderamus? Etiamne consules et tribunos pl. in biennium quos ille voluit? Nullo modo reperio quem ad modum possim* πολιτεύεσθαι. Suet. *Iul.* 76.3: *eadem licentia spreto patrio more magistratus in pluris annos ordinavit.* App. *BCiv.* 2.138/574: ὁ δ᾽ ἐπὶ ἄλλην στρατείαν χρόνιον ἀπιὼν ἐς πενταετὲς ὑμῶν τὰ ἀρχαιρέσια προελάμβανε, ποία ταῦτα ἦν ἐλευθερία, ἧς οὐδ᾽ ἐλπὶς ὑπεφαίνετο ἔτι. Dio 43.47.1 adds that Caesar was given the formal right to choose only half of the future magistracies for the next three years, but "in reality he chose them all."

[270] Nic. Dam. *Bios* 67: μάλιστα δὲ τῶν ἐψηφισμένων ἐλύπει τοὺς ἐν τέλει τὸ καὶ τῶν ἀρχῶν ἄκυρον γενέσθαι τῆς καταστάσεως τὸν δῆμον, ἐκείνῳ δ᾽ αὐτὰς ἀποδεδόσθαι οἷς βούλοιτο διδόναι.

[271] On the phrase see Toher 2017: 286.

"honor" at all.[272] In Ser. Sulpicius Rufus's famous letter of consolation to Cicero on the death of his beloved daughter Tullia, whose basic theme might be crudely summarized as "she's lucky to have died when she did" (February 45), he declares that Tullia really had no reason to want to live in a world in which she would not be able to take satisfaction in sons who "would canvass for office in sequence and enjoy their freedom in political life and supporting their friends in the courts."[273] The famous passage shows better than most that "canvass[ing] for office in sequence" was an essential part of a noble's identity and sense of "freedom," without which life was hardly worth living, not just for the nobles themselves but for their families.

Yet, as we have seen (n. 189), it would be facile to conclude that senators were the only ones who resented the loss of the People's effective freedom to choose their leaders. The recent trouble with the tribunes itself shows that the Roman People were not indifferent to their ancient political rights. We surely have here another source of the grave popular alienation from Caesar that we have traced. Perhaps those who wrote in the names of Flavus and Marullus at the first consular election held after their banishment were not senators but ordinary citizens.[274]

A review of the results of these remarkable elections will help to bring the fissures in the Caesarian faction into focus. At the time of the assassination, as we noted, all magistrates had been chosen for 43, only consuls and tribunes for 42 and apparently none for 41.[275] The consuls for 43 were two prominent Caesarian administrators: C. Vibius Pansa of a minor senatorial family, who had already governed two provinces for Caesar but had limited military experience and is not known with certainty to have been elected to *any* urban magistracy beyond the tribunate,[276] and the *novus* A. Hirtius,

---

[272] See Morstein-Marx 2009: 115–122. For important discussion of the popular assemblies as a "third party" (*dritte Instanz*) necessary for the adjudication of aristocratic competition see Hölkeskamp 2010: 103–105.

[273] Cic. *Fam.* 4.5.3, with Bruhns 1978: 138, 164.   [274] See nn. 147, 263.   [275] See n. 25.

[276] Pansa and Hirtius are placed first in the list of *Caesaris familares* at Cic. *Fam.* 6.12.2; both appear to have been scorned by Caesar's former officers (Q. Cicero, [Cic.] *Fam.* 16.27.1) and objects of Cicero's veiled contempt (Shackleton Bailey 1998: 111–114). Pansa's father had been proscribed by Sulla (Dio 45.17.1). Although most scholars have assumed that the C. Vibius Pansa who was tr. pl. in 51 was the same man, Hinard 1985: 408–410 rejects this and stands firm against Ryan's argument that he had recovered his right to office not through the lifting of the ban on sons of the proscribed holding office (on which see Bruhns 1978: 72–75: perhaps by a law of 49) but through adoption, like M. Brutus/Servilius Caepio (Ryan 1996b; Hinard 2008: 126–129). In any case, neither Vibii or Caetronii were of notable senatorial stock (Fündling, *BNP* Vibius I 2; Wiseman 1971: no. 490). For his further offices see *MRR* 2. 274, 290, 299, 310, 3.220–221. Pansa was also distinguished by Caesar with the augurate, probably in 45: Rüpke 2005: 1368. Whether or not he held the praetorship in 48, which is plausible though not yet established with certainty (*MRR* 3.220–221. Jehne 1987a: 387), he

praetor in 46 and then placed in charge of Narbonese Gaul together with Caesar's new conquests – a most sensitive duty.[277] For the next year, 42, the consuls-designate were the noble Dec. Iunius Brutus, one of Caesar's most capable marshals, to whom Transalpine Gaul had been entrusted in 47–46 (or 48–46) and then, probably after a praetorship in the last months of 45, the crucial province of Cisalpine Gaul – a man close enough to Caesar personally to be named as secondary heir in his will;[278] and the *homo novus* from Tibur, L. Munatius Plancus, one of the several prefects left in charge of the City in 45, perhaps praetor in that year or already in 47, and appointed by Caesar to command recently conquered Gaul in 44 as Hirtius's successor.[279]

What stands out in these choices is their solid prior record of reliable service to Caesar, which is no more than we would expect since they would be the chief officials in Rome during the Dictator's planned absence. However, according to traditional standards of pedigree, military leadership, and public service, a number of other eligible candidates also probably considered themselves more deserving than most of those Caesar favored for the consulships of 43 and 42 (excepting Dec. Brutus, whose nobility and service were indeed unimpeachable). For example, the quite senior noble Ser. Sulpicius Galba, who had reached the praetorship as far back as 54 and had been disappointed in his consular run just before the Civil War, may still have been waiting for his due (he would in due course turn up among the conspirators); another eligible candidate, P. Sulpicius

---

was a Caesarian "creature" through and through. According to Vell. 2.57.1, Pansa and Hirtius advised Caesar to maintain by arms the domination he had won by arms.

[277] W. Will, *BNP* Hirtius, Aulus; Jehne 1987a: 401n54; Wiseman 1971: no. 206 (Ferentinum?); *MRR* 2.295, 3.102; possibly tr. pl. 48 (*MRR* 2.274). Also elevated to the augural college in 46, perhaps even simultaneously to the pontificate: so, on the basis of *RRC* 466/1 (also the only testimony to the praetorship), Rüpke 2005: 1035–1036 with n. 5 (contra Bruhns 1978: 154n63, who accepts that Caesar's appointments to the pontificate were exclusively noble). In letters of 44 Cicero refers to him by a Greek epithet which perhaps means either "five-gullet" (referring to his gourmandizing: cf. Shackleton Bailey 1965: 6.241) or "lick-all" (ditto, or perhaps worse: Shackleton Bailey 1998: 112).

[278] Dettenhofer 1992: 72–78, 183–192, 256–262. Dec. Brutus had been prefect of Caesar's fleet against the Veneti, prefect in the Alesia campaign, *praefectus classis* against Massilia in 49, then legate in charge of Transalpine Gaul, where he suppressed a rebellion in 46 (*MRR* 2.213, 239, 267, 281, 291, 301, 328; 3.112–113; note, however, Dettenhofer pp. 76, 257, dating the quaestorship to 54 or 53). For the praetorship see *MRR* 3.313. For the will, dated September 13, 45, see esp. Suet. *Iul.* 83.1–2; cf. Dio 44.35.2; Plut. *Caes.* 64.1; App. 2.143/597, 146/611 thinks Decimus was also adopted under the will (generally rejected). The position of secondary heir was not very exclusive, and Dio makes clear that a number of the conspirators were named among them.

[279] *MRR* 2.307, 313, 329; 3.146; see Bruhns 1978, 156n69. Again, however, the praetorship is not explicitly attested. Septemvir Epulonum probably 45 (Rüpke 2005: 1162). Wiseman 1971: no. 262 (Tibur).

Rufus, who had held the praetorship in 48, had a distinguished record under Caesar culminating in an acclamation as *imperator* in Illyricum, which should have positioned him well for the consulships of 43, 42, or 41.[280] If we move down to the praetorian level, where we happen to know ten names of the sixteen men appointed for 43, we again observe signs of Caesar's preference for a less illustrious and more partisan group than those for 44: there are only a few noble names, a high proportion of *homines novi*, and no ex-Pompeians, at least so far as we can tell from the admittedly thin evidence.[281]

This suggests that the sequential elections Caesar held shortly before his departure for the Parthian War signaled a step back from the inclusive policy of integrating former enemies and attention to pedigree and *dignitas* that had graced the *fasti* for 44, the first post–Civil War year.[282] Closeness to the Dictator and a proven record of loyal and effective service rather than pedigree or *merita in rem publicam* would now be determinative, at least for the near future. That was no doubt unsurprising given the huge undertaking being launched, but it came at a bad time given the already fraught nature of the "advance elections" themselves and the increasingly invidious position in which the Dictator had found himself early in 44. And there is good reason to think that the advance consular elections for 43 and 42 would have provoked friction even among loyal Caesarians. Why should Dec. Brutus, for example, wait in the queue behind those mere

---

[280] Caesar had supported Galba, great-grandfather of the future emperor, for the consulship of 49 [Chapter 6, n.72]): Cic. *Phil.* 13.33. P. Sulpicius Rufus: Sumner 1971: 249–250, proposed to distinguish between two men of the same name differing only in its patronymic (*MRR* 3.202–203), one (*RE* 93 and P.f.) the praetor of 48, the *imperator* in Illyricum, and the future censor of 42 (*MRR* 2.299), the other (Q.f. on the basis of an uncertain legend on a coin of Sinope) procos. Bithynia and Pontus 46–45. This is far from certain, however, and if these offices belong to one man rather than two, his qualifications would appear even more impressive. Note that since Sulpicius reached the censorship in 42 without having held the consulship, he was probably one of ten ex-praetors elevated by Caesar to consular status without holding the office (Suet. *Iul.* 76.3; cf. Dio 43.47.3; Jehne 1987a: 406n72). However, we cannot be sure that this occurred in 45 (so Bruhns 1978: 152), and it is probably best seen as consolation for those passed over in the "advance elections" of 44.

[281] Nobles: only L. Marcius Censorinus and (presumably) M'. Aquillius Crassus. Probable *novi* include L. Cestius (Wiseman 1971: no. 117; *MRR* 3.53), L. Plotius Plancus, natural brother of L. Munatius Plancus (Wiseman, no. 328) and member of the land commission, P. Rupilius Rex, tr. pl. by 45 (Wiseman, no. 366, although Badian suggests descent from the consul of 132), and P. Ventidius Bassus (Wiseman, no. 474). Lower-ranking senatorial families fielded Q. Gallius, perhaps q. or leg. Cilicia 47–46 (*MRR* 3.98–99) and possibly son of homonymous *novus* (cf. Wiseman, no. 192), and C. Norbanus Flaccus, probably grandson of the famous Marian *novus* (Frigo, *BNP* Norbanus I 2). Only Rupilius is known to have served on the Pompeian side (Porphyrio on Hor. *Sat.* 1.7). By comparison, fully half of the praetorian college of 44 (all sixteen are known) were nobles, and at least four (one-fourth) were former Pompeians (Bruhns 1978: 156). Broughton now deletes L. Aelius Lamia from the praetorian college of 43 (*MRR* 3.4).

[282] Bruhns 1978: 153, 156.

placeholders Hirtius and Pansa? Another possible source of friction was the implied subordination of the consuls of 44 after Caesar's departure and the consuls-elect of 43 to Caesar's designated Masters of the Horse (second in command to a Dictator), M. Valerius Messalla Rufus and Cn. Domitius Calvinus – the two elected consuls of 53 who almost certainly were soon convicted of electoral corruption and sent into exile before the Civil War, from which purgatory Caesar had restored them, putting them to good use in Africa and Pharsalus, respectively. It is hard to believe that they would not have been tainted in the eyes of their peers and especially of the consuls they would be expected to keep in line during Caesar's absence.[283]

In addition to the sharp intensification of competition for Caesar's favor just before his expected departure, the flurry of extraordinary "advance elections" produced two dangerous further effects: it threw into doubt Caesar's policy of reconciliation as recent Pompeians and in general those without strong ties to the Dictator appeared to be disfavored to act as his surrogates during the long projected absence; and, even more ominously, it set up a situation in which loyal *Caesarians* were "forced" to compete with each other all at once for the top positions available over the next few years. We might expect this to lead to serious fragmentation within what had been the victorious Caesarian "party," and as we shall see there is good evidence for this. Taking these two effects together one can see the emergence of the possibility of common ground between men who had been on opposite sides of the recent fighting, expressed by shared resentment and indignation toward the man who had taken these heavily freighted decisions into his own hands.

Caesar's policy of leniency toward the defeated had ruled out wholesale confiscations of property to reward his supporters for risking their lives and fortunes by taking up his cause. Thus what was left in his hands to

---

[283] The newly published fragment of the Privernum Fasti shows that Caesar's choice for *magister equitum* after Lepidus's imminent departure for Spain was Messalla, not the future Octavian, as has been often supposed (*MRR* 2.319, Jehne 1987a: 381–383); Domitius Calvinus was to succeed him in turn. Messalla had been convicted in 51 and Calvinus may have also fallen victim to the purge under the *lex Pompeia* (Alexander 1990: nos. 301, 331, with Caes. *BCiv.* 3.1.4–5; cf. Syme 1964: 217; Bruhns 1978: 40 no. 1). Caes. loc. cit. shows that notwithstanding the sweeping statements of Dio 41.36.2 and App. *BCiv.* 2.48/198, he proceeded cautiously in restoring those "unjustly" condemned under Pompey's law; Bruhns (pp. 64–70) explains this caution by noting the fraught politics of the measure at a time when Caesar still hoped to avoid offending senatorial sentiment. Calvinus had after his restoration by Caesar played important roles in the Pharsalus and Pharnaces campaigns (*MRR* 2.277, 289; 3.84), and would later (40) be awarded a second consulship by the triumvirs; Messalla had served with distinction in the African and Munda campaigns (*MRR* 2.291, 302, 312). Clearly they were being rehabilitated, and Pompey's "housecleaning" of 52–51 correspondingly impugned.

distribute to them as rewards, and also to co-opt former Pompeians, were *honores* – magistracies and priesthoods – of which he freely availed himself as victor.[284] Dio clearly links this motivation with the increase (ultimately the doubling) of the number of magistracies except for the consulship, although by keeping such a constraint on the number of consuls while ultimately doubling the number of praetors, Caesar also greatly intensified competition for the highest office. This was moderated only slightly by the novel practice, conspicuous since late 45, of electing suffect consuls to take his own place as consul (Trebonius and Fabius in 45, Dolabella in 44), particularly since Caesar himself held the consulship himself four times during the years 48–44.[285] Thus, even Caesar's generosity in dispersing *honores* was bound to create bitterness in those who were disappointed in their petitions[286] – especially since place had also to be found for the specially favored ex-Pompeians M. Brutus and Cassius, who had both been given prestigious praetorships for 44.[287]

An interesting anecdote about these two men's praetorships (probably deriving from Pollio) illustrates the dangerous dynamic set in motion by these kinds of decisions. Brutus, as we have seen, had shortly after his pardon become a trusted and prominent Caesarian – a valuable bridge between the defeated former Pompeians such as Cicero and M. Marcellus and Caesar, as well as governor of the key province of Cisalpine Gaul, even as his uncle Cato disemboweled himself at Utica.[288] As recently as August 45 Brutus had assured Cicero that Caesar had joined the *boni* – that is, the "loyal patriots" of the Republic as Cicero styled himself.[289] Brutus's praetorship in 44 along with that of another ex-Pompeian who

---

[284] Dio 43.47.2, 51.9.

[285] Dio 42.51.3–4; 43.47. Bruhns 1978: 155: doubling the number of praetors halved the expected probability of reaching the consulship afterward from about 1 in 4 to 1 in 8.

[286] Dio 43.47.6.

[287] Two other ex-Pompeians were also given praetorships in 44: Chapter 8, n. 259 (but see n. 331). Other notable ex-Pompeians who received honor from Caesar before his assassination include the antiquarian Varro (a special case, admittedly), P. Sestius (pr. inc. ann.), C. Messius (aed. 55), C. Ateius Capito (tr. pl. 55), and the noble A. Terentius Varro Murena. Pelling 2011: 429.

[288] Chapter 8, #33. Dettenhofer 1992: 194–211 offers a plausible account of Brutus as "committed Caesarian" in 46 and still an active agent in 45. In his encomium of Cato Brutus seems to have criticized his suicide even while eulogizing him (Plut. *Brut.* 40.7–8), thus performing his familial duty while avoiding giving offense to Caesar (Dettenhofer, pp. 206–207) and implicitly validating his own and Cicero's different choice – which was in keeping with Caesar's policy. His marriage to Cato's daughter, Porcia, need not signal disaffection from Caesar so much as Caesar's magnanimous treatment of former enemies.

[289] Cic. *Att.* 13.40.1: *nuntiat Brutus illum ad bonos viros?* The ms. *ut fultum est*, explicated by Shackleton Bailey (1965: 5:388) as equivalent to "As the cushions lie, so he sits," implies the criticism that Brutus was adapting himself comfortably to the situation.

had won special favor from Caesar, C. Cassius, was probably meant to send a celebratory signal of peace and reconciliation.[290] But the two former Pompeians immediately fell into contention with each other over the prize appointment as urban praetor, and naturally they took the matter straight to Caesar:

> Brutus had little more than his honourable reputation and his record for upright dealings to set against Cassius's many brilliant exploits during Crassus's campaign against the Parthians. However, when Caesar had listened to each man's claims and was discussing the affair with his friends, he summed it up by saying: "Cassius has the stronger case, but we must give Brutus the first praetorship." Cassius was appointed to another praetorship, but he was more resentful about the post he had lost than grateful for the one he received.[291]

Note how the two men's "claims" are first measured by moral, "republican" standards: "honorable reputation," integrity, military deeds. By these traditional standards, Caesar is made to acknowledge that Cassius had the better claim. Nevertheless, he gives the position to Brutus as a *personal favor* – thus showing that those traditional claims meant nothing, or were not determinative. But if an office was an *honor*, it was so precisely because it was bestowed in recognition of *dignitas* according to that traditional standard. Seen in this light, it becomes obvious why Cassius was "more resentful about the post he had lost than grateful for the one he received." And even the recipients of Caesar's bounty could be offended by the blatant use of *honores* as personal gifts. How could Brutus regard as an *honor* an office that he didn't deserve on the basis of *dignitas* but only as a personal gift? (This gives added point to the story that among the graffiti written on Brutus's tribunal was the question "Brutus, are you taking bribes?"[292]) Thus, with this one decision regarding what was intended on its face as a *beneficium*, Caesar managed to offend both Cassius and Brutus, though both were conspicuous recipients of his favor and leniency toward former enemies. The story brings out the risk he ran of

---

[290] See Chapter 8, pp. 476ff. Caesar had made Brutus his legate before October 46 (Cic. *Fam.* 6.6.10). Dettenhofer 1992: 218–222 plausibly explicates the relatively optimistic tone of Cassius's epistolary exchange with Cicero in late 46 and early 45.

[291] Plut. *Brut.* 7.4 (Scott-Kilvert tr.): ʽδικαιότερα μὲν λέγει Κάσσιος, Βρούτῳ δὲ τὴν πρώτην δότεον'; very similar language at *Caes.* 62.4–5 (αὐτὸς μέντοι Βροῦτον οὐκ ἂν παρέλθοι) and App. *BCiv.* 2.112/466–467 (Βρούτῳ δ' αὐτὸς χαρίζοιτο). Cf. Vell. Pat. 2.56.3, who attaches the idea of double failure to the expectation of a consulship: *quorum alterum promittendo consulatum non obligauerat, contra differendo Cassium offenderat*. Both may be right: Pelling 2011: 461–462, and see later in this chapter. Pollionic origin for the story seems likely (Chapter 5, n. 19.).

[292] App. *BCiv.* 2.112/469: "Βροῦτε δωροδοκεῖς."

alienating the *recipients* of "handouts" of *honores*, for even those who benefited from Caesar's "generosity" in this way were likely to resent the giver. Was it a token of *honor* or the bribe of a tyrant? In an effort to reward supporters and co-opt former enemies, Caesar had removed the only clear marker between the two – thereby, for those with any "republican" feeling, moral scruples, or self-regard, subverting his very purpose.

When the assassination came, it became clear that the members of the conspiracy were largely former Pompeians, including its leaders, Gaius Cassius and Marcus Brutus.[293] Yet several disgruntled Caesarians were among the assassins, most notably Dec. Brutus, the consul-designate for 42, also the suffect consul for 45, Gaius Trebonius, and some lesser figures such as Ser. Galba, L. Minucius Basilus (pr. 45), L. Tillius Cimber (pr. 45?), and C. (or P.?) Servilius Casca (tr. pl. 44 or 43?).[294] Why? Suetonius explicitly writes that Galba, despite his service to Caesar as his legate in Gaul, joined the conspiracy *ob repulsam consulatus*, presumably therefore out of disappointment suffered either in the "advance elections" of 44 or in one of those during the Civil War years.[295] Basilus, a legate of Caesar's in Gaul and again in the Adriatic during the first phases of the Civil War, felt insulted according to Dio when after his praetorship in late 45 Caesar did not give him a province (he probably did not have any more provinces to give, for there were fourteen praetors in this year alone), but "a great deal of money" instead. To judge from Dio's wording, Basilus was not appeased "but held out against him" – presumably by nursing his sense of alienation

---

[293] List of conspirators at Drumann and Groebe 1906: 627–643, Groebe, *RE* 10 (1918), 254–255, conveniently also in Lintott 2009: 77. Ten of the twenty known conspirators were former Pompeians. Cn. Domitius Ahenobarbus the Younger should also be on the list: Cic. *Phil.* 2.27 with Ramsey's comment ad loc. Brutus was sensitive to the charge that the assassination would be regarded as a continuation of the Civil War or a political coup, and therefore argued against the killing of Antony or any other Caesarians: App. *BCiv.* 2.114/478; Dio 44.19.2. (This important consideration is muddied or omitted by Plut. *Brut.* 18.3–6, *Ant.* 13.2–3, Vell. Pat. 2.58.2.) Cicero was to complain incessantly about this strategic decision (*Att.* 14.21.3, *Fam.* 12.4.1, *Phil.* 2.34 with Ramsey ad loc., etc.), but in fact the alternative would have mobilized Caesarian forces immediately against the assassins. Thus Brutus's plan was not less "realistic" than Cassius's alternative (Vell. Pat. 2.58.2), pace Dettenhofer 1992: 254.

[294] App. *BCiv.* 2.113/474 provides a list of notable Caesarians in the conspiracy, omitting Galba, however. It has been conjectured that Appian or his source confuses the praenomen and that Publius Casca, the tribune of 43 and better-known conspirator, is meant instead of Gaius, the tribune of 44, who denied any connection to the conspirator other than his cognomen and therefore was perhaps not Publius's brother. See *MRR* 3.194–195. L. Staius Murcus, possibly praetor in 45 (see *MRR* 3.200), is another Caesarian officer who joined the conspirators at least after the assassination, if not before (*MRR* 2.282, 302).

[295] Suet. *Galba* 3, with Bruhns 1978, 152n57: his loss in 50, when he was perceived as Caesar's candidate (Chapter 6, n. 72), could hardly have been held against the proconsul at the time, but Caesar had not corrected the apparent injustice by 44, although he was now fully in control of the elections.

openly or covertly – and he turns up among the killers on the Ideas of March.[296] These two known examples encourage us to suspect that other Caesarians in the conspiracy had similar motives of disappointed expectations that induced them ultimately to turn against their former commander. Trebonius, who had served the Triple Alliance spectacularly as tribune in 55, then had performed well under Caesar in Gaul, seems to have won most of the credit for the Civil War victory at Marseilles in 49 and as praetor had held the line against the rebellious Caelius in Rome the next year, may have been less than thrilled with his three-months' "suffect" consulship, which, as we saw, was a constitutional novelty that attracted popular derision.[297] He would be the only consular to participate in the conspiracy. Dec. Brutus may well have thought that with his pedigree and important military contributions both in the Gallic campaigns and in the Civil War, he deserved better than to wait for his consulship in 42 behind the undistinguished likes of Hirtius and Pansa.[298]

We are told that Caesar had intended to hold elections for 41 – at least for the consulship – as well, and since time was running out this particular prize will have loomed especially heavily over the Ides of March. As it happens, a remarkable number of men who would have been eligible and worthy candidates for the consulship in 41 end up on the list of Caesar's assassins, starting with Brutus and Cassius themselves, who as praetors in 44 would have been legally eligible for the consulship in 41. A passage in Cicero's *Philippics* explicitly indicates that there was some expectation that the pair were seen as the favored candidates.[299] Velleius thinks that Caesar had promised Brutus a consulship for 41, but disappointed Cassius, thus again failing to win the gratitude of one while further offending the

---

[296] Dio 43.47.5: καὶ ὅτι προπηλακισθεὶς ἐν τῇ στρατηγίᾳ ὑπ' αὐτοῦ ἀντεκαρτέρησε. Nic. Dam. *Bios* 89; cf. App. *BCiv.* 2.113/474.

[297] Trebonius's record may be traced at MRR 2.217, 226, 232, 239, 245, 253, 269–270, 273–274; summary by Fündling, *BNP* Trebonius I 1. He was evidently the ranking commander of the siege of Marseilles (Dettenhofer 1992: 186–188) and was rewarded with a praetorship the very next year, while the victor at sea, the *praefectus classis* Dec. Brutus, had to wait until 45 (n. 278). Trebonius may, however, have been held partly responsible for the Caesarian loss of Spain in 47–46: MRR 2.289, 299. At *Phil.* 2.34 Cicero refers to (or fabricates) a rumor that Trebonius had discussed killing Caesar with Antony at Narbo during the return from Spain in 45, before his attenuated consulship: Ramsey 2003: 212–213. (Plut. *Ant.* 13.2 surely derives from Cicero.)

[298] See nn. 276–278. Dettenhofer 1992: 258–262 plausibly speculates that Dec. Brutus was driven by his noble heritage to prove that he was not Caesar's servant. This is not inconsistent with the suggestion made in the text.

[299] Cic. *Phil.* 8.27: *dum M. Brutus C. Cassius consules prove coss. provincias obtinebunt* with Manuwald 2007: 1014–1015; see also Dettenhofer 1992: 249–250; Pelling 2011: 461. Cf. *Fam.* 12.2.2 (to Cassius) *vestro anno*, referring to 41. A consulship for two pardoned ex-Pompeians would send a very strong message. Sumner 1971: 370 shows that Caesar generally respected the *lex annalis*.

other.[300] Some anecdotes (which of course may be apocryphal, the product of hindsight) suggest that Caesar saw Brutus as one of Rome's likely future leaders; the story that he may have been the Dictator's illegitimate son was surely invented to explain Caesar's peculiar favoritism toward him.[301] But the hopes of his former enemies were not all Caesar had to worry about. An obvious "Caesarian" contender for a consulship of 41 was Mark Antony's brother Gaius (pr. 44), one of three brothers who were such a powerful force at this time. All three held office in this year – Antony as consul, Gaius as praetor, and Lucius as tribune – and it was only to be expected that they would exert whatever influence they had to further the chances of another consulship as soon as possible. Other persons who should have been strong candidates by reason of their service or connection to Caesar and a praetorship held no later than 44 were the nobles Ser. Sulpicius Galba (pr. 54), P. Sulpicius Rufus (pr. 48), both briefly discussed earlier in connection with the elections for 43 and 42 (p. 551f.); Caesar's own nephew Q. Pedius (pr. 48), who had been given the high (and surprising) honor of a triumph "over Spain" in just the previous year; Caesar's former legate L. Minucius Basilus (pr. 45), also discussed previously, of whose resentment at being "bought off" from a province we happen to be informed; and L. Marcius Philippus (pr. 44), a noble and stepson to Caesar's niece Atia (thus stepbrother to Caesar's heir, C. Octavius).[302]

Among this group of well-qualified contenders for the remaining consulships to be settled, two of the Civil War Caesarians – Sulpicius Galba and

[300] See n. 291. Possibly, given its similarity to the story of their praetorships, only a conflation. But cf. Plut. Caes. 62.4 "he [Brutus] was also going to be consul in three years' time" perhaps in contrast to Cassius?

[301] Plut. Brut. 8.3, Caes. 62.6 (n. 213); cf. Brut. 5.2; App. BCiv. 2.112/467–468. On Caesar's famous lines "whatever he wants, he wants it with a will" (Cic. Att. 14.1.1; cf. Plut. Brut. 6.7) and "you too, my son?" (Suet. Iul. 82.2; Dio 44.19.5) see Dettenhofer 1992: 199, Pelling 2011: 482–483, and Tempest 2017: 101–104. If, as is most widely accepted, Brutus was born in 85 (see now Tempest 2017: 262–263n28; cf. Dettenhofer 1992: 100–101), the story of Caesar's paternity is refuted by Servilia's age (about fifteen at the time): all prudery aside, a newly married patrician girl aged about fifteen would have been closely watched, and rumors would have left a stronger trace. Tempest (p. 102) reaches a similar conclusion.

[302] A "zealous" Caesarian named Curtius Postumus had in 45 supposedly been pondering his chances at the consulship (Cic. Att. 12.49.2, with 14.9.2 [obelized: Shackleton Bailey 1965: 6:220]) and thus may have been another hopeful for the consulship in 43, 42, or 41. Cf. Att. 9.2a.3, 3.2, 5.1, 6.2, Fam. 2.16.7 and 6.12.2, which reveals him to be a member of Caesar's innermost circle in late 46. Curtius seems to be accused of being a Caesarian war profiteer at Att. 14.10.2; it is unclear whether his name should be printed at 14.9.2 (Shackleton Bailey 1965: 6:220; Cristofoli 2011: 105–106: M'. Curius?). Most scholars accept the identification of Curtius Postumus with C. Rabirius Postumus, Cicero's client in an extant speech of 54 (see Shackleton Bailey 1965: 4:361–362, 1977: 2:450; Sumner 1971: 254–255; Siani Davies 1996: 239; MRR 2.273, 3.80), but like Bruhns 1978: 56, 57 (nos. 8, 32), White 1995 (who doubts Curtius was even a senator), and Cristofoli 2011: 115, I am inclined to distinguish the two because of the consistency of Cicero's references in his letters to "Curtius (Postumus)" while other sources in the Civil War refer to C. Rabirius or Rabirius Postumus.

Minucius Basilus – turn up subsequently among the conspirators against Caesar's life as do, of course, the Pompeian competitors for the positions, M. Brutus and Cassius. If we widen the circle to include not only those who are likely to have the strongest claim in Caesar's eyes but also those who had held the praetorship in time to *consider themselves* eligible for the remaining consulships (of 41), we find at least five more known to have participated in the conspiracy or who soon aligned themselves with the assassins. P. (Sextius?) Naso (pr. 44) was probably another pardoned ex-Pompeian.[303] Three Caesarian ex-praetors had obtained important provincial assignments for 44 that betoken relatively high standing with Caesar and probable consular ambitions: L. Tillius Cimber (pr. 45?), about to depart as proconsul of Bithynia-Pontus, which would be a frontline province in the first phase of the Parthian War; Q. Cornificius (pr. prob. 45), an invaluable officer in the recent wars now assigned to govern Africa, and Q. Hortensius (pr. by 45), a noble, son of the great orator, who had preceded Caesar across the River Rubicon in 49 and was now assigned to govern Macedonia.[304] In the Caesarian column we may also add the brother of Caesar's second (or first?) wife, L. Cornelius Cinna, favored at this time with a praetorship for 44, but who would swiftly remove the insignia of his office after Caesar's assassination on the grounds that they were "the gift of a tyrant."[305]

The majority of those listed were naturally partisans of Caesar in the Civil War, which prompts the reflection that competition and resentment *among ambitious Caesarians* still climbing their way to the top may have been an important factor in recruiting so many of them to the plot against Caesar's life. Of the seven Caesarians known to have been in the plot (or who immediately joined it) at least four and possibly six were eligible contenders in the rapid-fire advance consular elections held in 44 for the years 43–41.[306] If we now include the two ex-Pompeian leaders of the conspiracy and Sextius Naso, it is evident that a disproportionately high number of eligible

---

[303] Naso: chapter 8, #70.

[304] Tillius (a *novus*): *MRR* 2.330, 3.205; Wiseman 1971: 266. Cornificius: *MRR* 2.276, 297, 306, 327–328, 3.76; Sumner 1971: 358. Hortensius: *MRR* 2.267, 328, 3.103.

[305] App. *BCiv.* 2.121/509: τήν τε ἐσθῆτα τὴν στρατηγικὴν ἀπεδύσατο, ὡς παρὰ τυράννου δεδομένης ὑπερορῶν. Other sources for his *contio* denouncing Caesar as a tyrant in *MRR* 2.320. This was the Cinna for whom the crowd mistook poor "Cinna the poet." L. Cinna is generally excluded from membership in the conspiracy despite the explicit statement of Dio 44.50.4; this is unduly fussy since he certainly immediately and publicly threw in his lot with the cause. On the enumeration of Caesar's wives, see Pelling 2011: 133.

[306] Dec. Brutus, Ser. Galba, Minucius Basilus, Tillius Cimber (pp. 556-57, 559). In addition, Staius Murcus (n. 294) and L. Cinna (n. 305) quickly joined the conspirators. Cimber and Murcus were likely praetors in 45; all the rest are known to have held that office no later than 44 and thus were eligible for a consulship by 41. The seventh, Trebonius, was already cos. suff. 45.

candidates for those elections are found among the conspirators against Caesar's life.[307] By contrast, consider as a kind of control that of the perhaps seventeen active consulars sitting in the Senate in early 44 (nearly all of them now of course also "Caesarians") only one – Trebonius, whose consulship was, as we have noted, of a second-rate (*suffectus*) kind – is found in the ranks of the assassins.[308] These men, of course, would have had no expectations in the distribution of consulships for the next three years before Caesar's departure.

Such arguments are suggestive rather than decisive, but they encourage the thought (not implausible in itself) that disappointed ambition for *honores* as rewards for good service, which we would expect now to be much heightened by the burst of prospective consular elections, was a significant factor favoring the coalescence of the conspiracy, especially among recent Caesarians.[309] This aspect of the rising discontent with Caesar resides mostly below the surface of our texts, but it is certainly not difficult to find if we read between the lines, and sometimes it emerges into plain view, as when Dio, discussing various "gifts" both in the form of *honores* and money, sums up as follows:

> All this suited those citizens who were receiving or even expected to receive something, since they had no regard for the public good in comparison with the chance of the moment for their own advancement by such means. But all the rest took it greatly to heart and had much to say about it to each other and also – as many as felt safe in so doing – in outspoken utterances and the publication of anonymous pamphlets. (43.47.6)[310]

[307] Dettenhofer 1992: 317–318 makes a similar argument but emphasizes the generational aspect while leaving consular ambitions out of account. I suggest, on the other hand, that the statistically overrepresented subgroup of plausible consular contenders goes far to explain the generational focus. See also recently Tempest 2017: 97–100.

[308] Famously, Cicero himself surely did not participate: Cic. *Phil.* 2.25–32, with Ramsey 2003: 198. The seventeen consulars besides Caesar: L. Cotta (cos. 65), L. Caesar (64), Cicero and C. Antonius Hybrida (63), L. Piso (58), L. Marcius Philippus (56), M. Valerius Messalla Rufus and Domitius Calvinus (53, both of them now Masters of the Horse-designate: n. 283), Ser. Sulpicius Rufus (51), L. Aemilius Paulus and C. Marcellus (50), P. Servilius Isauricus (48), Q. Fufius Calenus and P. Vatinius (three-month consulship in 47), Aemilius Lepidus (46), Trebonius, and Caninius Rebilus (suff. 45). (See Bruhns 1978: 37–42.) Left out of the count are P. Servilius Vatia (cos. 79), who died aged ninety in this year, thus surely too old to play a role, M'. Lepidus, and Volcacius Tullus (both cos. 66), both of whom may have died during the Civil War years. Also omitted are the new consuls Antony and Dolabella, neither of whom participated in the conspiracy.

[309] Cf. the arguments of Bruhns and Dettenhofer that the conspirators sought to restore their "republican" freedom of action and independence ("Handlungsspielraum"). This is not inconsistent with the motives I have suggested but a slightly more respectable way of describing them.

[310] Tr. after E. Cary. Pamphlets: in a painstaking study of the phenomenon and its associated language Angius 2015: 260–270 argues persuasively that the phrase βιβλία ἐκτιθέναι / *libellum proponere* sometimes, perhaps often, refers to the production of graffiti rather than "pamphlets." This particular case, however, is hard to decide; perhaps the epithet ἀνώνυμα tilts the balance in favor

For some, the dishonor of receiving *honores* that were hardly even disguised as recognition of superior *virtus* by the Roman People, for others the disappointment and resentment that came from seeing the *honores* they desired go to others, coalesced into an explosive brew, heightening their own sense of groveling subservience to a "tyrant" – a *rex*. No wonder the Dictator gave consular *ornamenta* to fully ten ex-praetors in what looks like a consolation prize.[311] Yet, as we saw in the Brutus-Cassius story, this kind of "gift" of a sham honor was as likely to offend in the current atmosphere as to appease. Thus men who had been on opposing sides in the late Civil War were made more receptive to the idea that Caesar was in fact a "tyrant."

Ronald Syme opined that "Caesar was slain for what he was, not for what he might become."[312] Syme, however, rather uncharacteristically put misplaced emphasis on what was in itself little more than a change of title. Not the change to *dictator perpetuo*, which, as we have seen, our sources (with the exception of Plutarch) hardly single out as the major precipitant of the conspiracy, but Caesar's iron shackles on the political ambitions of former enemies and followers alike – even to the extent of setting the *fasti* of the near future in stone – are likely to have been the major precipitant of a broad consensus (some sixty senators) that he had to be removed immediately and their future reclaimed before he was out of reach.

Mark Antony and the Spoiled Election

This analysis of the advance elections suggests that the victorious "Caesarian party" was fragmenting now that the Civil War was won. That was only to be expected. Their side had not been unified by any political program. This had been no organized revolt against "the Republic" or the Senate. On its best showing, the war had been fought against those who had sought to destroy a Roman "hero" and were ready to cast various republican institutions and principles overboard in order to perform this service for the Republic; for some, however, like Caelius, Antony, and Dolabella, it was probably much more a matter of making an opportunistic grab for the power and riches that fell to the victors in the

---

of the latter, especially since the agents seem to be members of the political elite (op. cit., pp. 270–271 for this distinction).

[311] Suet. *Iul.* 76.3 notes this breach of tradition almost in the same breath as the "advance elections" (*eadem licentia spreto patrio more*). Cf. the offense taken by Basilus at a gift of money in place of a proconsular province: Dio 43.47.5.

[312] Syme 1939: 56.

Civil War.[313] By its very nature, the "Caesarian party" resisted consolidation and was bound to fragment quickly by the force of its constituents' boundless ambitions, especially as there is no reason to suppose that they (many of them Roman nobles) wanted a master enthroned over themselves. Historians have tended to think too much about what Caesar may or may not have dreamed of in the private space of his mind, and too little about what his supporters – without whom he not only could not have won the Civil War but could hardly carry on his regime – would have wanted or been willing to tolerate. And one thing they surely did want was the freedom to advance their ambitions. True, thus far Caesar had been instrumental toward that end. What would happen, though, if he got in the way?

An important clue has been staring us in the face for a very long time. At the meeting of the Senate on the Ides of March at which Julius Caesar was struck down, what was the agenda? The answer given by some of our late narrative sources, which, as we have seen, are fixated on the "kingship" controversy, is, as famously rendered by Shakespeare, "the Senate have concluded / To give this day a crown to mighty Caesar."[314] Shortly before the assassination a rumor had emerged that the *quindecimviri sacris faciundis*, the priests in charge of the interpretation of the Sibylline books of oracles, had found therein the warning that the Romans would prevail over the Parthians only if led by a king, and that a proposal to confer the title on Caesar (perhaps intended only for non-Romans outside Italy) was about to be made at the next meeting of the Senate.[315] That there was such a rumor is validated by no less an authority than Cicero – who adds, however, that it

---

[313] Bruhns 1978: 168–170, and Dettenhofer's observations (1992: 227–228) on the lifting of hierarchical constraints as the military crisis reached its end. See n. 254.

[314] *Julius Caesar*, II.2.93–94. Bonnefond-Coudry 1989: 166–167, like most scholars, looks no further than the story of the royal title (see Plut. *Caes.* 64.3 with Pelling 2011: 475). Dettenhofer 1992: 255 asserts without evidence that funeral games *for Pompey* were to be held in his theater on the Ides of March. This is surely impossible in the absence of Pompey's sole surviving son. We seem to have no explicit evidence of the nature of the gladiatorial games scheduled for that day or their sponsor (ἀγωνοθέτην: Nic. Dam. *Bios* 98 with Horsfall 1974: 194–196 and Toher 2017: 328; cf. Plut. *Brut.* 12.5; App. *BCiv.* 2.118/495; Dio 44.16.2; Vell. Pat. 2.58.2; Nic. Dam. *Bios* 81, 92, 94) – not, apparently, Dec. Brutus himself, who owned some of the gladiators rented for the show and who was in fact about to stage his own *munera* (Nic. Dam. *Bios* 98), most likely funeral games for his homonymous father, the consul of 77, husband of Sallust's famous Sempronia, who had died sometime after 63 (last appearance at Sall. *Cat.* 40.5; cf. Cic. *Att.* 12.22.2). The interval would have been shorter than the twenty-year delay in Caesar's own case; presumably it was often necessary to await accumulation of the requisite financial resources.

[315] Cf. Dio 44.15.3–4 (λόγου γάρ τινος, εἴτ᾽ οὖν ἀληθοῦς εἴτε καὶ ψευδοῦς); App. *BCiv.* 2.110/460–461 (λόγος ἄλλος ἐφοίτα); Plut. *Caes.* 60.2 (λόγον τινὰ κατέσπειραν εἰς τὸν δῆμον), 64.3, *Brut.* 10.3. Appian and Plutarch (*Caes.* 64.3) add the restriction of the title to outside Italy. Dio says that the rumor was spread *by* the *quindecimviri* themselves, which is notable given that C. Cassius, the

was false.[316] Some of our sources claim that the rumor compelled the conspirators to hasten their plans for assassination when the fateful meeting was called for the Ides (or the Kalends [the 1st], in one source).[317] That claim does not stand up well to scrutiny. Caesar was to depart within three days anyway; the meeting on the Ides was in any case the last, best opportunity to do the deed in the Senate, so there was no need for a rumor to speed things up. Moreover, Caesar's practice with other honorific decrees had been to absent himself from such meetings in order to maintain the appearance of autonomous judgment on the part of the Senate (n. 113); if the conspirators thought this was in the works, then their whole purpose would have been foiled because Caesar himself should have been absent.[318] Finally, it has apparently escaped notice in this context that the real leader of the conspiracy, C. Cassius, was almost certainly himself one of the *quindecimviri*.[319] He would have known very well what the *quindecimviri* were about to do, for the simple reason that he was one of them. One could try to save the argument by supposing that he lied to his fellow conspirators. Yet Appian says that the rumor had anyway been

---

apparent head of the conspiracy, was almost certainly himself a member of that priestly board (n. 319).

[316] Cic. *Div.* 2.110: *quorum* [sc. *versuum*] *interpres nuper falsa quadam hominum fama dicturus in senatu putabatur eum, quem re vera regem habebamus, appellandum quoque esse regem si salvi esse vellemus.* Suet. *Iul.* 79.3: *quin etiam varia* [see Kaster 2016: 82–83] *fama percrebruit . . . proximo autem senatu Lucium Cottam* [Caesar's first cousin and cos. 65] *quindecimvirum sententiam dicturum ut quoniam fatalibus libris contineretur, Parthos nisi a rege non posse vinci, Caesar rex appellaretur. Quae causa maturandi fuit, ne destinata negotia assentiri necesse esset.* L. Cotta was probably the senior *quindecimvir*; the only two other known members at this time (n. 319) were a full generation younger.

[317] Suet. *Iul.* 79.3; Dio 44.15.4; cf. Plut. *Brut.* 10.3 for the meeting on the Kalends (14.3 appears to prove that he understood that this was *not* the meeting at which Caesar was assassinated), which contradicts the implication of *Caes.* 64.3.

[318] A further difficulty is that Dio thinks that the conspirators chose the Ides because they feared that Brutus and Cassius, as magistrates, would be forced to state their opinion on such an important matter (44.15.4). Mommsen objected that magistrates could not give *sententiae* (1887: 3:944n2), which seems true enough for the past, though Dio does suggest that the fear was precisely for a breach in this tradition because of the importance of the matter (καὶ τοῖς ἄρχουσιν . . . ἡ ψῆφος ἅτε καὶ ὑπὲρ τηλικούτου βουλεύματος ἐπαχθήσοιτο); Bonnefond-Coudry 1989: 166 accepts Dio, but in the absence of any plausible precedent for Brutus and Cassius's alleged fear the point cannot carry much weight. (Dio 44.8.1 claims that Cassius and some others won credit for not *voting* for Caesar's culminating package of honors [n. 50 above]; whether this is true or an accretion to the Liberators' legend, whether magistrates normally voted, and even whether the date is 44, when Cassius held the praetorship, or 45, are all unclear.)

[319] See now Rüpke 2005: no. 1103. The evidence is the series of *aurei* and *denarii* of 43–42 bearing Apollo's tripod in association with Cassius's name in a way that corresponds with Brutus's advertisement of the symbols of his pontificate: *RRC* 498–500; see *MRR* 2: 369 and *RRC* 2.74n6. Rüpke and Glock suggest that Cassius had been appointed in 50 or alternatively [n. 4] in 46–45, after making his peace with Caesar.) It defies credulity to assume that Cassius was elected only after the Ides of March, shortly after which he had been forced to flee the City. Another notable member of the college of *quindecimviri* was Dolabella: Caelius [Cic.] *Fam.* 8.4.1; Rüpke, no. 1324.

scotched by Caesar's rejection of the alleged proposal *before* the meeting on the Ides; in fact, for Appian, the main effect of the rumor is to hasten *Caesar's* plans to leave since he had become the object of such powerful resentment.[320] In sum, the rumor story looks like simply another manifestation of the monarchical conjectures swirling about Caesar through the early months of 44 which he had been at pains repeatedly to suppress or control, yet could apparently not make go away even after their symbolic rejection at the Lupercalia. The tight connection it forged with the assassins' justification of tyrannicide made it only too seductive in retrospect for those who later crafted the canonical narratives of the event. Historians should cast a sober eye on the story, not base remarkable conjectures on it, such as Weinstock's suggestion that Caesar was about to "try again" for monarchy by springing the proposal on the Senate at the meeting on the Ides.[321]

It is better to give our attention to Cicero's *Second Philippic*, where he states the agenda with perfect clarity: "But let us return to the auspices, about which Caesar was going to take action on the Ides of March" (*sed ad auspicia redeamus, de quibus rebus Idibus Martiis fuit in senatu Caesar acturus*, 88). The meeting, that is, was summoned to consider Antony's religious obstruction of P. Dolabella's election to the consulship to take Caesar's place as the latter prepared to depart for an extended campaign against the Parthians.[322] The backstory to this moment is particularly illuminating in our present context.

The essentials of the narrative Cicero tells in the *Second Philippic* are as follows. The story goes back to Caesar's return from the Munda campaign late in 45. Antony was "recommended" to the voters for the consulship of 44 along with Caesar himself, assuring his election.[323] Cicero presents Antony's election as an indirect slap at P. Dolabella, whom Caesar had allegedly first promised an "ordinary" consulship for 44 before usurping that position himself, now putting Dolabella off to take over as suffect consul only after he, Caesar, stepped down. The claim regarding the

[320] App. *BCiv.* 2.110/461: ὁ δὲ καὶ τόδε παρῃτεῖτο καὶ τὴν ἔξοδον ὅλως ἐπετάχυνεν, ἐπίφθονος ὢν ἐν τῇ πόλει.

[321] Weinstock 1971: 340–341; Bonnefond-Coudry 1989: 166–167. Appropriately skeptical: Malitz 1984: 42 with n. 108 (his view that Caesar was *expeditionem Parthicam meditans* [Flor. 2.13.94] is not inconsistent with the emphasis here on the electoral quarrel, which he overlooks); Ramsey 2000: 449 with n. 42; Lintott 2009: 78.

[322] The fact is occasionally noted (e.g. Gelzer 1968: 325n1; Horsfall 1974: 192) but little is made of it. Horsfall suggests that the edict which announced the meeting may have contained the agenda (194).

[323] "Ordered" in Cicero's tendentious language: *Phil.* 2.79: *iussus es renuntiari consul et quidem cum ipso.*

"ordinary" consulship is dubious, but that Caesar had promised his young friend a consulship seems consistent with his practice at this time.[324] Yet Antony's claims appear to have been far greater. The favor Caesar showed to Dolabella is indeed rather hard to explain, particularly after the debacle of Dolabella's attempt as tribune in 47 to overturn his debt legislation. Dio is mystified by Caesar's leniency on that occasion:

> He spared them all [i.e. those responsible for the tumult and violence] and even honoured some of them, including Dolabella. For he owed the latter some kindness, which he did not see fit to forget; in other words, in place of overlooking that favour because he had been wronged, he pardoned him in consideration of the benefit he had received, and besides honouring him in other ways he not long afterward appointed him consul, though he had not yet even served as praetor.[325]

In both Dolabella's and Antony's case Caesar overlooked the stipulations of the *lex annalis*, which he otherwise largely respected, at least for the consulship. Neither man had even held the praetorship (although Antony had twice served as Caesar's Master of the Horse), and Dolabella had held no further public office beyond that disastrous tribunate of 47; both men were considerably underage according to the law, for Antony had probably just turned thirty-nine while Dolabella was probably not older than about thirty-six (roughly the usual minimum age for the aedileship).[326] "Caesar's predilection for Dolabella is enigmatic," commented Syme, who went so far as to speculate that he may even have been Caesar's illegitimate son.[327] (Yet Dio's wording discourages that particular hypothesis.)[328] At any rate, Antony was senior to him in age and much more accomplished. A distant cousin of Caesar through his mother Iulia's line, Antony was one of the Dictator's closest male relatives and was widely thought to have been the

---

[324] Cic. *Phil.* 2.79, with Ramsey, ad loc., 275.   [325] Dio 42.33.2–3, tr. Cary.

[326] Bruhns 1978: 129; Dettenhofer 1992: 119–122, 165–182. App. *BCiv.* 2.129/511 (consulship at age twenty-five!) is generally acknowledged to be a mistake and Dolabella's age as consul is now put nearer thirty-six (Sumner 1971: 261–262; Syme 1980: 431–433 (= *RP* 3.1244–1247); Dettenhofer, p. 119). After 47 Caesar seems to have kept the volatile young man by his side; he was wounded in Spain (Cic. *Phil.* 2.75–76). Antony's age: Pelling 1988: 323. Dettenhofer (p. 179) speculates that Antony's early consulship may have been justified by an adlection among the patricians, giving him, like Caesar, a two-year boost (Badian 1964). However, like Dolabella, he had not held the praetorship.

[327] Syme 1986: 27n103; see 1980, 433–435, with a devastating portrait of the young man's antecedent career: "P. Dolabella was one of those sharp little men whose exorbitant pretensions provoke annoyance or disruption" (435). Syme made the same suggestion about Dec. Brutus (p. 430).

[328] As Syme 1980: 433 himself saw. Dio speaks of Caesar "owing some favor to him" (εὐεργεσίαν γάρ τινα αὐτῷ ὀφείλων), which surely refers to a debt for some unknown, perhaps even secret, *beneficium*. Speculation is rife. Dettenhofer 1992: 170–171 cautiously notes that Caesar's own freedom of action vis-à-vis his misbehaving tribune was constrained at the moment, yet nothing prevented him from stopping his further advancement.

natural candidate to become his heir.[329] Antony had been with Caesar in
Gaul probably as far back as 54 and was backed by him in 52 and 50 in his
successful bids for the quaestorship and augurate; he was the more prominent of the two tribunes forced to flee Rome because of their forceful
defense of Caesar's position in January 49, thereby precipitating the Civil
War. He had been left in command in Italy when Caesar was engaged in
Spain in 49, and again, now as Master of Horse, in 47; he had displayed
conspicuous bravery and military competence in the Dyrrachium campaign and at Pharsalus he had commanded Caesar's left wing. In 47,
however, he had taken a back seat after his bloody suppression of the
violent agitation for debt relief – led by none other than Dolabella, as it
happens – and he took no part in the African and final Spanish campaigns,
while M. Lepidus now held the fort in Rome as Caesar's consular colleague
in 46 and Master of the Horse in 46–45.[330] Yet, as Ramsey has shown, the
Dictator's offer of a consulship, especially of a full-year consulship, for 44
must be a sign that Antony was still (or had come back) in favor.[331] Soon,
however, it emerged that Dolabella would be his colleague after Caesar's
departure. Given the history between Antony and Dolabella, it is hard to
imagine what Caesar was thinking.[332] It was even rumored that Dolabella
had committed adultery with Antony's wife.[333] Can a more explosive
combination within the Caesarian party be imagined? In a story iterated

---

[329] Antony's mother was a Julia, daughter of L. Caesar (cos. 90), and thus he was a third cousin to the
Dictator. (See Cic. *Phil.* 2.14 with Ramsey's note.) Antony was therefore probably among the two
closest male blood relatives in Rome at the time of the assassination (the other being Caesar's
nephew Q. Pedius), which partly explains why the will was opened at his house (*Iul.* 83.1) and he
delivered the notorious eulogy. Cic. *Phil.* 2.71; Nic. Dam. *Bios* 74; App. *BCiv.* 3.16/60 indicate that
there was some expectation that Caesar might adopt Antony as his son (Dettenhofer 1992: 183); Dio
44.35.2, 36.2 reports that he was appointed guardian to Octavian and second heir in Caesar's will.
Toher 2017: 314 suggests that Antony had been named as Caesar's primary heir in the will that was
in force through the Civil War (replaced on September 13, 45: Suet. *Iul.* 83.2).

[330] See *MRR* 2.236, 242, 258, 272, 280, 286–287; with corrections in 3.19–20. Dettenhofer 1992: 65–72,
166–175.

[331] Ramsey 2004: 161–173. However, the notion on the basis of Cic. *Phil.* 2.76 that Antony made an
old-style electoral campaign tour of Cisalpina to further his consular prospects for 44 (repeated
recently by Ramsey, p. 166) is probably a misunderstanding of Cicero's sarcasm: he *asked* (*rogare*, sc.
Caesarem) for the office rather than canvassing for it (*petere*). (Cf. Bruhns 1978: 146n32; Jehne 1987a:
125n72.) On the (possibly false) rumor that Trebonius had sounded out Antony against Caesar
during the return from Spain see n. 297.

[332] Bruhns 1978: 147, 165, 177 sees the problem and supposes that the intention was to balance out the
two by means of an "eingeplante Rivalität." (Dettenhofer 1992: 180 agrees.) It looks to me more like
tossing a match into a tinderbox. But, as often, speculation on Caesar's motive seems fruitless
beyond the obvious: that he was settling his debts to two important nobles in his faction.

[333] Cic. *Phil.* 2.99; Plut. *Ant.* 9.2–3 places the affair at the time of the tumults of 47 (despite Pelling ad
loc., it would be hard to find a better time, especially since Cicero makes Antony claim that this was
the *causa odi*).

four times by Plutarch (but unfortunately absent from our other sources) and made famous by Shakespeare, Antony and Dolabella are both denounced to Caesar as intending a coup – a perfectly plausible risk after the Dictator's departure, judging on their prior record.[334]

It did not take long for sparks to fly. On the traditionally celebratory meeting of the Senate on New Year's Day (January 1, 44), Dolabella attacked Antony fiercely (so at least claims Cicero). When Caesar tried to smooth ruffled feathers by indicating that he would "order" Dolabella elected to the suffect consulship in his place when he set out on campaign,[335] Antony, tracing their quarrel back to 47 and allegedly even adducing Dolabella's penetration of his domestic sphere, responded that, as an augur, he was in a position to prevent the assembly from voting or vitiate its result by means of announcing unfavorable auspices; moreover, he promised to carry out the threat.[336] This already seems a remarkably aggressive intervention in opposition to Caesar's express wishes, hardly consistent with the image of an all-powerful Caesar but quite in keeping with Bruhns's picture of centrifugally dissolving Civil War coalition.[337] Perhaps Cicero is exaggerating; these were mere words. But when the election came (probably in early March) Antony's actions were as good as his words.[338] According to Cicero's hostile

---

[334] They were the "fat, long-haired ones" whom Caesar famously feared less than the "thin and pale ones" (Plut. *Caes.* 62.10; *Ant.* 11.6; *Brut.* 8.2; *Mor.* 206e; cf. Shakespeare *JC* 1.ii.191–194). In the two more specific passages (*Caes.*, *Brut.*) they are said to be plotting to νεωτερίζειν.

[335] Note Cic. *Phil.* 2.80: *Dolabellam consulem esse iussurum* (cf. *iussus es renuntiari consul* §79), prompting the aside, "Yet they say he was not a tyrant/king (*rex*), although he always used to do and say something of this kind!" (Cf. Ramsey 2003: 277). Here the arbitrary determination of elections is made a basic criterion of "tyranny" (*regnum*).

[336] Cic. *Phil.* 2.79–80; cf. 99: *frequentissimo senatu Kalendis Ianuariis*, with Ramsey's note. Plut. *Ant.* 11.34 probably offers no independent information: Pelling 1988 ad loc. Cicero goes on to make much of Antony's ostensible ignorance of the difference between *obnuntiatio* and *spectio*, only the first of which he had by virtue of his augurate while the second he possessed as consul. Since Cicero cannot dispute that Antony did in fact hold both powers, his objection is technical and immaterial for our purposes: rhetorically, its point is to make Antony look ignorant of basic rules of Roman public life (§80). The passage has recently come in for close examination from the point of view of religious law (Santangelo 2013: 273–278; Dreidiger-Murphy 2019: 138–143). Not surprisingly, Cicero has been unfair (Santangelo, p. 278).

[337] Bruhns 1978: 177: "A conflict arose over the consulate such as would be unimaginable under a 'monarch.'"

[338] Date: Ramsey 2000: 447 thinks the date of the election was not more than about two weeks after February 15 on the assumption that it came at "approximately the same time" as the prospective elections for future magistrates. Yet the precise chronological relationship between these elections is quite unclear, and in the absence of direct evidence it is surely best to assume that Dolabella's disputed election came very shortly before the meeting of the Senate that was called to debate its validity. (So too Jehne 1987a: 119n34.) This sort of thing could hardly be left to fester for weeks. There was a string of comitial days from March 9 to March 12 (the 13th was only half-comitial: *endotercisus*). That was to leave the matter rather late, but despite Antony's outburst on January 1 Caesar surely thought that he would have his way in a matter of such importance.

presentation, Antony stood by as the first and second "classes" were summoned to vote, and then apparently after a majority of centuries had been reached (*confecto negotio*) in this rather formal, one-candidate election, Antony suddenly gave the formal augural pronouncement, *alio die* ("another day"), which, if respected, would traditionally have brought the proceedings to an abrupt end.[339]

What did Caesar do – *dictator perpetuo* and thus, as many scholars would have it, the declared autocrat of Rome – after his plans were thus directly flouted under the eyes of all?[340] He who had taken such pains to preside personally over elections in order to assert complete control over them, even three years into the future? He did not overrule Antony on the spot by means of his superior *imperium* but behaved as any ordinary consul would have done: apparently allowing the objection to stand for the present, he scheduled a meeting of *the Senate* to discuss the matter. Cicero says that he had heard that Antony had come to the meeting prepared to defend himself against an attack he anticipated from Cicero, an augur himself, for falsifying the auspices. Cicero himself makes the point that false as Antony's pronouncement was, it was still necessary to respect an augural pronouncement.[341] (Which apparently had been Caesar's view as well.) In the chaos that followed Caesar's assassination, the issue was not actually forgotten but simply caught up in the sweep of much larger events. Dolabella was not yet formally *consul suffectus* but simply seized the trappings of the office upon Caesar's assassination, at first actually joining the conspirators on the Capitol, presumably because he saw Antony as his main threat. (Dolabella seems not to have considered that his consulship was itself the gift of the "tyrant," and it must be said that very few, if any, of those who took the conspirators' side seem to have been willing to lay aside the *honores* they had received from the "tyrant.")[342] At the "amnesty" meeting of March 17, however, he was brought over by Antony's implicit

---

[339] It is unclear whether elections of *suffecti* were always or normally contested. In this case it is unlikely that many voters turned up for what was more of a legal ceremony rather than an exercise of choice, so it can easily be supposed that the affair did not in fact take very long (§82 *omnia sunt citius facta quam dixi*).

[340] A. Thein's (2006) reassessment of Sulla as a "weak tyrant" offers a thought-provoking point of comparison.

[341] Cic. *Phil.* 2.88. Plut. *Ant.* 11.5 probably adds nothing, although he may not be altogether wrong in understanding Caesar to have "yielded [to Antony] and abandoned [Dolabella]" by not overriding Antony's resistance and leaving the matter to be resolved in the Senate. This after all must have been Dolabella's perception, as is further suggested by his immediate reaction to Caesar's assassination.

[342] L. Cinna had made a gesture of laying aside his magistrate's *toga praetexta* (n. 305), and others did so as well at the "amnesty debate" of March 17 before Antony skillfully called their bluff by proposing new elections (App. *BCiv.* 2.129/538–541).

concession of the consulship (as being among Caesar's *acta*), and immediately began to attack the conspirators as "murderers" and their supporters in the Senate as men willing to debase their offices to protect them.[343] Cicero in the *First* and *Second Philippics* mocks Antony's reversal and even claims that the issue would still have to be referred to the augural college for proper judgment.[344] But in practice the matter seems then to have been shelved, since neither Antony nor his enemies wished to alienate Dolabella during the delicate maneuvering over the rest of the year.[345]

Now it is true that nearly all our evidence about Antony's obstruction of Dolabella's election and its background (especially the *altercatio* between Antony and Dolabella at the senatorial meeting of January 1) comes from Cicero's *Second Philippic* – not a source to which one can lend unqualified credence on the subject of Antony.[346] It may be that Cicero enhances the story somewhat in order to embarrass Antony with allegations of opposition to Caesar and of hostility to Dolabella, with whom he seems to have been in a tense alliance at the time of writing. Yet such considerations hardly justify the conclusion that he fabricated the quarrel utterly. Dolabella's vitiated election and Antony's auspicial intervention were a public event which was hardly conducive to wholesale invention.[347] Although Cicero is surely going too far when he suggests that Antony had actually been brought into the conspiracy by Trebonius, even this allegation may bank on contemporary awareness that relations between Caesar and Antony were dangerously fraught by the time of the Dictator's assassination.[348] Antony's willingness to defy Caesar's will openly with

---

[343] App. *BCiv.* esp. 2.129/539–540; cf. 119/500, 122/511, 132/553–554. Vell. Pat. 2.58.3; Dio 44.22.1, 53.1.

[344] Cic. *Phil.* 1.31: *oblitus auspiciorum a te ipso augure populi Romani nuntiatorum, illo primum die collegam tibi esse voluisti*; 2.88: *num etiam tuum de auspiciis iudicium interitus Caesaris sustulit?* 2.83: *nolo plura, ne acta Dolabellae videar convellere, quae necesse est aliquando ad nostrum collegium deferantur.*

[345] Cic. *Att.* 14.15.1–2, 19.1; *Fam.* 9.14 = *Att.* 14.17A; *Fam.* 12.1.1; *Phil.* 1.5. Cicero himself does not press the point of Dolabella's technical illegitimacy even after he has turned against him, perhaps because this would entail legitimizing Antony's augural intervention (*Phil.* 3.9, 5.9, 11, 13.36). Cf. Santangelo 2013: 278.

[346] Plut. *Ant.* 11.3–5 presumably derives from Cicero, although as Pelling notes, the biographer "adds some circumstantial detail" (Pelling 1988: 143). Some confirmation of Cicero's story is provided by the fact that Dolabella's entry into office as *cos. suff* does indeed seem to have been arrested pending adjudication by the Senate.

[347] This is not to say that every detail of Cicero's invective is credible. For instance, the assertion that Caesar had initially promised the full-year consulship to Dolabella may be a plausible fabrication about a private event whose real purpose is to develop the idea of Caesar's perfidiousness; also, it strains credulity to believe that Antony himself raised Dolabella's humiliating seduction of his wife in the Senate.

[348] *Phil.* 2.34, with Plut. *Ant.* 13.2: see Ramsey and Pelling ad loc., who agree that the story in Plutarch is probably merely a dramatic elaboration of Cicero. See also n. 297.

regard to the election of Dolabella may lend more credence than is usually given to the various reports that the conspirators considered approaching him, and help to explain their decision not to assassinate him as well.[349]

The immediate context of the assassination, then, was an intensely public clash with the Dictator himself at the highest level of state, one that emerges from the directly opposed ambitions of two men at the heart of the "Caesarian party." Surprisingly little has been made of Antony's spectacular act of defiance on the very eve of the Dictator's departure on a campaign expected to keep him away from Rome for a full three years.[350] The very fact of Antony's "veto" and the respect Caesar accorded it demonstrate that the Dictator possessed no statutory right of "naming" the consuls. It is intriguing that Antony used religious obstructionism against Caesar just as Bibulus had tried in his consulship (in a technically different form, of course). But Caesar does not respond as an "autocrat"; he does not even respond with the uncompromising determination he showed against Bibulus in 59. Instead, he takes the respectful or cautious step of summoning the Senate to debate the matter. Such a question would traditionally be discussed first in the Senate, then most likely passed on to the college of augurs for their religious interpretation: that is why in the *Second Philippic* Cicero insists that an augural ruling is still needed.[351] Caesar didn't have time for that. Whatever plan he may have had for resolving the dispute died with him.

From the conspirators' point of view, this explosion within Caesar's "inner circle" must have seemed a godsend. Antony had demonstrated an unheard of disregard for the Dictator's will, spoiling his plans at least temporarily and surely deeply offending him, while he and the man Caesar had chosen to succeed himself as consul were in open conflict.[352] Even if he managed to patch the matter up for the present, another explosion was more than likely. The Civil War having been won, the Caesarian "party" was in disarray and to some extent at each others'

---

[349] Plut. *Ant.* 13, *Brut.* 18.4–6 (cf. 29.10 and *Cic.* 43.1); App. 2.114/478; Dio 44.19.1–2; Vell. Pat. 2.58.2; Cic. *Phil.* 2.34. To be sure, the decision was also defensible as an attempt to avoid civil war (n. 293).

[350] Gelzer buries the controversy in a subordinate clause in a footnote (1968: 325n1); even Bruhns 1978: 146–147 is surprisingly muted. Dettenhofer 1992: 178–183 pays more attention. Ramsey 2004 rejects the common inference that Antony fell out of favor with Caesar in 46–45, but does not take up the question what Antony was doing on these fateful days. Santangelo rightly stresses the forcefulness of Antony's objection (n. 336) but does not delve further into its political significance.

[351] See n. 344.

[352] It is tempting to speculate that Antony's power play had something to do with furthering his brother's candidacy in the expected advance consular election for 41. Ferrary 2010: 21–22 speculates that Antony's inauguration as flamen *Divi Iuli* may have been delayed by this quarrel (see n. 92).

throats. Caesar's lack of control over his fellow consul and powerful supporter would have emboldened others. In such a situation, it was a fair bet that at least some Caesarians could be detached from the others, bolstering the conspiracy, giving it nonpartisan "cover," and preventing an effective, coordinated response to the successful execution of the plot.

Nor, given the recent signs of popular displeasure, did the conspirators expect trouble from the side of the Roman People. The accounts of the assassination make clear that in fact the conspirators expected to be met with a significant show of popular *support*. After the killing, Plutarch describes how the assassins marched out of Pompey's Theater and up to the Capitol, "not like fugitives, but with glad faces and full of confidence, summoning the multitude to freedom."[353] Appian tells us that the conspirators emerged from the Curia in the Theater of Pompey with their daggers still bloody, one of them carrying the "cap of freedom" on the end of a spear, calling upon the People to restore the traditional constitution and to remember Lucius Brutus and the ancient oath he had administered against the kings; they appear to have expected that the People (ὁ δῆμος) would immediately flock to them.[354] They "still thought that the Roman People were exactly as they had heard they had been in the time of the Brutus of old, who had brought down the monarchy."[355] Modern scholars typically describe the conspirators as having almost inexplicably misread the popular mood, projecting their own "wishful thinking" upon the People.[356] Yet Roman senators' success in general, and in this case (as they must have known) the conspirators' very lives, depended on their accurately reading the signs of the "judgment and will of the Roman People" (Cic. *Sest.* 106) in the dense and extensive network of communication that characterized republican politics in the city of Rome. Those signs – palpable anger and confusion at the deposing of the tribunes, graffiti calling for a Brutus, somewhat more ambiguously the applause

---

[353] Plut. *Caes.* 67.3. For a concise summary of the known facts of the assassination see Lintott 2009. Woolf 2007 and Strauss 2015 are both insightful treatments for a popular readership; see also Tempest 2017: 78–104 (but Suetonius's account of the killing itself cannot be certainly traced to L. Balbus, who is cited only for the story of the tomb of Capys [p. 101]: Suet. *Iul.* 81.1–2 with *FRHist* 1.383–384, no. 41, F1, with 3.486).

[354] App. *BCiv.* 2.119/499, 501.

[355] App. *BCiv.* 2.120/504 (strictly speaking, Ῥωμαῖον is in the predicative position, which apparently emphasizes the point that the citizenry had fallen away from their pristine state of consummate "Roman-ness"). In Appian, the conspirators and their supporters repeatedly allude to the expulsion of the ancient kings in their attempts to rally popular support (121/509, 122/514): the Brutus theme of the graffiti is thus continued, but this time it is the populace rather than the praetor who must recover their ancestors' spirit.

[356] See n. 179.

that greeted Caesar's rejection of the diadem – will have suggested that the People were alienated from their former hero, and on perfectly traditional grounds. There is abundant evidence of popular dismay and anger over the suppression of the power of the tribunes, the traditional defenders of the People, and while our evidence is less explicit (though still not negligible) about the People's reaction to the loss of their fundamental electoral rights, this is likely due to the pervasively elite perspective of our sources.[357]

This is not to say, of course, that our evidence of popular reactions to Caesar at this time is *unanimous*; it certainly is not.[358] It is often tempting to attribute a single will to the countless minds that make up "the multitude," but a moment's reflection upon the absurdity of interpreting real phenomena in this way encourages caution. Modern survey methods have allowed us to see that "public opinion" is a gross abstraction that tends to be shaped by the very methods used to measure it. Careful analysis of our sources' habit of attributing unanimity to the Roman People or the urban plebs *when* this supports the interpretation they favor indicates that this is typically a rhetorical move driven by the tendentious aim to lend republican legitimacy to certain figures and divest it from their opponents.[359] The "fundamental indeterminacy of the Popular Will" prevailed no less before the trauma of Caesar's assassination as after it. Over the tense few days immediately after the killing, a strong show of public support for the self-proclaimed "Liberators" failed to materialize before the demonstration of public grief at Caesar's funeral, which then proved to be the tipping point in the other direction.[360] Bruhns observed that "the plebs' reverence for Caesar was much stronger after his death than during his life."[361] This is in fact entirely understandable. His resistance to the *pauci* in 59 and his brilliant record of victory in Gaul in the name of the *imperium populi*

[357] See n. 189.
[358] For instance, "some" did address Caesar as *rex* on his return from the Latin festival, and "some" did applaud the offer of the diadem (App. *BCiv.* 2.108/450, 109/457; Plut. *Caes.* 60.3, 61.5–6; Dio 44.10.1; Suet. *Iul.* 79.2). Nicolaus by contrast represents these as the unanimous voice of ὁ δῆμος (*Bios* 70, 72–73).
[359] Morstein-Marx 2004: 119–159.
[360] The phrase: Morstein-Marx 2004: 151. My analysis of the contional crowds *after* Caesar's assassination at ibid., 150–159 (cf. 2012: 212–213) has been criticized by Wiseman 2009: 216–234. To my mind he suppresses the tensions and contradictions in our evidence for popular opinion immediately after the killing and omits altogether the evidence for anti-Caesarian popular sentiment beforehand, without which the conspirators' actions become implausibly clueless. See now the detailed examination by Rosillo López 2017: 188–194, broadly consistent with my analysis; cf. also Walter 2009: 48n75; Strauss 2015: 148–153; Tempest 2017: 109–110. For detailed narrative see Dettenhofer 1992: 263–276, Gotter 1996: 21–29, and in English, the books of Strauss and Tempest just cited.
[361] Bruhns 1978: 179n46.

Romani were followed by a more mixed record from the plebs' point of view over the Civil War years, but the treacherous, bloody murder of one widely recognized as one of the greatest Romans in history, on the very floor of the Senate, by men whose lives he himself had spared – that was quite another matter.[362]

Tyrannicide?

F. Pina Polo and T. P. Wiseman have rightly questioned whether the "theory of preemptive tyrannicide" which we meet at so many key moments in Cicero's voluminous oeuvre was widely accepted by Roman citizens.[363] None of Cicero's most stirring passages on the duty of "tyrannicide" was delivered in a *contio* before the Roman People.[364] They had good reason to be skeptical when they remembered what had been done under this name to their heroes, starting with the Gracchi, most recently with P. Clodius. It is not clear how much they would have known about or admired the "heroic" tyrant slayers Cicero likes to adduce when safely away from the Rostra. It is surprising, for instance, that Cicero of all people *never* mentions in his extant works the supposed "Oath of Brutus" that no man should ever "reign" in Rome, yet Appian – on the whole, perhaps our best source for the immediate aftermath of the assassination – does cite the oath when he says that the conspirators called upon the Roman People to "remember" it, surely implying that the story was well known.[365] The

---

[362] Compare the widespread anger against King Charles I in the 1640s with the equally widespread and swift revulsion against his execution in 1649.

[363] Pina Polo 2006, 2017: 21–29; Wiseman 2009: 177–210; cf. Arena 2012: 214–218. On popular reaction to the death of C. Gracchus, see also Morstein-Marx 2012: 197–201.

[364] Most notably Cic. *Cat.* 1.2–4 and esp. *Mil.* 72–82. (Admittedly, there was a secondary popular audience surrounding the primary audience of jurors at the trial of Milo, but it is doubtful that they could follow the speech verbatim, and there is of course the further question of how much of the published version Cicero actually delivered at the trial.) In a more philosophical (and clearly polemical) vein after Caesar's assassination, *De off.* 3.32; cf. 1.76, 2.43 (n.b. *iure caesorum*, a phrase that seems to have grown out of the Gracchan crisis [*De or.* 2.106, *Mil.* 8, etc. = *ORF* pp. 131–132] and was applied to Caesar by Suet. *Iul.* 76.1 *iure caesus*), 3.83. Scipio Nasica, who led the lynch mob against Ti. Gracchus, deserved statues for "killing the tyrant" (Cic. *Rep.* 6.12, app. = Mac. *In Somn. Scip.* 1.4.2); similarly, Cicero laments the "lonely tomb" of Opimius abroad, a "man who had served the Republic splendidly" by savagely executing the *s.c.u.* against C. Gracchus and his followers (*Sest.* 140).

[365] Cicero: unfortunately there is a long lacuna at one obvious place where a mention could have been made (*Rep.* 2.52–53). App. *BCiv.* 2.119/499: Βρούτου τοῦ πάλαι καὶ τῶν τότε σφίσιν ὁμωμοσμένων ἐπὶ τοῖς πάλαι βασιλεῦσιν ἀνεμίμνησκον; cf. 2.107/444: τὴν τῶν προγόνων ἀράν. Livy 2.1.9 is, strictly speaking, our earliest citation, as also for the law confiscating the property of any who *planned regnum* (2.8.1–2). Mommsen 1887: 2.16n2 was prepared to accept both, Ogilvie 1965: 252 at least the law, but Wiseman 2009: 186n63 makes a good point against the culpability of "mere intention."

legend of C. Servilius Ahala's summary killing of Sp. Maelius for seeking tyranny in the fifth century was very likely put to political use to justify the murder of Tiberius Gracchus and other "aspiring tyrants," yet it also looks like the story in all tyrannicidal essentials had been told as early as circa 200 BC by Rome's second historian, Cincius Alimentus.[366] So little survives of Roman historical "memory" before Cicero that it would be bold to presume that either or both of these historical *exempla* were unfamiliar at least to those Roman citizens who attended the occasional *contio* or aristocratic funeral in the Forum at the time of Caesar. An extraordinary issue of denarii struck about 54 BC by the state moneyer, M. Brutus – none other than the future assassin – still bears on one side the portrait of Lucius Brutus, the founder of the Republic, and on the other, Ahala, another ancestor on his mother's side, while a second issue bore the image of the goddess "Freedom" (*Libertas*) on the obverse, Brutus walking with his lictors on the reverse.[367] The use of such imagery implies that the stories were reasonably familiar to those into whose hands the coins would come, and moreover that Ahala was hardly a blot on Brutus's family tree. When we learn in addition that only about two years later the young Brutus wrote and published a mock oration of defense of T. Annius Milo, the murderer of P. Clodius, taking the line that his killing was justified by the good of the Republic, we have good reason to think that the future Caesaricide was strongly identifying himself with the doctrine that Cicero had espoused more than once.[368]

Yet for all Cicero's memorable fulminations, the "tyrannicide" argument had failed, or was hardly even taken seriously, first against Catiline and then in his defense of Milo. The conclusion most consistent with the evidence is that these legends were all familiar, but distant in time and in practice impossible to apply arbitrarily to an individual without any kind of formal authorization by Senate or People. A very high bar would have to be cleared by anyone who hoped for peace and impunity after declining recourse to the laws and courts and resorting instead to extrajudicial killing. In his defense of Milo in 52, Cicero knew he still had to offer a legal argument, not simply rest upon the extralegal "tyrannicide" justification that Brutus preferred to write up in a fictional speech he published as a pamphlet.[369]

---

[366] *FRHist* no. 2 F4, cf. 3.51–53.
[367] Crawford, *RRC* 433/1–2; cf. Cic. *Att.* 13.40.1. See Dettenhofer 1992: 105–106, 210.
[368] Ascon. 41C: *interfici Clodium pro re publica fuisse.* Dettenhofer 1992: 109.
[369] Ascon. 36C: *Ciceroni id non placuit ut, quisquis bono publico damnari, idem etiam occidi indemnatus posset.*

Be that as it may, the conspirators actually had no good Roman precedent or compelling *exemplum* to appeal to. Tarquin the Proud and the Decemvirs had been overthrown, not assassinated; Sp. Cassius and Manlius Capitolinus had been tried, not cut down in cold blood; Maelius was a mere rich plebeian, not a patrician hero of the Republic, five times consul and quintuple *triumphator*, and anyway his killing had been preceded by some kind of legitimate, or ostensibly legitimate, formal process.[370] The *popularis* tribunes of recent history (Ti. Gracchus, C. Gracchus, and Saturninus) were killed in what could be considered riotous upheavals, the last two targeted by a formal, if somewhat controversial, constitutional process (the "Final Decree" or *s.c.u.*); even Catiline had been allowed to leave Rome "voluntarily." Thus the conspirators' success would entirely depend on successfully framing Caesar as truly a "tyrant," as the kind of illegitimate, unjust, or downright "monstrous" *rex* who was so destructive of the civil order that his death was necessary to save it.[371] Under such dire circumstances, of course, underhanded and bloody means might be legitimate since they were more or less unavoidable: if you can bring a "tyrant" to justice in a court of law, he can hardly be a tyrant.[372] Could Caesar be made out to be a "tyrant" in this strong sense?

It was not an easy argument to make, and clearly some outright denied it.[373] A crucial part of the construction of the tyrant in Greek and Roman thought is his cruelty. Caesar's leniency toward his former enemies and

---

[370] The earliest *attested* version, related by the early historians Cincius and Piso, said nothing of Cincinnatus's dictatorship and Ahala's being made his Master of the Horse, by virtue of which he delivered the Dictator's summons to Maelius (as in Livy and Dionysius of Halicarnassus); instead, they had the Senate formally authorize the killing in advance (*FRHist* no. 2, fr. 4, with vol. 3, 51–53). It is not certain which version is actually earlier, since we have no evidence of Fabius Pictor's position on the matter, indeed whether he told the story at all.

[371] Cic. *Rep.* 2.48–49 notes the Greek distinction between "king" and "tyrant" and acknowledges that Latin *rex* covered both. Yet it would seem that only the *rex iniustus* – that is, one who has turned *in dominatum iniustiorem* – is identifiable as the man than whom "no animal can be imagined that is more awful or foul or more hateful to gods and men alike" (Zetzel tr.). Since tyrannicide doctrine was itself a Greek import it rested on this distinction, suggesting that only the *rex iniustus* could be killed with impunity. For an introduction to Cicero's philosophically inflected thinking on tyranny, and his efforts so to categorize Caesar, see Gildenhard 2011: 85–98. On the history of "tyrannicide theory" in Rome, Lintott 1999: 53–66, 182–203; but cf. Pina Polo 2006.

[372] The Athenian "tyrannoktonoi," Harmodius and Aristogeiton, were the classic *exempla*, well known also in Rome, to judge from Cic. *Mil.* 80 and the extant statue group on the Capitol: recently Pina Polo 2006: 88–92. The killing of Hipparchus was universally praised, though ineffective in actually overthrowing the tyranny, as Thucydides pointed out.

[373] Cic. *Phil.* 2.80 : *quem negant regem, qui et faceret semper eius modi aliquid et diceret!* (n. 335). See Pelling 2011: 421 on Plutarch's struggle with the Platonic stereotype of "the tyrant" in these late chapters of the *Caesar*. Sedley 1997 clarifies and emphasizes Brutus's possible adherence to a specifically Platonic argument for tyrannicide, but we should not assume that the purported descendant of Ahala and L. Brutus was motivated primarily by philosophy.

encouragement to them to return to political life was the very antithesis of tyrannical "cruelty." Nor were the other nightmare visions of tyrannical cruelty in evidence: secret trials and executions, torture, Phalaris's bronze bull bellowing with the cries of the poor innocents roasted within. Tyrants (and their families) were also notorious for their sexual crimes, rapes of matrons, aristocrats' wives, and children: legends of the rape of Lucretia and attempted rape of Verginia emphasized this theme in the Roman tradition. But while Caesar was a man well known for his love affairs well into middle age (all the world knows the Cleopatra story, and Dio remarks that "even at this time, though fifty [plus!] years old, he still had numerous mistresses"), no sexual crimes or even broken homes seem to have been alleged against him.[374] The use of a bodyguard was a traditional litmus test of tyranny, but Caesar had dismissed the Spanish military guard that had attended him during the wars and had agreed instead to be protected informally "by the senators and equites."[375] Unlike that paradigmatic tyrant, Dionysius II of Syracuse, who lived in perpetual anxiety because of the fear he inspired in others, Caesar "always used to say that he preferred to die rather than to fear."[376]

---

[374] Dio 44.7.3, where he also claims that a proposal was made shortly before Caesar's death to legalize polygamy for him (presumably to accommodate Cleopatra and perhaps others during his long absence, and to raise the chances of a legitimate heir). Suet. *Iul.* 52.3, however, shows that this depends on a rumor spread by the unfortunate Helvius Cinna, who supposedly had drawn up the relevant legislation before he was notoriously lynched by mistake. After his middle-aged romance with the twenty-one-year-old Cleopatra, which some scholars have been at pains to deny, Caesar's affair with his contemporary, Servilia, is most famous; there is no evidence that it lasted beyond his first consulship (Suet. 50.2), although if the amusing anecdote in Plut. *Cat. Min.* 24.1–3 be plausible it was adulterous, since her husband, Dec. Iunius Silanus (cos. 62), was more or less alive at that time (Chapter 3, n. 35). Plut. *Brut.* 5.2, however, dates the affair to their teens in the mid-80s (n. 301). Scandalized rumor of an affair with Servilia's daughter Junia Tertulla at a very young age is implied by Suet. 50.2; she would have been about fifteen at the time of Caesar's first consulship (cf. Syme 1986: 199), just before his nine-year absence in Gaul. It is not known when exactly Tertulla married the future Caesaricide Cassius (contra Syme, p. 19n33, the evidence is consistent with a date much later than 61), but somewhat surprisingly no source cites sexual tension as a motive for Cassius's hatred.

[375] Dio 44.7.4 (cf. 15.2); App. *BCiv.* 2.107/44 (cf. 109/455); Plut. *Caes.* 57.7; Nic. Dam. *Bios* 80, with Toher 2017: 323–324. Dobesch 2001: 1.427-432 (originally published 1971); Jehne 1987a: 256–257, 453–454; Pelling 2011: 430. The "friends" who urged Caesar to employ a bodyguard in the last two passages are probably Hirtius and Pansa: Vell. Pat. 2.57.1. The pledge to protect him was probably made in a formal oath by senators and perhaps representatives of the *equites*: Suet. *Iul.*: 86.1 *confisum eum . . . iure iurando*, with 84.2: *ius iurandum, quo se cuncti pro salute unius astrinxerant.* In December 45 Caesar had brought two thousand men with him to Cicero's villa in Puteoli (Cic. *Att.* 13.52.1 with Shackleton Bailey 1965: 5:395). For a list of Greek sources emphasizing the link between bodyguards and tyranny see Pelling 2011: 429. As he there observes, "A 'monarchy without bodyguards,' as here, thus becomes a paradox."

[376] Vell. Pat. 2.57.1: *ille dictitans mori se quam timer* (mss. *timeri*) *malle.* The emendation is confirmed by Plut. *Caes.* 57.7; Suet. *Iul.* 86.2; App. *BCiv.* 2.109/455: clearly a well-known and well-remembered

There was, of course, one important way in which Caesar could be defined as a "tyrant": his de jure and de facto political domination, which, whatever its causes and rationale, whatever its excuses and even arguably benign effects for the short term, "robbed" Romans both elite (senators) and non-elite (voters) of their cherished freedom to debate and determine policy, laws, verdicts, and elections – that is, to play their traditional constitutional role in ruling themselves.[377] Since our evidence is clear that neither the Senate or the People had exercised that role freely since at least the victory at Thapsus in 46 and arguably since the beginning of the military crisis in 49, it will not do to say, with T. P. Wiseman, that "Caesar's power ... was held by right, freely voted to him by the people Cicero pretends he had enslaved."[378] Caesar may in his own mind, or privately to friends, have plausibly asserted that his monopoly on power was necessary for the foreseeable future (at least the Parthian expedition) to keep the avaricious, ambitious, and frustrated in check. Suetonius writes that

> Some say that he was even in the habit of remarking that his safety was more a matter of concern for the republic than it was for him. After all, he had long ago achieved outstanding powers and honours. However, if anything happened to him, the republic would not remain at peace but in a far worse state it would soon suffer civil war.[379]

Since events proved this prediction so resoundingly correct, it is tempting to see this as an interpolation made from hindsight. Yet the clash between

---

remark. Contrast the famous "sword of Damocles" and Dionysius's wretched shaving routine, both stories told by Cicero in his *Tusculan Disputations* written in 45 (5.57–63).

[377] The sources (including Cicero) generally subsume the constitutional details under the more general charge of seeking to be *rex* (or *regnare*). Cicero specifically equates this with robbing the Roman People of their "freedom" (Cic. *Phil.* 2.116: *attulerat iam liberae civitati partim metu partim patientia consuetudinem serviendi*; *Off.* 3.84: *ei regi ... qui exercitu populi Romani populum ipsum Romanum oppressisset, civitatemque non modo liberam sed etiam gentibus imperantem servire sibi coegisset?*), but at times is more specific about the forms of exercising such domination and in such cases tends to cite electoral domination in particular (*Phil.* 2.80: the promise to "order" Dolabella elected; *Att.* 14.6.2: *etiamne consules et tribunos pl. in biennium quos ille voluit?*). For such complaints also in the later sources cf. Nic. Dam. *Bios* 67 (n. 269), Suet. *Iul.* 76.3: *eadem licentia spreto patrio more magistratus in pluris annos ordinavit* (both discussed earlier). To be sure, Suetonius stresses more generally a variety of manifestations of *impotentia* and *arrogantia* (76–79), which is probably why, even writing under the (Trajanic-Hadrianic) Principate, Suetonius (*Iul.* 76.1) could comment that Caesar's words and deeds were such that "it is thought" (n.b. present tense, in Suetonius's own time) that Caesar "exercised (illegitimate) domination and was justly killed" (*et abusus dominatione et iure caesus*).

[378] Wiseman 2009: 207. Cf. idem, p. 198: "Caesar's power was not usurped, but granted constitutionally by the only competent authority to do so."

[379] *Iul.* 86.2: *Rem publicam, si quid sibi eveniret, neque quietam fore et aliquanto deteriore condicione civilia bella subituram.* (Trans. after C. Edwards). On the surfeit of "powers and honours," see the famous *satis diu vel naturae vixi vel gloriae*: n. 213.

Antony and Dolabella brought the fragmentation of the Caesarian "party" and the instability of the peace fully out into the open: Caesar would not have had to be a prophet to see this in the early months of 44.[380] On the other hand, if this was indeed his view, it is certainly true that he did little to send a clear, public message that he did not, in fact, intend permanently to rob the Roman Senate and People of their constitutional "freedom." Persistent verbal denials of *regnum*, combined somewhat mysteriously with the assumption of a "continuous Dictatorship," implicitly at least "for life," sent a confused signal. Perhaps, focused on his imminent patriotic war to redeem Rome's honor from the Parthians, Caesar assumed that the logic of his position was plain, or that further pronouncements might be interpreted as "protesting too much."

To justify Caesar's killing as a "tyrannicide" before the Roman People, the conspirators and the ex post facto allies such as Cicero would have to make his definition as a *rex* or "tyrant" stick. As we have seen, this was no easy matter, and in the event the mass of the People soon came to reject the identification. Tacitus recognized the deep cleft in opinion when he refers to senators' memory (in AD 14) of "that day when servitude was still young and freedom had been unsuccessfully taken back, when the killing of Caesar the Dictator seemed *to some the worst of crimes*, to others the most splendid deed."[381] Cicero's old friend – and Caesar's too – the equestrian Gaius Matius also vehemently rejected the justification of the assassination as legitimate "tyrannicide," a justification he well knew his correspondent, Cicero, enthusiastically approved. Supporters of the "tyrannicide" complained that Matius mourned the "tyrant" and was "indignant that the man [he] loved has been destroyed. They say that country should come before friendship – as though they have already proved that his death was to the public advantage (*rei publicae fuisse utilem*)."[382] Far from celebrating the death of "the tyrant," Matius replies with solemn dignity,

> I want every man's heart to be sore for Caesar's death. But I shall be told that as a citizen I ought to wish the good of the Commonwealth (*rem publicam velle salvam*). Unless my past life and hopes for the future prove that I so desire without words of mine, then I do not ask anyone to accept it because I say so. ([Cic.] *Fam.* 11.28.4, tr. Shackleton Bailey)

---

[380] Matius probably saw it too: Cic. *Att.* 14.1.1: *etenim si ille tali ingenio exitum non reperiebat, quis nunc reperiet?*

[381] Tac. *Ann.* 1.8.6: *diem illum crudi adhuc servitii et libertatis inprospere repetitae, cum occisus Dictator Caesar aliis pessimum aliis pulcherrimum facinus videretur.*

[382] Matius, [Cic.] *Fam.* 11.28.2 (tr. Shackleton Bailey). On the letter see Chapter 7, p. 369. Rice Holmes 1923: 349 considered it "the noblest that has come from antiquity." Poor Cicero!

Matius pleads guilty to following a friend in the Civil War, and not deserting him "even though I did not like what he was doing." He had, so he claims, disapproved both of civil war in general and of the outbreak of this one; he had tried to prevent it, and once his friend was victorious he had declined to exploit the victory for personal benefit, unlike some others, while he had strained every nerve that his defeated fellow citizens be spared.[383] "Well then," he goes on, "can I, who desired every man's preservation, help feeling indignant at the slaughter of the man who granted it – all the more when the very persons who brought him unpopularity were responsible for his destruction?"[384] Cicero, no doubt, was appalled.[385] But Matius was telling him no more than what he might have heard on any street corner in the City.

---

[383] Matius, [Cic.] *Fam.* 11.28.2.

[384] Matius, [Cic.] *Fam.* 11.28.3: *cum praesertim idem homines illi et invidiae et exitio fuerunt?* The identification of these people is uncertain. Shackleton Bailey 1977: 2:489 thinks of "Caesarians among the conspirators who *praemiis immoderate sunt abusi,*" but perhaps more likely Matius is referring to those who had brought *odium* on him by their excessive honors and flattery only to join the conspiracy against his life.

[385] As he certainly was by Matius's sentiments immediately after the killing: *inimicissimum oti, id est Bruti* (Cic. *Att.* 14.2.3); *nam cum Matius, quid censes ceteros?* (14.4.1). Cf. the whole series, 14.1–4.

CHAPTER 10

Conclusion

Teleologies dominate the received narratives of Gaius Julius Caesar's life: the outbreak and end of the Civil War, the end of his life, the end of the Republic. In the absence of good information about a stage of his career when he had not amounted to very much, the ancient writers wrote a beginning for their story to match its end. But contemporaries and Caesar himself could not see that end. Like all people, but perhaps even more so given the Roman reverence for their ancestors and their ways (the *mos maiorum*), they took the measure of themselves and their leaders against the distinguished figures of the past. Caesar, a patrician war hero already in his youth, had worthy models in the Scipiones both in military glory and in "popular" though by no means "seditious" politics combined with a proud aristocratic pedigree. Despite his family connection, he was no "Marian" in the strong sense of reviving and refighting the battles of the 80s. By the time of his entry on the highest stage of politics in 63, he was known as a *popularis* of a particular sort: one exceptionally skilled at cultivating the support of the Roman People but not a demagogue or a street fighter, or even as a significant player in the classic *popularis* proposals for land redistribution, debt relief, or the like. (Certainly he was no "democrat," as he has sometimes been called: such exotic creatures did not exist in Roman public life.)[1] Caesar's reputation for "largesse" may have been well earned, and yet it does not seem to have exceeded the norms of his day, or perhaps even what many of his contemporaries considered to be simple necessity given the growth of the City's populations and the mass-oriented politics that had developed over the course of several generations. The best evidence suggests that his objective at this time, as Sallust famously declared (*Cat.* 54.4), was to make his way to a position where he could obtain "a great command, an army, a new war in which his excellence could shine forth." But that path lay through the Senate. Like many

[1] Morstein-Marx 2014: 3.

aristocrats Caesar did not shy away from a feud with a powerful figure (Q. Catulus, the senior consular and leading senator after Sulla's death), but that did not set him at odds with the aristocracy as a whole – not even the dominant faction of the aristocracy that had emerged on the winning side of the Sullan-Marian civil wars of the 80s (Chapter 2).

Caesar's famous intervention in the Catilinarian Debate of December 5, 63, too often viewed through a Ciceronian lens as a kind of insidious, demagogic attempt to make trouble for the Senate or, worse, to save the conspirators from their just deserts, instead illustrates the kind of patrician republicanism discernable in his early career. His apparent objective in Sallust's version of the speech (the best evidence we have) is to avoid the kind of popular backlash that was inevitable if traditional, cherished Roman rights, such as those encompassed by the term *provocatio*, were violated, and thus to secure and strengthen the Senate's paternalistic leadership of the Republic. Yet Cato, Cicero, and others had a different idea of how to deal with the conspirators, and of how best to strengthen the authority of the Senate. Cicero thought it restored rather than undermined by the Catilinarian executions – a questionable conclusion in view of the coming backlash of 58, which Caesar may have anticipated.[2] Over the next few years a series of clashes followed between Cato and Caesar, but it would be superficial to characterize this opposition as one between the Senate and People (or "popular" politics). Cato's harrying of Caesar did not always carry the majority of the Senate (consider his filibuster in 60 by which he frustrated Caesar's hopes of a praetorian triumph probably already granted by that body), nor should Caesar's feuds with Cato and Catulus be characterized as anti-senatorial as such rather than a fairly aggressive self-defense targeting those who had sought to incriminate him in the Catilinarian purges. His role in the Metellan rogation of 62 calling on Pompey to take over the job of eliminating Catiline was a subordinate one. His avoidance of the Bona Dea imbroglio that erupted toward the end of his praetorship as he made a dash for Spain is also indicative of his continued preference for the traditional model of Roman aristocratic achievement over "popular politics" in its now-familiar form, complete with "rabble-rousing" *contiones* (Caesar is not known to have delivered even one accusatory speech in a *contio* in this period, even after the execution of the conspirators) and uproarious assemblies (he disappears quickly from the one known instance at the vote for the Metellan rogation). On the eve of his consulship Cicero clearly still had suspicions of

---

[2] Cic. *Att.* 1.16.7; cf. 1.18.3; *Fam.* 1.9.12; *Leg.* 3.37.

him – inevitably, given his opposition in the Catilinarian Debate – but could still contemplate working with him as an ally (Chapter 3).[3]

Caesar's tumultuous first consulship in 59 is often regarded as the beginning of the end of the Roman Republic: the moment when Caesar's hostile or at least dangerously reckless attitude toward constitutional norms set the Republic on a course which would predictably, if not necessarily inevitably, result in the outbreak of civil war ten years later. Yet let us first recall how Caesar's consular year had begun: with a respectful presentation of his first agrarian bill to the Senate in a manner that appears to reflect the natural inclinations of a Roman aristocrat. There is no denying that the conflicts that subsequently exploded in 59 between Caesar and his associates on one side and Bibulus and Cato on the other to a great extent defined the oppositions that characterize the following decade and provide the fundamental background to the Civil War. Yet scholars have been too impressed with Bibulus's and Cato's obstructionist tactics and too ready to concede that they were "correct" from a traditional republican perspective. Far from representing an established republican constitutional tradition, Bibulus, Cato, and those who followed their lead pushed the obstructive devices available to them far beyond their customary limits and attempted to use them to suppress the People's sovereign right to effect its will through the voting assemblies without so much as articulating an alternative position either before the People or even, it seems, the Senate. No senator, not even Bibulus and Cato, had actually been able to bring forth any rational objection to the law; these two had simply declared that they would not allow it to pass.[4] This was absurd in any republic deserving the name, and we may interpret the overwhelmingly positive response of voters to the bill and its subsequent persistent survival, despite the angry complaints of Bibulus and others, as the Roman People's verdict on such bloody-minded obstructionism. No revered republican norm dictated that a law which was unimpeachable on its merits and strongly approved by the Roman People could be resolutely blocked from consideration simply on the grounds that it risked enhancing the proposer's influence or authority. If all conservative opponents had to

---

[3] Cic. *Att.* 2.1.7, 2.3.3–4.
[4] Cato: Dio 38.3.1: "M. Cato, however, did not criticize anything in the text of the bill but urged them in general terms to hold fast to the status quo and not to take any step outside of it" (τοῖς μὲν γεγραμμένοις οὐδὲν οὐδ' αὐτὸς ἐπεκάλει, τὸ δ' ὅλον ἠξίου τῇ τε παρούσῃ σφᾶς καταστάσει χρῆσθαι καὶ μηδὲν ἔξω αὐτῆς ποιεῖν). Bibulus: Dio 38.4.3 (sc. to citizens in a *contio*): "You won't get this law this year even if you *all* should want it!" ("οὐχ ἕξετε ... τὸν νόμον τοῦτον ἐν τῷ ἔτει τούτῳ, οὐδ' ἂν πάντες ἐθελήσητε").

do to stop *popularis* rogations was to "watch the skies," obnuntiate, or ignore the result of a vote, we would hardly be able to enumerate more than thirty examples of such proposals that actually became law over the ninety years that preceded the Civil War despite strong opposition from the majority of the Senate.[5] Again and again before 59 BC the Roman People had asserted its will successfully over strong senatorial resistance, which was no doubt often driven by similar concerns about the boost success would give to a law's proposer, although it appears that substantive objections were still normally expected to be made by a bill's opponents (compare most recently Q. Catulus's arguments against the *lex Gabinia* and *lex Manilia*, ineffectual though they were) rather than simply a blanket "no."[6] A common modern perception of the year 59 is that by rejecting Bibulus's attempted obnuntiation and continuous *servatio* Caesar demolished the constitutional constraints on executive and popular power that defined the Republic. Roman voters, however, are likely to have felt that Bibulus's mute obstinacy had forced Caesar to exploit the full power of the assembly if he was not to allow "the voice and will of his single colleague from overcoming that of the entire People," as Cicero himself had put it in 65 while praising Aulus Gabinius's dismissal of a fellow tribune's veto.[7]

The notion that Caesar (and Pompey) simply imposed their will in the assemblies through violence overlooks both the weakness and paucity of the evidence for the pervasive use of violence in the passage of these laws and the self-evident fact that no violence should have been necessary for them to prevail in the assemblies in the normal course of events given that the bills were overwhelmingly popular. Rather, the violence for which we have the best and most detailed evidence (i.e. that which attended voting on Caesar's first agrarian law) was manifestly provoked by the aggressive tactics of the opposition, in part at least intentionally in order to lay a foundation for the annulment of the assembly, as well as by the extreme unpopularity of their stand in the midst of an excited assembly overwhelmingly favorable to the bill on offer. Furthermore, when Bibulus sought to have the law annulled by the Senate, it *refused*, in sharp contrast to what had been done on some earlier occasions.[8] Other incidents about which we

---

[5] Morstein-Marx 2013; 2019: 526–529.

[6] Catulus and Hortensius on the *leges Gabinia et Manilia*: Steel 2001: 114–123; Morstein-Marx 2004: 181–183; Rodgers 2008; Yakobson 2009: 49–54; Arena 2012: 186–189, 194–200.

[7] Corn. I 31: *neque … passus est plus unius collegae sui quam universae civitatis vocem valere et voluntatem.*

[8] See Chapter 4, nn. 87, 89, and De Libero's sifting of precedents in the annulment of legislation of Saturninus, Titius, Livius Drusus, Sulpicius, and Manilius (1992: 88–99). De Libero acknowledges that in practice the Senate could only succeed in such an effort when the proposer had lost his strong

have less complete information may have been broadly similar in their dynamics. Bibulus's unprecedented and clearly unreasonable expansion of the practice of "watching the skies" also conspicuously failed to receive senatorial sanction after the termination of Caesar's consulship and thereafter, while by the *lex Clodia* passed in the very next year it was explicitly repudiated by the Roman People. Caesar's *acta* of 59 remained formally valid even while some senators, such as Bibulus himself, continued to try to cast doubt on their legitimacy. This need not be taken too seriously.[9]

To the extent that, whatever Caesar's and Bibulus's motives and intentions, the traditional republican norm of constraints on executive and popular power was in fact damaged by their forceful actions in 59, this was of course a blow to the traditional "constitution," potentially pointing the way to outright democracy or charismatic personal domination. Coached by our knowledge of what was soon to come, it is easy to suppose that this is exactly what had happened in Caesar's first consulship. But troublesome facts get in the way of such a conclusion. Two hard-line opponents (L. Domitius and C. Memmius) were voted into the praetorship in the elections for 58, who immediately upon taking office raised the issue of the legal validity of Caesar's *acta* in the Senate. Allies of Caesar and Pompey had indeed been elected consuls for 58, yet with their record and other assets they were likely to win election anyway. Caesar and Pompey both found audiences at *contiones* resistant to their rhetoric against their opponents. Nor was the Senate reduced to a rump of Caesarian or Pompeian partisans, as we saw both in its response to the potentially explosive "Vettius affair" and in the heckling by *adversarii*. If the voting assemblies had truly been under Caesar's control he should have included in the *lex Vatinia* the prize military province for his purposes, Transalpine Gaul; instead, whether by necessity or design, he left that province at the Senate's disposal, giving that body something close to a veto power over his pursuit of military glory from the time he had committed himself to central Gaul in early 58 until the eventual passage of the *lex Pompeia Licinia* of 55. This may be an example of Caesar's aristocratic respect for the Senate as an institution, or it may be nothing more than a realistic political compromise – which would be worth noting in itself. Moreover, the annual rhythms of Roman political life and the advantages of presence in the City meant that whatever influence Caesar had been able to exert during his consulship

support among the city plebs (p. 90). Obstructionism was in practice itself constrained by the political reality of the power of the People: see Morstein-Marx 2019 on "Fear of the People."
[9] See Chapter 4, p. 181–191.

would dissipate quickly upon his departure for extended military operations in the provinces. The continued presence of his allies, Pompey and Crassus, could not ensure the election of friendly consuls: even in their notoriously heavy-handed joint consulship of 55 they were unable to prevent the election of Caesar's great enemies, L. Domitius and M. Cato.[10]

The year 59 may be viewed as a constitutional crisis of a sort, but for too long the story has been told in a one-sided way, largely, it seems, under the overpowering influence of Cicero. If we take seriously the theory of the republican "constitution" as laid out by Polybius and the tradition of popular sovereignty revealed empirically by the behavior of the assemblies over some eight decades previous, along with prior history of the limitations of purely obstructive tactics (which would have put an end to virtually all "popular" legislation if they were as absolute as Bibulus had hoped, and many scholars appear to believe), we are forced to conclude that it was Caesar who better represents the historical republican tradition in this struggle, not those who are so often held up as the hard-line defenders of the "constitution." Rather, it is Cato and his followers who seem bent, at least from the execution of the "Catilinarian" conspirators in 63, on breaking from long-standing republican tradition and intent on creating, by the novel exploitation of traditional obstructive devices such as the veto, obnuniation, and *servatio*, a new kind of republic (perhaps inspired by Sulla's reforms) in which despite the restoration of the tribunician power popular sovereignty would be effectively suppressed and the institutions of the People subordinated in practice to senatorial authority. Cato and his associates appear to have been strongly motivated in their push for war with Caesar in late 50 by the fear that if he escaped a reckoning for his refusal to accept the constraint they tried to impose in 59 he would no longer have to obey the Senate's rules, and nothing said here is intended to dismiss this anxiety as an entirely frivolous concern.[11] My point is rather that there were two legitimate sides to this debate, not just one as is usually supposed, and it seems clear that the Roman People – an essential constituent of the SPQR on an equal basis with the Senate according to the ancient phrase, but in practice superior to it as the final, sovereign arbiter – did not stand with the Catos and Bibuluses in the argument over republican legitimacy (Chapter 4).

Caesar decamped to Gaul to fulfill his high military ambition and at last to win as ex-consul the triumph taken from him after his praetorship, but the notion that this was simply an open ticket to escape from a date with

---

[10] Chapter 5, p. 230.   [11] Chapter 6, p. 311ff.

the *maiestas* (or any other) court ignores the fact that until 55, every time the consular provinces were determined in preparation for the midsummer elections he was subject to swift removal from Transalpine Gaul, the province where he had fully invested his military resources, by a simple decree of the Senate that was not subject to tribunician interference. The five-year term of the *lex Vatinia* has tended to give a misleading impression that Caesar's position enjoyed ironclad security when in March 58 he launched the first of a series of campaigns that would turn out to effect the conquest of "Gaul in its entirety" (*Gallia omnis*, BGall. 1.1.1). Every decree "on the consular provinces" according to the *lex Sempronia* between 58 and 55 could therefore be seen as an implicit senatorial referendum on Caesar's actions in Gaul. He had to show results quickly and he had to be sure that every campaigning season ended victoriously. This doubtless explains his swift commitment already in 58 (after the more traditional border-policing action against the Helvetii, recent troublemakers, which scholars too often perversely regard as an actual violation of his remit as proconsul) to high-stakes, aggressive action against Ariovistus in eastern Gaul far beyond the boundaries of "the Province," followed by his army's winter encampment also well outside the province among the Sequani and the extraordinarily risky invasion of the Belgae in the northeast extremity of Gaul the following year. The inevitable murmurs of "unauthorized warfare" waged to satisfy a commander's ambition were in the event quelled by victory, and at the end of the campaigning season of 57 the Senate put its imprimatur on the campaigns thus far by voting Caesar a *supplicatio* of unparalleled length "since the whole of Gaul had been pacified" (*omni Gallia pacata*, BGall. 2.35.1).

Unsurprisingly, this turned out almost immediately to be a wildly optimistic claim. Already in 56 Caesar's opponents in the Senate began to mobilize to wrest the key province away from him, as it was entirely within their rights to do. Yet his successes had also already won over other key senators such as Cicero, and the reinvigoration of the Triple Alliance in 56–55 enabled him to ward off the immediate danger. The rest of his time in Gaul down to the decisive victory at Alesia in 52 may be seen as an effort actually to realize his extravagantly exaggerated claim in 57 that he had "pacified the whole of Gaul." This proved to be a tough fight marked by memorable disasters (the loss of a fleet in Britain and the *clades Tituriana* both in 54, Gergovia in 52) as well as magnificent victories, but luckily for Caesar his position in Transalpina had by now been secured by the *lex Pompeia Licinia*, putting it outside the Senate's reach until the successful conclusion of the war. Having lost his chance to triumph after the praetorship, Caesar staked everything on the Gallic venture, and it is rarely appreciated how delicately poised on the knife's edge his final success had been. But victory brought the acclaim not only of the People but also of the Senate (fifty-five days of *supplicationes* in toto, celebrated in three well-spaced and well-timed bursts in 57, 55, and 52). When Cato called for Caesar to be handed over to the enemy, far from making a dent in his adversary's reputation he achieved nothing: "No decree was passed" (Plut. *Cat. Min.* 51.4). In the end Caesar, who as the sole commander in the effort was given the credit for bringing to its knees Rome's oldest remaining enemy, had won a place among the greatest heroes in the annals of Rome: "the Fabii, Scipios and Metelli . . . Caesar's achievements outdo them all."[12]

Obviously, then, Caesar had a vital interest in making sure that Roman senators and the Roman People received a flow of positive news about his campaigns in Gaul. But the chief media for this communication probably did not even include the *Gallic War Commentaries* that we read today, as seems to be universally supposed. A plethora of news passed from the army of Gaul to Rome through a dense network of "letters, rumor, [and] reports" (Cic. *Prov. cons.* 22), not to mention face-to-face meetings among the principals in Cisalpine Gaul, soldiers sent home to vote, or the celebrations of Caesar's victories during those fifty-five days of supplications, no doubt accompanied by plenty of conversation and chatter. Nor did this network converge at either end at a single point, with Caesar at one end and the Roman Senate at the other. Many senators and even ordinary citizens will have known men serving under Caesar or his lieutenants and thus will have had their independent sources of information about what was going on in the war zone. Caesar's control over this multifocal network of communication is often greatly overstated. "Propaganda" is a misleading term for the *Gallic War Commentaries*, particularly if one concludes, as I do, that they are not to be understood as a shot fired in contemporary, partisan information wars or even as an effort at current "image-building" back home in the capital, but Caesar's attempt to secure indirectly the *sempiterna gloria* he doubtless longed for by the pen of some future historian worthy of his subject. This objective provides more than sufficient motivation for Caesar's, shall we say, careful writing about the more problematic moments of his military leadership in Gaul.

Just as Caesar could not control the flow of information between the Army of Gaul and Italy, he also could not control political events in Rome.

---

[12] Plut. *Caes.* 15.2–4, quoted Chapter 5, p. 257.

Two particularly hazardous moments for his standing – when his continued command in Transalpina and then ultimately throughout "his" provinces was under threat in 56 and 55 – were successfully negotiated through a combination of renewed cooperation with his powerful allies, Pompey and Crassus, and his own growing esteem among senators and citizens for his military achievements. But not until 54, when his position in Transalpina was at last safely secured, could Caesar begin to invest his Gallic winnings to augment his political influence in Rome on a large scale. Even then, the idea suggested by some of our sources, that Caesar simply "bought" a number of friendly senators at this time through sweetheart loans or even outright bribery, seems likely to be an exaggerated rhetorical charge that was particularly useful for political rivals to explain sudden reversals of behavior (notably Curio's) that in truth can readily be accounted for otherwise. This is not to say that money did not change hands, as had happened in Roman politics for generations, but rather that the scale of the phenomenon and its effectiveness in determining events are open to question. Cicero himself, despite an interest-free, open-ended loan of 800,000 sesterces, regarded this as an intense embarrassment when fears of a conflict with Caesar emerged but does not appear to have altered his political attitude or actions. As is clear from the very run-up to the Civil War itself, after the conquest of Gaul Caesar had a formidable political presence in Rome, but for all that, there is little concrete evidence to support Plutarch's rhetorical suggestion that in effect he had bought much of the Senate with his profits from the conquest of Gaul – and of course the crisis of 50–49 would have gone very differently had that been the case (Chapter 5).

The Civil War of 49–45, which often goes by Caesar's name (the "Caesarian Civil War") is inevitably central to any assessment of the life and career of Gaius Julius Caesar, and also, indeed, to analyses of the "End of the Republic" in which it played such a profound part. The story of the "Coming of Civil War" (Gruen) in the late 50s has long been part of the traditional indictment of Caesar as a rebel against the "legitimate government" or even "the Republic." Many scholars have signed on to the theory that in order to prevent a trial and probable conviction for his supposedly outrageous violations of the law and constitution in his consulship and afterward in Gaul, Caesar sought to exploit the legal immunity of magistrates and those engaged in public service (*rei publicae causa*) to escape judgment for his "crimes," engineering through the Law of the Ten Tribunes a path whereby he could slip directly from his military command into the consulship without exposing himself in the interim (if any) to criminal prosecution, which, it is further supposed, he would not be able to escape (although it is rarely acknowledged just how far the scales would have to be tipped to achieve that result). I have shown how weakly founded this theory is in our copious evidence for this period: a couple of brief allusions, without concrete detail and no external warrant of their weight, standing against the unaccountable silence of Cicero and nearly all of our witnesses. But as it happens, there is no need to resort to clever, legalistic schemes like this to explain the outbreak of the Civil War. Put simply, Caesar demanded an honorific return from his (ultimately) victorious campaigns against Rome's oldest enemy in keeping with Roman traditions, while his inveterate enemies, now joined in increasing anxiety by Pompey, rejected his demands for fear that, if they did not do so and failed to force him to pay a high price for his refusal to yield to their radical obstructionism in 59, not only would he survive and be stronger than ever but the lesson would be passed to the future, and a central buttress for their vision of a Senate-dominated Republic would perhaps be toppled forever. Memories of Scipio Africanus and Cato the Elder's humbling of that hero, not to mention of Sulla's victory, whose fruits (from a certain, "optimate" point of view) had been squandered from the time of Pompey's and Crassus's joint consulship in 70 BC, all probably played their part. Fears of *regnum* activated by the Marian-Sullan Civil War no doubt also underlay it all.

But to quash Caesar's plans his enemies were "forced" to jettison overboard various core principles of the Roman republican tradition: not simply the tribunician veto (clearly a late pretext for Caesar, though not lacking in force for all that), but the principles that the *dignitas* of Rome's heroes, who had (ostensibly) devoted their lives to the service of the state, should be protected and rewarded; that the will of the Roman People, as expressed by its laws (the Law of the Ten Tribunes), its protectors (the tribunes), and public discussion in *contiones* must be respected; and that they, the Roman People, had the exclusive and fundamental right to choose their consuls with their votes. Caesar considered himself "constitutionally" (i.e. *more maiorum*) in the right and it seems likely that many, probably most, Roman citizens would have agreed with him. He did not shy away from declaring that he was fighting for his *dignitas*, for this was an *honorable* motivation, and due to his adversaries' contemptuous disregard for popular rights and demands he could plausibly assert that his *dignitas* was completely bound up with the honor and freedom of the Roman People. So the Caesarian Civil War was not a merely "personal" conflict provoked by an astonishing and unconscionable assertion of megalomaniacal pride, nor should it be interpreted simplistically as a showdown between a treasonous rebel and "the Republic" (or "die Regierung") tottering on its last legs. Egos, pride, and emotions (including, not least, the "war madness" which so upset Cicero) were all of course engaged, as is ever the case in the run-up to war, and yet this civil war was also about principles and politics – in fact, in important respects it was about the very nature of the Republic. Like Cato and his crowd, Caesar, his followers, and his army could convince themselves and others that they were trying to save the Republic, not destroy it.

Nevertheless, a good case can be made that neither of the two main principals, Caesar or Pompey, actually sought this war (although the same does not appear to be true of the Catos, Bibuluses, and Domitiuses). As the question of Caesar's return began to emerge in 51–50 as the chief problem confronting Rome's political leaders, Pompey appears to have sought at first to give his former ally and father-in-law room in which to make his actions in pursuit of his goal of an honorific return politically acceptable to skeptics in Rome. Right down to the first week of January 49 and again later in the month, Caesar offered concessions that, had cooler heads prevailed, could have provided an acceptable basis for stepping back from the brink. Pompey showed himself amenable and came within a hair's breadth, it seems, of accepting both of them. (Technically he *did* accept the second.) It might have been possible to head off the looming disaster; perhaps that could have happened if Cicero had been present in the Senate in the fall and early winter of 50–49 to serve as a trusted intermediary during the great escalation that took place after Caesar bypassed the elections of 50. But Cicero was away, and as matters came to a head he was in no hurry to rush to the scene of deliberation in Rome. By the time he was able to engage in the Senate early in January 49 both Caesar and Pompey were even more deeply entrenched in their positions. Ultimately it was too much, especially with Cato and the consul Lentulus pressing Pompey "not to be fooled again."[13] The Civil War that broke out in 49 was a classic example of a conflict brought on by an incremental but steady erosion of mutual trust in the manner predicted by the Prisoner's Dilemma, not by naked aggression on either side (Chapter 6).

A long tradition that originated in the *History* of Asinius Pollio makes the Rubicon a kind of trip wire, a "point of no return" whose crossing irrevocably launched the Civil War. That is in fact what the phrase "crossing the Rubicon" *means* in modern parlance.[14] Yet the reality, which we can trace through Caesar's own *Commentaries* and particularly

---

[13] Plut. *Pomp.* 59.6. See Chapter 6, p. 306f. and Appendix 4.   [14] *OED* s.v. Rubicon (n.), 1.

Cicero's nearly day-to-day correspondence, was that Caesar's entry into Italy on or about January 11, 49, was followed by a military pause accompanied by various gestures backing up a flurry of communications to friendly senators that professed the desire for an immediate settlement if Pompey could only be induced to agree to a meeting. Having crossed into Italy, Caesar did not begin a "blitzkrieg" march on Rome as is so often imagined by moderns and even by some of the later sources. He paused in the vicinity of Ariminum for at least a week, perhaps two, having sent forward detachments to Arretium, Iguvium and Ancona which, though they could serve as the leading edge of a renewed advance, also defensively screened the approaches from the south during the pause. Although like Pompey he did not suspend military preparations during this time – he began recruitment around Ariminum while his four legions in Cisalpina strained to catch up, and the occupation of Iguvium on the most direct route (via Flaminia) to Rome was awkwardly late – he did in fact pause after making an offer for peace whose seriousness, too often dismissed, is proven by its swift initial acceptance by Pompey and the consuls (though they were to spoil it by adding unacceptable conditions) and Cicero's optimism that a settlement was in fact likely. After the peace talks collapsed Caesar resumed his march, but pointedly *not* down the Via Flaminia toward the capital but down the "back" of the peninsula and through the Appenines toward Pompey at Luceria and Brundisium, while frequently communicating his hopes for a meeting and a settlement either directly or through intermediaries, even with supposedly "enemy" commanders such as Cicero. Unwarlike gestures of good faith such as the release of all those captured at Corfinium, including one of his bitterest enemies, L. Domitius, together with his war treasury, or that of Pompey's captured prefect, N. Magius, with instructions to encourage negotiation, made a great impact, so that right down to the eve of Pompey's setting sail from Italy Cicero continued to nurse hopes that a full-scale war could be averted. Cicero's unusually copious correspondence in this anxious period reveals his continual swings between optimism that war could still be averted and pessimism that it could no longer be stopped. This valuable source offers us a truer picture of these first three months of 49 than that which any of our retrospective, narrative sources produces (although Caesar's own narrative comes close): what has come to be seen as the opening "Italian Campaign" of the Caesarian Civil War is revealed as not so much the opening military campaign of a war in the normal sense, but a confusing prelude, a series of stops and starts, contradictory messages, and signs both belligerent and conciliatory that left Cicero and surely many others, including some of those who unlike him made their way back to a peaceful Rome not even (it seems) occupied by a substantial military force, in a state of uncertainty whether there really was a war on.

It is commonplace to describe Caesar's opponents in the Civil War as Pompey and "the Senate" (or even, tendentiously, "the Republicans"). After all, it was a decree of the Senate that had tried to force him to yield his command, and it was the Senate who had on January 7 passed the "Final Decree" against him (though not, strictly speaking, by name) which precipitated the war. No doubt this fact, combined with the widespread notion that the essence of the republican political system was senatorial *dominance* ("Senatsherrschaft"), encourages many to interpret the opposition at this crucial moment as one between Caesar and "the Republic" tout court. Yet careful prosopographical analysis shows that the Senate and the Roman nobility who held such authority therein were both deeply divided, if not evenly between the two sides, still far from one-sidedly. The consulars, the top of the senatorial hierarchy, were much less "Pompeian" than has been appreciated: fewer than half of them actually joined Pompey, while remaining in Italy was in practice a discreetly pro-Caesarian position for them, as both sides recognized; the lower ranks of senators on the other hand tended to favor Caesar. According to Dio, only one-third (or perhaps a bit more) of all senators physically joined Pompey in the ersatz Senate that met at Thessalonica. Dire Pompeian threats against those who did not actively take their side must have accounted for part of this number. Our sources are unanimous on the other hand that the ordinary citizens of Rome and Italy, including many *equites* and local officials, were favorable to Caesar, or at least not on board with a war fought to deprive him of his hero's welcome. If the People should count as central constituents of the SPQR as well as the Senate, then it would seem that "the Republic" was largely in Caesar's camp in January–March 49.

Given the nature of the quarrel that led to the war this division within the Republic and within the Senate itself should be no surprise. It is clear that Caesar's defiance of the "Final Decree," and especially his decision in response to march right into Italy before serious preparations for war had been made by either side, caused a huge initial shock. Cicero asked incredulously whether a "Hannibal" (or a Sulla) was coming to put Rome to the sword and torch. Many senators who had previously been sympathetic to Caesar's demands (as even Cicero was, within limits) must now have seen him in a very different, far more threatening light. This probably also accounts for some of the senatorial numbers on Pompey's side along with the latter's harsh threats against neutrality. But Caesar's behavior once he was in Italy, especially his avoidance of bloodshed and of any hostile advance on Rome itself, calmed nerves and allowed for more sober reflection about the evils represented by both sides – as well, for many younger senators and nobles, as the opportunities presented by Caesar's success – and there is no reason to think senators were in general eager to set a *rex* over themselves. Hermann Strasburger's attempt to show that even Caesar's own people disapproved of him and his actions was fundamentally flawed by his failure to take sufficient account of the rhetorical strategies Cicero's correspondents and friends employed. Caesar was now a highly polarizing figure, of course, but then so had been Sulla, and this had not prevented him from donning the mantle of "the Republic."

Many senators, including quite a few senior consulars, made their way back to Rome once they saw there was no danger there after all. Even as late as March 5, 49, Cicero was being advised by his wealthy equestrian friend, Atticus, to keep his options open: "If Caesar continues as he has begun, with sincerity, moderation, and prudence, I shall think hard and look attentively to our interests" (Cic. *Att.* 9.10.9). Cicero himself had not tried very hard to join Pompey in his dash to Brundisium, misled, he later acknowledged to Atticus, by the belief that a settlement would be reached. Even after Pompey slipped out of Italy on March 17 (~ ca. January 25, Jul.) he was far from resolute in joining his commander in chief. Atticus's advice to remain in Italy to use his influence for peace, his beloved daughter's similar sentiments, anxiety over how Pompey would receive him, increasingly clear signs of Caesar's disapproval, alternative plans for a dignified exit to a neutral place like Malta, as well of course as the winter season, all tugged him in the opposite direction and conspired to detain him to all appearances down to the last weeks before he was able to set sail from Caieta on June 7 (~ April 15, Jul.). It seems unfair to view Cicero's lack of resolution simply as a failure of character; rather, it is further evidence of the large political ambiguities of the situation – not to mention its sheer enormity – in the first quarter of the year 49 (Chapter 7).

Caesar's repeatedly deferred but ultimately decisive victory in the Civil War left him – so it is often suggested – in a position to reshape Roman politics in conformity to his will. His famous *clementia*, or more broadly, leniency in dealing with his former enemies has frequently in modern times been interpreted as an assertion of lordly mastery, establishing a quasi-monarchic supremacy over the recipients of his pardon that trampled aristocratic, "republican" sensibilities and prefigured the Principate. Even this prima facie most attractive aspect of Caesar's policy is used as a stick to beat him with. But this view is misguided. As Konstan showed some time ago, "clemency was a virtue," and an unimpeachably "republican" one at that. While often urged upon kings in Hellenistic ethical literature, Cicero's writings copiously attest that the virtues of "forgiveness" and leniency toward one's political opponents (so long as they were not outright enemies of the state) were highly valued also in the rough-and-tumble civic life of republics or democracies. There was therefore nothing peculiarly monarchical about Caesar's remarkable and impressive acts of leniency in the civil wars, which began long before any realistic expectation of his enemies' ultimate defeat was possible. Caesar's letter to his advisors about his leniency at Corfinium was no thinly veiled blueprint for *regnum* but in its historical context it appears, just as its words openly claim, to be an attempt to prevent the catastrophe of civil war if possible and, if not, to minimize bloodshed and restore a deeply divided community. The same can be said also for the many pardons after Pharsalus and even after Thapsus, although unsurprisingly they diminished in frequency with the emergence and intensification over the years of what Caesar viewed as *pertinacia* by "diehards." The idea that "clemency" was little more than a way to break the spirit of proud nobles is reminiscent more of Lucan's over the top and, frankly, rather absurd portrayal of Domitius's frantic terror of being pardoned than of the actual historical circumstances. After all, as we saw, when facing defeat Caesar's enemies rushed to avail themselves of it in great numbers, and never refused it (Cato notwithstanding) when it was actually offered. Nor were its recipients tightly bound to Caesar in chains of reciprocity once they had availed themselves of his pardon: the record of "recidivists" like Domitius, Lentulus Spinther, Afranius, Petreius, Varro, and others shows that whatever gratitude they may have felt to Caesar lay very lightly on their conscience. When the wars were over and the character of the exchange had changed accordingly – from giving up the fight against Caesar to obtaining his permission to return from de facto exile – it stands to reason that those who had obtained pardon would now feel that they had less hope of escaping their defeated state. Yet that regime lasted only a few months until the Dictator's assassination, so evidence is lacking for just how heavy a moral burden of reciprocity actually weighed on the recipients of Caesar's pardons – except, that is, in the brutal fact that the leaders of the assassination were themselves among the most prominent examples of Caesar's leniency. The defeated naturally felt resentment, but there is no reason to assume that what they resented was the pardon itself (which as a rule they had sought), rather than the fact that they had been defeated and had therefore needed it in the first place. Cicero himself worked hard to encourage remaining Pompeian stragglers or holdouts to make use of Caesar's "clemency," which would be puzzling if it were in itself such an offensive thing to senatorial or aristocratic sentiment. The new cult of *Clementia Caesaris* seems likely to have been intended both to reassure ex-Pompeians about their future and to encourage the Dictator himself to be as good as his word about his desire to "win back the good will of all" (Chapter 8).

The narrative of the final months of Caesar's life from his return to Rome late in September 45 to the Ides of March 44 has traditionally been dominated by the question whether "he wanted to be king." This sharp focusing of the story clearly dates back to antiquity, for it is present in all of our (late) narrative sources from the near-contemporary Nicolaus through (most emphatically) Plutarch and Suetonius, Appian, and finally Dio in the third century. The reason is clear and simple: on this very question depended the moral assessment of the action of the assassins as "liberators" and "tyrannicides," which as the very civil wars to come showed was highly controversial;[15] and after the first assassination of a reigning emperor, another Gaius Caesar in AD 41, the ideology of "tyrannicide" was once again extremely salient for writers in the Principate. Framing the story in this way almost ineluctably forces us to make the story one about *the assassination*, pro or con, and equally inevitably draws us to view the matter through the perspective of the conspirators and their sympathizers (or, less commonly in our democratic age, of those like Matius who reacted to it with abhorrence). This approach, however, tends to obscure or suppress the perspective of Caesar and his own partisans in the leadup to the Ides of March – their objectives and preoccupations at this fraught time – as well as any other circumstances that are less straightforwardly related to the dominant "assassination narrative." Most notable among these are the massive preparations launched at this time for a great war of vengeance against the Parthians on a truly extraordinary scale. This rarely bulks very large in accounts of Caesar's final months, yet it was obviously not only his chief political priority at the time but arguably that of most Romans, who had, according to Dio, authorized the campaign in a burst of enthusiasm.

Caesar and Rome were in the midst of extensive military preparations for a multiyear campaign to be fought by what might have been the largest army assembled in a single theater of operations in Roman history. Not surprisingly, therefore, the knock-on effects of the mobilization effort were themselves disruptive, above all the decision to choose all magistrates for at least

---

[15] Tac. *Ann.* 1.8.6: *diem illum ... cum occisus dictator Caesar aliis pessimum aliis pulcerrimum facinus videretur.*

the three years to come in a rapid-fire series of high-stakes elections just before Caesar's scheduled departure date of March 18. Political payoffs, rewards for loyalty or (in the case of select Pompeians) for coming to terms at a seasonable hour, all had to be settled in a matter of a few months, then set in stone for the expected years of the Dictator's absence. Given the constraint under which he had placed himself by his own policy of sparing his former enemies' lives and property, Caesar's followers can only have been put in a state of great excitement by this abrupt reckoning of their rewards, while the expectations of a few favored Pompeians such as Brutus and Cassius were surely no less intense. The Caesarian coalition was coming apart, even at times in explosive fashion, as may be glimpsed in the remarkable clash between two key loyalists, Mark Antony and Dolabella, on the very eve of Caesar's scheduled departure. Ultimately it is the agenda for the meeting of the Senate on the Ides of March that gives the crucial clue: not the false rumor that Caesar would be made king, which neatly echoes the apologetic tradition on the assassins' motives, but the seemingly mundane information Cicero offers in the *Second Philippic* that it was Antony's attempt at religious obstruction of Caesar's will at Dolabella's election that was to be discussed in the Senate that day. This tells us much about the atmosphere in Rome at the end of Caesar's life – not least, that one of Caesar's most loyal and valuable supporters saw himself not as a mere minion of the "permanent Dictator" but as a Roman consul with political independence. This explosive atmosphere is likely to have encouraged the conspirators to make their move, which in view of Caesar's recent grave alienation of the politically active segment of the Roman plebs by his arbitrary treatment of their tribunes and his usurpation of the authority of their voting assemblies no longer seems like merely "wishful thinking" after all. There may not have been many left to defend his recent actions, although after his bloody, treacherous murder on the Senate floor many more would be prepared to cry out for vengeance. If Caesar's solution to the division of civil war was a "great patriotic war" against the Parthian enemy, it is ironic that it was his forceful pursuit of that cause that created the most favorable, perhaps even necessary conditions for his assassination.

Caesar made little to no effort to create a new political system out of the ruins of civil war during the short period he spent in Rome before his scheduled departure for the East, much less to oversee a transition to a whole new kind of politics. Civil war by its very nature always brings with it severe violations of the norms and rules of peacetime political life; these do not just spring to life again in full health after the fighting is over. Caesar had made things much more complicated for himself by his mild treatment of his enemies and his invitation to some of them to resume their proper place in political life. His followers and their recent adversaries would have to relearn habits of peacetime, of regarding and treating each other not as deadly enemies but as fellow citizens who might legitimately oppose one's projects with impunity save for the limits laid down by the political system and the law. (This is, in fact, more or less equivalent to the civic version of *clementia*.) Sulla had taken the easier route (in a sense) of simply eliminating his enemies by massacre, proscription, confiscation, and banishment from public life; even so, he spent a year in Rome legislating a quite elaborate series of reforms and remained at the helm as consul after laying down the dictatorship in order to launch the new order and see it through its first full year. It is doubtful that Caesar actually thought his work of "winning the peace" was done simply by making himself (or letting others make him) "Continuous Dictator," choosing the magistrates in advance for the next few years and leaving for a multiyear expedition only five and a half months after his return to Rome. A glorious campaign of some years and the anticipated victory might have been the first step toward a definitive political solution, or simply a way to buy more time while habituating Romans to fighting on the same side again. We cannot know. (Chapter 9)

* * *

Caesar's very assassination, together with its (partisan) justification, have done much to fix the central teleology of Caesar's story by setting the seal of "tyrannicide" upon it. Had Caesar for whatever reason not been assassinated on March 15, 44, but, say, succumbed one month later to a gangrenous broken leg suffered while dismounting from his horse at Brundisium on his way eastward, would he have been remembered as a tyrant and destroyer of the Republic? That is at least doubtful. The fact that, Cicero included, the texts that portray Caesar as the destroyer of the Republic virtually all postdate the assassination (one might argue about some of Cicero's Civil War letters and writings, but none is so vehement as the *Philippics* or *De officiis*) should put us on our guard. Continuing with our counterfactual hypothetical, absent vengeful veterans and an outraged citizenry, could Octavian have amounted to anything more than a "boy" to be "praised, honored, and gotten out of the way" (Cic. *Fam.* 11.20.1)? And without an Octavian to take up the Caesarian torch, could Caesar ever have become the first of "the Caesars," the founder figure not only of an imperial dynasty but of the monarchic Principate itself? Caesar's historical significance is substantially not something of his own making or even of his own time.

The justification of tyrannicide requires a tyrant, and the most plausible kind of tyrant, as Tacitus knew, was one who had really always been thus. A desire to subvert the Republic and establish an autocracy was imputed to Caesar from an early age and traced back with great interest through his every move, betraying itself ever more clearly as it unfolded step by step to its natural end. Moderns have not entirely shed the habit. But I have tried to show here that the hypothesis that Caesar's disposition was fundamentally alien to the Republic, that it somehow looked forward to the imperial future that would only be firmly established by his heir, is entirely unnecessary to explain his actions. A historical character's innermost thoughts and plans cannot be directly known to us; we can only infer intent from reasonably well-substantiated public actions.[16] But if we restrict ourselves to Caesar's public actions we have no great difficulty interpreting them as determined by the traditional republican ends and values of the Roman "meritocracy." As we have noted, in the pre–Civil War years Caesar never behaves as an ideologue, activist, or great reformer; his actions never compel us to suppose that he was doing anything more than operating according to the values, ideology, expectations, and traditional patterns of aristocratic ambition that are familiar from the history of the past century and a half or so. What seems such a distinctive characteristic of Caesar – the relentless pursuit of *honor* through *virtus* proven by "services to the Republic" (*merita in rem publicam*) – was already inspiringly exemplified by admired figures such as the Scipiones who, patricians like Caesar, were renowned for their military achievements but also adept at their use of "popular" methods to advance their *dignitas*. And like Sulla, Caesar had resorted to arms to defend his *dignitas* against his enemies, who had also arguably torn up the "constitution" in their zeal to destroy him.[17]

Once the Civil War was on, the civil institutions of peacetime inevitably suffered enormous damage. Republican institutions with their characteristic division of power were not designed for civil war, which had an irresistible tendency to consolidate power in the hands of a supreme commander. Hence Caesar's sequence of dictatorships and usurpation of the traditional rights both of Senate and People. That in the not quite six months he spent in Rome while preparing to launch the greatest military expedition of his life and age he did not "restore the Republic" or even turn in earnest to Cicero's more limited agenda to "set the courts in order, restore good credit, repress sexual excess, increase the birthrate, and bind everything which has collapsed and washed away with tough laws,"[18]

---

[16] Chapter I, p. 28ff.   [17] Sulla: see Morstein-Marx 2011.   [18] Cic. *Marc.* 27; Chapter 9, n. 2.

should hardly occasion great surprise under the circumstances. Even his assumption of a "Continuous Dictatorship" does not suffice to make clear whatever plans Caesar may have had for the future political structure of the Republic, which therefore remain, like so many of the other "final plans" conjectured or fabricated by contemporaries and later generations, the stuff of uncontrolled and sometimes wild speculation.[19] Whatever the import of the "Continuous Dictatorship," however – and it is probably best understood as one of an avalanche of extravagant honors showered over him at this time by the Senate – it hardly reveals his pursuit of autocracy over a lifetime, any more than would Oliver Cromwell's transformation into an autocrat after the Parliamentary victory in the English Civil War and the execution of King Charles I.[20]

Interpreting Caesar not as a subversive or disaffected "outsider" to the republican system but as a culmination of its aristocratic, meritocratic traditions (if ultimately an explosive one) casts further doubt on the assumption that the Roman Republic had lost or forfeited the allegiance of many or most of its constituents. Central to that assumption is the even more widespread idea that the Roman People themselves had given up on the Republic.[21] But this is inconsistent with the story we have traced of the role of the Roman People in Caesar's rise and the ultimate erosion of their support through the Civil War years and especially in the last months before the assassination. In reinterpreting Julius Caesar as a republican political leader, I have sought to give due recognition to the political role of the Roman People, which has long been suppressed due to prevailing

---

[19] Dio 44.34.3; App. *BCiv.* 2.135; Cic. *Phil.* 1.16–26, 2.100, etc. Some of Caesar's "final plans" (e.g. the conferral of Latin rights upon Sicily) may have been smuggled in among his *acta*, which the Senate had ratified en masse in the immediate aftermath of the assassination. Other grandiose "final plans" are recounted by Suet. *Iul.* 44, Plut. *Caes.* 58.8–10, Dio 44.5.1, with Pelling 2011: 434–440: compiling an authoritative edition of the civil law, collecting a library of Greek and Roman works under Varro's direction, draining the Pomptine Marshes and the Fucine Lake, building a road through the Appenines from the Adriatic directly to the Tiber, punching a canal through the Isthmus of Corinth and another alongside the coast of Latium from Rome to Tarracina, and building a great harbor at Ostia. These projects must be in good part products of rank speculation drawn to a famous name or imputed to Caesar by later emperors who took them in hand (Suet. *Claud.* 20.1: *a Divo Iulio saepius destinatum ac propter difficultatem omissum*). What did such "planning" actually entail? I can well imagine that Caesar "wanted" (*voluit*, Cic. *Phil.* 5.7) to drain the marshes, which many others after him wanted as well. In my view Caesar's "final plans" are taken much too seriously by many leading authorities, e.g. Gelzer 1968: 314 ("his grandiose concept of government is also illustrated by the following plans"); Yavetz 1983: 159–160; Billows 2009: 244; Pelling 2011: 439–440. Yet the diversion of the Tiber and the intended redesign of the Campus Martius seem well enough attested (Chapter 9, n. 37).

[20] Chapter 1, p. 28.

[21] The classic statement of the theory is that of Peter Brunt (n. 32), but it is implied in any statement along the lines of "Rome was ready for a monarch."

assumptions that identified "the Republic" too closely with the Senate. The Roman People gave the crucial push to the *leges agrariae*, Caesar's Gallic command, and other important legislation in 59; they repudiated the Senate's decision to execute the "Catilinarian" conspirators in 58 yet also restored Cicero from exile the next year; they elected candidates of the Caesarian-Pompeian alliance to the consulships of 58 yet also chose "sound" conservatives for the consulships of 57, 56, and again in 54, after a temporary assertion of "triumviral" raw power in 55; they largely fell in line behind Pompey's restoration of law and order in 52, passing a variety of reformist laws that ended the endemic violence of 54–52; they applauded Caesar's victories in Gaul with enthusiasm and reacted badly when the proconsul's enemies sought to destroy him politically and pushed for civil war in a manner that would brook no opposition from the People and their officers, the tribunes. The Roman People, whose great-grandfathers had perhaps been among those who shouted that "the People were masters of the elections" and thus elected Scipio Aemilianus to the consulship of 147 before he had served even as aedile, did not take kindly to the push by Caesar's enemies to prevent him even from standing for the consulship on his return from Gaul, arguably in violation of a law of the Roman People that gave him exactly that right. Despite a deep fear of civil war founded on their experience or memory of the horrors of the 80s, the urban plebs of Rome along with town councils and townspeople up and down the peninsula largely welcomed Caesar's return, even if he were forced to do so under arms, and hardly leapt to defend senatorial decisions made by the very men who, though they had offered no contrary argument against Caesar's overwhelmingly popular agrarian legislation in 59, had nevertheless tried to suppress the People's voice.

Yet the regime that took charge of Rome during the Civil War years mostly in Caesar's absence was hardly in fact "popular" in the traditional sense, aligning itself in the public eye most notably with creditors, renters, and savage forces of repression (including the "Final Decree of the Senate") mobilized by Caesar's deputies and the Caesarian wartime Senate to confront serious outbreaks of rioting and violence in 48 and 47.[22] City residents and those who could make their way to the capital no doubt enjoyed the unparalleled extravagance of the triumphal celebrations of September–October 46, yet the festal relief was short-lived as Pompey's sons proved in Spain that the war was not yet over. We hear nothing that suggests much in the way of authentic celebration by the Roman populace

[22] Chapter 9, p. 528ff.

upon Caesar's ultimate return in October 45, and soon the public mood was deeply soured by the Dictator's high-handed and seemingly arbitrary deposition of their own officers, the tribunes Flavus and Marullus. Some public demonstrations and an "underground" graffiti campaign sent the signal that at least "the People" who actively engaged in urban politics were running out of patience with their former hero. Even the urban plebs, then, had not given up their attachment to the Republic, and far from enlisting in a personality cult of Caesar they appear to have been seriously troubled by their former hero's arbitrary, un-republican actions at the cost of cherished popular rights. Caesar's demobilized veterans were more staunchly loyal – at least to his memory once he was dead (for their mutinies should not be forgotten) – but the common assumption that legionary soldiers had long since abandoned any real allegiance to the Republic is open to serious question, especially once it is acknowledged that there were in fact arguable republican reasons for crossing the Rubicon. Those who did are likely to have considered themselves defenders of the Republic.[23] Note that the conspirators clearly counted on a wave of public support for the Dictator's assassination. They failed to appreciate the difference between political resistance or opposition and the treacherous, bloody slaughter of one of the most celebrated military and political leaders in the annals of Rome, in the very midst of a meeting of the august council of state, by men he had trusted and favored, including some he had generously spared and advanced.[24]

It has always served the teleological narrative of a "Rome ready for monarchy" to pay little attention to the ways in which Rome in the 60s and 50s still functioned *as a republic* – as a political system in which "the People" played an important role in their self-government through elections, legislation, and an ideology of "popular sovereignty" – rather than as an oligarchy that depended on habits of deference and consensus, relatively closed to outward influence and relatively invulnerable to external pressure, presiding over a "frozen waste" devoid of authentic politics.[25] The

---

[23] Chapter 6, p. 319f. For the persistence of civic values among the soldiery see Chapter 1, n. 79 and Chapter 9, n. 190.

[24] This is not to deny the "fundamental indeterminacy of the Popular Will" (Chapter 1, n. 38) but simply to highlight what appears to have been a widespread sentiment that prevailed from the time of the tumultuous funeral (March 20): Morstein-Marx 2004: 157–158.

[25] The tendency of many scholars to emphasize the importance of "consensus" for governmental functioning in general and in particular to define Rome's Republic as one based on "consensus" (see e.g. Lundgreen 2011: 277–285, "Rom als Konsenssystem," with reference to Flaig's theory that the assemblies functioned as "Konsensorgan(e)" and Jehne's description of their "Konsensklima") is notably divergent from the perspective of Polybius, with his theory of the fundamental and

idea that the Roman Republic of the 60s and 50s was "on life support," as it were, and ready to collapse under the slightest pressure has been a reliable buttress for the idea that Caesar was able to see beyond the Republic and envision an autocratic future for himself. Yet not only is this an unnecessary conclusion from the evidence of Caesar's actions and decisions that we have reviewed, but the assumption of the Republic's frailty is itself doubtful.

Already in 1974 Erich Gruen made a strong case that the vitality of the republican system remained strong even in these last two decades of its existence. While, as in any political system in which the People have a voice, tensions between the haves and have-nots posed a challenge to the political order, while major security threats demanded serious attention and competing political leaders frequently stirred the pot, the Senate and People – not always in tandem, of course, but sometimes in the competitive fashion Polybius described in the second century – rose to the occasion and carried on the functions of government.[26] Through the 50s, the Senate deliberated and laws were passed, including important reforms (one might note in particular, besides Caesar's agrarian laws and Clodius's grain law, Caesar's law on extortion in the provinces and Pompey's laws on electoral bribery or on magistrates and their provincial assignments). Forty-four regular magistrates were chosen every year in at least five separate elections, sometimes tainted or delayed by the pressure exerted by powerful figures (as in 55) or violence and bribery (as became briefly endemic from 54 to 52).[27] Dominant figures, especially the three-way alliance of Pompey, Crassus, and Caesar, sometimes managed to have their way when they were able to coordinate effectively (as in 59, 56, and 55), but even now this was not the norm. There is still a tendency among some scholars to treat the important interventions of the People – for instance, the *leges Gabinia* and *Manilia* by which the pirate threat and Mithridates were dealt with, Caesar's *leges agrariae*, Clodius's grain law, all great successes in fact – as if these were

---

adversarial division of the Roman *politeia*, a view profoundly developed by Machiavelli in his famous chapter of the *Discorsi* (1.4) in which he attributes Rome's greatness to its structural tendency toward *discord* rather than concord (Morstein-Marx 2013: 47 with n82; cf. however, Atkins 2013: 83–85 for Machiavelli's divergence from Polybius). Most scholars' bias toward the ideology of *concordia ordinum* may be another case of implicit Ciceronian bias; recall too the tendentious use to which the rhetoric of *concordia* was put by those seeking to preserve the *auctoritas senatus* in public discourse (Morstein-Marx 2012: 197–199; 2004: 54–56).

[26] Gruen 1974, neatly summarized at pp. 499–503.

[27] This was the number of regular magistrates down to the quaestorian level, including tribunes of the plebs, through the 50s. (It is unclear in the state of the evidence whether twenty-four military tribunes were still elected annually by the People.)

somehow extraneous interruptions of the "proper" senatorial business of politics (i.e. something contrary to the way the Republic, seen simply as "senatorial rule," was *supposed* to work) rather than illuminating examples of a perfectly proper "popular" role in the administration of the Republic.[28] Politics in the City veered dangerously toward anarchy at times in the middle years of the decade, from the tumultuous tribunate of P. Clodius in 58 through the heavy-handed consulship of Pompey and Crassus in 55 to the murder of the same Clodius on the Appian Way in 52 followed by mob rioting in Rome. Elections were repeatedly postponed, their results vitiated by massive bribery, and violence not infrequently raged across the Forum, as described most vividly in a letter of Cicero's (*Att.* 4.3, 57 BC), which probably has done as much as anything to taint the last decade of the Republic in its readers' minds.[29] Yet less familiar is the story of the Senate's collaboration with Pompey as sole consul in 52 to clean up the mess, not merely by restoring order in the City by previously unthinkable police methods (bringing units of the military within the bounds of the City), but also by passing a raft of reform legislation ranging from novel trial procedures that emphasized testimony over rhetorical fireworks to updating laws on electoral corruption, political violence, magistracies, and provincial assignments. The rest of the year 52 as well as 51 and even 50, despite the developing crisis over Caesar's return, saw no repeat of the dismaying violence and anarchy of the mid-50s. Pompey's housecleaning did not in the event get a long enough probationary period for us to judge its effectiveness definitively, but it simply cannot plausibly be asserted in the face of this evidence that the Senate and People of Rome were no longer able to take difficult political problems in hand and to deal with them with every appearance of success. Indeed, the readiness of Caesar's enemies to mount

---

[28] See Morstein-Marx 2015: 304–306. Cf. the contrary view of Mouritsen 2017: esp. 67–72: the popular assemblies typically functioned as ritual generators of consent, and their "ritual status ... was challenged only in exceptional instances, when dissident members of the elite brought their disagreements into a realm that was normally insulated from political strife. In those instances it was a question of politics 'spilling over' into the ratification procedure, which was usually kept separate. The taboo associated with such behaviour is underlined not just by the rarity with which it happened but also by the consternation it appears to have caused" (68–69). An older generation of scholars tended to discount popular participation as a matter of course: Syme struck the keynote with his famous description of the Roman Republic as "a feudal order of society" with an oligarchy lurking behind the façade (1939: 11–12; cf. Morstein-Marx 2004: 4–11).

[29] The violence and corruption that attended the elections of the mid-to-late 50s are often cited as evidence that the Republic was collapsing. However, the connection is not a simple one. In the modern world many "emerging democracies" and even quite well-established ones such as India's (often cited as a model example of democratization) are plagued by widespread and severe electoral violence. Indeed, electoral violence to some extent correlates with the value placed on elections: see, e.g., Staniland 2014. For India in particular, Kumar 2015.

a vigorous push for a showdown in late 50 and the beginning of 49 may well have been brought on by a renewed sense of confidence now that they had succeeded in unifying Pompey and the dominant voices in the Senate, rather than despair.

This is not however intended to be a comprehensive study of why the Roman Republic "fell," or, better, "transformed" into a monarchy.[30] That is a much larger question that would take us far beyond the limits set for this book, a study of Caesar as a republican leader, to answer adequately. However, the findings of this book should offer material for future attempts to tackle the problem.

Most obviously, this study raises the question why the Republic destroyed itself if no one actually sought to destroy it, and it was by no means bereft of its traditional allies at the elite and more "popular" levels of society. The paradoxical answer I propose is that what tore the Republic apart was not that anyone was seeking to overthrow or undermine it, but that important agents convinced themselves that the other side was intent on doing so, leading to an erosion of mutual trust to the point where each side, acting on this conviction, was determined to prevent that result by any means necessary – civil war.

A "great event," we often feel, demands an equally "great" explanation. In modern times this most often means a search for causes at a deeper structural level rather than among often transitory and aberrant human choices: a decisive failure of institutions, say, or socioeconomic disruption, leading to deep alienation from the contemporary political order by groups or classes in a position to effect change (here, e.g. perhaps a disaffected soldiery). But in the case of the Caesarian Civil War, neither of these shows a convincing link to the outbreak of the war itself. We have already cited Gruen's challenge to the theory of general institutional failure. More specifically, scholars have often cited "extraordinary commands" like Caesar's in Gaul, which placed immense state resources into the hands of individual generals who were thereby enabled (so the theory goes) to slip from senatorial control and even turn against "the Republic."[31] The first fully realized example of the phenomenon would in fact be the Caesarian case – but since this was preceded by *extraordinaria imperia* held by Pompey and others, with no comparable result, the conclusion is far from cogent. I have argued that the Caesarian Civil War is not to be

---

[30] For "transformation" as the better term see Morstein-Marx and Rosenstein 2006: 625–626.

[31] On the debates and constitutional issues see Arena 2012: 179–200 and Straumann 2016: 100–117, with references to earlier work. Gruen 1974: 534–543 remains a bracing challenge to the traditional pessimistic diagnosis.

attributed simplistically to an unchecked, overweening proconsul, but to a great extent instead to Caesar's enemies who, having managed at last to get their way in the Senate, were driven (as they saw it) to make a desperate and very risky gamble to destroy him *before* he became too strong. How far this fear was justifiable in view of Caesar's past and present behavior is open to reasonable debate. I have tried to show, however, that the Civil War was substantially a war of choice initiated not by Caesar ("crossing the Rubicon") but by his enemies, who have no unique claim to be acting in defense of the Republic. Caesar's "extraordinary command" in Gaul, then, seems in itself no more responsible for the catastrophic civil war that ensued than those who in their partisan zeal brushed aside the various institutions through which the popular will was expressed (law, elections, tribunes) in order to destroy the man whom the Roman People certainly would have elected consul for the second time if they had only been given the chance to do so. The crisis of 50–49 saw the abuse or failure of various institutions (one might start with the Senate, tribunes, and powerful pro-consular commands and go on to examine the law itself and elections), but it is unconvincing to attribute these failures to the institutions themselves rather than to those seeking to make them do things they could not do.

Similarly, the attempt to explain the Civil War as the result of essentially social and economic factors – for instance, by emphasizing the soldiering class's supposed (but unproven) disaffection from the "Republic" due to a "crisis of the peasantry" across rural Italy – again downplays the signifi-cance of human decisions that brought on the tragedy and overlooks the central ideological dispute between those intent on "saving the Republic" from Caesar and others intent on "saving the Republic" from an oligarchic clique who had trampled on the rights of the People, as represented by their tribunes, by the Law of the Ten Tribunes, and by their right to choose whom they wanted to be their consul.[32] There is reason to suppose that Caesar's army was in fact moved by such violations of norms and trad-itional rights: in his own account he motivates the 13th Legion to march under arms into Italy by means of a speech detailing these wrongs.[33] The

---

[32] Cf. Brunt 1988: 273–274: "It was the wretchedness of the population from which the army was recruited that enabled leaders whose primary concern was their own enrichment or aggrandizement to threaten and finally to subvert the Republic . . . [T]heir designs could not have been accomplished if they had failed to find followers, and we need also to consider why the soldiers showed so little attachment to the old order." Yet Brunt's famous article on "the Army and the Land" is notably free of evidence of rural distress pertaining to the 50s or to the crisis leading to the Caesarian Civil War (see pp. 250–253, 258, 269–270); cf. Gruen 1974: 400–404. Cf. Morstein-Marx and Rosenstein 2006: 627–629, and n. 23 of this chapter.

[33] Caes. *BCiv.* 1.7. Cf. Sulla's appeal to his army in 88: Morstein-Marx 2011.

soldiering class of Italy appears to have sympathized with Caesar, *tantis rebus gestis*, rather than with his enemies: even Pompey's recruits cried out for peace.[34] This in itself suggests that we look for the explanation not in some kind of quasi-clientelistic relationship of soldiers with their commanders or a revolutionary alienation from an indifferent government but in the recognition, perhaps especially widespread among soldiers and the soldiering class, that "the Republic" was with Caesar rather than against him. Our sources seem to show no evidence of significant or novel rural discontent in Italy throughout the 50s, our best-documented period in Roman history (this in sharp contrast to the 70s and 60s) – perhaps precisely because of the success of Caesar's own agrarian laws. In sum, there is no clear and convincing causal line to be drawn between the outbreak of the Caesarian Civil War and contemporary conditions in rural Italy.

The civil war that began in 49 BC was, more than most, a war of choice. But this does not mean that it was a random choice. Just as in chess one move leads to another, and the twenty possible first moves typically narrow down as the game develops to one, two, or three good moves, so too the choices that led to the final ones of early 49 can be traced back to earlier, less constrained choices at key decision points made by human agents who could have chosen differently. The sharp opposition between Caesar and Cato and their allies is traceable at least back to the late 60s (the Catilinarian Debate, the bill of Nepos, and the forfeited triumph), but it was a series of choices and retaliations that incrementally narrowed the range of possible and probable outcomes until by March or April 49 civil war had become the only likely option. Yet at each stage before the final step – even as late as Pompey's flight from Italy, or perhaps even a few weeks later when Caesar requested that the Senate open negotiations with Pompey – other choices could have been made. Looking back in the other direction, as far back as 62 Marcus Cato and his allies were not *forced* to try to frustrate Pompey at every turn, thus driving him to seek out new alliances and new methods. Cato was also not *forced* to try to take Caesar down a few pegs (by blocking Caesar's in absentia request, leading to his forfeit of the Spanish triumph) and simultaneously – in a spectacular failure of political *nous* of which Cicero himself complained sharply in private – to frustrate Crassus's project on behalf of the *publicani*, thus pushing these three men to pool their extraordinary assets in a virtually unstoppable new coalition (if a somewhat unstable one, as time would

---

[34] Plut. *Pomp.* 59.4: Chapter 7, n. 366.

prove).[35] Cato's principled but inept way of shoring up senatorial authority, a goal he shared with Cicero, was of course not the only one. He could
have taken Cicero's own counsel: to bring Pompey on board with the
"right-minded citizens" (*boni*) and draw him away from "popular" demagogy (*aliquid de populari levitate deponeret*), and perhaps as well "to make
Caesar, who is riding on the crest of the wave [sc. of 'popularity'] just now,
a better citizen."[36] Politically powerful military heroes had been successfully accommodated in the past: the Scipios again, who had hardly posed
an existential threat to senatorial leadership of the Republic. Nor did
Bibulus and Cato need to try to expand beyond all recognition the potency
of the available obstructive devices in an attempt not merely to stop an
overwhelmingly popular agrarian law against which they themselves, and
the rest of the senators, could find no substantive objection, but to try to
cast doubt on the legality or legitimacy of nearly an entire year of legislation
(some of it immensely popular) and consular acts. And when they failed in
their efforts to erase virtually everything done in 59, they were hardly *forced*
to eye the proconsul's return as their last, best opportunity to bring him
down. "He was weak then," they pointed out, "and yet stronger than the
entire state. What do you think he will be like now?"[37] Caesar and his
adversaries had now become committed enemies, a predictable consequence of this kind of no-holds-barred political warfare. Caesar for his
part could rationally believe that it would be political suicide to settle for
anything less than a splendid honorific return from Gaul, including (at
last) a triumph and a second consulship to secure his position and vindicate
him in a great demonstration of popular support. This can only have been
anathema to Cato and his ilk, who instead were looking for "payback" and
an object lesson for anyone in the future who might wish to emulate the
"consulship of Julius and Caesar" – and try to get away with it.

One might sympathize at least with the goals of those who chose in the
course of that fraught year 50 to opt, quite consciously, for civil war in
preference to giving in to Caesar's "impudent demands." It is possible
(though the Republic had no real experience of this) that with his remarkable record of victory and the backing of a mass of (presumably demobilized) veterans in numbers that had not been seen since Sulla, unchastened

---

[35] Cic. *Att.* 2.1.8: *ille optimo animo utens et summa fide nocet interdum rei publicae* (cf. *Off.* 3.88). This is
the famous passage where Cicero remarks that "Cato speaks in the Senate as though he were living in
Plato's Republic instead of Romulus' cesspool." See now Drogula 2019: 102–127.

[36] Cic. *Att.* 2.1.6: *quid si etiam Caesarem, cuius nunc venti valde sunt secundi, reddo meliorem?*

[37] Cic. *Att.* 7.9.3: *"at tum imbecillus plus"* inquit [sc. *aliquis*] *"valuit quam tota res publica. quid nunc
putas?"*

and perhaps emboldened by his escape from any devastating consequences for his actions in 59, Caesar in his second consulship would have been for all practical purposes a *rex* – elevated so far above his former peers in the Senate that arbitrary assertions of his will could no longer realistically be checked. But their choice to risk the horrors of civil war to avert that possibility "by any means necessary" was one that turned out in the event very badly for the Republic. Under the circumstances, no reasonable person could have expected Caesar simply to yield quietly.[38] Under such circumstances, as Thucydides had written long before, the formerly unthinkable becomes "prudent" and "necessary."[39]

Alternative choices existed. Caesar's enemies might have respected the People's right to elect whom they wished to the consulship, and accepted Caesar's right to a triumphal reentry to the City after his extraordinary military achievements. Caesar might have been more reassuring to Pompey about his plans, he might not have let slip the last good opportunity to exercise his electoral privilege in the elections of 50, he might not have held his army in Gaul over the heads of his adversaries as a form of political blackmail (to him, however, an "insurance policy"). Pompey might have resisted being drawn so far to the side of his former enemies – *mutual* enemies long shared with Caesar; he might have seen that he probably had less reason to trust them than he did Caesar. And the principals were not the only ones making crucial choices: the consuls of 50 might have thought better of ominously holding the "Parthian legions" in Italy, or not have raised the alarm of imminent invasion on dubious rumors and handed over supreme command to Pompey. The mass of senators might have insisted that their 370–22 vote in favor of mutual disarmament only six weeks or so before the Rubicon was crossed was the one that the consul should recognize. And early in January 49, when pressure for a decisive move by the Senate against Caesar intensified to its peak, Pompey might not have listened to Cato and the consul when they warned him not to accept Caesar's offer of almost complete demobilization until the upcoming consular election. Indeed, later in January, when Pompey's war council at Capua had accepted Caesar's terms in principle and Cicero was convinced that the two old allies were about to resolve their differences

---

[38] When at the end of December 50 Cicero lays out all the possible sequences of moves and countermoves he could envision (Cic. *Att.* 7.9.2–4), he reluctantly acknowledges that Caesar would never agree to leave his army and come to Rome to try his chances in the election of 49 without the reassurance of his *ratio absentis*.

[39] Thuc. 3.82–83, a passage that was very much on Sallust's mind in the aftermath. Syme noted that "a single chapter so captivated Sallust that he put it under contribution a dozen times" (1964: 246).

peacefully, a settlement with Caesar was indeed in sight and might well have come about had the Pompeians not now tacked on new conditions that he could be expected to refuse. A host of highly contingent choices make up this causal chain, none of them apparently determined by circumstance or structural constraints.

An extended confrontation of this kind makes its own history, and this history plays a powerful role in making the future. To draw again on the Prisoner's Dilemma, once one party to the "game" has firmly opted for "defection," retaliation by the other party is the most rational response. There may be some question about the first player's *intent* – that is, whether the move truly reveals a clear commitment to defect in future – in which case it may be reasonable for the second player, if he is not himself intent on conflict, to make some exploratory moves or even change the game in the hope of "resetting" it and moving away from the tragic pathology of a tit-for-tat cycle of retaliation. This in fact looks like what Caesar sought to do with his verbal and diplomatic efforts to avert catastrophe in January (two peace proposals), February (the remarkable debut of the "leniency" policy at Corfinium), and even March (Caesar's freeing and return of N. Magius to Pompey) of the year 49.[40] It was reasonable, by no means hopeless, for Caesar to try to detach Pompey from his new and unreliable friends. Yet these efforts failed each time as the hard-liners on the Pompeian side prevailed. With the departure of Pompey and the consuls from Italy the chances for averting a full-scale war become very slender indeed. All of these steps were *choices* among alternatives, and even if the range of options progressively narrowed between 59 and 49 they were not determined in any very meaningful sense by institutional or socioeconomic structures or any other structure in fact than the logic of strategic interaction.

In such a riot of choice to blame institutions or other underlying structural causes seems deeply unsatisfying, for this tends to make the responsibility of human agents disappear from view. There is a real danger of too easily letting the men who made these choices off the hook.[41]

---

[40] See Appendix 4.

[41] Badian 1990: 38–39 (the culmination of his trenchant critique of Meier's *Caesar*): "We have stepped over the line that separates history from (dare we after all call it?) theology. The process has become fate, and human responsibility is discarded as irrelevant, along with human choice. Yet there were innumerable points where things might have taken a different turn . . . [If] some of those mistakes had not been made, and if the luck of the game had been different, the *res publica* would have been saved at that time, and quite possibly for a long time." Badian continues with the wry but not unjust comment quoted in Chapter 1, p. 14. My own interpretation of Caesar, it need hardly be said, is very different from Badian's.

Certainly criticism of the choices made by the human agents on each side is warranted. Readers may feel that I have spent a lot more time criticizing the choices of Cato, Bibulus, and other enemies of Caesar than those of Caesar himself, and explaining the legitimacy of the latter's political moves while giving much shorter shrift to his opponents; my defense is that historical scholarship has mostly tended to be quite indulgent of the faults and errors of Caesar's enemies (often cloaked in the mantle of "the Republic's defenders," however blinkered) and typically fixated on those of the latter, whom history and our own democratic tradition have long been pleased to paint as the villain of the story.[42] In order to open our eyes to the issues in play I have spent more time elucidating the responsibility of Caesar's enemies and the legitimacy of Caesar's responses than a rigidly even-handed approach might call for. This allows us to see that both sides of the Caesarian controversy of the fifties BC were equally animated by their own vision of political legitimacy, and equally convinced that the other side was out to destroy it and therefore must be crushed first. Such convictions do not excuse the self-serving motivations that can typically be assumed to lurk underneath the public justifications of all political action, but they do help to explain why disputes that might have been controlled had they remained solely on the plane of arguments over mere self-interest became so explosive that they issued in civil war. This civil war, I contend, did not come about because either side had given up on the existing political framework but because both sides were strongly commit-ted to their vision of it – and determined to save it from each other.

These observations have thus far been derived from the logic of strategic interaction; a useful systemic perspective is provided by an important, recent book by political scientists Steven Levitsky and Daniel Ziblatt on the failures of democracy in our own times (*How Democracies Die*, 2018). Ziblatt and Levitsky show that democratic/republican institutions and constitutions do not fail necessarily because they are simply badly designed or ill suited to their functions but also, quite often, by the erosion of democratic *norms*, in the absence of which institutions can be co-opted with remarkable speed and finality, and then put in the service of creeping authoritarianism.[43] Well-designed constitutions, constitutional safeguards, the much-vaunted "checks and balances" of the United States and also of course the Roman republican constitution (on Polybius's showing) are not

---

[42] Christ 1994; Baehr 1998; Wyke 2008.

[43] Levitsky and Ziblatt 2018: 7–8 and passim. On Roman norms see the recent volume of Itgenshorst and Le Doze 2017.

enough to maintain and secure a democracy or republic.[44] Levitsky and Ziblatt note that

> Constitutions are always incomplete. Like any set of rules, they have countless gaps and ambiguities ... Constitutional rules are also always subject to competing interpretations ... Because of the gaps and ambiguities inherent in all legal systems, we cannot rely on constitutions alone to safeguard democracy against would-be authoritarians. "God has never endowed any statesman or philosopher, or any body of them," wrote former U.S. president Benjamin Harrison, "with wisdom enough to frame a system of government that everybody could go off and leave."[45]

The "unwritten rules" of any political system are its norms, "shared codes of conduct that become common knowledge within a particular community or society – accepted, respected, and enforced by its members."[46] Because they are unwritten, norms are largely invisible except by their effects (or the effects of their absence).

> Like oxygen or clean water, a norm's importance is quickly revealed by its absence. When norms are strong, violations trigger expressions of disapproval, ranging from head-shaking and ridicule to public criticism and outright ostracism. And politicians who violate them can expect to pay a price.[47]

While a huge number of established political practices can be described as norms of widely varying importance, Levitsky and Ziblatt put special emphasis on the fundamental importance of two higher-order, systemic norms – namely, "mutual toleration" and "institutional forbearance." "Mutual toleration," they write, "refers to the idea that as long as our rivals play by constitutional rules, we accept that they have an equal right to exist, compete for power, and govern."[48] "Institutional forbearance," on the other hand,

> can be thought of as avoiding actions that, while respecting the letter of the law, obviously violate its spirit. Where norms of forbearance are strong, politicians do not use their institutional prerogatives to the hilt, even if it is technically legal to do so, for such action could imperil the existing system.[49]

These two super-norms imply each other: where one is present, the other is almost certain to exist, and in the absence of one, the other cannot long

---

[44] Ibid., 98–99.
[45] Ibid., 99. Even Polybius thought that the remarkable equilibrium of the Roman constitution would eventually fail, causing it to change to "democracy" and at last enter the cycle of constitutional corruption (6.57).
[46] Ibid., 101. [47] Ibid., 102. [48] Ibid., 102. [49] Ibid., 106.

survive. When our political rivals use "any means necessary" to gain dominance and thus throw "institutional forbearance" overboard, we are apt to withdraw our "toleration" of them as merely political rivals and begin to regard them instead as "enemies" – of the state as well as of ourselves – against whom any "institutional forbearance" would only be self-defeating folly. When these norms fail, institutions turn into partisan political weapons, at which point they no longer command the wide societal consensus needed to sustain them as institutions, thus leading to a death spiral of institutional failure. Levitsky and Ziblatt supply a mass of convincing modern historical examples of such death spirals in which institutions have been captured by authoritarianism, from Juan Perón's Argentina in the 1950s to Hugo Chávez's Venezuela, the overthrow of Chilean president Salvador Allende in 1972, and other cases, such as the contemporary United States, where at the time of writing such a fate might well be feared.

It may be instructive to view the increasingly explosive partisan atmosphere of the last decade before the Caesarian Civil War, from Caesar's first consulship to the crossing of the Rubicon, as an ancient precedent for the kind of death spiral of norm-breaking that Ziblatt and Levitsky describe. Cato's unprecedented use of the filibuster to block Caesar's praetorian triumph, capped by Bibulus's explosive, unprecedented use of *servatio* to seek to invalidate the legislative accomplishments of an entire year, were certainly norm-breaking in the narrow sense of their unprecedented exploitation of obstructive devices, but also as a clear rejection of the systemic norm of "institutional forbearance." Predictably, Caesar responded with an almost equal lack of restraint, at which point the second super-norm of "mutual toleration," itself the underlying foundation of institutional forbearance, had clearly cracked. It is clear that throughout the 50s Cato, Bibulus, Domitius, and other like-minded senators eagerly sought to right what they viewed as the "constitutional" violations of 59 by hastening a final reckoning with Caesar, who at first had seemingly slipped from their grasp to build up a nearly unassailable record of achievement in Gaul; it is equally clear that the proconsul warmly reciprocated their hatred and was more determined than ever to avoid the fate they planned for him. His extended command in Gaul (protected at first by a neutral Senate, then by a law of the Roman People) will have seemed to Caesar's enemies to be yet a further violation of institutional restraint on his part, exacerbated by the use once again of the popular assembly to secure his honorific return and a second consulship by means of the Law of the Ten Tribunes. The horrific realization dawned that

Caesar was not only about to get away with it all but even to lord it over them for a second time: what kind of precedent would that set for future consuls? And so a correspondingly gross violation of norms on their part (of respect for the law and for the People's exclusive electoral rights) must have seemed to them nothing more than what was necessary in order to "save the Republic" from one whom they had come to see as the enemy not only of themselves but also of the state and Rome itself. What was left of mutual toleration was exhausted, a state from which civil war is simply the logical next step. I have argued that Caesar and those who marched with him, and those who supported his claims overtly or quietly, will have felt much the same.

Human choices, then, made in a state of radical uncertainty and therefore frequently leading to unintended and paradoxical results, meaningfully constrained by the logic of strategic interaction and the systemic dynamics of a fundamentally divided political system, offer the best explanation for the Caesarian Civil War.[50] The view presented here is that the two sides in the Civil War did not come to blows randomly or because of some new taste for risk-taking but because both sides felt "forced" to defend themselves *and* the Republic. The Caesarian Civil War did not occur because one side sought to subvert the Republic while the other tried to defend it, but because *both* sides had reason – *good* reason, as they saw it – to contemplate the almost unthinkable in order to defend the Republic from the other. The political system ultimately had come to be locked into a "death spiral" in which civic norms like "mutual tolerance" and "institutional restraint" were eventually tossed overboard like so much superfluous baggage. Yet it did not have to be this way. Although each hostile move between the principals made a subsequent hostile counter-move more likely, still there were earlier points in the story where Caesar and his enemies could well have taken a different path without existential risk to themselves. If we unwind the spool back to the beginnings of the animosity between Cato and Caesar, the more degrees of freedom are discernable for the future course of the relationship. Had Cato not simultaneously taken up the cudgels against both Caesar and Pompey in 60–59 there is no very persuasive reason, and certainly no reliable evidence, to conclude that civil war would have been the likely outcome – in ten years,

---

[50] Not, then, a (presumably new) dispositional tendency in favor of extremely risky undertakings, as in Walter 2009: 49–51 (cf. Jehne 2009a: 152, also 2009, a brief, engaging study of Caesar's decisions). Nor was it a relatively unaccountable, random accident ("Betriebsunfall," rightly rejected by Meier 1970: 142 and Jehne 2009a: 159–160). But as suggested in the text, these are not the only two possible explanations that might be offered on the level of human decision-making.

twenty, or more. The fact that he presumably did so in order to "save the Republic" is one of the many ironies of history that pique our tragic sensibility while we contemplate this grand spectacle for posterity.

The view here taken is fully consistent with Erich Gruen's aphorism that "civil war caused the fall of the Republic, not vice versa."[51] Note that he did not write "*the* (single) Civil War of 49–45": Rome was ravaged by a cycle of intermittent civil wars that spanned nearly two decades from 49 to the Battle of Actium in 31. If Levitsky and Ziblatt are right in seeing institutional and systemic political norms as the heart and soul of the constitution, it is not difficult to see how the nearly two decades of intermittent but bloody and often savage civil wars that began in January 49 would have been quite enough to disrupt the civic practices and ravage the institutions and constitutional norms of the republican political system to the point where it became impossible to turn the clock back. If we look back over these years and earlier we note a series of "lasts" that cluster in the late 50s or the very early 40s: the last major reforming legislation (Pompey's laws of 52), the last free consular election (51 or 50, depending on whether we accept Hirtius's serious allegation: Chapter 6, n. 72), the last old-style tribunician vetoes (50–49), the last examples of good old *popularis* urban agitation (Caelius in 48, Dolabella in 47), while the last gasp of senatorial independence might be pushed down at the latest (after extended dormancy due to the Caesarian Civil War) to Cicero's rallying of that body and the consuls for the war of Mutina against Mark Antony (44–43). These represent the final noteworthy instances of republican institutional restraints exercised by the People and Senate upon the powerful magistrates and generals who transform into warlords to dominate the field of civil war. Even a decade of civil war seems to have been enough to put an end to the norms that animated and governed the key institutions of the Republic to produce the complex diffusion of power characteristic of it. The further cycle of savagery that would continue intermittently for most of a generation until Actium, together with the changed conditions that resulted, destroyed them – forever, as it would turn out. The names of the institutions remained the same, but the norms that defined the Republic had profoundly changed: "everyone had abandoned the idea of political equality and awaited the orders of a Leader."[52]

[51] Gruen 1974: 504. Chapter 1, p. 24ff.
[52] Tac. *Ann.* 1.3.7–4.1: *eadem magistratuum vocabula; iuniores post Actiacam victoriam, etiam senes plerique inter bella civium nati: quotus quisque reliquus qui rem publicam vidisset? Igitur verso civitatis statu nihil usquam prisci et integri moris: omnes exuta aequalitate iussa principis aspectare.*

Paradoxically perhaps, of all the acts perpetrated in those cruel civil wars, it may have been Caesar's assassination that at a key moment did the most to fuel the cycle of destruction that would in time tear the life out of the Republic. The killing unleashed extraordinarily powerful emotions – a lust for bloody vengeance opposed by exultation in reclaimed freedom. Through the works of Cicero we are well acquainted with the exultation. At this distance the lust for revenge is less familiar, but I think Mark Antony in Shakespeare's play catches the right tone:

> *Woe to the hand that shed this costly blood!*
> *Over thy wounds now do I prophesy*
> *(Which like dumb mouths do ope their ruby lips*
> *To beg the voice and utterance of my tongue)*
> *A curse shall light upon the limbs of men;*
> *Domestic fury and fierce civil strife*
> *Shall cumber all the parts of Italy;*
> *Blood and destruction shall be so in use,*
> *And dreadful objects so familiar,*
> *That mothers shall but smile when they behold*
> *Their infants quartered with the hands of war;*
> *All pity chok'd with custom of fell deeds;*
> *And Caesar's spirit, ranging for revenge,*
> *With Ate by his side come hot from hell,*
> *Shall in these confines with a monarch's voice*
> *Cry "Havoc!" and let slip the dogs of war,*
> *That this foul deed shall smell above the earth*
> *With carrion men, groaning for burial.*
>
> (Shakespeare, *Julius Caesar*, III.i.254–275)

Appendices

APPENDIX I

Caesar's Profits in Gaul

Appian claims that when Caesar departed for Gaul he was deeply in debt (*BCiv.* 2.13/49), but his reference to the extravagant spectacles given in his consulship (sic) suggests that this is simply a reemergence in the wrong place of a tired Caesarian theme (for which see Chapter 2).[1] At his death Caesar's private fortune was thought to amount to 100 million denarii = HS 400,000,000 (Plut. *Cic.* 43.8, *Ant.* 15.1 with Pelling 1988: 155). This is clearly an astronomical sum: the wealth of Pompey and Crassus is thought to have been "only" about half that amount each (Kay 2014: 296 and Chapter 8, n. 134). In addition (apparently) he is alleged to have had control over some HS 700,000,000 of public money in the Temple of Ops (Cic. *Phil.* 2.93a, 5.11, 12.12; cf. Vell. 2.60.4) – probably, as Jehne and Woytek have persuasively argued, the cumulative amount appropriated from unrepentant Pompeians in the Civil War (Chapter 8, n. 135). Velleius claims that *manubiae* evaluated at more than HS 600,000,000 were carried in his five triumphs (2.56.2). The sums are enormous (compare the annual tribute Caesar set for all of conquered Gaul: HS 40,000,000 [Suet. *Iul.* 25.1]), but it is unclear how much of all this came from Gaul and how much from the civil wars (the latter of which accounted for four out of the five triumphs). And of course whatever remained in his pocket in 46 or 44 had *not* been spent on cultivating political influence in Rome during the 50s.

Suetonius relates a number of shocking anecdotes (*Iul.* 54) about Caesar's lack of *abstinentia* as proconsul in Spain, as consul, and in Gaul,

---

[1] The following summary differs in some details from Woytek 2003: 15–28, the fullest survey of Caesar's financial position at the outbreak of the Civil War, including the accumulated profits from his Gallic campaigns.

the last of which claims that he plundered Gallic shrines and sacked cities more often for the sake of plunder than for their misdeeds, with the result that he became awash in gold and thus sold it in Italy and the provinces at a rate of (only) HS 3,000/lb. (perhaps one-third the normal price), presumably due to flooding of the market. Stories of the fabulous wealth in Gallic shrines just ready for the taking go back to the second century and the fabled "Tolosan Gold" (Cic. *ND* 3.74; Gell. 3.9.7; Posid. Fr. 273 E–K), yet one can reasonably wonder whether, like the rumored British gold and silver in which the Cicero brothers were so disappointed (Cic. *Fam.* 7.7.1; cf. Tac. *Agr.* 12.6 with Ogilvie and Richmond 1967: 329–333), this may have been more anticipated than real. (See, however, Haselgrove 1984 for the rapid stripping of much of what *was* there.) For what it's worth, note that Caesar's soldiers sang at his triumph in 46 that he had to *borrow* gold *in Rome* to lavish on his paramours in Gaul! (Suet. *Iul.* 51, *aurum in Gallia effutuisti, hic sumpsisti mutuum*). One would think that the depredations alleged by Suetonius in chapter 54 would have given hope of a successful extortion or peculation charge on Caesar's return to Rome, and yet none of the references to his enemies' hopes to prosecute him refer to his behavior in the wars, focusing instead, if they give any specific indication at all, on his ostensible illegal/unconstitutional actions as consul (Suet. *Iul.* 30.3 *ne eorum, quae primo consulatu adversus auspicia legesque et intercessiones gessisset, rationem reddere cogeretur*).[2] (See Appendix 2.)

Regarding the plundering (including mass enslavement) of Gallic cities, Suetonius's assertion plainly contradicts Caesar's own account in the *BGall.*, where he carefully justifies such action either implicitly (as when the systematic sacking of the Atuatuci [2.29–33] is clearly presented as retaliation for abuse of his *clementia* and "mildness" [2.14.5, 31.4]; cf. also 7.11 [Cenabum] with 7.1–3; 6.3.2, 6.6.1 [Nervii and Menapii]) or explicitly (the massacre at Avaricum is explicitly motivated by revenge [7.28.4] – the soldiers', however, not Caesar's own). Given the hostile nature of this charge of violating even the relaxed norms of Roman warfare we must wonder whether it derives from the invective tradition developed by Caesar's enemies, as does so much of what Suetonius preserves in his biography (e.g. *Iul.* 49). The Roman invective tradition included standard *topoi* of debt, avarice, and extravagance (Craig 2004), so caution is clearly in order. As for the "infection" of Suetonius's biography by such stories (which are taken much too seriously by

---

[2] The peculation charge was rare in the Late Republic, but the disaster that befell M. Cotta (cos. 74) may well have exercised a deterrent effect: Rosenstein 2011: 152.

Badian 1968: 89 – "the greatest brigand of them all" – and even Gelzer 1968, 168), consider Suetonius's bland assertion (54.3) that in his consulship Caesar stole 3,000 lb. of gold from the Capitol, replacing it with gilded bronze (see Cary and Butler 1924: 113). This is hardly credible, and if Pliny *HN* 33.14 is a reference to the same scandal, Caesar stands acquitted, since he dates it to 52. Compare also the dubious story Suetonius relates (on the authority of *multi*) about Caesar's extravagant building and immediate destruction of a fine Alban villa at §46 (Chapter 2, n. 81), apparently attested by the same sober critics who charged Caesar with invading Britain for its pearls – this latter perhaps an amusing riff on Caesar's dedication in his temple of Venus Genetrix of a marvelous breastplate of British pearls (Plin. *HN* 9.116), or the story of his extravagant gift to his mistress Servilia of a single pearl valued at 6 million sesterces (Suet. *Iul.* 50.2, apparently dated, however, to 59).

It does seem that Caesar and his soldiers were awash in *slaves*: fifty-three thousand men, women, and children of the Atuatuci were sold off on the spot to slave dealers in 57 (*BGall.* 2.33.7). Yet these kinds of mass sales can only have drastically depressed prices: compare the small price Cicero received for his captives at Pindenissum (*Att.* 5.20.5: only HS 120,000, unless we resort to emendation [contra, Shackleton Bailey 1965: 228-229.]) or the drop in the price of a male slave to four drachmae during Lucullus's march through Galatia (Plut. *Luc.* 14.1; Rosenstein 2011: 142–148). This probably explains why after Alesia Caesar opted to distribute one slave each to his soldiers instead of cash prizes (*BGall.* 7.89.5). Suet. *Iul.* 28.1 mentions "thousands of captives" given, evidently as slaves, to "kings and provinces throughout the world"; however, there is nothing to say that this preceded the Civil War, if indeed it be true (Butler and Cary 1927: 79). Slaves may have been the biggest source of the funds Caesar realized in Gaul, just as they were in Britain (Cic. *Att.* 4.16.7; Caes. *BGall.* 5.23.2; Goudineau 1990: 311–313). Caesar claimed to have captured about 1 million persons (Plut. *Caes.* 15.5, App. *Celt.* 1.2; cf. however Vell. 2.47.1 and Pelling 2011: 210–212), many of whom will have been sold as slaves. (But not all – some *captivi* were returned to their people for "diplomatic" reasons: *BGall.* 7.90.3.) If so, note that of the mass enslavements listed in the previous paragraph, all but one date to the later years of campaigning.

In the early years of Caesar's campaigning in Gaul he appears to have been forced to "pay" his troops out of plunder: that at least appears to be the necessary inference from the fact that the Senate refused to cough up the funds to pay his legions' *stipendium* for the first two years of campaigning (Chapter 5, p. 220ff.; the bill may have amounted to as much as

36 million sesterces: ibid., n. 122). This may have left little remainder to put to political use in Rome in the early years. However, by 54 Catullus 29 attests well enough to the poet's perception that enormous wealth was now flowing from Gaul and Britain into the pockets of Caesar and thence to his favorites. (See Badian 1977; Thomson 1997: 281; cf. Cic. *Att.* 7.7.6, explicitly mentioning Mamurra as well as Labienus and Balbus. The date of the poem [pace Thomson] is probably late 55 or early 54, in view of *socer generque* [line 24] and Julia's death in summer 54; note that the last datable reference in the entire corpus is Calvus's prosecution of Vatinius in August 54 [Wiseman 1985: 188].) Although we know from the Cicero brothers' disappointment in the poverty of Britain that such ideas did not always correspond with reality, the large loan given to M. Cicero and the huge sum of money already invested in the monuments planned in the Forum and Campus roughly coincide about 54 (Chapter 5, p. 246ff.; Cicero values the initial purchase in the Forum at 60 million sesterces [Chapter 5, n. 229], and note that Caesar's financing of Paullus's only somewhat less extravagant building in the Forum [36 million sesterces, Plut. *Caes.* 29.3 with Pelling 2011: 297–298] was approximately simultaneous [Cic. *Att.* 4.16.8]; see below). This suggests that it was after the famous successes of 55 that the riches from Gaul really started pouring in. A further impulse was probably later given by the crushing of the Alesia revolt, soon followed by the large loan/gift made to C. Curio.

These large expenditures may in turn have come at the cost of keeping up his obligations to his soldiers, or at least of meeting their expectations.[3] Although Caesar gave a large cash handout to the army in 50 BC (Hirt. [Caes.] *BGall.* 8.4.1), presumably realized from the sale of booty, including slaves, and he was careful to reward handsomely the two legions the Senate recalled from his control in that same year (HS 1,000 each, probably more than double their annual pay: App. *BCiv.* 2.29/115 and Plut. *Caes.* 29.4 with Pelling's note), his difficulty paying his troops in the Civil War is notorious and this certainly was an important factor in the legionary mutinies of 49 and 47 (App. *BCiv.* 2.47/191, 92/387; Dio 41.26.1, 42.52.1; Chrissanthos 2001: 68, 70; Woytek 2003: 46, 171–173) despite his having extracted a huge sum from the treasury ostensibly precisely for this purpose during his brief visit to Rome in April 49 (Chapter 7, p. 408). Wild stories were told of the promises he had made to his men when he led his men into Italy (the wealth of an equestrian for all – rejected even by Suet., *Iul.* 33).

---

[3] Cf. contra, however, Woytek 2003: 38–41.

Another source of funds for Caesar in the 50s *may* have been the bribe/ gift, allegedly amounting to 6,000 talents (~ HS 144,000,000), pledged by King Ptolemy Auletes of Egypt to both Caesar and Pompey (presumably equally) in return for confirming his right to the Egyptian throne (Suet. *Iul.* 54.3, perhaps alluded to at Cic. *Rab. Post.* 4, with Siani-Davies 2001: 120; cf. Dio 39.12.1). This came, however, not in cold, hard cash but in the form of an IOU, on which Caesar claimed upon his arrival in Egypt in 48 that 17,500,000 drachmas (~ HS 70,000,000) were still owed (Plut. *Caes.* 48.8), though he had remitted all but 10,000,000 drachmas (~ HS 40,000,000). Since the HS 70,000,000 balance apparently still outstanding in 48 constitutes only a little less than Caesar's (maximal) original share of the loan, it looks as though little of the principal had actually been repaid in the interim and perhaps not much, if any, of the interest either. This would be consistent with Ptolemy's straitened finances after his expulsion from Egypt in 58, requiring further borrowing to finance the royal establishment in exile as well as to bribe influential people and assassins (Cic. *Prov. cons.* 4–6; Dio 39.12–13), and ultimately the necessity to contract a much bigger loan (allegedly 10,000 talents) in order to secure Gabinius's (and Pompey's) help in his restoration by force. (For a concise summary of the most relevant evidence see Pelling 2011: 384; for details of Ptolemy's complicated financial arrangements and the involvement of Roman financier C. Rabirius Postumus see Siani-Davies 2001: 8–38 and her commentary. See also Alexander 2002: 110–118; Morrell 2017: 174–176; and for a good summary of Ptolemy's vicissitudes see Hekster 2012: 193–199, with some confusion, however, between M. and C. Cato).

Suet *Iul.* 27.1 claims that at some point shortly before the Civil War most of the Senate had become indebted to Caesar with interest-free or cut-rate loans; this is doubtless exaggerated, yet it prompts the idea that such loans as those to Cicero, which in a cash-strapped economy like Rome's tended to be paid back slowly if at all, may be the basis for the allegations of large-scale "bribes" about which we hear late in the decade, notably of C. Curio (tr. 50) and L. Aemilius Paullus (cos. 50: brother of the future triumvir): esp. Plut. *Caes.* 29.3; Dio 40.60.3; App. *BCiv.* 2.26/101; Val. Max. 9.1.6, with Shatzman 1975: 127–128, 289, 396–397, and Pelling 2011: 296–297; more skeptically, Gruen 1974: 475n91. (See also Chapter 6, nn. 55, 70.) Lacey 1961: 318–319 is right to be concerned about the carelessness with which such allegations could be tossed about and the lack of good contemporary testimony; Velleius's *non liquet* regarding Curio (2.48.4) is in itself notable, especially given his inclination to blame him for provoking the Civil War (Chapter 6, n. 178). But if instead of an outright gift, Caesar gave loans like that tendered to Cicero, perhaps interest-free and evidently quite indefinite as to payoff date, this could easily have given rise to such allegations. Paullus's loan/"bribe," though our sources bring it into relation to his consulship in 50, probably goes back to 54, since his public buildings in the Forum, mentioned by Cic. *Att.* 4.16.8 in mid-54, were supposed to have been financed with T1,500 = HS 36 million of Caesar's money (Plut. *Caes.* 29.3 and see above).

The "Prosecution Theory" Revisited

This appendix supplements the argument presented in Morstein-Marx 2007.

1. As noted in the main text, none of our sources remark on the significance of the electoral privilege granted in 52 by the Law of the Ten Tribunes to any alleged plan to try Caesar during his window of vulnerability. (Girardet 2017: 49 notes this but is untroubled.) We know that Cato objected vociferously to the proposed law in the Senate (Caes. *BCiv.* 1.32.3) but we do not know on precisely what grounds; if Plut. *Pomp.* 56.3 belongs in this context (the law is not mentioned) then Cato's objection was that Caesar should not be able to receive any benefit from the citizens (the consulship) before he had become a private citizen and given up his army (ἰδιώτην γενόμενον καὶ τὰ ὅπλα καταθέμονον εὑρίσκεσθαί τι παρὰ τῶν πολιτῶν ἀγαθόν). This may look like an allusion to the strategy hypothesized in the "prosecution theory," but no trial is mentioned and it is most obviously explicable as a warning against possible electoral intimidation by Caesar (that is, by on holding on to his army and province as a kind of insurance policy for his election, as in fact was eventually to occur). This clearly was an aggravating factor in the development of the crisis in that year, and there is no reason Caesar's bitterest enemies could not have anticipated this possibility already in 52. But if it had been their long-standing plan to bring him to trial upon his return from Gaul our sources should have *something* to say about the decisive foiling of this expectation by means of the Law of the Ten Tribunes already in 52, nor does it seem possible that the law would have been backed by a powerful show of consensus including not only Pompey and the entire college of tribunes but also M. Caelius (also tribune in this year) and Cicero, neither of whom was in Caesar's pocket.

2. So long as Caesar's electoral privilege under the Law of the Ten Tribunes was still respected, as a practical matter it was impossible to bring him to trial either before his seemingly inevitable election to a second consulship or after it (see #4) when, among other reasons, he was likely to remain outside the City preparing for a triumphal entry until the last possible moment – perhaps on the last day of the year before he would enter office. Therefore when our best sources, Caelius and Cicero, ponder in 50 the steps likely to be taken by Caesar's adversaries, the *only* strategy they consider is not a trial, but the denial of Caesar's candidacy in absentia if he did not first leave his army and provinces to which, arguably, he would no longer have a legitimate claim. (Cael. [Cic.] *Fam.* 8.11.3, 14.2; Cic. *Att.* 7.1.4, 7.7.6, 7.9.2 and 4 "*Habe meam rationem.*") The absence from Cicero's exhaustive consideration of the options at *Att.* 7.9.2–4 (cf. 7.4.3) of any consideration of some sort of prosecution strategy that could interrupt Caesar's march to a second consulship sufficiently proves that this was simply not a realistic possibility (and indeed no source actually articulates any causal connection between that goal and a trial). True, if Caesar's election could somehow be averted, his enemies might dream of follow-up moves against him (but see ## 3, 4). But their dominant and primary objective in 50 was to stop Caesar's anticipated second consulship – that was their greatest fear (Cic. *Att.* 7.8.5, 7.9.3). Thus the "prosecution theory" is a fifth wheel, superfluous for an explanation of the coming of the Civil War in 52–49.

3. Suet. *Iul.* 30.3–4 states that M. Cato often declared under oath that he would prosecute Caesar as soon as he dismissed his army, and that his officer and later historian Asinius Pollio quoted Caesar as declaring on the battlefield at Pharsalus that his enemies would have condemned him in the courts if he had not appealed to his army (cf. *FRHist* 56 F3 with Drummond's comments). It is important to note that neither of these statements (assuming they are true) actually attests to or implies a realistic plan to deprive Caesar of a consulship by means of a prosecution. At most, they are evidence for what Cato and Caesar's other enemies *would have liked to do* if they got the chance (Morstein-Marx 2007: 162–164). Cato's threats were hardly constrained by political reality (for a recent instance see Chapter 5, p. 237f.), and we do not even know whether they were made before or after Caesar declared his intention to seek a second consulship. Of course, if Cato ever did say any such thing, no matter how unrealistic the threat it would have

given Caesar all he needed to justify the words that Pollio puts in his mouth at Pharsalus.

4. Suet. *Iul.* 30.3 alone is at all specific about what charges might have been brought against Caesar: he is *said by some* to have feared (note the vagueness of this assertion) that he might be compelled to stand trial for "what he had done in his first consulship contrary to the auspices, the laws, and vetoes" (*alii timuisse dicunt, ne eorum, quae primo consulatu adversus auspicia legesque et intercessiones gessisset, rationem reddere cogeretur*). In view of his enemies' persistent failure to get his acts and laws overturned even by the Senate (twice) and their retreat to ineffective sniping through the 50s, the idea that he would be indicted much less convicted in a *maiestas* court for these lacks any foundation in precedent and seems to be nothing more than a pipe dream. (Pompey could hardly have approved!) In fact the most promising charge on the merits in 50–49 might have been extortion or peculation in Gaul (Appendix 1), yet this potential line of attack is not so much as mentioned by Suetonius, who, cursory as his comments are, remains our most informative source about this matter. (App. *BCiv.* 2.23/87–88 [cf. 25/96] reports the suspicions of Caesar's friends that Pompey's retroactive law on *ambitus* may have been intended to ensnare him, but if so they were surely overreacting: even Cato objected to the retroactive clause [Plut. *Cat. Min.* 48.5–6], and no one was in fact prosecuted under this law for acts before 54 [Gruen 1974: 106].) The only mechanism for preventing a consul-elect from taking up office appears to have been conviction on an *ambitus* charge pertaining to that very election (as in 66: Morstein-Marx 2007: 165n26); but Caesar will not have had to rely on illegal methods to win a fair election, *tantis rebus gestis*. It must be underscored that there is no known precedent for the kind of election-defying chicanery envisioned by the theory.

Some Important Dates in the Crisis Year 50 BC

The effort to understand the complex moves of the year 50 is bedeviled by an obscure chronology that depends on various undated letters in the Ciceronian correspondence whose chronology is quite debatable. The letters Caelius wrote in this year to Cicero, then on provincial duty in the east, are by far our most vivid and rich source for reconstructing events in Rome down to the time of Cicero's approach to the City in December (when the letters to Atticus pick up and become more informative), but none of these are explicitly dated or even inferentially datable with much precision. On the other hand, the late narratives by Appian, Plutarch, and Dio provide much important information but very few chronological pegs on which to hang their stories. Further, modern accounts have shied away from reexamining most of the inferences made in the nineteenth and early twentieth centuries, which, once adopted as fact and used in turn to estimate dates for the letters themselves, threaten to ensnare the modern researcher in a *petitio principii*. This appendix is intended to warn of this danger and to show that unfortunately we must allow for greater chronological imprecision in reconstructing the narrative of 50 than many scholars acknowledge. Finally, of course (though this is the least of our worries), because of the pontifices' disinclination to give Curio (and Caesar) an extra month to work with, the Roman civil calendar was now well out of alignment with the solar year: by New Year's Day of 49 (civil) the misalignment amounted to more than six weeks (~ ca. November 13, 50, Jul.). (All ancient dates given in this appendix follow the civil calendar unless otherwise specified.)

A recurring problem is that, at least since Nissen (1881), scholars have tended to regard it as a fixed axiom that (1) the consuls "held the *fasces*" in monthly alternation, (2) that the consul listed first in the *fasti* "held' the *fasces*" in all odd months, along with its corollary that the consul listed second "held" them on even months, and (3) that only the consul "holding the *fasces*" in a particular month could preside over the Senate, make a formal *relatio*, or indeed play a major role in a meeting in that month. In view of Vervaet's recent painstaking examination of the question (2014), #1 seems secure, but it is less clear what exactly this meant;[1] #2 is less so (since the privilege could be transferred to a more senior consul) while #3 is quite fallible and subject to circumstance (Vervaet 2014: 40–41; cf. Drummond 1978; Pina Polo 2011: 192–207, 288), and thus appears to be at most a matter of custom rather than strict legality. In fact, our own narrative reveals the weakness of #3, for although L. Lentulus Crus is listed second in the consular *fasti* for 49 and thus should have "held the *fasces*" in the even months, we find that in Caesar's narrative of the senatorial meetings at the beginning of the year *both* consuls are said to have referred the question to the body (*BCiv.* 1.1.2 *referunt consules de re publica infinite*) and indeed that it is Lentulus who plays the starring role (1.1.2–3, 1.2.4–6, 1.4.2, 1.14.1) while his colleague plays a very quiet second fiddle (1.6.4. 1.14.2). Another anomaly arises in the year 50: according to #1 and #2, the presiding consul in March, the month when debate on Caesar's provinces had been scheduled to resume, should have been the relatively friendly L. Paullus, and yet Appian, our single source for the resumption of the debate, gives C. Marcellus the chief role at that moment, advocating a motion hostile to Caesar while Paullus merely "was silent" (App. *BCiv.* 2.27/103–104). Appearances have been saved in the past by the simple but dubious hypothesis that in fact debate did not resume in March but only in April, when Marcellus should again have "held the *fasces*."[2] But surely this is special pleading; a letter of Cicero's makes clear that Curio had already begun his persistent veto threat by March 7 (*Att.* 6.2.6). Moving back earlier to that tumultuous year 59, Caesar presided over the tribal assembly that passed the first agrarian law yet when Bibulus tried to stop the proceedings he was attended by *fasces* (which were then broken: Chapter 4, n. 82), and the next day he summoned and apparently presided over a meeting of the Senate. Strictly speaking we do not know *who* "held the *fasces*" in the formal sense at this time, but if it was Bibulus, then the non-holding consul was evidently able to conduct business with the popular

---

[1] "It should not be doubted that every other month … one consul was preceded by twelve lictors carrying the *fasces*, while his colleague was followed by twelve lictors without *fasces*" (Vervaet 2014: 30–33 at 31). This is a reasonable interpretation of the somewhat contradictory evidence, but note that if *fasces habere* is a technical term indicating (temporary) priority (#3), signaled symbolically chiefly by being *preceded* by the lictors with their *fasces* (cf. Cic. *Rep.* 2.55), then Suet. *Iul.* 20.1 may not after all attest to the paradoxical spectacle of a consul attended by *fasces*-less lictors, whose chief purpose was after all to carry (and if necessary to use) the *fasces*.
[2] The hypothesis, found already in Nissen 1881: 66, is never to my knowledge explicitly challenged, and uncritically accepted by Shackleton Bailey 1977: 1:419.

assembly, while if it was Caesar, then the non-holding consul was competent to summon and preside over a meeting of the Senate. These circumstances therefore do not suffice to show whether this incident occurred in January or February (or even April).[3] We should therefore recognize that exceptions to #3 are not uncommon – that is, that even the consul who did not "hold the *fasces*" could at least intervene significantly in senatorial meetings by making a *relatio* (perhaps together with his colleague) or by offering a motion and otherwise participating quite vigorously in the debate, and that he was probably not strictly barred even from presenting legislation to the assembly.

If, then, we relinquish premise #3, the dates for a number of events in 50, along with Shackleton Bailey's dates of some of the very letters that serve as our chief chronological markers, must be spread over a slightly wider interval than is usually assigned them. So, for instance:

(a) The failed motion in the Senate that pressure should be put on the tribunes to yield their veto is described in Cael. [Cic.] *Fam.* 8.13.2 (cf. *Att.* 7.7.5). The letter manifestly belongs sometime in the summer of 50, but Shackleton Bailey dates it to June (probably the Kalends) on the assumption that C. Marcellus presided over the session as consul, hence supposedly in an even month (1965: 1.424). In view of our earlier discussion this holds little water. Cicero replied to this letter (as well as two earlier ones probably written in April) from Side in Pamphylia on August 3 or 4 (*Fam.* 2.15); thus a date in May cannot be excluded.

(b) Cael. [Cic.]*Fam.* 8.14 presupposes completion of the consular elections (cf. Hirt. [Caes.] *BGall.* 8.50.1–4), and Shackleton Bailey lays out the case for dating the letter shortly before August 12 (1977: 1:429). Cicero learned the results of the various elections by September 29 (*Att.* 6.8.2, at Ephesus); since the news should have taken around a month to reach him (cf. Cic. *Att.* 6.9.1: twenty-five days from Rome to Athens) the date of the consular elections should be not very much earlier than the latest possible date of August 12. However, late July cannot be excluded with certainty (Raaflaub and Ramsey 2017: 69 with n. 204), at least not on the grounds that C. Marcellus would have "held the *fasces*" in the even-numbered months (Girardet 2000:

---

[3] Chapter 4, n. 73. Cf. Vervaet 2014: 40–41 who, building on the work of Drummond 1978 and Ferrary 1996, denies that *only* the *consul maior* (= "holding the *fasces*") could preside over a voting assembly, contra Taylor and Broughton 1949: 12n22.

705, 2017: 118). Since the election only provides a *terminus post quem*, however, *Fam.* 8.14 still may be dated "early August" with little chance of error as long as the range of uncertainty is recognized.

(c)   Modern scholars universally adopt December 1–2 as the date of the senatorial meetings that led to the "Schwertübergabe," for the most part without supporting arguments, for which one is generally referred to Bardt 1910: 339 (himself dependent on Nissen 1881: 71–72 with notes; summary in Ottmer 1979: 63n243); but note also Sanford 1911: 318–319; Rice Holmes 1923: 2:324–326, and esp. now Raaflaub and Ramsey 2017: 70–71. Unfortunately upon examination the evidence turns out to be thin, suggesting a somewhat broader range of possible dates between late November and very early December. Caesar's intermediary Hirtius arrived in Rome on December 6 but failed to meet with Pompey or Metellus Scipio that night as expected, which Pompey took as a very hostile sign (Cic. *Att.* 7.4.2). While it is widely agreed that Hirtius's rebuff was a response to the troubling new developments in the Senate connected with the "Schwertübergabe," we do not actually know whether he had been sent by Caesar (then in Cisalpine Gaul) only *after* Caesar had learned of the transfer of military command to Pompey, or already before he had learned of it (in which case Hirtius's response would be an improvisation based on information he received en route or when he arrived in Rome). If the former, the necessary travel time pushes the meetings that resulted in the "Schwertübergabe" back into November, possibly as early as November 25 (Sanford). (Note that some indeterminate but short period of time intervened between the famous vote and the "Schwertübergabe" [App. *BCiv.* 2.30–31/119–120], and that Caesar's return to Cisalpine Gaul in November may have prompted the rumor of his march on the City [Raaflaub and Ramsey 2017: 70].) But if the latter, as is thought to suit Pompey's complaint of an abrupt change of plans (now Raaflaub and Ramsey), then the meetings could have occurred any time between December 1 and the 6th itself. Raaflaub and Ramsey believe that Caesar must have been prompted to summon the 8th and 12th Legions into Cisalpine Gaul already by this news, and since they think that moment can be independently dated to December 7–8, by subtracting a travel time of "just over four days" for a messenger to travel from Rome to Ravenna we reach about December 2 for the "Schwertübergabe." Yet, as noted in Appendix 5, we do not actually know when those legions were ordered into Cisalpine Gaul (Caesar himself seems to put the summons only about January 11, but the more likely scenario is that the legions had been brought into the province already sometime in the fall), nor in fact is there any need to assume that only the "Schwertübergabe" could have motivated Caesar to bring up the legions, so the argument, while not to be ruled out, is hardly cogent. Rice Holmes's objection (following Nissen and Bardt) to any date in November (Rice Holmes 1923: 2:326n9) on the grounds that Marcellus held the *fasces* in the even months is, as we have seen, insecure; nor do we know for certain whether the meeting was summoned by one of the consuls or by Curio. While December 1 remains a plausible midpoint in the range of dates open for the "Schwertübergabe" itself (the series of senatorial votes must have preceded it by at least a few days), when precision is desired we should allow a range of perhaps as much as ten days between November 25 and December 6 (~ ca. October 10–20, Jul.), certainly before Pompey left the environs of the City for Campania on December 7 or 8 to check in on the legions (Cic. *Att.* 7.4.2).

Three other important events of 50 that are frequently dated by inference, and though not dependent on the premises questioned earlier still deserve brief consideration, are:

(d) The date of the senatorial decree which ordered Caesar and Pompey each to contribute a legion for the Parthian War depends on calculations from references to the imminence of the Parthian threat at Cic. *Att.* 6.1.14 (February 20 ~ ca. January 12, Jul., from Laodicea in Cilicia), its subsidence around the beginning of July (*Att.* 6.5.3 with *Fam.* 2.17.5), and Cicero's awareness of the decree demonstrated in the last letter, written at Tarsus in Cilicia. If some fifty days were needed for the news to reach Cicero at Tarsus, the *latest* likely date for the decree is roughly mid-May (~ early April, Jul.: Raaflaub and Ramsey 2017: 65–66; cf. Shackleton Bailey 1977: 1:460; Rice Holmes 1923 2:323). If that is correct, this *terminus ante quem* can in turn probably be moved back to about April 15 (~ early March, Jul.) in view of the senatorial spring recess, which appears to have regularly taken place between mid-April and mid-May (Sanford 1911: 329 and Stein 1930: 59, 103 with 110–111 [cf. Stevens 1938: 199n128]). Since given the bad season for road and especially sea travel Cicero's alarming missive sent from Cilician Laodicea on February 20 probably took *at least* a month to reach Rome, it is reasonable to place the decree, with Sanford and Stein, in the first half of April. (Raaflaub and Ramsey opt for ca. April 15.)

The legions would have been well spaced out: the 15th had been posted in Cisalpine Gaul whereas the 1st seems to have been no nearer than the land of the Aedui in central Transalpina (Chapter 6, n. 100). Even the 1st must have arrived in central Italy in the summer given that it doubtless made haste. Sanford 1911: 328–332 thought both reached the environs of Rome by late July, but it is uncertain whether they actually marched through Rome or down the "back" of Italy, the quickest route to Brundisium. Raaflaub and Ramsey estimate that the legions could have been projected to arrive at Brundisium around July 30 (Raaflaub and Ramsey 2017: 66n191: predicated on ca. April 15 as the date of the decree); there is no evidence, however, that they had actually reached their embarkation point before the threat dissipated. Note that Caelius in Rome ca. August 12 ([Cic.] *Fam.* 8.14.4) treats a Parthian campaign as still possibly in the cards, suggesting that the decision to keep the legions in Italy had not yet definitively been taken by that time even though news of the Parthian withdrawal must have (just) reached Rome.

(e) Curio's proposal for mutual disarmament is first mentioned in the contemporary sources by Caelius at [Cic.] *Fam.* 8.14.2 (late July/early August). Since it goes unmentioned in Caelius's earlier surviving letters, which contain references to Curio's Caesarian intervention but entirely in the character of a persistent veto (8.11.3, 8.13.2: Section [a] of this Appendix), it is tempting to date the proposal relatively late – perhaps late June or July – more or less just before the elections, when the move makes good sense as an attempt to deflect pressure from Caesar onto Pompey, potentially either to lay the diplomatic groundwork for Caesar's refusal to compete in the election despite expectations or even (though probably much less likely) to prompt a breakthrough by which Caesar could actually accept Pompey's condition of prior disarmament. Appian seems to imply that Curio made the offer as soon as the debate on Caesar's provinces was opened, thus as early as March 1 (so Raaflaub 1974: 28 with 1974a: 302–306), yet this is hardly a necessary inference. It helps little that Appian (*BCiv.* 2.27–28) (quite reasonably) places the original proposal before Pompey's dangerous illness since the beginning and duration of this illness are even less clearly datable.

(f) Pompey's illness (or at least its most serious phase) was dated by Shackleton Bailey around the time of Cael. [Cic.] *Fam.* 8.13.2, viz. June by his reckoning, though May can hardly be excluded ([a] above). Yet Caelius's reference to Pompey's *stomacho ... languenti* is set in a purely political context and so may (as *stomacho* often does) refer only to emotional/political dismay rather than his "actual state of health" (so Shackleton Bailey). Cicero's concerns about Pompey's health expressed as early as *Att.* 6.3.4 (written between May 7 and June 5 en route to Tarsus) might point to some report dated as early as April, yet it is so vaguely expressed that it may refer to some long prelude to the disease or even to another illness altogether. In the current state of the evidence the period during which Pompey's illness raged must be regarded as quite indefinite within the broad range of late spring through summer.

(g) According to Raaflaub and Ramsey's calculations (2017: 67–68), as late as mid-July 50 (~ June 3–4, Jul.) Caesar was still at Nemetocenna (= Arras) among the Belgae, where he had spent the winter. But this is not stated in the text – in fact on the contrary the natural reading of the text is that he was in haste to reach Cisalpine Gaul as soon as winter was over (Hirtius [Caes.] *BGall.* 8.50.1 *ipse hibernis peractis contra consuetudinem in Italiam quam maximis itineribus est profectus*). Even if June (Jul.) would be in line with the usual opening of the military campaigning season, the normal seasonal patterns of major military movements did not constrain Caesar's own personal travel to and from Cisalpina. In view of the looming political crisis and various important elections upcoming in July and August for which his presence in Cisalpina well before-hand would have been helpful since voters had quite a distance to travel (see Hirt. [Caes.] *BGall.* 8.50.1–4, 52.2 for some electioneering efforts in Cisalpina, though he conspicuously leaves out any effort on behalf of Antony's essential run for the tribunate), it is hard to credit the idea that Caesar himself would not even have begun returning from the far extremity of Gaul until June (Jul.), a trip that would have taken more than two weeks at a high rate of speed (Raaflaub and Ramsey 2017: 68n203).

(h) Finally, there is a conflict between Plutarch and Appian on the timing of Caesar's dramatic concessions shortly before the passage of the *s.c. u.* In two separate places, and with mutually and internally consistent circumstantial detail, Plutarch dates the initiative to early January, between January 1 and the passage of the *s.c.u.* on January 7 (*Caes.*

31.1–2, *Pomp.* 59.5–6); App., *BCiv.* 2.32/125–127, however, places it just *before* the meeting of January 1.[4] One major objection to Plutarch is based on the impossibility of making a round trip to Ravenna in time (Rice Holmes), but Plutarch and App. both make clear that "Caesar's friends" were empowered to negotiate on his behalf (Plut. *Pomp.* 59.6, *Caes.* 31.2; App. *BCiv.* 2.32/126), thus obviating the need to refer back to Caesar for further instructions at such a critical juncture. Plutarch provides the detail that Cicero was directly engaged in the negotiation; since he did not arrive at the outskirts of the City until January 4 (*Fam.* 16.11.2), at least the second stage of the discussion should not have taken place before then. (Girardet 2017: 309 places the entire negotiation on January 4.) Plutarch also in both references explicitly names the consul Lentulus, whereas Appian refers vaguely to "the consuls" who would in his view have been the consuls of 50, hardly any longer relevant. Finally, such an extraordinary concession by Caesar only makes sense as a last-ditch effort to ward off the *s.c.u.*; if offered *before* the letter delivered to the Senate on January 1 or even at the same time (Pelling), it would have seriously undermined Caesar's public negotiating position. I am inclined to think that Appian inserted the account of Caesar's concession he found elsewhere *just before* his description of Caesar's somewhat threatening letter to the Senate delivered on January 1 because this ordering fits best his claim, made immediately before, that Caesar chose not to follow Curio's advice and initiate hostilities but to make a final try at a settlement (*BCiv.* 2.32/125).

---

[4] Raaflaub 1974a: 312–321 (cf. 1974: 66–67) supports Plutarch's chronology (so too Pelling 2011: 306–307: January 1); Gruen 1974: 488n133, following Rice Holmes 1923: 2:331–333, prefers Appian.

The Civil War Crisis as a Prisoner's Dilemma

It always sounds a bit dubious when a historian claims that a war broke out that nobody wanted. Surely these things do not come about by sheer accident, and often both sides appear to have been playing with fire with a lot of kindling lying about. *Of course* even the most belligerent bullies (e.g. Adolf Hitler at Munich in 1938) prefer to win by posturing without having to pay the price of real armed conflict. One party's calculation that the other would "see reason" rather than fight, therefore, hardly proves that its intentions were peaceful. Yet the most elementary conundrum of game theory, the Prisoner's Dilemma, shows how, merely as a product of competitive strategic interaction, two parties hopeful for the peaceful resolution of a confrontation, but willing to chance a fight rather than capitulate, may well end up fighting a war that neither wanted.[1]

The fundamental problem can be illustrated by means of the matrix shown on the following page. Red Country's options are given in the rows: to negotiate cooperatively or to order an attack. Blue Country's options are presented in the columns: again, it can negotiate cooperatively or launch an attack. The convergence of each country's options on a given quadrant results in an outcome that is given in numerical form, the higher the better, with Red Country's outcome given first. Now, for each country, the biggest prize (five points in this example) comes from attacking the unsuspecting rival who is still pinning his hopes on negotiation; second best (three points) is peaceful coexistence; third best (and second worst at only two points) is the costly outcome of war; worst of all, however, is to be

---

[1] A good, readable, and philosophically informed introduction to the Prisoner's Dilemma and elementary game theory in general is Hargreaves Heap and Varoufakis 1995. An up-to-date exploration of the Prisoner's Dilemma by a variety of authors with diverse points of view about its application is Peterson 2015. Axelrod 1984 remains an eye-opening exploration of the implications of the Iterated Prisoner's Dilemma for social interaction and norms, while Ridley 1996 provides a fascinating "popular" review of the use of the game to account for the diversity of cooperation across many species.

fooled into thinking the other is negotiating in good faith while the tanks
are actually rolling over the border (zero points).

	Blue: negotiate	Blue: attack
Red: negotiate	3,3 (peace)	0,5 (Blue attacks while Red is negotiating)
Red: attack	5,0 (Red attacks while Blue is negotiating)	2,2 (war)

The "dilemma" of the game's name (it need have nothing to do with
prisoners) is that strategic rationality requires *both* Red and Blue in this
game to choose "attack," even though this results in an outcome that is
(1) the *second-worst for each* of them individually out of the four possible
outcomes, and above all (2) *worse for each of them* than peace, and
therefore finally (3) worse than peace also *for the pair of them collectively.*
Why? Because *each country* must rationally fear that if they choose to
negotiate they will be "suckered" by an unscrupulous opponent lunging
for the big win, and thus end up with the worst result of all. Each must
choose what is individually preferable no matter what the adversary
chooses: if Blue negotiates, Red will gain more by attacking; if Blue
attacks, Red will also gain more by attacking than negotiating. The same
goes for Blue.

The Prisoner's Dilemma has given rise to an enormous literature,
swelled considerably by those who object to using the sacred word
"rationality" to force our assent to an outcome so obviously "irrational"
from a larger perspective. It is important to note that the dilemma does
not pretend to describe real human behavior (except, perhaps, for econo-
mists!). It describes an abstract relationship of interactive choices, which
however can be identified as an underlying structure in an enormous
variety of human and even animal scenarios where the participants may
opt for cooperation, at some potential risk to themselves, or competition/
aggression. In fact, however, human beings are probably genetically
predisposed to cooperate with kin and socialized (or morally accultur-
ated) to cooperate to varying degrees even with larger, more anonymous
groups – the village, the tribe, the nation, sometimes even "the human
race."[2] So of course, if there is some prior foundation for a cooperative

---

[2] See Ridley 1996. As Ridley and others have suggested, the emergence of emotions may have provided
an evolutionary advantage to humans by "solving" the Prisoner's Dilemmas that pervade our social
life.

relationship between the two players in a Prisoner's Dilemma, the outcome need not follow the tragic pathology illustrated by the paradigm
case.[3] The great value of the Prisoner's Dilemma (I suggest) is that as an
abstract model it recognizes that, in a very common kind of interaction
between participants who are free to choose either cooperation or noncooperation, cooperation cannot be simply presumed as a given but is
a *problem* (intellectually) that needs some explanation. The explanation
for cooperation must come from factors *external to the game* that encourage or discourage cooperation in specific environments: sometimes these
are relatively fixed determinants such as kinship relation or societal
norms, but they can also be constituted by contingent factors such as
a past and known history of reliable cooperation or anything that similarly
encourages the parties reasonably to expect cooperation rather than
adversarial competition in the future.[4] The reverse, on the other hand –
a history of noncooperation, or good reason to believe that cooperation
will cease – will clearly intensify or exaggerate the incentive to "defect" –
that is, to make an exploitative or aggressive move instead of
a cooperative one.

Returning to our historical problem, it is possible to interpret the
strategic "game" between Pompey and Caesar as a Prisoner's Dilemma of
the following form:

	Pompey: *allow Caesar's election to second consulship* ("Cooperate")	Pompey: *block Caesar's election to second consulship* ("Defect")
Caesar: *give up provinces and army* ("Cooperate")	Peace: Caesar elected consul for second time while Pompey departs for his provinces in Spain	Caesar humiliated, "cheated" of his second consulship
Caesar: *hold on to provinces and army* ("Defect")	Caesar gets second consulship, triumph	War: grave risks for both sides

---

[3] Strictly speaking, such cases are no longer actually Prisoner's Dilemmas (Binmore 2015: 21–22).
However, Binmore's dismissive comments on those pages about the game's heuristic value for
examining "the essence of the problem of human cooperation" seem to miss the point. Flexible
use of the concept helps to focus attention on the factors that enable "players" to *escape* the tragic
pathology, and these factors are of the greatest interest to anthropologists, sociologists, and
historians.

[4] This converts the game into the Iterated Prisoner's Dilemma, which can serve as a basic model for the
evolution and operation of social norms. The classic study is Axelrod 1984.

The game table suggests that, despite the grave, even existential risks of war for both men, *and despite the (at least arguable) preference of each man individually for peaceful parity,* in the absence of a convincing reason why each party should be prepared to entrust his fate to the other, each *must* "defect" out of fear that the other will simply exploit to the fullest any cooperative move. By the end of 50 BC the result – not inevitable, of course, but "natural" under the circumstances – is that Caesar insists on holding on to his provinces and army, while Pompey rejects Caesar's election in absentia: civil war.

What we gain by looking at the coming of the Caesarian Civil War as a Prisoner's Dilemma is the appropriate emphasis on the importance of the problem of trust: specifically, the role of mutual (dis)trust in determining the outcome although arguably neither side was intent on provoking a conflict, whose cost both sides could see would be great.[5] I argue that the Civil War did not come about because either Caesar or Pompey was particularly eager to resort to armed force, but because neither side found a way to *prevent* it on terms in which they had good reason to trust.

Moreover, when we recall that in an Iterated Prisoner's Dilemma, each uncooperative move is likely to prompt a "defensive" defection in return because the basis for judgment that the other will respond cooperatively has been further undermined, the model also shows convincingly how over the course of 51 to the beginning of 49 the ability of each side to trust the other and thus to bridge the gap between them was progressively eroded. Considering the effects of *history* (past "moves" in the game) on expectations of future cooperation, we can see more clearly how a spiral of mistrust shifted both parties progressively toward defection rather than cooperation over the course of the year, with each move adding to a recent history of defection that in turn made further defection more and more rational. Thus Pompey's willingness late in 51 to give the Senate a free hand to dispose of Caesar's provinces predictably aroused suspicion in Caesar, which helped to determine the uncooperative move of Curio's veto on March 1. That in turn may have influenced Pompey to resort to the "sharp practice" of giving the Senate, as his own contribution to the expected Parthian campaign, a legion currently commanded by Caesar, and to signal clearly that, the Law of the Ten Tribunes notwithstanding, he expected him to give up his provinces and army if he wanted his second consulship as agreed. Those moves in turn eroded Caesar's trust in Pompey further so

---

[5] See already Raaflaub's observations (1975: 299–300) on the cumulative effect of mistrust in the coming of the Caesarian Civil War.

that he may well have felt he had legitimate reasons to fear a "stolen election" if he did leave his army and provinces to compete in the near election in summer 50. And of course, Caesar's failure to use his *ratio absentis* at the last moment that could be unproblematically defended (summer 50) then suggested to Pompey and others that he would never give up his command until a time of his arbitrary choosing. And so on, until by December 50 it seems (as Cicero said) that Pompey no longer really wanted to avoid war if that was what it would take to bring Caesar to heel. Progressive iterations of the Prisoner's Dilemma had driven the two men farther and farther apart, to the point where by December 50 Pompey at least preferred war to cooperation.

Early in January, however, Caesar surprised Pompey with a remarkable concession in this deteriorating environment: his offer to give up the Gallic provinces and all but two, and finally one, legion. This can be seen in game-theoretic terms as an attempt to "reset" the spiral of defection by a cooperative move that gives some hope of breaking the cycle. One obvious way to avoid the "natural," noncooperative outcome is, of course, to adjust the choices radically. That is what Caesar did in very early January with his offer to give up all but one province and nine-tenths of his army. The game then changes to this:

	Pompey: *accept Caesar's proposal (and almost certainly withdraw to Spain)*[6] ("Cooperate")	Pompey: *reject Caesar's proposal* ("Defect")
Caesar: *give up provinces and army except Illyricum + one legion until next election* ("Cooperate")	Peace: Caesar gets second consulship but Pompey is left with seven legions in Spain	Pompey has military advantage but impasse continues
Caesar: *remain in Gaul in command of more than eleven legions* ("Defect")	Caesar has military advantage but impasse continues	War: grave risks for both sides

We see that now the payoff structure of the top row has changed quite a bit and therefore the game has changed substantially, making the mutual cooperation outcome (upper-left quadrant) more attractive in comparison

[6] Chapter 6, n. 206.

to its alternatives in the same row (upper-right quadrant) or same column (lower-left). Caesar's offer makes the "peace" outcome (upper-left quadrant) far from a nonstarter for Pompey because the impasse is resolved and Caesar now gives up nearly his entire victorious army, removing a major source of tension surrounding his election (for Caesar's "insurance policy" was surely seen on the other side as military intimidation and extortion of "impudent" demands), leaving Pompey with double Caesar's number of legions in Italy at the time of the election and until he moves off to Spain, with more than parity thereafter once Pompey joined his seven legions there (Chapter 7, n. 70). On the other hand, both players are now in a better position to countenance a non-cooperative move by the other side, especially since in practice neither side is likely to disarm unilaterally without convincing evidence of cooperation by the other party. (Thus the upper-right and lower-left quadrants are in practice highly unlikely.) In fact, with these major revisions the game is no longer actually a Prisoner's Dilemma with a single "dominant" solution in the lower-right quadrant (mutual defection = "war"): Caesar's best move (as is also suggested by the fact that he initiated the proposal) is now probably the "cooperative" one, and it is no longer a given that Caesar's "cooperative" move would result in "defection" by Pompey – which would perpetuate the crisis but hardly resolve it in Pompey's favor.[7]

Although we are told that Pompey came very close to accepting the proposal (Chapter 6, n. 208), success was far from certain even without the intervention of others extraneous to the game (Cato and consul Lentulus). Much would depend on actual implementation of the de-escalating trade-off, yet if both parties saw mutual cooperation as the more attractive option for themselves individually, then with the help of mutually trusted intermediaries such as Cicero it should have been possible for them to climb down from the increasingly aggressive positions they had taken up since Caesar's bypassing of the elections of 50. Pompey had a history of trusted cooperation with Caesar (founded on at least nine years of mutual services, more than half of the time while linked as son- and father-in-law through Julia), and as we shall see, even as late as early February 49, Cicero thought it a real possibility that the two men were about to reach a settlement.[8] Accepting Caesar's offer would have meant repudiating Pompey's recent cooperation with Cato and his followers, but how much trust had been established in *that* relationship?

---

[7] I do not propose here to elaborate further and specifically to identify the new game among the other double-matrix games commonly employed for the analysis of such conflicts (see Snyder 1977: 41–48). I believe it is an "asymmetric" one.

[8] Chapter 7, n. 86. Also Dio 41.5.3.

To judge from the sequel (the evacuation of Italy, the Corfinium debacle, and the demoralizing sniping during the Pharsalus campaign), the answer appears to be: "not very much."

There was a realistic possibility that civil war could still have been averted in early January 49. The two sides again came close to a settlement later in the same month (Chapter 7, p. 341ff.). There was nothing inevitable about this catastrophe. And if it was indeed "civil war [that] caused the fall of the Republic, not vice versa" (Gruen) these moments give a glimpse of a significantly different counterfactual future.

Where Were the 8th and 12th Legions When Caesar Marched into Italy?

Ottmer 1979: 27–38 has shown that despite Hirtius's report of the entirely transalpine disposition of the winter camps of Caesar's army in 50–49 ([Caes.] *BGall.* 8.54.3–4) Caesar may have brought the equivalent of four additional legions into Cisalpine Gaul by the beginning of 49 (supplementing the 13th Legion then already posted at Ravenna). This may be inferred from the fact that the 8th and 12th Legions, plus twenty-two recently recruited cohorts, are able to catch up to Caesar during his march through Italy in early-to-mid February (Caes. *BCiv.* 1.15.3, 18.5). If we believe Caesar's assertion that he gave them the order to begin their march to join him only after his entry into Ariminum (1.7.8–8.1), then their (ultimate) winter quarters must have been in Cisalpina, perhaps Placentia (cf. the rumor mentioned at Cic. *Att.* 6.9.5). (Girardet 2017: 144–147 agrees, although his further speculation is unconvincing [pp. 246–256] that by the time Caesar summoned them to join him they had again been moved up to closer camps, perhaps Mutina or Bononia, only two to three days rather than five days of forced marches from Ariminum, while the 13th was "with Caesar," not at Ravenna, as usually supposed, but much closer, at Caesena just north of the Rubicon [about 29 km rather than 50 km from Ariminum].) Since this, however, conflicts with the dispositions Hirtius describes at [Caes.] *BGall.* 8.54.3–4, either these forces (or parts of them) were moved across the Alps in the fall (which could give some substance to the rumors noted later in this appendix as well as the others which reached Rome in November: Chapter 6, nn. 157, 158), or they are simply not mentioned by Hirtius. Plut. *Caes.* 32.1 (similarly but not explicitly, App. *BCiv.* 2.34/134 with 2.32/124) asserts that the 13th Legion, which had been brought into Cisalpina perhaps in late May to replace one of the two legions handed over for the Parthian crisis (Raaflaub and Ramsey 2017: 66n191), was Caesar's *only* force south of the Alps at the beginning of the campaign. However, this tidbit is probably not worth very much; it is likely a careless inference based on nothing more than that Caesar first entered Italy proper at Ariminum with only this one legion.[1]

The older view is that Caesar is not to be taken too literally (or is caught out in yet another lie: Carter 1991: 166) about the timing of his summons for reinforcements (it would have been awkward for him to put this too early), and that this order must actually have gone out to them sometime early in December (according to Raaflaub and Ramsey 2017: 71 with n. 217, no later than December 8) presumably then in response to the arrival at Ravenna of the alarming news of the "Schwertübergabe" (Appendix 3(c)). On this hypothesis, the 12th Legion *could* have had time to march directly from its winter quarters in Aeduan country far across the Alps (according to Raaflaub and Ramsey, at minimum ca. 1,175 km from Ravenna, but strictly speaking we do not know whether some of the legions might have been shifted south, perhaps somewhere in the vicinity of Aquae Sextiae, "only" about 800 km away: Carter 1991: 165–166 and Ottmer 1979: 32–34) to join Caesar about February 8 around Firmum near Asculum (a further 265 km from Ravenna). Ottmer's solution seems preferable in view of the rapid marches to which Caesar promptly subjects the two legions once they do join him after having covered an immense journey at a rate of some 35 km/day.

Ottmer's theory also fits well with the rumor reported by Atticus to Cicero about September 19 ~ ca. August 5, Jul. that Caesar would be moving four legions to Placentia on October 15 (Cic. *Att.* 6.9.5; cf. 6.8.2, 7.1.1; Ottmer 1979: 36–37). They may have been led into Cisalpina by Caesar's trusted legate, T. Labienus (Hirt. [Caes.] *BGall.* 8.52.2). For Girardet 2017: 144–147, this clearly demonstrates Caesar's intention to use force, "zu Putsch und Krieg gegen die Regierung," if it rejected his demands. But this goes too far: Caesar himself had *left* Cisalpina around September 1 (~ July 18, Jul.) to undertake a formal review of his legions in the territory of the Treveri virtually at the far end of Gaul, and the review itself can hardly have taken place before mid-October (Hirt. [Caes. *BGall.* 8.52.1, with Raaflaub and Ramsey 2017: 69–70), precisely when the four legions according to rumor were supposed to march to Placentia. Caesar himself can hardly therefore have reentered Cisalpina before late in November (ibid., p. 70), perhaps *then* giving rise to the "false" rumor which arrived in the midst of the "Schwertübergabe" meetings (ca. late

---

[1] Pace Pelling 1982. Pelling himself accepts the common view that the twenty-two newly recruited cohorts had been levied in Cisalpina in the fall of 50, which in itself would contradict Plutarch.

November/early December, civil calendar) that he had "crossed the Alps and was marching on the City" (App. *BCiv.* 2.31/120).

Whether one accepts Ottmer's theory or not, there was apparently real anxiety in Rome about Caesar's movements and those of his troops. But they hardly prove that he was now committed to war (so Ottmer 1979: 79, 98; cf. 36; contra Pelling 1982; Morstein-Marx 2007: 176n82). The disposition of the 8th and 12th Legions at the time of Caesar's entry into Italy shows that he had prepared for the possibility of conflict; he would have been an utter fool to have reached this point in the crisis without having done so. But it does not prove that he had resolved upon initiating a war.

Among the forces that took part in the Italian campaign were twenty-two cohorts *ex novis Galliae dilectibus* subsequently supplemented en route to constitute three legions (Caes. *BCiv.* 1.18.5, 25.1). On the strength of the term *novi* (recent), these are often supposed to be distinct from the twenty-two cohorts Caesar explicitly says he had levied in "the province" in 52 (*BGall.* 7.65.1), which would imply that they were recruited in Cisalpina in the fall of 50 (see Girardet 2017: 145–147, following Ottmer and apparently Kraner-Hofmann ad 1.25.1; likewise Pelling 1982: 212), but the repetition of the numeral is curious and may indicate identity with the twenty-two Transalpine cohorts (so Raaflaub in Raaflaub [ed.] 2017: 324n9.18i). The word *novi* can be quite flexible, so on the whole the latter hypothesis seems better. Omission of these twenty-two cohorts, whatever their provenance, may explain the discrepancy between the nine legions which, Hirtius says, Caesar sent into winter quarters in 50 (*BGall.* 8.54.3–4) and the eleven legions cited by Cic. *Att.* 7.7.6 in mid-December, but Ottmer in effect doubles the twenty-two cohorts by assuming that the "new" ones (recruited in Cisalpina on his view) were not included in *Cicero's* number, thus pushing the total size of Caesar's army to the equivalent of thirteen-plus legions (or fourteen once the twenty-two newly recruited cohorts were consolidated). (For objections see Pelling 1982: 212; Botermann 1989a: 411n5; and Raaflaub, loc. cit.) It should be remembered that Caesar brought the equivalent of (not quite) six of these legions into Italy (*BCiv.* 1.25.1).

"Caesar's Passion to Be King": Relative and Absolute Chronology

The following table illustrates the variations among our major narrative sources in the sequence of the four key events of the narrative that they all share focusing on the question whether Caesar wanted to be king.

	Dio, Bk 44	App., *BCiv.* 2	Suet., *Iul.*	Plut., *Caesar*	Nic. Dam. *Bios*
A) Forum Iulium	1 (ch. 8)	1 (107/445)	1 (78.1)	2 (60.4)	4 (78)
B) Diadem on statue	2 (9.2)	2 (108/449)	2 (79.1)[1]	4 (61.8)	1 (69)
C) Acclamation on return from Latin Festival	3 (10.1)	3 (108/450)	3 (79.2)[2]	1 (60.3)	?2 (70)[3]
D) Lupercalia	4 (11)	4 (109/456–458)	4 (79.2)	3 (61.1)	3 (71–75)

The sequence A-B-C-D is common to Dio (on the whole our most complete source for this narrative), Appian, and Suetonius (though the last is not unambiguously ordered as a sequential narrative). This may therefore

---

[1] Note: Here synchronized with the return from the Latin Festival. Suet. also mentions in this connection *immodicas ac novas populi acclamationes*, although he mentions the explicit royal address, along with Caesar's response, several lines later (79.2). Since that seems to be introduced under the rubric of Caesar's inability to cut off speculation about his desire for kingship (*neque ex eo infamiam affectati etiam regii nominis discutere valuit*) it seems best to suppose that here he steps back slightly in time to give a notable example of the *immodicae ac novae populi acclamationes*. That in turn would imply that Suet. sees B and C as more or less simultaneous, which I now prefer to the idea that he "conflates" the two (Morstein-Marx 2012: 208n63).

[2] No explicit mention here of the return to the City from the Latin Festival, though Suet. has mentioned *immodicae ac novae populi acclamationes* in that connection just a few lines earlier (79.1). See previous note.

[3] A plausible but not certain reference to the acclamations at the Latin Festival.

be called the "canonical" sequence.[4] Plutarch's variations from it are readily explained away (Pelling 2011: 422–423). This leaves Nicolaus, whose divergence from the canonical order may be seen as lying simply in moving the Forum Iulium incident to the end and placing it shortly before the assassination. In no account, however, is this incident as tightly woven into the logic of the narrative as is the B-C-D sequence, all of which circulate explicitly around the question of "kingship." The Forum Iulium story is best seen as "free-floating" (Pelling 2011: 448), attached tightly to the assassination by Nicolaus most likely because he sees it as a particularly powerful stimulus to the conspirators (78: κατόπιν δὲ τούτου καὶ ἕτερον ἐπράχθη, ὃ σφόδρα ἤγειρε τοὺς συνεστῶτας; see Toher 2017: 319). The canonical sequence therefore appears to be far preferable than any rival combination.

A few absolute dates can be attached to the canonical sequence. The *Fasti Triumphales* give VII Kal. Feb. (= January 26) as the date of Caesar's *ovatio* on his return from the celebration of the Latin Festival on the Alban Mount, which would give us the absolute date of C. Dio and Appian both place B before C, but since Suetonius appears to synchronize them (nn. 1, 2), we should probably assume that the gap between them was small, probably so small as to be almost negligible (perhaps in sequence on the same day).[5] The date of the Lupercalia, of course, was February 15. There remains the date of A (Forum Iulium incident).

Dio and Appian both imply that the episode in the Forum Iulium was the climax of a series of ever more extravagant honors voted for Caesar after his return from Spain in late September 45.[6] There were a number of possible occasions for an outpouring of such enthusiasm before the *terminus ante quem* established by the date of his *ovatio*: his initial arrival in Rome (*adventus*), the Spanish triumph at most a few weeks later, the Kalends of January (New Year's Day, typically a celebratory day for the new consuls: Pina Polo 2011: 17–18).[7]

Some support for a date in January may be found in the fact that Caesar assumed the *dictatura perpetua* for the first time between

---

[4] Contra Toher 2017: 291, who seems to think that *all* these events were "free-floating." See also Dobesch 2001: 1.205-273 (1978), who argues that the chronological consistency that underlies most of these sources is due to the influence of an influential primary source that established a basic chronological framework. In a later paper (2001: 1.275-361 [1988]) Dobesch identifies this "chronological" source as Pollio.

[5] Cf. Weinstock 1971: 319–320. I fail to understand his warning about the possibility of a "duplication."

[6] Pp. 500ff.

[7] Date of Spanish triumph: only "a few days" before that of Q. Fabius Maximus, which took place on October 13 (*I.It.* 13.1, pp. 86–87, 562; Quint. 6.3.61). It follows that Caesar must have celebrated this triumph very shortly after his arrival in the City – perhaps even on the very day.

February 9 and 15 (i.e. not long before D).[8] This implies that the proposal was made fairly close to those dates. Now, Appian (*BCiv.* 2.106/442) thinks that the continuous dictatorship was among the honors "offered" to Caesar by the procession to the Forum Iulium, while Dio says, in a brief comment appended to his account of that event, that he was "elected" to the office shortly thereafter (44.8.4).[9] These two statements can be harmonized if we suppose that the Senate's decree on the matter was presented to Caesar at the Forum Iulium but that the formal election, presumably by a vote of the People, followed soon afterward. It is reasonable to suppose that this vote would have come to the People in the form of a legislative bill, which ought for form's sake to have been promulgated a *trinundinum* of three market days (seventeen to twenty-five days) earlier.[10] Thus on this hypothesis the Forum Iulium incident likely belongs in January, most probably before the return from the Alban Mount on January 26.[11]

A date in January would be consistent with the version of Nicolaus of Damascus, in which the senatorial procession to the Forum Iulium is headed by "*the* [single] consul, Caesar's colleague at the time" (*Bios* 78 τούτων δ᾽ ἡγεῖτο μὲν ὁ ὕπατος, συνάρχων τότε αὐτῷ ὤν): Mark Antony, then, pointing to a date in 44.[12] It is true, however, that the (synoptic, as

---

[8] Caesar held the "continuous" dictatorship already on February 15 (Cic. *Phil.* 2.87) but is only "*designatus*" in a document cited by Josephus and dated February 9 (Joseph. *AJ* 14.211 δικτάτωρ τὸ τέταρτον ὕπατός τε τὸ πέμπτον, δικτάτωρ ἀποδεδειγμένος διὰ βίου, with 222, Jehne 1987a: 32–33. (Pucci Ben Zeev 1996 and 1996a add little.) Because the *Fasti Triumphales* refer to Caesar as *DICT IIII* but not *dict. perp. des.*, it seems probable but not certain that Caesar had not yet been *elected* by January 26 (*I.It.* 13.1, pp. 86–87, 567).

[9] Chapter 9, n. 79 Dio 44.8.4 δικτάτωρ διὰ βίου μετὰ ταῦτα ἀποδειχθείς. For ἀποδείκνυμι as "elect," see e.g. Dio 43.51.2, 4, and the apparent use of Roman technical language by Josephus (ἀποδεδειγμένος = *designatus*, Chapter 9, n. 224.; Wilcken 1940: 24).

[10] On the length of the *trinundinum*, I follow Lintott: see Morstein-Marx 2004: 8n36. In favor of the continued observation of due formalities even now, note that Caesar had to abdicate his former serial dictatorship in order to take up the continuous dictatorship (*Fasti Cons.* an. 44, Zevi and Cassola 2016: 295, line 10). Possible evidence of a vote: Dio 46.17.4–5 (Chapter 9, n. 196).

[11] Pelling 2011: 448 is uncertain whether we can trust Dio's relative chronology here, but his account does not otherwise suffer from the "floating" phenomena to which Pelling alludes.

[12] It must be acknowledged that Nicolaus wrongly places the Forum Iulium episode *after* the other key events and just before the assassination; it might therefore be objected that Nicolaus's one-consul version is simply a consequence of this mistaken relative chronology. But he can be mistaken about the sequence of these events without being wrong about the somewhat counterintuitive detail of the single consul, and the texture of circumstantial detail in Nicolaus's account is greater than that of Plutarch and Appian. Dobesch 2001: 1. 416–1.417 (cf. 1966: 32–33), also objects that Cicero would not have kept silence in the *Philippics* about such an act of grotesque servility by Antony. Yet Cicero declines to mention the incident in the Forum Iulium altogether, which prompts the suspicion that he found it counterproductive to raise such a distasteful example of *senatorial* servility. As one of Caesar's most prominent "honorers" himself (Chapter 9, n. 100), he may have had something to hide. Gelzer 1968: 317n1 accuses Nicolaus of "deliberate bias" against Antony.

often) accounts of Appian (2.107/445) and Plutarch (*Caes.* 60.4) put *two* consuls at the head of the procession: thus Q. Fabius Maximus and C. Trebonius, which would put the event late in 45. But the egregious error shared by both Appian and Plutarch about the location of the event (the Rostra, ἔμβολοι, apparently confusing the setting with that of the Lupercalia) weakens their credibility regarding circumstantial details, even if Pollio may be assumed to be their ultimate common source, and it is possible that their two-consul version is nothing but an imagined "default" scenario.[13] Most, but not all, historians have assumed that the implied sequence in Dio's narrative appears to favor 45 for the incident, yet it is actually quite unclear whether the honors listed by Dio at 44.4–7 all belong strictly to one year or the other, or were spread across both.[14]

The main effect of putting the contre-temps at the Forum Iulium somewhat later than usual would be to bring it into closer proximity to the other unfortunate events that undermined Caesar's public position during the time when the conspiracy was gathering around him. The atmosphere becomes even more oppressive, the tinderbox even more explosive.

[13] They do not simply conflate the Forum Iulium incident with the Lupercalia story, which they both have slightly later and correctly place at the Rostra (61.4; 2.109/456). Their congruence is still best seen as evidence of joint dependence on the *History* of C. Asinius Pollio (Pelling 2011: 44–47, but see contra Drummond, *FRHist* 1.439–140), which again reminds us that Pollio cannot be considered infallible. He may not even have been in Rome at the time but en route to his praetorian province of Hispania Ulterior.

[14] Balsdon 1967: 152 thought they belonged "clearly" to 44, most others to December 45 (e.g. Dobesch 1966: 31ff.; 2001: 1.412–421; Gelzer 1968: 316–317; Weinstock 1971: 275. Pelling 2011: 448 and perhaps Toher 2017: 320–321 are agnostic. Tempest 2017: 80 offers February 14, presumably inferred from Nicolaus; but see above, p. 644. See also Chapter 9, n. 75.

Works Cited

Adams, J. N. 1982. *The Latin Sexual Vocabulary*. Baltimore.

Adcock, F. E. 1956. *Caesar as Man of Letters*. Cambridge.

Alexander, M. 1990. *Trials in the Late Roman Republic, 149 BC to 50 BC*. Toronto.

2002. *The Case for the Prosecution in the Ciceronian Era*. Ann Arbor.

Alföldi, A. 1985. *Caesar in 44 v. Chr. Vol. 1: Studien zu Caesars Monarchie und ihren Wurzeln*. Bonn.

Amsterdam, A. G., and J. Bruner. 2000. *Minding the Law*. Cambridge and London.

Anderson, R. D., P. J. Parsons, and R. G. M. Nisbet. 1979. "Elegiacs by Gallus from Qasr Ibrîm." *JRS* 69: 125–155.

Andreau, J. 1999. *Banking and Business in the Roman World*. Cambridge.

Angius, A. 2014. "Le fonti dell'opinione pubblica nella tarda Repubblica Romana." Diss. U. Roma III.

2015. "Graffiti e pamphlet. Lessico e sociologia di un fenomeno politico." *BIDR* 109: 247–277.

2018. *La Repubblica delle opinioni. Informazione politica e partecipazione popolare a Roma tra II e I secolo a. C.* Milan.

Arena, V. 2012. *Libertas and the Practice of Politics in the Late Roman Republic*. Cambridge.

Ashrafian, H., and F. M. Galassi. 2016. *Julius Caesar's Disease: A New Diagnosis*. South Yorkshire.

Astin, A. E. 1958. *The* lex annalis *before Sulla*. Coll. Latomus 32. Brussels.

1967. *Scipio Aemilianus*. Oxford.

Atkins, J. W. 2013. *Cicero on Politics and the Limits of Reason: The* Republic *and* Laws. Cambridge.

Austin, R. G. 1960. *Cicero:* Pro M. Caelio Oratio. 3rd ed. Oxford.

Axelrod, R. 1984. *The Evolution of Cooperation*. New York.

Badian, E. 1959. "The Early Career of A. Gabinius (cos. 58 BC)." *Philologus* 103: 87–99.

1964. *Studies in Greek and Roman History*. Oxford.

1968. *Roman Imperialism in the Late Republic*. Ithaca.

1972. "Tiberius Gracchus and the Roman Revolution." *ANRW* 1.1: 668–731.

1974. "The Attempt to Try Caesar." In J. A. S. Evans (ed.), *Polis and imperium. Studies in Honour of Edward Togo Salmon*. Amsterdam. 145–166.

1977. "Mamurra's Fourth Fortune." *CPh* 72: 320–322.

1990. Rev. of Meier, *Caesar. Gnomon* 62: 22–39.

2009. "From the Iulii to Caesar." In M. T. Griffin (ed.), *A Companion to Julius Caesar*. Malden, MA, and Oxford. 11–22.

Baehr, P. 1998. *Caesar and the Fading of the Roman World: A Study in Republicanism and Caesarism*. New Brunswick and London.

Balsdon, J. P. V. D. 1939. "Consular Provinces under the Late Republic – II. Caesar's Gallic Command." *JRS* 29: 167–183.

1962. "Roman History, 65–50 B.C.: Five Problems." *JRS* 52: 134–141.

1967. Rev. of Dobesch, *Caesars Apotheose. Gnomon* 39: 150–156.

1967a. *Julius Caesar: A Political Biography*. New York.

Bardt, C. 1910. "Die Übergabe des Schwertes an Pompeius im December 50 v. Chr." *Hermes* 45: 337–346.

Barwick, K. 1938. *Caesars* Commentarii *und das* Corpus Caesarianum. Mainz.

Bastien, J.-L. 2007. *Le triomphe romain et son utilisation politique à Rome aux trois derniers siècles de la république*. Rome.

Batstone, W. 1991. "A Narrative Gestalt and the Force of Caesar's Style." *Mnemosyne* 44: 126–136.

Batstone, W., and C. Damon. 2006. *Caesar's Civil War*. Oxford.

Bauman, R. A. 1963. *A Study of the* Crimen Maiestatis Imminutae *in the Roman Republic*. Johannesburg.

Beagon, M. 2005. *The Elder Pliny on the Human Animal*. Natural History Book 7. Oxford.

Beard, M. 2007. *The Roman Triumph*. Cambridge, MA.

Beard, M., and M. Crawford. 1985. *Rome in the Late Republic: Problems and Interpretations*. London. 2nd ed. 1999.

Beard, M., J. North, and S. Price. 1998. *Religions of Rome*. 2 vols. Cambridge.

Bearzot, C. 2000. "Cesare e Corinto." In G. Urso (ed.), *L'ultimo Cesare*. Rome. 35–53.

Beck, H. 2005. *Karriere und Hierarchie. Die römische Aristokratie und die Anfänge des cursus honorum in der mittleren Republik*. Berlin.

Beck. H., A. Duplá, M. Jehne, and F. Pina Polo (eds.) 2011. *Consuls and Res Publica*. Cambridge.

Bellemore, J. 2005. "Cato's Opposition to Caesar in 59 B.C." In K. Welch and T. Hillard (eds.), *Roman Crossings*. Swansea. 225–257.

Beneker, J. 2011. "The Crossing of the Rubicon and the Outbreak of Civil War in Cicero, Lucan, Plutarch, and Suetonius." *Phoenix* 65: 74–99.

Bennett, C. 2003–2012. "Roman Dates." www.instonebrewer.com/TyndaleSites/Egypt/ptolemies/chron/roman/roman_civil.htm. [Accessed February 13, 2021.]

Bennett, M. 2006. *Oliver Cromwell*. London and New York.

Bennett, W. L., and M. S. Feldman. 1981. *Reconstructing Reality in the Courtroom: Justice and Judgment in American Culture*. New Brunswick.

Bergmann, B. 2010. *Der Kranz des Kaisers. Genese und Bedeutung einer römischen Insignie*. Berlin and New York.

Bernstein, F. 1998. Ludi publici. *Untersuchungen zur Entstehung und Entwicklung der öffentlichen Spiele im republikanischen Rom*. Historia Einzelschriften 119. Stuttgart.

Berry, D. H. 1996. *Cicero:* Pro P. Sulla Oratio. Cambridge.

Bicknell, P., and D. Nielsen. 1998. "Five Cohorts against the World." In C. Deroux (ed.), *Studies in Latin Literature and Roman History IX*. Collection Latomus 244. Brussels. 138–166.

Billows, R. 2009. *Julius Caesar: The Colossus of Rome*. London.

Binmore, K. 2015. "Why All the Fuss? The Many Aspects of the Prisoner's Dilemma." In M. Peterson (ed.), *The Prisoner's Dilemma*. Cambridge. 16–34.

Bleicken, J. 1998. "Gedanken zum Untergang der römischen Republik." *Gesammelte Schriften* 2 (Stuttgart): 683–704.

Blom, H. van der. 2016. *Oratory and Political Career in the Late Roman Republic*. Cambridge.

Blom, H. van der, C. Gray, and C. Steel (eds.) 2018. *Institutions and Ideology in Republican Rome: Speech, Audience and Decision*. Cambridge.

Blösel, W. 2016. "Provincial Commands and Money in the Late Roman Republic." In H. Beck, M. Jehne, and J. Serrati (eds.), *Money and Power in the Roman Republic*. Coll. Latomus v. 355. Brussels. 68–81.

Bömer, F. 1953. "Der Commentarius: Zur Vorgeschichte und literarischen Form der Schriften Caesars." *Hermes* 81: 210–250.

Bonnefond-Coudry, M. 1989. *Le sénat de la République romaine de la guerre d'Hannibal à Auguste. Pratiques délibératives et prise de décision*. Rome.

Bosworth, A. B. 1972. "Asinius Pollio and Augustus." *Historia* 21: 441–473.

Botermann, H. 1989. "Cato und die sogenannte Schwertübergabe im Dezember 50 v. Chr. Ein übersehenes Zeugnis für die Vorgeschichte des Bürgerkrieges (Sen. ep. mor. 14, 12 f.; 95.69 f; 104, 29–33)." *Hermes* 117: 62–85.

1989a. "Denkmodelle am Vorabend des Bürgerkrieges (Cic. *Att.* 7.9): Handelsspielraum oder unausweichliche Notwendigkeit?" *Historia* 38: 410–430.

Bourdieu, P., and L. J. D. Wacquant. 2002. *An Invitation to Reflexive Sociology*. Cambridge.

Braund, S. M. 2009. *Seneca*, de Clementia. Oxford.

2012. "The Anger of Tyrants and the Forgiveness of Kings." In C. L. Griswold and D. Konstan (eds.), *Ancient Forgiveness: Classical, Judaic, and Christian*. Cambridge. 79–96.

Brennan, T. C. 2000. *The Praetorship in the Roman Republic*. 2 vols. Oxford.

Brind'Amour, P. 1983. *Le Calendrier Romain. Recherches Chronologiques*. Ottawa.

Briscoe, J. 2008. *A Commentary on Livy, Books 38–40*. Oxford.

Brooks, P., and P. D. Gewirtz. 1996. *Law's Stories: Narrative and Rhetoric in the Law*. New Haven.

Broughton, T. R. S. 1946. "Notes on Roman Magistrates." *TAPhA* 77: 35–43.

1948. "More Notes on Roman Magistrates." *TAPhA* 79: 63–78.

1991. "Candidates Defeated in Roman Elections: Some Ancient Roman 'Also Rans.'" *Transactions of the American Philosophical Society* 81.4.

Bruhns, H. 1978. *Caesar und die römische Oberschicht in den Jahren 49–44.* Göttingen.

Brunt, P. 1957. "Three Passages from Asconius." *CR* 71: 193–195.

——— 1971. *Social Conflicts in the Roman Republic.* London.

——— 1971a. *Italian Manpower: 225 B.C.–A.D. 14.* Oxford.

——— 1979. "*Laus Imperii.*" In P. D. A. Garnsey and C. R. Whittaker (eds.), *Imperialism in the Ancient World.* Cambridge. 159–191.

——— 1986. "Cicero's *Officium* in the Civil War." *JRS* 76: 12–32.

——— 1988. *The Fall of the Roman Republic and Related Essays.* Oxford.

Burden-Strevens, C. 2018. "Reconstructing Republican Oratory in Cassius Dio's Roman History." In C. Gray, A. Balbo, R. M. A. Marshall, and C. E. W. Steel (eds.), *Reading Republican Oratory: Reconstructions, Contexts, Receptions.* Oxford. 111–134.

Butler, H. E., and M. Cary. 1924. *M. Tulli Ciceronis De Provinciis Consularibus Oratio ad Senatum.* Oxford.

——— 1927/1982. *Suetonius: Divus Iulius.* Oxford.

Buttrey, T. V. 2015. "Caesar at Play: Some Preparations for the Parthian Campaign, 44 BCE." *JAH* 3: 220–241.

Cadario, M. 2006. "Le statue di Cesare a Roma tra il 46 e il 44 a.C.: la celebrazione della vittoria e il cofronto con Alessandro e Romolo." *Acme* 59: 25–70.

Cairns, F., and E. Fantham (eds.) 2003. *Caesar against Liberty? Papers of the Langford Latin Seminar.* Leeds.

Canfora, L. 2007. *Julius Caesar: The Life and Times of the People's Dictator.* Berkeley.

Cape, R. 1995. "The Rhetoric of Politics in Cicero's Fourth Catilinarian." *AJPh* 116: 255–277.

——— 2002. "Cicero's Consular Speeches." In J. M. May (ed.), *Brill's Companion to Cicero: Oratory and Rhetoric.* Leiden. 113–158.

Carlyle, T. 1911. *On Heroes, Hero-Worship and the Heroic in History.* Ed. by G. Wherry. Cambridge.

Carsana, C. 2007. *Commento storico al libro II delle Guerre Civili di Appiano (parte I).* Pisa.

Carter, J. M. 1991. *Julius Caesar: The Civil War, Books I & II.* Warminster.

——— 1993. *Julius Caesar: The Civil War, Book III.* Warminster.

Cavarzere, A. 1994. "Note alla *In Pisonem* di Cicerone." *MD* 33: 157–176.

Chrissanthos, S. 2001. "Caesar and the Mutiny of 47 B.C." *JRS* 91: 63–75.

——— 2019. *The Year of Julius and Caesar: 59 BC and the Transformation of the Roman Republic.* Baltimore.

Christ, K. 1974. "Caesar und Ariovistus." *Chiron* 4: 251–292.

——— 1994. *Caesar. Annäherungen an einen Diktator.* Munich.

Clarendon, Edward Hyde, Earl of, 1857. *The Life of Edward, Earl of Clarendon, in Which Is Included a Continuation of His History of the Grand Rebellion.* Oxford.

Clark, C. 2013. *The Sleepwalkers: How Europe Went to War in 1914.* New York.

Coarelli, F. 1992. *Il Foro Romano: periodo arcaico.* 3rd ed. Rome.

——— 1992a. *Il Foro Romano: periodo repubblicano e augusteo.* 2nd ed. Rome.

——— 1997. *Il Campo Marzio dalle origini alla fine della Repubblica.* Rome.

Cole, S. 2013. *Cicero and the Rise of Deification at Rome*. Cambridge.

Collins, J. H. 1972. "Caesar as Political Propagandist." *ANRW* 1.1: 922–966.

Conroy, J. 2014. *Our One Common Country: Abraham Lincoln and the Hampton Roads Peace Conference of 1865*. Guildford, CT.

Cornwell, H. 2018. Rev. of Wiseman 2016, Mouritsen 2017, and Haake and Harders (eds.) 2017. *JRS* 108: 200–202.

Cordier, P. 1994. "M. Caelius Rufus, le préteur récalcitrant." *MEFRA* 106: 533–577.

Cornell, T. J. (ed.) 2014. *Fragments of the Roman Historians*. 3 vols. Oxford.

Costa-García, J. M. 2018. "Rediscovering the Roman Conquest of the Northwestern Iberian Peninsula." In M. Fernández-Götz and N. Roymans (eds.), *Conflict Archaeology: Materialities of Collective Violence from Prehistory to Late Antiquity*. London and New York. 141–151.

Courrier, C. 2014. *La plèbe de Rome et sa culture (fin de IIe siècle av. J.-C.-fin du Ier siècle ap. J.-C.)*. Rome.

Courtney, E. 1993. *The Fragmentary Latin Poets*. Oxford.

Craig, C. 1986. "Cato's Stoicism and the Understanding of Cicero's Speech for Murena." *TAPhA* 116: 229–239.

2004. "Audience Expectations, Invective, and Proof." In J. Powell and J. Patterson (eds.), *Cicero the Advocate*. Oxford. 187–213.

Crawford, J. 1994. *M. Tullius Cicero, the Fragmentary Speeches*. Oxford.

Crawford, M. H. 1976. "Hamlet without the Prince" (rev. of Gruen 1974). *JRS* 66: 214–217.

1989. "The *lex Iulia Agraria*." *Athenaeum* 67: 179–190.

Cristofoli, R. 2011. *Cicerone e l'ultima vittoria di Cesare. Analisi storica del XIV libro delle Epistole ad Attico*. Bari.

Damon, C. 2018. *Studies on the text of Caesar's* Bellum civile. New York and Oxford.

Damon, C., and C. Mackay. 1995. "On the Prosecution of C. Antonius in 76 BC." *Historia* 44: 37–55.

David, J.-M. 1992. *Le patronat judiciaire au dernier siècle de la république romaine*. Rome.

Davies, P. J. E. 2017. *Architecture and Politics in Republican Rome*. Cambridge.

De Libero, L. 1992. *Obstruktion. Politische Praktiken im Senat und in der Volksversammlung der ausgehenden römischen Republik (70–49 v. Chr.)*, Stuttgart.

1998. "Der Raub des Staatsschatzes durch Caesar." *Klio* 80: 111–133.

De Ligt, L. 2012. *Peasants, Citizens, and Soldiers: Studies in the Demographic History of Roman Italy, 225 BC–AD 100*. Cambridge.

De Ligt, L., and S. Northwood (eds.) 2008. *People, Land, and Politics: Demographic Developments and the Transformation of Roman Italy, 300 BC–AD 14*. Boston.

Degrassi, A. 1947. *Inscriptiones Italiae 13/1: Fasti Consulares et Triumphales*. Rome.

Dettenhofer, M. H. 1992. *Perdita Iuventus. Zwischen den Generationen von Caesar und Augustus*. Munich.

Deutsch, M. E. 1914. "The Year of Caesar's Birth." *TAPhA* 45: 17–28.

Devillers, O., and K. Sion-Jenkis (eds.) 2012. *César sous Auguste*. Bordeaux.

Dighton, A. 2017. "Mutatio Vestis: Clothing and Political Protest in the Late Roman Republic." *Phoenix* 71: 345–369.

Dobesch, E. 1966. *Caesars Apotheose zu Lebzeiten und sein Ringen um den Königstitel. Untersuchungen über Caesars Alleinherrschaft*. Vienna.

1980. *Die Kelten in Österreich nach den ältesten Berichten der Antike*. Vienna.

1994. "Zur Chronologie des Dakerkönigs Burebista." In R. Göbl (ed.), *Die Hexadrachmenprägung der Gross-Boier*. Vienna. 51–68.

1998. "Der Weltreichsgedanke bei Caesar." In *L'ecumenismo politico nella coscienza dell'occidente*. Rome. 195–263.

2000. "Caesars monarchische Ideologie." In G. Urso (ed.), *L'ultimo Cesare*. Rome. 89–123.

2001. *Ausgewählte Schriften*. Cologne.

Dowling, M. B. 2006. *Clemency and Cruelty in the Roman World*. Ann Arbor.

Driediger-Murphy, L. G. 2018. "Falsifying the Auspices in Republican Politics." In H. van der Blom, C. Gray, and C. Steel (eds.), *Institutions and Ideology in Republican Rome: Speech, Audience and Decision*. Cambridge. 183–202.

2019. *Roman Republican Augury. Freedom and Control*. Oxford.

Drogula, F. 2015. *Commanders and Command in the Roman Republic and Early Empire*. Chapel Hill.

2019. *Cato the Younger: Life and Death at the End of the Roman Republic*. Oxford.

Drumann, W., and P. Groebe. 1906. *Geschichte Roms in seinem Übergange von der republikanischen zur monarchischen Verfassung*. Vol. 3. Leipzig.

Drummond, A. 1978. "Some Observations on the Order of Consuls' Names." *Athenaeum* 56: 80–108.

1994. Rev. of Libero, *Obstruktion.CR* 44: 123–124.

1995. *Law, Politics and Power: Sallust and the Execution of the Catilinarian Conspirators*. Stuttgart.

1999. "Tribunes and Tribunician Programs in 63 B.C." *Athenaeum* 87: 121–167.

2013. "C. Asinius Pollio." In T. J. Cornell (ed.), *Fragments of the Roman Historians*. 3 vols. Oxford. 1:430–435.

Dugan, J. 2013. "Cicero and the Politics of Ambiguity: Interpreting the *Pro Marcello*." In C. Steel and H. van der Blom (eds.), *Community and Communication: Oratory and Politics in Republican Rome*. Oxford. 211–225.

Duplá, A., G. Fatás, and F. Pina. 1994. Rem publicam restituere*: una propuesta popularis para la crisis republicana: las* Epistulae ad Caesarem de Salustio. Zaragoza.

Dyck, A. 1996. *A Commentary on Cicero, De Officiis*. Ann Arbor.

2008. *Cicero: Catilinarians*. Cambridge.

Dyer, R. R. 1990. "Rhetoric and Intention in Cicero's *Pro Marcello*." *JRS* 80: 17–30.

Dyson, S. L. 1985. *The Creation of the Roman Frontier*. Princeton.

2010. *Rome. A Living Portrait of an Ancient City*. Baltimore.

Dzino, D. 2010. *Illyricum in Roman Politics, 229 BC–AD 68*. Cambridge.

Eberle, L. P. 2018. Rev. of Hölkeskamp 2017. *JRS* 108: 204–205.

Ebert, C. 1909. *Über die Entstehung von Caesars "Bellum Gallicum."* Nürnberg.

Eckstein, A. 1987. *Senate and General: Individual Decision-Making and Roman Foreign Relations, 264–194.* Berkeley.

Ehrhardt, C. 1987. "Caesar's First Triumph?" *Prudentia* 19: 50–58.

Elkins, N. T. 2007. Rev. of Hölkeskamp 2004. *JRS* 97: 268–270.

Elster, M. 2003. *Die Gesetze der mittleren römischen Republik: Text und Kommentar.* Darmstadt.

Erskine, A. 2001. *Troy between Greece and Rome.* Oxford.

Evans, J. D. 1990. "Statues of the Kings and Brutus on the Capitoline." *Opuscula Romana* 18: 99–105.

Evans, R. J. 1994. *Gaius Marius: A Political Biography.* Pretoria.

Farney, G. 2007. *Ethnic Identity and Aristocratic Competition in Republican Rome.* Cambridge.

Feig Vishnia, R. 1996. *State, Society, and Popular Leaders in Mid-Republican Rome: 241–167 B.C.* London.

Ferguson, N. 1997. "Virtual History: Towards a 'Chaotic' Theory of the Past." In N. Ferguson (ed.), *Virtual History: Alternatives and Counterfactuals.* London. 1–90.

⸻ 1999. *The Pity of War.* London.

⸻ 2006. "Political Risk and the International Bond Market between the 1848 Revolution and the Outbreak of the First World War." *Economic History Review* 59: 70–112.

Fernández-Götz, M., and N. Roymans (eds.) 2018. *Conflict Archaeology: Materialities of Collective Violence from Prehistory to Late Antiquity.* London and New York.

Ferrary, J.-L. 1988. "Rogatio Servilia Agraria." *Athenaeum* 66: 141–164.

⸻ 1996. "*Princeps legis et adscriptores*: la collégialité des magistrats romains dans la procedure de proposition des lois." *RevPhil* 70: 217–246.

⸻ 2010. "À propos des pouvoirs et des honneurs décernés à César entre 48 et 44." In G. Urso (ed.), *Cesare: Precursore o visionario?* Pisa. 9–30.

Fezzi, L. 1997. "Lex Clodia de iure et tempore legum rogandarum." *Studi Classici e Orientali* 45: 297–328.

⸻ 2019. *Crossing the Rubicon: Caesar's Decision and the Fate of Rome.* Tr. R. Dixon. New Haven.

Fischer, F. 1985. "Caesar und die Helvetier." *Bonner Jahrbücher* 185: 1–26.

⸻ 2004. "Caesars strategische Planung für Gallien. Zum Verhältnis von Darstellung und Wirklichkeit." In H. Heftner and K. Tomaschitz (eds.), *Ad Fontes! Festschrift G. Dobesch.* Vienna. 305–315.

⸻ 2009. "Caesars Griff nach Gallien." *Klio* 91: 435–442.

Flaig, E. 1995. "Entscheidung und Konsens. Zu den Feldern der politischen Kommunikation zwischen Aristokratie und Plebs." In M. Jehne (ed.), *Demokratie in Rom? Die Rolle des Volkes in der Politik der römischen Republik.* Stuttgart. 77–127.

⸻ 2002. *Ritualisierte Politik: Zeichen, Gesten und Herrschaft im Alten Rom.* Göttingen.

Flamerie de Lachapelle, G. 2011. Clementia. *Recherches sur la notion de clémence à Rome, du début du Ier siècle a.C. à la mort d'Auguste.* Bordeaux.

Flower, H. I. 1996. *Ancestor Masks and Aristocratic Power in Roman Culture.* Oxford.

——— 2006. *The Art of Forgetting: Disgrace and Oblivion in Roman Political Culture.* Chapel Hill.

——— 2010. *Roman Republics.* Princeton.

——— 2013. "Beyond the *Contio*: Political Communication in the Tribunate of Tiberius Gracchus." In C. Steel and H. van der Blom (eds.), *Community and Communication: Oratory and Politics in Republican Rome.* Oxford. 85–100.

Foxley, R. 2013. "Democracy in 1659: Harrington and the Good Old Cause." In S. Taylor and G. Tapsell (eds.), *The Nature of the English Revolution Revisited.* Woodbridge. 175–196.

Fränkel, E. 1956. "Eine Form römischer Kriegsbulletins." *Eranos* 54: 189–194.

Frederiksen, M. W. 1966. "Caesar, Cicero and the Problem of Debt." *JRS* 56: 128–141.

Gabba, E. 1967. *Appiani Bellorum civilium liber primus.* 2nd ed. Florence.

Gagliardi, L. 2011. *Cesare, Pompeo e la lotta per le magistrature, anni 52–50 a.C.* Milan.

Gagliardi, P. 2014. "Il poeta, Cesare, il trionfo." *Papyrologica Lupiensia* 23: 31–52.

Gallagher, C. 2018. *Telling It Like It Wasn't: The Counterfactual Imagination in History and Fiction.* Chicago and London.

Gardner, J. F. 2009. "The Dictator." In M. T. Griffin (ed.), *A Companion to Julius Caesar.* Malden, MA, and Oxford. 57–71.

Gazzaniga, M. 2011. *Who's In Charge?* New York.

Gelzer, M. 1963. "Die *lex Vatinia de imperio Caesaris*." *Kleine Schriften* 2: 206–228. (= *Hermes* 63 [1928] 113–137.)

——— 1968. *Caesar: Politician and Statesman.* Cambridge, MA.

——— 2008. *Caesar: Der Politiker und Staatsmann.* New ed. Stuttgart.

Gentles, I. J. 2011. *Oliver Cromwell: God's Warrior and the English Revolution.* Basingstoke and New York.

Gesche, H. 1976. *Caesar.* Darmstadt.

Gildenhard, I. 2006. "Reckoning with Tyranny: Greek Thoughts on Caesar in Cicero's Letters to Atticus in Early 49." In S. Lewis (ed.), *Ancient Tyranny.* Edinburgh: 197–209.

——— 2011. *Creative Eloquence: The Construction of Reality in Cicero's Speeches.* Oxford.

Gill, C. 1983. "The Question of Character-Development: Plutarch and Tacitus." *CQ* 33: 469–487.

Giovannini, A. 1983. *Consulare Imperium.* Basel.

——— 1995. "Catilina et le problème des dettes." In I. Malkin and Z. W. Rubinsohn (eds.), *Leaders and Masses in the Roman World: Studies in Honor of Zvi Yavetz.* Leiden. 15–34.

Girardet, K. M. 2000. "Caesars Konsulatsplan für das Jahr 49: Gründe und Scheitern." *Chiron* 30: 679–710. (= *Rom auf dem Weg von der Republik zum Prinzipat* [Bonn 2007] 121–158.)

2001. "*Imperia* und *provinciae* des Pompeius 82 bis 48 v. Chr." *Chiron* 31: 153–209.

2017. *Januar 49 v. Chr.: Vorgeschichte, Rechtslage, politische Aspekte.* Bonn.

Göbl, R. (ed.) 1994. *R. Die Hexadrachmenprägung der Gross-Boier.* Vienna.

Golden, G. 2013. *Crisis Management during the Roman Republic.* Cambridge.

Goldsworthy, A. 2006. *Caesar: Life of a Colossus.* New Haven.

Goltz, A. 2000. "*Maiestas sine viribus*: Die Bedeutung der Lictoren für die Konfliktbewältigungsstrategien römischer Magistrate." In B. Linke and M. Stemmler (eds.), *Mos Maiorum. Untersuchungen zu den Formen der Identitätsstiftung und Stabilisierung in der römischen Republik.* Historia ES 141. Stuttgart. 237–267.

Gomme, A. W., and F. H. Sandbach. 1973. *Menander: A Commentary.* Oxford.

Gotter, U. 1996. *Der Diktator ist tot! Politik in Rom zwischen den Iden des März und der Begründung des zweiten Triumvirats.* Historia ES 110. Stuttgart.

Goudineau, C. 1990. *César et la Gaule.* Paris.

Goudineau, C., and C. Peyre. 1993. *Bibracte et les Eduens: à la découverte d'un peuple gaulois.* Paris.

Gray, C., A. Balbo, R. M. A. Marshall, and C. E. W. Steel. 2018. *Reading Republican Oratory: Reconstructions, Contexts, Receptions.* Oxford.

Greenidge, A. H. J. 1901. *The Criminal Procedure of Cicero's Time.* Oxford.

Greenidge, A. H. J., and A. M. Clay. 1960. *Sources for Roman History 133–70 B.C.* Oxford.

Gregori, G. L. 2015. "Forgeries and Fakes: Historical and Documentary Forgeries." In C. Bruun and J. C. Edmondson (eds.), *The Oxford Handbook of Roman Epigraphy.* Oxford. 54–65.

Grethlein, J. 2013. *Experience and Teleology in Ancient Historiography: "Futures Past" from Herodotus to Augustine.* Cambridge and New York.

Griffin, M. T. 1976. *Seneca, a Philosopher in Politics.* Oxford and New York.

2003. "*Clementia* after Caesar: From Politics to Philosophy." In F. Cairns and E. Fantham (eds.), *Caesar against Liberty? Papers of the Langford Latin Seminar.* Leeds. 154–182.

Griffin, M. T. (ed.) 2009. *A Companion to Julius Caesar.* Malden, MA, and Oxford.

Griffin, M. T., and E. M. Atkins (eds.) 1991. *Marcus Tullius Cicero: On Duties.* Cambridge.

Griffiths, D. M. 2008. "Changing Life Expectancy throughout History." *Journal of the Royal Society of Medicine* 101: 577.

Grillo, L. 2012. *The Art of Caesar's* Bellum Civile: *Literature, Ideology, and Community.* Cambridge.

2015. *Cicero's* De provinciis consularibus oratio. Oxford.

Grillo, L., and C. Krebs (eds.) 2018. *The Cambridge Companion to the Writings of Julius Caesar.* Cambridge.

Grisart, A. 1981. "L'Atuatuca césarienne au Fort de Chaudfontaine?" *L'antiquité classique* 50: 367–381.

Griswold, C. L., and D. Konstan (eds.) 2012. *Ancient Forgiveness: Classical, Judaic, and Christian.* Cambridge.

Gruen, E. 1966. "Publius Clodius, Instrument or Independent Agent?" *Phoenix* 20: 120–130.

1968. "Pompey and the Pisones." *CSCA* 1: 155–170.

1969. "Notes on the 'First Catilinarian Conspiracy.'" *CPh* 64: 20–24.

1969a. "Pompey, the Roman Aristocracy, and the Conference of Luca." *Historia* 28: 71–108.

1973. "The Trial of C. Antonius." *Latomus* 32: 301–310.

1974. *The Last Generation of the Roman Republic*. Berkeley.

1992. *Culture and National Identity in Republican Rome*. Ithaca, NY.

1995. "The 'Fall' of the Scipios." In I. Malkin and Z. W. Rubinsohn (eds.), *Leaders and Masses in the Roman World: Studies in Honor of Zvi Yavez.* Leiden. 59–90.

1996. "The Expansion of the Empire under Augustus." *CAH*² 10: 147–197.

2009. "Caesar as a Politician." In M. T. Griffin (ed.), *A Companion to Julius Caesar*. Malden, MA, and Oxford. 23–36.

Haake, M., and A.-C. Harders (eds.) 2017. *Politische Kultur und Soziale Struktur der römischen Republik*. Stuttgart.

Habicht, C. 1990. *Cicero the Politician*. Baltimore.

Halkin, L. 1953. *La supplication d'action de grâces chez les Romains (Bibliothèque de la Faculté de Philosophie et Lettres de l'Université de Liège* 128). Paris.

Hall, J. 2009. *Politeness and Politics in Cicero's Letters*. Oxford.

2009a. "Serving the Times: Cicero and Caesar the Dictator." In W. J. Dominik, J. Garthwaite, and P. A. Roche (eds.), *Writing Politics in Imperial Rome*. Leiden. 89–110.

Haller, B. 1967. "C. Asinius Pollio als Politiker und zeitkritischer Historiker. Ein Beitrag zur Geschichte des Übergangs von der Republik zum Prinzipat in Rom (60 bis 30 v. Chr.)." Diss. Münster.

Hammer, D. 2014. *Roman Political Thought*. Cambridge.

Hammersley, R. 2012. "James Harrington's *The Commonwealth of Oceana* and the Republican Tradition." In L. Lunger Knoppers (ed.), *The Oxford Handbook of Literature and the English Revolution*. Oxford. 534–550.

Hardy, E. G. 1924. *The Catilinarian Conspiracy in Its Context*. Oxford.

Hargreaves Heap, S. P., and Y. Varoufakis. 1995. *Game Theory: A Critical Introduction*. London and New York.

Harrington, J. 1656/1992. *The Commonwealth of Oceana* and *A System of Politics*. Ed. by J. G. A. Pocock. Cambridge.

Harris, W. V. 1979. *War and Imperialism in Republican Rome, 327–70 B.C.* Oxford.

2001. *Restraining Rage: The Ideology of Anger Control in Classical Antiquity*. Cambridge, MA.

2009. *Dreams and Experience in Classical Antiquity*. Cambridge, MA.

Harrison, I. 2008. "Catiline, Clodius, and Popular Politics at Rome during the 60s and 50s BC." *BICS* 51: 95–118.

Harrison, S. 2017. *Horace, Odes Book II*. Cambridge.

Haselgrove, C. 1984. "Warfare and Its Aftermath as Reflected in the Precious Metal Coinage of Belgic Gaul." *OJA* 3: 81–105.

Hastrup, T. 1957. "On the Date of Caesar's *Commentaries of the Gallic War.*" *C&M* 18: 59–74.

Havener, W. 2014. "A Ritual against the Rule? The Representation of Civil War Victory in the Late Republican Triumph." In C. H. Lange and F. J. Vervaet (eds.), *The Roman Republican Triumph: Beyond the Spectacle.* Rome. 165–179.

Heftner, H. 1995. *Plutarch und der Aufstieg des Pompeius. Ein historischer Kommentar zu Plutarchs Pompeiusvita Teil I: Kap. 1–45.* Frankfurt.

Hegel, G. W. F. 1847/2001. *The Philosophy of History.* Tr. J. Sebree. Kitchener.

Heikkilä, K. 1993. "*Lex non iure rogata*: Senate and the Annulment of the Laws in the Republic." In U. Paananen (ed.), *Senatus Populusque Romanus: Studies in Roman Republican Legislation.* Helsinki. 117–142.

Hekster, H. 2012. "Kings and Regime Change in the Roman Republic." In C. Smith and L. M. Yarrow (eds.), *Imperialism, Cultural Politics, and Polybius.* Oxford. 184–204.

Henderson, J. 1998. *Fighting for Rome: Poets and Caesars, History and Civil War.* Cambridge.

Hickson-Hahn, F. 2000. "Pompey's *Supplicatio Duplicata*: A Novel Form of Thanksgiving." *Phoenix* 54: 244–254.

Hillard, T. 2013. "Graffiti's Engagement: The Political Graffiti of the Late Roman Republic." In G. Sears, P. Keegan, and R. Laurence (eds.), *Written Space in the Latin West, 200 BC to AD 300.* London. 105–122.

Hillman, T. P. 1988. "Strategic Reality and the Movements of Caesar, January, 49 BC." *Historia* 37: 248–252.

1996. "Pompeius ad Parthos?" *Klio* 78: 380–399.

Hinard, F. 1985. *Les proscriptions de la Rome républicaine.* Rome.

2008. *Syllana Varia. Aux sources de la première guerre civile romaine.* Paris.

Hodgson, L. 2017. Res Publica *and the Roman Republic: "Without Body or Form."* Oxford.

Hoffmann, W. 1952. "Zur Vorgeschichte von Caesars Eingreifen in Gallien." *AU* 4: 5–22.

Hölkeskamp, K.-J. 2004. Senatus populusque Romanus. *Die politische Kultur der Republik – Dimensionen und Deutungen.* Stuttgart.

2008. Rev. of Pittenger, *Contested Triumphs. Gnomon* 82: 714–720.

2010. *Reconstructing the Roman Republic: An Ancient Political Culture and Modern Research.* Princeton.

2017. Libera res publica. *Die politische Kultur des antiken Rom – Positionen und Perspektiven.* Stuttgart.

Hölkeskamp, K.-J. (ed.) 2009. *Eine politische Kultur (in) der Krise? Die "letzte Generation" der römischen Republik.* Munich.

Hollis, A. S. 2007. *Fragments of Roman Poetry.* Oxford.

Holzer, H. 2014. *Lincoln and the Power of the Press: The War for Public Opinion.* New York.

Hopkins, K., and G. Burton. 1983. "Political Succession in the Late Republic" and "Ambition and Withdrawal: The Senatorial Aristocracy under the Emperors." In K. Hopkins (ed.), *Death and Renewal.* Cambridge. 31–200.

Horsfall, N. 1974. "The Ides of March. Some New Problems." *G&R* 21: 191–199.

Hume, D. 1778/1983. *The History of England: From the Invasion of Julius Caesar to the Revolution in 1688.* Vol. 5. London.

Humphreys, A. R. (ed.) 1984. *Shakespeare: Julius Caesar.* Oxford.

Hutchinson, G. O. 1998. *Cicero's Correspondence: A Literary Study.* Oxford.

Itgenshorst, T. 2005. *Tota illa pompa: Der Triumph in der römischen Republik.* Göttingen.

Itgenshorst, T., and P. Le Doze (eds.) 2017. *Le norme sous la République et le Haut-Empire romains. Élaboration, diffusion et contournements.* Bordeaux.

Jahn, J. 1970. *Interregnum und Wahldiktatur.* Kallmünz.

Jal, P. 1961. "Remarques sur la cruauté à Rome pendant les guerres civiles (de Sylla à Vespasien)." *BAGB* 475–501.

Jehne, M. 1987. "Caesars Bemühungen um die Reintegration der Pompeianer." *Chiron* 17: 313–341.

1987a. *Der Staat des Dictators Caesar.* Cologne.

2000. "Caesar und die Krise von 47 v. Chr." In G. Urso (ed.), *L'ultimo Cesare.* Rome: 151–173.

2001. *Caesar.* Munich.

2005. "Über den Rubicon. Caesars Eröffnung des Bürgerkrieges am 10. Januar 49 v. Chr." In W. Krieger (ed.), *Und keine Schlacht bei Marathon. Große Ereignisse und Mythen der europäischen Geschichte.* Stuttgart. 25–49, 325–336.

2006. "Who Attended Roman Assemblies? Some Remarks on Political Participation in the Roman Republic." In F. M. Simón, F. Pina Polo, and J. R. Rodríguez (eds.), *Repúblicas y ciudadanos: modelos de participación cívica en el mundo antiguo.* Barcelona. 221–234.

2006a. "Methods, Models, and Historiography." In N. Rosenstein and R. Morstein-Marx (eds.), *A Companion to the Roman Republic.* Malden, MA. 3–28.

2009. *Der große Trend, der kleine Sachzwang und das handelnde Individuum: Caesars Entscheidungen.* Munich.

2009a. "Caesars Alternative(n): das Ende der römischen Republik zwischen autonomem Prozess und Betriebsunfall." In K.-J. Hölkeskamp (ed.), *Eine politische Kultur (in) der Krise? Die "letzte Generation" der römischen Republik.* Munich. 141–160.

2010. "Erfahrungsraum und Erwartungshorizont bei Julius Caesar." In G. Urso (ed.), *Cesare: Precursore o visionario?* Pisa. 311–332.

2011. "Blaming the People in Front of the People." In C. Smith and R. Covino (eds.), *Praise and Blame in Roman Republican Rhetoric.* Swansea. 111–125.

2013. "Feeding the Plebs with Words: The Significance of Senatorial Public Oratory in the Small World of Roman Politics." In C. Steel and H. van der Blom (eds.), *Community and Communication: Oratory and Politics in Republican Rome.* Oxford. 49–62.

2017. "Why the Anti-Caesarians Failed: Political Communication on the Eve of Civil War (51 to 49 BC)." In C. Rosillo-López (ed.), *Political Communication in the Roman World.* Leiden and Boston. 201–227.

Jones, C. P. 1970. "Cicero's Cato." *RhM* 113: 188–196.

Kahneman, D. 2011. *Thinking Fast and Slow*. New York.

Kallet-Marx, R. M. 1995. *Hegemony to Empire: The Development of the Roman Imperium in the East from 148 to 62 BC*. Berkeley.

Kantor, G. 2014. "Roman Treaty with Lycia (*SEG* LV 1452) and the Date of Caesar's Third Dictatorship." *ZPE* 190: 135–136.

Kaster, R. 2006. *Marcus Tullius Cicero: Speech on Behalf of Publius Sestius*. Oxford.

2016. *Studies on the Text of Suetonius' "De vita Caesarum."* Oxford.

Kay, P. 2014. *Rome's Economic Revolution*. Oxford.

Keaveney, A. 1982. "Young Pompey, 106–79 B.C." *AC* 51: 111–139.

1984. "Who Were the *Sullani?*" *Klio* 66: 114–150.

2005. *Sulla: The Last Republican*. Rev. ed. London.

2007. *The Army in the Roman Revolution*. London and New York.

2018. "Notes on the First Mithridatic War in Macedonia and Greece." *SyllClass* 29: 29–65.

Keppie, L. G. F. 1983. *Colonisation and Veteran Settlement in Italy, 47–14 B.C.* London.

King, A. 1990. *Roman Gaul and Germany*. Berkeley.

Koestermann, E. 1970. "Ps.-Sall. *Epistula ad Caesarem senem*. I." *Historia* 19: 216–223.

1971. *C. Sallustius Crispus:* Bellum Iugurthinum. Heidelberg.

Konstan, D. 2005. "Clemency as a Virtue." *CPh* 100: 337–346.

2007. "The Contemporary Political Context." In M. B. Skinner (ed.), *A Companion to Catullus*. Malden, MA. 108–144.

Koortbojian, M. 2013. *The Divinization of Caesar and Augustus: Precedents, Consequences, Implications*. Cambridge.

Kornemann, E. 1896. *Die historische Schriftstellerei des Consuls Asinius Pollio*. Leipzig.

Kraft, K. 1969. *Der goldene Kranz Caesars und der Kampf um die Entlarvung des "Tyrannen."* 2nd ed. Darmstadt.

Kraner, F., W. Dittenberger, and H. Meusel. 1964. *C. Iulii Caesaris Commentarii de bello gallico*. 20th ed. 3 vols. Zürich and Berlin.

Kraus, C. 2005. "Hair, Hegemony, and Historiography: Caesar's Style and Its Earliest Critics." *PBA* 129: 97–115.

2009. "Bellum Gallicum." In M. T. Griffin (ed.), *A Companion to Julius Caesar*. Malden, MA, and Oxford. 159–175.

Krebs, C. 2006. "Imaginary Geography in Caesar's *Bellum Gallicum*." *AJPh* 127: 111–136.

2013. "Caesar, Lucretius and the Dates of the *De rerum natura* and the *Commentarii*." *CQ* 63: 751–758.

2017. "Caesar the Historian." In K. Raaflaub (ed.), *The Landmark Julius Caesar*. New York. Web Essay DD, pp. 210–213. http://thelandmarkcaesar.com/La ndmarkCaesarWebEssays_5Jan2018.pdf

2018. "More than Words: The Commentarii in Their Propagandistic Context." In L. Grillo and C. Krebs (eds.), *The Cambridge Companion to the Writings of Julius Caesar*. Cambridge. 29–42.

2018a. "A Style of Choice." In L. Grillo and C. Krebs (eds.), *The Cambridge Companion to the Writings of Julius Caesar*. Cambridge. 110–130.

Kumar, C. 2015. "Electoral Violence, Threats and Security: Problems and Prospects for Indian Democracy." *American Journal of Social Science Research* 1: 38–51.

Kunkel, W., and R. Wittmann. 1995. *Staatsordnung und Staatspraxis der Römischen Republik*. Munich.

Lacey, W. K. 1961. "The Tribunate of Curio." *Historia* 10: 318–329.

Lange, C. H., and F. J. Vervaet (eds.) 2014. *The Roman Republican Triumph: Beyond the Spectacle*. Rome.

Laurence, R. 1999. *The Roads of Roman Italy: Mobility and Cultural Change*. New York.

1999a. "Tourism, Townplanning and *romanitas:* Rimini's Roman heritage." In M. D. Biddiss and M. Wyke (eds.), *The Uses and Abuses of Antiquity*. Bern and Berlin. 187–205.

Le Bohec, Y. 1998. "Vercingétorix." *RSA* 28: 85–120.

Levick, B. 1998. "The *Veneti* Revisited: C. E. Stevens and the Tradition on Caesar the Propagandist." In K. Welch and A. Powell (eds.), *Caesar as Artful Reporter*. Swansea. 61–83.

Levitsky, S., and D. Ziblatt. 2018. *How Democracies Die*. New York.

Levithan, J. 2013. *Roman Siege Warfare*. Ann Arbor.

Lewis, S. (ed.) 2006. *Ancient Tyranny*. Edinburgh.

Linderski, J. 1965. "Constitutional Aspects of the Consular Elections in 59 B.C." *Historia* 14: 423–442.

1966. "Were Pompey and Crassus Elected in Absence to Their First Consulship?" In M.-L. Bernhard (ed.), *Mélanges offerts à Kazimierz Michalowski*. Warsaw. 523–526.

1995. *Roman Questions: Selected Papers 1958–1993*. Stuttgart.

Lindley, D. V. 2012. *Understanding Uncertainty*. Hoboken.

Lintott, A. W. 1968/1999. *Violence in Republican Rome*. Oxford.

1972. "*Provocatio*: From the Struggle of the Orders to the Principate." *ANRW* 1.2: 226–267.

1990. "Electoral Bribery in the Roman Republic." *JRS* 80: 1–16.

1993. Imperium Romanum: *Politics and Administration*. London.

1999. *The Constitution of the Roman Republic*. Oxford.

2008. *Cicero as Evidence*. Oxford.

2009. "The Assassination." In M. T. Griffin (ed.), *A Companion to Julius Caesar*. Malden, MA, and Oxford. 72–82.

2013. *Plutarch*: Demosthenes *and* Cicero. Oxford.

Liverani, P. 2008. "Cesare urbanista." In G. Gentili (ed.), *Giulio Cesare: L'uomo, le imprese, il mito*. Milan. 42–51.

Lott, J. B. 2001. *The Neighborhoods of Augustan Rome*. New York.

Lundgreen, C. 2011. *Regelkonflikte in der römischen Republik. Geltung und Gewichtung von Normen in politischen Entscheidungsprozessen*. Stuttgart.

Macfarlane, R. T. 1996. "*Ab inimicis incitatus*: On Dating the Composition of Caesar's *Bellum Civile*." *SyllClass* 7: 107–132.

MacGillivray, R. 1974. *Restoration Historians and the English Civil War.* The Hague.

Mackay, C. 2000. "Sulla and the Monuments: Studies in His Public Persona." *Historia* 49: 161–210.

Mackie, N. 1992. "*Popularis* Ideology and Popular Politics at Rome in the First Century BC." *RhM* 135: 49–73.

Maier, U. 1978. *Caesars Feldzüge in Gallien (58–51 v. Chr.) in ihrem Zusammenhang mit der stadtrömischen Politik.* Bonn.

Malitz, J. 1984. "Caesar's Partherkrieg." *Historia* 33: 21–59.

———. 1987. " Die Kanzlei Caesars: Herrschaftsorganisation zwischen Republik und Prinzipat." *Historia* 36: 51–72.

Manuwald, G. 2007. *Cicero: Philippics 3–9.* 2 vols. Berlin.

Marshall, B. A. 1974. "Cicero and Sallust on Crassus and Catiline." *Latomus* 33: 804–813.

———. 1975. "The Date of the Delivery of Cicero's *in Pisonem.*" *CQ* 25: 88–93.

———. 1985. *A Historical Commentary on Asconius.* Columbia, MO.

———. 1987. "Pompeius' Fear of Assassination." *Chiron* 17: 119–133.

McDermott, W. 1970. "In Ligarianam." *TAPhA* 101: 317–347.

———. 1972. "Cicero's Publication of His Consular Orations." *Philologus* 116: 277–284.

———. 1982/1983. "Caesar's Projected Dacian-Parthian Expedition." *AncSoc* 13/14: 223–231.

McDonnell, M. 2006. *Roman Manliness: Virtus and the Roman Republic.* Cambridge.

McGushin, P. 1977. Bellum Catilinae: *A Commentary.* Leiden.

———. 1992–1994. *Sallust:* The Histories. 2 vols. Oxford.

Meier, C. 1961. "Zur Chronologie und Politik in Caesars erstem Konsulat." *Historia* 10: 68–98.

———. 1965. "*Populares.*" *RE* Suppl. 10: 549–615.

———. 1970. "Caesars Bürgerkrieg." In C. Meier, *Entstehung des Begriffs "Demokratie." Vier Prolegomena zu einer historischen Theorie.* Frankfurt. 70–150.

———. 1975. "Das Kompromiss-Angebot an Caesar i. J. 59 v. Chr., ein Beispiel senatorischer 'Verfassungspolitik.'" *MH* 32: 197–208.

———. 1982. *Caesar.* English tr. D. McClintock. New York.

Mensching, E. 1984. "Zu den Auseinandersetzungen um den Gallischen Krieg und der Considius-Episode (BG I 21–22)." *Hermes* 112: 53–65.

Meyer, E. 1919. *Caesars Monarchie und das Principat des Pompeius.* Stuttgart.

Meyer, P. N. 2014. *Storytelling for Lawyers.* Oxford and New York.

Miles, G. 1995. *Livy: Reconstructing Early Rome.* Ithaca and London.

Millar, F. 1998. *The Crowd in Rome in the Late Republic.* Ann Arbor.

———. 2002. *Rome, the Greek World, and the East.* Chapel Hill.

Milnor, K. 2012. "Gender and Forgiveness in the Early Roman Empire." In C. L. Griswold and D. Konstan (eds.), *Ancient Forgiveness: Classical, Judaic, and Christian.* Cambridge. 97–114.

Mitchell, T. 1979. *Cicero: The Ascending Years.* New Haven.

———. 1991. *Cicero: The Senior Statesman.* New Haven.

Moatti, C. 2017. "*Res publica, forma rei publicae* and *SPQR*." *Essays in Honour of Fergus Millar. BICS* 60: 34–48.

2018. Res publica. *Histoire romaine de la chose publique.* Paris.

Moles, J. 1982. "Plutarch, *Crassus* 13.4–5 and Cicero's *De Consiliis Suis.*" *LCM* 7: 136–137.

1988. *The Life of Cicero.* Warminster.

1997. "Plutarch, Brutus and Brutus' Greek and Latin Letters." In J. M. Mossman (ed.), *Plutarch and His Intellectual World: Essays on Plutarch.* London. 141–168.

Mommsen, T. 1887. *Römisches Staatsrecht.* 3 vols. Leipzig.

1894/1996. *The History of Rome.* 5 vols. Tr. W. P. Dickson. London.

Montlahuc, P. 2019. *Le pouvoir des bons mots. "Faire rire" et politique à Rome du milieu du IIIe siècle a.C. à l'avènement des Antonins.* Rome.

Montesquieu, Charles de Secondat (Baron de). 1734/1965. *Considerations on the Causes of the Greatness of the Romans and Their Decline.* Tr. D. Lowenthal. New York.

Morgan, L. 1997. "Julius Caesar as Tyrant and Pedant." *JRS* 87: 23–40.

2000. "The Autopsy of C. Asinius Pollio." *JRS* 90: 51–69.

Morrell, K. 2017. *Pompey, Cato, and the Governance of the Roman Empire.* Oxford.

2018. "'Certain Gentlemen Say . . . .': Cicero, Cato, and the Debate on the Validity of Clodius' Laws." In C. Gray, A. Balbo, R. M. A. Marshall, and C. E. W. Steel (eds.), *Reading Republican Oratory: Reconstructions, Contexts, Receptions.* Oxford. 191–210.

Morstein-Marx, R. 1998. "Publicity, Popularity and Patronage in the *Commentariolum Petitionis.*" *CA* 17: 259–288.

2004. *Mass Oratory and Political Power in the Late Republic.* Cambridge.

2007. "Caesar's Alleged Fear of Prosecution and His *ratio absentis* in the Approach to the Civil War." *Historia* 56: 159–178.

2009. "*Dignitas* and *res publica*: Caesar and Republican Legitimacy." In K.-J. Hölkeskamp (ed.), *Eine politische Kultur (in) der Krise? Die "letzte Generation" der römischen Republik.* Munich. 115–140.

2011. "Consular Appeals to the Army in 88 and 87: The Locus of Legitimacy in Late-Republican Rome." In H. Beck, A. Duplá, M. Jehne, and F. Pina Polo (eds.), *Consuls and* Res Publica. Cambridge. 259–278.

2012. "Political Graffiti in the Late Roman Republic: Hidden Transcripts and Common Knowledge." In C. Kuhn (ed.), *Politische Kommunikation und öffentliche Meinung in der antiken Welt.* Heidelberg. 191–217.

2013. "'Cultural Hegemony' and the Communicative Power of the Roman Elite." In C. Steel and H. van der Blom (eds.), *Community and Communication: Oratory and Politics in Republican Rome.* Oxford. 29–48.

2014. Rev. of Arena 2012. *CJ-Online* 2014.03.07.

2015. "Persuading the People in the Roman Participatory Context." In D. Hammer (ed.), *A Companion to Greek Democracy and the Roman Republic.* Malden, MA. 294–309.

2019. "Fear of the People." *RSI* 131: 515–533.

Forthcoming. "Values and Ideology." In V. Arena and J. Prag (eds.), *Companion to Roman Republican Political Culture.*

Morstein-Marx, R., and N. Rosenstein. 2006. "The Transformation of the Republic." In N. Rosenstein and R. Morstein-Marx (eds.), *A Companion to the Roman Republic.* Malden, MA. 625–637.

Mouristen, H. 2001. *Plebs and Politics in the Late Roman Republic.* Cambridge.

2017. *Politics in the Roman Republic.* Cambridge.

Muccioli, F. 1994. "Dopo la vittoria dei *Campi Raudi:* Mario Terzo Fondatore di Rome? (Su Plut., *Mar.* 27, 8–10)." *Atene e Roma* 39: 192–205.

Müller, C. 1972. *Untersuchungen zu Caesars italischem Feldzug 49 v. Chr.* Munich.

Mundt, F. 2004. "Cicero's '*Commentarioli belli Ciliciensis*': Fam. 15.4 and other letters from Cilicia." *Philologus* 148: 255–273.

Muntz, C. E. 2017. *Diodorus Siculus and the World of the Late Roman Republic.* Oxford.

Nicolet, C. 1966/1974. *L'ordre équestre à l'époque républicaine (312–43 av. J.-C.).* 2 vols. BEFAR 207. Paris.

Nippel, W. 1995. *Public Order in Ancient Rome.* Cambridge.

Nisbet, R. G. M. 1961. *Cicero* in L. Calpurnium Pisonem. Oxford.

Nisbet, R. G. M., and M. Hubbard. 1978. *A Commentary on Horace, Odes, Book II.* Oxford.

Nissen, H. 1881. "Der Ausbruch des Bürgerkriegs 49 v. Chr." *HZ* 46: 48–105.

Noreña, C. F. 2011. *Imperial Ideals in the Roman West: Representation, Circulation, Power.* Cambridge.

North, J. A. 1990. "Politics and Aristocracy in the Roman Republic." *CPh* 85: 277–287.

2008. "Caesar at the Lupercalia." *JRS* 98: 144–160.

2010. Rev. of Flower, *Roman Republics. JRA* 23: 469–472.

2011. "*Lex Domitia* Revisited." In J. H. Richardson and F. Santangelo (eds.), *Priests and State in the Roman World.* Stuttgart. 39–61.

Nousek, D. 2018. "Genres and Generic Contaminations: The *Commentarii.*" In L. Grillo and C. Krebs (eds.), *The Cambridge Companion to the Writings of Julius Caesar.* Cambridge. 97–109.

Odelman, E. 1972. "Études sur quelques reflets du style administratif chez César." Diss. Stockholm.

Ogilvie, R. M. 1965. *A Commentary on Livy, Books I–V.* Oxford.

Ogilvie, R. M., and I. A. Richmond. 1967. *Tacitus:* De vita Agricolae. Oxford.

Osgood, J. 2006. *Caesar's Legacy.* Cambridge.

2007. Rev. of Wyke (ed.) 2006, Kamm, *Julius Caesar,* and Goldsworthy 2006. *CR* 57: 466–469.

2008. "Caesar and Nicomedes." *CQ* 58: 687–691.

2009. "The Pen and the Sword: Writing and Conquest in Caesar's Gaul." *ClAnt* 28: 328–358.

2014. "Julius Caesar and Spanish Triumph-Hunting." In C. H. Lange and F. J. Vervaet (eds.), *The Roman Republican Triumph: Beyond the Spectacle*. Rome. 149–162.

Östenberg, I. 2009. *Staging the World: Spoils, Captives, and Representations in the Roman Triumphal Procession*. Oxford.

2014. "Triumph and Spectacle. Victory Celebrations in the Late Republican Civil Wars." In C. H. Lange and F. J. Vervaet (eds.), *The Roman Republican Triumph: Beyond the Spectacle*. Rome. 181–193.

Ottmer, H. M. 1979. *Die Rubikon-Legende. Untersuchungen zu Caesars und Pompeius' Strategie vor und nach Ausbruch des Bürgerkrieges*. Boppard.

Panayotakis, C. 2010. *Decimus Laberius: The Fragments*. Cambridge.

Parkin, T. G. 1992. *Demography and Roman Society*. Baltimore and London.

Pascucci, C. 2007. "*Fluvius Rubico, quondam finis Italiae*. Osservazioni sul corso del Rubicone in epoca romana." *Orizzonti* 8: 79–85.

Peer, A. 2015. *Julius Caesar's* Bellum Civile *and the Composition of a New Reality*. Dorchester.

Pelling, C. 1982. Rev. of Ottmer 1979. *Gnomon* 54: 212–213.

1988. *Life of Antony*. Cambridge.

2002. *Plutarch and History: Eighteen Studies*. Swansea.

2004. "Plutarch on the Outbreak of the Roman Civil War." In H. Heftner and K. Tomaschitz (eds.), *Ad Fontes! Festschrift für G. Dobesch*. Vienna. 317–327.

2006. "Judging Julius Caesar." In M. Wyke (ed.), *Julius Caesar in Western Culture*. Malden, MA. 3–26.

2006a. "Breaking the Bounds: Writing about Julius Caesar." In B. C. McGing and J. M. Mossman (eds.), *The Limits of Ancient Biography*. 255–280.

2011. *Plutarch: Caesar*. Oxford.

Pennacini, A. (ed.) 1993. *Gaio Giulio Cesare, Opera omnia*. Tr. A. La Penna and A. Pennacini. Commentary by M. Faraguna, A. Garzetti, and D. Vottero. Turin.

Pepe, C. 2018. "Fragments of Epideictic Oratory: The Exemplary Case of the Laudatio Funebris for Women." In C. Gray, A. Balbo, R. M. A. Marshall, and C. E. W. Steel (eds.), *Reading Republican Oratory: Reconstructions, Contexts, Receptions*. Oxford. 281–296.

Petersmann, G. 1983. "Cornelius Gallus und der Papyrus von Qasr Ibrim." *ANRW* II.30.3: 1649–1655.

Peterson, M. (ed.) 2015. *The Prisoner's Dilemma*. Cambridge.

Pettinger, A. 2012. *The Republic in Danger*. Oxford.

Phillips, E. J. 1974. "The Prosecution of C. Rabirius in 63 BC." *Klio* 56: 87–101.

Pina Polo, F. 1989. "Las contiones civiles y militares en Roma." Diss. Saragossa.

2006. "The Tyrant Must Die: Preventive Tyrannicide in Roman Political Thought." In F. M. Simón, F. Pina Polo, and J. R. Rodríguez (eds.), *Repúblicas y ciudadanos: modelos de participación cívica en el mundo antiguo*. Barcelona. 71–101.

2011. *The Consul at Rome: The Civil Functions of the Consuls in the Roman Republic*. Cambridge.

2017. "The 'Tyranny' of the Gracchi and the Concordia of the Optimates: An Ideological Construct." In R. Cristofori, A. Galimberti, and F. R. Vio (eds.), *Costruire la memoria*. Rome. 5–33.

2018. "Political Alliances and Rivalries in Contiones in the Late Roman Republic." In H. van der Blom, C. Gray, and C. Steel (eds.), *Institutions and Ideology in Republican Rome: Speech, Audience and Decision*. Cambridge. 107–127.

2018a. "Magistrates without Pedigree: The *Consules Suffecti* of the Triumviral Age." *JRS* 108: 99–114.

Pittenger, M. R. Pelikan. 2008. *Contested Triumphs: Politics, Pageantry, and Performance in Livy's Republican Rome*. Berkeley.

Pocock, L. G. 1926/1967. *A Commentary on Cicero* in Vatinium. London. (Repr. Amsterdam 1967.)

Powell, A. 1998. "Julius Caesar and the Presentation of Massacre." In K. Welch and A. Powell (eds.), *Caesar as Artful Reporter*. Swansea. 111–137.

Powell, A. (ed.) 2013. *Hindsight in Greek and Roman History*. Swansea.

Powell, H. J. 2016. *Targeting Americans: The Constitutionality of the U.S. Drone War*. Oxford.

Price, S. R. F. 1984. *Rituals and Power: The Roman Imperial Cult in Asia Minor*. Cambridge.

Pucci Ben Zeev, M. 1996. "When Was the Title '*Dictator perpetuus*' Given to Caesar?" *AC* 65: 251–253.

1996a. "Caesar's Decrees in the *Antiquities*: Josephus' Forgeries or Authentic Roman *senatus consulta*?" *Athenaeum* 84: 71–91.

Purcell, N. 1993. "*Atrium Libertatis*." *PBSR* 61: 125–155.

Putnam, M. C. J. 1980. "Propertius and the New Gallus Fragment." *ZPE* 39: 49–56.

Raaflaub, K. 1974. *Dignitatis contentio. Studien zur Motivation und politischen Taktik im Bürgerkrieg zwischen Caesar und Pompeius*. Munich.

1974a. "Zum politischen Wirken der caesarfreundlichen Volkstribunen am Vorabend des Bürgerkrieges." *Chiron* 4: 293–326.

1975. "Caesar und die Friedensverhandlungen zu Beginn des Bürgerkrieges von 49 v. Chr." *Chiron* 5: 247–300.

2003. "Caesar as Liberator? Factional Politics, Civil War, and Ideology." In F. Cairns and E. Fantham (eds.), *Caesar against Liberty? Papers of the Langford Latin Seminar*. Leeds. 35–67.

2010. "Creating a Grand Coalition of True Roman Citizens." In B. Breed, C. Damon, and A. Rossi (eds.), *Citizens of Discord*. Oxford. 159–170.

2010a. "Between Tradition and Innovation: Shifts in Caesar's Political Propaganda and Self-Representation." In G. Urso (ed.), *Cesare: Precursore o visionario?* Pisa. 141–157.

2017. "The Roman Commentarius and Caesar's Commentaries." In K. Raaflaub (ed.), *The Landmark Julius Caesar*. New York. Web Essay CC, pp. 203–209. http://thelandmarkcaesar.com/LandmarkCaesarWebEssays_5 Jan2018.pdf

Raaflaub, K. (ed.) 2017. *The Landmark Julius Caesar*. New York.

Raaflaub, K., and J. T. Ramsey. 2017. "Reconstructing the Chronology of Caesar's Gallic Wars." *Histos* 11: 1–74.

———. 2017a. "The Chronology of Caesar's Campaigns." In K. Raaflaub (ed.), *The Landmark Julius Caesar*. New York. Web Essay BB. http://thelandmarkcaesar.com/LandmarkCaesarWebEssays_5Jan2018.pdf

Racine, F. 2012. "Review of Billows 2009, Gelzer 2008, and Canfora 2007." *CR* 62: 241–243.

Rambaud, M. 1966. "Note sur l'armée des gaules de 58 à 54." *IL* 18: 21–25.

———. 1966a. *L'art de la déformation historique dans les commentaires de César*. 2nd ed. Paris.

Ramsey, J. T. 2000. "'Beware the Ides of March': An Astronomical Prediction?" *CQ* 50: 440–454.

———. 2003. *Cicero: Philippics I–II*. Cambridge.

———. 2004. "Did Julius Caesar Temporarily Banish Mark Antony from His Inner Circle?" *CQ* 54: 161–173.

———. 2007. *Sallust's Bellum Catilinae*. 2nd ed. Oxford.

———. 2009. "The Proconsular Years: Politics at a Distance." In M. T. Griffin (ed.), *A Companion to Julius Caesar*. Malden, MA, and Oxford. 37–56.

———. 2013. *Sallust: The War with Catiline, the War with Jugurtha*. (Rev. Loeb ed.) Cambridge, MA.

———. 2016. "How and Why Was Pompey Made Sole Consul in 52 B.C.?" *Historia* 65: 298–324.

———. 2019. "The Date of the Consular Elections in 63 and the Inception of Catiline's Conspiracy." *HSCPh* 110: 213–269.

———. Forthcoming. *Asconius: Commentaries on Speeches of Cicero* (rev.). Oxford.

Ramsey, J. T., and A. Lewis Licht. 1997. *The Comet of 44 B.C. and Caesar's Funeral Games*. Atlanta.

Ramsey, J. T., and K. Raaflaub. 2017. "Chronological Tables for Caesar's Wars (58–45 BCE)." *Histos* 11: 162–217.

Rauh, S. 2012. "Suicide in the Roman Republic." Diss. UCSB.

———. 2018. "Cato at Utica: The Emergence of a Roman Suicide Tradition." *AJPh* 139: 59–91.

Rawson, E. 1975. "Caesar's Heritage. Hellenistic Kings and Their Roman Equals." *JRS* 65: 148–159.

———. 1982. "History, Historiography, and Cicero, *Expositio Consiliorum Suorum*." *LCM* 7: 121–124.

———. 1991. *Roman Culture and Society: Collected Papers*. Oxford.

Renehan, R. 1969. *Greek Textual Criticism: A Reader*. Cambridge, MA.

Rice Holmes, T. 1911. *Caesar's Conquest of Gaul*. 2nd ed. Oxford.

———. 1923. *The Roman Republic and the Founder of the Empire*. 3 vols. Oxford.

Rich, J. W. 1976. *Declaring War in the Roman Republic in the Period of Transmarine Expansion*. Coll. Latomus 149. Brussels.

———. 2014. "The Triumph in the Roman Republic: Frequency, Fluctuation and Policy." In C. H. Lang and F. J. Vervaet (eds.), *The Roman Republican Triumph beyond the Spectacle*. Rome. 197–258.

Richardson, J. S. 1996. *The Romans in Spain*. Oxford and Cambridge, MA.

2008. *The Language of Empire: Rome and the Idea of Empire from the Third Century BC to the Second Century AD*. Cambridge.

Rickman, G. 1980. *The Corn Supply of Ancient Rome*. Oxford.

Ridley, M. 1996. *The Origins of Virtue: Human Instincts and the Evolution of Cooperation*. New York.

Ridley, R. 2000. "The Dictator's Mistake. Caesar's Escape from Sulla." *Historia* 49: 211–229.

2004. "Attacking the World with Five Cohorts." *AS* 34: 127–152.

Riggsby, A. 2006. *Caesar in Gaul and Rome: War in Words*. Austin, TX.

Rising, T. 2013. "Senatorial Opposition to Pompey's Eastern Settlement. A Storm in a Teacup?" *Historia* 62: 196–221.

2015. "Caesar's Offer, Cicero's Rebuff, and the Two Land Commissions of 59 B.C." *Historia* 64: 419–427.

Robb, M. A. 2010. *Beyond* Populares *and* Optimates: *Political Language in the Late Republic*. Stuttgart.

Robinson, O. 1992. *Ancient Rome: City Planning and Administration*. New York.

Rodgers, B. S. 2008. "Catulus' Speech in Cassius Dio 36.31–36." *GRBS* 48: 295–318.

Roller, M. B. 2001. *Constructing Autocracy: Aristocrats and Emperors in Julio-Claudian Rome*. Princeton.

Rondholz, A. 2009. "Crossing the Rubicon: A Historiographical Study." *Mnemosyne* 62: 432–450.

Roselaar, S. T. 2010. *Public Land in the Roman Republic: A Social and Economic History of* Ager Publicus *in Italy, 396–89 BC*. Oxford.

Rosenblitt, J. A. 2016. "Hostile Politics: Sallust and the Rhetoric of Popular Champions in the Late Republic." *AJPh* 137: 655–688.

2019. *Rome after Sulla*. London and New York.

Rosenstein, N. 1995. "Sorting Out the Lot in Republican Rome." *AJPh* 116: 43–75.

2004. *Rome at War: Farms, Families, and Death in the Middle Republic*. Chapel Hill.

2006. "Aristocratic Values." In N. Rosenstein and R. Morstein-Marx (eds.), *A Companion to the Roman Republic*. Malden, MA. 365–382.

2011. "War, Wealth and Consuls." In H. Beck, A. Duplá, M. Jehne, and F. Pina Polo (eds.), *Consuls and* Res Publica. Cambridge. 133–158.

2012. *Rome and the Mediterranean, 290 to 146 BC: The Imperial Republic*. Edinburgh.

Rosenstein, N., and R. Morstein-Marx (eds.) 2006. *A Companion to the Roman Republic*. Malden, MA.

Rosillo López, C. 2010. *La corruption à la fin de la République romaine (IIe-Ier s. av. J.-C.) aspects politiques et financiers*. Stuttgart.

2017. *Public Opinion and Politics in the Late Roman Republic*. Cambridge.

Rotondi, G. 1912. Leges publicae populi Romani. Milan.

Roymans, N. 2018. "A Roman Massacre in the Far North: Caesar's Annihilation of the Tencteri and Usipetes in the Dutch River Area." In M. Fernández-Götz and N. Roymans (eds.), *Conflict Archaeology: Materialities of Collective Violence from Prehistory to Late Antiquity*. London and New York. 167–181.

Rüpke, J. 2005. *Fasti Sacerdotum: Die Mitglieder der Priesterschaften und das sakrale Funktionspersonal römischer, griechischer, orientalischer und jüdisch-christlicher Kulte in der Stadt Rom von 300 v. Chr. bis 499 n. Chr.* 3 vols. Stuttgart.

Ryan, F. X. 1996. "Bibulus as President of the Senate." *Latomus* 55: 384–388.

1996a. "Four Republican Senators." *C&M* 47: 207–215.

1996b. "C. Vibius Pansa Caetronianus and His Fathers." *Mnemosyne* 49: 186–188.

1997. "The Praetorship of L. Roscius Otho." *Hermes* 125: 236–240.

1998. *Rank and Participation in the Republican Senate.* Stuttgart.

Sanford, F. W. 1911. "The Narrative in the Eighth Book of the 'Gallic War,' Chapters 50–55; A Study in Chronology." *University of Nebraska Studies* 11: 293–342.

Santangelo, F. 2006. "Sulla and the Senate: A Reconsideration." *CCG* 17: 7–22.

2010. Rev. of Tatum 2008. *JRS* 100: 253–254.

2012. "'Sullanus' and 'Sullani.'" *Arctos* 46: 187–191.

2013. *Divination, Prediction and the End of the Republic.* Cambridge.

2014. "Roman Politics in the 70s B.C.: A Story of Realignments?" *JRS* 104: 1–27.

2016. "Caesar's Aims in Northeast Italy." *PBSR* 84: 101–129.

2018. "Theophanes of Mytilene, Cicero and Pompey's Inner Circle." In H. van der Blom, C. Gray, and C. Steel (eds.), *Institutions and Ideology in Republican Rome: Speech, Audience and Decision.* Cambridge. 128–146.

Schleussner, B. 1978. *Die Legaten der römischen Republik; decem legati und ständige Hilfsgesandte.* Munich.

Schmid, W. 1993. *Frühschriften Sallusts im Horizont des Gesamtwerkes.* Neustadt.

Schneider, W. C. 2004. "A 'Neque' and the Roman Republic: A Text-Critically Abridged Compromise Proposal of the Senate of June 50 in a Letter of the Caelius Rufus." *WS* 117: 115–150.

Scholz, P. 2011. *Den Vätern folgen: Sozialisation und Erziehung der republikanischen Senatsaristokratie.* Berlin.

Schulz, R. 2002. "Caesars Statthalterschaft in Spanien." In J. Spielvogel (ed.), *Res publica reperta: zur Verfassung und Gesellschaft der römischen Republik und des frühen Prinzipats: Festschrift für Jochen Bleicken zum 75. Geburtstag.* Stuttgart. 263–278.

Scullard, H. 1981. *Festivals and Ceremonies of the Roman Republic.* London.

Seager, R. 1964. "The First Catilinarian Conspiracy." *Historia* 13: 338–347.

1972. "Cicero and the Word *Popularis.*" *CQ* 1972: 328–338.

1973. "Iusta Catilinae." *Historia* 22: 240–248.

1994. "Sulla." *CAH²* 9: 165–207.

2002. *Pompey the Great: A Political Biography.* 2nd ed. Malden, MA.

2003. "Caesar and Gaul: Some Perspectives on the *Bellum Gallicum.*" In F. Cairns and E. Fantham (eds.), *Caesar against Liberty? Papers of the Langford Latin Seminar.* Leeds. 19–34.

Sedley, D. 1997. "The Ethics of Brutus and Cassius." *JRS* 87: 41–53.

Segal, N. 2019. "Military Achievement and Late-Republican Aristocratic Values, 81–49 B.C.E." Diss. UCSB.

Sehlmeyer, M. 1999. *Stadtrömische Ehrenstatuen der republikanischen Zeit.* Stuttgart.

Shackleton Bailey, D. R. 1960. "The Roman Nobility in the Second Civil War." *CQ* 10: 253–267.

——— 1965. *Cicero: Letters to Atticus.* 7 vols. Cambridge.

——— 1971. *Cicero.* New York.

——— 1977. *Cicero: Epistulae ad Familiares.* 2 vols. Cambridge.

——— 1980. *Cicero: Epistulae ad Quintum fratrem et M. Brutum.* Cambridge.

——— 1986. *Cicero: Philippics.* Chapel Hill.

——— 1991. *Two Studies in Roman Nomenclature.* Atlanta.

——— 1998. "Caesar's Men in Cicero's Correspondence." *Ciceroniana* 10: 107–118.

Sharpe, K. 2013. *Rebranding Rule: The Restoration and Revolution Monarchy, 1660–1714.* New Haven and London.

Shatzman, I. 1975. *Senatorial Wealth and Roman Politics.* Coll. Latomus 142. Brussels.

Sherwin-White, A. N. 1983. *Roman Foreign Policy in the East, 168 B.C. to A.D. 1.* Norman, OK.

Siani-Davies, M. 1996. "Gaius Rabirius Postumus: A Roman Financier and Caesar's Political Ally." *Arctos* 30: 207–240.

——— 2001. *Marcus Tullius Cicero: Pro Rabirio Postumo.* Oxford.

Silver, N. 2012, *The Signal and the Noise,* New York.

Simón, F. M., F. Pina Polo, and J. R. Rodríguez (eds.) 2006. *Repúblicas y ciudadanos: modelos de participación cívica en el mundo antiguo.* Barcelona.

Sklenář, R. 1998. "La République des Signes: Caesar, Cato and the Language of Sallustian Morality." *TAPhA* 128: 205–220.

Skořepa, M. 2011. *Decision-Making: A Behavioral Economic Approach.* New York.

Smith, C., and L. M. Yarrow. 2012. *Imperialism, Cultural Politics, and Polybius.* Oxford.

Snyder, G. H. 1977. *Conflict among Nations: Bargaining, Decision Making, and System Structure in International Crises.* Princeton.

Sommer, M. 2010. "Le ragioni della guerra: Roma, i Parti e l'ultimo imperativo di Cesare." In G. Urso (ed.), *Cesare: Precursore o visionario?* Pisa. 123–140.

Sordi, M. 1969. "Ottaviano patrono di Taranto nel 43 a.C." *Epigraphica* 31: 79–83.

——— 1999. "L'opposizione a Cesare e i Lupercali." *CISA* 25: 151–160.

——— 2000. "I poteri dell'ultimo Cesare." In G. Urso (ed.), *L'ultimo Cesare.* Rome. 305–313.

——— 2003. "Caesar's Powers in His Last Phase." In F. Cairns and E. Fantham (eds.), *Caesar against Liberty? Papers of the Langford Latin Seminar.* Leeds. 190–199. (English trans. of Sordi 2000.)

Stacey, P. 2014. "The Princely Republic." *JRS* 104: 133–154.

Staniland, P. 2014. "Violence and Democracy (Review Article)." *Comparative Politics* 47: 99–118.

Steel, C. 2001. *Cicero, Rhetoric, and Empire.* Oxford.

2010. "Tribunician Sacrosanctity and Oratorical Performance in the Late Republic." In D. H. Berry and A. Erskine (eds.), *Form and Function in Roman Oratory*. Cambridge. 37–50.

2012. "The *Lex Pompeia de Provinciis* of 52 B.C.: A Reconsideration." *Historia* 61: 83–93.

2013. *The End of the Roman Republic, 146 to 44 B.C.* Edinburgh.

2014. "Rethinking Sulla: The Case of the Roman Senate." *CQ* 64: 657–668.

2014a. Rev. of Arena 2012. *CPh* 109: 86–88.

2014b. "The Roman Senate and the Post-Sullan *res publica*." *Historia* 63: 323–339.

Steel, C., and H. van der Blom (eds.) 2013. *Community and Communication: Oratory and Politics in Republican Rome*. Oxford.

Stein, P. 1930. "Die Senatssitzungen der Ciceronischen Zeit (68–43)." Diss. Münster.

Stevens, C. E. 1938. "The Terminal Date of Caesar's Command." *AJPh* 59: 169–208.

1953. "Britain and the *Lex Pompeia Licinia*." *Latomus* 12: 14–21.

Stevenson, T. 2015. *Julius Caesar and the Transformation of the Republic*. London and New York.

Stockton, D. L. 1977. Rev. of Gruen, *Last Generation of the Roman Republic*. *Gnomon* 49: 216–218.

Stone, M. 2018. "Gaius Verres Troubleshooter." In H. van der Blom, C. Gray, and C. Steel (eds.), *Institutions and Ideology in Republican Rome: Speech, Audience and Decision*. Cambridge. 299–313.

Strasburger, H. 1938. *Caesars Eintritt in die Geschichte*. Munich.

1968. *Caesar im Urteil seiner Zeitgenossen*. 2nd ed. Darmstadt.

Straumann, B. 2016. *Crisis and Constitutionalism: Roman Political Thought from the Fall of the Republic to the Age of Revolution*. Oxford.

Strauss, B. 2015. *The Death of Caesar: The Story of History's Most Famous Assassination*. New York.

Sumi, G. 2011. "Ceremony and the Emergence of Court Society in the Augustan Principate." *AJPh* 132: 81–102.

Sumner, G. 1971. "The *lex annalis* under Caesar." *Phoenix* 25: 246–271, 357–371.

1976. "A Note on Julius Caesar's Great-Grandfather." *CPh* 71: 341–344.

Syme, R. 1938. "The Allegiance of Labienus." *JRS* 28: 113–125 = *Roman Papers* 1.62–75.

1939. *The Roman Revolution*. Oxford.

1958. "Pseudo-Sallust." *MH* 15: 46–55 = *Roman Papers* 6.55–64.

1958a. *Tacitus*. 2 vols. Oxford.

1961. "Who Was Vedius Pollio?" *JRS* 51: 23–30 = *Roman Papers* 2.518–529.

1964. *Sallust*. Berkeley.

1980. "No Son for Caesar?" *Historia* 29: 422–437 = *Roman Papers* 3.1236–1250.

1980a. "The Sons of Crassus." *Latomus* 39: 403–408 = *Roman Papers* 3.1220–1225.

1986. *The Augustan Aristocracy*. Oxford.

Taleb, Nassim Nicholas. 2010. *The Black Swan: The Impact of the Highly Improbable.* New York.

Tatum, W. J. 1999. *The Patrician Tribune: Publius Clodius Pulcher.* Chapel Hill.

2008. *Always I Am Caesar.* Malden, MA.

2018. *Quintus Cicero: A Brief Handbook on Canvassing for Office.* Oxford.

Täubler, E. 1924. Bellum Helveticum, *eine Caesarstudie.* Zürich.

Taylor, L. R. 1941. "Caesar's Early Career." *CPh* 36: 113–132.

1942. "Caesar's Colleagues in the Pontifical College." *AJPh* 63: 385–412.

1942a. "The Election of the *Pontifex Maximus* in the Late Roman Republic." *CPh* 37: 421–424.

1942b. "Caesar and the Roman Nobility." *TAPhA* 73: 1–24.

1951. "On the Chronology of Caesar's First Consulship." *AJPh* 72: 254–268.

1957. "The Rise of Julius Caesar." *G & R* 4: 10–18.

1966. *Roman Voting Assemblies from the Hannibalic War to the Dictatorship of Caesar.* Ann Arbor.

1968. "The Dating of Major Legislation and Elections in Caesar's First Consulship." *Historia* 17: 173–193.

Taylor, L. R., and T. R. S. Broughton. 1949. "The Order of the Two Consuls' Names in the Yearly Lists." *MAAR* 19: 3–14.

Tempest, K. 2017. *Brutus: The Noble Conspirator.* New Haven and London.

Thein, A. 2006. "Sulla the Weak Tyrant." In S. Lewis (ed.), *Ancient Tyranny.* Edinburgh: 238–249.

2014. "Reflecting on Sulla's Clemency." *Historia* 63: 166–186.

Thommen, L. 1989. *Das Volkstribunat der späten römischen Republik.* Historia ES 59. Stuttgart.

Thomson, D. F. S. 1997. *Catullus.* Toronto.

Thorne, J. 2007. "The Chronology of the Campaign against the Helvetii: A Clue to Caesar's Intentions?" *Historia* 56: 27–36.

Tiersch, C. 2018. "Political Communication in the Late Republic." In H. van der Blom, C. Gray, and C. Steel (eds.), *Institutions and Ideology in Republican Rome: Speech, Audience and Decision.* Cambridge. 35–68.

Till, C. 2003. *Die republikanischen Grundlagen der Ehrungen und der Selbstdarstellung Caesars.* Göttingen.

Timpe, D. 1965. "Caesars Gallischer Krieg und das Problem des römischen Imperialismus." *Historia* 14: 189–214.

Toher, M. 2017. *Nicolaus of Damascus: The Life of Augustus and The Autobiography.* Cambridge.

Toland, J. (ed.) 1700/1737. *Oceana of James Harrington and His Other Works.* Dublin.

Townend, B. G. 1987. "C. Oppius on Julius Caesar." *AJPh* 108: 325–342.

Treggiari, S. 2007. *Terentia, Tullia and Publilia: The Women of Cicero's Family.* London and New York.

Treu, M. 1948. "Zur *Clementia Caesaris.*" *MH* 5: 197–217.

Tschiedel, H. J. 1981. *Caesars Anticato.* Darmstadt.

Tyrrell, W. B. 1978. *A Legal and Historical Commentary to Cicero's* Oratio pro C. Rabirio perduellionis reo. Amsterdam.

Uggeri, G. 1984. "La via Popilia e i collegamenti stradali tra Rimini e Ravenna in età romana." In P. Delbianco (ed.), *Culture figurative e materiali tra Emilia e Marche.* Rimini. 401–417.

Ungern-Sternberg, J. 1970. *Untersuchungen zum spätrepublikanischen Notstandsrecht.* Munich.

Urso, G. (ed.) 2000. *L'ultimo Cesare.* Rome.

2010. *Cesare: Precursore o visionario?* Pisa.

Vanderbroeck, P. J. J. 1987. *Popular Leadership and Collective Behavior in the Late Roman Republic (ca. 80–50 BC).* Amsterdam.

Várhely, Z. 2012. "'To Forgive Is Divine.'" In C. L. Griswold and D. Konstan (eds.), *Ancient Forgiveness: Classical, Judaic, and Christian.* Cambridge. 115–133.

Vervaet, F. J. 2006. "The Scope of the *Lex Sempronia* concerning the Assignment of the Consular Provinces (123 BCE)." *Athenaeum* 94: 625–654.

2014. *The High Command in the Roman Republic. The Principle of the* summum imperium auspiciumque *from 509 to 19 BCE.* (*Historia* ES 232) Stuttgart.

Von Fritz, K. 1941. "The Mission of L. Caesar and L. Roscius in January 49 BC." *TAPhA* 72: 125–156.

Vretska, K. 1976. *De Catilinae Coniuratione.* 2 vols. Heidelberg.

Walter, U. 2004. Memoria *und* res publica*: zur Geschichtskultur im republikanischen Rom.* Frankfurt.

2009. "Struktur, Zufall, Kontingenz? Überlegungen zum Ende der römischen Republik." In K.-J. Hölkeskamp (ed.), *Eine politische Kultur (in) der Krise? Die "letzte Generation" der römischen Republik.* Munich. 27–51.

Walter, U., J. Geisweid, G. Hellweg, S. Pollpeter, T. Reiz, A. van Ross, and G. Siemoneit. 2013. *Cicero: Zweite Rede an das Volk gegen den Volkstribunen Publius Servilius Rullus über das Ackergesetz. Einführung, Kommentar zu §§1–46, Appendices.* Bielefeld.

Wardle, D. 2009. "Caesar and Religion." In M. T. Griffin (ed.), *A Companion to Julius Caesar.* Malden, MA, and Oxford. 100–111.

2014. *Suetonius: Life of Augustus.* Oxford.

Watkins, O. D. 1987. "*Caesar Solus?* Senatorial Support for the *Lex Gabinia.*" *Historia* 36: 120–121.

Weggen, K. 2011. *Der lange Schatten von Carrhae: Studien zu M. Licinius Crassus.* Hamburg.

Weinstock, S. 1971. *Divus Julius.* Oxford.

Welch, K. 1995. "Antony, Fulvia, and the Ghost of Clodius in 47 B.C." *G&R* 42: 182–201.

2012. *Magnus Pius: Sextus Pompeius and the Transformation of the Roman Republic.* Swansea.

Welch, K. (ed.) 2015. *Appian's* Roman History: *Empire and Civil War.* Swansea.

Welch, K., and A. Powell (eds.) 1998. *Caesar as Artful Reporter.* Swansea.

Welwei, K.-W. 2000. "Lucius Iunius Brutus: ein fiktiver Revolutionsheld." In K.-J. Hölkeskamp and E. Stein-Hölkeskamp (eds.), *Von Romulus zu Augustus: große Gestalten der römischen Republik.* Munich. 48–57.

Wensler, A. F. 1989. "Lucan und Livius zum Januar 49 v. Chr.: Quellenkundliche Beobachtungen." *Historia* 38: 250–254.

Westall, R. W. 1996. "The Forum Iulium as Representation of Imperator Caesar." *MDAIR* 103: 198–224.

2018. *Caesar's* Civil War: *Historical Reality and Fabrication.* Mnemosyne Suppl. 410. Leiden.

White, P. 1995. "Postumus, Curtius Postumus, and Rabirius Postumus." *CPh* 90: 151–161.

2003. "Tactics in Caesar's Correspondence with Cicero." In F. Cairns and E. Fantham (eds.), *Caesar against Liberty? Papers of the Langford Latin Seminar.* Leeds. 68–95.

2010. *Cicero in Letters: Epistolary Relations of the Late Republic.* Oxford.

Wilcken, U. 1940. *Zur Entwicklung der römischen Diktatur.* Berlin.

Will, W. 1992. *Julius Caesar: eine Bilanz.* Stuttgart.

Williams, J. H. C. 2001. *Beyond the Rubicon: Romans and Gauls in Republican Italy.* Oxford.

Wiseman, T. P. 1971. *New Men in the Roman Senate, 139 B.C.–A.D. 14.* Oxford.

1974. *Cinna the Poet and Other Roman Essays.* Leicester.

1985. *Catullus and His World: A Reappraisal.* Cambridge.

1998. "The Publication of the De Bello Gallico." In K. Welch and A. Powell (eds.), *Caesar as Artful Reporter.* Swansea. 1–9.

1998a. *Roman Drama and Roman History.* Exeter.

2008. *Unwritten Rome.* Exeter.

2009. *Remembering the Roman People.* Oxford.

2016. *Julius Caesar.* Stroud.

Wistrand, M. 1979. *Cicero Imperator: Studies in Cicero's Correspondence 51–47 B.C.* Göteborg.

Woodman, A. J. 2003. "Poems to Historians: Catullus 1 and Horace, Odes 2.1." In D. C. Braund and C. Gill (eds.), *Myth, History, and Culture in Republican Rome: Studies in Honour of T. P. Wiseman.* Exeter. 191–216.

Woolf, G. 1998. *Becoming Roman: The Origins of Provincial Civilization in Gaul.* Cambridge.

2007. *Et tu, Brute? The Murder of Caesar and Political Assassination.* Cambridge, MA.

Wootten, D. (ed.) 1994. *Republicanism, Liberty, and Commercial Society, 1649–1776.* Stanford.

Worden, B. 1994. "Harrington's 'Oceana': Origins and Aftermath, 1651–1660." In D. Wootton (ed.), *Republicanism, Liberty, and Commercial Society, 1649–1776.* Stanford. 111–138.

1994a. "Republicanism and the Restoration, 1660–1683." In D. Wootton (ed.), *Republicanism, Liberty, and Commercial Society, 1649–1776.* Stanford. 139–193.

Woytek, B. 2003. Arma et nummi. *Forschungen zur römischen Finanzgeschichte und Münzprägung der Jahre 49 bis 42 v. Chr.* Vienna.

Woytek, E. 2004. "Klärendes zu den pseudo-sallustischen 'epistulae'." In H. Heftner and K. Tomaschitz (eds.), *Ad fontes: Festschrift für G. Dobesch.* Vienna. 329–341.

Wyke, M. 2008. *Caesar: A Life in Western Culture.* Chicago and London.

Wyke, M. (ed.) 2006. *Julius Caesar in Western Culture.* Malden, MA, and Oxford.

Yakobson, A. 1999. *Elections and Electioneering in Rome: A Study in the Political System of the Late Republic.* Stuttgart.

2004. Rev. of Mouritsen 2001 and Morstein-Marx 2004. *SCI* 23: 201–206.

2006. "Popular Power in the Roman Republic." In N. Rosenstein and R. Morstein-Marx (eds.), *A Companion to the Roman Republic.* Malden, MA. 383–400.

2009. "Public Opinion, Foreign Policy and "Just War" in the Late Republic." In C. Eilers (ed.), *Diplomats and Diplomacy in the Roman World.* Mnemosyne Suppl. 304. Leiden and Boston. 45–72.

2010. "Traditional Political Culture and the People's Role in the Roman Republic." *Historia* 59: 282–302.

2011. Review of Flower, *Roman Republics. AJPh* 132: 153–156.

2012. Review of Robb, *Beyond Populares and Optimates, SCI* 31: 212–214.

2014. "Marius Speaks to the People: 'New Man,' Roman Nobility and Roman Political Culture." *SCI* 33: 283–300.

2017. "*Optimates, populares.*" *OCD* (updated August 22, 2017).

Yarrow, L. M. 2012. "*Decem Legati*: A Flexible Institution, Rigidly Perceived." In L. M. Yarrow and C. J. Smith (eds.), *Imperialism, Cultural Politics, and Polybius.* Oxford. 168–183.

Yavetz, Z. 1983. *Julius Caesar and His Public Image.* London.

Zampieri, E. 2016. Rev. of Stevenson 2015. *CR* 66: 210–212.

Zarecki, J. 2014. *Cicero's Ideal Statesman in Theory and Practice.* London.

Zecchini, G. 1982. "Asinio Pollione: Dall'attività politica alla riflessione storiografica." *ANRW* II.30.2: 1265–1296.

2000. "Cesare e Cartagine." In G. Urso (ed.), *L'ultimo Cesare.* Rome. 353–362.

2001. *Cesare e il mos maiorum.* Stuttgart.

Zetzel, J. E. G. 1995. *Cicero:* De re publica. Cambridge.

2013. "Political Philosophy." In C. Steel (ed.), *Cambridge Companion to Cicero.* Cambridge. 181–195.

Zevi, F., and F. Cassola 2016. "I Fasti di Privernum." *ZPE* 197: 287–309.

Ziolkowski, A. 1993. "*Urbs Disrepta* or How the Romans Sacked Cities." In J. Rich and G. Shipley (eds.), *War and Society in the Roman World.* London. 69–91.

Zippel, G. 1877. *Die römische Herrschaft in Illyrien bis auf Augustus.* Leipzig.

Select Index of Passages Cited

The passages listed here have been selected either for their inherent importance or for their significance in my interpretation. Many passages not listed here will be found by using the General Index.

675

General Index

third consulship of, 247, 249, 250, 259,
530n189, 603–604, 614, 622
three triumphs of, 246
wealth of, 167, 443n134
See also Alliance, Three-Way; Caesar, Gaius
Julius, as consul: agrarian laws of, *and*
other legislation; Caesar, Gaius Julius,
early career: support for Pompey; Caesar,
Gaius Julius, in Civil War: final proposals
to avert war, *and* proposes peace terms;
Cicero, Marcus Tullius, attitude in 59
toward Three-Way Alliance; Julia
(Caesar's daughter); Luca, "Conference"
at; Laws, Pompeian: on electoral
corruption, on magistracies, *and* on
province assignments; Metellus Nepos,
Quintus Caecilius, proposed law of;
Vettius, Lucius, "Vettius Affair" of 59
Pomptinus, Gaius, 171, 173, 176, 246, 264n17
Pontius Aquila, 515, 520
popularis, 8, 13, 614
See also Caesar, Gaius Julius, as *popularis*
Prisoner's Dilemma, 259n3, 291n133, 302n188,
315n241, 345, 590, 609, 633–639
Ptolemy XII Auletes, king of Egypt, 162, 199,
430n78, 479, 620
Pupius Piso, Marcus (pr. 44), 431, 476, 483
Pupius, Lucius (centurion), 347, 449, 478

Quinctilius Varus, Sextus, 433, 445, 479,
484
Quinctius Scapula, Titus, 447

Rabirius Postumus, Gaius, 620
Rabirius, Gaius (defendant 63), 69–71
Regnum See People, Roman; Republic, Roman:
opposed to *regnum*
Republic, Roman
agrarian and demographic problems of, 24n79,
605–606
alleged disaffection of soldiers from, 24n79,
531n190, 601, 606
constitutional norms of, 132–133, 315–320,
612–614
end of, 14, 20–21, 601–615
imperia extraordinaria ("extraordinary
commands"), 177, 604
nature of, 2, 3–14, 601, 603
opposed to *regnum* (monarchy/tyranny),
318–319
still functioning in 50s, 6n16, 601–604,
See also People, Roman.
Rubicon River. *See* Caesar, Gaius Julius, in the
Civil War: crosses the Rubicon
Rubrius, Lucius, 479

Rupilius Rex, Publius, 552n281
Rutilius Lupus, Publius, 229, 230, 358n154

Sallust (Sallustius Crispus, Gaius), 378
Sallustius, Gnaeus, 483
Scipio Aemilianus, Publius Cornelius, 11, 250,
600, 607
as plausible model for Caesar, 58, 60, 80–82,
249, 257, 537, 580, 598
Scipio Africanus, Publius Cornelius, 12n32, 256,
288, 312, 589, 607
as plausible model for Caesar, 58, 60, 80–82,
249, 257, 580, 598
sella aurea, 540
Senate
change into mourning dress (*mutatio vestis*),
305, 411n418
Final or Emergency Decree of (*senatus
consultum ultimum*), 69–70, 94–95, 107,
139, 575
passed against Caesar, 308–309, 310–311, 322,
331, 333, 351, 364, 365, 388n297, 400,
592, 631
passed in 47, 407n396, 529
size of, after Sulla, 358n157
votes in 50 for disarmament of both parties,
292–294, 608
senators
life expectancy of, 535n211
servatio ("watching the skies"), 136n75, 142–145,
150, 182–188, 583, 612
Servilia (mother of Brutus), 90n35, 558n301,
576n374, 618
Servilius Isauricus, Publius (cos. 48), 359,
367n189, 406, 545n253
Servilius Rullus, Publius (tr. pl. 63), 69
Servilius Vatia Isauricus, Publius (cos. 79), 42, 64,
358, 361, 362
Sestius, Publius, 209n67, 295, 344n83, 431, 476,
481, 489, 496, 554n287
Sextius Naso, Publius, 476, 487, 559
Silanus, Decimus Iunius, 89–90, 93n53, 576n374
Silius, Publius, 481
Sittius, Publius, 434, 447, 480
soldiers
mutinies of, in 49 and 47, 407n396, 437, 443,
601, 619
Staius Murcus, Lucius, 556n294
Subernius Calenus, Gaius, 486
Sulla, Faustus Cornelius (son of dictator), 42,
295, 384, 434
execution of, 435–436, 447n144, 487
Sulla, Lucius Cornelius (Dictator 82), 320, 598
cruelty of, 424–426, 460–461, 597
dictatorship of, 535

Printed in the USA
CPSIA information can be obtained
at www.ICGtesting.com
LVHW010732161223
766604LV00018B/1291